Introduction to Law and the Legal System

Introduction to Law and the Legal System

Eighth Edition

Frank A. Schubert

Professor Emeritus
NORTHEASTERN UNIVERSITY

Houghton Mifflin Company   Boston   New York

To Taylor Grace

—F.A.S.

Editor-in-chief: Jean Woy
Sponsoring Editor: Katherine Meisenheimer
Editorial Associate: Tonya Lobato
Senior Project Editor: Bob Greiner
Editorial Assistant: Wendy Thayer
Senior Production/Design Coordinator: Jodi O'Rourke
Senior Manufacturing Coordinator: Priscilla Bailey
Marketing Manager: Nicola Poser

Printed in the U.S.A.

Library of Congress Catalog Number: 2002109668

ISBN: 0-618-31202-1

789-MV-07 06

Contents

III   THE JUDICIAL SYSTEM   118

IV   CIVIL PROCEDURE   157

V INSTITUTIONAL SOURCES OF AMERICAN LAW 198

VII   JUDICIAL REMEDIES   277

VIII   CRIMINAL LAW AND PROCEDURE   316

X   CONTRACTS   457

Preface

This book provides an introduction to a topic every educated citizen should know about—law and the American legal system. A basic understanding of law's philosophical, historical, and cultural antecedents and its fundamentals promotes a better understanding of the role law plays in a complex, modern society. From this understanding, students can decide for themselves whether lawmaking institutions—the legislative, judicial, and administrative agencies—are adequately addressing our society's problems.

Suited for undergraduate or graduate programs, this text is a survey of the American legal system and can be used in a variety of courses such as Survey of Law, Introduction to Law and the Legal System, Law and Society, Legal Environment and Business, and Legal Process. This text could be an integral part of business, criminal justice, political science, interdisciplinary, paralegal, or other similar courses in an institution of higher learning.

This textbook is designed to stimulate students to exercise their powers of reasoning and provides an interesting and exciting means of developing an understanding of the strengths and weaknesses of the law. Students read case reports of real-world problems along with textual and appellate court discussions of alternative approaches to and theories of resolving the underlying disputes. Case analysis also helps students develop an understanding of legal method and reasoning.

New to the Eighth Edition

The Eighth Edition has been updated with forty-two new cases including many that have recently inspired debate, such as *Ethyl Corporation v. Environmental Protection Agency, Cronin v. Sierra Medical Center, Brent v. Ashley,* and *Charles T. Dickerson v. United States.* Comments from reviewers and users have been carefully considered as decisions were made with respect to the replacement or retention of particular cases. As always, the goal has been to select cases that are interesting, teachable, controversial, and that illustrate the theory being discussed in the corresponding chapter section. Some of the selected cases are classics and have proven to be useful for many years. Traditional favorites such as *DuPont v. Christopher, Cruzan v. Director, Missouri Department of Health, Katko v. Briney, Strunk v. Strunk,* and *Campbell Soup Company v. Wentz,* have been retained. Other cases were chosen because they illustrate a problem in a contemporary factual setting.

The Eighth Edition breaks new ground in that it is supported by an Internet site, accessible at *college.hmco.com*. The text was written with the website in mind. Each chapter contains one or more "Internet Tips" which direct the reader to the website where additional material relevant to the textbook's discussion can be found. This website will be updated periodically with new and relevant cases, and will include concurring and dissenting opinions that would be too lengthy to include in the textbook itself. Additional resources such as chapter outlines, helpful web links, and more, will be available to both students and instructors.

Teaching and Learning Aids

Law, like other disciplines, has a language all its own. A glossary of selected terms from *The Law Dictionary* (*Cochran's Law Lexicon,* Sixth Edition) is included at the end of the book to help students. The Constitution of the United States is also reprinted for easy reference.

In addition to the website discussed above, *Introduction to Law and the Legal System* is accompanied by a *Study Guide* and an *Instructor's Resource Manual.* The *Study Guide* provides students with case summaries and a series of review exercises to test comprehension. For instructors, case summaries and case questions appear in the *Instructor's Resource Manual* along with a section of test items for each chapter, including completion, true-false, multiple choice, and essay questions.

All cases have been edited to frame issues for classroom discussion, and for length and readability. Most case footnotes have been deleted. Many citations have similarly been omitted, as well as less important portions of majority opinions. Ellipses have been inserted to indicate such omissions. Academic works that were relied upon as sources within each chapter have been acknowledged with endnotes. Case citations are occasionally provided so that interested students can consult the official reports for unedited cases.

Acknowledgments

This revision would not have been possible without the valuable contributions of many people. The following reviewers were instrumental in shaping the Eighth Edition: Douglas R. Davenport, Truman State University; Susan M. DeMatteo, Boston University; Michael Fitch, Edmonds Community College; Tracey C. McCarthy, Webster University; and Richard Poland, Flagler College.

The manuscript for the Eighth Edition was significantly improved by the dedicated professionals at Houghton Mifflin. Special thanks are extended to Katherine Meisenheimer, Tonya Lobato, Bob Greiner, and Wendy Thayer.

I would also like to thank my wife, Barbara, for helping me throughout this long, lonely, and seemingly at times, endless process. Her love, encouragement, patience, and fantastic cookies, really made all the difference.

This edition is dedicated to my fabulous granddaughter, Taylor Grace. Every time I see her it's a sunny day.

F.A.S.

Introduction to Law and the Legal System

I Introduction

The study of legal philosophy is called *jurisprudence*. Many of the world's greatest philosophers have theorized about the nature and meaning of law. Jurisprudential philosophers ask questions such as, "What is law?" "Is bad law, law?" "Is custom law?" "Is law what it says in the statute books or what really happens in practice?" Philosophers have debated the essential nature of law for centuries, yet there is no single commonly accepted definition. This chapter begins by summarizing some of the schools of legal philosophy in order to introduce students to different ways of answering this fundamental question: "What is law?"[1]

Law as Power

Some philosophers argued that laws are nothing more than the will of those who hold power. In totalitarian regimes, military power often controls governmental institutions, and laws are essentially edicts. In a democracy, political majorities control legislative bodies and determine who exercises executive authority, and appellate court majorities determine legal precedents.

According to this view, the validity of a law does not depend on whether it is socially good or bad. It is apparent, for example, that tyrannies, monarchies, and democracies have produced socially beneficial laws. They have also produced laws that are unjust and "wrongful." What these different forms of government have in common is that each is based on power and that possessing the power to enforce its laws is central to each government's existence. This philosophy can be criticized for ignoring arbitrariness, abuses of power, and tyranny, and for producing bad law.

Natural Law

Natural law philosophers argued that law is that which reflects, or is based on, the built-in sense of right and wrong that exists within every person at birth. This moral barometer, which operates through the functioning of conscience, gives each person the capacity to independently discover moral truth. Some believed that this sense was God-given; others believed it was an intrinsic part of human nature.[2] Natural law philosophers argued that moral goodness is conceptually independent of individual or institutional views of goodness or evil. Thus no government can make a morally evil law good or a morally good law evil. Moral goodness exists prior to institutional lawmaking, and sets a moral standard against which positive law should be measured. Thus, even though during apartheid the all-white, South African government may have had the power to enact racially discriminatory statutes, such statutes were not truly "law" because they were morally abhorrent.

This natural law philosophy was very influential in seventeenth- and eighteenth-century Europe. Revolutionaries who sought to overthrow established monarchies were attracted to natural law because it established a philosophical foundation for political reform.

Natural law thinking has greatly influenced American law as well. American civil rights advocates currently use time-tested natural law arguments that were used thirty and forty years ago to oppose racial discrimination. They argue that discriminatory statutes should not be respected as law because they are so blatantly unfair. Constitutional provisions that require government to treat all persons fairly and impartially (the due process and equal protection clauses) are other examples.

Our tort system is also a reflection of natural law thinking. It is "right" that people who intend no harm but who carelessly cause injury to other people should have to pay compensation for the damages. Similarly, if two people voluntarily enter into a contract, it is "right" that the parties comply with its terms or pay damages for the breach. (However, our law confers power in our judges to refuse to enforce contractual provisions that are too one-sided.) Finally, it is "right" to punish persons who commit crimes for those acts.

When there is no consensus in society about what is morally right and wrong, natural law loses its effectiveness as a basis for law. Current examples of this problem include issues such as abortion, physician-assisted suicide, and capital punishment.

Historical Jurisprudence

Historical jurisprudence evolved in response to the natural law philosophy. Aristocrats were attracted to this school because it provided a justification for preserving the status quo and the preferential treatment of powerful elites that was deeply rooted in cultural tradition. The historical philosophy of law integrated the notion that law is the will of the sovereign with the idea of the "spirit of the people."[3] That is, law is only valid to the extent that the will of the sovereign is compatible with long-standing social practices, customs, and values. Law, according to this view, could not be arbitrarily imposed by legislators whose legal source was "right" reasoning. Instead, the historical school insisted that only practices that have withstood the test of time could be thought of as law.[4] Further, these philosophers believed that law changes slowly and invisibly as human conduct changes.

A major advantage of historical jurisprudence is that it promotes stability in law. In fact, much law is largely grounded in judicially approved custom. Our contemporary American real estate law,[5] property law,[6] and contract law[7] are some of the areas in which long-standing practices continue to be recognized as law. Custom has also played an important role in determining the meaning of the Constitution. Appellate courts such as the United States Supreme Court trace provisions of the Bill of Rights to their historical statutory and case law antecedents. They do this because they recognize that some beliefs, practices, procedures, and relationships between people and the state have become fundamental to our culture.

Occasionally a sovereign will enact legislation that significantly contravenes long-standing custom. A few years ago the Massachusetts legislature enacted a mandatory seat belt law. Many citizens believed that the state was infringing on a matter of personal choice. They insisted that the matter be placed on the ballot, and the law was repealed in a statewide referendum.[8]

A major problem with historical jurisprudence is determining at what point a practice has become a custom. How long must a practice have been followed and how widespread must it be accepted to be recognized as customary?

Utilitarian Law

The utilitarian school of law concentrated on the social usefulness of legislation rather than on metaphysical notions of goodness and justice.[9] Utilitarians thought that government was responsible for enacting laws that promote the general public's happiness. They believed that the desire to maximize pleasure and minimize pain is what motivates people, and that legislatures were responsible for inducing people to act in socially desirable ways through a legislated system of incentives and disincentives.[10] For example, if the pain imposed by a criminal sentence exceeds the gain realized by an offender in committing the offense, future criminal actions will be deterred. Additionally, they thought that law should focus on providing people with security and equality of opportunity. They maintained that property rights should be protected because security of property is crucial to attaining happiness. People, they thought, should perform their contracts because increased commercial activity and economic growth produce socially beneficial increases in employment.

Utilitarians also favored the simplification of legal procedures. They opposed checks and balances, legal technicalities, and complex procedures. They believed that these "formalities" increased the costs and length of the judicial process and made the justice system ineffective and unresponsive to the needs of large numbers of average people. Instead, utilitarians would favor small claims courts, with their simplified pleading requirements, informality, low cost, and the optional use of lawyers.

Utilitarian influence can be found in legislative enactments that require the nation's broadcasters to operate "in the public interest," in "lemon laws," and in other consumer protection legislation. A major problem with utilitarianism is that everyone does not agree about what is pleasurable and what is painful. And many, if not most, political scientists would dispute that legislators actually make decisions according to the pleasure-pain principle.

Analytical Positivism

Analytical positivists asserted that law was a self-sufficient system of legal rules that the sovereign issues in the form of commands to the governed. These commands do not depend for legitimacy on extraneous considerations such as reason, ethics, morals, or even social consequences.[11] However, the sovereign's will was law only if it was developed according to duly established procedures, such as the enactments of a national legislature.

Thus the apartheid laws passed by the previously all-white South African legislature were "the law" of that country at that time to the same extent that civil rights legislation enacted by the United States Congress was the law of this country. Each of these lawmaking bodies was exercising sovereign power in accordance with provisions of a national constitution. Individuals and governmental officials would have no right to disobey laws with which they personally disagree due to moral, ethical, or policy objections. Positivists would also maintain that trial jurors have a legal obligation to apply the law according to the judge's instructions, even if that means disregarding strongly held personal beliefs about the wisdom of the law or its application in a particular factual dispute.

Members of this philosophical school would view disputes about the goodness or badness of legal rules as extra-legal.[12] They would maintain that such issues do not relate to the law *as it is*. This approach promotes stability and security. It also legitimizes governmental line drawing (such as laws that specify the age at which people can lawfully drink and vote, or those that determine automobile speed limits).

In the United States, people often disagree with governmental decisions about foreign policy as well as about such issues as housing, the financing of public education, health care, abortion, environmental protection, and the licensing of nuclear power plants. Many contend that governmental officials are pursuing wrongful, and sometimes immoral, objectives. Such concerns, however, are generally unpersuasive in our courts. If governmental officials are authorized to make decisions, act within constitutional limitations, and follow established procedures, even decisions that are unpopular with some segments of society are nevertheless law.

But is law really just a closed system of rules and the product of a sovereign? Doesn't international law exist despite the absence of a sovereign? Don't contracting parties routinely create their own rules without any sovereign's involvement unless a dispute arises that results in litigation? And is law really morally neutral? Shouldn't the positivist approach be criticized if it protects governmental officials who act unfairly?

SOCIOLOGICAL JURISPRUDENCE, LEGAL REALISM, AND LEGAL SOCIOLOGY

After the Civil War, the nation's economy rapidly expanded and America moved toward a market economy. Along with this expansion came new technologies, new products, and changing legal attitudes about government's rights to interfere with private property. Laissez-faire was in vogue, and although it contributed to expanding the economy, it also produced monopolies, political corruption, environmental pollution, hazardous working conditions, and labor-management conflict. The United States Supreme Court often opposed social reforms initiated by state governments. In *Lochner v. New York,* for example, the Court struck down a reform statute that limited bakers to ten-hour workdays and sixty-hour work weeks.[13] The majority ruled that this statute unreasonably infringed on the rights of employees and employers to negotiate their own contracts. The Court also declared the *Erdman Act* unconstitutional in *Adair v. United States.*[14] Congress enacted the Erdman Act to stop the railroad monopolies from discharging employees who joined labor unions. Congress, said the Supreme Court, had no right under the interstate commerce clause to regulate labor relations in the railroad industry.

The excesses of laissez-faire produced social and economic unrest among farmers and laborers in particular, and produced political pressure for reforms. These factors culminated in the rise of the Progressive movement. The Progressives sought an expanded governmental role in the economy. They wanted government to pay attention to reforming government and to enacting reforms that would regulate the special interests. The Progressives rejected the notion that law is based on immutable principles and deductive reasoning, and is therefore unrelated to political, social, and economic factors in society. Too often, they contended, the court had ignored what Benjamin Cardozo would call the "pursuit of social justice."[15]

Roscoe Pound, of Harvard Law School, published an article in the 1911 *Harvard Law Review* that picked up on Progressive themes and announced a philosophy of law called Sociological Jurisprudence.[16] Pound argued against what he called "mechanical jurisprudence" with its backwardness and unjust outcomes in individual cases. He advocated that governments become proactive in working to promote social and economic reforms and that judges become more socially aware of the impact of their decisions on society.[17]

Early sociologists were interested in examining jurisprudence from a social scientific perspective. They focused on what they called the living law—not just the law declared by legislatures and courts, but the informal rules that actually influence social behavior. The sociological school maintains that law can only be understood when the formal system of rules is considered in conjunction with social realities (or facts). In this sense, it is similar to the historical school. However, the historical school approached time in terms of centuries, whereas the sociological school focused on ten- or twenty-year segments.

Sociological jurisprudents, for example, would note that during the last thirty years the courts and legislatures have made many attempts to eliminate racial discrimination in voting, housing, employment, and education and that the law on the books has significantly changed. It is equally clear from scholarly studies, however, that discrimination continues. The written law provides for equal opportunity, and on the surface racial discrimination is not as obvious as it once was. But the social facts continue to reveal subtle forms of racism that law has not been able to legislate or adjudicate away. Similarly, employment discrimination against women, older workers, and the disabled continues despite the enactment of federal and state legislation that legally puts an end to such practices. Informally enforced social norms that condone bigotry and inflict personal indignities and economic inequities on targeted segments of society are not easily legislated away.

Although this approach effectively points out the discrepancies between the promise and the reality of enacted law, it often fails to produce practical solutions to the problems. Should judges be encouraged to consider social consequences in addition to legal rules in reaching decisions? If so, might this not result in arbitrary, discretionary decisions that reflect only the personal preferences of one particular jurist or group of jurists?

Legal Realists

During the early decades of the twentieth century, the social sciences were emerging. Academics and judges were attempting to borrow the scientific methods, which had been used to study the natural and physical sciences, and use them to examine social institutions. From the late 1920s through the middle 1930s, juries and judges in particular were subjected to empirical scrutiny by reformists like Jerome Frank and Karl Llewellyn, who called themselves legal realists. The realists focused on the extent to which actual practices varied from the formal legal rules.[18] They believed that judges were more influenced by their personal convictions than by established and immutable rules. Llewellyn made a very important distinction between the legal rules and precedent-setting cases that were often cited as the basis for deciding why cases were won and lost (which he called "paper" rules) and the "real" rules of decisions that were undisclosed unless revealed by behavioral research.[19] Llewellyn believed that judges made law instead of discovering it, and he went so far as to proclaim that law was merely "what officials do about disputes."[20] Rules, they pointed out, do not adequately account for witness perjury and bias, nor do they compensate for the differing levels of ability, knowledge, and prejudice in individual lawyers, judges, and jurors. Because the realists produced little theory and research, they primarily blazed a trail for the legal sociologists to follow.

Legal Sociologists

Legal sociologists such as Donald Black have gone beyond the legal realists. Using quantitative methodological tools, they examine such factors as the financial standing, race, social class, respectability, and cultural differences of those involved in disputes.[21] In addition, they evaluate the social facts of the lawyers and judges working on the case as well as those of the parties. In theory, legal outcomes should not be affected by differences in the socioeconomic status of the litigants, because all are "equal" before the law. Individual plaintiffs, for example, should be able to win when suing multinational corporations. But legal sociologists claim that the facts do not support this theory.[22] The rule of law is a myth, they say, because legal rules fail to take into account the impact of social diversity on litigation. Discrimination is a fact of modern life, and different combinations of social factors will produce disparate legal outcomes.[23] Donald Black points out that disputes between friends, neighbors, and family members are rarely litigated because "law varies directly with relational distance."[24] It can be persuasively argued that well-trained lawyers should decide whether to settle a case or go to trial, whether to try a case to a judge or a jury, and whether to appeal only after carefully considering the relevant social factors and relationships.[25]

Legal sociologists raise issues that challenge fundamental postulates of our society. If people become convinced that legal outcomes are largely a function of sociological considerations, rather than the application of impartial rules, the integrity of the judicial process itself will be undermined, as will the legitimacy of government. If research, however, can reveal more precisely how various combinations of sociological factors influence legal outcomes, this information could be used either to eliminate the bias or to develop alternative mechanisms for resolving particular types of disputes.

OBJECTIVES OF LAW

One of the foundations of our society is the belief that ours is a nation committed to the rule of law. No person is above the law. Our shared legal heritage binds us together as Americans. We use law to regulate people in their relationships with each other, and in their relationships with government. Law reflects our societal aspirations, our culture, and our political and economic beliefs. It provides mechanisms for resolving disputes and for controlling government officials. Private law includes property, family, tort, probate, and corporate law. Public law includes constitutional, criminal, and administrative law. Common to both, however, are certain legal objectives.

Continuity and Stability

It is important that established laws change gradually. Litigants have greater confidence that justice has been done when preexisting rules are used to determine legal outcomes. Laws work best when people become aware of them and learn how they work and why they are necessary. Stable laws are also more likely to be applied uniformly and consistently throughout a jurisdiction, and will be better understood by those charged with enforcement.

Stable laws are also very important to creating and maintaining a healthy economy because they are predictable and serve as a guide for conduct. Businesspeople, for example, are not likely to incur risk in a volatile legal and political environment. They are likely to feel more comfortable in making investments and taking economic risks where it appears likely that the future will resemble the present and the recent past. This stability is threatened by society's appetite for producing rules. Various state and federal legislative and administrative rule-making bodies are currently promulgating so many regulations that it is difficult, if not impossible, for affected citizens to stay current.

Adaptability

In one sense it would be desirable if society could create a great big "legal cookbook" that contained a prescribed law or rule for every conceivable situation. We would then only have to look in the cookbook for definitive answers to all legal problems. In reality, there is no such cookbook. Legislators produce statutes that have a broad scope and are designed to promote the public health, safety, welfare, and morals. Judges make law in conjunction with resolving disputes that have been properly brought before the court. Experience has shown that legislative enactments and judicial opinions produce imperfect law. Lawmakers cannot anticipate every factual possibility. Courts, in particular, often feel compelled to recognize exceptions to general rules in order to provide justice in individual cases. Judges often find that there are gaps in the law that have to be filled in order to decide a case, or that a long-standing rule no longer makes any sense, given current circumstances and societal values. In this way law adapts to social, environmental, and political changes within our evolving society.

Justice, Speed, and Economy

Although most people would agree with the preamble to the United States Constitution that it is the role of the government "to establish justice," there is no consensus about what that means. Some see justice as a natural law type settlement, which means each party to a dispute receives what he or she is due. To other people justice means that a specified process was followed by governmental institutions. In some situations, justice requires the elimination of discretion so that law is applied more equally. In other situations, justice requires the inclusion of discretion (equity) in order that the law not be applied too mechanically. In this respect, it is helpful to look at recent history. Our current notions of justice with respect to race, gender, and class differ from the views of many of our forebears. Posterity will probably have a concept of justice that differs from our own.

Rule One of the Federal Rules of Civil Procedure provides that procedural rules should be construed "to secure the just, speedy and inexpensive determination of every action." Although it would be desirable if our judicial systems could satisfy all three of these objectives, they are often in conflict. As a society, we continually have to make choices about how much justice we desire and can afford.

Consider a society dedicated to achieving the highest possible levels of justice in its judicial system. Elaborate measures would be required to ensure that all relevant evidence has been located and all possible witnesses identified and permitted to testify. In such a society, all litigants would be entitled to the services of investigators, thorough pretrial discovery procedures, and qualified and experienced trial attorneys. Great care would have to be taken to ensure that jurors were truly unbiased and competent to render a fair verdict. Only highly probative evidence would be permitted as proof, and various levels of appellate review would be required to carefully consider whether significant substantive or procedural errors were made at trial. Obviously, such a process would be very slow and very expensive. Denying deserving plaintiffs a recovery until the process had run its course could itself be unfair because a recovery would be denied for several years.

Instead, some judicial systems build in cost-cutting measures such as six-person juries instead of twelve-person juries. They also make it easier for juries to reach decisions by permitting less-than-unanimous verdicts. Although each cost-cutting step risks more error in the system, there are limits to how much justice society is willing to provide. People have a multitude of needs including medical care, housing, education, and defense, as well as a limited interest in paying taxes. These competing needs have to be prioritized. In recent years, governmental funding of poverty lawyers has been greatly reduced. This has occurred at a time when the costs of litigating average cases have risen substantially. As the costs of using the legal system increase, fewer persons will be able to afford to use litigation to resolve their disputes. Some private attorneys will decline to represent a potential client if the likely recovery in the case will not produce an acceptable profit.

An example of how law balances the desire for justice with a concern for cost is seen in the Internet case *Goss v. Lopez*. In that case the United States Supreme Court determined that public school administrators only have to provide rudimentary procedural due process to students who face short suspensions. The Supreme Court explained that requiring schools to provide students with extensive trial-type procedures would make the disciplinary process too expensive. In Chapter 14 we will examine alternative lower-cost methods for resolving disputes.

Determining Desirable Public Policy

Historically, law is used to determine desirable public policy. It has been used to establish and then abolish discrimination on the basis of race, gender, age, and sexual preference. Law has been used to promote environmental protection and to permit resource exploitation. Through law, society determines whether capital punishment is permissible and whether women have the right to obtain abortions.

ORIGIN OF LAW IN THE UNITED STATES

The British victory over the French in the French and Indian War and the signing of the Treaty of Paris (1763) concluded the competition between the two nations for domination of North America. A French victory might well have resulted in the establishment of the civil law system of France in the colonies along the Atlantic seaboard. The British victory, however, preserved the English common law system for what would become the United States. The following discussion highlights some of the important milestones in the development of the common law.

The Origins of English Common Law

Anglo-Saxon kings ruled England prior to 1066. During the reign of Edward the Confessor (1042–1066), wealthy landowners and noblemen, called earls, gained power over local affairs. There was no central legislature or national judicial court. Instead, the country was organized into communal units, based on population. Each was called the hundred, and was headed by an official called the reeve. The primary function of the hundred was judicial; it held court once each month and dealt with routine civil and criminal matters. Local freemen resolved these cases in accordance with local custom.[26]

The hundreds were grouped into units called shires (counties) that had in earlier times often been Anglo-Saxon kingdoms. The shire was of much greater importance than the hundred. The king used it for military, administrative, and judicial purposes. The king administered the shires through the person of the shire reeve (sheriff). Royal sheriffs existed in each of the shires throughout the country. The sheriff was the king's principal judicial and administrative officer at the local level. Sheriffs collected taxes, urged support of the king's administrative and military policies, and performed limited judicial functions.[27] The shire court, composed of all the freemen in the county, was held twice a year and was presided over by the bishop and the sheriff.[28] It handled criminal, civil, and religious matters that were too serious or difficult for the hundred court as well as disputes about land ownership.[29] The freemen in attendance used local custom as the basis for making decisions, even in religious matters, resulting in a variety of regional practices throughout the country. Anglo-Saxon law did not permit a person to approach the king to appeal the decisions of these communal courts.[30]

The Anglo-Saxon king had a number of functions. He raised armies and a navy for the defense of the kingdom. He issued writs, which were administrative letters containing the royal seal.[31] The writs were used to order courts to convene, the sheriffs to do justice, and to award grants of land and privileges.[32] The king administered the country with the assistance of the royal household, an early form of king's council.[33] He also declared law (called dooms),[34] sometimes after consulting with the Witan, a national assembly of important nobles.[35]

When Edward the Confessor died childless in 1066, the candidates to succeed him were his brother-in-law Harold, the Earl of Wessex, and his cousin, William, Duke of Normandy (a French duchy). Harold was English and the most powerful baron in the country. William was French. Each claimed that

Edward had selected him as the next king. William also claimed that Harold had agreed to support William's claim to the throne.[36] Harold, however, was elected king by the Witan and was crowned. William's response was to assemble an army, cross the English Channel, and invade England.

The Norman Invasion

In 1066, Duke William of Normandy with 5,000 soldiers and 2,500 horses defeated the Anglo-Saxons and killed King Harold at the Battle of Hastings.[37] William became King of England and the Normans assumed control of the country. Although the Anglo-Saxons had implemented a type of feudalism before the invasion, the Normans developed and refined it. *Feudalism* was a military, political, and social structure that ordered relationships between people. Under feudalism, a series of duties and obligations existed between a lord and his vassals. In England, the Normans merged feudalism with the Anglo-Saxon institution of the national king. William insisted, for example, that all land in England belonged ultimately to the king, and in 1086 he required all landholders to swear allegiance to him.[38] In this way, all his barons and lords and their vassals were personally obligated to him by feudal law. At his coronation, King William decreed that Englishmen could keep the customary laws that had been in force during the reign of the Anglo-Saxon King Edward the Confessor. This meant that the communal, hundred, and shire courts could continue to resolve disputes between the English as they had in the past.[39] William did, however, make one significant change in the jurisdiction of the communal courts: he rejected the Anglo-Saxon practice of allowing church officials to use the communal courts to decide religious matters. Instead, he mandated that the church should establish its own courts and that religious matters should be decided according to canon (church) law, rather than customary law.[40] William also declared that the Normans would settle their disputes in the courts of the lords and barons in agreement with feudal law.

England at that time consisted of two societies, one French and the other English.[41] French was the language spoken by the victorious Normans, as well as by the king, the upper classes, the clergy, and scholars.[42] English was only spoken by the lower classes following the invasion, and it did not achieve prominence and become the language of the courts and the "common law" until 1362.[43] The French legacy can be seen in many words used by lawyers today. *Acquit, en banc, voir dire, demurrer, embezzle,* and *detainer* are some examples of "English" words that were borrowed from the French. Although the Normans spoke French, formal written documents were written in Latin. This may help to explain why students reading law in the twenty-first century encounter Latin words such as *certiorari, subpoena, mens rea, actus reus, in camera, mandamus, capias,* and *pro se.*

The Development of the Common Law

Over time, marriages between Norman and English families blurred the old class system. William's son Henry (who became Henry I), for example, married a descendant of the Anglo-Saxon royal house.[44] It was not until after 1453, when the French drove the English out of France (except for Calais), however, that the Normans and English were unified as one nation.

William died in 1100. The most important of his successors—in terms of the development of the common law—were Henry I and Henry's grandson, Henry II. After the death of the very unpopular William II, the nobles elected Henry I as king. Henry I had promised the nobles that if elected he would issue a charter in which he pledged to respect the rights of the nobles.[45] He also promised to be a fair ruler in the manner of William I. This charter is significant because it was a model for the most famous of all charters, *Magna Carta*.[46]

Henry I ruled during a prosperous period and strengthened the king's powers while making peace with the church and feudal barons. He also strengthened the judiciary by requiring members of his council, the *Curia Regis,* to ride circuit occasionally throughout the country listening to pleas and supervising the local courts. During this period, the communal courts, the religious courts, and the feudal courts of the barons were still meeting and there was much confusion over jurisdiction.[47] Henry I encouraged people who distrusted the local courts to turn to the king for justice.

Henry II was the king most involved in the development of the central judiciary and the common law.[48] He created a professional royal court to hear civil litigation between ordinary parties (common pleas) and staffed this court with barons who had learned how to judge from working as members of the *Curia Regis*.[49] The king had some of his judges sit with him at Westminster (in London), and others traveled throughout the country listening to pleas and supervising local courts.[50] These royal judges applied the same law in each of the jurisdictions in which they held court.[51] They did not treat each case as if it were a case of first impression, or apply the customary law of the particular region. Decisions were not based on abstract principles and theories. The royal judges decided disputes in a consistent manner throughout the country, based on slowly evolving legal rules adopted by the members of the court.[52]

There were important procedural incentives for bringing suit in the court of common pleas rather than in local courts. One was that the losing party in a communal or feudal court could have the decision reviewed by common pleas. Another was that the king enforced royal court judgments. Lastly, royal courts used juries instead of trials by battle and ordeal.[53]

One problem that was often brought to the king involved land disputes between neighboring nobles. One noble would claim part of his neighbor's land and seize it without bringing the matter to the attention of any court. Henry II's response was to allow victims to petition him for issuance of a *writ of right*. This writ was purchased from the king and directed the communal courts to do full justice without delay or to appear in a royal court and give an explanation.[54] The development of the writ of right resulted in a law making it illegal to dispossess someone of land without a trial conducted according to a royal writ.

The Normans became very creative in the way they used writs. Under the Norman kings, suitors had to obtain writs in order to litigate any claim. As the demand for writs increased, the responsibility for issuing them was transferred from the king to the chancellor,[55] and in later years to the courts themselves.

Each writ conferred jurisdiction on a designated court to resolve a particular dispute. It also specified many of the procedures to be followed since there was no general code of civil procedure to regulate the conduct of litigation.[56] A writ, for example, would often be addressed to the sheriff and would require him to summons in the defendant and convene a jury. In Henry I's era, there were very few writs. By Henry III's reign, many writs existed, including entry, debt, detinue, account, replevin, covenant, and novel disseisin (wrongful ejection).[57] A few master registers of writs were developed to form a primitive "law library."

By roughly 1200 the principal components of the common law system were in place. National law had replaced local and regional customs of the shire and hundred. A body of royal judges applied a common law throughout the nation, a tradition of respecting precedent was established, and the writ system was functioning.[58]

The development of legal literature was important to the development and improvement of the common law.[59] Henry Bracton, a thirteenth-century English lawyer, wrote commentaries on the writs of the day during the reign of Henry III (Henry II's grandson) and collected cases from the preceding twenty years.[60] During the fourteenth and fifteenth centuries, lawyers and law students began a series of "Year Books," a collection of the cases that had been heard in the most important courts for each year. The Year Books were discontinued in 1535 and were replaced by case reports, informal collections by various authors. Some of these authors, such as Chief Justice Edward Coke (pronounced "cook"), were well known and highly respected.[61] Coke published thirteen volumes of cases between 1572 and 1616. The reports established a process that in 1865 resulted in the publication of official law reports. In 1765, Sir William Blackstone, an Oxford professor, published a collection of his lectures in a book entitled *Commentaries on the Laws of England,* which was immensely popular in the American colonies. The first American judicial reports were published in 1789, and James Kent's influential *Commentaries on American Law* was published between 1826 and 1830.[62]

The common law came to what is now the United States as a result of Britain's colonization policies. In the early 1600s British monarchs began awarding charters to merchants and proprietors who would establish colonies along the Atlantic coast of North America. Over the next 150 years, a steady flow of immigrants, most of whom were British, crossed the Atlantic, bringing the English language, culture, law books, and the English legal tradition. The common law was one major component of that tradition; another was the court of equity.

The Origin of the English Equitable Court

Until the fourteenth century, the common law courts were willing to consider arguments based on conscience as well as law. The judges were concerned with equity (fairness and mercy), as well as legality. By the fifteenth century, however, the common law courts were sometimes less concerned with justice than with technicalities. Common law pleading was complex and jury tampering was common.[63] The courts often refused to allow parties to testify, and there were no procedures for discovering an opponent's evidence. Although the common law courts were able to act against land and would award money judgments, they refused to grant injunctive relief (court orders directing individuals to perform or refrain from engaging in certain acts).[64] Unusual situations arose for which there was no common law relief, or where the relief available was inadequate as a remedy. In addition, the law courts were often slow, and litigation was very costly. Increasingly, dissatisfied parties began to petition the king and his council to intervene in the name of justice. As the number of petitions rose, the king and council forwarded the petitions to the chancellor.[65]

The *chancellor*, originally a high-ranking member of the clergy, was part of the royal household. He was the king's leading advisor in political matters and was a professional administrator. The chancellor's staff included people with judicial experience who issued the writs that enabled suitors to litigate in the common law courts.[66] Because they were ecclesiastics, the early chancellors were not trained as common law lawyers. They were well educated,[67] however, and were familiar with the canon law of the Roman Catholic Church.[68] As a result, the chancellors were often more receptive to arguments based on morality than to arguments based exclusively on legality.

As chancellors began to hear petitions, the *court of chancery,* or equity court, came into being. It granted relief based on broad principles of right and justice in cases in which the restrictions of the common law prevented it. Chancellors began to use the *writ of subpoena* to speed up their hearings and the *writ of summons* to require people to appear in the chancery.[69] Chancery trials were conducted before a single judge who sat without a jury. The chancellor, who exercised discretion and did not rely on precedent in granting relief, would only act where extraordinary relief was required, because no writ applied to the wrong from which the petitioner sought relief. One such area was specific performance of contracts. Although a suit for what we would call breach of contract could be maintained in a common law court, that court could not require a contracting party to perform his bargain. The chancellor, however, could issue such an order directed to the nonperforming person and could enforce it with the contempt power.

The equity court became very popular and was very busy by the middle 1500s. For centuries, common law and equity were administered in England by these two separate courts. Each court applied its own system of jurisprudence and followed its own judicial rules and remedies. Much of traditional equity is based on concepts such as adequacy, practicality, clean hands, and hardship (matters we will discuss in Chapter 7). The equity court's workload continued to grow, as did the chancellor's staff. By the seventeenth century, the most important of the chancellor's staff clerks were called masters in chancery. The chief master was called the Master of the Rolls. Masters in chancery helped the chancellor conduct the equity court, particularly while the chancellor was performing nonjudicial duties for the king.

Initially, despite their differing aims, the common law courts and the equity court cooperated with each other. Starting with Henry VIII's reign, common law lawyers rather than ecclesiastics were named chancellor, which improved relations between law and equity.[70] Sir Thomas More, as chancellor, invited the common law judges to incorporate the notion of conscience into the common law, but the judges declined, preferring to stand behind the decisions of the juries. Gradually, however, this dual-court system created a competition for business, and the common law courts became more flexible by borrowing from equity. The equitable courts were also changing, and chancellors began to identify jurisdictional boundaries between the equitable and common law courts. Equity, for example, agreed to furnish a remedy only when the common law procedure was deficient or the remedy at common law was inadequate.[71]

Beginning in 1649, the decisions of the chancellors were sporadically collected and published, a process that led to the establishment of equitable precedent.[72] Eventually, equitable precedent made the equity courts as formalistic and rigid as the common law courts had been in equity's early days.[73] This dual-court system continued in England until the passage by Parliament of the Judicature Acts of 1873 and 1875, which merged the equitable and common law courts into a unified court.

The North American colonies along the Atlantic coast differed from British precedent when it came to the establishment of equity courts. Massachusetts never established an equity court, and its trial courts were not permitted to exercise the equitable powers of the chancellor until 1870. Maryland, New York, New Jersey, Delaware, North Carolina, and South Carolina established separate courts for common law and equity. However, by 1900 common law and equity had merged into a single judicial system in most states.

As you read the cases that follow, you will notice that plaintiffs often request legal and equitable relief in the same complaint. A plaintiff may demand money damages (common law relief), a declaratory judgment (equitable relief), and an injunction (equitable relief) in the complaint. This creates no problem for the courts. The legal issues will be tried by a jury (unless the parties prefer a bench trial) and the equitable issues will be decided by the judge sitting as a chancellor according to the rules of equity. In Chapter 6 we will look more closely at the differences between the common law and equitable remedies.

A PROCEDURAL PRIMER

The following highly simplified overview of litigation is intended to give you a sense of the big picture before we examine each stage of the process in more detail. Like a trial attorney's opening statement in a jury trial, it is intended to help you to see how the various procedural stages fit together. Obviously, this abbreviated treatment omits many of the details and is intentionally very limited in scope.

Every lawsuit is based on some event that causes a person to feel that he or she has been legally injured in some manner by another. The injured party will often contact an attorney to discuss the matter. The attorney will listen to the facts, make a determination about whether the client has a case, and present the client with a range of options for pursuing a claim. These options will often include informal attempts to settle the claim, alternative dispute resolution methods such as those discussed in Chapter 14, and filing suit in court. After weighing the costs and benefits of each option and listening to the advice of the attorney, the client will make a decision as to how to proceed. If the decision is made to file suit, the lawyer will draft a document called a *complaint* and a *writ of summons*, and serve them on the defendant in accordance with the law. The complaint will explain the plaintiff's claims and requested relief. The summons will inform the defendant to serve a document called an *answer* on the plaintiff's attorney by a statutorily determined date. If the defendant's attorney finds any legal defects in jurisdiction, venue, form, or substance in either the summons or the complaint, he or she can make motions seeking modification or dismissal of the action. Assuming that the motions are denied and any defects are corrected, the defendant will then draft and serve a timely answer to prevent the plaintiff from winning the case by default due to the defendant's inaction.

Once the complaint has been properly served and filed with the court, the *discovery* phase begins. This is where each party learns as much as possible about the case. Virtually all relevant information can be obtained from sources who are friendly, neutral, or adverse, such as the opposing party. Obviously, some information is not discoverable, such as an attorney's trial strategy, research notes (work product), and other material that is classified as privileged. Later in the chapter, we will learn specific techniques lawyers use during the discovery phase.

After the facts have been sufficiently investigated, one or both parties will frequently request the court to dispose of the case and award a *judgment* (the court's final decision in a case), rather than proceeding to trial. This request, called a *motion for summary judgment*, is properly granted when the plaintiff and defendant substantially agree about the important facts in the case. If there is no dispute about the significant facts, there is no reason to conduct a trial. In that situation, the judge can resolve any dispute about what legal rule applies to this particular set of facts and award a judgment to the deserving party.

It is important to note that informal discussions between the attorneys often take place at all stages of the process, up to and even during the course of the trial, in an effort to settle the case. These discussions usually intensify once motions for summary judgment have been denied and it appears that the case will be tried. Assuming that summary judgment is denied and there is no negotiated settlement, what usually follows is the pretrial conference.

At a *pretrial conference,* the court and the attorneys will meet to define the issues, prepare for the trial, and discuss the possibility of settlement. At this meeting the parties can indicate how many days they believe it will take to try the case, try to resolve evidentiary and discovery problems, and schedule any necessary pretrial hearings. After the meeting, a pretrial order will be signed by the judge which records the decisions that were made at the conference.

Before proceeding to trial, many jurisdictions will require or encourage the litigating parties to participate in *alternative dispute resolution* (ADR). The majority of state legislatures have approved some form of ADR, and over one-third of the federal courts participate to some degree.[74]

Alternative dispute resolution is an umbrella concept for a variety of procedures designed to help parties resolve their disputes without trials. Jurisdictions participate in ADR to differing degrees. Some mandate cooperation, and others make participation optional. In Chapter 14 we explain such ADR techniques as mediation, arbitration, summary jury trials, and mini-trials, but we emphasize that any party dissatisfied with the ADR process can insist on proceeding to trial. There is a continuing dispute as to whether ADR is living up to its proponents' claims and producing faster, less expensive, and higher-quality justice than litigation.[75]

Only 3 to 4 percent of all lawsuits filed actually are decided at trial. Non-jury trials, where a judge decides the factual issues (also known as *bench trials*), are conducted differently from trials in which juries render a verdict. In bench trials, for example, there are no jurors to select, the attorneys generally do not make opening statements, the rules of evidence are often relaxed, and there are no jury instructions to prepare and deliver. The judge will consider the evidence presented by each party and determine whether the plaintiff has satisfied the burden of proof. At the end of a bench trial, the judge will announce findings of fact, state conclusions of law, and award a judgment.

Additional procedures are necessary for jury trials. The jurors have to be carefully selected, and in major trials the lawyers may seek help from trial consultants. Because jurors generally know little about rules of evidence and the applicable law, the lawyers do not present their cases as they would in a bench trial. Judges must keep the lawyers in check and ensure that the jury is exposed only to evidence that is relevant, material, and competent (legally adequate). After each side has had the opportunity to present evidence and cross-examine opposing witnesses, the attorneys will conclude by arguing their case to the jury. After the closing arguments, the judge instructs the jury on the law and sends it out to deliberate. The jury deliberates until it reaches a verdict, which it reports to the court. After deciding any postverdict motions, the court will enter a judgment in favor of one of the parties and award relief accordingly. Normally, any party dissatisfied with the judgment will have a specified number of days after the entry of judgment in which to make an appeal, provided timely objections were made during the trial.

READING CASES

The application of law to factual situations is necessary when there is a controversy between two or more people or when parties seek guidance concerning the consequences of their conduct or proposed conduct. The court cases in this text involve disputes that the parties were unable to resolve by themselves and that were brought to the trial and appellate courts for a decision. Most disputes, however, are settled by the parties outside court based on professional predictions of what a court would do.

Students learn to understand the legal process and the relationship between judicial theories and practical legal problems by analyzing actual court cases.

The cases in this text illustrate particular points of law. They also convey current legal theory. These cases should serve as points of departure for discussions about the legal response to current social problems. It is important to understand the strengths and weaknesses of law as an instrument of social change.

Case reports are official explanations of a court's decision-making process. They explain which legal principles are applicable and why they are controlling under the particular circumstances of each case. Thus, in analyzing each case decision, students should focus attention on the underlying factual situation, the law that the court applied, whether the decision was just, and the future impact of the decision when it is used as precedent.

The first case concerns private law and shows how law affects business morality. Note how the court has to balance competing social values in reaching its decision. Commercial morality has become a vital interest of society because of the size and power of modern business organizations.

One last tip is in order before reading the first case. Students in their first law course should expect to use the glossary or a legal dictionary frequently. Law has its own language, and understanding legal jargon is essential to understanding the cases.

E. I. Du Pont de Nemours & Co., Inc. v. Christopher

431 F.2d 1012
U.S. Court of Appeals, Fifth Circuit
August 25, 1970

Goldberg, Circuit Judge

This is a case of industrial espionage in which an airplane is the cloak and a camera the dagger. The defendants-appellants, Rolfe and Gary Christopher, are photographers in Beaumont, Texas. The Christophers were hired by an unknown third party to take aerial photographs of new construction at the Beaumont plant of E. I. Du Pont de Nemours & Company, Inc. Sixteen photographs of the Du Pont facility were taken from the air on March 19, 1969, and these photographs were later developed and delivered to the third party.

Du Pont employees apparently noticed the airplane on March 19 and immediately began an investigation to determine why the craft was circling over the plant. By that afternoon the investigation had disclosed that the craft was involved in a photographic expedition and that the Christophers were the photographers. Du Pont contacted the Christophers that same afternoon and asked them to reveal the name of the person or corporation requesting the photographs. The Christophers refused to disclose this information, giving as their reason the client's desire to remain anonymous.

Having reached a dead end in the investigation, Du Pont subsequently filed suit against the Christophers, alleging that the Christophers had wrongfully obtained photographs revealing Du Pont's trade secrets which they then sold to the undisclosed third party. Du Pont contended that it had developed a highly secret but unpatented process for producing methanol, a process that gave Du Pont a competitive advantage over other producers. This process, Du Pont alleged, was a trade secret developed after much expensive and time-consuming research, and a secret that the company had taken special precautions to safeguard. The area photographed by the Christophers was the plant designed to produce methanol by this secret process, and because the plant was still under construction parts of the process were exposed to view from directly above the construction area. Photographs of that area, Du Pont alleged, would enable a skilled person to deduce the secret process for making methanol. Du Pont thus contended that the Christophers had wrongfully appropriated Du Pont trade secrets by taking the photographs and delivering them to the undisclosed third party. In its suit Du Pont asked for damages to cover the loss it had already sustained as a result of the wrongful disclosure of the trade secret and sought temporary and permanent injunctions prohibiting any further circulation of the photographs already taken and prohibiting any additional photographing of the methanol plant.

The Christophers answered with . . . [a motion] to dismiss for lack of jurisdiction and failure to state a claim upon which relief could be granted. Depositions were taken during which the Christophers again refused to disclose the name of the person to whom they had delivered the photographs. Du Pont then filed a motion to compel an answer to this question and all related questions.

On June 5, 1969, the trial court held a hearing on the pending motions . . . [and] granted Du Pont's motion to compel the Christophers to divulge the name of their client. . . . Agreeing with the trial court's determination that Du Pont had stated a valid claim, we affirm the decision of that court.

This is a case of first impression, for the Texas courts have not faced this precise factual issue, and sitting as a diversity court we must sensitize our *Erie* antennae to decide what the Texas courts would do if such a situation were presented to them. The only question involved in this interlocutory appeal is whether Du Pont has asserted a claim upon which relief can be granted. The Christophers argued both at trial and before this court that they committed no "actionable

wrong" in photographing the Du Pont facility and passing these photographs on to their client because they conducted all of their activities in public airspace, violated no government aviation standard, did not breach any confidential relation, and did not engage in any fraudulent or illegal conduct. In short, the Christophers argue that for an appropriation of trade secrets to be wrong there must be a trespass, other illegal conduct, or breach of a confidential relationship. We disagree.

It is true, as the Christophers assert, that the previous trade secret cases have contained one or more of these elements. However, we do not think that the Texas courts would limit the trade secret protection exclusively to these elements. On the contrary, in *Hyde Corporation v. Huffines*, 1958, 314 S.W.2d 763, the Texas Supreme Court specifically adopted the rule found in the Restatements of Torts which provides:

> "One who discloses or uses another's trade secret, without a privilege to do so, is liable to the other if
> "a. he discovered the secret by improper means, or
> "b. his disclosure or use constitutes a breach of confidence reposed in him by the other in disclosing the secret to him." . . .

Thus, although the previous cases have dealt with a breach of a confidential relationship, a trespass, or other illegal conduct, the rule is much broader than the cases heretofore encountered. Not limiting itself to specific wrongs, Texas adopted subsection (a) of the Restatement which recognizes a cause of action for the discovery of a trade secret by any "improper" means. . . .

The question remaining, therefore, is whether aerial photography of plant construction is an improper means of obtaining another's trade secret. We conclude that it is and that the Texas courts would so hold. The Supreme Court of that state had declared that "the undoubted tendency of the law has been to recognize and enforce higher standards of commercial morality in the business world." *Hyde Corporation v. Huffines*, at 773. That court has quoted with approval articles indicating that the *proper* means of gaining possession of a competitor's secret process is "through inspection and analysis" of the product in order to create a duplicate. Later another Texas court explained:

> "The means by which the discovery is made may be obvious, and the experimentation leading from known factors to presently unknown results may be simple and lying in the public domain. But these facts do not destroy the value of the discovery and will not advantage a competitor who by unfair means obtains the knowledge *without paying the price expended by the discoverer.*" (*Brown v. Fowler*, 316 S.W.2nd 111.)

We think, therefore, that the Texas rule is clear. One may use his competitor's secret process if he discovers the process by reverse engineering applied to the finished product; one may use a competitor's process if he discovers it by his own independent research; but one may not avoid these labors by taking the process from the discoverer without his permission at a time when he is taking reasonable precautions to maintain its secrecy. To obtain knowledge of a process without spending the time and money to discover it independently is *improper* unless the holder voluntarily discloses it or fails to take reasonable precautions to ensure its secrecy.

In the instant case the Christophers deliberately flew over the Du Pont plant to get pictures of a process which Du Pont had attempted to keep secret. The Christophers delivered their pictures to a third party who was certainly aware of the means by which they had been acquired and who may be planning to use the information contained therein to manufacture methanol by the Du Pont process. The third party has a right to use this process only if he obtains this knowledge through his own research efforts;

but thus far all information indicates that the third party has gained this knowledge solely by taking it from Du Pont at a time when Du Pont was making reasonable efforts to preserve its secrecy. In such a situation Du Pont has a valid cause of action to prohibit the Christophers from improperly discovering its trade secret and to prohibit the undisclosed third party from using the improperly obtained information.

We note that this view is in perfect accord with the position taken by the authors of the Restatement. In commenting on improper means of discovery, the savants of the Restatement said:

> "f. *Improper Means of Discovery.* The discovery of another's trade secret by improper means subjects the actor to liability independently of the harm to the interest in the secret. Thus, if one uses physical force to take a secret formula from another's pocket, or breaks into another's office to steal the formula, his conduct is wrongful and subjects him to liability apart from the rule stated in this Section. Such conduct is also an improper means of procuring the secret under this rule. But means may be improper under this rule even though they do not cause any other harm than that to the interest in the trade secret. Examples of such are fraudulent misrepresentations to induce disclosure, tapping of telephone wires, eavesdropping or other espionage. A complete catalogue of improper means is not possible. In general they are means which fall below the general accepted standards of commercial morality and reasonable conduct."

In taking this position, we realize that industrial espionage of the sort here perpetrated has become a popular sport in some segments of our industrial community. However, our devotion to freewheeling industrial competition must not force us into accepting the law of the jungle as the standard of morality expected in our commercial relations. Our tolerance of the espionage game must cease when the protections required to prevent another's spying cost so much that the spirit of inventiveness is dampened. Commercial privacy must be protected from espionage that could not have been reasonably anticipated or prevented. We do not mean to imply, however, that everything not in plain view is within the protected vale, nor that all information obtained through every extra optical extension is forbidden. Indeed, for our industrial competition to remain healthy there must be breathing room for observing a competing industrialist. A competitor can and must shop his competition for pricing and examine his products for quality, components, and methods of manufacture. Perhaps ordinary fences and roofs must be built to shut out incursive eyes; but we need not require the discoverer of a trade secret to guard against the unanticipated, the undetectable, or the unpreventable methods of espionage now available.

In the instant case Du Pont was in the midst of constructing a plant. Although after construction the finished plant would have protected much of the process from view, during the period of construction the trade secret was exposed to view from the air. To require Du Pont to put a roof over the unfinished plant to guard its secret would impose an enormous expense to prevent nothing more than a schoolboy's trick. We introduce here no new or radical ethic, since our ethos has never given moral sanction to piracy. The marketplace must not deviate far from our mores. We should not require a person or corporation to take unreasonable precautions to prevent another from doing that which he ought not to do in the first place. Reasonable precautions against predatory eyes we may require; but an impenetrable fortress is an unreasonable requirement, and we are not disposed to burden industrial inventors with such a duty in order to protect the fruits of their efforts. "Improper" will always be a word of many nuances, determined by time, place, and circumstances. We therefore need not proclaim a catalogue of commercial improprieties. Clearly, however, one of its commandments does say, "Thou shalt not appropriate a trade secret through deviousness under circumstances in which countervailing defenses are not reasonably available."

Having concluded that aerial photography, from whatever altitude, is an improper method of discovering the trade secrets exposed during construction of the Du Pont plant, we need not worry about whether the flight pattern chosen by the Christophers violated any federal aviation regulations. Regardless of whether the flight was legal or illegal in that sense, the espionage was an improper means of discovering Du Pont's trade secret.

The decision of the trial courts is affirmed and the case remanded to that court for proceedings on the merits.

Case Questions

1. The court in *Hyde Corporation v. Huffines*, cited in the *Du Pont* opinion, stated that the law has tended to "recognize and enforce higher standards of commercial morality." Should the law perform that function?

2. Which philosophies of law does the court appear to rely upon in determining the outcome of this case? Which does it reject?

3. Most disputes are settled outside of court by the parties to the dispute based on a prediction of what the court would do if the case went before it. Would a lawyer be able to predict the result of the *Du Pont* case with a high degree of certainty?

4. Explain the extent to which the objectives of law were addressed in the *Du Pont* case.

 What were the competing social values presented in this case?
Do you agree with the way the appellate court balanced these values?

CASE ANALYSIS

Since the *Du Pont* case is the first reported judicial decision of this book, a brief analysis of it is appropriate. The heading consists of four items. The first line contains the names of the parties to the suit. E. I. Du Pont de Nemours & Company, Inc., the party that brought the suit, is the *plaintiff*. Rolfe and Gary Christopher are the *defendants*. When there is more than one plaintiff or defendant, it is appropriate to include only one name. This is why the heading reads "Christopher" rather than "Christophers." The Christophers are the *appellants*, the parties who appealed to a higher court from the decision of a lower court. The other party to an appeal is called the *appellee*.

The next item in the heading describes the volume and page where the case can be found. The *Du Pont* case is reported in volume 431 of the second series of the *Federal Reporter*, on page 1012. The name of the court that decided the dispute is next in the heading, followed by the date the decision was reached. The first item in the body of the court opinion is the name of the judge who wrote the court opinion. Usually only one judge is selected to write the majority opinion, even though several judges may have participated in reaching the decision.

In the suit, Du Pont asked for *damages* (money to cover the loss sustained as a result of the defendant's action) and for an *injunction* (an order by the court prohibiting the action of the defendants). What the plaintiff really wanted was to know for whom the defendants were taking the pictures. The defendants asked that the court dismiss the complaint against them for the plaintiff's failure to state a claim, meaning that there was no legal basis for granting relief. The court denied the motion. Since the case was on *appeal*, a judicial review of a decision rendered by a lower court, the appellate court could have affirmed, remanded, reversed, or dismissed the appeal. The court rejected the motion to dismiss and chose to affirm and remand the case. By *affirming*, the appellate court rules that the lower court's decision is valid and reasserts the judgment. To render a judgment of *reversal* is to vacate and set aside the lower court's judgment. Note that reversals can be in part. When a case is *remanded*, it is returned to the lower court, generally with instructions, so that further proceedings may be taken.

The *issue* that the court had to decide in this case was whether aerial photography of plant construction is an improper means of obtaining another's trade secret. This was a case of *first impression*, meaning that no decision in Texas had been reached on the point at issue. The federal court tried to determine the law

for the state of Texas. The court searched for factual situations in previously decided Texas cases comparable to the factual situation of the case before it. The
court extracted from the previously decided comparable cases the principle on
which those cases were decided and applied those principles of law to the case
at hand.

In order to reap the benefits of the case study method, one must read each
case accurately and pay close attention to detail. After reading a case, one
should have not merely a general sense or the gist of what the case says, but a
precise understanding of what the court did. Careful attention should be given
to the *holding* of the case—what the court decided on the facts of the case.

Opinions are often discursive. Judges often discuss issues they need not decide. Their statements on these issues are labeled *dicta*. Although these statements
may be important, they lack the authority of the case's holding.

Most students find it helpful to *brief* a case. After careful reading and analysis of a case, one should be able to write a brief without referring to the case
again. Briefing with the case aside provides a check on understanding as well
as an incentive to careful reading. A brief should contain the parts of the case
selected as important, organized for the purpose at hand rather than in the haphazard order in which they may be reported.

The following brief of the *Du Pont* case illustrates one way of briefing. The
elements in the example are usually found in most briefs, though writing style
is often a matter of individual preference. It is usually desirable to keep copying
from the text of the case to a minimum; briefs are not exercises in stenography.
This brief was written to help students who have not previously read a case report. It is intended to help these students understand what is important in the
material they have read.

Sample Brief

E. I. Du Pont de Nemours & Co., Inc. v. Christopher
431 F.2d 1012 (1970)

Facts:

Du Pont had developed a highly secret but as-yet-unpatented process for producing methanol that would give it a competitive advantage in the methanol-
producing market. Du Pont had taken special precautions to safeguard
disclosure of this secret process, which was developed after much expensive
and time-consuming research. Du Pont had also designed a plant, which was
under construction, where the methanol would be produced by the secret
process. Because the plant was still under construction, part of the process was
exposed to view from above the construction area. A skilled person would have
been able to determine the nature of the trade secret from aerial photographs of
the construction area.

Rolfe and Gary Christopher were photographers who were hired by an
undisclosed third party to take aerial photographs of the Du Pont plant. The
Christophers took photographs from the air, developed them, and delivered
them to the third party.

Issues Presented or Questions of Law:

Did Du Pont state a claim upon which relief could be granted under Texas law?

Was the taking of aerial photographs of the Du Pont plant an improper method of discovering a trade secret?

Holding/Rule of Law:

The taking of aerial photographs to obtain knowledge of a trade secret without spending the time and money to discover it independently is improper.

Rationale:

(A) Texas courts have never previously decided this issue. Previous Texas cases on trade secrets have only addressed situations in which parties have trespassed on another's property to obtain a trade secret, or have performed some illegal conduct, or have violated a confidential relationship. These three conditions should not be viewed, however, as an exhaustive listing of improper methods of obtaining trade secrets.

(B) The rule that provides that a party is liable for trade secrets discovered by improper means was adopted in *Hyde v. Huffines.*

(C) "Proper means" involves paying the price for the information by either spending time and money or obtaining permission from the discoverer. The only exceptions to this rule are when the discoverer gives the information voluntarily or fails to take reasonable precautions to prevent its disclosure.

(D) Although our society encourages competition in industry, this must be weighed against the standards of morality and ethics expected in commercial relations. Industrial espionage tactics must stop when the cost of guarding against them is so high as to prevent or deter inventiveness. Simply because an espionage tactic could not have been reasonably anticipated or prevented does not mean that it should be tolerated or that the party victimized should bear the cost.

(E) Requiring Du Pont to put a roof over the unfinished plant would be unreasonable.

CONSTITUTIONAL POLICYMAKING

The second case illustrates the difficult policymaking role of the judiciary in a case involving public law. This case involves the balancing of interests: those of the state in protecting life and the constitutionally protected "liberty" rights of the individual (whether presently competent or incompetent) to refuse death-prolonging procedures.

Here, the devoted parents of an incompetent person in a persistent vegetative state sought to stop her life-support systems. They sought and obtained judicial authorization at the trial court level for termination. The Missouri Supreme Court reversed the decision of the trial court. It interpreted state law as requiring in substituted judgment cases that the parents of an incompetent clearly and convincingly prove that the incompetent would have wanted the life-support systems withdrawn under such circumstances. The United States Supreme Court was asked to decide whether Missouri's requirement of clear and convincing evidence of the incompetent's wishes violated the U.S. Constitution. The Supreme Court also had to decide whether the U.S. Constitution requires states, in cases such as this, to accept the substituted judgment of close family members.

Cruzan v. Director, Missouri Dept. of Health
110 S.Ct. 2841
U.S. Supreme Court
June 25, 1990

Chief Justice Rehnquist delivered the opinion of the Court.

Petitioner Nancy Beth Cruzan was rendered incompetent as a result of severe injuries sustained during an automobile accident. Co-petitioners Lester and Joyce Cruzan, Nancy's parents and co-guardians, sought a court order directing the withdrawal of their daughter's artificial feeding and hydration equipment after it became apparent that she had virtually no chance of recovering her cognitive faculties. The Supreme Court of Missouri held that because there was no clear and convincing evidence of Nancy's desire to have life-sustaining treatment withdrawn under such circumstances, her parents lacked authority to effectuate such a request. We granted certiorari, . . . and now affirm.

On the night of January 11, 1983, Nancy Cruzan lost control of her car as she traveled down Elm Road in Jasper County, Missouri. The vehicle overturned, and Cruzan was discovered lying face down in a ditch without detectable respiratory or cardiac function. Paramedics were able to restore her breathing and heartbeat at the accident site, and she was transported to a hospital in an unconscious state. An attending neurosurgeon diagnosed her as having sustained probable cerebral

contusions compounded by significant anoxia (lack of oxygen). The Missouri trial court in this case found that permanent brain damage generally results after 6 minutes in an anoxic state; it was estimated that Cruzan was deprived of oxygen from 12 to 14 minutes. She remained in a coma for approximately three weeks and then progressed to an unconscious state in which she was able to orally ingest some nutrition. In order to ease feeding and further the recovery, surgeons implanted a gastrostomy feeding and hydration tube in Cruzan with the consent of her then husband. Subsequent rehabilitative efforts proved unavailing. She now lies in a Missouri state hospital in what is commonly referred to as a persistent vegetative state: generally, a condition in which a person exhibits motor reflexes but evinces no indications of significant cognitive function. The State of Missouri is bearing the cost of her care.

After it had become apparent that Nancy Cruzan had virtually no chance of regaining her mental faculties her parents asked hospital employees to terminate the artificial nutrition and hydration procedures. All agree that such a removal would cause her death. The employees refused to honor the request without court approval. The parents then sought and received authorization from the state trial court for termination. The court found that a person in Nancy's condition had a fundamental right under the State and Federal Constitutions to refuse or direct the withdrawal of "death prolonging procedures." The court also found that Nancy's "expressed thoughts at age twenty-five in somewhat se-rious conversation with a housemate friend that if sick or injured she would not wish to continue her life unless she could live at least halfway normally suggests that given her present condition she would not wish to con-tinue on with her nutrition and hydration."

The Supreme Court of Missouri reversed by a divided vote. . . .

We granted certiorari to consider the ques-tion of whether Cruzan has a right under the United States Constitution which would re-quire the hospital to withdraw life-sustaining treatment from her under these circumstances.

At common law, even the touching of one person by another without consent and without legal justification was a battery. . . .

This notion of bodily integrity has been embodied in the requirement that informed consent is generally required for medical treat-ment. Justice Cardozo, while on the Court of Appeals of New York, aptly described this doctrine: "Every human being of adult years and sound mind has a right to determine what shall be done with his own body; and a sur-geon who performs an operation without his patient's consent commits an assault, for which he is liable in damages." . . .

The logical corollary of the doctrine of in-formed consent is that the patient generally possesses the right not to consent, that is, to refuse treatment. Until about 15 years ago and the seminal decision in *In re Quinlan*, . . . the number of right-to-refuse-treatment decisions were relatively few. . . . More recently, how-ever, with the advance of medical technology capable of sustaining life well past the point where natural forces would have brought cer-tain death in earlier times, cases involving the right to refuse life-sustaining treatment have burgeoned. . . .

In the *Quinlan* case, young Karen Quinlan suffered severe brain damage as the result of anoxia, and entered a persistent vegetative state. Karen's father sought judicial approval to disconnect his daughter's respirator. The New Jersey Supreme Court granted the relief,

holding that Karen had a right of privacy grounded in the Federal Constitution to ter-minate treatment. . . . The court . . . concluded that the "only practical way" to prevent the loss of Karen's privacy right due to her in-competence was to allow her guardian and family to decide "whether she would exercise it in these circumstances."

After *Quinlan*, however, most courts have based a right to refuse treatment either solely on the common law right to informed con-sent or on both the common law right and a constitutional privacy right. . . .

As these cases demonstrate, the common law doctrine of informed consent is viewed as generally encompassing the right of a compe-tent individual to refuse medical treatment. Beyond that, these decisions demonstrate both similarity and diversity in their approach to a decision of what all agree is a perplexing question with unusually strong moral and ethical overtones. State courts have available to them for decision a number of sources—state constitutions, statutes, and common law—which are not available to us. In this Court, the question is simply and starkly whether the United States Constitution pro-hibits Missouri from choosing the rule of de-cision which it did. This is the first case in which we have been squarely presented with the issue of whether the United States Con-stitution grants what is in common parlance referred to as a "right to die." . . .

The Fourteenth Amendment provides that no State shall "deprive any person of life, liberty, or property, without due process of law." The principle that a competent person has a constitutionally protected liberty inter-est in refusing unwanted medical treatment may be inferred from our prior decisions. . . .

But determining that a person has a "lib-erty interest" under the Due Process Clause does not end the inquiry; "whether respon-dent's constitutional rights have been vio-lated must be determined by balancing his liberty interests against the relevant state interests." . . .

Petitioners insist that under the general holdings of our cases, the forced administration of life-sustaining medical treatment, and even of artificially-delivered food and water essential to life, would implicate a competent person's liberty interest. . . .

Petitioners go on to assert that an incompetent person should possess the same right in this respect as is possessed by a competent person. . . .

The difficulty with petitioners' claim is that in a sense it begs the question: an incompetent person is not able to make an informed and voluntary choice to exercise a hypothetical right to refuse treatment or any other right. Such a "right" must be exercised for her, if at all, by some sort of surrogate. Here, Missouri has in effect recognized that under certain circumstances a surrogate may act for the patient in electing to have hydration and nutrition withdrawn in such a way as to cause death, but it has established a procedural safeguard to assure that the action of the surrogate conforms as best it may to the wishes expressed by the patient while competent. Missouri requires that evidence of the incompetent's wishes as to the withdrawal of treatment be proved by clear and convincing evidence. The question, then, is whether the United States Constitution forbids the establishment of this procedural requirement by the State. We hold that it does not.

Whether or not Missouri's clear and convincing evidence requirement comports with the United States Constitution depends in part on what interests the State may properly seek to protect in this situation. Missouri relies on its interest in the protection and preservation of human life, and there can be no gainsaying this interest. As a general matter, the States—indeed, all civilized nations—demonstrate their commitment to life by treating homicide as [a] serious crime. Moreover, the majority of States in this country have laws imposing criminal penalties on one who assists another to commit suicide. We do not think a State is required to remain neutral in the face of an informed and voluntary decision by a physically-able adult to starve to death.

But in the context presented here, a State has more particular interests at stake. The choice between life and death is a deeply personal decision of obvious and overwhelming finality. We believe Missouri may legitimately seek to safeguard the personal element of this choice through the imposition of heightened evidentiary requirements. It cannot be disputed that the Due Process Clause protects an interest in life as well as an interest in refusing life-sustaining medical treatment. Not all incompetent patients will have loved ones available to serve as surrogate decisionmakers. . . .

A State is entitled to guard against potential abuses in such situations. Similarly, a State is entitled to consider that a judicial proceeding to make a determination regarding an incompetent's wishes may very well not be an adversarial one, with the added guarantee of accurate factfinding that the adversary process brings with it. Finally, we think a State may properly decline to make judgments about the "quality" of life that a particular individual may enjoy, and simply assert an unqualified interest in the preservation of human life to be weighed against the constitutionally protected interests of the individual.

In our view, Missouri has permissibly sought to advance these interests through the adoption of a "clear and convincing" standard of proof to govern such proceedings. . . .

We believe that Missouri may permissibly place an increased risk of an erroneous decision on those seeking to terminate an incompetent individual's life-sustaining treatment. An erroneous decision not to terminate results in a maintenance of the status quo; the possibility of subsequent developments such as advancements in medical science, the discovery of new evidence regarding the patient's intent, changes in the law, or simply the unexpected death of the patient despite the administration of life-sustaining treatment, at least create the potential that a wrong decision will eventually be corrected or its impact mitigated. An erroneous decision to withdraw life-sustaining treatment, however, is not susceptible of correction. . . .

In sum, we conclude that a State may apply a clear and convincing evidence standard in proceedings where a guardian seeks to discontinue nutrition and hydration of a person diagnosed to be in a persistent vegetative state. . . .

The Supreme Court of Missouri held that in this case the testimony adduced at trial did not amount to clear and convincing proof of the patient's desire to have hydration and nutrition withdrawn. In so doing, it reversed a decision of the Missouri trial court which had found that the evidence "suggest[ed]" Nancy Cruzan would not have desired to continue such measures, but which had not adopted the standard of "clear and convincing evidence" enunciated by the Supreme Court. The testimony adduced at trial consisted primarily of Nancy Cruzan's statements made to a housemate about a year before her accident that she would not want to live should she face life as a "vegetable," and other observations to the same effect. The observations did not deal in terms with withdrawal of medical treatment or of hydration and nutrition. We cannot say that the Supreme Court of Missouri committed constitutional error in reaching the conclusion that it did.

Petitioners alternatively contend that Missouri must accept the "substituted judgment" of close family members even in the absence of substantial proof that their views reflect the views of the patient. . . .

No doubt is engendered by anything in this record but that Nancy Cruzan's mother and father are loving and caring parents. If the State were required by the United States Constitution to repose a right of "substituted judgment" with anyone, the Cruzans would surely qualify. But we do not think the Due

Process Clause requires the State to repose judgment on these matters with anyone but the patient herself. Close family members may have a strong feeling—a feeling not at all ignoble or unworthy, but not entirely disinterested, either—that they do not wish to witness the continuation of the life of a loved one which they regard as hopeless, meaningless, and even degrading. But there is no automatic assurance that the view of close family members will necessarily be the same as the patient's would have been had she been confronted with the prospect of her situation while competent. All of the reasons previously discussed for allowing Missouri to require clear and convincing evidence of the patient's wishes lead us to conclude that the State may choose to defer only to those wishes, rather than confide the decision to close family members.

The judgment of the Supreme Court of Missouri is Affirmed.

Justice Brennan, with whom Justice Marshall and Justice Blackmun join, dissenting

> "Medical technology has effectively created a twilight zone of suspended animation where death commences while life, in some form, continues. Some patients, however, want no part of a life sustained only by medical technology. Instead they prefer a plan of medical treatment that allows nature to take its course and permits them to die with dignity."

Nancy Cruzan has dwelt in that twilight zone for six years. She is oblivious to her surroundings and will remain so. . . . Her body twitches only reflexively, without consciousness. The areas of her brain that once thought, felt, and experienced sensations have degenerated badly and are continuing to do so. The cavities remaining are filling with cerebrospinal fluid. The "cerebral cortical atrophy is irreversible, permanent, progressive and ongoing." . . . "Nancy will never interact meaningfully with her environment again. She will remain in a persistent vegetative state until her death." Because she cannot swallow, her nutrition and hydration are delivered through a tube surgically implanted in her stomach.

A grown woman at the time of the accident, Nancy had previously expressed her wish to forgo continuing medical care under circumstances such as these. Her family and her friends are convinced that this is what she would want. A guardian ad litem appointed by the trial court is also convinced that this is what Nancy would want. Yet the Missouri Supreme Court, alone among state courts deciding such a question, has determined that an irreversibly vegetative patient will remain a passive prisoner of medical technology— for Nancy, perhaps for the next 30 years.

Today the Court, while tentatively accepting that there is some degree of constitutionally protected liberty interest in avoiding unwanted medical treatment, including life-sustaining medical treatment such as artificial nutrition and hydration, affirms the decision of the Missouri Supreme Court. The majority opinion, as I read it, would affirm that decision on the ground that a State may require "clear and convincing" evidence of Nancy Cruzan's prior decision to forgo life-sustaining treatment under circumstances such as hers in order to ensure that her actual wishes are honored. Because I believe that Nancy Cruzan has a fundamental right to be free of unwanted artificial nutrition and hydration, which right is not outweighed by any interests of the State, and because I find that the improperly biased procedural obstacles imposed by the Missouri Supreme Court impermissibly burden that right, I respectfully dissent. Nancy Cruzan is entitled to choose to die with dignity. . . .

II A

The right to be free from unwanted medical attention is a right to evaluate the potential benefit of treatment and its possible consequences according to one's own values and to make a personal decision whether to subject oneself to the intrusion. For a patient like Nancy Cruzan, the sole benefit of medical treatment is being kept metabolically alive. Neither artificial nutrition nor any other form of medical treatment available today can cure or in any way ameliorate her condition. Irreversibly vegetative patients are devoid of thought, emotion and sensation; they are permanently and completely unconscious. . . .

There are also affirmative reasons why someone like Nancy might choose to forgo artificial nutrition and hydration under these circumstances. Dying is personal. And it is profound. For many, the thought of an ignoble end, steeped in decay, is abhorrent. A quiet, proud death, bodily integrity intact, is a matter of extreme consequence. . . .

Such conditions are, for many, humiliating to contemplate, as is visiting a prolonged and anguished vigil on one's parents, spouse, and children. A long, drawn-out death can have a debilitating effect on family members. For some, the idea of being remembered in their persistent vegetative states rather than as they were before their illness or accident may be very disturbing. . . .

B

Although the right to be free of unwanted medical intervention, like other constitutionally protected interests, may not be absolute, no State interest could outweigh the rights of an individual in Nancy Cruzan's position. Whatever a State's possible interests in mandating life-support treatment under other circumstances, there is no good to be obtained here by Missouri's insistence that Nancy Cruzan remain on life-support systems if it is indeed her wish not to do so. Missouri does not claim, nor could it, that society as a whole will be benefited by Nancy's receiving medical treatment. No third party's situation will be improved and no harm to others will be averted. . . .

III D

A State's inability to discern an incompetent patient's choice still need not mean that a State is rendered powerless to protect that choice. But I would find that the Due Process Clause prohibits a State from doing more than that. A State may ensure that the person who makes the decision on the patient's behalf is the one whom the patient himself would have selected to make that choice for him. And a State may exclude from consideration anyone having improper motives. But a State generally must either repose the choice with the person whom the patient himself would most likely have chosen as proxy or leave the decision to the patient's family.

IV

As many as 10,000 patients are being maintained in persistent vegetative states in the United States, and the number is expected to increase significantly in the near future. Medical technology, developed over the past 20 or so years, is often capable of resuscitating people after they have stopped breathing or their hearts have stopped beating. Some of those people are brought fully back to life. Two decades ago, those who were not and could not swallow and digest food, died. Intravenous solutions could not provide sufficient calories to maintain people for more than a short time. Today, various forms of artificial feeding have been developed that are able to keep people metabolically alive for years, even decades. . . .

The 80% of Americans who die in hospitals are "likely to meet their end . . . 'in a sedated or comatose state; betubed nasally, abdominally and intravenously; and far more like manipulated objects than like moral subjects.'" A fifth of all adults surviving to age 80

will suffer a progressive dementing disorder prior to death. . . .

The new medical technology can reclaim those who would have been irretrievably lost a few decades ago and restore them to active lives. For Nancy Cruzan, it failed, and for others with wasting incurable disease it may be doomed to failure. In these unfortunate situations, the bodies and preferences and memories of the victims do not escheat to the State; nor does our Constitution permit the State or any other government to commandeer them. . . . Yet Missouri and this Court have displaced Nancy's own assessment of the processes associated with dying. They have discarded evidence of her will, ignored her values, and deprived her of the right to a decision as closely approximating her own choice as humanly possible. They have done so disingenuously in her name, and openly in Missouri's own. That Missouri and this Court may truly be motivated only by concern for incompetent patients makes no matter. As one of our most prominent jurists warned us decades ago: "Experience should teach us to be most on our guard to protect liberty when the government's purposes are beneficent. . . . The greatest dangers to liberty lurk in insidious encroachment by men of zeal, well meaning but without understanding." *Olmstead v. United States*, 277 U.S. 438, 479 (1928) (Brandeis, J., dissenting).

I respectfully dissent.*

---

*Editor's Note: Following the U.S. Supreme Court's decision in the *Cruzan* case, her parents asked the County Probate Court Judge for a second hearing. They claimed to have new evidence that would prove that Nancy would not have wanted to live in a vegetative state. The hearing was held on November 1, 1990. At that time, three of Nancy's former coworkers testified as did her doctor. The state of Missouri did not participate in this hearing, having established the legal standard before the U.S. Supreme Court. On December 14, 1990, the judge ruled that clear and convincing evidence of Nancy's intentions had been shown and that the feeding tube could be removed. Nancy Cruzan died on December 26, 1990.

Case Questions

1. Why do you think that the state of Missouri opposed the parents' efforts to disconnect the life-support systems?
2. Does the U.S. Supreme Court majority believe that an incompetent person possesses the same rights as a competent person to refuse food and water?
3. What might competent persons do who wish to avoid the problems encountered by the Cruzans?
4. Why do justices Brennan, Marshall, and Blackmun dissent?
5. Was justice done in this case?

DUE PROCESS

The due process clauses of the Fifth and Fourteenth Amendments to the U.S. Constitution provide that no person shall be "deprived of life, liberty or property without due process of law." These clauses are deeply embedded in Anglo-American legal history, going back to 1215. In June of that year, English barons decided that King John had been acting arbitrarily and in violation of their rights. They sought protection from the king in the Magna Carta, a charter containing sixty-three chapters that limited the king's powers.[76] Chapter 39 of the Magna Carta is the predecessor of our due process clauses. It provided that "no man shall be captured or imprisoned or disseised or outlawed or exiled or in any way destroyed, nor will we go against him or send against him, except by the lawful judgment of his peers or by the law of the land."[77]

The barons amassed an army, confronted the king, and forced him to agree to the Magna Carta. Subsequent monarchs reissued the Magna Carta many times over the next two centuries.[78] In 1354 the words "by the law of the land" (which were initially written in Latin) were translated into English to mean "by due process of the law."[79] In the seventeenth century these words were interpreted to include the customary rights and liberties of Englishmen.[80] English legal commentators further expanded the scope of due process by arguing that it included what philosopher John Locke called each individual's natural right to "life, liberty, and property."[81]

The Magna Carta's influence in this country is apparent in the 1776 constitutions of Maryland and North Carolina, which contain verbatim due process language taken from the Magna Carta. In 1791 the due process clause was included in the Fifth Amendment to the U.S. Constitution. Every person in our society has an inherent right to due process of law, which protects him or her from arbitrary, oppressive, and unjust governmental actions. If a proceeding results in the denial of fundamental fairness and shocks the conscience of a court, a violation of due process has occurred. In addition, under both the Fifth and

Fourteenth Amendments, a corporation, as well as a partnership or unincorporated association, is a person to whom that protection applies.

Due process of the law focuses on deprivations of "life, liberty, and property." "Life" refers to deprivation of biological life and to a person's right to have a lifestyle. "Liberty," as will be further explained below, covers a vast scope of personal rights. It also infers the absence of arbitrary and unreasonable governmental restraints on an individual's person, as well as the freedom to practice a trade or business and the right to contract, and to establish a relationship with one's children. "Property" is everything that may be subject to ownership, including real and personal property, obligations, rights, legal entitlements such as a public education, and other intangibles.

Determining what due process means in a given factual situation has been a matter for the judiciary. In this, the courts are influenced by procedures that were established under English common law prior to the enactment of our Constitution. They are also influenced by contemporary events, values, and political and economic conditions.

The following case of *Washington v. Glucksberg* illustrates conflicting approaches to the meaning of substantive due process. In this case, Dr. Harold Glucksberg and four other doctors brought suit for declaratory and injunctive relief against the state of Washington. They sought to enjoin a Washington statute that made it a crime for the doctors to assist three of their mentally competent but terminally ill patients to commit suicide. Chief Justice Rehnquist first explains his views on the proper scope of substantive due process under the Fourteenth Amendment. Associate Justice David Souter then explains that although he agrees with Rehnquist on the correct decision in the case, he profoundly disagrees with the Chief Justice about the proper scope of substantive due process.

Washington et al., Petitioners, v. Harold Glucksberg et al.
521 U.S. 702
U.S. Supreme Court
June 26, 1997

Chief Justice Rehnquist delivered the opinion of the Court.

The question presented in this case is whether Washington's prohibition against "caus[ing]" or "aid[ing]" a suicide offends the Fourteenth Amendment to the United States Constitution. We hold that it does not.

It has always been a crime to assist a suicide in the State of Washington. In 1854, Washington's first Territorial Legislature outlawed "assisting another in the commission of self murder." Today, Washington law provides: "A person is guilty of promoting a suicide attempt when he knowingly causes or aids another person to attempt suicide." . . . "Promoting a suicide attempt" is a felony, punishable by up to five years' imprisonment and up to a $10,000 fine. . . . At the same time, Washington's Natural Death Act, enacted in 1979, states that the "withholding or withdrawal of life sustaining treatment" at a patient's direction "shall not, for any purpose, constitute a suicide." . . .

Petitioners in this case are the State of Washington and its Attorney General. Respondents Harold Glucksberg, M. D., Abigail Halperin, M. D., Thomas A. Preston, M. D., and Peter Shalit, M. D., are physicians who practice in Washington. These doctors occasionally treat terminally ill, suffering patients, and declare that they would assist these patients in ending their lives if not for Washington's assisted suicide ban. In January 1994, respondents, along with three gravely ill, pseudonymous plaintiffs who have since died and Compassion in Dying, a nonprofit organization that counsels people considering physician assisted suicide, sued in the United States District Court, seeking a declaration that Wash Rev. Code 9A.36.060(1) (1994) is, on its face, unconstitutional. . . .

The plaintiffs asserted "the existence of a liberty interest protected by the Fourteenth Amendment which extends to a personal choice by a mentally competent, terminally ill adult to commit physician assisted suicide." . . . Relying primarily on *Planned Parenthood v. Casey*, 505 U.S. 833 (1992), and *Cruzan v. Director, Missouri Dept. of Health*, 497 U.S. 261 (1990), the District Court agreed, . . . and concluded that Washington's assisted suicide ban is unconstitutional because it "places an undue burden on the exercise of [that] constitutionally protected liberty interest." . . . The District Court also decided that the Washington statute violated the Equal Protection Clause's requirement that "'all persons similarly situated . . . be treated alike.'" . . .

A panel of the Court of Appeals for the Ninth Circuit reversed, emphasizing that "[i]n the two hundred and five years of our existence no constitutional right to aid in killing oneself has ever been asserted and upheld by a court of final jurisdiction." . . . The Ninth Circuit reheard the case en banc, reversed the panel's decision, and affirmed the District Court. . . . Like the District Court, the en banc Court of Appeals emphasized our *Casey* and *Cruzan* decisions. . . . The court also discussed what it described as "historical" and "current societal attitudes" toward suicide and assisted suicide, . . . and concluded that "the Constitution encompasses a

due process liberty interest in controlling the time and manner of one's death—that there is, in short, a constitutionally recognized 'right to die.'" . . . After "[w]eighing and then balancing" this interest against Washington's various interests, the court held that the State's assisted suicide ban was unconstitutional "as applied to terminally ill competent adults who wish to hasten their deaths with medication prescribed by their physicians." . . . The court did not reach the District Court's equal protection holding. . . . We granted certiorari, . . . and now reverse.

I

We begin, as we do in all due process cases, by examining our Nation's history, legal traditions, and practices. . . . In almost every State—indeed, in almost every western democracy—it is a crime to assist a suicide. The States' assisted suicide bans are not innovations. Rather, they are long-standing expressions of the States commitment to the protection and preservation of all human life. . . . Indeed, opposition to and condemnation of suicide—and, therefore, of assisting suicide—are consistent and enduring themes of our philosophical, legal, and cultural heritages. . . .

More specifically, for over 700 years, the Anglo American common law tradition has punished or otherwise disapproved of both suicide and assisting suicide. . . . In the 13th century, Henry de Bracton, one of the first legal treatise writers, observed that "[j]ust as a man may commit felony by slaying another so may he do so by slaying himself." . . . The real and personal property of one who killed himself to avoid conviction and punishment for a crime were forfeit to the king; however, thought Bracton, "if a man slays himself in weariness of life or because he is unwilling to endure further bodily pain . . . [only] his movable goods [were] confiscated." . . . Thus, "[t]he principle that suicide of a sane person, for whatever reason, was a punishable felony was . . . introduced into English common law." Centuries later, Sir William Blackstone, whose *Commentaries on the Laws of England* not only provided a definitive summary of the common law but was also a primary legal authority for 18th and 19th century American lawyers, referred to suicide as "self murder" and "the pretended heroism, but real cowardice, of the Stoic philosophers, who destroyed themselves to avoid those ills which they had not the fortitude to endure. . . ." . . . Blackstone emphasized that "the law has . . . ranked [suicide] among the highest crimes," . . . although, anticipating later developments, he conceded that the harsh and shameful punishments imposed for suicide "borde[r] a little upon severity." . . .

For the most part, the early American colonies adopted the common law approach. . . .

Over time, however, the American colonies abolished these harsh common law penalties. William Penn abandoned the criminal forfeiture sanction in Pennsylvania in 1701, and the other colonies (and later, the other States) eventually followed this example. . . .

Nonetheless, although States moved away from Blackstone's treatment of suicide, courts continued to condemn it as a grave public wrong. . . .

That suicide remained a grievous, though nonfelonious, wrong is confirmed by the fact that colonial and early state legislatures and courts did not retreat from prohibiting assisting suicide. . . . And the prohibitions against suicide never contained exceptions for those who were near death. . . .

The earliest American statute explicitly to outlaw assisting suicide was enacted in New York in 1828, . . . and many of the new States and Territories followed New York's example. . . . In this century, the Model Penal Code also prohibited "aiding" suicide, prompting many States to enact or revise their assisted suicide bans. The Code's drafters observed that "the interest in the sanctity of life that are represented by the criminal homicide

laws are threatened by one who expresses a willingness to participate in taking the life of another, even though the act may be accomplished with the consent, or at the request, of the suicide victim." . . .

Though deeply rooted, the States' assisted suicide bans have in recent years been reexamined and, generally, reaffirmed. Because of advances in medicine and technology, Americans today are increasingly likely to die in institutions, from chronic illnesses. . . . Public concern and democratic action are therefore sharply focused on how best to protect dignity and independence at the end of life, with the result that there have been many significant changes in state laws and in the attitudes these laws reflect. Many States, for example, now permit "living wills," surrogate health care decisionmaking, and the withdrawal or refusal of life sustaining medical treatment. . . . At the same time, however, voters and legislators continue for the most part to reaffirm their States' prohibitions on assisting suicide.

The Washington statute at issue in this case, . . . was enacted in 1975 as part of a revision of that State's criminal code. Four years later, Washington passed its Natural Death Act, which specifically stated that the "withholding or withdrawal of life sustaining treatment . . . shall not, for any purpose, constitute a suicide" and that "[n]othing in this chapter shall be construed to condone, authorize, or approve mercy killing. . . ." . . . In 1991, Washington voters rejected a ballot initiative which, had it passed, would have permitted a form of physician assisted suicide. Washington then added a provision to the Natural Death Act expressly excluding physician assisted suicide. . . . Wash. Rev. Code § 70.122.100 (1994). . . .

Attitudes toward suicide itself have changed since Bracton, but our laws have consistently condemned, and continue to prohibit, assisting suicide. Despite changes in medical technology and notwithstanding an increased emphasis on the importance of end of life decisionmaking, we have not retreated from this prohibition. Against this backdrop of history, tradition, and practice, we now turn to respondents' constitutional claim.

II

The Due Process Clause guarantees more than fair process, and the "liberty" it protects includes more than the absence of physical restraint. . . . The Clause also provides heightened protection against government interference with certain fundamental rights and liberty interests. . . . In a long line of cases, we have held that, in addition to the specific freedoms protected by the Bill of Rights, the "liberty" specifically protected by the Due Process Clause includes the rights to marry, *Loving v. Virginia,* 388 U.S. 1 (1967); to have children, *Skinner v. Oklahoma ex rel. Williamson,* 316 U.S. 535 (1942); to direct the education and upbringing of one's children, *Meyer v. Nebraska,* 262 U.S. 390 (1923); *Pierce v. Society of Sisters,* 268 U.S. 510 (1925); to marital privacy, *Griswold v. Connecticut,* 381 U.S. 479 (1965); to use contraception, . . . *Eisenstadt v. Baird,* 405 U.S. 438 (1972); to bodily integrity, *Rochin v. California,* 342 U.S. 165 (1952), and to abortion. . . . We have also assumed, and strongly suggested, that the Due Process Clause protects the traditional right to refuse unwanted lifesaving medical treatment. *Cruzan,* 497 U.S., at 278–279.

But we "ha[ve] always been reluctant to expand the concept of substantive due process because guideposts for responsible decisionmaking in this unchartered area are scarce and open ended." . . . By extending constitutional protection to an asserted right or liberty interest, we, to a great extent, place the matter outside the arena of public debate and legislative action. We must therefore "exercise the utmost care whenever we are asked to break new ground in this field," . . . lest the liberty protected by the Due Process Clause be subtly transformed into the policy preferences of the members of this Court. . . .

Our established method of substantive due process analysis has two primary features: First, we have regularly observed that the Due Process Clause specially protects those fundamental rights and liberties which are, objectively, "deeply rooted in this Nation's history and tradition," . . . "so rooted in the traditions and conscience of our people as to be ranked as fundamental," and "implicit in the concept of ordered liberty," such that "neither liberty nor justice would exist if they were sacrificed." . . . Second, we have required in substantive due process cases a "careful description" of the asserted fundamental liberty interest. . . . Our Nation's history, legal traditions, and practices thus provide the crucial "guideposts for responsible decisionmaking," . . . that direct and restrain our exposition of the Due Process Clause. As we stated recently, . . . the Fourteenth Amendment "forbids the government to infringe . . . 'fundamental' liberty interests at all, no matter what process is provided, unless the infringement is narrowly tailored to serve a compelling state interest." . . .

Justice Souter, relying on Justice Harlan's dissenting opinion in *Poe v. Ullman,* would largely abandon this restrained methodology, and instead ask "whether [Washington's] statute sets up one of those 'arbitrary impositions' or 'purposeless restraints' at odds with the Due Process Clause of the Fourteenth Amendment," . . . (quoting *Poe* . . . [1961] [Harlan, J., dissenting]). In our view, however, the development of this Court's substantive due process jurisprudence, described briefly above, . . . has been a process whereby the outlines of the "liberty" specially protected by the Fourteenth Amendment—never fully clarified, to be sure, and perhaps not capable of being fully clarified—have at least been carefully refined by concrete examples involving fundamental rights found to be deeply rooted in our legal tradition. This approach tends to rein in the subjective elements that are necessarily present in due process judicial review. In addition, by establishing a threshold requirement—that a challenged state action implicate a fundamental right— before requiring more than a reasonable relation to a legitimate state interest to justify the action, it avoids the need for complex balancing of competing interests in every case.

Turning to the claim at issue here, the Court of Appeals stated that "[p]roperly analyzed, the first issue to be resolved is whether there is a liberty interest in determining the time and manner of one's death," . . . or, in other words, "[i]s there a right to die?." . . . Similarly, respondents assert a "liberty to choose how to die" and a right to "control of one's final days," . . . and describe the asserted liberty as "the right to choose a humane, dignified death," . . . and "the liberty to shape death." . . . As noted above, we have a tradition of carefully formulating the interest at stake in substantive due process cases. For example, although *Cruzan* is often described as a "right to die" case, . . . we were, in fact, more precise: we assumed that the Constitution granted competent persons a "constitutionally protected right to refuse life-saving hydration and nutrition." . . . The Washington statute at issue in this case prohibits "aid[ing] another person to attempt suicide," . . . and, thus, the question before us is whether the "liberty" specially protected by the Due Process Clause includes a right to commit suicide which itself includes a right to assistance in doing so.

We now inquire whether this asserted right has any place in our Nation's traditions. Here, as discussed above, . . . we are confronted with a consistent and almost universal tradition that has long rejected the asserted right, and continues explicitly to reject it today, even for terminally ill, mentally competent adults. To hold for respondents, we would have to reverse centuries of legal doctrine and practice, and strike down the considered policy choice of almost every State. . . .

Respondents contend, however, that the liberty interest they assert is consistent with this Court's substantive due process line of cases, if not with this Nation's history and practice. Pointing to *Casey* and *Cruzan,* respondents read our jurisprudence in this area as reflecting a general tradition of "self sovereignty," . . . and as teaching that the "liberty" protected by the Due Process Clause includes "basic and intimate exercises of personal autonomy." . . . According to respondents, our liberty jurisprudence, and the broad, individualistic principles it reflects, protects the "liberty of competent, terminally ill adults to make end of life decisions free of undue government interference." . . . The question presented in this case, however, is whether the protections of the Due Process Clause include a right to commit suicide with another's assistance. With this "careful description" of respondents' claim in mind, we turn to *Casey* and *Cruzan.*

Respondents contend that in *Cruzan* we "acknowledged that competent, dying persons have the right to direct the removal of life sustaining medical treatment and thus hasten death," . . . and that "the constitutional principle behind recognizing the patient's liberty to direct the withdrawal of artificial life support applies at least as strongly to the choice to hasten impending death by consuming lethal medication." . . . Similarly, the Court of Appeals concluded that "*Cruzan,* by recognizing a liberty interest that includes the refusal of artificial provision of life sustaining food and water, necessarily recognize[d] a liberty interest in hastening one's one death." . . .

The right assumed in *Cruzan,* however, was not simply deduced from abstract concepts of personal autonomy. Given the common law rule that forced medication was a battery, and the long legal tradition protecting the decision to refuse unwanted medical treatment, our assumption was entirely consistent with this Nation's history and constitutional traditions. The decision to commit suicide with the assistance of another may be just as personal and profound as the decision to refuse unwanted medical treatment, but it has never enjoyed similar legal protection. Indeed, the two acts are widely and reasonably regarded as quite distinct. . . . In *Cruzan* itself, we recognize that most States outlawed assisted suicide—and even more do today—and we certainly gave no intimation that the right to refuse unwanted medical treatment could be somehow transmuted into a right to assistance in committing suicide. . . .

Respondents also rely on *Casey.* There, the Court's opinion concluded that "the essential holding of *Roe v. Wade* should be retained and once again reaffirmed." . . . We held, first, that a woman has a right, before her fetus is viable, to an abortion "without undue interference from the State"; second, that States may restrict post-viability abortions, so long as exceptions are made to protect a woman's life and health; and third, that the State has legitimate interests throughout a pregnancy in protecting the health of the woman and the life of the unborn child. . . . In reaching this conclusion, the opinion discussed in some detail this Court's substantive due process tradition of interpreting the Due Process Clause to protect certain fundamental rights and "personal decisions relating to marriage, procreation, contraception, family relationships, child rearing, and education," and noted that many of those rights and liberties "involv[e] the most intimate and personal choices a person may make in a lifetime." . . .

The Court of Appeals, like the District Court, found *Casey* " 'highly instructive' "and " 'almost prescriptive' " for determining " 'what liberty interest may inhere in a terminally ill person's choice to commit suicide' ":

"Like the decision of whether or not to have an abortion, the decision how and when to die is one of 'the most intimate and personal choices a person may make in a lifetime,' a choice 'central to personal dignity and autonomy.' " . . .

By choosing this language, the Court's opinion in *Casey* described, in a general way

and in light of our prior cases, those personal activities and decisions that this Court has identified as so deeply rooted in our history and traditions, or so fundamental to our concept of constitutionally ordered liberty, that they are protected by the Fourteenth Amendment. . . . That many of the rights and liberties protected by the Due Process Clause sound in personal autonomy does not warrant the sweeping conclusion that any and all important, intimate, and personal decisions are so protected, . . . and *Casey* did not suggest otherwise.

The history of the law's treatment of assisted suicide in this country has been and continues to be one of the rejection of nearly all efforts to permit it. That being the case, our decisions lead us to conclude that the asserted "right" to assistance in committing suicide is not a fundamental liberty interest protected by the Due Process Clause. The Constitution also requires, however, that Washington's assisted suicide ban be rationally related to legitimate government interests. . . . This requirement is unquestionably met here. As the court below recognized, . . . Washington's assisted suicide ban implicates a number of state interests. . . .

First, Washington has an "unqualified interest in the preservation of human life." . . . The State's prohibition on assisted suicide, like all homicide laws, both reflects and advances its commitment to this interest. . . .

Respondents admit that "[t]he State has a real interest in preserving the lives of those who can still contribute to society and enjoy life." . . . The Court of Appeals also recognized Washington's interest in protecting life, but held that the "weight" of this interest depends on the "medical condition and the wishes of the person whose life is at stake." . . . Washington, however, has rejected this sliding scale approach and, through its assisted suicide ban, insists that all persons' lives, from beginning to end, regardless of physical or mental condition, are under the full protection of the law. . . . As we have previously affirmed, the States "may properly decline to make judgments about the 'quality' of life that a particular individual may enjoy." . . . This remains true, as *Cruzan* makes clear, even for those who are near death.

Relatedly, all admit that suicide is a serious public health problem, especially among persons in otherwise vulnerable groups. . . . The State has an interest in preventing suicide, and in studying, identifying, and treating its causes. . . .

The State also has an interest in protecting the integrity and ethics of the medical profession. In contrast to the Court of Appeals' conclusion that "the integrity of the medical profession would [not] be threatened in any way by [physician assisted suicide]," . . . the American Medical Association, like many other medical and physicians' groups, has concluded that "[p]hysician assisted suicide is fundamentally incompatible with the physician's role as healer." American Medical Association, Code of Ethics §2.211 (1994). . . . And physician assisted suicide could, it is argued, undermine the trust that is essential to the doctor-patient relationship by blurring the time honored line between healing and harming. . . .

Next, the State has an interest in protecting vulnerable groups—including the poor, the elderly, and disabled persons—from abuse, neglect, and mistakes. The Court of Appeals dismissed the State's concern that disadvantaged persons might be pressured into physician assisted suicide as "ludicrous on its face." . . . We have recognized, however, the real risk of subtle coercion and undue influence in end of life situations. . . . Similarly, the New York Task Force warned that "[l]egalizing physician assisted suicide would pose profound risks to many individuals who are ill and vulnerable. . . . The risk of harm is greatest for the many individuals in our society whose autonomy and well being are already compromised by poverty, lack of ac-

cess to good medical care, advanced age, or membership in a stigmatized social group." . . . If physician assisted suicide were permitted, many might resort to it to spare their families the substantial financial burden of end of life health care costs.

The State's interest here goes beyond protecting the vulnerable from coercion; it extends to protecting disabled and terminally ill people from prejudice, negative and inaccurate stereotypes, and "societal indifference." . . . The State's assisted suicide ban reflects and reinforces its policy that the lives of terminally ill, disabled, and elderly people must be no less valued than the lives of the young and healthy, and that a seriously disabled person's suicidal impulses should be interpreted and treated the same way as anyone else's. . . .

Finally, the State may fear that permitting assisted suicide will start it down the path to voluntary and perhaps even involuntary euthanasia. The Court of Appeals struck down Washington's assisted suicide ban only "as applied to competent, terminally ill adults who wish to hasten their deaths by obtaining medication prescribed by their doctors." . . . Washington insists, however, that the impact of the court's decision will not and cannot be so limited. . . . If suicide is protected as a matter of constitutional right, it is argued, "every man and woman in the United States must enjoy it." . . . See *Kevorkian*, . . . 527 N. W. 2d, at 727-728, n. 41. The Court of Appeals' decision, and its expansion reasoning, provide ample support for the State's concerns. The court noted, for example, that the "decision of a duly appointed surrogate decision maker is for all legal purposes the decision of the patient himself," . . . that "in some instances, the patient may be unable to self administer the drugs and . . . administration by the physician . . . may be the only way the patient may be able to receive them," . . . and that not only physicians, but also family members and loved ones, will inevitably participate in assisting suicide. . . . Thus, it turns out that what is couched as a limited right to "physician assisted suicide" is likely, in effect, a much broader license, which could prove extremely difficult to police and contain. . . . Washington's ban on assisting suicide prevents such erosion.

We need not weigh exactly the relative strengths of these various interests. They are unquestionably important and legitimate, and Washington's ban on assisted suicide is at least reasonably related to their promotion and protection. We therefore hold that Wash. Rev. Code § 9A.36.060(1) (1994) does not violate the Fourteenth Amendment, either on its face or "as applied to competent, terminally ill adults who wish to hasten their deaths by obtaining medication prescribed by their doctors." . . .

Justice Souter, concurring in the judgment

. . . When the physicians claim that the Washington law deprives them of a right falling within the scope of liberty that the Fourteenth Amendment guarantees against denial without due process of law, they are . . . [claiming] that the State has no substantively adequate justification for barring the assistance sought by the patient and sought to be offered by the physician. Thus, we are dealing with a claim to one of those rights sometimes described as rights of substantive due process and sometimes as unenumerated rights, in view of the breadth and indeterminacy of the "due process" serving as the claim's textual basis. The doctors accordingly arouse the skepticism of those who find the Due Process Clause an unduly vague or oxymoronic warrant for judicial review of substantive state law, just as they also invoke two centuries of American constitutional practice in recognizing unenumerated, substantive limits on governmental action. . . . The persistence of substantive due process in our cases points to the legitimacy of the modern justification for such judicial review, . . . while the acknowl-

edged failures of some of these cases point with caution to the difficulty raised by the present claim. . . .

Respondents claim that a patient facing imminent death, who anticipates physical suffering and indignity, and is capable of responsible and voluntary choice, should have a right to a physician's assistance in providing counsel and drugs to be administered by the patient to end life promptly. . . .

This liberty interest in bodily integrity was phrased in a general way by then Judge Cardozo when he said, "[e]very human being of adult years and sound mind has a right to determine what shall be done with his own body" in relation to his medical needs. . . . The familiar examples of this right derive from the common law of battery and include the right to be free from medical invasions into the body, . . . as well as a right generally to resist enforced medication. . . . Thus "[i]t is settled now . . . that the Constitution places limits on a State's right to interfere with a person's most basic decisions about . . . bodily integrity." . . . Constitutional recognition of the right to bodily integrity underlies the assumed right, good against the State, to require physicians to terminate artificial life support, . . . and the affirmative right to obtain medical intervention to cause abortion. See . . . *Roe v. Wade.* . . .

It is, indeed, in the abortion cases that the most telling recognitions of the importance of bodily integrity and the concomitant tradition of medical assistance have occurred. In *Roe v. Wade,* the plaintiff contended that the Texas statute making it criminal for any person to "procure an abortion," . . . for a pregnant woman was unconstitutional insofar as it prevented her from "terminat[ing] her pregnancy by an abortion 'performed by a competent, licensed physician, under safe, clinical conditions,'" . . . and in striking down the statute we stressed the importance of the relationship between patient and physician. . . .

The analogies between the abortion cases and this one are several. Even though the State has a legitimate interest in discouraging abortion, . . . the Court recognized a woman's right to a physician's counsel and care. Like the decision to commit suicide, the decision to abort potential life can be made irresponsibly and under the influence of others, and yet the Court has held in the abortion cases that physicians are fit assistants. Without physician assistance in abortion, the woman's right would have too often amounted to nothing more than a right to self mutilation, and without a physician to assist in the suicide of the dying, the patient's right will often be confined to crude methods of causing death, most shocking and painful to the decedent's survivors.

There is, finally, one more reason for claiming that a physician's assistance here would fall within the accepted tradition of medical care in our society, and the abortion cases are only the most obvious illustration of the further point. While the Court has held that the performance of abortion procedures can be restricted to physicians, the Court's opinion in *Roe* recognized the doctors' role in yet another way. For, in the course of holding that the decision to perform an abortion called for a physician's assistance, the Court recognized that the good physician is not just a mechanic of the human body whose services have no bearing on a person's moral choices, but one who does more than treat symptoms, one who ministers to the patient. . . . This idea of the physician as serving the whole person is a source of the high value traditionally placed on the medical relationship. Its value is surely as apparent here as in the abortion cases, for just as the decision about abortion is not directed to correcting some pathology, so the decision in which a dying patient seeks help is not so limited. The patients here sought not only an end to pain (which they might have had, although perhaps at the price of stupor) but an end to

their short remaining lives with a dignity that they believed would be denied them by powerful pain medication, as well as by their consciousness of dependency and helplessness as they approached death. In that period when the end is imminent, they said, the decision to end life is closest to decisions that are generally accepted as proper instances of exercising autonomy over one's own body, instances recognized under the Constitution and the State's own law, instances in which the help of physicians is accepted as falling within the traditional norm. . . .

I take it that the basic concept of judicial review with its possible displacement of legislative judgment bars any finding that a legislature has acted arbitrarily when the following conditions are met: there is a serious factual controversy over the feasibility of recognizing the claimed right without at the same time making it impossible for the State to engage in an undoubtedly legitimate exercise of power; facts necessary to resolve the controversy are not readily ascertainable through the judicial process; but they are more readily subject to discovery through legislative factfinding and experimentation. It is assumed in this case, and must be, that a State's interest in protecting those unable to make responsible decisions and those who make no decisions at all entitles the State to bar aid to any but a knowing and responsible person intending suicide, and to prohibit euthanasia. How, and how far, a State should act in that interest are judgments for the State, but the legitimacy of its action to deny a physician the option to aid any but the knowing and responsible is beyond question. . . .

. . . The principal enquiry at the moment is into the Dutch experience, and I question whether an independent front line investigation into the facts of a foreign country's legal administration can be soundly undertaken through American courtroom litigation. While an extensive literature on any subject can raise the hopes for judicial understanding, the literature on this subject is only nascent. Since there is little experience directly bearing on the issue, the most that can be said is that whichever way the Court might rule today, events could overtake its assumptions, as experimentation in some jurisdictions confirmed or discredited the concerns about progression from assisted suicide to euthanasia.

Legislatures, on the other hand, have superior opportunities to obtain the facts necessary for a judgment about the present controversy. Not only do they have more flexible mechanisms for factfinding than the Judiciary, but their mechanisms include the power to experiment, moving forward and pulling back as facts emerge within their own jurisdictions. There is, indeed, good reason to suppose that in the absence of a judgment for respondents here, just such experimentation will be attempted in some of the States. . . .

I do not decide here what the significance might be of legislative foot dragging in ascertaining the facts going to the State's argument that the right in question could not be confined as claimed. Sometimes a court may be bound to act regardless of the institutional preferability of the political branches as forums for addressing constitutional claims. . . . Now, it is enough to say that our examination of legislative reasonableness should consider the fact that the Legislature of the State of Washington is no more obviously at fault than this Court is in being uncertain about what would happen if respondents prevailed today. We therefore have a clear question about which institution, a legislature or a court, is relatively more competent to deal with an emerging issue as to which facts currently unknown could be dispositive. The answer has to be, for the reasons already stated, that the legislative process is to be preferred. There is a closely related further reason as well.

One must bear in mind that the nature of the right claimed, if recognized as one constitutionally required, would differ in no essential way from other constitutional rights guaranteed by enumeration or derived from some more definite textual source than "due process." An unenumerated right should not therefore be recognized, with the effect of displacing the legislative ordering of things, without the assurance that its recognition would prove as durable as the recognition of those other rights differently derived. To recognize a right of lesser promise would simply create a constitutional regime too uncertain to bring with it the expectation of finality that is one of this Court's central obligations in making constitutional decisions. . . .

Legislatures, however, are not so constrained. The experimentation that should be out of the question in constitutional adjudication displacing legislative judgments is entirely proper, as well as highly desirable, when the legislative power addresses an emerging issue like assisted suicide. The Court should accordingly stay its hand to allow reasonable legislative consideration. While I do not decide for all time that respondents' claim should not be recognized, I acknowledge the legislative institutional competence as the better one to deal with that claim at this time.

Case Questions

1. What was Doctor Glucksberg's argument in the U.S. Supreme Court?
2. On what grounds did Chief Justice Rehnquist justify his conclusion that Washington's statute did not violate the Due Process Clause?

How does Justice Souter answer the respondent's argument that a patient fac-ing "imminent death after physical suffering and indignity" has a moral right to a physician's assistance in ending life and is entitled to Supreme Court recognition that such a right is fundamental to due process?

The due process guarantee protects people from unfairness in the operation of both substantive and procedural law. Substantive law refers to the law that creates, defines, and regulates rights. It defines the legal relationship between the individual and the state and among individuals themselves and is the primary responsibility of the legislative branch of the government. Procedural law prescribes the method used to enforce legal rights. It provides the machinery by which individuals can enforce their rights or obtain redress for the invasion of such rights.

The Fifth and Fourteenth Amendments

The Fifth Amendment guarantee of due process of law was included in the Bill of Rights in order to place limits on the federal government. It was intended to control the Congress, and prior to the Civil War it was primarily used to protect property rights from governmental regulation. The due process clause was also interpreted by the Supreme Court to overrule those parts of the Missouri Compromise that prohibited slavery. In the *Dred Scott* case (60 U.S. 393 [1861]), the Supreme Court ruled that slaves were property and thus the due process clause prohibited Congress from making slavery illegal. This is a historical irony, given the role due process has played in promoting civil rights in recent decades. Even during the Civil War era, many abolitionists interpreted due process differently and identified this Fifth Amendment clause as the basis for their convictions, maintaining that states had no right to deny slaves, or any other person, the right to life, liberty, or property without due process of law.

The addition of the Fourteenth Amendment to the Constitution in 1868 reflected the abolitionists' position. From that point forward, state governments were constitutionally required to provide due process of law and equal protection of the law to *all* people.

The Meaning of Substantive Due Process

The Bill of Rights contains many specifics regarding procedural fairness, particularly in criminal cases, but the meaning of substantive due process is less obvious. In our system of government, the U.S. Supreme Court has historically borne the responsibility for determining the degree to which the concept of due process includes a substantive dimension.

In substantive due process cases, the claimant challenges a statute on the grounds that the law excessively intrudes on individual decision making. The claimant argues that the infringement is against that person's due process, liberty interest. When the Court examines the facts, it often discovers that the government has no legitimate interest in the matter and is acting arbitrarily, and the claimant has an important, historically validated interest (a "fundamental right" in legalese) to make the decision. The Court decides these claims on a case-by-case basis, and the claimant wins when a majority of justices conclude that the claimed right should be classified as fundamental given these particular circumstances.

An example of such a case is found in Chapter Eight of this textbook in a case decided by the U.S. Supreme Court in 1967, entitled *Loving v. Virginia*. Richard Loving, who was white, and his wife, Mildred, who was black, brought suit challenging Virginia's antimiscegenation laws (statutes making it illegal for white people to marry black people). The U.S. Supreme Court ruled in favor of the Lovings. It concluded that the decision as to whether to enter into an interracial marriage was a matter for Richard and Mildred, and not the Commonwealth of Virginia. Virginia, said the Court, had no legitimate interest in the races of married people, and could not categorically prohibit black and white people from marrying one another.

But most persons seeking federal due process protection are unsuccessful. You may recall in the case of *Washington v. Glucksberg,* that Dr. Glucksberg and other doctors unsuccessfully argued before the U.S. Supreme Court that they had a constitutionally protected due process right to assist their terminally ill patients to commit suicide. The Supreme Court justices ultimately decided that the doctors' claim was not within the scope of due process protection.

U.S. Supreme Court Justice David H. Souter, commented on substantive due process in his concurring opinion in *Glucksberg*. Souter, although voting with the majority to sustain Washington's statute, recognized the conceptual legitimacy of substantive due process. He referred to substantive due process as the longstanding " . . . American constitutional practice . . . [of] recognizing unenumerated,* substantive limits on governmental action. . . ."†

We recently saw another example of this "American constitutional practice" in the *Cruzan* case. There, Chief Justice Rehnquist acknowledged that "the principal that a competent person has a constitutionally protected liberty interest in refusing unwanted medical treatment may be inferred from our prior decisions. . . ." In *Cruzan,* as in *Glucksberg* and *Loving,* the fact that the due process clauses were textually silent about a substantive due process claim did not preclude the Court from recognizing that such an unenumerated right is protected as within the scope of substantive due process.

Substantive Due Process and Economic and Social Regulation

In the years following the enactment of the Fourteenth Amendment, the U.S. Supreme Court began a slow process of expanding the substantive meaning of due process. As we learned in the earlier discussion of sociological jurisprudence,

---

*rights not actually explicitly identified in the text of the Constitution
†From *Washington v. Glucksberg,* 521 U.S. 702 (1997).

the Supreme Court in the 1890s was unsympathetic to the Progressives and state reform legislation. In the early cases, the states usually won if they were legislating to protect the public's health, welfare, safety, and morals. Gradually, however the Court began using the Fourteenth Amendment to strike down state social and economic legislation. The justices often concluded that these laws exceeded the state's legislative power because they infringed upon the individual's due process right to contract. They maintained that the individual had the right to determine how many hours he or she wanted to work, at least in nonhazardous occupations. And legislative attempts to set minimum wages for women hospital workers were viewed by the Court as "price fixing." The Court was, in effect, sitting in judgment on the legislative policies themselves. The Court used the due process clause as an instrument for striking down social and economic legislation with which it disagreed.

The depression of the 1930s resulted in New Deal legislative initiatives that were intended to stimulate the economy. Congress created numerous agencies and programs in order to benefit industry, labor, savers and investors, farmers, and the needy. However, the Supreme Court struck down many of these New Deal laws between 1934 and 1936. This made the Court very unpopular in the "court" of public opinion, and the president responded by proposing that Congress increase the size of the Court, presumably so that he could nominate people for the new seats who were sympathetic to New Deal legislation. In 1936, the Supreme Court began to reverse itself and uphold New Deal legislation. The Court's majority, in 1937, began using the commerce clause to sustain federal legislation, and they were no longer using the due process clause to overturn state reforms. The Court replaced the dual federalism doctrine, which attempted to enforce strict boundaries around the federal and state "zones of interest," with a general policy of deference to legislative preferences with respect to social and economic policies that are neither arbitrary nor irrational.

The Scope of Substantive Due Process

In the 1920s the Supreme Court had begun to recognize that an individual's liberty rights included more than just property rights. Individual "liberty" also required the constitutional protection of certain kinds of conduct. The justices of the U.S. Supreme Court differed, however, about whether such rights could be "found" within the meaning of due process. Although various justices on the Court proposed limits on the scope of substantive due process, the majority on the Court adopted what is called the selective incorporation approach. This approach recognizes that all rights that the Court deems to be fundamental are included in the concept of due process.

Fundamental rights include those that have historically been part of our legal tradition, such as the First Amendment freedoms. Other fundamental rights include intimate decisions relating to marriage, procreation, contraception, family relations, child rearing, and education. The determination of whether a right is fundamental is made by the U.S. Supreme Court on a case-by-case basis.

It is important to emphasize that the Fifth and Fourteenth Amendment due process clauses operate only as restraints on government. One of the consequences of this limitation is that private schools have considerably more procedural latitude than public schools. Private elementary and secondary schools can regulate what students wear, substantially restrict student expression and behavior, enforce a common moral code, and enforce rules that are so vague that they would not be constitutionally acceptable in a public school. If private schools contract with their students to provide due process, or if they violate public policy, commit torts, or act inequitably, courts have been increasingly willing to intervene. Over the years there has been an expansion of the concept of "state action" and a closer relationship between private schools and government in the forms of grants, scholarships, and research funds to institutions of higher education. Courts are beginning to require procedural due process in actions of those private colleges and universities that have such governmental involvement.

The next case in this chapter, *City of Chicago v. Morales*, illustrates another aspect of substantive due process. Here, the Supreme Court determined that the due process clause required that the Chicago ordinance be overturned because it was too vague. *Vague* legislation fails to provide citizens with *fair notice* of what the ordinance/law prohibits. In *Morales*, however, the Court explains that there is a more important reason than providing fair notice for striking down vague laws. The reason is that vague laws fail to control police discretion. Uncontrolled police discretion, according to the Court, can lead to arbitrary police decision making.

City of Chicago v. Jesus Morales, et al.
No. 97-1121
U.S. Supreme Court
June 10, 1999

Justice Stevens announced the judgment of the Court and delivered the opinion of the Court with respect to Parts I, II, and V, and an opinion with respect to Parts III, IV, and VI, in which Justice Souter and Justice Ginsberg join.

In 1992, the Chicago City Council enacted the Gang Congregation Ordinance, which prohibits "criminal street gang members" from "loitering" with one another or with other persons in any public place. The question presented is whether the Supreme Court of Illinois correctly held that the ordinance violates the Due Process Clause of the Fourteenth Amendment to the Federal Constitution.

I

Before the ordinance was adopted, the city council's Committee on Police and Fire conducted hearings to explore the problems created by the city's street gangs, and more particularly, the consequences of public loitering by gang members. . . .

The council found that a continuing increase in criminal street gang activity was largely responsible for the city's rising murder rate, as well as an escalation of violent and drug related crimes. . . . Furthermore, the council stated that gang members "establish control over identifiable areas . . . by loitering in those areas and intimidating others from entering those areas; and . . . [m]embers of criminal street gangs avoid arrest by committing no offense punishable under existing laws when they know the police are present. . . ." . . . It further found that "loitering in public places by criminal street gang members creates a justifiable fear for the safety of persons and property in the area" and that "[a]ggressive action is necessary to preserve the city's streets and other public places so that the public may use such places without fear." Moreover, the council concluded that the city "has an interest in discouraging all persons from loitering in public places with criminal gang members." . . .

The ordinance creates a criminal offense punishable by a fine of up to $500, imprisonment for not more than six months, and a requirement to perform up to 120 hours of community service. Commission of the offense involves four predicates. First, the police officer must reasonably believe that at least one of the two or more persons present in a "public place" is a "criminal street gang membe[r]." Second, the persons must be "loitering," which the ordinance defines as "remain[ing] in any one place with no apparent purpose." Third, the officer must then order "all" of the persons to disperse and remove themselves "from the area." Fourth, a person must disobey the officer's order. If any person, whether a gang member or not, disobeys the officer's order, that person is guilty of violating the ordinance. . . .

Two months after the ordinance was adopted, the Chicago Police Department promulgated General Order 92-4 to provide guidelines to govern its enforcement. That order purported to establish limitations on the enforcement discretion of police officers "to ensure that the anti-gang loitering ordinance is not enforced in an arbitrary or discriminatory way." . . . The limitations confine the authority to arrest gang members who violate the ordinance to sworn "members of the Gang Crime Section" and certain other designated

officers, and establish detailed criteria for defining street gangs and membership in such gangs. . . . In addition, the order directs district commanders to "designate areas in which the presence of gang members has a demonstrable effect on the activities of law abiding persons in the surrounding community," and provides that the ordinance "will be enforced only within the designated areas." . . . The city, however, does not release the location of these "designated areas" to the public.

II

During the three years of its enforcement, the police issued over 89,000 dispersal orders and arrested over 42,000 people for violating the ordinances. In the ensuing enforcement proceedings, two trial judges upheld the constitutionality of the ordinance, but eleven others ruled that it was invalid. In respondent Youkhana's case, the trial judge held that the "ordinance fails to notify individuals what conduct is prohibited, and it encourages arbitrary and capricious enforcement by police." . . .

We granted certiorari, . . . and now affirm. . . . [W]e conclude that the ordinance enacted by the city of Chicago is unconstitutionally vague.

III

The basic factual predicate for the city's ordinance is not in dispute. . . . We have no doubt that a law that directly prohibited . . . intimidating conduct would be constitutional, but this ordinance broadly covers a significant amount of additional activity. Uncertainty about the scope of that additional coverage provides the basis for respondents' claim that the ordinance is too vague.

. . . [T]he freedom to loiter for innocent purposes is part of the "liberty" protected by the Due Process Clause of the Fourteenth Amendment. We have expressly identified this "right to remove from one place to another according to inclination" as "an attribute of personal liberty" protected by the Constitution. . . . Indeed, it is apparent that an individual's decision to remain in a public place of his choice . . . or the right to move "to whatsoever place one's own inclination may direct" is identified in Blackstone's *Commentaries.* (W. Blackstone, *Commentaries on the Laws of England,* 130 [1765]) . . .

Vagueness may invalidate a criminal law for either of two independent reasons. First, it may fail to provide the kind of notice that will enable ordinary people to understand what conduct it prohibits; second, it may authorize and even encourage arbitrary and discriminatory enforcement. . . . Accordingly, we first consider whether the ordinance provides fair notice to the citizen and then discuss its potential for arbitrary enforcement.

IV

"It is established that a law fails to meet the requirements of the Due Process Clause if it is so vague and standardless that it leaves the public uncertain as to the conduct it prohibits. . . ." The Illinois Supreme Court recognized that the term "loiter" may have a common and accepted meaning . . . but the definition of that term in this ordinance—"to remain in any one place with no apparent purpose"—does not. It is difficult to imagine how any citizen of the city of Chicago standing in a public place with a group of people would know if he or she had an "apparent purpose." If she were talking to another person, would she have an apparent purpose? If she were frequently checking her watch and looking expectantly down the street, would she have an apparent purpose?

Since the city cannot conceivably have meant to criminalize each instance a citizen stands in public with a gang member, the vagueness that dooms this ordinance is not the product of uncertainty about the normal meaning of "loitering," but rather about what loitering is covered by the ordinance and what is not. . . .

The city's principal response to this concern about adequate notice is that loiterers are not subject to sanction until after they have failed to comply with an officer's order to disperse. "[W]hatever problem is created by a law that criminalizes conduct people normally believe to be innocent is solved when persons receive actual notice from a police order of what they are expected to do." We find this response unpersuasive for at least two reasons.

First, the purpose of the fair notice requirement is to enable the ordinary citizen to conform his or her conduct to the law. "No one may be required at peril of life, liberty, or property to speculate as to the meaning of penal statutes." . . . Because an officer may issue an order only after prohibited conduct has already occurred, it cannot provide the kind of advance notice that will protect the putative loiterer from being ordered to disperse. Such an order cannot retroactively give adequate warning of the boundary between the permissible and the impermissible applications of the law.

Second, the terms of the dispersal order compound the inadequacy of the notice afforded by the ordinance. It provides that the officer "shall order all such persons to disperse and remove themselves from the area." . . . After such an order issues, how long must the loiterers remain apart? How far must they move? If each loiterer walks around the block and they meet again at the same location, are they subject to arrest or merely being ordered to disperse again? . . .

Lack of clarity in the description of the loiterer's duty to obey a dispersal order might not render the ordinance unconstitutionally vague if the definition of the forbidden conduct were clear, but it does buttress our conclusion that the entire ordinance fails to give the ordinary citizen adequate notice of what is forbidden and what is permitted. The Constitution does not permit a legislature to "set a net large enough to catch all possible offenders, and leave it to the courts to step inside and say who could be rightfully detained, and who should be set at large." . . . This ordinance is therefore vague "not in the sense that it requires a person to conform his conduct to an imprecise but comprehensible normative standard, but rather in the sense that no standard of conduct is specified at all." . . .

V

The broad sweep of the ordinance also violates "the requirement that a legislature establish minimal guidelines to govern law enforcement." . . . In any public place in the city of Chicago, persons who stand or sit in the company of a gang member may be ordered to disperse unless their purpose is apparent. The mandatory language in the enactment directs the police to issue an order without first making any inquiry about their possible purposes. It matters not whether the reason that a gang member and his father, for example, might loiter near Wrigley Field is to rob an unsuspecting fan or just to get a glimpse of Sammy Sosa leaving the ballpark; in either event, if their purpose is not apparent to a nearby police officer, she may—indeed, she "shall"—order them to disperse.

Recognizing that the ordinance does reach a substantial amount of innocent conduct, we turn, then, to its language to determine if it "necessarily entrusts law-making to the moment-to-moment judgment of the policeman on his beat." . . . [T]he principal source of the vast discretion conferred on the police in this case is the definition of loitering as "to remain in any one place with no apparent purpose."

As the Illinois Supreme Court interprets that definition, it "provides absolute discretion to police officers to determine what activities

constitute loitering." . . . We have no authority to construe the language of a state statute more narrowly than the construction given by that State's highest court. . . .

. . . [W]e find . . . [t]hat the ordinance does not . . . even address the question of how much discretion the police enjoy in deciding which stationary persons to disperse under the ordinance. Similarly, . . . [t]he "no apparent purpose" standard for making [the] decision [to order persons to disperse] is inherently subjective because its application depends on whether some purpose is "apparent" to the officer on the scene.

Presumably an officer would have discretion to treat some purposes—perhaps a purpose to engage in idle conversation or simply to enjoy a cool breeze on a warm evening—as too frivolous to be apparent if he suspected a different ulterior motive. . . .

It is true, as the city argues, that the requirement that the officer reasonably believe that a group of loiterers contains a gang member does place a limit on the authority to order dispersal. That limitation would no doubt be sufficient if the ordinance only applied to loitering that had an apparently harmful purpose or effect, or possibly if it only applied to loitering by persons reasonably believed to be criminal gang members. But this ordinance, for reasons that are not explained in the findings of the city council, requires no harmful purpose and applies to non-gang members as well as suspected gang members. It applies to everyone in the city who may remain in one place with one suspected gang member as long as their purpose is not apparent to an officer observing them. Friends, relatives, teachers, counselors, or even total strangers might unwittingly engage in forbidden loitering if they happen to engage in idle conversation with a gang member. . . .

. . . [W]e must assume that the ordinance means what it says and that it has no application to loiterers whose purpose is apparent. The relative importance of its application to harmless loitering is magnified by its inapplicability to loitering that has an obviously threatening or illicit purpose.

Finally, in its opinion striking down the ordinance, the Illinois Supreme Court refused to accept the general order issued by the police department as a sufficient limitation on the "vast amount of discretion" granted to the police in its enforcement. We agree . . . that the police have adopted internal rules limiting their enforcement to certain designated areas in the city that would not provide a defense to a loiterer who might be arrested elsewhere. Nor could a person who knowingly loitered with a well-known gang member anywhere in the city safely assume that they would not be ordered to disperse no matter how innocent and harmless their loitering might be.

VI

In our judgment, the Illinois Supreme Court correctly concluded that the ordinance does not provide sufficiently specific limits on the enforcement discretion of the police "to meet constitutional standards for definiteness and clarity." . . . We recognize the serious and difficult problems testified to by the citizens of Chicago that led to the enactment of this ordinance. . . . However, in this instance the city has enacted an ordinance that affords too much discretion to the police and too little notice to citizens who wish to use the public streets.

Accordingly, the judgment of the Supreme Court of Illinois is Affirmed.

Justice Thomas, with whom The Chief Justice and Justice Scalia join, dissenting.

The duly elected members of the Chicago City Council enacted the ordinance at issue as part of a larger effort to prevent gangs from establishing dominion over the public streets. By invalidating Chicago's ordinance, I fear that the Court has unnecessarily sentenced law-abiding citizens to lives of terror and mis-

ery. The ordinance is not vague. "[A]ny fool would know that a particular category of conduct would be within [its] reach." . . . Nor does it violate the Due Process Clause. The asserted "freedom" to loiter for innocent purposes . . . is in no way "'deeply rooted in the Nation's history and tradition.'" . . . I dissent.

I

The human costs exacted by criminal street gangs are inestimable. In many of our Nation's cities, gangs have "[v]irtually overtake[n] certain neighborhoods, contributing to the economic and social decline of these areas and causing fear and lifestyle changes among law-abiding residents." . . . Gangs fill the daily lives of many of our poorest and most vulnerable citizens with a terror that the Court does not give sufficient consideration, often relegating them to the status of prisoners in their own homes. . . .

In 1996, the Chicago Police Department estimated that there were 132 criminal street gangs in the city. . . . Between 1987 and 1994, these gangs were involved in 63,141 criminal incidents, including 21,689 nonlethal violent crimes and 894 homicides. . . .

As part of its ongoing effort to curb the deleterious effects of criminal street gangs, the citizens of Chicago sensibly decided to return to basics. The ordinance does nothing more than confirm the well-established principle that the police have the duty and the power to maintain the public peace, and, when necessary, to disperse groups of individuals who threaten it. . . .

A

We recently reconfirmed that "[o]ur Nation's history, legal traditions, and practices . . . provide the crucial 'guideposts for responsible decisionmaking' that direct and restrain our exposition of the Due Process Clause." . . . Only laws that infringe "those fundamental rights and liberties which are, objectively, 'deeply rooted in this Nation's history and tradition'" offend the Due Process Clause. . . .

The plurality's sweeping conclusion that this ordinance infringes upon a liberty interest protected by the Fourteenth Amendment's Due Process Clause withers when exposed to the relevant history: Laws prohibiting loitering and vagrancy have been a fixture of Anglo-American law at least since the time of the Norman Conquest. . . . Vagrancy laws were common in the decades preceding the ratification of the Fourteenth Amendment, and remained on the books long after. . . .

. . . [We] should be extremely reluctant to breathe still further substantive content into the Due Process Clause so as to strike down legislation adopted by a State or city to promote its welfare." . . . When "the Judiciary does so, it unavoidably preempts for itself another part of the governance of the country without express constitutional authority." . . .

B

The Court concludes that the ordinance is also unconstitutionally vague because it fails to provide adequate standards to guide police discretion and because, in the plurality's view, it does not give residents adequate notice of how to conform their conduct to the confines of the law. I disagree on both counts.

At the outset, it is important to note that the ordinance . . . penalizes loiterers' failure to obey a police officer's order to move along. A majority of the Court believes that this scheme vests too much discretion in police officers. Nothing could be further from the truth. . . . [T]he ordinance merely enables police officers to fulfill one of their traditional functions. Police officers are not, and never have been, simply enforcers of the criminal law. . . . Nor is the idea that the police are also peace officers simply a quaint anachronism. In most American jurisdictions, police officers

continue to be obligated, by law, to maintain public peace.

In order to perform their peace-keeping responsibilities satisfactorily, the police inevitably must exercise discretion. Indeed, by empowering them to act as peace officers, the law assumes that the police will exercise that discretion responsibly and with sound judgement. . . . Just as we trust officers to rely on their experience and expertise in order to make spur-of-the-moment determinations about amorphous legal standards such as "probable cause" and "reasonable suspicion," so we must trust them to determine whether a group of loiterers contains individuals (in this case members of criminal street gangs) whom the city has determined threaten the public peace. . . .

II

The plurality's conclusion that the ordinance "fails to give the ordinary citizen adequate notice of what is forbidden and what is permitted," . . . is similarly untenable. There is nothing "vague" about an order to disperse. While "we can never expect mathematical certainty from our language," . . . it is safe to assume that the vast majority of people who are ordered by the police to "disperse and remove themselves from the area" will have little difficulty understanding how to comply. . . .

As already explained, . . . the ordinance does not proscribe constitutionally protected conduct—there is no fundamental right to loiter. The term "loiter" is no different from terms such as "fraud," "bribery," and "perjury." We expect people of ordinary intelligence to grasp the meaning of such legal terms despite the fact that they are arguably imprecise. Here, we are asked to determine whether the ordinance is "vague in all of its applications." . . . The answer is unquestionably no. . . .

Today, the Court focuses extensively on the "rights" of gang members and their companions. It can safely do so— . . . the people who will suffer from our lofty pronouncements are people like Ms. Susan Mary Jackson; people who have seen their neighborhoods literally destroyed by gangs and violence and drugs. . . . As one resident described, "There is only about maybe one or two percent of the people in the city causing these problems maybe, but it's keeping ninety-eight percent of us in our houses and off the streets and afraid to shop." . . . By focusing exclusively on the imagined "rights" of the two percent, the Court today has denied our most vulnerable citizens the very thing that Justice Stevens, . . . elevates above all else—the "freedom of movement." And that is a shame. I respectfully dissent.

Case Questions

1. What standards did the U.S. Supreme Court use in determining whether the Chicago ordinance was unconstitutionally vague?
2. What is the essence of the dispute between Justices Stevens and Thomas?
3. Which opinion more reflects your own views of this debate, and why?

Procedural Due Process

American law is very much concerned with procedure. The underlying premise is that justice is more likely to result when correct procedures have been followed. All states and the federal government have extensive rules that govern criminal and civil litigation; these are subject to modification by federal and state legislative and judicial bodies. Although some rules are essentially arbitrary— for instance, one that requires a defendant to file an answer within twenty days of being served with a summons and complaint—other procedures are thought to be essential to due process and have been given constitutional protection. This latter category of rules promotes accurate fact-finding and fairness and is used in all jurisdictions in every case.

Procedural due process rules play a major role in criminal cases, placing limits on police investigative techniques and prosecutorial behavior, and outlining how criminal trials should be conducted.

Even when the Supreme Court has interpreted the due process clause of the Fourteenth Amendment to require a procedural right, however, it sometimes permits states to deviate from practices followed in federal courts. Procedural due process, for example, guarantees criminal defendants who are subject to more than six months' incarceration upon conviction the right to a jury trial. A defendant who stands trial in a state court, however, may not receive the same type of jury trial as in a federal court. Due process has been interpreted to permit states to accept nonunanimous jury verdicts in criminal cases where a unanimous verdict would be required in a federal court. Similarly, states are not constitutionally mandated to provide twelve-member juries even though twelve jurors are required in federal court.

In civil cases, due process rules are less extensive. They ensure that the court has jurisdiction over the parties, that proper notice has been given to defendants, and that the parties have an equal opportunity to present evidence and argument to the decision maker. In both types of litigation, procedural due process rules help ensure that decisions are made in a fair and reasonable manner.

As mentioned earlier, however, accuracy and fairness are not the only considerations. Elaborate procedural requirements are costly in terms of time, money, and utility. When the Supreme Court decides that a procedural right is fundamental to due process, there are often financial costs imposed on government, society, and individual litigants. Due process requirements can also lengthen the time it takes to conclude litigation, adding to the existing backlogs in many jurisdictions. Courts therefore generally try to balance accuracy against its cost on a case-by-case basis. In criminal cases the need for accurate decision making is paramount, and the requirements of due process are quite extensive.

In recent years, state legislatures throughout the country have enacted controversial statutes intended to protect the public from future attacks by convicted sexual offenders. These statutes require convicted sexual offenders to register with one or more governmental agencies (often the police or state attorney general) and supply detailed information of the type shown in Figure 1-1. Convicted sex offenders have been challenging these registration and notification laws on procedural due process grounds and the reviewing federal and state courts are very divided as to whether these notification requirements are constitutional. The following case, *State v. Bani,* involves a challenge to Hawai'i's registration and notification statute, more popularly known as "Megan's Law."*

*"Megan's Law" was named after a seven-year-old New Jersey girl who was sexually attacked and murdered by a neighbor in 1994.

State v. Bani
No. 22196
Hawai'i Supreme Court
November 21, 2001

Factual Summary

The convicted sex offender in *State v. Bani,* Eto Bani, entered a no contest plea to misdemeanor sexual assault. He was alleged to have twice grabbed a 17-year-old female on her buttocks while he was intoxicated. He was fined, incarcerated for two days, and placed on probation for one year. He appealed claim-

ing that Hawai'i's statute unconstitutionally deprived him of procedural due process.

Opinion of the Court by Ramil, J.

This appeal involves a challenge to the constitutionality of Hawai'i's sex offender registration and notification statute. . . . The arguments advanced implicate the inherent tensions between safety and freedom that exist in any democracy. The question ultimately raised is how the people of Hawai'i may protect themselves against future offenses by those prone to recidivism without jeopardizing the constitutional rights of persons who have already

---

HRS. Section 846E-3.

(a) Registration information shall be disclosed as follows:

    (1) The information shall be disclosed to law enforcement agencies for law enforcement purposes;

    (2) The information shall be disclosed to government agencies conducting confidential background checks;

    (3) The attorney general and any county police department shall release relevant information that is necessary to protect the public concerning a specific person required to register under this chapter; provided that the identity of a victim of an offense that requires registration under this chapter shall not be released.

(b) For purposes of this section, "relevant information that is necessary to protect the public" means:

    (1) Name and all aliases used by the sex offender or under which the sex offender has been known;

    (2) The street name and zip code where the sex offender resides and how long the sex offender has resided there;

    (3) The street name and zip code where the sex offender is staying for more than ten days, if other than the stated residence;

    (4) The future street name and zip code, if known, where the sex offender is planning to reside, if other than the stated residence;

    (5) The street name and zip code of the sex offender's current locations of employment;

    (6) The year, make, model, color, and license number of all vehicles currently owned or operated by the sex offender;

    (7) A brief summary of the criminal offenses against victims who were minors and the sexually violent offenses for which the sex offender has been convicted or found unfit to proceed or acquitted pursuant to chapter 704; and a recent photograph of the sex offender.

(c) Relevant information that is necessary to protect the public shall be collected for purposes of making it available to the general public, and a sex offender shall have a diminished expectation of privacy in the information. . . .

FIGURE 1-1   Hawai'i Revised Statutes 846E-3   Access to registration information

---

paid the price imposed by law for their crimes. Resolving the issues and arguments raised in this appeal requires us to discern and delineate the sensitive and difficult balance between these tensions embodied in the United States and Hawai'i Constitutions.

Defendant-appellant Eto Bani ("Bani") pled no contest to the charge of sexual assault in the fourth degree. . . . (1) Following Bani's plea, the district court ordered Bani, as part of his sentence, . . . to register as a sex offender pursuant to the sex offender registration and notification law, . . . commonly known as "Megan's Law."

On appeal, Bani contends, under the United States and Hawai'i Constitutions, that the statute violates: (1) the constitutional right to procedural due process. . . .

HRS chapter 846E . . . [Megan's Law] imposes certain registration requirements on "sex offender[s]." HRS 846E-1 defines a "sex offender" as "[a]ny person convicted of a 'sexually violent offense' or a 'criminal offense against a victim who is a minor[.]'" . . .

HRS 846E-2(a) requires sex offenders to register with the attorney general and comply with the provisions of HRS chapter 846E "for life." Nothing in HRS chapter 846E provides for the possibility of an offender ever obtaining relief from the requirements of the statute.

HRS 846E-3 mandates the registration information be disclosed to law enforcement agencies for law enforcement purposes and to government agencies conducting confidential background checks. Moreover, the attorney general and county police departments must publicly release "relevant information that is necessary to protect the public." . . . Such release provides for public access at the Hawai'i Criminal Justice Data Center and at designated county police stations, during business hours. . . . Registration information on any offender "may" also be released by the respective law enforcement agencies through an "interactive computer-based system," i.e., the Internet. . . .

HRS 846E-3 does not specify any limitations as to who can access the registration information, what information may be accessed, or the purpose for which the registration information may be accessed. . . .

Within three days of release from custody or arrival in a county where the sex offender expects to reside or be present for more than ten days, the offender is required to register in person with the county police chief. HRS 846E-4(e). . . .

846E subjects the offender to all of these requirements for life, regardless of the gravity of the offense committed. Failure to comply

with the requirements of HRS chapter 846E constitutes a substantive criminal offense. . . .

There is nothing inherent in the act of registering that imposes on any of Bani's protected liberty interests. The vast majority of federal and state courts . . . confronted with the issue of the validity of have found . . . [sex-offender registration statutes] constitutional on procedural due process grounds. . . .

Bani contends that HRS chapter 846E violated his procedural due process rights by failing to provide him with adequate procedural protections prior to depriving him of a protected liberty interest. Specifically, Bani argues that he was entitled to notice and an opportunity to be heard before being subjected to HRS chapter 846E's public notification provisions.

The fourteenth amendment to the United States Constitution and article I, section 5 of the Hawai'i Constitution provide in relevant part that no person shall be deprived of "life, liberty, or property without due process of law[.]" . . .

Hawai'i appellate courts have not had occasion to consider whether a person's reputation alone constitutes a "liberty interest" protected by the Hawai'i Constitution. However, the United States Supreme Court has previously recognized that a person's reputation is a protected liberty interest under the federal due process clause. . . . The Court . . . held that a protectible liberty interest is implicated "[w]here a person's good name, reputation, honor, or integrity is at stake because of what the government is doing to him [or her.]" . . .

However, in . . . *Paul v. Davis* . . . (1976), the Court clarified that "reputation alone, apart from some more tangible interests such as employment, is [n]either 'liberty' [n]or 'property' by itself sufficient to invoke the procedural protection of the Due Process Clause." . . . In other words, an allegation that government dissemination of information or government defamation has caused damage to reputation, even with all the attendant emotional anguish and social stigma, does not in itself state a cause of action for violation of a constitutional right; infringement of more 'tangible interests' . . . must be alleged as well. . . .

For the reasons discussed below, we conclude that Bani has shown substantial injury to both his reputation and other "tangible interests." . . . Suffice it to say that Bani has established that the public notification provisions of HRS chapter 846E implicate a liberty interest protected by the due process clause of the Hawai'i Constitution. First, Bani has demonstrated that the public notification provisions of HRS chapter 846E will likely cause harm to his reputation. The statute effectively brands Bani a "sex offender," i.e., a public danger, for life. . . .

Second, Bani will foreseeably suffer serious harm to other "tangible interests" as a result of registration as a sex offender. Potential employers and landlords will foreseeably be reluctant to employ or rent to Bani once they learn of his status as a "sex offender." . . . Indeed, the public disclosure provisions of HRS chapter 846E can adversely affect an offender's personal and professional life, employability, associations with neighbors, and choice of housing. . . .

In addition, public disclosure may encourage vigilantism and may expose the offender to possible physical violence. . . .

Under these circumstances, we are persuaded . . . that Bani has a liberty interest protected by the Hawai'i Constitution that entitles him to procedural due process. . . .

Having held that HRS chapter 846E operated to deprive Bani of a protected liberty interest, we review the underlying objectives of HRS chapter 846E in order to ascertain whether the statute afforded Bani the due process of law guaranteed him by article I, section 5 of the Hawai'i Constitution.

The minimum requirements of due process are notice and the opportunity to be heard.

. . . However, we have repeatedly recognized that "[d]ue process is not a fixed concept requiring a specific procedural course in every situation." . . . Instead, "due process is flexible and calls for such procedural protections as the particular situation demands." . . .

A review of the process, or lack thereof, . . . reveals that Bani was denied the minimum requirements of due process: notice and the opportunity to be heard. . . .

Undoubtedly, Bani's interest in the protected "liberty" denied him by HRS 846E is great. As discussed at length above, the public notification provisions adversely affect a person's interests in reputation, employment and earning opportunities, housing, and personal safety. . . . As the United States Court of Appeals for the Third Circuit observed:

> Notification puts the registrant's livelihood, domestic tranquility, and personal relationships all around him in grave jeopardy. This jeopardy will not only extend to virtually every aspect of the registrant's everyday life, it will also last [a lifetime]. . . .

The current procedures under the public notification provisions of HRS chapter 846E are extremely broad and contain absolutely no safeguards to prevent erroneous deprivations of a registrant's liberty interests. Without any preliminary determination of whether and to what extent an offender represents a danger to society, the level of danger to the public posed by any particular sex offender, if any, remains unknown. Surely, not all offenders present a significant danger to the public. Yet, HRS chapter 846E currently deprives all offenders—including those who present no danger to the community and are not likely to recidivate—of these interests automatically, for life. Therefore, persons convicted of crimes listed under HRS chapter 846E who do not pose a significant danger to the community are at substantial risk of being erroneously deprived of their liberty interests. . . .

The State generally has a compelling interest in protecting its citizens inasmuch as sex offenders pose a threat to the community.

[T]he legislature intended to provide for sex offender registration and public dissemination of relevant information about a sex offender to protect the public from sex offenders who present an "extreme threat to public safety." Thus, the State also has an interest in assuring that the information disclosed to the public, which carries a label that a person is a danger to the community, is accurate. Accordingly, the State itself has an interest in affording procedural safeguards to ensure against erroneous deprivations of registrant liberty interests. . . .

A weighing of these factors leads us to conclude that, at a minimum, Bani was entitled to notice and an opportunity to be heard prior to public notification of his status as a sex offender. In other words, the State must allow a registered sex offender a meaningful opportunity to argue that he or she does not represent a threat to the community and that public notification is not necessary, or that he or she represents only a limited threat such that limited public notification is appropriate. Because HRS 846E-3 provided Bani with neither notice nor an opportunity to be heard prior to notifying the public of his status as a convicted sex offender, HRS 846E-3 denied Bani the due process of law guaranteed him by article I, section 5 of the Hawai'i Constitution. Accordingly, we hold that the public notification provisions of HRS chapter 846E are void and unenforceable. . . .

For the reasons discussed above, we vacate the portion of Bani's sentence ordering him to submit to the notification requirements of HRS chapter 846E and remand this case for proceedings consistent with this opinion.

Case Questions

1. How did Bani satisfy the requirement that he demonstrate the infringement of a "life, liberty, or property" interest in order to be entitled to seek relief under the Fourteenth Amendment Due Process Clause?
2. What exactly was Bani's procedural due process claim?
3. How did the Hawai'i Supreme Court rule? How did the Court justify its decision?

You may have noticed that the Hawai'i Supreme Court based its decision exclusively on the due process clause of the Hawai'i Constitution and made no mention of the Fourteenth Amendment Due Process Clause. They did this because the supreme court of each state is the highest authority on the meaning of its own state constitution. The U.S. Supreme Court cannot stop Hawai'i from establishing a higher lever of due process protections as a matter of state law than are required by the federal constitution. This decision is in effect not subject to review by the U.S. Supreme Court. If the Hawai'i Supreme Court had based its decision on the Fourteenth Amendment Due Process Clause, that decision would be reviewable in a federal court. The U.S. Supreme Court ultimately has the last word on the meaning of the U.S. Constitution. Ironically, the U.S. Supreme Court has agreed to review Connecticut's version of Megan's

Law which was decided by lower courts on the basis of the Fourteenth Amendment's Due Process Clause.

INTERNET TIP

The text of the U.S. Supreme Court's opinion in the Connecticut case (*Doe v. Lee*) will be posted on the textbook's website once the justices have reached their decision. Also available on the website is a case entitled *People v. Malchow,* in which the Illinois Supreme Court upheld the constitutionality of that state's version of "Megan's Law" from a challenge that was based on the same grounds as the Hawai'i case.

CRIMINAL AND CIVIL LAW

The distinction between criminal and civil law is a very important concept in our legal system (see Figure 1-2). This text deals primarily with civil law. A civil suit involves a dispute between private individuals involving either a breach of an agreement or a breach of a duty imposed by law. A criminal action is brought by the government against an individual who has allegedly committed a crime. Crimes are classified as treason, felonies, and misdemeanors, depending on the punishment attached to the crime. *Treason* is a crime defined only by the Constitution, Article III, Section 3, Clause 1. To commit treason—levying war against the United States, or adhering to or giving aid or comfort to its enemies—there must be an overt act and the intent to commit treason. A *felony* is a crime that is classified by statute of the place in which it is committed. That is, the severity of the punishment for a felony varies from place to place. A felony is generally regarded as being any criminal offense for which a defendant may be imprisoned for more than one year, or executed. One determines whether a crime is a felony according to the sentence that might lawfully be imposed, not according to the sentence actually ordered. Felonies do not include *misdemeanors*, which are offenses that are generally punishable by a maximum term of imprisonment of less than one year.

In a civil suit, the court attempts to remedy the dispute between individuals by determining their legal rights, awarding money damages to the injured party, or directing one party to perform or refrain from performing a specific act. Since a crime is an act against society, the criminal court punishes a guilty defendant by imposing a fine or imprisonment or both.

In a criminal prosecution, the rules of court procedure differ. In order to meet the burden of proof to find a person guilty of a crime, guilt must be proved beyond a reasonable doubt, a stricter standard than the preponderance of evidence usually required in a civil case.

As we will see in the next case, when the same act gives rise to both a criminal proceeding and a civil suit, the actions are completely independent of each other. *Katko v. Briney* involves a civil suit for damages brought against the victim of a criminal larceny, by the person convicted of committing the crime.

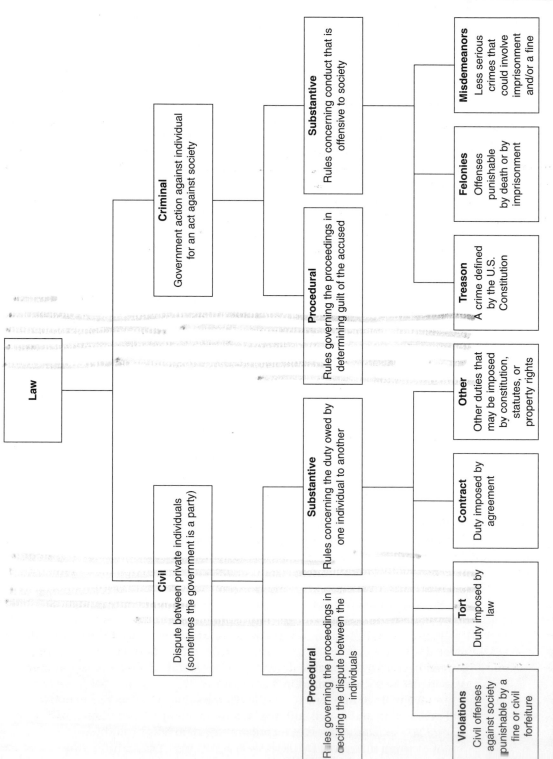

FIGURE 1-2   Criminal and Civil Law

Katko v. Briney
183 N.W.2d 657
Supreme Court of Iowa
February 9, 1971

Moore, Chief Justice

The primary issue presented here is whether an owner may protect personal property in an unoccupied boarded-up farmhouse against trespassers and thieves by a spring gun capable of inflicting death or serious injury.

We are not here concerned with a man's right to protect his home and members of his family. Defendants' home was several miles from the scene of the incident to which we refer *infra*.

Plaintiff's action is for damages resulting from serious injury caused by a shot from a 20-gauge spring shotgun set by defendants in a bedroom of an old farmhouse which had been uninhabited for several years. Plaintiff and his companion, Marvin McDonough, had broken and entered the house to find and steal old bottles and dated fruit jars which they considered antiques.

At defendants' request, plaintiff's action was tried to a jury consisting of residents of the community where defendants' property was located. The jury returned a verdict for plaintiff and against defendants for $20,000 actual and $10,000 punitive damages.

After careful consideration of defendants' motions for judgment notwithstanding the verdict and for a new trial, the experienced and capable trial judge overruled them and entered judgment on the verdict. Thus we have this appeal by defendants. . . .

Most of the facts are not disputed. In 1957 defendant Bertha L. Briney inherited her parents' farmland in Mahaska and Monroe Counties. For about ten years, 1957 to 1967, there occurred a series of trespassing and housebreaking events with loss of some household items, the breaking of windows, and "messing up of the property in general."

The latest occurred June 8, 1967, prior to the event on July 16, 1967, herein involved.

Defendants through the years boarded up the windows and doors in an attempt to stop the intrusions. They had posted "no trespass" signs on the land several years before 1967. The nearest one was 35 feet from the house. On June 11, 1967, defendants set a "shotgun trap" in the north bedroom. After Mr. Briney cleaned and oiled his 20-gauge shotgun, the power of which he was well aware, defendants took it to the old house where they secured it to an iron bed with the barrel pointed at the bedroom door. It was rigged with wire from the doorknob to the gun's trigger so that it would fire when the door was opened. Briney first pointed the gun so an intruder would be hit in the stomach but at Mrs. Briney's suggestion it was lowered to hit the legs. He admitted he did so "because I was mad and tired of being tormented" but "he did not intend to injure anyone." He gave no explanation of why he used a loaded shell and set it to hit a person already in the house. Tin was nailed over the bedroom window. The spring gun could not be seen from the outside. No warning of its presence was posted.

Plaintiff lived with his wife and worked regularly as a gasoline station attendant in Eddyville, seven miles from the old house. He had observed it for several years while hunting in the area and considered it as being abandoned. He knew it had long been uninhabited. In 1967 the area around the house was covered with high weeds. Prior to July 16, 1967 plaintiff and McDonough had been to the premises and found several old bottles and fruit jars which they took and added to their collection of antiques. On the latter date about 9:30 P.M. they made a second trip to the Briney property. They entered the old house by removing a board from a porch window which was without glass. While McDonough was looking around the kitchen area, plaintiff went to another part of the house. As he started to open the north bedroom door the shotgun went off, striking him in the right leg above the ankle bone. Much of his leg, including part of the tibia, was blown away. Only by McDonough's assistance was plaintiff able to get out of the house and after crawling some distance, he was put in his vehicle and rushed to a doctor and then to a hospital. He remained in the hospital 40 days.

Plaintiff's doctor testified he seriously considered amputation but eventually the healing process was successful. Some weeks after his release from the hospital plaintiff returned to work on crutches. He was required to keep the injured leg in a cast for approximately a year and wear a special brace for another year. He continued to suffer pain during this period.

There was undenied medical testimony that plaintiff had a permanent deformity, a loss of tissue, and a shortening of the leg.

The record discloses plaintiff to trial time had incurred $710 for medical expenses, $2056.85 for hospital service, $61.80 for orthopedic service and $750 as loss of earnings. In addition thereto the trial court submitted to the jury the question of damages for pain and suffering and for future disability.

Plaintiff testified he knew he had no right to break and enter the house with intent to steal bottles and fruit jars therefrom. He further testified he had entered a plea of guilty to larceny in the nighttime of property of less than $20 value from a private building. He stated he had been fined $50 and costs and paroled during good behavior from a 60-day jail sentence. Other than minor traffic charges, this was plaintiff's first brush with the law. On this civil case appeal, it is not our prerogative to review the disposition made of the criminal charge against him.

The main thrust of defendants' defense in the trial court and on this appeal is that "the law permits use of a spring gun in a dwelling or warehouse for the purpose of preventing the unlawful entry of a burglar or thief." . . . [T]he court referred to the early case history

of the use of spring guns and stated under the law their use was prohibited except to prevent the commission of felonies of violence and where human life is in danger. The instruction included a statement that breaking and entering is not a felony of violence.

Instruction 5 stated: "You are hereby instructed that one may use reasonable force in the protection of his property, but such right is subject to the qualification that one may not use such means of force as will take human life or inflict great bodily injury. Such is the rule even though the injured party is a trespasser and is in violation of the law himself."

Instruction 6 stated: "An owner of premises is prohibited from willfully or intentionally injuring a trespasser by means of force that either takes life or inflicts great bodily injury; and therefore a person owning a premise is prohibited from setting out 'spring guns' and like dangerous devices which will likely take life or inflict great bodily injury, for the purpose of harming trespassers. The fact that the trespasser may be acting in violation of the law does not change the rule. The only time when such conduct of setting a 'spring gun' or a like dangerous device is justified would be when the trespasser was committing a felony of violence or a felony punishable by death, or where the trespasser was endangering human life by his act."

Instruction 7, to which defendants made no objection or exception, stated:

"To entitle the plaintiff to recover for compensatory damages, the burden of proof is upon him to establish by a preponderance of the evidence each and all of the following propositions:

"1. That defendants erected a shotgun trap in a vacant house on land owned by defendant, Bertha L. Briney, on or about June 11, 1967, which fact was known only by them, to protect household goods from trespassers and thieves.

"2. That the force used by defendants was in excess of that force reasonably necessary and which persons are entitled to use in the protection of their property.

"3. That plaintiff was injured and damaged and the amount thereof.

"4. That plaintiff's injuries and damages resulted directly from the discharge of the shotgun trap which was set and used by defendants."

The overwhelming weight of authority, both textbook and case law, supports the trial court's statement of the applicable principles of law.

Prosser on Torts, third edition, pages 116–118, states that:

"the law has always placed a higher value upon human safety than upon mere rights in property[. I]t is the accepted rule that there is no privilege to use any force calculated to cause death or serious bodily injury to repel the threat to land or chattels, unless there is also such a threat to the defendant's personal safety as to justify a self-defense. . . . [S]pring guns and other man-killing devices are not justifiable against a mere trespasser, or even a petty thief. They are privileged only against those upon whom the landowner, if he were present in person, would be free to inflict injury of the same kind."

Restatement of Torts, §85, page 180, states that:

"the value of human life and limbs, not only to the individual concerned but also to society, so outweighs the interest of a possessor of land in excluding from it those whom he is not willing to admit thereto that a possessor of land has, as is stated in §79, no privilege to use force intended or likely to cause death or serious harm against another whom the possessor sees about to enter his premises or meddle with his chattel, unless the intrusion threatens death or serious bodily harm to the occupiers or users of the premises. . . . A possessor of land cannot do indirectly and by a mechanical device that which, were he present, he could not do immediately and in person. Therefore, he cannot gain a privilege to install, for the purpose of protecting his

land from intrusions harmless to the lives and limbs of the occupiers or users of it, a mechanical device whose only purpose is to inflict death or serious harm upon such as may intrude, by giving notice of his intention to inflict, by mechanical means and indirectly, harm which he could not, even after request, inflict directly were he present." . . .

In *Hooker v. Miller*, 37 Iowa 613, we held defendant vineyard owner liable for damages resulting from a spring gun shot although plaintiff was a trespasser and there to steal grapes. At pages 614, 615, this statement is made: "This court has held that a mere trespass against property other than a dwelling is not a sufficient justification to authorize the use of a deadly weapon by the owner in its defense; and that if death results in such a case it will be murder, though the killing be actually necessary to prevent the trespass. . . ." At page 617 this court said: "[T]respassers and other inconsiderable violators of the law are not to be visited by barbarous punishments or prevented by inhuman inflictions of bodily injuries."

The facts in *Allison v. Fiscus*, 156 Ohio 120, decided in 1951, are very similar to the case at bar. There plaintiff's right to damages was recognized for injuries received when he feloniously broke a door latch and started to enter defendant's warehouse with intent to steal. As he entered, a trap of two sticks of dynamite buried under the doorway by defendant owner was set off and plaintiff seriously injured. The court held the question whether a particular trap was justified as a use of reasonable and necessary force against a trespasser engaged in the commission of a felony should have been submitted to the jury. The Ohio Supreme Court recognized the plaintiff's right to recover punitive or exemplary damages in addition to compensatory damages. . . .

In *United Zinc & Chemical Co. v. Britt*, 258 U.S. 268, 275, the Court states: "The liability for spring guns and mantraps arises from the fact that the defendant has . . . expected the trespasser and prepared an injury that is no more justified than if he had held the gun and fired it."

In addition to civil liability many jurisdictions hold a landowner criminally liable for serious injuries or homicide caused by spring guns or other set devices. . . .

In Wisconsin, Oregon and England the use of spring guns and similar devices is specifically made unlawful by statute. . . .

The legal principles stated by the trial court in instructions 2, 5 and 6 are well established and supported by the authorities cited and quoted *supra*. There is no merit in defendants' objections and exceptions thereto. Defendants' various motions based on the same reasons stated in exceptions to instructions were properly overruled.

Plaintiff's claim and the jury's allowance of punitive damages, under the trial court's instructions relating thereto, were not at any time or in any manner challenged by defendants in the trial court as not allowable. We therefore are not presented with the problem of whether the $10,000 award should be allowed to stand.

We express no opinion as to whether punitive damages are allowable in this type of case. If defendants' attorneys wanted that issue decided, it was their duty to raise it in the trial court.

The rule is well established that we will not consider a contention not raised in the trial court. In other words, we are a court of review and will not consider a contention raised for the first time in this court. . . .

Under our law punitive damages are not allowed as a matter of right. When malice is shown or when a defendant acted with wanton and reckless disregard of the rights of others, punitive damages may be allowed as punishment to the defendant and as a deterrent to others. Although not meant to compensate a plaintiff, the result is to increase his recovery. He is the fortuitous beneficiary of

such an award simply because there is no one else to receive it.

The jury's findings of fact including a finding that defendants acted with malice and with wanton and reckless disregard, as required for an allowance of punitive or exemplary damages, are supported by substantial evidence. We are bound thereby.

This opinion is not to be taken or construed as authority that the allowance of punitive damages is or is not proper under circumstances such as exist here. We hold only that a question of law not having been properly raised cannot in this case be resolved.

Study and careful consideration of defendants' contentions on appeal reveal no reversible error.

Affirmed.

Larson, Justice, dissenting

I respectfully dissent, first because the majority wrongfully assumes that by installing a spring gun in the bedroom of their unoccupied house the defendants intended to shoot any intruder who attempted to enter the room. Under the record presented here, that was a fact question. Unless it is held that these property owners are liable for any injury to an intruder from such a device regardless of the intent with which it is installed, liability under these pleadings must rest on two definite issues of fact, i.e., did the defendants intend to shoot the invader, and if so, did they employ unnecessary and unreasonable force against him?

It is my feeling that the majority oversimplifies the impact of this case on the law, not only in this but other jurisdictions, and that it has not thought through all the ramifications of this holding.

There being no statutory provisions governing the right of an owner to defend his property by the use of a spring gun or other like device, or of a criminal invader to recover punitive damages when injured by such an instrumentality while breaking into the building of another, our interest and attention are directed to what should be the court determination of public policy in these matters. On both issues we are faced with a case of first impression. We should accept the task and clearly establish the law in this jurisdiction hereafter. I would hold there is no absolute liability for injury to a criminal intruder by setting up such a device on his property, and unless done with an intent to kill or seriously injure the intruder, I would absolve the owner from liability other than for negligence. I would also hold the court had no jurisdiction to allow punitive damages when the intruder was engaged in a serious criminal offense such as breaking and entering with intent to steal. . . .

Case Questions

1. Suppose that, instead of a spring gun, the Brineys had unleashed on the premises a vicious watchdog that severely injured Katko's leg? Would the result have been different? What if the watchdog had been properly chained?
2. When may one set a spring gun and not be subject to liability? What can one legally do to protect property or life?
3. What do you think the consequences would be if the dissenting judge's suggestions had become law?
4. A case involving breaking and entering and shooting a gun might appear to be a criminal matter. What factors make this a civil lawsuit?

EQUAL PROTECTION OF THE LAW

The Equal Protection Clause of the Fourteenth Amendment has been used to strike down legislation that was enacted for the purpose of discriminating against certain groupings of people (called "classifications" in legalese). The Jim Crow laws, used to discriminate against African Americans, are one notorious example of an invidious (legally impermissible) classification scheme.

Earlier in this chapter we saw how the U.S. Supreme Court ruled in the 1967 case of *Loving v. Virginia* that Virginia's miscegenation statute was found to violate substantive due process. We return to that case at this time because the Lovings had an additional ground for challenging the statute. They maintained that it also violated the Equal Protection Clause of the Fourteenth Amendment. The Supreme Court agreed. It ruled that the statute had deprived the Lovings of equal protection because " . . . Virginia prohibit[ed] only interracial marriages involving white persons . . ." and because . . . "There is no legitimate overriding purpose independent of invidious racial discrimination which justifies [such a] classification."

The Equal Protection Clause has also been invoked to invalidate discriminatory classification schemes that are based on national origin, alienage, religion, and gender (in some situations).

TORT AND CONTRACT LAW

A person has a right to bring a civil action against another for a wrongful act or omission that causes injury to him or her. The basis of the suit is a violation of some duty owed to the injured person. This duty arises either from an agreement of the persons or by operation of the law.

Torts

Tort law establishes standards of conduct that all citizens must meet. A plaintiff sues in tort to recover money damages for injuries to his or her person, reputation, property, or business caused by a breach of a legal duty.

A tort is any wrongful act, not involving a breach of an agreement, for which such a civil action may be maintained. The wrongful act can be intentional or unintentional. Intentional torts are based on the defendant's willful misconduct or intentional wrongdoing. This does not necessarily mean the defendant had a hostile intent, only that he or she had a belief that a particular harmful result was substantially likely to follow. *Katko v. Briney* was such a case. When Briney rigged the spring gun, he did so believing that serious bodily injury was very likely to occur to any intruder who opened the door. Briney was civilly found to have violated the standard of care owed by a property owner to a trespasser such as Katko under the circumstances of that case. A person who commits an intentional tort may also be committing a criminal act, for which the government may bring criminal charges. As we saw in *Katko v. Briney*, the tort and criminal actions would be independent of each other.

An unintentional tort occurs when a person acts negligently. That is, he or she unintentionally fails to live up to the community's ideal of reasonable care. Every person has a legal duty to act toward other people as a reasonable and prudent person would have acted under the circumstances. Torts will be discussed more fully in Chapter 11.

Contracts

A contract is a promissory agreement between two or more people that creates, modifies, or destroys a legally enforceable obligation. People voluntarily enter into a contract in order to create private duties for mutual advantage. Thus, under ordinary conditions, contractual terms are not imposed by law. There are exceptions to this rule; however, the essence of contract law is the enforcement of a promise voluntarily made.

Although contract law is more thoroughly discussed in Chapter 10, it will be helpful to introduce it here. In the legal sense, the term *contract* does not mean the tangible document that contains evidence of an agreement. Rather, a contract is the legally enforceable agreement itself. There are three parts to every contract: *offer, acceptance,* and *consideration.* An offer is a communication of a promise, with a statement of what is expected in return. An offer is made with the intention of creating an enforceable legal obligation. Acceptance is the evidence of assent to the terms of the offer. Consideration is the inducement each party has to enter into an agreement. Only legally enforceable obligations are called contracts.

A person who fails to perform a contractual obligation has breached the contract. The plaintiff brings a suit in contract to obtain legal relief from the breaching party. The normal remedy for a breach of contract is monetary damages, although in appropriate circumstances, the breaching party may be ordered to perform his or her agreement.

Contracts may be oral, written, express (explicit terms), implied in fact (inferred from the person's actions), or implied in law. In *Suggs v. Norris*, which follows, the trial court permitted the jury to find an implied-in-law agreement from the facts of the case, even though there was no proof of an oral agreement or written document evidencing a contract.

Suggs v. Norris
364 S.E.2d 159
Court of Appeals of North Carolina
February 2, 1988

Wells, Judge

The overriding question presented by this appeal is whether public policy forbids the recovery by a plaintiff partner to an unmarried but cohabiting or meretricious relationship, from the other partner's estate, for services rendered to or benefits conferred upon the other partner through the plaintiff's work in the operation of a joint business when the business proceeds were utilized to enrich the estate of the deceased partner.

Defendant argues under her first three assignments of error that any agreement between plaintiff and the decedent providing compensation to plaintiff for her efforts in the raising and harvesting of produce was void as against public policy because it arose out of the couple's illegal cohabitation. While it is well-settled that no recovery can be had under either a contractual or restitutionary (*quantum meruit*) theory arising out of a contract or circumstances which violate public policy, . . . defendant's application of the rule to the present case is misplaced.

This Court has made it clear that we do not approve of or endorse adulterous meretricious affairs, *Collins v. Davis*, 68 N.C.App. 588. . . . We made it clear in *Collins*, however, that cohabiting but unmarried individuals are capable of "entering into enforceable express or implied contracts for the purchase and improvement of houses, or for the loan and repayment of money." . . . Judge Phillips, writing for the majority, in *Collins* was careful to point out that if illicit sexual intercourse had provided the consideration for the contract or implied agreement, all claims arising therefrom, having been founded on illegal consideration, would then be unenforceable.

While our research has disclosed no other North Carolina cases which address this specific issue, we do find considerable guidance in the decisional law of other states. Most notable is Justice Tobriner's landmark decision in *Marvin v. Marvin*, 18 Cal.3d 660, . . . (1976) which held that express contracts between unmarried cohabiting individuals are enforceable unless the same are based solely on sexual services. . . .

The *Marvin* Court also held that an unmarried couple may, by words and conduct, create an implied-in-fact agreement regarding the disposition of their mutual properties and money as well as an implied agreement of partnership or joint venture. . . . Finally, the court endorsed the use of constructive trusts wherever appropriate and recovery in *quantum meruit* where the plaintiff can show that the services were rendered with an expectation of monetary compensation. . . .

Other jurisdictions have fashioned and adhered to similar rules. In *Kinkenon v. Hue*, 207 Neb. 698 . . . (1981), the Nebraska Supreme Court confirmed an earlier rule that while bargains made in whole or in part for consideration of sexual intercourse are illegal, any agreements not resting on such consideration, regardless of the marital status of the two individuals, are enforceable. . . .

Likewise, the New Jersey Supreme Court held as enforceable an oral agreement between two adult unmarried partners where the agreement was not based "explicitly or inseparably" on sexual services. *Kozlowski v. Kozlowski*, 80 N.J. 378 . . . (1979). In *Fernandez v. Garza*, 88 Ariz. 214, (1960), the Arizona Supreme Court held that plaintiff's meretricious or unmarried cohabitation with decedent did not bar the enforcement of a partnership agreement wherein the parties agreed to share their property and profits equally and where such was not based upon sexual services as consideration. . . .

We now make clear and adopt the rule that agreements regarding the finances and property of an unmarried but cohabiting couple, whether express or implied, are enforceable as long as sexual services or promises thereof do not provide the consideration for such agreements. . . .

In the present case, the question is before this Court on an appeal of the trial court's denial of defendant's Motion for Judgment Notwithstanding the Verdict; therefore, our standard of review is whether the evidence viewed in the light most favorable to plaintiff is sufficient to support the jury verdict. *Wallace v. Evans*, 60 N.C.App. 145, . . . (1982). Applying the foregoing standard, we find that plaintiff's

evidence that she began work for the decedent in his produce business several years before she began cohabiting with him and that at the time she began work she believed the two of them were "partners" in the business, was sufficient evidence for the jury to have inferred that plaintiff's work comprised a business relationship with decedent which was separate and independent from and of their cohabiting relationship. Therefore, the jury may have inferred that sexual services did not provide the consideration for plaintiff's claim. We therefore hold that plaintiff's claim for a *quantum meruit* recovery was not barred as being against public policy. Defendant's first three assignments of error are overruled.

Defendant next argues under assignments of error 4 and 5 that the trial court erred in submitting a *quantum meruit* recovery issue to the jury because any services rendered by plaintiff were either gratuitous or incidental to an illegal relationship. As we have already addressed the issue of illegality we are concerned here only with the question of whether there existed sufficient evidence to submit the issue of recovery in *quantum meruit* to the jury.

The trial court placed the following issue regarding a quasi-contract or *quantum meruit* recovery before the jury:

> *Issue Four:*
> 4. Did DARLENE SUGGS render services to JUNIOR EARL NORRIS involving the raising, harvesting and sale of produce under such circumstances that the Estate of JUNIOR EARL NORRIS should be required to pay for them?
> ANSWER: Yes

Recovery on *quantum meruit* requires the establishment of an implied contract. . . . The contract may be one implied-in-fact where the conduct of the parties clearly indicates their intention to create a contract or it may be implied-in-law based on the restitutionary theory of quasi-contract which operates to prevent unjust enrichment. . . . An implied-in-law theory required the plaintiff to establish that services were rendered and accepted between the two parties with the mutual understanding that plaintiff was to be compensated for her efforts. . . . Moreover, plaintiff's efforts must not have been gratuitous as is generally presumed where services are rendered between family or spousal members. . . .

In the present case, the evidence clearly showed that the plaintiff had from 1973 until the death of the decedent in 1983 operated a produce route for and with the decedent. According to several witnesses' testimony, plaintiff had worked decedent's farm, disced and cultivated the soil, and harvested and marketed the produce. Plaintiff, working primarily without the decedent's aid, drove the produce to various markets over a 60-mile route. She handled all finances and deposited them in the couple's joint banking account. Finally, the evidence showed that the decedent, an alcoholic, depended almost entirely on plaintiff's work in the produce business and as well her care of him while he was ill. Because of plaintiff's efforts the couple had amassed seven vehicles valued at $20,000; some farm equipment valued at $4,000; $8,000 in cash in the account, and all debts which had attached to the farm when plaintiff began working with decedent in 1973 were paid—all due to plaintiff's efforts. Additionally, plaintiff testified that when she began work with the decedent in 1973 she believed they were partners and that she was entitled to share in one-half the profits.

The foregoing evidence clearly establishes a set of facts sufficient to have submitted a quasi-contractual issue to the jury and from which the jury could have inferred a mutual understanding between plaintiff and the decedent that she would be remunerated for her services. Plaintiff's efforts conferred many years of benefits on the decedent and the decedent, by all accounts, willingly accepted those benefits.

Because the evidence viewed in the light most favorable to plaintiff was clearly sufficient to permit the jury to find a mutual understanding between plaintiff and decedent that plaintiff's work in the produce business was not free of charge and because plaintiff's work in the produce business was not of the character usually found to be performed gratuitously, . . . defendant's Motions for Directed Verdict and Judgment Notwithstanding the Verdict were properly denied.

No Error.

Case Questions

1. Darlene Suggs's suit against the estate of Junior E. Norris was based on what legal theories?
2. Under what circumstances does the court indicate that the contracts between unmarried but cohabiting persons would not be enforceable?
3. Why should a court be able to create a contract after a dispute arises for parties who never signed a binding contract?

 Do you see any moral principles reflected in the court's opinion in this case?

Chapter Questions

1. Define the following terms:

affirm	injunction
analytical positivism	legal realism
appeal	Magna Carta
appellant	misdemeanor
appellee	money damages
canon law	natural law
case of first impression	plaintiff
chancellor	procedural due process
civil suit	public policy
common law	*quantum meruit*
contract	quasi-contract
court of equity	remand
criminal law	reeve
Curia Regis	reverse
damages	shire
defendant	sociological jurisprudence
dicta	substantive due process
due process clause	tort
equity	trade secret
express contract	trespass
felony	trial court instructions
feudalism	unjust enrichment
hearing	utilitarian law
holding	void-for-vagueness doctrine
historical jurisprudence	writ
hundred	writ of right
implied contract	Year Books

2. Inmates in a state reformatory brought suit against the state department of corrections because corrections officials refused to permit certain persons to visit inmates. The inmates brought suit because receiving visitors is so essential to inmates' morale and to maintaining contacts with their families. They argued that the state had established regulations to guide prison officials in making visitation decisions. Thus the court should recognize that inmates have a constitutionally protected liberty right to a hearing whenever prison officials deny a visitation. Convening such a hearing would make it possible for inmates to determine whether prison officials had complied with the guidelines or had acted arbitrarily in denying a visitation. Should the inmates have a due process right to a hearing?

   Kentucky Department of Corrections v. Thompson, 490 U.S. 454 (1989)

3. Terry Foucha, a criminal defendant, was charged with aggravated burglary and a firearms offense. On October 12, 1904, Foucha was found not guilty

by reason of insanity and was ordered committed to a mental institution until medically discharged or released pursuant to a court order. In March of 1988, doctors evaluated Foucha and determined that he was "presently in remission from mental illness, [but] [w]e cannot certify that he would not constitute a menace to himself or to others if released." There was testimony from one doctor that Foucha had "an antisocial personality, a condition that is not a mental disease, and that is untreatable." Based on these opinions, the court ordered that Foucha remain in the mental institution because he posed a danger to himself as well as others. Under state law, a person who has been acquitted of criminal charges because of insanity but who is no longer insane can only be released from commitment if he can prove that he is not a danger to himself or to society. Does the statutory scheme violate Foucha's liberty rights under the due process clause?
Foucha v. Louisiana, 504 U.S. 71 (1992)

4. Rhode Island's legislature enacted laws that prevented liquor retailers from advertising the retail prices of their merchandise at sites other than their retail stores. It feared that allowing package stores to freely and honestly advertise their prices would lower the cost to consumers and increase the use of alcoholic beverages. 44 Liquormart, a liquor retailer, brought suit seeking a declaratory judgment on the grounds that Rhode Island's laws violated the store's First Amendment right to freedom of speech. The U.S. District Court made a finding of fact that Rhode Island's law had "no significant impact on levels of alcohol consumption" and concluded that the law was unconstitutional. The district judge's rationale was that the statute in question did not further the goal of reducing alcohol consumption, and further, that its restrictions on commercial freedom of speech were unnecessary and excessive. The First Circuit U.S. Court of Appeals reversed, however, and the U.S. Supreme Court granted certiorari. Do you believe that Rhode Island's statute violates the package store's First Amendment and due process right to engage in commercial speech?
44 Liquormart, Inc. v. Rhode Island, No. 94-1140, __U.S.__ (1996)

5. Margaret Gilleo is a homeowner in a St. Louis suburb. In December 1990, she placed a 24- by 36-inch sign on her lawn expressing opposition to Operation Desert Storm. She contacted police after her sign was stolen on one occasion and knocked down on another occasion. Police officials told Margaret that her signs were prohibited by city ordinance. Margaret unsuccessfully petitioned the city council for a variance, and then filed suit. In her civil rights action, she maintained that the city ordinance violated her First Amendment right of freedom of speech, which was applicable to the state through the Fourteenth Amendment due process clause. The U.S. District Court agreed and enjoined the enforcement of the ordinance. Margaret then placed an 8½- by 11-inch sign in an upstairs window indicating her desire for "Peace in the Gulf." The city, in the meantime, repealed its original ordinance and replaced it with an ordinance that prohibited all signs that did not fit within ten authorized exemptions. The ordinance's preamble indicated that its purpose

was to improve aesthetics and protect property values within the city. Margaret's peace sign did not fit within any of the authorized exemptions. She amended her complaint and challenged the new ordinance because it prohibited her from expressing her opposition to the war. The city defended by arguing that its ordinance was content neutral and its purposes justified the limited number of exemptions. It noted that alternative methods of communication, such as hand-held signs, pamphlets, flyers, etc., were permissible under the ordinance. How would you decide this case?

City of Ladue v. Gilleo, No. 92-1856 __U.S.__ (1994)

6. Keen Umbehr was in the trash collection business. He had an exclusive contract with Wabaunsee County and six of the county's seven cities to collect the trash from the 1985 to 1991. Throughout his term as the primary trash collector he publicly criticized the county board and many of its policies, successfully sued the board for violating the state open meeting law, and tried, unsuccessfully, to be elected to the board. The board's members retaliated against Umbehr by voting to terminate his contract with the county. Umbehr, however, successfully negotiated new agreements with five of the six cities whose trash he had previously collected. In 1992, Umbehr sued the two county board members who had voted to terminate his contract. He alleged that his discharge/nonrenewal was in retaliation for having exercised his right to freedom of speech. The U.S. District Court ruled that only public employees were protected by the First Amendment from retaliatory discharge. The U.S. Court of Appeals disagreed and reversed. Should independent contractors who have government contracts be protected by the Fourteenth Amendment's due process clause from retaliatory contract discharges resulting from a contractor's exercise of speech? Should the well-known system of patronage, a practice followed by politicians of all stripes by which they reward their supporters with contracts and discharge those who are their political adversaries or who criticize their policies, take precedence over First Amendment considerations?

Board of County Commissioners, Wabaunsee County, Kansas v. Umbehr, No. 94-1654, __U.S.__ (1996)

7. A Cincinnati, Ohio, ordinance makes it a criminal offense for "three or more persons to assemble, except at a public meeting of citizens, on any of the sidewalks, street corners, vacant lots, or mouths of alleys, and there conduct themselves in a manner annoying to persons passing by, or occupants of adjacent buildings." Coates, a student involved in a demonstration, was arrested and convicted for the violation of this ordinance. His argument on appeal was that the ordinance on its face violated the Fourteenth Amendment. Is this a valid contention?

Coates v. City of Cincinnati, 402 U.S. 611 (1971)

8. Fuentes purchased a stove and stereo from Firestone Tire and Rubber Company. Payment was to be made in monthly installments over a period of time. After two-thirds of the payments were made, Fuentes defaulted. Firestone filed an action for repossession and at the same time instructed the sheriff to seize the property pursuant to state law. The sheriff seized the

property before Fuentes even knew of Firestone's suit for repossession. Fuentes claims that she was deprived of due process because her property was taken without notice or a hearing. What should the result be?

Fuentes v. Shervin, 407 U.S. 67 (1972)

9. Plaintiff brought a class action on behalf of all female welfare recipients residing in Connecticut and wishing divorces. She alleged that [members of the class were] prevented from bringing divorce suits by Connecticut statutes that require[d] payment of court fees and costs of service of process as a condition precedent to access to the courts. Plaintiff contended that such statutes violate basic due process considerations. Is her argument valid?

Boddie v. Connecticut, 401 U.S. 371 (1970)

10. Like many other states, Connecticut requires nonresidents of the state who are enrolled in the state university system to pay tuition and other fees at higher rates than residents of the state who are so enrolled. A Connecticut statute defined as a nonresident any unmarried student if his or her "legal address for any part of the one-year period immediately prior to his application for admission . . . was outside of Connecticut," or any married student if his or her "legal address at the time of his application for admission . . . was outside of Connecticut." The statute also provided that the "status of a student, as established at the time of his application for admission . . . shall be his status for the entire period of his attendance." Two University of Connecticut students who claimed to be residents of Connecticut were by the statute classified as nonresidents for tuition purposes. They claimed that the due process clause does not permit Connecticut to deny an individual the opportunity to present evidence that he or she is a *bona fide* resident entitled to state rates and that they are being deprived of property without due process. Is this a valid argument?

Vlandis v. Kline, 412 U.S. 441 (1973)

Notes

1. Special recognition goes to Bruce D. Fisher and Edgar Bodenheimer. Students seeking more extensive treatment of this material should see Fisher, *Introduction to the Legal System* (St. Paul, MN: West Publishing Co., 1977); and Bodenheimer, *Jurisprudence* (Cambridge, MA: Harvard University Press, 1967).
2. Murphy and Coleman, *An Introduction to Jurisprudence* (Totowa, NJ: Rowman and Allenheld Publishers, 1984), p. 13.
3. Bodenheimer, p. 71; and Fisher, p. 7.
4. Bodenheimer, p. 72.
5. Examples are adverse possession, delivery of a deed, the concept of escheat, estate, and the covenant of seisin, and the rule against restraints on alienation.
6. Property law addresses the notion that property equals rights, the rights of a finder vis-à-vis everyone but the true owner, the importance of delivery in the making of a gift, or the right of survivorship in joint tenancies.

7. The concept of consideration, silence as acceptance, and the Statute of Frauds are addressed by contract law.

8. The Massachusetts legislature has again enacted a mandatory seat belt law. An attempt to repeal this statute was unsuccessful.

9. G. Sabine, *A History of Political Theory*, 3rd ed. (New York: Holt, Rinehart and Winston, 1961), pp. 681–684; and Bodenheimer, p. 85.

10. Bodenheimer, p. 84; and B. H. Levy, *Anglo-American Philosophy of Law* (New Brunswick, NJ: Transaction Publishers, 1991), pp. 19–23.

11. Bodenheimer, pp. 94, 99; and Levy, pp. 29–36.

12. Bodenheimer, p. 96; and Fisher, p. 11.

13. *Lochner v. New York*, 198 U.S. 45 (1905).

14. *Adair v. United States*, 208 U.S. 161 (1908).

15. B. Cardozo, *The Nature of Judicial Process* (New Haven, CT: Yale University Press, 1921), p. 65–66.

16. R. Pound, *The Scope and Purpose of Sociological Jurisprudence,* 24 *Harvard L.R.* 591 (1911).

17. Ibid., pp. 510–514.

18. Bodenheimer, p. 116.

19. K. Llewellyn, "A Realistic Jurisprudence—The Next Step," 30 *Columbia Law Review*, 431 (1930) 12.

20. K. Llewellyn, *The Bramble Bush* (1930), p. 12.

21. D. Black, *Sociological Justice* (New York: Oxford University Press, 1989), p. 5.

22. Ibid., p. 21.

23. Ibid., pp. 24–25 and Chapter 2 "Sociological Litigation."

24. Ibid., pp. 9–13, 21–22.

25. Ibid., p. 24–25, 95–96.

26. F. Marcham, *A History of England* (New York: Macmillan, 1937), p. 62.

27. G. Keeton, *The Norman Conquest and the Common Law* (London: Ernest Benn Limited, 1966), p. 14.

28. Ibid., p. 128; and Marcham, pp. 60–61.

29. T. F. F. Plucknett, *A Concise History of the Common Law* (Little, Brown and Co., 1956), p. 102.

30. Marcham, p. 62; and Ibid., p. 144.

31. Keeton, p. 23.

32. F. Barlow, *The Feudal Kingdom of England,* 4th ed. (Longman, 1988), p. 51; P. Loyn, *The Making of the English Nation* (Thames & Hudson, 1991), p. 78; C. Brooke, *From Alfred to Henry III* (Norton, 1961), p. 78.

33. Plucknett, p. 139.

34. A. K. R. Kiralfy, *Potter's Historical Introduction to English Law,* 4th ed. (London: Sweet and Maxwell Ltd., 1962), p. 11.

35. Plucknett, p. 141; and Keeton, p. 13.

36. Marcham, p. 80.

37. Plucknett, p. 11; and Barlow, p. 81.

38. Marcham, p. 83.

39. Ibid., p. 86.

40. Ibid., p. 90; and Plucknett, p. 12.

41. Marcham, pp. 110–111.

42. Keeton, p. 160.

43. A. C. Baugh and T. Cable, *A History of the English Language*, 3rd ed. (Englewood Cliffs, NJ: Prentice Hall, 1978), pp. 145, 148–149.

44. Brooke, pp. 160, 192.

45. Ibid., p. 156; and Plucknett, p. 14.
46. Marcham, p. 118; and Plucknett, p. 22.
47. Plucknett, p. 15.
48. Brooke, pp. 182–185; and Loyn, p. 128.
49. Marcham, pp. 156–157.
50. Plucknett, p. 103.
51. Keeton, p. 125.
52. Ibid., p. 201.
53. Loyn, p. 139.
54. Marcham, p. 131; and Plucknett, p. 355.
55. Marcham, p. 295.
56. Plucknett, p. 408.
57. Plucknett, p. 357.
58. R. Walsh, *A History of Anglo-American Law* (Indianapolis: Bobbs-Merrill Co., 1932), p. 65.
59. P. H. Winfield, *Chief Sources of English Legal History* (Cambridge, MA: Harvard University Press, 1925).
60. Plucknett, p. 259.
61. Ibid., pp. 280–281.
62. M. Grossberg, *Governing the Hearth* (Chapel Hill: University of North Carolina Press, 1985), p. 15.
63. Marcham, p. 295.
64. Plucknett, p. 178.
65. Ibid., p. 180.
66. Ibid., p. 280; and Marcham, p. 295.
67. Cardinal Wolsey was educated at Oxford, and Becket was educated at the Universities of Paris and Bologna (Brooke, p. 64).
68. Brooke, p. 64.
69. D. Roebuck, *The Background of the Common Law*, 2nd ed. (Oxford University Press, 1990), p. 64; and Marcham, p. 295.
70. Plucknett, p. 688.
71. Ibid., p. 689; and Potter, pp. 581–584.
72. Potter, p. 280; and Plucknett, pp. 693–694.
73. Roebuck, p. 68.
74. M. L. Shaw, "Courts Point Justice in a New Direction," *The National Law Journal* C1 (April 11, 1994).
75. J. D. Rosenberg, "Court Studies Confirm That Mandatory Mediation Works," *The National Law Journal* C7 (April 11, 1994); D. R. Hensler, "Does ADR Really Save Money? The Jury's Still Out," *The National Law Journal* C2–5 (April 11, 1994).
76. Loyn, p. 141; and Brooke, pp. 220–223.
77. Marcham, p. 143; and Brooke, p. 221.
78. Brooke, p. 223.
79. C. A. Miller, "The Forest of Due Process of Law: The American Constitutional Tradition," in J. R. Pennock and J. W. Chapman, *Due Process* (New York: New York University Press, 1977), p. 6.
80. Ibid.
81. Ibid., p. 9.

II Ethics and Law

This chapter builds on themes introduced in the philosophy section of Chapter 1. Its primary purpose is to show students why people need to be sensitive to ethical issues. A second objective is to illustrate some of the problems that arise because our complex and diverse society is unable to agree on the proper boundaries of law and ethics. It is only possible to give the reader a taste of this rich and intricate subject. However, this discussion can expand our understanding and hopefully encourage students to pursue courses that are devoted exclusively to ethics.

All human beings face ethical challenges in their personal, professional, and public lives. Ethical questions permeate our society. In charting public policy, for example, legislators choose from among competing alternative courses of action as part of the lawmaking process. Similarly, when appellate judges construe constitutions and statutes and review the decisions of lower courts in contract and tort cases, they also make choices about public policy. Is it morally right for the Supreme Judicial Court of Maine to rule in a medical malpractice unintended pregnancy case that "a parent cannot be said to have been damaged by the birth and rearing of a healthy, normal child?"[1] Is the Massachusetts legislature morally justified in enacting an extremely short statute of limitations for the commencement of skiers' personal injury actions against ski area operators, to the detriment of injured skiers?[2] Reasonable people can differ about whether the ethical judgments embodied in these legislative and judicial decisions should be legally sanctioned as the public policy of the state. It is no wonder that there is great public concern about the morality of governmental policies regarding such topics as capital punishment, abortion, assisted suicide, same-sex marriages, homosexuality, interracial adoptions, the rights of landowners versus environmental protection, the meaning of cruel and unusual punishment, and the right of indigents to appellate counsel in capital cases.

The following case is an example of an ethical debate over public policy. The petitioner was a convicted robber and murderer who was sentenced to death pursuant to a Georgia statute. He failed to convince the courts in Georgia to overturn his sentence, but he did successfully petition the U.S. Supreme Court for certiorari.

In the case of *Gregg v. Georgia,* the Supreme Court justices debated the ethics and the legality of capital punishment. The case of *Gregg v. Georgia* was decided in 1976. In that case, seven justices ruled that Georgia's statute authorizing capital punishment was not inherently cruel and unusual under the Eighth and Fourteenth Amendments to the U.S. Constitution. The following excerpts from Gregg have been edited to focus on the argument about the morality of capital punishment. In the opinions below, you will find several references to an earlier case, *Furman v. Georgia. Furman* was a 1972 case in which the Supreme Court prohibited states from imposing the death penalty in an arbitrary manner. The justices wrote extensively on the ethical issue of capital punishment in *Furman,* and only summarized their views in *Gregg.* Because of limitations of space, *Gregg* has been excerpted below. However, you are encouraged to read the *Furman* case on the Internet.[3] You will better understand the following discussion of *Gregg* if you do so.

Gregg v. Georgia
428 U.S. 153
United States Supreme Court
July 2, 1976

Opinion of Justices Stewart, Powell, and Stevens

C

. . . We now consider specifically whether the sentence of death for the crime of murder is a per se violation of the Eighth and Fourteenth Amendments to the Constitution. We note first that history and precedent strongly support a negative answer to this question.

The imposition of the death penalty for the crime of murder has a long history of acceptance both in the United States and in England. The common-law rule imposed a mandatory death sentence on all convicted murderers. . . . And the penalty continued to be used into the 20th century by most American States, although the breadth of the common-law rule was diminished, initially by narrowing the class of murders to be punished by death and subsequently by wide-spread adoption of laws expressly granting juries the discretion to recommend mercy. . . .

It is apparent from the text of the Constitution itself that the existence of capital punishment was accepted by the Framers. At the time the Eighth Amendment was ratified, capital punishment was a common sanction in every State. Indeed, the First Congress of the United States enacted legislation providing death as the penalty for specified crimes. . . . The Fifth Amendment, adopted at the same time as the Eighth, contemplated the continued existence of the capital sanction by imposing certain limits on the prosecution of capital cases:

> "No person shall be held to answer for a capital, or otherwise infamous crime, unless on a presentment or indictment of a Grand Jury . . . ; nor shall any person be subject for the same offense to be twice put in jeopardy of life or limb; . . . nor be deprived of life, liberty, or property, without due process of law. . . ."

And the Fourteenth Amendment, adopted over three-quarters of a century later, similarly contemplates the existence of the capital sanction in providing that no State shall deprive any person of "life, liberty, or property" without due process of law.

For nearly two centuries, this Court, repeatedly and often expressly, has recognized that capital punishment is not invalid per se. . . .

. . . [I]n *Trop v. Dulles*, . . . Mr. Chief Justice Warren, for himself and three other Justices, wrote:

> "Whatever the arguments may be against capital punishment, both on moral grounds and in terms of accomplishing the purposes of punishment . . . the death penalty has been employed throughout our history, and, in a day when it is still widely accepted, it cannot be said to violate the constitutional concept of cruelty."

Four years ago, the petitioners in *Furman* . . . predicated their argument primarily upon the asserted proposition that standards of decency had evolved to the point where capital punishment no longer could be tolerated. The petitioners in those cases said, in effect, that the evolutionary process had come to an end, and that standards of decency required that the Eighth Amendment be construed finally as prohibiting capital punishment for any crime regardless of its depravity and impact on society. This view was accepted by two Justices. Three other Justices were unwilling to go so far; focusing on the procedures by which convicted defendants were selected for the death penalty rather than on the actual punishment inflicted, they joined in the conclusion that the statutes before the Court were constitutionally invalid.

The petitioners in the capital cases before the Court today renew the "standards of decency" argument, but developments during the four years since *Furman* have undercut substantially the assumptions upon which their argument rested. Despite the continuing debate, dating back to the 19th century, over the morality and utility of capital punishment, it is now evident that a large proportion of American society continues to regard it as an appropriate and necessary criminal sanction.

The most marked indication of society's endorsement of the death penalty for murder is the legislative response to *Furman*. The legislatures of at least 35 States have enacted new statutes that provide for the death penalty for at least some crimes that result in the death of another person. And the Congress of the United States, in 1974, enacted a statute providing the death penalty for aircraft piracy that results in death. These recently adopted statutes have attempted to address the concerns expressed by the Court in *Furman* primarily (i) by specifying the factors to be weighed and the procedures to be followed in deciding when to impose a capital sentence, or (ii) by making the death penalty mandatory for specified crimes. But all of the post-*Furman* statutes make clear that capital punishment itself has not been rejected by the elected representatives of the people. . . .

As we have seen, however, the Eighth Amendment demands more than that a challenged punishment be acceptable to contemporary society. The Court also must ask whether it comports with the basic concept of human dignity at the core of the Amendment. . . . Although we cannot "invalidate a category of penalties because we deem less severe penalties adequate to serve the ends of penology," . . . the sanction imposed cannot be so totally without penological justification that it results in the gratuitous infliction of suffering. . . .

The death penalty is said to serve two principal social purposes: retribution and deterrence of capital crimes by prospective offenders.

In part, capital punishment is an expression of society's moral outrage at particularly offensive conduct. This function may be unappealing to many, but it is essential in an ordered society that asks its citizens to rely on legal processes rather than self-help to vindicate their wrongs.

"The instinct for retribution is part of the nature of man, and channeling that instinct in the administration of criminal justice serves an important purpose in promoting the stability of a society governed by law. When people begin to believe that organized society is unwilling or unable to impose upon criminal offenders the punishment they "deserve," then there are sown the seeds of anarchy—of self-help, vigilante justice, and lynch law." *Furman v. Georgia,* . . . (STEWART, J., concurring).

"Retribution is no longer the dominant objective of the criminal law," *Williams v. New York,* . . . but neither is it a forbidden objective nor one inconsistent with our respect for the dignity of men. . . . Indeed, the decision that capital punishment may be the appropriate sanction in extreme cases is an expression of the community's belief that certain crimes are themselves so grievous an affront to humanity that the only adequate response may be the penalty of death.

Statistical attempts to evaluate the worth of the death penalty as a deterrent to crimes by potential offenders have occasioned a great deal of debate. The results simply have been inconclusive. . . .

. . . In sum, we cannot say that the judgment of the Georgia Legislature that capital punishment may be necessary in some cases is clearly wrong. Considerations of federalism, as well as respect for the ability of a legislature to evaluate, in terms of its particular State, the moral consensus concerning the death penalty and its social utility as a sanction, require us to conclude, in the absence of more convincing evidence, that the infliction of death as a punishment for murder is not without justification and thus is not unconstitutionally severe. . . .

We hold that the death penalty is not a form of punishment that may never be imposed, regardless of the circumstances of the offense, regardless of the character of the offender, and regardless of the procedure followed in reaching the decision to impose it.

Mr. Justice Brennan, dissenting

. . . In *Furman v. Georgia,* . . . I said:

"From the beginning of our Nation, the punishment of death has stirred acute public controversy. Although pragmatic arguments for and against the punishment have been frequently advanced, this longstanding and heated controversy cannot be explained solely as the result of differences over the practical wisdom of a particular government policy. At bottom, the battle has been waged on moral grounds. The country has debated whether a society for which the dignity of the individual is the supreme value can, without a fundamental inconsistency, follow the practice of deliberately putting some of its members to death. In the United States, as in other nations of the western world, "the struggle about this punishment has been one between ancient and deeply rooted beliefs in retribution, atonement or vengeance on the one hand, and, on the other, beliefs in the personal value and dignity of the common man that were born of the democratic movement of the eighteenth century, as well as beliefs in the scientific approach to an understanding of the motive forces of human conduct, which are the result of the growth of the sciences of behavior during the nineteenth and twentieth centuries." It is this essentially moral conflict that forms the backdrop for the past changes in and the present operation of our system of imposing death as a punishment for crime."

That continues to be my view. For the Clause forbidding cruel and unusual punishments under our constitutional system of government embodies in unique degree moral principles restraining the punishments that our civilized society may impose on those persons who transgress its laws. Thus, I too say: "For myself, I do not hesitate to assert the proposition that the only way the law has progressed from the days of the rack, the screw, and the wheel is the development of moral concepts, or, as stated by the Supreme Court . . . the application of 'evolving standards of decency'. . . ."

This Court inescapably has the duty, as the ultimate arbiter of the meaning of our Constitution, to say whether, when individuals condemned to death stand before our Bar, "moral concepts" require us to hold that the law has progressed to the point where we should declare that the punishment of death, like punishments on the rack, the screw, and the wheel, is no longer morally tolerable in our civilized society. My opinion in *Furman v. Georgia* concluded that our civilization and the law had progressed to this point and that therefore the punishment of death, for whatever crime and under all circumstances, is "cruel and unusual" in violation of the Eighth and Fourteenth Amendments of the Constitution. I shall not again canvass the reasons that led to that conclusion. I emphasize only the foremost among the "moral concepts" recognized in our cases and inherent in the Clause is the primary moral principle that the State even as it punishes, must treat its citizens in a manner consistent with their intrinsic worth as human beings—a punishment must not be so severe as to be degrading to human dignity. A judicial determination whether the punishment of death comports with human dignity is therefore not only permitted but compelled by the Clause. . . .

I do not understand that the Court disagrees that "[i]n comparison to all other punishments today . . . the deliberate extinguishment of human life by the State is uniquely degrading to human dignity." . . . For three of my Brethren hold today that mandatory infliction of the death penalty constitutes the penalty cruel and unusual punishment. I perceive no principled basis for this limitation. Death for whatever crime and under all circumstances "is truly an awesome punishment. The calculated killing of a human being by the State involves, by its very nature, a denial of the executed person's humanity. . . . An executed person has indeed 'lost the right to have rights.'" Death is not only an unusually severe punishment, unusual in its pain, in its finality, and in its enormity, but it serves no penal purpose more effectively than a less severe punishment; therefore the principle inherent in the Clause that prohibits pointless infliction of excessive punishment when less severe punishment can adequately achieve the same purposes invalidates the punishment. . . .

The fatal constitutional infirmity in the punishment of death is that it treats "members of the human race as nonhumans, as objects to be toyed with and discarded. [It is] thus inconsistent with the fundamental premise of the Clause that even the vilest criminal remains a human being possessed of common human dignity." . . . As such it is a penalty that "subjects the individual to a fate forbidden by the principle of civilized treatment guaranteed by the [Clause]." I therefore would hold, on that ground alone, that death is today a cruel and unusual punishment prohibited by the Clause. "Justice of this kind is obviously no less shocking than the crime itself, and the new 'official' murder, far from offering redress for the offense committed against society, adds instead a second defilement to the first."

I dissent from the judgments in . . . *Gregg v. Georgia,* . . . *Proffitt v. Florida,* and . . . *Jurek v. Texas,* insofar as each upholds the death sentences challenged in those cases. I would set aside the death sentences imposed in those cases as violative of the Eighth and Fourteenth Amendments.

Mr. Justice Marshall, dissenting

In *Furman v. Georgia,* 408 U.S. 238, 314 (1972) (concurring opinion), I set forth at some length my views on the basic issue presented to the Court in these cases. The death penalty, I concluded, is a cruel and unusual punishment prohibited by the Eighth and Fourteenth Amendments. That continues to be my view. . . .

In *Furman* I concluded that the death penalty is constitutionally invalid for two reasons. First, the death penalty is excessive. . . . And second, the American people, fully informed as to the purposes of the death penalty and its liabilities, would in my view reject it as morally unacceptable. . . .

. . . [A]ssuming . . . that the post-*Furman* enactment of statutes authorizing the death penalty renders the prediction of the views of an informed citizenry an uncertain basis for a constitutional decision, the enactment of those statutes has no bearing whatsoever on the conclusion that the death penalty is unconstitutional because it is excessive. An excessive penalty is invalid under the Cruel and Unusual Punishments Clause "even though popular sentiment may favor" it. . . . The inquiry here, then, is simply whether the death penalty is necessary to accomplish the legitimate legislative purposes in punishment, or whether a less severe penalty—life imprisonment—would do as well. . . .

The two purposes that sustain the death penalty as nonexcessive in the Court's view are general deterrence and retribution. In *Furman*, I canvassed the relevant data on the deterrent effect of capital punishment. . . .

The available evidence, I concluded . . . , was convincing that "capital punishment is not necessary as a deterrent to crime in our society." . . . The evidence I reviewed in *Furman* remains convincing, in my view, that "capital punishment is not necessary as a deterrent to crime in our society." . . . The justification for the death penalty must be found elsewhere. . . .

The other principal purpose said to be served by the death penalty is retribution. The notion that retribution . . . can serve as a moral justification for the sanction of death finds credence in the opinion of my Brothers Stewart, Powell, and Stevens, and that of my Brother White. . . . It is this notion that I find to be the most disturbing aspect of today's unfortunate decisions.

The concept of retribution is a multifaceted one, and any discussion of its role in the criminal law must be undertaken with caution. On one level, it can be said that the notion of retribution or reprobation is the basis of our insistence that only those who have broken the law be punished, and in this sense the notion is quite obviously central to a just system of criminal sanctions. But our recognition that retribution plays a crucial role in determining who may be punished by no means requires approval of retribution as a general justification for punishment. It is the question whether retribution can provide a moral justification for punishment—in particular, capital punishment—that we must consider.

My Brothers Stewart, Powell, and Stevens offer the following explanation of the retributive justification for capital punishment:

> "'The instinct for retribution is part of the nature of man, and channeling that instinct in the administration of criminal justice serves as important purpose in promoting the stability of a society governed . . . by law. When people begin to believe that organized society is unwilling or unable to impose upon criminal offenders the punishment they 'deserve,' then there are sown the seeds of anarchy—of self-help, vigilante justice, and lynch law.'" . . .

This statement is wholly inadequate to justify the death penalty. As my Brother Brennan stated in *Furman*, "[t]here is no evidence whatever that utilization of imprisonment rather than death encourages private blood feuds and other disorders." . . . It simply defies belief to suggest that the death penalty is necessary to prevent the American people from taking the law into their own hands.

In a related vein, it may be suggested that the expression of moral outrage through the imposition of the death penalty serves to reinforce basic moral values—that it marks some crimes as particularly offensive and therefore to be avoided. The argument is akin to a deterrence argument, but differs in that it contemplates the individual's shrinking from antisocial conduct, not because he fears punishment, but because he has been told in the strongest possible way that the conduct is wrong. This contention, like the previous one, provides no support for the death penalty. It is inconceivable that any individual concerned about conforming his conduct to what society says is "right" would fail to realize that murder is "wrong" if the penalty were simply life imprisonment.

The foregoing contentions—that society's expression of moral outrage through the imposition of the death penalty preempts the citizenry from taking the law into its own hands and reinforces moral values—are not retributive in the purest sense. They are essentially utilitarian in that they portray the death penalty as valuable because of its beneficial results. These justifications for the death penalty are inadequate because the penalty is, quite clearly I think, not necessary to the accomplishment of those results.

There remains for consideration, however, what might be termed the purely retributive justification for the death penalty—that the death penalty is appropriate, not because of its beneficial effect on society, but because the taking of the murderer's life is itself morally good. Some of the language of the opinion of my Brothers Stewart, Powell, and Stevens . . . appears positively to embrace this notion of retribution for its own sake as a justification for capital punishment. They state:

> "[T]he decision that capital punishment may be the appropriate sanction in extreme cases is an expression of the community's belief that certain crimes are themselves so grievous an affront to humanity that the only adequate response may be the penalty of death." . . .

They then quote with approval from Lord Justice Denning's remarks before the British Royal Commission on Capital Punishment:

> "'The truth is that some crimes are so outrageous that society insists on adequate punishment, because the wrong-doer deserves it, irrespective of whether it is a deterrent or not.'" . . .

Of course, it may be that these statements are intended as no more than observations as to the popular demands that it is thought must be responded to in order to prevent anarchy. But the implication of the statements appears to me to be quite different—namely, that society's judgment that the murderer "deserves" death must be respected not simply because the preservation of order requires it, but because it is appropriate that society make the judgment and carry it out. It is this latter notion, in particular, that I consider to be fundamentally at odds with the Eighth Amendment. . . . The mere fact that the community demands the murderer's life in return for the evil he has done cannot sustain the death penalty, for as Justices Stewart, Powell, and Stevens remind us, "the Eighth Amendment demands more than that a challenged punishment be acceptable to contemporary society." . . . To be sustained under the Eighth Amendment, the death penalty must "compor[t] with the basic concept of human dignity at the core of the Amendment," . . . the objective in imposing it must be "[consistent] with our respect for the dignity of [other] men." . . . Under these standards, the taking of life "because the wrongdoer deserves it" surely must fall, for such a punishment has as its very basis the total denial of the wrongdoer's dignity and worth.

The death penalty, unnecessary to promote the goal of deterrence or to further any legitimate notion of retribution, is an excessive penalty forbidden by the Eighth and Fourteenth Amendments. I respectfully dissent from the Court's judgment upholding the sentences of death imposed upon the petitioners in these cases. . . .

Case Questions

1. How does Justice Stewart justify his conclusion that capital punishment is a permissible form of punishment?
2. What is the moral principle that is the fundamental basis of Justice Brennan's dissent?
3. Does Justice Marshall believe that retribution provides a moral justification for capital punishment? Why or why not?
4. In your opinion, is the fact that capital punishment is popular with a majority of society a sufficient fact to conclude the debate about whether the death penalty is cruel and unusual under the Eighth Amendment?

People are also affected by ethical considerations in their professional interactions with others. Although we may not realize it as the time, our actions and inactions at work and school are often interpreted by others as evidence of our personal values and character—who we are and what we stand for. A person whose behavior is consistent with moral principles is said to have integrity. It is common for people to try to create at least the illusion that they have integrity. Integrity is prized by employers, who try to avoid hiring persons known to lie, cheat, and steal. Many companies also try to avoid doing business with firms that are reputed to engage in fraudulent practices, who try to take unfair advantage of those with whom they contract, who negotiate in bad faith, or are otherwise unscrupulous to their business partners. Students applying to professional schools quickly learn that integrity is important to members of admissions committees. Such committees generally require recommenders to include an evaluation of an applicant's character in their letters. People are also concerned about ethical behavior in their personal lives. They worry about whether a person with whom they have shared a confidence is trustworthy.

But it is often difficult to know the parameters of ethical behavior in particular situations. Is it ever permissible to break a promise not to tell? Are there any rules about lying? Who determines the rules? How are they enforced? Are there any circumstances when it is morally permissible to lie to a total stranger? A family member? A best friend? A business partner? When is it acceptable for other people to lie to you? What are the social and legal consequences of lying?[4]

In your role as a student you may have encountered situations in which you and/or some classmates have cheated on a test or paper. Have you ever seriously thought about the ethics of cheating? Is it always morally wrong for a student to cheat? Can circumstances make a difference? Does it make a difference if the teacher makes no effort to prevent dishonesty and virtually every other student in the class is cheating on a test or written assignment? Would it make a difference if you believed the teacher had been unfair to you on a previous assignment and cheating would enable you to get the final grade that you "really deserved"? If you observe classmates cheat, do you have any duty to tell the instructor? What would you think about some other student who did tell? What is the basis for your positions?

Who makes the rules for you? Is it up to you to decide, your peer group, your parents, or other significant people in your life? Perhaps you look for guidance to religious leaders. Religious groups have historically assumed a major role in setting moral standards, and religious leaders frequently take firm positions on contemporary ethical issues. How can anyone tell who is "right"? Thomas Jefferson in the Declaration of Independence said, "We hold these truths to be self evident. . . ." Is that sufficient proof of the proposition that all people are created equal?

Philosophers have argued for centuries about the answers to questions such as those raised above. The following mini-introduction will help to provide some background and structure for the discussion of the cases that follow.

ETHICS

Ethics is one of the five traditional branches of study within philosophy, as can be seen in Table 2-1. It is the study of morality. Ethicists are concerned with what makes conduct morally right or wrong and the essential nature of moral responsibility. They also investigate the application of ethical principles to the practice of professions such as law, medicine, and business.

We see in Table 2-2 that ethical theories are often classified as being either metaethical or normative in their approach.[5]

Metaethical scholars have centered on defining ethical terms and developing theories. They have tended to focus on abstract topics, such as identifying the fundamental characteristics of moral behavior. These discussions have tended to be extremely theoretical and have been often criticized for not having many practical applications.[6] The following example is intended to raise philosophical questions about the essential nature of integrity under circumstances when it is acknowledged that all of the actors have engaged in "correct" actions.

Karen, Keisha, & Kelly

Assume that Karen is a "goody-goody" and always tries to do the "right" thing in order to comply with what she perceives to be her moral duty. Assume that Keisha does the "right" thing, at least in part for selfish reasons (being seen doing the right thing will make the newspapers and will be good for business). What if Kelly selectively does the "right" thing only when she feels a personal connection with some other person in need, under circumstances when she feels she can help without putting herself at risk? Does Karen have more integrity than Keisha and Kelly?

Ethics	The study of morality
Metaphysics	The study of the nature of reality or being
Aesthetics	The study of beauty
Logic	The study of correct reasoning
Epistemology	The study of knowledge

TABLE 2-1   Branches of Philosophy

Normative ethnicians have been more concerned with answering practical questions such as "Is killing in self-defense wrong?" or "What ought a physician do when a patient dying of a terminal disease asks for assistance in committing suicide?" Modern ethnicians primarily focus on normative moral issues rather than metaethical, although this tendency is of recent origin and primarily began in the 1970s.[7]

Philosophers disagree about whether ethical judgments about right and wrong can be conclusively proven.[8] Some have argued that ethical judgments can be scientifically proven. Others have rejected science and insisted that such judgments be based on natural law, sounding intuitive notions of right and wrong,[9] or based on the logical soundness of the reasons underlying the ethical judgment.[10]

Another area of disagreement involves where those making ethical judgments should focus their attention. *Teleological* philosophers believe that whether an action is "good" or "bad" can only be determined after an act has occurred by examining the outcomes. Only by looking backwards can the relative costs and benefits of an action be weighed and its worth assessed.[11] *Utilitarianism,* which was discussed in Chapter 1, is such a theory. Thus publicly and brutally caning one prisoner for a given criminal offense, from a utilitarian perspective, would be moral if it could be proven later that it has deterred thousands of others from engaging in that same offense.

Deontologists would reject a focus on aftermaths in favor of studying the role of moral duty. Immanuel Kant, for example, argued that, to be ethical, an actor's *deeds* should be evaluated based on the reasoning that led to the act.[12] Kant believed that intent mattered and that an ethical actor should be motivated only by a desire to comply with a universally accepted *moral duty.* He did not view actions motivated by feelings of love, sympathy, or the potential for personal gain, as being ethically principled.[13] Caning a convicted person could not be a moral act if it amounted to torture. *Egoists* had yet a different approach.

| Metaethics | Theoretical foundations of ethics |
| Normative ethics | Applied ethics |

TABLE 2-2   Ethics

They believed that individuals were ethically "right" to act in their own self-interest, without regard for the consequences to other people.[14]

Many theorists have argued that conduct is moral only if it coincides with religious mandates such as the Ten Commandments or the Golden Rule. Society, however, has been unable to agree on any single, universally acceptable ethical theory. Serious disagreements exist about what constitutes ethical conduct in specific contexts. "Right" answers are not always obvious, and rules, interpretive opinions, and guidelines are needed to direct individuals toward "good" conduct.

Law and Morality

One of the unresolved debates revolves around what role law should play in making ethical rules. Should law supply the enforcement mechanism for enforcing moral norms? What should an ethical person do when confronted with "bad" laws? Should decisions about morality in some contexts be reserved to the individual?

Although law can contribute rules that embody moral norms, law in our democracy is not expected to play the primary role in promoting ethical behavior in society. Parents, churches, schools, youth organizations, athletic teams, and business, professional, and fraternal groups of all types are expected to fill the void. They often establish ethical codes, rules (such as those prohibiting "unsportsmanlike conduct" or "conduct unbecoming an officer"), and discipline and even expel members who violate their terms. A precise calculus of law's relationship to morality, however, remains illusive.

You may recall from reading Chapter 1 that there is a fundamental and unresolved disagreement between philosophers who are *natural law* adherents and the *analytical positivists* regarding the true nature of law. From the positivist point of view, laws are merely the rules that political superiors develop pursuant to duly established procedures that are imposed on the rest of the polity. Laws are viewed as being intrinsically neither good nor bad. They do establish norms of legal behavior, but such efforts sometimes amount to little more than arbitrary line drawing. Positivists would point out that law establishes a floor but not a ceiling. Individuals who satisfy their legal obligations always retain the right to self-impose additional restrictions on their conduct in order to satisfy a deeply felt moral duty. But law does not depend for its authority on an ad hoc assessment of whether the government *ought* to follow a different policy. It is clear, however, that defying the law can result in state-imposed sanctions. Assume, for example, that a taxpayer takes an unauthorized "deduction" off her income tax obligation and makes an equivalent dollar donation to a charity rather than to the Internal Revenue Service. The fact that her conscience tells her that it is self-evident that the U.S. government is morally wrong to spend our dollars on some disfavored program is unlikely to save her from criminal and civil sanctions.

In the following passage, Martin Luther King, Jr., distinguishes between just and unjust laws and argues that immoral laws should be civilly disobeyed.

Letter from a Birmingham Jail*

You express a great deal of anxiety over our willingness to break laws. This is certainly a legitimate concern. Since we so diligently urge people to obey the Supreme Court's decision of 1954 outlawing segregation in the public schools, it is rather strange and paradoxical to find us consciously breaking laws. One may well ask, "How can you advocate breaking some laws and obeying others?" The answer is found in the fact that there are two types of laws: there are *just* and there are *unjust* laws . . .

. . . A just law is a man-made code that squares with the moral law or the law of God. An unjust law is a code that is out of harmony with the moral law. To put it in the terms of Saint Thomas Aquinas, an unjust law is a human law that is not rooted in eternal and natural law. Any law that uplifts human personality is just. Any law that degrades human personality is unjust. All segregation statutes are unjust because segregation distorts the soul and damages the personality. It gives the segregator a false sense of superiority, and the segregated a false sense of inferiority. . . .

So segregation is not only politically, economically and sociologically unsound, but it is morally wrong and sinful. . . .

. . . I submit that an individual who breaks a law that conscience tells him is unjust and willingly accepts the penalty by staying in jail to arouse the conscience of the community over its injustice, is in reality expressing the very highest respect for law. . . .

We can never forget that everything Hitler did in Germany was "legal" and everything that Hungarian freedom fighters did in Hungary was "illegal." It was "illegal" to aid and comfort a Jew, in Hitler's Germany. But I am sure that if I had lived in Germany during that time I would have aided and comforted my Jewish brothers even though it was illegal. . . .

Positive Law Rules

In our republic, the people are sovereign, but there is no law higher than the U.S. Constitution.[15] We have adopted the analytical positivist view that bills that have been enacted in conformity with constitutional requirements are the law. Individuals, for reasons of conscience, may defy these duly enacted laws, but they are lawfully subject to prosecution.

It is important to note, however, that political majorities in federal and state legislatures often enact statutes that reflect widely held moral beliefs in the electorate. Examples include the Civil Rights Act of 1964, the Americans with Disabilities Act, the Clean Air Act, the Clean Water Act, and the Sherman Act, to name just a few. Legislative bodies have also taken the ethical views of political minorities into consideration when drafting legislation. Congress, for example, exempted conscientious objectors from having to register with the Selective Service System. Similarly, Congress's 1998 omnibus spending bill contained a

---

provision that permitted doctors opposed to birth control to refuse on moral grounds to write prescriptions for contraceptives requested by federal employees.[16] But one need only look at Article I, Section 9, of the U.S. Constitution to see an example of political expediency taking precedence over moral considerations. In that article, antislavery founders compromised their moral principles in order to win ratification of the Constitution in southern states.

Federal and state judicial bodies also impart moral views when they construe constitutions and statutes. Examples include the U.S. Supreme Court's opinions in *Cruzan v. Missouri* (right to refuse life-sustaining medical treatment), *Loving v. Virginia* (interracial marriages), and *Moore v. City of East Cleveland* (meaning of the term family), three famous cases involving interpretations of the due process clause, which are included elsewhere in this textbook.

It is obvious that there are many instances in which moral rules and legal rules overlap. Our criminal laws severely punish persons convicted of murder, rape, and robbery, and they *ought* to do so. Such acts simultaneously violate legal and moral principles. Tort law provides another example. Damages in negligence cases should be borne by the parties based on the extent to which each was responsible for the damages. Because this decision is, with some exceptions, based on the relative fault of the parties, it can also be argued both on teleological and deontological grounds to be an ethical rule. We saw another example of legal and ethical harmony in the *Iacomini* case (Chapter 7). In that case the court ruled that the law would permit a mechanic to claim an equitable lien in a motor vehicle that he had repaired, under circumstances when no other relief was possible. The court said that such a remedy was legally appropriate in proper circumstances to prevent *unjust enrichment.* The following materials raise interesting legal and moral questions about legal and moral duties as they relate to members of one's family.

Aiding and Abetting, Misprision, Informing, and the Family

Imagine how difficult it must be for a person to learn to pick up bits and pieces of information and ultimately conclude that a member of his or her family is probably involved in criminal activity. Suppose that the crimes involved are a series of premeditated murders, and that the offender will probably be sentenced to the death penalty upon conviction of the charges. Assume further that you have to admit that, unless you inform authorities, other innocent persons may well become additional victims. Suppose there is a million dollar cash award that will be paid to the person who provides the information that ultimately leads to the conviction of the offender. What would you do? Would you tell authorities and run the risk of being viewed as being disloyal to your family? Would you stay silent and hope that nobody else is harmed?[17]

If you were writing a statute to prevent people from harboring fugitive felons, would you carve out an exception for people protecting members of their own families? Examine the following New Mexico statute from the ethical and legal perspectives.

New Mexico Statutes Annotated 30–22–4.
Harboring or Aiding a Felon.

Harboring or aiding a felon consists of any person, not standing in the relation of husband or wife, parent or grandparent, child or grandchild, brother or sister, by consanguinity or affinity, who knowingly conceals any offender or gives such offender any other aid, knowing that he has committed a felony, with the intent that he escape or avoid arrest, trial conviction or punishment. Whoever commits harboring or aiding a felon is guilty of a fourth degree felony. In a prosecution under this section it shall not be necessary to aver, or on the trial to prove, that the principal felon has been either arrested, prosecuted or tried.

Do you agree with the way the legislature defined the scope of the legal duty? Should the scope of the moral duty be the same as the scope of the legal duty?

The above statute has its roots in the common law crime of accessory after the fact. With the exceptions indicated above, it creates a legal duty on everyone else to refrain from helping a known felon escape apprehension by authorities. You can see how this statute was applied in the following case. Read the case and think about whether you agree with the opinion of the court majority or the dissenting judges. What is the basis for your choice?

State v. Mobbley
650 P.2d 841
Court of Appeals of New Mexico,
August 3, 1982

Wood, Judge

The criminal information charged that defendant did "knowingly aid Andrew Needham knowing that he had committed a felony with the intent that he escape arrest, trial, conviction and punishment. . . . The issue is whether the agreed upon facts are such that defendant may not be prosecuted for the offense of aiding a felon.

Defendant is married to Ricky Mobbley. Police officers went to a house and contacted defendant; they advised defendant that felony warrants had been issued for Ricky Mobbley and Andrew Needham. The officers asked defendant if "both were there." Defendant denied that the men were there, although she knew that both men were in the house. Hearing noises, the officers entered the house and discovered both men. Defendant could not have

revealed Needham without also revealing her husband. The criminal charge was based on the failure to reveal Needham. . . .

The power to define crimes is a legislative function. . . .

Section 30–22–4, *supra*, applies to "any person, not standing in the relation of husband or wife, parent or grandparent, child or grandchild, brother or sister by consanguinity or affinity. . . ." There is no claim that any of the exempted relationships applies as between defendant and Needham. As enacted by the Legislature, § 30–22–4, *supra*, applies to the agreed facts.

Defendant contends that such a result is contrary to legislative intent because statutes must be interpreted in accord with common sense and reason, and must be interpreted so as not to render the statute's application absurd or unreasonable. . . . We give two answers to this contention.

First, where the meaning of the statutory language is plain, and where the words used by the Legislature are free from ambiguity, there is no basis for interpreting the statute.

. . . Section 30–22–4, *supra*, applies to "any person" not within the relationship exempted by the statute. Defendant is such a person.

Second, if we assume that the statute should be interpreted, our holding that § 30–22–4, *supra*, applies to the agreed facts accords with legislative intent. Statutes proscribing harboring or aiding a felon grew out of the common law of accessories after the fact. LaFave & Scott, Criminal Law § 66 (1972). However:

> At common law, only one class was excused from liability for being accessories after the fact. Wives did not become accessories by aiding their husbands. No other relationship, including that of husband to wife, would suffice. Today, close to half of the states have broadened the exemption to cover other close *relatives*. . . . This broadening of the exemption [*sic*] may be justified on the ground that it is unrealistic to expect persons to be deterred from giving aid to their close *relations*. (Our emphasis.)

LaFave & Scott, *supra*, at 523–24.

New Mexico legislative history accords with the discussion in LaFave & Scott, *supra*. In 1875 New Mexico adopted the common law. . . . The present statute . . . was a part of the Criminal Code enacted in 1963. . . .

Limiting the exemptions in § 30–22–4, *supra*, to *relatives* named in that statute accords with the legislative intent as shown by legislative history. In light of the limited exemption at common law, and legislation limited to relatives, it is not absurd and not unreasonable to hold that if defendant aided Needham, § 30–22–4, *supra*, applies to that aid.

Except for one fact, there would have been no dispute as to the applicability of § 30–22–4, *supra*. That one fact is that defendant could not have revealed Needham without also revealing her husband. The statute does not exempt a defendant from prosecution when this fact situation arises; to judicially declare such an additional exemption would be to improperly add words to the statute. . . . Also, such a judicial declaration would be

contrary to the rationale for this type of statute; it is unrealistic to expect persons to be deterred from giving aid to their close relations. LaFave & Scott, *supra*.

We recognize that defendant was placed in a dilemma; if she answered truthfully she revealed the presence of her husband; if she lied she took the chance of being prosecuted. . . .

Defendant contends we should follow two Arkansas decisions which support her position. . . . We decline to do so. Our duty is to apply the New Mexico statute, not the Arkansas law of accomplices.

The order of the trial court, which dismissed the information, is reversed. The cause is remanded with instructions to reinstate the case on the trial court's docket.

IT IS SO ORDERED.

Hendley, J., concurs.

Lopez, J., dissents.

Lopez, Judge (dissenting)

I respectfully dissent. The majority holds that the defendant can be charged with the offense of harboring or aiding Andrew Needham . . . because she does not qualify under any of the exemptions listed in the statute with respect to Needham. It arrives at this holding in spite of the fact that the defendant could not have revealed the presence of Needham in the house without also revealing the presence of her husband. This holding negates the legislative intent of the statute to exempt a wife from being forced to turn in her husband. Under the majority ruling, the defendant would have had to turn in Needham to escape being charged under § 30–22–4, which would have been tantamount to turning in her husband.

Whether the rationale underlying the legislative exemption is a recognition "that it is unrealistic to expect persons to be deterred from giving aid to their close relations," LaFave and Scott, Criminal Law § 66 (1972), or an acknowledgment of human frailty, Torcia, Wharton's Criminal Law § 35 (14th ed. 1978), that rationale is ignored by requiring a wife to turn in her husband if he is with another suspect. Such a result requires a proverbial splitting of analytic hairs by attributing the defendant's action, in denying that Needham was at the house, to an intent to aid Needham rather than her husband. . . .

The practical effect of the majority opinion, which requires a wife to turn in her husband if he is with a co-suspect, is to deny the wife's exemption in § 30–22–4. The reasons for refusing to force a wife to inform on her husband are the same whether or not he is alone. The statute should not be construed so narrowly as to frustrate the legislative intent

to exempt a wife from turning in her husband. . . . Although the court should not add to the provisions of a statute, it may do so to prevent an unreasonable result. . . . Given the wife's exemption from turning in her husband contained in § 30–22–4, it would be unreasonable to require her to do just that by revealing Needham.

For the foregoing reasons, I cannot agree that the defendant in this case can be charged under § 30–22–4 for refusing to tell the police that Needham was in the house. I would affirm the action of the trial court in dismissing the information against the defendant.

Case Questions

1. Given the wording of the statute, did the majority have any flexibility in applying this law to the facts of this case? Do you think that Andrew Needham's presence in the house with Ricky Mobbley *ought* to warrant application of this legal rule?
2. Do you believe the statute should be amended to exempt individuals in Pam Mobbley's predicament from prosecution?
3. What would you have done if you had been in Pam's situation? Why?

Misprision of a felony is another common law crime. It makes it criminal for a person to fail to tell authorities of the commission of a felony of which he or she has knowledge. The history and rationale for this crime are explained in the following excerpt from the case of *Holland v. State*. In *Holland*, the court had to decide whether misprision is a crime in Florida.

Holland v. State of Florida
302 So.2d 806
Supreme Court of Florida
November 8, 1974

McNulty, Chief Judge

. . . As far as we know or are able to determine, this is the first case in Florida involving the crime of misprision of felony.

As hereinabove noted, we chose to decide this case on the fundamental issue of whether misprision of felony is a crime in Florida.

In any case, we now get on to the merits of the question we decide today. We begin by pointing out that almost every state in the United States has adopted the Common Law of England to some extent. Many of these states have done so by constitutional or statutory provisions similar to ours. But the nearly universal interpretation of such provisions is that they adopt the common law of England only to the extent that such laws are consistent with the existing physical and social conditions in the country or in the given state.

To some degree Florida courts have discussed this principle in other contexts. In *Duval v. Thomas,* for example, our Supreme Court said:

> "[W]hen grave doubt exists of a true common law doctrine . . . we may, . . . exercise a 'broad discretion' taking 'into account the changes in our social and economic customs and present day conceptions of right and justice.' It is, to repeat, only when the common law is plain that we must observe it."

Moreover, our courts have not hesitated in other respects to reject anachronistic common law concepts.

Consonant with this, therefore, we think that the legislature in enacting § 775.01, *supra,* recognized this judicial precept and intended to grant our courts the discretion necessary to prevent blind adherence to those portions of the common law which are not suited to our present conditions, our public policy, our traditions or our sense of right and justice.

With the foregoing as a predicate, we now consider the history of the crime of misprision of felony and whether the reasons therefor have ceased to exist, if indeed they ever did exist, in this country. The origin of the crime is well described in 8 U. of Chi.L.Rev. 338, as follows:

> "[M]isprision of felony as defined by Blackstone is merely one phase of the system of communal responsibility for the apprehension of criminals which received its original impetus from William I, under pressure of the need to protect the invading Normans in hostile country, and which endured up to the Seventeenth Century in England. In order to secure vigilant prosecution of criminal conduct, the vill or hundred in which such conduct occurred was subject to fine,

as was the tithing to which the criminal belonged, and every person who knew of the felony and failed to make report thereof was subject to punishment for misprision of felony. Compulsory membership in the tithing group, the obligation to pursue criminals when the hue and cry was raised, broad powers of private arrest, and the periodic visitations of the General Eyre for the purpose of penalizing laxity in regard to crime, are all suggestive of the administrative background against which misprision of felony developed. With the appearance of specialized and paid law enforcement officers, such as constables and justices of the peace in the Seventeenth Century, there was a movement away from strict communal responsibility, and a growing tendency to rely on professional police. . . ."

In short, the initial reason for the existence of misprision of felony as a crime at common law was to aid an alien, dictatorial sovereign in his forcible subjugation of England's inhabitants. Enforcement of the crime was summary, harsh and oppressive; and commentators note that most prosecutors in this country long ago recognized the inapplicability or obsolescence of the law and its harshness in their contemporary society by simply not charging people with that crime. . . .

Many courts faced with this issue have also found, though with varying degrees of clarity, that the reasons for the proscription of this crime do not exist. Moreover, as early as 1822 in this country Chief Justice John Marshall states in *Marbury v. Brooks:*

> "It may be the duty of a citizen to accuse every offender, and to proclaim every offense which comes to his knowledge; but the law which would punish him in every case, for not performing this duty, is too harsh for man." . . .

We agree with Chief Justice Marshall . . . that the crime of misprision of felony is wholly unsuited to American criminal law. . . . While it may be desirable, even essential, that we encourage citizens to "get involved" to help reduce crime, they ought not be adjudicated criminals themselves if they don't. The fear of such a consequence is a fear from which our traditional concepts of peace and quietude guarantee freedom. We cherish the right to mind our own business when our own best interests dictate. Accordingly, we hold that misprision of felony has not been adopted into, and is not a part of, Florida substantive law.

Case Questions.

1. The majority in *Holland* noted that American judges going back to the esteemed John Marshall have concluded that it is "un-American" for citizens to be criminally prosecuted for not reporting the commission of known felonies to the authorities. Is this position morally justifiable in your opinion?
2. Justice John Marshall is quoted in an 1822 case as follows: "It may be the duty of a citizen to accuse every offender, and to proclaim every offense which comes to his knowledge. . . ." Do you think Marshall was referring to a moral duty, a legal duty, or both?

Traditionally, individuals have not been legally obligated to intervene to aid other persons in the absence of a judicially recognized duty owed to that person. Courts have recognized the existence of a duty where a special relationship exists. The special relationships generally fall within one of the following categories: a) where a *statutory duty* exists (such as the obligation parents have to support their children), b) where a *contractual duty* exists (lifeguards are employed to try to make rescues on the beach), or c) where a *common law duty* exists (such as when an unrelated adult *has voluntarily assumed* primary responsibility for bringing food to an isolated, incapacitated, elderly neighbor, and then stops without notifying authorities). In the absence of a legal duty to act, the law has generally left the decision as to whether or not to be a Good Samaritan up to each individual's conscience.

Good Samaritan Laws

Many people feel that Americans today are less willing than in times past to play the role of Good Samaritan. But do bystanders, who have no special relationship to a person in need, have a moral obligation to intervene? Should they have a legal duty to either intervene or inform authorities if they can do so without placing themselves in jeopardy? You may have read about the 18-year-old young man who in May 1997 enticed a 7-year-old girl into a ladies' room stall in a Las Vegas casino and sexually assaulted and murdered her. You may remember that the attacker had a male friend who allegedly watched some of the events in that stall and presumably knew that the little girl was in danger. The friend made no attempt to dissuade the attacker, save the girl, or tell authorities. He was not subject to prosecution under the laws of Nevada.

Should a person who is a passive observer, as in the above situation, be subjected to criminal prosecution for failing to act? The following Massachusetts statute was enacted in 1983 in response to a brutal rape at a tavern. This crime was the basis for the movie *The Accused.*

Massachusetts General Law Chapter 268, Section 40.
Reports of Crimes to Law Enforcement Officials.

Whoever knows that another person is a victim of aggravated rape, rape, murder, manslaughter or armed robbery and is at the scene of said crime shall, to the extent that said person can do so without danger or peril to himself or others, report said crime to an appropriate law enforcement official as soon as reasonably practicable. Any person who violates this section shall be punished by a fine of not less than five hundred nor more than two thousand and five hundred dollars.

Why do you believe the Massachusetts legislature limited the scope of this duty to only these four crimes? Do you see any potential problems that may result because of this statute? Do you think that such laws will influence more bystanders to intervene? Should society enact such laws irrespective of whether they change any minds, if only to make a moral statement and put society on record as expecting citizens to act as members of a larger community? Do you agree with Lord Patrick Devlin that our society would disintegrate if we didn't criminalize immoral conduct? Devlin argues that such statutes encourage citizens to think similarly about questions of right and wrong and that this helps to bind us together as a people.[18] The following discussion focuses on the society's right to promote a common morality by enacting statutes that prohibit certain types of private sexual conduct between consenting adults.

Individual Choice Versus Social Control: Where Is the Line?

Our society continues to have a difficult time determining the extent to which the states have the constitutional right to criminalize conduct that offends prevailing moral norms. In legal jargon, this is a question about the scope of the state's police power. The supreme courts of Pennsylvania and Kentucky addressed this issue in cases challenging the constitutionality of their respective deviant sexual intercourse statutes. In each state the legislature enacted a criminal statute that prescribed specified sexual conduct to be morally unacceptable. The following two cases have been edited to focus on the rationales that the supreme court majorities in both states used to justify their decisions. In both instances, the majorities relied on a doctrine developed by the philosophy of John Stuart Mill in 1859.

Although both state supreme court majorities used the philosophy of John Stuart Mill to support their conclusions, they used different constitutional theories to reach their conclusions. The constitutional right of the federal and states legislatures to enact laws is discussed more thoroughly on pages 199–209; however, since the Pennsylvania Supreme Court based its decision in *Commonwealth v. Bonadio* on a legal concept known as the *"police power,"* it is necessary to provide readers with some additional information about that topic prior to reading the case.

In general, the police power is a term that refers to each state's inherent right as a sovereign ("autonomous") government to enact laws to protect the public's health, welfare, safety, and morals. You will recall that the states were in existence prior to the adoption of the U.S. Constitution, and that they had traditionally exercised broad lawmaking powers to protect the citizens of their states. Congress's right to legislate, however, has no such historical underpinning. Congress does not have the right to legislate based on the police power because it derives all of its authority from powers granted in the federal constitution. Because the states retained their right to exercise the police power when the U.S. Constitution was adopted, they continue to enact laws pursuant to this right today.

In *Bonadio*, the state supreme court had to determine whether the enactment of Pennsylvania's deviant sexual intercourse statutes constituted a proper exercise of the police power. If not, the statute would be constitutionally invalid and an infringement of individual liberty rights.

Commonwealth of Pennsylvania v. Bonadio
Pennsylvania Supreme Court
415 A.2d 47
May 30, 1980

Flaherty, Justice

This is an appeal from an Order of the Court of Common Pleas of Allegheny County granting appellees' Motion to Quash an Information on the ground that the Voluntary Deviate Sexual Intercourse Statute is unconstitutional. Appellees were arrested at an "adult" pornographic theater on charges of voluntary deviate sexual intercourse and/or conspiracy to perform the same.

The Commonwealth's position is that the statute in question is a valid exercise of the police power pursuant to the authority of states to regulate public health, safety, welfare, and morals. . . .

The threshold question in determining whether the statute in question is a valid exercise of the police power is to decide whether it benefits the public generally. The state clearly has a proper role to perform in protecting the public from inadvertent offensive displays of sexual behavior, in preventing people from being forced against their will to submit to sexual contact, in protecting minors from being sexually used by adults, and in eliminating cruelty to animals. To assure these protections, a broad range of criminal statutes constitute valid police power exercises, including proscriptions of indecent exposure, open lewdness, rape, *involuntary* deviate sexual intercourse, indecent assault, statutory rape, corruption of minors, and cruelty to animals. The statute in question serves none of the foregoing purposes and it is nugatory to suggest that it promotes a state interest in the institution of marriage. The Voluntary Deviate Sexual Intercourse Statute has only one possible purpose: to regulate the private conduct of consenting adults. Such a purpose, we believe, exceeds the valid bounds of the police power while infringing the right to equal protection of the laws guaranteed by the Constitution of the United States and of this Commonwealth.

With respect to regulation of morals, the police power should properly be exercised to protect each individual's right to be free from interference in defining and pursuing his own morality but not to enforce a majority morality on persons whose conduct *does not harm others*. . . . Many issues that are considered to be matters of morals are subject to debate, and no sufficient state interest justifies legislation of norms simply because a particular belief is followed by a number of people or even a majority. Indeed, what is considered to be "moral" changes with the times and is dependent upon societal background. Spiritual leadership, not the government, has the responsibility for striving to improve the morality of individuals. Enactment of the Voluntary Deviate Sexual Intercourse Statute, despite the fact that it provides punishment for what many believe to be abhorrent crimes against nature and perceived sins against God, is not properly in the realm of the temporal police power.

The concepts underlying our view of the police power in the case before us were once summarized as follows by the great philosopher, John Stuart Mill, in his eminent and apposite work, ON LIBERTY (1859):

> [T]he sole end for which mankind are warranted, individually or collectively, in interfering with the liberty of action of any of their number, is self-protection . . . [T]he only purpose for which power can be rightfully exercised over any member of a civilised community, against his will, is to prevent harm to others. His own good, either physical or moral is not a sufficient warrant. He cannot rightfully be compelled to do or forbear because it will be better for him to do so, because it will make him happier, because, in the opinions of others, to do so would be wise, or even right. These are good reasons for remonstrating with him, or reasoning with him, or persuading him, or entreating him, but not for compelling him, or visiting him with any evil in case he do otherwise. To justify that, the conduct from which it is desired to deter him must be calculated to produce evil to some one else. *The only part of the conduct of any one, for which he is amenable*

> *to society, is that which concerns others. In the part which merely concerns himself, his independence is, of right, absolute. Over himself, over his own body and mind, the individual is sovereign.*
>
> It is, perhaps, hardly necessary to say that this doctrine is meant to apply to human beings in the maturity of their faculties. . . .
>
> But there is a sphere of action in which society as distinguished from the individual, has, if any, only an indirect interest; comprehending all that portion of a person's life and conduct which affects only himself, or if it also affects others, only with their free, voluntary, and undeceived consent and participation. . . .
>
> This, then, is the appropriate region of human liberty. It comprises, first, the inward domain of consciousness; demanding liberty of conscience, in the most comprehensive sense; liberty of thought and feeling; absolute freedom of opinion and sentiment on all subjects, practical or speculative, scientific, *moral,* or *theological* . . . Secondly, the principle requires liberty of tastes and pursuits; of framing the plan of our life to suit our own character; of doing as we like, subject to such consequences as may follow: without impediment from our fellow-creatures, *so long as what we do does not harm them, even though they should think our conduct foolish, perverse, or wrong.* Thirdly, from this liberty of each individual, follows the liberty, within the same limits of combination among individuals; freedom to unite, for any purpose not involving harm to others: the persons combining being supposed to be of full age, and not forced or deceived.
>
> No society in which these liberties are not, on the whole, respected, is free, whatever may be its form of government; . . . *The only freedom which deserves the name, is that of pursuing our own good in our own way, so long as we do not attempt to deprive others of theirs,* or impede their efforts to obtain it. Each is the proper guardian of his own health, whether bodily, or mental or spiritual. Mankind are greater gainers by suffering each other to live as seems good to themselves, than by compelling each to live as seems good to the rest. (Emphasis Supplied)

This philosophy, as applied to the issue of regulation of sexual morality presently before the Court, or employed to delimit the police power generally, properly circumscribes state power over the individual.

Order affirmed.

Case Questions

1. What is the position of the Commonwealth of Pennsylvania regarding the constitutionality of the statute?
2. How does the Pennsylvania Supreme Court define the limits of the state's police power?
3. Do you see any problems with John Stuart Mill's privacy doctrine?

The Kentucky Supreme Court majority in *Commonwealth v. Wasson,* while still relying on Mill's philosophy, however, chose a different approach in deciding that Kentucky's sodomy statute was unconstitutional. It interpreted the Kentucky Constitution as providing greater privacy rights than are required by the U.S. Constitution. It is important that students understand, however, that the U.S. Constitution establishes a constitutional floor which is binding of the states, but not a ceiling. States cannot legally enact laws that contradict the national constitution. But states are not violating the federal constitution if they provide their inhabitants with more freedom from government than is required by the U.S. Constitution. The U.S. Constitution may only require that states provide six-person jury trials and yet states can decide to require twelve-person juries in criminal cases. The U.S. Constitution may permit states to criminalize acts of sodomy between consenting adults and yet a state supreme court, such as Kentucky's, may decide that the state constitution leaves that decision to the individuals themselves, in some circumstances, and not to the state.

Commonwealth of Kentucky v. Wasson
842 S.W.2d 487
Supreme Court of Kentucky
September 24, 1992

Lambert, Justice, dissenting

The issue here is not whether private homosexual conduct should be allowed or prohibited. The only question properly before this Court is whether the Constitution of Kentucky denies the legislative branch a right to prohibit such conduct. Nothing in the major- ity opinion demonstrates such a limitation on legislative prerogative.

To justify its view that private homosexual conduct is protected by the Constitution of Kentucky, the majority has found it necessary to disregard virtually all of recorded history, the teachings of the religions most influential on Western Civilization, the debates of the delegates to the Constitution Convention, and the text of the Constitution itself. Rather than amounting to a decision based upon precedent as is suggested, this decision reflects the value judgment of the majority and its view that public law has no right to prohibit the conduct at issue here.

The majority concedes that "'proscriptions against that conduct [sodomy] have ancient roots.'" . . . It fails, however, to describe the depth of such roots as was done in *Bowers v. Hardwick*, 478 U.S. 186, (1986):

> Sodomy was a criminal offense at common law which was forbidden by the laws of the original 13 States when they ratified the Bill of Rights. 478 U.S. at 192. . . .

In his concurring opinion in *Bowers*, Chief Justice Burger elaborated upon the historical condemnation of sodomy as follows:

> "Decisions of individuals relating to homosexual conduct have been subject to state intervention throughout the history of Western Civilization. Condemnation of those practices is firmly rooted in Judeao-Christian moral and ethical standards. Homosexual sodomy was a capital crime under Roman law. During the English Reformation when powers of the ecclesiastical courts were transferred to the King's Courts, the first English statute criminalizing sodomy was passed. Blackstone described 'the infamous crime against nature' as an offense of 'deeper malignity' than rape, a heinous act 'the very mention of which is a disgrace to human nature' and 'a crime not fit to be named.' . . . To hold that the act of homosexual sodomy is somehow protected as a fundamental right would be to cast aside millennia of moral teaching." 478 U.S. at 196–197. . . .

The history and traditions of this Commonwealth are fully in accord with the Biblical, historical and common law view. Since at least 1860, sodomy has been a criminal offense in Kentucky and this fact was well known to the delegates at the time of the 1890 Constitutional Convention.

Embracing "state constitutionalism," a practice in vogue among many state courts as a means of rejecting the leadership of the Supreme Court of the United States, the majority has declared its independence from even the influence of this nation's highest court. The majority cannot, however, escape the logic and scholarship of *Bowers* which reached the conclusion that nothing in the Due Process Clause of the United States Constitution prevented a state from punishing sodomy as a crime. While I do not advocate the view that state courts should march in lock step with the Supreme Court of the United States, on those occasions when state courts depart from that Court's reasoned interpretations, it should be for compelling reasons, usually text or tradition, and only in clearly distinguishable circumstances, none of which are present here. . . .

The major premise in the majority opinion is that the Constitution forbids any legal restriction upon the private conduct of adults unless it can be shown that such conduct is harmful to another. This view represents the essence of the philosophy of John Stuart Mill in his essay *On Liberty*. While espousing such a view, however, Mill recognized the difficulty of distinguishing that part of a person's life which affected only himself from that which affected others. He recognized that one who by deleterious vices harmed himself indirectly harmed others and that society suffered indirect harm by the mere knowledge of immoral conduct. Nevertheless, Mill clung to his philosophy by insisting that society was without power to punish gambling or drunkenness. He made a ringing defense of the right of persons so disposed to practice polygamy.

While the philosophy of John Stuart Mill as adopted by this Court in *Campbell v. Commonwealth, supra*, exalts individuality in the extreme, it has, nevertheless, a superficial appeal. It rejects majoritarian morality as a basis for law and imposes legal limits on the conduct of man only insofar as it may harm others. Unfortunately for the purposes of the majority, the philosophy of Mill and the views contained in the *Campbell* case, if logically applied, would necessarily result in the eradication of numerous other criminal statutes. For example, if majoritarian morality is without a role in the formulation of criminal law and the only standard is harm to another, all laws proscribing the possession and use of dangerous or narcotic drugs would fall. Likewise incest statutes which proscribe sexual intercourse between persons of close kinship regardless of age or consent would be rendered invalid. Laws prohibiting cruelty to animals, the abuse of dead human bodies, suicide and polygamy would be held unconstitutional. Despite the majority's disingenuous departure from Mill based on "an enlightened paternalism" to prevent self-inflicted harm, many prevailing criminal statutes would nevertheless fail the "harm to another" test. While the majority of this Court manifestly sees the proposition otherwise, the Supreme Court of the United States has addressed the role of morality as a rationale to support criminal law and found no impediment.

> "The law, however, is constantly based on notions of morality, and if all laws representing essentially moral choices are to be invalidated under the Due Process Clause, the courts will be very busy indeed." *Bowers, supra,* 478 U.S. at 196. . . .

From my study of this case, I have concluded that the privacy right found in the Constitution of Kentucky does not apply to claimed rights not remotely envisioned by the delegates to the Constitutional Convention or reasonably emerging from our history and traditions. As such, the right to determine whether sodomy should be a criminal offense belongs to the people through their elected representatives. We should not deprive the people of that right. As the majority has observed, many states have already decriminalized consensual sodomy. Appellee should take his case to the Kentucky General Assembly and let that branch of government say whether the crime shall remain or be abolished. . . .

As persons who engage in homosexual sodomy have never been held to constitute a suspect classification to be upheld, the statute at issue need only satisfy the lowest level of judicial scrutiny and demonstrate that it bears a rational relationship to a legitimate legislative objective. Protection of public "health, safety and morality" was held to be such an objective in *Bosworth v. City of Lexington* . . . (1930). This objective found new vitality with the emergence of the AIDS epidemic which indisputably originated in this country in the homosexual community. Moreover, *Bowers v. Hardwick, supra,* held forthrightly that the rational basis standard was satisfied by majority sentiments as to the immorality of homosexuality. . . .

In final analysis, the question is whether a rational distinction may be drawn between acts of sodomy committed by heterosexuals and homosexuals. As cases such as *Griswold v. Connecticut,* . . . *Eisenstadt v. Baird,* . . . *Loving v. Virginia,* . . . and *Roe v. Wade,* . . . demonstrate, there is a heightened protection of the right of persons with respect to conduct in the context of marriage, procreation, contraception, family relationships, and child rearing and education. As such considerations are without any application as to acts of homosexual sodomy, the distinction is manifest.

"We do not condone the immorality of such activity," says the majority. Despite this statement, it should not be doubted that this decision will be regarded as the imprimatur of Kentucky's highest court upon homosexual conduct. The moral opprobrium of the majority will be lost and the popular perception will be that if the Constitution protects such conduct, it must be okay. While this is not an accurate line of thought, it is a natural one. Those who wish to urge that homosexual conduct is immoral and those who oppose the portrayal of homosexuality as an acceptable alternative lifestyle will encounter the majority opinion as a powerful argument to the contrary. . . .

I conclude with the view that this Court has strayed from its role of interpreting the Constitution and undertaken to make social policy. This decision is a vast extension of judicial power by which four Justices of this Court have overridden the will of the Legislative and Executive branches of Kentucky State Government and denied the people any say in this important social issue. No decision cited by the majority has ever gone so far and certainly none comes to mind. Where this slippery slope may lead is anybody's guess, but the ramifications of this decision will surely by profound.

For these reasons, I dissent.

Wintersheimer, Justice, dissenting

There is a long history of laws against sodomy in Kentucky and elsewhere. Of course it has been considered morally wrong since the beginning of time, but this is a secular legal question here. The very word "sodomy" is derived from the biblical name of the city of Sodom which was destroyed by God for its perverse behavior. In 1533, it became a statutory crime in England under King Henry VIII. In the early English colonies, laws were enacted against sodomy, which punished the crime by death. . . .

. . . It is foolish and fruitless to ignore morality in our society and in our governmental function. Every political decision of consequence reflects a moral judgment. In response to the oft-heard claim that you can't legislate morality, it needs to be said that legislation is always based on someone's morality. It is based on someone's notion of what is right or wrong, just or unjust, fair or unfair. The claim that we cannot legislate morality is a deception intended to exclude from the democratic process those citizens who frankly acknowledge that their motivation is moral in nature. The majority opinion has reached the conclusion that Kentucky Constitution supports a right of privacy that permits consensual sodomy. The majority opinion treats with favor a federal constitutional analysis which proceeds from so-called "emanations" and "penumbras" in its discussion of the First, Third, Fourth and Fifth Amendments to the Federal Bill of Rights. "Emanations and penumbras" are more suited to a seance or a psychic experience rather than to a judicial opinion at any level in any court. . . .

The majority opinion . . . ecstatically embraces the philosophy of John Steward [sic] Mill, an English philosopher of the mid–19th Century. Absolute adoption of the philosophy of Mill is not required by the Kentucky Constitution in any respect. Mill and his disciples express a kind of "anything goes" or laissez-faire attitude towards what they construed as individual liberty. . . . If the Mill concept was ever valid, it had been totally overcome by the development of the interconnection of modern society. If Mill's philosophy that "a man's conduct affects himself alone" was ever true it was not so today. The English–Irish poet, John Dunne [sic], expressed it marvelously when he wrote:

> No man is an island. Ask not for whom the bell tolls, it tolls for you.

No individual is permitted to opt out of any system of comprehensive social legislation even when harm could only come to the individual. If a person lives in society, it is not just the concern of that person whether they can operate a motorcycle safely. The safety of the motorcyclist is directly related to the safety of others using the highway. Contemporary society strongly indicates that the medical bills and the danger to others clearly require precautions that reduce the number of highway accidents.

Proscribing sodomy is clearly within the legitimate authority of the police power of the state and this Court should not infringe on that authority. Justice Lewis Powell in a concurring opinion in *Zablocki v. Redhail*, 434

U.S. 374, . . . (1978) stated that the State represents the collective expression of moral aspirations and has an undeniable interest in insuring that its rules reflect the widely held values of its people. Former U.S. Chief Justice Warren Burger in *Paris Theatre I v. Slaton,* 413 U.S. 49, . . . (1973), quoting former Chief Justice Earl Warren, . . . said that there is a right of the nation and of the states to maintain a decent society.

Clearly the Court should not usurp the power of the legislature and create or invent fundamental constitutional rights. Such a procedure is not contemplated in any way by the Kentucky Constitution. Any change in the Kentucky sodomy statute must be made in the legislature, the duly elected representatives of all the citizens of Kentucky.

It is beyond question that the Kentucky Constitution does not guarantee unlimited privacy in any regard. The state has a rightful concern for the moral welfare of all its citizens and a correct commitment to examining criminal activities wherever they may be committed whether concealed in the home or elsewhere. . . .

Kentucky's fourth-degree sodomy statute is a valid exercise of legitimate police power by the legislature. The constitutional basis of any statute enacted pursuant to the legislative police power is that it appears that the provisions have some substantial tendency to benefit the public or the general welfare. . . . The benefit to be derived from the enactment of the statute is primarily a question for determination by the legislature and such determination will not be set aside by the courts unless it manifestly appears to be arbitrary or not based upon substantial grounds.

K.R.S. 510.100 is a constitutionally permissible decision by the Kentucky General Assembly to protect the public and general welfare; it is essentially the kind of statutory enactment that has been recognized by a plurality of the U.S. Supreme Court . . . in a case involving an Indiana statute prohibiting nude dancing. Justice Antonin Scalia noted that our society prohibits certain activities, not because they harm others but because they are considered in the traditional phrase, *contra bonos mores,* that is, immoral. He notes that in American society such prohibitions have included sadomasochism, cock-fighting, bestiality, suicide, drug use, prostitution and sodomy.

The question of public health cannot be ignored in this situation. The contemporary plague of the AIDS virus supports the legitimate exercise of governmental police power by the legislature in banning sodomy. The majority opinion warmly embraces some of the *amicus* briefs, and condones the testimony of the defendant's expert witnesses in an effort to diminish the impact of the curse of AIDS in our society.

Based on data available in 1986, defense witness, Dr. Martin Raff, testified that AIDS is more readily transmitted by homosexual activity than by heterosexual behavior. . . . Dr. Raff stated that AIDS is primarily a homosexual disease and that 73 percent of all AIDS patients are homosexuals while drug use and prostitution account for most of the AIDS cases among heterosexuals. Dr. Raff also testified that venereal diseases and parasitic infections are more prevalent among homosexuals than among heterosexuals and that Kentucky, which outlaws homosexual sodomy, has "relatively few cases of AIDS in comparison with other states in the Union." . . .

The practice of consensual homosexual sodomy is not a fundamentally protected right as specifically determined in the Federal *Bowers* case. Homosexuals are not a suspect class, and consequently, K.R.S. 510.100 is constitutional because Kentucky has a legitimate and rational interest in protecting the health, safety and morality of its citizens.

The judgment of the Fayette Circuit Court should be reversed. . . .

Case Questions

1. What are the principal arguments made by the dissenting judges in support of the Kentucky legislature's legal right to criminalize private homosexual conduct through the auspices of a deviant sexual intercourse statute?
2. What do the dissenters think about John Stuart Mill's philosophy?
3. What do you think is the proper scope of the state's police power, and why?

Business Ethics

Business managers often encounter ethical questions as they attempt to increase profits, lower costs, and secure and preserve markets in their never-ending quest to maximize earnings and the return that stockholders receive on their investments. One of the most interesting debates presently taking place in academic and professional circles involves ethical challenges to the traditional definition of the role of the corporation in society. The question, which encompasses both legal and ethical dimensions, is "Do corporations have ethical obligations beyond increasing stockholder equity?" Do corporations, for example, have any ethical obligations to such other stakeholders as employees, suppliers, customers, and the community?[19] To what extent should law attempt to influence business decision makers to expand their perspectives and include in their calculus the concerns of a broad range of constituencies? Some authors argue that ethical managers are more likely to flourish where businesses view themselves as a "corporate community." In such an environment, it is suggested, the need to weigh and balance the corporate community's competing needs and interests will naturally lead policymakers to make ethical choices.[20]

Businesspeople often employ lawyers to help them monitor legal developments in such highly relevant subject areas as contract, tort, property, and employment law. You may be familiar with traditional common law doctrines such as *privity of contract* and *caveat emptor,* the preference traditionally shown to landlords over tenants, and the *at-will* employment doctrine. Implicit in these judicial doctrines are assumptions about what constitutes ethical business conduct. The trend in recent decades has been for legislatures and courts to use law as a catalyst for influencing companies to change or modify their business practices. Their apparent goal has been to encourage businesses to become more aware of the ethical implications and the societal consequences resulting from their business choices.

Between 1890 and 1914, Congress enacted a series of antitrust statutes to counter the perceived abuses of economic power by the dominant national monopolies of that era. The Sherman Act (1890), the Clayton Act (1914), and the Federal Trade Commission Act (1914) were intended to redress price discrimination and other monopolistic practices. Unethical business practices in the securities industry in the early 1930s led to the creation of the Securities and

Exchange Commission. More recently, legal initiatives have produced implied warranty statutes, lemon laws, strict liability in tort, affirmative action requirements linked to federal contracts, state and federal environmental protection standards, and legislation protecting people from discrimination in employment because of their age or disabilities. Prior to the passage of the National Labor Relations Act (the Wagner Act) in 1935, employers were allowed to pursue almost any business tactic that served to inhibit or destroy the collective bargaining power of employees. In their struggle against the union movement, companies used discharges, blacklisting, lockouts (withholding work from employees), injunctions that prohibited employees from picketing, and violence. Although some legislation had been passed to protect the rights of employees, the first act that dealt comprehensively with employer-employee relations was the Wagner Act. This act stated the right of a union to exist and the rights of employees to associate with and bargain collectively through a union without interference from the employer. The law gave employees the power to legally engage in group activities, and it helped to equalize the bargaining positions of companies and laborers by outlawing employers' practices that constituted "unfair labor practices." In the following case, an employer allegedly tried to permanently close its plant after employees elected to join a union. The employees filed a complaint with the National Labor Relations Board (NLRB), accusing the company of engaging in an unfair labor practice to prevent them from collectively bargaining over wages, hours, and working conditions.

Textile Workers v. Darlington Manufacturing Company
380 U.S. 263
U.S. Supreme Court
March 25, 1965

Mr. Justice Harlan delivered the opinion of the Court.

We here review judgments of the Court of Appeals setting aside and refusing to enforce an order of the National Labor Relations Board which found respondent Darlington guilty of an unfair labor practice by reason of having permanently closed its plant following petitioner union's election as the bargaining representative of Darlington's employees.

Darlington Manufacturing Company was a South Carolina corporation operating one textile mill. A majority of Darlington's stock was held by Deering Milliken, a New York "selling house" marketing textiles produced by others. Deering Milliken in turn was controlled by Roger Milliken, president of Darlington, and by other members of the Milliken family. The National Labor Relations Board found that the Milliken family, through Deering Milliken, operated 17 textile manufacturers, including Darlington, whose products, manufactured in 27 different mills, were marketed through Deering Milliken.

In March 1956 petitioner Textile Workers Union initiated an organizational campaign at Darlington which the company resisted vigorously in various ways, including threats to close the mill if the union won a representation election. On September 6, 1956, the union won an election by a narrow margin. When Roger Milliken was advised of the union victory, he decided to call a meeting of the Darlington board of directors to consider closing the mill. . . .

The board of directors met on September 12 and voted to liquidate the corporation, action which was approved by the stockholders on October 17. The plant ceased operations entirely in November, and all plant machinery and equipment were sold piecemeal at auction in December. The union filed charges with the Labor Board claiming that Darlington had violated §§ 8(a)(1) and (3) of the National Labor Relations Act by closing its plant, and § 8(a)(5) by refusing to bargain with the union after the election. The Board, by a divided vote, found that Darlington had been closed because of the antiunion animus of Roger Milliken, and held that to be a violation of § 8(a)(3). The Board also found Darlington to be part of a single integrated employer group controlled by the Milliken family through Deering Milliken; therefore Deering Milliken could be held liable for the unfair labor practices of Darlington. Alternatively, since Darlington was a part of the Deering Milliken enterprise, Deering Milliken had violated the Act by closing part of its business for a discriminatory purpose. The Board ordered back pay for all Darlington employees until they obtained substantially equivalent work or were put on preferential hiring lists at other Deering Milliken mills. Respondent Deering Milliken was ordered to bargain with the union in regard to details of compliance with the Board order. . . .

On review, the Court of Appeals, sitting *en banc,* set aside the order and denied enforcement by a divided vote. We granted certiorari . . . to consider the important questions involved. We hold that so far as the Labor Relations Act is concerned, an employer has the absolute right to terminate his entire business for any reason he pleases, but disagree with the Court of Appeals that such right includes the ability to close part of a business no matter what the reason. We conclude that the cause must be remanded to the Board for further proceedings. . . .

We consider first the argument, advanced by the petitioner union but not by the Board, and rejected by the Court of Appeals, that an employer may not go completely out of business without running afoul of the Labor Relations Act if such action is prompted by a desire to avoid unionization. . . . A proposition that a single businessman cannot choose to go out of business if he wants to would represent such a startling innovation that it should not be entertained without the clearest manifestation of legislative intent or unequivocal judicial precedent so construing the Labor Relations Act. We find neither.

So far as legislative manifestation is concerned, it is sufficient to say that there is not the slightest indication in the history of the Wagner Act or of the Taft-Hartley Act that Congress envisaged any such result under either statute. . . .

The courts of appeals have generally assumed that a complete cessation of business will remove an employer from future coverage by the Act. . . .

The AFL-CIO suggests in its *amicus* brief that Darlington's action was similar to a discriminatory lockout, which is prohibited "'because designed to frustrate organizational efforts, to destroy or undermine bargaining representation, or to evade the duty to bargain.'" One of the purposes of the Labor Relations Act is to prohibit the discriminatory use of economic weapons in an effort to obtain future benefits. The discriminatory lockout designed to destroy a union, like a "runaway shop," is a lever which has been used to discourage collective employee activities in the future. But a complete liquidation of a business yields no such future benefit for the employer, if the termination is bona fide. It may be motivated more by spite against the union than by business reasons, but it is not the type of discrimination which is prohibited by the Act. The personal satisfaction that such an employer may derive from standing on his beliefs and the mere possibility that other employers will follow his example are surely too remote to be considered dangers at which the labor statutes were aimed. Although employees may be prohibited from engaging in a strike under certain conditions, no one would consider it a violation of the Act for the same employees to quit their employment *en masse*, even if motivated by a desire to ruin the employer. The very permanence of such action would negate any future economic benefit to the employees. The employer's right to go out of business is no different.

We are not presented here with the case of a "runaway shop," whereby Darlington would transfer its work to another plant or open a new plant in another locality to replace its closed plant. Nor are we concerned with a shutdown where the employees, by renouncing the union, could cause the plant to reopen. Such cases would involve discriminatory employer action for the purpose of obtaining some benefit from the employees in the future. We hold here only that when an employer closes his entire business, even if the liquidation is motivated by vindictiveness toward the union, such action is not an unfair labor practice.*

While we thus agree with the Court of Appeals that viewing Darlington as an independent employer the liquidation of its business was not an unfair labor practice,

we cannot accept the lower court's view that the same conclusion necessarily follows if Darlington is regarded as an integral part of the Deering Milliken enterprise.

The closing of an entire business, even though discriminatory, ends the employer-employee relationship; the force of such a closing is entirely spent as to that business when termination of the enterprise takes place. On the other hand, a discriminatory partial closing may have repercussions on what remains of the business, affording employer leverage for discouraging the free exercise of § 7 rights among remaining employees of much the same kind as that found to exist in the "runaway shop" and "temporary closing" cases. . . . Moreover, a possible remedy open to the Board in such a case, like the remedies available in the "runaway shop" and "temporary closing" cases, is to order reinstatement of the discharged employees in the other parts of the business. No such remedy is available when an entire business has been terminated. By analogy to those cases involving a continuing enterprise we are constrained to hold, in disagreement with the Court of Appeals, that a partial closing is an unfair labor practice under § 8 (a) (3) if motivated by a purpose to chill unionism in any of the remaining plants of the single employer and if the employer may reasonably have foreseen that such closing would likely have that effect.

*Nothing we have said in this opinion would justify an employer's interfering with employee organizational activities by threatening to close his plant, as distinguished from announcing a decision to close already reached by the board of directors or other management authority empowered to make such a decision. We recognize that this safeguard does not wholly remove the possibility that our holding may result in some deterrent effect on organizational activities independent of that arising from the closing itself. An employer may be encouraged to make a definitive decision to close on the theory that its mere announcement before a representation election will discourage the employees from voting for the union, and thus his decision may not have to be implemented. Such a possibility is not likely to occur, however, except in a marginal business, a solidly successful employer is not apt to hazard the possibility that the employees will call his bluff by voting to organize. We see no practical way of eliminating this possible consequence of our holding short of allowing the Board to order an employer who chooses so to gamble with his employees not to carry out his announced intention to close. We do not consider the matter of sufficient significance in the overall labor-management relations picture to require or justify a decision different from the one we have made.

While we have spoken in terms of a "partial closing" in the context of the Board's finding that Darlington was part of a larger single enterprise controlled by the Milliken family, we do not mean to suggest that an organizational integration of plants or corporations is a necessary prerequisite to the establishment of such a violation of § 8 (a) (3). If the persons exercising control over a plant that is being closed for antiunion reasons (1) have an interest in another business, whether or not affiliated with or engaged in the same line of commercial activity as the closed plant, of sufficient substantiality to give promise of their reaping a benefit from the discouragement of unionization in that business; (2) act to close their plant with the purpose of producing such a result; and (3) occupy a relationship to the other business which makes it realistically foreseeable that its employees will fear that such business will also be closed down if they persist in organizational activities, we think that an unfair labor practice has been made out.

Although the Board's single employer finding necessarily embraced findings as to Roger Milliken and the Milliken family which, if sustained by the Court of Appeals, would satisfy the elements of "interest" and "relationship" with respect to other parts of the Deering Milliken enterprise, that and the other Board findings fall short of establishing the factors of "purpose" and "effect" which are vital requisites of the general principles that govern a case of this kind.

Thus, the Board's findings as to the purpose and foreseeable effect of the Darlington closing pertained only to its impact on the Darlington Employees. No findings were made as to the purpose and effect of the closing with respect to the employees in other plants comprising the Deering Milliken group. It does not suffice to establish the unfair labor practice charged here to argue that the Darlington closing necessarily had an adverse impact upon unionization in such other plants. We have heretofore observed that employer action which has a foreseeable consequence of discouraging concerted activities generally does not amount to a violation of § 8 (a) (3) in the absence of a showing of motivation which is aimed at achieving the prohibited effect. . . . In an area which trenches so closely upon otherwise legitimate employer prerogatives, we consider the absence of Board findings on this score a fatal defect in its decision. The Court of Appeals for its part did not deal with the question of purpose and effect at all, since it concluded that an employer's right to close down his entire business because of distaste for unionism, also embraced a partial closing so motivated.

Apart from this, the Board's holding should not be accepted or rejected without court review of its single employer finding, judged, however, in accordance with the general principles set forth above. Review of that finding, which the lower court found unnecessary on its view of the cause, now becomes necessary in light of our holding in this part of our opinion, and is a task that devolves upon the Court of Appeals in the first instance. . . .

In these circumstances, we think the proper disposition of this cause is to require that it be remanded to the Board so as to afford the Board the opportunity to make further findings on the issue of purpose and effect. . . . This is particularly appropriate here since the cases involve issues of first impression. If such findings are made, the cases will then be in a posture for further review by the Court of Appeals on all issues. Accordingly, without intimating any view as to how any of these matters should eventuate, we vacate the judgments of the Court of Appeals and remand the cases to that court with instructions to remand them to the Board for further proceedings consistent with this opinion.

It is so ordered.

Case Questions

1. According to the Supreme Court, is it an unfair labor practice for an employer to close his entire business to prevent the unionization of his former employees?
2. Does it make any difference if an employer closes only one of several plants for the purpose of discouraging unionism in the employer's remaining plants?
3. How would teleological philosophers differ from deontologists in their evaluation of the morality of Darlington's decision to close its plant?

Professional Ethics

We have learned that law is only one of society's resources for developing standards of ethical conduct. Professional associations also make significant contributions. It is common for persons in a trade or profession who share a common concern about competency, quality, and integrity to organize an association. Such an association typically will develop a code of ethics to which the members will subscribe. In this fashion many of the do's and don'ts of a profession become codified, at least as far as the members are concerned. Theoretically, a member who fails to comply with the code will be expelled from membership. This process has the twin advantages of distinguishing the membership from predatory competitors, and enables the members to establish and maintain a positive image with consumers. Real estate brokers, undertakers, social workers, engineers, doctors, police chiefs, and lawyers, to name but a few, have formed associations, at least in part, to establish and maintain standards of ethical behavior for their memberships. In some of the regulated professions, membership in an association is required as a condition of licensure. This is true in the legal profession, where thirty states require attorneys to be dues-paying members of the state's bar association.[21]

The American Bar Association and many state bar associations have standing committees on ethics that issue advisory opinions at the request of members. These opinions are often highly respected and can be influential when used in conjunction with disciplinary proceedings. Bar associations are also heavily involved in developing proposed rules for consideration by the state supreme courts, and they often sponsor courses in continuing legal education for the benefit of the membership.

Ethics and Professional Responsibility Codes for Lawyers

The supreme court of each state is normally responsible for overseeing the practice of law within its jurisdiction. It fulfills this obligation in part by promulgating standards of professional conduct to protect the public from incompetent and/or unethical lawyers. Supreme courts also create an administrative board to investigate complaints and enforce the rules and increasingly require that all licensed attorneys participate in continuing legal education programs.

An examination of typical codes of conduct for lawyers will demonstrate concerns with competency, confidentiality, loyalty, honesty, candor, fairness, and avoiding conflicts of interest.

S. G., the juvenile in the following case, was accused of committing murder. The Sufrin law firm was retained to defend S. G. in what began as a juvenile action and, after a waiver hearing, was subsequently transferred into the criminal court. When the government discovered that the Sufrin law firm had also previously represented the deceased murder victim, Theodore Hilton, they asked the trial court to disqualify S. G.'s lawyers because of an alleged conflict of interest.

State of New Jersey in the Interest of S. G.
791 A.2d 285, A-1542-01T2
Superior Court of New Jersey, Appellate Division
February 14, 2002

Per Curiam

The State . . . appeals . . . from an order . . . denying its motion to disqualify the law firm of Sufrin, Zucker, Steinberg, Waller & Wixted and its individual attorneys, Saul Steinberg (Steinberg) and Dennis Wixted (Wixted) (collectively "Sufrin firm"), from representing the juvenile, S. G., in the State's murder prosecution.

The State contends that in a criminal prosecution for murder in which the juvenile has privately retained counsel, a conflict of interest under the Rules of Professional Conduct (R.P.C.) 1.9(a)(2) or an appearance of impropriety under R.P.C. 1.7(c)(2) exists requiring the disqualification of defense counsel where that counsel also represented the murder victim on unrelated criminal charges. . . .

The . . . Camden County juvenile delinquency complaint . . . charge[s] S. G. with purposely or knowingly causing death or serious bodily injury resulting in death by the shooting of Theodore J. Hilton. . . . The shooting occurred on August 1, 2001, at Morton Street and Mt. Ephraim Avenue in Camden. According to the testimony of John Grier, an investigator in the homicide unit of the Camden County Prosecutor's Office, a group of people were standing around the corner of Morton Street and Mt. Ephraim Avenue for approximately two hours when a verbal confrontation erupted between a . . . male identified as Woo and a female identified as Shirley. Incensed, Shirley left and returned twenty minutes later with five males, one of whom is alleged to be S. G. The five males descended upon the group and demanded that Woo apologize to Shirley. Woo apologized and the five males retreated. Approximately thirty minutes later, the person alleged to be S. G. returned with a firearm. He shot several times into the group still standing on the corner. The victim suffered a gun shot wound to the neck. The Camden Police reported the incident as an aggravated assault. The police report did not identify the shooter, but described him as five feet five inches and wearing dark clothes. The victim died seven days later in the hospital. . . . The Prosecutor's office conducted an investigation into the shooting and arrested S. G.

On August 13, 2001, the State filed a motion . . . for prosecution of S. G. as an adult. The Chancery Division granted that motion on October 23, 2001.

In the interim, on August 14, 2001, Steinberg . . . entered an appearance on behalf of S. G. Concomitantly, the State filed a motion to disqualify the Sufrin firm as defense counsel, alleging that the firm had a conflict of interest in the defense of this case because that firm previously represented the victim in a criminal case, and the firm was currently representing the victim in another criminal case. Apparently, the victim was indicted in 1996 and 2001 on unrelated criminal charges prior to his murder. On September 13, 1996, Steinberg entered an appearance on behalf of the victim. Presumably, the 1996 charges were resolved before August 1, 2001. On May 18, 2001, Wixted entered an appearance on behalf of the victim. The 2001 charges against the victim were pending at the time of the victim's murder. The Camden County Prosecutor's Office was involved in the prosecution of both cases.

On August 16, 2001, the court conducted a hearing and denied the State's motion to disqualify the Sufrin firm. In doing so, the judge had this to say:

> . . . I assume that since defense counsel has entered their appearance that in fact, this is the attorney of [S. G.'s] choosing. As such, and the fact that the . . . victim, defense counsel's former client is now obviously deceased. I don't perceive any specific direct conflict. . . . As such the Court will simply deny the application at this time . . . I don't see, . . . that the appearance of impropriety outweighs the fundamental Sixth Amendment right to have an attorney of one's choosing. . . .

After the disqualification hearing, the court held a waiver hearing at which time the juvenile and his family waived the potential conflict. . . .

On August 20, 2001, the judge entered a written order specifically denying the State's

motion to disqualify and denied the State's request for a stay of the proceedings pending an interlocutory appeal. . . .

On November 14, 2001, the Supreme Court granted leave to the State to appeal and summarily remanded the matter to this court for consideration of the appeal on the merits. The Supreme Court stayed all further proceedings . . . in the trial court pending resolution of the disqualification issue.

On appeal, the State argues that the Sufrin firm's representation of S. G., when that firm previously represented the murder victim, constitutes a conflict of interest. . . . The State maintains that the Sufrin firm's continued representation of S. G. will "place a cloud of doubt on any future proceedings," and will raise questions as to S. G.'s right to effective assistance of trial counsel.

The pertinent provisions of the Rules of Professional Conduct in terms of a lawyer's duty to maintain the confidences of a former client and to avoid conflicts of interest are R.P.C. 1.9(a)(2) and R.P.C. 1.7(c)(2).

Rule 1.9 provides:

(a) A lawyer who has represented a client in a matter shall not thereafter:
   (1) represent another client in the same or a substantially related matter in which that client's interests are materially adverse to the interests of the former client unless the former client consents after a full disclosure of the circumstances and consultation with the former client; or
   (2) use information relating to the representation to the disadvantage of the former client except as RPC 1.6 would permit with respect to a client or when the information has become generally known. [R.P.C. 1.9]

Rule 1.7 provides the general rule that a lawyer shall not represent a client, without full disclosure to and consultation with the client, if the lawyer believes that representation of that client will be directly adverse to another client, or if the representation of that client may be materially limited by other responsibilities or interests of the lawyer. R.P.C. 1.7(a) and (b). Subsection (c) contains the "appearance of impropriety" language, which reads:

> (c) This rule shall not alter the effect of case law or ethics opinions to the effect that:
>   (1) in certain cases or categories of cases involving conflicts or apparent conflicts, consent to continued representation is immaterial, and
>   (2) in certain cases or situations creating an appearance of impropriety rather than an actual conflict, multiple representation is not permissible, that is, in those situations in which an ordinary knowledgeable citizen acquainted with the facts would conclude that the multiple representation poses substantial risk of disservice to either the public interest or the interest of one of the clients. [R.P.C. 1.7(c)]

According to the State, the concern is that the Sufrin firm's attorney-client relationship with the victim gave rise to a continuing obligation of confidentiality and that (1) if the confidences are not kept, the Sufrin firm will use that information to benefit S. G.; or (2) if the confidences are kept, the representation of S. G. might prove to be ineffective due to the inability of the Sufrin firm to conduct a thorough cross examination, or that the public may perceive that S. G. gained advantages through the Sufrin firm's representation. . . .

. . . The possibilities and risks here, at best, are weak and hypothetical. The obvious concern of a conflict, . . . focuses on the former client's participation in the trial where defense counsel may engage in cross examination of that client. Clearly, that prime concern is absent where the deceased client will not be a witness.

Regardless, the State contends that . . . Steinberg may use confidential information to decide "whether to place [the victim's] con-

duct and character at issue, or simply investigate ways to do so at trial." However, the rules of evidence limit the ways in which the character of a victim may be introduced at trial. . . . In order to be introduced, evidence of a victim's character must be relevant to the substantive issue of guilt. . . . Here, the character of the victim is irrelevant.

The facts, as presently known, disclose that the murder occurred when a male, alleged to be S. G., shot a firearm several times into a group of people standing on a street corner. The State has not alleged facts that would lead one to believe that the victim was the intended target of the bullet. Instead, it appears that someone shot into the group and a bullet aimlessly struck the victim. The victim was simply in the wrong place at the wrong time. As such, the victim's character is not relevant to the crime. . . .

The State maintains it "may choose to call" a family member or friend of the victim to vouch for his character or to testify as to the events leading up to the day of his murder. In this regard, the State argues that an appearance of impropriety . . . exists because Steinberg will be less likely to engage in an objective and vigorous cross examination of any such witness, or because he may use the confidences gained during the representation of the victim to S. G.'s advantage. Thus, the State contends that the public will perceive that S. G. unfairly benefited from the Sufrin firm's prior representation. This mere possibility lacks a reasonable basis and is insufficient to constitute an . . . appearance of impropriety. . . .

. . . The facts, as presently alleged, indicate that someone shot randomly into a group, and that the shooter did not seek out the victim. As such, the State's proposed family/friend character testimony is not relevant. For the same reason, the proposed testimony concerning the "events leading up to" the day of the victim's death is irrelevant. . . .

This is a case of successive representation where the former client is deceased. The Sufrin firm did not simultaneously represent the juvenile and the victim. Steinberg represented the victim for the 1996 charge. At the time of the shooting, Wixted represented the victim for the 2001 charge. However, the victim died on August 8, 2001, at which time the charges became moot. The Sufrin firm's representation of the victim terminated on August 8, 2001. The Sufrin firm . . . was no longer representing the victim on August 14, 2001, when Steinberg entered an appearance on behalf of S. G. . . .

The United States Supreme Court has recognized that defendants who retain their own lawyers are entitled to the same protections as the defendants for whom the state appoints counsel. . . . As such there is no reason to draw a distinction between retained and appointed counsel that denies equal justice to defendants who have retained private counsel. . . . It borders on the unconstitutional to [rule] that private attorneys, because of their pecuniary interests, cannot represent successive clients in criminal matters. To do so would deprive a defendant with retained counsel from the protections of the Sixth Amendment while affording that right to a defendant with appointed counsel. Instead, it is constitutionally principled to . . . conclude that where defense . . . counsel has no relevant confidential information there is no conflict, and where defense counsel does have such information he or she cannot use it.

. . . [T]here is no possibility that an issue of privilege would arise requiring a waiver of the victim's attorney-client privilege where the victim is deceased. The State, who prosecuted the victim's prior charges, has not furnished any evidence to indicate that its murder prosecution has any relationship to the former prosecution of the victim or that the victim's death has any relationship to that prosecution. Out of extreme caution, S. G. has indicated, at a hearing, that he wants his present attorney to continue his representation and has waived any potential conflict.

The State next argues that the prior representation is an actual conflict because "nothing would be more disadvantageous to [the victim], the [Sufrin firm's] former client, than to have his killer go free." That statement impermissibly presumes S. G.'s guilt. . . . It also amounts to a contention that the Sufrin firm's previous representation of the murder victim, in and of itself, is an actual and apparent conflict that warrants disqualification. While we agree that it looks bad for privately retained counsel to represent the person alleged to have killed that counsel's former client, the Rules of Professional Conduct do not prohibit that representation.

All lawyers are bound to retain the confidences of their clients, . . . and their former clients, . . . and are obligated to refrain from engaging in representation that would appear inappropriate, . . . They are also prohibited from engaging in conduct that is prejudicial to the administration of justice, . . . and are required to refrain or withdraw from the representation of a client if that representation will result in a violation of the Rules of Professional Conduct, . . . There is, however, no rule that prohibits a lawyer from representing a client because of a subjective belief that the representation will look bad. Indeed, courts have recognized that even where representation "looks bad" in some indeterminate way, "the appearance of impropriety alone is 'simply too slender a reed on which to rest a disqualification order except in the rarest of cases.'" . . .

Even where defense counsel had a personal relationship with the murder victim, courts have refused to find an actual conflict on that basis alone. . . . (no actual conflict where defense counsel was high school classmate of victim's father, whom defense counsel had not seen for thirty years); . . . (no actual conflict where defense counsel was related by blood to victim where defense counsel conducted thorough cross examination of victim); . . . (no actual conflict in murder prosecution where two members of defense counsel's law firm had personal association with victim's family) . . . ; (no actual conflict where defense counsel was former husband of the victim's mother); . . . (no actual conflict where defense counsel had personal relationship with the murder victim); . . . (no actual conflict where defense counsel had friendship with murder victim), . . .

The decisions of the lower federal courts . . . make it clear that defense counsel's representation of the defendant against a murder prosecution where that defense counsel has previously represented the murder victim is not an actual conflict per se. Instead, those circumstances present only the potential for a conflict that requires a hearing before the trial court. In this case, an actual conflict does not exist and the trial court conducted a hearing to consider the potential conflict and found disqualification is unwarranted.

The foregoing authority teaches that courts are to determine, on a case-by-case basis, whether defense counsel has divided interests that prevent the effective representation of a defendant. If the conflict could cause defense counsel to improperly use privileged communications during cross examination, then disqualification is appropriate. Disqualification is also appropriate if the conflict could deter defense counsel from conducting a vigorous cross examination. In this particular case, for the reasons discussed . . . disqualification is not appropriate, and, . . . in the absence of an actual conflict or potentially serious conflict it would be unconstitutional to establish a presumption in favor of disqualification.

Disqualification of a criminal defendant's chosen counsel is a harsh remedy that should be invoked infrequently because it raises problems of a constitutional dimension. . . . The Sixth Amendment to the United States Constitution provides that a criminal defendant has a right to have the assistance of counsel for his or her defense. . . . A similar right to counsel is found in the New Jersey Constitution, N.J. Const. art. 1, P 10; . . .

Thus, the Sixth Amendment recognizes a presumption in favor of the defendant's chosen counsel, . . . and encompasses the right to assistance of counsel unhindered by a conflict of interest. . . . A trial court must recognize a presumption in favor of a defendant's counsel of choice, but that presumption may be overcome by a demonstration of actual conflict or a showing of a serious potential for conflict. . . . Disqualification in such cases is necessary because when a defendant is represented by an attorney who has an actual or potentially serious conflict, the defendant may be deprived of effective assistance of counsel. . . .

A defendant can waive his or her right to assistance of counsel unhindered by a conflict of interest, provided that the waiver is knowing and intelligent . . . a court is not required to accept a defendant's waiver in all circumstances. . . . Therefore, the right to counsel of choice is not absolute. . . . This is so because the Supreme Court has also recognized an independent interest of the courts in ensuring that criminal trials are conducted within the ethical standards of the profession and that legal proceedings appear fair to all who observe them. . . . Therefore, when determining whether or not to disqualify defense counsel, courts must balance the defendant's Sixth Amendment right to counsel of choice against his right to representation free from conflicts.

As discussed . . . , this is a case of successive representation that does not involve an actual conflict of interest. A potentially serious conflict is also not present. The Supreme

Court has stated that the seriousness of any potential conflict depends on its "likelihood and dimensions." . . . Here, the State did not present evidence to suggest that the Sufrin firm obtained any relevant confidential information from the victim. Even if it is assumed that the Sufrin firm was privy to confidential information, . . . , there is no evidence to conclude that the confidential information would be relevant to the charges in the present case. . . .

[Nor is there] . . . evidence that S. G.'s attorney is privy to confidential information that will compromise any ethical duty to the victim, or that will deprive S. G. of effective assistance of counsel.

In sum, the judicial system's interest in safeguarding the criminal proceedings is not threatened. When an actual or apparent conflict does not exist and where any potential conflict is improbable, the interests of the judicial system will not be undermined. . . . To the contrary, in a case such as this where the potential conflict is a mere possibility, the disqualification of a juvenile's counsel of choice would compromise the judicial system by denying the juvenile his constitutional right to his attorney of choice. Ibid.

The order denying disqualification of the Sufrin firm is affirmed.

Case Questions

1. The court balances conflict of interest and appearance of impropriety against what other consideration?
2. Did the fact that Hilton, the former client, was deceased influence the court in reaching its decision?

---

www   *INTERNET TIPS*

1. The Camden County Prosecutor is appealing the decision to the New Jersey Supreme Court. That court's decision will be posted on the textbook's website.
2. This was a split decision with Judge Richard Newman in dissent. The dissent will be posted on the textbook's website.

The number of lawyer-lawyer marriages is increasing as more and more women enter the legal profession. This social phenomenon has resulted in ethical issues such as we see in the case of *DCH Health Services Corp. v. Waite*. The defendant, Waite, selected Attorney Randy Kramer to be his lawyer. However, Kramer's wife, Ana, who also happens to be a judge in a different county, had been a member of plaintiff DCH Health Services' board of directors. The trial court ruled that Kramer should be disqualified from representing Waite because of "an appearance of impropriety." Waite appealed that decision to the state court of appeals.

DCH Health Services Corp. v. Waite
G026285/ 95 Cal.App.4th 829
California Court of Appeals (Fourth District,.
   Div. Three)
Jan. 28, 2002

Rylaarsdam, Acting P. J.

Defendant Verner Waite and his lawyer Randy Kramer appeal from the trial court's order disqualifying Kramer from representing or assisting defendant in the underlying actions. They contend plaintiffs Carl Westerhoff, Sheldon Zinberg, and Abram Zinberg lacked standing to bring the motion for disqualification. Further, they contend that, even had the motion been made by a proper party, the court abused its discretion in ordering Kramer's disqualification. . . .

Facts

The cases in which the court recused Kramer consist of three consolidated actions. The plaintiffs in these actions are DCH Health Services Corporation (the hospital), Downey Community Hospital Foundation (the foundation), Westerhoff, the Zinbergs, and several other parties not pertinent to this appeal. They sued Waite, an anonymous organization denominated "Concerned Citizens of Downey," and some 1000 Does [unidentified persons]. The complaints in these actions are for defamation in connection with a very public dispute in the Downey community concerning the operations of the hospital and the foundation. . . .

When the first of these actions was commenced in 1996, Los Angeles Superior Court Judge Ana Luna was a member of the foundation's board of directors and was engaged to marry Kramer. Almost two years later, Luna resigned from the board. Shortly thereafter, she and Kramer married and, some time later, Kramer was retained to represent Waite

after Waite's counsel became ill. Westerhoff, a former officer of the foundation, requested Kramer voluntarily withdraw as counsel for Waite because of his marital relationship with Luna. When Kramer refused to do so, Westerhoff moved to disqualify him. The Zinbergs joined in the motion.

The court granted the motion, stating, "The record establishes that Judge Luna received confidential information while serving on the hospital board. Despite Mr. Kramer's declaration stating that he has not received any confidential information regarding this lawsuit, the Court believes that because of the unique nature of the marital relationship this Court should apply a prophylactic rule to avoid the appearance of impropriety."

Discussion

Code of Civil Procedure section 128, subdivision (a)(5) gives courts the power to order a lawyer's disqualification. . . . On appeal, a trial court's decision concerning a disqualification motion will not be disturbed . . . absent an abuse of discretion. . . .

Only a party with an expectation of confidentiality can disqualify a lawyer

Luna never acted as a lawyer for the foundation; but the trial court assumed, and none of the parties dispute, that as a corporate director she owed the corporation a duty of confidentiality. The trial court's conclusion that Luna's relationship with Kramer created an appearance of impropriety must have been based on an assumed likelihood that Luna would breach her duty of confidentiality or that Kramer would prevail on her to do so. But to whatever extent Luna owed a duty of confidentiality to the foundation, she owed no such duty to the parties who sought Kramer's disqualification. Nor did Kramer. Kramer and Waite assert Westerhoff and the Zinbergs do not have "any legally recognizable expectation of confidentiality" and thus lack standing to bring the motion to disqualify Kramer.... This overstates the case. Standing arises from a breach of the duty of confidentiality owed to the complaining party, regardless of whether a lawyer-client relationship existed. Thus, for example, a lawyer may be disqualified after improper contacts with an opposing party's expert witness....

Had the foundation brought the motion to disqualify Kramer, it would have had standing based on the duty of confidentiality Luna owed to it despite the absence of attorney-client relationship between Kramer and the foundation. As discussed below, this does not mean it would have prevailed. But a lawyer owes no general duty of confidentiality to nonclients.... Neither does a corporate director owe such a duty to anyone but the corporation....

The motion to disqualify Kramer was based solely on confidential information allegedly imparted to Luna while she served as a director of the foundation. None of the plaintiffs assert the existence of a current or former lawyer-client relationship with Kramer or a confidential relationship between themselves and Luna. Absent the existence of a lawyer-client relationship or other relationship imposing a duty of confidentiality, neither Westerhoff nor the Zinbergs were entitled to seek Kramer's disqualification....

No Basis for Disqualification

Though the court concluded Luna had received confidential information pertinent to the underlying action while she served on the foundation's board, it had no evidence, and did not make any factual determinations, that she disclosed such information to Kramer. The court did not find or suggest that Luna or Kramer had engaged in any impropriety. Instead, to support Kramer's disqualification, the court sought to "avoid the

appearance of impropriety" arising from the "unique nature of the marital relationship." This is an inadequate basis for the order disqualifying Kramer.

As distinguished from judicial recusals which may be required on the basis of a mere "appearance of impropriety" ... such an appearance of impropriety by itself does not support a lawyer's disqualification.... Speculative contentions of conflict of interest cannot justify disqualification of counsel.... "A lawyer whose husband or wife is also a lawyer must, like every other lawyer, obey all disciplinary rules, for the disciplinary rules apply to all lawyers without distinction as to marital status. We cannot assume that a lawyer who is married to another lawyer necessarily will violate any particular disciplinary rule, such as those that protect a client's confidences, that proscribe neglect of a client's interest, and that forbid representation of differing interests." (ABA Com. on Ethics and Prof. Resp., opn. No. 340 (Sept. 23, 1975) p. 2.)

Currently, women constitute approximately 23 percent of the lawyers in California.... Those numbers will inevitably rise, considering that almost 50 percent of today's law students are women.... As this trend increases, there undoubtedly will be more marriages between lawyers. Consequently, factual situations similar to the one before us will become more commonplace, giving way to issues previously unanticipated in an era when the practice of law was dominated by men.

We concede that marriages between lawyers create a variety of novel issues concerning a lawyer's duty of confidentiality as well as whether lawyer-client conflicts arise. At the same time, we reject the suggestion that such issues should be resolved solely by reference to the marriage relationship. Is the likelihood of disclosure any less when two lawyers are sharing a household without being married or when they are involved in a dating relationship? Does the gender of the lawyers affect the analysis?

These issues should not be decided mechanically on the basis of the precise relationship between the lawyers. Rather, the court should start with the presumption that, unless proven otherwise, lawyers will behave in an ethical manner. Society has entrusted lawyers with confidences, and we should not assume that lawyers will violate these confidences when involved in particular relationships. Neither the marital relationship between Luna and Kramer nor any "appear-ance of impropriety" is sufficient to deprive Waite of his right to be represented by a lawyer of his choice. The trial court abused its discretion in disqualifying Kramer based solely on what it considered to be an appear-ance of impropriety.

Disposition

The order is reversed and the matter is re-manded. We direct the trial court to enter a new order consistent with the findings herein. . . .

Case Questions

1. Why did the trial court conclude that Kramer should be disqualified from representing Waite?
2. Why did the appeals court reverse the trial court? With which court do you agree?
3. After reading the case we know that the appellate court determined that Kramer had violated no rule of *professional ethics* in defending Waite. Might an attorney in Kramer's situation decide, as a matter of *personal morality,* that it is not *right* for him or her to represent this client?

Chapter Questions

1. Define the following terms:

analytical positivism	misprision
deontology	moral duty
egoist	natural law
ethics	normative ethics
integrity	teleology
legal duty	unjust enrichment
metaethics	utilitarianism

2. Michael and Patricia Sewak bought a house from Charles and Hope Lock-hart. Prior to the sale, the Lockharts had employed a contractor for $12,000 to renovate their basement. Somehow, the main structural support which held up the house was removed during the renovations. Shortly after mov-ing in, the Sewaks noticed that the kitchen floor was not level, that doors

were not in alignment, and that the first and second floors were sagging. They hired a consultant, who investigated and determined that the support column was missing and that an illegal jack, found in the back of a heater closet, was used to provide the needed structural support. The consultant predicted that the absence of the structural column would ultimately result in the collapse of the house. The Sewaks filed suit, alleging fraud and a violation of the Pennsylvania Unfair Trade Practices and Consumer Protection Law (UTPCPL). The Sewaks maintained that the Lockharts should have informed them that the support column had been removed. The trial evidence, according to the appellate court, permitted the jury to find that the Lockharts not only had knowledge of the column's removal, but also took steps to conceal its replacement with the illegal jack, and that they had not obtained the proper building permits before undertaking the renovations. Did the Lockharts act ethically in their dealings with the Sewaks? Should the law impose a legal duty on the Sewaks to investigate and discover the absence of the structural support column for themselves?

Sewak v. Lockhart, 699 A.2d 755 (1997)

3. Jonas Yoder and Wallace Miller, members of the Amish religion, withdrew their daughters, Frieda Yoder and Barbara Miller, from school after they had completed the eighth grade. This refusal violated a Wisconsin compulsory school attendance law which required Frieda and Barbara to be in school until their sixteenth birthdays. The U.S. Supreme Court ruled that the Amish parents had a constitutionally protected right to control the religious education of their children under the First and Fourteenth Amendments. The Court's majority concluded that to require the children to attend public high school would undermine fundamental Amish values and religious freedoms. Frieda and Barbara were not parties to the lawsuit, and there is no record as to their positions on the issue in this case. Given the Supreme Court's holding in *Wisconsin v. Yoder*, what posture should the law take in a situation where Amish children desire to attend high school over the objections of their parents?

Wisconsin v. Yoder, 406 U.S. 205 (1972)

4. Raymond Dirks worked for a New York City broker-dealer firm. He specialized in analyzing insurance company investments. Dirks received a tip from a former officer at Equity Funding of America (an insurance company) named Ronald Secrist that Equity Funding had fraudulently overstated its assets. Dirks decided to investigate. Although neither Dirks nor his employer traded in Equity Funding shares, he told others in the securities industry about the tip, and soon thereafter Equity Funding's shares dropped precipitously in value. The Security and Exchange Commission (SEC) investigated Dirk's role in disclosing the existence of the fraud and charged him with being a "tipee" who had aided and abetted violations of the Securities Act of 1933. This statute makes it illegal for persons with inside knowledge (nonpublic information) to unfairly take advantage of Equity Funding's shareholders by trading in the affected securities before the news has become public. Can you make an argument supporting the conclusion that it would

be unethical for Dirks to share the information he obtained from Secrist with other people in the industry? Can you make an argument that Dirk's conduct was not unethical?

Dirks v. Securities and Exchange Commission, 463 U.S. 646 (1983)

5. Three separate federal suits were brought by homosexual men and women who had been discharged from their jobs. One plaintiff, a schoolteacher, alleged that his firing was because he wore an earring to school. The second suit was brought by two lesbians who alleged that they were terminated from their jobs because of their sexual orientation. The third suit was filed by three homosexual plaintiffs, who alleged that they were in one case denied employment and in two cases fired from employment because their employer had a corporate policy of not employing homosexuals. The U.S. District Court dismissed the complaints on the grounds that Title VII does not protect employees from discharges based on effeminacy or homosexuality. The U.S. Court of Appeals affirmed the decision of the District Court. Does the fact that two federal courts ruled that the plaintiffs were not entitled to legal relief affect the ethical merits of their claims?

De Santis v. Pacific Tel. & Tel. Co., Inc., 608 F.2d 327 (1979)

6. In many regions of the country, it is customary for schools to take a break for school vacations during February. Many families arrange their schedules so that families can take very special trips to remote destinations. The airlines are beneficiaries of this tradition, and flights to popular vacation spots are often totally booked. In 1999, airline pilots involved in collective bargaining disputes with their employer engaged in a "sick-out" during the school vacation period. Analyze this scenario from the *egoist* perspective.

7. The Massachusetts Supreme Judicial Court has interpreted a statute to require injured skiers who wish to sue ski area operators to give the operators notice of the skier's claims within ninety days of the injury and establishes a one-year statute of limitations. Failure to give timely notice of the claims will preclude bringing the suit at all. Both the court majority and the dissenting justices attributed these unusually short limitations to bringing actions to a legislative policy. Both concluded that the legislature evidently placed a higher value on the economic vitality of the Massachusetts ski industry than on the rights of injured skiers to seek recoveries in tort and contract from ski area operators. Analyze this case from a *utilitarian* perspective.

Atkins v. Jiminy Peak, Inc. 514 N.E.2d 850 (1987)

Notes

1. See *Macomber v. Dillman* in Chapter 6.
2. See *Marybeth Atkins v. Jiminy Peak, Inc.* in Chapter 5.
3. You can find this case on the Internet at www.Findlaw.com. The case citation is *Furman v. Georgia*, 408 U.S. 238 (1972).

4. Telling a lie about a material fact while under oath is a crime called perjury. Theft by false pretense is another crime that is based on a fraudulent, actual, factual misrepresentation. In contracts, fraud in the formation of an agreement can result in rescission and an award of damages to the injured party.

5. GE Moore in Hancock, p. 2.

6. An example is the debate about whether the concept we call "good" is composed of parts or is essentially indefinable (G. Moore, *Principia Ethica*, 1903; Battin and Francis in *Applied Ethics and Ethical Theory*).

7. James Rachels in Rosenthal and Shehad, "Applied Ethics," and Kant in David Lyons, pp. 8–14. ("The Elements of Moral Philosophy," 2nd Ed.)

8. Hancock, p. 12.

9. Ibid., p. 12.

10. Rachels, pp. 12–24; Kant, pp. 8–14.

11. You will recall from Chapter 1, for example, that utilitarians sought to produce the greatest good for the greatest number of people. This kind of calculation can only be undertaken by examining aftermaths.

12. Carol Gilligan and Jane Attanucci maintain that all people think about the morality of their relations with others from two perspectives. One perspective is based on a concern for treating people fairly (which they call the "justice perspective"), and the other focuses on responding to persons who are in need (which they call the "care perspective"). The authors suggested that males are more oriented toward concerns for "justice" and "females" toward caring. See Gilligan, Ward, Taylor, and Bardige, *Mapping the Moral Domain* (Cambridge, MA: Harvard University Graduate School of Education, 1988), Chapter 4.

13. Cite to Kant's ethical imperatives.

14. *Egoism* (Benedict Spinoza, 1632–1677): "The virtues that ethics seeks to inculcate are the qualities we require to have personally fulfilled lives." These he said included "courage, temperance, harmonious, cooperative and stable relations with others."

15. Under Article VI's supremacy clause, the federal Constitution is the ultimate authority as to matters arising under it, but the state constitutions are the ultimate authority as to matters that do not amount to federal questions.

16. *Boston Globe*, October 16, 1998, p. A17.

17. Note that these facts parallel the facts in the Unabomber case and that Ted Kaczynski's brother did tell authorities of his suspicions, he did receive a large cash reward, and he gave it all to charity.

18. P. Devlin, "Morals and the Criminal Law," in *The Enforcement of Morals* (Oxford University Press, 1965), pp. 9–10.

19. David Millen refers to this as a dispute between the "contractarians" and the "communitarians." See David Millon, "Communitarians, Contractarians, and the Crisis in Corporate Law," 50 *Washington & Lee Review*, 1373 (1993).

20. See J. Nesteruk, "Law, Virtue, and the Corporation," 33 *American Business Journal*, 473 (1996).

21. For a brief and critical history of the development of bar associations, see Howard Abadinsky, *Law and Justice* (Chicago: Nelson-Hall, 1991), p. 102.

III The Judicial System

COURTS

A court is a governmental body that is empowered to resolve disputes according to law. Courts are reactive institutions. They do not undertake to adjudicate disputes by themselves, and can only act when someone files suit.

Courts are created in accordance with constitutional provisions and legislative acts. The legislative branch of the government usually has the right to establish and change courts, to regulate many of their procedures, and to limit their jurisdiction.

In the United States, we have a separate judicial system for each of the states and the federal government. These systems vary in size and complexity, although they usually have hierarchical structures as illustrated in Figure 3-1 (see page 121). Since federal and state judicial systems function simultaneously throughout the nation, conflicts can arise with respect to jurisdictional issues, substantive law, supremacy, and the finality of decisions.

Although each of the states has developed its own unique structure, substantive law, rules, and procedures, there is an underlying common law heritage. In our nation's formative years we were greatly influenced by English structures, procedures, and substantive law. Yet from the earliest days, the states modified or replaced both substantive law and legal structures when necessary, and created new ones. Each of the various states was independently charged with dispensing justice in its courts. Each system had the capacity to adapt, reform, and experiment. From those early days down to the present, the states have borrowed from each other in order to improve the administration of justice.

Even though fifty-one judicial systems are available to resolve disputes, very few cases actually go to trial. Disputes are usually settled outside the courtroom on the basis of the lawyer's predictions of what would happen if the case were tried. Litigation is very expensive and time consuming, which encourages litigants to settle cases without a trial.

Trial Courts

Courts are classified by function: there are trial courts and appellate courts. A trial court hears and decides controversies by determining facts and applying appropriate rules. The opposing parties to a dispute establish their positions by introducing evidence of the facts and by presenting arguments on the law.

The right of a trial by jury provides litigants with a choice of trying the case to a single judge or to a jury of peers. When a case is litigated before a judge instead of a jury, it is called a *bench trial.* The judge controls the entire trial and determines the outcome. In a jury trial, the decision-making functions are divided between the judge and the jury, which provides a safeguard of checks and balances. The judge rules on the admissibility of evidence, decides questions of law, and instructs the jury. The jury listens to the testimony, evaluates the evidence, and decides what facts have been proven. In many instances, the testimony of witnesses is contradictory. In such cases, the jury can determine the facts only after deciding which witnesses should be believed. It then applies the law to those facts in accordance with the judge's instructions. The judge supervises the entire litigation. This includes ruling on pretrial motions, supervising discovery, and conducting the trial, matters that will be addressed in Chapter 4.

When the jury's verdict is submitted, the jury decides who wins and what the recovery will be. Over half of the states permit a less-than-unanimous verdict in civil cases. The usual requirement in such states is five jurors in agreement out of six. Unless the parties stipulate otherwise, the rule in federal civil trials is that the jury verdict must be unanimous.

The law may authorize the jury to use a *special verdict.* This means that the jury answers specific questions related to certain factual issues in the case. A special verdict is used to focus the jury's attention on the evidence and the factual disputes in the case. It discourages jurors from determining the case's outcome by deciding which party they would like to see win the lawsuit. When the jury returns a special verdict, the judge applies the law to the jury's answers and reaches a final judgment.

It is often said that questions of fact are for the jury and questions of law are for the judge. A factual issue is presented when reasonable people could arrive at different results in deciding what happened in an actual event. When an inference is so certain that all reasonable people must draw the same conclusion, it becomes a question of law for the judge. It is often difficult to make a distinction between questions of fact and questions of law.

There is no need for a trial (either to a jury or to the court) unless there is a factual dispute between the parties. If the parties agree about the facts, but disagree about the law, the judge can determine the applicable law and dispose of the case by *motion for summary judgment.*

A jury was traditionally composed of twelve people. Today, many jurisdictions have authorized six-person juries. Jurors are chosen from the community, and their qualifications are reviewed before they are seated. At trial, they make their decision in private.

Although federal and state constitutions guarantee the right to a trial by jury, there is some dispute about the effectiveness of the jury system. Jury trials take more time to conduct than bench trials and contribute to the congestion of court dockets. Jury trials also are expensive. Because jurors do not know how to evaluate evidence, rules of evidence and trial procedures have been developed so that they are exposed only to competent evidence and permissible argument. In a bench trial, many of these procedures and rules can be eliminated or relaxed.

In addition, juries are known to be very unpredictable, sometimes arbitrary, and add uncertainty to the adjudication process. Lawyers deal with this uncertainty by attempting to discover jurors' hidden tendencies, biases, and attitudes. More and more trial attorneys employ jury research firms in big cases to help them select the jury and prepare and present their clients' cases. Attorneys who try such cases develop special skills and strategies that they would be unlikely to use in a bench trial before an experienced judge.

One of the most important benefits of the jury system is that it allows citizens to participate in the legal process. A jury is supposed to represent a cross section of the public, whereas a judge does not. Despite the weaknesses of the jury system, it is not likely that the right to a trial by jury will be eliminated in the near future.

Appellate Courts

Appellate courts review the decisions of trial courts. Usually, an appeal can only be taken from a lower court's judgment. In the case of *Du Pont v. Christopher*, however, we saw that some jurisdictions permit a limited interlocutory appeal to be made prior to a trial in some circumstances. That is, appellate review may determine a controlling question of law before the case itself is decided. In a civil action, any dissatisfied party generally may appeal to a higher court. In criminal cases, the defendant usually may appeal, but the prosecution generally may not.

The appellate court reviews the proceedings of the trial court and decides whether the trial court acted in accordance with the law, and whether the appellant properly preserved the error. This means that an attorney cannot observe error occurring in a trial court and do nothing. The attorney must inform the judge of the error and request specific relief. Failure to object results in a waiver of the right to subsequently raise the matter on appeal.

An appellate court bases its decision solely on the theories argued and evidence presented in the lower court. There are no witnesses or jury at the appellate level. The appellate court does not retry the facts of the case, and no new arguments or proof are permitted. The appellate court reaches its decision by using only the record of the proceedings in the lower court, the written briefs filed by both parties to the appeal, and the parties' oral arguments given before the appellate judges. The record of the proceedings in the lower court includes the pleadings, pretrial papers, depositions, and a transcript of the trial proceedings and testimony.

STATE COURT SYSTEMS

The power to create courts is an attribute of every sovereignty. The various states of the United States have exercised this power either by constitutional provisions or by statutory enactments. The power to create courts includes the authority to organize them, including the establishment of judgeships, and to regulate their procedure and jurisdiction.

Although judicial systems vary considerably from state to state, a state court system usually consists of probate courts, a large number of courts with limited jurisdiction, courts with residual jurisdiction, and appellate courts, as illustrated in Figure 3-1.

Courts of limited jurisdiction—inferior courts—are limited as to subject matter and territory. For example, the justice of the peace court administers justice in minor matters at the local level such as civil cases involving small

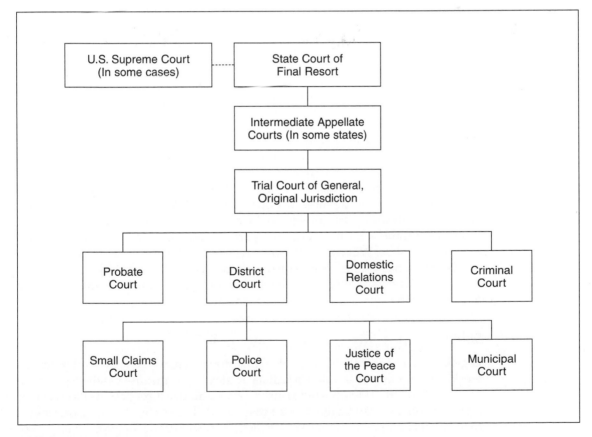

FIGURE 3-1   A State Court System

Source: Adapted from Arnold J. Goldman and William D. Sigismond, *Business Law: Principles & Practices,* 2nd Ed. Copyright © 1988 by Houghton Mifflin Company. Used with permission.

sums of money and minor criminal matters. A state judicial system also usually includes a probate court to handle deceased persons' estates. The jurisdiction of local courts, such as municipal, city, and county courts, is limited to a specified territory. The jurisdiction of small claims and municipal courts is also limited to relatively low maximum amounts of damages that may be awarded. In small claims proceedings, representation by attorney and ordinary court procedure may be dispensed with.

Trial courts of residual jurisdiction in the state court system may bear the name of common pleas, district, superior, circuit, or even—in New York State—supreme court. These courts have the power to hear all types of cases. The primary function of trial courts is to exercise original jurisdiction. (Original jurisdiction is the power to take note of a suit at its beginning, try it, and pass judgment on the law and the facts of the controversy.) Generally, they also exercise appellate jurisdiction over decisions of courts of limited jurisdiction.

A state's judicial system may provide an intermediate appellate court analogous to the court of appeals in the federal system. Not all states provide this intermediate step. A final appellate court, analogous to the U.S. Supreme Court, serves as the highest court in the state. It reviews appeals of major questions emanating from the lower state courts, and at the state level its decision is final.

JURISDICTION

Jurisdiction is the power or authority of a court to determine the merits of a dispute and to grant relief. A court has jurisdiction when it has this power both over the subject matter of the case and over the persons of the plaintiff and defendant or the property that is in dispute. The court itself must determine whether it has jurisdiction over a controversy presented before it. This is true even if neither party questions the court's jurisdiction. Once a court has acquired jurisdiction, it keeps it throughout the case, even if a party changes domicile or removes property from the state. When more than one court has a basis for jurisdiction, the first to exercise it has exclusive jurisdiction until the case is concluded. Questions about jurisdiction should be resolved before the court concerns itself with other matters involved in the case.

Subject Matter Jurisdiction in State Court

Legislatures, in accordance with state constitutions, have the right to allocate the workload throughout the state's judicial system. This means that the legislature enacts statutes that define each court's subject matter jurisdiction (the types of controversies that can be litigated in that court). The parties to a lawsuit cannot by consent confer subject matter jurisdiction on a court.

Courts of general jurisdiction are authorized to handle most types of controversies. Other judicial systems are structured around courts of specialized jurisdiction, for example, housing courts, juvenile courts, probate courts, and land courts. Occasionally, subject matter jurisdiction is determined by the dollar amount involved in the controversy, such as in small claims courts and municipal courts.

In the following case, a petitioner attempts to litigate two breach of contract claims in a court that only has subject matter jurisdiction over land.

In the Matter of the Application of Arthur Hyde RICE to Register and Confirm Title to Land Situated in Kailua, District of Koolaupoko, Oahu, City and County of Honolulu, State of Hawai'i
713 P.2d 426
Supreme Court of Hawai'i
February 3, 1986

Wakatsuki, Justice

Appellees Richard A. Breton and Margaret Mary Breton, as Sellers, filed a petition in the land court against Appellant Central Pacific Supply Corporation (hereinafter "CPS"), as Buyer, seeking to cancel the Agreement of Sale of a leasehold interest and for damages. The Bretons alleged that CPS had breached the Agreement by defaulting on the payment due thereon and by vacating the premises. CPS timely answered the complaint and counter-claimed against the Bretons for the breach of the Agreement and sought a rescission of the Agreement and damages. The land court, after trial, found in favor of the Bretons against CPS on both the complaint and the counterclaim. Thereafter, CPS filed a motion to set aside the findings of fact, conclusions of law and judgment, and to set the matter for a jury trial. The land court denied the motion, and CPS filed timely notices of appeal.

I.

In answer to the Breton's petition to cancel Agreement of Sale, one of CPS's defenses was that the land court lacked jurisdiction over the subject matter of the petition. The land court, after trial, concluded that it had "jurisdiction of the parties and this cause of action."

Although the issue of jurisdiction of the land court over the subject matter was not questioned at the trial level nor raised in this appeal, we hold, *sua sponte*, that the land court lacked jurisdiction over the subject matter of the Breton's petition.

"The lack of jurisdiction over the subject matter cannot be waived by the parties." . . . If the parties do not raise the issue, "a court *sua sponte* will, for unless jurisdiction of the court over the subject matter exists, any judgment rendered is invalid." . . . "Such a question is in order at any stage of the case, and though a lower court is found to have lacked jurisdiction, we have jurisdiction here on appeal, not of the merits, but for the purpose of correcting an error in jurisdiction." . . .

II.

The land court derives its jurisdiction from section 501–1 of the Hawai'i Revised Statutes (HRS).* "The land court is a court of limited

*HRS § 501-1 in relevant part reads: A court is established, called the land court, which shall have exclusive original jurisdiction of all applications for the registration of title to land and easements or rights in land held and possessed in fee simple within the State, with power to hear and determine all questions arising upon such applications, *and also have jurisdiction over such other questions as may come before it under this chapter,* subject to the rights of appeal under this chapter. The proceedings upon the applications shall be proceedings in rem against the land, and the decrees shall operate directly on the land and vest and establish title thereto. (Emphasis added.)

jurisdiction, created for a special purpose, that of carrying into effect what is known as the Torrens title scheme, derives all of its power from the statutes relating to it, and can exercise no power not found within those statutes." . . .

The Bretons' petition to cancel the Agreement of Sales and for damages and CPS's counterclaim for rescission of the Agreement and for damages are both causes of action arising out of alleged breaches of the Agreement. Both are breach of contract actions over which the land court does not have jurisdiction under any of the provisions of chapter 501 of the Hawai'i Revised Statutes, as amended.

The judgment of the land court is void for lack of jurisdiction. This appeal is dismissed.

Case Questions

1. Why is subject matter jurisdiction so crucial that any court, including the Hawai'i Supreme Court, should raise such an issue on its own initiative when the parties failed to make it an issue at trial or on appeal?
2. Why was the land court unable to render a judgment with respect to the breach of contract actions?

Jurisdiction over the Person

Imagine what would happen in our country if there were no jurisdictional limits on a state judicial system's ability to exercise personal jurisdiction over nonresidents. Every state would try to maximize its power and total chaos would result. It was for this reason that jurisdictional rules were created that prevent courts from deciding the merits of a case unless they have jurisdiction over the particular parties to the suit.

In the 1860s there were two methods of establishing a basis for jurisdiction over a person (*in personam* jurisdiction). The first involved showing that the party had been served within the boundaries of the state in which the lawsuit was filed (called the *forum state*) with a summons originating from within the state (see Figure 3-2). The constitutionality of this method was upheld by the U.S. Supreme Court in the 1990 case of *Burnham v. Superior Court*. The Court rejected Burnham's argument that basing personal jurisdiction on someone's mere presence within the forum state when served is unfair where minimum contacts between the person and the forum state do not exist. California, said the Court, was entitled to exercise personal jurisdiction over a nonresident from New Jersey, who voluntarily traveled to California and was served with a California summons while he was in San Francisco for the weekend to visit his children.[1] The summons had nothing to do with his actions within California.[2]

A second traditional method of establishing personal jurisdiction not involving the existence of "sufficient minimum contacts" was based on consent. For example, a plaintiff implicitly consents to personal jurisdiction (*in personam*

STATE OF WISCONSIN   _____ Court   _____ County

_____ , Plaintiff

        v.   Summons File No.   _____

_____ , Defendant

The State of Wisconsin

To each person named above as a defendant:

    You are hereby notified that the plaintiff named above has filed a lawsuit or other legal action against you. The complaint, which is attached, states the nature and basis of the legal action.

    Within 45 days of receiving this summons, you must respond with a written answer, as that term is used in chapter 802 of the Wisconsin Statues, to the complaint. The court may reject or disregard an answer that does not follow the requirements of the statutes. The answer must be sent or delivered to the court, whose address is . . . . , and to . . . . , plaintiff's attorney, whose address is . . . . . You may have an attorney help or represent you.

    If you do not provide a proper answer within 45 days, the court may grant judgment against you for the award of money or other legal action requested in the complaint, and you may lose your right to object to anything that is or may be incorrect in the complaint. A judgment may be enforced as provided by law. A judgment awarding money may become a lien against any real estate you own now or in the future, and may also be enforced by garnishment or seizure of property.

Dated: . . . . . . , 20 . . .

                           [signed] _____
                                       Attorney for Plaintiff

                           Address: _____

FIGURE 3-2   **State of Wisconsin Statutory Form of Summons [Sec. 801.095]**

jurisdiction) in a state when he or she files a lawsuit with a clerk of court. Defendants can also consent to personal jurisdiction in the following circumstances:

1. The defendant makes a *general appearance* in a case. If the defendant argues the substantive facts of the case, he or she is implicitly consenting to personal

jurisdiction. Thus a defendant wishing to challenge *in personam* jurisdiction would notify the Court that she or he is making a *special appearance* for the limited purpose of contesting jurisdiction.

2. A nonresident defendant allegedly commits a tortious act within the forum state.

3. A nonresident drives a motor vehicle on the roads of the forum state and becomes involved in a collision. Under the laws of most states, the motorist impliedly appoints an official of the forum state to be his agent for receiving service of the plaintiff's summons arising from the accident.

Because nonresident defendants rarely consent to being sued, and can avoid being served within the forum state by never going there, a new theory for jurisdiction was necessary. To remedy this problem, the U.S. Supreme Court developed its "sufficient minimum contacts" rule. The following brief case excerpt explains the early history of this rule, and its underlying rationale.

Case Excerpt

Kerry Steel, Inc., v. Paragon Industries, Inc.
No. 95-1334
U.S. Court of Appeals, Sixth Circuit
February 7, 1997

II

At the time of the adoption of the Fourteenth Amendment, it was widely understood that the nature of our federal system implied significant limits on the authority of state courts to exercise jurisdiction over out-of-state defendants. . . .

. . . [I]n the landmark case of *International Shoe Co. v. Washington,* 326 U.S. 310 (1945) . . . [the U.S. Supreme Court adopted] . . . a requirement that the defendant "have certain minimum contacts" with the forum state, such that the exercise of personal jurisdiction "does not offend 'traditional notions of fair play and substantial justice.'" 326 U.S. at 316.

The requirement of such contacts . . . serves two important purposes: "It protects the defendant against the burdens of litigating in a distant or inconvenient forum," . . . and it protects the defendant against attempts by states to "reach out beyond the limits imposed on them by their status as coequal sovereigns in a federal system." . . . In 1968 . . . [the 6th Circuit U.S. Court of Appeals,] . . . surveyed the case-law on the [minimum] "contacts" doctrine and identified three prerequisites for the exercise of personal jurisdiction: "First, the defendant must purposely avail himself of the privilege of acting in the forum state or causing a consequence in the forum state. Second, the cause of action [must arise from the defendant's activities there. Finally, the acts of the defendant or consequences caused by the defendant must have a substantial enough connection with the forum state to make the exercise of jurisdiction over the defendant reasonable." . . .

The sufficiency of the defendant's contacts with the forum state is determined by looking at the particular facts of each case. Sufficient minimum contacts, for example, exist in the state in which the defendant is domiciled. A person's domicile in the state in which the defendant has established his or her permanent home and to which the defendant returns after temporary absences. Factors such as where a person is licensed to drive, votes, and is employed are considered in determining domicile.

The plaintiff in the following case claimed that sufficient minimum contacts for *in personam* jurisdiction existed where it was established that a defendant had operated an internet website.

David Mink v. AAAA Development LLC
U.S. Court of Appeals for the 5th Circuit
No. 98-20770
September 17, 1999

Robert M. Parker, Circuit Judge:

David Mink appeals the district court's dismissal of his complaint for lack of personal jurisdiction. We affirm.

I. Facts and Proceedings

David Mink is a Texas resident who works in the retail furniture business. In January 1997, Mink claims that he began to develop a computer program, the Opportunity Tracking Computer System ("OTC"), designed to track information on sales made and opportunities missed on sales not made. On May 13, 1997, Mink submitted a patent application for the computer software and hardware that he developed to the United States Patent and Trademark Office. He also submitted a copyright application for the OTC to the United States Copyright Office.

Mink claims that in June 1997 he was approached by a Colorado resident named Richard Stark at a trade show. Stark allegedly asked Mink if he would be interested in marketing the OTC product with Stark's software at an upcoming computer seminar. Mink gave Stark a full demonstration of the OTC system, including its written material. While Mink initially declined Stark's offer to market the software together, Mink later contacted Stark to discuss the possibility of Stark marketing his product.

Between June 1997 and October 1997, Stark allegedly shared all of Mink's ideas and information on the OTC system with David Middlebrook. According to Mink's complaint, Middlebrook and two companies, AAAA Development and Profitsystems, conspired to copy Mink's copyrighted and patent-pending OTC system and create an identical system of their own for financial gain. AAAA Development is a Vermont corporation with its principal place of business in Vermont. Middlebrook is a Vermont resident. Neither AAAA Development nor Middlebrook own property in Texas. Mink is silent concerning where his contacts with the defendants occurred. However, we infer that the contacts were not in Texas based on the statement in Middlebrook's affidavit that AAAA has not made any sales in Texas nor has it had any agents or employees travel to Texas or represent it in Texas. The company has advertised in a national furniture trade journal and maintains a website advertising its sales management software on the Internet.

On November 7, 1997, Mink filed his original complaint in the United States District Court for the Southern District of Texas against AAAA Development and David Middlebrook, alleging that they conspired to copy Mink's computer program in violation of federal copyright and patent pending rights. AAAA Development and Middlebrook moved to dismiss for lack of personal jurisdiction. The district court granted their motions. Mink filed a motion for reconsideration of the order dismissing AAAA and Middlebrook, adding allegations that the defendants had been actively targeting customers in Texas with cold calls and asserting for the first time that AAAA's Internet website, accessible from Texas, could fulfill the minimum contacts requirement for the exercise of personal jurisdiction. The district court denied the motion for reconsideration. . . .

II. Discussion

The sole issue on appeal is whether the district court erred in dismissing defendants AAAA and Middlebrook for a lack of personal jurisdiction. . . . When a nonresident defendant challenges personal jurisdiction, the plaintiff bears the burden of establishing the district court's jurisdiction over the defendant. . . .

The Due Process Clause of the Fourteenth Amendment permits the exercise of personal jurisdiction over a nonresident defendant when (1) that defendant has purposefully availed himself of the benefits and protections of the forum state by establishing "minimum contacts" with the forum state; and (2) the exercise of jurisdiction over that defendant does not offend "traditional notions of fair play and substantial justice." . . .

The "minimum contacts" aspect of the analysis can be established through "contacts that give rise to 'specific' personal jurisdiction or those that give rise to 'general' personal jurisdiction." . . . Specific jurisdiction exists when the nonresident defendant's contacts with the forum state arise from, or are directly related to, the cause of action. . . . General jurisdiction exists when a defendant's contacts with the forum state are unrelated to the cause of action but are "continuous and systematic." . . . Because we conclude that Mink has not established any contacts directly related to the cause of action required for specific jurisdiction, we turn to the question of whether general jurisdiction has been established.

At the outset, we note that Mink has not met his burden of establishing that the district court had personal jurisdiction over defendant Middlebrook. Mink, however, contends

that the district court could exercise personal jurisdiction over AAAA because its World Wide Website is accessible by Texas residents. The issue of exercising personal jurisdiction over a defendant who operates an Internet website without other contacts with the forum state is a question of first impression in the Fifth Circuit.

Courts addressing the issue of whether personal jurisdiction can be constitutionally exercised over a defendant look to the "nature and quality of commercial activity that an entity conducts over the Internet." . . . The *Zippo* [*Manufacturing Co. v. Zippo Dot Com Inc.*, 952 F.Supp.1119 (W.D. Pa 1997)] decision categorized Internet use into a spectrum of three areas. At the one end of the spectrum, there are situations where a defendant clearly does business over the Internet by entering into contracts with residents of other states which "involve the knowing and repeated transmission of computer files over the Internet. . . ." . . . In this situation, personal jurisdiction is proper. . . . At the other end of the spectrum, there are situations where a defendant merely establishes a passive website that does nothing more than advertise on the Internet. With passive websites, personal jurisdiction is not appropriate. . . . In the middle of the spectrum, there are situations where a defendant has a website that allows a user to exchange information with a host computer. In this middle ground, "the exercise of jurisdiction is determined by the level of interactivity and commercial nature of the exchange of information that occurs on the Website." . . . We find that the reasoning of Zippo is persuasive and adopt it in this Circuit.

Applying these principles to this case, we conclude that AAAA's website is insufficient to subject it to personal jurisdiction. Essentially, AAAA maintains a website that posts information about its products and services. While the website provides users with a printable mail-in order form, AAAA's toll-free telephone number, a mailing address and an electronic mail ("e-mail") address, orders are not taken through AAAA's website. This does not classify the website as anything more than passive advertisement which is not grounds for the exercise of personal jurisdiction. . . .

This case does not fall into the spectrum of cases where a defendant clearly conducted business over the Internet nor does it fall into the middle spectrum of interactivity where the defendant and users exchange information through the Internet. There was no evidence that AAAA conducted business over the Internet by engaging in business transactions with forum residents or by entering into contracts over the Internet. . . .

We note that AAAA's website provides an e-mail address that permits consumers to interact with the company. (1) There is no evidence, however, that the website allows AAAA to do anything but reply to e-mail initiated by website visitors. In addition, AAAA's website lacks other forms of interactivity cited by courts as factors to consider in determining questions of personal jurisdiction. For example, AAAA's website does not allow consumers to order or purchase products and services on-line. . . . In fact, potential customers are instructed by the website to remit any completed order forms by regular mail or fax.

In this case, the presence of an electronic mail access, a printable order form, and a toll-free phone number on a website, without more, is insufficient to establish personal jurisdiction. Absent a defendant doing business over the Internet or sufficient interactivity with residents of the forum state, we cannot conclude that personal jurisdiction is appropriate.

III. Conclusion

Based on the foregoing, the district court's decision to dismiss Defendants Middlebrook and AAAA Development for lack of personal jurisdiction is AFFIRMED.

Case Questions

1. The Court classifies contacts that are used to establish *in personam* jurisdiction as being either "general" or "specific." What is the distinction?
2. Why did the Court conclude that Mink, the plaintiff, had not established sufficient minimum contacts to form the basis for the exercise of *in personam* jurisdiction over the defendants?
3. Under what circumstances would a company's website probably constitute a sufficient basis to satisfy the minimum contacts rule?

The consequences of not establishing personal jurisdiction are significant. Assume, for example, that a plaintiff has won a lawsuit and been awarded a *judgment* (the court document declaring the plaintiff the victor and specifying the remedy) entitling the plaintiff (now called the *judgment creditor*), to collect money damages from the defendant (now called the *judgment debtor*) and the judgment debtor fails to pay the plaintiff. If the judgment-issuing court had proper personal jurisdiction over the defendant, the judgment creditor would be entitled to take the judgment to any state in which the judgment debtor owns property and there have it enforced. If the court issuing the judgment lacked *in personam* jurisdiction over the defendant, however, that judgment would be unenforceable.

Long-Arm Statutes

Every state has enacted what are called long-arm statutes (see Figure 3-3) that permit the exercise of personal jurisdiction over nonresident defendants who have had sufficient minimum contacts with the forum state. A long-arm statute allows the plaintiff to serve the forum state's summons on the defendant in some other state. When a plaintiff successfully uses the long-arm statute, the defendant can be required to return to the forum state and defend the lawsuit. If the defendant fails to do so, he or she risks the entry of a default judgment.

The defendants in the following medical malpractice case sought dismissal of the action on the grounds that the courts in New Mexico had no right to exercise *in personam* jurisdiction over the defendant doctors pursuant to the state's long-arm statute due to a lack of sufficient minimum contacts between themselves and the forum state.

Cronin v. Sierra Medical Center
New Mexico Court of Appeals
2000-NMCA-082
June 19, 2000

Pickard, Chief Judge.

Kenneth Cronin and Brigitte Cronin (Plaintiffs) filed a medical malpractice lawsuit against Sierra Medical Center, El Paso Southwestern Cardiovascular Associates, P.A., Dr. Kenneth Eisenberg, Dr. Felice Bruno, Dr. Jerry Miller, and Dr. Joe Kidd (Defendants) after Mr. Cronin (Patient) experienced certain health complications arising out of heart bypass surgery. Plaintiffs, who reside in New Mexico, traveled to Texas so that Patient could undergo the surgery. Dr. Eisenberg performed the surgery at Sierra Medical Center (Hospital). The surgery was successful; however, Patient developed a staphylococcus aureus infection in his surgical wound. Dr. Eisenberg asked Dr. Bruno and Dr. Miller to help him treat the staph infection. Both doctors agreed to do so. Dr. Bruno performed mediastinal debridement and sternal rewiring, and Dr. Miller prescribed

certain antibiotics. In the course of his antibiotic treatment, Patient experienced vertigo and loss of equilibrium.

Plaintiffs subsequently formed the belief that Patient's health complications were caused by Dr. Miller's failure to adequately monitor the administration of the antibiotic therapy, so they filed suit. In their complaint, Plaintiffs asserted claims of medical negligence, battery, negligent infliction of emotional distress, and loss of consortium. Plaintiffs claimed they were entitled to damages because Defendants knew or should have known that the antibiotics prescribed by Dr. Miller can cause bilateral weakness in the inner ear labyrinthine systems, which results in vertigo and loss of equilibrium, and yet they allowed Patient to take the antibiotics until he sustained severe and permanent damage.

Defendants responded to Plaintiffs' complaint by filing motions to dismiss for lack of personal jurisdiction. In their motions, Defendants claimed the trial court lacked the authority to assert personal jurisdiction over them because (1) they did not transact business in New Mexico, (2) they did not commit a

New Mexico Statutes § 38-1-16 (1971).
Personal service of process outside state

A. Any person, whether or not a citizen or resident of this state, who in person or through an agent does any of the acts enumerated in this subsection thereby submits himself or his personal representative to the jurisdiction of the courts of this state as to any cause of action arising from:

   (1) the transaction of any business within this state;

   (2) the operation of a motor vehicle upon the highways of this state;

   (3) the commission of a tortious act within this state;

   (4) the contracting to insure any person, property or risk located within this state at the time of contracting; [or]

   (5) with respect to actions for divorce, separate maintenance or annulment, the circumstance of living in the marital relationship within the state, notwithstanding subsequent departure from the state, as to all obligations arising from alimony, child support or real or personal property settlements under Chapter 40, Article 4 NMSA 1978 if one party to the marital relationship continues to reside in the state.

B. Service of process may be made upon any person subject to the jurisdiction of the courts of this state under this section by personally serving the summons upon the defendant outside this state and such service has the same force and effect as though service had been personally made within this state.

C. Only causes of action arising from acts enumerated in this section may be asserted against a defendant in an action in which jurisdiction is based upon this section.

D. Nothing contained in this section limits or affects the right to serve any process in any other manner now or hereafter provided by law.

FIGURE 3-3   New Mexico Long-Arm Statute § 38-1-16 (1971)

tort in New Mexico, and (3) they lack minimum contacts with New Mexico such that due process considerations would be offended if the trial court were to assert personal jurisdiction over them. The trial court accepted Defendants' arguments and dismissed Plaintiffs' complaint without prejudice. Plaintiffs now appeal. . . .

Discussion

Plaintiffs failed to serve process upon Defendants within the territorial limits of New Mexico. Nevertheless, they contend that the trial court had the authority to assert personal jurisdiction over the non-resident Defendants. In order for this contention to hold true, the conduct Plaintiffs complain of must meet a three-part test: (1) Defendants must have done at least one of the acts enumerated in our long-arm statute, (2) Plaintiffs' causes of action must have arisen from the act or acts, and (3) Defendants must have had minimum contacts with New Mexico sufficient to satisfy constitutional due process. . . .

A. Long-Arm Statute and Causes of Action

Plaintiffs claim Defendants' conduct satisfies the requirements of our long-arm statute. . . .

[New Mexico Statutes Annotated] NMSA 1978, § 38-1-16 (1971). Section 38-1-16(A) provides that any party, whether or not a resident of New Mexico, who does one or more of our long-arm statute's enumerated acts submits to the jurisdiction of the courts of this State so long as the complainant's cause of action arises from:

(1) the transaction of any business within this state;
(2) the operation of a motor vehicle upon the highways of this state;
(3) the commission of a tortious act within this state;
(4) the contracting to insure any person, property or risk located within this state at the time of contracting; [or]
(5) with respect to actions for divorce, separate maintenance or annulment, . . . if one party to the marital relationship continues to reside in the state.

Section 38-1-16(A). The parties agree that based on the facts presented in this case, we need only consider whether Defendants' conduct falls within subsections (1) and (3) of our long-arm statute.

1. Business
   Plaintiffs claim Defendants transacted business in New Mexico. The determination of whether a party has transacted business within the meaning of our State's long-arm statute must be made on a case-by-case basis. . . .
   Plaintiffs contend that Hospital transacted business in New Mexico because it placed advertisements in several New Mexico telephone directories, produced television commercials that could be and were viewed by New Mexico customers, and previously performed health care services for other New Mexico customers. In support of their contention, Plaintiffs provided the trial court with copies of Hospital's written ads, which appeared in the white and yellow pages of the Roswell,

Alamogordo, Silver City, and Las Cruces telephone directories for the years 1994 to 1997. Plaintiffs also produced Patient's affidavit in which he stated that he was aware of and had seen Hospital's commercial advertisements on his television. In his affidavit, Patient averred that he decided to have the surgery performed at Hospital based on its general solicitations, as well as on the recommendation from some of his fellow employees who apparently had received medical care at Hospital in the past.

We agree with Plaintiffs that the evidence they produced at the trial court level supports their contention that Hospital intentionally initiated commercial activities in New Mexico for the purpose of realizing pecuniary gain. . . . This determination is further compelled by the fact that Patient was not the first New Mexico resident to receive medical care at Hospital on account of its commercial activities within this State. . . .

Plaintiffs also contend that their causes of action arise from Hospital's transaction of business in New Mexico. This contention is based on Plaintiffs' allegation that, but for Hospital's solicitations, Patient would not have sought treatment at Hospital nor would he have endured certain health complications arising from Dr. Miller's prescription and Defendants' negligent failure to monitor the administration of potentially ototoxic antibiotics. Again, we agree with Plaintiffs. . . .

2. Tort
   Plaintiffs contend that Defendants committed a tortious act in New Mexico. This contention is based on Plaintiffs' theory that, although Defendants' negligent conduct may have occurred in Texas, a tort is not complete until there is injury. . . . Plaintiffs assert that Patient did not sustain a cognizable injury until he began to experience vertigo and loss of equilibrium.

Inasmuch as Patient experienced these health problems in New Mexico, and not in Texas, Plaintiffs assert that the allegedly tortious act occurred in New Mexico. . . .

The proper two-step analysis for determining issues of personal jurisdiction is set forth in *Aetna Casualty & Surety Co. v. Bendix Control Division*, . . . (. . . 1984), wherein we stated:

> In reviewing challenges to jurisdiction under our state's long-arm statute, two levels of analysis are necessary. First, the court must determine whether plaintiff has alleged an event in New Mexico, . . . so as to subject defendant to that statute. Secondly, if the threshold requirements have been met, the court must determine whether the exercise of personal jurisdiction over the defendant is consistent with the requirements of due process. . . .

B. Minimum Contacts

In order for a non-resident defendant to be subjected to the personal jurisdiction of an out-of-state court, he must have "certain minimum contacts with [the forum state] such that the maintenance of the suit does not offend 'traditional notions of fair play and substantial justice.'" . . . "[I]t is essential in each case that there be some act by which the defendant purposefully avails itself of the privilege of conducting activities within the forum State, thus invoking the benefits and protections of its law." *Hanson v. Denckla,* 357 U.S. 235, 253 (1958). . . .

For the reasons stated above, we believe that Hospital established certain minimum contacts with this State by intentionally, purposefully, and persistently soliciting the business of New Mexico customers. It placed advertisements in several New Mexico telephone directories, produced television commercials that could be and were viewed by potential customers in New Mexico, and previously performed health care services for other New Mexico customers. Hospital's ad-

vertisements support the conclusion that it intentionally initiated commercial activities in New Mexico for the purpose of realizing pecuniary gain. . . .

We believe, however, that [the defendant doctors] . . . lack minimum contacts with New Mexico because they did not purposefully initiate any activities in this State. This is true even though technically they may have committed a tortious act in New Mexico. . . .

In *Valley Wide Health Servs., Inc. v Graham,* . . . (1987), the New Mexico Supreme Court addressed the issue of whether a Colorado physician had subjected himself to the jurisdiction of our state courts by giving a New Mexico patient allegedly negligent medical advice in a telephone call. Answering in the negative, our Supreme Court stated that prior to the physician's telephone call, a doctor-patient relationship had already been established in Colorado. . . . The Supreme Court determined that the physician had not purposely initiated activity in this State, but instead had simply responded to his patient's call for help as the patient's treating physician. . . . It was mere happenstance that the patient lived in New Mexico.

In our view, the case at bar falls under the rubric set forth in *Valley Wide Health Services, Inc.* Although *Valley Wide Health Services, Inc.* involved a phone call and this case involved discharge instructions including the continuation of the antibiotic therapy that allegedly hurt Patient, the Supreme Court's underlying rationale in *Valley Wide Health Servs., Inc.* still holds true. It is determinative that other than Hospital, Defendants acted in New Mexico only after Patient had unilaterally initiated a doctor-patient relationship in Texas. This type of action does not constitute purposeful action. As one court so aptly put it:

> The case at bar does not involve a product which was deliberately or foreseeably shipped into the forum state's markets. It focuses on a service, not performed in the forum state but in a foreign state, rendered

after the plaintiff voluntarily traveled to the foreign state so that he could benefit from that service which was available there only.

When one seeks out services which are personal in nature, such as those rendered by attorneys, physicians, dentists, hospitals or accountants, and travels to the locality where he knows the services will actually be rendered, he must realize that the services are not directed to impact on any particular place, but are directed to the needy person himself. While it is true that the nature of such services is that if they are negligently done, their consequences will thereafter be felt wherever the client or patient may go, it would be fundamentally unfair to permit a suit in whatever distant jurisdiction the patient may carry the consequences of his treatment, or the client the consequences of the advice received.

Unlike a case involving voluntary interstate or international economic activity, which is directed at the forum state's markets, the residence of a recipient of personal services rendered elsewhere is irrelevant and totally incidental to the benefits provided by the defendant at his own location. It is clear that when a client or a patient travels to receive professional services without having been solicited (which is prohibited by most professional codes of ethics), then the client, who originally traveled to seek services apparently not available at home, ought to expect that he will have to travel again if he thereafter complains that the services sought by him in the foreign jurisdiction were therein rendered improperly.

Any other rule would seem to be not only fundamentally unfair, but would inflict upon the professions the obligation of traveling to defend suits brought in foreign jurisdictions, sometimes very distant jurisdictions, there brought solely because the patient or client upon his return to his own home decided to sue at home for services sought by himself abroad. *Gelineau v. New York Univ. Hosp.*, 375 F. Supp. 661, 667 (D.N.J.1974) . . .

We acknowledge Plaintiffs' argument that their case differs from *Gelineau* . . . in that they allege a continuing tort, whereas the other cited cases involve a discrete set of services that could be said to have been rendered strictly outside the patient's home state. This point notwithstanding, we fail to see why the case at bar falls outside the purview of *Valley Wide Health Services, Inc.* When a person unilaterally seeks speciality care, which Patient no doubt did by traveling to Texas to undergo heart bypass surgery and then again to receive treatment for his staph infection, follow-up care, including medical prescriptions, are almost sure to follow. This type of follow-up care, without any evidence that the non-resident physician reached into the forum state in order to attract the patient's business, simply does not constitute the purposeful availment that is both contemplated in and required by our due process analysis. Nor are we impressed by Patient's conclusory affidavit that all doctors "provided medical services to me . . . at Mountain Shadows." The 600-page record in this case is replete with case notes, discharge summaries, and specific information, and all it shows is the transfer of follow-up care, including prescriptions, to New Mexico. . . .

The citizens of New Mexico would be ill-served if we were to establish a rule that effectively compelled non-resident specialist physicians to prescribe only so much medicine as would get patients home. . . . We instead choose to reiterate the longstanding rule that a non-resident defendant will not be subjected to the jurisdiction of the courts of this State unless his or her activities are properly characterized as purposeful availment, rather than incidental. . . .

Conclusion

For the reasons stated, we affirm in part and reverse in part and remand with instructions to the trial court to reinstate Plaintiffs' complaint against Hospital only. . . .

Case Questions

1. How did the plaintiff satisfy the minimum contacts requirement with respect to the defendant, Sierra Medical Center?
2. Why did the New Mexico Court of Appeals conclude that the plaintiff had not established sufficient minimum contacts to form the basis for the exercise of *in personam* jurisdiction over the doctors?
3. Does New Mexico's decision mean that defendant doctors cannot be sued anywhere?

In Personam Jurisdiction over Corporations

Every corporation has been incorporated by one of the fifty states and is therefore subject to the *in personam* jurisdiction in that state's courts. A corporation may also consent to *in personam* jurisdiction in other states. Generally a state will require that all corporations doing business within its borders register with it and appoint a state government official as its agent. This official will be authorized to receive service of process relating to litigation arising in the wake of its presence and its business activities conducted within that state. Soliciting orders, writing orders, and entering into contracts would establish a corporate presence that would be sufficient for *in personam* jurisdiction. The mere presence of corporate officers within the forum state or the occasional shipping of orders into the forum is not sufficient for personal jurisdiction.

Jurisdiction over Property—*In Rem* Jurisdiction

A state has jurisdiction over property located within the state. The property may be real (land and buildings) or personal (clothes, cars, televisions, checking accounts, antique clocks, etc.). This is called *in rem* jurisdiction, or jurisdiction over things. An *in personam* decision imposes liability on a person and is personally binding. A decision *in rem*, however, is directed against the property itself and resolves disputes about property rights. A court can determine the rights to property that is physically located within the forum state regardless of whether the court has personal jurisdiction over all interested individuals. For example, if two parties—one of whom is from out of state—dispute the ownership of a piece of land in Montana, the courts of Montana can determine ownership because it relates to property located within that state.

Procedural Due Process Requirements

In addition to establishing a basis for jurisdiction over the person or the property that is in dispute, a court must give proper notice to a defendant. The statutes of each jurisdiction often make distinctions between the type of notice required for *in personam* actions and *in rem* actions. This subject is covered in more detail in Chapter 4.

Venue

Venue requirements determine the place where judicial authority should be exercised. Once personal jurisdiction has been established, a plaintiff has to litigate in a court that has subject matter jurisdiction over the controversy and in a place that the legislature says is a permissible venue.

State legislatures enact venue statutes to distribute the judicial workload throughout the system. They often provide for venue in the county or district where the cause of action arose, the county or district in which the defendant resides, and the county or district in which the plaintiff resides. In cases where the venue requirements can be satisfied in more than one district, the plaintiff's choice will usually prevail.

Parties wishing to challenge venue must assert their objections promptly, or they may be waived. In both civil and criminal cases, venue may be considered improper for several reasons. A court may decline to hear a case for fear of local prejudice, for the convenience of litigants and witnesses, or in the interests of justice.

In a civil case, the most common reason given for a court to decline to exercise jurisdiction is that it believes the case can proceed more conveniently in another court. This is known as the *doctrine of forum non conveniens*. The doctrine is applied with discretion and caution. One frequent ground for applying the doctrine occurs when the event that gave rise to the suit took place somewhere other than in the forum state. The difficulties of securing the attendance of out-of-state witnesses and applying foreign law may make decision making inconvenient. The court balances the conveniences between the forum court and another court and weighs the obstacles to a fair proceeding and advantage.

 INTERNET TIP ────────────────────────────────

You can see an example of a venue statute and read *Massey v. Mandell,* a Michigan venue case, on the textbook's website.

──

THE FEDERAL COURT SYSTEM

Article III, Section 1, of the U.S. Constitution is the basis of our federal court system. It provides that "the judicial power of the United States shall be vested in one supreme court, and in such inferior courts as the Congress may, from time to time, ordain and establish." Congress first exercised this power by passing the Judiciary Act of 1789, which has been amended and supplemented many times in order to establish the various federal courts as well as their jurisdiction and procedures.

The federal court system consists of the district courts, exercising original federal jurisdiction; the courts of appeals, exercising intermediate federal jurisdiction; and the U.S. Supreme Court, sitting as the highest court for both federal and state cases involving federal questions. Alongside these courts of general jurisdiction, there are the U.S. Court of Federal Claims, which decides nontort claims filed against the United States; the U.S. Tax Court, which reviews decisions of the Secretary of the Treasury with respect to certain provisions of the Internal Revenue Code; the U.S. Court of International Trade, which has jurisdiction over civil actions relating to embargoes on imports, customs duties, and revenues from imports or tonnage; the Federal Bankruptcy Court, which hears bankruptcy cases; and the Court of Appeals for the Armed Forces, which is a court of last resort in military criminal Appeals. (See Figure 3-4.)

THE U.S. DISTRICT COURTS

There are ninety-four federal district courts, at least one in each state and territory in the United States. They are the courts of original jurisdiction and serve as the trial court in the federal court system. The federal district courts are given *limited subject matter jurisdiction* by the Constitution and by Congress. Article III provides that federal courts have jurisdiction over "all cases . . . arising under . . . the laws of the United States." The limited nature of federal subject matter jurisdiction is emphasized in the following excerpt from a recent case decided by the U.S. Circuit Court of Appeals for the Fifth Circuit. Notice how the court explains that subject matter jurisdiction and *in personam* jurisdiction are grounded in different parts of the U.S. Constitution.

Marathon Oil Company v. A. G. Ruhrgas
No. 96-20361
U.S. Court of Appeals, Fifth Circuit
June 22, 1998

Smith, Circuit Judge

I.

"Federal courts, as opposed to state trial courts of general jurisdiction, are courts of limited jurisdiction marked out by Congress. ". . . The Constitution provides that "[t]he judicial Power of the United States, shall be vested in one supreme court, and in such inferior Courts as the Congress may from time to time ordain and establish." . . . "This language reflects a deliberate compromise . . . reached at the Constitutional Convention between those who thought that the establishment of lower federal courts should be constitutionally mandatory and those who thought there should be no federal courts at all except for a Supreme Court with, . . . appellate jurisdiction to review state court judgments." . . .

The effect of the compromise is this: "Only the jurisdiction of the Supreme Court is derived directly from the Constitution. Every

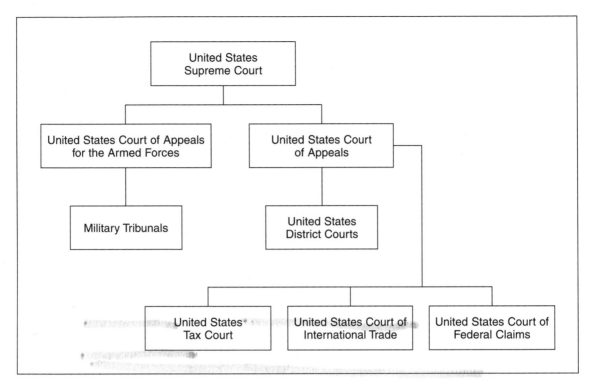

FIGURE 3-4   The Federal Court System

Source: Adapted from Arnold J. Goldman and William D. Sigismond, *Business Law: Principles & Practices,* 2nd Ed. Copyright © 1988 by Houghton Mifflin Company. Used with permission.

other [federal] court . . . derives its jurisdiction wholly from the authority of Congress. That body may give, withhold or restrict such jurisdiction at its discretion, provided it be not extended beyond the boundaries fixed by the Constitution." Accordingly . . . the Constitution leaves Congress the policy choice concerning how far the federal courts' jurisdiction should extend.

Under our federal constitutional scheme, the state courts are assumed to be equally capable of deciding state and federal issues. To the extent that Congress elects to confer only limited jurisdiction on the federal courts, state courts become the sole vehicle for obtaining initial review of some federal and state claims. . . . Where Congress has given the lower fed-

eral courts jurisdiction over certain controversies, "'[d]ue regard for the rightful independence of state governments, which should actuate federal courts, requires that they scrupulously confine their own jurisdiction to the precise limits which [a federal] statute has defined.'" . . .

The importance of both the lower federal courts' constitutional and statutory subject-matter jurisdiction should not be underestimated. "Because of their unusual nature, and because it would not simply be wrong but indeed would be an unconstitutional invasion of the powers reserved to the states if federal courts were to entertain cases not within their jurisdiction, the rule is well settled that the party seeking to invoke the jurisdiction of a federal court must demonstrate that the case is within the competence of that court." . . .

When a federal court acts outside its statutory subject-matter jurisdiction, it violates the fundamental constitutional precept of limited federal power. . . . "Federal courts are courts of limited jurisdiction by origin and design, implementing a basic principle of our system of limited government." . . .

[T]he Supreme Court has reminded us that our jurisdiction must be considered at the outset of a case. This term, the Court rejected what the Ninth Circuit had labeled the . . . "'doctrine of hypothetical jurisdiction'"—the process of "'assuming' [Article III] jurisdiction for the purpose of deciding the merits" of a case. . . . *Steel Co. v. Citizens for a Better Env't,* (1998) (majority opinion). . . . The *Steel Co.* Court remarked:

> This is essentially the position embraced by several Courts of Appeals, which find it proper to proceed immediately to the merits question, despite jurisdictional objections, at least where (1) the merits question is more readily resolved, and (2) the prevailing party on the merits would be the same as the prevailing party were jurisdiction denied. . . .

We decline to endorse such an approach because it carries the courts beyond the bounds of authorized judicial action and thus offends fundamental principles of separation of powers. This conclusion should come as no surprise, since it is reflected in a long and venerable line of our cases. "Without jurisdiction the court cannot proceed at all in any cause. Jurisdiction is power to declare the law, and when it ceases to exist, the only function remaining to the court is that of announcing the fact and dismissing the cause." . . . The requirement that jurisdiction be established as a threshold matter "spring[s] from the nature and limits of the judicial power of the United States" and is "inflexible and without exception." . . .

"[E]very federal appellate court has a special obligation to 'satisfy itself not only of its own jurisdiction, but also that of the lower courts in a cause under review,' . . ." The rule that we first address our jurisdiction is so fundamental that "we are obliged to inquire sua sponte whenever a doubt arises as to the existence of federal jurisdiction." . . . "The general rule is that the parties cannot confer on a federal court jurisdiction that has not been vested in that court by the Constitution and Congress. This means that the parties cannot waive lack of [subject matter] jurisdiction by express consent, or by conduct, . . . ; the subject matter jurisdiction of the federal courts is too basic a concern to the judicial system to be left to the whims and tactical concerns of the litigants." . . .

III.

Ruhrgas does not dispute that a federal district court must determine its jurisdiction before proceeding to the merits of the case. It contests only the proposition that the federal court must reach the issue of subject-matter jurisdiction before reaching a challenge to personal jurisdiction. Ruhrgas argues that the district court may decide the personal jurisdiction challenge first, because "jurisdiction is jurisdiction is jurisdiction."

Because a federal district court must have both subject-matter jurisdiction over the . . . controversy and personal jurisdiction over the defendant, so the argument goes, the court should have discretion to decide the easier jurisdictional challenge first, to save judicial resources and to avoid tougher legal issues. . . .

A.

Although the personal jurisdiction requirement is a "fundamental principl[e] of jurisprudence," . . . without which a court cannot

adjudicate, the requirement of personal jurisdiction unlike that of subject-matter jurisdiction, "may be intentionally waived, or for
various reasons a defendant may be estopped
from raising the issue." . . . The defendant's
ability to waive the defense arises from the
reality that "[t]he requirement that a court
have personal jurisdiction flows not from Art.
III, but from the Due Process Clause. . . . It
represents a restriction on the judicial power
not as a matter of sovereignty, but as a matter
of individual liberty." . . .

The Supreme Court has carefully eluci-
dated the distinctions between subject-matter
and personal jurisdiction:

> Subject-matter jurisdiction, then, is an Art. III
> as well as a statutory requirement; it func-
> tions as a restriction on federal power, and
> contributes to the characterization of the fed-
> eral sovereign. Certain legal consequences
> directly follow from this. For example, no
> action of the parties can confer subject-matter
> jurisdiction upon a federal court. Thus, the
> consent of the parties is irrelevant, principles
> of estoppel do not apply, and a party does

not waive the requirement by failing to challenge jurisdiction early in the proceedings.
Similarly, a court, including an appellate
court, will raise lack of subject-matter jurisdiction on its own motion. "[T]he rule, spring-
ing from the nature and limits of the judicial
power of the United States is inflexible and
without exception, which requires this court,
of its own motion, to deny its jurisdiction,
and, in the exercise of its appellate power,
that of all other courts of the United States,
in all cases where such jurisdiction does not
affirmatively appear in the record. . . ."

None of this is true with respect to personal
jurisdiction. . . . The Court therefore has indicated that "jurisdiction" is not always "jurisdiction." The distinction is that subject-matter
jurisdictional requirements prevent our overreaching into the powers that the Constitution
and Congress have left to the state courts,
while personal jurisdiction requirements
prevent both state and federal courts from
upsetting the defendant's settled expectations as to where it can reasonably anticipate
being sued. . . .

Case Questions

1. Where does a plaintiff assert a basis for federal subject matter jurisdiction?
2. In what way does the constitutional basis for federal subject matter jurisdiction differ from the basis for federal *in personam* jurisdiction?

Because there are no federal common law crimes, all federal criminal actions
must be based on federal statutes. In civil actions, the federal courts have subject matter jurisdiction over two categories of cases:

1. *Federal question jurisdiction* exists where the case involves claims based on
   the Constitution, laws, or treaties of the United States. Such claims would
   include suits by the United States and civil rights, patent, copyright, trademark, unfair competition, and admiralty suits.
2. *Diversity of citizenship jurisdiction* exists if a suit is between citizens of different states or between a citizen of a state and an alien, and if the amount

in controversy exceeds $75,000 (*the jurisdictional amount*). Diversity jurisdiction provides qualifying plaintiffs with a choice of a federal or state forum for many types of civil actions. However, federal courts have traditionally declined to exercise diversity jurisdiction in divorce actions, child custody cases, and probate matters.

State citizenship is a key concept in diversity cases. For natural citizens, state citizenship is closely related to the establishment of a principal residence (domicile). Thus a person who presently makes her home in Texas is a citizen of Texas. If she spends the summer working in Colorado and plans to return to Texas in September, she would still be a citizen of Texas.

Federal diversity jurisdiction requires that the diversity of citizenship be complete. This means that in a multiple-party suit, no one plaintiff and one defendant can be citizens of the same state. Thus, if a citizen of New York brings suit against two defendants, one a citizen of Wisconsin and one a citizen of Michigan, there would be total diversity of citizenship. A federal district court would have jurisdiction over the subject matter if the plaintiff is suing in good faith for over $75,000. If, however, one of the defendants was a citizen of New York, there would not be complete diversity of citizenship necessary for jurisdiction.

Congress has provided special citizenship rules for corporations. A corporation is considered a citizen in the state where it is incorporated as well as in the state of its principal place of business. For example, a corporation incorporated in Delaware with its principal place of business in New York cannot sue or be sued by citizens of either of the two states in a diversity case in a federal district court.

Diversity jurisdiction avoids exposing the defendant to possible prejudice in the plaintiff's state court. There are many who argue against diversity jurisdiction, however, claiming that the fear of possible prejudice does not justify the expense of the huge diversity case load in federal courts. See Figure 3-5 for data regarding the number of and types of cases commenced and pending in U.S. District Courts.

The Plaintiff's Choice of Forum

There are various factors that influence plaintiffs in their choice of a federal or state forum. One forum may be more attractive than another because it is closer and more convenient for the plaintiff. The plaintiff's attorney may be influenced by the reputation of the county or court in terms of the size of verdicts awarded there, by whether the forum is rural or urban, by socioeconomic factors, and by the reputations of the plaintiff and defendant within the forum. Plaintiffs may also be influenced to file in a federal forum if the federal procedural rules are more liberal than the corresponding state rules.

In the following case, a plaintiff who's diversity suit was dismissed by a federal district court for failing to satisfy the jurisdictional amount requirement, appeals that decision to the U.S. Court of Appeals for the Eighth Circuit.

Type of Case	Cases Commenced				
	1996	1997	1998	1999	2000
Cases total	269,132	272,027	256,787	260,271	259,517
Contract actions	35,688	40,836	42,292	50,676	53,625
Recovery of overpayments					
Real property actions	6,254	5,473	5,663	5,972	6,711
Tort actions	59,661	58,289	50,362	44,426	36,586
Personal injury	55,647	53,940	46,496	40,497	32,621
Personal injury product liability, Total	27,584	32,856	26,886	18,781	14,428
Asbestos	7,289	7,143	9,111	8,948	7,187
Other personal injury	19,555	24,972	17,092	9,189	6,602
Personal property damage	4,014	4,349	3,866	3,929	3,965
Actions under statutes					
Civil rights	42,007	43,278	42,354	41,304	40,908
Employment	23,152	23,796	23,735	22,490	21,032
Commerce	1,624	502	503	672	891
Environmental matters	1,131	958	997	895	886
Prisoner petitions	68,235	62,966	54,715	56,603	58,257
Forfeiture and penalty	2,235	2,384	2,331	2,258	2,320
Labor laws	15,073	15,508	14,650	14,372	14,142
Protected property rights (Copyright, patent, trademark)	7,028	7,559	7,748	8,242	8,738
Securities commodities and exchanges	1,704	1,669	2,358	2,563	2,678
Social security laws	9,347	13,605	14,552	13,920	15,829
Tax suits	2,122	2,272	1,524	1,179	907
Freedom of Information Act	463	371	397	352	341

FIGURE 3-5   U.S. District Courts—Civil Cases Commenced: 1996–2000

Source: Administrative Office of the U.S. Courts, *Annual Report of the Director, 2001.*

Kopp v. Kopp
00-3965
U.S. Court of Appeals for the Eighth Circuit
February 19, 2002

Morris Sheppard Arnold, Circuit Judge

Donna Kopp appeals from the order of the district court dismissing her tort claim for lack of subject-matter jurisdiction. . . .

I

Ms. Kopp was attacked, restrained, and sexually assaulted in her own home by her ex-husband, Donald Kopp. When Mr. Kopp . . . pleaded guilty . . . and was sentenced to four years in prison, Ms. Kopp then sued Mr. Kopp in federal court, claiming violations of the Violence Against Women Act of 1994 . . . and of state tort law as well. After the district court dismissed the federal claim because of the decision in *United States v. Morrison,* 529 U.S. 598 (2000) [declaring the Violence Against Women Act unconstitutional], it also dismissed the state law claims because it concluded that they did not satisfy the requirements for diversity jurisdiction.

II

When the two parties to an action are citizens of different states, as they are here, a federal district court's jurisdiction extends to "all civil actions where the matter in controversy exceeds the sum or value of $75,000, exclusive of interest and costs," 28 U.S.C. § 1332(a). Although Ms. Kopp's medical bills fall well below the requisite amount, she argues that in the circumstances of this case she could well recover punitive damages and damages for emotional distress that would exceed $75,000.

We have held that "a complaint that alleges the jurisdictional amount in good faith will suffice to confer jurisdiction, but the complaint will be dismissed if it 'appear[s] to a legal certainty that the claim is really for less than the jurisdictional amount.'" *Larkin v. Brown* . . . (8th Cir. 1994). . . . If the defendant challenges the plaintiff's allegations of the amount in controversy, then the plaintiff must establish jurisdiction by a preponderance of the evidence. *McNutt v. General Motors Acceptance Corp.,* 298 U.S. 178 (1936); . . .

. . . The district court has subject matter jurisdiction in a diversity case when a fact finder could legally conclude, from the pleadings and proof adduced to the court before trial, that the damages that the plaintiff suffered are greater than $75,000. We emphasize that McNutt does not suggest that . . . damages in some specific amount must be proved before trial by a preponderance of the evidence. . . .

Confusion may arise because the relevant jurisdictional fact, that is, the issue that must be proved by the preponderance of evidence, is easily misidentified. The jurisdictional fact in this case is not whether the damages are greater than the requisite amount, but whether a fact finder might legally conclude that they are: In other words, an amount that a plaintiff claims is not "in controversy" if no fact finder could legally award it. In one of our more extensive discussions of this issue, we upheld jurisdiction even though the jury ultimately awarded less than the statutory minimum, because jurisdiction is "measured by the amount properly pleaded or as of the time of the suit, not by the end result." . . . "If access to federal district courts is to be further limited it should be done by statute and not by court decisions that permit a district court judge to prejudge the monetary value of [a] . . . claim." . . .

As we see it, the federal court has jurisdiction here unless, as a matter of law, Ms. Kopp, could not recover punitive damages or damages for emotional distress, the amount of damages that she could recover is somehow fixed below the jurisdictional amount, or no reasonable jury could award damages totaling more than $75,000 in the circumstances that the case presents.

Under Missouri law, which is applicable here, punitive damages "may be awarded for conduct that is outrageous, because of the defendant's evil motive or reckless indifference to the rights of others. . . . We have no trouble reconciling the facts of this case with those criteria, as the defendant admitted in his pre-trial deposition that he attacked, restrained, and raped his ex-wife who ultimately had to flee to a neighbor's house for safety. Furthermore, we have discovered no statutory or judicially created limits on punitive damages or damages for emotional distress in Missouri, nor has the defendant directed our attention to any. Finally, we conclude that an award of damages of more than $75,000 would not have to be set aside as excessive under Missouri law, nor would such an award be so "grossly excessive" as to violate the due process clause of the United States Constitution. . . .

Based on the present record, therefore, it seems clear to us that Ms. Kopp has demonstrated that her case falls within the diversity jurisdiction of the federal courts.

III

For the foregoing reasons, the order of the district court is reversed and the case is remanded to that court for further proceedings not inconsistent with this opinion.

Case Questions

1. Inasmuch as Ms. Kopp's medical bills were well below the jurisdictional amount, how could she make a good faith claim that she had enough damages to satisfy the jurisdictional amount requirement?
2. How closely do you believe federal district court judges should scrutinize a plaintiff's assertions in the complaint about having sufficient damages to satisfy the jurisdictional amount in cases in which federal subject matter jurisdiction is based on diversity of citizenship (i.e., brings a diversity action)?
3. Assume that a plaintiff brings a diversity action in federal district court. Assume further, that the plaintiff is ultimately awarded a money judgment for $60,000. Is the fact that plaintiff's damage award was for less than the jurisdictional amount of any jurisdictional significance if the case is appealed to a federal court of appeals?

In Rem and *In Personam* Jurisdiction

In order for a district court to hear a civil case, it must have, in addition to jurisdiction over the subject matter, jurisdiction over the property in an *in rem* proceeding or over the person of the defendant in an *in personam* proceeding. Jurisdiction over the person is normally acquired by serving a summons within the territory. In an ordinary civil action, the summons may be properly served anywhere within the territorial limits of the state in which the district court is located. A federal summons may also be served anywhere that a state summons could be served pursuant to the state's long-arm statute.

Venue in Federal Courts[3]

Congress has provided that venue generally exists in the federal district where any defendant resides, if all defendants reside in the same state. Or it exists where the claim arose or the property is located. If neither of these choices is appropriate, in a diversity case venue will exist in the federal district in which the defendant is subject to personal jurisdiction at the time the action is filed. In federal question cases, the alternative venue is the federal district in which any defendant can be found.

A corporation-defendant is subject to suit in any federal district in which it is subject to personal jurisdiction when the suit is filed.

Removal from State to Federal Courts (Removal Jurisdiction)

Except in those areas in which federal courts have exclusive jurisdiction, a suit does not have to be brought in a federal district court just because that court could exercise jurisdiction over the subject matter and over the person or property. A plaintiff may bring a dispute in any state or federal court that has jurisdiction.

A defendant sued in a state court may have a right to have the case removed to the federal district court. (Any civil action brought in a state court that could originally have been filed in a district court is removable. Federal statutes contain some limitations to removal jurisdiction. One statute limits a defendant who is a citizen of the state in which the lawsuit is filed to removing claims that raise a federal question.) For example, if a citizen of New York sues a citizen of Ohio in a state court in Ohio for breach of contract or tort, the defendant could not have the case removed. (Where the basis of removal jurisdiction is diversity of citizenship, that basis must exist at the time of filing the original suit and also at the time of petitioning for removal. To initiate the removal process, the defendant must file notice of removal with the federal court within thirty days after service of the complaint.)

The plaintiff in the following case sought to prevent Wal-Mart from removing her tort action from the Louisiana court system to federal district court.

Catherine Gebbia v. Wal-Mart Stores, Inc.
No. 00-30386/233 F.3d 880
U.S. Court of Appeals for the Fifth Circuit
December 4, 2000

Background

Plaintiff brought this action on September 23, 1998, in the Twenty-First Judicial District Court of Louisiana, alleging claims arising from her injuries suffered in one of Defendant-Appellee Wal-Mart Stores, Inc.'s ("Defendant") stores in Hammond, Louisiana, on October 5, 1997. Plaintiff suffered her injuries when she went into the produce section of the store and slipped and fell in liquid, dirt, and produce on the floor. Plaintiff alleged in her original state court petition that she sus-

tained injuries to her right wrist, left knee and patella, and upper and lower back. . . . Plaintiff alleged damages for medical expenses, physical pain and suffering, mental anguish and suffering, loss of enjoyment of life, loss of wages and earning capacity, and permanent disability and disfigurement. . . . Consistent with Article 893 of the Louisiana Code of Civil Procedure, which prohibits the allegation of a specific amount of damages, Plaintiff did not pray for a specific amount of damages.

Defendant removed this action to the district court on October 13, 1998, pursuant to diversity jurisdiction as provided by 28 U.S.C. § 1332. It is undisputed that the parties are completely diverse, as Plaintiff is a citizen of Louisiana and Defendant is a citizen of Delaware with its principle place of business in Arkansas. Defendant stated in its Notice of Removal that the $75,000 amount in controversy requirement was satisfied because Plaintiff's alleged injuries and damages, exclusive of interests and costs, exceeded that amount.

The district court scheduled this action for trial on March 20, 2000, and the parties proceeded with pre-trial discovery until March 2, 2000, when Plaintiff questioned the court's diversity jurisdiction by filing a motion to remand arguing that the $75,000 amount in controversy requirement was not satisfied. In the motion, accompanied by Plaintiff's affidavit, Plaintiff argued that due to continuing medical treatment of her injuries, Plaintiff was unable to confirm the amount of damages claimed. Plaintiff added that only after conducting discovery and receiving information from her treating physicians was she able to ascertain that the amount of claimed damages would be less than $75,000. In light of such information, Plaintiff argued that the amount in controversy was less than $75,000, and that the district court should remand this action for lack of subject-matter jurisdiction.

The district court denied the motion to remand on March 14, 2000, finding that the court had subject-matter jurisdiction because Plaintiff's petition at the time of removal alleged injuries that exceeded the $75,000 requirement. In the Revised Joint Pretrial Order filed on March 16, 2000, Plaintiff again disputed the court's jurisdiction because Plaintiff stipulated, based on medical evidence, that her claims did not amount to $75,000. Plaintiff then filed a motion to reconsider the district court's denial of her motion to remand in light of the stipulation, and re-urged the district court to remand for lack of subject-matter jurisdiction. On March 16, 2000, the district court denied Plaintiff's motion for reconsideration, restating its finding that because Plaintiff's claims at the time of removal alleged claims in excess of $75,000,

the court was not inclined to reconsider its previous denial of the motion to remand.

Thereafter, this action was tried on March 20, and a jury found for Defendant on Plaintiff's claims. On March 22, the district court entered a judgment in favor of Defendant and dismissing Plaintiff's claims with prejudice. Plaintiff timely appealed the judgment, and now argues that the district court erred in denying her motion to remand.

Analysis

. . . Any civil action brought in a state court of which the district courts have original jurisdiction may be removed to the proper district court. 28 U.S.C. § 1441(a). District courts have original jurisdiction of all civil actions where the matter in controversy exceeds the sum or value of $75,000, exclusive of interests and costs, and is between citizens of different states. . . . §1332(a)(1). As noted above, . . . the only issue on this appeal is whether the district court erred in deciding that the amount in controversy exceeded the sum or value of $75,000, exclusive of interests and costs.

We have established a clear analytical framework for resolving disputes concerning the amount in controversy for actions removed from Louisiana state courts pursuant to § 1332(a)(1). . . . Because plaintiffs in Louisiana state courts, by law, may not specify the numerical value of claimed damages, . . . the removing defendant must prove by a preponderance of the evidence that the amount in controversy exceeds $75,000. . . . The defendant may prove that amount either by demonstrating that the claims are likely above $75,000 in sum or value, or by setting forth the facts in controversy that support a finding of the requisite amount. . . .

Moreover, once the district court's jurisdiction is established, subsequent events that reduce the amount in controversy to less than $75,000 generally do not divest the court of diversity jurisdiction. . . . The jurisdictional facts that support removal must be judged at the time of the removal. . . . Additionally, if it is facially apparent from the petition that the amount in controversy exceeds $75,000 at the time of removal, post-removal affidavits, stipulations, and amendments reducing the amount do not deprive the district court of jurisdiction. . . .

In this action, the district court properly denied Plaintiff's motion to remand. It is "facially apparent" from Plaintiff's original petition that the claimed damages exceeded $75,000. In *Luckett* [*v. Delta Airlines, Inc.*, 171 F.3d 295, (5th Cir. 1999)], we held that the district court did not err in finding that the plaintiff's claims exceeded $75,000 because the plaintiff alleged damages for property, travel expenses, an emergency ambulance trip, a six-day stay in the hospital, pain and suffering, humiliation, and temporary inability to do housework after hospitalization. . . .

In this action, Plaintiff alleged in her original state court petition that she sustained injuries to her right wrist, left knee and patella, and upper and lower back. Plaintiff alleged damages for medical expenses, physical pain and suffering, mental anguish and suffering, loss of enjoyment of life, loss of wages and earning capacity, and permanent disability and disfigurement. Such allegations support a substantially large monetary basis to confer removal jurisdiction . . . , and therefore the district court did not err in denying Plaintiff's motion to remand. Because it was facially apparent that Plaintiff's claimed damages exceeded $75,000, the district court properly disregarded Plaintiff's post-removal affidavit and stipulation for damages less than $75,000, and such affidavit and stipulation did not divest the district court's jurisdiction. . . .

AFFIRMED.

Case Questions

1. In this case, which party had to prove that the jurisdictional amount requirement was met?
2. How did the court in this case assure itself as to the extent and nature of the plaintiff's damages?
3. What provision of the Louisiana Code of Civil Procedure makes it more difficult for litigants to determine the amount of a plaintiff's damages?

The *Erie* Doctrine

In adjudicating state matters, a federal court is guided by a judicial policy known as the *Erie* doctrine. In the 1938 landmark case of *Erie Railroad Company v. Tompkins*, 304 U.S. 64, the U.S. Supreme Court decided that federal questions are governed by federal law. In other cases, however, the substantive law that should generally be applied in federal courts is the law of the state. The law of the state was defined as including judicial decisions as well as statutory law. In addition, there is no federal general common law governing state matters. A federal district court is bound by the statutes and precedents of the state in which it sits.

This restriction prevents a federal court and a state court from reaching different results on the same issue of state law. You will recall that the federal judge in our first case, *Du Pont v. Christopher*, tried to determine what the Texas state courts would do if that case had been litigated in a state court. The court "applied" Texas substantive law because the question of whether aerial photography is an improper method of discovering a trade secret is a matter of state tort law. It does not raise any federal constitutional or statutory issues.

The *Erie* doctrine, which went to the heart of relations between the state and federal courts, is one of the most important judicial policies ever adopted by the U.S. Supreme Court. Many of the civil cases brought subsequent to this landmark case have been affected by the decision.

Where state and federal procedural rules differ, the *Erie* doctrine does not generally require that federal courts apply state procedural rules. Instead, the Federal Rules of Civil Procedure apply in federal courts unless they would: significantly affect a litigant's substantive rights, encourage forum shopping, or promote a discriminatory application of the law. The Federal Rules of Civil Procedure were not designed to have any effect upon the rules of decision.

In the following case, the district court relied on the *Erie* doctrine in deciding whether the plaintiff had stated a claim upon which relief could be granted.

Carson v. National Bank
501 F.2d 1082
U.S. Court of Appeals, Eighth Circuit
July 30, 1974

Per Curiam*

This case is before the Court upon appeal . . . from an order granting . . . judgment in favor of defendants on the first count of a two-count complaint.

The count which was dismissed was based on diversity of citizenship and alleged that defendants, in advertising a travel tour, used the name and image of the plaintiff without his permission, thereby damaging him. The District Court . . . dismissed the count on the ground that, under Nebraska law, it failed to state a claim upon which relief could be granted.

The facts are undisputed. Defendants, a bank and its wholly owned subsidiary travel agency, placed an advertisement bearing the name and picture of Mr. Carson, the well-known television personality and nightclub performer, in several newspapers and in a pamphlet distributed to bank customers. The advertisement concerned a travel tour to Las Vegas organized by defendant Travel Unlimited, Inc., which was called "Nebraskan Johnny Carson's Tour of Las Vegas." Mr. Carson was to be performing at a Las Vegas nightclub during the time scheduled for the tour, and tickets to his show were included in the tour package. Mr. Carson did not approve the use of his name and photograph, nor was he connected in any way with the travel venture.

. . . [T]he federal courts must apply the law of the state wherein the United States District Court is located. Here, the applicable principles must, therefore, be determined from an examination of the law of the state of Nebraska. The District Court, after examining that law, determined that Count I of the complaint failed to state a claim upon which relief could be granted. The only issue on appeal is whether the trial court was correct in that interpretation of Nebraska law. . . .

---

*An opinion written by the entire court rather than by just one judge. —*Ed.*

We therefore have undertaken our own review of Nebraska law, and particularly the case of *Brunson v. Ranks Army Store*, 161 Neb. 519, 73 N.W.2d 803 (1955). This case . . . formed the basis for the District Court's conclusion that plaintiff's first cause of action did not state a claim upon which relief could be granted.

Plaintiff Brunson was an actor who was hired by Ranks Army Store to re-enact the Brinks armed robbery as a publicity device. The Store failed to warn the local police of the planned re-enactment, and Mr. Brunson was arrested and jailed during the staged robbery. Thereafter, the Store ran advertisements setting forth the story of Brunson's arrest and incarceration, using Brunson's name and picture. Brunson sued the Store, charging in one count that his right to privacy, which he had not waived, was violated by the use of the picture and story without his consent and he had thereby been subjected to ridicule, embarrassment, and humiliation. The Nebraska Supreme Court affirmed the lower court's dismissal of the action, stating:

> "Our research develops no Nebraska case holding that this court has in any form or manner adopted the doctrine of the right of privacy, and there is no precedent in this state establishing the doctrine. Nor has the Legislature of this state conferred such a right of action by statute. . . . We therefore hold that the action of the trial court in sustaining the defendant's demurrer to plaintiff's action based on the right of privacy was correct and needs no further comment."

Brunson, argues plaintiff here, sought damages not for his loss of the opportunity to sell his name for commercial purposes, but for the mental suffering he underwent as a result of the revelation of an embarrassing incident. . . . All these actions stem from the initial recognition of a right to control the use of one's own name and image, which the Nebraska Supreme Court explicitly rejected in *Brunson*. Plaintiff's characterization of his action as one seeking damages for "misappropriation" cannot serve as a means to escape the rule of the *Brunson* case. If the Nebraska court had intended to recognize an action for "misappropriation," *Brunson* would certainly have been an appropriate place for some indication of such intention, since Brunson, like Carson, alleged that his picture and name had been used without his permission in an advertising scheme. (Brunson had agreed that his picture could be used in connection with the re-enactment of the robbery, but had not contracted for the use of his name and picture in connection with his actual arrest and incarceration.)

Such a result might seem anomalous today where the vast majority of states have recognized a "right to privacy" by court decision or statute, and where the plaintiff's first cause of action, in most jurisdictions, would clearly state a claim upon which relief could be granted. However, the fact that Nebraska has followed a different course from that of other states is not reason for this court to determine that Nebraska would now wish to judicially change its law. This court must look to Nebraska law as it is and not as one might believe it ought to be.

Plaintiff argues that we need not slavishly adhere to the last ruling of the Nebraska Supreme Court in a similar case, but should determine what the present Supreme Court would do if faced with this case now. We have done so, but we believe that the best method of ascertaining what the Nebraska court would do with this case is to examine what it has done with similar cases in the past. The *Brunson* case has not been overruled, nor has any subsequent case we have found cast any doubt on its continuing authority. . . . [T]he learned District Judge, familiar with the law of Nebraska, has concluded that *Brunson* states the current law of Nebraska. We conclude that his interpretation was, and is, correct.

Affirmed.

Case Questions

1. Why did the federal district court have jurisdiction in this case?
2. Since the case was heard in federal court, why didn't the judge apply the law as generally applied in the nation, rather than the law of Nebraska?
3. Since the Brunson case was decided so long ago (1955), and most other states have recognized a "right to privacy," why didn't the federal court overturn Nebraska's "outdated" substantive tort law regarding these types of cases?

THE THIRTEEN U.S. COURTS OF APPEALS

The United States has been divided by Congress into eleven circuits (clusters of states), and a court of appeals has been assigned to each circuit. A court of appeals has also been established for the District of Columbia. In 1982, Congress created a new court of appeals with broad territorial jurisdiction and with very specialized subject matter jurisdiction. This court is called the Court of Appeals for the Federal Circuit. Its job is to review appeals from the U.S. district courts throughout the nation in such areas as patent, trademark, and copyright cases; cases in which the United States is the defendant; and cases appealed from the U.S. Court of International Trade and the U.S. Court of Federal Claims. Figure 3-6 shows the boundaries of the thirteen circuits.

These appellate courts hear appeals on questions of law from decisions of the federal district courts in their circuits and review findings of federal administrative agencies. For most litigants, they are the ultimate appellate tribunals of the federal system. Appeal to these courts is a matter of right, not discretion, so long as proper procedures are followed.

When attorneys wish to appeal decisions of lower tribunals, they must follow such procedures to get the cases before a court of appeals. Notice of appeal must be filed within thirty days from the entry of judgment, sixty days when the United States or an officer or agent thereof is a party. A cost bond (in civil cases) may be required to ensure payment of the costs of the appeal. Both the record on appeal and a brief must be filed.

Attorneys must then persuade the judges that the lower tribunals committed errors that resulted in injustices to their clients. On appeal, the court of appeals does not substitute its judgment for that of the lower tribunal's finding of fact. It does reverse the lower court's decision if that decision was clearly erroneous as a matter of law. See Figure 3-7 for statistical information regarding the types and number of cases decided by U.S. Courts of Appeals between 1995 and 2000.

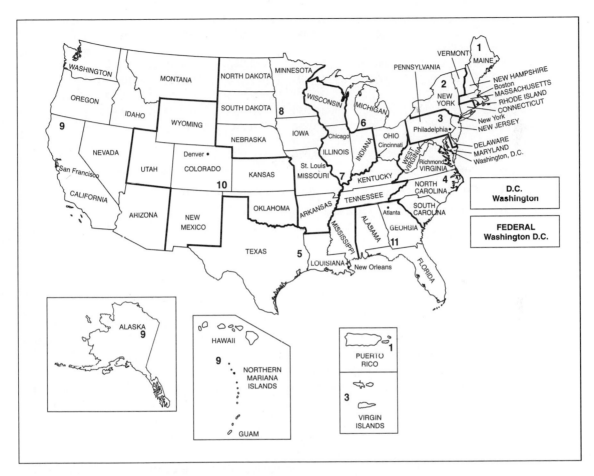

FIGURE 3-6   The Thirteen Federal Judicial Circuits

THE U.S. SUPREME COURT

The U.S. Supreme Court has existed since 1789. Today the Court consists of a chief justice and eight associate justices. It exercises both appellate and original jurisdiction. Its chief function is to act as the last and final court of review over all cases in the federal system and some cases in the state system.

Supreme Court review is not a matter of right. A party wishing to have its case reviewed by the Supreme Court (called a *petitioner*) is required by statute to file a petition for a *writ of certiorari* with the Court. The other party, called the *respondent,* will have the right to oppose the granting of the writ. The Court grants *certiorari* only where there are special and important reasons for so doing. If four or more justices are in favor of granting the petition, the writ issues and the case is accepted. The Court thus controls its docket, reserving its

	2000	1999	1998	1997	1996	1995
Total Appeals Filed	54,697	54,693	53,805	52,319	51,991	50,072
Prisoner Appeals Filed	17,252	17,191	17,422	16,188	16,996	14,985
All Other Civil Appeals Filed	23,501	23,971	22,055	21,198	21,279	21,630
Criminal Appeals Filed	10,707	10,251	10,535	10,521	10,889	10,162
Administrative Appeals Filed	3,237	3,280	3,793	4,412	2,827	3,295
Total Appeals Terminated	56,512	54,088	52,002	51,194	50,413	49,805

FIGURE 3-7   U.S. Court of Appeals—Judicial Caseload profile, National Totals 1995–2000

Source: Administrative Office of the U.S. Courts, *Annual Report of the Director, 2000.*

time and efforts for the cases that seem to the justices to deserve consideration. Figure 3-8 illustrates the number of cases the Supreme Court addressed over a twelve-month period.

The U.S. Supreme Court is the only court specifically created in the Constitution. All other federal courts are statutorily created by the Congress. The Constitution provides for the Court's original jurisdiction. Original jurisdiction is the power to take note of a suit at its beginning, try it, and pass judgment on the law and the facts of the controversy. The Constitution has given the Court the power to perform the function of trial court in cases affecting ambassadors, public ministers, and consuls, and in controversies in which a state is a party. Usually the power is not exclusive, nor is the Court required to hear all cases over which it has original jurisdiction.

Article III authorizes Congress to determine the Court's appellate jurisdiction. A history-making example occurred in 1983 when Congress enacted the

Nature of Proceeding	Pending 10/1/99	Filed	Granted	Denied	Dismissed	Pending 9/30/00
Total	2,498	5,633	99	5,236	45	2,751
Criminal	778	1,786	12	1,779	0	773
U.S. Civil	455	956	29	935	12	435
Private Civil	1,175	2,763	51	2,416	32	1,439
Administrative Appeals	90	128	7	106	1	104

FIGURE 3-8   Petitions for Review on Writ of Certiorari to the U.S. Supreme Court Commenced, Terminated, and Pending During the 12-Month Period Ending 9/30/2000.

Source: Administrative Office of the U.S. Courts, *Annual Report of the Director, 2001.*

Military Justice Act. This act conferred jurisdiction on the Supreme Court to directly review designated categories of appeals from the Court of Military Appeals. These appeals are brought to the Court pursuant to the writ of certiorari procedure. This marked the first time in the history of the United States that any Article III court was authorized to review the decisions of military courts.

Chapter Questions

1. Define the following terms:

bench trial	jurisdictional amount
doctrine of *forum non conveniens*	limited jurisdiction
domicile	long-arm statutes
diversity of citizenship jurisdiction	minimum contacts requirement
Erie doctrine	motion for summary judgment
federal question jurisdiction	original jurisdiction
forum state	quash
general appearance	residual jurisdiction
general jurisdiction	removal jurisdiction
intermediate appellate court	special appearance
in personam jurisdiction	special verdict
in rem jurisdiction	subject matter jurisdiction
judgment creditor	summons (also called process)
judgment debtor	venue
jurisdiction	writ of *certiorari*

2. A plaintiff airline company sought to establish *in personam* jurisdiction over defendant, a resident of Washington state, who was alleged by plaintiff to have sent defamatory e-mails into Minnesota. Plaintiff served defendant within Washington state with a Minnesota summons, arguing that this was permissible under Minnesota's long-arm statute. The defendant sought dismissal of the suit on jurisdictional grounds. Were defendant's contacts with Minnesota sufficient to satisfy the Fourteenth Amendment Due Process Clause's minimum contacts requirement for establishing *in personam* jurisdiction?

   Northwest Airlines, Inc., v. H. Louise Friday, C1-00-528, Minnesota Court of Appeals (2000)

3. Plaintiff Watertronics, Inc., a Wisconsin corporation manufacturing pumping equipment, filed suit in Wisconsin against defendant Flanagan's Inc., a New Jersey general contractor, for the unpaid balance due on a pumping system. These parties had prior business dealings, and in the past, Flanagan's had always purchased equipment through a New Jersey supplier. When the pumping system didn't work, Flanagan's stopped making payments and the lawsuit ensued. Flanagan's sought dismissal on the grounds that its only connection with Wisconsin was a 4.4 minute telephone call that it

had made to the plaintiff's Wisconsin headquarters. Was that contact sufficient to establish "sufficient minimum contacts"?

Watertronics Inc. v. Flanagan's Inc., No. 00-2924, Wisconsin Court of Appeals, (2001)

4. Bensusan Restaurant Corporation owns and operates a popular, large New York City jazz club called "The Blue Note." Richard King owns and has operated a small cabaret also called "The Blue Note" in Columbia, Missouri, since 1980. King's establishment features live music and attracts its customers from central Missouri. In 1996, King decided to establish a website for the purpose of advertising his cabaret. King included a disclaimer on his website in which he gave a plug to Bensusan's club and made it clear that the two businesses were unrelated. He later modified this disclaimer by making it even more explicit and said that his "cyberspot was created to provide information for Columbia, Missouri area individuals only."

Bensusan brought suit in the U.S. District court for the Southern District of New York against King seeking monetary damages and injunctive relief. The plaintiff maintained that King had infringed on his federally protected trademark by calling his cabaret "The Blue Note." King moved to dismiss the complaint for lack of personal jurisdiction. He contended that he had neither engaged in business within New York nor committed any act sufficient to confer *in personam* jurisdiction over him by New York. The U.S. District Court agreed with King, and the case was appealed to the United States Court of Appeals for the Second Circuit. Should the Second Circuit affirm or reverse the District Court? Why?

Bensusan Restaurant Corporation v. Richard B. King, Docket No. 96-9344 (1997)

5. Mr. and Mrs. Woodson instituted a product liability action in an Oklahoma state court to recover for personal injuries sustained in Oklahoma in an accident involving a car that they had bought in New York while they were New York residents. The Woodsons were driving the car through Oklahoma at the time of the accident. The defendants were the car retailer and its wholesaler, both New York corporations, who did no business in Oklahoma. The defendants entered a special appearance, claiming that the Oklahoma state court did not have personal jurisdiction. Would there be enough "minimum contacts" between the defendants and the forum state for the forum state to have personal jurisdiction over the defendants?

World-Wide Volkswagen Corp. v. Woodson, 444 U.S. 286 (1980)

6. Dorothy Hooks brought a class action suit against Associated Financial Services, Inc. and others for breach of contract, fraud, and conspiracy. In her complaint, Hooks stipulated for the members of the class that the plaintiffs would waive both the right to recover more than $49,000 in damages and any right to recover punitive damages. The defendant nevertheless sought removal predicated on diversity of citizenship jurisdiction. Should the U.S. District Court grant the plaintiff's petition to remand this case back to the state courts?

Hooks v. Associated Financial Services Company, Inc. et al. 966 F. Supp. 1098 (1997)

7. David Singer was injured when his automobile was struck by an uninsured motorist. David was insured against this type of accident up to a policy limit of $30,000 by State Farm Mutual Automobile Insurance Company. When State Farm stalled on paying on his insurance claim, David filed suit in state court, alleging breach of contract and breach of good faith and fair dealing. David did not demand any specified amount of money damages in his complaint because state law prohibited him from so doing. State Farm filed a removal petition in U.S. District Court, alleging that the federal court had subject matter jurisdiction based on diversity of citizenship. The defendant alleged that damages existed in excess of $50,000 (the jurisdictional amount at the time the suit was filed). Has the defendant followed the correct procedure, under these circumstances, for establishing the existence of the jurisdictional amount? How should the U.S. Ninth Circuit Court of Appeals rule?

   Singer v. State Farm, No. 95-55441 (1997)

8. In this hypothetical diversity of citizenship case, federal law requires complete diversity of citizenship between plaintiffs and defendants and an amount in controversy greater than $75,000 in order for federal courts to entertain jurisdiction of an action. Tom Jones and Leonard Woodrock were deep-shaft coal miners in West Virginia, although Leonard lived across the border in Kentucky. Tom purchased a new Eureka, a National Motors car, from Pappy's Auto Sales, a local firm. National Motors Corporation is a large auto manufacturer with its main factory in Indiana, and is incorporated in Kentucky. When Tom was driving Leonard home from the mine, the Eureka's steering wheel inexplicably locked. The car hurtled down a 100-foot embankment and came to rest against a tree. The Eureka, which cost $17,100, was a total loss. Tom and Leonard suffered damages of $58,000 apiece for personal injuries. Can Tom sue National Motors for damages in a federal court? Why? Can Leonard? Can Leonard and Tom join their claims and sue National Motors in federal court?

9. National Mutual Insurance Company is a District of Columbia corporation. It brought a diversity action in the U.S. District Court of Maryland against Tidewater Transfer Company, a Virginia corporation doing business in Maryland. National Mutual contends that, for diversity purposes, a D.C. resident may file suit against the resident of a state. Tidewater Transfer disagrees. What should be taken into consideration in deciding whether the District of Columbia can, for diversity purposes, be regarded as a state?

   National Mutual Insurance v. Tidewater Transfer Co., 337 U.S. 582 (1949)

10. Several Arizona citizens brought a diversity suit in a federal district court against Harsh Building Company, an Oregon corporation. All parties involved in the suit stipulated that the defendant had its principal place of business in Oregon. During the trial, evidence showed that the only real business activity of Harsh Building Co. was owning and operating the Phoenix apartment complex, which was the subject of the suit. The plaintiffs

lost the suit. On appeal, they claimed that the district court did not have jurisdiction because of lack of diversity of citizenship. Did the plaintiffs waive their right to challenge jurisdiction?

Bialac v. Harsh Building Co., 463 F.2d 1185 (9th Cir. 1972)

Notes

1. *In personam* jurisdiction will generally not be recognized where someone is duped into entering the state for the purpose of making service. *Townsend v. Smith,* 3 N.W.439 (1879). *Jacobs/Kahan & Co. v. Marsh,* 740F.2d 587 (7th Cir. 1984). Similarly, a person who enters a state to challenge jurisdiction cannot be validly served. *Stewart v. Ramsay,* 242 U.S. 128 (1916).
2. *Burnham v. Superior Court,* 495 U.S. 604 (1990).
3. 28 U.S.C 1391.

IV Civil Procedure

As a passive adjudicator of disputes, courts neither initiate nor encourage litigation. The court system does nothing until one of the parties has called on it through appropriate procedures. Procedural rules create the process that is used to decide the merits of a dispute. At the beginning of the process, these rules explain what a plaintiff must do to start a lawsuit and how the plaintiff can assert a legal claim against a defendant. Defendants are similarly told how to raise defenses and claims once they have been notified of suit. Procedural rules govern what documents must be prepared, what each must contain, and how they should be presented to the court and the defendant. Once the lawsuit has been initiated, procedures govern how the parties discover relevant information and evidence, especially when it is in the possession of one's opponent. Rules also govern the conduct of trials, any enforcement procedures necessary after trial, the conduct of appeals, and the imposition of sanctions on rule violators. The principal objective of procedural law is to give the parties to a dispute an equal and fair opportunity to present their cases to a nonprejudiced and convenient tribunal. If procedural rules are correctly drafted and implemented, both parties to the dispute should feel that they have been fairly treated.

Although all procedures must satisfy constitutional due process requirements, the state and federal governments, as separate sovereigns, have promulgated separate rules of civil procedure that govern the litigation process in their respective forums. This means, for example, that Oregon lawyers have to learn two sets of procedural rules. If they are litigating in the state courts of Oregon, they comply with the *Oregon Rules of Civil Procedure,* and when litigating in the U.S. District Court for Oregon, they follow the provisions of the *Federal Rules of Civil Procedure* (FRCP).

The purpose of this chapter is to explain the procedures that govern a civil suit from the time a litigant decides to sue until final court judgment. Indispensable to an understanding of these systems is a familiarity with the various stages and terms that are encountered in a civil proceeding.

PROCEEDINGS BEFORE A CIVIL TRIAL

The first step in civil litigation involves a triggering event that injures the plaintiff or damages his or her property (see Figure 4-1). The second step usually involves the plaintiff selecting an attorney. It is important to understand that, in general, each party pays for his or her attorney's fee irrespective of who ultimately prevails in the substantive dispute. This is subject to exceptions where statutory law provides otherwise and where common law judicial doctrines permit the court to order the loser to pay the winner's attorney fees.

Hiring a Lawyer

The period between the event that gives rise to the suit (the triggering event) and the filing of a complaint is known as the *informal discovery* period. The court has neither knowledge of nor interest in the plaintiff's cause of action against the defendant.

During this time, the plaintiff contacts an attorney and describes the circumstances that led to the injury. The attorney discusses in general terms the legal alternatives available and usually asks for an opportunity to conduct an independent investigation to assess the value of the claim. This meeting is known as an exploratory conversation. At this point, the plaintiff and the attorney are not contractually bound to each other.

After the exploratory conversation and further investigation, the plaintiff meets once again with the attorney to determine which course of action should be taken. The attorney presents an evaluation of the case in terms of the remedies available, the probability of achieving a favorable verdict, and the nature and probability of the award likely to be granted. At this point, the plaintiff retains the attorney as a representative in the judicial proceedings that are likely to follow.

Attorney's fees may be determined in several ways. Attorneys may charge the client by the hour. They may take a percentage of the damages collected (*contingent fee*), in which case they receive nothing if the client loses. They may be on a retainer, in which case they are paid a certain sum per year to handle all their client's legal problems. Or they may charge a flat rate for their services.

When the plaintiff's lawyer has been officially retained, the defendant is so informed. This information puts the defendant on notice that the plaintiff is preparing to seek an adjudicative settlement of the claim. If the defendant has not already retained an attorney, this is the time to do so. The attorneys meet, with or without their clients, to discuss a reasonable settlement. These discussions are referred to as *settlement conferences*. If they prove unsuccessful, the judicial machinery is set in motion.

Clients retain the power to discharge their lawyers at any time. In the following case, the Supreme Court of Colorado weighs this right against the rule of damages.

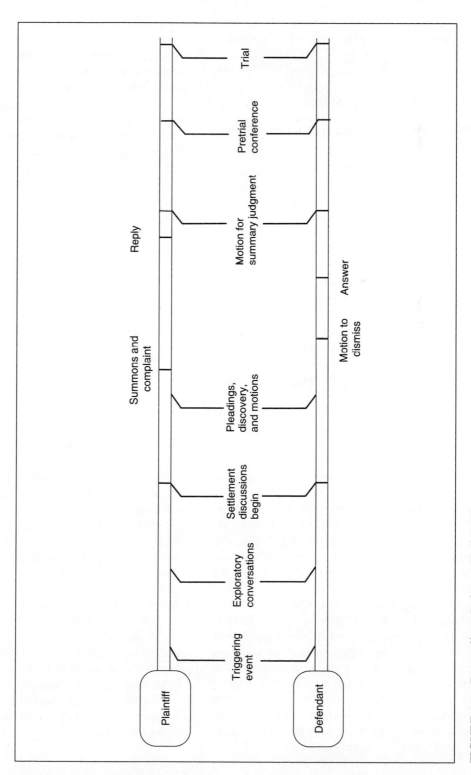

FIGURE 4-1   Proceedings Before a Civil Trial

Olsen and Brown v. City of Englewood
889 P.2d 673
Supreme Court of Colorado
January 30, 1995

Chief Justice Rovira delivered the opinion of the Court.

We granted certiorari to determine whether an attorney may recover damages for a client's breach of a non-contingency contract for legal services without cause; whether the court of appeals can reverse a trial court's judgment on an issue not appealed when it expands the rights of a party; and whether an attorney's claims resulting from operation of a municipal sanitation facility are barred by the doctrine of sovereign immunity.

We affirm the court of appeals' determination that an attorney may not recover damages under a non-contingency contract for services not rendered prior to such discharge. Because we determine that under the circumstances of this case the claims of misrepresentation and equitable estoppel are barred, it is not necessary to reach issues two and three.

The City of Englewood (Englewood) entered into an oral agreement with Olsen & Brown (Olsen), a law partnership, whereby Olsen was to represent Englewood in toxic litigation to its conclusion, including all appeals. Englewood agreed to compensate Olsen for the work by a set monthly fee commencing in October 1989.

The litigation required Olsen to devote substantially all of its time to the case and to forgo other employment in doing so. Olsen made further arrangements in connection with the agreement including retention of outside counsel to assist with the litigation.

Subsequently, Englewood terminated the attorney-client relationship without cause. Olsen then sued Englewood for damages al-leging inter alia breach of contract, . . . Englewood filed a motion to dismiss all of the claims, contending Olsen could not recover attorneys' fees for legal services not rendered. . . .

The trial court ruled that a client has the right to terminate the attorney-client relationship at any time, with or without cause, and in so doing is not bound to pay for services not yet rendered. Accordingly, it granted the motion in part "with respect to any purported fees not earned for services rendered" as to the claims for breach of contract, . . . and denied the motion as to any "claims for fees earned for services rendered." . . .

The court of appeals affirmed dismissal of the breach of contract claim, concluding an attorney who "is employed under a fixed fee contract to render specific legal services and is discharged by the client without cause is entitled only to compensation for the reasonable value of the services rendered up to the time of the discharge." . . .

A

Historically, courts have been in disagreement as to the measure of compensation owed an attorney who has a non-contingency contract with a client and is discharged without cause. . . .

There is no question that an attorney who withdraws for a justifiable reason or is terminated by a client without cause is entitled to compensation for services rendered. . . . Generally, courts are in agreement that *quantum meruit* is an appropriate measure of recovery in such circumstances.

A divergence in opinion, however, results from a consideration of whether recovery of damages under traditional breach of contract principles is also permitted.

Under the traditional "contract rule," courts allow recovery of damages for breach of contract. . . .

The rationale for the contract rule is based upon assumptions that (1) the full contract price is the most logical measure of damages as it reflects the value placed on the services at the time of the contract's formation; (2) awarding damages prohibits a client from profiting from his own breach of contract; and (3) it lessens the difficult task of valuing a lawyer's partially completed work. . . .

However, a modern view has emerged and has been adopted in many jurisdictions, which permits quantum meruit as the sole basis for recovery in such situations. . . . The "quantum meruit rule" is premised upon the special confidence and trust existing between an attorney and client which sets the relationship apart from other employment relationships. . . .

B

The relationship between an attorney and client is a distinct fiduciary affiliation which arises as a matter of law. . . . The foundation of this relationship is grounded upon a special trust and confidence, . . . and requires that a client have the utmost faith in chosen counsel.

To this end, attorneys are governed by and must adhere to specific rules of conduct which this court has the exclusive jurisdiction to oversee. . . . Thus, the attorney-client relationship may initially be distinguished from other business relationships by virtue of these specific rules and the uniqueness of the governing body under which attorney conduct is regulated.

These rules are not designed to alter civil liability nor do they serve a basis for such liability. Code of Professional Responsibility, Preliminary Statement; Colorado Rules of Professional Conduct, Preamble, Scope and Terminology. . . .

Rather, such rules are in place to provide guidance in the attorney-client relationship and to serve as a mechanism of internal professional discipline. Code of Professional Responsibility, Preliminary Statement; Colorado Rules of Professional Conduct, Preamble, Scope and Terminology.

Although not controlling of the issue before us, we must be mindful of these rules and the influence they necessarily have in situations involving the attorney-client relationship.

R.P.C. [Rules of Professional Conduct] 1.16 requires an attorney's withdrawal from representation upon discharge by the client. The Comment to this rule states, in pertinent part: "[a] client has a right to discharge a lawyer at any time, with or without cause, subject to liability for payment for the lawyer's services."

In order to assure no compulsion to retain an attorney where trust between attorney and client has been broken, and to further guarantee a client may always be confident with such representation, a client must, and does, have the right to discharge the attorney at any time and for whatever reason. . . . An attorney may not rely upon an indefinite continuation of employment but instead enters an attorney-client relationship with knowledge that the relationship may be terminated at any time and for any reason.

The unique relationship between attorney and client prevents the agreement between them from being considered as an ordinary contract because doing so would ignore the special fiduciary relationship. . . .

The right to terminate the attorney-client relationship "is a term of the contract implied by public policy because of the peculiar relationship between attorney and client." . . . A client's discharge of chosen counsel is not a breach of contract but merely an exercise of this inherent right. . . .

The position which Olsen asks us to adopt would have a profound effect on the power and inherent right of the client to discharge the attorney. To allow an attorney to recover damages for services not actually rendered prior to termination of the attorney-client relationship would penalize the client in direct contravention of the client's absolute right to discharge his attorney. . . .

The right to discharge is obviously meaningless if the client is penalized by having to pay for services that have not been rendered. The client could conceivably be required to pay duplicate charges consisting of fees to the discharged attorney for services not rendered, in addition to those incurred by a newly appointed attorney for the same work. This does not comport with the rights a client must be accorded in the attorney-client relationship, which this court has recognized, pursuant to our duty to regulate that relationship. . . .

We are guided by the same principles in both contingency and non-contingency fee cases, . . . and find any difference would serve only to confuse the principles set forth in this opinion. . . .

We believe it necessary to adopt a rule of law which balances the important interests of (1) protecting the special fiduciary nature of the attorney-client relationship and the client's inherent right to discharge and (2) assuring fair and adequate compensation to an attorney.

Accordingly, we hold an attorney, who is discharged without cause, may not recover damages under a non-contingency contract for services not rendered prior to such discharge. The attorney's remedy is the recovery of the reasonable value of services rendered before discharge on the basis of *quantum meruit*. . . .

The judgment of the court of appeals is affirmed.

Case Questions

1. How do contracts between attorneys and their clients differ from other contracts?
2. List the pros and cons of contingent fees.
3. Should a court uphold a contingent fee contract between attorney and client that prohibits a settlement by the client?
4. If an attorney's client decides not to prosecute the claim, should the attorney be allowed to continue to prosecute the cause to secure the contingent fee?
5. A criminal defendant is accorded the right to have a court-appointed attorney. Should civil litigants be accorded a similar right to court-appointed counsel? Are prepaid legal services—for example, group insurance coverage for litigation expenses—the solution? Are legal services such as public defender systems and legal aid societies the solution?
6. Should an attorney who fits the description of an "ambulance chaser" be disbarred? What if the attorney solicits professional employment by advertising?

 Assume Attorney Smith orally contracted to represent a client in a real estate transaction and had performed satisfactorily for six months. Assume further that the client, who had been completely satisfied with Smith's work until this point, discharged him from employment without legal cause after

learning that Attorney Brown would perform the remaining legal work for 30 percent less than the client was currently obligated to pay Smith. Should the rule of Olsen *control the facts in this hypothetical case in your estimation? What position would you take if you were a member of the Colorado Supreme Court?*

The Pleadings

The pleading stage begins after the client has chosen a lawyer and decides to bring suit. The role of pleadings in Anglo-American law goes back to the earliest days of the English common law system and writ system.[1] In the twelfth century, persons wishing to litigate in the royal courts had to purchase an original writ (such as the Writ of Right) from the king or chancellor in order to establish the court's jurisdiction. Each writ specified the procedures and substantive law to be followed in deciding the dispute.[2] The writ would often require the plaintiff to make an oral recitation (a pleading) in which the claims would be stated, after which the defendant would be entitled to respond orally. In this way the parties would inform the court of the nature of the dispute.[3] In time, the practice of oral pleadings was replaced with written documents, and the common law and equitable pleading process became very complex, overly technical, cumbersome, and long.

In 1848, New York merged the common law and equity courts and replaced its writ system with a newly enacted Code of Civil Procedure. Thus began a reform movement that swept the country and produced modern code pleading at the state level. The popularity of code pleading convinced Congress to enact the Rules Enabling Act in 1934, which led to the development and adoption in 1938 of the Federal Rules of Civil Procedure.

Modern pleadings are much less complex than in earlier times and are somewhat less important because of liberal discovery rules. They continue, however, to establish the basis for jurisdiction, briefly state facts giving rise to the complaint, aid in the formulation of the issues, and indicate the relief sought. Today, the pleadings consist of the plaintiff's complaint, the defendant's *answer*, and, rarely, the plaintiff's *reply*.

The *complaint* is a written document in which the plaintiff alleges jurisdiction, sets forth facts that he or she claims entitle the plaintiff to relief from the defendant, and demands relief. Figure 4-2 provides a sample of a federal complaint.

The complaint is the first pleading. It is filed with the court and served on the defendant with a *writ of summons*.[4] The writ of summons warns the defendant that a *default judgment* can be awarded unless the defendant responds with a pleading (usually an *answer*—see Figure 4-3) within a stated period of time (often between twenty and forty-five days).

UNITED STATES DISTRICT COURT
. . . . District of . . . .

:
. . . . Plaintiff   :
                                        :   Civil Action No. . . . .
         V.   :   COMPLAINT
. . . . Defendant   :
                                        :   JURY TRIAL DEMANDED

This is a civil action seeking damages under the laws of the State of . . . . . . for injuries to the person of the plaintiff, and to her automobile, caused by the defendant's negligent and/or willful, wanton, or reckless conduct.

   1. The court has jurisdiction of this matter by virtue of the fact that the plaintiff is a citizen of the State of . . . . . , and the defendant, ... is a citizen of the State of . . . . . and the amount in controversy exceeds $75,000 exclusive of interest and costs.

   2. This suit is brought pursuant to Section . . . . . . of the Revised Statutes.

   3. The plaintiff . . . . is, and at all times material to this action was, a resident of the City of . . . . , State of . . . .

   4. The defendant, ... is, and at all times material to this action was, a resident of the City of . . . . , State of . . . .

   5. At all times hereinafter mentioned, plaintiff was in the exercise of all due care and caution for her own safety and the safety of others.

   6. On January . . . . . . 200 . . . . at or about . . . . P.M., plaintiff . . . . was operating her automobile in a northerly direction along United States Route . . . . at or about . . . . miles north of . . . .

   7. On January . . . . . . 200 . . . . at or about . . . . P.M., defendant was operating her motor automobile in a southerly direction along United States Route . . . . at or about . . . . miles north of . . . .

   8. At that date and time, defendant, ... , negligently operated her vehicle in one or more of the following ways:

     a. Improperly failed to give a signal of her intention to make a turn.

     b. Negligently made an improper left-handed turn, without yielding the right-of-way to traffic coming in the opposite direction.

     c. Negligently failed to yield the right-of-way.

     d. Operated her vehicle on the wrong side of the road.

     e. Negligently failed to keep said vehicle under proper control.

     f. Operated her vehicle in a negligent manner.

     g. Negligently failed to stop her vehicle when danger to the plaintiff was imminent.

   9. As a result of one or more of the acts or omissions complained of, the vehicle driven by . . . . . . was caused violently to collide with the vehicle driven by . . . . . .

10. As a direct and proximate result thereof, the plaintiff suffered painful, severe and permanent injuries, loss of income, and has incurred, and will continue to incur expenses for medical care and further was caused to expend the sum of $ . . . . to repair the damages to her automobile caused by the accident.

    WHEREFORE, plaintiff prays for judgment against the defendant, ... in the sum of dollars ($ . . . .) plus costs.

    Plaintiff requests a jury trial.

. . . .
Attorney for Plaintiff
Office and P.O. Address

. . . .

FIGURE 4-2   Complaint Document

Methods of Service

The *summons* (see Figure 3-2) must be served to the defendant in time for the person to take action in defense. This right is constitutionally guaranteed by the *due process clauses*. The several methods to serve the summons can be found in the statute books of each state. These requirements must be precisely followed and *in personam* may differ from *in rem* actions. Clearly the most desirable method is to deliver the summons personally to the defendant. Some jurisdictions require that the summons be served within a specified period of time. The Federal Rules of Civil Procedure, for example, require service within 120 days

---

UNITED STATES DISTRICT COURT

. . . . District of . . . .

. . . . Plaintiff   :

:   Civil Action No. . . . .

V.   :   ANSWER

:

. . . . Defendant   :

:   JURY TRIAL DEMANDED

Now comes the defendant in the above-captioned action and gives the following answers to the plaintiff's complaint:

1. Denies the allegations of paragraphs 1 and 2 of the complaint.
2. Admits the allegations of paragraphs 3 and 4 of the complaint.
3. Denies the allegations of paragraphs 5 through 10 of the complaint.

FIRST AFFIRMATIVE DEFENSE

This court lacks subject matter jurisdiction as the amount in controversy does not exceed $75,000, exclusive of interest and cost.

SECOND AFFIRMATIVE DEFENSE

Plaintiff was guilty of negligence which was a contributing cause of the accident in that the plaintiff was negligently operating her automobile at the time that same collided with defendant's automobile. The plaintiff is therefore barred from recovery.

WHEREFORE, the defendant demands that the plaintiff's complaint be dismissed and that the costs of this action be awarded the defendant.

Defendant claims a trial by jury.

. . . .
Attorney for Defendant
Office and P.O. Address

. . . .
. . . .

FIGURE 4-3   Complaint Document

of the filing of the complaint. The summons, sometimes called *process*, is generally served by a process server or sheriff.

As previously mentioned, the recently amended federal rules provide incentives that encourage defendants to voluntarily waive their right to be formally served with process. For defendants in federal court who agree to waive, the benefit is the right to take 60 days to respond to the complaint rather than the normal 20 days. The benefit to plaintiffs is in not having to pay someone to serve the summons and complaint. Defendants who refuse to honor a requested waiver of service can be required to pay the service costs unless they can show good cause for the refusal.

In addition to having the summons personally served on a defendant, many states permit service by certified or registered mail, return receipt requested. This method is increasingly preferred because it is inexpensive and generally effective.

When personal service of a summons and the complaint to a defendant is not possible, the law often permits what is called *substituted or alternative service*. This method involves mailing the summons and complaint to the defendant by certified mail and leaving these documents at the defendant's home with a person who resides there and who is of "suitable age and discretion." Traditionally, this means someone aged fourteen or over. If the plaintiff is suing a corporation, the statutes usually authorize the use of substituted service on a designated agent or even a state official such as the secretary of state or the commissioner of insurance. The agent or official then sends a copy of the documents to the corporation. In some circumstances, the statutes provide for *constructive service*, which means publishing the notice of summons in the legal announcements section of newspapers. Traditionally, the law has required that the summons be published for three weeks.

The *answer* is a responsive written document in which the defendant makes admissions or denials, asserts legal defenses, and raises counterclaims. An *admission* means that there is no need to prove that fact during the trial. A denial creates a factual issue to be proved. Facts that may bar the plaintiff from recovery constitute a *defense*. The defendant may also make a claim for relief against the plaintiff by raising a *counterclaim* in the answer. A counterclaim is appropriate when the defendant has a *cause of action* against a plaintiff arising out of essentially the same set of events that gave rise to the plaintiff's claim. For example, assume that P observes D fishing without permission on P's land and tells D to vacate. If P kicks D in the back as D leaves the property, P is committing a battery against D. P could bring suit against D for trespass, and D could counterclaim against P for the battery. P could file a *reply* to the defendant's counterclaim raised in the answer. In this reply, the plaintiff may admit, deny, or defend against the factual allegations raised in the counterclaim.

A defendant who has been properly served with a summons and complaint defaults by failing to file a written answer in a timely manner. The court can then award judgment to the plaintiff for the award of money or other legal relief that was demanded in the complaint. In a default judgment, the defendant loses the right to object to anything that is incorrect in the complaint.

In the following case, the plaintiff was awarded a default judgment against the defendant. The defendant in *Dorsey v. Gregg* sought to vacate the default judgment because the trial court lacked jurisdiction over his person because of the inadequacy of the service.

Dorsey v. Gregg
784 P.2nd 154
Court of Appeals of Oregon
January 13, 1988

Richardson, Presiding Judge

Defendant seeks vacation of a default judgment, contending that the trial court lacked jurisdiction over him. We reverse.

Plaintiff's complaint was filed on December 5, 1985. Defendant, a student of the University of Oregon, lived in Eugene. He was a member of a fraternity but did not reside at the fraternity house. Personal service was attempted at the fraternity house from December 29 through February 19, 1986. No attempt was made to serve defendant at his residence even though his address was available from the university. On March 4, the trial court granted plaintiff's motion for alternative service. The motion was supported by the affidavit of Hoyt, which states:

> "I am an employee of Barristers' Aid, Inc., a civil process service corporation engaged in delivery of documents among attorneys and in serving civil process in the Lane County area. From on or about December 29, 1985, [to] February 18, 1986, I have made numerous attempts to serve the Defendant, Joseph Gregg, at his fraternity. On various occasions I would call in advance and find that his vehicle was there, or that they expected him to eat dinner at the fraternity that evening. However, upon arriving there in the evening for purposes of serving Mr. Gregg, various individuals there would profess that he no longer resides at the fraternity, nor that he ever eats at the facility nor visits.

> "It has become apparent to me and other individuals in our office who have attempted service upon Mr. Gregg, that the members of the fraternity are 'covering' for him, and are not cooperating in allowing us to learn his whereabouts at any given time.

> "It is my opinion that, if service was made upon a member of the fraternity, due notice of that would be conveyed to Mr. Gregg from earlier statements of members that he remained in the Eugene-Springfield area, and attended fraternity house functions."

The trial court authorized service "upon a person in charge or other resident member present" at the fraternity and by certified mail, return receipt requested, addressed to defendant's father at a Beaverton address.

Defendant first contends that the trial court erred in ordering the alternative service, because Hoyt's supporting affidavit was insufficient under ORCP 7D(6)(a). That rule provides, in relevant part:

> "On motion upon *a showing by affidavit that service cannot be made by any method otherwise specified in these rules* or other rule or statute, the court, at its discretion, may order service by any method or combination of methods which under the circumstances is most reasonably calculated to apprise the defendant of the existence and pendency of the action, including but not limited to: publication of summons; mailing without publication to a specified post office address of defendant, return receipt requested, deliver to addressee only; or posting at specified locations." (Emphasis supplied.)

In *Dhulst and Dhulst*, 657 P.2d 231 (1983), the trial court ordered alternative service on the husband by publication and registered mail.

The supporting affidavit addressed the reasons why the husband could not be personally served, but it was silent about the other types of service authorized by ORCP 7D(3)(a)(i). We held that, because the affidavit was insufficient to support alternative service under ORCP 7D(6)(a), "the trial court [had] erred in ordering [the alternative service]. Because [the alternative service] was improper, the trial court lacked personal jurisdiction over [the] husband." The default decree against the husband was therefore set aside.

Here, Hoyt's affidavit makes no mention of any attempt to locate and serve defendant at his "dwelling house or usual place of abode." ORCP 7D(3)(a)(i). It only details attempts to serve defendant at the fraternity house where he had not resided for at least a year before the filing of this action. . . . The affidavit fails to comply with the requirement of ORCP 7D(6)(a), and the trial court erred in ordering alternative service. The alternative service was therefore invalid, and the trial court lacked personal jurisdiction over defendant.

Reversed and remanded with instruction to vacate the judgment.

Case Questions

1. Why is the law so concerned with proper service of process?
2. Why did the Oregon Court of Appeals rule that the alternative service of process was invalid?
3. If the circumstances allow a court in the plaintiff's state to assert jurisdiction over an out-of-state defendant, what is the proper method of serving process?

Pretrial Motions

The second stage of the litigation process involves decisions about whether motions are filed prior to trial. Sometimes a defendant's lawyer, after receiving the plaintiff's complaint, will decide to challenge the complaint because of legal insufficiency. For example, the complaint might be poorly drafted and so vague that the defendant can't understand what is being alleged, whether the venue might be wrong, or whether there might be some problem with service. In such situations the attorney may choose to file a *motion to dismiss* (sometimes also called a *demurrer* or a "12(b) motion" in some jurisdictions) prior to preparing the answer. In *Du Pont v. Christopher,* we saw a *motion to dismiss* made by the defendant on the grounds that the plaintiff's complaint failed to state a claim upon which relief could be granted under Texas law. The motion to dismiss is decided by a judge, and jurisdictions differ about permitting the attorneys to argue orally the merits of the motion. If the judge grants the motion, the plaintiff will often try to cure any defect by amending the complaint. If the judge denies the motion, the defendant will normally submit an answer. Alleged defects in the answer and reply can also be raised through a motion to dismiss or an equivalent motion used for that purpose in a particular jurisdiction.

The *motion for summary judgment* can be made by either or both parties. It is intended to dispose of controversies when no genuine issues of material fact exist, or when the facts necessary to prove the other party's case are not provable or are not true. The motion is supported with proof in the form of affidavits and depositions. This proof is used to illustrate that there is no need to conduct a trial because there is no factual dispute between the parties. The party opposing the motion will present affidavits and depositions to prove the existence of contested issues of fact. Such proof may also be used to show the impossibility of certain facts alleged by an opposing party. For example, a complaint might accuse a defendant of various counts of negligence in operating a car. However, if the defendant was in jail that day, it could be proved that he or she could not possibly have committed the acts in question. The defendant in this instance would move for a summary judgment. Motions for summary judgment are disfavored by courts because, when granted, a party is denied a trial.

Summary judgment should not be granted if there is a genuine issue of material fact because it would deprive the parties of their right to a trial.

Discovery and Pretrial Conference

To prevent surprise at the trial, each party is provided with tools of *discovery* before trial in order to identify the relevant facts concerning the case. Discovery is based on the premise that prior to a civil action each party is entitled to information in the possession of others. This includes the identity and location of persons, the existence and location of documents, known facts, and opinions of experts.

There is a distinction between the right to obtain discovery and the right to use in court the statements or information that are the product of discovery. The restrictions that are made concerning the admissibility in court of the product of discovery will be discussed later in the chapter. The requirements for discovery are as follows: the information sought cannot be privileged, it must be relevant, it cannot be the "work product" of an attorney, and good cause must be shown to require a physical or mental examination.

The tools of discovery are depositions, written interrogatories to parties, production of documents, physical and mental examinations, and requests for admissions. In an *oral deposition* a witness is examined under oath outside court before an official of the court. The party wishing the deposition must give notice to the opposing party to the suit so that that person may be present to cross-examine the witness. The questioning of the witness at an oral deposition is thus much the same as it would be in a courtroom. Alternatively, an attorney may prepare a list of written questions to be answered by a witness. This report is called a *written deposition. Written interrogatories to the parties* are similar to written depositions in that both are lists of questions that must be answered in writing and under oath. Interrogatories are simpler, however, and can be submitted only to the parties to the case, not to witnesses. Because the rules of discovery can differ in federal and state courts, lawyers may take this into consideration in making a choice of forum. A state court, for example, might only permit an attorney to ask a party to answer thirty questions by written interrogatories, whereas fifty questions might be permissible under the federal rules.

One party to the suit may compel the *production of documents* or things in the possession of the other party for inspection. When the mental or physical condition of a party is at issue, a court may order the party to submit to an examination by a physician. Finally, one party may send to the other party a *request for admissions or denials* to certain specified facts or to the genuineness of certain documents. If no reply is made to such a request, the matters are considered admitted for the purpose of the suit.

All discovery except for physical examinations can be done without a court order. In case of noncompliance, the discovering party may request a court order to compel compliance. Failure to comply with the court order results in sanctions provided in the discovery statute.

Discovery may begin after the filing of the complaint, but usually commences after the answer is filed and continues until trial. In addition, a pretrial conference may be called by the judge to discuss the issues of the case. A judge and the two opposing lawyers discuss and evaluate the controversy informally. They consider the simplification and sharpening of the issues, the admissions and disclosure of facts, possible amendments to the pleadings, the limitation of the number of witnesses, the possibility of reaching an out-of-court settlement, and any other matters that may aid in the speedy and just disposition of the action.

The importance of discovery cannot be overestimated. Discovery results in the disclosure of unknown facts, the strengths and weaknesses of each side's proof, and is an educational process for the lawyers and their clients. Each side is, in sports terminology, "scouting" their opponent and learning what they plan to prove and how they intend to do it if the case goes to trial. Justice is not supposed to be determined based on surprise witnesses, trickery, and deceit. Discovery allows the parties to identify the core issues, pin witnesses down so they can't easily change their views at trial, determine witness credibility, especially in the case of experts, and clarify where impeachment and cross-examination will be effective.

Lawyers who fail to comply with discovery rules can gain an outcome determining tactical advantage over their opponents when a case comes to trial. When this occurs, the injured party has the right to ask for judicial intervention and seek the imposition of sanctions against the offending party. The plaintiff/appellants in the following case argued on appeal that they were entitled to a new trial because an expert witness called by the defendant/appellee violated the discovery rules and should not have been allowed to testify to the jury.

Debra Clark v. Frederick J. Klein,
Idaho Supreme Court
No. 26652
March 5, 2002

Ayres (Ayres) (collectively "Appellants") involving the death of their son, Corey Ayres, in which a jury rendered a verdict in favor of Respondent Frederick J. Klein, M.D. (Klein). . . .

Trout, Chief Justice

This is an appeal from a medical malpractice action by Debra A. Clark (Clark) and Allen

Factual and Procedural History

During the late evening of August 3, 1997, or early morning of August 4, 1997, Corey Ayres

(Corey) was injured on Pleasant Valley Road, south of Boise. Corey, who was nineteen-years-old at the time, was apparently kneeling on the back bumper of a pickup truck one of his friends was driving on a dirt road, pretending that he was running behind the pickup, when the pickup hit a bump causing Corey to strike his abdomen on the tailgate of the pickup. After the incident, Corey complained to his friends that he was in pain and they took him to St. Alphonsus Hospital.

At the hospital, Klein examined Corey and requested a CT scan and X-rays. The tests were negative and about two hours after arriving, during the early morning of Sunday, August 4, Klein released Corey to his mother, Clark. Klein told them that Corey would be sore for a couple of days, but that he could return to work when he felt better. The discharge nurse gave Clark instructions as directed by Klein at the time of his release. Corey was given a sample packet of Tylenol with codeine for pain and the nurse told Clark to contact the hospital if Corey vomited, his fever worsened, or his pain increased.

Corey slept most of Sunday and apparently he ate and drank intermittently. On Monday, August 5, at approximately 5:00 a.m., Clark checked on Corey and found that he was still asleep. Clark went to work and called Corey about half an hour later from work and he told her that he was not feeling any better. She told him to take his medication and if that did not help, she would come home. About forty-five minutes later, Clark's daughter called Clark at work and told her Corey had collapsed on the floor and she did not know whether he was breathing. The paramedics were called but were unable to revive Corey, and he died on Monday, August 5, 1997.

An autopsy was performed following Corey's death, which revealed that he had a small tear in his intestine . . . , resulting in an infection (peritonitis), which was the cause of his death.

On March 9, 1998, Clark and Corey's father, Ayres, filed a complaint and demand for a jury trial . . . , seeking damages for wrongful death against Klein and St. Alphonsus Medical Center. . . . The claim against St. Alphonsus was subsequently settled and the claim against Klein was tried before a jury, commencing on May 9, 2000.

At trial, Dr. Renee Bourquard (Bourquard) was allowed to testify as an expert, over Clark's objection. Clark objected that Bourquard, and the substance of her testimony was not properly disclosed [made known to Clark during discovery], despite the fact that Clark had asked Klein in one of her interrogatories to identify any expert witnesses he planned to call at trial and the substance of their testimony. . . .

At the conclusion of the trial, the jury found in favor of Klein, and final judgment was entered on May 18, 2000. Appellants filed a timely notice of appeal thereafter. . . .

The Trial Judge Erred by Allowing Bourquard to Testify

Idaho Rule of Civil Procedure [IRCP] 26(b)(4) provides that a party can request that the opposing party set forth the identity of the opposing party's expert witnesses and the substance of the experts' opinions. Rule 26(e) imposes a duty on parties to seasonably update interrogatory responses and provides that the "trial court may exclude the testimony of witnesses or the admission of evidence not disclosed by a required supplementation of the responses of the party."

This Court has previously held that a trial court abused its discretion and committed reversible error by allowing expert testimony, which was not properly disclosed in violation of Rule 26. *Radmer v. Ford Motor Co.,* . . . (1991). . . . In its analysis . . . , this Court quoted the language of I.R.C.P. 26(e)(1), stating that the rule "unambiguously imposes a continuing duty to supplement responses to discovery with respect to the substance and subject matter of an expert's testimony where the initial responses have been rejected, modified, expanded upon, or otherwise altered in some manner." . . . This Court then quoted the advisory committee to the federal rules, which in reference F.R.C.P. 26 provides:

> In cases of this character [involving expert testimony], a prohibition against discovery of information held by expert witnesses produces in acute form the very evils that discovery has been created to prevent. Effective cross-examination of an expert witness requires advance preparation. . . . Similarly, effective rebuttal requires advance knowledge of the line of testimony of the other side. If the latter is foreclosed by a rule against discovery, the narrowing of issues and elimination of surprise which discovery normally produces are frustrated. . . .

This Court also quoted one scholar for the proposition that:

> It is fundamental that opportunity be had for full cross-examination, and this cannot be done properly in many cases without resort to pretrial discovery, particularly when expert witnesses are involved. . . . Before an attorney can even hope to deal on cross-examination with an unfavorable expert opinion he [or she] must have some idea of the bases of that opinion and the data relied upon. If an attorney is required to await examination at trial to get this information, he [or she] often will have too little time to recognize and expose vulnerable spots in the testimony.

. . . [quoting Friedenthal, Discovery and Use of an Adverse Party's Expert Information, 14 Stan.L.Rev. 455, 485 (1962)] (ellipses in original); . . .

In *Radmer*, . . . [t]his Court thus concluded that "[the plaintiffs] breached their obligation to supplement their discovery responses prior to trial, as required by Rule 26, and as a result Ford was unprepared to meet and effectively challenge [the plaintiffs'] new theory of liability and was prejudiced thereby. Accord-

ingly, we hold that the trial judge committed reversible error in allowing the testimony to come in and remand the case for a new trial." . . .

In the present action, Appellants made a Rule 26(b)(4) request about two years before the trial began, and Klein responded that he had not yet decided which expert witnesses he would call, but he reserved the right to update his response. Klein did not update his response to Appellants' 26(b)(4) request to include Bourquard until after the trial had begun, but Bourquard was allowed to testify over Appellants' objection. Klein asserts that Appellants had notice that Bourquard might be called as an expert witness because she was disclosed by Klein as an expert witness in accordance with the court's scheduling order on January 3, 2000. Even though she was disclosed as a possible expert, however, the substance of Bourquard's testimony was not disclosed at that time as required by Appellants' Rule 26(b)(4) interrogatory. Moreover, the substance of her testimony was not ever disclosed in compliance with Rule 26(b)(4), even at trial within days of her testimony. The transcript reveals that in open court Klein's counsel indicated that Bourquard would serve as an anatomical expert and a causation witness; however, he did not disclose that Bourquard would testify that:

> It would appear to me that what I was describing earlier of a piece of intestine that is bruised, crushed, beginning to leak some bacteria and/or fluid across the wall, but it is not burst apart, was what happened to him in his injury, and that allows him to go along for the whole next day and night without a whole lot of change. And then suddenly something happens to cause the intestine to be torn open, and the only thing time-wise in the discussion was that I believe he vomited in the morning when he thought he was coming apart, somewhere in that time frame.
>
> My assumption would be that the two-centimeter hole tore open at that time. . . .

This was the first time anyone had suggested that the tear in Corey's intestine was not present when Klein discharged him from the hospital. Whether Corey was released from the hospital with a two-centimeter tear in his intestine goes beyond causation and it goes to the standard of care. Whether releasing Corey was a breach of the standard of care, of course, depends on the condition he was in at the time of his release from Klein's care. Because this was the first time that this theory was advanced that Corey did not have the hole in his intestine at the time of his release, Appellants did not have an opportunity to prepare cross-examination or to offer rebuttal testimony. In fact, when Bourquard testified, Appellants' expert witnesses had been excused and had apparently left town, so, Appellants were prejudiced by the ruling that allowed the testimony. Although the trial judge perceived the issue of the testimony as one of discretion, his indication that the burden was on Appellants to file a motion to compel the substance of the testimony was outside the bounds of his discretion. . . . We therefore reverse and order a new trial on that basis. . . .

Conclusion

It was reversible error for the trial judge to allow Bourquard to testify and, therefore, we reverse and remand for a new trial. We award costs to Appellants on appeal.

Case Questions

1. What should a party do when an opponent fails to follow the rules of civil procedure with respect to discovery?
2. The media often depict courtroom lawyers using surprise witnesses and evidence. In reality, thorough discovery usually destroys any possibility of surprise. Is this good or bad? Exhaustive discovery is very expensive. One party will frequently be able to afford more discovery than his or her opponent. Does that change your mind about the value of discovery?

 How do the discovery rules seek to encourage ethical conduct in the context of an adversarial process of litigation?
The Court attempted to balance what two policy considerations in this case?

CIVIL TRIALS

A trial is a legal procedure that is available to parties who have been otherwise unwilling or unable to resolve their differences through negotiations, settlement offers, and even mediation attempts. Trials involve the staging of a confrontation between the plaintiff and the defendant as contradicting witnesses and arguments collide in a courtroom in accordance with procedural and evidentiary rules. The trial process may, as a result of appeals and/or new trials, take many years, but it will ultimately result in a dismissal of the complaint or in a judgment.

In some cases, parties with a right to present their evidence to a jury prefer instead to try their case to a judge. This is called a *bench trial*. Bench trials can be scheduled more quickly, and they take less time to conclude because the procedures associated with the jury are eliminated. Bench trials also cost the parties less money than would the same case tried to a jury.

The right to a federal jury trial is provided by the Seventh Amendment to the U.S. Constitution to parties involved in a common law civil action. The right to a jury trial in the state judicial system is determined by state law and may not exist for some types of actions, such as equitable claims and small claims cases. Federal rules permit parties to stipulate to less than twelve jurors, and local court rules often provide for six.

The judge is responsible for making sure that (1) the jury is properly selected in a jury trial; (2) due process requirements for a fair trial are satisfied; (3) proper rulings are made with respect to the admissibility of evidence; (4) the rules of procedure are followed by the parties; and (5) the judgment is awarded in accordance with law.

Selection of the Jury

The procedure discussed here applies only to jury trials (see Figure 4-4). Jurors are selected at random from a fair cross section of the community and summoned to the courthouse for jury duty.[5] After a case has been assigned to a courtroom, the judge calls in a group of prospective jurors, who take their seats in the jury box. A *voir dire* (literally, "to speak the truth") examination is conducted to determine each juror's qualifications for duty under the appropriate statute, and any grounds for a challenge for cause, or information on which to base a peremptory challenge. A challenge for cause may be based on prejudice or bias. A juror's relationship, business involvement, or other close connection with one of the parties or attorneys may also be considered cause for replacing a juror. Attorneys for both sides may make as many challenges for cause as they wish, and it is within the judge's sound discretion to replace a juror for cause. In addition to the challenges for cause, each party is given a limited number of peremptory challenges that may be exercised for any reason other than race (*Batson v. Kentucky*, 476 U.S. 79 (1986)) or gender (*J. E. B. v. Alabama* ex rel. T.B., 511 U.S. 127 (1994)).

Opening Statements and Examination of Witnesses

After a jury has been selected and sworn, the trial begins with an opening statement by the plaintiff's attorney. The opening statement explains the case in general, including the attorney's legal theories and what he or she intends to prove. The defendant's lawyer may also present an opening statement introducing legal theories of the case and the facts the defense intends to prove.

In order for the plaintiff to win the case, the disputed allegations of the complaint must be proved by presenting evidence. Witnesses and exhibits are produced by both parties to the suit. If witnesses do not voluntarily appear to testify, they may be ordered by means of a *subpoena* (see Figure 4-5) to appear in court. A *subpoena duces tecum* issued by the court commands a witness to produce a document that is in his or her possession. If witnesses refuse to appear, to testify, or to produce required documents, or if they perform any act that disrupts the judicial proceedings, they may be punished for contempt of court.

Judges have much discretion with respect to the order of production of evidence. Normally, a plaintiff's attorney presents the plaintiff's case first. The attorney presents witnesses, documents, and other evidence, and rests the case when he or she decides that enough evidence has been produced to substantiate the allegations. Defendant's lawyer then presents the defendant's case in the same manner. When the defense is finished, the plaintiff's attorney may introduce additional witnesses and exhibits in rebuttal of the defense's case. If new matters are brought out by the rebuttal, the defendant may introduce evidence in rejoinder, limited to answering the new matters.

Both attorneys introduce their own witnesses and question them. This is called *direct examination*. The opposing attorney *cross-examines* the witnesses after the direct examination is completed. Attorneys may conduct *redirect examinations* of their own witnesses following the cross-examinations. Attorneys generally may not ask their own witnesses leading questions (except for preliminary questions to introduce a witness or questions to a hostile witness). A leading question is one that suggests the answer to the witness. For instance, if an attorney asks, "You've never seen this gun before, have you?" the witness is almost told to answer no. Leading questions are permissible on cross-examination because they promote the purpose of cross-examination: testing the credibility of witnesses. Upon cross-examination, for example, an attorney could ask a witness the following question: "Isn't it true, Mr. Smith, that you are a firearms expert?"

RULES OF EVIDENCE

Since 1975, federal trials have been conducted pursuant to the Federal Rules of Evidence (FRE). Although each state is entitled to promulgate its own rules, most states have chosen to adopt the federal rules as their "state rules." Rules of evidence apply to jury and nonjury trials, although they are applied less strictly in the latter. Many of the so-called "rules" are actually more like policy statements because many provide judges with considerable discretion in their application. Trial judges use the rules to control the admissibility of evidence, and their decisions are generally upheld on appeal unless there has been a clear abuse of discretion. Judges will instruct jurors to disregard evidence that has been improperly presented to them, but it is difficult to evaluate the effect that this excluded evidence has on the jurors' decision-making process. Once jurors have heard testimony, they may not be able simply to forget what they have seen and heard. In some situations, the judge may conclude that significant prejudice has occurred and that instructing the jury is an inadequate remedy. Consequently, a mistrial will be declared.

Relevance and Materiality

Evidence, whether it be testimony, demonstrative evidence (such as photographs, charts, and graphs), or physical evidence, is admissible only if it is relevant. That is, it must logically tend to prove or disprove some issue of consequence that is in dispute at the trial. Irrelevant evidence confuses the jury, wastes court time, and is often prejudicial. Relevancy is sometimes confused with materiality, which has to do with the probative value of evidence. Probative evidence tends to prove something of importance to the case. Relevant evidence that has little

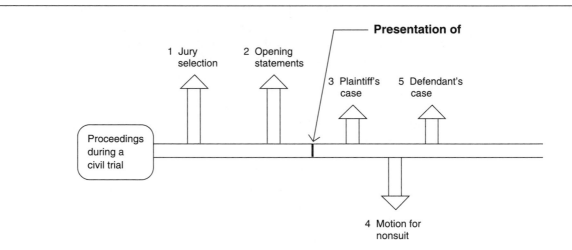

1   Prospective jurors are questioned by attorneys and judge. A prospective juror is dismissed if an attorney successfully makes a challenge for cause or exercises a peremptory challenge.

2   Attorneys explain facts of case in general to judge and jury. Plaintiff's attorney's opening argument usually precedes defendant's.

3   Plaintiff's attorney presents witnesses, documents, and other evidence to substantiate allegations in complaint.

4   Defendant's attorney moves for an involuntary dismissal (motion for nonsuit) if it is felt that plaintiff failed to prove allegations. If judge agrees, motion is granted and plaintiff loses. If judge disagrees, motion is denied and trial continues.

5   Defendant's attorney presents witnesses, documents, and other evidence to rebut plaintiff's case.

6   Plaintiff's attorney presents evidence to rebut evidence brought out during presentation of defendant's case.

7   Defendant's attorney presents evidence to rebut any new matters brought out during plaintiff's rebuttal.

8   After both parties rest their case, either or both parties may move for a directed verdict. If judge feels that reasonable persons could not disagree that the moving party should win, judge grants motion. If motion is granted, moving party wins and trial is over. If motion is denied, trial continues.

FIGURE 4-4   Proceedings During a Civil Trial

probative value is immaterial. Evidence that is either immaterial or irrelevant should be excluded.

Competency

Evidence must be competent (legally adequate) to be admissible. Competency is a broad concept. To be competent, witnesses have to take an oath or affirm that they will testify truthfully. A nonexpert witness is limited to testimony

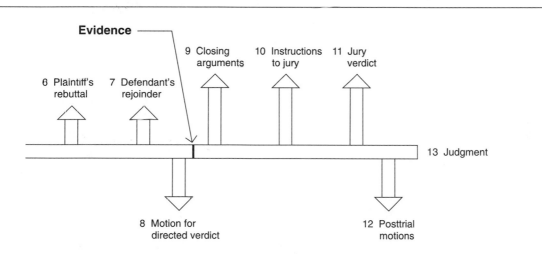

9   Both attorneys sum up evidence for jury. They suggest how the jury should resolve specific disputed items. Plaintiff's attorney argues first, but may reserve time to rebut defendant's attorney's closing argument.

10 Judge explains substantive law to jury, and tells how it should be applied to facts. Both attorneys may suggest specific instructions to judge, but final instructions are left to judge's discretion.

11 After deliberation, jury returns either a general or special verdict or both. A general verdict is simply a declaration of winner and amount of recovery. A special verdict answers specific factual questions requested by judge.

12 After jury returns its verdict, either or both parties may move to have verdict set aside by filing a motion for a new trial or a motion for a judgment notwithstanding verdict of jury or relief from judgment. If the judge grants the motion, judge renders judgment in accordance with jury verdict.

13 By rendering judgment, judge declares who prevailed at trial and amount of recovery. If losing party does not voluntarily pay prescribed amount, winning party can force payment by obtaining an order of execution.

UNITED STATES DISTRICT COURT
FOR THE . . . . . DISTRICT OF . . . . .
. . . . DIVISION

. . . .
Plaintiff,

v.   Civil Action No. . . . .

. . . .
Defendant.

To: . . . . *[name and address of witness]*
    You are commanded to appear in the United States District Court for
the . . . . District of . . . . , at . . . . in the City of . . . . ,
State of . . . . . on the . . . . . day of . . . . . , 20 . . . . . at . . . . . o'clock
. . . . . .M. to testify on behalf of . . . . . in the above pending action.
Dated . . . . . , 20 . . . . . .
[Name and address of attorney]

[Signature and title of clerk]

[Seal]

FIGURE 4-5   Subpoena—For Attendance of Witness [FRCP 45(a)]

about what he or she has heard or seen firsthand; the opinions and conclusions
of such a witness are "incompetent."

As fact-finder, the jury must draw its own conclusions from the evidence.
However, where special expertise is required to evaluate a fact situation, a jury
may not be competent to form an opinion. In that case, a person with special
training, knowledge, or expertise may be called to testify as an expert witness.
Doctors, for example, are frequently called as expert witnesses in personal injury
cases. The qualifications and expertise of such witnesses must be established to
the court's satisfaction before an expert witness's opinion is admissible.

The Best Evidence Rule

The best evidence rule requires that, unless they are unobtainable, original documents rather than copies be introduced into evidence. Even when the original

writing is unobtainable, secondary evidence of the contents is admissible only if the unavailability is not the fault of the party seeking to introduce the evidence. In this situation, the best available alternative proof must be presented. For example, a carbon copy of a writing is preferred over oral testimony as to its contents.

The Hearsay Rule

The Hearsay evidence rule excludes proceeding not from the personal knowledge of the witness but from the repetition of what was said or written outside court by another person, and which is offered for the purpose of establishing the truth of what was written or said. The person who made the out-of-court statement may have been lying, joking, or speaking carelessly. The witness reporting the statement in court may have a poor memory. This exclusionary rule guarantees the opportunity to cross-examine the person who made the out-of-court statement and prevents highly unreliable evidence from being considered.

The hearsay rule contains many exceptions. The *spontaneous declarations exception* (in legalese called *res gestae*) permits courts to admit in court spontaneous declarations uttered simultaneously with the occurrence of an act. The basis for the admission is the belief that a statement made instinctively at the time of an event, without the opportunity for formulation of a statement favorable to one's own cause, is likely to be truthful. In the next case, Storytown U.S.A. Inc. appeals a trial court's ruling that testimony benefitting the plaintiff was admissible under the spontaneous declarations exception to the hearsay evidence rule.

Terry L. LaGuesse v. Storytown U.S.A. Inc.

Supreme Court of New York, Appellate Division, Third Department
91112
July 25, 2002

Spain, J.

. . . Plaintiff Terry L. LaGuesse (hereinafter plaintiff) and her husband, . . . commenced this action to recover damages for personal injuries sustained by plaintiff on August 23, 1996 while visiting defendant Great Escape, an amusement park located in the Town of Lake George, Warren County. According to plaintiff's unrefuted testimony, when she bent over to look at something in a western jailhouse exhibit, a grate made of iron bars which was affixed to the top half of the wall came loose and struck her on her head, back and shoulder. Following a trial, a jury awarded plaintiffs $283,062.60, of which $175,000 was designated for future pain and suffering. [The trial court] . . . entered judgment and subsequently denied defendants' motion to set aside the verdict. Defendants appeal from the judgment and the order denying their motion to set aside the verdict. . . .

. . . [D]efendants argue that [the trial court] . . . committed reversible error by admitting hearsay evidence at trial on the issue of defendants' notice of the alleged unreasonably unsafe condition. Plaintiff testified that after she was struck, she left the exhibit with the assistance of her husband and immediately stopped two park employees and described the accident to them. Over defendants' objection, [the trial court] . . . permitted plaintiff to testify further that, after the employees inspected the jailhouse, one of them told plaintiff that a screw had broken. Defendants also objected to testimony given by plaintiff's husband to the effect that, at the first aid station just a few minutes after the accident, one of the employees told him that they had tried to fix the grate the day before but it had broken again.

[The trial court] . . . found these statements to be spontaneous declarations admissible as an exception to the hearsay rule because they were made by defendants' employees within minutes of a startling event— i.e., the appearance of a seriously injured, distressed patron of the facility. . . . Following [the trial court's] . . . ruling on this issue, the Court of Appeals decided *Tyrrell v. Wal-Mart Stores* (. . . 762 N.E.2d 921) in which it rejected as inadmissible hearsay a statement allegedly made by an unidentified Wal-Mart employee immediately after a patron fell. There, the Court made clear that more is required to demonstrate a spontaneous declaration than the mere fact that at the time he or she made the statement, the employee was assisting a patron of his or her employer immediately after an accident. As in *Tyrrell v. Wal-Mart Stores* (supra), here the declarant [the person making a declaration] was not a witness to the accident and "plaintiffs failed to show that at the time of the statement the declarant was under the stress of excitement caused by an external event sufficient to still [his] reflective faculties and had no opportunity for deliberation." . . . Accordingly, plaintiffs failed to meet their burden of demonstrating that the statements allegedly made by the employees fell within the spontaneous declaration exception to the hearsay rule. . . .

The statements, therefore, were inadmissible hearsay and improperly admitted. Defendants contend that reversal is necessary as the improperly admitted statements were the only direct evidence that they had notice of the dangerous condition. We disagree. The first statement—simply that "a screw broke"— is a fact conceded in the testimony of an assistant general manager of the amusement park and nowhere contested by defendants. Although the second hearsay statement—that the grate had been repaired the day before—clearly goes to the issue of notice, at trial plaintiffs submitted expert testimony on that issue from a civil engineer who inspected the scene. Relying on the condition of the wooden frame where the iron grate had been affixed to the wall—specifically a series of holes and gouges in the wood—the expert was able to opine that "the grate had been attached several times with screws or nails and that these had pulled out, and that as they pulled out, they ripped portions of the wood." Relying on the condition of the wooden frame and the fact that sheetrock screws had improperly been used to attach the bars to the frame, creating a risk that the bars would fall, the expert also testified that the grate had not been properly maintained. Given this evidence that the screws had repeatedly failed in the past and that the grate thereafter had been improperly reattached to the wall, we find ample admissible and credible evidence upon which the jury could have based its conclusion that defendants, in the exercise of reasonable care, knew or should have known of the dangerous condition. Thus, we find the error in improperly admitting hearsay evidence to be harmless inasmuch as the statements were cumulative to other evidence presented at trial. . . .

ORDERED that judgment and order are affirmed. . . .

Case Questions

1. Why did the appellate court rule that the employee statements did not qualify for admission into evidence under the spontaneous exclamation exception to the hearsay rule?
2. Why, then, did the court refuse to set aside the verdict and affirm the entry of judgment on behalf of the plaintiff?

Privileges

Evidence may also be excluded because a privilege exists. Witnesses cannot be forced to give testimony that might expose them to a criminal prosecution. Confidential communications between husband and wife are often privileged in judicial proceedings, as well as information given by a patient to a doctor for the purpose of treatment. All jurisdictions recognize the attorney-client privilege in order to encourage informed legal services. The privilege applies to all communications from a client to a lawyer in the course of professional consultation. In addition, the attorney's work product, including all matters considered to be part of the preparation of a case, is privileged. These privileges may be waived by the witness for whose protection they are intended.

The following case involves the physician-patient privilege. This privilege permits a patient to prevent his or her physician from disclosing confidential medical information the patient has revealed to the doctor while receiving professional services.

Raymond Binkley v. Georgette Allen
Case No. 2000CA00160
Ohio Court of Appeals, Fifth Appellate District
February 5, 2001

Opinion: Reader, V. J.

. . . The relevant facts leading to this appeal are as follows. On October 19, 1999, appellee filed a personal injury action against appellant regarding an automobile collision which occurred in July 1999. The complaint sought compensatory and punitive damages from appellant, as well as underinsured motorist benefits from appellee's own insurance company, Ohio Casualty Group, Inc.

On December 30, 1999, appellee propounded his set of interrogatories and a request for production of documents to appellant. Appellant's responses were not to appellee's satisfaction, which resulted in the appellee's filing of a motion to compel discovery on April 24, 2000. Appellant filed a brief in opposition on May 1, 2000.

On May 3, 2000, the trial court issued a judgment entry granting appellee's motion in part, and denying it in part. The entry effectively ordered, inter alia, that appellant furnish her social security number, her unlisted telephone number, the names of any drug and alcohol treatment centers she had utilized, and any prescription drugs appellant may have taken on the day of the accident.

Appellant filed her notice of appeal therefrom on June 2, 2000, and herein raises the following two Assignments of Error:

I. The Trial Court Erred in Ordering Defendant to Disclose Her Prescription Drug Use and Prior Medical Treatment since Such Information Is Privileged Pursuant to R.C. 2317.

II. [omitted] . . .

I. Appellant, in her First Assignment of Error, contends that the trial court improperly ordered her to disclose privileged medical information during discovery. . . .

Turning to the specifics of [this] case . . . , we start with the interrogatories in dispute, which request appellant to "state whether you were taking any prescription medications at the time of the collision, [and] to state any visits to treatment for drug or alcohol abuse." . . . We commence with the prescription medication issue.

Our initial task is to determine whether the disclosure of a patient's status as a user of prescription medication results in the effective disclosure of a privileged communication between the patient and the physician. The necessary definition is found in [Revised Code] R.C. 2317.02(B): (4)(a) As used in divisions (B)(1) to (3) of this section, "communication" means acquiring, recording, or transmitting any information, in any manner, concerning any facts, opinions, or statements necessary to enable a physician or dentist to diagnose, treat, prescribe, or act for a patient. A "communication" may include, but is not limited to, any medical or dental, office, or hospital communication such as a record, chart, letter, memorandum, laboratory test and results,

x-ray, photograph, financial statement, diagnosis, or prognosis.

In applying the above provision, we take historical note that there is no physician-patient privilege under Ohio common law. . . . "Because the privilege is entirely statutory and in derogation of the common law, it must be strictly construed against the party seeking to assert it." . . . Other jurisdictions have equally ascertained: "Since the protection against privileged communications often leads to a suppression of the truth and to a defeat of justice, the tendency of the courts is toward a strict construction of such statutes." . . . Even as strictly construed against appellant, however, we find that the broad definition of "communication" recited in Ohio's statute would include the requested answer to the prescription medication interrogative. In *State v. Spencer* (1998), . . . the Eighth District Court of Appeals broached this issue in a physician's appeal of a judgment which found him in contempt for failing to produce medical records relating to his prescriptions of anabolic steroids. Because the facts revealed "a suspicion of criminality", the Court affirmed the trial court's refusal to allow the physician to use privilege as a shield: "When the unrebutted evidence supports the contention that prescribed pharmaceuticals far exceed the dosage levels generally accepted in the medical community, that circumstance takes the claimed 'communication' outside the realm of 'privilege.'" . . . What is important in *Spencer*, for our present purposes, is the apparent underlying presumption that the prescription information would have been considered privileged, but for the suspicious nature of the dosages involved. Thus, questions during discovery in a civil action pertaining to a party's use of prescription medications are presumptively part of privileged communication between the party and his or her physician, absent a waiver.

Our next step is therefore determining the existence of any waiver to appellant's privileged information. . . . A review of the record on appeal reveals [no] . . . waiver. Appellee nonetheless argues in his brief that appellant incorrectly "took a simple request for the identity of the medications she was taking on the day of the collision and mutated it into a request for her medical records." . . . However, the evidence in the record simply does not demonstrate that privilege was waived, whether the requested information is voluminous or meager. As one Indiana court has succinctly observed: "Clearly, the method or means by which a physician treats his patient is so intimately connected with the nature of the patient's illness, malady or injury, the mere revelation thereof may tacitly reveal the patient's illness, injury, or malady." *Sharp v. State* (Ind. App. 1991), . . . We therefore find merit in appellant's position that the compelling of her prescription medication information was improper under the facts and circumstances of this case.

We next turn to appellant's argument regarding the compelled disclosure of her drug and alcohol treatment visits. Appellant first asserts that appellant's history is protected as confidential under R.C. 3793.13. We are unpersuaded by this argument. The statute, by its clear language, applies to "records or information . . . pertaining to the identity, diagnosis, or treatment of any patient which are maintained in connection with the performance of any drug treatment program. . . ." The requested information in [this case] . . . is not the maintained records of a licensed drug treatment program, but instead merely seeks appellant's recollection of the names of any treatment centers she has utilized, if any. We therefore find the specific confidentiality statute inapplicable to the disputed interrogatory. Appellant also argues that the compelled drug treatment information, i.e., the name of any treatment center ever utilized, is privileged. We disagree. Unlike the medication list discussed previously, this basic request for information cannot be legitimately classified as a physician-patient communication. One court has noted the following in regard to this type of general question: "On a rudimentary level, R.C. 2317.02 does not prevent the physician from testifying under oath that he was consulted in a professional capacity by a person on a certain date." *State v. Spencer,* supra, . . . We reiterate that the issue herein is that of privilege; the issue of relevancy is not presently under appeal. The trial court did not err, as urged by appellant, in compelling her to answer the drug and alcohol treatment interrogatory. Appellant's First Assignment of Error is sustained in part and overruled in part. . . .

For the reasons stated in the foregoing opinion, the decision of the Court of Common Pleas, Stark County, is hereby affirmed in part and reversed in part. The trial court's order to compel disclosure of appellant's prescription medications is hereby vacated. In all other respect, the judgment is affirmed, and the matter is remanded to the trial court for any and all remaining proceedings.

Case Questions

1. The Ohio Court of Appeals indicated that the doctor-patient privilege is strictly statutory and has no common law basis in Ohio. As such, said the court, it should be strictly construed against the party claiming it. That means the privilege should be applied only when the statute clearly provides for its use. Ambiguities should be resolved against its application. What policy reason supports this narrow application?

2. Why did the appellate court agree with the plaintiff that she did not have to answer the interrogatory question requiring her to disclose any prescription medications she was taking at the time her vehicle collided with the vehicle of the defendant?

3. Why did the appellate court agree with the defendant that the plaintiff should have to answer the interrogatory requesting disclosure of the names of treatment centers the plaintiff had visited?

Trial Motions

If, after the plaintiff's attorney presents plaintiff's case, the defendant's attorney believes that the plaintiff was unable to substantiate the essential allegations adequately, the defendant may make a *motion for nonsuit*. The judge grants the motion only if a reasonable person could not find in favor of the plaintiff after considering the evidence most favorable to the plaintiff. If the motion is granted, the case is over and the plaintiff loses.

If the motion for a nonsuit is denied or not made at all, the defendant's lawyer then presents the defendant's case and tries to disprove the plaintiff's evidence or substantiate the defendant's arguments. Witnesses and exhibits are presented, following the same procedure as the plaintiff's—direct examination followed by cross-examination. After the defendant rests his or her case, the plaintiff then may produce evidence to rebut the defendant's evidence.

At the end of the presentation of evidence, but before the issues are submitted to the jury, either or both parties may make a motion for a directed verdict. The motion is granted for the party making the motion if the judge decides that the case is perfectly clear and that reasonable people could not disagree on the result. If the motion is granted, the moving party wins the dispute without the jury deciding the case. If no motion for a directed verdict is made, or if made and denied, the case is submitted to the jury.

Jury Verdict and Posttrial Motions

Both attorneys have an opportunity to make oral arguments to the jury summarizing their cases. The judge then instructs the members of the jury as to how they should proceed. Although jury deliberations are secret, certain restrictions must be observed to avoid possible grounds for setting aside the verdict. These include prohibitions on juror misconduct, such as drunkenness; the use of unauthorized evidence, such as secretly visiting the scene of an accident; or disregarding the judge's instructions, such as discussing the merits of the case over lunch with a friend.

After the verdict has been rendered, a party not satisfied with it may move for judgment notwithstanding the verdict, a new trial, or relief from judgment.

A motion for *judgment notwithstanding the verdict* (j.n.o.v.) is granted when the judge decides that reasonable people could not have reached the verdict that the jury has reached. A *new trial* before another jury may be granted by a judge for a variety of reasons, including excessive or grossly inadequate damages, newly discovered evidence, questionable jury verdict, errors in the production of evidence, or simply the interest of justice. A motion for *relief from judgment* is granted if the judge finds a clerical error in the judgment, newly discovered evidence, or fraud that induced the judgment.

The appellant in the following case made a motion for a directed verdict at the close of all the evidence. She also made postverdict motions for j.n.o.v. and a new trial. She appealed from the court's denial of all three motions.

Cody v. Atkins
658 P.2d 59
Supreme Court of Wyoming
February 4, 1983

Raper, Justice

This appeal arose from a negligence action brought by Lois M. Cody (appellant) against Alfred Atkins (appellee) for injuries she allegedly sustained in an automobile collision between her car and appellee's pickup. Appellant appeals from the judgment on a jury verdict entered by the district court in favor of appellee. . . .

At about 7:00 o'clock A.M. on the morning of November 13, 1980, appellant's car was struck from behind by a pickup driven by appellee. At the time of the accident appellant was stopped for a red light in the right-hand, west-bound lane of 16th Street at the intersection of 16th Street and Snyder Avenue in Cheyenne, Wyoming. The right front corner of appellee's vehicle struck the left rear corner of appellant's car. In the words of a police officer who investigated the accident, the lane of traffic in which the accident occurred was ice covered and "very slick." It was overcast and snowing lightly at the time the accident occurred but visibility was not impaired. Neither party complained of injuries when questioned by the investigating officer at the accident scene; however, later that day appellant complained of injuries and was taken to the emergency room at Memorial Hospital where she was examined and released. Appellant was subsequently hospitalized and treated for numerous physical complaints that she alleged resulted from the accident.

Appellant brought suit June 5, 1981, complaining that appellee's negligent operation of his vehicle had caused harm to her. On March 1, 1982, appellant filed an amended complaint against appellee. Appellee answered the complaints by admitting that his pickup collided with appellant's car but denying appellant's remaining allegations of negligence, etc.; there were no counterclaims made nor affirmative defenses asserted by appellee. The matter was tried before a six-person jury May 10 and 11, 1982, in the district court in Cheyenne. At the close of appellee's case, appellant made a motion for directed verdict. . . . The district court denied the motion. The jury then, after receiving its instructions and deliberating on the matter, returned a verdict in favor of appellee. Following the trial, appellant made timely motions for a new trial . . . and for a judgment notwithstanding the verdict. . . . The district court denied both motions; this appeal followed.

I

The first issue appellant raises for our consideration is the propriety of the district court's denial of his motion for a directed verdict. . . . We . . . have held that since a directed verdict deprives the parties of a determination of the facts by a jury, such motion should be cautiously and sparingly granted. . . .

In the majority of our decisions in which directed verdicts are at issue, we have dealt with directed verdicts sought by the defendant; here we are faced with the opposite situation of a plaintiff seeking a directed verdict. In general, the standard in directing a verdict for a plaintiff is similar to the standard used to direct one against him. . . . It is proper to direct a verdict for the plaintiff in those rare cases where there are no genuine issues of fact to be submitted to a jury. . . . In a negligence action a verdict may be directed for the plaintiff when there is no evidence that would justify a jury verdict for the defendant. . . . A directed verdict for the plaintiff is proper when there is no dispute as to a material fact, and when reasonable jurors cannot draw any other inferences from the facts than that propounded by the plaintiff. . . . In a negligence action, then, we need only determine that there was sufficient evidence to permit a reasonable jury to find that the defendant acted without negligence to hold that appellant's motion was properly denied. We so hold.

In this case appellee presented evidence that the roadway he was traveling on was slippery due to snow and ice; that he had been attempting to slow down and to stop to avoid a collision for some 400 feet prior to impact; that he had slowed from 20 m.p.h. to 5 m.p.h. in the 400 feet prior to impact; that he had attempted to drive to the left and avoid the collision; that his ability to stop was further complicated because he was traveling downhill; and that he was in control of his vehicle at all times prior to the collision. Although we were unable to find where appellee had testi-

fied in so many words that he had not been negligent, the jury could have properly inferred as much from the evidence we have outlined. Although appellant contends otherwise, the concept of an automobile accident occurring without a finding of negligence is not novel in our jurisprudence. . . . The district court could not have, in the face of appellee's evidence showing an absence of negligence, directed a verdict for appellant. Therefore, we hold the district court properly denied appellant's motion for directed verdict.

II

Appellant next argues that the district court erred in denying her motion for a judgment notwithstanding the verdict (J.N.O.V.). . . . As previously noted, appellant had sought and had been denied a directed verdict at the close of the evidence; therefore, we reach this issue. Before deciding the issue, however, we first set out the standard of review we shall employ. . . .

J.N.O.V. can only be granted where there is an absence of any substantial evidence to support the verdict entered. . . . The test then for granting a J.N.O.V. is virtually the same as that employed in determining whether a motion for directed verdict should be granted or denied. . . .

The logic behind similar standards of review is that it allows the district court another opportunity to determine the legal question of sufficiency of the evidence raised by the motion after the jury has reached a verdict. . . . In close cases the J.N.O.V. procedure promotes judicial economy. When a J.N.O.V. is reversed, for example, an appellate court can remand for reinstatement of the original verdict, where a new trial is generally required when a directed verdict is reversed. . . .

In the case before us, we have, in ruling on the directed verdict question, already held that there was sufficient evidence presented to create a question of fact for the jury to determine on the issue of appellee's negligence. For those same reasons we must also hold that the district court correctly denied appellant's motion for a J.N.O.V.

III

We next reach appellant's final argument that the district court erred in denying her motion for a new trial. . . . Appellant's motion set forth the following grounds for obtaining a new trial:

"1. That the Verdict is not Sustained by sufficient Evidence and is Contrary to Law.
"2. That Errors of Law were Committed at the Trial."

Appellant then centers her argument around the first ground. The position appellant takes is that she was entitled to a new trial because the jury's verdict was not consistent with the evidence. We disagree. . . .

A court's exercise of the power to grant a new trial is not a derogation of the right of a jury trial but is one of that right's historic safeguards. . . . The power to grant a new trial gives the trial court the power to prevent a miscarriage of justice. . . . Trial courts should grant new trials whenever, in their judgment, the jury's verdict fails to administer substantial justice to the parties. . . .

"The right of trial by jury includes the right to have the jury pass upon questions of fact by determining the credibility of witnesses and the weight of conflicting evidence. The findings of fact, however, are subject to review by the trial judge who, like the jury, has had the benefit of observing the demeanor and deportment of the witnesses. If he concludes that the evidence is insufficient to support the verdict, he should grant a new trial. . . ."

This court has acknowledged that when a court could have properly granted a J.N.O.V. for insufficient evidence, it was not error to

grant a motion for a new trial. . . . That does not mean, however, that the same standards apply for granting a new trial and a J.N.O.V.; the standard must be more lenient for exercising the power to grant new trials to preserve that power's historic role as a safety valve in our system of justice. . . .

"When the evidence is wholly insufficient to support a verdict, it is the duty of the trial court to direct a verdict or enter a judgment n.o.v., and the court has no discretion in that respect. But, the granting of a new trial involves an element of discretion which goes further than the mere sufficiency of the evidence. It embraces all the reasons which inhere in the integrity of the jury system itself. . . ."

It is well settled in Wyoming that trial courts are vested with broad discretion when ruling on a motion for new trial, and that on review we will not overturn the trial court's decision except for an abuse of that discretion. . . .

In this case, appellant argues there was not sufficient evidence before the jury to entitle them to find in favor of appellee. As we pointed out in our discussion of appellant's first issue, appellee presented sufficient evidence to permit the jury to reach the issue of negligence. Also, as we said earlier, the mere fact that the collision occurred does not in itself indicate negligence. Therefore, after hearing the testimony of the witnesses and observing their demeanor, the district court exercised its discretion and denied appellant's motion for a new trial. The district court thereby indicated its belief that under the circumstances of the case no substantial injustice would occur in upholding the jury's verdict. Appellant has presented no convincing argument that would persuade us that the district court abused its discretion. Therefore, we hold that the district court did not err when it denied appellant's motion for a new trial.

Affirmed.

Case Questions

1. Does granting a new trial because the jury awarded excessive damages infringe on the plaintiff's constitutional right to a jury trial?
2. Does a reduction of the amount of damages by the court as a condition for denying a new trial invade the province of the jury?
3. When is it proper for a judge to grant a directed verdict motion?
4. What is the purpose of the motion for judgment notwithstanding the verdict (j.n.o.v.)?

Additur and Remittitur

On occasion, juries award money damages that are, in the view of the trial or appellate courts, insufficient as a matter of law. When a jury finds for the plaintiff and the money damage award is grossly excessive, the defendant is entitled to ask the trial and appellate courts to reduce the size of the award by awarding the defendant a *remittitur*. Both state and federal judges, with the consent of the plaintiff, can reduce unreasonably high jury verdicts. If the trial court awards a remittitur, the plaintiff can agree to accept a reduced sum in an amount determined by the court, refuse to remit any of the jury's award, in which case the trial court will order a new trial on damages, or appeal to a higher court. The appellant in the following case, Carl and Vera Griggs, successfully requested the Missouri Court of Appeals to award a remittitur, after the trial judge entered judgment for the plaintiff in accordance with the jury's verdict.

Armon v. Griggs
Missouri Court of Appeals, Western District
WD59138
11/20/2001

William E. Turnage, Senior Judge

Carl and Vera Griggs appeal from the judgment entered on a jury verdict in favor of Michael Armon in his action for wrongful eviction and conversion. Mr. Armon sued the Griggses after Mr. Griggs changed the locks on the building Mr. Armon was leasing for use as a bar. On appeal, Mr. and Mrs. Griggs raise several arguments, only one of which is of import. . . .

Facts

Carl and Vera Griggs leased a building to Michael Jarman for use as a bar. At some point, Mr. Jarman decided to put his bar up for sale. Jeff Williams, hearing of the sale, contacted Mr. Jarman and, after negotiation, entered into an agreement for the purchase of the bar. The agreement between Mr. Jarman and Mr. Williams was contingent upon Mr. Williams' acquisition of a liquor license. When the City of Excelsior Springs denied Mr. Williams a liquor license, Mr. Williams contacted a friend, Michael Armon, and proposed that Mr. Armon purchase and manage the bar, using Mr. Williams as his advisor. Mr. Armon agreed and thereafter purchased the business from Mr. Jarman. Mr. Armon also entered into a lease agreement with Mr. and Mrs. Griggs for the building that housed the bar.

In April of 1998, Mr. Armon was cited for a liquor violation and as a result was ordered to shut down the bar. Soon afterwards, Mr. Armon and Mr. Williams met with Mr. Griggs to inform him that they would be late in making payment on rent but that they would pay as soon as possible and continue paying rent thereafter. Mr. Armon then left town for two weeks to visit his father. Upon his return, Mr. Armon discovered that the locks had been changed at the bar. After several attempts to contact Mr. and Mrs. Griggs, Mr. Armon filed suit. . . . Eventually, the Griggses permitted Mr. Armon to go back into the bar, by this time, however, "[a]lmost every item of value was missing."

The case was submitted and the jury returned verdicts in favor of Mr. Armon awarding him $52,290 on count I for wrongful eviction, $92,365 on count III for conversion, and $1 in punitive damages on count III for conversion. The trial court entered judgment consistent with the verdicts. Mr. and Mrs. Griggs then filed a motion for new trial or in the alternative for remittitur, which the trial court overruled. . . . This appeal followed. . . .

. . . Mr. and Mrs. Griggs assert that the trial court erred in denying their motion for new trial or remittitur because the verdict . . . for conversion was excessive.

The assessment of damages is primarily a function of the jury. . . . A trial court has great discretion in approving a verdict or setting it aside as excessive. . . . An appellate court, therefore, "will interfere only when the verdict is so grossly excessive that it shocks the conscience of the court and convinces the

court that both the jury and the trial court abused their discretion." . . .

This court now considers whether the trial court erred in overruling the Griggses motion for remittitur. Remittitur may be ordered where the jury errs by awarding a verdict that is simply too bountiful under the evidence. . . . A new trial is not required because the jury made an honest mistake as to the nature and extent of damages. . . . Remittitur is appropriate "if, after reviewing the evidence in support of the jury's verdict, the court finds that the jury's verdict is excessive because the amount of the verdict exceeds fair and reasonable compensation for plaintiff's . . . damages." . . .

In this case, Mr. Armon prayed for "a money judgment equal to the amount of property . . . converted." Several dollar figures were adduced from the witnesses at trial. Based on this court's review of the record, the only one of any significance, however, was $37,365, the amount Mr. Williams, plaintiff's witness, testified was the total sum for the property that was either not recovered or was beyond economic repair as a result of the conversion. Thus, $37,365 was the maximum amount that Mr. Armon could recover in an action for conversion, as it was the "reasonable market value [of the property] at the time of conversion." . . . Mr. Armon was not entitled to any consequential damages because he did not present evidence to support such damages. . . . The jury awarded Mr. Armon $92,365 in actual damages . . . for conversion, an amount in excess of that actually supported by the evidence. Remittitur, therefore, was necessary. Thus, it was an abuse of discretion for the trial court to deny Mr. and Mrs. Griggs' motion for remittitur. . . .

In conclusion, the verdict . . . for conversion of $92,365 exceeds fair and reasonable compensation for Mr. Armon's damages. Section 537.068. The award is excessive in the amount of $55,000. An appellate court may not compel remittitur; it may only order a party plaintiff to remit or experience the burden and expense of a new trial. . . . If Mr. Armon, therefore, enters a remittitur of $55,000 of the judgment against Mr. and Mrs. Griggs within fifteen days after the filing of this court's mandate, that judgment will stand affirmed for $37,365 as of the date of its original entry; otherwise, that judgment is reversed and the cause remanded for a new trial on the issue of damages only.

Case Questions

1. What is the purpose of the remittitur process?
2. Why did the Missouri Court of Appeals conclude that remittitur was appropriate in this case?
3. What options did the plaintiff have after the appellate court's ruling?

When a jury's award is grossly inadequate, a prevailing party in state court is often entitled to ask the trial court to award the plaintiff an additional sum of money (called *additur*). If the trial court agrees it will specify an additional amount for the defendant to pay the plaintiff. In that event, the defendant can agree to pay the additur, refuse to pay, in which case the trial court will order a new trial on damages, or appeal to a higher court. Federal judges cannot award additur because of the Seventh Amendment. It provides that "no fact tried by a jury shall be otherwise reexamined . . . than according to the rules of the common law." This means that no federal judge can award money damages in an amount above the sum awarded by the jury.

 INTERNET TIP ─────────────────────────────

Students wishing to read a case in which additur was awarded are invited to visit the textbook's website for the case of *Ruben Dilone v. Anchor Glass Container Corporation.*

Judgment and Execution

The trial process concludes with the award of a *judgment.* The judgment determines the rights of the disputing parties and decides what relief is awarded (if any). A judgment is awarded after the trial court has ruled on posttrial motions. Appeals are made from the court's entry of judgment. Either party (or both) may appeal from a trial court's judgment to an appellate court.

A person who wins a judgment is called a judgment creditor, and the person who is ordered to pay is called a judgment debtor. Many times the judgment debtor will comply with the terms of the judgment and deliver property or pay a specified sum of money to the judgment creditor. If necessary, however, the judgment creditor can enforce the judgment by obtaining a writ of execution from the clerk of court where the judgment is filed. The writ will be directed to the sheriff who can then seize the judgment creditor's nonexempt personal property and sell it to satisfy the judgment. An example of a statute exempting specified property from seizure can be seen in Figure 4-6. The statute authorizing judicial sale includes safeguards to prevent abuse of the defendant's rights.

Alternatively, the plaintiff may have a lien placed against the judgment debtor's real property. It is created when the clerk of courts records the judgment (officially informing interested persons of the existence of the lien). The

---

Vermont Statutes Annotated §§ 2740.
GOODS AND CHATTELS; EXEMPTIONS FROM

The goods or chattels of a debtor may be taken and sold on execution, except the following articles, which shall be exempt from attachment and execution, unless turned out to the officer to be taken on the attachment or execution, by the debtor:

(1) the debtor's interest, not to exceed $2,500.00 in aggregate value, in a motor vehicle or motor vehicles;

(2) the debtor's interest, not to exceed $5,000.00 in aggregate value, in professional or trade books or tools of the profession or trade of the debtor or a dependent of the debtor;

(3) a wedding ring;

(4) the debtor's interest, not to exceed $500.00 in aggregate value, in other jewelry held primarily for the personal, family or household use of the debtor or a dependent of the debtor;

(5) the debtor's interest, not to exceed $2,500.00 in aggregate value, in household furnishings, goods or appliances, books, wearing apparel, animals, crops or musical instruments that are held primarily for the personal, family or household use of the debtor or a dependent of the debtor;

(6) growing crops, not to exceed $5,000.00 in aggregate value;

(7) the debtor's aggregate interest in any property, not to exceed $400.00 in value, plus up to $7,000.00 of any unused amount of the exemptions provided under subdivisions (1), (2), (4), (5) and (6) of this section;

(8) one cooking stove, appliances needed for heating, one refrigerator, one freezer, one water heater, sewing machines;

(9) ten cords of firewood, five tons of coals or 500 gallons of oil;

(10) 500 gallons of bottled gas;

(11) one cow, two goats, 10 sheep, 10 chickens, and feed sufficient to keep the cow, goats, sheep or chickens through one winter;

(12) three swarms of bees and their hives with their produce in honey;

(13) one yoke of oxen or steers or two horses kept and used for team work;

(14) two harnesses, two halters, two chains, one plow, and one ox yoke;

FIGURE 4-6   Vermont Statute Exempting Goods and Chattels from Execution

(15) the debtor's interest, not to exceed $700.00 in value, in bank deposits or deposit accounts of the debtor;

(16) the debtor's interest in self-directed retirement accounts of the debtor, including all pensions, all proceeds of and payments under annuity policies or plans, all individual retirement accounts, all Keogh plans, all simplified employee pension plans, and all other plans qualified under sections 401, 403, 408, 408A or 457 of the Internal Revenue Code. However, an individual retirement account, Keogh plan, simplified employee pension plan, or other qualified plan, except a Roth IRA, is only exempt to the extent that contributions thereto were deductible or excludable from federal income taxation at the time of contribution, plus interest, dividends or other earnings that have accrued on those contributions, plus any growth in value of the assets held in the plan or account and acquired with those contributions. A Roth IRA is exempt to the extent that contributions thereto did not exceed the contribution limits set forth in section 408A of the Internal Revenue Code, plus interest, dividends or other earnings on the Roth IRA from such contributions, plus any growth in value of the assets held in the Roth IRA acquired with those contributions. No contribution to a self-directed plan or account shall be exempt if made less than one calendar year from the date of filing for bankruptcy, whether voluntarily or involuntarily. Exemptions under this subdivision shall not exceed $5,000.00 for the purpose of attachment of assets by the office of child support pursuant to 15 V.S.A. §§ 799;

(17) professionally prescribed health aids for the debtor or a dependent of the debtor;

(18) any unmatured life insurance contract owned by the debtor, other than a credit life insurance contract;

(19) property traceable to or the debtor's right to receive, to the extent reasonably necessary for the support of the debtor and any dependents of the debtor:

(A) Social Security benefits;

(B) veteran's benefits;

(C) disability or illness benefits;

(D) alimony, support or separate maintenance;

(E) compensation awarded under a crime victim's reparation law;

(F) compensation for personal bodily injury, pain and suffering or actual pecuniary loss of the debtor or an individual on whom the debtor is dependent;

(G) compensation for the wrongful death of an individual on whom the debtor was dependent;

(H) payment under a life insurance contract that insured the life of an individual on whom the debtor was dependent on the date of that individual's death;

(I) compensation for loss of future earnings of the debtor or an individual on whom the debtor was or is dependent;

(J) payments under a pension, annuity, profit-sharing, stock bonus, or similar plan or contract on account of death, disability, illness, or retirement from or termination of employment.

FIGURE 4-6   Vermont Statute Exempting Goods and Chattels from Execution (*continued*)

judgment debtor's property cannot be transferred until the lien is satisfied. This often means that when the judgment debtor's property is sold, part of the sale proceeds are paid to the judgment creditor to satisfy the lien. Garnishment is another remedy for judgment creditors. It is a process that results in the debtor's employer being ordered to deduct a percentage of the debtor's earnings from each paycheck. These payments are first credited against the debt and then forwarded to the judgment creditor.

Chapter Questions

1. Define the following terms:

additur	motion for directed verdict
alternative dispute resolution	motion for new trial
alternative service	motion for nonsuit
answer	motion for relief from judgment
bench trial	motion for summary judgment
complaint	motion to dismiss
constructive service	oral deposition
contingent fee	personal service
counterclaim	petition
default	pleading
deposition	pretrial conference
direct examination	privilege
directed verdict	process
discovery	production of documents
execution	remittitur
garnishment	reply
general verdict	request for admissions
hearsay	request for waiver of service
judgment	settlement conference
judgment creditor	substituted service
judgment debtor	voir dire
judgment notwithstanding the verdict (j.n.o.v.)	writ of summons
	written deposition
lien	written interrogatories

2. The Stars' Desert Inn Hotel filed suit against Richard Hwang, a citizen of Taiwan, to collect on a $1,885,000 gambling debt. The parties were unable to cooperate in scheduling a date for taking defendant Hwang's deposition. The court, aware of the scheduling problem, entered an order requiring that the deposition be taken no later than November 29, 1994. Stars requested that Hwang provide at least two dates prior to the deadline when he would be available to be deposed. When Hwang failed to respond to this request, Stars set the date for November 23. Hwang's lawyers responded on November 21

with a proposal that Hwang be deposed in Taiwan prior to November 29. Stars rejected this proposal and filed a motion asking the court to strike Hwang's answer and enter a default judgment in favor of the plaintiff. Hwang's attorneys explained that their client was not cooperating with them and that he refused to be deposed in Nevada. The court imposed a $2,100 fine against Hwang and ordered him to either be deposed in Nevada or to prepay the plaintiff's expenses (estimated by the plaintiff to be between $20,000 and $40,000), for taking the deposition in Taiwan, no later than February 10, 1995. Hwang failed to pay the fine, asserted that the plaintiff's estimate of the costs of taking the deposition in Taiwan were excessive, and refused to comply with either option contained in the court's order. The plaintiff again requested that the court impose the sanctions. Should the court strike the answer and award a default judgment to the plaintiff in the amount of $1,885,000 (plus interest, costs, attorney's fees, and postjudgment interest)? Are there any less drastic steps that should be taken before imposing such a drastic sanction?

Stars' Desert Inn Hotel & Country Club v. Hwang, 105 F.3d 521 (9th Cir. 1997)

3. Colin Cody, a Connecticut resident, invested $200,000 in the common stock of Phillips Company, a firm that installs video gambling machines in Louisiana casinos. Cody brought suit against the defendant, Kevin Ward, a resident of California, alleging that Ward had used an Internet website called "Money Talk " to perpetrate a fraud on potential investors. The gist of Cody's complaint was that Ward had engaged in false and fraudulent misrepresentations about the Phillips' impending financial prospects. Cody claimed to have made decisions about whether to buy and hold Phillips stock in partial reliance on Wade's misrepresentations on the Internet and on telephone calls made by Wade that encouraged Cody to buy and hold Phillips stock. Cody further claimed that the Phillips stock was essentially worthless. Ward sought to dismiss the complaint, alleging that he could not be sued in Connecticut because there were insufficient grounds for personal jurisdiction. Cody maintains that a defendant who orally or in writing causes information to enter Connecticut by wire is committing a tortious act within Connecticut and is subject to suit pursuant to the Connecticut long-arm statute. Do you believe that Ward has committed a tortious act within the forum state, which would satisfy the requirements of the long-arm statute? Do you believe that there is a constitutional basis for Connecticut to exercise *in personam* jurisdiction over Ward?

Cody v. Ward, 954 F.Supp 43 (D. Conn. 1997)

4. The Stars' Desert Inn Hotel filed suit against Richard Hwang, a citizen of Taiwan, to collect on a $1,885,000 gambling debt. Stars unsuccessfully tried to serve Hwang on six occasions at a guarded and gated housing complex in Beverly Hills. The process server, after verifying with the guard that Hwang was inside, left the summons and complaint with the gate attendant. Hwang moved to quash the service. Was Hwang properly served?

Stars' Desert Inn Hotel & Country Club v. Hwang, 105 F.3d 521 (9th Cir. 1997)

5. Colm Nolan and others brought suit against two City of Yonkers police officers and the City of Yonkers, New York, for alleged brutality and false arrest. The plaintiff's process server alleged that he had served both defendants at Police Headquarters (rather than at their place of residence), and also mailed copies of the summons and complaint to each officer at Police Headquarters. New York law provides that a summons can be delivered to "the actual place of business of the person to be served and by mailing a copy to the person to be served at his actual place of business." One defendant admitted receiving a copy of the summons and complaint at his police mailbox; the second officer denied ever receiving either document at Police Headquarters. Neither officer suffered any prejudice because both defendants did receive the summons and complaint and both filed answers in a timely manner. Rule 4 of the Federal Rules of Civil Procedure permits service "pursuant to the law of the state in which the district court is located." The two police officers asked the court to dismiss the complaint for lack of personal jurisdiction. Was the service at Police Headquarters sufficient to confer *in personam* jurisdiction over these defendants?
   Nolan v. City of Yonkers, 168 F.R.D. 140 (S.D.N.Y. 1996)

6. A car driven by James Murphy struck a boy and injured him. Immediately after the accident, according to the boy's mother, Murphy told her "that he was sorry, that he hoped her son wasn't hurt. He said he had to call on a customer and was in a bit of a hurry to get home." At trial, Murphy denied telling the boy's mother that he was involved in his employment at the time of the accident. It was shown, however, that part of his normal duties for his employer, Ace Auto Parts Company, included making calls on customers in his car. Can the mother have the statement admitted in court as a spontaneous exclamation?

7. Wilkinson was a resident of California and an officer of the now defunct St. Paul Transportation Company. In June, Wilkinson was served in California with a criminal summons from a Minnesota court for a misdemeanor allegedly committed when Wilkinson was in Minnesota. The arraignment for the misdemeanor charge was scheduled for September 25. Wilkinson flew to Minnesota to attend the arraignment. As he ascended the courthouse steps, a U.S. marshal approached him and handed him a summons to appear in a civil action brought against him by the Interstate Commerce Commission (ICC) for activities involving the St. Paul Transportation Company. Consider policy questions arising from Wilkinson's appearance in response to the criminal summons. Was the service of summons and complaint on Wilkinson sufficient to give the Minnesota court jurisdiction in the civil action?
   Interstate Commerce Commission v. St. Paul Transportation Co., 39 F.R.D. 309 (D.C. Minn. 1966)

8. James Duke filed a suit against Pacific Telephone & Telegraph Company (PT&T) and two of its employees for invasion of privacy through unauthorized wiretapping. Duke claimed that defendant's employees installed

an interception device on his telephone line without his knowledge or consent for the sole purpose of eavesdropping. Through the use of the bugging devices, defendants acquired information that they communicated to the police department, resulting in his arrest. Although the charges were dismissed, he was discharged from his job. As part of the plaintiff's discovery, oral depositions were taken of the employees. The defendants refused to answer (1) questions relating to the procedure used in making unauthorized tapes of phone conversations (training of personnel, equipment, authority among employees), (2) questions relating to the deponent's knowledge of the illegality of unauthorized monitoring, (3) questions relating to a possible working relationship between the police and PT&T, and (4) questions relating to the monitoring of telephone conversations of subscribers other than the plaintiff. The defendants claimed that these questions were irrelevant to the litigation and therefore not proper matters for discovery. Do you agree?

Pacific Telephone & Telegraph Co. v. Superior Court, 2 Cal.3d 161, 465 P.2d 854, 84 Cal. Rptr. 718 (1970)

9. W. R. Reeves filed suit under the Federal Employers Liability Act against his employer, Central of Georgia Railway Company, seeking damages he allegedly suffered when the train on which he was working derailed near Griffin, Georgia. The liability of the defendant railroad was established at trial, and the issue of damages remained to be fixed. Several physicians testified regarding the injuries received by Reeves. Reeves also testified. On the witness stand, he said that an examining physician had told him that he would be unable to work because of a weakness in his right arm, a dead place on his arm, stiffness in his neck, and nerve trouble in his back. Why did admission of this testimony into evidence constitute reversible error?

Central of Georgia Ry. Co. v. Reeves, 257 So.2d 839 (Ga. 1972)

10. On December 10, 1962, Rosch obtained a judgment against Kelly from the superior court of Orange County, California. The California Code permits execution of a judgment only within ten years after entry of a judgment. If this is not done, the judgment may be enforced only by leave of court, after notice to the judgment debtors, accompanied by an affidavit setting forth the reasons for the failure to proceed earlier. The plaintiff made no attempt to enforce the judgment in California before Kelly moved to Texas in 1970. On February 15, 1974, the plaintiff attempted to execute on the California judgment in Texas. Does the Texas court have to allow execution under the full faith and credit clause?

Rosch v. Kelly, 527 F.2d 871 (5th Cir. 1976)

Notes

1. T. F. F. Plucknett, *A Concise History of the Common Law*, 5th ed. (Boston: Little, Brown and Co., 1956), p. 408.
2. Ibid., pp. 408–409.

3. Ibid., p. 400.
4. Recent amendments to the Federal Rules of Civil Procedure have significantly altered the service requirement in federal court. Rule 4(d) requires plaintiffs to send a copy of the complaint and a request for waiver of service to the defendant. A defendant who signs the waiver of service is allowed sixty days from the date of the notice to file an answer. If the defendant fails to sign the waiver and has no good cause for such refusal, the defendant can be required to pay for the service costs and the plaintiff's costs in going to court to obtain enforcement.
5. Jurors are generally selected from rosters containing lists of taxpayers, licensed drivers, and/or registered voters.

V Institutional Sources of American Law

It is important to understand that the rules constituting American law derive from several authoritative sources. The most important of these are the federal and state constitutions; legislation produced at the federal, state, and local levels of government; decisions of federal and state courts; and the regulations and adjudicatory rulings of federal, state, and local administrative agencies. In this chapter we shall preview each of these major sources of law and focus on the legislative and judicial branches of government.

COMMON LAW AND CIVIL LAW LEGAL SYSTEMS

From your reading of Chapter 1, you have already seen how the English common law system developed over many centuries.[1] You know that as judges decided cases, rules slowly evolved and became recognized as judicial precedents, which began to be written down and followed. These practices made it possible for cases raising a particular issue to be decided in essentially the same way throughout England. With its emphasis on judge-made law, this approach differs markedly from the legal systems found in France, Germany, and Italy. Those countries follow a different approach, often referred to as the civil law system.[2]

Civil law systems are based upon detailed legislative codes rather than judicial precedents. Such a code is a comprehensive, authoritative collection of rules covering all the principal subjects of law. Civil law codes are often developed by academicians and then enacted by legislative bodies. They are based on philosophy, theory, and abstract principles. Civil law systems usually reject the use of precedent, dispense with juries in civil cases, and avoid complex rules of evidence. In civil law countries, judges are expected to base their decisions on the appropriate provisions of the relevant code, and they do not treat the decisions of other judges as authoritative sources.

The civil law tradition traces its roots to historically famous codes of law such as ancient Rome's *Corpus Juris Civilis* and the *Code Napoleon*. At present, Europe, Central and South America, the Province of Quebec, and the former French colonies of Africa have adopted the civil law system.

Although the common law system has had much more impact on American law, the civil law system has been of increasing influence. For example, early nineteenth-century American legislatures wanted to replace the complex and ponderous system of common law pleading, and reformers campaigned in favor of replacing the traditional approach with legislated codes. Today, codes of civil procedure regulate litigation in all federal and state courts. Many states have taken a similar approach with respect to probate law, criminal law, and commercial law. State legislatures in forty-nine states, for example, have adopted the Uniform Commercial Code to replace the common law with respect to the sale of goods. (Louisiana is the holdout.)

CONSTITUTIONS

Each of the fifty states and the federal government are sovereignties. Each is a complete government with a legislative, an executive, and a judicial branch, and each has a written constitution. The written constitution is the fundamental source of the rule of law within each jurisdiction. It creates a framework for the exercise of governmental power and allocates responsibility among the branches of government. It authorizes and restrains the exercise of governmental authority, protects fundamental rights, and provides an orderly vehicle for legal change. Laws and governmental actions that violate its terms are unconstitutional.

The Federal Constitution grants certain powers to the federal government in Article I, such as the rights to regulate interstate commerce, operate post offices, declare war, and coin money. The states, however, retain many important powers and can implement significant change by enacting statutes and by amending their state constitutions. One strength of our federal form of government is that states can innovate and experiment without having to obtain permission from other states. Nebraska's constitution, for example, provides for a unicameral legislature (the only state to do so), and Louisiana is unique in that it does not confer common law powers on its judges. State constitutions can even provide greater protections for individual liberties than are required under the United States Constitution.

 INTERNET TIP ————————————————————————————

Vermont is an example of a state exercising its sovereign right to chart its own course. It was the first state to legally recognize same-sex relationships in a way that is essentially equivalent to marriage. The Vermont Supreme Court decided the case of *Baker v. State* in 1998. It decided in that case that ". . . the State is constitutionally required to extend to same-sex couples the common benefits and protections that flow from marriage under Vermont law. . . ." This decision ultimately led to the enactment of a "Civil Union" statute in Vermont. Students can read this ground-breaking case on the textbook's website.

LEGISLATION

To maintain social harmony, society needs uniformly operating rules of conduct. The responsibility for determining the rules lies primarily with legislative bodies. The legislative branch creates law by enacting statutes. An examination of legislation reveals the problems and moods of the nation. Legislatures write history through the legislative process. There have been legislative reactions to almost all political, social, and business problems that have faced society. Laws have been passed in response to wars, depressions, civil rights problems, crime, and concern for cities and the environment. Checks and balances have been built into the system in order to prevent overreaction by the legislature and to promote wise and timely legislation.

The process of enacting statutes is lengthy and complex. At the federal level, it is a procedure that involves 535 persons in the House and Senate who represent the interests of their constituents, themselves, and the country. A proposed bill may encounter numerous obstacles. Mere approval by the legislative bodies does not ensure passage, for at both federal and state levels the executive branch has the power to veto a bill. Another check on legislation can come once a bill becomes law. At that point, the constitutionality of the legislative act may be challenged in court.

With the exception of bills for raising revenue, which must originate in the House (Article I, Section 7 of the Constitution), it makes no difference in which body a bill is introduced, because a statute must be approved by both houses of the legislature. However, the legislative process varies slightly between the Senate and House. If differences exist between the House and Senate versions of a bill, a joint conference committee meets to reconcile the conflicts and draft a compromise bill.

After a bill has been approved by both houses and certain formalities have been completed, it must be approved and signed by the president of the United States to become effective. If the president vetoes a bill—which rarely occurs—it does not become law unless the veto is overridden by a two-thirds vote of both houses.

Defeat of a bill is far more common than passage. More than 95 percent of all legislation introduced is defeated at some point. Still, much legislation *is* signed into law each year. Legislative death can result at any stage of the process, and from many sources. For legislation to be successful in passing, assignment to the proper committee is crucial. However, committees can be cruel. They may refuse to hold hearings. They may alter a bill completely. Or they may kill it outright. If a proposed statute survives the committee stage, the House Rules Committee or the Senate majority leaders determine the bill's destiny. Once a bill reaches the floor of the House or Senate, irrelevant proposals—known as *riders*—may be added to it. Or drastic amendments can so alter it that it is defeated. The possibilities are almost endless.

The need for certainty and uniformity in the laws among the states is reflected in federal legislation and uniform state laws. A great degree of uniformity has been accomplished among the states on a number of matters. An important example is the Uniform Commercial Code. With increased interstate business operations, business firms pressured for uniform laws dealing with commercial transactions among states. Judges, law professors, and leading members of the bar drafted the Uniform Commercial Code for adoption by the individual states. The UCC was first adopted by the Pennsylvania legislature in 1953, and has now been adopted at least partially in all fifty states. The UCC covers sales, commercial paper, bank collection processes, letters of credit, bulk transfers, warehouse receipts, bills of lading, other documents of title, investment securities, and secured transactions.

The Power to Legislate

Legislative bodies are organized in accordance with the provisions of the U.S. and state constitutions, and are entrusted with wide-ranging responsibilities and powers. These powers include enacting laws, raising taxes, conducting investigations, holding hearings, and determining how public money will be appropriated. Legislatures play a major role in determining public policy. It is widely understood, however, that today's legislatives actually share policy-making duties with the executive and judicial branches and with administrative agencies.

Federal Government

The federal government cannot exercise any authority that is not granted to it by the Constitution, either expressly or by implication. The U.S. Constitution, in Article I, Section 8 and in authorizing sections contained in various constitutional amendments, enumerates the powers granted to the Congress. The powers that the Constitution delegates to the federal government are comprehensive and complete. They are limited only by the Constitution. The power to regulate interstate commerce is one of the most important of the expressly delegated powers.

From 1900 until 1937, the U.S. Supreme Court often followed a formalistic approach in its interpretations of the commerce clause. The justices severely limited the scope of this clause in a series of controversial cases. The Court, for example, rejected Congress's claim that Article I, Section 8 permitted the federal government to address problems resulting from indirect as well as direct impacts on interstate commerce,[3] and it defined interstate commerce very narrowly in cases in which Congress sought to regulate mining,[4] protect workers wishing to join labor unions,[5] and discourage the use of child labor in factories.[6]

The Supreme Court reversed its direction in 1937 and began to defer to Congress in cases where a rational connection existed between the legislation and commerce. The Court often used the necessary and proper clause in conjunction with the commerce clause to justify extensions of federal authority.[7] In one case it upheld a federal act that was jurisdictionally based on indirect effects on interstate commerce and that authorized the use of injunctions against companies engaging in unfair labor practices,[8] and in a second case it upheld minimum wage legislation.[9] The continued viability of the "deferential" standard was called into question because of the Court's decision in *United States v. Lopez*, the case we are about to read. The question confronting the Court concerns whether Congress has the right, under the commerce clause, to enact the Gun-Free School Zones Act of 1990.

United States v. Lopez
No. 93-1260
U.S. Supreme Court
April 26, 1995

Chief Justice Rehnquist delivered the opinion of the Court.

In the Gun-Free School Zones Act of 1990, Congress made it a federal offense "for any individual knowingly to possess a firearm at a place that the individual knows, or has reasonable cause to believe, is a school zone." . . . The Act neither regulates a commercial activity nor contains a requirement that the possession be connected in any way to interstate commerce. We hold that the Act exceeds the authority of Congress "[t]o regulate Commerce . . . among the several States. . . ." U.S. Const., Art. 1, 8, cl. 3.

On March 10, 1992, respondent, who was then a 12th-grade student, arrived at Edison High School in San Antonio, Texas, carrying a concealed .38 caliber handgun and five bullets. Acting upon an anonymous tip, school authorities confronted respondent, who admitted that he was carrying the weapon. He was arrested and charged under Texas law with firearm possession on school premises. . . . The next day, the state charges were dismissed after federal agents charged respondent by complaint with violating the Gun-Free School Zones Act of 1990. . . .

A federal grand jury indicted respondent on one count of knowing possession of a firearm at a school zone, in violation of 922(q). Respondent moved to dismiss his federal indictment on the ground that 922(q) "is unconstitutional as it is beyond the power of Congress to legislate control over our public schools." The District Court denied the motion, concluding that 922(q) "is a constitutional exercise of Congress' well-defined power to regulate activities in and affecting commerce, and the 'business' of elementary, middle and high schools . . . affects interstate commerce." . . . Respondent waived his right to a jury trial. The District Court conducted a bench trial, found him guilty of violating 922(q), and sentenced him to six months' imprisonment and two years' supervised release.

On appeal, respondent challenged his conviction based on his claim that 922(q) exceeded Congress' power to legislate under the Commerce Clause. The Court of Appeals for the Fifth Circuit agreed and reversed respondent's conviction. It held that, in light of what it characterized as insufficient congressional findings and legislative history, "section 922(q), in the full reach of its terms, is invalid as beyond the power of Congress under the Commerce Clause." . . . Because of the importance of the issue, we granted certiorari, . . . and we now affirm.

We start with first principles. The Constitution creates a Federal Government of enumerated powers. See U.S. Const., Art. 1, 8. As James Madison wrote, " [t]he powers delegated by the proposed Constitution to the federal government are few and defined. Those which are to remain in the State governments are numerous and indefinite." . . . This constitutionally mandated division of authority "was adopted by the Framers to ensure protection of our fundamental liberties." . . . "Just as the separation and independence of the coordinate branches of the Federal Government serves to prevent the accumulation of excessive power in any one branch, a healthy balance of power between the States and the Federal Government will reduce the risk of tyranny and abuse from either front." . . .

The Constitution delegates to Congress the power " [t]o regulate Commerce with foreign Nations, and among the several States, and with the Indian Tribes." . . . U.S. Const., Art. 1, 8, cl. 3. The Court, through Chief Justice Marshall, first defined the nature of Congress' commerce power in *Gibbons v. Ogden*, . . . (1824):

> "Commerce, undoubtedly, is traffic, but it is something more: it is intercourse. It describes the commercial intercourse between nations, and parts of nations, in all its branches, and is regulated by prescribing rules for carrying on that intercourse."

The commerce power "is the power to regulate; that is, to prescribe the rule by which commerce is to be governed. This power, like all others vested in Congress, is complete in itself, may be exercised to its utmost extent, and acknowledges no limitations, other than are prescribed in the constitution." The *Gibbons* Court, however, acknowledged that limitations on the commerce power are inherent in the very language of the Commerce Clause.

"It is not intended to say that these words comprehend that commerce, which is completely internal, which is carried on between man and man in a State, or between different parts of the same State, and which does not extend to or affect other States. Such a power would be inconvenient, and is certainly unnecessary.

"Comprehensive as the word 'among' is, it may very properly be restricted to that commerce which concerns more States than one. . . . The enumeration presupposes something not enumerated; and that something, if we regard the language or the subject of the sentence, must be the exclusively internal commerce of a State." . . .

For nearly a century thereafter, the Court's Commerce Clause decisions dealt but rarely with the extent of Congress' power, and almost entirely with the Commerce Clause as a limit on state legislation that discriminated against interstate commerce. . . . In 1887, Congress enacted the Interstate Commerce Act, . . . and in 1890, Congress enacted the Sherman Antitrust Act, . . . These laws ushered in a new era of federal regulation under the commerce power. When cases involving these laws first reached this Court, we imported from our negative Commerce Clause cases the approach that Congress could not regulate activities such as "production," "manufacturing," and "mining." . . . Simultaneously, however, the Court held that, where the interstate and intrastate aspects of commerce were so mingled together that full regulation of interstate commerce required incidental regulation of intrastate commerce, the Commerce Clause authorized such regulation. . . .

In *A. L. A. Schecter Poultry Corp. v. United States*, . . . (1935), the Court struck down regulations that fixed the hours and wages of individuals employed by an intrastate business because the activity being regulated related to interstate commerce only indirectly. In doing so, the Court characterized the distinction between direct and indirect effects of intrastate transactions upon interstate commerce as "a fundamental one, essential to the maintenance of our constitutional system." . . . Activities that affected interstate commerce directly were within Congress' power; activities that affected interstate commerce indirectly were beyond Congress' reach. . . . The justification for this formal distinction was rooted in the fear that otherwise "there would be virtually no limit to the federal power and for all practical purposes we should have a completely centralized government." . . .

Two years later, in the watershed case of *NLRB v. Jones & Laughlin Steel Corp.*, . . . (1937), the Court upheld the National Labor Relations Act against a Commerce Clause challenge, and in the process, departed from the distinction between "direct" and "indirect" effects on interstate commerce. . . . ("The question [of the scope of Congress' power] is necessarily one of degree"). The Court held that intrastate activities that "have such a close and substantial relation to interstate commerce that their control is essential or appropriate to protect that commerce from burdens and obstructions" are within Congress' power to regulate. . . .

In *Wickard v. Filburn*, the Court upheld the application of amendments to the Agricultural Adjustment Act of 1938 to the production and consumption of home-grown wheat. . . . The *Wickard* Court explicitly rejected earlier distinctions between direct and indirect effects on interstate commerce, stating:

> "[E]ven if appellee's activity be local and though it may not be regarded as commerce, it may still, whatever its nature, be reached by Congress if it exerts a substantial economic effect on interstate commerce, and this irrespective of whether such effect is what might at some earlier time have been defined as 'direct' or 'indirect.'" . . .

The *Wickard* Court emphasized that although Filburn's own contribution to the demand for wheat may have been trivial by itself, that was not "enough to remove him from the scope of federal regulation where, as here, his contribution, taken together with that of many others similarly situated, is far from trivial." . . .

Jones & Laughlin Steel, . . . and *Wickard* ushered in an era of Commerce Clause jurisprudence that greatly expanded the previously defined authority of Congress under that Clause. In part, this was a recognition of the great changes that had occurred in the way business was carried on in this country. Enterprises that had once been local or at most regional in nature had become national in scope. But the doctrinal change also reflected a view that earlier Commerce Clause cases artificially had constrained the authority of Congress to regulate interstate commerce.

But even these modern-era precedents which have expanded congressional power under the Commerce Clause confirm that this power is subject to outer limits. In *Jones & Laughlin Steel*, the Court warned that the scope of the interstate commerce power "must be considered in the light of our dual system of government and may not be extended so as to embrace effects upon interstate commerce so indirect and remote that to embrace them, in view of our complex society, would effectually obliterate the distinction between what is national and what is local and create a completely centralized government." . . . Since that time, the Court has heeded that warning and undertaken to decide whether a rational basis existed for concluding that a regulated activity sufficiently affected interstate commerce. . . .

Consistent with this structure, we have identified three broad categories of activity that Congress may regulate under its commerce power. . . . First, Congress may regulate the use of the channels of interstate commerce. . . . Second, Congress is empowered to regulate and protect the instrumentalities of interstate commerce, or persons or things in interstate commerce, even though the threat may come only from intrastate activities. . . . Finally, Congress' commerce authority includes the power to regulate those activities having a substantial relation to interstate commerce, . . .

Within this final category, admittedly, our case law has not been clear whether an activity must "affect" or "substantially affect" interstate commerce in order to be within Congress' power to regulate it under the Commerce Clause. . . . We conclude, consistent with the great weight of our case law, that the proper test requires an analysis of whether the regulated activity "substantially affects" interstate commerce.

We now turn to consider the power of Congress, in the light of this framework, to enact 922(q). The first two categories of authority may be quickly disposed of—922(q) is not a regulation of the use of the channels of interstate commerce, nor is it an attempt to prohibit the interstate transportation of a commodity through the channels of commerce; nor can 922(q) be justified as a regulation by which Congress has sought to protect an instrumentality of interstate commerce or a thing in interstate commerce. Thus, if 922(q) is to be sustained, it must be under the third category as a regulation of an activity that substantially affects interstate commerce.

First, we have upheld a wide variety of congressional Acts regulating intrastate economic activity where we have concluded that the activity substantially affected interstate commerce. Examples include the regulation of intrastate coal mining; . . . intrastate extortionate credit transactions, . . . restaurants utilizing substantial interstate supplies, . . . inns and hotels catering to interstate guests, . . . and production and consumption of homegrown wheat, *Wickard v. Filburn*, . . . (1942). These examples are by no means exhaustive, but the pattern is clear. Where economic activity sub-

stantially affects interstate commerce, legislation regulating that activity will be sustained.

Section 922(q) is a criminal statute that by its terms has nothing to do with "commerce" or any sort of economic enterprise, however broadly one might define those terms. Section 922(q) is not an essential part of a larger regulation of economic activity, in which the regulatory scheme could be undercut unless the intrastate activity were regulated. It cannot, therefore, be sustained under our cases upholding regulations of activities that arise out of or are connected with a commercial transaction, which viewed in the aggregate, substantially affects interstate commerce. Second, 922(q) contains no jurisdictional element which would ensure, through case-by-case inquiry, that the firearm possession in question affects interstate commerce. . . .

Although as part of our independent evaluation of constitutionality under the Commerce Clause we of course consider legislative findings, and indeed even congressional committee findings, regarding effect on interstate commerce, . . . the Government concedes that "[n]either the statute nor its legislative history contain[s] express congressional findings regarding the effects upon interstate commerce of gun possession in a school zone." . . . We agree with the Government that Congress normally is not required to make formal findings as to the substantial burdens that an activity has on interstate commerce. . . . But to the extent that congressional findings would enable us to evaluate the legislative judgment that the activity in question substantially affected interstate commerce, even though no such substantial effect was visible to the naked eye, they are lacking here. . . .

The Government's essential contention, . . . is that we may determine here that 922(q) is valid because possession of a firearm in a local school zone does indeed substantially affect interstate commerce. . . . The Government argues that possession of a firearm in a school zone may result in violent crime and that violent crime can be expected to affect the functioning of the national economy in two ways. First, the costs of violent crime are substantial, and, through the mechanism of insurance, those costs are spread throughout the population. . . . Second, violent crime reduces the willingness of individuals to travel to areas within the country that are perceived to be unsafe. . . . The Government also argues that the presence of guns in schools poses a substantial threat to the educational process by threatening the learning environment. A handicapped educational process, in turn, will result in a less productive citizenry. That, in turn, would have an adverse effect on the Nation's economic well-being. As a result, the Government argues that Congress could rationally have concluded that 922(q) substantially affects interstate commerce.

We pause to consider the implications of the Government's arguments. The Government admits, under its "costs of crime" reasoning, that Congress could regulate not only all violent crime, but all activities that might lead to violent crime, regardless of how tenuously they relate to interstate commerce. . . . Similarly, under the Government's "national productivity" reasoning, Congress could regulate any activity that it found was related to the economic productivity of individual citizens: family law (including marriage, divorce, and child custody), for example. Under the theories that the Government presents in support of 922(q), it is difficult to perceive any limitation on federal power, even in areas such as criminal law enforcement or education where States historically have been sovereign. Thus, if we were to accept the Government's arguments, we are hard-pressed to posit any activity by an individual that Congress is without power to regulate. . . .

Justice Breyer focuses, . . . on the threat that firearm possession in and near schools poses to the educational process and the potential economic consequences flowing from that threat. . . . Specifically, the dissent reasons that (1) gun-related violence is a serious problem; (2) that problem, in turn, has an adverse effect on classroom learning; and (3) that adverse effect on classroom learning, in turn, represents a substantial threat to trade and commerce. . . . This analysis would be equally applicable, if not more so, to subjects such as family law and direct regulation of education.

For instance, if Congress can, pursuant to its Commerce Clause power, regulate activities that adversely affect the learning environment, then, a fortiori, it also can regulate the educational process directly. Congress could determine that a school's curriculum has a "significant" effect on the extent of classroom learning. As a result, Congress could mandate a federal curriculum for local elementary and secondary schools because what is taught in local schools has a significant "effect on classroom learning," . . . and that, in turn, has a substantial effect on interstate commerce.

Justice Breyer rejects our reading of precedent and argues that "Congress . . . could rationally conclude that schools fall on the commercial side of the line." . . . Again, Justice Breyer's rationale lacks any real limits because, depending on the level of generality, any activity can be looked upon as commercial. Under the dissent's rationale, Congress could just as easily look at child rearing as "fall[ing] on the commercial side of the line" because it provides a "valuable service— namely, to equip [children] with the skills they need to survive in life and, more specifically, in the workplace." . . . We do not doubt that Congress has authority under the Commerce Clause to regulate numerous commercial activities that substantially affect interstate commerce and also affect the educational process. That authority, though broad, does not include the authority to regulate each and every aspect of local schools.

Admittedly, a determination whether an intrastate activity is commercial or noncommercial may in some cases result in legal uncertainty. But, so long as Congress' authority is limited to those powers enumerated in the Constitution, and so long as those enumerated powers are interpreted as having judicially enforceable outer limits, congressional legislation under the Commerce Clause always will engender "legal uncertainty.". . . As Chief Justice Marshall stated in *McCulloch v. Maryland*, . . . (1819): "The [federal] government is acknowledged by all to be one of enumerated powers. The principle, that it can exercise only the powers granted to it . . . is now universally admitted. But the question respecting the extent of the powers actually granted, is perpetually arising, and will probably continue to arise, as long as our system shall exist." . . . The Constitution mandates this uncertainty by withholding from Congress a plenary police power that would authorize enactment of every type of legislation. . . . Congress has operated within this framework of legal uncertainty ever since this Court determined that it was the judiciary's duty "to say what the law is." *Marbury v. Madison*, . . . (1803) . . . Any possible benefit from eliminating this "legal uncertainty" would be at the expense of the Constitution's system of enumerated powers.

In *Jones & Laughlin Steel*, . . . we held that the question of congressional power under the Commerce Clause "is necessarily one of degree." . . . These are not precise formulations, and in the nature of things they cannot be. But we think they point the way to a correct decision of this case. The possession of a gun in a local school zone is in no sense an economic activity that might, through repetition elsewhere, substantially affect any sort of interstate commerce. Respondent was a local student at a local school; there is no indication that he had recently moved in interstate commerce, and there is no requirement that his possession of the firearm have any concrete tie to interstate commerce.

To uphold the Government's contentions here, we would have to pile inference upon inference in a manner that would . . . convert congressional authority under the Commerce Clause to a general police power of the sort retained by the States. Admittedly, some of our prior cases have taken long steps down that road, giving great deference to congressional action. . . . The broad language in these opinions has suggested the possibility of additional expansion, but we decline here to proceed any further. To do so would require us to conclude that the Constitution's enumeration of powers does not presuppose something not enumerated, . . . and that there never will be a distinction between what is truly national and what is truly local, . . . This we are unwilling to do.

For the foregoing reasons the judgment of the Court of Appeals is Affirmed.

Case Questions

1. Why does the Supreme Court conclude that the statute exceeds Congress's authority under the Commerce Clause?
2. Assume that the Supreme Court had sustained the constitutionality of this statute. What impact might such a ruling have on the states?
3. What is your appraisal of Justice Breyer's defense of the statute as it was summarized in the Court's opinion?

State Government

The authority that resides in every sovereignty to pass laws for its internal regulation and government is called *police power*. It is the power inherent in the state to pass reasonable laws necessary to preserve the public health, safety, morals, and welfare. Police power of the states is not a grant derived from a written constitution; the federal Constitution assumes the preexistence of the police power. The Tenth Amendment to the Constitution reserves to the states any power not delegated to the federal government. Police power exists without any reservation in the Constitution, although both federal and state constitutions set limits in the exercise of this power.

The basis of the police power is the state's obligation to protect its citizens and provide for the safety and order of society. This yields a broad, comprehensive authority. The definition of crimes and the regulating of trades and professions are examples of this vast scope of power. A mandatory precondition to the exercise of police power is the existence of an ascertainable public need for a particular statute, and the statute must bear a real and substantial relation to the end that is sought. The possession and enjoyment of all rights may be limited under the police power, provided that it is reasonably exercised.

Limitations on the police power have never been drawn with exactness or determined by a general formula. The power may not be exercised for private purposes or for the exclusive benefit of a few. Its scope has been declared to be greater in emergency situations. Otherwise its exercise must be in the public interest, must be reasonable, and may not be repugnant to the rights implied or secured in the Constitution.

Powers delegated by the federal government and individual state constitutions also serve as a basis for state legislation. Any activity solely attributable to the sovereignty of the state may not be restrained by Congress.

Federal Supremacy

The U.S. Constitution divides powers between the federal government and the states. Certain powers are delegated to the federal government alone. Others are reserved to the states. Still others are exercised concurrently by both. The Tenth Amendment to the Constitution specifies that the "powers not delegated to the United States by the Constitution . . . are reserved to the states . . . or to the people." Unlike the federal power, which is granted, the state already has its power, unless expressly or implicitly denied by the state or federal constitutions. Each state has the power to govern its own affairs, except where the Constitution has withdrawn that power.

The powers of both the federal and state governments are to be exercised so as not to interfere with each other's exercise of power. Whenever there is a conflict, state laws must yield to federal acts to the extent of the conflict. This requirement is expressed by the supremacy clause in Article VI of the Constitution.

Under the supremacy clause, Congress can enact legislation that may supersede state authority and preempt state regulations. The preemption doctrine is based on the supremacy clause. Hence state laws that frustrate or are contrary to congressional objectives in a specific area are invalid. In considering state law, one takes into account the nature of the subject matter, any vital national interests that may be involved, or perhaps the need for uniformity between state and federal laws, and the expressed or implied intent of Congress. It is necessary to determine whether Congress has sought to occupy a particular field to the exclusion of the states. All interests, both state and federal, must be examined.

Constitutionality of Statutes

The power to declare legislative acts unconstitutional is the province and the duty of the judiciary, even though there is no express constitutional grant of the power. It is generally presumed that all statutes are constitutional and that a statute will not be invalidated unless the party challenging it clearly shows that it is offensive to either a state or federal constitution. When a court encounters legislation that it believes to be unconstitutional, it first tries to interpret the statute in a narrow way with what is called a limiting construction. An act of the legislature is declared invalid only as a last resort if it is clearly incompatible with a constitutional provision.

The right and power of the courts to declare whether the legislature has exceeded the constitutional limitations is one of the highest functions of the judiciary. The Supreme Court declared in *Marbury v. Madison*, 5 U.S. (1 Cranch) 137 (1803) that the judicial branch has the power to declare void an act of the legislature that conflicts with the Constitution. The issue of the supremacy of the U.S. Constitution, and the right of individuals to claim protection thereunder whenever they were aggrieved by application of a contrary statute, was decided in *Marbury*. Chief Justice John Marshall wrote the opinion for the Court, stating in part:

> The question, whether an act, repugnant to the Constitution, can become the law of the land, is a question deeply interesting to the United States; but, happily, not of an intricacy proportioned to its interest. It seems only necessary to recognize certain principles, supposed to have been long and well established, to decide it.
>
> That the people have an original right to establish, for their future government, such principles as, in their opinion, shall most conduce to their own happiness, is the basis on which the whole American fabric has been erected. The exercise of this original right is a very great exertion; nor can it, nor ought it, to be frequently repeated. The principles, therefore, so established, are deemed fundamental. And as the authority from which they proceed is supreme, and can seldom act, they are designated to be permanent.
>
> . . . It is a proposition too plain to be contested, that the Constitution controls any legislative act repugnant to it; or that the legislature may alter the Constitution by an ordinary act.
>
> Between these alternatives there is no middle ground. The Constitution is either a superior paramount law, unchangeable by ordinary means, or it is on a level with ordinary legislative acts, and, like other acts, is alterable when the legislature shall please to alter it.
>
> If the former part of the alternative be true, then a legislative act, contrary to the Constitution, is not law; if the latter part be true, then written constitutions

are absurd attempts, on the part of the people, to limit a power, in its own nature illimitable. . . .

It is, emphatically, the province and duty of the judicial department to say what the law is. Those who apply the rule to particular cases must of necessity expound and interpret that rule. If two laws conflict with each other, the courts must decide on the operation of each.

So, if a law be in opposition to the Constitution; if both the law and the Constitution apply to a particular case, so that the court must either decide that case, conformable to the law, disregarding the Constitution, or conformable to the Constitution, disregarding the law; the court must determine which of the conflicting rules governs the case. This is of the very essence of judicial duty.

If, then, the courts are to regard the Constitution—and the Constitution is superior to any ordinary act of the legislature—the Constitution, and not such ordinary act, must govern the case to which they both apply.

Ex Post Facto Laws

Article I, Section 9, of the federal Constitution prohibits Congress from enacting *ex post facto* laws or *bills of attainder.* The state legislatures are likewise prohibited by Article I, Section 10.

An *ex post facto* law is a law that makes acts criminal that were not criminal at the time they were committed. Statutes that make a crime greater than when committed, impose greater punishment, or make proof of guilt easier have also been held to be unconstitutional *ex post facto* laws. Laws are unconstitutional when they alter the definition of a penal offense or its consequence to people who commit that offense, to their disadvantage. An accused is deprived of a substantial right provided by the law that was in force at the time when the offense was committed.

The *ex post facto* clause restricts legislative power and does not apply to the judicial function. The doctrine applies exclusively to criminal or penal statutes. The impact of *ex post facto* may not be avoided by disguising criminal punishment in a civil form. When a law imposes punishment for certain activity of the past and future, even though it is void for the punishment of past activity, it is valid insofar as the law acts prospectively. A law is not *ex post facto* if it "mitigates the rigor" of the law or simply reenacts the law in force when the crime was done.

To determine if a legislative act unconstitutionally punishes past activity, courts examine the intent of the legislature. The court, after examining the text of the law and its legislative history, makes a determination as to whether an act that imposes a present disqualification is, in fact, merely the imposition of a punishment for a past event. The principle governing the inquiry is whether the aim of the legislature was to punish an individual for past activity, or whether a restriction on a person is merely incident to a valid regulation of a present situation, such as the appropriate qualifications for a profession.

A constitutionally prohibited bill of attainder involves the singling out of an individual or group for punishment. Bills of attainder are acts of a legislature that apply either to named individuals or to easily ascertainable members of a group in such a way as to impose punishments on them without a trial. For example, an act of Congress that made it a crime for a member of the Communist party to serve as an officer of a labor union was held unconstitutional as a bill of attainder (*United States v. Brown*, 381 U.S. 437, 1965).

Statutory Construction

To declare what the law shall be is a legislative power; to declare what the law *is* is a judicial power. The courts are the appropriate body for construing acts of the legislature. Since courts decide only real controversies and not abstract or moot questions, a court does not construe statutory provisions unless required for the resolution of a case before it. A statute is open to construction only when the language used in the act is ambiguous and requires interpretation. Where the statutory language conveys a clear and definite meaning, there is no occasion to use rules of statutory interpretation.

Courts have developed rules of statutory construction to determine the meaning of legislative acts. For interpreting statutes, the legislative will is the all-important and controlling factor. In theory, the sole object of all rules for interpreting statutes is to discover the legislative intent; every other rule of construction is secondary.

It is the duty of the judiciary in construing criminal statutes to determine whether particular conduct falls within the intended prohibition of the statute. Criminal statutes are enforced by the court if worded so that they clearly convey the nature of the proscribed behavior. Legislation must be appropriately tailored to meet its objectives. Therefore it cannot be arbitrary, unreasonable, or capricious. A court holds a statute void for vagueness if it does not give a person of ordinary intelligence fair notice that some contemplated conduct is forbidden by the act. The enforcement of a vague statute would encourage arbitrary and erratic arrests and convictions.

Penal statutes impose punishment for offenses committed against the state. They include all statutes that command or prohibit certain acts and establish penalties for their violation. Penal statutes are enacted for the benefit of the public. They should receive a fair and reasonable construction. The words used should be given the meaning commonly attributed to them. Criminal statutes are to be strictly construed, and doubts are to be resolved in favor of the accused. *Strict construction* means that the statute should not be enlarged by implication beyond the fair meaning of the language used. However, the statute should not be construed so as to defeat the obvious intention of the legislature.

A literal interpretation of statutory language can lead to unreasonable, unjust, or even absurd consequences. In such a case, a court is justified in adopting a construction that sustains the validity of the legislative act, rather than one that defeats it.

Courts do not have legislative authority and should avoid "judicial legislation." To depart from the meaning expressed by the words of the statute so as to alter it is not construction—it is legislative alteration. A statute should not be construed more broadly or given greater effect than its terms require. Nothing should be read into a statute that was not intended by the legislature. Courts, however, don't always adhere to the principle.

Statutes are to be read in the light of conditions at the time of their enactment. A new meaning is sometimes given to the words of an old statute because of changed conditions. The scope of a statute may appear to include conduct that did not exist when the statute was enacted—for example, certain activity related to technological progress. Such a case does not preclude the application of the statute thereto.

ADMINISTRATIVE AGENCIES

As we will see in more detail in Chapter 13, legislative bodies often delegate some of their authority to governmental entities called agencies, boards, authorities, and commissions. Legislatures do this when they lack expertise in an area requiring constant oversight and specialized knowledge. Agencies such as the Environmental Protection Agency; the Securities and Exchange Commission; the boards that license doctors, attorneys, and barbers; and public housing authorities are other examples.

Legislative bodies often permit the agencies to exercise investigative and rule-making powers. Administrative rules, if promulgated according to law, have the same force as statutes. Some agencies also are delegated authority to conduct adjudicatory hearings before administrative law judges who will determine whether agency rules have been violated.

JUDICIAL DECISION MAKING

Our society is not able to legislate laws that address every societal problem. Sometimes a court encounters a case that presents a problem that has not been previously litigated within the jurisdiction. In such a case, the court will try to base its decision on a statute, ordinance, or administrative regulation. If none can be found, it will base its decision on general principles of the common law (principles that have been judicially recognized as precedent in previous cases). This judge-made law has an effect similar to a statute in such situations. Legislatures can modify or replace judge-made law either by passing legislation or through constitutional amendment.

In this portion of the chapter we will learn about the use of common law precedents and how judges determine which body of substantive law to apply when the facts of a case involve the laws of more than one state.

One of the most fundamental principles of the common law is the *doctrine of stare decisis*. A doctrine is a policy, in this case a judicial policy, that guides courts in making decisions. The doctrine normally requires lower-level courts to follow the legal precedents that have been established by higher-level courts. Following precedent helps to promote uniformity and predictability in judicial decision making. All judges within a jurisdiction are expected to apply a rule of law the same way until that rule is overturned by a higher court.

Following Precedent

Literally, *stare decisis* means that a court will "stand by its decisions" or those of a higher court. This doctrine originated in England and was used in the colonies as the basis of their judicial decisions.

A decision on an issue of law by a court is followed in that jurisdiction by the same court or by a lower court in a future case presenting the same—or substantially the same—issue of law. A court is not bound by decisions of courts of other states, although such decisions may be considered in the decision-making process. A decision of the U.S. Supreme Court on a federal question is absolutely binding on state courts as well as on lower federal courts. Similarly, a decision of a state court of final appeal on an issue of state law is followed by lower state courts and federal courts in the state dealing with that issue.

The doctrine of *stare decisis* promotes continuity, stability, justice, speed, economy, and adaptability within the law. It helps our legal system to furnish guidelines so that people can anticipate legal consequences when they decide how to conduct their affairs. It promotes justice by establishing rules that enable many legal disputes to be concluded fairly. It eliminates the need for every proposition in every case to be subject to endless relitigation. Public faith in the judiciary is increased where legal rules are consistently applied and are the product of impersonal and reasoned judgment. In addition, the quality of the law decided on is improved, as more careful and thorough consideration is given to the legal questions than would be the case if the determinations affected only the case before the court.

Stare decisis is not a binding rule, and a court need not feel absolutely bound to follow previous cases. However, courts are not inclined to deviate from it, especially when the precedents have been treated as authoritative law for a long time. The number of decisions announced on a rule of law also has some bearing on the weight of the precedent. When a principle of law established by precedent is no longer appropriate because of changing economic, political, and social conditions, however, courts should recognize this decay and overrule the precedent to reflect what is best for society.

The Holding and Rule of the Case

Under the doctrine of *stare decisis*, only a point of law necessarily decided in a reported judicial opinion is binding on other courts as precedent. A question of fact determined by a court has no binding effect on a subsequent case involving similar questions of fact. The facts of each case are recognized as being unique.

Those points of law decided by a court to resolve a legal controversy constitute the *holding* of the case. In other words, the court holds that a certain rule of law applies to the given factual situation of the case and renders its decision accordingly. The rule of law as applied to the facts of the case expresses the *rule of the case*. Under *stare decisis*, the rule of the case is applied to future cases with the same or closely analogous factual situations. The rule of the case as expressed in a court's holding becomes a precedent that guides courts in their decisions and is generally considered to be the law.

Sometimes, in their opinions, courts make comments that are not necessary to support the decision. These extraneous judicial expressions are referred to as *dictum*. They have no value as precedent because they do not fit the facts of the case. The reason for drawing a distinction between holding and *dictum* is that only the issues before the court have been argued and fully considered. Even though *dictum* is not binding under the doctrine of *stare decisis*, it is often considered persuasive. Other judges and lawyers can determine what the decision makers are thinking and gain an indication of how the problem may be handled in the future.

It is the task of the lawyer and judge to find the decision or decisions that set the precedent for a particular factual situation. In court, lawyers argue about whether a prior case should or should not be recognized as controlling in a subsequent case.

The Ohio Supreme Court had to make such a decision in the following 1969 case. Did the prosecution violate Butler's federal due process rights when it used his voluntary, in-custody statement (that was obtained without prior *Miranda* warnings) to *impeach* his trial testimony? The U.S. Supreme Court had ruled in a 1954 case (*Walder v. United States*) that prosecutors could impeach a testifying defendant with illegally obtained evidence once the defendant had "opened the door" with false testimony. The U.S. Supreme Court's *Miranda v. Arizona* (1966) opinion seemed to suggest that constitutional due process prevented the government from using such statements for any purpose. In *Miranda*, however, the prosecution had used the defendant's statement to prove guilt, not to impeach the defendant's testimony. Butler's lawyer argued to the Ohio Supreme Court that (1) the language contained in *Miranda* applied to impeachment uses, (2) *Miranda* should be recognized as controlling, and (3) Butler's statement was inadmissible. The lawyers for the State of Ohio disagreed. They argued (1) *Miranda* was not controlling, because Butler's facts were distinguishable from the facts in *Miranda*, (2) the *Walder* case was controlling, and (3) Butler's statement was admissible for purposes of impeachment.

State v. Butler
19 Ohio St. 2d 55, 249 N.E.2d 818
Supreme Court of Ohio
July 9, 1969

Schneider, Justice

. . . The offense for which appellant was indicted, tried, and convicted occurred on August 30, 1964. He struck Annie Ruth Sullivan with a jack handle, causing an injury which resulted in loss of sight of her left eye. Appellant was apprehended and arrested by the Cincinnati police, and while in custody he was interrogated by police officers. Prior to the questioning, the police gave no explanation to appellant as to his rights to remain silent and have an attorney present. The interrogation was recorded and reduced to writing. Over objection by appellant's counsel, these questions and answers were repeated by the prosecutor at trial to impeach statements made by appellant during cross-examination.

Appellant appeared before the municipal court of Hamilton County on November 22, 1965. Probable cause was found and appellant was bound over to the Hamilton County grand jury. Bond was set at $500, which appellant posted. The grand jury returned an indictment for the offense of "maiming." Appellant was arraigned and pleaded not guilty, after which the court appointed counsel. Trial was set. A jury was waived and appellant was found guilty by the court of the lesser included offense of aggravated assault. The court of appeals affirmed the judgment of conviction.

Appellant raises [the question in this appeal as to] whether, in cross-examination of a defendant the prosecutor may use prior inconsistent statements of the defendant, made to police without *Miranda* warnings, in order to impeach his credibility. . . .

Appellant's . . . contention is that the prosecution violated his Fifth Amendment right against self-incrimination by using statements of his which were made to police during in-custody interrogation with no warning of his right to silence or to counsel. . . . The United States Supreme Court . . . in *Miranda v. Arizona* [1966], . . . held there that the prosecution's use of statements of an accused, made to police without prior warnings of his rights to remain silent, to counsel and appointed counsel if indigent, was a violation of the accused's Fourteenth and Fifth Amendment right against self-incrimination. . . .

The appellant took the stand and, on cross-examination by the prosecution, he made assertions as to the facts surrounding the crime. A recorded statement appellant made to a detective after arrest was then read to him to show a prior inconsistent statement. Counsel objected, but the court allowed the statement to be used as evidence to impeach the witness's credibility. Appellant contends that this use of the statements, made without cautionary warnings, violated his Fifth Amendment rights as defined by *Miranda v. Arizona, supra.* . . .

We cannot agree. First, the statements used by the prosecution were not offered by the state as part of its direct case against appellant, but were offered on the issue of his credibility after he had been sworn and testified in his own defense. Second, the statements used by the prosecution were voluntary, no claim to the contrary having been made.

The distinction between admissibility of wrongfully obtained evidence to prove the state's case in chief and its use to impeach the credibility of a defendant who takes the stand was expressed in *Walder v. United States* [1954] . . . "It is one thing to say that the government cannot make an affirmative use of evidence unlawfully obtained. It is quite another to say that the defendant can turn the illegal method by which evidence in the Government's possession was obtained to his own advantage, and provide himself with a shield against contradiction of his untruths. . . ."

Those words of Justice Frankfurter were uttered in regard to evidence inadmissible under the Fourth Amendment exclusionary rule. In the case of the Fifth Amendment, even greater reason exists to distinguish between statements of an accused used in the prosecution's direct case and used for impeachment in cross-examining the accused when he takes the stand. We must not lose sight of the words of the Fifth Amendment: ". . . nor shall be compelled to be a witness against himself. . . ." This is a privilege accorded an accused not to be compelled to testify, nor to have any prior statements used by the prosecution to prove his guilt. We cannot translate those words into a privilege to lie with impunity once he elects to take the stand to testify. . . .

We do not believe that . . . *Miranda* . . . dictates a conclusion contrary to ours. In *Miranda*, the court indicated that statements of a defendant used to impeach his testimony at trial may not be used unless they were taken with full warnings and effective waiver. However, we note that in all four of the convictions reversed by the decision, statements of the accused, taken without cautionary warnings, were used by the prosecution as direct evidence of guilt in the case in chief.

We believe that the words of Chief Justice Marshall regarding the difference between holding and *dictum* are applicable here. "It is a maxim not to be disregarded, that general expressions, in every opinion, are to be taken in connection with the case in which those expressions are used. If they go beyond the case, they may be respected, but ought not to control the judgment in a subsequent suit when the very point is presented for decision. The reason of this maxim is obvious. The question actually before the court is investigated with care, and considered in its full extent. Other principles which may serve to illustrate it are considered in their relation to the case decided, but their possible bearing on all other cases is seldom completely investigated." . . .

The court, in *Miranda*, was not faced with the facts of this case. Thus, we do not consider ourselves bound by the *dictum* of *Miranda*.

The "linch pin" (as Mr. Justice Harlan put it . . .) of *Miranda* is that police interrogation is destructive of human dignity and disrespectful of the inviolability of the human personality. In the instant case, the use of the interrogation to impeach the voluntary testimony of the accused is neither an assault on his dignity nor disrespectful of his personality. He elected to testify, and cannot complain that the state seeks to demonstrate the lack of truth in his testimony.

Finally, we emphasize that the statements used by the prosecution were voluntarily made. The decision in *Miranda* did not discard the distinction between voluntary and involuntary statements made by an accused and used by the prosecution. . . . Lack of cautionary warnings is one of the factors to consider in determining whether statements are voluntary or not. However, appellant here has never claimed that the statements used to impeach were involuntary. Thus, we assume they were voluntary, and hold that voluntary statements of an accused made to police without cautionary warnings are admissible on the issue of credibility after defendant has been sworn and testifies in his own defense. . . .

Judgment affirmed.*

Duncan, Justice, dissenting

. . . The use of statements made by the defendant for impeachment without the warnings set forth in *Miranda v. Arizona* . . . having been given, is reversible error.

In *Miranda*, Chief Justice Warren stated . . .

> "The warnings required and the waiver necessary in accordance with our opinion today are, in the absence of a fully effective equivalent, prerequisites to the admissibility of *any statement made by a defendant.* No distinction can be drawn between statements which are direct confessions and statements which amount to 'admissions' of part or all of an offense. The privilege against self-incrimination protects the individual from being compelled to incriminate himself in any manner; it does not distinguish degrees of incrimination. Similarly, for precisely the same reason, *no distinction may be drawn between inculpatory statements and statements alleged to be merely 'exculpatory.'* If a statement made were in fact truly exculpatory, it would, of course, never be used by the prosecution. *In fact, statements merely intended to be exculpatory by the defendant are often used to impeach his testimony at trial or to demonstrate untruths in the statement given under interrogation and thus to prove guilt by implication.* These statements are incriminating in any meaningful sense of the word and may not be used without the full warnings and effective waiver required for any other statement." . . . [Emphasis supplied.]

This *specific* reference to impeachment, I believe, forecloses the use of defendant's in-custody statement in the instant case.

*The U.S. Supreme Court addressed this issue in a 1971 case, *Harris v. New York* (401 U.S. 222). The Court declared that the *Miranda* rule did not require suppression. Due process permitted the prosecution's use of a defendant's voluntary, in-custody statement (obtained without prior *Miranda* warnings) to impeach a testifying defendant's credibility.

The United States Court of Appeals for the Second Circuit . . . arrived at a decision contrary to that arrived at by the majority in this case. Judge Bryan . . . stated:

"These pronouncements by the Supreme Court may be technically *dictum.* But it is abundantly plain that the court intended to lay down a firm general rule with respect to the use of statements unconstitutionally obtained from a defendant in violation of *Miranda* standards. The rule prohibits the use of such statements whether inculpatory or exculpatory, whether bearing directly on guilt or on collateral matters only, and whether used on direct examination or for impeachment." . . .

I would reverse.

Case Questions

1. Explain the difference between holding and *dictum.*
2. Can the holding of a case be broader than the precedent relied on?
3. Why should *dictum* not be considered binding under the doctrine of *stare decisis*?
4. Was *Miranda* properly relied on by the majority in the *Butler* case?
5. If this same case had been decided by the United States Court of Appeals for the Second Circuit, would the decision have been different or the same? Why?

Requirements for a Precedent

Only a judicial opinion of the majority of a court on a point of law can have *stare decisis* effect. A dissent has no precedential value, nor does the fact that an appellate court is split make the majority's decision less of a precedent. When judges are equally divided as to the outcome of a particular case, no precedent is created by that court. This is true even though the decision affirms the decision of the next-lower court.

In addition, in order to create precedent, the opinion must be reported. A decision by a court without a reported opinion does not have *stare decisis* effect. In the great majority of cases, no opinion is written. Appellate courts are responsible for practically all the reported opinions, although occasionally a trial judge will issue a written opinion relating to a case tried to the court. Trial judges do not write opinions in jury cases. There are over three million reported U.S. judicial decisions.

Once a reported judicial precedent-setting opinion is found, the effective date of that decision has to be determined. For this purpose, the date of the court decision, not the date of the events that gave rise to the suit, is crucial.

The Retroactive Versus Prospective Application Question

A court has the power to declare in its opinion whether a precedent-setting decision should have retroactive or prospective application. *Retroactive effect* means that the decision controls the legal consequences of causes of action arising before the announcement of the decision. *Prospective effect* means that the new rule will apply to all questions subsequently coming before that court and the lower courts of the jurisdiction. In general, unless the precedent-setting court has expressly indicated otherwise, or unless special circumstances warrant the denial of retroactive application, the decision is entitled to retroactive as well as prospective effect to all actions that are neither *res judicata* nor barred by a *statute of limitations* as of the date of the precedent-setting decision.

The next case illustrates how courts make this decision. The court examines three factors in determining whether to grant retroactive application: (1) the degree of reliance on the rule of law being overruled, (2) the extent to which prospective application would advance or retard the purpose of the new rule, and (3) the extent to which retroactivity would be substantially inequitable. Courts decide this issue on a case-by-case basis.

Adkins v. Sky Blue, Inc.
702 P.2d 549
Supreme Court of Wyoming
May 24, 1985

Cardine, Justice

During the evening of May 4, 1982, Christopher Kennedy became intoxicated as a result of drinking liquor at a bar known as "The Lounge." On leaving "The Lounge" that evening he purchased and consumed more liquor before departing Casper, Wyoming. Approximately twenty miles north of Medicine Bow, Wyoming, the automobile being driven by Christopher Kennedy struck plaintiff Leland Adkins's vehicle head-on in Mr. Adkins's lane of travel. Christopher Kennedy was killed, as were his two passengers. Leland Adkins and his passenger suffered personal injuries in the accident resulting in Adkins being left a quadriplegic. Some time after the accident a blood sample, taken from the body of Christopher Kennedy, determined his blood alcohol level to be .11%. Leland Adkins filed suit in the United States District Court for the District of Wyoming against "The Lounge," its owners and employee to recover damages for the personal injuries suffered by him.

The United States District Court found that Adkins's case involved a question of law of the State of Wyoming which might be determinative of the action and that there was no clear and controlling precedent in the decisions of the Supreme Court of the State of Wyoming; it therefore certified for instruction, pursuant to § 1–13–106, W.S.1977, the following question.

> "Do third persons injured by an intoxicated patron of a liquor vendor state a claim for relief against the liquor vendor for causes of action that arose prior to *McClellan v. Tottenhoff,* . . . (Wyo.1983)?"

We answer the certified question in the negative.

In *Parsons v. Jow,* . . . the bar owner sold intoxicating liquor to McCall, a minor, who became drunk and crashed his car into a building. Plaintiff, a passenger in the car at the time, sued the bar owner to recover damages resulting from his personal injuries. The trial court dismissed plaintiff's complaint for failure to state a claim upon which relief could be granted. We affirmed stating that

> " . . . it cannot be denied there was no cause of action at common law against a vendor of liquor in favor of one injured by a vendee who becomes intoxicated—this for the reason

that the proximate cause of injury was deemed to be the patron's consumption of liquor and not its sale. . . .

"Statutes, in a number of states, have changed the common law rule and subjected a tavern keeper to liability to a third party, where injury results from the furnishing of intoxicating liquor. The statutes are called civil damage or dramshop acts.

*   *   *   *   *   *

"The legislature of Wyoming has not seen fit to change the common law rule as it applies in this case. Whether legislation in the nature of a dramshop act or a civil damage statute should be included as part of our liquor control code is within the province of the legislature." . . .

Thus, the Wyoming Supreme Court issued a clear pronouncement that it would not undertake to adopt a dramshop law by judicial decision but would leave that to the legislature. When the question of liability for sale of liquor to an intoxicated person was next considered in *Snyder v. West Rawlins Properties, Inc.* . . . (D.Wyo.1982), the United States District Court, relying upon the pronouncements of the Wyoming Supreme Court stated:

"The general rule is that in the absence of a civil damage or dramshop act enacted by the state legislature, the common law provided that no remedy existed against a tavern owner or vendor of liquor for injuries to a [third] party. Wyoming does not have a civil damages or dramshop act."

Thus, as late as February 1982, there was no reason for anyone to suspect that the Wyoming Supreme Court would, at the next opportunity, impose liability upon the vendors of liquor by an overruling decision rather than leaving the matter to the legislature.

McClellan v. Tottenhoff, decided June 28, 1983, involved the sale of alcoholic beverage to a minor who became intoxicated and drove a car so as to fatally injure the plaintiff. Without prior warning or suggestion of what was to occur, the court in *McClellan v. Tottenhoff*, supra, stated:

"The rule that there is no cause of action when a vendor sells liquor to a consumer who injures a third party was created by the courts. We see no reason to wait any longer for the legislature to abrogate it, Common law created by the judiciary can be abrogated by the judiciary." . . .

The common law has served us well because it is flexible, able to grow and meet the requirements of changing conditions and a different society. There are times when change is necessary; but the doctrine of *stare decisis* is also important in an organized society. Change, therefore, should occur slowly, deliberately after much experience, and if possible so as not to affect vested rights or things in the past. Thus, it is said that:

"[T]he courts may apply or effectuate common law principles in the light of altered or new conditions, and when the circumstances and conditions are different, in that the common law principles are unsuitable to new circumstances or conditions, the needs of society, or in conflict with public policy, the courts may make such changes or modifications as the situation requires." (Footnotes omitted.) 15A C.J.S. Common Law § 13. . . .

Acknowledging that there ought to be an extreme reluctance to change the common law and recognizing the obvious benefits of the doctrine of *stare decisis*, yet on occasion it does become eminently clear that society has long passed beyond the point where an ancient doctrine remains viable. This court believed it had arrived at that place in deciding *McClellan v. Tottenhoff*, supra—now the law of this state—and in stating:

"We hereby overrule *Parsons v. Jow*, supra.

*   *   *   *   *   *

"*Henceforth,* cases involving vendors of liquor and injured third parties will be approached in the same manner as other negligence cases.

*   *   *   *   *   *

"We hold that a vendor of liquor owes a duty to exercise the degree of care required of a reasonable person in light of all the circumstances." (Emphasis added.) . . .

The rule of *McClellan v. Tottenhoff*, supra, became effective with the issuance of the court's opinion on June 28, 1983. The accident in which plaintiff was involved and which is the subject of this case, occurred May 5, 1982, more than a year prior to the court's pronouncement in *McClellan v. Tottenhoff*. If the rule announced in *McClellan v. Tottenhoff*, supra, applies prospectively only—that is in the future, *henceforth* and from now on—then plaintiff's case is subject to the common-law rule of nonliability for sellers of intoxicating liquor as stated in *Parsons v. Jow*. And, as was held in *Parsons v. Jow*, it must be dismissed.

Initially it was held that a court issuing an overruling decision had merely discovered and announced existing law; since the overruling case did not create new law, but merely recognized what had always been the law, such law would operate both retrospectively and prospectively:

> "'[B]ut the modern decisions, taking a more pragmatic view of the judicial function, have recognized the power of a court to hold that an overruling decision is operative prospectively only and is not even operative upon the rights of the parties to the overruling case. As a matter of constitutional law, retroactive operation of an overruling decision is neither required nor prohibited.'"

Where an overruling decision announces a change in the common law, some guidelines are set forth in *Chevron Oil Company v. Huson*, 404 U.S. 97 (1971), for whether its operation should be retrospective or prospective only:

> "In our cases dealing with the nonretroactivity question, we have generally considered three separate factors. First, the decision to be applied nonretroactively must establish a new principle of law, either by overruling clear past precedent on which litigants may

have relied, . . . or by deciding an issue of first impression whose resolution was not clearly foreshadowed. . . . Second, it has been stressed that 'we must . . . weigh the merits and demerits in each case by looking to the prior history of the rule in question, its purpose and effect, and whether retrospective operation will further or retard its operation.' . . . Finally, we have weighed the inequity imposed by retroactive application, for '[w]here a decision of this Court could produce substantial inequitable results if applied retroactively, there is ample basis in our cases for avoiding the "injustice or hardship" by a holding of nonretroactivity.'" Id., 92 S.Ct. at 355.

This court has on several occasions considered whether a change in law should operate retrospectively or prospectively. In *Nehring v. Russell*, . . . (1978), we stated that

> " . . . the determination is ours to make, [and] we conclude that in consideration of all the factors and any prior reliances involved, our holding should be applied prospectively only, i.e., to this action and all causes of action accruing after 30 days following the date of this decision." . . .

It has been repeatedly stated that where a decision might produce substantial inequitable results if applied retroactively, it is appropriate to avoid such hardship or injustice by providing for prospective operation only. *Chevron Oil Company v. Huson*, supra. Vendors of liquor in this state had no reason to suspect that this court would adopt a dramshop-type law placing liability on vendors of liquor. There were no cases following *Parsons v. Jow*, supra, suggesting an imminent change in the law. The court had given its firm assurance in *Parsons v. Jow*, . . . that this was a matter for the legislature. As late as 1982, in *Snyder v. West Rawlins Properties, Inc.*, . . . the United States District Court, District of Wyoming, reaffirmed the rule of *Parsons v. Jow*, . . . which provided nonliability to third persons injured by an intoxicated patron of a liquor vendor. Liquor vendors had no reason to obtain insurance or otherwise protect themselves against liability that did not exist. Insuring against this kind of broad liability is expensive, and they surely were justified in relying upon the pronouncement of this court in not purchasing insurance coverage.

The public policy of *McClellan v. Tottenhoff* and the purpose to be served by imposing civil liability upon vendors of liquor are to cause them (a) to exercise care in dispensing liquor, (b) to refuse liquor to intoxicated persons or refuse to sell in violation of law; and (c) to provide financial responsibility for negligence. Those purposes are not served or affected by retroactive operation of the law, for the incident complained of had already occurred—nothing could be done to change it. The stated public policy would not be promoted by holding the vendor retroactively liable for damages. We note here also that the legislature, at its 1985 general session, was concerned about this area of the law and enacted legislation on this subject.

It is suggested that the case for prospective operation of the rule of *McClellan v. Tottenhoff* is weak because vendors of alcoholic beverage cannot seriously and in good conscience contend that they violated the liquor laws relying upon *Parsons v. Jow* to escape civil liability. We do not suggest they violated the law relying upon *Parsons v. Jow*. We do suggest they may not have purchased expensive insurance or otherwise obtained financial protection against this newly-created liability in reliance upon *Parsons v. Jow*. That is the reliance of which we speak. With respect to the violation of the liquor laws in reliance upon *Parsons v. Jow*, that is not likely, for severe criminal sanctions are imposed as are procedures resulting in the loss of a liquor license whether by revocation or refusal to renew.

There was no series of cases following *Parsons v. Jow* that suggested or even intimated that the court might overrule *Parsons v. Jow*. The vendors of liquor justifiably relied

upon the law as we stated it to be. To hold now that a vendor of liquor, not liable for damages under the law existing at the time of the accident involved nevertheless, a year later, became liable because of a change in the law by an overruling case would be manifestly unfair.

We find comfort in the language of the court in *McClellan v. Tottenhoff* wherein we stated that *"henceforth"* this type of case would be determined upon ordinary negligence principles. It is held that such terms as "hereafter," "thereafter," and "shall be" speak to prospective operation. 82 C.J.S. Statutes § 413. Henceforth is in the same category. It is defined as:

> "A word of futurity, which, as employed in legal documents, statutes, and the like, always imports a continuity of action or condition from the present time forward, but excludes all the past." Black's Law Dictionary (5th ed. 1979).

We, therefore, hold that the rule of *McClellan v. Tottenhoff*, supra, applies prospectively only, to claims or causes of action that accrue after the date of its publication, to wit, June 28, 1983.

Brown, Justice, dissenting

In holding that *McClellan v. Tottenhoff*, . . . (1983), has only prospective application, the majority bases its decision on language in the *McClellan* case, and the notion that vendors of liquor relied on *Parsons v. Jow*, . . . (1971) to insulate them from civil liability in the illegal sale of liquor. . . .

There is no clear prohibition in *McClellan* against retrospective application nor is there a clear mandate requiring only prospective application. The general rule is that, in civil cases, decisions are to be applied retroactively. . . .

In *Malan v. Lewis*, . . . (1984), the court stated:

> "The *general rule* from time immemorial is that the ruling of a court is deemed to state

the true nature of the law both retrospectively and prospectively. In civil cases, at least, constitutional law neither requires nor prohibits retroactive operation of an overruling decision, [Citations] but in the vast majority of cases a decision is effective both prospectively and retrospectively, even an overruling decision. [Citations.] Whether the *general rule* should be departed from depends on whether a substantial injustice would otherwise occur. [Citation.]" (Emphasis added.) . . .

These cases, of course, are not without exception:

> "Although there is a traditional general rule in favor of giving retroactive effect to an overruling decision, it has become recognized that this rule is subject to various exceptions, for example, where there has been justifiable reliance on decisions which are subsequently overruled and those who have so relied may be substantially harmed if retroactive effect is given to the overruling decision. . . ." Annot., 10 A.L.R.3d 1384 (1966).

The case before us, however, is the weakest case imaginable for an exception from the general rule. How can vendors of alcoholic beverages seriously and in good conscience contend that they violated the liquor laws, relying on *Parsons v. Jow* to escape civil liability? . . .

Brannigan v. Raybuck, . . . (1983), has elements of both the case before us and the *McClellan* case. In *Brannigan,* the surviving parents of minor passengers and the driver killed in an automobile accident brought a wrongful death action against tavern operators for negligently furnishing liquor to the decedents. The court en banc held, among other things, that where violation of a statute pertaining to furnishing liquor to those who are underage or who are already intoxicated is shown, negligence exists as a matter of law and the rule may be retroactively and prospectively applied. . . .

Both the majority and this dissent strive mightily albeit circuitously to arrive at divergent views. Both argue that logic, precedent, and justice support their position. Both avoid the real basis of how the decision was made or, from the dissent's view, should have been made.

> ". . . [M]ost courts now treat the question of how an overruling decision should operate as one of judicial policy rather than of judicial power, and recognize that varying results may be reached, depending on the particular circumstances presented and the particular rule affected." Annot., 10 A.L.R.3d 1378 (1966).

I would hold that *McClellan* should be applied retroactively as well as prospectively.

Case Questions

1. Why should there be a strong presumption in favor of retroactivity in civil cases?
2. Why did the Wyoming Supreme Court apply the three tests established in the *Chevron* case?
3. Why did the Wyoming Supreme Court conclude that the *McClellan* precedent should apply only prospectively?

 Did ethical considerations play a role in the Wyoming Supreme Court's decision to not apply retroactively the rule of McClellan v. Tottenhoff?

Absence of Precedent

When judges are confronted by a novel fact situation, they must rely on their own sense of justice and philosophy of law. The public interest, tradition, prevailing customs, business usage, and moral standards are important considerations in the decision-making process. Judges encountering a case of first impression first look for guidance within the forum state (as was done by the court in the *Du Pont* case in Chapter 1). When precedent is lacking in the forum state, decisions of other state and federal courts, as well as English decisions, may be considered persuasive on the legal point at issue.

The trial court in the following case encountered a problem that was unique. The trial and appellate courts were required to make decisions without being able to benefit from the experience of others as reflected in statutory law and common law opinions. They had to create new law when life and death were at stake. Note that three of the seven members of the appellate court dissented.

Strunk v. Strunk
445 S.W.2d 145
Court of Appeals of Kentucky
September 26, 1969

Osborne, Judge

The specific question involved upon this appeal is: Does a court of equity* have power to permit a kidney to be removed from an incompetent ward of the state upon petition of his committee, who is also his mother, for the purpose of being transplanted into the body of his brother, who is dying of a fatal kidney disease? We are of the opinion it does.

The facts of the case are as follows: Arthur L. Strunk, 54 years of age, and Ava Strunk, 52 years of age, of Williamstown, Kentucky, are the parents of two sons. Tommy Strunk is 28 years of age, married, an employee of the Penn State Railroad and a part-time student at the University of Cincinnati. Tommy is now suffering from chronic glomerus nephritis, a fatal kidney disease. He is now being kept alive by frequent treatment on an artificial

kidney, a procedure that cannot be continued much longer.

Jerry Strunk is 27 years of age, incompetent, and through proper legal proceedings has been committed to the Frankfort State Hospital and School, which is a state institution maintained for the feeble-minded. He has an IQ of approximately 35, which corresponds with the mental age of approximately six years. He is further handicapped by a speech defect, which makes it difficult for him to communicate with persons who are not well acquainted with him. When it was determined that Tommy, in order to survive, would have to have a kidney, the doctors considered the possibility of using a kidney from a cadaver if and when one became available, or one from a live donor if this could be made available. The entire family, his mother, father, and a number of collateral relatives, were tested. Because of incompatibility of blood type or tissue, none was medically acceptable as a live donor. As a last resort, Jerry was tested and found to be highly acceptable. This immediately presented the legal problem as to what, if anything, could be done by the family, especially the mother and the father, to procure a transplant from Jerry to Tommy.

---

*Equity is discussed in Chapters 1 and 7—Ed.

The mother as a committee petitioned the county court for authority to proceed with the operation. The court found that the operation was necessary, that under the peculiar circumstances of this case, it would not only be beneficial to Tommy but also beneficial to Jerry because Jerry was greatly dependent on Tommy, emotionally and psychologically, and that his well-being would be jeopardized more severely by the loss of his brother than by the removal of a kidney.

Appeal was taken to the Franklin Circuit Court where the chancellor reviewed the record, examined the testimony of the witnesses, and adopted the findings of the county court.

A psychiatrist, in attendance to Jerry, who testified in the case, stated in his opinion the death of Tommy under these circumstances would have "an extremely traumatic effect upon him [Jerry]."

The Department of Mental Health of this commonwealth has entered the case as *amicus curiae* and on the basis of its evaluation of the seriousness of the operation as opposed to the traumatic effect on Jerry as a result of the loss of Tommy, recommended to the court that Jerry be permitted to undergo the surgery. Its recommendations are as follows: "It is difficult for the mental defective to establish a firm sense of identity with another person. The acquisition of this necessary identity is dependent on a person whom one can conveniently accept as a model and who at the same time is sufficiently flexible to allow the defective to detach himself with reassurances of continuity. His need to be social is not so much the necessity of a formal and mechanical contact with other human beings as it is the necessity of a close intimacy with other men, the desirability of a real community of feeling, an urgent need for a unity of understanding. Purely mechanical and formal contact with other men does not offer any treatment for the behavior of a mental defective; only those who are able to communicate intimately are of value to hospital treatment in these cases. And this generally is a member of the family.

"In view of this knowledge, we now have particular interest in this case. Jerry Strunk, a mental defective, has emotions and reactions on a scale comparable to that of a normal person. He identifies with his brother Tom. Tom is his model, his tie with his family. Tom's life is vital to the continuity of Jerry's improvement at Frankfort State Hospital and School. The testimony of the hospital representative reflected the importance to Jerry of his visits with his family and the constant inquiries Jerry made about Tom's coming to see him. Jerry is aware he plays a role in the relief of this tension. We the Department of Mental Health must take all possible steps to prevent the occurrence of any guilt feelings Jerry would have if Tom were to die.

"The necessity of Tom's life to Jerry's treatment and eventual rehabilitation is clearer in view of the fact that Tom is his only living sibling and at the death of their parents, now in their fifties, Jerry will have no concerned, intimate communication so necessary to his stability and optimal functioning.

"The evidence shows that at the present level of medical knowledge, it is quite remote that Tom would be able to survive several cadaver transplants. Tom has a much better chance of survival if the kidney transplant from Jerry takes place."

Upon this appeal, we are faced with the fact that all members of the immediate family have recommended the transplant. The Department of Mental Health has likewise made its recommendation. The county court has given its approval. The circuit court has found that it would be to the best interest of the ward of the state that the procedure be carried out. Throughout the legal proceedings, Jerry has been represented by a guardian *ad litem*, who has continually questioned the power of the state to authorize the removal of an organ from the body of an incompetent who is a ward of the state. We are fully cognizant of the fact that the question before us is unique. Insofar as we have been able to learn, no similar set of facts has come before the highest court of any of the states of this nation or the federal courts. The English courts have apparently taken a broad view of the inherent power of the equity courts with regard to incompetents. *Ex parte Whitebread* (1816), . . . holds that courts of equity have the inherent power to make provisions for a needy brother out of the estate of an incompetent. . . . The inherent rule in these cases is that the chancellor has the power to deal with the estate of the incompetent in the same manner as the incompetent would if he had his faculties. This rule has been extended to cover not only matters of property but also to cover the personal affairs of the incompetent. . . .

The right to act for the incompetent in all cases has become recognized in this country as the doctrine of substituted judgment and is broad enough not only to cover property but also to cover all matters touching on the well-being of the ward. . . .

The medical practice of transferring tissue from one part of the human body to another (autografting) and from one human being to another (homografting) is rapidly becoming a common clinical practice. In many cases, the transplants take as well when the tissue is dead as when it is alive. This has made practicable the establishment of tissue banks where such material can be stored for future use. Vascularized grafts of lungs, kidneys, and hearts are becoming increasingly common. These grafts must be of functioning, living cells with blood vessels remaining anatomically intact. The chance of success in the transfer of these organs is greatly increased when the donor and the donee are genetically related. It is recognized by all legal and medical authorities that several legal problems can arise as a result of the operative techniques of the transplant procedure. . . .

The renal transplant is becoming the most common of the organ transplants. This is be-

cause the normal body has two functioning kidneys, one of which it can reasonably do without, thereby making it possible for one person to donate a kidney to another. Testimony in this record shows that there have been over 2500 kidney transplants performed in the United States up to this date. The process can be effected under present techniques with minimal danger to both the donor and the donee. . . .

Review of our case law leads us to believe that the power given to a committee under KRS 387.230 would not extend so far as to allow a committee to subject his ward to the serious surgical techniques here under consideration unless the life of his ward be in jeopardy. Nor do we believe the powers delegated to the county court by virtue of the above statutes would reach so far as to permit the procedure which we [are] dealing with here.

We are of the opinion that a chancery court does have sufficient inherent power to authorize the operation. The circuit court having found that the operative procedures are to the best interest of Jerry Strunk and this finding having been based on substantial evidence, we are of the opinion the judgment should be affirmed. We do not deem it significant that this case reached the circuit court by way of an appeal as opposed to a direct proceeding in that court.

Judgment affirmed.

Hill, C.J., Milliken, and Reed, JJ., concur.

Neikirk, Palmore, and Steinfeld, JJ., dissent.

Steinfeld, Judge, dissenting

Apparently because of my indelible recollection of a government which, to the everlasting shame of its citizens, embarked on a program of genocide and experimentation with human bodies, I have been more troubled in reaching a decision in this case than in any other. My sympathies and emotions are torn between a compassion to aid an ailing young man and a duty to fully protect unfortunate members of society.

The opinion of the majority is predicated on the authority of an equity court to speak for one who cannot speak for himself. However, it is my opinion that in considering such right in this instance, we must first look to the power and authority vested in the committee, the appellee herein. KRS 387.060 and KRS 387.230 do nothing more than give the committee the power to take custody of the incompetent and the possession, care, and management of his property. Courts have restricted the activities of the committee to that which is for the best interest of the incompetent. . . . The authority and duty have been to protect and maintain the ward, to secure that to which he is entitled and preserve that which he has. . . .

The wishes of the members of the family or the desires of the guardian to be helpful to the apparent objects of the ward's bounty have not been a criterion. "A curator or guardian cannot dispose of his ward's property by donation, even though authorized to do so by the court on advice of a family meeting, unless a gift by the guardian is authorized by statute." . . .

Two Kentucky cases decided many years ago reveal judicial policy. In *W. T. Sistrunk & Co. v. Navarra's Committee*, . . . 105 S.W.2d 1039 (1937), this court held that a committee was without right to continue a business which the incompetent had operated prior to his having been declared a person of unsound mind. More analogous is *Baker v. Thomas*, . . . 114 S.W.2d 1113 (1938), in which a man and woman had lived together out of wedlock. Two children were born to them. After the man was judged incompetent, his committee, acting for him, together with his paramour, instituted proceedings to adopt the two children. In rejecting the application and refusing

to speak for the incompetent, the opinion stated: "The statute does not contemplate that the committee of a lunatic may exercise any other power than to have the possession, care, and management of the lunatic's or incompetent's estate." . . .

The majority opinion is predicated on the finding of the circuit court that there will be psychological benefits to the ward but points out that the incompetent has the mentality of a six-year-old child. It is common knowledge beyond dispute that the loss of a close relative or a friend to a six-year-old child is not of major impact. Opinions concerning psychological trauma are at best most nebulous. Furthermore, there are no guarantees that the transplant will become a surgical success, it being well known that body rejection of transplanted organs is frequent. The life of the incompetent is not in danger, but the surgical procedure advocated creates some peril.

It is written in *Prince v. Massachusetts*, 321 U.S. 158 (1944), that "Parents may be free to become martyrs themselves. But it does not follow they are free, in identical circumstances, to make martyrs of their children before they have reached the age of full and legal distinction when they can make the choice for themselves." The ability to fully understand and consent is a prerequisite to the donation of a part of the human body. . . .

Unquestionably, the attitudes and attempts of the committee and members of the family of the two young men whose critical problems now confront us are commendable, natural, and beyond reproach. However, they refer us to nothing indicating that they are privileged to authorize the removal of one of the kidneys of the incompetent for the purpose of donation, and they cite no statutory or other authority vesting such right in the courts. The proof shows that less compatible donors are available and that the kidney of a cadaver could be used, although the odds of operational success are not as great in such cases as they would be with the fully compatible donor brother.

I am unwilling to hold that the gates should be open to permit the removal of an organ from an incompetent for transplant, at least until such time as it is conclusively demonstrated that it will be of significant benefit to the incompetent. The evidence here does not rise to that pinnacle. To hold that committees, guardians, or courts have such awesome power, even in the persuasive case before us, could establish legal precedent, the dire result of which we cannot fathom. Regretfully I must say no.

Neikirk and Palmore, JJ., join with me in this dissent.

Case Questions

1. The Court of Appeals of Kentucky is the court of last resort in that state. The *Strunk* decision is now Kentucky law. Does the decision make mental institutions a storehouse of human bodies available for distribution to the more productive members of society whenever the state decides that someone's need outweighs the danger to the incompetent?
2. Which opinion, the majority or dissent, was more persuasive?
3. Where no legal cases have a direct bearing on the issue of a case, should the court turn to other disciplines for authority?

 What ethical considerations do you think convinced the dissenters in this case to oppose the operation on Jerry Strunk?

RECOGNIZING LAWS OF OTHER STATES

Conflict of Laws

Every person within the territorial limits of a government is bound by its laws. However, it is well recognized that law does not of its own force have any effect outside the territory of the sovereignty from which its authority is derived. Since each of the fifty states is an individual sovereignty that creates its own common and statutory law, there are often inconsistencies among the laws of the various states. When the facts of a case under consideration have occurred in more than one state or country, and a court must make a choice between the laws of different states or nations, a conflict case is presented.

Another type of conflict-of-laws case involves a situation in which an event occurred in one state and the suit is brought in another state. For example, a driver from Michigan might bring suit in Kentucky regarding an automobile collision in Ohio involving a driver from Kentucky. In this situation, the court must decide whether to apply its own substantive law, the law of the state in which the events occurred, or possibly the law of some other state.

Conflict-of-laws rules have been developed by each state to assist its courts in determining whether and when foreign substantive law should be given effect within the territory of the forum. (Remember that a state court follows that state's procedural law.) The rules afford some assurance that a case will be treated in the same way under the appropriate substantive law, no matter where the suit is brought. Foreign law may be enforced or given effect when the conflict-of-laws rule determining such enforcement or recognition is part of the law of the local jurisdiction.

It is important to remember that the *Erie* doctrine (see *Carson* case in Chapter 3) applies to conflict cases. Federal judges will follow the conflict-of-laws rules that would be applied in the courts of the state in which the federal court is located.

Tort Cases

The traditional approach in tort cases is to apply the law of the place where the wrong was committed—*lex loci delicti commissi*. The place of the wrong is where the last event necessary to make the actor liable takes place or where the person or thing harmed is situated at the time of the wrong. The following case exemplifies a trend that had been occurring in recent years. The Indiana Supreme Court used the *Hubbard* case to replace the traditional *lex loci delicti commissi* rule with the *significant relationship rule*. The significant relationship approach is more flexible than a rigid *lex loci* approach. A court following the significant relationship rule can apply the law of the place that has the most significant contacts with the incident or event in dispute.

Hubbard Manufacturing Co., Inc., v. Greeson
515 N.E.2d 1071
Supreme Court of Indiana
December 1, 1987

Shepard, Chief Justice

The question is whether an Indiana court should apply Indiana tort law when both parties are residents of Indiana and the injury occurred in Illinois.

Plaintiff Elizabeth Greeson, an Indiana resident, filed a wrongful death action in Indiana against defendant Hubbard Manufacturing Co., Inc., an Indiana corporation.

The defendant corporation built lift units for use in cleaning, repairing, and replacing streetlights.

On October 29, 1979, Donald Greeson, plaintiff's husband and also a resident of Indiana, happened to be working in Illinois maintaining street lights. He died that day while using a lift unit manufactured by Hubbard in Indiana.

Elizabeth Greeson's suit alleged that defective manufacture of Hubbard's lift unit caused her husband's death. When she raised the possibility that Illinois products liability law should be applied to this case, Hubbard moved the trial court for a determination of the applicable law. The trial court found that Indiana had more significant contacts with the litigation but felt constrained to apply Illinois substantive law because the decedent's injury had been sustained there. The Court of Appeals expressed the opinion that Indiana law should apply but concluded that existing precedent required use of Illinois law. . . .

We grant transfer to decide whether Indiana or Illinois law applies.

Greeson's complaint alleged two bases for her claim: "the defective and unreasonably dangerous condition of a lift type vehicle sold . . . by the defendant" and "the negligence of the defendant." Both theories state a cause for liability based on Hubbard's manufacture of the vehicle in Indiana.

The differences in Indiana law and Illinois law are considerable. First, in Indiana a finding that the product represented an open and obvious danger would preclude recovery on the product liability claim. . . . to impress liability on manufacturers the defect must be hidden and not normally observable. Under Illinois law, the trier of fact may find product liability even if the danger is open and obvious. . . . Second, under Indiana law misuse would bar recovery. . . . In Illinois misuse merely reduces a plaintiff's award. . . . These differences are important enough to affect the outcome of the litigation.

Choosing the applicable substantive law for a given case is a decision made by the courts of the state in which the lawsuit is pending. An early basis for choosing law applicable to events transversing several states was to use the substantive law of the state "where the wrong is committed" regardless of where the plaintiff took his complaint seeking relief. . . .

The historical choice-of-law rule for torts, . . . was *lex loci delicti commissi*, which applied the substantive law where the tort was committed. *Burns v. Grand Rapids and Indiana Railroad Co.* (1888). . . . The tort is said to have been committed in the state where the last event necessary to make an actor liable for the alleged wrong takes place.

Rigid application of the traditional rule to this case, however, would lead to an anomalous result. Had plaintiff Elizabeth Greeson filed suit in any bordering state the only forum which would not have applied the substantive law of Indiana is Indiana. . . . To avoid this inappropriate result, we look elsewhere for guidance.

Choice-of-law rules are fundamentally judge-made and designed to ensure the appropriate substantive law applies. In a large number of cases, the place of the tort will be significant and the place with the most contacts. . . . In such cases, the traditional rule serves well. A court should be allowed to evaluate other factors when the place of the tort is an insignificant contact. In those instances where the place of the tort bears little connection to the legal action, this Court will permit the consideration of other factors such as:

1. the place where the conduct causing the injury occurred;
2. the residence or place of business of the parties; and
3. the place where the relationship is centered.

Restatement (Second) of Conflicts of Laws § 145(2) (1971). These factors should be evaluated according to their relative importance to the particular issues being litigated.

The first step in applying this rule in the present case is to consider whether the place of the tort "bears little connection" to this legal action. The last event necessary to make Hubbard liable for the alleged tort took place in Illinois. The decedent was working in Illinois at the time of his death and the vehicle involved in the fatal injuries was in Illinois. The coroner's inquest was held in Illinois, and the decedent's wife and son are receiving benefits under the Illinois Workmen's Compensation Laws. None of these facts relates to the wrongful death action filed against Hubbard. The place of the tort is insignificant to this suit.

After having determined that the place of the tort bears little connection to the legal action, the second step is to apply the additional factors. Applying these factors to this wrongful death action leads us to the same conclusion that the trial court drew: Indiana has the more significant relationship and contacts. The plaintiff's two theories of recovery relate to the manufacture of the lift in Indiana. Both parties are from Indiana; plaintiff Elizabeth Greeson is a resident of Indiana

and defendant Hubbard is an Indiana corporation with its principal place of business in Indiana. The relationship between the deceased and Hubbard centered in Indiana. The deceased frequently visited defendant's plant in Indiana to discuss the repair and maintenance of the lift. Indiana law applies.

The Court of Appeals decision is vacated and the cause remanded to the trial court with instructions to apply Indiana law.

Case Questions

1. Under *lex loci delicti commissi*, how should a court determine where a tort was committed?
2. Why did the Indiana Supreme Court decide to replace the traditional *lex loci delicti commissi* approach?
3. What contacts were evaluated by the court in determining which state had a more significant relationship with the occurrence and with the parties?

Contract Cases

All states have developed their own conflict-of-laws rules for contractual disputes, which differ from the rules that apply to tort cases. In contractual disputes, depending on the facts involved and jurisdictional preferences, courts have historically applied the law of place in any of the following ways: (1) where the action was instituted (*lex fori*), (2) where the contract was to be performed (*lex loci solutionis*), (3) which law the parties intended to govern their agreement, (4) the law of the state where the last act necessary to complete the contract was done and which created a legal obligation (*lex loci contractus*), and (5) the law of the state that has the greatest concern with the event and the parties (significant relationship rule). A court may choose to follow its own substantive law of contracts and will do so if the application of the foreign law would offend its public policy.

Courts often honor the law intended by the parties to be controlling. The state chosen usually has a substantial connection with the contract, but courts have held that no such connection is necessary if the parties intended that that state's laws govern the agreement. For example, automobile and house insurance contracts generally included a choice-of-law clause, usually a forum selected by the lawyers for the insurance company, and "agreed to" by the insured. If a contract fails to include a choice-of-law clause, courts may still determine the parties' intent by examining the facts surrounding the contract.

One of the important developments in contract law has been the enactment by all states of at least some provisions of the Uniform Commercial Code (UCC). This code was created in order to enhance the uniformity of state laws regulating certain commercial transactions. The UCC does not apply to all types of contracts. It does not apply, for example, to employment contracts, services, or to the sale of real property. With respect to conflicts of law, the UCC basically follows the significant relationship rule when parties to contracts have not specified a choice of law.

Full Faith and Credit

Since each state in the United States is a distinct sovereignty, each of the states is entitled to disregard the constitutions, statutes, records, and judgments of other states. Thus the refusal of some states to recognize and enforce the judgments issued by other states would deny justice to those who had taken their disputes to court. Judgment debtors could flee to a state that refuses to recognize and enforce judgments from the issuing state, undermining public confidence in the law.

The authors of the U.S. Constitution anticipated this problem and addressed it in Article IV, Section 1, which provides that "full faith and credit shall be given in each state to the public acts, records, and judicial proceedings of every other state." Thus the Constitution requires the states to cooperate with each other and binds them together into one nation. Since final judgments of each state are enforceable in every other state, irrespective of differences in substantive law and public policy, the full faith and credit requirement also helps to preserve the legal differences that exist from state to state.

Another important benefit of the full faith and credit requirement is that it puts teeth into the doctrine of *res judicata*. Once a valid judgment has been rendered in one state, the claims adjudicated in that lawsuit cannot be relitigated by the same parties in some other state.

A state can justifiably refuse to grant full faith and credit to another state's judgment under limited circumstances: for example, when the issuing court has failed to follow the mandates of the federal Constitution regarding due process of law. Full faith and credit can be denied when the issuing court did not have minimum contacts with the person of the judgment debtor, or when the judicial proceedings denied the judgment debtor the constitutionally required elements of notice and an opportunity for a hearing.

Article IV, Section 1, only requires that the states provide full faith and credit to other states. The federal Full Faith and Credit Act (28 USC Section 1738), however, requires all federal courts to afford full faith and credit to state court judgments.

Although a properly authenticated judgment of an issuing state is presumptively valid and binding in all other states, it is not self-implementing. A judgment creditor who has to go to some other state to enforce a judgment will have to begin an action against the judgment debtor in the nonissuing state. The courts of the nonissuing state will then have to enforce the foreign judgment in the same manner as they would one of their own judgments, even if enforcing the judgment would contravene the enforcing state's public policy.

In the following case, the U.S. Supreme Court has to decide whether Missouri courts are required by the full faith and credit clause to respect an injunction issued by a Michigan court. Under the terms of the injunction, a "whistleblower" would have been prevented from giving testimony against General Motors Corporation in a Missouri product liability lawsuit.

Baker et al. v. General Motors
No. 96-653
U.S. Supreme Court
January 13, 1998

Justice Ginsburg delivered the opinion of the Court.

This case concerns the authority of one State's court to order that a witness's testimony shall not be heard in any court of the United States. In settlement of claims and counterclaims precipitated by the discharge of Ronald Elwell, a former General Motors Corporation (GM) engineering analyst, GM paid Elwell an undisclosed sum of money, and the parties agreed to a permanent injunction. As stipulated by GM and Elwell and entered by a Michigan County Court, the injunction prohibited Elwell from "testifying, without the prior written consent of [GM], . . . as . . . a witness of any kind . . . in any litigation already filed, or to be filed in the future, involving [GM] as an owner, seller, manufacturer and/or designer." . . . GM separately agreed, however, that if Elwell were ordered to testify by a court or other tribunal, such testimony would not be actionable as a violation of the Michigan court's injunction or the GM-Elwell agreement. After entry of the stipulated injunction in Michigan, Elwell was subpoenaed to testify in a product liability action commenced in Missouri by plaintiffs who were not involved in the Michigan case. The question presented is whether the national full faith and credit command bars Elwell's testimony in the Missouri case. We

hold that Elwell may testify in the Missouri action without offense to the full faith and credit requirement.

I

Two lawsuits, initiated by different parties in different states, gave rise to the full faith and credit issue before us. One suit involved a severed employment relationship, the other, a wrongful-death complaint. . . .

II
A

The Constitution's Full Faith and Credit Clause provides: "Full Faith and Credit shall be given in each State to the public Acts, Records, and judicial Proceedings of every other State. And the Congress may by general Laws prescribe the Manner in which such Acts, Records and Proceedings shall be proved, and the Effect thereof." U.S. Const., Art.IV, § 1.3.

Pursuant to that Clause, Congress has prescribed: "Such Acts, records and judicial proceedings or copies thereof, so authenticated, shall have the same full faith and credit in every court within the United States and its Territories and Possessions as they have by law or usage in the courts of such State, Territory or Possession from which they are taken."

The animating purpose of the full faith and credit command, as this Court explained . . . "was to alter the status of the several states as independent foreign sovereignties, each free to ignore obligations created under the laws or by the judicial proceedings of the others, and to make them integral parts of a single nation throughout which a remedy upon a just obligation might be demanded as of right, irrespective of the state of its origin." . . . See also *Estin v. Estin,* . . . (1948) (the Full Faith and Credit Clause "substituted a command for the earlier principles of comity and thus basically altered the status of the States as independent sovereigns").

Our precedent differentiates the credit owed to laws (legislative measures and common law) and to judgments. "In numerous cases this Court has held that credit must be given to the judgment of another state although the forum would not be required to entertain the suit on which the judgment was founded." . . . The Full Faith and Credit Clause does not compel "a state to substitute the statutes of other states for its own statutes dealing with a subject matter concerning which it is competent to legislate." . . . Regarding judgments, however, the full faith and credit obligation is exacting. A final judgment in one State, if rendered by a court with adjudicatory authority over the subject matter and persons governed by the judgment, qualifies for recognition throughout the land. For claim and issue preclusion (res judicata) purposes, in other words, the judgment of the rendering State gains nationwide force. . . .

A court may be guided by the forum State's "public policy" in determining the law applicable to a controversy. . . .

But our decisions support no roving "public policy exception" to the full faith and credit due judgments . . . . See *Estin,* . . . (Full Faith and Credit Clause "ordered submission . . . even to hostile policies reflected in the judgment of another State, because the practical operation of the federal system, which the Constitution designed, demanded it."). . . . In assuming the existence of a ubiquitous "public policy exception" permitting one State to resist recognition of another State's judgment, the District Court in the Bakers' wrongful-

death action, . . . misread our precedent. "The full faith and credit clause is one of the provisions incorporated into the Constitution by its framers for the purpose of transforming an aggregation of independent, sovereign States into a nation." . . . We are "aware of [no] considerations of local policy or law which could rightly be deemed to impair the force and effect which the full faith and credit clause and the Act of Congress require to be given to [a money] judgment outside the state of its rendition." . . .

The Court has never placed equity decrees outside the full faith and credit domain. Equity decrees for the payment of money have long been considered equivalent to judgments at law entitled to nationwide recognition. . . .

Full faith and credit, however, does not mean that States must adopt the practices of other States regarding the time, manner, and mechanisms for enforcing judgments. Enforcement measures do not travel with the sister state judgment . . . ; such measures remain subject to the even-handed control of forum law. See . . . Restatement (Second) of Conflict of Laws §99 (1969) ("The local law of the forum determines the methods by which a judgment of another state is enforced"). . . .

B

With these background principles in view, we turn to the dimensions of the order GM relies upon to stop Elwell's testimony. Specifically, we take up the question: What matters did the Michigan injunction legitimately conclude?

As earlier recounted, . . . the parties before the Michigan County Court, Elwell and GM, submitted an agreed-upon injunction, which the presiding judge signed.

. . . Michigan's judgment, however, cannot reach beyond the Elwell-GM controversy to control proceedings against GM brought in other States, by other parties, asserting claims the merits of which Michigan has not considered. Michigan has no power over those parties, and no basis for commanding them to become intervenors in the Elwell-GM dispute. . . . Most essentially, Michigan lacks authority to control courts elsewhere by precluding them, in actions brought by strangers to the Michigan litigation, from determining for themselves what witnesses are competent to testify and what evidence is relevant and admissible in their search for the truth. . . .

As the District Court recognized, Michigan's decree could operate against Elwell to preclude him from volunteering his testimony. . . . But a Michigan court cannot, by entering the injunction to which Elwell and GM stipulated, dictate to a court in another jurisdiction that evidence relevant in the Bakers' case—a controversy to which Michigan is foreign—shall be inadmissible. This conclusion creates no general exception to the full faith and credit command, and surely does not permit a State to refuse to honor a sister state judgment based on the forum's choice of law or policy preferences. Rather, we simply recognize that, just as the mechanisms for enforcing a judgment do not travel with the judgment itself for purposes of Full Faith and Credit, . . . and just as one State's judgment cannot automatically transfer title to land in another State, . . . similarly the Michigan decree cannot determine evidentiary issues in a lawsuit brought by parties who were not subject to the jurisdiction of the Michigan court. . . .

In sum, Michigan has no authority to shield a witness from another jurisdiction's subpoena power in a case involving persons and causes outside Michigan's governance. Recognition, under full faith and credit, is owed to dispositions Michigan has authority to order. But a Michigan decree cannot command obedience elsewhere on a matter the Michigan court lacks authority to resolve. For the reasons stated, the judgment of the Court of Appeals for the Eighth Circuit is reversed, and the case is remanded for further proceedings consistent with this opinion.

Case Questions

1. Why, according to the U.S. Supreme Court, did the authors of the Constitution create the full faith and credit clause?

2. The Supreme Court in the *Baker* case makes a distinction between final court judgments and statutes when it comes to the requirements of the full faith and credit clause. What is the nature of the distinction?

3. Congress enacted the Defense of Marriage Act on 9/21/96, in anticipation that the state of Hawai'i might legalize same-sex marriages. The act reads as follows:

   28 USC Sec. 1738C. Certain acts, records, and proceedings and the effect thereof

   No State, territory, or possession of the United States, or Indian tribe, shall be required to give effect to any public act, record, or judicial proceeding of any other State, territory, possession, or tribe respecting a relationship between persons of the same sex that is treated as a marriage under the laws of such other State, territory, possession, or tribe, or a right or claim arising from such relationship.

   Do you see any potential constitutional problems with this statute? Explain your reasoning.

Chapter Questions

1. Define the following terms:

comity	*lex fori*
common law	*lex loci contractus*
conflict of laws	*lex loci delicti commissi*
dictum	*lex loci solutionis*
doctrine of substituted judgment	police power
ex post facto	*prima facie* evidence
foreign law	prospective effect
forum	retroactive effect
full faith and credit	significant relationship rule
guardian *ad litem*	sovereignty
holding	*stare decisis*
impeach	supremacy clause

2. Elizabeth Fedorczyk slipped and fell in a bathtub in her cabin on board the M/V *Sovereign,* a cruise ship sailing in navigable waters. She brought a negligence suit against the ship's owners and operators in a state court in New Jersey. The defendants removed the case to the U.S. District Court for the District of New Jersey on the basis of diversity jurisdiction. Neither party addressed the admiralty issue in their pleadings. The trial court entered summary judgment in favor of the defendants. The plaintiffs appealed to the U.S. Court of Appeals. The appeals court, in order to rule on the appeal, had to determine whether it should apply admiralty law to this dispute or follow instead the substantive law of the state of New Jersey. Which option should the Court of Appeals choose and why?
   Fedorczyk v. Caribbean Cruise Lines, LTD, No. 95-5462, (3rd Cir. 1996)

3. Sludge, Inc., entered into a contract with XYZ, Inc., whereby Sludge was to build a building for XYZ in Detroit, Michigan, at the price of $1 million. Sludge was incorporated in Ohio; its principal place of business was in Chicago, Illinois. XYZ is a Delaware corporation with its home office in New York. The contract was negotiated primarily in Chicago but became effective when it was signed at XYZ's home office. There was a dispute concerning the agreement, and XYZ sued Sludge in a federal district court in Ohio. Which state law would govern the dispute if the court follows (1) the *lex fori* approach, (2) the *lex loci contractus* approach, or (3) the *lex loci solutionis* approach?

4. Lorretta Klump, at the time a resident of Illinois, was injured in an automobile collision in which her vehicle was struck by a vehicle driven by Curt Eaves, also an Illinois resident. This incident occurred in Illinois. After the accident, Lorretta moved to North Carolina, where she retained a local attorney, J. David Duffus, Jr., to represent her in a lawsuit she wanted to file in Illinois against Mr. Eaves. She subsequently moved back to Illinois, where

she maintained regular contact with Attorney Duffus. Lorretta's doctor and her insurance carrier were both situated in Illinois. She filed a malpractice suit against Duffus when he failed to file her Illinois suit prior to the lapsing of the Illinois Statute of Limitations. The jury awarded a judgment in plaintiff's favor in the amount of $424,000, but the defendants appealed on the grounds that the trial court did not have *in personam* jurisdiction over them. Duffus argued on appeal that since his allegedly negligent acts occurred in North Carolina, he could not be subject to personal jurisdiction in Illinois. Is Duffus correct? Why or why not?

Klump v. Duffus, Jr., No. 90-C-3772, U.S. Court of Appeals (7th Circuit 1995)

5. Evian Waters of France, Inc., a New York corporation, was an importer of natural spring water from France. Evian contracted in 1987 with Valley Juice Limited, of Boston, to become Evian's exclusive New England distributor. Valley came to believe that Evian was violating its exclusivity rights in New England and filed breach of contract and other claims in a suit it filed in Massachusetts State Court. Evian, believing that Valley had not paid it for contract water it had delivered, also filed suit in Connecticut. Both suits were removed to federal court on the basis of diversity jurisdiction, and the two suits were consolidated in the U.S. District Court for the District of Connecticut. The case was tried to a jury which found in favor of Evian. Valley appealed to the U. S. Court of Appeals for the Second Circuit. Before reviewing the appellant's claims, the appeals court had to determine what state's law applied when two suits, which were initially filed in different states, were consolidated for trial, as in this case. Evian argued that a provision in its agreement with Valley provided that New York law should apply. Valley contended that if the states' laws conflict, Massachusetts law should apply. How should the court of appeals resolve this dispute?

Valley Juice Ltd., Inc. v. Evian Waters of France, Inc., Nos. 94-7813, 94-7817,95-7709, U.S. Court of Appeals (2nd Circuit 1996)

6. On May 20, Arnie Walters' car crashed into a train owned and operated by the Regional Transit Authority at its crossing in Smithville. As a matter of law, the court found that the "Smithville crossing is extremely hazardous." On December 1 of that same year, Ole and Anna Hanson ran into a RTA train at the same crossing while George was driving them home from a party. Does the doctrine of *stare decisis* require that the court in *Hanson* accept the conclusion announced in the *Walters* case?

7. While en route to jury duty, Evans sustained a personal injury as a result of carelessness on the part of the county commissioners in permitting the concrete steps at the El Paso County Courthouse to deteriorate. The lower court dismissed the complaint under the doctrine of governmental immunity. On appeal, the Supreme Court of Colorado, in its opinion dated March 22, 1971, decided to abolish governmental immunity for that state. The courts stated, "Except as to the parties in this proceeding the ruling here shall be prospective only and shall be effective only as to causes of action

arising after June 30, 1972." Why might a court make its decision effective as a precedent some fifteen months after the date of its decision?

Evans v. Board of County Commissioners, 174 Colo. 97, 482 P.2d 968 (1971)

8. P. Whitney, a West Virginia contractor, was under contract with the state of West Virginia to construct State Route 2 near East Steubenville, just across the border from Steubenville, Ohio. Since the area was very hilly, Whitney used high explosives, such as dynamite and nitroglycerin, to clear the way for the road. One particularly large blast damaged a storeroom of the Steubenville Plate and Window Glass Company, located across the border in Ohio. The damage was extensive, and most of the stored glass was broken and unusable. Keeping in mind that the blasting was done in West Virginia and the damage occurred in Ohio, which state's law will govern the action brought in a West Virginia court by Steubenville Plate Glass against Whitney?

Dallas v. Whitney, 118 W. Va. 106 (1936)

Notes

1. You might want to refresh your memory and review this material in conjunction with your current reading.
2. L. Fuller, *Anatomy of the Law* (New York: Praeger, 1968), p. 85.
3. *Schechter Poultry Corp. v. United States*, 295 U.S. 495 (1935).
4. *Carter v. Carter Coal Co.*, 298 U.S. 495 (1936).
5. *Adair v. United States*, 208 U.S. 161 (1908).
6. *Hammer v. Dagenhart*, 247 U.S. 251 (1981).
7. *Heart of Atlanta Hotel, Inc. v. United States*, 379 U.S. 241 (1964).
8. *National Labor Relations Board v. Jones & Laughlin Steel Corp.*, 301 U.S. 1 (1937).
9. *West Coast Hotel v. Parrish*, 300 U.S. 379 (1937).

VI Limitations in Seeking Relief

People with grievances have a variety of options for obtaining relief. Nonjudicial alternatives such as mediation and arbitration, for example, are discussed in Chapter 14. Access to the public courts, however, is not available to every litigant who would like to have a dispute decided in the public courts. We have already seen in Chapter Three, for example, that jurisdictional requirements prevent or limit courts from deciding many cases. In this chapter we learn about other constitutional, statutory, and common law limitations that have been created to determine if suits should be litigated in the public courts.

In some lawsuits courts are asked to provide legal answers to theoretical questions. These suits will generally be dismissed for failure to state a "case or controversy." Cases can also be dismissed for inappropriateness. This occurs, for example, when a plaintiff sues prematurely, takes "too long" to initiate litigation, or tries to relitigate a matter that had been previously decided in a prior suit. Similarly, courts don't want to waste time on cases that are not truly adversarial (such as where *collusion* exists and one party is financing and controlling both sides of the litigation) or where the person bringing the suit has no personal stake in the litigation (such as where the plaintiff is suing on behalf of a friend who is reluctant to sue).

Later in the chapter we will learn that, in some circumstances, the public interest requires that certain defendants receive immunity (preferential protection) from lawsuits. Immunities have historically been granted to governments, certain public officials, and charitable institutions. In some jurisdictions immunities also limit lawsuits between family members.

CASE OR CONTROVERSY REQUIREMENT

To be within the federal judicial power, a matter must be a "case" or "controversy" as required by Article III, Section 2, of the U.S. Constitution. The U.S. Supreme Court has always construed the *case or controversy* requirement as precluding the federal courts from advising the other branches of the government or anyone else.

Assume that a police chief has devised a new search and seizure strategy for identifying and apprehending terrorists. Assume further that the chief, wishing to know whether this strategy, if implemented, would violate the Fourth Amendment's reasonableness clause regarding searches and seizures, sends a letter posing the question to the U.S. Supreme Court. Will the Court answer the question? No, it will not. The police chief is asking for a legal opinion. The question posed is based on a set of assumed facts. The facts are limited and entirely "hypothetical" and there are no true adversaries here. The entire matter is entirely premature. The case or controversy requirement would be satisfied, however, if the police chief were to implement the strategy, seize evidence, and make an arrest that results in a criminal prosecution.

Many state constitutions follow the U.S. Constitution and do not permit courts to render advisory opinions. The executive and legislative branches may seek advice from the attorney general when the constitution does not provide for judicial advisory opinions or when the question is outside the scope of authorization. Generally, courts do not have the power to decide questions that do not affect the rights of the litigants before them. However, the constitutions of some states specifically permit the state supreme court to issue advisory opinions to government officials concerning certain matters of law. In this capacity, the court acts only as an adviser; its opinion does not have the effect of a judicial decision.

JUSTICIABILITY

Only cases that are *justiciable* can be decided by courts on their merits. To be justiciable, a case must be well-suited for judicial determination. Courts use judicial doctrines (policies), such as standing, ripeness, and *res judicata* to weed out cases that lack justiciability. One of the cornerstones of our judicial system is the notion that the parties to a lawsuit must be true adversaries. The underlying assumption is that the best way to determine the truth and do justice in a lawsuit is to require disputing parties to use their full faculties against each other in court. Their interests must collide and they must be seeking different relief. The ripeness and standing doctrines help courts preserve this essential aspect of the litigation process.

The concepts of *ripeness* and *standing*, although distinguishable, are similar and can overlap. A ripeness inquiry focuses on whether a case has developed sufficiently to be before a court for adjudication. A challenge to a party's standing differs in that it focuses on whether the plaintiff who filed the lawsuit is the right person or entity to be bringing this particular claim before the court.

A lawsuit is not ripe for adjudication, and is therefore nonjusticiable, if it has been filed prematurely. The adversary system works best when the litigant's positions are definite and distinct and unambiguously adverse. In such a situation the consequences of ruling for or against each party are more apparent. Where the full facts of a case are unknown or obscured, making a decision becomes much more difficult because the decision maker in such situations has to make too many assumptions in order to reach a well-reasoned conclusion. A just outcome is more likely if more certainty is required.

To have standing, a plaintiff must have a legally sufficient personal interest in the dispute and must be adversely affected by the defendant's conduct. With a few notable exceptions (such as for parents of minor children and guardians of incompetents), one person cannot sue to recover for another person who has been legally injured. Most people actually refuse to bring lawsuits against individuals they have a legal right to sue. They choose not to take legal action because the persons who have caused them harm are their friends, relatives, neighbors, and acquaintances. The standing requirement ensures that the injured person is in control of the decision to sue, prevents undesired and unnecessary suits, and prevents people who have marginal or derivative interests from filing multiple suits.

The following case, from the state of Alaska, discusses both ripeness and standing in a case brought by landlords who were religiously opposed to renting to cohabiting but unmarried male-female couples.

Thomas v. Anchorage Equal Rights Commission
U.S. 9th Circuit Court of Appeals
9735220
August 4, 2000

McKeown, Circuit Judge:

This is a case in search of a controversy. Several landlords mount a First Amendment free exercise of religion and free speech challenge to the Alaska housing laws prohibiting discrimination on the basis of marital status. We do not address this constitutional question, however, because this pre-enforcement challenge presents a threshold issue of justiciability. . . .

Background

Kevin Thomas and Joyce Baker, (the "landlords"), individually own residential rental properties in Anchorage, Alaska. Both are devout Christians who are committed to carrying out their religious faith in all aspects of their lives, including their commercial activities as landlords. Central to their faith is a belief that cohabitation between an unmarried man and an unmarried women is a sin. The landlords also believe that facilitating the cohabitation of an unmarried couple is tantamount to committing a sin themselves. Based on this religious belief, the landlords claim that they have refused to rent to unmarried couples in the past and that they intend to continue to do so in the future.

Both that State of Alaska and the City of Anchorage have adopted laws the outlaw certain forms of discrimination in rental housing and prohibit any refusal to rent on the basis of marital status. The Alaska statute makes it unlawful "to refuse to sell, lease or rent . . . real property to a person because of . . . marital status." Alaska Stat. § 18.80.240(1), (2). The Anchorage ordinance is parallel in this respect. See Anchorage Mun. Code § 5.20.020(A), (B). The laws further prohibit landlords from inquiring about the marital status of prospective tenants or representing to prospective tenants that property is not available because of the tenants' marital status. . . . , (E). Finally, the ordinance, but not the state statute, prohibits publication or advertisement in the leasing of property that indicates a preference based on marital status. . . . The Alaska Supreme Court has construed the marital status provisions of the laws to prohibit landlords from refusing to rent their properties to unmarried couples. . . .

The landlords brought this action against Paula Haley, the Executive Director of the Alaska State Commission for Human Rights, the Anchorage Equal Rights Commission, and the Municipality of Anchorage, seeking declaratory and injunctive relief under 42 U.S.C. § 1983 and 28 U.S.C. S 2201. They claimed that the threat of enforcement of the marital status provisions of the anti-discrimination laws infringed their First Amendment rights to free exercise of religion and free speech. Specifically, they argued that their religious beliefs precluded them from renting to unmarried couples and that the laws restricted their ability to communicate those beliefs through advertising or by inquiring about the marital status of prospective tenants. On cross-motions for summary judgment, the district court held that the landlords' claims were justiciable. In a subsequent order, the court concluded that the marital status provisions substantially burdened the landlords' free exercise rights. The court declared the provisions unconstitutional as applied and permanently enjoined the State and the City from enforcing the provisions against the landlords. A divided panel of this court affirmed, and we voted to consider this matter en banc. . . .

Discussion

This case presents a threshold question of ripeness. The Supreme Court instructs that ripeness is "peculiarly a question of timing," . . . designed to "prevent the courts, through avoidance of premature adjudication, from entangling themselves in abstract disagree-

ments." . . . Our role is neither to issue advisory opinions nor to declare rights in hypothetical cases, but to adjudicate live cases or controversies consistent with the powers granted the judiciary in Article III of the Constitution. See U.S. Const. art. III. Although ripeness, like other justiciability doctrines, is "not a legal concept with a fixed content or susceptible of scientific verification," . . . the Supreme Court has observed that the doctrine "is drawn both from Article III limitations on judicial power and from prudential reasons for refusing to exercise jurisdiction," . . . We consider each component in turn.

A. Constitutional Component

The constitutional component of the ripeness inquiry is often treated under the rubric of standing and, in many cases, ripeness coincides squarely with standing's injury in fact prong. Sorting out where standing ends and ripeness begins is not an easy task. Indeed, because the focus of our ripeness inquiry is primarily temporal in scope, ripeness can be characterized as standing on a timeline. . . . The overlap between these concepts has led some legal commentators to suggest that the doctrines are often indistinguishable. . . .

Whether the question is viewed as one of standing or ripeness, the Constitution mandates that prior to our exercise of jurisdiction there exist a constitutional "case or controversy," that the issues presented are "definite and concrete, not hypothetical or abstract." . . . In assuring that this jurisdictional prerequisite is satisfied, we consider whether the plaintiffs face "a realistic danger of sustaining a direct injury as a result of the statute's operation or enforcement," . . . , or whether the alleged injury is too "imaginary" or "speculative" to support jurisdiction. . . . We need not delve into the nuances of the distinction between the injury in fact prong of standing and the constitutional component of ripeness: in this case, the analysis is the same.

We have held that neither the mere existence of a proscriptive statute nor a generalized threat of prosecution satisfies the "case or controversy" requirement. . . . In a somewhat circular argument, the landlords contend that they are presently injured because they must violate the housing laws to remain true to their religious beliefs, even though their beliefs counsel against violating secular law. This argument is essentially another way of saying that the mere existence of a statute can create a constitutionally sufficient direct injury, a position that we have rejected before and decline to adopt now. . . . (" '[t]he mere existence of a statute . . . is not sufficient to create a case or controversy within the meaning of Article III.' " . . . Rather, there must be a "genuine threat of imminent prosecution." . . .

In evaluating the genuineness of a claimed threat of prosecution, we look to whether the plaintiffs have articulated a "concrete plan" to violate the law in question, whether the prosecuting authorities have communicated a specific warning or threat to initiate proceedings, and the history of past prosecution or enforcement under the challenged statute. . . . Applying these three factors here, we conclude that the landlords' claimed injury—their fear of enforcement or prosecution—fails the constitutional component of the ripeness inquiry. . . .

Turning to the first prong, it is clear that even if "concrete plan" does not mean cast in stone, the Constitution requires something more than a hypothetical intent to violate the law. Thomas and Baker claim that they have refused to rent to unmarried couples in the past, yet they cannot say when, to whom, where, or under what circumstances. They pledge their intent to do so in the future, yet again they cannot specify when, to whom, where, or under what circumstances.

A general intent to violate a statute at some unknown date in the future does not rise to the level of an articulated, concrete plan. . . .

The landlords' expressed "intent" to violate the law on some uncertain day in the future—if and when an unmarried couple attempts to lease one of their rental properties—can hardly qualify as a concrete plan. Because their free speech claims are similarly contingent on such "some day" intentions and are inextricably linked with the prohibited conduct, they suffer the same infirmity. . . .

As for the second factor, a specific threat of enforcement, the record is devoid of any threat—generalized or specific—directed toward Thomas and Baker. Although we do not always require plaintiffs to await arrest or prosecution before entertaining a challenge to the constitutionality of a statute, . . . the threat of enforcement must at least be "credible," not simply "imaginary or speculative." Id. "When plaintiffs 'do not claim that they have ever been threatened with prosecution, that a prosecution is likely, or even that a prosecution is remotely possible,' they do not allege a dispute susceptible to resolution by a federal court." . . . No action has ever been brought against the landlords to enforce the marital status provision. There has been no specific threat or even hint of future enforcement or prosecution. Nor could there be, as neither Thomas nor Baker can identify any tenants turned away due to their marital status and no prospective tenant has ever complained to the state or municipal authorities, formally or informally. In fact, appellant Haley never heard of either Thomas or Baker before this action was filed. The threat of enforcement based on a future violation—which may never occur—is beyond speculation.

The third factor to be considered is the history of enforcement under the statute. In the twenty-five years that these housing laws have been on the books, the record does not indicate even a single criminal prosecution, and of the two reported instances of civil enforcement, only one raised the freedom of religion issue presented here. . . . See *Swanner v.*

Anchorage Equal Rights Comm., . . . (Alaska 1994) (holding that enforcement of the anti-discrimination provisions did not violate right to free exercise of religion); *Foreman v. Anchorage Equal Rights Comm.,* . . . (Alaska 1989) (holding that the marital status provision was intended to protect unmarried couples). . . . These enforcement actions stemmed from complaints filed by actual, prospective tenants. Unlike other cases in which we have held that the government's "active enforcement" of a statute rendered the plaintiff's fear of prosecution reasonable, . . . here the record of past enforcement is limited, was civil only, not criminal, and in any event was in each case precipitated by the filing of complaints by potential tenants. . . . In *Swanner* and *Foreman,* the enforcement agency was faced with real people involved in a real controversy, not hypothetical requests for an advisory opinion. Indeed, the agencies are now surely aware of these landlords and still have launched no enforcement proceedings. At most, the past prosecution factor is a neutral one in this case.

Considering the applicable factors, we hold that any threat of enforcement or prosecution against the landlords in this case—though theoretically possible—is not reasonable or imminent. The asserted threat is wholly contingent upon the occurrence of unforeseeable events: whether the landlords retain their rental properties; whether an unmarried couple will seek to lease available property; whether the couple, having been denied tenancy, will file a complaint or communicate the alleged discrimination to the enforcement agencies; and whether the enforcement agencies will decide to prosecute. The landlords do not at this time confront "a realistic danger of sustaining a direct injury as a result of the statute's operation or enforcement," . . . , and thus this "dispute is not justiciable, because it is not ripe for court review." . . .

B. Prudential Component

Even were we to conclude that Thomas and Baker present a ripe case or controversy in the constitutional sense, we would decline to exercise jurisdiction under the prudential component of the ripeness doctrine. In evaluating the prudential aspects of ripeness, our analysis is guided by two over-arching considerations: "the fitness of the issues for judicial decision and the hardship to the parties of withholding court consideration." . . .

The manner in which the intersection of marital status discrimination and the First Amendment is presented here, devoid of any specific factual context, renders this case unfit for judicial resolution. The record before us is remarkably thin and sketchy, consisting only of a few conclusory affidavits. "A concrete factual situation is necessary to delineate the boundaries of what conduct the government may or may not regulate." . . . And yet, the landlords ask us to declare Alaska laws unconstitutional, in the absence of any identifiable tenants and with no concrete factual scenario that demonstrates how the laws, as applied, infringe their constitutional rights. This case is a classic one for invoking the maxim that we do not decide "'constitutional questions in a vacuum.'" . . .

. . . [T]he First Amendment challenge presented in this case requires an adequately developed factual record to render it ripe for our review. That record, at this point, does not exist. . . .

Turning to the second consideration—the hardship to the parties if jurisdiction is withheld—the landlords have not persuaded us that any hardship will result from deferring resolution of this matter to a time when a real case arises. The hardship analysis of our ripeness jurisprudence dovetails, in part, with the constitutional consideration of injury. Although the constitutional and prudential considerations are distinct, the absence of any real or imminent threat of enforcement, particularly criminal enforcement, seriously undermines any claim of hardship. Moreover, by being forced to defend the housing laws in a vacuum and in the absence of any particular victims of discrimination, the State and the City would suffer hardship were we to adjudicate this case now.

Prudential considerations of ripeness are discretionary, and here we exercise our discretion to decline jurisdiction over a dispute that is too remote. At this juncture, neither landlord has been charged with violating either the statute or the ordinance. Nor is there any reasonable or imminent threat of enforce-

ment. If and when an enforcement action is brought against Thomas or Baker, that will be the appropriate time to raise the constitutional arguments. Postponing judicial review to a time when the landlords actually face an enforcement proceeding, or at least an imminent threat of one, poses insufficient hardship to justify the exercise of jurisdiction now.

Conclusion

Because this action is not ripe for judicial review, we vacate the district court's decision and remand this case to the district court with the instruction to dismiss the action without prejudice.

Case Questions

1. Why do courts refuse to decide cases unless and until they are ripe?
2. Explain how Article III's case or controversy requirement includes aspects both of ripeness and standing.

 INTERNET TIP ————————————————————————————

Students wishing to read a case focusing on standing can read *American Postal Workers v. Frank* on the textbook's website.

MOOTNESS

Moot cases are outside the judicial power because there is no case or controversy. Mootness is an aspect of ripeness, in that there is no reason to try a case unless there has been some direct adverse effect on some party. Deciding when a case is moot is sometimes difficult. An actual controversy must not only exist at the date the action was filed, but it also must exist at the appellate stage. Courts recognize an exception to the mootness rule when the issue is capable of repetition. If a defendant is "free to return to his or her old ways," the public interest in determining the legality of the practices will prevent mootness. In the following case, the passage of time made a case "moot" in the eyes of the U.S. Supreme Court.

DeFunis v. Odegaard
416 U.S. 312
U.S. Supreme Court
April 23, 1974

Per Curiam

In 1971 the petitioner Marco DeFunis, Jr., applied for admission as a first-year student at the University of Washington Law School, a state-operated institution. The size of the incoming first-year class was to be limited to 150 persons, and the Law School received some 1600 applications for these 150 places. DeFunis was eventually notified that he had been denied admission. He thereupon commenced this suit in a Washington trial court, contending that the procedures and criteria employed by the Law School Admissions Committee invidiously discriminated against him on account of his race in violation of the equal protection clause of the Fourteenth Amendment to the United States Constitution.

DeFunis brought the suit on behalf of himself alone, and not as the representative of any class, against the various respondents, who are officers, faculty members, and members of the Board of Regents of the University of Washington. He asked the trial court to issue a mandatory injunction commanding the respondents to admit him as a member of the first-year class entering in September 1971, on the grounds that the Law School admissions policy had resulted in the unconstitutional denial of his application for admission. The trial court agreed with his claim and granted the requested relief. DeFunis was, accordingly, admitted to the Law School and began his legal studies there in the fall of 1971. On appeal, the Washington Supreme Court reversed the judgment of the trial court and held that the Law School admissions policy did not violate the Constitution. By this time, DeFunis was in his second year at the Law School.

He then petitioned this Court for a writ of certiorari, and Mr. Justice Douglas, as Circuit Justice, stayed the judgment of the Washington Supreme Court pending the "final disposition of the case by this Court." By virtue of this stay, DeFunis has remained in law school, and was in the first term of his third and final year when this Court first considered his . . . petition in the fall of 1973. Because of our concern that DeFunis' third-year standing in the Law School might have rendered this case moot, we requested the parties to brief the question of mootness before we acted on the petition. In response, both sides contended that the case was not moot. The respondents indicated that, if the decision of the Washington Supreme Court were permitted to stand, the petitioner could complete the term for which he was then enrolled, but would have to apply to the faculty for permission to continue in the school before he could register for another term.

We granted the petition for certiorari on November 19, 1973. . . . The case was orally argued on February 26, 1974. . . .

The starting point for analysis is the familiar proposition that "federal courts are without power to decide questions that cannot affect the rights of litigants in the case before them." . . . The inability of the federal judiciary "to review moot cases derives from the requirement of Art. III of the Constitution under which the exercise of judicial power depends on the existence of a case or controversy." . . . Although as a matter of Washington state law, it appears that this case would be saved from mootness by "the great public interest in the continuing issues raised by this appeal," the fact remains that under Art. III, "[e]ven in cases arising in the state courts, the question of mootness is a federal one which a federal court must resolve before it assumes jurisdiction." . . .

The respondents have represented that, without regard to the ultimate resolution of the issues in this case, DeFunis will remain a student in the law school for the duration of any term in which he has already enrolled. Since he has now registered for his final term, it is evident that he will be given an opportunity to complete all academic and other requirements for graduation and, if he does so, he will receive his diploma regardless of any decision this Court might reach on the merits of this case. . . . The controversy between the parties has thus clearly ceased to be "definite and concrete" and no longer "touch[es] the legal relations of parties having adverse legal interests." . . .

There is a line of decisions in this Court standing for the proposition that the "voluntary cessation of allegedly illegal conduct does not deprive the tribunal of power to hear and determine the case, i.e., does not make the case moot." . . . These decisions and the doctrine they reflect would be quite relevant if the question of mootness here had arisen by reason of unilateral change in the *admissions procedures* of the Law School. For it was the admissions procedures that were the target of this litigation, and a voluntary cessation of the admissions practices complained of could make this case moot only if it could be said with assurance "that 'there is no reasonable expectation that the wrong will be repeated.'" . . . But mootness in the present case depends not at all upon a "voluntary cessation" of the admissions practices that were the subject of this litigation. It depends, instead, upon the simple fact that DeFunis is now in the final quarter of the final year of his course of study, and the settled and unchallenged policy of the Law School to permit him to complete the term for which he is now enrolled.

It might also be suggested that this case presents a question that is "capable of repetition" . . . and is thus amenable to federal adjudication even though it might otherwise be considered moot. But DeFunis will never again be required to run the gauntlet of the

Law School's admission process, and so the question is certainly not "capable of repetition" so far as he is concerned. . . .

Because the petitioner will complete his law school studies at the end of the term for which he has now registered regardless of any decision this Court might reach on the merits of this litigation, we conclude that the Court cannot, consistently with the limitations of Art. III of the Constitution, consider the substantive constitutional issues tendered by the parties. Accordingly, the judgment of the Supreme Court of Washington is vacated, and the cause is remanded for such proceedings as by the Court may be deemed appropriate.

It is so ordered. . . .

Mr. Justice Brennan, with whom Mr. Justice Douglas, Mr. Justice White, and Mr. Justice Marshall concur, dissenting

I respectfully dissent. Many weeks of the school term remain, and petitioner may not receive his degree despite respondents' assurances that petitioner will be allowed to complete this term's schooling regardless of our decision. Any number of unexpected events—illness, economic necessity, even academic failure—might prevent his graduation at the end of the term. Were that misfortune to befall, and were petitioner required to register for yet another term, the prospect that he would again face the hurdle of the admissions policy is real, not fanciful; for respondents warn that "Mr. DeFunis would have to take some appropriate action to request continued admission for the remainder of his law school education, and *some discretionary action by the university on such request would have to be taken.*" . . . [P]etitioner might once again have to run the gauntlet of the University's allegedly unlawful admissions policy. The Court therefore proceeds on an erroneous premise in resting its mootness holding on a supposed inability to render any judgment that may affect one way or the other petitioner's completion of his law studies. For surely if we were to reverse the Washington Supreme Court, we could insure that, if for some reason petitioner did not graduate this spring, he would be entitled to re-enrollment at a later time on the same basis as others who have not faced the hurdle of the University's allegedly unlawful admissions policy.

In these circumstances, and because the University's position implies no concession that its admissions policy is unlawful, this controversy falls squarely within the Court's long line of decisions holding that the "[m]ere voluntary cessation of allegedly illegal conduct does not moot a case." . . . Since respondents' voluntary representation to this Court is only that they will permit petitioner to complete this term's studies, respondents have not borne the "heavy burden," . . . of demonstrating that there was not even a "mere possibility" that petitioner would once again be subject to the challenged admissions policy. On the contrary, respondents have

positioned themselves so as to be "free to return to [their] old ways.". . .

Moreover, in endeavoring to dispose of this case as moot, the Court clearly disserves the public interest. The constitutional issues that are avoided today concern vast numbers of people, organizations, and colleges and universities, as evidenced by the filing of twenty-six *amicus curiae* briefs. Few constitutional questions in recent history have stirred as much debate, and they will not disappear. They must inevitably return to the federal courts and ultimately again to this Court. . . . Although the Court should, of course, avoid unnecessary decisions of constitutional questions, we should not transform principles of avoidance of constitutional decisions into devices for side-stepping resolution of difficult cases.

On what appears in this case, I would find that there is an extant controversy and decide the merits of the very important constitutional questions presented.

Case Questions

1. If the plaintiff had been in his second-to-last term of law school when the Supreme Court heard the case, would its decision have been different?
2. The dissenting justices feel that the majority disserved the public interest. Why? Do you agree?
3. In the first paragraph of the decision, the court notes that the University of Washington Law School is a state-operated institution. Why is this an important fact?
4. Did the U.S. Supreme Court decide the merits of this case?

POLITICAL QUESTIONS

The courts can also decline to decide cases that raise *political questions*. The federal Constitution allocates separate governmental power to the legislative, executive, and judicial branches. As members of the judicial branch of government, the courts exercise judicial powers. As the political departments, the executive and legislative branches are entrusted with certain functions, such as conducting foreign relations, making treaties, or submitting our country to the jurisdiction of international courts. Such issues fall outside the jurisdiction of the courts. Courts classify an issue as justiciable or as a nonjusticiable political question on a case-by-case basis.

In the following case, Americans formerly held hostage by Iran filed suit against the United States, claiming that provisions of the agreement President Carter negotiated with Iran infringed on their property rights. The hostages argued that the U.S. government had taken their property rights when it agreed to extinguish the hostages' claims against their Iranian captors. The U.S. Court of Appeals affirmed the U.S. Claims Court's application of the political questions doctrine.

Belk v. United States
858 F.2d 706
U.S. Court of Appeals, Federal Circuit
September 22, 1988

Friedman, Circuit Judge

This is an appeal from a judgment of the United States Claims Court granting summary judgment dismissing a complaint by former hostages held in the United States Embassy in Tehran, Iran. The appellants seek just compensation for the alleged taking by the United States of their property right to sue Iran for injuries sustained while held hostage—a right the United States extinguished in connection with obtaining the release of the hostages. The Claims Court dismissed the complaint on alternative grounds: (1) that the government's action did not constitute a taking, and (2) that the complaint would require the resolution of political questions, which the court could not do. . . .

I

The appellants are 15 United States citizens, 13 of whom were held hostage in the United States Embassy in Tehran from November 4, 1979 to January 20, 1981, and the wives of two of the hostages. The United States had attempted unsuccessfully to obtain the release

of the hostages in various ways. . . . The hostages finally were released by agreements arranged through the government of Algeria.

The United States signed these agreements (commonly referred to as the Algiers Accords) on January 19, 1981. . . .

The relevant provision of the Algiers Accords prohibits United States nationals from prosecuting claims related to the seizure of the hostages, their detention, and injuries to them or their properties that arose out of events that occurred before the date of the Accords. . . . The day after the United States signed the Algiers Accords, the hostages were released.

Following the appellants' release, they filed the present suit against the United States in the Claims Court. The complaint alleged that the appellants had "valid and valuable causes of action against the Islamic Republic of Iran, its officials, agents, instruments, and employees" resulting from the mistreatment the appellants suffered while being held hostage; that before the Accords were executed, the appellants "were entitled to prosecute their valid and valuable causes of action and to collect upon their claims" in the "federal district courts of the United States" and "in Iran itself"; and that by executing the Accords the United States "barred plaintiffs from prosecuting any and all of their existing and potential causes of action against Iran in any court or forum anywhere in the world" and thereby "extinguished plaintiffs' valid causes of action."

According to the complaint, these causes of action "constituted valuable private property rights," which the United States has "taken for public use without just compensation." The complaint asserted that the appellants are entitled to recover from the United States just compensation "equivalent to the damages they could have recovered from Iran had defendant not extinguished their claims."

The United States moved for summary judgment. The Claims Court granted the motion, and dismissed the complaint. . . . The court held that the complaint raised a political question because "[t]his case involves a policy decision made by the President during a crisis situation." . . . The court noted that "'[a] judicial inquiry into whether the President could have extracted a more generous settlement from another country would seriously interfere with his ability to carry on diplomatic relations.'" . . . The court concluded that the President's extinguishment of the plaintiffs' claim could not ground a cause of action for a taking "because such an action is not susceptible to judicial review." . . .

III

On the undisputed facts, the Claims Court correctly held that the appellants have not stated a valid or judicially cognizable claim for a taking of private property for a public use, for which the United States is required to pay just compensation.

A

Assuming without deciding that the appellants' claims against Iran constituted "property" under the Fifth Amendment's takings clause, the extinguishment of those claims pursuant to the Algiers Accords did not constitute a taking of that property. . . . Although

the Algiers Accords did not provide any alternative forum in which the hostages could assert their claims, that fact is not sufficient to establish a taking.

The President's action in implementing the Algiers Accords was primarily designed to benefit the hostages. It followed their imprisonment for 14 months and various unsuccessful attempts by the United States to obtain their release. The day after the Accords were signed, the hostages were released. The President's authority to extinguish the kind of claims against Iran that the appellants seek to assert is no more novel, done as it was "in return for" the hostages' freedom and perhaps their very lives. As the Claims Court pointed out in its ruling from the bench following argument in which it granted summary judgment for the government: "there's no doubt that if the question was put by the President in some hypothetical world that you want to be released from Iran as of today or would you want to go on indefinitely preserving your right to sue Iran at some late date, there wouldn't have been a millionth of a second pause on the part of the hostages or their spouses, as to which way to go on that." . . .

B

We also agree with the Claims Court's alternative holding that adjudication of the appellants' taking claim would involve the court in the resolution of a political question. The President is "the sole organ of the federal government in the field of international relations." . . . Issues involving foreign relations frequently present questions not meet for judicial determination. In *Baker v. Carr*, 369 U.S. 186, . . . the Court explained:

> "Prominent on the surface of any case held to involve a political question is found a textually demonstrable constitutional commitment of the issue to a co-ordinate political department; or a lack of judicially discoverable and manageable standards for

resolving it; or the impossibility of deciding without an initial policy determination of a kind clearly for nonjudicial discretion; or the impossibility of a court's undertaking independent resolution without expressing lack of the respect due coordinate branches of government; or an unusual need for unquestioning adherence to a political decision already made; or the potentiality of embarrassment from multifarious pronouncements by various departments on one question."

Most, if not all, of those concerns are present in this case. It involves a policy decision made by the President during a time of crisis. The appellants apparently contend that the President should not have entered into the Algiers Accords because he could have obtained better terms, and that the Accords themselves were illegal because the President was coerced into agreeing to them. The determination whether and upon what terms to settle the dispute with Iran over its holding of the hostages and obtain their release, necessarily was for the President to make in his foreign relations role. That determination was "of a kind clearly for nonjudicial discretion," and there are no "judicially discoverable and

manageable standards" for reviewing such a Presidential decision. A judicial inquiry into whether the President could have extracted a more favorable settlement would seriously interfere with the President's ability to conduct foreign relations. . . .

C

Although the appellants underwent an agonizing experience, they have not stated a valid claim for a taking by the United States of their causes of action against Iran that, as they frame their case, is appropriate for judicial resolution. If there is to be any compensation of the appellants for the mistreatment and suffering they underwent during their captivity as hostages in Iran, it must be provided by one of the other "coordinate branches of government."

Conclusion

The judgment of the United States Claims Court granting summary judgment dismissing the complaint is
    Affirmed.

Case Questions

1. What might have been the ramifications if the *Belk* court had decided the merits of this case?
2. A cause of action (or a right to sue) is a property right under the due process clause of the Fifth Amendment. What are some other property rights?

THE ACT OF STATE DOCTRINE

The judicially created Act of State doctrine's roots go back to England in 1674. It provides that American courts should not determine the validity of public acts committed by a foreign sovereign within its own territory. The doctrine is pragmatic: it prevents our courts from making pronouncements about matters over which they have no power. Judicial rulings about such matters could significantly interfere with the conduct of foreign policy—a matter that the Constitution assigns to the political branches of government. The Constitution does not require the Act of State doctrine; it is based on the relationships among the three branches of the federal government.

Assume, for example, that a foreign dictator confiscates a warehouse containing merchandise belonging to an American corporation. The American corporation subsequently files suit in an American court to challenge the foreign nation's laws and procedures, alleging that the dictator did not have a valid right to confiscate the merchandise. The American court can apply the Act of State doctrine and refuse to make any pronouncements about the foreign nation's laws or procedures. The law presumes the public acts of a foreign sovereign within its own territory to be valid.

STATUTE OF LIMITATIONS

There is a time period, established by the legislature, within which an action must be brought upon claims or rights to be enforced. This law is known as the *statute of limitations* (see Figure 6-1). The statute of limitations compels the exercise of a right of action within a reasonable time, so that the opposing party has a fair opportunity to defend and will not be surprised by the assertion of a stale claim after evidence has been lost or destroyed. With the lapse of time, memories fade and witnesses may die or move. The prospects for impartial and comprehensive fact-finding diminish.

The statutory time period begins to run immediately on the accrual of the cause of action, that is, when the plaintiff's right to institute a suit arises. If the plaintiff brings the suit after the statutory period has run, the defendant may plead the statute of limitations as a defense. Although jurisdictions have differing definitions, a cause of action can be generally said to exist when the defendant breaches some legally recognized duty owed to the plaintiff and thereby causes some type of legally recognized injury to the plaintiff.

Generally, once the statute of limitations begins to run, it continues to run until the time period is exhausted. However, many statutes of limitation contain a "saving clause" listing conditions and events that "toll" or suspend the running of the statute. The occurrence of one of these conditions may also extend the limitations period for a prescribed period of time. In personal injury cases, for example, the statute may start to run from the date of the injury or from the date when the injury is discoverable, depending on the jurisdiction. Conditions that may serve to toll the running of the statute or extend the time period include infancy, insanity, imprisonment, court orders, war, and fraudulent concealment of a cause of action by a trustee or other fiduciary. The statute of limitations often starts to run in medical malpractice cases on the day that the doctor or patient stops the prescribed treatment or on the day that the

| | Contract | | | | Tort | | | | | | | | | | | |
| | | | | | Negligence | | | Intentional Torts | | | | | | | | |
	Breach of Sales Contract	Breach of Warranty	Oral	Written	Personal Injury	Wrongful Death	Medical Malpractice	Assault and Battery	Fraud and Deceit	Libel	Slander	Trespass	Damage to Personal Property	Conversion	False Imprisonment	Malicious Prosecution
Alabama	4	4	6	6	1	2	2	6	2	1	1	6	1	6	6	1
Alaska	4	4	6	6	2	2	2	2	2	2	2	6	6	6	2	2
Arizona	4	4	3	6	2	2	2	2	3	1	1	2	2	2	1	1
Arkansas	4	4	3	5	3	3	2	1	5	3	1	3	3	3	1	5
California	4	4	2	4	1	1	3	1	3	1	1	3	3	3	1	1
Colorado	4	4	3	3	2	2	2	1	1	1	1	2	2	3	1	2
Connecticut	4	4	3	6	2	2	2	3	3	2	2	3	3	3	3	3
Delaware	4	4	3	3	2	2	2	2	3	2	2	3	2	3	2	2
District of Columbia	4	4	3	3	3	1	3	1	3	1	1	3	3	3	1	1
Florida	4	4	4	5	4	2	2	4	4	2	2	4	4	4	4	4
Georgia	4	4	4	6	2	2	2	2	4	1	1	4	4	4	2	2
Hawaii	4	4	6	6	2	2	2	2	6	2	2	2	2	6	6	6
Idaho	4	4	4	5	2	2	2	2	3	2	2	3	3	3	2	4
Illinois	4	4	5	10	2	2	2	2	5	1	1	5	5	5	2	2
Indiana	4	4	6	10	2	2	2	2	6	2	2	6	2	6	2	2
Iowa	5	5	5	10	2	2	2	2	5	2	2	5	5	5	2	2
Kansas	4	4	3	5	2	2	2	1	2	1	1	2	2	2	1	1
Kentucky	4	4	5	15	1	1	1	1	5	1	1	5	2	2	1	1
Louisiana	10	1	10	10	1	1	1	1	1	1	1	1	1	1	1	1
Maine	4	4	6	6	6	2	2	2	6	2	2	6	6	6	2	6
Maryland	4	4	3	3	3	3	3	1	3	1	1	3	3	3	3	3
Massachusetts	4	4	6	6	3	3	3	3	3	3	3	3	3	3	3	3
Michigan	4	4	6	6	3	3	2	2	6	1	1	3	3	3	2	2
Minnesota	4	4	6	6	6	3	2	2	6	2	2	6	6	6	2	2
Mississippi	6	6	3	6	6	2	2	1	6	1	1	6	6	6	1	1
Missouri	4	4	5	10	5	3	2	2	5	2	2	5	5	5	2	5
Montana	4	4	5	8	3	3	3	2	2	2	2	2	2	2	2	5
Nebraska	4	4	4	5	4	2	2	1	4	1	1	4	4	4	1	1
Nevada	4	4	4	6	2	2	2	2	3	2	2	3	3	3	2	2
New Hampshire	4	4	3	3	3	3	2	3	3	3	3	3	3	3	3	3
New Jersey	4	4	6	6	2	2	2	2	6	1	1	6	6	6	2	2

FIGURE 6-1   Statutes of Limitations for Civil Actions (in Years)

| | Contract | | | | Tort | | | | | | | | | | | |
| | | | | | Negligence | | | Intentional Torts | | | | | | | | |
	Breach of Sales Contract	Breach of Warranty	Oral	Written	Personal Injury	Wrongful Death	Medical Malpractice	Assault and Battery	Fraud and Deceit	Libel	Slander	Trespass	Damage to Personal Property	Conversion	False Imprisonment	Malicious Prosecution
New Mexico	4	4	4	6	3	3	3	3	4	3	3	4	4	4	3	3
New York	4	4	6	6	3	2	2½	1	6	1	1	3	3	3	1	1
North Carolina	4	4	3	3	3	2	3	1	3	1	1	3	3	3	1	3
North Dakota	4	4	6	6	6	2	2	2	6	2	2	6	6	6	2	6
Ohio	4	4	6	15	2	2	1	1	4	1	1	4	2	4	1	1
Oklahoma	5	5	3	5	2	2	2	1	2	1	1	2	2	2	1	1
Oregon	4	4	6	6	2	3	2	2	2	1	1	6	6	6	2	2
Pennsylvania	4	4	4	4	2	2	2	2	2	1	1	2	2	2	2	2
Rhode Island	4	4	10	10	3	2	3	10	10	10	1	10	10	10	3	10
South Carolina	6	6	6	6	6	6	3	2	6	2	2	6	6	6	2	6
South Dakota	4	4	6	6	3	3	2	2	6	2	2	6	6	6	2	6
Tennessee	4	4	6	6	1	1	1	1	3	1	½	3	3	3	1	1
Texas	4	4	2	4	2	2	2	2	2	1	1	2	2	2	2	1
Utah	4	4	4	6	4	2	2	1	3	1	1	3	3	3	1	1
Vermont	4	4	6	6	3	2	3	3	6	3	3	6	3	6	3	3
Virginia	4	4	3	5	2	2	2	2	1	1	1	5	5	5	2	1
Washington	4	4	3	6	3	3	3	2	3	2	2	3	3	3	2	3
West Virginia	4	4	5	10	2	2	2	2	2	1	1	2	2	2	1	1
Wisconsin	6	6	6	6	3	3	3	2	6	2	2	6	6	6	2	6
Wyoming	4	4	8	10	4	2	2	1	4	1	1	4	4	4	1	1

FIGURE 6-1   Statutes of Limitations for Civil Actions (in Years) (*continued*)

patient becomes aware (or should have become aware) of the malpractice and subsequent injury. The commencement of an action almost universally tolls the running of the statute of limitations. Thus once an action is commenced on a claim within the statutory time period, it does not matter if judgment is ultimately rendered after the period of limitations has expired.

In the following case the interests of consumers were pitted against the economic welfare of an important industry (and a major regional employer) within the state. The state legislature used the statute of limitations and a ninety-day notification requirement to further the economic interests of the state's ski industry at the expense of consumers.

Marybeth Atkins v. Jiminy Peak, Inc.
514 N.E.2d 850
Massachusetts Supreme Judicial Court
November 5, 1987

O'Connor, Justice

This case presents the question whether an action by an injured skier against a ski area operator is governed by the one-year limitation of actions provision of G.L.c. 143, § 71P, where the plaintiff's theories of recovery are negligence and breach of warranty, as well as breach of contract, in the renting of defective ski equipment.

In her original complaint, filed on December 5, 1984, the plaintiff alleged that on March 20, 1982, she sustained serious injuries while skiing at the defendant's ski resort, and that those injuries were caused by defective ski equipment she had rented from the rental facility on the premises. She further alleged that the defendant had not inspected or adjusted the equipment, and this failure amounted to negligence and breach of contract. In an amended complaint filed on February 14, 1986, the plaintiff added counts alleging that the defendant had breached warranties of merchantability and fitness for a particular purpose.

The defendant moved for summary judgment on the ground that the plaintiff's action was barred by the statute of limitations. A judge of the Superior Court granted the motion, and the plaintiff appealed. We transferred the case to this court on our own motion, and now affirm.

The statute we must interpret, G.L.c. 143, § 71P, imposes a one-year limitation on actions "against a ski area operator for injury to a skier." There is no contention that the defendant is not a "ski area operator," or that this action is not "for injury to a skier." The text of the statute, then, seems fully to support the decision of the Superior Court judge.

The plaintiff argues, however, that the statute should be construed as governing only actions based on a defendant ski area operator's violation of those duties prescribed by G.L.c.143, § 71N. Section 71N requires that ski areas be maintained and operated in a reasonably safe manner, and prescribes methods by which skiers must be warned about the presence of equipment and vehicles on slopes and trails. The plaintiff thus contends that the statute does not bar her lawsuit because her action does not assert a violation of § 71N but rather was brought against the defendant solely in its capacity as a lessor of ski equipment. We do not interpret the statute in this limited way. Rather, we conclude that the one-year limitation in § 71P applies to all personal injury actions brought by skiers against ski area operators arising out of skiing injuries.

If the Legislature had intended that the one-year limitation apply only to actions alleging breach of a ski area operator's duties under § 71N, it easily could have employed language to that effect instead of the sweeping terms contained in the statute. Nothing in § 71P suggests that its reach is so limited.

The plaintiff contends that there is no sound basis for applying the one-year limitation to her action, because if she "had rented skis from an independently operated ski rental shop which leased space in the Defendant's base lodge, such an independent rental shop could not defend against the Plaintiff's action by relying upon Section 71P." Hence, she argues, it makes no sense to afford special protection to lessors of ski equipment who happen also to be ski operators. We assume for purposes of this case that the plaintiff's assertion that § 71P would not apply to an independent ski rental shop is correct. But we cannot say that, in enacting § 71P, the Legislature could not reasonably have decided that ski area operators require more protection than do other sectors of the ski industry. "Personal injury claims by skiers . . . may be myriad in number, run a whole range of harm, and constitute a constant drain on the ski industry." . . . The Legislature appears to have concluded that, in view of this perceived threat to the economic stability of owners and operators of ski areas, not shared by those who simply rent ski equipment, a short period for the commencement of skiers' personal injury actions against ski operators, regardless of the fault alleged, is in the public interest. . . .

Because § 71P applies to the plaintiff's action, the Superior Court judge correctly concluded that the plaintiff's action was time barred.

Judgment affirmed.

Liacos, J. (dissenting, with whom Wilkins and Abrams, JJ., join)

I respectfully dissent. The court's interpretation of G.L.c. 143, § 71P (1986 ed.), is too broad. The general purpose of G.L.c. 143, § § 71H–71S (1986 ed.), is to set the terms of responsibility for ski area operators and skiers in a sport which has inherent risks of injury or even death. This legislative intent to protect ski area operators was designed, as the court indicates, not only to decrease the economic threat to the ski industry, but also to enhance the safety of skiers.

An examination of the whole statutory scheme reveals, however, that the Legislature did not intend to protect the ski area operators from claims for all harm which occurs in connection with skiing accidents, regardless of where the negligence that caused the harm takes place. Indeed, this court decided not long ago that G.L.c. 143, § 71P, on which it relies to rule adversely on this plaintiff's claim, did not apply to wrongful death actions arising from injuries on the ski slope. *Grass v. Catamount Dev. Corp.*, 390 Mass. 551 (1983) (O'Connor, J.). The court now ignores the wisdom of its own words in *Grass*, supra at 553: "Had the Legislature intended that

G.L.c. 143, § 71P, should apply to claims for wrongful death as well as to claims for injuries not resulting in death, we believe it would have done so expressly. . . ." Here, however, the court extends the protective provisions of § 71P to ordinary commercial activity simply because it occurred at the base of a ski area and was conducted by the operator of the ski slope. No such intent can be perceived in this statute. To the contrary, the statute clearly manifests an intent to promote safety on ski slopes by regulating, through the creation of a recreational tramway board and otherwise, the operation of tramways, chair lifts, "J bars," "T bars," and the like (§ § 71H–71M). The statute defines the duties both of ski area operators and skiers (§ § 71K–71O).

In § 71O, liability of ski area operators for ski slope accidents is sharply limited: "A skier skiing down hill shall have the duty to avoid any collision with any other skier, person or object on the hill below him, and, except as otherwise provided in this chapter, the responsibility for collisions by any skier *with any other skier or person shall be solely that of the skier or person involved and not that of the operator*, and the responsibility for the collision with an obstruction, man-made or otherwise, shall be solely that of the skier and not that of the operator, provided that such obstruction is properly marked pursuant to the regulations promulgated by the board" (emphasis supplied). Clearly, then, the statutory scheme is designed not only to enhance the safety of skiers, but also to limit the liability of a ski area operator for his negligent activities which cause injuries (but not deaths, see *Grass*, supra) on the ski slopes. It is in this context that the court ought to consider the additional protection of a ninety-day notice requirement, as well as the short statute of limitations of one year found in § 71P.

General Laws c. 143, § 71P, imposes a ninety-day notice requirement and a one-year statute of limitations on a party who brings suit against a ski area operator. The imposition in § 71P of the ninety-day notice requirement as a condition precedent to recovery confirms, I think, my view that this statute is designed only to protect the ski area operator as to claims arising from conditions on the ski slope. But there is an even stronger argument against the court's position—that is in the very language of the statute. A "[s]ki area operator" is defined in G.L.c. 143, § 71I(6), as "the owner or operator of a ski area." In the same subsection, a "[s]ki area" is defined as: "[A]ll of the slopes and trails under the control of the ski area operator, including cross-country ski areas, slopes and trails, and any recreational tramway in operation on any such slopes or trails administered or operated as a single enterprise *but shall not include base lodges, motor vehicle parking lots and other portions of ski areas used by skiers when not actually engaged in the sport of skiing*" (emphasis supplied).

The alleged negligence and breach of warranty that occurred in this case happened in the rental shop in the base lodge area. It was there that the defendant rented allegedly defective equipment to the plaintiff and failed to check and to adjust that equipment. The injury was not due to ungroomed snow or exposed rocks or any condition on the slopes or trails under the control of the ski area operator. Rather, the injury allegedly was the result of a transaction in the rental shop, not of a defect on the slope. The rental shop is an area excluded from the purview of G.L.c. 143, § 71P, and thus the ninety-day notice requirement and the one-year statute of limitations do not apply.

The Legislature intended to separate the many functions of a ski area operator so as to focus on the business of operating ski slopes and trails. The statute does not apply where the alleged negligent behavior occurs when the ski area operator is acting as a restauranteur, barkeeper, parking lot owner, souvenir vendor, or, as is the case here, rental agent. For this reason, I would reverse the judgment of the Superior Court.

Case Questions

1. Marybeth Atkins severely broke her leg while using skis and ski bindings rented from a shop at a ski resort. The shop was owned and operated by the owners of the resort. What argument did Atkins make to the court in an effort to avoid the one-year statute of limitations?

2. Do you agree with the dissenters, who feel that the negligent action that caused the harm occurred in the rental shop (an area not covered by the statute), or with the majority, who feel that the accident occurred on the slopes (an area covered by the statute)?

 The state supreme court stated in its opinion that "The Legislature appears to have concluded that, . . . a short period for the commencement of skiers' personal injury actions against ski operators . . . was in the public interest." It denied recovery to a plaintiff who alleged that she was seriously injured as a result of the defendant's negligence in fitting her with defective ski equipment at its on-premises rental facility. Do you see any utilitarian aspects in the making of public policy in this instance?

RES JUDICATA

Res judicata literally means that the matter has been already decided. A final decision by a competent court on a lawsuit's merits concludes the litigation of the parties and constitutes a bar (puts an end to) a new suit. When a plaintiff wins his or her lawsuit, the claims that he or she made (and could have made, but didn't) merge into the judgment and are extinguished. Thus no subsequent suit can be maintained against the same defendant based on the same claim. This is known as the principle of *bar and merger*. Once a claim has been judicially decided, it is finally decided. The loser may not bring a new suit against the winner for the same claim in any court. The loser's remedy is to appeal the decision of the lower court to a higher court.

The *res judicata* doctrine reduces litigation and prevents harassment of or hardship on an individual who otherwise could be sued twice for the same cause of action. In addition, once the parties realize that they have only one chance to win, they will make their best effort.

For *res judicata* to apply, two conditions must be met. First, there must be an identity of parties. Identity means that parties to a successive lawsuit are the same as, or in privity with, the parties to the original suit. Privity exists when there is a relationship between two people that allows one not directly involved in the case to take the place of the one who is a party. Thus if a person dies during litigation, the executor of the estate may take the deceased person's place in the lawsuit. Privity exists between the person who dies and the executor, so that as far as this litigation is concerned, they are the same person.

Second, there must be an identity of claims. In other words, for *res judicata* to bar the suit, the claim—or cause of action—in the first case must be the same the second time the litigation is attempted. For instance, if A sues B for breach of contract and loses, *res judicata* prohibits any further action on that same contract by A and B (except for appeal). A could, however, sue B for the breach of a different contract, because that would be a different cause of action.

The appellant in the following case, Henry Shin, appealed a trial judge's dismissal of Shin's breach of contract action against the Portals Confederation Corporation because it was *res judicata*.

Henry B. Y. Shin v. Portals Confederation Corporation
728 A.2d 615/No. 96-CV-618
District of Columbia Court of Appeals
April 22, 1999

Terry, Associate Judge

The trial court dismissed appellant's action for fraudulent misrepresentation and breach of contact on the ground of res judicata. On appeal he contends that the court erred in granting appellees' motion to dismiss because res judicata does not apply to claims that were previously dismissed without prejudice. . . .

This case arises from a retail lease agreement dated July 16, 1992, between appellant, Henry Shin, and appellees, Portals Confederation Corporation and Republic Properties Corporation (collectively "the landlords").

Appellant agreed to lease 580 square feet of retail space in a large office building at 1250 Maryland Avenue, S.W., in which he intended to operate a dry-cleaning business. . . . The lease provided that it would become effective on "the first date on which at least twenty percent of the rentable area of the Office Space is leased and occupied by tenants" and that the landlords would partially abate the rent until "at least fifty percent of the rentable area of the Office Space is leased and occupied by tenants." On June 7, 1993, the landlords notified Mr. Shin that twenty percent of the building had been leased, and he began to pay the reduced rent. In February 1994 the landlords advised him that they had leased more than fifty percent of the office space, which meant that he was then obliged to pay the full rent, beginning in March 1994. Mr. Shin, however, failed to pay the full rent, continuing instead to pay only the reduced rent, and in January and February 1995 he did not pay any rent at all.

On November 30, 1994, Republic Properties Corporation, the general partner in the partnership which managed the building, filed a complaint against Mr. Shin in the Landlord and Tenant Branch of the Superior Court, seeking payment of the partially unpaid rent and possession of the leased premises. Shin filed an answer to the complaint, along with a counterclaim alleging misrepresentation. After Republic orally moved to strike the counterclaim . . . appellant voluntarily withdrew it without prejudice. A bench trial was then held before Judge Henry Kennedy, in which the main issue was the meaning of the phrase "leased and occupied" in the lease agreement. Judge Kennedy found that . . . a reasonable person would interpret "leased and occupied" to refer to the time at which the tenants have a legal right to possess the property, not when the property is actually physically occupied. . . . Therefore, on May 24, 1995, Judge Kennedy granted a judgment of possession for Republic and entered a monetary judgment against Mr.

Shin in the amount of $26,058.62, representing unpaid rent and related charges.

On December 19, 1995, almost seven months after resolution of the landlord-tenant dispute, Mr. Shin filed the instant action against the landlords, alleging fraudulent misrepresentation and breach of contract . . . and seeking rescission of the lease agreement and money damages. The landlords filed a motion to dismiss on the ground of *res judicata*, and Shin filed an opposition. The trial court, concluding that Shin's claim arose from the same "common nucleus of facts" as the landlord-tenant proceeding and that appellant could have raised his claim as a defense in that proceeding, granted the motion. Shin then noted this appeal. . . .

. . . Under the doctrine of *res judicata*, or claim preclusion, "a prior judgment on the merits raises an absolute bar to the relitigation of the same cause of action between the original parties or those in privity with them." . . . The doctrine bars relitigation "not only as to every ground of recovery or defense actually presented in the action, but also as to every ground which might have been presented. . . ."

> A defendant seeking dismissal of a complaint on *res judicata* grounds bears the burden of persuasion on two separate issues. First, he must demonstrate that the prior decision on which he bases his *res judicata* claim was a decision on the merits; second, he must establish that the earlier litigation was based on the same cause of action [as the current claim]. . . .

Appellant contends that *res judicata* does not apply to this case because his counterclaim in the landlord-tenant action was dismissed (by him) without prejudice. It is certainly true that "the crucial element of *res judicata* is a final judgment on the merits . . . and it is beyond dispute that . . ."a dismissal of a claim without prejudice does not bar a subsequent suit of issues arising out of the same cause of action." Therefore, because it was not a final adjudication, Mr. Shin's voluntary dismissal of his earlier counter-claim does not, in itself, bar his present claim.

But our inquiry does not end there. A dismissal without prejudice does not forever protect a claim from dismissal in a later proceeding on the ground of *res judicata.* If there is subsequent litigation resulting in a decision on the merits, in which a party has the opportunity to litigate an issue and fails to do so, that party may not rely on an earlier dismissal without prejudice to shield his later claim from a *res judicata*-based dismissal. Such a result would violate the principle that a "final judgment embodies all of a party's rights arising out of the transaction involved, and a party will be foreclosed from later seeking relief on the basis of issues which might have been raised in the prior action." . . .

In this case, after Mr. Shin voluntarily dismissed his counterclaim, there was a trial in Landlord and Tenant court, in which his present claims could have been litigated as part of his general denial of liability for rent. As challenges to the contract itself . . . , a defendant always has the right to present any legal defense as part of a general denial of liability. . . . Even though Shin's allegations of fraudulent misrepresentation and breach of contract may not have been presentable in the form of a counterclaim . . . [because of re-strictive procedural rules in landlord-tenant cases], he still could have raised them as legal defenses to the landlord's claim for back rent. . . . These allegations are challenges to the lease itself and, if true, would have made the lease void and unenforceable, or at least would have markedly affected the total amount of the money judgment.

Shin contends nevertheless that *res judicata* does not bar his claim because it is not based on the same cause of action as the landlord-tenant proceeding. . . . In determining whether two cases are based on the same cause of action, "the courts have considered the nature of the two actions and the facts sought to be proved in each one." . . . We have specifically held that claims for fraudulent misrepresentation arise out of the same cause of action as an earlier proceeding based on the contract. . . . In this case, Mr. Shin's claim arose out of the same contract and surrounding negotiations as the landlord-tenant proceeding. We conclude, therefore, that it could and should have been offered as a defense in the landlord-tenant case, and hence that the present action is barred by *res judicata*. . . .

Because the trial court correctly applied the doctrine of *res judicata* to the facts of this case, its order of dismissal is
Affirmed.

Case Questions

1. What must a defendant prove in order to establish a *res judicata* defense?
2. Why does that appellate court agree that Mr. Shin's December 19, 1995 action should have been dismissed?

IMMUNITY FROM LEGAL ACTION

The law provides immunity from tort liability when to do so is thought to be in the best interest of the public. Immunities are an exception to the general rule that a remedy must be provided for every wrong, and they are not favored by courts. They make the right of the individual to redress a private wrong subservient to what the law recognizes as a greater public good. Immunity does not mean that the conduct is not tortious in character, but only that for policy reasons the law denies liability resulting from the tort. Today, many courts are willing to abolish or limit immunities when it becomes apparent that the public is not actually deriving any benefit from their existence.

Sovereign Immunity

It is a basic principle of common law that no sovereign may be sued without its express consent. When a person sues the government, the person is actually suing the taxpayers and themselves, because any judgment is paid for out of public revenues. The payment of judgments would require the expenditure of funds raised to provide services to the public.

The doctrine of governmental immunity from liability originated in the English notion that "the king can do no wrong." (Ironically, although most U.S. courts have retained the doctrine, England has repudiated it.) Congress consented to be sued in contract cases in the 1887 Tucker Act. In 1946 the federal government passed the Federal Tort Claims Act, in which the U.S. government waived its immunity from tort liability. It permitted suits against the federal government in federal courts for negligence or wrongful acts committed by its employees within the scope of their employment. Liability is based on the applicable local tort law. Thus the government may be sued in its capacity as a landlord and as a possessor of land, as well as for negligent acts and omissions (concepts explained in Chapter 11). Immunity was not waived for all acts of federal employees, however. Acts within the discretionary function of a federal employee or acts of military and naval forces in time of war are examples of situations in which immunity has not been waived. In addition, members of the armed forces who have suffered a service-related injury due to governmental negligence are denied the right to sue. Permitting such suits has been thought to undermine military discipline. State governments also enjoy sovereign immunity.

Courts have made a distinction between governmental and *proprietary functions*. When a public entity is involved in a governmental function, it is generally immune from tort liability. When the government engages in activity that is usually carried out by private individuals or that is commercial in character, it is involved in a proprietary function, and the cloak of immunity is lost. For example, a state is not immune when it provides a service that a corporation may perform, such as providing electricity.

Courts currently favor limiting or abolishing sovereign immunity. Their rationale is the availability of liability insurance and the perceived inequity of denying relief to a deserving claimant. Many jurisdictions have replaced blanket sovereign immunity with tort claims acts that limit governmental liability. For example, they can reduce exposure to suit by restricting recoveries to the limits of insurance policies or by establishing ceilings on maximum recoveries (often ranging from $25,000 to $100,000). Many states continue to immunize discretionary functions and acts.

Immunity of Governmental Officials

As described in the previous section, executive, legislative, and judicial officers are afforded immunity when the act is within the scope of their authority and in the discharge of their official duties. Immunity increases the likelihood that government officials will act impartially and fearlessly in carrying out their public duties. Thus it is in the public interest to shield responsible government officers from harassment or ill-founded damage suits based on acts they committed in the exercise of their official responsibilities. Prosecutors, for example, enjoy immunity when they decide for the public who should be criminally prosecuted. Public defenders, however, are not immunized, because their clients are private citizens and not the general public.

This immunity applies only when public officers are performing discretionary acts in conjunction with official functions. Officials are not immune from liability for tortious conduct when they transcend their lawful authority and invade the constitutional rights of others. They are legally responsible for their personal torts.

Some argue that granting immunity to officials does not protect individual citizens from harm resulting from oppressive or malicious conduct on the part of public officers. A governmental official may in some jurisdictions lose this protection by acting maliciously or for an improper purpose, rather than honestly or in good faith.

High-level executive, legislative, and judicial officials with discretionary functions enjoy more immunity than lower-level officials. Judges, for example, are absolutely immune when they exercise judicial powers, regardless of their motives or good faith. We will see in the next case that police officers are entitled to *"qualified immunity,"* a much less generous form of protection.

Brent v. Ashley
No. 99-12169
U.S. Court of Appeals, Eleventh Circuit
April 19, 2001

Barkett, Circuit Judge

In this interlocutory appeal, Prospero Ellis and Seymour Schor, both United States Customs Service inspectors, appeal the denial of their motion for summary judgment based on qualified immunity in an action filed by Rhonda Brent alleging violation of her Fourth Amendment rights during a strip search and x-ray examination. Brent cross-appeals the district court's grant of summary judgment on the basis of qualified immunity to Ellis and Schor's subordinates, Odesta Ashley, Carl Pietri, Francine Williams, Ricky Grim, Kathryn Dellane, and Lee Sanchez-Blair. We affirm.

Facts

In reviewing summary judgment, we are bound to consider all of the evidence and the inferences drawn in the light most favorable to the non-moving party. . . . On July 20, 1991, Rhonda Brent, a United States citizen, was returning home to Houston, Texas, aboard

Alitalia Flight 618 from a vacation in Nigeria. During the Rome to Miami leg of her return flight, Brent met Kehinde Elbute, a black Nigerian man who was also en route to Houston. Brent and Elbute were the only black persons on the flight. The flight arrived at Miami International Airport and the passengers disembarked from the plane. As Brent entered the baggage claim area at the airport, she noticed Customs Agent Ricky Grim and his inspection dog with Elbute. Brent stopped briefly, observed Grim searching Elbute and his luggage, and shook her head in disapproval. Based on this look and gesture, Inspector Seymour Schor instructed Inspector Carl Pietri to detain Brent and escort her to the examination area where Elbute had been taken. Pietri seized Brent's passport and other documents, isolated her from other passengers and took her to the examination area for interrogation. Brent protested Pietri's actions, alleging that she was being singled out because she was black.

Schor questioned both Brent and Elbute about the nature of their trips and personally conducted a thorough search of both of their luggage, in which he took every item out of their bags and examined each item separately and carefully. He found no narcotics, nor did he find any items commonly associated with drug couriers. Brent continued to protest the search stating that she was aware of her rights and that she was being treated this way because she was black. Despite finding no objective evidence that she was a drug courier, Schor continued to detain Brent for further questioning.

Shortly thereafter, Schor was joined by Supervisor Inspector Prospero Ellis. Ellis reexamined Brent's travel documents, clothing and luggage, and questioned her. Both Ellis and Schor then decided to conduct a full body pat-down and strip search. The report form filed by the agents at the time of the search indicated that the reasons for conducting the search were Brent's nervousness and her

arrival from a source country. Female customs agents Odesta Ashley, Lee Sanchez-Blair and Kathryn Dellane were called in to assist.

The body pat-down and strip search, conducted by Blair and witnessed by Ashley and Dellane, . . . revealed none of the typical indicators of internal drug smuggling. There was no rigid or distended abdomen, no girdle to hold up the abdomen, no synthetic lubricants, and no contraband could be seen in her body cavities. After the strip search, Brent asked if she could use the bathroom. She was allowed to use the bathroom, but was watched closely by the female agents and told not to flush the toilet. After she had gone to the bathroom, the agents examined Brent's urine for signs of contraband. None were found. At some point during her detention, Brent's name was entered into the Treasury Enforcement Computer Systems to search for frequent travels or past arrests. The inquiry returned nothing suspicious.

Although the pat-down, strip search, and electronic record search revealed nothing, Ellis and Schor nonetheless decided that an x-ray and pelvic examination at the hospital should be performed. The search report form filed the day after the x-ray listed the reasons for conducting the examination as Brent's nervousness and her arrival from a source country. Dellane handcuffed Brent and transported her to Jackson Memorial Hospital. Prior to transport, Brent was presented with a consent form and told that if she refused to sign it she could be held for 35 days or indefinitely until a judge ordered the x-ray. She requested to speak with an attorney and to call home. Both requests were denied. She signed the consent form and waived her Miranda rights after being told she had no choice. Upon arrival at the prison ward of the hospital, Brent was told to sign another consent form. Inspector Francine Williams escorted Brent to the x-ray room and remained with Brent throughout the examination. The examination revealed a complete absence of drugs. Dellane drove Brent back to the airport and, ten hours after she was first detained, made arrangements for Brent to return home to Houston. Brent filed this suit against the United States under the Federal Tort Claims Act ("FTCA") and against nine named customs employees, alleging the commission of common law torts and constitutional violations pursuant to *Bivens v. Six Unknown Named Agents of Federal Bureau of Narcotics*, 403 U.S. 338 (1971). The district court dismissed with prejudice Brent's FTCA claim for failure to file the action within the statutory time limits. The individual defendants then moved for summary judgment on Brent's Bivens claims based on qualified immunity. The district court granted the motion with regard to Ashley, Pietri, Williams, Grim, Dellane, and Sanchez-Blair, and denied the motion as to Ellis and Schor. This appeal followed. . . .

We review de novo a district court's ruling on summary judgment, applying the same legal standards as the district court. . . . Summary judgment is appropriate only when the evidence before the court demonstrates that "there is no genuine issue of material fact and that the moving party is entitled to judgment as a matter of law." . . .

Discussion

"A court evaluating a claim of qualified immunity must first determine whether the plaintiff has alleged the deprivation of an actual constitutional right at all, and if so, proceed to determine whether that right was clearly established at the time of the alleged violation." . . . Thus, we address initially the question of whether Ellis and Schor's actions violated Brent's constitutional rights.

1. Was there a violation of Brent's Fourth Amendment rights?

Rather than viewing the initial stop, strip search and x-ray examination of Brent as a single incident, the facts of this case compel that each progressive stage of the search be viewed as a discrete occurrence. Accordingly, in determining whether Brent has met her burden to demonstrate the existence of a constitutional violation, we examine the constitutionality of the initial stop, the strip search and the x-ray examination separately.

a. Was the initial stop constitutional under the Fourth Amendment?

During the initial stop of Brent, the customs agents isolated Brent from the other passengers, asked her questions about the nature of her trip, and searched her luggage. The decision to stop and search Brent was based upon the fact that she shook her head in disapproval upon seeing the way customs agents were treating a co-passenger. Brent argues that a simple expression of disapproval cannot provide reasonable suspicion sufficient to justify the stop and search and thus the initial stop is constitutionally infirm.

We agree with Brent that her simple disapproving head movement is insufficient to raise reasonable suspicion; however, the law is clear that "[r]outine [border] searches of the persons and effects of entrants are not subject to any requirement of reasonable suspicion, probable cause, or warrant. . . ." Because the initial stop did not constitute more than a routine border search, Brent has failed to demonstrate that the initial stop violated her Fourth Amendment rights.

b. Was the strip search constitutional under the Fourth Amendment?

The Supreme Court has held that "detention of a traveler at the border, beyond the scope of routine customs search and inspection, is justified at its inception if customs agents considering all the facts surrounding the traveler and her trip, reasonably suspect that the traveler is smuggling contraband. . . ." Reasonable suspicion is "more than an inchoate and unparticularized suspicion or hunch," . . . and requires that officials have a "'particularized and objective basis for suspecting the particular person' of . . . smuggling." . . ." Accordingly,

> [r]easonable suspicion to justify a strip search can only be met by a showing of articulable facts which are particularized as to the place to be searched. . . .

Moreover, as a search progresses from a stop, to a pat-down search, to a strip search, an agent must reevaluate whether reasonable suspicion to justify the next level of intrusion exists in light of the information gained during the encounter. . . . Under . . . Supreme Court and Eleventh Circuit standards, the strip search of Brent, on the basis of the generalized and unparticularized reasons given in either the contemporaneously filed search report forms or in the affidavits filed six years later, constitutes a Fourth Amendment violation.

This Court has previously applied these standards in an analogous setting and found that a strip search violated the Fourth Amendment. . . .

Here, . . . Ellis and Schor based their decision to strip search Brent upon the fact that Brent fit a general profile of arrival from a source country, and she was nervous. However, in making this determination, they . . . disregarded the fact that: (1) a non-intrusive search of Brent's person and her luggage revealed nothing to support the suspicion that she was smuggling narcotics; (2) Brent presented verifiable residence and employment information; and (3) a check of Brent's name in the Treasury Enforcement Computer System revealed nothing suspicious. . . . [U]pon these facts, the strip search of Brent was unconstitutional.

. . . [R]ecent cases further compel this conclusion. In *Reid v. Georgia*, 448 U.S. 438 (1980) (per curiam), a DEA agent stopped a traveler in the Atlanta Airport because his characteristics and actions fit the "drug courier profile": (1) the defendant arrived from Fort Lauderdale, a city the agent knew to be a principal source of cocaine; (2) he arrived early in the morning, when law enforcement activity is diminished; (3) he and his companion appeared to be concealing the fact that the two were traveling together; and (4) he and his companion had no luggage except for their shoulder bags. . . . The Supreme Court concluded that "the agent could not, as a matter of law, have reasonably suspected the petitioner of criminal activity on the basis of these observed circumstances." . . . The only fact that related to the individuals' conduct, the Court found, was that the defendant preceded his companion and occasionally looked backward at him. The Court found that the other circumstances, including arrival from a source location, describe a large number of "presumably innocent travelers, who would be subject to virtually random seizures were the Court to conclude that as little foundation as there was in this case could justify a seizure." . . .

In this case, the facts known to Ellis and Schor were far less suspicious than the ones found insufficient as a matter of law by the Supreme Court in *Reid*. Even in combination, the articulated characteristics here could be ascribed generally to a great number of innocent travelers. Indeed, the only fact that relates to Brent's conduct is that she was nervous. However, this general observation of Brent's nervousness, standing alone, cannot provide "reasonable suspicion" to justify the strip search. See *United States v. Tapia*, . . . (11th Cir. 1990) (holding that no reasonable suspicion existed to support detention when suspect appeared visibly nervous during confrontation with officers, and had few pieces of luggage). . . . The initial stop and questioning of Brent, with the attendant search of her luggage, failed to produce particularized and objective evidence that would raise reasonable suspicion that she was a drug courier.

Accordingly, we conclude that the strip search of Brent violated the Fourth Amendment.

c. Was the x-ray examination constitutional under the Fourth Amendment?

. . . The agents listed the same reasons for conducting the x-ray examination as they did for conducting the strip search. As discussed above, these types of general observations, without more, can never give rise to reasonable suspicion sufficient to justify an intrusive search such as an x-ray examination. Moreover, the unconstitutionality of the x-ray examination is more apparent than the strip search, because at the time of the x-ray, in addition to the significant exculpatory factors of which they had knowledge prior to strip search, Ellis and Schor were also aware that Brent's urine had no traces of contraband and that the strip search revealed nothing to suggest that Brent was carrying drugs internally. Accordingly, we conclude that the x-ray examination of Brent also violated the Fourth Amendment.

2. Are Ellis and Schor entitled to qualified immunity?

Having determined that the strip search and x-ray violated the Fourth Amendment, we turn to examine whether Ellis and Schor can be held personally liable for their actions. Our cases hold that a law enforcement officer who conducts an unconstitutional search based upon a reasonable but mistaken conclusion that reasonable suspicion exists is entitled to qualified immunity. . . . Thus, "[w]hen an officer asserts qualified immunity, the issue is not whether reasonable suspicion existed in fact, but whether the officer has 'arguable' reasonable suspicion." . . . In determining whether Ellis and Schor had "arguable reasonable suspicion" to justify the strip search and x-ray examination, we analyze whether "a reasonable officer could have believed that the search[es] comported with the Fourth Amendment." . . . This inquiry ensures that law enforcement officials "'reasonably can anticipate when their conduct may give rise to liability.'" . . . With these standards in mind, we now consider whether Ellis and Schor had "arguable reasonable suspicion" to support either the strip search or x-ray examination.

a. Was there "arguable reasonable suspicion" for the strip search?

In 1978, well before the strip search of Brent, our precedent clearly established that even if Brent fit a drug courier profile, the "fruitless search of [her] luggage and the failure to elicit suspicious information [from her] on questioning would . . . preclude . . . justification for a strip search." . . . Moreover, at the time of the incident, Supreme Court precedent had made clear that a law enforcement official must have "reasonable suspicion" to justify any stop at the border beyond a routine non-intrusive search. . . . The Supreme Court had held that reasonable suspicion must be based upon "more than an inchoate and unparticularized suspicion or hunch," . . . but rather, requires "particularized and objective" facts. . . .

Here, the two factors Ellis and Schor relied upon in justifying the search—Brent's arrival from a source location and her nervousness—were not particularized to the place to be searched and had been expressly rejected by the Supreme Court and the Eleventh Circuit as factors that, standing alone, give rise to reasonable suspicion.

Based upon the foregoing, we conclude that a reasonable customs agent at the time of the incident would have known that a strip search under the facts of this case was a violation of Brent's Fourth Amendment rights. Thus, Ellis and Schor did not have "arguable reasonable suspicion" to support the strip search and are not entitled to qualified immunity from liability arising from their alleged unconstitutional conduct.

b. Was there "arguable reasonable suspicion" for the x-ray examination?

. . . Here, as with the strip search, the only undisputed reasons for the x-ray examination are Brent's nervousness and her arrival from a source location. For the reasons stated above, these factors not only fail to raise reasonable suspicion to justify the x-ray examination, but also fail to raise even "arguable reasonable suspicion." Based on the foregoing, we conclude that because a reasonable customs agent would have understood that the x-ray examination, based only upon an observation of nervousness and a general profile, violated Brent's constitutional rights, there was not "arguable reasonable suspicion" to support the x-ray examination, and therefore Ellis and Schor are not protected by qualified immunity from civil liability arising from the x-ray examination.

3. Are Ellis and Schor's subordinates protected by qualified immunity?

The district court determined that only Schor and Ellis made decisions to conduct the intrusive searches of Brent, and that Ashley, Pietri, Williams, Grim, Dellane, and Sanchez-Blair had no discretionary authority and no reason to suspect that Brent's constitutional rights were being violated. Accordingly, the district court concluded that Ashley, Pietri, Williams, Grim, Dellane, and Sanchez-Blair acted reasonably in following Ellis and Schor's orders and that qualified immunity shielded them from civil liability. On appeal, Brent argues that whether a gov-

ernment agent is acting in a supervisory role is not determinative of . . . liability and that following orders does not immunize government agents from civil rights liability. While we agree with Brent's general summary of the law, we do not agree that the district court erred in granting summary judgment in favor of Ashley, Pietri, Williams, Grim, Dellane, and Sanchez-Blair.

. . . Here, the record is devoid of any evidence that would support the conclusion that Ashley, Pietri, Williams, Grim, Dellane, and Sanchez-Blair acted unreasonably.

The record reflects that Grim merely inspected Elbute and had no contact with Brent. Pietri, under orders of Schor, asked Brent a few routine questions, obtained her documents and walked her to the secondary examination area. Dellane, on orders of Schor and Ellis, witnessed the strip search, traveled with Brent to the hospital, and returned with her to the airport. Ashley, on orders of Schor and Ellis, witnessed the strip search. Williams, on orders of Schor and Ellis, took Brent to the x-ray room, and arranged her return to the airport. Sanchez-Blair, at the direction of Schor and Ellis, conducted the strip search. Each of these individuals acted at the order of a superior and the record reflects no reason why any of them should question the validity of that order. We, therefore, affirm the district court's grant of qualified immunity to Ashley, Pietri, Williams, Grim, Dellane, and Sanchez-Blair.

For all of the above reasons, the rulings of the district court are

Affirmed.

Case Questions

1. Why do police officers receive any form of immunity from civil suit?
2. Why did U.S. Court of Appeals conclude that some of the officers should receive qualified immunity, but that others should not?

Charitable Immunity

The judicial doctrine that excuses charitable institutions from tort liability was created in England in 1846 and was recognized in this country in the 1870s. In the late 1800s and early 1900s, when many of the charitable immunity precedents were established, charitable institutions were often financially weak. The courts feared that they would not financially survive if people who accepted charity were permitted to sue in tort the institutions that provided them with care. They feared that donors would refuse to make donations if funds intended to be used to provide care were used to pay tort claims. Others argued that people who accepted charity had assumed the risk of negligent care from the charitable institutions.

The most important argument against charitable immunity is that it is unjust to victims. Indigents, who are least able to assume the risk, are made to assume all the costs resulting from the charitable institution's negligence. In addition, the doctrine of charitable immunity helps to perpetuate the delivery of inferior care to the poor. It is argued that, if the doctrine were abolished, such institutions would be forced to take greater precautions to avoid judgments and that the quality of care provided to indigents would significantly improve. In addition, injured victims would be able to obtain compensation for their injuries.

In the following case, a hospital invoked the charitable immunity defense, despite receiving less than 1 percent of its annual revenues in the form of charitable donations.

Thompson v. Mercy Hospital
483 A.2d 706
Supreme Judicial Court of Maine
October 29, 1984

Nichols, Justice

The narrow issue presented in this appeal is whether a hospital which derives less than one percent of its annual revenue from charitable sources is entitled in a tort action to the defense of charitable immunity. We conclude that it is not.

On February 22, 1982, the Plaintiff, Dorothy A. Thompson, entered a complaint against the Defendant, Mercy Hospital, in Superior Court, Cumberland County; the complaint alleged that the Plaintiff was mentally retarded and that the Defendant had negligently given her inadequate training and supervision in the operation of a press-ing machine in its Portland facility. It was further alleged that the Plaintiff's left hand was drawn into the machine and sustained "partial permanent impairment." The Plaintiff sought damages for medical expenses and for pain and suffering.

The Defendant filed a motion to dismiss, invoking the defense of charitable immunity. Hearing on this motion was continued to allow the Plaintiff to conduct discovery limited to the issue of whether the Defendant was a charitable institution for purposes of immunity from tort liability. Following a hearing on the Plaintiff's motion to compel, it was determined that the Plaintiff could discover the sources of the Defendant's revenue by percentages but not by amounts. The Plaintiff drafted its interrogatories accordingly, and the Defendant answered them on December 6, 1982.

These answers revealed that unrestricted gifts and bequests comprised .6%, .5% and

.1%, respectively, of the Defendant's annual revenues in the fiscal years 1980, 1981, and 1982, while specific donations constituted .3%, .1% and .1%, respectively, of its revenues for these same years.

. . . After the hearing, the Superior Court granted the motion. . . .

On appeal, the Plaintiff argues that the Superior Court erred in applying the doctrine of charitable immunity to the Defendant. . . .

The doctrine of charitable immunity is a creation of our common law. Except for one significant restriction imposed by statute, its applicability in Maine is controlled entirely by the precedents of this Court. Under the leading cases, in order to qualify for charitable immunity, an institution must, *inter alia*, derive its funds "mainly from public and private charity." . . . This requirement is one of the "constituent elements" of charitable institutions for tort immunity purposes. . . . In its absence, charitable immunity is not available. . . .

We have recognized two rationales for this immunity: "(1) that funds donated for charitable purposes are held in trust to be used exclusively for those purposes, and (2) that to permit the invasion of these funds to satisfy tort claims would destroy the sources of charitable support upon which the enterprise depends." . . . Neither rationale justifies extending immunity to an organization which derives only a modicum of its fi-

nancial support from charitable sources. The small fraction of the Defendant's revenues donated for charitable purposes need not be depleted to satisfy tort claims. Even where its insurance coverage may be insufficient to satisfy such claims fully, the Defendant can draw exclusively upon its noncharitable revenues. The second rationale is inapplicable because the Defendant's survival does not depend on its sources of charitable support.

The Defendant proposes an additional justification for charitable immunity: "that to permit tort actions against an uninsured nonprofit hospital would have a serious and dramatic effect upon the quality of that facility's health care." We have never approved this rationale, and we decline to do so now. It is based on unfounded supposition.

The defense of charitable immunity is unavailable to an institution in the Defendant's financial position. We decline to extend the scope of this much criticized doctrine to shield the Defendant in the tort case before us. . . .

The entry, therefore, must be:

Appeal sustained.

Judgment vacated.

Remanded for entry of a summary judgment for the Plaintiff against the Defendant on the defense of charitable immunity and further proceedings consistent with the opinion herein.

All concurring.

Case Questions

1. What does it mean when the court states, "The doctrine of charitable immunity is a creation of our common law," and why is this fact significant?
2. Did the Supreme Judicial Court of Maine find the defendant guilty of negligence?

 What moral duty does the hospital have in your view? Does the court's decision coincide with your views of the hospital's moral duty?

Immunity Among Family Members

American courts have traditionally recognized two types of immunities among family members. *Interspousal immunity* has prevented suits in tort between husbands and wives, and parental immunity has severely limited the types of suits children can bring against their parents.

According to traditional common law principles, husbands and wives were immune from liability for torts committed against their spouses, because they were legally considered to be one person. Today, only Georgia, Hawai'i, Illinois, Louisiana, and the District of Columbia still recognize the doctrine in whole or in part. The remaining jurisdictions have abolished spousal immunity for the reasons given by the South Carolina Supreme Court in the following case, *Boone v. Boone*. The *Boone* case procedurally revolves around a topic we studied in Chapter 5—conflicts of law in tort cases. The trial court in this case followed South Carolina's established precedent and applied *lex loci delicti commissi,* and dismissed the case. The plaintiff on appeal, argued to the state supreme court that its precedent should be overruled.

Juanita Boone v. Freddie Boone
No. 25283
Supreme Court of South Carolina
April 23, 2001

Justice Burnett

The question presented by this appeal is whether interspousal immunity from personal injury actions violates the public policy of South Carolina. . . .

Facts

Appellant Juanita Boone (Wife) was injured in a car accident in Georgia. At the time of the accident, Wife was a passenger in a vehicle driven by her husband Respondent Freddie Boone (Husband). Wife and Husband reside in South Carolina.

Wife brought this tort action against Husband in South Carolina. Concluding Georgia law which provides interspousal immunity in personal injury actions was applicable, the trial judge granted Husband's motion to dismiss. Wife appeals. . . .

Issue

Does Georgia law providing interspousal immunity in personal injury actions violate the public policy of South Carolina?

Discussion

I. Interspousal Immunity

Interspousal immunity is a common law doctrine based on the legal fiction that husband and wife share the same identity in law, namely that of the husband. . . . Accordingly, at common law, it was "both morally and conceptually objectionable to permit a tort suit between two spouses." . . .

With the passage of Married Women's Property Acts in the mid-nineteenth century, married women were given a legal estate in their own property and the capacity to sue and be sued. Under this legislation, a married woman could maintain an action against her husband for any tort against her property interest such as trespass to land or conversion. Since the legislation destroyed the "unity of persons," a husband could also maintain an action against his wife for torts to his property. . . .

For a long time, however, the majority of courts held Married Women's Property Acts did not destroy interspousal immunity for personal torts. Courts adopted two inconsistent arguments in favor of continued immunity. First, they theorized suits between spouses would be fictitious and fraudulent, particularly against insurance companies. Second, they claimed interspousal suits would destroy domestic harmony. . . .

In the twentieth century, most courts either abrogated or provided exceptions to interspousal immunity. . . . South Carolina has abolished the doctrine of interspousal immunity from tort liability for personal injury. . . . see S.C. Code Ann. §§ 15-5-170 (1976) ("[a] married woman may sue and be sued as if she were unmarried. When the action is between herself and her husband she may likewise sue or be sued alone.").

Very few jurisdictions now recognize interspousal tort immunity. . . . [District of Columbia, Georgia, Hawai'i, Illinois, and Louisiana].

Georgia continues to recognize the common law doctrine of interspousal immunity. . . . Under Georgia law, interspousal tort immunity bars personal injury actions between spouses, except where the traditional policy reasons for applying the doctrine are absent, i.e., where there is no marital harmony to be preserved and where there exists no possibility of collusion between the spouses. . . .

II. Choice of Law

Under traditional South Carolina choice of law principles, the substantive law governing a tort action is determined by lex loci delicti, the law of the state in which the injury occurred. . . . However,

> foreign law may not be given effect in this State if 'it is against good morals or natural justice . . .' . . . . The 'good morals or natural justice' of our State are not violated when foreign law is applied to preclude a tort

action for money damages, whether against an individual or the State, even if recovery may be had upon application of South Carolina law. '[T]he fact that the law of two states may differ does not necessarily imply that the law of one state violates the public policy of the other.'

Dawkins v. State, . . . (1991) citing *Rauton v. Pullman Co.,* . . . (1937) (court will refuse to follow law of lex loci when it is against good morals or natural justice, or "for some other such reason the enforcement of it would be prejudicial to the general interests of our own citizens."). Accordingly, under the "public policy exception," the Court will not apply foreign law if it violates the public policy of South Carolina.

Although South Carolina had abolished the doctrine of interspousal immunity from tort liability for personal injury thirty years before, this Court held it would apply the law of the foreign state even if it recognized interspousal immunity. *Oshiek v. Oshiek,* . . . (1964). If a spouse had no right of action against her spouse where the tort occurred, the action would not be enforced in South Carolina. . . .

In *Algie v. Algie,* . . . (1973), the Court expressly declined to overrule *Oshiek v. Oshiek,* . . . In Algie, the parties lived in Florida. The wife was injured in an airplane accident in South Carolina. Her husband had piloted the airplane. The husband urged the Court to apply Florida law which, at that time, recognized interspousal immunity. The Court declined, noting "[w]e are not persuaded that this result would be in furtherance of justice." . . .

III. Analysis

It is the public policy of our State to provide married persons with the same legal rights and remedies possessed by unmarried persons. . . . Had the parties to this action not been married to each other, Wife could have maintained a personal injury action against Husband. We find it contrary to "natural justice," . . . , to hold that because of their marital status, Wife is precluded from maintaining this action against Husband. Accordingly, we conclude application of the doctrine of interspousal immunity violates the public policy of South Carolina.

Moreover, the reasons given in support of interspousal immunity are simply not justified in the twenty-first century. There is no reason to presume married couples are more likely than others to engage in a collusive action. Whether or not parties are married, if fraudulent conduct is suspected, insurers can examine and investigate the claim and, at trial, cross-examine the parties as to their financial stakes in the outcome of the suit. Fraudulent claims would be subject to the trial court's contempt powers and to criminal prosecution for perjury and other crimes. It is unjustified to prohibit all personal injury tort suits between spouses simply because some suits may be fraudulent.

Additionally, we do not agree that precluding spouses from maintaining a personal injury action against each other fosters domestic harmony. Instead, we find marital harmony is promoted by allowing the negligent spouse, who has most likely purchased liability insurance, to provide for his injured spouse. . . .

Furthermore, in Georgia, spouses may maintain an action against each other for torts committed against their property. . . . If suits encompassing one type of tort are permitted between spouses, we fail to see how suits encompassing a different tort should be prohibited under the guise of protecting domestic tranquility. In our opinion, marital disharmony will not increase because married persons are permitted to maintain a personal injury action against each other.

Finally, we recognize the Court previously declined to overrule the *lex loci delicti* doctrine with regard to interspousal personal injury suits. . . . However, in *Algie*, the *lex loci delicti* (South Carolina) permitted personal injury suits between spouses. Accordingly, South Carolina's public policy was not violated by continuation of the *lex loci delicti* doctrine in that case. Unlike *Algie*, declining to apply interspousal immunity here "would be in the furtherance of justice." . . .

Because interspousal immunity violates the public policy of South Carolina, we will no longer apply the *lex loci delicti* when the law of the foreign state recognizes the doctrine. *Oshiek v. Oshiek,* . . . , is overruled.

Reversed.

Case Questions

1. What was the traditional rationale for recognizing interspousal immunity?
2. Why did the South Carolina Supreme Court decide to reverse the trial court?
3. If interspousal immunity violates the public policy of South Carolina and 45 other states, what, if anything, does that say about the remaining four states that continue to support it?

Parental immunity was created by U.S. courts in 1891. Many courts thought it in society's interest to prohibit unemancipated minor children from maintaining actions for negligence or intentional torts against their parents. At common law, children remained minors until they reached the age of twenty-one. Today, legislation has reduced this age to eighteen. A child is unemancipated until the parents surrender the right of care, custody, and earnings of such child and renounce their parental duties. Many courts believed that subjecting the parent to suit by the child might interfere with domestic harmony, deplete family funds at the expense of the other family members, encourage fraud or collusion, and interfere with the discipline and control of children. However, unemancipated minor children have always been able to enforce contracts or property rights against their parents. The parental immunity doctrine has been significantly eroded in the United States.

INTERNET TIP

Students wishing to read a case in which the state supreme court creates an exception to the doctrine of parental immunity so that children can sue their parents for sexual abuse can read *Hurst v. Capitell* on the textbook's website.

Immunity Through Contract

In addition to the immunities imposed by law, parties can create their own immunities by agreeing not to sue. Because policy favors freedom of contract, the agreement may be enforced in a court of law. However, courts are often reluctant to do so. An immunity provision in a contract is construed against the party asserting the contract and is held invalid if the contract is against public policy or is a result of unfair negotiations. Factors that the court considers in determining whether to enforce the agreement are the subject matter involved, the clause itself, the relation of the parties, and the relative bargaining power of the parties.

A basic tenet of freedom of contract is that both parties are free to negotiate the terms of the contract. As a result, the contract should reflect a real and voluntary meeting of the minds. Therefore the equality of bargaining power is an important consideration for courts in determining unfair negotiations. Different courts may accord different degrees of importance to such elements as superior bargaining power, a lack of meaningful choice by one party, take-it-or-leave-it propositions, or exploitation by one party of another's known weaknesses.

The trial court in the following case enforced a bicycle rental agreement that contained an exculpatory clause. The plaintiff signed the agreement without carefully reading its terms. The defendant, who allegedly rented a bicycle with defective brakes to the plaintiff, was granted summary judgment.

Gimpel v. Host Enterprises, Inc.
640 F.Supp. 972
U.S. District Court, Eastern District of Pa.
July 24, 1986
Memorandum and Order

Troutman, Senior District Judge

On August 25, 1985, plaintiff Reuben Gimpel was injured when he fell from a bicycle rented at the Host Enterprises, Inc., resort in Lancaster, Pennsylvania. Gimpel was allegedly unable to stop the bicycle because of a malfunction of its brakes due to Host's failure to properly maintain and inspect it.

Defendant Host has moved for summary judgment, contending that the rental agreement which Gimpel signed contains an exculpatory clause releasing Host from any liability arising from the rental and use of the bicycle....

Turning to the merits of the motion for summary judgment, we look first to the law of Pennsylvania to determine the effect of exculpatory clauses in general before examining the clause at issue here.

In *Employers Liability Assurance Corp., Ltd. v. Greenville Business Men's Association,* . . . 224 A.2d 620 (1966), the Pennsylvania Supreme Court set forth the conditions under which such clauses are valid and enforceable:

> "Generally speaking, an exculpatory clause is valid if: (a) 'it does not contravene any policy of the law, that is, if it is not a matter of interest to the public or State; . . .' (b) 'the contract is between persons relating entirely to their own private affairs'; . . . (c) 'each party is a free bargaining agent' and the clause is not in effect 'a mere contract of adhesion, whereby [one party] simply adheres to a document which he is powerless to alter having no alternative other than to reject the transaction entirely.' . . .
>
> "Assuming, *arguendo*, that the instant exculpatory clause satisfies all three conditions and is valid, our case law requires that, even if valid, an exculpatory clause must meet certain standards [to be enforceable]. . . .
>
> "Such standards are: (1) contracts providing for immunity from liability for negligence must be construed strictly since they are not favorites of the law; . . . (2) such contracts 'must spell out the intentions of the parties with the greatest of particularity'; . . . and show the intent to release from liability 'beyond doubt by express stipulation' and '[n]o inference from words of general import can establish it'; . . . (3) such contracts must be construed with every intendment against the party who seeks the immunity from liability; . . . (4) the burden to establish immunity from liability is upon the party who asserts such immunity." . . .

As noted, the exculpatory clause at issue here was contained in the rental agreement for the bicycle, called the "Ride Charge Agreement," and reads as follows:

> "User agrees to return said item in the same condition as when received, ordinary wear and tear excepted. *User agrees to indemnify and hold Host free and harmless from all injuries to person or persons, including death, damages to property, loss of time, and/or any and all other loss or damages, whether caused or occasioned by the negligence of Host, its employees or servants, or any other person whatsoever, arising or flowing from the use, operation or rental of the said item by User.* User agrees to pay or reimburse Host for all charges incidental to all breakages, shortages, damages, or losses other than such ordinary wear to said item caused by User."

In the case of *Zimmer v. Mitchell and Ness,* . . . 385 A.2d 437 (1978), the court considered and found valid and enforceable a very similar exculpatory clause. There, as here, the plaintiff was injured when sports equipment which he had rented at a resort allegedly malfunctioned.

Despite Gimpel's efforts to distinguish *Zimmer* on the basis of the nature of the resort, we are not persuaded that the Superior Court was responding to a need for heightened protection for ski resorts as compared to other kinds of resorts when it upheld the exculpatory clause at issue in that case. Rather, we believe that guests at all types of resorts are in essentially the same position when they seek to rent equipment. Thus, we conclude, as did the Pennsylvania Superior Court, that the contract at issue here, which concerns a preprinted rental agreement containing the exculpatory clause, contravenes no policy of the law, was between private parties and that each party was a free bargaining agent. Consequently, the clause is valid.

Next, we consider whether the clause expressly provides for Host's immunity from liability and whether Host has borne its burden of proof in the matter. It is clear that the language of the clause is both detailed and unequivocal in releasing Host from liability for negligence in connection with the rental of the bicycle. Moreover, Host has produced the "Ride Charge Agreement" which Gimpel identified at his deposition as the agreement he signed before he obtained the bicycle. . . .

Therefore, we conclude that the exculpatory clause is enforceable against the plaintiff. . . .

We find no merit in Gimpel's argument that he "couldn't" read the contract before he signed it. Although he did not have his reading glasses with him when he arrived at the rental office, he could have requested that either the friend who accompanied him or Host's employee read the agreement to him before he signed it. Having already concluded that he was a free bargaining agent, we can find no basis for Gimpel's argument that Host's employee was obliged to call his attention to the exculpatory clause and its implications.

In summary, we conclude that the exculpatory clause at issue here meets the conditions set forth by the Pennsylvania Supreme Court for both validity and enforceability. Moreover, we reject plaintiff's attempt to engraft additional conditions onto the plain requirements of Pennsylvania law. For the foregoing reasons, we will grant Host's motion for summary judgment.

Case Questions

1. What three conditions are necessary for exculpatory clauses to be valid under Pennsylvania law?
2. What conditions are necessary for valid exculpatory clauses to be enforceable?

Chapter Questions

1. Define the following terms:

Act of State doctrine	property right
advisory opinion	public policy
cases and controversies	*res judicata*
collusion	small claims action
insurance	sovereign immunity
moot	speech or debate clause
political question	statute of limitations
privity	standing

2. The city of Jacksonville, Florida, sought to increase the percentage of municipal contracts awarded to minority business enterprises (MBEs) and enacted an ordinance containing a 10 percent set aside. Members of the Association of General Contractors brought suit against the city because they thought the set aside program impermissibly favored one race over another. Such a race-based classification system in the awarding of municipal construction contracts, they contended, violated the equal protection clause of the Fourteenth Amendment. The trial court granted summary judgment in favor of the contractor's association; however, the U.S. Court of Appeals for the 11th Circuit vacated the judgment on the grounds that the contractors

lacked standing to sue. The appeals court concluded that the contractor's association had "not demonstrated that, but for the program, any member would have bid successfully for any of the contracts." After the U.S. Supreme Court granted the contractor's association's petition for a writ of certiorari, the city repealed its MBE ordinance and enacted a second ordinance that was very similar in that it provided for contractual set asides favoring women and black contractors. Is this case moot, inasmuch as the ordinance complained about has been repealed?

Association of General Contractors v. City of Jacksonville, 508 U.S. 656 (1993)

3. Assume the same facts as in question 2. Assume further that the city argued in the Supreme Court that the contractor's association lacked standing in that no member of the association alleged that he would have been awarded a city contract but for the set aside ordinance. Did the contractor's association have standing to sue? Why? Why not?

Association of General Contractors v. City of Jacksonville, 508 U.S. 656 (1993)

4. Paula Piper was a public defender assigned to defend William Aramy. Prior to William's trial, Paula told the judges she thought William was crazy. Bail was set and William was placed in a mental institution. Paula failed to tell William how he could arrange bail. Claiming that his prolonged stay in the mental institution was caused by Paula's negligence, William sued Paula for malpractice. Paula claims that her position as an officer of the court gives her the defense of judicial immunity. Who wins? Why?

5. On February 1, 1999, John Smith bought a car for $10,000. He paid $1,000 down and signed a promissory note for $9,000, due in three years. Assume that the note was never paid and that the applicable statute of limitations is five years. The plaintiff could wait until what date to bring a civil suit for nonpayment of the note?

6. The Endangered Species Act of 1973 authorizes citizens to bring suits against the government to protect threatened wildlife and plantlife. When the U.S. Fish and Wildlife Service decided to restrict the amount of water released from an irrigation project along the Oregon-Washington border, Oregon ranchers brought suit against the federal government. The ranchers maintained that their businesses would be severely damaged as a result of this decision. They also alleged that the government had not used the "best scientific and commercial data available" as required by the federal statute. The U.S. Court of Appeals for the 9th Circuit ruled that the ranchers did not have standing because the statute only provided for citizen suits brought on behalf of endangered species. Should citizens who believe that the government has been overly pro-environment and insufficiently sensitive to the economic consequences of environmental protection have standing to sue the government?

Bennett v. Spear, No. 95–813, U.S. Supreme Court, (1997)

7. In 1942, Congress amended the Nationality Act of 1940 to make it easier for noncitizens who had fought in World War II and who had been honorably

discharged from the U.S. Armed Services to become American citizens. The 1942 act specifically provided that the noncitizen servicemen could complete the naturalization before a designated immigration and naturalization officer and while outside the border of the United States. This procedure was in lieu of requiring the applicant to come to the United States and appear before a U.S. district court judge. In August of 1945, the U.S. Vice Consul in Manila was designated by the Immigration and Naturalization Service to perform this responsibility. The government of the Philippines, concerned that too many of its nationals would take advantage of this law, soon prevailed on the United States to restrict this opportunity. The U.S. Attorney General responded by revoking the Vice Consul's authority to process citizenship applications from October 1945 until October 1946. Congress also proceeded to limit the window of opportunity to those filing petitions by December 1946. Filipino war veterans brought suit, contending that they were entitled to become citizens under the amended Nationality Act. The INS responded by asserting that the plaintiffs' claims were nonjusticiable because they were political questions. Should the political questions doctrine apply in cases such as this?

Pangilinan v. Immigration and Naturalization Service, 796 F2d. 1091, U.S. Court of Appeals (9th Circuit 1986)

8. Judge Stump of a circuit court in Indiana, a court of general jurisdiction, approved a mother's petition to have her "somewhat retarded" fifteen-year-old daughter sterilized. The judge approved the mother's petition the same day, without a hearing and without notice to the daughter or appointment of a *guardian ad litem*. The operation was performed on Linda Sparkman, but she was told that she was having her appendix removed. A few years later, after Sparkman married and discovered that she had been sterilized, she and her husband brought suit against Judge Stump. Should Judge Stump be immune under the circumstances?

Stump v. Sparkman, 435 U.S. 349 (1978)

VII Judicial Remedies

Before addressing the power of the court to award various types of relief, we should establish that courts do not have a monopoly on resolving private disputes. Many disputes within families, for example, are settled without resort to the judiciary by grandparents, parents, or an older sibling. Other peacemakers include religious leaders, coaches, teachers, and other respected persons. Arbitrators, mediators, and private courts, as discussed in Chapter 14 on alternative dispute resolution (ADR), also offer disputants nonjudicial procedures for resolving disagreements without involving the public court systems.

Some readers would better understand remedies if they took a few minutes to review the material in Chapter 1 regarding the development of the English common law and equitable courts. If readers also take another look at Article III, Section 2, of the U.S. Constitution and the Seventh Amendment, they will see that notions of law and equity are specifically mentioned within the text of our Constitution. Lastly, reviewing this historical material will remind readers of the reasons for the traditional rule that a plaintiff who has an adequate legal remedy is not entitled to equitable relief.

We now turn to a discussion of judicial remedies. Once a person has established a substantive right through judicial procedures, the court will award relief. Judicial relief can assume many different forms, called remedies (see Figure 7-1). The most common remedy is awarding money damages in the form of *compensatory damages* and, where permissible, *punitive damages.* Additional remedies include *injunctive relief* (requiring someone to do or refrain from doing something), *restitution* (restoring a person to a previous position to prevent *unjust enrichment*), *declaratory judgment* (a judicial determination of the parties' rights), and *reformation* (judicially rewriting a written instrument to reflect the real agreement of the parties).

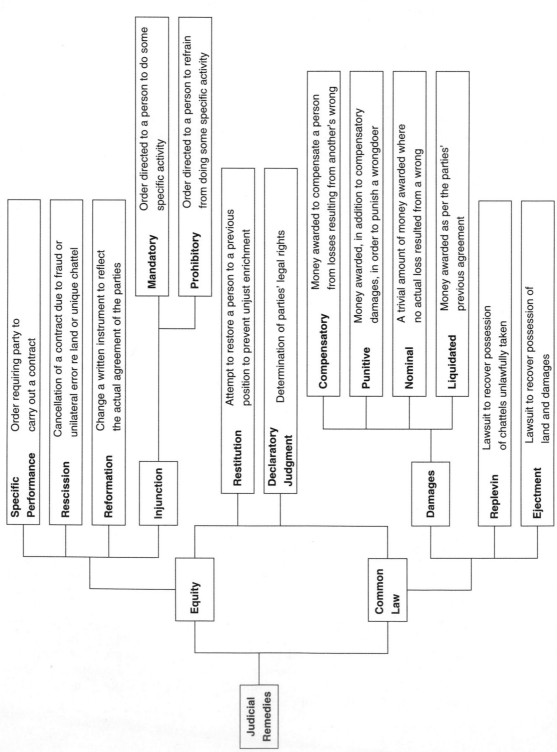

FIGURE 7-1   Judicial Remedies

COMMON LAW REMEDIES

Common law remedies are generally limited to the court's determination of some legal right and the award of money damages. There are some exceptions. For example, when parties want the court's opinion concerning their legal rights, without seeking damages or injunctive relief, they seek a declaratory judgment. In addition, both the common law remedies of ejectment and replevin seek restitution. An *ejectment* occurs when a trespasser secures full possession of the land and the owner brings an action to regain possession as well as damages for the unlawful detention of possession. Usually this process involves a title dispute between plaintiff and defendant, and the ejectment action settles this dispute. *Replevin* is an action used to recover possession of personal property wrongfully taken. Once the action is brought, the goods are seized from the defendant after proper notice has been given.

Usually, however, a common law court grants relief in the form of damages, a sum of money awarded as compensation for an injury sustained as the consequence of either a tortious act or a breach of a legal obligation. Damages are classified as compensatory, punitive, nominal, and liquidated.

Compensatory Damages

Compensatory damages are awarded to compensate the plaintiff for pecuniary losses that have resulted from the defendant's tortious conduct or breach of contract. Although the permissible damage elements vary by jurisdiction, they typically include awards for loss of time or money, bodily pain and suffering, permanent disabilities or disfigurement, injury to reputation, and mental anguish. Future losses are also recoverable; however, recovery is not allowed for consequences that are remote, indirect, or uncertain (i.e., where speculative). Damages are usually limited to those reasonably foreseeable by the defendant as a result of the breach. Assume that two plaintiffs have a contract to buy some equipment needed to open their new business, and a defendant breaches by nondelivery. If the plaintiffs sue for lost profits from the delay in opening because they have to procure alternative goods, they would probably not recover, because the defendant could not have foreseen this, not knowing that the opening depended on the delivery. Also, future profits are very difficult to measure with any degree of certainty.

In awarding compensatory damages, the court's objective is to put the plaintiff in the same financial position as existed before the commission of the tort or, in a contract case, in the financial position that would have resulted had the promise been fulfilled. In the absence of circumstances giving rise to an allowance of punitive damages, the law will not put the injured party in a better position than the person would have been in had the wrong not been done.

A person who is injured must use whatever means are reasonable to avoid or minimize damages. This rule is called by most the *rule of mitigation* (and by others the avoidable harm doctrine). It prevents recovery for damages that could have been foreseen and avoided by reasonable effort without undue risk, expense, or humiliation. For example, P sues to recover the loss of a crop, because

D removed some rails from P's fence, and as a result, cattle escaped and destroyed the crop. Since P, knowing the rails were missing, did not repair the fence, only the cost of repairing the fence is recoverable, because the loss of the crop could have been avoided.

When the defendant's misconduct causes damages but also operates directly to confer some benefit on the plaintiff, then the plaintiff's damage claim may be diminished by the amount of the benefit conferred. This policy is called the *benefit rule.* For example, a trespasser digs on plaintiff's land, but the digging works to drain swampy areas and improves the value. The plaintiff may recover for the trespass and any damage it caused, but the defendant gets a credit for the value of the benefit conferred. However, this credit exists only for clear benefits and not for those that are remote and uncertain. Problems arise in deciding what is a benefit and by what standard to measure it.

Compensatory damages may be categorized as either general or special. This distinction is very important to lawyers because general damages do not have to be specifically pleaded, whereas special damages must be listed in the pleadings. *General damages* are those that are the natural and necessary result of the wrongful act or omission, and thus can normally be expected to accompany the injury. Pain and suffering, mental anguish, and the loss of enjoyment of life are damages that occur so frequently in the tort of battery that they do not have to be specifically pleaded. *Special damages* are awarded for injuries that arise from special circumstances of the wrong. A plaintiff in a battery case, for example, would have to specifically plead such special damages as medical and hospital expenses, loss of earnings, and a diminished ability to work.

Putting a dollar value on the plaintiff's loss for the purpose of compensation often becomes a difficult task. Because the amount of damages is a factual question and decisions on factual issues do not create precedent, previous case decisions are not binding. The amount of damages is decided by a jury, unless a jury trial has been waived.

The next case involves a plaintiff who seeks to recover a variety of damages for medical malpractice. The court rules that the state's public policy prohibits her from recovering for all that she claims. The concurrence contains a discussion of the benefits rule and the rule requiring the mitigation of damages.

Macomber v. Dillman
505 A.2d 810
Supreme Judicial Court of Maine
February 27, 1986

Glassman, Justice

I

In April of 1984, the plaintiffs, Roxanne and Steven Macomber, filed a complaint against the defendants, Carter F. Dillman and the Webber Hospital Association. The complaint alleged, *inter alia,* that as a proximate result of the defendants' negligent and careless failure to comply with the standard of care of medical practice in the performance of a tubal ligation on Roxanne for the purpose of permanent sterilization, Roxanne was not permanently sterilized and had conceived and given birth to a child, Mazie. Although the plaintiffs did not allege in their complaint that Mazie is a healthy, normal child, they did not allege otherwise, and the parties have agreed to these facts. Plaintiffs sought damages from defendants "including, but not limited to, the cost of raising and educating Mazie May Macomber, the medical and other expenses of the pregnancy and childbirth, the medical and other expenses of a subsequent hysterectomy for purposes of sterilization, lost wages, loss of consortium, the medical and other expenses of the unsuccessful tubal ligation, permanent physical impairment to Roxanne Macomber resulting from bearing Mazie May, her sixth child, and physical and mental pain and suffering resulting [therefrom]."

Defendants filed motions for dismissal or summary judgment on the grounds that the plaintiffs by their complaint failed to state a claim for which relief could be granted and could not recover damages for the cost of rearing and educating a healthy, normal child. After hearing, the Superior Court entered its order denying the defendants' motions and adopting the analysis that should the plaintiffs prevail they would be entitled to recover "all reasonable, foreseeable, and proximately caused damages, including the expenses of child rearing." The court refused to rule on whether damages so recoverable by plaintiffs "should be offset by benefits" of parenthood.

On a joint motion of the parties, the Superior Court reported the case to this court thereby posing the following questions of law: (1) Did the Superior Court by its order properly deny the defendants' motion to dismiss the plaintiff's complaint for failure to state a claim against the defendants for which relief can be granted? (2) Did the Superior Court by its order properly set forth the damages that the plaintiffs could recover should they prevail in their action against the defendants?

II

We first address the question of whether the plaintiffs have by their complaint stated a claim against the defendants. Contrary to the defendants' contention, the plaintiffs' action does not represent a new cause of action in the state of Maine. "Since the early days of the common law a cause of action in tort has been recognized to exist when the negligence of one person is the proximate cause of damage to another person." . . . When a plaintiff claims he has suffered a personal injury as the result of medical mistreatment, his remedy lies in a complaint for negligence. . . . The necessary elements of a cause of action for negligence are a duty owed, a breach of that duty proximately causing the plaintiff's injuries and resulting damages. . . . Applying these principles to the allegations in the plaintiffs' complaint, it is clear that the necessary elements of a cause of action in negligence have been set forth against the defendants.

III

We next consider whether the Superior Court correctly established the scope of recoverable damages. We are aware that the courts which have considered this type of case have not reached a consensus as to damages, if any, that may be recoverable. . . .

We hold for reasons of public policy that a parent cannot be said to have been damaged or injured by the birth and rearing of a healthy, normal child. Accordingly, we limit the recovery of damages, where applicable, to the hospital and medical expenses incurred for the sterilization procedures and pregnancy, the pain and suffering connected with the pregnancy and the loss of earnings by the mother during that time. Our ruling today is limited to the facts of this case, involving a failed sterilization procedure resulting in the birth of a healthy, normal child.

We also must address whether the plaintiff, Steven Macomber, may recover for loss of consortium of his wife, Roxanne. For centuries courts have recognized a husband's right to recover damages for the loss of consortium when a tortious injury to his wife detrimentally affects the spousal relationship.

. . . Because his wife's cause of action is for negligence, Steven Macomber may recover proven damages for loss of consortium.

The entry is:

The order of the Superior Court is modified to limit the scope of recoverable damages, and as so modified, affirmed. Remanded to the Superior Court for further proceedings consistent with the opinion herein.

McKusik, Nichols, and Roberts, J.J., concurring.

Scolnik, Justice, concurring in part and dissenting in part

Although I concur that a cause of action exists for medical malpractice in the performance of a tubal ligation, I am unable to agree with the Court's judicially imposed limitation on the damages that are recoverable. The Court reasons that in no circumstances can a parent be said to have been damaged by the birth and rearing of a healthy, normal child. This rationale, however, is not only plainly inconsistent with the Court's recognition of a cause of action but also totally ignores the fact that many individuals undergo sterilization for the very purpose of avoiding such a birth. Moreover, the Court's opinion is an unwarranted departure from the fundamental principle of tort law that once a breach of duty has been established, the tortfeasor is liable for all foreseeable damages that proximately result from his acts. I dissent because, in my view, the jury should be permitted to consider awarding damages for child rearing costs.

By finding that a parent is not harmed by the birth of a healthy child, the Court's opinion is logically inconsistent. In the first part of its opinion, the Court applies traditional tort principles to recognize a cause of action for negligence resulting in an unwanted conception and subsequent birth of a normal, healthy child. Although the opinion is noticeably silent as to what the required harm is to support the cause of action, . . . the Court has in effect concluded that the birth of a normal child is recognized as an injury that is directly attributable to the health-care provider's negligence. In the second part of its opinion, however, the Court states that based on unarticulated reasons of public policy, the birth of a normal, healthy child cannot be said to constitute an injury to the parents. As a result, the Court limits the damages that a parent can recover to the hospital and medical expenses incurred for the sterilization procedure and the pregnancy, the pain and suffering connected with the pregnancy and the loss of earnings sustained by the mother during that time. If, however, the birth of a child does not constitute an injury, no basis exists for any award of damages. Damages for "pain and suffering" and medical expenses incidental to child birth cannot be recoverable if the birth itself is not an injury. Similarly, if the parent is to be compensated for the loss of earnings that result from the pregnancy, should she not equally be compensated for the identical loss following the birth of the child? The Court's opinion fails to reconcile these obvious inconsistencies.

Not only is the Court's opinion internally inconsistent, but its stated rationale to support an artificial limitation on the scope of recoverable damages ignores reality. To hold that a parent cannot be said to have been damaged or injured by the birth and rearing of a normal, healthy child is plainly to overlook the fact that many married couples, such as the plaintiffs, engage in contraceptive practices and undergo sterilization operations for the very purpose of avoiding the birth of [a] child. Many of these couples resort to such conception avoidance measures because, in their particular circumstances, the physical or financial hardships in raising another child are too burdensome. Far from supporting the view that the birth of a child is in all situations a benefit, the social reality is that, for many, an unplanned and unwanted child can be a clear detriment. . . . "[W]hen a couple has chosen not to have children, or not to have any more children, the suggestion arises that for them, at least, the birth of a child would not be a net benefit." . . . This is not to say that there are not many benefits associated with the raising of a child. The point is that it is unrealistic universally to proclaim that the joy and the companionship a parent receives from a healthy child always outweigh the costs and difficulties of rearing that child. As one judge explained:

> "A couple privileged to be bringing home the combined income of a dual professional household may well be able to sustain and cherish an unexpected child. But I am not sure the child's smile would be the most memorable characteristic to an indigent couple, where the husband underwent a vasectomy or the wife underwent a sterilization procedure, not because they did not desire a child, but rather because they faced the stark realization that they could not afford to feed an additional person, much less clothe, educate and support a child when that couple had trouble supporting one another. The choice is not always giving up personal amenities in order to buy a gift for the baby; the choice may only be to stretch necessities beyond the breaking point to provide for a child that the couple had purposely set out to avoid having." . . .

I know of no instance where we have strayed from the common law principle that a tortfeasor is liable for every foreseeable injury proximately caused by his negligent act and we should avoid doing so here. The Court states that public policy dictates the result it reaches without explaining the source from which it was derived or the foundation on which it rests. This is not a case where change is required in the common law, without legislative help, because of a conflict between an outdated judicially crafted policy and contemporary legal philosophy. . . . In

fact, I am sure that the Court realizes that substantial disagreement exists among the courts as to whether a parent is harmed by the birth of an unexpected child. This fact coupled with the empirical reality that many individuals choose to forego parenthood for economic or other reasons demonstrates that the Court's unexplained judicial declaration of public policy is unwarranted. . . .

In my view, it is the duty of this Court to follow public policy, not to formulate it, absent a clear expression of public opinion. Moreover, it has always been the public policy of this State to provide relief to those injured by tortfeasors and to allow for compensation for damages caused by their acts. To deprive the plaintiffs in this case of the opportunity to recover compensation for all their damages contravenes this basic policy. Any limitation on the scope of recoverable damages in such cases is best left to the Legislature where the opportunity for wide ranging debate and public participation is far greater than in the Law Court. . . .

Rather than to rely on unstated notions of public policy, the better approach to determine what damages may be recoverable is to apply traditional common-law rules. It is certainly foreseeable that a medical health professional's failure properly to perform a tubal ligation will result in the birth of an unplanned child. As a result of the tortfeasor's act, the parents, who had chosen not to have a child, find themselves unexpectedly burdened both physically and financially. They seek damages not because they do not love and desire to keep the child, but because the direct and foreseeable consequences of the health-care provider's negligence has forced burdens on them that they sought and had a right to avoid.

In assessing damages for child rearing costs, I would follow those jurisdictions that have adopted the "benefit rule" of the Restatement (Second) of Torts § 920 (1979). . . . The benefit rule recognizes that various tangible and intangible benefits accrue to the parents of the unplanned child and therefore to prevent unjust enrichment, their benefits should be weighed by the factfinder in determining damages associated with the raising of the unexpected child. The rule provides that "[w]hen the defendant's tortious conduct has caused harm to the plaintiff or to his property and in so doing has conferred a special benefit to the interest of the plaintiff that was harmed, the value of the benefit conferred is considered in mitigation of damages, to the extent that this is equitable." . . . The assessment of damages, if any, should focus on the specific interests of the parents that were actually impaired by the physician's negligence. An important factor in making that determination would be the reason that sterilization was sought, whether it was economic, genetic, therapeutic or otherwise. . . . The advantages of this approach were succinctly stated by the Arizona Supreme Court.

> "By allowing the jury to consider the future costs, both pecuniary and non-pecuniary, of rearing and educating the child, we permit it to consider all the elements of damage on which the parents may present evidence. By permitting the jury to consider the reason for the procedure and to assess and offset the pecuniary and non-pecuniary benefits which will inure to the parents by reason of their relationship to the child, we allow the jury to discount those damages, thus reducing speculation and permitting the verdict to be based upon the facts as they actually exist in each of the unforeseeable variety of situations which may come before the court. We think this by far the better rule. The blindfold on the figure of justice is a shield from partiality, not from reality." . . .

Although the benefit rule approach requires the jury to mitigate primarily economic damages by weighing them against primarily noneconomic factors, I reject the view that such a process is "an exercise in prophecy, an undertaking not within the specialty of our factfinders." . . . The calculation of the benefits a parent could expect to receive from the child is no more difficult than similar computations of damages in wrongful death actions, for extended loss of consortium or for pain and suffering. . . .

As a final note, the parents should not be forced to mitigate their damages by resorting to abortion or to adoption. A doctrine of mitigation of damages known as the avoidable consequences rule requires only that reasonable measures be taken. . . . Most courts that have considered the matter have held, as a matter of law, neither course of action would be reasonable. . . . I agree. The tortfeasor takes the injured party as he finds him and has no right to insist that the victims of his negligence have the emotional and mental make-up of a woman who is willing to undergo an abortion or offer her child for adoption. Moreover, the parents should not be precluded from recovering damages because they select the most desirable alternative and raise the child. Accordingly, the avoidable consequences rule is not relevant to the issue of the recovery of child rearing expenses.

Damages recoverable under the cause of action recognized today by this Court should not be limited by unstated notions of public policy so as arbitrarily to limit recovery of proximately caused and foreseeable damages. I recognize that this is an extremely difficult case but I find no public policy declaring that physicians should be partially immunized from the consequences of a negligently performed sterilization operation nor declaring that the birth of a healthy child is in all circumstances a blessing to the parents. Accordingly, I see no justification for supporting a departure from the traditional rules that apply to tort damages.

I would affirm, without modification, the order of the Superior Court and permit the recovery of the potential costs of rearing the child.

Case Questions

1. Why does the court majority hold that the parents could recover damages for hospital and medical expenses, pain and suffering connected with the unwanted pregnancy, the loss of earnings by the mother during the pregnancy, and loss of consortium but denies a recovery for the cost of rearing and educating a healthy, normal child?

2. The dissenting justice argues that the majority opinion is inconsistent. Explain the inconsistencies.

3. After carefully reading the majority and dissenting opinions, how would you rule?

 Do you agree with the Court that "a parent cannot be said to have been damaged or injured by the birth and rearing of a healthy, normal child"?

Plaintiffs in recent years have increasingly been seeking compensation for what are called *hedonic damages,* the loss of enjoyment of life. Adding hedonic damages as an element of compensatory awards has proven to be extremely controversial with each state having to decide whether or not to recognize losses of this type as compensable.

The Mississippi Supreme Court was recently faced with deciding whether that state should permit compensation for hedonic damages to a plaintiff who survived a train-truck accident and was permanently confined to a wheelchair.

Kansas City Southern Railway Co., Inc. v. J. C. Johnson and Kerry Lynn Johnson
798 So.2d 374
Mississippi Supreme Court
February 8, 2001

Smith, Justice, for the Court . . .

Statement of the Facts

Viewed in the light most favorable to the Johnsons, the facts are as follows. On July 18, 1995, the vehicle driven by J. C. Johnson ("Johnson") was struck by KCS's eastbound 40-mile-per-hour freight train operated by its engineer, Cook. Before turning off to his right from U.S. Highway 80 some 68 feet north of the railroad crossing, Johnson had been traveling east on Highway 80, heading parallel with and in the same direction as the train, which, unknown to Johnson, was overtaking him from behind.

As Johnson headed up the steep, rough roadway slope of Johnson Quarters Road to the humpbacked summit of the crossing, unable to see oncoming vehicles on the other side of the tracks because of the severe grade, his view both up and down the tracks was seriously impaired by trees, bushes and other vegetation growing on KCS's right-of-way, which extended out 50 feet on either side of the track. There were no flashing lights or gates, or any other form of active protection, to warn motorists that a train was approaching this crossing at about 60 feet per second.

KCS's conductor seated on the left side of the locomotive cab testified that he saw Johnson as he turned off Highway 80 onto Johnson Quarters Road, when the train was about 300 feet away from impact. The engineer on the right side of the cab never saw Johnson's truck until somewhere between 100 to 150 feet. There was evidence that the train's horn was blown before the collision, but it was alleged that KCS's engineer had failed to blow his horn at a sufficient distance away from the crossing to give Johnson adequate warning that the 40-mph(60-feet-per-second) train was coming.

It is also alleged that KCS had not maintained the crossing nor adopted any reasonable policy relative to vegetation control to provide a clear sight distance to the motoring public to detect approaching high speed trains. As a result of the railroad's negligence, in both crossing maintenance and train operation, Johnson contends he sustained severe and permanent injuries, consisting of a closed-head injury which has left him little more than a child. Johnson had a long history of employment and alleges he has suffered significant economic loss and medical expenses. Additionally, his wife suffered substantial loss of consortium.

After hearing the evidence, the jury found in favor of the Johnsons. KCS appeals to this Court and presented a number of issues for discussion. . . .

III. Whether the Circuit Court Erred in Allowing Recovery of Hedonic Damages.

The loss of one's enjoyment of life continues to be an area of confusion in the state of Mississippi. The issue to be decided here is whether our state will or will not recognize this type of recovery in a personal injury action, and if so to what extent? Jurisdictions around the country have chosen either; 1) not to recognize the loss of enjoyment of life, 2) recognize the loss of enjoyment of life as a completely separate element considered in addition to pain and suffering, or 3) recognize the loss of enjoyment of life but only as integrated into pain and suffering. . . . Today we decide to follow the jurisdictions which recognize the loss of enjoyment of life.

The Court of Appeals has pointed out that there are no Mississippi cases directly on point on the question of whether loss of enjoyment of life is an element of damages in a survival personal injury action. . . . While we have not declared how to classify the loss of enjoyment of life, we have made clear that the damages to a particular plaintiff in a personal injury action should be decided on a case-by-case basis. . . .

Furthermore, we said that an injured plaintiff enjoys the right to damages such as will compensate him for all of his losses, past and future and is entitled to the present worth of all that has been forced upon him. . . . It was not, however, specified as to whether damages for loss of enjoyment of life were to be considered as part of or separate from those for pain and suffering.

The loss of enjoyment of life should be fully compensated and should be considered on its own merits as a separate element of damages, not as a part of one's pain and suffering. We decide to follow other jurisdictions which have held that damages for loss of enjoyment of life compensate the injured person for the limitations placed on his or her ability to enjoy the pleasures and amenities of life. . . . This type of damage relates to daily life activities that are common to most people. There are numerous activities that courts have held constitute daily life activities: going on a first date, reading, debating politics, the sense of taste, recreational activities, and family activities. . . . Pain and suffering encompasses the physical and mental discomfort caused by an injury, such as anguish, distress, fear, humiliation, grief, shame, and worry. . . . A permanent injury differs from pain and suffering in that it is an injury from which the plaintiff cannot completely recover. . . .

Evidence was presented at trial that prior to the accident Mr. Johnson enjoyed hunting, fishing, and yard work. As a result of the accident, Johnson suffered brain injury, a cracked pelvis, bruised lungs, pneumonia, and was forced to move to an inpatient rehabilitation center for close to a year. Johnson also testified as to his inability to enjoy those activities in which he participated prior to the accident. His wrist has been damaged and one of his fingers remains crooked. Furthermore, there is evidence that Johnson has a diminished ability to speak. We find that the testimony of Mr. Johnson, Ms. Johnson, the physical therapist, the rehab specialist, the speech therapist, are ample to support damages for Johnson's lost ability to enjoy his prior life style. Johnson has demonstrated that he is conscious of his lost enjoyment of life's pleasures, and our tort system should compensate him for these losses. Perhaps most telling about the effects of the accident on Johnson's life is this testimony from Johnson's daughter, Angela: "I watched an active man sit in a wheelchair all day. I watched an articulate man who took pride in his vocabulary struggle to get one word out. And I have watched a person that was always happy look sullen and sad, stare out into space."

It is apparent that Johnson is no longer the person he was prior to the accident. We hold today that these restrictions are significant enough to warrant compensation as a separate and distinct element of damages.

We believe jury instruction P-11A was correctly given. The instruction at issue reads as follows:

> The Court instructs the jury that "damages" is the word which expresses in dollars and cents the injuries sustained by a plaintiff. The damages to be assessed by a jury in a personal injury case cannot be assessed by any fixed rule, but you are the sole judges as to the measure of damages in any case. Should your verdict be for the plaintiffs, you may consider the following factors in determining the amount of damages to be awarded as may be shown by a preponderance of the evidence: . . . 5.) Loss of enjoyment of life, and 6.) The value of past, present and future physical pain and suffering and resulting mental anguish, if any.

This instruction adequately separates loss of enjoyment of life damages from pain and suffering. The instruction was a simple, appropriate way to place before the jury the issue of loss of the enjoyment of life as a distinct and separate element of damages which cannot be considered as pain and suffering.

The trial court did not err in granting this instruction. . . .

Conclusion

Having held that damages for loss of enjoyment of life are recoverable as a separate form of damages . . . we affirm the judgment of the trial court.

Affirmed. . . .

Case Questions

1. How does the Mississippi appellate court distinguish hedonic damages from pain and suffering?
2. Johnson was awarded hedonic damages because he could no longer engage in what activities?
3. How could one argue, as a matter of public policy, against awarding hedonic damages as a separate damage element?

INTERNET TIP

Students wishing to read another case focusing on hedonic damages can read *Overstreet v. Shoney's, Inc.,* a case from Tennessee, on the textbook's website.

Punitive Damages

Damages can also be awarded to punish defendants for their conduct and to deter others from similar conduct. These are called *punitive* or *exemplary* damages, and are awarded to the plaintiff beyond the compensatory amount. They are additional damages for a civil wrong and are not imposed as a substitute for criminal punishment. An award of punitive damages also may include an award of attorneys' fees. We will see in the next case, *Volz v. Coleman,* that any type of negligence, even gross or extreme, is insufficient to award punitive damages. Such an award is appropriate only when a defendant has engaged in aggravated, wanton, reckless, malicious, or oppressive conduct. This includes all acts done with an evil disposition, or a wrong and unlawful motive, or the willful doing of an injurious act without a lawful excuse. Punitive damages are generally available only for intentional torts and for some statutory wrongs.

Some of the actions that may result in punitive damage awards are copyright and trademark infringement, corporate crimes such as antitrust violations, insurers not paying off on their policies, wrongful discharge by an employer, libel and slander, wrongful death, trespass, conversion, battery, and securities fraud. Traditionally, punitive damages have not been awarded in contract cases, even in situations in which there has been a malicious breach. Some jurisdictions have modified this rule in some situations. If a breach of contract is accompanied by a malicious tort, exemplary damages will be awarded for the tort.

In *Volz v. Coleman,* the appellate court reviewed a trial jury's $1.06 million punitive damages award. The court had to decide whether reasonable jurors, as a matter of law, could have found Coleman's actions to have been malicious, spiteful, outrageous, oppressive, or intolerable.

Volz v. Coleman Co., Inc.
748 P.2d 1191
Supreme Court of Arizona
December 17, 1987

Cameron, Justice

I. Jurisdiction

This is a petition for review, filed by The Coleman Co., Inc. (Coleman), of an opinion of the court of appeals which affirmed a trial court judgment and award in favor of the respondents Sharon Volz and Valley National Bank, co-conservators of the Plaintiff, Shannon Haddix. . . .

II. Question Presented

We granted the petition for review to consider whether punitive damages were properly awarded. . . .

III. Facts

On 15 August 1983, while camping with her family, five-year-old Shannon Haddix (plaintiff) was severely burned by ignited gasoline.

Her stepfather, Ron Volz, was pumping the fuel tank on his Coleman stove when, according to his testimony, a stream of fuel, without warning, ejected through the filler cap, crossed the campfire, ignited, and landed on Shannon, some 10–12 feet away. Volz testified that, after refueling the tank, he had screwed the cap on tightly before pressurizing the tank for the morning meal. He added that he did not pour any more fuel into the tank for the evening meal, and that he had checked the cap to make sure that it was tight before pumping the tank in the evening. Volz testified that because the pump was "pretty stiff" after only three to six pumps, he knew that the tank had retained pressure from the morning use.

The plaintiff presented expert testimony concerning the design of the cap and alternative cap designs that Coleman could have utilized. John B. Sevart, an engineer with a private consulting practice and with two engineering companies, testified that, in his opinion, the design of a gas tank using a cap with a vent-hole is defective with respect to safety. Kenneth John Saczalski, a professor of engineering at Northern Arizona University and the owner of a private consulting company, testified that there were alternative cap designs that Coleman could have utilized to accomplish ventilation of the tank without the cap having any of the vent-hole characteristics.

Coleman has manufactured camp stoves for over forty-five years. During this time, Coleman has introduced 25–50 million stoves into the marketplace. From the early 1940s through 1963, Coleman equipped its camp stoves with a vent-hole filler cap used in this case. This same cap was used on fuel-burning lanterns also manufactured by Coleman.

In using the Coleman stove, the fuel must be pressurized so that it will flow from the tank to the burner. Pressurization is accomplished by pumping the sealed tank until the plunger handle becomes resistant. To refuel a Coleman tank, the cap on the end of the tank opposite the plunger handle is unscrewed and removed. The cap, however, needs to have some type of ventilation capacity in order to equalize the interior pressure of the tank with that of the exterior atmosphere as the cap is removed. If the cap is removed without a ventilation feature, then removal of the cap will create a sudden pressure surge causing a discharge of fuel in a stream-like manner.

In 1963, the vent-hole filler cap for use in the stove was discontinued by Coleman and was replaced with a cap referred to as the "Plamann patent." The Plamann patent cap, because it is internally broached, directs any type of pressurized discharge from the tank in a downward direction, rather than in an outward direction as in the vent-hole filler cap. In 1963, however, several hundred thousand stoves were already in the marketplace equipped with the vent-hole filler cap. The Volz's received the stove in question as a Christmas gift in 1982. The stove, however, contained the old cap and not the newer "Plamann Patent" cap. Coleman never issued warnings to users about the old caps nor did it recall any of the stoves or lanterns containing these caps.

A 1963 internal Coleman document and a 1967 patent application were introduced into evidence that discussed the defects in the vent-hole filler cap and improvements that would be gained by redesigning the venting system. However, Coleman employees, both engineers and management-level, repeatedly testified that no warning on the use of Coleman fuel in the tank and stove was necessary because "common sense" would indicate to a person that the "hazardous substance" of the Coleman fuel should not be used in such a way that a stream would be emitted from the tank. Those employees also testified that Coleman redesigned the original cap into the "Plamann patent" cap because it was more functional to use and economical to produce, and *not* because of safety reasons. Indeed, testimony was introduced at trial indicating that there was no safety advantage to the "Plamann patent" cap when compared to the vent-hole filler cap.

The 1963 Coleman internal memorandum stated: "[b]ecause, under many circumstances the gasoline . . . tends to foam when the pressure is relieved, . . . [such] gasoline froth [can blow] out through this vent hole." Furthermore, the memo stated that it was not possible to control the direction in which the stream traveled.

Additionally, the testimony of Coleman employees Randy May, director of technical services, William Marsh, director of design engineering for the outgoing products division, Jerry Koontz, national service manager, and William Townsend, a technical research engineer, indicated that Coleman had notice since 1960 of the tendency of the cap to spray fuel. However, Coleman's head of outgoing products division, Elwood Little, did not believe it was hazardous to loosen the cap and believed the instructions were clear that the tank needed to be kept level. Koontz testified that fuel sprayed only if the tank was not level and the cap was loose. He also testified that if the stove were operated in the proper manner a person could not "pump enough pressure into it to shoot fuel 12 feet."

Despite Coleman's knowledge of the possibility of fuel spraying through the vent hole of the filler cap, no warnings were issued advising the user not to open the cap except when the tank was level and not near a flame. Coleman's design project manager, Frank Schmidt, testified that there were no instructions on how to relieve pressure from the tank. Relieving pressure would prevent the possibility of fuel spraying out if the tank were not level or if the cap were loose. Testimony of other Coleman employees emphasized that Coleman only had notice of fuel spraying when the cap was unscrewed. In the present case, Volz testified that he had not unscrewed the cap and that the fuel was released "spontaneously."

The jury awarded plaintiff $6.8 million in compensatory damages and $1.06 million in punitive damages. The defendant appealed and the court of appeals affirmed the awards. Defendant petitioned this court for review. We granted the petition only on the issue of punitive damages.

IV. Punitive Damages

In both its motion for a new trial and on appeal, Coleman contends that it was an error for the trial court to give a punitive damages instruction. We agree.

Punitive damages are awarded in order to punish the wrongdoer and deter others from emulating the same conduct. . . . The focus is on the wrongdoer's attitude and conduct. . . . The punitive damages standard in Arizona requires "something more" than gross negligence. . . . The "something more" is the evil mind, which is satisfied by evidence "that defendant's wrongful conduct was motivated by spite, actual malice, or intent to defraud" or defendant's "conscious and deliberate disregard of the interest and rights of others." . . .

To obtain punitive damages, a plaintiff must prove that "defendant's evil hand was guided by an evil mind." . . . This "evil mind" element may be shown by either (1) evil actions; (2) spiteful motives; or (3) outrageous, oppressive or intolerable conduct that creates substantial risk of tremendous harm to others. . . . The fact that a manufacturer continues to market a product is not in itself enough to show the evil mind necessary for punitive damages. . . .

This court has expressly rejected awarding punitive damages based on gross negligence or mere reckless disregard of the circumstances. . . . We have stated that such terms as "gross," "reckless," and "wanton conduct" convey little and fail to focus the jury's attention on the important question—the defendant's motives. . . .

As one court has noted:

"It is quite clear, we think, from the evidence, that the jury could well have found negligence or even gross negligence on the part of this defendant. But negligent conduct, no matter how gross or wanton, cannot be equated with the conduct required for punitive damages. We hold, therefore, that plaintiff's evidence in this case was insufficient as a matter of law to demonstrate that type of "outrageous conduct" on which an award of punitive damages must depend. *Thomas v. American Cytoscope Makers, Inc.,* 414 F.Supp. 255, 267 (E.D.Pa. 1976) (applying Pennsylvania law in a products liability action)."

This is a case of negligence, or even gross negligence, and the jury so found in awarding compensatory damages. It is not, however, a case of punitive damages or the "something more" than gross negligence. . . .

V. Disposition

The award of punitive damages is reversed and set aside. The judgment as amended is affirmed.

Case Questions

1. What must be present to justify an award of punitive damages?
2. What kinds of activities did the court indicate that plaintiffs should offer to prove that the defendant's "evil hand was guided by an evil mind"?

 The Arizona Supreme Court stated in its opinion that "punitive damages are awarded in order to punish the wrongdoer and deter others from emulating the same conduct. . . . The focus is on the wrongdoer's attitude and conduct. . . ." Why do they deny this remedy to persons found to have been negligent or even grossly negligent?

Nominal Damages

If a defendant breaches a legal duty owed to the plaintiff and injures that person, compensatory damages may be awarded. The compensatory damages are measured by the amount of the loss. *Nominal damages* are awarded when there has been a breach of an agreement or an invasion of a right but there is no evidence of any specific harm. This occurs, for example, if a person trespasses on your land but causes no actual harm. In such a situation, the plaintiff would only be entitled to a judgment for a trivial amount, such as one dollar or fifty dollars. The judge awards this token sum to vindicate the plaintiff's claim or to establish a legal right. Nominal damages also are awarded when a plaintiff proves breach of duty and harm but neglects to prove the value of the loss. They are also allowable when the defendant's invasion of the plaintiff's rights produces a benefit.

Courts award nominal damages because a judgment for money damages is the only way a common law court can establish the validity of the plaintiff's claim. Students should be careful not to confuse nominal charges with small compensatory damage awards, which are awarded when the actual loss was minor.

Liquidated Damages

Parties may agree, in advance, about the amount to be paid as compensation for loss in the event of a breach of contract. *Liquidated damages* are the stipulated sum contained in such an agreement. An example can be seen in the *Campbell Soup* case (page 300), where Campbells' contract with the Wentz brothers included a provision for damages of $50 per acre if the contract were breached. If the court determines that the amount stipulated in the agreement is a punishment used to prevent a breach rather than an estimate of actual damages, it will deem that sum a penalty and refuse to enforce it. Traditionally, the court upholds a liquidated damage clause only when (1) the damages in case of breach are uncertain or difficult to compute, (2) the parties have agreed in advance to liquidate the damages, and (3) the amount agreed on is reasonable and not disproportionate to the probable loss. Another form of liquidated damages results when money is deposited to guarantee against future damages.

Occasionally, a plaintiff who has suffered no actual damages can recover substantial liquidated damages; however, this occurs only rarely. Some courts require plaintiffs to prove some actual loss before the liquidated damage clause is triggered.

EQUITABLE REMEDIES

An equitable remedy would have been dealt with by a court of equity before the merger of equity and the common law courts. Today, most courts in the United States are empowered to grant both equitable and legal relief as required to achieve justice. However, the availability of equitable remedies is a matter for judges and not juries. Traditionally, courts only grant equitable remedies when the common law remedies are inadequate.

Injunctions

An injunction is an equitable remedy in the form of a judicial order directing the defendant to act or refrain from acting in a specified way. An order compelling one to do an act is called a *mandatory injunction*, whereas one prohibiting an act is called a *prohibitory injunction*. An injunction may be enforced by the contempt power of a court, and a defendant may be fined, sent to jail, or deprived of the right to litigate issues if he or she disobeys an injunction. This order must be obeyed until it is reversed, even if it is issued erroneously or the court lacks jurisdiction.

Injunctions may be divided into three classes: (1) permanent, (2) preliminary or interlocutory, and (3) temporary restraining orders. A permanent injunction is a decree issued after a full opportunity to present evidence. It is permanent only in the sense that it is supposed to be a final solution to a dispute. It may still be modified or dissolved later. A preliminary or interlocutory injunction is granted as an emergency measure before a full hearing is held. There must be notice to the defendant and a hearing, usually informal. This remedy is generally limited to situations in which there is a serious need to preserve the status quo until the parties' rights have finally been decided. Thus a preliminary injunction continues only until a further order of the court is issued.

The temporary restraining order, known as a TRO, is an *ex parte* injunction. This means that it is granted without notice to the defendant. The trial judge has heard only the plaintiff's side of the case. Because of the potential for abuse, certain procedures protect a defendant. A TRO may not be granted unless irreparable harm would result and there is no time for notice and a hearing. There must be clear evidence on the merits of the case. The court should look at any damage to the defendant that would be noncompensable in money if the plaintiff's relief is later shown to be improper. This consideration must be balanced with the plaintiff's harm if the TRO is not granted. Factors weigh more heavily against the plaintiff, since there is no notice to defendant.

Certain classes of cases are not considered proper subject matter for injunctions. In general, an injunction is not issued to stop a criminal prosecution or to prevent crimes. However, this law has been modified in recent years by regulatory statutes or civil rights statutes. Injunctions are usually not proper in defamation cases because they would intrude on the defendant's constitutional right of free speech and would be considered prior restraint.

The following case illustrates how a judge deciding an equity case makes a decision to grant or deny injunctive relief. The judge's balancing of the interests and the harm is a hallmark of equity.

Gano v. School District No. 411 of Twin Falls County, Idaho

674 F.Supp. 796
U.S. District Court for the District of Idaho
November 5, 1987

Callister, Chief Judge

Memorandum Decision

The Court has before it the plaintiff's motion for preliminary injunction. The Court held an evidentiary hearing on October 30, 1987, and ruled from the bench that the motion would be denied. This memorandum decision will constitute the Court's written findings pursuant to Fed.R.Civ.P. 52(a).

The plaintiff, Rod Gano, Twin Falls High School student, was requested by members of the senior class to draw a caricature of three administrators: (1) Twin Falls High School Principal Frank Charlton; (2) Vice-Principal Norman Thomas; and (3) Dean of Men Richard Baun. The plaintiff drew the caricature and it was transferred to T-shirts to be sold to other students during homecoming week.

One of those T-shirts was made a part of the record in this case. It shows the three administrators sitting against a fence labeled "Bruin Stadium, Home of the Bruins." Each administrator is holding a different alcoholic beverage and is acting drunk. While one administrator holds aloft a beer mug, another holds a wine cooler, while the third grasps a bottle of whiskey. A case of "light beer" sits nearby. A phrase, "It doesn't get any better than this," not coincidentally lifted from a television beer commercial, appears just below the caricature.

When the administrators discovered the T-shirts, and the plan to sell them to the students, they suspended the plaintiff. The suspension lasted two days, October 5 and 6, 1987, and the plaintiff returned to school on October 7, 1987. The unrebutted affidavits of the administrators establish that this disciplinary action has been removed from the plaintiff's file. For attendance purposes, the plaintiff was not cited for being absent on October 5 and 6, 1987. He is noted as being absent during second period on October 8, 1987. On that date he wore the T-shirt to school, and was told to go home and change shirts during second period. He wore the T-shirt again on October 15, 1987, and was sent home to change it. Although he was free to return to school without the T-shirt, he failed to return on October 16, 1987, and is listed as being absent on that date. If the plaintiff continues to wear the T-shirt, he will be sent home to change it. For the purposes of this case, there are no other absences or disciplinary actions at issue.

On October 16, 1987, the plaintiff filed this action along with a motion for preliminary injunction. The motion seeks to enjoin defendants "from suspending or interfering with the plaintiff's attendance at Twin Falls High School for wearing a T-shirt with the caricature on it until such time as those matters alleged by way of the verified complaint filed herein have been litigated or otherwise resolved." . . .

There are two alternative tests, one of which must be met in order to grant a preliminary injunction. The first test requires that the Court find (1) the moving party will suffer irreparable injury if the injunctive relief is not granted; (2) there is a substantial likelihood that the moving party will succeed on the merits; (3) in balancing the equities the nonmoving party will not be harmed more than the moving party is helped; and (4) granting injunctive relief is in the public interest.

The second test requires the moving party to demonstrate either (1) a combination of probable success on the merits and the possibility of irreparable harm; or (2) that serious questions are raised and the balance of hardship tips sharply in his favor. These two tests are not separate; they are the outer reaches of a single continuum. . . .

The Court will employ the second test, and will examine first the plaintiff's chance for success on the merits. The plaintiff argues that his First Amendment freedom of speech right will be abridged if he is disciplined for wearing the T-shirt. Unfortunately, neither the plaintiff, nor plaintiff's counsel, was able to articulate the expression which was in danger of suppression. Did the T-shirt represent a political protest? Was it a criticism of administration policies? Testimony and argument from the plaintiff, his counsel, and other witnesses, indicated that the T-shirts were not intended to criticize or be disrespectful to the administrators. What message is conveyed by the T-shirts?

The T-shirt portrays the three administrators with alcoholic beverages on school property during a homecoming activity. It is a misdemeanor to consume alcoholic beverages on school property at any school activity. . . . There is no evidence in the record that the three administrators have ever so imbibed. The plaintiff's T-shirt thus falsely accuses the three administrators of committing a misdemeanor. For this expression, the plaintiff demands protection. Is he so entitled? The United States Supreme Court has stated that students cannot be disciplined for wearing black armbands to protest the Vietnam War, but can be disciplined for making sexually explicit speeches at school assemblies. . . . *Bethel School Dist. No. 403 v. Fraser.* . . . To understand these cases, one must first understand that discipline and debate are equally effective teaching tools. A robust exchange of ideas can only occur effectively within a civilized context. The school is actively engaged in teaching when it sets the bounds for proper conduct. As the United States Supreme Court stated in the *Bethel* case:

> "The process of educating our youth for citizenship in public schools is not confined to books, the curriculum, and the civics class; school must teach by example the shared values of a civilized social order. Consciously or otherwise, teachers—and indeed the older students—demonstrate the appropriate form of civil discourse and political expression by their conduct and deportment in and out of class. Inescapably, like parents, they are role models. The schools, as instruments of the state, may determine that the essential lessons of civil, mature conduct cannot be conveyed in a school that tolerates lewd, indecent, or offensive speech and conduct such as that indulged in [here]."

In the present case, the school has determined that the T-shirt—which is clearly offensive—cannot be tolerated. In this state, the schools are statutorily charged with teaching about the "effects of alcohol." . . . When the school disciplines the plaintiff for wearing a T-shirt falsely depicting the administrators in an alcoholic stupor, it is engaged in its statutory duty. It is teaching the students that falsely accusing one of being drunk is not acceptable. The administrators are role models, as stated by the United States Supreme Court, and their position would be severely compromised if this T-shirt was circulated among the students. This case appears to clearly fall within the *Bethel* precedent, and thus the Court finds that the plaintiff has only a minuscule chance of success on the merits.

With regard to the balance of harm, the plaintiff would be effectively prevented from falsely accusing the administrators of being drunks. The Court cannot find that the plaintiff suffers much harm by being so prevented. When this case is examined in its entirety, the plaintiff has so little success on the merits and would suffer so little harm that the Court finds that a preliminary injunction is not warranted. The Court will therefore deny the motion for preliminary injunction.

Case Questions

1. Why did the court deny the plaintiff's claim for injunctive relief?
2. What basis did the court give for rejecting the plaintiff's First Amendment freedom-of-speech claims?
3. How was the public interest protected by the court's denial of the plaintiff's claim for injunctive relief?
4. What type of injunctive relief was requested and granted in the *Gano* case?

Reformation and Rescission

The equitable remedy of reformation is granted when a written agreement fails to express accurately the parties' agreement because of mistake, fraud, or the drafter's ambiguous language. Its purpose is to rectify or reform a written instrument in order that it may express the real agreement or intention of the parties.

The equitable remedy of rescission is granted when one of the parties' consent to a contract is obtained through duress, undue influence, fraud, or innocent misrepresentation, or when either or both of the parties made a mistake concerning the contract. Rescission means the court cancels the agreement. If a court orders rescission, each party normally has to return any property or money received from the other party in performance of the agreement (*restitution*). This topic, with an illustrative case (*Carter v. Matthews*), is addressed in Chapter 10.

The following case involves a contractor who was the successful bidder on a public construction contract. The contractor made a unilateral error in computing his bid and subsequently brought suit seeking the equitable remedy of reformation. The appellate court majority ruled that the plaintiff was not entitled to reformation. The dissenting judge disagreed on the basis of the defendant's inequitable conduct. The majority opinion also discusses the equitable remedy of rescission and explains why the plaintiff has waived any claim to that remedy.

Department of Transportation v. Ronlee, Inc.

518 So.2d 1326
District Court of Appeal of Florida,
Third District
December 22, 1987

Per Curiam

The threshold question presented is whether the successful bidder for a government road construction contract is entitled to reformation of the contract to increase the price by $317,463 based on a unilateral mistake, after the competing bids are all opened, where the new contract price would still be lower than the second lowest bid.

The Department of Transportation (DOT) solicited bids pursuant to section 337.11, Florida Statutes (1985), for the construction of an interchange at the intersection of State Road 826 and Interstate 75 in Hialeah. On December 7, 1983, DOT declared Ronlee, Inc. the apparent low bidder with a bid of $15,799,197.90. The second lowest bid exceeded Ronlee's bid by $610,148.

On February 13, 1984, DOT entered into a contract with Ronlee to construct the project based on the bid, and on March 7, 1984, gave Ronlee notice to proceed with the project. Five days later, Ronlee advised DOT that the bid contained a "stupid mistake" in the amount of $317,463. The letter alleged an error with respect to the unit price for concrete culverts which occurred when an employee of Ronlee erroneously transcribed a phone quote of $525 for each culvert as $5.25 each. By letter dated March 21, 1984, DOT informed Ronlee that it was aware of the apparently unbalanced unit price for the concrete culverts, but that it was unable, as a matter of state policy, to permit an increase in the contract price.

Nevertheless, on March 22, 1984, having made no effort to withdraw the bid, Ronlee began construction of the project. Twenty-one months later, with the project seventy-five percent completed, Ronlee filed suit against DOT seeking reformation of the contract. Both sides moved for a summary judgment, agreeing that the material facts were not in dispute. Ronlee's motion for summary judgment was granted, the trial court holding that

DOT's silence about Ronlee's apparent error in price calculations constituted inequitable conduct and that reformation of the contract would not undermine the competitive bidding process. In addition to the $317,463, the court awarded Ronlee $60,000 in prejudgment interest and costs. We reverse.

Where a contractor makes a unilateral error in formulating his bid for a public contract, the remedy is rescission of the contract. . . . Florida courts have permitted a contractor to *withdraw* a bid on a public contract, subject to certain equitable conditions. In *State Board of Control v. Clutter Construction Corp.,* . . . a contractor was permitted to withdraw a bid on a showing of the following equitable factors: (1) the bidder acted in good faith in submitting the bid; (2) in preparing the bid there was an error of such magnitude that enforcement of the bid would work severe hardship upon the bidder; (3) the error was not a result of gross negligence or willful inattention; (4) the error was discovered and communicated to the public body, *along with a request for permission to withdraw the bid,* before acceptance.

No reported Florida decision has permitted reformation by belated request of a bid contract for a public project in order to make it profitable to the contractor. *Graham v. Clyde,* . . . is the only case presented by the parties where reformation was even sought as relief for a mistaken bid. There a building contractor was low bidder on a proposal to construct a public school building and was awarded the contract. The following day he notified public officials that he had made a mistake of $5,000 in computing items in his bid and asked to be relieved of his obligation to perform according to the contract terms. He offered to perform the contract for $5,000 more, which was still less than the next low bidder. The circuit court did not grant a reformation but did rescind the contract and enjoined the school board from attempting to enforce it.

The Florida Supreme Court, citing a number of cases from other jurisdictions, reversed, holding that unilateral errors are not generally relieved and that there was no equitable basis for relief. In an opinion by Justice Terrell the court stated the reason for the firm rule:

> "If errors of this nature can be relieved in equity, our system of competitive bidding on such contracts would in effect be placed in jeopardy and there would be no stability whatever to it. It would encourage careless, slipshod bidding in some cases and would afford a pretext for the dishonest bidder to prey on the public. . . . After the bid is accepted, the bidder is bound by his error and is expected to bear the consequence of it." . . .

The prevailing view is that reformation is not the appropriate form of relief for unilateral mistakes in public contract bids where the bidder is negligent. . . . The reason for not permitting reformation of bid contracts for public projects based on unilateral mistake is the same in other jurisdictions—to prevent collusive schemes between bidders, or between bidders and awarding officials, or multiple claims from contractors asserting mistake and claiming inequity at taxpayers' expense. . . .

A written instrument may be reformed where it fails to express the intention of the parties as a result of mutual mistake, or unilateral mistake accompanied by inequitable conduct by the other party. . . . Because the mistake in this instance was admittedly unilateral, in order to obtain reformation of the contract, Ronlee was obligated to show by clear and convincing evidence that DOT's conduct in not calling Ronlee's attention to a possible error in the bid tabulations was fraudulent or otherwise inequitable. . . . That burden was not carried. The Department's failure to call Ronlee's attention to the error in calculation was of no consequence since Ronlee discovered its own error shortly after the Department learned of the miscalculation.

Competitive bidding statutes are enacted to protect the public and should be construed to avoid circumvention. . . . A government unit is not required to act for the protection of a contractor's interest; it is entitled to the bargain obtained in accepting the lowest responsible bid and is under no obligation to examine bids to ascertain errors and to inform bidders accordingly. . . . Absent an obligation to do so, failure of the government in this case to call the bidder's attention to a relatively minor two percent error in its calculations, after the bids were opened, was not such fraud or imposition as would entitle the bidder to reformation of the contract.

Further, Ronlee forfeited any right it may have had to reformation or rescission. It had knowledge of its own mistake at least ten days before commencement of construction. Ronlee's conduct in performing according to the terms of the agreement for twenty-one months instead of seeking to withdraw the bid, after DOT had advised that it could not administratively correct the error, effected a waiver of rights. *See Farnham v. Blount,* . . . (any unreasonable or unnecessary delay by a party seeking to cancel an instrument based on fraud or other sufficient cause will be construed as a waiver or ratification). . . .

Reversed and remanded with instructions to enter judgment for the Department of Transportation.

Hendry and Ferguson, JJ., concur.

Schwartz, Chief Judge, dissenting

With respect, I must dissent. The majority does not say that the record shows and the trial judge found just the inequitable conduct by the DOT which, under principles it acknowledges, renders reformation an entirely appropriate remedy; although the DOT was aware of the mistake when the bids were opened and well before construction commenced, it deliberately failed to inform the contractor of this fact. The final judgment under review

contains, among others, the following, essentially undisputed determinations:

"(e) The Defendant acknowledged receipt of notice, *prior* to commencement of construction, of the existence of the error and further acknowledged that the Plaintiff's bid 'error was unintentional' and 'resulted from inexperienced personnel' generating a simple mathematical error by misplacing a decimal point and 'not comprehending the reasonableness of the money figures being used.' (Exhibit 'D' to Plaintiff's Motion).

"(f) Indeed, the Defendant even admitted that *prior* to the Plaintiff's March 12, 1984 notification to the Defendant, the Defendant had already been 'aware of the apparent unbalanced unit price of the item of Class II Concrete Culverts' (Exhibits 'D' and 'C' to Plaintiff's Motion; Plaintiff's Motion at 5–6, 9). Exhibit 'C', a December 19, 1983 computer print-out (entitled 'summary of bids') produced by Defendant during discovery, demonstrates that the 'apparent unbalanced unit price' with respect to the bids 'opened at Tallahassee, Florida on December 7, 1983' was known to Defendant promptly upon examination of the bids.

"3. The Court is therefore of the view that plaintiff has proved inequitable conduct by the Defendant by clear and convincing proof. Clearly, the Defendant was aware, or certainly should have been aware, that the unit item bid price for 400–2–1 Class II Concrete Culverts was one hundred (100) times less than the nearest unit price for the same item. However, the Defendant chose wrongfully to remain silent as to the existence of this error and, further, refused to act equitably after the Plaintiff had discovered the error and promptly acted to notify the Defendant of the error."

On this basis, the trial court held:

"4. While the Court is not unmindful of the fact that competitive bidding statutes should be construed to avoid circumvention, under the unique facts of the case *sub judice,* the integrity of the competitive bidding process will not be undermined with the granting of contract reformation. Where, as here, the differential between the mistaken bid and the second lowest bid exceeds the amount of the error sought to be reformed, no frustration or harm to beneficial purpose can fairly be demonstrated."

I entirely agree.

It is undisputed that, through a simple mistake in decimal point transcription, Ronlee was out and the DOT was in over $300,000 in material expenses. Short of reliance on the well-known playground maxim about keepers and weepers, there is no reason why the state should be entitled to retain this found money. Under ordinary reformation law, the combination of a unilateral mistake and inequitable conduct fully justifies that relief, . . . and no bases exist or are advanced for the application of a different rule merely because a process of competitive bidding is involved. Since the correction of the mistake would still bring the appellee under the next highest bid, no administratively difficult process of rebidding would be required and none of the purported horribles—"collusive schemes between bidders, or between bidders and awarding officials, or multiple claims from contractors asserting mistake and claiming inequity at taxpayers' expense," . . . are even arguably implicated. . . . I would not refuse to reach a just result here because of the mechanical application of an unsupportable rule or out of a necessarily unjustified fear that someone may in the future misapply our holding in a materially different situation.

The very salutary Florida rule of unilateral mistake—which represents a minority view on the question, . . .—is that the courts will relieve one of the consequences of such an error and the opposite party should be deprived of any consequent windfall whenever there is neither a detrimental reliance upon the mistake nor an inexcusable lack of due care which led to its commission. . . . Neither is present in this case. While the law of our state says otherwise, the majority has permitted DOT successfully to play "gotcha" with Ronlee's money. The state, perhaps even more and certainly no less than a private party, should not be permitted to do so. . . . I would affirm.

Case Questions

1. Why did the trial court grant the plaintiff's summary judgment motion and order reformation in this case?
2. What is the difference between reformation and rescission of a contract?
3. Could Ronlee have rescinded the contract?

 What ethical consideration motivates Chief Judge Schwartz to dissent in this case?

Court of Conscience

In equity's early period, chancellors were almost always members of the clergy attempting to attain justice between parties to a dispute. A court of equity has always been considered to be a court of conscience in which natural justice and moral rights take priority over precedent. For example, a chancellor may decline to grant a plaintiff relief because of the plaintiff's wrongdoing in connection with the dispute. A chancellor may also decline to enforce a contract clause that is too unfair or one-sided. Such a clause would be declared to be unconscionable. To enforce it by granting equitable remedies would "shock the conscience of the court."

In the two cases that follow, the plaintiffs/appellants acted inequitably. Why did the courts in these cases decide that equitable relief is inappropriate?

Campbell Soup Company v. Wentz
172 F.2d 80
U.S. Court of Appeals, Third Circuit
December 23, 1948

Goodrich, Circuit Judge

These are appeals from judgments of the District Court denying equitable relief to the buyer under a contract for the sale of carrots. . . .

The transactions which raise the issues may be briefly summarized. On June 21, 1947, Campbell Soup Company (Campbell), a New Jersey corporation, entered into a written contract with George B. Wentz and Harry T. Wentz, who are Pennsylvania farmers, for delivery by the Wentzes to Campbell of *all* the Chantenay red-cored carrots to be grown on fifteen acres of the Wentz farm during the 1947 season. . . . The contract provides . . . for delivery of the carrots at the Campbell plant in Camden, New Jersey. The prices specified in the contract ranged from $23 to $30 per ton according to the time of delivery. The contract price for January 1948 was $30 a ton.

The Wentzes harvested approximately 100 tons of carrots from the fifteen acres covered by the contract. Early in January, 1948, they told a Campbell representative that they would not deliver their carrots at the contract price. The market price at that time was at least $90 per ton, and Chantenay red-cored carrots were virtually unobtainable.

On January 9, 1948, Campbell, suspecting that [defendant] was selling it[s] "con-

tract carrots," refused to purchase any more, and instituted these suits against the Wentz brothers . . . to enjoin further sale of the contract carrots to others, and to compel specific performance of the contract. The trial court denied equitable relief. We agree with the result reached, but on a different ground from that relied upon by the District Court. . . . A party may have specific performance of a contract for the sale of chattels if the legal remedy is inadequate. Inadequacy of the legal remedy is necessarily a matter to be determined by an examination of the facts in each particular instance.

We think that on the question of adequacy of the legal remedy the case is one appropriate for specific performance. It was expressly found that at the time of the trial it was "virtually impossible to obtain Chantenay carrots in the open market." This Chantenay carrot is one which the plaintiff uses in large quantities, furnishing the seed to the growers with whom it makes contracts. It was not claimed that in nutritive value it is any better than other types of carrots. Its blunt shape makes it easier to handle in processing. And its color and texture differ from other varieties. The color is brighter than other carrots. . . . It did appear that the plaintiff uses carrots in fifteen of its twenty-one soups. It also appeared that it uses these Chantenay carrots diced in some of them and that the appearance is uniform. The preservation of uniformity in appearance in a food article marketed throughout the country and sold under the manufacturer's name is a matter of considerable commercial significance and one which is properly considered in determining whether a substitute ingredient is just as good as the original.

The trial court concluded that the plaintiff had failed to establish that the carrots, "judged by objective standards," are unique goods. This we think is not a pure fact conclusion like a finding that Chantenay carrots are of uniform color. It is either a conclusion of law or of mixed fact and law and we are bound to exercise our independent judgment upon it. That the test for specific performance is not necessarily "objective" is shown by the many cases in which equity has given it to enforce contracts for articles—family heirlooms and the like—the value of which was personal to the plaintiff.

Judged by the general standards applicable to determining the adequacy of the legal remedy we think that on this point the case is a proper one for equitable relief. There is considerable authority, old and new, showing liberality in the granting of an equitable remedy. We see no reason why a court should be reluctant to grant specific relief when it can be given without supervision of the court or other time-consuming processes against one who has deliberately broken his agreement. Here the goods of the special type contracted for were unavailable on the open market, the plaintiff had contracted for them long ahead in anticipation of its needs, and had built up a general reputation for its products as part of which reputation uniform appearance was important. We think if this were all that was involved in the case, specific performance should have been granted.

The reason that we shall affirm instead of reversing with an order for specific performance is found in the contract itself. We think it is too hard a bargain and too one-sided an agreement to entitle the plaintiff to relief in a court of conscience. For each individual

grower the agreement is made by filling in names and quantity and price on a printed form furnished by the buyer. This form has quite obviously been drawn by skillful draftsmen with the buyer's interests in mind.

Paragraph 2 provides for the manner of delivery. Carrots are to have their stalks cut off and be in clean sanitary bags or other containers approved by Campbell. This paragraph concludes with a statement that Campbell's determination of conformance with specifications shall be conclusive.

The defendants attack this provision as unconscionable. We do not think that it is, standing by itself. We think that the provision is comparable to the promise to perform to the satisfaction of another and that Campbell would be held liable if it refused carrots which did in fact conform to the specifications.

The next paragraph allows Campbell to refuse carrots in excess of twelve tons to the acre. The next contains a covenant by the grower that he will not sell carrots to anyone else except the carrots rejected by Campbell nor will he permit anyone else to grow carrots on his land. Paragraph 10 provides liquidated damages to the extent of $50 per acre for any breach by the grower. There is no provision for liquidated or any other damages for breach of contract by Campbell.

The provision of the contract which we think is the hardest is paragraph 9. . . . It will be noted that Campbell is excused from accepting carrots under certain circumstances. But even under such circumstances, the grower, while he cannot say Campbell is liable for failure to take the carrots, is not permitted to sell them elsewhere unless Campbell agrees. This is the kind of provision which the late Francis H. Bohlen would call "carrying a good joke too far." What the grower may do with his product under the circumstances set out is not clear. He has covenanted not to store it anywhere except on his own farm and also not to sell to anybody else.

We are not suggesting that the contract is illegal. Nor are we suggesting any excuse for the grower in this case who has deliberately broken an agreement entered into with Campbell. We do think, however, that a party who has offered and succeeded in getting an agreement as tough as this one is, should not come to a chancellor and ask court help in the enforcement of its terms. That equity does not enforce unconscionable bargains is too well-established to require elaborate citation.

The plaintiff argues that the provisions of the contract are separable. We agree that they are, but do not think that decisions separating out certain provisions from illegal contracts are in point here. As already said, we do not suggest that this contract is illegal. All we say is that the sum total of its provisions drives too hard a bargain for a court of conscience to assist. . . .

The judgments will be affirmed.

Case Questions

1. If the plaintiff had sued for damages, would the result of the suit have been different?
2. Campbell Soup Company lost this case in its attempt to get equitable relief. May it now sue for money damages?
3. If the contract between Campbell Soup Company and Wentz were not unconscionable, would specific performance of the contract be an appropriate remedy? What is necessary before specific performance will be granted?

 Why did the court hold the contract to be unconscionable and therefore unenforceable in equity?

Equitable Maxims

Instead of using rules of law in reaching decisions, courts of equity used *equitable maxims*, which are short statements that contain the gist of much equity law. These maxims were developed over the years (with no agreement as to the number or order) and today are used as guides in the decision-making process in disputes in equity. The following are some of the equitable maxims:

Equity does not suffer a wrong to be without a remedy.
Equity regards substance rather than form.
Equality is equity.
Equity regards as done that which should be done.
Equity follows the law.
Equity acts *in personam* rather than *in rem*.
Whoever seeks equity must do equity.
Whoever comes into equity must do so with clean hands.
Delay resulting in a prejudicial change defeats equity (laches).

Isbell v. Brighton Area Schools
No. 136310
Court of Appeals of Michigan
April 5, 1993

Taylor, Judge

Defendants appeal as of right a December 1990 order denying defendants' motion for summary disposition and granting plaintiff's motion for summary disposition, both brought pursuant to MCR 2.116(C)(10). We reverse.

During each semester of the 1988–89 school year, plaintiff's senior year at Brighton High School, plaintiff was absent without excuse on more than six occasions. She was denied course credit under the school's attendance policy, and was ultimately denied a diploma.

Plaintiff sued defendants alleging constitutional, contract, and tort theories, and also raising equitable claims. The trial court ruled that plaintiff lacked an adequate remedy at law and was entitled to equitable relief (issuance of a diploma) because the school attendance policy was unreasonable. Accordingly, the trial court granted plaintiff's (and denied defendants') motion for summary disposition.

Because we conclude that plaintiff is barred from equitable relief by the clean hands doctrine, we need not and do not reach the question whether defendants' attendance policy was reasonable.

One who seeks the aid of equity must come in with clean hands. This maxim is an integral part of any action in equity, and is designed to preserve the integrity of the judiciary. The . . . Court [has] described the clean hands doctrine as "a self-imposed ordinance that closes the doors of a court of equity to one tainted with inequitableness or bad faith relative to the matter in which he seeks relief, however improper may have been the behavior of the defendant. That doctrine is rooted in the historical concept of the court of equity as a vehicle for affirmatively enforcing the requirements of conscience and good faith. This presupposes a refusal on its part to be "the abettor of iniquity." . . .

Plaintiff admittedly forged excuse notes, so she does not have clean hands. In determining whether the plaintiffs come before this Court with clean hands, the primary factor to be considered is whether the plaintiffs sought to mislead or deceive the other party, not whether that party relied upon plaintiff's misrepresentations. . . . Thus, it is plaintiff's deceit, not defendants' reliance on the forged notes, that determines whether the clean hands doctrine should be applied. As Justice Cooley wrote:

> [I]f there are any indications of overreaching or unfairness on [equity plaintiff's] part, the court will refuse to entertain his case, and turn him over to the usual remedies.

We find that the clean hands doctrine applies to prevent plaintiff from securing the relief she requests. In view of our resolution of this matter, we do not reach the other issues raised.

Reversed.

Case Questions

1. Why did the trial court believe that the plaintiff was entitled to an equitable remedy?
2. Why did the appellate court reverse the trial court?

What is the practical significance of the equitable maxim called the clean hands doctrine?

Specific Performance

Specific performance is an equitable remedy that is identified with breaches of contract. The plaintiff brings suit to obtain a court order that requires the defendant to fulfill his or her contractual obligations. Specific performance will only be granted where there is a valid contract.[1] It is enforced through the use of the contempt power.

Like all equitable relief, specific performance is limited to situations in which there is no adequate remedy at common law. This means that under the particular circumstances of the case, the plaintiff can establish that a breach of contract action for money damages is inadequate. We saw an example of this in the *Campbell* case. Campbell wanted the court to order the Wentz brothers to live up to their contractual obligations to deliver Chantenay carrots to Campbell. Campbell argued that requiring the Wentz brothers to pay Campbell $50 per acre in liquidated damages for breach of contract was an inadequate remedy. Campbell contended that it couldn't go out on the open market and purchase Chantenay carrots from another seller. There was no alternative source of supply.

Specific performance is usually applied in situations involving contracts for the sale of land and unique goods. Common law relief is often inadequate for unique goods, because one cannot take money damages and go out and purchase the same item. A similar item might be purchased, but that is not what the parties had bargained. The buyer had an agreement to purchase a particular, unique property item. Thus, if a seller and buyer have contracted for the sale of land, a painting, sculpture, an antique car, or a baseball card collection, money damages are just not a substitute for the item. The Chantenay carrot was unique for Campbell soup. It was the only carrot that would work in the machinery. Consumers of Campbell soups were accustomed to that particular carrot's firmness, consistency, color, and taste.

A plaintiff must have substantially performed, or be ready to perform, his or her obligations under the contract in order to be entitled to specific performance. This is referred to as a condition precedent for specific performance.

In addition, equity courts are concerned with practicality. For example, an equitable court generally will not order one person to fulfill a personal service contract and perform work for another. Such a decree would be tantamount to involuntary servitude. It is also impractical for a court to require one person to work for another. Such an order could involve the court in a never-ending series of employer-employee spats.

A defendant can assert various equitable defenses in response to a plaintiff's claim for specific performance. These include (1) unclean hands (see page 302), (2) hardship, and (3) *laches*. Hardship involves sharp practices where the contractual terms are entirely one-sided and where there is a gross inadequacy of consideration. Hardship exists because one party is attempting to take unfair advantage of the other party. *Laches* is an equitable defense that is used to deny equitable relief where a plaintiff's unreasonable delay in bringing the action has caused prejudicial harm to the defendant. This defense is similar to the common law defense of statute of limitations. The equitable defense of *laches* does not involve any specific period of time.

Contracts for the sale of goods are governed by the Uniform Commercial Code (UCC).[2] The UCC provides buyers with a right to specific performance in 2-716, and sellers with an equivalent remedy in 2-709.

The court in the following case explains why specific performance is not granted where a contract calls for the performance of personal services.

Bloch v. Hillel Torah North Suburban Day School
426 N.E.2d 976
Appellate Court of Illinois,
First District, Third Division
September 9, 1981

McNamara, Justice

Plaintiffs appeal from an order of the trial court granting summary judgment in favor of defendant Hillel Torah North Suburban Day School. Helen Bloch is a grade school child who was expelled from defendant, a private Jewish school, at mid-year in 1980. Her parents brought this action seeking to enjoin expulsion and for specific performance of defendant's contract to educate Helen.

The complaint alleged that defendant arbitrarily and in bad faith breached its contract, and that Helen's expulsion was motivated by defendant's disapproval of plaintiff's leadership role in combatting an epidemic of head lice at the school. The complaint also alleged that the school uniquely corresponded exactly to the religious commitments desired by plaintiffs. Defendant's answer stated that Helen was expelled, pursuant to school regulations, for excessive tardiness and absences. The parties also disputed the duration of the contractual obligation to educate. Defendant contended that the contract was to endure only for a school year since tuition for only that period of time was accepted by it. Plaintiffs maintained that the contract, as implied by custom and usage, was to endure for eight years, the first year's tuition creating irrevocable option contracts for the subsequent school years, provided that Helen conformed to defendant's rules.

After the trial court denied plaintiff's request for a preliminary injunction, both sides moved for summary judgment. The trial court denied plaintiff's motion and granted the motion of the defendant. In the same order, the trial court gave plaintiffs leave to file an amended complaint for money damages.

Whether a court will exercise its jurisdiction to order specific performance of a valid contract is a matter within the sound discretion of the court and dependent upon the facts of each case. . . . Where the contract is one which establishes a personal relationship calling for the rendition of personal services, the proper remedy for a breach is generally not specific performance but rather an action for money damages. . . . The reasons for denying specific performance in such a case are as follows: the remedy at law is adequate; enforcement and supervision of the order of specific performance may be problematic and could result in protracted litigation; and the concept of compelling the continuance of a personal relationship to which one of the parties is resistant is repugnant as a form of involuntary servitude. . . .

Applying these principles to the present case, we believe that the trial court properly granted summary judgment in favor of defendant. It is beyond dispute that the relationship between a grade school and a student is one highly personal in nature. Similarly, it is apparent that performance of such a contract requires a rendition of a variety of personal services. Although we are cognizant of the difficulties in duplicating the personal services offered by one school, particularly one like defendant, we are even more aware of the difficulties pervasive in compelling the continuation of a relationship between a young child and a private school which openly resists that relationship. In such a case, we believe the trial court exercises

sound judgment in ruling that plaintiffs are best left to their remedy for damages. . . .

Illinois law recognizes the availability of a remedy for monetary damages for a private school's wrongful expulsion of a student in violation of its contract. . . . And especially, where, as here, the issue involves a personal relationship between a grade school and a young child, we believe plaintiffs are best left to a remedy for damages for breach of contract.

For the reasons stated, the judgment of the circuit court of Cook County is affirmed, and the cause is remanded for further proceedings permitting plaintiffs to file an amended complaint for money damages.

Affirmed and remanded.

Rizzi, P. J., and McGillicuddy, J., concur.

Case Questions

1. What problems might have been encountered in court-ordered specific performance?
2. In what types of cases would specific performance be granted?

Restitution

The remedy of restitution is in some situations an equitable remedy and in other cases a common law remedy. *Restitution* means restoration to the plaintiff of property in the possession of the defendant. The purpose of restitution is to prevent unjust enrichment, which means that a person should not be allowed to profit or be enriched inequitably at another's expense. Thus a person is permitted recovery when another has received a benefit and retention of it would be unjust.

The restoration may be *in specie*, in which a specific item is recovered by the plaintiff from the defendant. In many situations, an *in specie* recovery is impossible or impractical. In such instances, the remedy might have to be "substitutionary," whereby the defendant is ordered to return to the plaintiff as restitution the dollar value of any benefit he or she has received. If so, the amount is determined by the defendant's gain, not by the plaintiff's loss, as in the case of money damages. So if D takes P's car, worth $4,000, and sells it to someone else at $8,000, D may be liable to make restitution to P for the full amount of $8,000. P never had $8,000, only a car worth half as much, but is still entitled to the total amount. If there was cash in the glove compartment, P would be entitled to recover that also.

The following case discusses restitution in both the common law and equitable contexts. The court first determines whether the plaintiff was entitled to a statutory mechanics lien or a common law lien. It is only after ruling the plaintiff ineligible for a lien under the common law that the court turns to equity. The balancing of interests and harm to produce a just result is clearly evidenced here. Observe how damages are computed in an unjust enrichment case. The court said the mechanic's recovery would be limited to the difference in a vehicle's value before and after it was repaired and he would not receive damages reflecting his hourly rate.

Iacomini v. Liberty Mutual Insurance Company
497 A.2d 854
Supreme Court of New Hampshire
August 7, 1985

Douglas, Justice

The issue presented in this case is whether a party may subject an owner's interest in an automobile to a lien for repair and storage charges, without the owner's knowledge, acquiescence, or consent. We hold that no common law or statutory lien may be created under such circumstances but that equitable relief for unjust enrichment may be appropriate.

On August 10, 1983, the plaintiff, Richard Iacomini, d/b/a Motor Craft of Raymond, contracted with one Theodore Zadlo for the towing, storage, and repair of a 1977 Mercedes Benz 450-SL. Mr. Zadlo represented himself to be the owner of the car and presented the plaintiff with a New Hampshire registration certificate for the car bearing Zadlo's name. In fact, the car did not belong to Mr. Zadlo but had been stolen in 1981 from a car lot in New Jersey. The defendant, Liberty Mutual Insurance Company, had earlier fulfilled its policy obligations by reimbursing the owner of the stolen car $22,000. It thereby had gained title to the vehicle.

Extensive damage was done to the car after its theft, and Zadlo brought the car to Mr. Iacomini for the purpose of repairing this damage. The plaintiff kept the car at his garage, where he disassembled it in order to give a repair estimate. He apparently never fully reassembled it. Mr. Zadlo periodically returned to the plaintiff's garage to check the status of the repair work.

In October 1983, the Raymond Police Department notified the plaintiff that the Mercedes was a stolen car and also notified Liberty Mutual of the location of the car. Mr. Iacomini at that point moved the vehicle from the lot to the inside of his garage where it remained for the next several months. Liberty Mutual contacted the plaintiff soon after it learned of the vehicle's location to arrange its pick-up. The plaintiff refused to relinquish the car until he had been reimbursed for repair and storage fees.

. . . Liberty Mutual instituted a replevin action . . . seeking return of the car. . . . On the basis of facts presented at a hearing . . . in the replevin action, the Court . . . found that the plaintiff (defendant in that action) did not have a valid statutory lien since the vehicle was brought to the plaintiff by one other than the owner. The court then ordered Mr. Iacomini to make the vehicle available forthwith to Liberty Mutual with the proviso that Liberty Mutual retain the vehicle in its possession and ownership for a period of at least ninety days in order to allow Mr. Iacomini the opportunity to file an action against Liberty Mutual relating to repairs.

The plaintiff petitioned for an *ex parte* attachment, . . . claiming approximately $10,000, most of which was for storage fees. . . . [T]he same court entered judgment in Liberty Mutual's favor finding that "the plaintiff was not authorized or instructed by the legal or equitable owner of the automobile to perform any repair work on the vehicle." On either the day before, or the day of, the hearing, . . . the plaintiff filed a Motion to Specify Claim to include an action for unjust enrichment. Liberty Mutual objected to the plaintiff's attempt to amend his cause of action at that date, and the court denied the motion. It also denied the plaintiff's requests for findings that the value of the car had been enhanced by the plaintiff and that denial of the plaintiff's claim would result in unjust enrichment. This appeal followed.

The law generally recognizes three types of liens: statutory, common law, and equitable. . . . The statutes provide as follows:

> For Storage. "Any person who maintains a public garage, public or private airport or hangar, or trailer court for the parking, storage or care of motor vehicles or aircraft or house trailers brought to his premises or placed in his care *by or with the consent of the legal or equitable owner* shall have a lien upon said motor vehicle or aircraft or house trailer, so long as the same shall remain in his possession, for proper charges due him for the parking, storage or care of the same." . . .

> For Labor. "Any person who shall, by himself or others, perform labor, furnish materials, or expend money, in repairing, refitting or equipping any motor vehicle or aircraft, *under a contract expressed or implied with the legal or equitable owner,* shall have a lien upon such motor vehicle or aircraft, so long as the same shall remain in his possession, until the charges for such repairs, materials, or

accessories, or money so used or expended have been paid." . . .

"[I]n the case of a statutory lien, the specified requisites must be strictly observed." . . . By the language of the statute, no lien may be created on an automobile as to the owner without the owner's knowledge, acquiescence, or consent. Under the present circumstances, where the repairman contracted with the possessor of a stolen vehicle for the repair of the car, it is difficult to imagine how the owner could have consented to, or acquiesced in, the repair of the vehicle. The owner in this case had no idea even where the car was located. Whether the plaintiff was reasonable in believing Mr. Zadlo to be the true owner is irrelevant to whether a contract existed between him and Liberty Mutual.

Prior to the passage of a statute on the subject of mechanics' liens, . . . "there existed here and elsewhere a lien at common law in favor of anyone who upon request expended labor and materials upon another's property." . . . The statutory lien does not supplant, but supplements, the common law mechanics lien, so that we must also look to the rights of the plaintiff under the common law. . . .

As with the statutory liens, common law liens on property for repair costs could be created only by the owner or by a person authorized by him. "By common law, every person, who employs labor and skill upon the goods of another, *at the request of the owner,* without a special contract, is entitled to retain the goods until a proper recompense is made." . . . New Hampshire common law is consistent with the common law of other jurisdictions which also require the owner's consent or acquiescence before a lien may be established on the property of the owner. . . .

The necessity of the owner's consent is consistent with the contractual relationship between the lienor and the lienee which underlies the establishment of a lien. . . . As discussed previously, no such contractual relationship may be inferred where a possessor of a stolen vehicle turns it over to a garageman for repairs; accordingly, no lien is created against the owner. This is the correct result under the common law even though hardships may result to a good faith repairman. "There are many hard cases . . . of honest and innocent persons, who have been obliged to surrender goods to the true owners without remedy. . . . But these are hazards to which persons in business are continually exposed." . . . Of course, the repairman would always have a cause of action against the third party who contracted with him for repairs without the owner's consent.

Although the facts of this case do not establish either a statutory or common law lien, the plaintiff may be entitled to restitution under principles of equity. An equitable lien may be imposed to prevent unjust enrichment in an owner whose property was improved, for the increased value of the property. . . . "In the absence of a contractual agreement, a trial court may require an individual to make restitution for unjust enrichment if he has received a benefit which would be unconscionable to retain." . . . The trial court must determine whether the facts and equities of a particular case warrant such a remedy. . . .

We here note that "when a court assesses damages in an unjust enrichment case, the focus is not upon the cost to the plaintiff, but rather it is upon the value of what was actually received by the defendants." . . . In this case, the damages would thus be the difference between the value of the vehicle before and after the plaintiff worked on it, regardless of its worth when stolen.

Reversed and remanded.

Case Questions

1. Why should the defendant insurance company be required to pay the plaintiff repairman for services that the plaintiff performed without the defendant's knowledge or consent?
2. What is an equitable lien? How does it work?
3. How does a judge determine the amount of an award in an unjust enrichment case?

Declaratory Judgment

When someone seeks a judicial determination of the rights and obligations of the parties, that person is seeking the remedy of *declaratory judgment*. The court determines what the law is, or the constitutionality or the meaning of the law. For example, if a legislative body passes a statute making your business activity illegal, you could continue to operate the business and be arrested. You could also try to prevent the enforcement of the law by seeking a declaratory judgment. This action asks a court to determine whether the statute in question is constitutional. Because a judge granting declaratory judgment does not issue any orders telling anyone to act or refrain from acting, people who are seeking declaratory relief often ask for injunctive relief as well.

Declaratory judgment is considered by some courts to be an equitable remedy and by other courts to be a legal remedy.

Jury Trial

Cases are set for a jury trial only if a right to jury trial exists and one or both of the parties properly asserts this right. For the most part, trial by jury is a constitutional right. The Seventh Amendment to the U.S. Constitution guarantees litigants in federal court a jury trial in suits at common law, and most state constitutions make similar provisions. However, there is no constitutional right to a jury trial in equity cases because jury trials were not a part of chancery procedure.

Parties in most U.S. courts may join common law and equitable remedies in the same action without giving up their right to a jury trial. A jury decides the legal issues, and the judge decides the equitable issues. In the following case the appellant objected when the trial court classified the action as exclusively in equity.

State v. Yelsen Land Company
185 S.E.2d 897
Supreme Court of South Carolina
January 5, 1972

Littlejohn, Justice

This action was commenced by the State of South Carolina to settle a dispute concerning ownership and control of certain tidelands, submerged lands, and waters adjacent to Morris Island in Charleston Harbor. The State seeks to enjoin the defendants from trespassing upon the property involved, and seeks confirmation of title to the land in the State.

By way of answer and counterclaim, defendants assert title to the area in question, and allege that the State has trespassed upon it. They seek judgment confirming title in themselves, and seek monetary damages for wrongful taking, forbidden by the constitution. They also seek attorney fees and an injunction against the State. Their claim of title to the area stems from grants by the state of South Carolina to their predecessors in title.

After the case had been placed on the calendar for a jury trial, and the case reached for trial on the roster, the judge, on his own motion and over the objection of the State, referred all issues for trial to the Master in Equity for Charleston County. The State duly excepted to this order of reference and has appealed.

The sole question raised on this appeal is whether the judge erred in ordering the issues tried by the master instead of a jury.

The complaint in this action asserts that "Plaintiff has no adequate remedy at law and therefore brings this action in equity. . . ." Defendants Yelsen Land Company, Inc. and Dajon Realty Company likewise assert in their answer and counterclaim that "Defendants have no adequate remedy at law to prevent further trespass. . . ." Defendants contend that all parties have alleged this to be a matter in equity, and that a trial by jury has therefore been waived.

The State's assertion that it "has no adequate remedy at law" was, perhaps, unfortunate. Obviously, it referred to the injunctive relief sought, which is purely equitable. But the character of an action is not necessarily determined by such recitations in the pleadings. Rather, it is the nature of the issues and the remedies which are sought that is determinative.

A great many actions are of a hybrid nature. They involve not only issues normally tried by a jury, but also issues normally tried in equity without a jury.

This court noted . . .

"Under our Code practice legal and equitable issues and rights may be asserted in the same complaint, and legal and equitable remedies and relief afforded in the same action. In such event the legal issues are for determination by the jury, and the equitable issues for the judge sitting as a chancellor. The legal and equitable issues should be separated and each tried by the appropriate branch of the court." . . .

Both the State and the defendants seek injunctive relief in this action. An action for such relief is equitable. . . .

But both the State and the defendants assert title to the tidelands here in question. And when an issue of title to real estate is raised, such issue is generally triable by jury. . . .

Bryan v. Freeman . . . was a suit to remove a cloud on and quiet title to land. The complaint alleged that plaintiffs had title to land. Defendants, by answers, asserted paramount title. The issue there was whether the action should have been referred to a master. In hold-ing that the trial court acted properly in refusing to refer the action to a master, we said:

"An action to remove a cloud on and quiet title to land is one in equity. . . . However, when the defendant's answer raises an issue of paramount title to land, such as would, if established, defeat plaintiff's action, it is the duty of the court to submit to a jury the issue of title as raised by the pleadings." . . .

The facts before us require the same holding as the *Bryan* case. All parties seek equitable relief, and all parties seek relief triable at law. We do not think that the allegation in the complaint that this is an action in equity warrants the conclusion, as argued by defendants, that the plaintiff waived its right to a jury trial. To hold that the State voluntarily relinquished its right to a jury trial of the law issues involved would require a strained construction of the allegation in the complaint. It was the duty of the lower court to submit the law issues to a jury.

Reversed.

Case Questions

1. What was the common law part of the case? What was the equity part of the case?
2. Who will decide the equity claims? Who will decide the common law claims?
3. Suppose a party has a single claim of relief but demands various remedies, some available at law and some available only in equity. Will the case be tried before a jury?

Chapter Questions

1. Define the following terms:

avoidable harm doctrine	compensatory damages
benefit rule	declaratory judgment
common law lien	ejectment

equitable lien

equitable remedy

ex parte

exemplary damages

general damages

injunctive relief

in specie

jurisprudence

laches

liquidated damages

maxims

nominal damages

punitive damages

reformation

remedy

replevin

rescission

restitution

special damages

specific performance

statutory lien

unjust enrichment

waiver

2. Richard and Darlene Parker leased an apartment from Sun Ridge Investors for $465 per month. The lease provided that the Parkers would be charged a $20 late fee if the rent was not paid by the third day of the month, and $5 per day for each additional day until the account was paid in full. The Parkers were late in making their February 1995 rental payment, for which the landlord assessed the monthly and per diem late fees. The Parkers made their subsequent monthly rental payments in a timely manner, but the landlord, after informing the Parkers, applied their payments to the amount that was past due. The Parkers refused to pay the $5 per diem fee. Sun Ridge brought suit in state court seeking the rights to forcibly enter and repossess the apartment and $330 in past due rent. The trial court granted judgment to the landlord, and the Parkers unsuccessfully appealed to the intermediate court of appeals. The Parkers appealed to the Supreme Court of Oklahoma. The landlord argued that the per diem fees were additional rent, but the Parkers contended the fees amounted to an unenforceable penalty. Should the Oklahoma Supreme Court affirm or reverse the lower court? Explain your reasoning.

Sun Ridge Investors, Ltd v. Parker, 956 P.2d 876 (1998)

3. El Paso Gas Company transports natural gas through pipelines to points throughout the country. TransAmerican is a natural gas producer. The two companies and their predecessors negotiated various contracts during the 1970s and 1980s. TransAmerica brought suit in 1988 against El Paso when the parties were unable to resolve several disagreements about their respective contractual rights and duties. The trial court entered judgment in favor of TransAmerica. While El Paso's appeal was pending, the parties negotiated a settlement agreement which resulted in the termination of all litigation by both sides, the payment of compensation to TransAmerica by El Paso, and a restructuring of their relationship. The agreement also included a choice of forum clause which provided that a party, in the event of a breach, would have to bring suit in the Delaware Court of Chancery. In 1993, TransAmerica filed suit against El Paso, in Texas, alleging, among other claims, breach of the settlement contract. El Paso responded by filing suit against TransAmerica in the Delaware Court of Chancery. The Delaware

Chancery Court dismissed the petition on the grounds that it did not have jurisdiction, and the Delaware Supreme Court agreed. What was the fundamental problem that caused the court to rule that it did not have subject matter jurisdiction?

El Paso Natural Gas Company v. TransAmerican Natural Gas Company, 669 A.2d 36 (1995)

4. Plaintiff Whalen discovered upon his return from a trip that someone had left a message on his answering machine from an anonymous caller, to the effect that his dog had been found roaming at large, had been given poison, and would die within 24 hours unless the dog were treated immediately. Whalen took the dog to the veterinarian, who examined the animal and concluded that the dog had not ingested poison. Whalen filed suit for damages against Isaacs (the anonymous caller) for intentional infliction of emotional distress, believing that the story about the dog poisoning was a hoax. Under Georgia law, the question as to whether the facts supporting the plaintiff's claim are sufficiently outrageous to constitute the tort of intentional infliction of emotional distress is decided by the trial judge. Both parties moved for summary judgment. The plaintiff's evidence primarily consisted of incidents of conduct in which the defendant demonstrated hostility toward the plaintiff's dog when it was unleashed and allowed to run onto the defendant's property. The defendant, in a deposition, admitted making the telephone call, but explained that he was acting as a good Samaritan and made the call to help save the life of the dog. The defendant further claimed that he was only relaying what he had been told about the dog by an unknown bicyclist. Which party should be awarded judgment? Why?

Whalen v. Isaacs, 504 S.E. 2d. 214 (1998)

5. Chris Titchenal, the plaintiff, and Diane Dexter, the defendant, both women, were in an intimate relationship from 1985 until they broke up in 1994. Their home, cars, and bank accounts were jointly owned, and they had jointly acted as caretakers to Dexter's adopted daughter Sarah (who was named Sarah Ruth Dexter-Titchenal). The plaintiff had not sought to jointly adopt the child. Titchenal alleged that she was a defacto parent and had provided 65 percent of Sarah's care prior to the demise of her personal relationship with Dexter. Titchenal brought suit when Dexter severely cut off Titchenal's visitation opportunities with Sarah. The trial court granted Dexter's motion to dismiss the plaintiff's suit, because it concluded that Titchenal had no common law, statutory, constitutional, or compelling public policy right to visitation with Sarah. Titchenal appealed, contending that the trial court had equitable jurisdiction, in the best interest of the child, to grant "nontraditional" family members visitation rights where a parentlike situation existed, as in this instance. Do you agree with the trial court and the Vermont Supreme Court that equity has no jurisdiction in this case?

Titchenal v. Dexter, 693 A.2d 682 (1997)

6. Pet Ponderosa Memorial Gardens leased ten acres of land from Memory Gardens to be used as a pet cemetery. This land was adjacent to Memory

Gardens' human cemetery. As part of the lease, the pet cemetery was allowed to use all available water each evening for two hours to develop and maintain its landscaping. Then Memory Gardens abruptly cut off the water supply, and as a result the grass and other plantings died. The pet cemetery tried to renegotiate the lease without success. It found that hiring a water truck to haul in water was too expensive. Other water supplies could not be obtained. The pet cemetery instituted a suit and sought a preliminary injunction. Should this relief be granted?

Memory Gardens of Las Vegas v. Pet Ponderosa M.G., 492 P.2d 123 (Nev. 1972)

7. Inez Vacarro, who had had two miscarriages, received injections of a hormone to prevent miscarriages throughout the third pregnancy. A child was born with severe birth defects. The child's deformity was the result of the ingestion of the drug Delalutin, manufactured and sold by Squibb Corporation to prevent miscarriages. In a suit against Squibb, should the father, mother, and/or child be allowed recovery for emotional distress?

Vacarro v. Squibb Corp., 71 A.D.2d 270, 422 N.Y.2d 679 (1979)

8. Flowers, a senior college football player, wanted to play in the Sugar Bowl, which required him to refrain from signing with a professional team. Nevertheless, Flowers entered into a contract with the Giants with the tacit understanding that the contract would be concealed until after the game. The Giants reneged on the understanding when Flowers discussed withdrawing from the contract. In the meantime, Flowers got a better offer from the Los Angeles Chargers and formally tried to cancel the New York agreement. The Giants brought suit for specific performance to force Flowers to play for New York. Should the court order specific performance?

New York Football Giants v. Los Angeles Chargers Football Club, 291 F.2d 471 (1961)

9. Since 1950, Harris-Walsh, Inc., has been engaged in the removal of anthracite coal by strip-mining within the limits of the Borough of Dickson City, Pennsylvania. On June 28, 1963, the borough adopted an ordinance requiring that strip-mine operators furnish bonds sufficient to reclaim stripped land in all future mining operations. The Dickson City ordinance also provides for certain criminal penalties for violation of the above ordinance. Since Harris-Walsh has been mining the area for many years, it feels it should be able to continue to mine in its old fashion. Can Harris-Walsh invoke the jurisdiciton of a court of equity?

Harris-Walsh, Inc. v. Dickson City, 216 A.2d 329 (Pa. 1966)

10. For a number of years, a gambling establishment and saloon called the Sycamore Cafe was conducted on Central Avenue in Louisville, Kentucky, in an industrial and residential district. The proprietors, the Goose brothers, had been arrested numerous times for gambling, disorderly conduct, malicious assault, and other crimes. Records show that these charges were "filed away," or stooges were employed to "take the rap." The record of the Goose brothers and the Sycamore Cafe is a sordid one of flagrant violations of the law occurring at all times of the day and night. Can the commonwealth's

attorney enjoin the continuation of these activities at the Sycamore Cafe by invoking the jurisdiction of a court of equity for injunctive purposes?
Goose v. Commonwealth, 305 Ky 644, 205 S.W.2d 326 (1947)

11. During the summer of 1961, Harry Kapchuk and other stockholders reorganized the capital structure of Seashore Food Products, Inc., by creating an issue of no-par common stock with voting rights. The Kapchuk group retained 15 percent of this issue for themselves on the basis of three shares for every dollar of contributed capital. In August 1962, Seashore Food Products became heavily indebted to Seymour Friend and other creditors, some being close affiliates of the corporation. The debts were so large that the corporation faced bankruptcy. Acting as officers of the corporation, the Kapchuk group explained the situation to Friend and the creditors' group, and proposed that bankruptcy could be averted if the creditors would accept corporate stock in payment of their claims against the corporation. This was agreed to, and the transfer of stock to the creditors was made on the basis of one share of stock for every three dollars of corporate debt. Primarily because of the Kapchuk's skillful management, the corporation regained its solvency and began to prosper. In February 1966, Friend and other creditors filed suit, asking that a constructive trust be imposed on the stock acquired by Kapchuk during corporate reorganization because Kapchuk failed to disclose during the 1962 negotiations that he obtained this stock at three shares for one dollar. What equitable doctrine bars such relief to Friend and the creditors' group? Why?
    Friend v. Kapchuk, 216 So.2d 783 (Fla. 1968)

12. Prisoners sued their jailers for money damages for cruel and unusual punishment by the state prison authorities in violation of their constitutional rights. Included among these practices were the imposition of a bread-and-water diet; arbitrary use of tear gas; taping, chaining, or handcuffing of inmates to cell bars; extended periods of confinement in solitary confinement cells; placing prisoners naked in a hot, roach-infested cell; and arbitrary removal of good conduct time, thereby extending a man's compulsory prison term by months, and in the case of one of the plaintiffs, by years. Is the computation of damages possible?
    Landman v. Royster, 354 F.Supp. 1302 (E.D. Va. 1973)

Notes

1. You can learn about the requirements of a valid contract by reading Chapter 4. In general, a valid contract must be clear, the terms must be reasonably certain, and there must have been an agreement between competent parties supported by consideration, which does not contravene principles of law and which in some circumstances must be in writing.
2. Please see the discussion on the Uniform Commercial Code in Chapter 10 and in the glossary.

VIII Criminal Law and Procedure

This chapter introduces students to some of the fundamental principles of criminal law and criminal procedure. Each of these subjects could be a course in itself; in one chapter it is only possible to examine the major issues associated with each topic, and even then it is necessarily in cursory form.

CRIMINAL LAW

William Blackstone, an English judge and author of *Commentaries on the Laws of England* (1765–1769), defined a crime as a wrong committed against the public,[1] a definition that is today still widely recognized as appropriate. Because the general public is injured when a crime is committed, as well as the person who was the perpetrator's targeted victim, the government and not the victim has the primary responsibility to initiate a response. It is government's responsibility to investigate, prosecute, and punish those found by the courts to be responsible for the commission of crimes. In criminal cases, unlike in most civil cases, the government, not the victim, brings the action. This public character of criminal prosecutions means that irrespective of the targeted victim's financial condition the government will pay the costs of the action. The government and not the victim will pay for the investigation of the crime and for the prosecutors. If evidence requires scientific analysis, the government pays for the services of forensic scientists, and if expert witnesses are needed, they, too, are paid for by the government. If the individual accused of committing the crime is convicted and sentenced to incarceration, state-funded correctional institutions will become involved. If the court sentences the accused to probation, probation officers will be assigned to supervise the probationer, again at public expense.

This massive involvement of the government is generally not found in civil cases. Although governmental bodies can both sue and be sued in civil actions, most civil suits are between private parties. The private parties may be businesses, associations, or individuals. In civil cases, the parties are generally responsible for determining whether to pursue a lawsuit or seek some other nonjudicial resolution (see Chapter 14 for examples of nonjudicial dispute resolution alternatives). In a civil suit, each party is responsible for any costs incurred in conjunction with the suit such as investigative costs, lawyer fees, and expert witnesses fees. In the civil justice system, a party's financial condition can make an enormous difference. Many people feel shut out of the civil justice system because of the cost involved in litigation.

Civil remedies, burdens of proof, and court procedures, however, differ significantly from those in criminal cases. Readers might benefit from reviewing Figure 1-2 in Chapter 1 and refreshing their memories as to other ways in which the civil and criminal systems differ. Because the actions that are defined as criminal also are recognized as violations of the civil law, it is not uncommon for the victims in criminal cases to maintain separate civil suits against their attackers. You may remember that there were two O. J. Simpson cases. In the criminal prosecution brought by the State of California, Simpson was found not guilty of the criminal charges. In the subsequent civil action, however, he was found liable for significant monetary damages.

Sources of American Criminal Law

You will recall from the discussion in Chapter 1 that the colonists along the eastern seaboard of North America were very influenced by the English common law, which defined offenses both judicially and legislatively. Although the influence of common law diminished following the American Revolution because of public opposition to things English,[2] many of the states that abolished common law crimes converted most of them into statutes.[3] Although these "American" statutes deviated in some respects from the common law, they retained significant aspects of that heritage. In addition, some states continued to recognize common law crimes without statutes, and judges with common law authority could use this to augment the criminal statutes. They also could rely on well-established legal principles to define new offenses in the absence of precedent.

In the twentieth century, the legislative branch has replaced the judiciary as the dominant criminal law policymaker. The inventions of the automobile, fax machine, copying machines, airplanes, and computers, and the growth of sophisticated banking/finance companies and the securities industry produced as a by-product new and previously unforeseen criminal opportunities. Legislative bodies responded by enacting prodigious numbers of new criminal laws. Some of these laws were well thought out; others were enacted on a piecemeal basis to appease voters without sufficient attention to detail or to appropriate constitutional limitations such as vagueness and overbreadth.

The complexities of modern society and the common law's imprecision led reformers, among them the drafters of the influential Model Penal Code, to call for its abolishment. Today, most states define criminal offenses only through statutes, an approach that is consistent with federal law. In 1812, the U.S. Supreme

Court decided that Article I, Section 8, of the U.S. Constitution does not include among the enumerated powers the power to adopt the common law. Thus, all federal crimes had to be statutory. Both the federal and state courts, however, turn to common law definitions for help in statutory construction.

Classification of Crimes

The common law classified crimes as either *mala in se* or *mala prohibita*. *Mala in se* crimes were offenses that were intrinsically bad, such as murder, rape, arson, and theft. Acts that were criminal only because the law defined them as such were classified as *mala prohibita*. A second way of categorizing crimes is in terms of the harm they cause to society. Today, state statutes are often organized so that crimes of a particular type are clustered, for example, crimes against persons (rape, kidnapping, battery, murder, etc.), crimes against property (larceny, robbery, burglary, arson, etc.), and crimes against government (contempt, perjury, bribery, etc.).

Crimes can also be classified as felonies and misdemeanors, and the distinction between the two is essentially a decision of each state's legislature. In some states, felonies are crimes that are served in state prisons and misdemeanors are offenses served in county jails. Other jurisdictions provide that crimes authorizing a sentence of incarceration of over one year are felonies, whereas those authorizing sentences of one year or less are misdemeanors. The distinction between misdemeanor and felonious theft is usually based on the value of the stolen article. Felony thresholds in theft cases range from $20 in South Carolina to $2,000 in Pennsylvania. In recent years, other classification schemes have gained popularity, for example, white-collar crime (tax evasion, insider trading, kickbacks, defrauding governmental agencies, etc.) and victimless crimes (smoking marijuana, loitering, sodomy, etc.). Other crimes have been reclassified: driving while intoxicated, a misdemeanor twenty years ago, is today a felony.

Constitutional Limitations on Criminalization

The Constitution limits the imposition of criminal liability and criminal punishments. A criminal statute, for example, must be reasonably precise, since one that is too vague or overly broad violates substantive due process. In *Kolender v. Lawson*, for example, the U.S. Supreme Court ruled that a California statute was too vague, explaining that due process requires that a penal statute define the criminal offense "with sufficient definiteness that ordinary people can understand what conduct is prohibited and in a manner that does not encourage arbitrary and discriminatory enforcement." A statute suffers from overbreadth if its terms are so general that it could be used to arrest a person engaged in activities protected by the First Amendment.

Article I, Sections 9 and 10, of the Constitution prohibit federal and state legislative bodies from enacting *ex post facto* laws—laws that make acts criminal that were not criminal at the time they were committed. Statutes that make a crime greater than when committed, impose greater punishment, or make proof of guilt easier have also been held to be unconstitutional *ex post facto* laws. Laws also are unconstitutional if they alter the definition of a penal offense or its consequence to the disadvantage of people who have committed that offense. A law is not *ex post facto* if it "mitigates the rigor" of the law or simply reenacts the law in force when the crime was done. The *ex post facto* clause restricts only legislative power and does not apply to the judiciary. In addition, the doctrine applies exclusively to penal statutes, whether civil or criminal in form [see *Hiss v. Hampton*, 338 F.Supp. 1141 (1972)].

The Constitution also prohibits bills of attainder—acts of a legislature that apply either to named individuals or to easily ascertainable members of a group in such a way as to impose punishments on them without a trial. In *United States v. Brown*, 381 U.S. 437 (1965), for example, an act of Congress that made it a crime for a member of the Communist party to serve as an officer of a labor union was held unconstitutional as a bill of attainder by the Supreme Court.

Although no specific provision in the federal Constitution guarantees a general right of personal privacy, the U.S. Supreme Court has recognized that a limited privacy right is implicit in the due process guarantees of life, liberty, and property in the Fourth and Fifth amendments, and in the First, Ninth, and Fourteenth amendments. The Court also has recognized that certain fundamental liberties are inherent in the concept of ordered liberty as reflected in our nation's history and tradition and has selected them for special protection. These rights include personal intimacies relating to the family, marriage, motherhood, procreation, and child rearing. The Court has also recognized that a person's home is entitled to special privacy protection. For example, it has prevented the enforcement of state obscenity laws within the home where the conduct in question involved protected First Amendment rights.

The limited constitutionally recognized right of privacy is not absolute and is subject to limitations when the government's interest in protecting society becomes dominant. However, a statute affecting a fundamental constitutional right will be subjected to strict and exacting scrutiny, and the statute will fail to pass constitutional muster unless the state proves a compelling need for the law and shows that its goals cannot be accomplished by less restrictive means. If a challenged statute does *not* affect a fundamental constitutional right, the law will be upheld if it is neither arbitrary nor discriminatory, and if it bears a rational relation to a legitimate legislative purpose—protecting the public health, welfare, safety, or morals. A state can satisfy this rational basis test if it can show that there is some conceivable basis for finding such a rational relationship.

The *Equal Protection Clause* of the Fourteenth Amendment provides that "No state shall . . . deny to any person within its jurisdiction the equal protection of the laws." This clause was included in the Fourth Amendment in the aftermath of the Civil War for the purpose of securing freedom for black people. On its face, the clause might seem to guarantee individuals as well as groups not only the equal application of the laws, but also equal outcomes. The Supreme Court has rejected such an expansive interpretation and has ruled that the Equal Protection Clause only requires that the laws be applied equally and leaves issues associated with the existence of unequal outcomes to the political branches of government.

The Supreme Court has ruled that classification schemes are *inherently suspect* if they are based on race, national origin, or alienage, or if they hamper the exercise of fundamental personal rights. When an inherently suspect classification scheme is challenged in court on equal protection grounds, it is subject to "*strict scrutiny.*" This means that the classification scheme will be overturned unless the government can demonstrate that its discriminatory impact is narrowed as much as possible and that the remaining discrimination is necessary to achieve a "compelling" governmental interest.

Discriminatory classifications that are neither suspect, nor based on gender, will be sustained only if they are rationally related to a legitimate governmental interest. When a challenged classification scheme involves gender, the Supreme Court applies a special rule. In these cases, the discriminatory scheme must bear a "substantial relationship to "important governmental objectives."[4]

Although the Equal Protection Clause has rarely been relied upon to strike down criminal statutes, it has played a small, but important role in preventing legislatures from defining crimes in ways that target groups on the basis of race and gender. Examples of criminal statutes that were overturned by the Supreme Court on Equal Protection grounds include a Massachusetts statute that made it a crime for unmarried adults to use birth control[5] and an Oklahoma statute that allowed females 18 years or older to consume beer containing 3.2% alcohol, while withholding this right from males until they were 21 years of age.[6]

Classifications based on race have received the closest scrutiny in recent decades, and the case we are about to read, involves a challenge to a Virginia criminal statute that prohibited interracial marriages.

Loving v. Commonwealth of Virginia
388 U.S. 1
U.S. Supreme Court
June 12, 1967

Mr. Chief Justice Warren delivered the opinion of the Court.

This case presents a constitutional question never addressed by this Court: whether a statutory scheme adopted by the State of Virginia to prevent marriages between persons solely on the basis of racial classifications violates the Equal Protection and Due Process Clauses of the Fourteenth Amendment. For reasons which seem to us to reflect the central meaning of those constitutional commands, we conclude that these statutes cannot stand consistently with the Fourteenth Amendment.

In June 1958, two residents of Virginia, Mildred Jeter, a Negro woman, and Richard Loving, a white man, were married in the District of Columbia pursuant to its laws. Shortly after their marriage, the Lovings returned to Virginia and established their marital abode in Caroline County. At the October Term, 1958, of the Circuit Court of Caroline County, a grand jury issued an indictment charging the Lovings with violating Virginia's ban on interracial marriages. On January 6, 1959, the Lovings pleaded guilty to the charge and were sentenced to one year in jail; however, the trial judge suspended the sentence for a period of 25 years on the condition that the Lovings leave the State and not return to Virginia together for 25 years. He stated in an opinion that:

> "Almighty God created the races white, black, yellow, malay and red, and he placed them on separate continents. And but for the interference with his arrangement there would be no cause for such marriages. The fact that he separated the races shows that he did not intend for the races to mix."

After their convictions, the Lovings took up residence in the District of Columbia. On November 6, 1963, they filed a motion in the state trial court to vacate the judgment and set aside the sentence on the ground that the statutes which they had violated were repugnant to the Fourteenth Amendment. The motion not having been decided by October 28, 1964, the Lovings instituted a class action in the United States District Court for the Eastern District of Virginia requesting that a three-judge court be convened to declare the Virginia antimiscegenation statutes unconstitutional and to enjoin state officials from enforcing their convictions. On January 22, 1965, the state trial judge denied the motion to vacate the sentences, and the Lovings perfected an appeal to the Supreme Court of Appeals of Virginia. On February 11, 1965, the three-judge District Court continued the case to allow the Lovings to present their constitutional claims to the highest state court.

The Supreme Court of Appeals upheld the constitutionality of the antimiscegenation statutes and, after modifying the sentence, affirmed the conviction. The Lovings appealed this decision. . . .

The two statutes under which appellants were convicted and sentenced are part of a comprehensive statutory scheme aimed at prohibiting and punishing interracial marriages. The Lovings were convicted of violating § 20–58 of the Virginia Code:

> *"Leaving State to evade law.*—If any white person and colored person shall go out of this State, for the purpose of being married, and with the intention of returning, and be married out of it, and afterwards return to and reside in it, cohabiting as man and wife, they shall be punished as provided in § 20–59."

Section 20–59, which defines the penalty for miscegenation, provides:

> *"Punishment for marriage.*—If any white person intermarry with a colored person, or any colored person intermarry with a white person, he shall be guilty of a felony and

shall be punished by confinement in the penitentiary for not less than one nor more than five years." . . .

The Lovings have never disputed in the course of this litigation that Mrs. Loving is a "colored person" or that Mr. Loving is a "white person" within the meanings given those terms by the Virginia statutes.

Virginia is now one of 16 States which prohibit and punish marriages on the basis of racial classifications. Penalties for miscegenation arose as an incident to slavery and have been common in Virginia since the colonial period. The present statutory scheme dates from the adoption of the Racial Integrity Act of 1924, passed during the period of extreme nativism which followed the end of the First World War. The central features of this Act, and current Virginia law, are the absolute prohibition of a "white person" marrying other than another "white person," a prohibition against issuing marriage licenses until the issuing official is satisfied that the applicants' statements as to their race are correct, certificates of "racial composition" to be kept by both local and state registrars, and the carrying forward of earlier prohibitions against racial intermarriage.

I

In upholding the constitutionality of these provisions in the decision below, the Supreme Court of Appeals of Virginia referred to its 1955 decision in *Naim v. Naim*, . . . as stating the reasons supporting the validity of these laws. In *Naim*, the state court concluded that the State's legitimate purposes were "to preserve the racial integrity of its citizens," and to prevent "the corruption of blood," "a mongrel breed of citizens," and "the obliteration of racial pride," obviously an endorsement of the doctrine of White Supremacy. . . . The court also reasoned that marriage has traditionally been subject to state regulation without federal intervention, and, consequently, the regulation of marriage should be left to exclusive state control by the Tenth Amendment.

While the state court is no doubt correct in asserting that marriage is a social relation subject to the State's police power, . . . the State does not contend in its argument before this Court that its powers to regulate marriage are unlimited notwithstanding the commands of the Fourteenth Amendment. . . . Instead, the State argues that the meaning of the Equal Protection Clause, as illuminated by the statements of the Framers, is only that state penal laws containing an interracial element as part of the definition of the offense must apply equally to whites and Negroes in the sense that members of each race are punished to the same degree. Thus, the State contends that, because its miscegenation statutes punish equally both the white and the Negro participants in an interracial marriage, these statutes, despite their reliance on racial classifications, do not constitute an invidious discrimination based upon race. The second argument advanced by the State assumes the validity of its equal application theory. The argument is that, if the Equal Protection Clause does not outlaw miscegenation statutes because of their reliance on racial classifications, the question of constitutionality would thus become whether there was any rational basis for a State to treat interracial marriages differently from other marriages. On this question, the State argues, the scientific evidence is substantially in doubt and, consequently, this Court should defer to the wisdom of the state legislature in adopting its policy of discouraging interracial marriages.

Because we reject the notion that the mere "equal application" of a statute containing racial classifications is enough to remove the classifications from the Fourteenth Amendment's proscription of all invidious racial discriminations, we do not accept the State's contention that these statutes should be upheld if there is any possible basis for concluding that they serve a rational purpose. . . .

In the case at bar, we deal with statutes containing racial classifications, and the fact of equal application does not immunize the statute from the very heavy burden of justification which the Fourteenth Amendment has traditionally required of state statutes drawn according to race. . . .

There can be no question but that Virginia's miscegenation statutes rest solely upon distinctions drawn according to race. The statutes proscribe generally accepted conduct if engaged in by members of different races. Over the years, this Court has consistently repudiated "[d]istinctions between citizens solely because of their ancestry" as being "odious to a free people whose institutions are founded upon the doctrine of equality." . . . At the very least, the Equal Protection Clause demands that racial classifications, especially suspect in criminal statutes, be subjected to the "most rigid scrutiny," . . . and, if they are ever to be upheld, they must be shown to be necessary to the accomplishment of some permissible state objective, independent of the racial discrimination which it was the object of the Fourteenth Amendment to eliminate. Indeed, two members of this Court have already stated that they "cannot conceive of a valid legislative purpose . . . which makes the color of a person's skin the test of whether his conduct is a criminal offense." . . .

There is patently no legitimate overriding purpose independent of invidious racial discrimination which justifies this classification. The fact that Virginia prohibits only interracial marriages involving white persons demonstrates that the racial classifications must stand on their own justification, as measures designed to maintain White Supremacy. We have consistently denied the constitutionality of measures which restrict the rights of citizens on account of race. There can be no doubt that restricting the freedom to marry solely because of racial classifications violates the central meaning of the Equal Protection Clause.

These statutes also deprive the Lovings of liberty without due process of law in violation of the Due Process Clause of the Fourteenth Amendment. The freedom to marry has long been recognized as one of the vital personal rights essential to the orderly pursuit of happiness by free men.

Marriage is one of the "basic civil rights of man," fundamental to our very existence and survival. . . . To deny this fundamental freedom on so unsupportable a basis as the racial classifications embodied in these statutes, classifications so directly subversive of the principle of equality at the heart of the Fourteenth Amendment, is surely to deprive all the State's citizens of liberty without due process of law. The Fourteenth Amendment requires that the freedom of choice to marry not be restricted by invidious racial discriminations. Under our Constitution, the freedom to marry or not marry a person of another race resides with the individual and cannot be infringed by the State.

These convictions must be reversed. It is so ordered.

Reversed.

Case Questions

1. Virginia argued to the Supreme Court that its miscegenation statute did not constitute an invidious classification scheme based on race. What was the basis for this position?
2. What response did the Supreme Court make to Virginia's restrictions on an individual's right to decide whether to marry a person of another race?

 When Loving v. Virginia *arrived at the U.S. Supreme Court, Virginia and fifteen other states had statutes on the books that made it a crime for blacks and whites to intermarry. These statutes, called antimiscegenation laws, were common in former slave states, and had existed in Virginia since Colonial times. The justices of the U.S. Supreme Court declared that "there is patently no legitimate overriding purpose independent of invidious racial discrimination which justifies this classification." Which ethical tradition is most reflected in the Court's opinion in this case?*

The Imposition of Punishment

It is a principle of U.S. law that people convicted of crimes receive only punishments that have been provided by law. Also, legislative bodies are limited in the types of sentences they can provide by the Eighth Amendment's protection against the imposition of cruel and unusual punishments. The Supreme Court has interpreted this provision as preventing the use of "barbaric punishments as well as sentences that are disproportionate to the crime committed." The meaning of "barbaric punishment" has been the subject of much recent discussion in debate over capital punishment. The majority of the Supreme Court has consistently rejected arguments that imposition of capital punishment is barbaric, emphasizing that capital punishment was known to the common law and was accepted in this country at the time the Eighth Amendment was adopted. They also point out that at least thirty-five states have enacted statutes providing for the death penalty, citing this as evidence that society continues to view capital punishment as appropriate and necessary.

The Eighth Amendment's proportionality requirement can be traced to the Virginia Declaration of Rights (1775), the English Bill of Rights (1689), the Statute of Westminster (1275), and even Magna Carta (1215). The Supreme Court has used this principle to strike down sentences imposed pursuant to (1) a statute authorizing a jail sentence for drug addiction (because it is cruel and unusual punishment to incarcerate a person for being ill), (2) a statute authorizing the death penalty for rapists, and (3) a statute authorizing a sentence of life imprisonment without parole for a recidivist who wrote a one-hundred-dollar check on a nonexisting account.

THE BASIC COMPONENTS OF A CRIMINAL OFFENSE

Criminal offenses traditionally consist of the following basic components: (1) the wrongful act, (2) the guilty mind, (3) the concurrence of act and intent, and, in some crimes, (4) causation. To obtain a conviction in a criminal case, the government has to establish each of these components beyond a reasonable doubt.

The Wrongful Act

The wrongful act, or *actus reus*, is most easily defined by example. The wrongful act of larceny includes an unlawful taking and carrying away of another person's property. The wrongful act in a battery is the unjustified, offensive, or harmful touching of another person. The law makes a distinction between acts that are classified as voluntary, and those that result from reflexive acts, epileptic seizures, or hypnotic suggestion (see the Model Penal Code in Figure 8-1). A voluntary act occurs when the accused causes his or her body to move in a manner that produces prohibited conduct. The following case illustrates the requirement that criminal acts be voluntary.

People v. Shaughnessy
319 N.Y.S.2d 626
District Court, Nassau County, Third District
March 16, 1971

Lockman, Judge

On October 9th, 1970, shortly before 10:05 p.m., the Defendant in the company of her boyfriend and two other youngsters proceeded by automobile to the vicinity of the St. Ignatius Retreat Home, Searingtown Road, Incorporated Village of North Hills, Nassau County, New York. The Defendant was a passenger and understood that she was headed for the Christopher Morley Park which is located across the street from the St. Ignatius Retreat Home and has a large illuminated sign, with letters approximately 8 inches high, which identifies the park. As indicated, on the

MODEL PENAL CODE*
Official Draft, 1985

Section 2.01. Requirement of Voluntary Act; Omission as Basis of Liability; Possession as an Act

(1) A person is not guilty of an offense unless his liability is based on conduct which includes a voluntary act or the omission to perform an act of which he is physically capable.

(2) The following are not voluntary acts within the meaning of this Section:

(a) a reflex or convulsion;

(b) a bodily movement during unconsciousness or sleep;

(c) conduct during hypnosis or resulting from hypnotic suggestion;

(d) a bodily movement that otherwise is not a product of the effort or determination of the actor, either conscious or habitual.

(3) Liability for the commission of an offense may not be based on an omission unaccompanied by action unless:

(a) the omission is expressly made sufficient by the law defining the offense; or

(b) a duty to perform the omitted act is otherwise imposed by law.

(4) Possession is an act, within the meaning of this Section, if the possessor knowingly procured or received the thing possessed or was aware of his control thereof for a sufficient period to have been able to terminate his possession.

*A collection of suggestions for reforming American criminal law, the Model Penal Code was prepared by a private association of professors, lawyers, and judges called the American Law Institute. Over two-thirds of the states have adopted at least some of its provisions and hundreds of courts have been influenced by its suggestions.

FIGURE 8-1   Model Penal Code Section 2.01

other side of the street the St. Ignatius Retreat Home has two pillars at its entrance with a bronze sign on each pillar with 4 to 5 inch letters. The sign is not illuminated. The vehicle in which the Defendant was riding proceeded into the grounds of the Retreat Home and was stopped by a watchman and the occupants including the Defendant waited approximately 20 minutes for a Policeman to arrive. The Defendant never left the automobile.

The Defendant is charged with violating Section 1 of the Ordinance prohibiting entry upon private property of the Incorporated Village of North Hills, which provides: "No person shall enter upon any privately owned piece, parcel or lot of real property in the Village of North Hills without the permission of the owner, lessee or occupant thereof. The failure of the person, so entering upon, or found to be on, such private property, to produce upon demand, the written permission of the owner, lessee or occupant to enter upon, or to be on, such real property, shall be and shall constitute presumptive evidence of the violation of this Ordinance."

The Defendant at the conclusion of the trial moves to dismiss on the grounds that the statute is unconstitutional. Since the Ordinance is Malum Prohibitum, in all likelihood the Ordinance is constitutional. . . . However, it is unnecessary to pass upon the constitutionality of the Ordinance since there is another basis for dismissal.

The problem presented by the facts in this case brings up for review the primary elements that are required for criminal accountability and responsibility. It is only from an accused's voluntary overt acts that criminal responsibility can attach. An overt act or a specific omission to act must occur in order for the establishment of a criminal offense.

The physical element required has been designated as the *Actus Reus*. The mental element is of course better known as the *Mens Rea*. While the mental element may under certain circumstances not be required as in crimes that are designated *Malum Prohibitum*, the *Actus Reus* is always necessary. It certainly cannot be held to be the intent of the legislature to punish involuntary acts.

The principle which requires a voluntary act or omission to act had been codified . . . and reads as follows in part: "The minimal requirement for criminal liability is the performance by a person of conduct which includes a *voluntary act or the omission to perform an act* which he is physically capable of performing. . . ."

The legislature may prescribe that an act is criminal without regard to the doer's intent or knowledge, but an involuntary act is not criminal (with certain exceptions such as involuntary acts resulting from voluntary intoxication).

In the case at bar, the People have failed to establish any act on the part of the Defendant. She merely was a passenger in a vehicle. Any action taken by the vehicle was caused and guided by the driver thereof and not by the Defendant. If the Defendant were to be held guilty under these circumstances, it would dictate that she would be guilty if she had been unconscious or asleep at the time or even if she had been a prisoner in the automobile. There are many situations which can be envisioned and in which the trespass statute in question would be improperly applied to an involuntary act. One might conceive of a driver losing control of a vehicle through mechanical failure and the vehicle proceeding onto private property which is the subject of a trespass.

Although the Court need not pass on the question, it might very well be proper to hold the driver responsible for his act even though he was under the mistaken belief that he was on his way to Christopher Morley Park. The legislature has provided statutes which make mistakes of fact or lack of knowledge no excuse in a criminal action. However, if the driver had been a Defendant, the People could have established an act on the part of the Defendant driver, to wit, turning his vehicle into the private property.

In the case of the Defendant now before the Court, however, the very first and essential element in criminal responsibility is missing, an overt voluntary act or omission to act and, accordingly, the Defendant is found not guilty.

Case Questions

1. Judge Lockman's opinion explains that a voluntary act is normally necessary for criminal liability. What would be an example of an involuntary act?

2. Under what conditions should people be criminally liable for having omitted to act?

Special Rules

When the law recognizes the existence of a legal duty, the failure to act is equivalent to a criminal act. The duty to act can be imposed by statute (filing income tax returns, registering with selective service, registering firearms), by contract (such as that between parents and a day care center), as a result of one's status (parent-child, husband-wife), or because one has assumed a responsibility (voluntarily assuming responsibility for providing food to a person under disability).

Another exception to the requirement of a physical act is recognized in possession offenses in which the law treats the fact of possession as the equivalent of a wrongful act. For example, a person found with a controlled substance in his jacket pocket is not actually engaging in any physical act. Possession can be actual, as when the accused is found with the contraband on his or her person, or constructive, as when the contraband is not on the suspect's person but is under the suspect's dominion and control.

Status Crimes

The Supreme Court has emphasized the importance of the wrongful act requirement in its decisions relating to status crimes, ruling that legislatures cannot make the status of "being without visible means of support" or "being ill as a result of narcotic addiction" into crimes. Selling a controlled substance can be made criminal because it involves a voluntary act. The condition of being an addict, however, is a status.

The Criminal State of Mind

The second requirement of a criminal offense (subject to a few exceptions) is that an alleged criminal offender possess a criminal state of mind (*mens rea*) at the time of the commission of the wrongful act. This is called a concurrence of a wrongful act with a wrongful state of mind. Concurrence is required because some people who commit wrongful acts do not have a wrongful state of mind. For example, if the student sitting next to you mistakenly picks up your copy of a textbook, instead of her copy, and leaves the classroom, there has been a wrongful act but no wrongful intent. While it is easy to theoretically make this distinction between accidental and criminal acts, it is often difficult to prove that a person acted with *mens rea*, and prosecutors often have to prove *mens rea* indirectly and circumstantially. In addition, judges routinely instruct jurors that the law permits them to find that a defendant intended the natural and probable consequences of his or her deliberate acts. This instruction is based on human experience: most people go about their daily affairs intending to do the things they choose to do.

In the United States, *mala in se* offenses require proof of criminal intent. *Mala prohibita* offenses may require criminal intent (in possession of a controlled substance, for instance), or they may involve no proof of intent at all (as in traffic offenses or sales of illegal intoxicating beverages to minors).

There are two major approaches to *mens rea*, one formed by the traditional common law approach, the other by the Model Penal Code. The common law approach recognizes three categories of intent: general intent, specific intent, and criminal negligence. *General intent* crimes include serious offenses such as rape and arson and less serious offenses such as trespass and simple battery. For conviction of a general intent crime, the prosecution has to prove that the accused intended to commit the *actus reus*. The common law permitted the trier of fact to infer a wrongful state of mind from proof that the actor voluntarily did a wrongful act. Thus a person who punches another person in anger (without any lawful justification or excuse) may be found to have possessed general criminal intent.

A *specific intent* crime requires proof of the commission of an *actus reus*, plus a specified level of knowledge or an additional intent, such as an intent to commit a felony. A person who possesses a controlled substance (the *actus reus*) and who at the time of the possession has an intent to sell (an additional specified level of intent beyond the commission of the *actus reus*) has committed a specific intent crime.

Criminal negligence results from unconscious risk creation. For example, a driver who unconsciously takes his or her eyes off the road to take care of a crying infant is in fact creating risks for other drivers and pedestrians. Thus the driver's unreasonable conduct created substantial and unjustifiable risks. If the driver is unaware of the risk creation, he or she is acting negligently.

The defendant in the following case was charged and convicted of the specific intent crime of robbery. He appealed his conviction on the ground that he did not have specific intent—the intent to permanently deprive the true owner of his property.

State v. Gordon
321 A.2d 352
Supreme Judicial Court of Maine
June 17, 1974

Wernick, Justice

An indictment returned (on June 27, 1972) by a Cumberland County Grand Jury to the Superior Court charged defendant, Richard John Gordon, with having committed the crime of "armed robbery" in violation of 17

M.R.S.A. § 3401–A. A separate indictment accused defendant of having, with intention to kill, assaulted a police officer, one Harold Stultz. Defendant was arraigned and pleaded not guilty to each charge. Upon motion by the State, and over defendant's objection, the residing Justice ordered a single trial on the two indictments. The trial was before a jury. On the "assault" the jury was unable to reach a verdict and as to that charge a mistrial was declared. The jury found defendant guilty of "armed robbery." From the judgment of conviction entered on the verdict defendant has appealed, assigning ten claims of error.

We deny the appeal.

The jury was justified in finding the following facts.

One Edwin Strode and defendant had escaped in Vermont from the custody of the authorities who had been holding them on a misdemeanor charge. In the escape defendant and Strode had acquired two hand guns and also a blue station wagon in which they had fled from Vermont through New Hampshire into Maine. Near Standish, Maine, the station wagon showed signs of engine trouble, and defendant and Strode began to look for another vehicle. They came to the yard of one Franklin Prout. In the yard was Prout's 1966 maroon Chevelle and defendant, who was operating the station wagon, drove it parallel to the Prout Chevelle. Observing that the keys were in the Chevelle, Strode left the station wagon and entered the Chevelle. At this time Prout came out of his house into the yard. Strode pointed a gun at him, and the defendant and Strode then told Prout that they needed his automobile, were going to take it but they "would take care of it and see he [Prout] got it back as soon as possible." With defendant operating the station wagon and Strode the Chevelle, defendant and Strode left the yard and proceeded in the direction of Westbrook. Subsequently, the station wagon was abandoned in a sand pit, and defendant and Strode continued their flight in the Chevelle. A spectacular series of events followed—including the alleged assault (with intent to kill) upon Westbrook police officer, Stultz, a shoot-out on Main Street in Westbrook, and a high speed police chase, during which the Chevelle was driven off the road in the vicinity of the Maine Medical Center in Portland where it was abandoned, Strode and defendant having commandeered another automobile to resume their flight. Ultimately, both the defendant and Strode were apprehended, defendant having been arrested on the day following the police chase in the vicinity of the State Police Barracks in Scarborough. . . .

[D]efendant maintains that the evidence clearly established that (1) defendant and Strode had told Prout that they "would take care of . . . [the automobile] and see [that] he [Prout] got it back as soon as possible" and (2) defendant intended only a temporary use of Prout's Chevelle. Defendant argues that the evidence thus fails to warrant a conclusion beyond a reasonable doubt that defendant had the specific intent requisite for "robbery." (Hereinafter, reference to the "specific intent" necessary for "robbery" signifies the "specific intent" incorporated into "robbery" as embracing "larceny.")

Although defendant is correct that robbery is a crime requiring a particular specific intent, . . . defendant wrongly apprehends its substantive content.

A summarizing statement appearing in defendant's brief most clearly exposes his misconception of the law. Acknowledging that on all of the evidence the jury could properly

> ". . . have inferred . . . that [defendant and Strode] . . . intended to get away from the authorities by going to New York or elsewhere *where they would abandon* the car . . .", (emphasis supplied)

defendant concludes that, nevertheless, the State had failed to prove the necessary specific intent because it is

> ". . . entirely irrational to conclude . . . that the defendant himself intended at the time he and Strode took the car, *to keep the car in their possession for any length of time.*" (emphasis supplied)

Here, defendant reveals that he conceives as an essential element of the specific intent requisite for "robbery" that the wrongdoer must intend: (1) an advantageous relationship between himself and the property wrongfully taken, and (2) that such relationship be permanent rather than temporary.

Defendant's view is erroneous. The law evaluates the "animus furandi" of "robbery" in terms of the detriment projected to the legally protected interests of the owner rather than the benefits intended to accrue to the wrongdoer from his invasion of the rights of the owner. . . .

[M]any of the earlier decisions reveal language disagreements, as well as conflicts as to substance, concerning whether a defendant can be guilty of "robbery" without specifically intending a gain to himself (whether permanent or temporary), so-called "lucri causa." In the more recent cases, there is overwhelming consensus that "lucri causa" is not necessary. . . .

We now decide, in confirmatory clarification of the law of Maine, that "lucri causa" is not an essential element of the "animus furandi" of "robbery." . . . [T]he specific intent requisite for "robbery" is defined solely in terms of the injury projected to the interests of the property owner:—specific intent "to deprive permanently the owner of his property." . . .

The instant question thus becomes: on the hypothesis, arguendo, that defendant here actually intended to use the Prout automobile "only temporarily" (as he would need it to achieve a successful flight from the authorities), is defendant correct in his fundamental contention that this, *in itself*, negates, *as a matter of law*, specific intent of defendant to deprive permanently the owner of his property? We answer that defendant's claim is erroneous.

Concretely illustrative of the point that a wrongdoer may intend to use wrongfully taken property "only temporarily" and yet, without contradiction, intend that the owner be deprived of his property permanently is the case of a defendant who proposes to use the property only for a short time and then to destroy it. At the opposite pole, and excluding (as a matter of law) specific intent to deprive permanently the owner of his property, is the case of a defendant who intends to make a temporary use of the property and then by his own act to return the property to its owner. Between these two extremes can lie various situations in which the legal characterization of the wrongdoer's intention, as assessed by the criterion of whether it is a specific intent to deprive permanently the owner of his property, will be more or less clear and raise legal problems of varying difficulty.

In these intermediate situations a general guiding principle may be developed through recognition that a "taking" of property is *by definition* "temporary" only if the possession, or control, effected by the taking is relinquished. Hence, measured by the correct criterion of the impact upon the interests of the owner, the wrongdoer's "animus furandi" is fully explored for its true legal significance only if the investigation of the wrongdoer's state of mind extends beyond his anticipated *retention* of possession and includes an inquiry into his contemplated manner of *relinquishing* possession, or control, of the property wrongfully taken.

On this approach, it has been held that when a defendant takes the tools of another person with intent to use them temporarily and then to leave them wherever it may be that he finishes with his work, the fact-finder is justified in the conclusion that defendant had specific intent to deprive the owner permanently of his property. . . .

Similarly, it has been decided that a defendant who wrongfully takes the property of another intending to use it for a short time and then to relinquish possession, or control, in a manner leaving to chance whether the owner recovers his property is correctly held specifically to intend that the owner be deprived permanently of his property.

The rationale underlying these decisions is that to negate, as a matter of law, the existence of specific intent to deprive permanently the owner of his property, a wrongful taker of the property of another must have in mind not only that his retention of possession, or control, will be "temporary" but also that when he will relinquish the possession, or control, he will do it in some manner (whatever, particularly, it will be) he regards as having affirmative tendency toward getting the property returned to its owner. In the absence of such thinking by the defendant, his state of mind is fairly characterized as *indifference* should the owner *never* recover his property; and such indifference by a wrongdoer who is the moving force separating an owner from his property is appropriately regarded as his "willingness" that the owner *never* regain his property. In this sense, the wrongdoer may appropriately be held to entertain specific intent that the deprivation to the owner be permanent. . . .

On this basis, the evidence in the present case clearly presented a jury question as to defendant's specific intent. Although defendant may have stated to the owner, Prout, that defendant

> "would take care of . . . [the automobile] and see [that] . . . [Prout] got it back as soon as possible,"

defendant himself testified that

> "[i]n my mind it was just to get out of the area. . . . Just get out of the area and leave the car and get under cover somewhere."

This idea to "leave the car" and "get under cover somewhere" existed in defendant's mind as part of an uncertainty about where it would happen. Because defendant was ". . . sort of desperate during the whole day," he had not "really formulated any plans about destination."

Such testimony of defendant, together with other evidence that defendant had already utterly abandoned another vehicle (the station wagon) in desperation, plainly warranted a jury conclusion that defendant's facilely uttered statements to Prout were empty words, and it was defendant's true state of mind to use Prout's Chevelle and abandon it in whatever manner might happen to meet the circumstantial exigencies of defendant's predicament—without defendant's having any thought that the relinquishment of the possession was to be in a manner having some affirmative tendency to help in the owner's recovery of his property. On this finding the jury was warranted in a conclusion that defendant was indifferent should the owner, Prout, *never* have back his automobile and, therefore, had specific intent that the owner be deprived permanently of his property.

Appeal denied.

Case Questions

1. What must a wrongful taker of property do to avoid legal responsibility for having specific intent to deprive the owner permanently of his property?
2. Does a wrongful taker of property have specific intent if the taker does not intend to keep the property for any particular period of time?

The Model Penal Code recognizes four categories of intent. To be criminally culpable, a person must act purposely, knowingly, recklessly, or negligently (see Figure 8-2).

A person acts *purposely* when he or she has a conscious desire to produce a prohibited result or harm, such as when one person strikes another in order to injure the other person.

MODEL PENAL CODE
Official Draft, 1985

Copyright 1985 by The American Law Institute.
Reprinted with the permission of The American Law Institute.

Section 2.02   General Requirements of Culpability

*   *   *

(2) *Kinds of Culpability Defined.*

(a) *Purposely.*

A person acts purposely with respect to a material element of an offense when:

(i)   if the element involves the nature of his conduct or a result thereof, it is his conscious object to engage in conduct of that nature or to cause such a result; and

(ii)   if the element involves the attendant circumstances, he is aware of the existence of such circumstances or he believes or hopes that they exist.

(b) *Knowingly.*

A person acts knowingly with respect to a material element of an offense when:

(i)   if the element involves the nature of his conduct or the attendant circumstances, he is aware that his conduct is of that nature or that such circumstances exist; and

(ii)   if the element involves a result of his conduct, he is aware that it is practically certain that his conduct will cause such a result.

(c) *Recklessly.*

A person acts recklessly with respect to a material element of an offense when he consciously disregards a substantial and unjustifiable risk that the material element exists or will result from his conduct. The risk must be of such a nature and degree that, considering the nature and purpose of the actor's conduct and the circumstances known to him, its disregard involves a gross deviation from the standard of conduct that a law-abiding person would observe in the actor's situation.

(d) *Negligently.*

A person acts negligently with respect to a material element of an offense when he should be aware of a substantial and unjustifiable risk that the material element exists or will result from his conduct. The risk must be of such a nature and degree that the actor's failure to perceive it, considering the nature and purpose of his conduct and the circumstances known to him, involves a gross deviation from the standard of care that a reasonable person would observe in the actor's situation.

FIGURE 8-2   Model Penal Code Section 2.02

A person acts *knowingly* when he or she is aware that a prohibited result or harm is very likely to occur, but nevertheless does not consciously intend the specific consequences that result from the act. If a person sets a building on fire, the person may be aware that it is very likely that people inside will be injured, and yet hopes that the people escape and that only the building is burned.

A person acts *recklessly* when he or she consciously disregards the welfare of others and creates a significant and unjustifiable risk. The risk has to be one that no law-abiding person would have consciously undertaken or created. A driver acts recklessly if he or she consciously takes his or her eyes off the road to take care of a crying infant, is aware that this conduct creates risks for other drivers and pedestrians, and is willing to expose others to jeopardy.

As seen in the common law approach, negligence involves unconscious risk creation. A driver acts *negligently* if he or she unconsciously takes his or her eyes off the road to take care of a crying infant, is unaware that this conduct creates substantial and unjustifiable risks for other drivers and pedestrians, and yet has not acted reasonably while operating a motor vehicle.

Strict Liability

A *strict liability* offense represents a major exception to the requirement that there be a concurrence between the criminal act and criminal intent. In such offenses, the offender poses a generalized threat to society at large. Examples include a speeding driver, a manufacturer who fails to comply with pure food and drug rules, or a liquor store owner who sells alcohol to minors. With respect to such *mala prohibita* offenses, the legislature may provide that the offender is strictly liable. The prosecution need only prove the *actus reus* to convict the accused; there is no intent element.

Vicarious Liability

Criminal law recognizes two conditions under which individuals and groups can be held criminally liable for actions committed by other people. Employers can be held responsible for the acts of their employees that occur within the course and scope of employment. For example, if a bartender illegally sells to minors, the bartender's employer (as well as the bartender) can be prosecuted. *Vicarious liability* helps to impress on employers the importance of insisting that employees comply with legal requirements. However, an employer can be held vicariously liable only for strict liability offenses. In addition, people convicted vicariously can only be subject to a fine or forfeiture.

Corporations can also be held vicariously liable for criminal acts, if employees authorized to act for the corporation commit criminal acts to enhance corporate profits. Such crimes might include price fixing, stock misrepresentation, theft, violations of environmental laws or the National Pure Food and Drug Act, and fraud. Corporations have even been indicted for murder. The punishment options for corporations are limited, however. The law permits the imposition of fines, but these are often inadequate in size, and it is obvious that corporations cannot go to jail.

Causation

There are some criminal offenses that require proof that the defendant's conduct caused a given result. In a homicide case, for example, the prosecution must prove that the defendant's conduct caused death. To be convicted of an assault, the defendant's actions must have caused the victim to fear an impending battery. In a battery, the defendant's conduct must have caused a harmful or offensive touching. In contrast, offenses such as perjury, reckless driving, larceny, and burglary criminalize conduct irrespective of whether any actual harm results.

The prosecution must establish *causation* beyond a reasonable doubt whenever it is an element of a crime. A key to establishing causation is the legal concept of "proximate cause." Criminal liability only attaches to conduct that is determined to be the proximate or legal cause of the harmful result. This includes both direct and indirect causation. Often the legal cause is the direct cause of harm. If the defendant strikes the victim with his fist and injures him, the defendant is the direct cause of the injury. If the defendant sets in motion a chain of events that eventually results in harm, the defendant may be the indirect cause of the harm.

Proximate cause is a flexible concept. It permits fact-finders to sort through various factual causes and determine whom should be found to be legally responsible for the result. In addition, an accused is only responsible for the reasonably foreseeable consequences that follow from his or her acts. The law provides, for example, that an accused is not responsible for consequences that follow the intervention of a new, and independent, causal force. The next case, *Commonwealth v. Berggren*, illustrates the legal principle that an accused is only responsible for consequences that are reasonably foreseeable.

Commonwealth v. Berggren
496 N.E.2d 660
Supreme Judicial Court of Massachusetts
August 26, 1986

Lynch, Justice

The defendant is awaiting trial before a jury of six in the Barnstable Division of the District Court on a complaint charging him with motor vehicle homicide by negligent opera-

tion of a motor vehicle so as to endanger public safety (G.L. c. 90, § 24G(*b*) [1984 ed.]). The District Court judge granted the joint motion to "report an issue" to the Appeals Court pursuant to Mass.R. Crim.P. 34, 378 Mass. 905 (1979). We transferred the report here on our own motion.

We summarize the stipulated facts. On March 29, 1983, about 8:28 P.M., Patrolman Michael Aselton of the Barnstable police department was on radar duty at Old Stage

Road in Centerville. He saw the defendant's motorcycle speed by him and commenced pursuit in a marked police cruiser with activated warning devices. The defendant "realized a cruiser was behind him but did not stop because he was 'in fear of his license.'" The pursuit lasted roughly six miles through residential, commercial and rural areas. At one point, the defendant had gained a 100-yard lead and crossed an intersection, continuing north. The patrolman's cruiser approached the intersection at about "76 m.p.h. minimal" and passed over a crown in the roadway which caused the patrolman to brake. The wheels locked and the cruiser slid 170 yards, hitting a tree. Patrolman Aselton died as a result of the impact. The defendant had no idea of the accident which had occurred behind him. "No other vehicles were in any way involved in the causation of the accident." The stipulation further states that the decision to terminate a high speed chase "is to be made by the officer's commanding officer." No such decision to terminate the pursuit had been made at the time of the accident. The Barnstable police department determined that patrolman Aselton died in the line of duty.

We understand the report to raise the question whether the stipulated facts would be sufficient to support a conviction of motor vehicle homicide by negligent operation under G.L. c. 90, § 24G(*b*). We hold that it is.

A finding of ordinary negligence suffices to establish a violation of § 24G.

The Appeals Court has observed: "It would seem to follow that if the jury's task is to find ordinary negligence, then the appropriate principles of causation to apply are those which have been explicated in a large body of decisions and texts treating the subject in the context of the law of torts." . . .

The defendant argues, however, that the "causation theory properly applied in criminal cases is not that of proximate cause." . . .

If this theory has any application in this Commonwealth, . . . it does not apply to a charge of negligent vehicular homicide. We adopt instead the suggestion of the Appeals Court and conclude that the appropriate standard of causation to be applied in a negligent vehicular homicide case under § 24G is that employed in tort law.

The defendant essentially contends that since he was one hundred yards ahead of the patrolman's cruiser and was unaware of the accident, his conduct cannot be viewed as directly traceable to the resulting death of the patrolman. The defendant, however, was speeding on a motorcycle at night on roads which his attorney at oral argument before this court characterized as "winding" and "narrow." He knew the patrolman was following him, but intentionally did not stop and continued on at high speed for six miles. From the fact that the defendant was "in fear of his license," it may reasonably be inferred that he was aware that he had committed at least one motor vehicle violation. Under these circumstances, the defendant's acts were hardly a remote link in the chain of events leading to the patrolman's death. . . . The officer's pursuit was certainly foreseeable, as was, tragically, the likelihood of serious injury or death to the defendant himself, to the patrolman, or to some third party. The patrolman's death resulted from the "natural and continuous sequence" of events caused by the defendant's actions. . . .

We conclude that the proper standard of causation for this offense is the standard of proximate cause enunciated in the law of torts. We further conclude that, should the jury find the facts as stipulated in the instant case, and should the only contested element of the offense of motor vehicle homicide by negligent operation be that of causation, these facts would support a conviction under G.L. c.90, §24G(*b*).

Report answered.

Case Questions

1. Explain the difference between factual and legal causation, based on the facts of this case.

 Berggren claims to have been unaware of the collision involving the officer's cruiser and tree and he insists that he never intended that the officer die. Why should this defendant be criminally responsible for causing the death of the officer?

Inchoate Crime

The criminal law recognizes society's need to protect itself from dangerous people who have not yet completed their intended criminal acts. Thus the law defines the preparatory activities of solicitation, attempt, and conspiracy as criminal offenses called inchoate crimes.

Solicitation is a specific intent crime committed by a person who asks, hires, or encourages another to commit a crime. It makes no difference whether the solicited person accepts the offer or not; the solicitation itself constitutes the *actus reus* for this offense. All jurisdictions treat solicitations to commit a felony as a crime, and some jurisdictions also criminalize solicitations to commit a misdemeanor.

The crime of *attempt* is committed by a person who has the intent to commit a substantive criminal offense and does an act that tends to corroborate the intent, under circumstances that do not result in the completion of the substantive crime. For example, assume that person Y intends to commit armed robbery of a bank. Y dresses in clothing that disguises his appearance, wears a police scanner on his belt, carries a revolver in his coat pocket, wears gloves, and drives to a bank. Y approaches the front door with one hand in his pocket and the other over his face. When he attempts to open the front door he discovers that the door is locked and that it is just after the bank's closing time. Y quickly returns to his car, leaves the bank, and is subsequently apprehended by police. Y had specific intent to rob the bank, and took many substantial steps to realize that intent; however, he was unable to complete the crime because of his poor timing. Y has committed the crime of attempted robbery.

The crime of *conspiracy* is committed when two or more people combine to commit a criminal act. The essential *actus reus* of conspiracy is the agreement to commit a criminal act, coupled with the commission of some overt act by one or more of the coconspirators that tends to implement the agreement. The prosecution can prove the existence of an unlawful agreement either expressly or inferentially. The crime of conspiracy is designed to protect society from group criminality. Organized groups bent on criminal activity pose a greater threat to the public than do the isolated acts of individuals. Conspiracy is a separate crime, and unlike attempt, does not merge into the completed substantive offense. Thus a person can be prosecuted both for murder and conspiracy to murder. If a member of the conspiracy wants to abandon the joint enterprise, he or she must notify every other coconspirator. Conspiracy is a powerful prosecutorial weapon.

The Racketeer Influenced and Corrupt Organization Act

In 1970, the federal government enacted a criminal statute called the Racketeer Influenced and Corrupt Organization Act (RICO). This statute and its state counterparts have been very important weapons in combatting organized criminal activity such as drug trafficking, the theft and fencing of property, syndicated gambling, and extortion. A very broad statute, RICO applies to all people and organizations, whether public or private. It focuses on patterns of racketeering activity, the use of money obtained from racketeering to acquire legitimate businesses, and the collection of unlawful debt. The act defines racketeering activity as involving eight state crimes and twenty-four federal offenses called the predicate acts. A person who has committed two or more of the predicate acts within a ten-year period has engaged in a pattern of racketeering activity. People convicted under RICO can be punished by the forfeiture of real and personal property acquired with money obtained through racketeering, fines, and up to twenty years' incarceration. Civil penalties, including the award of treble damages, can also be recovered.

Defenses

Because of the constitutional presumption of innocence, criminal defendants are not required to prove anything at trial. If the government cannot prove the defendant's guilt beyond a reasonable doubt with its own evidence, the law provides that the accused is not guilty.

One defense strategy, is therefore, to establish reasonable doubt exclusively through the use of the government's own witnesses. It is possible to challenge the credibility of prosecution witnesses on the grounds that their testimony is unbelievable. The defense attorney, for example, may through cross-examination be able to show that a prosecution witness was too far away to have clearly seen what he/she testified to have observed, to be biased against the defendant, or to not really be certain as to the identity of the attacker as was suggested on direct examination. The defense can also challenge the way in which the police obtained evidence by alleging that the police did not comply with the requirements of *Miranda v. Arizona* when they interrogated the defendant, or violated the requirements of the Fourth Amendment when they conducted a search of the defendant's home. Where the prosecution's evidence is insufficient to establish elements of the crime, the defense attorney can move to dismiss, and it is always possible to defend by arguing that the level of *mens rea* required for conviction was not proven or that the prosecution in some other respect has failed its burden of proving the defendant's guilt beyond a reasonable doubt.

Sometimes an accused can call witnesses to testify that the defendant was somewhere other than at the scene of the crime on the date and time that the offense allegedly occurred—thereby raising an *alibi* defense. Rarely, an accused will present a *good character defense.* When this occurs, a defendant, for example, who is charged with a crime of violence could introduce reputation or opinion testimony that the defendant is nonviolent and peace-loving. From this evidence the defense attorney could argue that the defendant's character is so sterling that he would never have committed the crime with which he was charged.

The law gradually began to recognize that in some situations it would be unfair to impose criminal responsibility on a criminal defendant because of the presence of factors that legitimately mitigated, justified, or excused the defendant's conduct. These special circumstances came to be known as *affirmative defenses.* The defendant always bears the burden of production with respect to affirmative defenses. Unless the defense affirmatively introduces some evidence tending to establish such a defense, the court will refuse to give the corresponding instruction. Because affirmative defenses do not negate any element of the crime(s) charged by the government, states are constitutionally permitted to decide for themselves whether or not the defendant should bear the burden of persuasion with respect to affirmative defenses. Although some states require the prosecution to disprove affirmative defenses beyond a reasonable doubt, many other jurisdictions refuse that burden and require that the defendant carry the burden of persuasion regarding such defenses. Jurisdictions differ as to the availability of particular defenses and as to their definitions. Affirmative defenses are often further subdivided into *justification defenses* and *excuse defenses.*

Justification Defenses

Criminal laws are often written in general terms and without limitations and exceptions. It is understood that exceptions will be made, on a case-by-case basis, where it becomes apparent that a defendant was justified in his/her actions given the then existing circumstances. Recognized justification defenses often include *self-defense, defense of others, defense of property, necessity/choice of evils,* and *duress/coercion.* In each of these defenses the accused admits to having committed the act which is alleged by the prosecution; however, in each instance the accused claims to have acted correctly.

The law recognizes an individual is justified in defending his or her person and property and others. A person is entitled to use reasonable force in *self-defense* to protect oneself from death or serious bodily harm. Obviously, the amount of force that can be used in defense depends upon the type of force being used by the attacker. An attack that threatens neither death nor serious bodily harm does not warrant the use of deadly force in defense. When the attack has been repelled, the defender does not have the right to continue using force to obtain revenge. Although the common law required one to "retreat to the wall" before using deadly force in self-defense, the modern rule permits a person to remain on his or her property and to use reasonable force (including the reasonable use of deadly force in *defense of others* who are entitled to act in self-defense). However, as we saw in *Katko v. Briney,* in Chapter 1, it is never justifiable to use force that could cause death or serious bodily injury solely in *defense of property.* *Necessity* (also known as the *choice of evils* defense), traces its lineage to the English common law. Over time it became apparent that in some limited circumstances, committing a criminal act would actually result in a less harmful outcome than would occur were the accused to strictly adhere to the requirements of the law. To be successful with this defense, the accused must be able to establish that there was no reasonable, legal alternative to violating the law.

 INTERNET TIP ───────────────────────────

In November of 2002, a New Jersey appellate court ruled that a defendant was entitled to a necessity/choice of evils instruction in a drunk driving prosecution. You can read this case on the textbook's website.

Excuse Defenses

In excuse defenses, the defendant admits to having acted unlawfully, but argues that no criminal responsibility should be imposed, given the particular circumstances accompanying the act. Examples of this type of affirmative defense include *duress, insanity,* and *intoxication.*

A person who commits a criminal act only because he or she was presently being threatened with death or serious bodily injury may assert the defense called *duress/coercion.* This defense is based on the theory that the person who committed the criminal act was not exercising free will. Most states do not allow the use of this defense in murder cases. In addition, coercion is difficult to establish. It fails, as we see in the next case, if there was a reasonable alternative to committing the crime, such as running away or contacting the police.

United States v. Scott
901 F.2d 871
U.S. Court of Appeals, Tenth Circuit
April 20, 1990

Seay, District Judge

Appellant, Bill Lee Scott, was found guilty by a jury and convicted of one count of conspiracy to manufacture methamphetamine in violation of 21 U.S.C. § 2, and one count of manufacturing methamphetamine in violation of 21 U.S.C. § 841(a)(1), and 18 U.S.C. § 2. Scott appeals his convictions contending that he was denied a fair trial when the dis-

trict court refused to instruct the jury on the defense of coercion. We disagree, and therefore affirm the judgment of the district court.

I

Between the middle of August 1987, and the early part of January 1988, Scott made approximately six trips to Scientific Chemical, a chemical supply company in Humble, Texas. Scott made these trips at the request of co-defendant Mark Morrow. These trips resulted in Scott purchasing various quantities of precursor chemicals and laboratory paraphernalia from Scientific Chemical. Some trips resulted in Scott taking possession of the items purchased, other trips resulted in the items being shipped to designated points to be picked up and delivered at a future date. These chemicals and laboratory items were purchased to supply methamphetamine laboratories operated by Morrow in New Mexico with the assistance of Silas Rivera and codefendants George Tannehill, Jerry Stokes, and Robert Stokes.

Scott first became acquainted with Morrow when Morrow helped him move from Portales, New Mexico, to Truth or Consequences, New Mexico, in late July or early August 1987. . . . Shortly thereafter, Morrow became aware that Scott was going to Houston, Texas, to sell some mercury and Morrow asked Scott if he could pick up some items from Scientific Chemical. . . . Scott made the trip to Scientific Chemical and purchased the items Morrow requested. . . . Scott subsequently made approximately five other trips to Scientific Chemical at Morrow's request to purchase various quantities of precursor chemicals and assorted labware. . . . During the course of one trip on August 31, 1987, Scott was stopped by Drug Enforcement Administration agents after he had purchased chemicals from Scientific Chemical. . . . The agents seized the chemicals Scott had purchased as well as $10,800 in U.S. currency and a fully loaded .38 Smith and Wesson. . . . Scott was not arrested at that time. . . . Scott, however, was subsequently indicted along with the codefendants after the seizure of large quantities of methamphetamine and precursor chemicals from a laboratory site in Portales in January 1988.

At trial Scott claimed that his purchase of the chemicals and labware on behalf of Morrow was the result of a well-established fear that Morrow would kill him or members of his family if he did not act as Morrow had directed. Scott further claimed that he did not have any reasonable opportunity to escape the harm threatened by Morrow. To support this defense of coercion Scott testified on his own behalf as to the nature and circumstances of the threats. Scott testified that approximately one month after the August 31, 1987, trip Morrow called him at his home in Truth or Consequences and talked him into a meeting in Houston to "get that straightened out." It was Scott's contention that Morrow might not have believed that the money and chemicals had been seized and that Morrow might have thought that he had merely kept the money. . . .

After the trip to Houston and Scientific Chemical to confirm Scott's story about the seizure of the chemicals and cash, Morrow contacted Scott at Scott's daughter's house in Portales to have Scott make another trip to Scientific Chemical to make another purchase. . . . After Scott declined to make another trip, Morrow responded by stating that Scott would not want something to happen to his daughter or her house. . . . Scott thereafter made the trip for Morrow. . . .

Approximately one week later, Morrow again came by Scott's daughter's house and wanted Scott to make another trip. . . . At some point during this discussion they decided to go for a ride in separate vehicles. . . . After travelling some distance, they both stopped their vehicles and pulled off to the side of the road. . . . Morrow pulled out a machine gun and two banana clips and emptied the clips at bottles and rocks. . . . Morrow stated "you wouldn't want to be in front of that thing would you?" and "you wouldn't want any of your family in front of that, would you?" . . . Scott responded negatively to Morrow's statements and thereafter made another trip to Scientific Chemical for Morrow. . . . On another occasion, Scott testified that Morrow threatened him by stating that he had better haul the chemicals if he knew what was good for him. . . .

Scott testified that Morrow not only knew his adult daughter living in Portales, but that he knew his wife and another daughter who were living in Truth or Consequences and that Morrow had been to the residence in

Truth or Consequences. . . . Scott testified that he made these trips for Morrow because he feared for the safety of his family in light of the confrontations he had with Morrow. . . . Scott stated he had no doubt that Morrow would have carried out his threats. . . . Scott was aware of information linking Morrow to various murders. . . . Scott further testified that he did not go to the police with any of this information concerning Morrow because he had gone to them before on other matters and they did nothing. . . . Further, Scott believed that Morrow had been paying a DEA agent in Lubbock, Texas, for information regarding investigations. . . .

On cross-examination Scott testified that all of Morrow's threats were verbal, . . . that he saw Morrow only a few times between August 1987 and January 1988, . . . that he had an acquaintance by the name of Bill King who was a retired California Highway Patrolman living in Truth or Consequences, . . . and that he could have found a law enforcement official to whom he could have reported the actions of Morrow. . . .

II

A coercion or duress defense requires the establishment of three elements: (1) an immediate threat of death or serious bodily injury, (2) a well-grounded fear that the threat will be carried out, and (3) no reasonable opportunity to escape the threatened harm. . . .

Scott proffered a coercion instruction to the district court in conformity with the above elements. Scott . . . contended that the testimony before the court concerning coercion was sufficient to raise an issue for the jury and that a coercion instruction should be given. The district court found that Scott had failed to meet his threshold burden as to all three elements of a coercion defense. Accordingly, the district court refused to give an instruction on the defense of coercion.

Scott contends that the district court committed reversible error by substituting its judgment as to the weight of his coercion defense rather than allowing the jury to decide the issue. Scott maintains that he presented sufficient evidence to place in issue the defense of coercion and that it was error for the district court to usurp the role of the jury in weighing the evidence. We disagree and find that the district court acted properly in requiring Scott to satisfy a threshold showing of a coercion defense, and in finding the evidence insufficient to warrant the giving of a coercion instruction. In doing so, we find the evidence clearly lacking as to the third element for a coercion defense—absence of any reasonable opportunity to escape the threatened harm.

Only after a defendant has properly raised a coercion defense is he entitled to an instruction requiring the prosecution to prove beyond a reasonable doubt that he was not acting under coercion when he performed the act or acts charged. . . .

The evidence introduced must be sufficient as to *all* elements of the coercion defense before the court will instruct the jury as to such defense. . . . If the evidence is lacking as to any element of the coercion defense the trial court may properly disallow the defense as a matter of law and refuse to instruct the jury as to coercion. . . . Consequently, a defendant who fails to present sufficient evidence to raise a triable issue of fact concerning the absence of any reasonable opportunity to escape the threatened harm is not entitled to an instruction on the defense of coercion. . . .

The evidence in this case as to Scott's ability to escape the threatened harm wholly failed to approach the level necessary for the giving of a coercion instruction. Scott's involvement with Morrow covered a period of time in excess of one hundred twenty-five days. Scott's personal contact with Morrow was extremely limited during this time. Scott had countless opportunities to contact law enforcement authorities or escape the perceived threats by Morrow during this time. Scott made no attempt to contact law enforcement officials regarding Morrow's activities. In fact, Scott even failed to take advantage of his acquaintance, King, a retired law enforcement official, to seek his assistance in connection with Morrow's threats and activities. Scott's failure to avail himself of the readily accessible alternative of contacting law enforcement officials is persuasive evidence of the hollow nature of Scott's claimed coercion defense. . . . Clearly, the record establishes that Scott had at his disposal a reasonable legal alternative to undertaking the acts on behalf of Morrow. . . .

Morrow did not accompany Scott when he made the purchases nor was there any evidence that Scott was under surveillance by Morrow. In fact, Scott's contact with Morrow was limited and he admitted he saw Morrow only a few times during the course of his involvement on behalf of Morrow between August 1987 and January 1988. Based on all of these circumstances, the district court was correct in finding that Scott had failed to establish that he had no reasonable opportunity to escape the threatened harm by Morrow.

III

In conclusion, we find that Scott failed to present sufficient evidence to establish that he had no reasonable opportunity to escape the harm threatened by Morrow. Accordingly, the district court properly refused to instruct the jury as to the defense of coercion. We affirm the judgment of the district court.

Case Questions

1. What must a defendant do to be entitled to a jury instruction on the defense of coercion?
2. Given the facts of this case, why did the trial court refuse to give the instruction?

The law also recognizes that occasionally police officers induce innocent people to commit crimes. When this occurs, the person so induced can raise an affirmative defense called *entrapment.* If an officer provides a person who is previously disposed to commit a criminal act with the opportunity to do so, that is not entrapment. If, however, an officer placed the notion of criminal wrongdoing in the defendant's mind, and that person was previously undisposed to commit the act, entrapment has occurred and the charges will be dismissed. In entrapment cases, the defendant admits to having committed a criminal act, but the law relieves him or her of criminal responsibility in order to deter police officers from resorting to this tactic in the future.

Intoxication is recognized as a defense in limited circumstances. Most jurisdictions distinguish *voluntary intoxication,* which is generally not a defense from involuntary intoxication, which generally is. A person who commits a crime while voluntarily intoxicated will only have a defense if the intoxication is quite severe. A defendant cannot be convicted of a specific intent crime if the intoxication was so severe that the person was incapable of forming specific intent.

Involuntary intoxication, however, completely relieves a defendant of all criminal responsibility. This could occur, for example, when a defendant inadvertently ingests incompatible medicines.

Insanity is one of the least used and most controversial defenses. A defendant who claims insanity admits to having committed the act, but denies criminal responsibility for that act. Because insanity is a legal and not a medical term, jurisdictions use different tests to define insanity. The *M'Naghten Rule* specifies that a defendant is not guilty if he or she had a diseased mind at the time of the act and was unable to distinguish right from wrong or was unaware of the nature and quality of his or her act due to a diseased mind. The *Irresistible Impulse Test* specifies that a defendant is not guilty if he or she knows that an act is wrong and is aware of the nature and quality of the act, but cannot refrain from committing the act. The Model Penal code specifies that a defendant is not criminally responsible for his or her conduct due to either mental disease or defect and if the defendant lacked substantial capacity to understand its criminality or comply with legal requirements. The states of Idaho, Utah, and Montana have elected not to recognize insanity as a defense.

CRIMINAL PROCEDURE

Criminal procedure is that area of the law that deals with the administration of criminal justice, from the initial investigation of a crime and the arrest of a suspect through trial, sentence, and release.

The goal of criminal justice is to protect society from antisocial activity without sacrificing individual rights, justice, and fair play. The procedures used to apprehend and prosecute alleged criminal offenders must comply with the requirements of the law. One objective of using the adversary system involving prosecutors and defense attorneys is to ensure that procedural justice is accorded the defendant. The judge umpires the confrontation between the litigants and tries to ensure that both parties receive a fair trial—one that accords with the requirements of the substantive and procedural law. The judge or jury determines the guilt or innocence of the accused by properly evaluating the facts presented in open court. Ideally, the truth emerges from adversarial proceedings conducted in a manner consistent with constitutional guarantees. (See Figure 8-3.)

The constitutional limitations on the way governmental officials procedurally go about investigating criminal offenses and prosecuting alleged criminal offenders are primarily contained in the very general statements of the Fourth, Fifth, Sixth, Eighth, and Fourteenth amendments to the U.S. Constitution. The U.S. Supreme Court as well as the other federal and state courts have played a significant role in determining what these amendments actually mean in practice. Does the Constitution mandate that arrested persons who are indigent be provided a court-appointed attorney? Does the Constitution require that twelve-person juries be convened in criminal cases, or are six-person juries sufficient?

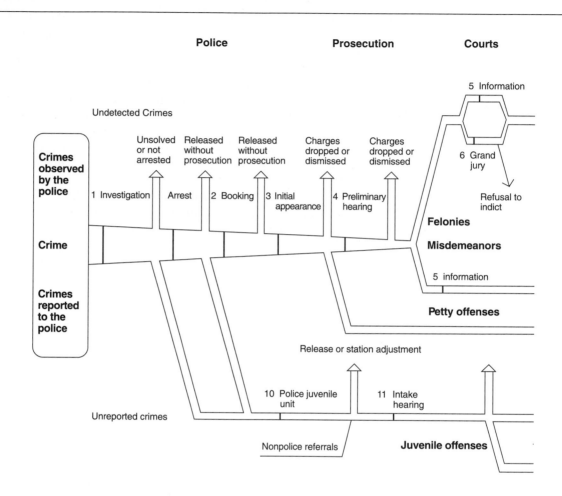

Police   **Prosecution**   **Courts**

5 Information

Undetected Crimes

Unsolved or not arrested | Released without prosecution | Released without prosecution | Charges dropped or dismissed | Charges dropped or dismissed

6 Grand jury

Crimes observed by the police

1 Investigation   Arrest   2 Booking   3 Initial appearance   4 Preliminary hearing

Refusal to indict

Felonies

Crime

Misdemeanors

5 information

Crimes reported to the police

Petty offenses

Release or station adjustment

10 Police juvenile unit   11 Intake hearing

Unreported crimes

Nonpolice referrals   **Juvenile offenses**

1 May continue until trial.

2 Administrative record of arrest. First step of which, temporary release on bail, may be available.

3 Before magistrate, commissioner, or justice of peace. Formal notice of charge, advice of rights. Bail set. Summary trials for petty offenses usually conducted here without further processing.

4 Preliminary testing of evidence against

defendant. Charge may be reduced. No separate preliminary hearing for misdemeanors in some systems.

5 Charge filed by prosecutor on basis of informatio submitted by police or citizens. Alternative to grand jury indictment; often used in felonies, almost always in misdemeanors.

A simple yet comprehensive view of the movement of cases through the criminal justice system. Procedures in individual jurisdictions may vary from pattern shown here. Differing widths of lines indicate relative volumes of cases disposed of at various points in system, but these are only suggestive, since no nationwide data of the sort exist.

FIGURE 8-3   General View of the Criminal Justice System

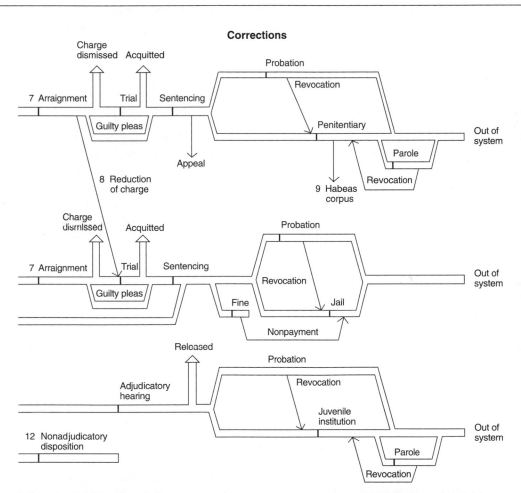

Corrections

Charge dismissed   Acquitted

7 Arraignment   Trial   Sentencing

Guilty pleas

Probation

Revocation

Penitentiary

Parole

Revocation

Out of system

Appeal

8 Reduction of charge

9 Habeas corpus

Charge dismissed   Acquitted

Probation

7 Arraignment   Trial   Sentencing

Guilty pleas

Revocation

Fine   Jail

Nonpayment

Out of system

Released

Adjudicatory hearing

Probation

Revocation

Juvenile institution

Parole

Revocation

Out of system

12 Nonadjudicatory disposition

6 Review whether government evidence is sufficient to justify trial. Some states have no grand jury system; others seldom use it.

7 Appearance for plea: defendant elects trial by judge or jury (if available); counsel for indigent usually appointed here.

8 Charge may be reduced at any time before trial in return for guilty plea or for other reasons.

9 Challenge on constitutional grounds to legality of detection. May be sought at any point in process.

10 Police often hold informal hearings and dismiss or adjust many cases without further processing.

11 Probation officer decides desirability of further court action.

12 Welfare agency, social services, counseling, medical care, etc. for cases where adjudicatory handling not needed.

Source: The Challenge of Crime in a Free Society, The President's Commission on Law Enforcement and Administration of Justice (Washington, D.C., 1967).

Do defendants have a constitutional right to be convicted beyond a reasonable doubt by a unanimous jury, or can a guilty verdict be received that is supported by nine out of twelve jurors?

PROCEEDINGS PRIOR TO TRIAL

A criminal trial occurs only after several preliminary stages have been completed. Although there are some jurisdictional variations in the way these stages occur, some generalizations can be made. The "typical" criminal prosecution originates with a police investigation of a crime that has been either reported to officers or that officers have discovered through their own initiatives. This investigation establishes if there really was a crime committed, and if so, determines the identity and whereabouts of the offender. In their investigations, officers are limited by federal and state constitutional and statutory law: (1) They are only permitted to make arrests if they have sufficient evidence to constitute probable cause; (2) they are similarly limited in undertaking searches and seizures; and (3) they are limited in the way they conduct custodial interrogations and line-ups. The failure to follow correct procedures in the preliminary stages of a criminal case can result in the suppression of evidence and the dismissal of the charges filed against the accused. Violations of a defendant's constitutional rights can also result in a civil and/or criminal lawsuit against the responsible police officers.

Arrest

An arrest occurs when an officer takes someone into custody for the purpose of holding the person to answer a criminal charge. The arrest must be made in a reasonable manner, and the force employed must be reasonable in proportion to the circumstances and conduct of the party being arrested. The traditional rule was that police officers could make arrests in felonies based on probable cause, but officers were required to observe the commission of a misdemeanor offense in order to make a valid arrest. Today, many states have repealed the in presence requirement and permit officers to make arrests for both misdemeanors and felonies, based on probable cause. Probable cause means that the arresting officer has a well-grounded belief that the individual being arrested has committed, or is committing, an offense.

If police officers intend to make a routine felony arrest in the suspect's home, the U.S. Supreme Court requires that they first obtain an arrest warrant. An arrest warrant is an order issued by a judge, magistrate, or other judicial officer commanding the arresting officer to take an individual into custody and to bring the person before the court to answer criminal charges. Before the court will issue a warrant, a written complaint containing the name of the accused, or a description of the accused, must be filed. The complaint must be supported by affidavits and contain a description of the offense and the surrounding circumstances. A *warrant* is then issued if the court magistrate decides that (1) the evidence supports the belief that (2) probable cause exists to believe that (3) a crime has been committed and that (4) the suspect is the probable culprit. Many times, the complaining party does not have firsthand information and is relying on hearsay. The warrant may still be issued if the court believes that there is substantial basis for crediting it.

Some policing agencies, such as the FBI, make a large number of arrests based on warrants. Most arrests, however, are made without a warrant, as illustrated in the following *Draper* case. This case also explains what constitutes probable cause to arrest.

Draper v. United States
358 U.S. 307
U.S. Supreme Court
January 26, 1959

Mr. Justice Whittaker delivered the opinion of the Court.

The evidence offered at the hearing on the motion to suppress was not substantially disputed. It established that one Marsh, a federal narcotic agent with 29 years' experience, was stationed at Denver; that one Hereford had been engaged as a "special employee" of the Bureau of Narcotics at Denver for about six months, and from time to time gave information to Marsh regarding violations of the narcotic laws, for which Hereford was paid small sums of money, and that Marsh had always found the information given by Hereford to be accurate and reliable. On September 3, 1956, Hereford told Marsh that James Draper (petitioner) recently had taken up abode at a stated address in Denver and "was peddling narcotics to several addicts" in that city. Four days later, on September 7, Hereford told Marsh "that Draper had gone to Chicago the day before [September 6] by train [and] that he was going to bring back three ounces of heroin [and] that he would return to Denver either on the morning of the 8th of September or the morning of the 9th of September also by train." Hereford also gave

Marsh a detailed physical description of Draper and of the clothing he was wearing, and said that he would be carrying "a tan zipper bag" and habitually "walked real fast."

On the morning of September 8, Marsh and a Denver police officer went to the Denver Union Station and kept watch over all incoming trains from Chicago, but they did not see anyone fitting the description that Hereford had given. Repeating the process on the morning of September 9, they saw a person, having the exact physical attributes and wearing the precise clothing described by Hereford, alight from an incoming Chicago train and start walking "fast" toward the exit. He was carrying a tan zipper bag in his right hand and the left was thrust in his raincoat pocket. Marsh, accompanied by the police officer, overtook, stopped and arrested him. They then searched him and found the two "envelopes containing heroin" clutched in his left hand in his raincoat pocket, and found the syringe in the tan zipper bag. Marsh then took him (petitioner) into custody. Hereford died four days after the arrest and therefore did not testify at the hearing on the motion. . . . [T]he Narcotic Control Act of 1956 . . . provides in pertinent part:

> "The Commissioner . . . and agents, of the Bureau of Narcotics . . . may— . . .
> "(2) Make arrests without warrant for violations of any law of the United States relating to narcotic drugs . . . where the

violation is committed in the presence of the person making the arrest or where such person had reasonable grounds to believe that the person to be arrested has committed or is committing such a violation."

The crucial question for us then is whether knowledge of the related facts and circumstances gave Marsh "probable cause" within the meaning of the Fourth Amendment, and "reasonable grounds" . . . to believe that petitioner had committed or was committing a violation of the narcotic laws. If it did, the arrest, though without warrant, was lawful. . . .

Petitioner . . . contends (1) that the information given by Hereford to Marsh was "hearsay" and, because hearsay is not legally competent evidence in a criminal trial, could not legally have been considered, but should have been put out of mind by Marsh in assessing whether he had "probable cause" and "reasonable grounds" to arrest petitioner without a warrant, and (2) that, even if hearsay could lawfully have been considered, Marsh's information should be held insufficient to show "probable cause" and "reasonable grounds" to believe that petitioner had violated or was violating the narcotic laws and to justify his arrest without a warrant.

Considering the first contention, we find petitioner entirely in error. *Brinegar v. United States*, 338 U.S. 160, . . . has settled the question the other way. There, in a similar situation, the convict contended "that the factors relating to inadmissibility of the evidence [for] *purposes of proving guilt at the trial*, deprive[d] the evidence as a whole of sufficiency to show probable cause for the search. . . ." But this Court, rejecting that contention, said: "[T]he so-called distinction places a wholly unwarranted emphasis upon the criterion of admissibility in evidence, to prove the accused's guilt, of facts relied upon to show probable cause. The emphasis, we think, goes much too far in confusing and disregarding the dif-

ference between what is required to prove guilt in a criminal case and what is required to show probable cause for arrest or search. It approaches requiring (if it does not in practical effect require) proof sufficient to establish guilt in order to substantiate the existence of probable cause. There is a large difference between the two things to be proved [guilt and probable cause], as well as between the tribunals which determine them, and therefore a like difference in the *quanta* and modes of proof required to establish them." . . .

Nor can we agree with petitioner's second contention that Marsh's information was insufficient to show probable cause and reasonable grounds to believe that petitioner had violated or was violating the narcotic laws and to justify his arrest without a warrant. The information given to narcotic agent Marsh by "special employee" Hereford may have been hearsay to Marsh, but coming from one employed for that purpose and whose information had always been found accurate and reliable, it is clear that Marsh would have been derelict in his duties had he not pursued it. And when, in pursuing that information, he saw a man, having the exact physical attributes and wearing the precise clothing and carrying the tan zipper bag that Hereford had described, alight from one of the very trains from the very place stated by Hereford and start to walk at a "fast" pace toward the station exit, Marsh had personally verified every facet of the information given him by Hereford except whether the petitioner had accomplished his mission and had the three ounces of heroin on his person or in his bag. And surely, with every other bit of Hereford's information being thus personally verified, Marsh had "reasonable grounds" to believe that the remaining unverified bit of Hereford's information—that Draper would have the heroin with him—was likewise true.

"In dealing with probable cause . . . as the very name implies, we deal with probabilities. These are not technical; they are the factual and practical considerations of everyday life on which reasonable and prudent men, not legal technicians, act." *Brinegar v. United States*. Probable cause exists where "the facts and circumstances within . . . [the arresting officer's] knowledge and of which they had reasonably trustworthy information [are] sufficient in themselves to warrant a man of reasonable caution in the belief that" an offense has been or is being committed. . . .

We believe that, under the facts and circumstances here, Marsh had probable cause and reasonable grounds to believe that petitioner was committing a violation of the laws of the United States relating to narcotic drugs at the time he arrested him. The arrest was therefore lawful, and the subsequent search and seizure, having been made incident to that lawful arrest, were likewise valid. It follows that petitioner's motion to suppress was properly denied and that the seized heroin was competent evidence lawfully received at the trial.

Affirmed.

Case Questions

1. Why did the Supreme Court allow hearsay evidence to be used to establish probable cause, when it would have been inadmissible at trial?
2. Do you believe that an officer who has time to obtain an arrest warrant should have to do so in lieu of making a warrantless arrest in a public place?

Custodial Interrogation

Part of the criminal investigative procedure involves questioning suspects with the aim of obtaining confessions and disclosures of crimes.

The privilege against self-incrimination applies to this questioning done outside the courtroom as well as at the trial. In general, only statements that are voluntarily made by a suspect are admissible. That is, statements must be the product of free and rational choice. The statements cannot be the result of promises, threats, inducements, or physical abuse. However, the U.S. Supreme Court has ruled that confessions that are neither voluntary nor intelligently made can in some instances be admissible if the coercion amounts to "harmless error."

In the case of *Miranda v. Arizona*, 384 U.S. 436 (1966), the Supreme Court required that people being interrogated while in police custody must first be informed in clear and unequivocal language that they have the right to remain silent, that anything they say can and will be used against them in court, that they have the right to consult with a lawyer and to have a lawyer with them during interrogation, and that they have the right to an appointed lawyer to represent them if they are indigent. If police officers conduct a custodial interrogation without giving these warnings, they violate an accused's Fifth Amendment privilege against self-incrimination. In such a situation, a court may suppress the prosecution's use of the accused's statement at trial to prove his or her guilt. Such statements may, however, be admissible at trial to impeach the credibility of a testifying defendant.

The protections afforded by the *Miranda* warnings may be waived in certain circumstances. The standard is whether a defendant in fact knowingly and voluntarily waived his or her rights.

The *Miranda* decision was very controversial during the late 1960s and Congress even went so far in 1968 as to enact a statute which was intended to "overrule" the Supreme Court's decision. The lower federal and state courts generally believed that the *Miranda* decision had been grounded in the U.S. Constitution. These courts essentially ignored the statute and went about applying *Miranda's* principles to the many cases that were brought forward for decision. Things changed, however, in 1999, when the U.S. Court of Appeals for the Fourth Circuit reversed a federal district court's suppression order based on the 1968 statute. The Supreme Court reviewed the Fourth Circuit's action in the following case of *Dickerson v. United States.*

Charles T. Dickerson v. United States
U.S. Supreme Court
No. 99-5525
June 26, 2000

Chief Justice Rehnquist delivered the opinion of the Court.

Petitioner Dickerson was indicted for bank robbery, conspiracy to commit bank robbery, and using a firearm in the course of committing a crime of violence, all in violation of the applicable provisions of Title 18 of the United States Code. Before trial, Dickerson moved to suppress a statement he had made at a Federal Bureau of Investigation field office, on the grounds that he had not received "*Miranda* warnings" before being interrogated. The District Court granted his motion to suppress, and the Government took an interlocutory appeal to the United States Court of Appeals for the Fourth Circuit. That court, by a divided vote, reversed the District Court's suppression order. It agreed with the District Court's conclusion that petitioner had not received *Miranda* warnings before making his statement. But it went on to hold that §§3501, which in effect makes the admissibility of statements such as Dickerson's

turn solely on whether they were made voluntarily, was satisfied in this case. It then concluded that our decision in *Miranda* was not a constitutional holding, and that therefore Congress could by statute have the final say on the question of admissibility. . . .

We begin with a brief historical account of the law governing the admission of confessions. Prior to *Miranda,* we evaluated the admissibility of a suspect's confession under a voluntariness test. The roots of this test developed in the common law, as the courts of England and then the United States recognized that coerced confessions are inherently untrustworthy. . . . Over time, our cases recognized two constitutional bases for the requirement that a confession be voluntary to be admitted into evidence: the Fifth Amendment right against self-incrimination and the Due Process Clause of the Fourteenth Amendment. . . .

. . . [F]or the middle third of the 20th century our cases based the rule against admitting coerced confessions primarily . . . on notions of due process. . . . The due process test takes into consideration "the totality of all the surrounding circumstances—both the characteristics of the accused and the details of the interrogation." . . .

We have never abandoned this due process jurisprudence, and thus continue to exclude confessions that were obtained involuntarily. But our decisions in *Malloy v. Hogan,* . . . (1964), and *Miranda* . . . (1966) changed the focus of much of the inquiry in determining the admissibility of suspects' incriminating statements. In *Malloy,* we held that the Fifth Amendment's Self-Incrimination Clause is incorporated in the Due Process Clause of the Fourteenth Amendment and thus applies to the States. . . . We decided *Miranda* on the heels of *Malloy.*

In *Miranda,* we noted that the advent of modern custodial police interrogation brought with it an increased concern about confessions obtained by coercion. . . . Because custodial police interrogation, by its very nature, isolates and pressures the individual, we stated that "[e]ven without employing brutality, the 'third degree' or [other] specific stratagems, . . . custodial interrogation exacts a heavy toll on individual liberty and trades on the weakness of individuals." . . . We concluded that the coercion inherent in custodial interrogation blurs the line between voluntary and involuntary statements, and thus heightens the risk that an individual will not be "accorded his privilege under the Fifth Amendment . . . not to be compelled to incriminate himself." . . . Accordingly, we laid down "concrete constitutional guidelines for law enforcement agencies and courts to follow." . . . Those guidelines established that the admissibility in evidence of any statement given during custodial interrogation of a suspect would depend on whether the police provided the suspect with four warnings. These warnings (which have come to be known colloquially as "*Miranda* rights") are: a suspect "has the right to remain silent, that anything he says can be used against him in a court of law, that he has the right to the presence of an attorney, and that if he cannot afford an attorney one will be appointed for him prior to any questioning if he so desires." . . .

Two years after *Miranda* was decided, Congress enacted §§3501. That section provides, in relevant part:

"(a) In any criminal prosecution brought by the United States or by the District of Columbia, a confession . . . shall be admissible in evidence if it is voluntarily given. Before such confession is received in evidence, the trial judge shall, out of the presence of the jury, determine any issue as to voluntariness. If the trial judge determines that the confession was voluntarily made it shall be admitted in evidence and the trial judge shall permit the jury to hear relevant evidence on the issue of voluntariness and shall instruct the jury to give such weight to the confession as the jury feels it deserves under all the circumstances.

"(b) The trial judge in determining the issue of voluntariness shall take into consideration all the circumstances surrounding the giving of the confession, including (1) the time elapsing between arrest and arraignment of the defendant making the confession, if it was made after arrest and before arraignment, (2) whether such defendant knew the nature of the offense with which he was charged or of which he was suspected at the time of making the confession, (3) whether or not such defendant was advised or knew that he was not required to make any statement and that any such statement could be used against him, (4) whether or not such defendant had been advised prior to questioning of his right to the assistance of counsel, and (5) whether or not such defendant was without the assistance of counsel when questioned and when giving such confession.

"The presence or absence of any of the above-mentioned factors to be taken into consideration by the judge need not be conclusive on the issue of voluntariness of the confession."

Given §§3501's express designation of voluntariness as the touchstone of admissibility, its omission of any warning requirement, and the instruction for trial courts to consider a nonexclusive list of factors relevant to the circumstances of a confession, we agree with the Court of Appeals that Congress intended by its enactment to overrule *Miranda*. . . . Because of the obvious conflict between our decision in *Miranda* and §§3501, we must address whether Congress has constitutional authority to thus supersede *Miranda*. . . .

The law in this area is clear. This Court has supervisory authority over the federal courts, and we may use that authority to prescribe rules of evidence and procedure that are binding in those tribunals. . . . Congress retains the ultimate authority to modify or set aside any judicially created rules of evidence and procedure that are not required by the Constitution. . . .

But Congress may not legislatively supersede our decisions interpreting and applying the Constitution. . . . This case therefore turns on whether the *Miranda* Court announced a constitutional rule or merely exercised its supervisory authority to regulate evidence in the absence of congressional direction. . . . [T]he Court of Appeals concluded that the protections announced in *Miranda* are not constitutionally required. . . .

We disagree with the Court of Appeals' conclusion. . . .

The *Miranda* opinion itself begins by stating that the Court granted certiorari "to explore some facets of the problems . . . of applying the privilege against self-incrimination to in-custody interrogation, and to give concrete constitutional guidelines for law enforcement agencies and courts to follow." . . . In fact, the majority opinion is replete with statements indicating that the majority thought it was announcing a constitutional rule. . . . Indeed, the Court's ultimate conclusion was that the unwarned confessions obtained in the four cases before the Court in *Miranda* "were obtained from the defendant under circumstances that did not meet constitutional standards for protection of the privilege." . . .

The dissent argues that it is judicial overreaching for this Court to hold §§3501 uncon-

stitutional unless we hold that the *Miranda* warnings are required by the Constitution, in the sense that nothing else will suffice to satisfy constitutional requirements. . . . But we need not go farther than *Miranda* to decide this case. In *Miranda*, the Court noted that reliance on the traditional totality-of-the-circumstances test raised a risk of overlooking an involuntary custodial confession, . . . , a risk that the Court found unacceptably great when the confession is offered in the case in chief to prove guilt. The Court therefore concluded that something more than the totality test was necessary. . . . As discussed above, §§3501 reinstates the totality test as sufficient. Section 3501 therefore cannot be sustained if *Miranda* is to remain the law.

Whether or not we would agree with *Miranda's* reasoning and its resulting rule, were we addressing the issue in the first instance, the principles of *stare decisis* weigh heavily against overruling it now. . . . While "'stare decisis* is not an inexorable command,'" . . . , particularly when we are interpreting the Constitution, . . . "even in constitutional cases, the doctrine carries such persuasive force that we have always required a departure from precedent to be supported by some 'special justification.'" . . .

We do not think there is such justification for overruling *Miranda*. *Miranda* has become embedded in routine police practice to the point where the warnings have become part of our national culture. . . . While we have overruled our precedents when subsequent cases have undermined their doctrinal underpinnings, . . . we do not believe that this has happened to the *Miranda* decision. If anything, our subsequent cases have reduced the impact of the *Miranda* rule on legitimate law enforcement while reaffirming the decision's core ruling that unwarned statements may not be used as evidence in the prosecution's case in chief.

The disadvantage of the *Miranda* rule is that statements which may be by no means involuntary, made by a defendant who is aware of his "rights," may nonetheless be excluded and a guilty defendant go free as a result. But experience suggests that the totality-of-the-circumstances test which §§3501 seeks to revive is more difficult than *Miranda* for law enforcement officers to conform to, and for courts to apply in a consistent manner. . . .

In sum, we conclude that *Miranda* announced a constitutional rule that Congress may not supersede legislatively. Following the rule of *stare decisis,* we decline to overrule *Miranda* ourselves. The judgment of the Court of Appeals is therefore
Reversed

Case Questions

1. Why did the Fourth Circuit believe the warnings could be dispensed with in Dickerson's case?
2. The Court's opinion defended the *Miranda* warnings requirement on legal grounds, but it went beyond such arguments to advance practical and cultural reasons for not abandoning *Miranda* warnings at this time—what were these arguments?

Searches and Seizures

Examinations of a person or premises are conducted by officers of the law in order to find stolen property or other evidence of guilt to be used by the prosecutor in a criminal action. With some exceptions, a warrant must be obtained by an officer before making a search. (See Figure 8-4).

As in the case of an arrest warrant, the Fourth Amendment requires probable cause for searches and seizures. Although the Fourth Amendment does not prescribe the forms by which probable cause must be established, evidence of probable cause has traditionally been presented to a magistrate in a written application for warrant supported by oath or affirmation, filed by someone who has personal information concerning items to be seized. Today it is increasingly common for statutes to provide for telephonic search warrants as seen in Figure 8-5.

A valid warrant must be specific and sufficiently descriptive. An officer conducting a search is prohibited from going outside the limits set by the warrant. Until recently officers were required, in the absence of reasonable suspicion that exigent circumstances required otherwise, to knock and announce their presence before entering by force to execute a search warrant. Exigent circumstances would exist, for example, where such notice could endanger an officer's safety or result in the destruction of evidence. However, following the attack on the World Trade Center and the enactment of the USA Patriot Act, an additional ground now exists for making unannounced entries. Officers are now authorized by Section 214 of the Act to "delay" giving notice when executing warrants where a magistrate has "reasonable cause" to believe that giving immediate notice might adversely effect the investigation.

SEARCH WARRANT

To . . . . *[specify official or officials authorized to execute warrant]:*
    Affidavit having been made before me by . . . . *[affiant]* that he has reason to believe that on the . . . . . [person of *or* premises known as] . . . . *[state name of suspect or specify exact address, including apartment or room number, if any, and give description of premises],* in the City of . . . . , State of . . . . , in the . . . . District of . . . . , there is now being concealed certain property, namely, ... *[specify, such as* certain dies, hubs, molds and plates, fitted and intended to be used for the manufacture of counterfeit coins of the United States, in violation of . . . . *(cite statute)],* and as I am satisfied that there is probable cause to believe that the property so described is being concealed on the . . . . [person *or* premises] above . . . . [named *or* described], and that grounds for issuance of a search warrant exist,
    You are hereby commanded to search within . . . . [ten] days from this date the . . . . [person *or* place] named for the property specified, serving this warrant and making the search . . . . [in the daytime *or* at any time in the day or night], and if the property be found there to seize it, leaving a copy of this warrant and a receipt for the property taken, and prepare a written inventory of the property seized, and promptly return this warrant and bring the property before me, as required by law.
Dated . . . . , 20. . . . .

[Signature and title]

FIGURE 8-4   Sample Search Warrant [FRCrP 41(c)]

Courts prefer that searches and seizures are undertaken pursuant to warrants. The warrant process permits a neutral and detached magistrate, in lieu of police officers, to determine if probable cause exists to support a requested search and/or seizure. But the Supreme Court has recognized that warrantless searches and/or seizures are constitutionally reasonable in some circumstances. In an introductory chapter, it is not possible to explain each of the circumstances in which an exception to the warrant requirement has been recognized. However, the most common of these recognized exceptions can be found in Figure 8-6. Interested students can look up the cases on the Internet or at the library using the case names and corresponding citations.

In 1914, the U.S. Supreme Court ruled that the Fourth Amendment prevented the use of evidence obtained from an illegal search and seizure in federal prosecutions. This exclusionary rule remedy was incorporated into the

968.12 Search warrant

(a) *General rule.* A search warrant may be based upon sworn oral testimony communicated to the judge by telephone, radio or other means of electronic communication, under the procedure prescribed in this subsection.

(b) *Application.* The person who is requesting the warrant shall prepare a duplicate original warrant and read the duplicate original warrant, verbatim, to the judge. The judge shall enter, verbatim, what is read on the original warrant. The judge may direct that the warrant be modified.

(c) *Issuance.* If the judge determines that there is probable cause for the warrant, the judge shall order the issuance of a warrant by directing the person requesting the warrant to sign the judge's name on the duplicate original warrant. In addition, the person shall sign his or her own name on the duplicate original warrant. The judge shall immediately sign the original warrant and enter on the face of the original warrant the exact time when the warrant was ordered to be issued. The finding of probable cause for a warrant upon oral testimony shall be based on the same kind of evidence as is sufficient for a warrant upon affidavit.

(d) *Recording and certification of testimony.* When a caller informs the judge that the purpose of the call is to request a warrant, the judge shall place under oath each person whose testimony forms a basis of the application and each person applying for the warrant. The judge or requesting person shall arrange for all sworn testimony to be recorded either by a stenographic reporter or by means of a voice recording device. The judge shall have the record transcribed. The transcript, certified as accurate by the judge or reporter, as appropriate, shall be filed with the court. If the testimony was recorded by means of a voice recording device, the judge shall also file the original recording with the court.

FIGURE 8-5 **Excerpt from the Wisconsin Search Warrant Statute [968.12]**

Fourteenth Amendment's due process clause and made binding on the states in the 1961 case of *Mapp v. Ohio* (367 U.S. 643). Although illegally obtained evidence may not be used by the government to prove the defendant's guilt, such evidence may be used to contradict (impeach) a defendant's trial testimony, thus showing that the defendant's testimony may be untruthful.

The exclusionary rule has not been applied in a rigid manner, and various exceptions have been recognized by the U.S. Supreme Court. When a recognized exception applies, the evidence can still be admitted as evidence of guilt, despite the violation of the Fourth Amendment. Examples are the independent source exception (when an untainted source of evidence unrelated to the illegal search and seizure is shown to exist) and the good faith exception (which applies if the police acted reasonably and relied on what subsequently turned out to be a defective warrant in obtaining evidence).

In the following case, a public hospital in conjunction with the local police, subjected maternity patients, without their knowledge or consent, to urine drug tests. The two public agencies acted pursuant to an inter-agency policy

Exception	Case	Citation
Abandoned Property	*California v. Greenwood*	486 U.S. 35
Booking Searches	*Illinois v. Lafeyette*	462 U.S. 640
Consent Searches	*Schnecloth v. Bustamonte*	412 U.S. 218
Hot Pursuit	*Warden v. Hayden*	387 U.S. 294
Open Fields	*Oliver v. United States*	466 U.S. 170
	United States v. Dunn	480 U.S. 294
Plain View	*Arizona v. Hicks*	480 U.S. 321
Mobile Vehicles	*Carroll v. United States*	267 U.S. 132
	Chambers v. Maroney	399 U.S. 42
	Ross v. Moffit	417 U.S. 600
	California v. Acevedo	500 U.S. 386
Incident to Arrest	*Chimel v. California*	395 U.S. 752
	United States v. Robinson	414 U.S. 218
	Maryland v. Buie	494 U.S. 325
Vehicle Inventories	*South Dakota v. Opperman*	428 U.S. 364
	Colorado v. Bertine	479 U.S. 367

FIGURE 8-6   Some Common Exceptions to the Search Warrant Requirement

and without a search warrant. Both agencies sought to identify which women were cocaine abusers so that the offenders could be criminally prosecuted for drug offenses, and coerced into participating in drug treatment programs.

Crystal M. Ferguson v. City of Charleston
No. 99-936
U.S. Supreme Court
March 21, 2001

Justice Stevens delivered the opinion of the Court.

In this case, we must decide whether a state hospital's performance of a diagnostic test to obtain evidence of a patient's criminal conduct for law enforcement purposes is an unreasonable search if the patient has not consented to the procedure. More narrowly, the question is whether the interest in using the threat of criminal sanctions to deter pregnant women from using cocaine can justify a departure from the general rule that an official nonconsensual search is unconstitutional if not authorized by a valid warrant.

In the fall of 1988, staff members at the public hospital operated in the city of Charleston by the Medical University of South Carolina (MUSC) became concerned about an apparent increase in the use of cocaine by patients who were receiving prenatal treatment. In response to this perceived increase, as of April 1989, MUSC began to order drug screens to be performed on urine samples from maternity patients who were suspected of using cocaine. If a patient tested positive, she was then referred by MUSC staff to the county substance abuse commission for counseling and treatment. However, despite the referrals, the incidence of cocaine use among the patients at MUSC did not appear to change.

Some four months later, Nurse Shirley Brown, the case manager for the MUSC obstetrics department, heard a news broadcast reporting that the police in Greenville, South Carolina, were arresting pregnant users of cocaine on the theory that such use harmed the fetus and was therefore child abuse. Nurse Brown discussed the story with MUSC's general counsel, Joseph C. Good, Jr., who then contacted Charleston Solicitor Charles Condon in order to offer MUSC's cooperation in prosecuting mothers whose children tested positive for drugs at birth. After receiving Good's letter, Solicitor Condon took the first steps in developing the policy at issue in this case. He organized the initial meetings, decided who would participate, and issued the invitations, in which he described his plan to prosecute women who tested positive for cocaine while pregnant. The task force that Condon formed included representatives of MUSC, the police, the County Substance Abuse Commission and the Department of Social Services. Their deliberations led to MUSC's adoption of a 12-page document entitled "POLICY M-7," dealing with the subject of "Management of Drug Abuse During Pregnancy." . . .

The first three pages of Policy M-7 set forth the procedure to be followed by the hospital staff to "identify/assist pregnant patients suspected of drug abuse." . . . The first section, entitled the "Identification of Drug Abusers," provided that a patient should be tested for cocaine through a urine drug screen if she met one or more of nine criteria. It also stated that a chain of custody should be followed when obtaining and testing urine samples, presumably to make sure that the results could be used in subsequent criminal proceedings. The policy also provided for education and referral to a substance abuse clinic for patients who tested positive. Most important, it added the threat of law enforcement intervention that "pro-

vided the necessary 'leverage' to make the [p]olicy effective." . . . That threat was, as respondents candidly acknowledge, essential to the program's success in getting women into treatment and keeping them there. . . .

The last six pages of the policy contained forms for the patients to sign, as well as procedures for the police to follow when a patient was arrested. The policy also prescribed in detail the precise offenses with which a woman could be charged, depending on the stage of her pregnancy. If the pregnancy was 27 weeks or less, the patient was to be charged with simple possession. If it was 28 weeks or more, she was to be charged with possession and distribution to a person under the age of 18—in this case, the fetus. If she delivered "while testing positive for illegal drugs," she was also to be charged with unlawful neglect of a child. . . . Under the policy, the police were instructed to interrogate the arrestee in order "to ascertain the identity of the subject who provided illegal drugs to the suspect." . . . Other than the provisions describing the substance abuse treatment to be offered to women who tested positive, the policy made no mention of any change in the prenatal care of such patients, nor did it prescribe any special treatment for the newborn.

Petitioners are 10 women who received obstetrical care at MUSC and who were arrested after testing positive for cocaine. . . . Respondents include the city of Charleston, law enforcement officials who helped develop and enforce the policy, and representatives of MUSC.

Petitioners' complaint challenged the validity of the policy . . . claim[ing] that warrantless and nonconsensual drug tests conducted for criminal investigatory purposes were unconstitutional searches. Respondents advanced two principal defenses . . . : (1) that, . . . petitioners had consented to the searches; and (2) that, . . . the searches were reasonable, even absent consent, because they were justified by special non-law-enforcement purposes. The District Court rejected the second defense because the searches in question "were not done by the medical university for independent purposes. [Instead], the police came in and there was an agreement reached that the positive screens would be shared with the police." . . . Accordingly, the District Court submitted the factual defense to the jury with instructions that required a verdict in favor of petitioners unless the jury found consent. The jury found for respondents.

Petitioners appealed, arguing that the evidence was not sufficient to support the jury's consent finding. The Court of Appeals for the Fourth Circuit affirmed. . . . Disagreeing with the District Court, the majority of the appellate panel held that the searches were reasonable as a matter of law under our line of cases recognizing that "special needs" may, in certain exceptional circumstances, justify a search policy designed to serve non-law-enforcement ends. . . . We granted certiorari, . . . to review the appellate court's holding on the "special needs" issue. Because we do not reach the question of the sufficiency of the evidence with respect to consent, . . . [w]e conclude that the judgment should be reversed and the case remanded for a decision on the consent issue.

Because MUSC is a state hospital, the members of its staff are government actors, subject to the strictures of the Fourth Amendment. . . . Moreover, the urine tests conducted by those staff members were indisputably searches within the meaning of the Fourth Amendment. . . . Neither the District Court nor the Court of Appeals concluded that any of the . . . criteria used to identify the women to be searched provided either probable cause to believe that they were using cocaine, or even the basis for a reasonable suspicion of such use. Rather, the District Court and the Court of Appeals viewed the case as one involving MUSC's right to conduct searches without warrants or probable cause. Furthermore, . . . we must assume for purposes of our decision that the tests were performed without the informed consent of the patients.

Because the hospital seeks to justify its authority to conduct drug tests and to turn the results over to law enforcement agents without the knowledge or consent of the patients, this case differs from . . . previous cases in which we have considered whether comparable drug tests "fit within the closely guarded category of constitutionally permissible suspicionless searches." . . . In three . . . cases, we sustained drug tests for railway employees involved in train accidents . . . , and for high school students participating in interscholastic sports. . . . In the fourth case, we struck down such testing for candidates for designated state offices as unreasonable. *Chandler v. Miller,* . . . (1997).

In each of those cases, we employed a balancing test that weighed the intrusion on the individual's interest in privacy against the "special needs" that supported the program. As an initial matter, we note that the invasion of privacy in this case is far more substantial than in those cases. In the previous four cases, there was no misunderstanding about the purpose of the test or the potential use of the test results, and there were protections against the dissemination of the results to third parties. The use of an adverse test result to disqualify one from eligibility for a particular benefit, such as a promotion or an opportunity to participate in an extracurricular activity, involves a less serious intrusion on privacy than the unauthorized dissemination of such results to third parties. The reasonable expectation of privacy enjoyed by the typical patient undergoing diagnostic tests in a hospital is that the results of those tests will not be shared with nonmedical personnel without her consent. . . . In none of our prior cases was there any intrusion upon that kind of expectation.

The critical difference between those four drug-testing cases and this one, however, lies in the nature of the "special need" asserted as justification for the warrantless searches. In each of those earlier cases, the "special need" that was advanced as a justification for the absence of a warrant or individualized suspicion was one divorced from the State's general interest in law enforcement. This point was emphasized both in the majority opinions sustaining the programs in the first three cases, as well as in the dissent in the *Chandler* case. In this case, however, the central and indispensable feature of the policy from its inception was the use of law enforcement to coerce the patients into substance abuse treatment. This fact distinguishes this case from circumstances in which physicians or psychologists, in the course of ordinary medical procedures aimed at helping the patient herself, come across information that under rules of law or ethics is subject to reporting requirements, which no one has challenged here. . . . Respondents argue in essence that their ultimate purpose—namely, protecting the health of both mother and child—is a beneficent one. In *Chandler,* however, we did not simply accept the State's invocation of a "special need." Instead, we carried out a "close review" of the scheme at issue before concluding that the need in question was not "special," as that term has been defined in our cases. . . . In this case, a review of the . . . policy plainly reveals that the purpose actually served by the MUSC searches "is ultimately indistinguishable from the general interest in crime control." . . .

In this case, as Judge Blake put it in her dissent below, "it . . . is clear from the record that an initial and continuing focus of the policy was on the arrest and prosecution of drug-abusing mothers. . . ." . . . Tellingly, the document codifying the policy incorporates the police's operational guidelines. It devotes its attention to the chain of custody, the range of possible criminal charges, and the logistics of police notification and arrests. Nowhere, however, does the document discuss different courses of medical treatment for either mother or infant, aside from treatment for the mother's addiction.

Moreover, throughout the development and application of the policy, the Charleston prosecutors and police were extensively involved in the day-to-day administration of the policy. Police and prosecutors decided who would receive the reports of positive drug screens and what information would be included with those reports. . . . Law enforcement officials also helped determine the procedures to be followed when performing the screens. . . . In the course of the policy's administration, they had access to Nurse Brown's medical files on the women who tested positive, routinely attended the substance abuse team's meetings, and regularly received copies of team documents discussing the women's progress. . . . Police took pains to coordinate the timing and circumstances of the arrests with MUSC staff, and, in particular, Nurse Brown. . . .

While the ultimate goal of the program may well have been to get the women in question into substance abuse treatment and off of drugs, the immediate objective of the searches was to generate evidence for law enforcement purposes in order to reach that goal. The threat of law enforcement may ultimately have been intended as a means to an end, but the direct and primary purpose of MUSC's policy was to ensure the use of those means. In our opinion, this distinction is critical. Because law enforcement involvement always serves some broader social purpose or objective, under respondents' view, virtually any nonconsensual suspicionless search could be immunized under the special needs doctrine by defining the search solely in terms of its ultimate, rather than immediate, purpose. Such an approach is inconsistent with the Fourth Amendment. Given the primary purpose of the Charleston program, which was to use the threat of arrest and prosecution in order to force women into treatment, and given the extensive involvement of law enforcement officials at every stage of the policy, this case simply does not fit within the closely guarded category of "special needs."

The fact that positive test results were turned over to the police does not merely provide a basis for distinguishing our prior cases applying the "special needs" balancing approach to the determination of drug use. It also provides an affirmative reason for enforcing the strictures of the Fourth Amendment. While state hospital employees, like other citizens, may have a duty to provide the police with evidence of criminal conduct that they inadvertently acquire in the course of routine treatment, when they undertake to obtain such evidence from their patients *for the specific purpose of incriminating those patients* [emphasis in original], they have a special obligation to make sure that the patients are fully informed about their constitutional rights, as standards of knowing waiver require. . . .

As respondents have repeatedly insisted, their motive was benign rather than punitive. Such a motive, however, cannot justify a departure from Fourth Amendment protections, given the pervasive involvement of law enforcement with the development and application of the MUSC policy. The stark and unique fact that characterizes this case is that Policy M-7 was designed to obtain evidence of criminal conduct by the tested patients that would be turned over to the police and that could be admissible in subsequent criminal prosecutions. While respondents are correct that drug abuse both was and is a serious problem, "the gravity of the threat alone cannot be dispositive of questions concerning what means law enforcement officers may employ to pursue a given purpose." . . . The Fourth Amendment's general prohibition against nonconsensual, warrantless, and suspicionless searches necessarily applies to such a policy. . . .

Accordingly, the judgment of the Court of Appeals is reversed, and the case is remanded for further proceedings consistent with this opinion.

It is so ordered.

Case Questions

1. On what grounds did the maternity patients challenge the Management of Drug Abuse During Pregnancy policy?
2. How did the U.S. Supreme Court distinguish the facts in this case from the facts in the four previous "special needs" cases?
3. Precisely why did the Supreme Court conclude that the Management of Drug Abuse During Pregnancy policy violated the Fourth Amendment?

Investigatory Detentions (Stop and Frisk)

The requirement that police officers have probable cause to arrest makes it difficult for them to investigate individuals whose conduct has aroused their suspicions. The Supreme Court was asked in 1968 to balance police investigative needs against citizen privacy rights in the famous case of *Terry v. Ohio*. In *Terry*, the Supreme Court ruled that it was reasonable under the Fourth Amendment for police officers to make brief seizures of individuals based on reasonable suspicion. The court interpreted the Fourth Amendment as permitting officers to detain suspiciously acting individuals so that their identity could be determined and so that officers could question them about their behavior. However, police officers must be able to articulate the specific facts and circumstances that created a reasonable suspicion in their minds that criminal activity has been, is being, or is about to be committed.

Further, the Supreme Court has ruled that officers who can articulate facts and circumstances that suggest that the stopped individual is armed have a right to make a "frisk." The frisk is less than a full search and consists of the pat-down of the outer clothing of a stopped individual in order to locate weapons that might be used against the officer. If an officer, while conducting the pat-down, feels an object that could be a weapon, the officer is entitled to reach inside the clothing and take the object. If a seized object or weapon is lawfully possessed, it must be returned upon the conclusion of the *investigatory detention*. If the weapon is unlawfully possessed, it can be seized and used in a criminal prosecution.

Stop and frisk is a very controversial technique in many communities. Police are frequently accused of making stops of individuals based on factors such as race, age, and choice of friends, rather than on actual evidence of impending criminal activity. Officers are also accused of making investigative stops and frisks for the purpose of conducting exploratory searches for evidence. The Supreme Court emphasized in the following case, *Adams v. Williams*, that the purpose of the frisk is to protect the officer, and not a pretext for an exploratory search for criminal evidence.

Adams v. Williams
407 U.S. 143
U.S. Supreme Court
June 12, 1972

Mr. Justice Rehnquist delivered the opinion of the Court.

Respondent Robert Williams was convicted in a Connecticut state court of illegal possession of a handgun found during a "stop and frisk," as well as of possession of heroin that was found during a full search incident to his weapons arrest. After respondent's conviction was affirmed by the Supreme Court of Connecticut, . . . this Court denied certiorari. . . . Williams' petition for federal habeas corpus relief was denied by the District Court and by a divided panel of the Second Circuit, . . . but on rehearing *en banc* the Court of Appeals granted relief. . . . That court held that evidence introduced at Williams' trial had been obtained by an unlawful search of his person

and car, and thus the state court judgments of conviction should be set aside. Since we conclude that the policeman's actions here conformed to the standards this Court laid down in *Terry v. Ohio*, 392 U.S. 1 (1968), we reverse.

Police Sgt. John Connolly was alone early in the morning on car patrol duty in a high-crime area of Bridgeport, Connecticut. At approximately 2:15 a.m. a person known to Sgt. Connolly approached his cruiser and informed him that an individual seated in a nearby vehicle was carrying narcotics and had a gun at his waist.

After calling for assistance on his car radio, Sgt. Connolly approached the vehicle to investigate the informant's report. Connolly tapped on the car window and asked the occupant, Robert Williams, to open the door. When Williams rolled down the window instead, the sergeant reached into the car and removed a fully loaded revolver from Williams' waistband. The gun had not been visible to Connolly from outside the car, but it was in precisely the place indicated by the informant. Williams was then arrested by Connolly for unlawful possession of the pistol. A search incident to that arrest was conducted after other officers arrived. They found substantial quantities of heroin on Williams' person and in the car, and they found a machete and a second revolver hidden in the automobile.

Respondent contends that the initial seizure of his pistol, upon which rested the later search and seizure of other weapons and narcotics, was not justified by the informant's tip to Sgt. Connolly. He claims the policeman's actions were unreasonable under the standards set forth in *Terry v. Ohio*. . . .

In *Terry* this Court recognized that "a police officer may in appropriate circumstances and in an appropriate manner approach a person for purposes of investigating possible criminal behavior even though there is no probable cause to make an arrest." . . . The Fourth Amendment does not require a policeman who lacks the precise level of information necessary for probable cause to arrest to simply shrug his shoulders and allow a crime to occur or a criminal to escape. On the contrary, *Terry* recognizes that it may be the essence of good police work to adopt an intermediate response. . . . A brief stop of a suspicious individual, in order to determine his identity or to maintain the status quo momentarily while obtaining more information, may be most reasonable in light of the facts known to the officer at the time. . . .

The Court recognized in *Terry* that the policeman making a reasonable investigatory stop should not be denied the opportunity to protect himself from attack by a hostile suspect. "When an officer is justified in believing that the individual whose suspicious behavior he is investigating at close range is armed and presently dangerous to the officer or to others," he may conduct a limited protective search for concealed weapons. . . . The purpose of this limited search is not to discover evidence of crime, but to allow the officer to pursue his investigation without fear of vio-

lence, and thus the frisk for weapons might be equally necessary and reasonable, whether or not carrying a concealed weapon violated any applicable state law. So long as the officer is entitled to make a forcible stop, and has reason to believe that the suspect is armed and dangerous, he may conduct a weapons search limited in scope to this protective purpose. . . .

Applying these principles to the present case, we believe that Sgt. Connolly acted justifiably in responding to his informant's tip. The informant was known to him personally and had provided him with information in the past. This is a stronger case than obtains in the case of an anonymous telephone tip. The informant here came forward personally to give information that was immediately verifiable at the scene. Indeed, under Connecticut law, the informant might have been subject to immediate arrest for making a false complaint had Sgt. Connolly's investigation proved the tip incorrect. Thus, while the Court's decisions indicate that this informant's unverified tip may have been insufficient for a narcotics arrest or search warrant . . . the information carried enough indicia of reliability to justify the officer's forcible stop of Williams.

In reaching this conclusion, we reject respondent's argument that reasonable cause for a stop and frisk can only be based on the officer's personal observation, rather than on information supplied by another person. Informants' tips, like all other clues and evidence coming to a policeman on the scene, may vary greatly in their value and reliability. One simple rule will not cover every situation. Some tips, completely lacking in indicia of reliability, would either warrant no police response or require further investigation before a forcible stop of a suspect would be authorized. But in some situations—for example, when the victim of a street crime seeks immediate police aid and gives a description of his assailant, or when a credible informant warns of a specific impending crime—the subtleties of the hearsay rule should not thwart an appropriate police response.

While properly investigating the activity of a person who was reported to be carrying narcotics and a concealed weapon and who was sitting alone in a car in a high-crime area at 2:15 in the morning, Sgt. Connolly had ample reason to fear for his safety. When Williams rolled down his window, rather than complying with the policeman's request to step out of the car so that his movements could more easily be seen, the revolver allegedly at Williams' waist became an even greater threat. Under these circumstances the policeman's action in reaching to the spot where the gun was thought to be hidden constituted a limited intrusion designed to insure his safety, and we conclude that it was reasonable. The loaded gun seized as a result of this intrusion was therefore admissible at Williams' trial. . . .

Once Sgt. Connolly had found the gun precisely where the informant had predicted, probable cause existed to arrest Williams for unlawful possession of the weapon. Probable cause to arrest depends "upon whether, at the moment the arrest was made . . . the facts and circumstances within [the arresting officers'] knowledge and of which they had reasonably trustworthy information were sufficient to warrant a prudent man in believing that the [suspect] had committed or was committing an offense." . . . In the present case the policeman found Williams in possession of a gun in precisely the place predicted by the informant. This tended to corroborate the reliability of the informant's further report of narcotics and, together with the surrounding circumstances, certainly suggested no lawful explanation for possession of the gun. Probable cause does not require the same type of specific evidence of each element of the offense as would be needed to support a conviction. . . . Rather, the court will evaluate generally the circumstances at the time of the arrest to decide if the officer had probable cause for his action. . . .

Under the circumstances surrounding Williams' possession of the gun seized by Sgt. Connolly, the arrest on the weapons charge was supported by probable cause, and the search of his person and of the car incident to that arrest was lawful. . . . The fruits of the search were therefore properly admitted at Williams' trial, and the Court of Appeals erred in reaching a contrary conclusion.

Reversed.

Case Questions

1. What facts and circumstances provided the reasonable suspicion for Sgt. Connolly's actions?
2. Why did the Supreme Court majority reject the defendant's argument that *Terry* stops should be based only on an officer's personal observations?

Bail

Although the U.S. Constitution does not guarantee criminal defendants the right to *bail*, at the present time, bail is authorized for all criminally accused persons except those charged with capital offenses (crimes for which punishment may be death). There is also much constitutional debate about whether legislatures can classify certain other noncapital offenses as nonbailable.

Under the traditional money bail system, the judge sets bail to ensure the defendant's attendance in court and obedience to the court's orders and judgment.

The accused is released after he or she deposits with a clerk cash, a bond, or a secured pledge in the amount of bail set by the judge. In 1951 the U.S. Supreme Court declared that the Eighth Amendment prevents federal judges and magistrates from setting bail at a figure higher than an amount reasonably calculated to ensure the defendant's appearance at trial. However, the Eighth Amendment's prohibition against excessive bail has been interpreted to apply only to the federal government and has not been incorporated into the Fourteenth Amendment. Thus it is not binding on the states.

During the early 1960s there was considerable dissatisfaction with the money bail system in this country because it discriminated against low-income people. Reform legislation was enacted in many states. The bail reform statutes made it easier for criminally accused people to obtain their release, since judges were required to use the least restrictive option that would ensure that the accused appeared for trial. In appropriate cases, a defendant could be released on his or her own recognizance (an unsecured promise to appear when required), upon the execution of an unsecured appearance bond, or upon the execution of a secured appearance bond. A judge or magistrate could impose appropriate limitations on the accused's right to travel as well as his or her contacts with other people. The judge's decision was based on the defendant's offense, family roots, and employment history. The court was empowered to revoke bail if the accused was found in possession of a firearm, failed to maintain employment, or disregarded the limitations.

Public fear about crimes committed by individuals out on bail resulted in the enactment of legislation authorizing preventive detention in the Bail Reform Act of 1984. Under these laws, people thought to be dangerous, who were accused of serious crimes, could be denied bail. The targeted crimes included violent crimes, offenses punishable by life imprisonment, and drug-related crimes punishable by a term of incarceration exceeding ten years. At a hearing a court would determine if the accused was likely to flee and if judicially imposed bail conditions would reasonably protect the public safety. In appropriate cases the court was authorized to deny bail and detain the accused until trial. The constitutionality of preventive detention was addressed by the U.S. Supreme Court in the following case.

United States v. Salerno
481 U.S. 739
U.S. Supreme Court
May 26, 1987

Chief Justice Rehnquist delivered the opinion of the Court.

The Bail Reform Act of 1984 allows a federal court to detain an arrestee pending trial if the Government demonstrates by clear and convincing evidence after an adversary hearing that no release conditions "will reasonably assure . . . the safety of any other person and the community." The United States Court of Appeals for the Second Circuit struck down this provision of the Act as facially unconstitutional, because, in that court's words, this type of pretrial detention violates "substantive due process."

I

Responding to "the alarming problem of crimes committed by persons on release," . . . Congress formulated the Bail Reform Act of 1984, . . . as the solution to a bail crisis in the federal courts. The Act represents the National Legislature's considered response to numerous perceived deficiencies in the federal bail process. By providing for sweeping changes in both the way federal courts consider bail applications and the circumstances under which bail is granted, Congress hoped [to] "give the courts adequate authority to make release decisions that give appropriate recognition to the danger a person may pose to others if released." . . .

To this end, § 3141(a) of the Act requires a judicial officer to determine whether an arrestee shall be detained. Section 3142(e) provides that "[i]f, after a hearing pursuant to the provisions of subsection (f), the judicial officer finds that no condition or combination of conditions will reasonably assure the appearance of the person as required and the safety of any other person and the community, he shall order the detention of the person prior to trial." Section 3142(f) provides the arrestee with a number of procedural safeguards. He may request the presence of counsel at the detention hearing, he may testify and present witnesses in his behalf, as well as proffer evidence, and he may cross-examine other witnesses appearing at the hearing. If the judicial officer finds that no conditions of pretrial release can reasonably assure the safety of other persons and the community, he must state his findings of fact in writing, . . . and support his conclusion with "clear and convincing evidence." . . .

The judicial officer is not given unbridled discretion in making the detention determination. Congress has specified the considerations relevant to that decision. These factors include the nature and seriousness of the charges, the substantiality of the Govern-

ment's evidence against the arrestee, the arrestee's background and characteristics, and the nature and seriousness of the danger posed by the suspect's release. . . . Should a judicial officer order detention, the detainee is entitled to expedited appellate review of the detention order. . . .

Respondents Anthony Salerno and Vincent Cafaro were arrested on March 21, 1986, after being charged in a 29-count indictment alleging various Racketeer Influenced and Corrupt Organizations Act (RICO) violations, mail and wire fraud offenses, extortion, and various criminal gambling violations. The RICO count alleged 35 acts of racketeering activity, including fraud, extortion, gambling, and conspiracy to commit murder. At respondents' arraignment, the Government moved to have Salerno and Cafaro detained pursuant to § 3142(e), on the ground that no condition of release would assure the safety of the community or any person. The District Court held a hearing at which the Government made a detailed proffer of evidence. The Government's case showed that Salerno was the "boss" of the Genovese Crime Family of La Cosa Nostra and that Cafaro was a "captain" in the Genovese Family. According to the Government's proffer, based in large part on conversations intercepted by a court-ordered wiretap, the two respondents had participated in wide-ranging conspiracies to aid their illegitimate enterprises through violent means. The Government also offered the testimony of two of its trial witnesses, who would assert that Salerno personally participated in two murder conspiracies. Salerno opposed the motion for detention, challenging the credibility of the Government's witnesses. He offered the testimony of several character witnesses as well as a letter from his doctor stating that he was suffering from a serious medical condition. Cafaro presented no evidence at the hearing, but instead characterized the wiretap conversations as merely "tough talk."

The District Court granted the Government's detention motion, concluding that the Government had established by clear and convincing evidence that no condition or combination of conditions of release would ensure the safety of the community or any person.

. . . Respondents appealed, contending that to the extent that the Bail Reform Act permits pretrial detention on the ground that the arrestee is likely to commit future crimes, it is unconstitutional on its face. Over a dissent, the United States Court of Appeals for the Second Circuit agreed. . . . The court concluded that the Government could not, consistent with due process, detain persons who had not been accused of any crime merely because they were thought to present a danger to the community. . . . It reasoned that our criminal law system holds persons accountable for past actions, not anticipated future actions. Although a court could detain an arrestee who threatened to flee before trial, such detention would be permissible because it would serve the basic objective of a criminal system—bringing the accused to trial.

II

. . . Respondents present two grounds for invalidating the Bail Reform Act's provisions permitting pretrial detention on the basis of future dangerousness. First, they rely upon the Court of Appeals' conclusion that the Act exceeds the limitations placed upon the Federal Government by the Due Process Clause of the Fifth Amendment. Second, they contend that the Act contravenes the Eighth Amendment's proscription against excessive bail. We treat these contentions in turn.

A

. . . Respondents first argue that the Act violates substantive due process because the pretrial detention it authorizes constitutes impermissible punishment before trial. . . .

As an initial matter, the mere fact that a person is detained does not inexorably lead to the conclusion that the government has imposed punishment. . . . To determine whether a restriction on liberty constitutes impermissible punishment or permissible regulation, we first look to legislative intent. . . .

The legislative history of the Bail Reform Act clearly indicates that Congress did not formulate the pretrial detention provisions as punishment for dangerous individuals. . . . Congress instead perceived pretrial detention as a potential solution to a pressing societal problem. . . . There is no doubt that preventing danger to the community is a legitimate regulatory goal. . . .

Nor are the incidents of pretrial detention excessive in relation to the regulatory goal Congress sought to achieve. The Bail Reform Act carefully limits the circumstances under which detention may be sought to the most serious of crimes. . . . The arrestee is entitled to a prompt detention hearing . . . and the maximum length of pretrial detention is limited by the stringent time limitations of the Speedy Trial Act. . . . Moreover, . . . the conditions of confinement envisioned by the Act "appear to reflect the regulatory purposes relied upon by the" Government. . . . [T]he statute at issue here requires that detainees be housed in a "facility separate, to the extent practicable, from persons awaiting or serving sentences or being held in custody pending appeal." . . . We conclude, therefore, that the pretrial detention contemplated by the Bail Reform Act is regulatory in nature, and does not constitute punishment before trial in violation of the Due Process Clause. . . .

The government's interest in preventing crime by arrestees is both legitimate and compelling. . . . The Bail Reform Act . . . narrowly focuses on a particularly acute problem in which the Government interests are overwhelming. The Act operates only on individuals who have been arrested for a specific category of extremely serious offenses. . . . Congress specifically found that these individuals are far more likely to be responsible for dangerous acts in the community after arrest. . . . Nor is the Act by any means a scattershot attempt to incapacitate those who are merely suspected of these serious crimes. . . . In a full-blown adversary hearing, the Government must convince a neutral decisionmaker by clear and convincing evidence that no conditions of release can reasonably assure the safety of the community or any person. . . . While the Government's general interest in preventing crime is compelling, even this interest is heightened when the Government musters convincing proof that the arrestee, already indicted or held to answer for a serious crime, presents a demonstrable danger to the community. Under these narrow circumstances, society's interest in crime prevention is at its greatest.

On the other side of the scale, of course, is the individual's strong interest in liberty. We do not minimize the importance and fundamental nature of this right. But, as our cases hold, this right may, in circumstances where the government's interest is sufficiently weighty, be subordinated to the greater needs of society. We think that Congress' careful delineation of the circumstances under which detention will be permitted satisfies this standard. When the Government proves by clear and convincing evidence that an arrestee presents an identified and articulable threat to an individual or the community, we believe that, consistent with the Due Process Clause, a court may disable the arrestee from executing that threat.

B

Respondents also contend that the Bail Reform Act violates the Excessive Bail Clause of the Eighth Amendment. . . .

The Eighth Amendment addresses pretrial release by providing merely that "[e]xcessive bail shall not be required." This Clause, of course, says nothing about whether bail shall be available at all. Respondents nevertheless contend that this Clause grants them a right to bail calculated solely upon considerations of flight. . . . Respondents concede that the right to bail they have discovered in the Eighth Amendment is not absolute. A court may, for example, refuse bail in capital cases. And . . . a court may refuse bail when the defendant presents a threat to the judicial process by intimidating witnesses. . . .

While we agree that a primary function of bail is to safeguard the courts' role in adjudicating the guilt or innocence of defendants, we reject the proposition that the Eighth Amendment categorically prohibits the government from pursuing other admittedly compelling interests through regulation of pretrial release. . . . Even if we were to conclude that the Eighth Amendment imposes some substantive limitations on the National Legislature's powers in this area, we would still hold that the Bail Reform Act is valid. Nothing in the text of the Bail Clause limits permissible government considertions solely to questions of flight. The only arguable substantive limitation of the Bail Clause is that the government's proposed conditions of release or detention not be "excessive" in light of the perceived evil. Of course, to determine whether the government's response is excessive, we must compare that response against the interest the government seeks to protect by means of that response. Thus, when the government has admitted that its only interest is in preventing flight, bail must be set by a court at a sum designed to ensure that goal, and no more. . . . We believe that when Congress has mandated detention on the basis of a compelling interest other than prevention of flight, as it has here, the Eighth Amendment does not require release on bail.

III

In our society liberty is the norm, and detention prior to trial or without trial is the carefully limited exception. We hold that the provisions for pretrial detention in the Bail

Reform Act of 1984 fall within that carefully limited exception. The Act authorizes the detention prior to trial of arrestees charged with serious felonies who are found after an adversary hearing to pose a threat to the safety of individuals or to the community which no condition of release can dispel. . . . [N]umerous procedural safeguards . . . must attend this adversary hearing. We are unwilling to say that this congressional determination, based as it is upon that primary concern of every government—a concern for the safety and indeed the lives of its citizens—on its face violates either the Due Process Clause of the Fifth Amendment or the Excessive Bail Clause of the Eighth Amendment.

The judgment of the Court of Appeals is therefore

Reversed.

Justice Marshall, with whom Justice Brennan joins, dissenting

This case brings before the Court for the first time a statute in which Congress declares that a person innocent of any crime may be jailed indefinitely, pending the trial of allegations which are legally presumed to be untrue, if the Government shows to the satisfaction of a judge that the accused is likely to commit crimes, unrelated to the pending charges, at any time in the future. Such statutes, consistent with the usages of tyranny and the excesses of what bitter experience teaches us to call the police state, have long been thought incompatible with the fundamental human rights protected by our Constitution. Today a majority of this Court holds otherwise. Its decision disregards basic principles of justice established centuries ago and enshrined beyond the reach of governmental interference in the Bill of Rights.

. . .

II

The majority approaches respondents' challenge to the Act by dividing the discussion into two sections, one concerned with the substantive guarantees implicit in the Due Process Clause, and the other concerned with the protection afforded by the Excessive Bail Clause of the Eighth Amendment. This is a sterile formalism, which divides a unitary argument into two independent parts and then professes to demonstrate that the parts are individually inadequate.

On the due process side of this false dichotomy appears an argument concerning the distinction between regulatory and punitive legislation. The majority concludes that the Act is a regulatory rather than a punitive measure. . . . The majority finds that "Congress did not formulate the pretrial detention provisions as punishment for dangerous individuals," but instead was pursuing the "legitimate regulatory goal" of "preventing danger to the community." . . . Concluding that pretrial detention is not an excessive solution to the problem of preventing danger to the community, the majority thus finds that no substantive element of the guarantee of due process invalidates the statute.

This argument does not demonstrate the conclusion it purports to justify. Let us apply the majority's reasoning to a similar, hypothetical case. After investigation, Congress determines (not unrealistically) that a large proportion of violent crime is perpetrated by persons who are unemployed. It also determines, equally reasonably, that much violent crime is committed at night. From amongst the panoply of "potential solutions," Congress chooses a statute which permits, after judicial proceedings, the imposition of a dusk-to-dawn curfew on anyone who is unemployed. Since this is not a measure enacted for the purpose of punishing the unemployed, and since the majority finds that preventing danger to the community is a legitimate regulatory goal, the curfew statute would, according to the majority's analysis, be a mere "regulatory" detention statute, entirely compatible with the substantive components of the Due Process Clause. . . .

The majority proceeds as though the only substantive right protected by the Due Process Clause is a right to be free from punishment before conviction. The majority's technique for infringing this right is simple: merely redefine any measure which is claimed to be punishment as "regulation," and, magically, the Constitution no longer prohibits its imposition. Because . . . the Due Process Clause protects other substantive rights which are infringed by this legislation, the majority's argument is merely an exercise in obfuscation.

IV

. . . Honoring the presumption of innocence is often difficult; sometimes we must pay substantial social costs as a result of our commitment to the values we espouse. But at the end of the day the presumption of innocence protects the innocent; the shortcuts we take

with those whom we believe to be guilty injure only those wrongfully accused and, ultimately, ourselves.

Throughout the world today there are men, women, and children interned indefinitely, awaiting trials which may never come or which may be a mockery of the word, because their governments believe them to be "dangerous." Our Constitution, whose construction began two centuries ago, can shelter us forever from the evils of such unchecked power. Over 200 years it has slowly, through our efforts, grown more durable, more expansive, and more just. But it cannot protect us if we lack the courage, and the self-restraint, to protect ourselves. Today a majority of the Court applies itself to an ominous exercise in demolition. Theirs is truly a decision which will go forth without authority, and come back without respect.

I dissent.

Case Questions

1. According to the Bail Reform Act of 1984, what factors must a judicial officer consider in making the decision to require that an accused person be denied bail?
2. What arguments were raised by the defendants against the Bail Reform Act?
3. Why did justices Marshall and Brennan dissent?

The Right to an Attorney

As said earlier, a defendant has an unqualified right to the assistance of retained counsel at all formal stages of a criminal case. An indigent defendant is entitled to a court-appointed attorney under much more limited circumstances. An indigent who is subjected to custodial interrogation by the police is entitled to an appointed attorney in order to protect the Fifth Amendment privilege against self-incrimination. His or her Sixth Amendment right to counsel does not arise until after adversarial judicial proceedings have begun, when the government has formally initiated criminal proceedings against a defendant—usually, after the defendant's initial appearance before a court.

The Supreme Court has ruled that an indigent defendant cannot be sentenced to a term of incarceration for a criminal offense unless appointed counsel was afforded to the defendant at all "critical stages" of a prosecution. Postindictment line-ups for identification purposes, initial appearances, and preliminary hearings, as well as trials and sentencing hearings, are examples of such critical stages. Finally, the Court has recognized that indigents convicted of criminal offenses who want to appeal the trial court's judgment only have a Fourteenth Amendment right to appointed counsel for purposes of a first appeal.

Line-ups

The police conduct *line-ups* before witnesses for the purpose of identifying a suspect. When formal charges are pending, an accused may not be in a line-up before witnesses for identification unless the accused and accused's counsel have been notified in advance. In addition, the line-up may not be conducted unless counsel is present, so that the defendant's counsel is not deprived of the right to effectively challenge the line-up procedures and any identifications that result. It is interesting to note that the U.S. Supreme Court has not required the presence of an attorney where an array of photographs is used in lieu of an actual line-up. Unlike a line-up, a photo array is not a trial-like confrontation that requires the presence of the accused.

Preliminary Hearing and Grand Jury

In order to weed out groundless or unsupported criminal charges before trial, a preliminary hearing is conducted or a grand jury is convened. In an informal *preliminary hearing*, the magistrate examines the facts superficially to determine whether there is a strong enough case to hold the arrestee for further proceedings. The prosecution presents evidence before the magistrate, without a jury, in order to determine if there is probable cause. The accused has a right to be present at the preliminary hearing and to present evidence. If there is no chance of conviction because of lack of evidence, the magistrate dismisses the charges.

A *grand jury*, composed of people selected at random from the list of registered voters, decides whether there is reason to believe an accused has committed an offense, not whether the person is guilty or innocent. Thus they determine whether a person should be brought to trial. The decision is based on evidence heard during a secret criminal investigation attended by representatives of the state and witnesses. The grand jury has the right to *subpoena* witnesses and documents for their investigation. The accused has no right to be present at the proceedings. A grand jury returns an *indictment* (an accusation in writing) to the court if it believes that the evidence warrants a conviction. (See Figure 8-7.)

For prosecutions involving crimes against the United States, the Fifth Amendment provides that all prosecution for *infamous crimes* (an offense carrying a term of imprisonment in excess of one year) must be commenced by a grand jury indictment. Virtually all states provide for a preliminary hearing for charges involving a felony. Approximately half of the states require a grand jury indictment, while the remainder use a bill of information (a formal charging document prepared by the prosecutor and filed with the court).

```
                    UNITED STATES DISTRICT COURT
                  FOR THE  . . . . . . DISTRICT OF . . . . . .
                         . . . . . . . DIVISION

United States of America,
          Plaintiff,                      Crim. No. . . . . . . . . . . . . .
             v.                           (. . . . .–USC § . . . . . . . . .
_____ )
          Defendant.

                              INDICTMENT
     The grand jury charges:
         On or about the . . . . . . day of . . . . . . , 20 . . . . . . . , in the . . . . . .
     District of . . . . . . . , . . . . . . . . [defendant] . . . . . . . [state essential facts
     constituting offense charged], in violation of . . . . . . . USC § . . . . . . . .
     Dated . . . . . . . , 20. . . . .

                              A True Bill.

                                                      [Signature],
                                                      Foreman

     . . . . . . . ,
     United States Attorney.
```

FIGURE 8-7   Sample Indictment [FRCrP 7(c)]

Arraignment

An arraignment follows a grand jury indictment or the judge's finding of probable cause at a preliminary hearing. At *arraignments,* accused people are advised of the formal charges against them as required by the Sixth Amendment. The description of the charges must be sufficiently clear so that the defendant may be able to enter an intelligent plea. The accused are also asked whether they understand the charges and whether they have an attorney. The court appoints counsel if the accused cannot afford an attorney. Finally, a trial date is set at the arraignment. Defendants and their counsel must be given adequate opportunity to prepare for trial.

The defendant is called on to enter a plea at the arraignment. This plea may be guilty, *nolo contendere,* or not guilty. The plea of *guilty* is entered in the great majority of situations; it is simply a confession of guilt. The plea of *nolo contendere* is the same as a guilty plea, except that it cannot be used later against the accused as an admission. It is a confession only for the purposes of the criminal prosecution and does not bind the defendant in a civil suit for the same wrong.

When the defendant pleads *not guilty*, the prosecution has the burden of proving him or her guilty beyond a reasonable doubt at the trial.

Plea bargaining is the process by which the accused agrees to enter a plea of guilty, often to a lesser offense, in exchange for a promise by the prosecuting attorney to recommend either a relatively light sentence or a dismissal of part of the charges. The judge does not have to accept the prosecutor's recommendations and will explain this to the defendant before accepting a negotiated plea.

THE CRIMINAL TRIAL

Every person who is charged with a crime has a constitutional right to a trial. In this way a defendant has the opportunity to confront and cross-examine the witnesses against him or her, testify and present evidence and arguments as a defense against the charges, have the assistance of an attorney in most cases, and take full advantage of the rights and protections afforded all people accused of crimes under the Constitution. Trial procedures are essentially the same in criminal and civil trials. The prosecution is the plaintiff and must initially present legally sufficient evidence of the defendant's criminal culpability with respect to each element of the crime or the judge will dismiss the charges and terminate the trial. A criminal defendant, unlike a civil defendant, has a constitutional right not to testify at trial. This privilege is often waived by defendants, however, because they wish to explain their version of the facts to the jury or to the judge in a bench trial. Every criminal defendant (and juvenile charged with a criminal offense) is additionally protected by the constitutional due process requirement that the prosecution prove guilt beyond a reasonable doubt in order to be entitled to a judgment of conviction.[7]

Before we read the case of *Sullivan v. Louisiana,* it is necessary to discuss two preliminary matters. In *Sullivan,* the trial judge's jury instruction defining reasonable doubt was almost identical to an instruction given in a previous case, *Cage v. Louisiana.*[8] Read the *Cage* instruction that follows and see whether you can identify any constitutional problems:[9]

> If you entertain a reasonable doubt as to any fact or element necessary to constitute the defendant's guilt, it is your duty to give him the benefit of that doubt and return a verdict of not guilty. Even where the evidence demonstrates a probability of guilt, if it does not establish such guilt beyond a reasonable doubt, you must acquit the accused. This doubt, however, must be a reasonable one; that is one that is founded upon a real tangible substantial basis and not upon mere caprice and conjecture. It must be such a doubt as would give rise to a grave uncertainty, raised in your mind by reasons of the unsatisfactory character of the evidence or lack thereof. A reasonable doubt is not a mere possible doubt. It is an actual substantial doubt. It is a doubt that a reasonable man can seriously entertain. What is required is not an absolute or mathematical certainty, but a moral certainty.

The U.S. Supreme Court in *Cage* determined that this instruction was unconstitutional. The Court noted that the trial court did at one point instruct the jury to convict only if guilt is proven beyond a reasonable doubt, "but it then equated a reasonable doubt with a 'grave uncertainty' and an 'actual substantial doubt' and stated that what was required was a 'moral certainty' that the defendant was guilty." The Court concluded, "It is plain to us that the words 'substantial' and 'grave,' as they are commonly understood, suggest a higher degree of doubt than is required for acquittal under the reasonable doubt standard. When those statements are then considered with the reference to 'moral certainty,' rather than evidentiary certainty, it becomes clear that a reasonable juror could have interpreted the instruction to allow a finding of guilt based on a degree of proof below that required by the Due Process Clause."[10]

In *Sullivan v. Louisiana*, the constitutionally erroneous *Cage* instruction was again given by the trial court. The defendant, relying on the *Cage* precedent, appealed to the Louisiana Supreme Court arguing that his murder conviction should be reversed. That court agreed that a constitutional error had occurred, but it refused to reverse Sullivan's conviction because, in its opinion, the error was harmless beyond a reasonable doubt.

According to the U.S. Supreme Court, a defendant's conviction need not be automatically reversed just because it has been proved that constitutional error occurred during the trial. In most instances, the Court has ruled there should be no reversal where the quantity and quality of the factual evidence introduced at trial is consistent with the jury's verdict and is so strong that appellate courts can conclude beyond a reasonable doubt that the constitutional error "did not contribute to the jury's verdict."[11]

In *Sullivan*, the U.S. Supreme Court granted *certiorari* to determine whether the giving of a constitutionally deficient instruction on the meaning of reasonable doubt can amount to harmless error.

Sullivan v. Louisiana
113 S.Ct. 2078
U.S. Supreme Court
June 1, 1993

Justice Scalia delivered the opinion of the Court.

The question presented is whether a constitutionally deficient reasonable-doubt instruction may be harmless error.

I

Petitioner was charged with first-degree murder in the course of committing an armed robbery at a New Orleans bar. His alleged accomplice in the crime, a convicted felon named Michael Hillhouse, testifying at the trial pursuant to a grant of immunity, identified petitioner as the murderer. Although several other people were in the bar at the time of the robbery, only one testified at trial. This witness, who had been unable to identify either Hillhouse or petitioner at a physical line-up, testified that they committed the robbery, and that she saw petitioner hold a gun to the victim's head. There was other circumstantial evidence supporting the conclusion that petitioner was the triggerman. . . . In closing argument, defense counsel argued that there was reasonable doubt as to both the identity of the murderer and his intent.

In his instructions to the jury, the trial judge gave a definition of "reasonable doubt" that was, as the State conceded below, essentially identical to the one held unconstitutional in *Cage v. Louisiana*, 498 U.S. 39, . . . (1990) (*per curiam*).

The jury found petitioner guilty of first-degree murder and subsequently recommended that he be sentenced to death. The trial court agreed. On direct appeal, the Supreme Court of Louisiana held . . . that the erroneous instruction was harmless beyond a reasonable doubt. It therefore upheld the conviction, though remanding for a new sentencing hearing because of ineffectiveness of counsel in the sentencing phase. We granted certiorari. . . .

II

The Sixth Amendment provides that "[i]n all criminal prosecutions, the accused shall enjoy the right to a speedy and public trial, by an impartial jury. . . ." In *Duncan v. Louisiana*, 391 U.S. 145, 149, (1968), we found this right to trial by jury in serious criminal cases to be "fundamental to the American scheme of justice," and therefore applicable in state proceedings. The right includes, of course, as its most important element, the right to have the jury, rather than the judge, reach the requisite finding of "guilty." Thus, although a judge may direct a verdict for the defendant if the evidence is legally insufficient to establish guilt, he may not direct a verdict for the State, no matter how overwhelming the evidence.

What the factfinder must determine to return a verdict of guilty is prescribed by the Due Process Clause. The prosecution bears the burden of proving all elements of the offense charged, . . . and must persuade the factfinder "beyond a reasonable doubt" of the facts necessary to establish each of those elements. . . .

This beyond-a-reasonable-doubt requirement, which was adhered to by virtually all common-law jurisdictions, applies in state as well as federal proceedings.

It is self-evident, we think, that the Fifth Amendment requirement of proof beyond a reasonable doubt and the Sixth Amendment requirement of a jury verdict are interrelated. It would not satisfy the Sixth Amendment to have a jury determine that the defendant is *probably* guilty, and then leave it up to the judge to determine . . . whether he is guilty beyond a reasonable doubt. In other words, the jury verdict required by the Sixth Amendment is a jury verdict of guilty beyond a reasonable doubt. Our opinion in *Cage* . . . held that an instruction of the sort given here does not produce such a verdict. Petitioner's Sixth Amendment right to jury trial was therefore denied.

III

In *Chapman v. California*, 386 U.S. 18, . . . (1967), we rejected the view that all federal constitutional errors in the course of a criminal trial require reversal. We held that the Fifth Amendment violation of prosecutorial comment upon the defendant's failure to testify would not require reversal of the conviction if the State could show "beyond a reasonable doubt that the error complained of did not contribute to the verdict obtained." . . . The *Chapman* standard recognizes that "certain constitutional errors, no less than other errors, may have been 'harmless' in terms of their effect on the factfinding process at trial." . . . Although most constitutional errors have been held amenable to harmless-error analysis, see *Arizona v. Fulminante*, 111 S.Ct. 1246, 1252, . . . some will always invalidate the conviction. *Gideon v. Wainwright*, 372 U.S. 335, . . . (1963) (total deprivation of the right to counsel); *Tumey v. Ohio*, 273 U.S. 510, . . . (1927) (trial by a biased judge); *McKaskle v. Wiggins*, 465 U.S.

168, . . . (1984) (right to self-representation). The question in the present case is to which category the present error belongs.

Chapman itself suggests the answer. Consistent with the jury-trial guarantee, the question it instructs the reviewing court to consider is not what effect the constitutional error might generally be expected to have upon a reasonable jury, but rather what effect it had upon the guilty verdict in the case at hand. . . . Harmless-error review looks, we have said, to the basis on which "the jury *actually rested* its verdict." *Yates v. Eatt*, 111 S.Ct. 1884, . . . (1991) (emphasis added). The inquiry, in other words, is not whether, in a trial that occurred without the error, a guilty verdict would surely have been rendered, but whether the guilty verdict actually rendered in *this* trial was surely unattributable to the error. That must be so, because to hypothesize a guilty verdict that was never in fact rendered—no matter how inescapable the findings to support that verdict might be—would violate the jury-trial guarantee.

Since, for the reasons described above, there has been no jury verdict within the meaning of the Sixth Amendment, the entire premise of *Chapman* review is simply absent. There being no jury verdict of guilty-beyond-a-reasonable-doubt, the question whether the *same* verdict of guilty-beyond-a-reasonable-doubt would have been rendered absent the constitutional error is utterly meaningless.

There is no *object*, so to speak, upon which harmless-error scrutiny can operate. The most an appellate court can conclude is that a jury *would surely have found* petitioner guilty beyond a reasonable doubt—not that the jury's actual finding of guilty beyond a reasonable doubt *would surely not have been different* absent the constitutional error. That is not enough. . . . The Sixth Amendment requires more than appellate speculation about a hypothetical jury's action, or else directed verdicts for the State would be sustainable on appeal; it requires an actual jury finding of guilty.

Denial of the right to a jury verdict of guilt beyond a reasonable doubt is certainly an error of the former sort, the jury guarantee being a "basic protectio[n]" whose precise effects are unmeasurable, but without which a criminal trial cannot reliably serve its function. . . . The right to trial by jury reflects, we have said, "a profound judgment about the way in which law should be enforced and justice administered." *Duncan v. Louisiana*, 391 U.S., at 155. . . . The deprivation of that right, with consequences that are necessarily unquantifiable and indeterminate, unquestionably qualifies as "structural error."

The judgment of the Supreme Court of Louisiana is reversed, and the case is remanded for proceedings not inconsistent with this opinion.

It is so ordered.

Case Questions

1. What is the essence of the harmless-error doctrine?
2. How does harmless error relate to the right to a jury trial?
3. Why does the U.S. Supreme Court reject application of harmless-error analysis where the reasonable doubt instruction is constitutionally defective?
4. What policy arguments can you make for and against the use of harmless-error analysis?

The Sixth and Fourteenth amendments guarantee accused people many important rights, including notice of the charges, trial by jury, a speedy and public trial, and representation by counsel. Also protected by these amendments are the right to present witnesses and evidence and to cross-examine opposing witnesses.

Trial by Jury

Accused people have a constitutional right to have their guilt or innocence decided by a jury composed of people representing a cross section of their community (this right to a jury trial does not extend to offenses traditionally characterized as petty offenses). The jury trial right is a safeguard against arbitrary and highhanded actions of judges.

Unless a jury trial is waived, the jury is selected at the beginning of the trial. The number of jurors ranges from six to twelve, depending on state law. A unanimous decision is not required for conviction in all states. However, twelve jurors are required in federal criminal courts, and a unanimous decision is necessary for a conviction. If a jury cannot agree on a verdict, it is called a *hung jury* and the judge dismisses the charges. In this situation, the prosecutor may retry the defendant before a new jury.

If a defendant pleads guilty, there are no questions of fact for a jury to decide, and the judge will proceed to the sentencing phase.

Fair and Public Trial

The right to be confronted by their accusers in an adversary proceeding protects accused people from being convicted by testimony given in their absence without the opportunity of cross-examination. The defendant also has a right to a public trial. This constitutional right prevents courts from becoming instruments of persecution through secret action. The right is not unlimited, however. It is subject to the judge's broad power and duty to preserve order and decorum in the courtroom. Judges may limit the number of spectators in order to prevent overcrowding or to prevent disturbances. Judges also have the power to impose sanctions on participants and observers for acts that hinder or obstruct the court in administering justice.

Right to a Speedy Trial and Cross-Examination

The accused's right to a speedy trial is interpreted as meaning that the trial should take place as soon as possible without depriving the parties of a reasonable period of time for preparation. This right, applicable to both the state and federal courts, protects an accused from prolonged imprisonment prior to trial, prevents long delay that could impair the defense of an accused person through the loss of evidence, and prevents or minimizes public suspicion and anxiety connected with an accused who is yet untried.

The right to speedy trial attaches when the prosecution begins, either by indictment or by the actual restraints imposed by arrest. How much time must elapse to result in an unconstitutional delay varies with the circumstances. The accused has the burden of showing that the delay was the fault of the state and that it resulted in prejudice.

The Prosecutor's Role

The sovereignty has the duty of prosecuting those who commit crimes; its attorney for this purpose is the prosecutor. As trial lawyer for the sovereignty, the prosecutor has extensive resources for investigation and preparation. The prosecutor is not at liberty to distort or misuse this information, and must disclose information that tends to relieve the accused of guilt. Any conduct of a prosecutor or judge that hinders the fairness of a trial to the extent that the outcome is adversely affected violates the defendant's right to due process.

Sentencing

Following conviction or a guilty plea, judges decide the punishment based on broad legislative guidelines. In reaching their decisions, they may consider unsworn or out-of-court information relevant to the circumstances of the crime and to the convicted person's life or prior record. Judges may spend days hearing testimony during a criminal trial, yet spend very little time deciding on a sentence. Their decisions may range from the maximum allowed by law to a suspended sentence. Parties found guilty may challenge the constitutionality of their sentences. They may argue that a sentence is "cruel and unusual" in violation of the Eighth Amendment, or that it violates the Equal Protection Clause of the Fourteenth Amendment.

Appeal

The federal and state constitutions guarantee defendants a fair trial, but not an error-free trial. In the federal and state judicial systems appellate courts determine if significant errors that warrant correction were committed by lower courts. The federal Constitution does not require states to provide for appellate review, although all defendants who enter a plea of not guilty are granted at least one appeal. The states differ in the number of discretionary appeals that are made available. A defendant who appeals has to exhaust all appellate opportunities at the state level and raise a federal question before petitioning the U.S. Supreme Court for a writ of *certiorari*. A person convicted of a crime in a federal district court can obtain review in the U.S. Court of Appeals, and then petition the U.S. Supreme Court for *certiorari*.

The prosecution is prohibited by the Fifth Amendment's double jeopardy clause, and by due process, from appealing a court's entry of a judgment of acquittal based on a jury verdict or on the insufficiency of the evidence. Statutes, however, may permit the prosecution to appeal (1) pretrial court orders suppressing evidence, (2) a trial judge's refusal to enter judgment on the jury's guilty verdict and the entry instead of judgment for the defendant (J.N.O.V.), (3) where the sentencing judge abused his or her discretion and imposed an "inadequate" sentence, and (4) from a judgment of acquittal for the sole purpose of clarifying the law.

Habeas Corpus

The writ of *habeas corpus* (Latin for "you have the body") is used to test the legality of a person's detention by government. It is frequently used by prisoners who have been unsuccessful in directly appealing their convictions and who are serving sentences of imprisonment. The writ of *habeas corpus* was recognized in Article 1, Section 9, of the U.S. Constitution. Congress extended the common law writ to federal prisoners in the Judiciary Act of 1789, and to state prisoners in 1867. Congress replaced the common law practices defining prisoner's use of the writ with legislation in 1948, and the U.S. Supreme Court expanded its scope during the 1960s and 1970s. In recent years both the Supreme Court and Congress have taken a different tack. Congress greatly limited the scope of *habeas corpus* by enacting procedural changes in the Antiterrorism and Effective Death Penalty Act of 1996 (AEDPA).[12]

Federal *habeas corpus* has much strategic importance because it permits convicted people, whether convicted in a federal or state court, to seek collateral review of their sentences in a federal court. The odds that a prisoner will be able to convince a U.S. District Court or U.S. Court of Appeals to order relief in a *habeas corpus* proceeding are much greater than the likelihood of successfully obtaining a writ of *certiorari* from the U.S. Supreme Court. However, the U.S. Supreme Court has severely limited the scope of federal *habeas corpus* review of prisoners convicted of drug offenses in state courts, and Congress has done likewise with petitions from persons convicted of capital offenses.

Chapter Questions

1. Define the following terms:

actus reus	due process
arraignment	duress
arrest	entrapment
attempt	Equal Protection Clause
bail	exclusionary rule
bill of attainder	*ex post facto*
causation	felony
conspiracy	fundamental liberties
cruel and unusual punishment	grand jury
custodial interrogation	*habeas corpus*

harmless-error doctrine

inchoate crime

indictment

insanity

intoxication

investigatory detentions (stop
   and frisk)

knowingly

larceny

line-ups

mala in se

mala prohibita

mens rea

misdemeanor

negligently

nolo contendere

pardon

parole

plea bargaining

preliminary hearing

preventive detention

probable cause

prosecutor

proximate cause

purposely

reasonable suspicion

recklessly

recognizance

solicitation

status crimes

strict liability

suspect classification

vicarious liability

warrant

writ

2. James Brogan was unexpectedly visited one evening at his home by federal investigators. The officers had records indicating that Brogan had received cash payments from a company whose employees were members of a union in which Brogan was an officer. Such an act would have violated federal bribery statutes. The officers asked Brogan if he had received any cash or gifts from the company. Brogan answered "no." Brogan was charged with violating federal bribery laws and with lying to a federal officer who was in the course of performing his or her duty to investigate criminal activity, as prohibited by 18 U.S. Code Section 1001. Do you see any potential for the possible abuse of prosecutorial discretion if persons in Brogan's situation can be convicted of a federal felony for untruthfully answering an incriminating question posed by federal officers in the course of an investigation?
Brogan v. United States, 96-1579 (1998)

3. Kalb County Police Officer Richardson stopped a motorist named Brown on Candler Road while it was raining for driving without using his headlights because he suspected that Brown might by DUI. Brown explained to the officer that he was not aware the lights were not on. When the officer asked Brown to produce his operator's license and evidence of insurance, Brown began a search for the requested documentation. While looking for the documents, Brown pulled an object out of one of his front pockets which the officer described as a "piece of paper" approximately one to two inches in diameter. When the paper fell in between Brown's legs onto the car seat, Brown immediately closed his legs. The officer asked Brown, "What are you trying to hide?" The trial testimony is silent as to Brown's reply. Officer Richardson then asked Brown to exit the car; however, Brown did not comply. He continued looking in the car for the documents until they were finally found. Brown appeared nervous and shaky while poking around the

car. This made Richardson suspicious that Brown was attempting to hide something. After Brown produced the documents, Officer Richardson asked him to step out of the car. Brown was given a Terry investigative pat-down, which produced neither weapons nor contraband, and he was then placed unarrested inside of Richardson's locked patrol car. The officer then proceeded to enter Brown's car to look for the piece of paper. Richardson found it, in plain view, on the car seat. This search disclosed the existence of several small plastic bags which were subsequently identified from field tests to be rock cocaine. Brown was then arrested for possession of cocaine. The officer did not know that anything was in the piece of paper at the time he conducted his search, and he did not see the cocaine in the paper until the officer subjected it to close examination. Did Officer Richardson have probable cause to make a warrantless search of Brown's car?

Brown v. State of Georgia, 504 S.E.2d 443 (1998)

4. Hillsborough County, New Hampshire, installed a teleconferencing system between the Nashua District Court and the Nashua Police Station. This system made it unnecessary to have police officers physically transport arrested persons to the courthouse for purposes of arraignment and setting bail. This procedure was intended to conserve time as well as money, and was approved by the state supreme court. Jay Larose and two other people were arraigned using this system and bail was set, but they were unable to make bail. They subsequently petitioned for a writ of *habeas corpus*. The petitioners argued that this high-tech approach to arraignments violated their due process rights under the state and federal constitutions. They also maintained that the teleconferencing procedure violated a state statute which required that arrested persons ". . . shall be taken before a district or municipal court without unreasonable delay, but not exceeding 24 hours, Sundays and holidays excepted, to answer for the offense." What due process rights could they have claimed were infringed upon, based on these facts? How might the state respond to the claimed infringement of the statutory right?

Larose v. Hillsborough County, 702 A.2d 326 (1997)

5. Bajakajian tried to take $357,000 in cash out of the United States without completing necessary paperwork. After his conviction, the federal government asked the court to order that the entire sum be forfeited, as called for by the federal statute. Would this punitive forfeiture violate the requirements of the excessive fines clause of the Eighth Amendment?

U.S. v. Bajakajian, 96-1487 (1998)

6. The Edmonds Police Department received an anonymous tip contained in a mailed note that Robert Young was growing marijuana in his house. A police detective went to the address. He noted that the windows of the house were always covered, bright lights never could be seen inside, and there was no apparent odor of marijuana detectable from the public sidewalk. The detective obtained records of Young's electric power consumption and believed it to be unusually high—a factor that his prior experience

suggested to him was consistent with the cultivation of marijuana. The detective contacted the federal DEA, which supplied an agent trained in the use of infrared thermal detection equipment. This equipment, when used at night, can detect manmade heat sources. Young's house was subjected to thermal surveillance, and the results suggested a pattern consistent with the growth of marijuana; the downstairs, for example, was warmer than the upstairs portion of the house. The detective used this information to establish probable cause for the issuance of a search warrant. Officers executing the search warrant found marijuana within the house, and Young was arrested and charged with possession of marijuana with intent to manufacture or deliver. Young sought to suppress the evidence on the grounds that the infrared surveillance of his home constituted an infringement of his rights under the Fourth Amendment to the U.S. Constitution and a corresponding right under the Washington State Constitution. Do you believe the suppression motion should be granted?

State of Washington v. Young, 867 P.2d 593 (1994)

7. Beckwith, a taxpayer, made certain statements to Internal Revenue agents. These statements were made during the course of a noncustodial interview in a criminal tax investigation. The interview was conducted in Beckwith's home after he voluntarily allowed the agents to enter. Beckwith was later tried for criminal tax fraud and, although he had not been given *Miranda* warnings before making the statements, his statements were admitted and used against him. What would be the court's reasoning in permitting these incriminating statements to be used?

Beckwith v. United States, 425 U.S. 341 (1976)

8. Defendant Butler moved to suppress evidence of his incriminating statements at his trial. These statements were made to a federal agent during custodial interrogation without counsel present. The agent testified that Butler had been advised of his rights at the time of his arrest and then taken to a local FBI office for interrogation. Butler had an eleventh-grade education. He was given an advice-of-rights form, which he read, and he stated that he understood his rights. However, Butler refused to sign a waiver provision at the bottom. After being told that he need not talk or sign anything, Butler stated that he would talk, but not sign anything. He said nothing when advised of his right to counsel. He never requested counsel or attempted to terminate the questioning. Did Butler effectively waive his rights under *Miranda*?

North Carolina v. Butler, 441 U.S. 369 (1979)

9. Police officers, armed with an arrest warrant but not a search warrant, were admitted to Chimel's home by his wife. They waited until Chimel arrived and served him with the warrant. Although he denied the officers' request to "look around," they conducted a search of the entire house "as incident to the lawful arrest." Are items taken from Chimel's home admissible at trial?

Chimel v. California, 395 U.S. 752 (1969)

10. Roosevelt Harris was convicted of possessing liquor on which no tax had been paid, in violation of federal law. The federal tax investigator's affidavit supporting the search warrant, the execution of which resulted in the discovery of the illicit liquor, stated the following: (1) Harris had a reputation with the investigator for over four years as being a trafficker in illicit distilled spirits. (2) During that time the local constable had located illicit whiskey in an abandoned house under Harris's control. (3) On the date of the affidavit, the affiant (tax investigator) had received sworn oral information from a person whom the affiant found to be a prudent person, and who feared for his life should his name be revealed, that the informant had purchased illicit whiskey from the residence described. Is the affidavit sufficient to establish probable cause for issuing a search warrant?
United States v. Harris, 403 U.S. 573 (1971)

Notes

1. G. Jones, *The Sovereignty of the Law* (Toronto: University of Toronto Press, 1973), pp. 189–191.
2. Schwartz, *The Law in America* (New York: McGraw-Hill, 1974), p. 9.
3. Schwartz, pp. 12–18, 72, 73.
4. *Craig v. Boren*, 429 U.S. 197 (1976).
5. *Eisenstadt v. Baird*, 405 U.S. 438 (1972).
6. *Craig v. Boren*, 429 U.S. 197 (1976).
7. *In re Winship*, 379 U.S. 358 (1970).
8. *Cage v. Louisiana*, 498 U.S. 38 (1990).
9. Ibid., p. 41.
10. Ibid.
11. See Chief Justice Rehnquist's concurrence in *Sullivan*.
12. The AEDPA was enacted by members of Congress who believed that the writ was being abused by desperate defendants seeking to postpone their execution dates.

IX Family Law

INTRODUCTION

The concept of what constitutes a family in the early 2000s differs greatly from that of earlier times. The seventeenth-century family had many more responsibilities. It was expected to provide members with food and shelter; to supply education, religious instruction, and discipline; and to nurse the injured and ill and care for the elderly.[1]

In contemporary America, many of these traditional family responsibilities are performed outside the family unit by public and private institutions such as schools, churches, prisons, hospitals, and nursing homes. The number of children under eighteen years of age living with a single parent has increased from 22 percent in 1980 to 28 percent in 1990 and in 2000 reached 31 percent of all family groups according to the U.S. Census Bureau.[2] Many of these families face enormous economic difficulties. They must struggle to meet even the most basic needs of their immediate members and have little ability to provide care for elders.[3] As children grow into adolescence, they become more mobile and independent than in the past, and parents often find themselves having less ability to exercise influence and control.[4]

These changes in families have been accompanied by changes in society's legal expectations about family life.[5] Family law, also called domestic relations law, has been recognized as a legal subfield only since the early 1900s.[6] Despite the rather recent formal recognition of family law, legal institutions have long been concerned with the rights and responsibilities of family members.

One of the most enduring features of the western tradition is the deference shown by the law to family self-governance, also called family autonomy.[7] This deference was recognized in Roman law[8] and was subsequently incorporated into Anglo-Saxon law,[9] canon law (the law applied in the English ecclesiastical courts, which historically handled domestic relations cases),[10] and the common law.[11]

383

Also dating from the time of the Roman emperors, however, is the legal recognition that society, through government, has a legitimate right to prevent the maltreatment and abuse of family members.[12] One example of this interest is the existence of laws in every state prohibiting child abuse and neglect. As the U.S. Supreme Court explained, governments today are expected to intervene to prevent "harm to the physical or mental health of [a] child . . ."[13]

These two legal principles accompanied the English immigrants who settled the eastern seaboard of North America and were widely accepted, although they were modified to meet the particular needs of each colony.[14]

In colonial America, the family was the most important unit of society. It was essential to preserving public order and producing economic stability.[15] After the Revolutionary War, the structure of the family was weakened by the ready availability of land, the shortage of labor, and the ease with which individuals could migrate.[16] Independence also brought a greater appreciation for the rights of individuals within the family and a corresponding decline in the outmoded view of a father's traditional rights (See Figure 9-1).[17] This trend has continued to the present time, and today mothers and fathers have equal rights and responsibilities.

Given the complexity of family law, the differences in the laws of the fifty states, and the limitations of available space, this chapter can provide only an introductory overview of the topic. This discussion will focus on how families are created, the nature of the rights and responsibilities of family members, how family relationships are terminated, and emerging issues such as the evolving dispute about the nature of the family.[18]

What Is a Family?

Although it is apparent that a *family* always includes people in a relationship, major disagreements exist about the precise meaning of the term. Traditionally, families have been based on kinship and defined as the "customary legal relationship established by birth, marriage, or adoption."[19] This definition has been challenged recently on the ground that it is too rigid. Critics argue that even if

---

From *Chapman v. Mitchell*, 44 A2d 392, 393 (1945)

" . . . the plaintiff [husband] is the master of his household. He is the managing head, with control and power to preserve the family relation, to protect its members and to guide their conduct. He has the obligation and responsibility of supporting, maintaining, and protecting the family and the correlative right to exclude intruders and unwanted visitors from the home despite the whims of the wife."

FIGURE 9-1   The Role of the Father—An Old-Fashioned View

they are unmarried, "two adult lifetime partners whose relationship is long term and characterized by an emotional and financial commitment and interdependence"[20] should receive the same rights and benefits as those who have been married. Anthropologists such as Collier, Rosaldo, and Yanagisako have favored such a functional approach. They think of families as "spheres of human relationships" that "hold property, provide care and welfare, and attend particularly to the young—a sphere conceptualized as a realm of love and intimacy," as contrasted with other more "impersonal" relationships.[21]

The legal definition of family becomes important because special rights, benefits, and privileges favor family membership. Some of these benefits are intangible, such as the societal approval that accompanies birth, marriage, and to some extent adoption. Another example is the sense of identity that family members have as to who they are and how they fit into the larger society.[22] Many other benefits are more tangible. Federal law, for example, favors married taxpayers who file jointly, and it provides social security benefits to family members in some circumstances. State legislatures also provide economic and noneconomic benefits favoring family members. Although states differ greatly as to the nature and scope of the benefits provided, they often include housing rights, homestead acts that protect some family property from creditors, statutory provisions that determine inheritance rights in the event a family member dies without leaving a will, mutual spousal support obligations, evidentiary privileges that prohibit adverse spousal testimony and that protect private spousal communications, and limited tort immunities. Many employers also favor families. Employee fringe benefit packages frequently provide family members with health and life insurance programs, as well as family leave and educational benefits.

Strong families perform essential tasks and help to create social and economic stability.[23] The family unit is expected to produce and care for the needs of the young. This includes raising children who will grow into responsible, well-adjusted adults. Family members are expected to care for each other from "cradle to grave," especially in times of crisis. When families do not or cannot meet the most basic responsibilities, they have to be met at public expense.

In the following case, the City of East Cleveland sought to enforce a housing ordinance that restricted the occupancy of a dwelling unit to a single family. The ordinance defined "family" so restrictively that it was criminal for a grandmother to live under the same roof with one of her grandsons. As written, the law prohibited a grandmother, her adult son and his child, Dale, Jr., and another grandson, John (who was a first cousin of Dale, Jr.), from living as a family. John had moved to his grandmother's house after the death of his mother. The grandmother, Inez Moore, was criminally convicted of the crime and sentenced to serve a jail term of five days and to pay a twenty-five-dollar fine. Mrs. Moore appealed her conviction, because she believed the statute violated her rights under the due process clause of the Fourteenth Amendment. Notice the Supreme Court's sympathy for the concept of the extended family, as well as the roles played by race, culture, and economics in defining the nature of a family.

Moore v. City of East Cleveland, Ohio
431 U.S. 494
U.S. Supreme Court
May 31, 1977

Mr. Justice Powell announced the judgment of the Court, and delivered an opinion in which Mr. Justice Brennan, Mr. Justice Marshall, and Mr. Justice Blackmun joined.

East Cleveland's housing ordinance, like many throughout the country, limits occupancy of a dwelling unit to members of a single family. . . . But the ordinance contains an unusual and complicated definitional section that recognizes as a "family" only a few categories of related individuals. . . . Because her family, living together in her home, fits none of those categories, appellants stand convicted of a criminal offense. The question in this case is whether the ordinance violates the Due Process Clause of the Fourteenth Amendment.

I

Appellant, Mrs. Inez Moore, lives in her East Cleveland home together with her son, Dale Moore, Sr., and her two grandsons, Dale, Jr., and John Moore, Jr. The two boys are first cousins rather than brothers; we are told that John came to live with his grandmother and with the elder and younger Dale Moores after his mother's death.

In early 1973, Mrs. Moore received a notice of violation from the city, stating that John was an "illegal occupant" and directing her to comply with the ordinance. When she failed to remove him from her home, the city filed a criminal charge. Mrs. Moore moved to dismiss, claiming that the ordinance was constitutionally invalid on its face. Her motion was overruled, and upon conviction she was sentenced to five days in jail and a $25 fine. The Ohio Court of Appeals affirmed after giving full consideration to her constitutional claims, and the Ohio Supreme Court denied review. . . .

II

The city argues that our decision in *Village of Belle Terre v. Boraas*, 416 U.S. 1, 94 (1974), requires us to sustain the ordinance attacked here.

But one overriding factor sets this case apart from *Belle Terre*. The ordinance there affected only *unrelated* individuals. It expressly allowed all who were related by "blood, adoption, or marriage" to live together, and in sustaining the ordinance we were careful to note that it promoted "family needs" and "family values." . . . East Cleveland, in contrast, has chosen to regulate the occupancy of its housing by slicing deeply into the family itself. This is no mere incidental result of the ordinance. On its face it selects certain categories of relatives who may live together and declares that others may not. In particular, it makes a crime of a grandmother's choice to live with her grandson in circumstances like those presented here.

When a city undertakes such intrusive regulation of the family, . . . the usual judicial deference to the legislature is inappropriate. "This Court has long recognized that freedom of personal choice in matters of marriage and family life is one of the liberties protected by the Due Process Clause of the Fourteenth Amendment." *Cleveland Board of Education v. LaFleur*. 414 U.S. 632, . . . (1974). . . . But when the government intrudes on choices concerning family living arrangements, this Court must examine carefully the importance of the governmental interests advanced and the extent to which they are served by the challenged regulation. . . .

When thus examined, this ordinance cannot survive. The city seeks to justify it as a means of preventing overcrowding, minimizing traffic and parking congestion, and avoiding an undue financial burden on East Cleveland's school system. Although these are legitimate goals, the ordinance before us serves them marginally, at best. For example, the ordinance permits any family consisting only of husband, wife, and unmarried children to live together, even if the family contains a half dozen licensed drivers, each with his or her own car. At the same time it forbids an adult brother and sister to share a household, even if both faithfully use public transportation. The ordinance would permit a grandmother to live with a single dependent son and children, even if his school-age children number a dozen, yet it forces Mrs. Moore to find another dwelling for her grandson John, simply because of the presence of his uncle and cousin in the same household. We need not labor the point. Section 1341.08 has but a tenuous relation to alleviation of the conditions mentioned by the city.

III

The city would distinguish the cases based on *Meyer* and *Pierce*. It points out that none of them "gives grandmothers any fundamental rights with respect to grandsons," . . . and suggests that any constitutional right to live together as a family extends only to the nuclear family—essentially a couple and their dependent children.

To be sure, these cases did not expressly consider the family relationship presented here. They were immediately concerned with freedom of choice with respect to childbearing, *e.g., LaFleur, Roe v. Wade, Griswold, supra,* or with the rights of parents to the custody and companionship of their own children, *Stanley v. Illinois, supra,* or traditional parental authority in matters of child rearing and education. *Yoder, Ginsberg, Pierce, Meyer, supra.* But unless we close our eyes to the basic reasons why certain rights associated

with the family have been accorded shelter under the Fourteenth Amendment's Due Process Clause, we cannot avoid applying the force and rationale of these precedents to the family choice involved in this case. . . .

Appropriate limits on substantive due process come not from drawing arbitrary lines but rather from careful "respect for the teachings of history [and], solid recognition of the basic values that underlie our society."

Our decisions establish that the Constitution protects the sanctity of the family precisely because the institution of the family is deeply rooted in this Nation's history and tradition. It is through the family that we inculcate and pass down many of our most cherished values, moral and cultural.

Ours is by no means a tradition limited to respect for the bonds uniting the members of the nuclear family. The tradition of uncles, aunts, cousins, and especially grandparents sharing a household along with parents and children has roots equally venerable and equally deserving of constitutional recognition. Over the years millions of our citizens have grown up in just such an environment, and most, surely, have profited from it. Even if conditions of modern society have brought about a decline in extended family households, they have not erased the accumulated wisdom of civilization, gained over the centuries and honored throughout our history, that supports a larger conception of the family. Out of choice, necessity, or a sense of family responsibility, it has been common for close relatives to draw together and participate in the duties and the satisfactions of a common home. Decisions concerning child rearing, which *Yoder, Meyer, Pierce* and other cases have recognized as entitled to constitutional protection, long have been shared with grandparents or other relatives who occupy the same household—indeed who may take on major responsibility for the rearing of the children. Especially in times of adversity, such as the death of a spouse or economic need, the broader family has tended to come together for mutual sustenance and to maintain or re-build a secure home life. This is apparently what happened here.

Whether or not such a household is established because of personal tragedy, the choice of relatives in this degree of kinship to live together may not lightly be denied by the State. *Pierce* struck down an Oregon law requiring all children to attend the State's public schools, holding that the Constitution "excludes any general power of the State to standardize its children by forcing them to accept instruction from public teachers only." . . . By the same token the Constitution prevents East Cleveland from standardizing its children—and its adults—by forcing all to live in certain narrowly defined family patterns.

Reversed.

Mr. Justice Brennan, with whom Mr. Justice Marshall joins, concurring

I join the plurality's opinion. I agree that the Constitution is not powerless to prevent East Cleveland from prosecuting as a criminal and jailing a 63-year-old grandmother for refusing to expel from her home her now 10-year-old grandson who has lived with her and been brought up by her since his mother's death when he was less than a year old. I do not question that a municipality may constitutionally zone to alleviate noise and traffic congestion and to prevent overcrowded and unsafe living conditions, in short to enact reasonable land-use restrictions in furtherance of the legitimate objectives East Cleveland claims for its ordinance. But the zoning power is not a license for local communities to enact senseless and arbitrary restrictions which cut deeply into private areas of protected family life. East Cleveland may not constitutionally define "family" as essentially confined to parents and the parents' own children. The plurality's opinion conclusively demonstrates that classifying family patterns in this eccentric way is not a rational means of

achieving the ends East Cleveland claims for its ordinance, and further that the ordinance unconstitutionally abridges the "freedom of personal choice in matters of . . . family life [that] is one of the liberties protected by the Due Process Clause of the Fourteenth Amendment." . . . I write only to underscore the cultural myopia of the arbitrary boundary drawn by the East Cleveland ordinance in the light of the tradition of the American home that has been a feature of our society since our beginning as a Nation—the "tradition" in the plurality's words, "of uncles, aunts, cousins, and especially grandparents sharing a household along with parents and children. . . ."

. . . The line drawn by this ordinance displays a depressing insensitivity toward the economic and emotional needs of a very large part of our society.

In today's America, the "nuclear family" is the pattern so often found in much of white suburbia. . . .

The Constitution cannot be interpreted, however, to tolerate the imposition by government upon the rest of us of white suburbia's preference in patterns of family living. The "extended family" that provided generations of early Americans with social services and economic and emotional support in times of hardship, and was the beachhead for successive waves of immigrants who populated our cities, remains not merely still a pervasive living pattern, but under the goad of brutal economic necessity, a prominent pattern—virtually a means of survival—for large numbers of the poor and deprived minorities of our society. For them compelled pooling of scant resources requires compelled sharing of a household.

The "extended" form is especially familiar among black families. We may suppose that this reflects the truism that black citizens, like generations of white immigrants before them, have been victims of economic and other disadvantages that would worsen if they were compelled to abandon extended, for nuclear, living patterns. . . .

I do not wish to be understood as implying that East Cleveland's enforcement of its ordinance is motivated by a racially discriminatory purpose: The record of this case would not support that implication. But the prominence of other than nuclear families among ethnic and racial minority groups, including our black citizens, surely demonstrates that the "extended family" pattern remains a vital tenet of our society. It suffices that in prohibiting this pattern of family living as a means of achieving its objectives, appellee city has chosen a device that deeply intrudes into family associational rights that historically have been central, and today remain central, to a large proportion of our population. . . . Indeed, *Village of Belle Terre v. Boraas,* 416 U.S. 1 . . . (1974), the case primarily relied upon by the appellee, actually supports the Court's decision. The Belle Terre ordinance barred only unrelated individuals from constituting a family in a single-family zone. The village took special care in its brief to emphasize that its ordinance did not in any manner inhibit the choice of *related* individuals to constitute a family, whether in the "nuclear" or "extended" form. This was because the village perceived that choice as one it was constitutionally powerless to inhibit. Its brief stated: "Whether it be the extended family of a more leisurely age or the nuclear family of today the role of the family in raising and training successive generations of the species makes it more important, we dare say, than any other social or legal institution. . . . *If any freedom not specifically mentioned in the Bill of Rights enjoys a 'preferred position' in the law it is most certainly the family.*" . . . The cited decisions recognized, as the plurality recognizes today, that the choice of the "extended family" pattern is within the "freedom of personal choice in matters of . . . family life [that] is one of the liberties protected by the Due Process Clause of the Fourteenth Amendment." . . .

Mr. Justice Stevens, concurring in the judgment

In my judgment the critical question presented by this case is whether East Cleveland's housing ordinance is a permissible restriction on appellant's right to use her own property as she sees fit. . . .

There appears to be no precedent for an ordinance which excludes any of an owner's relatives from the group of persons who may occupy his residence on a permanent basis. Nor does there appear to be any justification for such a restriction on an owner's use of his property. The city has failed totally to explain the need for a rule which would allow a homeowner to have two children live with her if they are brothers, but not if they are cousins. Since this ordinance has not been shown to have any "substantial relation to the public health, safety, morals, or general welfare" of the city of East Cleveland, and since it cuts so deeply into a fundamental right normally associated with the ownership of residential property—that of an owner to decide who may reside on his or her property . . . East Cleveland's unprecedented ordinance constitutes a taking of property without due process and without just compensation.

For these reasons, I concur in the Court's judgment.

Case Questions

1. What is the Supreme Court plurality's underlying criticism of the City of East Cleveland ordinance?
2. This case involves due process, a concept discussed in Chapter 1. How does due process apply in this instance?

3. Why does Justice Stevens write a concurring opinion?

 Justice Powell's plurality opinion links the legal meaning of substantive due process to moral values and the institution of the family. What is Powell's point?

CREATING FAMILY RELATIONSHIPS

An individual's family relationships are primarily created through marriage, the formation of a civil union/domestic partnership, and parenthood through birth or adoption and (to a much lesser extent) foster care placements. Each of these relationships will be examined in turn.

Marriage

When two people decide to marry, they are voluntarily seeking to enter into a number of relationships involving personal, economic, social, religious, and legal considerations. It is often said that marriage is a contract, and to an extent that is true, but it is unlike other civil contracts because of the extent of governmental regulation. In 1888 the United States Supreme Court noted that "[other] contracts may be modified, restricted, or enlarged, or entirely released upon the consent of the parties. Not so with marriage. The relation once formed, the law steps in and holds the parties to various obligations and liabilities. It is an institution, in the maintenance of which in its purity the public is deeply interested, for it is the foundation of the family and of society, without which there would be neither civilization nor progress."[24]

Marriage is regulated by the states, and each state determines who may marry, the duties and obligations of marriage, and how marriages are terminated. Although eligibility requirements for marriage differ from state to state, they generally include minimum age thresholds, prohibitions on marriage between close relatives, monogamy (it is illegal to marry someone who is already married), and competency (neither party can be mentally incompetent). Furthermore, the parties must not be of the same sex, and both must be entering the marriage voluntarily. The parties indicate their consent to the marriage by jointly applying for a license. Issuance of the license certifies that the applicants have complied with the relevant marriage eligibility requirements.

Although states have broad rights to regulate marriage, there are constitutional limitations on this power. This was demonstrated in 1967 in a case argued before the U.S. Supreme Court involving a Virginia criminal statute prohibiting interracial marriages. In the case of *Loving v. Virginia,* the Supreme Court was asked to determine whether such a statute was constitutionally permissible under the Fourteenth Amendment's due process and equal protection clauses.

The justices ruled that the "freedom to marry or not marry a person of another race resides with the individual and cannot be infringed by the state." You can find the *Loving* case in Chapter 8 on page 320. The following case offers another example of constitutional limitations. This case involves a 1978 constitutional challenge to a Wisconsin statute that prohibited persons who were behind on their child support payments from getting married.

Zablocki v. Redhail
434 U.S. 374
U.S. Supreme Court
January 18, 1978

Mr. Justice Marshall delivered the opinion of the Court.

At issue in this case is the constitutionality of a Wisconsin statute, Wis.Stat. §§ 245.10(1), (4), (5) (1973), which provides that members of a certain class of Wisconsin residents may not marry, within the State or elsewhere, without first obtaining a court order granting permission to marry. The class is defined by the statute to include any "Wisconsin resident having minor issue not in his custody and which he is under obligation to support by any court order or judgment." The statute specifies that court permission cannot be granted unless the marriage applicant submits proof of compliance with the support obligation and, in addition, demonstrates that the children covered by the support order "are not then and are not likely thereafter to become public charges." No marriage license may lawfully be issued in Wisconsin to a person covered by the statute, except upon court order; any marriage entered into without compliance with § 245.10 is declared void; and persons acquiring marriage licenses in violation of the section are subject to criminal penalties. . . .

I

Appellee Redhail is a Wisconsin resident who, under the terms of § 245.10, is unable to enter into a lawful marriage in Wisconsin or elsewhere so long as he maintains his Wisconsin residency. The facts, according to the stipulation filed by the parties in the District Court, are as follows. In January 1972, when appellee was a minor and a high school student, a paternity action was instituted against him in Milwaukee County Court, alleging that he was the father of a baby girl born out of wedlock on July 5, 1971. After he appeared and admitted that he was the child's father, the court entered an order on May 12, 1972, adjudging appellee the father and ordering him to pay $109 per month as support for the child until she reached 18 years of age. From May 1972 until August 1974, appellee was unemployed and indigent, and consequently was unable to make any support payments.

On September 27, 1974, appellee filed an application for a marriage license with appellant Zablocki, the County Clerk of Milwaukee County, and a few days later the application was denied on the sole ground that appellee had not obtained a court order granting him permission to marry, as required by § 245.10. . . .

II

In evaluating §§ 245.10(1), (4), (5) under the Equal Protection Clause, "we must first determine what burden of justification the classification created thereby must meet, by looking to the nature of the classification and the individual interests affected." . . . Since our past decisions make clear that the right to marry is of fundamental importance, and since the classification at issue here significantly interferes with the exercise of that right, we believe that "critical examination" of the state interests advanced in support of the classification is required. . . .

The leading decision of this Court on the right to marry is *Loving v. Virginia*, 388 U.S. 1, (1967). In that case, an interracial couple who had been convicted of violating Virginia's miscegenation laws challenged the statutory scheme on both equal protection and due process grounds. The Court's opinion could have rested solely on the ground that the statutes discriminated on the basis of race in violation of the Equal Protection Clause. . . . But the Court went on to hold that the laws arbitrarily deprived the couple of a fundamental liberty protected by the Due Process Clause, the freedom to marry. The Court's language on the latter point bears repeating:

> "The freedom to marry has long been recognized as one of the vital personal rights essential to the orderly pursuit of happiness by free men.
> "Marriage is one of the 'basic civil rights of man,' fundamental to our very existence and survival."

Although *Loving* arose in the context of racial discrimination, prior and subsequent decisions of this Court confirm that the right to marry is of fundamental importance for all individuals. Long ago, in *Maynard v. Hill*, 125 U.S. 190, . . . (1888), the Court characterized marriage as "the most important relation in life," . . . and as "the foundation of the family and of society, without which there would be neither civilization nor progress." . . . In *Meyer v. Nebraska*, 262 U.S. 390, . . . (1923), the Court recognized that the right "to marry, establish a home and bring up children" is a central part of the liberty protected by the Due Process Clause, . . . and in *Skinner v. Oklahoma* . . . 316 U.S. 535, . . . (1942), marriage was described as "fundamental to the very existence and survival of the race." . . .

More recent decisions have established that the right to marry is part of the fundamental "right of privacy" implicit in the Fourteenth Amendment's Due Process Clause. In *Griswold v. Connecticut*, 381 U.S. 479, . . . (1965), the Court observed:

> "We deal with a right of privacy older than the Bill of Rights—older than our political parties, older than our school system. Marriage is a coming together for better or for worse, hopefully enduring, and intimate to the degree of being sacred. It is an association that promotes a way of life, not causes; a harmony in living, not political faiths; a bilateral loyalty, not commercial or social projects. Yet it is an association for as noble a purpose as any involved in our prior decisions." . . .

It is not surprising that the decision to marry has been placed on the same level of importance as decisions relating to procreation, childbirth, child rearing, and family relationships. As the facts of this case illustrate, it would make little sense to recognize a right of privacy with respect to other matters of family life and not with respect to the decision to enter the relationship that is the foundation of the family in our society. The woman whom appellee desired to marry had a fundamental right to seek an abortion of their expected child, see *Roe v. Wade*, or to bring the child into life to suffer the myriad social, if not economic, disabilities that the status of illegitimacy brings. . . .

Surely, a decision to marry and raise the child in a traditional family setting must receive equivalent protection. And, if appellee's right to procreate means anything at all, it must imply some right to enter the only relationship in which the State of Wisconsin allows sexual relations legally to take place.

By reaffirming the fundamental character of the right to marry, we do not mean to suggest that every state regulation which relates in any way to the incidents of or prerequisites for marriage must be subjected to rigorous scrutiny. To the contrary, reasonable regulations that do not significantly interfere with decisions to enter into the marital relationship may legitimately be imposed. . . .

The statutory classification at issue here, however, clearly does interfere directly and substantially with the right to marry.

Under the challenged statute, no Wisconsin resident in the affected class may marry in Wisconsin or elsewhere without a court order, and marriages contracted in violation of the statute are both void and punishable as criminal offenses. Some of those in the affected class, like appellee, will never be able to obtain the necessary court order, because they either lack the financial means to meet their support obligations or cannot prove that their children will not become public charges. These persons are absolutely prevented from getting married. Many others, able in theory to satisfy the statute's requirements, will be sufficiently burdened by having to do so that they will in effect be coerced into forgoing their right to marry. And even those who can be persuaded to meet the statute's requirements suffer a serious intrusion into their freedom of choice in an area in which we have held such freedom to be fundamental.

III

When a statutory classification significantly interferes with the exercise of a fundamental right, it cannot be upheld unless it is supported by sufficiently important state interests and is closely tailored to effectuate only those interests. . . .

Appellant asserts that two interests are served by the challenged statute: the permission-to-marry proceeding furnishes an opportunity to counsel the applicant as to the necessity of fulfilling his prior support obligations; and the welfare of the out-of-custody children is protected. We may accept for present purposes that these are legitimate and substantial interests, but, since the means selected by the State for achieving these in-

terests unnecessarily impinge on the right to marry the statute cannot be sustained. . . .

First, with respect to individuals who are unable to meet the statutory requirements, the statute merely prevents the applicant from getting married, without delivering any money at all into the hands of the applicant's prior children. More importantly, regardless of the applicant's ability or willingness to meet the statutory requirements, the State already has numerous other means for exacting compliance with support obligations, means that are at least as effective as the instant statute's and yet do not impinge upon the right to marry. Under Wisconsin law, whether the children are from a prior marriage or were born out of wedlock, court-determined support obligations may be enforced directly via wage assignments, civil contempt proceedings, and criminal penalties. And, if the State believes that parents of children out of their custody should be responsible for ensuring that those children do not become public charges, this interest can be achieved by adjusting the criteria used for determining the amounts to be paid under their support orders.

There is also some suggestion that § 245.10 protects the ability of marriage applicants to meet support obligations to prior children by preventing the applicants from incurring new support obligations. But the challenged provisions of § 245.10 are grossly underinclusive with respect to this purpose, since they do not limit in any way new financial commitments by the applicants other than those arising out of the contemplated marriage. The statutory classification is substantially overinclusive as well: Given the possibility that the new spouse will actually better the applicant's financial situation, by contributing income from a job or otherwise, the statute in many cases may prevent affected individuals from improving their ability to satisfy their prior support obligations. And, although it is true that the applicant will incur support obligations to any children born during the contemplated marriage, preventing the marriage may only result in the children being born out of wedlock, as in fact occurred in appellee's case. Since the support obligation is the same whether the child is born in or out of wedlock, the net result of preventing the marriage is simply more illegitimate children.

The statutory classification created by §§ 245.10(1), (4), (5) thus cannot be justified by the interests advanced in support of it. The judgment of the District Court is, accordingly,
    Affirmed.

Mr. Justice Stewart, concurring in the judgment

I cannot join the opinion of the Court. To hold, as the Court does, that the Wisconsin statute violates the Equal Protection Clause seems to me to misconceive the meaning of that constitutional guarantee. The Equal Protection Clause deals not with substantive rights or freedoms but with invidiously discriminatory classifications. . . .

Like almost any law, the Wisconsin statute now before us affects some people and does not affect others. But to say that it thereby creates "classifications" in the equal protection sense strikes me as little short of fantasy. The problem in this case is not one of discriminatory classifications, but of unwarranted encroachment upon a constitutionally protected freedom. I think that the Wisconsin statute is unconstitutional because it exceeds the bounds of permissible state regulation of marriage, and invades the sphere of liberty protected by the Due Process Clause of the Fourteenth Amendment.

I

I do not agree with the Court that there is a "right to marry" in the constitutional sense. That right, or more accurately that privilege, is under our federal system peculiarly one to be defined and limited by state law. . . . A State may not only "significantly interfere with decisions to enter into marital relationship," but may in many circumstances absolutely prohibit it. Surely, for example, a State may legitimately say that no one can marry his or her sibling, that no one can marry who is not at least 14 years old, that no one can marry without first passing an examination for venereal disease, or that no one can marry who has a living husband or wife. But, just as surely, in regulating the intimate human relationship of marriage there is a limit beyond which a State may not constitutionally go. . . .

II

. . . Although the Court purports to examine the bases for legislative classifications and to compare the treatment of legislatively defined groups, it actually erects substantive limitations on what States may do. Thus, the effect of the Court's decision in this case is not to require Wisconsin to draw its legislative classifications with greater precision or to afford similar treatment to similarly situated persons. Rather, the message of the Court's opinion is that Wisconsin may not use its control over marriage to achieve the objectives of the state statute. Such restrictions on basic governmental power are at the heart of substantive due process.

Case Questions

1. The Supreme Court majority ruled that a statute preventing persons under support orders from marrying without judicial approval is a classification

that significantly interfered with the exercise of a fundamental privacy right. What is significant about classifying a right as *fundamental*?

2. Why does Justice Stewart agree with the majority on the judgment in this case, but disagree with the rationale?

Marriage Solemnization Ceremonies

States generally require that persons intending to marry solemnize their union with either a civil or a religious ceremony The solemnization ceremony provides tangible and public evidence that a marriage has occurred. It demonstrates that the parties mutually desire to marry and are legally qualified.[25]

Common Law Marriages

Some jurisdictions recognize privately created, informal marriages by agreement that dispense with licenses and solemnization ceremonies.[26] They are called *common law marriages.* Although each state that recognizes such marriages has its own particular requirements, most require that the parties be of age, and unmarried. Most importantly, the parties must have established the relationship of husband and wife, live together as a married couple, and present themselves to the world as being married. Living together, jointly owning property, and having a child are insufficient acts, in themselves, to establish a common law marriage. Montana and Pennsylvania have statutes protecting the validity of such marriages.[27] The other jurisdictions recognize their validity by court decisions. Georgia, Idaho, Kansas, and Ohio only recognize common law marriages that were formed prior to a specified date, and New Hampshire only recognizes such marriages in conjunction with probating an estate.

Civil Unions and Domestic Partnerships

During the 1990s, cases which sought to legalize marriages between persons of the same gender reached the supreme courts of Hawai'i[28] and Vermont.[29] Although the plaintiffs failed to convince either court to recognize a privacy right to marry a person of the same gender, both courts expressed concerns about whether other provisions in their respective state constitutions entitled the plaintiffs to relief. In Hawai'i, the court expressed its concern about perceived equal protection issues and remanded the case for trial. The case was tried on remand but before it could work its way back to the Hawai'i Supreme Court, a constitutional amendment was adopted that gave the legislature explicit power to restrict marriages to persons of different genders.

The Vermont Supreme Court determined that same-sex couples wishing to marry were being denied protections to which they were entitled under the

Common Benefits Clause of that state's constitution. The Court pointed to the many benefits and protections that accrued to married couples and questioned whether denying these benefits under these circumstances meaningfully contributed to advancing Vermont's "interest in promoting the link between procreation and child rearing."[30] Having identified the problem, the court essentially left it to the state legislature to figure out the appropriate remedy. Although the legislature decided that only male-female couples could receive marriage licenses, they created a functional equivalent status for same-sex couples called a "civil union." As can be seen in Figure 9-2, the benefits and

---

§§ 1204. Benefits, Protections and Responsibilities of Parties to a Civil Union

(a) Parties to a civil union shall have all the same benefits, protections and responsibilities under law, whether they derive from statute, administrative or court rule, policy, common law or any other source of civil law, as are granted to spouses in a marriage.

(b) A party to a civil union shall be included in any definition or use of the terms "spouse," "family," "immediate family," "dependent," "next of kin," and other terms that denote the spousal relationship, as those terms are used throughout the law.

(c) Parties to a civil union shall be responsible for the support of one another to the same degree and in the same manner as prescribed under law for married persons.

(d) The law of domestic relations, including annulment, separation and divorce, child custody and support, and property division and maintenance shall apply to parties to a civil union.

(e) The following is a nonexclusive list of legal benefits, protections and responsibilities of spouses, which shall apply in like manner to parties to a civil union:

   (1) laws relating to title, tenure, descent and distribution, intestate succession, waiver of will, survivorship, or other incidents of the acquisition, ownership, or transfer, inter vivos or at death, of real or personal property, including eligibility to hold real and personal property as tenants by the entirety (parties to a civil union meet the common law unity of person qualification for purposes of a tenancy by the entirety);

   (2) causes of action related to or dependent upon spousal status, including an action for wrongful death, emotional distress, loss of consortium, dramshop, or other torts or actions under contracts reciting, related to, or dependent upon spousal status;

   (3) probate law and procedure, including nonprobate transfer;

   (4) adoption law and procedure;

   (5) group insurance for state employees under 3 V.S.A. §§ 631, and continuing care contracts under 8 V.S.A. §§ 8005;

   (6) spouse abuse programs under 3 V.S.A. §§ 18;

FIGURE 9-2   Excerpt from Vermont Civil Union Statute Title 15 Vermont Statutes Annotated §§ 1204

protections afforded persons who enter into civil unions is exactly the same as those enjoyed by persons who marry.

It is interesting to note that Vermont had the right, as a sovereign state under the U.S. Constitution, to determine its own public policy with respect to marriage requirements. It chose to establish comprehensive, parallel, and separate procedures by which qualifying male-female and same-sex couples can have their relationships legally recognized by the state. The California Legislature has chosen a different course. It has adopted an a la carte approach in enacting its domestic partnership law. This law was signed by the governor on October 14, 2001, and provides qualifying same-sex couples who register with the state with

---

(7) prohibitions against discrimination based upon marital status;

(8) victim's compensation rights under 13 V.S.A. §§ 5351;

(9) workers' compensation benefits;

(10) laws relating to emergency and nonemergency medical care and treatment, hospital visitation and notification, including the Patient's Bill of Rights under 18 V.S.A. chapter 42 and the Nursing Home Residents' Bill of Rights under 33 V.S.A. chapter 73;

(11) terminal care documents under 18 V.S.A. chapter 111, and durable power of attorney for health care execution and revocation under 14 V.S.A. chapter 121;

(12) family leave benefits under 21 V.S.A. chapter 5, subchapter 4A;

(13) public assistance benefits under state law;

(14) laws relating to taxes imposed by the state or a municipality;

(15) laws relating to immunity from compelled testimony and the marital communication privilege;

(16) the homestead rights of a surviving spouse under 27 V.S.A. §§ 105 and homestead property tax allowance under 32 V.S.A. §§ 6062;

(17) laws relating to loans to veterans under 8 V.S.A. §§ 1849;

(18) the definition of family farmer under 10 V.S.A. §§ 272;

(19) laws relating to the making, revoking and objecting to anatomical gifts by others under 18 V.S.A. §§ 5240;

(20) state pay for military service under 20 V.S.A. §§ 1544;

(21) application for early voter absentee ballot under 17 V.S.A. §§ 2532;

(22) family landowner rights to fish and hunt under 10 V.S.A. §§ 4253;

(23) legal requirements for assignment of wages under 8 V.S.A. §§ 2235; and

(24) affirmance of relationship under 15 V.S.A. §§ 7.

(f) The rights of parties to a civil union, with respect to a child of whom either becomes the natural parent during the term of the civil union, shall be the same as those of a married couple, with respect to a child of whom either spouse becomes the natural parent during the marriage. (Added 1999, No. 91 (Adj. Sess.), §§ 3.)

FIGURE 9-2 **Excerpt from Vermont Civil Union Statute** (*continued*)

a limited menu of rights and benefits. What we are seeing take place in the country with respect to this most controversial issue is federalism at work in an area traditionally reserved to the states.

In the spring of 1996 there was considerable apprehension in Congress that Hawai'i might become the first state to sanction same-sex marriages and legislation entitled the "Defense of Marriage Act" was introduced and ultimately enacted into law (see Figure 9-3).

Full Faith and Credit Clause Issues

Although the parameters of the Constitution's Full Faith and Credit Clause (Article IV, Section I) remain very undefined, all states have traditionally recognized persons as married who were parties to a valid marriage in some other state. But in the aftermath of Vermont's Civil Union law, both Congress and many state legislatures are having second thoughts about this practice.

The federal Defense of Marriage Statute defines the term "effect," a term used in the U.S. Constitution's Full Faith and Credit Clause, as not requiring any state, against its will, to recognize same-sex marriages as valid. Some thirty states, not wishing to recognize same-sex unions that are legalized in other states, have also enacted parallel state legislation. It is likely that state and federal appellate courts will be determining whether such statutes are constitutional. In the following Georgia case of *Burns v. Burns*, the constitutionality of a defense of marriage statute is challenged.

Burns v. Burns
A01A1827
Court of Appeals of Georgia, Second Division
January 23, 2002

Miller, Judge.

The sole issue in this case is whether the trial court erred in enforcing a consent decree pursuant to a divorce between the parties in which they agreed that no child visitations would occur during any time the party being visited cohabited with or had overnight stays with any adult to whom that party was not legally married or related within the second degree. As we discern no error in enforcing this legally constituted consent order, we affirm.

Darian and Susan Burns were divorced on December 4, 1995, and Darian retained full custody of the couple's three minor children. Three years later Susan filed a motion for contempt, alleging that Darian refused to allow her visitation with the children. As a result the court issued a consent order modifying visitation rights. The modification required and the parties agreed that "there shall be no visitation nor residence by the children with either party during any time where such party cohabits with or has overnight stays with any adult to which such party is not legally married or to whom party is not related within the second degree."

On July 1, 2000, the State of Vermont enacted a civil union law, and on July 3, 2000, Susan Burns and a female companion (not related to Susan) traveled to Vermont where they received a "LICENSE AND CERTIFICATE OF CIVIL UNION." Two months later Darian filed a motion for contempt, alleging

> ### Defense of Marriage Act—28 USC §1738C
>
> §1738C. Certain acts, records, and proceedings and the effect thereof
>
> No State, territory, or possession of the United States, or Indian tribe, shall be required to give effect to any public act, record, or judicial proceeding of any other State, territory, possession, or tribe respecting a relationship between persons of the same sex that is treated as a marriage under the laws of such other State, territory, possession, or tribe, or a right or claim arising from such relationship.
>
> (Added Sept. 21, 1996, P. L. 104-199, '2(a), 110 Stat. 2419.)

FIGURE 9-3   Excerpt from the Defense of Marriage Act

that Susan violated the trial court's order by exercising visitation with the children "while cohabiting with her female lover." Susan opposed the motion for contempt, arguing that she was not in violation of the visitation requirements in that she had complied with the legally married requirement by virtue of her civil union with an adult female. No party argued that the consent decree was unenforceable.

The trial court found that the provisions of its order applied equally to both parties and to both sexes and that a "civil union" is not a marriage. The court further found that the provisions of the order were valid and enforceable.

On appeal Susan contends that she and her female companion were married in the State of Vermont and pursuant to "the full faith and credit doctrine they are married in Georgia as well." She argues further that she has a fundamental right to privacy which includes the right to define her own family and that the State of Georgia cannot place limitations on this right.

Susan's position, however, has a flawed premise: she and her female companion were not married in Vermont but instead entered into a "civil union" under 15 Vt. Stat. Ann. §§ 1201 et seq. The definitional section of that statute expressly distinguishes between "marriage," which is defined as "the legally recognized union of one man and one woman," and "civil union," which is defined as a relationship established between two eligible persons pursuant to that chapter. The next section reemphasizes this distinction, requiring that eligible persons must "be of the same sex and therefore excluded from the marriage laws of this state." Indeed, the legislative findings accompanying the enactment of the Vermont civil union statute noted that "a system of civil unions does not bestow the status of civil marriage. . . ."

Moreover, even if Vermont had purported to legalize same-sex marriages, such would not be recognized in Georgia, the place where the consent decree was ordered and agreed to by both parties (both of whom are Georgia residents), and more importantly the place where the present action is brought. O.C.G.A. §§ 19-3-3.1 (a) clearly states that it is the public policy of Georgia "to recognize the union only of man and woman. Marriages between persons of the same sex are prohibited in this state." Additionally, under O.C.G.A. §§ 19-3-3.1 (b) no marriage between persons of the same sex shall be recognized as entitled to the benefits of marriage. Any marriage entered into by persons of the same sex pursuant to a marriage license issued by another state or foreign jurisdiction or otherwise shall be void in this state. Any contractual rights granted by virtue of such license shall be unenforceable in the courts of this state and the courts of this state shall have no jurisdiction whatsoever under any circumstances to grant a divorce or separate maintenance with respect to such marriage or otherwise to consider or rule on any of the parties' respective rights arising as a result of or in connection with such marriage.

Moreover, Georgia is not required to give full faith and credit to same-sex marriages of other states. What constitutes a marriage in the State of Georgia is a legislative function, not a judicial one, and as judges we are duty bound to follow the clear language of the statute. The Georgia Legislature has chosen not to recognize marriage between persons of the same sex, and any constitutional challenge to Georgia's marriage statute should be addressed to the Supreme Court of Georgia. . . .

Simply put, the consent order signed by the presiding judge provides that visitation will not be allowed during the time that Darian or Susan cohabitates with an adult to whom he or she is not legally married, and as Susan and her companion are not legally married in the State of Vermont and clearly not legally married under Georgia law, any such activity by Susan is in violation of the court's order. Accordingly, the court did not err in its conclusion that the visitation order is valid and that such violation constitutes contempt.

Judgment affirmed. Andrews, P. J., and Eldridge, J., concur.

Case Questions

1. Upon what ground did Susan Burns appeal the trial court's finding that the consent order modifying her visitation rights with her three minor children was valid and that a violation of its terms would constitute contempt?
2. How did the Georgia Court of Appeals rule and why?

The parties to Vermont civil unions may experience great difficulty establishing subject matter jurisdiction in the courts of non-civil union states. The first such case to reach an appellate court encountered this jurisdictional hurdle in Connecticut. The Connecticut Court of Appeals, in July of 2002, affirmed a lower court's ruling that there was no subject matter jurisdiction in Connecticut to dissolve a civil union formed in Vermont between a same-sex couple. The appellate court concluded in *Rosengarten v. Downes* (802 A.2d 170 (2002), that it would be contrary to Connecticut public policy for any court to legally recognize same-sex unions in any manner. The Court of Appeals explained:

> "[a]lthough our General Assembly has on occasion adopted preambles to some of the enactments, it is not the usual case. . . . Section 45a-727a of the General Statutes is unusual in that it is completely devoted to a declaration of legislative policy. Subsection (4) of §§ 45a-727a provides: "It is further found that the current public policy of the state of Connecticut is now limited to a marriage between a man and a woman."

Adoption

Informal adoptions existed in this country from its earliest days, and into the 1860s orphans were often apprenticed to masters so that they could pay for their room and board.[31] Since adoption was unknown to the common law, adoption law in the United States is traced to 1851, when Massachusetts enacted the first statute.[32]

Although modern statutes permit the adoption of adults, subject to some exceptions,[33] most adoptions involve children. Adoption is primarily a social and a legal process by which the rights and duties accompanying the parent-child relationship are transferred from birth parents to adoptive parents. State adoption statutes were originally intended primarily to help qualified childless couples "normalize" their marriages,[34] but today the statutes provide families for many abandoned, abused, deserted, neglected, or unwanted children, who might otherwise need to be supported at public expense.

Adoptions can be classified as either independent or agency placements. In *agency adoptions,* the birth parents consent to the termination of their parental rights and surrender the child to an adoption agency to select the adoptive parent(s) and place the child. An *independent adoption* takes place when the birth parent(s) themselves interview prospective adoptive parents and make a selection without agency involvement. Some states prohibit independent adoptions and require that agencies participate in the process.

Becoming an adoptive parent is highly regulated, and the procedures vary by state and by the type of adoption. It often makes a difference whether the adoption involves an agency or is independent, is between relatives, or is of an adult. In adoptions between related persons, for example, where a stepparent wishes to adopt his or her spouse's child, the investigative process is often simplified or eliminated. In an independent adoption, the nature and scope of any investigation is left up to the birth parent(s). They interview prospective adoptive parents and place the child without agency participation. When a public or private agency licensed by the state places a child for adoption, the law usually requires close scrutiny. Adoptive parents who are unrelated to an adoptive child are carefully investigated to determine whether the placement is suitable and in the best interests of the child. This investigation is often very detailed and probes most areas of an applicant's life. The probe results in a report that includes information on the applicant's race, age, marital status, and financial condition, the "adequacy of the home environment," and information about very personal matters such as religious preferences, current romantic interests, and sexuality.[35]

Matching

The investigative process makes it possible for agencies to rank prospective adoptive parents in terms of how closely they match the agency's conception of the ideal family for the child. Those who most closely fit the profile are often matched with the most "desirable" adoptees.[36] Petitioners who are married generally rank higher than those who are unmarried, younger applicants ranked higher than older, able bodied higher than disabled, and heterosexuals higher than homosexuals.[37]

Agency placement decisions that hinge on considerations of race, religion, and sexual orientation have been challenged in the courts. Judicial bodies have struggled with the question of whether to support or oppose laws and policies prohibiting or disfavoring interracial adoptions. Although the U.S. Supreme Court decided in 1984 that race should not be used as the decisive factor in resolving child custody disputes,[38] it has made no comparable decision directly involving adoptions. Lower courts have declared as unconstitutional state statutes that prohibit interracial adoptions[39] and permit the consideration of race only as a "relevant but not a decisive factor," but this standard has not been generally implemented.[40] Race is still commonly considered in placement decisions.[41] Some states have responded to the constitutional ambiguity by enacting preference laws that favor adoptive parents who share the same ethnic or racial background of the adoptee. Reports persist that agencies continue the practice of making transracial placements only as a last resort.[42]

Interracial adoption is a topic heavily laden with emotion, most of the fury arising when whites seek to adopt nonwhite children. Questions are frequently raised about whether white adoptive parents have the ability to fully develop a nonwhite child's racial identity and appreciation for the richness of his or her culture.[43]

Congress enacted the Multiethnic Placement Act of 1994 (which was amended by the Interethnic Adoption Provisions of 1996), also known as the MEPA-IEP, to;

1. prohibit adoption agencies that receive federal funds from using an aspiring adoptive or foster parent's race, color, or national origin against him or her for purposes of denying such parent the placement of a child.
2. delay or deny a child an adoptive or foster care placement because of his or her race, color, or national origin.

However, this statute also contains language that allows agencies to consider a child's racial identity and cultural needs in making placement decisions (notice the language in California Statutes 8708 and 8709 in Figure 9-4).

The MEPA-IEP legislation intends that placement decisions be made on a case-by-case basis and cultural needs cannot routinely be used to prevent white adoptive parents, for example, from adopting nonwhite children. Congress's intent could not be more clear because it included a provision in the IEP which repealed language in the original MEPA that expressly permitted agencies to consider a "child's cultural, ethnic, and racial background and the capacity of the prospective foster or adoptive parents to meet the needs of a child from this background" in the making of placement decisions.

However, it is difficult to determine in individual cases whether the law is being followed. How can prospective white adoptive parents, who have been told that because of the child's cultural needs they will not be permitted to adopt a nonwhite child, know whether this justification is merely a pretext for invidious discrimination?

California Family Code § 8708

Neither the department nor a licensed adoption agency to which a child has been freed for adoption by either relinquishment or termination of parental rights may do any of the following:

(a) Categorically deny to any person the opportunity to become an adoptive parent, solely on the basis of the race, color, or national origin of the adoptive parent or the child involved.

(b) Delay or deny the placement of a child for adoption, or otherwise discriminate in making an adoptive placement decision, solely on the basis of the race, color, or national origin of the adoptive parent or the child involved.

(c) Delay or deny the placement of a child for adoption solely because the prospective, approved adoptive family resides outside the jurisdiction of the department or the licensed adoption agency. For purposes of this subdivision, an approved adoptive family means a family approved pursuant to the California adoptive applicant assessment standards. If the adoptive applicant assessment was conducted in another state according to that state's standards, the California placing agency shall determine whether the standards of the other state substantially meet the standards and criteria established in California adoption regulations.

California Family Code § 8709

The department or licensed adoption agency to which a child has been freed for adoption by either relinquishment or termination of parental rights may consider the cultural, ethnic, or racial background of the child and the capacity of the prospective adoptive parent to meet the needs of a child of this background as one of a number of factors used to determine the best interest of a child. The child's religious background may also be considered in determining an appropriate placement. As used in this section, "placement decision" means the decision to place, or to delay or deny the placement of a child, in an adoptive home, and includes the decision to seek termination of parental rights or otherwise make a child legally available for adoptive placement.

California Family Code § 8710

Where a child is being considered for adoption, the department or licensed adoption agency shall first consider adoptive placement in the home of a relative. However, if a relative is not available, if placement with an available relative is not in the child's best interest, or if placement would permanently separate the child from other siblings who are being considered for adoption or who are in foster care and an alternative placement would not require the permanent separation, the foster parent or parents of the child shall be considered with respect to the child along with all other prospective adoptive parents where all of the following conditions are present:

(a) The child has been in foster care with the foster parent or parents for a period of more than four months.

(b) The child has substantial emotional ties to the foster parent or parents.

(c) The child's removal from the foster home would be seriously detrimental to the child's well-being.

(d) The foster parent or parents have made a written request to be considered to adopt the child. This section does not apply to a child who has been adjudged a dependent of the juvenile court pursuant to Section 300 of the Welfare and Institutions Code.

FIGURE 9-4   California Family Code Sections 8708, 8709, 8710

But the potential for categorical placement practices is almost limitless. Religion, educational levels, and socioeconomic status are just a few of the areas in which informal "blanket" policies can be the norm.

The U.S. Supreme Court has strongly indicated that government should remain neutral in religious matters,[44] and later in this chapter we will see how the Court supported parental choice regarding the religious upbringing of children. But the Court has not attempted to answer, as a general proposition, whether religious matching is in the best interest of adoptive children.

State statutes, however, often express a preference that adoptive parents be of the same religion as the adoptee or birth parent(s).[45] Should adoptive parents who are of mixed religions, who adhere to obscure faiths or who are atheists, be legally disadvantaged in placement decisions?[46] Should adoptive parents have the right to choose the religion of their adoptive child, or must they raise the child in the faith chosen by the birth parents? Does it matter whether the adoptive child's religion differs from that of the other members of the adoptive family?[47] Questions like these are easy to ask, but they raise policy issues that are difficult to resolve.

Another area of current controversy involves the placement of adoptees with gay and lesbian adoptive parents. Some states, such as Florida and New Hampshire, have enacted statutes that explicitly prohibit such adoptions.[48] Where no statutes prevent them, they have been permitted, at least where the most difficult-to-place children are concerned.[49] However, the preference of agencies for married couples is sometimes used as a convenient justification for opposing placements that are really rejected because the adoptive parents are gays or lesbians.

Some courts have explicitly confronted the issue and have been reluctant to approve these placements. In 1986 an Arizona appellate court, in affirming the ruling of the trial court, commentated that it would be inconsistent for the state to declare sodomy to be criminal conduct and yet permit a bisexual man to become an adoptive parent.[50] The stated reasons for rejecting gays and lesbians as adoptive parents are often based on the perceived incompatibility of the "'gay lifestyle' with social mores and on a fear that an adoptive child would be exposed to an increased risk of contracting AIDS."[51] Other courts have been more flexible, as evidenced in the following Massachusetts case in which the Supreme Judicial Court had to decide whether two lesbians could jointly become adoptive parents.

Adoption of Tammy
619 N.E.2d 315
Supreme Judicial Court of Massachusetts
September 10, 1993

Greaney, Justice

In this case, two unmarried women, Susan and Helen, filed a joint petition in the Probate and Family Court Department . . . to adopt as their child Tammy, a minor, who is Susan's biological daughter. Following an evidentiary hearing, a judge of the Probate and Family Court entered a memorandum of decision containing findings of fact and conclusions of law. Based on her finding that Helen and Susan "are each functioning, separately and together, as the custodial and psychological parents of [Tammy]," and that "it is the best interest of said [Tammy] that she be adopted by both," the judge entered a decree allowing the adoption. Simultaneously, the judge reserved and reported to the Appeals Court the evidence and all questions of law. . . . We transferred the case to this court on our own motion. We conclude that the adoption was properly allowed under G. L. c. 210.

We summarize the relevant facts as found by the judge. Helen and Susan have lived together in a committed relationship, which they consider to be permanent, for more than ten years. In June, 1983, they jointly purchased a house in Cambridge. Both women are physicians specializing in surgery. At the time the petition was filed, Helen maintained a private practice in general surgery at Mount Auburn Hospital and Susan, a nationally recognized expert in the field of breast cancer, was director of the Faulkner Breast Center and a surgical oncologist at the Dana Farber Cancer Institute. Both women also held positions on the faculty of Harvard Medical School.

For several years prior to the birth of Tammy, Helen and Susan planned to have a child, biologically related to both of them, whom they would jointly parent. Helen first attempted to conceive a child through artificial insemination by Susan's brother. When those efforts failed, Susan successfully conceived a child through artificial insemination by Helen's biological cousin, Francis. The women attended childbirth classes together and Helen was present when Susan gave birth to Tammy on April 30, 1988. Although Tammy's birth certificate reflects Francis as her biological father, she was given a hyphenated surname using Susan and Helen's last names.

Since her birth, Tammy has lived with, and been raised and supported by, Helen and Susan. Tammy views both women as her parents, calling Helen "mama" and Susan "mommy." Tammy has strong emotional and psychological bonds with both Helen and Susan. Together, Helen and Susan have provided Tammy with a comfortable home, and have created a warm and stable environment which is supportive of Tammy's growth and over-all well being. Both women jointly and equally participate in parenting Tammy, and both have a strong financial commitment to her. During the work week, Helen usually has lunch at home with Tammy, and on weekends both women spend time together with Tammy at special events or running errands. When Helen and Susan are working, Tammy is cared for by a nanny. The three vacation together at least ten days every three to four months, frequently spending time with Helen's and Susan's respective extended families in California and Mexico. Francis does not participate in parenting Tammy and does not support her. His intention was to assist Helen and Susan in having a child, and he does not intend to be involved with Tammy, except as a distant relative. Francis signed an adoption surrender and supports the joint adoption by both women.

Helen and Susan, recognizing that the laws of the Commonwealth do not permit them to enter into a legally cognizable marriage, believe that the best interests of Tammy require legal recognition of her identical emotional relationship to both women. Susan expressed her understanding that it may not be in her own long-term interest to permit Helen to adopt Tammy because, in the event that Helen and Susan separate, Helen would have equal rights to primary custody. Susan indicated, however, that she has no reservation about allowing Helen to adopt. Apart from the emotional security and current practical ramifications which legal recognition of the reality of her parental relationships will provide Tammy, Susan indicated that the adoption is important for Tammy in terms of potential inheritance from Helen. Helen and her living issue are the beneficiaries of three irrevocable family trusts. Unless Tammy is adopted, Helen's share of the trusts may pass to others. Although Susan and Helen have established a substantial trust fund for Tammy, it is comparatively small in relation to Tammy's potential inheritance under Helen's family trusts.

Over a dozen witnesses, including mental health professionals, teachers, colleagues, neighbors, blood relatives and a priest and nun, testified to the fact that Helen and Susan participate equally in raising Tammy, that Tammy relates to both women as her parents, and that the three form a healthy, happy, and stable family unit. Educators familiar with Tammy testified that she is an extremely well-adjusted, bright, creative, cheerful child who interacts well with other children and adults. A priest and nun from the parties' church testified that Helen and Susan are active parishioners, that they routinely take Tammy to church and church-related activities, and that they attend to the spiritual and moral development of Tammy in an exemplary fashion. Teachers from Tammy's school testified that Helen and Susan both actively participate as volunteers in the school community and communicate frequently with school officials. Neighbors testified that they would have no hesitation in leaving their own children in the care of Helen or Susan. Susan's father, brother, and maternal aunt, and Helen's cousin testified in favor of the joint adoption. Members of both women's extended families attested to the fact that they consider Helen and Susan to be equal parents of Tammy. Both families unreservedly endorsed the adoption petition.

The Department of Social Services (department) conducted a home study in connection with the adoption petition which recommended the adoption, concluding that "the petitioners and their home are suitable for the proper rearing of this child." Tammy's pediatrician reported to the department that Tammy receives regular pediatric care and that she "could not have more excellent parents than Helen and Susan." A court-appointed guardian ad litem, Dr. Steven Nickman, assistant clinical professor of psychiatry at Harvard Medical School, conducted a clinical assessment of Tammy and her family with a view toward determining whether or not it would be in Tammy's best interests to be adopted by Helen and Susan. Dr. Nickman considered the ramifications of the fact that Tammy will be brought up in a "non-standard" family. As part of his report, he reviewed and referenced literature on child psychiatry and child psychology which supports the conclusion that children raised by lesbian parents develop normally. In sum, he stated that "the fact that this parent-child constellation came into being as a result of thoughtful planning and a strong desire on the part of these women to be parents to a child and to give that child the love, the wisdom and the knowledge that they possess . . . [needs to be taken into account]. . . . The maturity of these women, their status in the community, and their seriousness of purpose stands in contrast to the caretaking environments of a vast number of children who are born to heterosexual parents but who are variously abused, neglected and otherwise deprived of security and happiness." Dr. Nickman concluded that "there is every reason for [Helen] to become a legal parent to Tammy just as [Susan] is," and he recommended that the court so order. An attorney appointed to represent Tammy's interests also strongly recommended that the joint petition be granted.

Despite the overwhelming support for the joint adoption and the judge's conclusion that joint adoption is clearly in Tammy's best interests, the question remains whether there is anything in the law of the Commonwealth that would prevent this adoption. The law of adoption is purely statutory, . . . and the governing statute . . . is to be strictly followed in all its essential particulars. . . .

The primary purpose of the adoption statute, particularly with regard to children under the age of fourteen, is undoubtedly the advancement of the best interests of the subject child. . . .

With these considerations in mind, we examine the statute to determine whether adoption in the circumstances of this case is permitted.

1. The initial question is whether the Probate Court judge had jurisdiction under G.L.c.210 to enter a judgment on a joint petition for adoption brought by two unmarried cohabitants in the petitioners' circumstances. We answer this question in the affirmative.

There is nothing on the face of the statute which precludes the joint adoption of a child by two unmarried cohabitants such as the petitioners. . . .

In the context of adoption, where the legislative intent to promote the best interests of the child is evidenced throughout the governing statute, and the adoption of a child by two unmarried individuals accomplishes that goal, construing the term "person" as "persons" clearly enhances, rather than defeats, the purpose of the statute. Furthermore, it is apparent from the first sentence of G. L. c. 210, § 1, that the Legislature considered and defined those combinations of persons which would lead to adoptions in violation of public policy. Clearly absent is any prohibition of adoption by two unmarried individuals like the petitioners.

While the Legislature may not have envisioned adoption by same-sex partners, there is no indication that it attempted to define all possible categories of persons leading to adoptions in the best interests of children. . . .

The limitations on adoption that do exist derive from the written consent requirements contained in § 2, from specific conditions set forth in § 2A, which must be satisfied prior to the adoption of a child under the age of fourteen, and from several statutory and judicial directives which essentially restrict adoptions to those which have been found by a judge to be in the best interests of the subject child. . . .

In this case . . . [a]doption will not result in any tangible change in Tammy's daily life; it will, however, serve to provide her with a significant legal relationship which may be important to her future. At the most practical level, adoption will entitle Tammy to inherit from Helen's family trusts and from Helen and her family under the law of intestate succession . . . , to receive support from Helen, who will be legally obligated to provide such support . . . , to be eligible for coverage under Helen's health insurance policies, and to be eligible for social security benefits in the event of Helen's disability or death. . . .

Of equal, if not greater significance, adoption will enable Tammy to preserve her unique filial ties to Helen in the event that Helen and Susan separate, or Susan predeceases Helen.

Adoption serves to establish legal rights and responsibilities so that, in the event that problems arise in the future, issues of custody and visitation may be promptly resolved by reference to the best interests of the child within the recognized framework of the law. . . . There is no jurisdictional bar in the statute to the judge's consideration of this joint petition. The conclusion that the adoption is in the best interests of Tammy is also well warranted.

2. The judge also posed the question whether . . . Susan's legal relationship to Tammy must be terminated if Tammy is adopted. Section 6 provides that, on entry of an adoption decree, "all rights, duties and other legal consequences of the natural relation of child and parent shall . . . except as regards marriage, incest or cohabitation, terminate between the child so adopted and his natural parents and kindred." Although G. L. c. 210, § 2, clearly permits a child's natural parent to be an adoptive parent, § 6 does not contain any express exceptions to its termination provision. The Legislature obviously did not intend that a natural parent's legal relationship to its child be terminated

when the natural parent is a party to the adoption petition.

Section 6 clearly is directed to the more usual circumstances of adoption, where the child is adopted by persons who are not the child's natural parents (either because the natural parents have elected to relinquish the child for adoption or their parental rights have been involuntarily terminated). The purpose of the termination provision is to protect the security of the child's newly-created family unit by eliminating involvement with the child's natural parents. Although it is not uncommon for a natural parent to join in the adoption petition of a spouse who is not the child's natural parent, the statute has never been construed to require the termination of the natural parent's legal relationship to the child in these circumstances.

Reading the adoption statute as a whole, we conclude that the termination provision contained in § 6 was intended to apply only when the natural parents (or parent) are not parties to the adoption petition.

3. We conclude that the Probate Court has jurisdiction to enter a decree on a joint adoption petition brought by the two petitioners when the judge has found that joint adoption is in the subject child's best interests. We further conclude that, when a natural parent is a party to a joint adoption petition, that parent's legal relationship to the child does not terminate on entry of the adoption decree.

4. So much of the decree as allows the adoption of Tammy by both petitioners is affirmed. So much of the decree as provides in the alternative for the adoption of Tammy by Helen and the retention of rights of custody and visitation by Susan is vacated.

So ordered.

Case Questions

1. Why did the court rule that Tammy would significantly benefit from being jointly adopted by both Susan and Helen?
2. What role did the fact that the petitioners were persons of the same gender play in the court's decision? Can you construct an argument that would have led to a contradictory result if the court had been so inclined?

 How does the state supreme court respond to the following moral and legal question: Should gays and lesbians be categorically disqualified from becoming adoptive parents because of their sexual orientation?

Voluntary/Involuntary Adoption

Adoptions may be classified as voluntary or involuntary. Involuntary adoptions occur after a court has formally terminated the parental rights of the birth parent(s) on grounds such as abuse, abandonment, or neglect. In such a situation an agency is generally responsible for placement. If the adoption is voluntary, the birth parent(s) consent to the termination of their parental rights and surrender the child either to an agency for placement or to adoptive parents of their choosing.

The Adoption Petition

The adoption process starts with the filing of a petition for adoption by the adoptive parents and the serving of a summons on all affected parties (the child, the agency, birth parents, guardian, etc.). In voluntary adoptions, care must be taken to account for all relevant parties, and obtaining the consent of necessary third parties is a major consideration. When both birth parents have an intact marriage, they must jointly consent to a proposed adoption of their child. If the parents are not married to each other, and both the noncustodial and custodial parents have taken an active role in fulfilling parental obligations, each has the right to withhold or grant consent to the adoption of their child.

The following case discusses whether consent is required from a noncustodial parent who has only sporadically visited and supported his child and who has otherwise shown little or no interest in functioning as a parent. The biological father in the case filed a petition asking a state trial court to vacate its adoption order, claiming that his Fourteenth Amendment equal protection and due process rights had been violated. The trial court's denial of the motion was affirmed by two state appellate courts, and the matter was subsequently appealed to the U.S. Supreme Court.

Lehr v. Robertson
463 U.S. 248
U.S. Supreme Court
June 27, 1983

Justice Stevens delivered the opinion of the Court.

The question presented is whether New York has sufficiently protected an unmarried father's inchoate relationship with a child whom he has never supported and rarely seen in the two years since her birth. The appellant, Jonathan Lehr, claims that the Due Process and Equal Protection Clauses of the Fourteenth Amendment, . . . give him an absolute right to notice and an opportunity to be heard before the child may be adopted. We disagree.

Jessica M. was born out of wedlock on November 9, 1976. Her mother, Lorraine Robertson, married Richard Robertson eight months after Jessica's birth. On December 21, 1978, when Jessica was over two years old, the Robertsons filed an adoption petition in the Family Court of Ulster County, New York.

The court heard their testimony and received a favorable report from the Ulster County Department of Social Services. On March 7, 1979, the court entered an order of adoption. In this proceeding, appellant contends that the adoption order is invalid because he, Jessica's putative father, was not given advance notice of the adoption proceeding.

The State of New York maintains a "putative father registry." A man who files with that registry demonstrates his intent to claim paternity of a child born out of wedlock and is therefore entitled to receive notice of any proceeding to adopt that child. Before entering Jessica's adoption order, the Ulster County Family Court had the putative father registry examined. Although appellant claims to be Jessica's natural father, he had not entered his name in the registry.

In addition to the persons whose names are listed on the putative father registry, New York law requires that notice of an adoption proceeding be given to several other classes of possible fathers of children born out of wedlock—those who have been adjudicated to be the father, those who have been identified as the father on the child's birth certificate, those who live openly with the child and the child's mother and who hold themselves out to be the father, those who have been identified as the father by the mother in a sworn written statement, and those who were married to the child's mother before the child was six months old. Appellant admittedly was not a member of any of those classes. He had lived with appellee prior to Jessica's birth and visited her in the hospital when Jessica was born, but his name does not appear on Jessica's birth certificate. He did not live with appellee or Jessica after Jessica's birth, he has never provided them with any financial support, and he has never offered to marry appellee. . . .

Appellant has now invoked our appellate jurisdiction. He offers two alternative grounds for holding the New York statutory scheme unconstitutional. First, he contends that a putative father's actual or potential relationship with a child born out of wedlock is an interest in liberty which may not be destroyed without due process of law; he argues therefore that he had a constitutional right to prior notice and an opportunity to be heard before he was deprived of that interest. Second, he contends that the gender-based classification in the statute, which both denied him the right to consent to Jessica's adoption and accorded him fewer procedural rights than her mother, violated the Equal Protection Clause.

The Due Process Claim

The Fourteenth Amendment provides that no State shall deprive any person of life, liberty, or property without due process of law. When that Clause is invoked in a novel context, it is our practice to begin the inquiry with a determination of the precise nature of the private interest that is threatened by the State. . . .

Only after that interest has been identified, can we properly evaluate the adequacy of the State's process. . . . We therefore first consider the nature of the interest in liberty for which appellant claims constitutional protection and then turn to a discussion of the adequacy of the procedure that New York has provided for its protection.

I

The intangible fibers that connect parent and child have infinite variety. They are woven throughout the fabric of our society, providing it with strength, beauty, and flexibility. It is self-evident that they are sufficiently vital to merit constitutional protection in appropriate cases. In deciding whether this is such a case, however, we must consider the broad framework that has traditionally been used to resolve the legal problems arising from the parent-child relationship.

In the vast majority of cases, state law determines the final outcome. . . . Rules governing the inheritance of property, adoption, and child custody are generally specified in statutory enactments that vary from State to State. Moveover, equally varied state laws governing marriage and divorce affect a multitude of parent-child relationships. The institution of marriage has played a critical role both in defining the legal entitlements of family members and in developing the decentralized structure of our democratic society. In recognition of that role, and as part of their general overarching concern for serving the best interests of children, state laws almost universally express an appropriate preference for the formal family.

In some cases, however, this Court has held that the Federal Constitution supersedes state law and provides even greater protection for certain formal family relationships. . . . In these cases the Court has found that the relationship of love and duty in a recognized family unit is an interest in liberty entitled to constitutional protection. . . .

There are also a few cases in which this Court has considered the extent to which the Constitution affords protection to the relationship between natural parents and children born out of wedlock.

In this case, however, it is a parent who claims that the State has improperly deprived him of a protected interest in liberty. This Court has examined the extent to which a natural father's biological relationship with his child receives protection under the Due Process Clause in precisely three cases: *Stanley v. Illinois*, 405 U.S. 645, . . . (1972), *Quilloin v. Walcott*, 434 U.S. 246, . . . (1978), and *Caban v. Mohammed*, 441 U.S. 380, . . . (1979).

Stanley involved the constitutionality of an Illinois statute that conclusively presumed every father of a child born out of wedlock to be an unfit person to have custody of his children. The father in that case had lived with his children all their lives and had lived with their mother for 18 years. There was nothing in the record to indicate that Stanley had been a neglectful father who had not cared for his children. . . .

Under the statute, however, the nature of the actual relationship between parent and child was completely irrelevant. Once the mother died, the children were automatically made wards of the State. . . .

[T]he Court held that the Due Process Clause was violated by the automatic destruction of the custodial relationship without giving the father any opportunity to present evidence regarding his fitness as a parent.

Quilloin involved the constitutionality of a Georgia statute that authorized the adoption, over the objection of the natural father, of a child born out of wedlock. The father in that case had never legitimated the child. It was only after the mother had remarried and her new husband had filed an adoption petition that the natural father sought visitation

rights and filed a petition for legitimation. The trial court found adoption by the new husband to be in the child's best interests, and we unanimously held that action to be consistent with the Due Process Clause.

Caban involved the conflicting claims of two natural parents who had maintained joint custody of their children from the time of their birth until they were respectively two and four years old. The father challenged the validity of an order authorizing the mother's new husband to adopt the children; he relied on both the Equal Protection Clause and the Due Process Clause. Because this Court upheld his equal protection claim, the majority did not address his due process challenge. The comments on the latter claim by the four dissenting Justices are nevertheless instructive, because they identify the clear distinction between a mere biological relationship and an actual relationship of parental responsibility.

Justice Stewart correctly observed:

> "Even if it be assumed that each married parent after divorce has some substantive due process right to maintain his or her parental relationship, . . . it by no means follows that each unwed parent has any such right. *Parental rights do not spring full-blown from the biological connection between parent and child. They require relationships more enduring.*" . . .

When an unwed father demonstrates a full commitment to the responsibilities of parenthood by "com[ing] forward to participate in the rearing of his child," *Caban*, . . . , his interest in personal contact with his child acquires substantial protection under the Due Process Clause. At that point it may be said that he "act[s] as a father toward his children." . . . But the mere existence of a biological link does not merit equivalent constitutional protection. The actions of judges neither create nor sever genetic bonds. "[T]he importance of the familial relationship, to the individuals involved and to the society, stems from the emotional attachments that derive from the intimacy of daily association, and from the role it plays in 'promot[ing] a way of life' through the instruction of children . . . as well as from the fact of blood relationship." . . .

The significance of the biological connection is that it offers the natural father an opportunity that no other male possesses to develop a relationship with his offspring. If he grasps that opportunity and accepts some measure of responsibility for the child's future, he may enjoy the blessings of the parent-child relationship and make uniquely valuable contributions to the child's development. If he fails to do so, the Federal Constitution will not automatically compel a State to listen to his opinion of where the child's best interests lie.

In this case, we are not assessing the constitutional adequacy of New York's procedures for terminating a developed relationship. Appellant has never had any significant custodial, personal, or financial relationship with Jessica, and he did not seek to establish a legal tie until after she was two years old. We are concerned only with whether New York has adequately protected his opportunity to form such a relationship.

II

. . . Appellant argues, however, that even if the putative father's opportunity to establish a relationship with an illegitimate child is adequately protected by the New York statutory scheme in the normal case, he was nevertheless entitled to special notice because the court and the mother knew that he had filed an affiliation proceeding in another court. This argument amounts to nothing more than an indirect attack on the notice provisions of the New York statute. The legitimate state interests in facilitating the adoption of young children and having the adoption proceeding completed expeditiously that underlie the entire statutory scheme also justify a trial judge's

determination to require all interested parties to adhere precisely to the procedural requirements of the statute. The Constitution does not require either a trial judge or a litigant to give special notice to nonparties who are presumptively capable of asserting and protecting their own rights. Since the New York statutes adequately protected appellant's inchoate interest in establishing a relationship with Jessica, we find no merit in the claim that his constitutional rights were offended because the Family Court strictly complied with the notice provisions of the statute.

The Equal Protection Claim

The concept of equal justice under law requires the State to govern impartially. . . . The sovereign may not draw distinctions between individuals based solely on differences that are irrelevant to a legitimate governmental objective. . . . Specifically, it may not subject men and women to disparate treatment when there is no substantial relation between the disparity and an important state purpose. . . . The legislation at issue in this case . . . is intended to establish procedures for adoptions. Those procedures are designed to promote the best interests of the child, to protect the rights of interested third parties, and to ensure promptness and finality. To serve those ends, the legislation guarantees to certain people the right to veto an adoption and the right to prior notice of any adoption proceeding. The mother of an illegitimate child is always within that favored class, but only certain putative fathers are included. Appellant contends that the gender-based distinction is invidious.

As we have already explained, the existence or nonexistence of a substantial relationship between parent and child is a relevant criterion in evaluating both the rights of the parent and the best interests of the child. . . .

Because appellant, . . . has never established a substantial relationship with his daughter, . . . the New York statutes at issue in this case did not operate to deny appellant equal protection.

. . . Whereas appellee had a continuous custodial responsibility for Jessica, appellant never established any custodial, personal, or financial relationship with her. If one parent has an established custodial relationship with the child and the other parent has either abandoned or never established a relationship, the Equal Protection Clause does not prevent a state from according the two parents different legal rights.

The judgment of the New York Court of Appeals is

Affirmed.

Case Questions

1. What is the basis for the father's claim that his constitutionally protected liberty interest has been denied by the state of New York?
2. Why does the father claim that New York's adoption procedures violate the equal protection clause of the Fourteenth Amendment? Does the Supreme Court agree with him?
3. What does the Supreme Court decide in this case?

The birth parents and adoptive parents are not the only individuals who have legal interests in adoptions. The adoptee and grandparents, for example, also may have legal rights. An adoptee, if over a specified age (often twelve or fourteen), has a right to refuse to be adopted. Even the grandparents of a child born out of wedlock may have legally enforceable visitation rights when the birth father's parental rights may have been terminated.

In addition to providing notice to affected individuals, the petition for adoption will also indicate whether the parental rights have been voluntarily or involuntarily terminated and will allege that the adoption is in the best interests of the child.

Interim Orders

After the adoption petition has been filed, the parties properly served, and all necessary consents obtained, the court will frequently issue interim orders. In voluntary adoptions the court will order the birth parents' rights terminated and grant the adoptive parents temporary legal custody of the child, pending issuance of the final decree. A hearing can then be scheduled to take testimony about whether the final decree of adoption should be approved by the court. State statutes usually require that the adoptive parents have temporary custody of the adopted child for a statutorily determined minimum period of time so that the court will have evidence that the adoptive parents and child are making a successful adjustment. This waiting period is usually waived in related adoptions. After the waiting time has passed, the court will enter a final decree declaring that the adopted person is now the child of the petitioner(s), and a new birth certificate will be issued to reflect this change.[52]

Whether or not the adopted child will be able to learn the identity of the birth parents varies from state to state. In recent years there has been some movement away from permanently sealing such information. Today, although many states maintain the confidentiality of adoption records, the trend is toward more openness.[53] Over thirty states have some type of registry system whereby consenting birth parents and their subsequently adopted children can mutually indicate a desire for contact.[54] Adoptees frequently wish to learn more about their birth parents, not only out of curiosity, but also to gain information about their parents' medical histories.

Foster Care

There are an estimated 581,000 children presently in foster care in the United States[55] of whom 34 percent are white, 38 percent are black, and 15 percent are Hispanic.[56] Although parents can voluntarily choose to place their child in foster care while efforts are made to remedy a serious family problem, most placements result from court intervention because of alleged child abuse or neglect.[57] Once a court determines that a child is abused or neglected, it can determine that foster care is the most appropriate disposition under the circumstances.

In many situations, foster care is intended to provide temporary care for children while the biological parents work to fufill the requirements of a case plan. The objective in such situations is reunification of the family, once case workers have helped the family to work out its problems. If the birth parents address the problems that gave rise to the judicial intervention in the first place, the child will generally be returned to the parents. If the parents are uncooperative or fail to complete the intervention plan, the court may ultimately decide that it is in the best interests of the child to terminate the parental rights and place the child for adoption. It is reported that 16 percent of foster children are adopted and that over 69 percent are ordered returned to their birth parents or other relatives.[58] State governments license foster homes and federal and state resources financially support foster children. The foster care system is criticized as being underfunded, overwhelmed with cases, and staffed by persons who are not trained as social workers.[59]

The foster care system in this country is criticized for the length of time foster children often wait to be adopted. For example, for nearly 70 percent of foster children who become adopted, the wait between termination of parental rights and adoption takes at least two years, and for 25 percent, the wait is no less than five years.[60] Congress took action to improve this situation when it enacted the Adoption and Safe Families Act of 1997. This legislation created financial incentives and performance expectations for states in an effort to speed up the adoption process and increase the numbers of children placed for adoption. This act also provided for periodic Child and Family Services Reviews (CFSR) for each state. The states have responded, with the number of children adopted from public child welfare agencies during fiscal year 2000 increasing by 39 percent over the number adopted in fiscal year 1998.

Critics, however, claim that federal financial support to the states should increase, given that the states have moved increasing numbers of children from the foster care system into adoption placements. Concerns are also expressed about the impact of the foster care system on nonwhite families. One nationally respected scholar, for example, has pointed out that the foster care system is racially imbalanced and has not worked anywhere near as well for black children and their families as it has for whites.[61]

INTERNET TIP

To see a table summarizing the extent to which the seventeen states evaluated during 2001 were in substantial compliance with each of the CFSR's seven outcomes, please visit the textbook's website.

FAMILY RELATIONS IN ONGOING FAMILIES

Where families are intact, the law recognizes that spouses and children assume obligations to each other and are entitled to certain rights and benefits. Some of these rights, benefits, and obligations are economic and others are noneconomic.

Spousal Considerations

Although modern marriages are essentially partnerships, historically husbands and wives were legally considered to be a single unit with the husbands holding the preferred status as head of the household.[62] Before the enactment of married women's property statutes in the 1800s, wives did not generally own property in their own names. Upon marriage, a wife's property was generally controlled by her husband. An exception was created by equitable courts that allowed fathers to establish trusts for their daughters. This device was used to keep family assets out of the control of sons-in-law, but few women from the lower and middle classes were the beneficiaries of such arrangements. A husband, while benefitting from the preferred status as head to the household, was also legally obligated to provide economic support for his wife. The term traditionally associated with this responsibility for support is "necessaries," usually defined to include food, clothing, shelter, and medical care.[63] In earlier times this obligation only applied to husbands; however, it is now shared by both spouses.

Courts were initially resistant to statutory reforms expanding women's property rights and often construed them very narrowly.[64] Today, in common property law states, married women have essentially achieved legal equality. Both spouses retain title to property owned prior to marriage, have separate rights to their own earnings, and have title to property acquired separately during marriage.

In community property states (see Figure 9-5), each spouse is legally entitled to a percentage of what the state defines as *community property,* which will vary by jurisdiction. Although states differ, community property is usually defined as including the earnings of both spouses and property rights acquired with those earnings during the marriage. State statutes, however, usually exclude from community property rights acquired prior to marriage and spousal inheritances and gifts received during the marriage. These are classified as separate property. Community property states differ on whether earnings from separate property should be treated as community property.

Decision Making Within Traditional Families

The United States Supreme Court has reinforced family autonomy by ruling that married couples have the right to make decisions regarding the use of birth control[65] and whether they will become parents. If they do, it is they who will decide how many children they will have and how those children will be raised.[66] This right to raise children includes decisions about the nature and extent of their education and their religious upbringing.

Community property states

FIGURE 9-5   Community Property States

Spouses also have great latitude in deciding how their households will operate. Decisions about who is responsible for particular household chores, about how recreational time is used, and about having children and child rearing are often jointly made. Of course, a woman's decision to obtain an abortion early in a pregnancy can be made unilaterally—without regard to the wishes of the putative father. A married woman also has the right to retain her own surname, if she chooses.

Spouses also benefit from privileges contained within state and federal rules of evidence. Where the spousal privileges exists, a spouse may refuse to testify against his or her spouse in a criminal trial and may also refuse to testify about confidential communications that occurred between spouses during their marriage.

In the following case, Amish parents were prosecuted for violating a state-mandated compulsory school-attendance law by withdrawing their children from school after completion of the eighth grade. The parents appealed their convictions and claimed that the law infringed on their constitutionally protected right to determine the religious development of their children.

Wisconsin v. Yoder
406 U.S. 205
U.S. Supreme Court
May 15, 1972

Mr. Chief Justice Burger delivered the opinion of the Court.

On petition of the State of Wisconsin, we granted the writ of certiorari in this case to review a decision of the Wisconsin Supreme Court holding that respondents' convictions for violating the State's compulsory school-attendance law were invalid under the Free Exercise Clause of the First Amendment to the United States Constitution made applicable to the States by the Fourteenth Amendment. For the reasons hereafter stated we affirm the judgment of the Supreme Court of Wisconsin.

Respondents Jonas Yoder and Wallace Miller are members of the Old Order Amish religion, and respondent Adin Yutzy is a member of the Conservative Amish Mennonite Church. They and their families are residents of Green County, Wisconsin. Wis-

consin's compulsory school-attendance law required them to cause their children to attend public or private school until reaching age 16 but the respondents declined to send their children, ages 14 and 15, to public school after they complete the eighth grade. The children were not enrolled in any private school, or within any recognized exception to the compulsory-attendance law, and they are conceded to be subject to the Wisconsin statute.

On complaint of the school district administrator for the public schools, respondents were charged, tried, and convicted of violating the compulsory-attendance law in Green County Court and were fined the sum of $5 each. Respondents defended on the ground that the application of the compulsory-attendance law violated their rights under the First and Fourteenth Amendments. The trial testimony showed that respondents believed, in accordance with the tenets of Old Order Amish communities generally, that their children's attendance at high school, public or private, was contrary to the Amish religion and way of life. They believed that by sending their children to high school, they would not only expose themselves to the danger of the censure of the church community, but, as found by the county court, also endanger their own salvation and that of their children.

They object to the high school, and higher education generally, because the values they teach are in marked variance with Amish values and the Amish way of life; they view secondary school education as an impermissible exposure of their children to a "worldly" influence in conflict with their beliefs. The high school tends to emphasize intellectual and scientific accomplishments, self-distinction, competitiveness, worldly success, and social life with other students. Amish society emphasizes informal learning-through-doing; a life of "goodness, "rather than a life of intellect; wisdom, rather than technical knowledge; community welfare, rather than competition; and separation from, rather than integration with, contemporary worldly society.

Formal high school education beyond the eighth grade is contrary to Amish beliefs, not only because it places Amish children in an environment hostile to Amish beliefs with increasing emphasis on competition in class work and sports and with pressure to conform to the styles, manners, and ways of the peer group, but also because it takes them away from their community, physically and emotionally, during the crucial and formative adolescent period of life. During this period, the children must acquire Amish attitudes favoring manual work and self-reliance and the specific skills needed to perform the adult role of an Amish farmer or housewife. They must learn to enjoy physical labor. Once a child has learned basic reading, writing, and elementary mathematics, these traits, skills, and attitudes admittedly fall within the category of those best learned through example and "doing" rather than in a classroom. And, at this time in life, the Amish child must also grow in his faith and his relationship to the Amish community if he is to be prepared to accept the heavy obligations imposed by adult baptism. In short, high school attendance with teachers who are not of the Amish faith—and may even be hostile to it—interposes a serious barrier to the integration of the Amish child into the Amish religious community. . . .

The Amish do not object to elementary education through the first eight grades as a general proposition because they agree that their children must have basic skills in the "three R's" in order to read the Bible, to be good farmers and citizens, and to be able to deal with non-Amish people when necessary in the course of daily affairs. They view such a basic education as acceptable because it does not significantly expose their children to worldly values or interfere with their development in the Amish community during the crucial adolescent period. While Amish accept compulsory elementary education generally, wherever possible they have established their own elementary schools in many respects like the small local schools of the past. In the Amish belief higher learning tends to develop values they reject as influences that alienate man from God. . . .

Although the trial court in its careful findings determined that the Wisconsin compulsory school-attendance law "does interfere with the freedom of the Defendants to act in accordance with their sincere religious belief" it also concluded that the requirement of high school attendance until age 16 was a "reasonable and constitutional" exercise of governmental power, and therefore denied the motion to dismiss the charges. The Wisconsin Circuit Court affirmed the convictions. The Wisconsin Supreme Court, however, sustained respondents' claim under the Free Exercise Clause of the First Amendment and reversed the convictions. . . .

I

There is no doubt as to the power of a State, having a high responsibility for education of its citizens, to impose reasonable regulations for the control and duration of basic education. See, *e.g., Pierce v. Society of Sisters,* 268 U.S. 510 (1925). Providing public schools ranks at the very apex of the function of a State. Yet even this paramount responsibility was, in *Pierce,* made to yield to the right of parents to provide all equivalent education in a privately operated system. . . .

II

We come then to the quality of the claims of the respondents concerning the alleged encroachment of Wisconsin's compulsory school-attendance statute on their rights and the rights of their children to the free exercise of the religious beliefs they and their forbears have adhered to for almost three centuries.

. . . [T]he values of parental direction of the religious upbringing and education of their children in their early and formative years have a high place in our society. Thus, a State's interest in universal education, however highly we rank it, is not totally free from a balancing process when it impinges on fundamental rights and interests, such as those specifically protected by the Free Exercise Clause of the First Amendment, and the traditional interest of parents with respect to the religious upbringing of their children. . . .

It follows that in order for Wisconsin to compel school attendance beyond the eighth grade against a claim that such attendance interferes with the practice of a legitimate religious belief, it must appear either that the State does not deny the free exercise of religious belief by its requirement, or that there is a state interest of sufficient magnitude to override the interest claiming protection under the Free Exercise Clause. . . .

As the society around the Amish has become more populous, urban, industrialized, and complex, particularly in this century, government regulation of human affairs has correspondingly become more detailed and pervasive. The Amish mode of life has thus come into conflict increasingly with require-ments of contemporary society exerting a hydraulic insistence on conformity to majoritarian standards. So long as compulsory education laws were confined to eight grades of elementary basic education imparted in a nearby rural schoolhouse, with a large proportion of students of the Amish faith, the Old Order Amish had little basis to fear that school attendance would expose their children to the worldly influence they reject. . . . The conclusion is inescapable that secondary schooling, by exposing Amish children to worldly influences in terms of attitudes, goals, and values contrary to beliefs, and by substantially interfering with the religious development of the Amish child and his integration into the way of life of the Amish faith community at the crucial adolescent stage of development, contravenes the basic religious tenets and practice of the Amish faith, both as to the parent and the child. . . .

In sum, the unchallenged testimony of acknowledged experts in education and religious history, almost 300 years of consistent practice, and strong evidence of a sustained faith pervading and regulating respondents' entire mode of life support the claim that enforcement of the State's requirement of compulsory formal education after the eighth grade would gravely endanger if not destroy the free exercise of respondents' religious beliefs.

III

Neither the findings of the trial court nor the Amish claims as to the nature of their faith are challenged in this Court by the State of Wisconsin. Its position is that the State's interest in universal compulsory formal secondary education to age 16 is so great that it is paramount to the undisputed claims of respondents that their mode of preparing their youth for Amish life, after the traditional elementary education, is an essential part of their religious belief and practice. Nor does the State undertake to meet the claim that the Amish mode of life and education is inseparable from and a part of the basic tenets of their religion—indeed, as much a part of their religious belief and practices as baptism, the confessional, or a sabbath may be for others.

Wisconsin concedes that under the Religion Clauses religious beliefs are absolutely free from the State's control, but it argues that "actions," even though religiously grounded, are outside the protection of the First Amendment. But our decisions have rejected the idea that religiously grounded conduct is always outside the protection of the Free Exercise Clause. It is true that activities of individuals, even when religiously based, are often subject to regulation by the States in the exercise of their undoubted power to promote the health, safety, and general welfare, or the Federal Government in the exercise of its delegated powers. . . .

But to agree that religiously grounded conduct must often be subject to the broad police power of the State is not to deny that there are areas of conduct protected by the Free Exercise Clause of the First Amendment and thus beyond the power of the State to control, even under regulations of general applicability. . . .

This case, therefore, does not become easier because respondents were convicted for their "actions" in refusing to send their children to the public high school; in this context belief and action cannot be neatly confined in logic-tight compartments.

. . . Nor can this case be disposed of on the grounds that Wisconsin's requirement for school attendance to age 16 applies uniformly to all citizens of the State and does not, on its face, discriminate against religions or a particular religion, or that it is motivated by legitimate secular concerns. A regulation neutral on its face may, in its application, nonetheless offend the constitutional requirement for governmental neutrality if it unduly burdens the free exercise of religion. . . .

The State advances two primary arguments in support of its system of compulsory education. It notes, as Thomas Jefferson pointed out early in our history, that some degree of education is necessary to prepare citizens to participate effectively and intelligently in our open political system if we are to preserve freedom and independence. Further, education prepares individuals to be self-reliant and self-sufficient participants in society. We accept these propositions.

However, the evidence adduced by the Amish in this case is persuasively to the effect that an additional one or two years of formal high school for Amish children in place of their long-established program of informal vocational education would do little to serve those interests. Respondents' experts testified at trial, without challenge, that the value of all education must be assessed in terms of its capacity to prepare the child for life. It is one thing to say that compulsory education for a year or two beyond the eighth grade may be necessary when its goal is the preparation of the child for life in modern society as the majority live, but it is quite another if the goal of education be viewed as the preparation of the child for life in the separated agrarian community that is the keystone of the Amish faith.

The State attacks respondents' position as one fostering "ignorance" from which the child must be protected by the State. No one can question the State's duty to protect children from ignorance but this argument does not square with the facts disclosed in the record. Whatever their idiosyncrasies as seen by the majority, this record strongly shows that the Amish community has been a highly successful social unit within our society, even if apart from the conventional "mainstream." Its members are productive and very law-abiding members of society; they reject public welfare in any of its usual modern forms. The Congress itself recognized their self-sufficiency by authorizing exemption of such groups as the Amish from the obligation to pay social security taxes.

It is neither fair nor correct to suggest that the Amish are opposed to education beyond the eighth grade level. What this record shows is that they are opposed to conventional formal education of the type provided by a certified high school because it comes at the child's crucial adolescent period of religious development. . . .

The State, however, supports its interest in providing an additional one or two years of compulsory high school education to Amish children because of the possibility that some such children will choose to leave the Amish community, and that if this occurs they will be ill-equipped for life. The State argues that if Amish children leave their church they should not be in a position of making their way in the world without the education available in the one or two additional years the State requires. However, on this record, that argument is highly speculative. There is no specific evidence of the loss of Amish adherents by attrition, nor is there any showing that upon leaving the Amish community Amish children, with their practical agricultural training and habits of industry and self-reliance, would become burdens on society because of educational shortcomings. . . .

The independence and successful social functioning of the Amish community for a period approaching almost three centuries and more than 200 years in this country are strong evidence that there is at best a speculative gain, in terms of meeting the duties of citizenship, from an additional one or two years of compulsory formal education. Against this background it would require a more particularized showing from the State on this point to justify the severe interference with religious freedom such additional compulsory attendance would entail.

. . . Wisconsin's interests in compelling the school attendance of Amish children to age 16 emerges as somewhat less substantial than requiring such attendance for children generally. For, while agricultural employment is not totally outside the legitimate concerns of the child labor laws, employment of children under parental guidance and on the family farm from age 14 to age 16 is an ancient tradition that lies at the periphery of the objectives of such laws. There is no intimation that the Amish employment of their children on family farms is in any way deleterious to their health or that Amish parents exploit children at tender years. Any such inference would be contrary to the record before us. Moreover, employment of Amish children on the family farm does not present the undesirable economic aspects of eliminating jobs that might otherwise be held by adults. . . .

IV

Finally, the State, on authority of *Prince v. Massachusetts,* argues that a decision exempting Amish children from the State's requirement fails to recognize the substantive right of the Amish child to a secondary education, and fails to give due regard to the power of the State as *parens patriae* to extend the benefit of secondary education to children regardless of the wishes of their parents. Taken at its broadest sweep, the Court's language in *Prince,* might be read to give support to the State's position.

This case, of course, is not one in which any harm to the physical or mental health of the child or to the public safety, peace, order, or welfare has been demonstrated or may be properly inferred.

. . . [O]ur holding today in no degree depends on the assertion of the religious interest of the child as contrasted with that of the parents. It is the parents who are subject to prosecution here for failing to cause their children to attend school, and it is their right of free exercise, not that of their children, that must determine Wisconsin's power to impose criminal penalties on the parent. The dissent argues that a child who expresses a desire to attend public high school in conflict with the wishes of his parents should not be prevented from doing so. There is no reason for the Court to consider that point since it is not an issue in the case. The children are not parties to this litigation. The State has at no point tried this case on the theory that respondents were preventing their children from attending school against their expressed desires, and indeed the record is to the contrary. The State's position from the outset has been that it is empowered to apply its compulsory-attendance law to Amish parents in the same manner as to other parents—that is, without regard to the wishes of the child. That is the claim we reject today.

Our holding in no way determines the proper resolution of possible competing interests of parents, children, and the State in an appropriate state court proceeding in which the power of the State is asserted on the theory that Amish parents are preventing their minor children from attending high school despite their expressed desires to the contrary. Recognition of the claim of the State in such a proceeding would, of course, call into question traditional concepts of parental control over the religious upbringing and education of their minor children recognized in this Court's past decisions. It is clear that such an intrusion by a State into family decisions in the area of religious training would give rise to grave questions of religious freedom comparable to those raised here and those presented in *Pierce v. Society of Sisters*. . . . On this record we neither reach nor decide those issues. . . .

Indeed it seems clear that if the State is empowered, as *parens patriae*, to "save" a child from himself or his Amish parents by requiring an additional two years of compulsory formal high school education, the State will in large measure influence, if not determine, the religious future of the child. Even more markedly than in *Prince*, therefore, this case involves the fundamental interest of parents, as contrasted with that of the State, to guide the religious future and education of their children. The history and culture of Western civilization reflect a strong tradition of parental concern for the nurture and upbringing of their children. This primary role of the parents in the upbringing of their children is now established beyond debate as an enduring American tradition.

. . . Where nothing more than the general interest of the parent in the nurture and education of his children is involved, it is beyond dispute that the State acts "reasonably" and constitutionally in requiring education to age 16 in some public or private school meeting the standards prescribed by the State.

However read, the Court's holding in *Pierce* stands as a charter of the rights of parents to direct the religious upbringing of their children. And, when the interests of parenthood are combined with a free exercise claim of the nature revealed by this record, more than merely a "reasonable relation to some purpose within the competency of the State" is required to sustain the validity of the State's requirement under the First Amendment. To be sure, the power of the parent, even when linked to a free exercise claim, may be subject to limitation . . . if it appears that parental decisions will jeopardize the health or safety of the child, or have a potential for significant social burdens. But in this case, the Amish have introduced persuasive evidence undermining the arguments the State has advanced to support its claims in terms of the welfare of the child and society as a whole. . . .

V

For the reasons stated we hold, with the Supreme Court of Wisconsin, that the First and Fourteenth Amendments prevent the State from compelling respondents to cause their children to attend formal high school to age 16. . . .

It cannot be overemphasized that we are not dealing with a way of life and mode of education by a group claiming to have recently discovered some "progressive" or more enlightened process for rearing children for modern life.

Aided by a history of three centuries as an identifiable religious sect and a long history as a successful and self-sufficient segment of American society, the Amish in this case have convincingly demonstrated the sincerity of their religious beliefs, the interrelationship of belief with their mode of life, the vital role that belief and daily conduct play in the continued survival of Old Order Amish communities and their religious organization, and the hazards presented by the State's enforcement of a statute generally valid as to others. . . .

Nothing we hold is intended to undermine the general applicability of the State's compulsory school-attendance statutes or to limit the power of the State to promulgate reasonable standards that, while not impairing the free exercise of religion, provide for continuing agricultural vocational education under parental and church guidance by the Old Order Amish or others similarly situated. The States have had a long history of amicable and effective relationships with church-sponsored schools, and there is no basis for assuming that, in this related context, reasonable standards cannot be established concerning the content of the continuing vocational education of Amish children under parental guidance, provided always that state regulations are not inconsistent with what we have said in this opinion.

Affirmed.

Mr. Justice Douglas, dissenting in part

I

I agree with the Court that the religious scruples of the Amish are opposed to the education of their children beyond the grade schools, yet I disagree with the Court's conclusion that the matter is within the dispensation of parents alone. The Court's analysis assumes that the only interests at stake in the case are those of the Amish parents on the one hand, and those of the State on the other. The difficulty with this approach is that, despite the Court's claim, the parents are seeking to vindicate not only their own free exercise claims, but also those of their high-school-age children.

If the parents in this case are allowed a religious exemption, the inevitable effect is to impose the parents' notions of religious duty upon their children. Where the child is mature enough to express potentially conflicting desires, it would be an invasion of the child's rights to permit such an imposition without canvassing his views.

And, if an Amish child desires to attend high school, and is mature enough to have that desire respected, the State may well be able to override the parent's religiously motivated objections.

Religion is an individual experience. It is not necessary, nor even appropriate, for every Amish child to express his views on the subject in a prosecution of a single adult. Crucial, however, are the views of the child whose parent is the subject of the suit. Frieda Yoder has in fact testified that her own religious views are opposed to high-school education. I therefore join the judgment of the Court as to respondent Jonas Yoder. But Frieda Yoder's views may not be those of Vernon Yutzy or Barbara Miller. I must dissent, therefore, as to respondents Adin Yutzy and Wallace Miller as their motion to dismiss also raised the question of their children's religious liberty.

II

This issue has never been squarely presented before today. Our opinions are full of talk about the power of the parents over the child's education.

. . . [W]e have in the past analyzed similar conflicts between parent and State with little regard for the views of the child. See

Prince v. Massachusetts, supra. Recent cases, however, have clearly held that the children themselves have constitutionally protectible interests.

These children are "persons" within the meaning of the Bill of Rights. We have so held over and over again.

On this important and vital matter of education, I think the children should be entitled to be heard. While the parents, absent dissent, normally speak for the entire family, the education of the child is a matter on which the child will often have decided views. He may want to be a pianist or an astronaut or an oceanographer. To do so he will have to break from the Amish tradition.

It is the future of the student, not the future of the parents, that is imperiled by today's decision. If a parent keeps his child out of school beyond the grade school, then the child will be forever barred from entry into the new and amazing world of diversity that we have today. The child may decide that that is the preferred course, or he may rebel. It is the student's judgment, not his parents', that is essential if we are to give full meaning to what we have said about the Bill of Rights and of the right of students to be masters of their own destiny. If he is harnessed to the Amish way of life by those in authority over him and if his education is truncated, his entire life may be stunted and deformed. The child, therefore, should be given an opportunity to be heard before the State gives the exemption which we honor today.

The views of the two children in question were not canvassed by the Wisconsin courts. The matter should be explicitly reserved so that the new hearings can be held on remand of the case.

Case Questions

1. On what grounds did Wisconsin require school attendance until a child reaches sixteen years of age?
2. Why did respondents Yoder, Miller, and Yutzy refuse to allow their fourteen- and fifteen-year-old children to attend school?
3. What did the Supreme Court justices decide in this case?
4. Do you agree with Justice Douglas's dissent?

 The Supreme Court, in this case, reached a legal conclusion that is based on a moral conclusion. What is the underlying moral conclusion?

The Parent–Child Relationship

Historically, parents have been legally responsible for the financial costs of providing their children with food, clothing, shelter, medical care, and education. This duty exists irrespective of whether the parents are married, divorced, separated, living together, or living apart. The breach of this duty is treated by most states as a criminal offense and can also result in civil actions for nonsupport and child neglect. The government is most eager to identify and locate "deadbeat parents" and to hold them financially accountable for their children so that the public doesn't have to bear these costs. The facts in the following case are admittedly unusual, but they illustrate the lengths to which society will go to impose liability on parents for the support of their offspring.

State ex rel. Hermesmann v. Seyer
847 P.2d 1273
Supreme Court of Kansas
March 5, 1993

Holmes, Chief Justice

Shane Seyer *et al.*, appeal from an order of the district court granting the Kansas Department of Social and Rehabilitation Services (SRS) judgment for amounts paid for the birth and support of Seyer's daughter and ordering Seyer to pay monthly child support reimbursement to SRS.

The facts, as best we can determine them from an inadequate record, do not appear to be seriously in dispute.

Colleen Hermesmann routinely provided care for Shane Seyer as a baby sitter or day care provider during 1987 and 1988. The two began a sexual relationship at a time when Colleen was 16 years old and Shane was only 12. The relationship continued over a period of several months and the parties engaged in sexual intercourse on an average of a couple of times a week. As a result, a daughter, Melanie, was born to Colleen on May 30, 1989. At the time of the conception of the child, Shane was 13 years old and Colleen was 17. Colleen applied for and received financial assistance through the Aid to Families with Dependent Children program (ADC) from SRS.

On January 15, 1991, the district attorney's office of Shawnee County filed a petition requesting that Colleen Hermesmann be adjudicated as a juvenile offender for engaging in the act of sexual intercourse with a child under the age of 16, Shanandoah (Shane) Seyer, to whom she was not married, in violation of K.S.A.

Thereafter, Colleen Hermesmann entered into a plea agreement with the district attorney's office, wherein she agreed to stipulate to the lesser offense of contributing to a child's misconduct, K.S.A. On September 11, 1991, the juvenile court accepted the stipulation, and adjudicated Colleen Hermesmann to be a juvenile offender.

On March 8, 1991, SRS filed a petition on behalf of Colleen Hermesmann, alleging that Shane Seyer was the father of Colleen's minor daughter, Melanie. The petition also alleged that SRS had provided benefits through the ADC program to Colleen on behalf of the child and that Colleen had assigned support rights due herself and her child to SRS. The petition requested that the court determine paternity and order Shane to reimburse SRS for all assistance expended by SRS on Melanie's behalf. On December 17, 1991, an administrative hearing officer found Shane was Melanie's biological father. The hearing officer further determined that Shane was not required to pay the birth expenses or any of the child support expenses up to the date of the hearing on December 17, 1991, but that Shane had a duty to support the child from the date of the hearing forward.

Shane requested judicial review of the decision of the hearing officer, contending that the hearing officer "should have found a failure of consent would terminate rights." SRS sought review, asserting that the hearing officer correctly ruled that the issue of consent was irrelevant, but erred in allowing Shane to present evidence pertaining to the defense of consent. SRS also alleged that the hearing officer's denial of reimbursement to the State for funds already paid was arbitrary and capricious and contrary to the mandates of K.S.A. 1992 Supp. 39–718b.

The district judge, upon judicial review of the hearing officer's order, determined that Shane was the father of Melanie Hermesmann and owed a duty to support his child.

The court found that the issue of Shane's consent was irrelevant and ordered Shane to pay child support of $50 per month. The court also granted SRS a joint and several judgment against Shane and Colleen in the amount of $7,068, for assistance provided by the ADC program on behalf of Melanie through February 1992. The judgment included medical and other birthing expenses as well as assistance paid after Melanie's birth. Shane appeals the judgment rendered and the order for continuing support but does not contest the trial court's paternity finding. SRS has not cross-appealed from any of the orders or judgment of the district court.

This case was transferred from the Court of Appeals by this court's own motion. K.S.A. 20–3018(c).

Shane has designated three issues on appeal which he states as follows:

> "I. Can a minor, who is a victim of the crime of indecent liberties with a child, be responsible for any children conceived of the criminal union?
> "II. Is it sound public policy for a court to order child support when the order creates a clash of one minor's right to protection from being the victim of a crime with another minor's right to parental support?
> "III. Can a judgment ordering joint and several liability for child support be an adequate remedy when it fails to account for the wrongdoing of Plaintiff-appellee Hermesmann?"

Shane's argument on appeal is based on three basic premises. (1) Shane Seyer, as a minor under the age of 16, was unable to consent to sexual intercourse. (2) Because he was unable to consent to sexual intercourse, he cannot be held responsible for the birth of his child. (3) Because he cannot be held respon-

sible for the birth, he cannot be held jointly and severally liable for the child's support.

Shane asserts as his first issue that, because he was a minor under the age of 16 at the time of conception, he was legally incapable of consenting to sexual intercourse and therefore cannot be held legally responsible for the birth of his child. Shane cites no case law to directly support this proposition. Instead, he argues that Colleen Hermesmann sexually assaulted him, that he was the victim of the crime of statutory rape, and that the criminal statute of indecent liberties with a child should be applied to hold him incapable of consenting to the act.

Although the issue of whether an underage alleged "victim" of a sex crime can be held liable for support of a child born as a result of such crime is one of first impression in Kansas, other jurisdictions have addressed the question.

In *In re Paternity of J. L. H.,* . . . 441 N.W.2d 273 (1989), J. J. G. appealed from a summary judgment in a paternity proceeding determining that he was the father of J. L. H. and ordering him to pay child support equal to 17 percent of his gross income. J. J. G. was 15 years old when the child was conceived. On appeal, he asserted that the child's mother, L. H., sexually assaulted him, and that, as a minor, he was incapable of consent under the sexual assault law. The court rejected this argument and stated:

> "If voluntary intercourse results in parenthood, then for purposes of child support, the parenthood is voluntary. This is true even if a fifteen-year old boy's parenthood resulted from a sexual assault upon him within the meaning of the criminal law." . . .

Although the question of whether the intercourse with Colleen was "voluntary," as the term is usually understood, is not specifically before us, it was brought out in oral argument before this court that the sexual relationship between Shane and his baby sitter, Colleen, started when he was only 12 years old and lasted over a period of several months. At no time did Shane register any complaint to his parents about the sexual liaison with Colleen.

In *Schierenbeck v. Minor*, 367 P.2d 333 (1961), Schierenbeck, a 16-year-old boy, appealed the adjudication in a dependency proceeding that he was the father of a child born to a 20-year-old woman. On appeal, Schierenbeck cited a Colorado criminal statute which defined rape in the third degree by a female of a male person under the age of 18 years. In discussing the relevance of the criminal statute, the court stated:

> " 'The putative father may be liable in bastardy proceedings for the support and maintenance of his child, even though he is a minor. . . .' Bastards, 10 C.J.S. 152, § 53. If Schierenbeck is adjudged to be the father of [the child] after a proper hearing and upon sufficient evidence, he should support [the child] under this fundamental doctrine." 367 P.2d 333.

The trial court decision was reversed on other grounds not pertinent to the facts of our case and remanded for further proceedings.

The Kansas Parentage Act, K.S.A. 38–1110 *et seq.*, specifically contemplates minors as fathers and makes no exception for minor parents regarding their duty to support and educate their child. K.S.A. 38–1117 provides, in part:

> "If a man alleged or presumed to be the father is a minor, the court shall cause notice of the pendency of the proceedings and copies of the pleadings on file to be served upon the parents or guardian of the minor and shall appoint a guardian ad litem who shall be an attorney to represent the minor in the proceedings."

K.S.A.1992 Supp. 38–1121(c) provides, in part:

> "Upon adjudging that a party is the parent of a minor child, the court shall make provision for support and education of the child including the necessary medical expenses incident to the birth of the child. The court may order the support and education expenses to be paid by either or both parents for the minor child."

If the legislature had wanted to exclude minor parents from responsibility for support, it could easily have done so.

As previously stated, Shane does not contest that he is the biological father of the child. As a father, he has a common-law duty, as well as a statutory duty, to support his minor child.

We conclude that the issue of consent to sexual activity under the criminal statutes is irrelevant in a civil action to determine paternity and for support of the minor child of such activity. Consequently, Shane's reliance on the foregoing criminal case is misplaced.

For Shane's next issue, he asserts that it is not sound public policy for a court to order a youth to pay child support for a child conceived during the crime of indecent liberties with a child when the victim was unable to consent to the sexual intercourse. He claims that while the Kansas Parentage Act creates a State interest in the welfare of dependent relatives, the policy behind the Parentage Act is not to force a minor, who is unable to consent to sexual intercourse, to support a child born from the criminal act.

Shane provides no case law specifically on point, but once again relies upon the Kansas cases involving statutory rape.

Other jurisdictions have recognized the conflict between a State's interest in protecting juveniles and a State's interest in requiring parental support of children. In *In re Parentage of J.S.*, 550 N.E.2d 257 (1990), the trial court ordered a minor father to pay child support for his illegitimate son. The minor father appealed the order, but did not contest the trial court's paternity finding. In affirming the trial court's decision ordering support, the court stated:

> "In the instant case, *we find that the public policy mandating parental support of children overrides any policy of protecting a minor from improvident acts.* We therefore hold that the

trial court properly found that the respondent was financially responsible for his child." (Emphasis added.) 550 N.E.2d 257.

In *Commonwealth v. A Juvenile*, 442 N.E.2d 1155 (1982), a 16-year-old father was ordered to pay child support of $8 a week toward the support of his child born out of wedlock. The minor father admitted his paternity, but appealed the support order. On appeal, the court affirmed the judgment of the lower court and said:

> "The defendant's claim rests on an assertion that a support order is inconsistent with the statutory purpose of treating a juvenile defendant as a child 'in need of aid, encouragement and guidance.' [Citation omitted.] Although we acknowledge that purpose, we see no basis, and certainly no statutory basis, for concluding that a juvenile should be free from any duty to support his or her illegitimate child. The illegitimate child has interests, as does the Commonwealth." 442 N.E.2d 1155.

This State's interest in requiring minor parents to support their children overrides the State's competing interest in protecting juveniles from improvident acts, even when such acts may include criminal activity on the part of the other parent. Considering the three persons directly involved, Shane, Colleen, and Melanie, the interests of Melanie are superior, as a matter of public policy, to those of either or both of her parents. This minor child, the only truly innocent party, is entitled to support from both her parents regardless of their ages.

As his third issue, Shane asserts that the district court erred in finding he and Colleen were jointly and severally liable for the child support. He argues that, as Colleen was the perpetrator of the crime of statutory rape, she alone should be held responsible for the consequences of the act, and he requests this court to remand the case to the district court with instructions to order Colleen solely responsible for the support pursuant to K.S.A. 39–718a. He states that K.S.A. 39–701 *et seq.* does not require a judgment ordering joint and several liability for child support.

Nowhere does the law in this state suggest that the mother's "wrongdoing" can operate as a setoff or bar to a father's liability for child support. Under the facts as presented to this court, the district court properly held that Shane owes a duty of support to Melanie and properly ordered that Shane and Colleen were jointly and severally liable for the monies previously paid by SRS.

Finally, we call attention to the fact that no issue was raised as to the propriety of the judgment against a youngster who was still a full-time student when these proceedings were commenced. When questioned in oral argument about the policy of SRS in seeking a judgment in excess of $7,000, counsel replied with the surprising statement that SRS had no intention of ever attempting to collect its judgment. Under such circumstances, the reason for seeking that portion of the judgment still eludes us.

The judgment of the district court is affirmed.

Case Questions

1. What two state interests are in conflict in this case?
2. On what grounds did the Kansas Supreme Court reject Seyer's argument that a boy who was a thirteen-year-old victim at the time of his child's conception should not be held financially responsible for the birth of his child?
3. Do you believe this decision makes good public policy?

Child support. Another aspect of the parent–child relationship is the parental support obligation. The nature and extent of this obligation varies and depends on the child's needs as well as on the parent's financial condition. Though all states require that parents fulfill support obligations, some have gone so far as to require stepparents[67] and grandparents[68] to provide child support. When marriages break up, a court will usually require the noncustodial parent to pay child support until the child attains the age of majority, marries, becomes emancipated, or dies. Even after a child reaches the age of majority, parents often have a continuing support obligation if their offspring are disabled, haven't completed high school, or if such an obligation exists pursuant to a separation agreement.

One of the areas of recent conflict relates to a parent's duty to pay for a child's college education, an expense that usually isn't payable until after the child has passed the age of majority. Although parents in intact families have no legal duty to fund college educations for their children, as we see in the next case, some courts have ruled that a parent's support obligation can include funding their child's college education.

Nash v. Mulle
846 S.W.2d 803
Supreme Court of Tennessee
January 19, 1993

Daugherty, Justice

The essential facts in this case are not in dispute. What is contested is the extent of the child support obligation of Charles Mulle, who fathered Melissa Alice Matlock as the result of an extramarital affair with the appellant, Helen Nash, in 1981 but has since had nothing to do with mother or child. After an order was entered establishing his paternity in 1984, the Juvenile Court also ordered him to pay $200.00 each month in child support, in addition to other specified expenses. In 1990, Helen Nash filed this action seeking an increase in the amount of his payments because of Charles Mulle's dramatically increased income. The Juvenile Court then order Mulle to pay $3,092.62 per month, with $1,780.17 reserved for a trust fund established for Melissa's college education. The Court of Appeals reversed, limiting the award to $1,312.00 per month, or exactly 21 percent of $6,250.00, the top monthly income to which

the child support guidelines explicitly apply. The Court of Appeals also disallowed the trust, finding that it improperly extended the parental duty of support beyond the age of majority. Because the facts are not disputed, we review *de novo* the questions of law presented on appeal.

Child support in Tennessee is statutorily governed by T.C.A. § 36–5–101. Section 86–5–101(e)(I) provides that "[i]n making its determination concerning the amount of support of any minor child . . . of the parties, the court shall apply as a rebuttable presumption the child support guidelines as provided in this subsection." The General Assembly adopted the child support guidelines promulgated by the Tennessee Department of Human Services in order to maintain compliance with the Family Support Act of 1988, codified in various sections of 42 U.S.C.

I

The first issue presented concerns the proper measure of child support to be awarded in this case in view of the fact that Charles Mulle's monthly income exceeds $6,250.00. The guidelines apply in *all* cases awarding financial support to a custodial parent for the maintenance of a child, whether or not the child is a welfare recipient, and whether or not the child's parents are married. The guidelines are based, however, on several goals; they make many assumptions; and they permit deviation in circumstances that do not always comport with the assumptions. In studying the goals, premises, and criteria for deviation, we are convinced that the guidelines permit a monthly award greater than $1,312.00 without a specific showing of need by the custodial parent.

One major goal expressed in the guidelines is "[t]o ensure that when parents live separately, the economic impact on the child(ren) is minimized and to the extent that either parent enjoys a higher standard of living, the child(ren) share(s) in that higher standard." . . . This goal becomes significant when, as here, one parent has vastly greater financial resources than the other. It reminds us that Tennessee does not define a child's needs literally, but rather requires an award to reflect both parents' financial circumstances. This goal is consistent with our long-established common law rule, which requires that a parent must provide support "in a manner commensurate with his means and station in life."

The guidelines are currently structured to require payment by the non-custodial parent of a certain percentage of his or her net income, depending upon the number of children covered by the support order (21 percent for one child, 32 percent for two children, etc.). The statute promulgating the use of the guidelines creates a "rebuttable presumption" that the scheduled percentages will produce the appropriate amounts to be awarded as monthly child support. However, they are subject to deviation upward or downward when the assumptions on which they are based do not pertain to a particular situation. For example, one assumption on which the percentages are based is that the "children are living primarily with one parent but stay overnight with the other parent as often as every other weekend . . . , two weeks in the summer and two weeks during holidays. . . ." The criteria for deviation provide that when this level of visitation does not occur, child support should be adjusted upward to provide for the additional support required of the custodial parent. Additionally, "[e]xtraordinary educational expenses and extraordinary medical expenses not covered by insurance" are given as reasons for deviation. The guidelines thus recognize that "unique case circumstances will require a court determination on a case-by-case basis."

Among the "unique cases" specifically anticipated in the guidelines are those cases in which the income of the parent paying support exceeds $6,250.00 per month. In the criteria for deviation the guidelines provide that among the "cases where guidelines are neither appropriate nor equitable" are those in which "the net income of the obligor exceeds $6,250 per month." In the present case, the Juvenile Court calculated Charles Mulle's net monthly income to be $14,726.98, a figure well above the $6,250.00 figure justifying deviation from the guidelines. Yet the total award of $3,092 ordered by the trial judge is exactly 21 percent of Mulle's monthly income.

Obviously, to treat the monthly income figure of $6,250.00 as a cap and automatically to limit the award to 21 percent of that amount for a child whose non-custodial parent makes over $6,250.00 may be "neither appropriate nor equitable." Such an automatic limit fails to take into consideration the extremely high standard of living of a parent such as Charles Mulle, and thus fails to reflect one of the primary goals of the guidelines, *i.e.,* to allow the child of a well-to-do parent to share in that very high standard of living. On the other hand, automatic application of the 21 percent multiplier to every dollar in excess of $6,250.00 would be equally unfair.

. . . [W]e conclude that the trial court should retain the discretion to determine—as the guidelines provide, "on a case-by-case basis"—the appropriate amount of child support to be paid when an obligor's net income exceeds $6,250.00 per month, balancing both the child's need and the parents' means.

II

As he did before the Court of Appeals, Charles Mulle contends that the establishment of an educational trust fund for his daughter unlawfully requires him to support her past her minority. Citing *Garey v. Garey*, 482 S.W.2d 133 (Tenn.1972), he argues that the trust fund is incompatible with Tennessee case law. In *Garey*, this Court held that "[b]y lowering the age of majority from 21 to 18 years of age the Legislature has completely emancipated the minor from the control of the parents and relieved the parents of their attendant legal duty to support the child." . . . Because the trust fund is intended for Melissa's college education, her father insists that it unlawfully requires postminority support.

We conclude, to the contrary, that the establishment of the trust fund in this case does not conflict with the holding in *Garey*. Although child support payments may not extend beyond the child's minority (except in extraordinary circumstances involving physical or mental disability), the benefits from such payments can. Hence, it is consistent with established rules of Tennessee law to hold, as we do here, that funds ordered to be accumulated during a child's minority that are in excess of the amount needed to supply basic support may be used to the child's advantage past the age of minority.

In reaching this conclusion, we must recognize the obvious fact that responsible parents earning high incomes set aside money for their children's future benefit and often create trusts for that purpose. They save for unforeseen emergencies; they accumulate savings for trips and other luxuries; and they may, and usually do, save for their children's

college educations. Melissa's mother has expressed her intention to send her daughter to college. As all parents realize, however, the goal of sending a child to college often requires the wise management of money through savings. For a child of Melissa's age, assumed to begin college in the fall of 2000, it has been estimated that a parent must invest $457.00 per month for a public college education, or $964.00 per month for a private education, in order to save the $61,571.00 or $129,893.00, respectively, that will be required to fund a college education beginning that year. Lacking the resources to write a check for the full amount of college tuition, room, board, and other expenses when that time arrives, Helen Nash must accumulate these savings over the course of the child's minority, or be forced to borrow the money later on. Such savings in this case would inevitably deplete Melissa's child support award. While in many cases parents undergo serious financial sacrifices to make college possible for their children, in this case, as the Juvenile Court found, Charles Mulle's income can afford Melissa a high standard of living that also includes savings for college.

We believe that an approach that refuses to recognize the laudable goal of postsecondary education and instead provides only for the child's immediate needs, would not be a responsible approach. If the most concerned, caring parents do not operate in such a haphazard way, surely the courts cannot be expected to award child support in such a fashion. Thus, we conclude that establishing a program of savings for a college education is a proper element of child support when, as in this case, the resources of the noncustodial parent can provide the necessary funds without hardship to that parent.

Moreover, the use of a trust fund for just such a purpose is explicitly approved by the guidelines. In the section on criteria for deviation, . . . [t]here are . . . cases where guidelines are neither appropriate nor equitable when a court so finds. Guidelines are inappropriate in cases including but not limited to, the following: (a) In cases where the net income of the obligor . . . exceeds $6,250 per month. *These cases may require such things as the establishment of educational or other trust funds* for the benefit of the child(ren) or other provisions as may be determined by the court. . . . Thus, the guidelines specifically recommend a trust fund in cases in which a large cash award may be inappropriate. Moreover, the guidelines do not limit expenditures from such trusts to the child's minority. We defer to the policy judgment of the legislature in adopting the guidelines and uphold the use of the trust in this case.

In addition to adhering to the guidelines and providing a mechanism for this laudable use of savings, a trust fund for college education achieves several other goals. First, in a case such as this one involving a large difference in the parents' incomes, the trust allows for equitable contributions from each parent while avoiding an immediate cash windfall to one of them. When a large award given to a custodial parent with a much lower income would result in a windfall to the custodial parent, a trust fund helps to ensure that money earmarked for the child actually inures to the child's benefit. Thus, the trust fund is properly used to minimize unintended benefits to the custodial parent.

We also note the need for a trust as protection for the child of an uncaring non-custodial parent.

When a non-custodial parent has shown normal parental concern for a child, a trust fund may be unnecessary to ensure that his or her feelings are reflected in spending. However, when a non-custodial parent shows a lack of care, the court may step in and require the parent to support his or her child. The establishment of a trust is simply one discretionary mechanism used in the endeavor.

Thus, Charles Mulle's argument that the absence of a relationship with Melissa ob-

viates the need to fund her college education is simply backwards. Child support is designed to prevent a non-custodial parent from shirking responsibility for the child he or she willingly conceived. It is precisely when natural feelings of care and concern are absent, and no parent-child relationship has been developed, that the court must award child support in a manner that best mirrors what an appropriate contribution from an interested parent would be. In fact, at least one court has gone beyond the acknowledgment of this lack of parental interest, and has spoken in terms of compensating the child for the parent's lack of concern.

While we do not adhere to this compensatory view of child support, we do believe that an appropriate child support award should reflect an amount that would normally be spent by a concerned parent of similar resources.

We thus find no merit to Charles Mulle's complaint that the order deprives him of the freedom to decide his daughter's educational fate, arguing that a requirement is being imposed upon him that does not exist for married parents. He contends in his brief that "some parents plan for the future education of their children and some do not"; he argues that "[s]urely a divorce decree or a paternity order should not give children rights that children who are living with their parents who are married do not have." This argument overlooks the obvious fact that divorced and unmarried parents face a substantial loss of parental autonomy whenever a court must step in to exercise responsibility for their children in the absence of parental cooperation. Married parents may choose to rear their children in an extravagant or miserly fashion; they may send their children to expensive private schools and universities; or they may require their children to make their ways in the world at age 18. Nevertheless, when children become the subject of litigation, courts must judge the children's needs. Long-standing

Tennessee law requires the courts to evaluate children's needs not in terms of life's essentials, but in terms of the parents' "means and station in life."

The guidelines' requirement that child support allow a child to share in the higher standard of living of a high-income parent continues this objective. Thus, Mulle's complaint about the alleged unfairness of the court's judgment concerning the benefits his standard of living should afford Melissa is misplaced.

. . . Given the public policy favoring higher education in Tennessee, likewise evidenced by our many colleges and universities, it would be highly improper in this case to cast the burden of Melissa's higher education entirely on her mother, or on the "bounty of the state," when her father can provide for her education without unduly burdening himself.

In ruling the trust in this case illegal because it "has no relation to the support of the child during minority," the Court of Appeals relied for authority on prior Tennessee case law discussed earlier in this section, as well as cases from other jurisdictions, primarily Illinois and Hawai'i. But, the Tennessee precedents predate the enactment of the Child Support Guidelines, which specifically authorize the use of trusts in cases involving non-custodial parents with high income, without limiting expenditures to the beneficiary's minority. Moreover the courts and legislatures of many other states have approved the funding of a college education by non-custodial parents who can afford such an expense. Indeed, several courts have done so without explicit statutory permission. In Pennsylvania, for example, the rule that a parent owes no duty of support for a child's college education is subject to an important exception. A parent may be ordered to provide such support if that parent has the "earning capacity or income to enable him to do so without undue hardship to himself."

See Commonwealth v. Thomas, 364 A.2d 410, 411 (1976); *see also Brake v. Brake*, 413 A.2d 422 (1979). Therefore, in appropriate cases, the Pennsylvania courts require college support even though the age of majority in that jurisdiction is 18. An Alabama court, similarly, has required the establishment of a trust during a child's minority for educational expenses incurred after the age of majority. *See Armstrong v. Armstrong*, 391 So.2d 124, (1980). The Iowa Supreme Court decreed in *Hart v. Hart*, 30 N.W.2d 748 (1948), that a non-custodial parent should provide his sons with four-year college educations despite the fact that college funding would likely require support beyond the 21-year-old age of majority in existence at that time. New Hampshire courts also have the discretion to award college support past the age of majority. . . . These courts have used their equitable powers to require wealthy non-custodial parents to fund their children's college educations past the age of majority.

In yet other states, the authority of the courts to require non-custodial parents to fund a college education for their children is provided by statute. In Washington, after the child support statute was amended to include support for "dependents," the Washington Supreme Court declared that a college education could be included in the duty of support in cases where it "works the parent no significant hardship and . . . the child shows aptitude." . . . Oregon, similarly, allows courts to award support to children until the age of 21, three years past the age of majority, if they attend school. Or.Rev.Stat. § 107.108 (1991). . . . Indiana allows child support for college expenses if the parent has the financial ability and the child has the aptitude. Ind.Code § 31–1–11.5–12(b) (1991). . . .

Other legislatures have taken the lead from court decisions allowing college support and now statutorily provide for such support. For example, Illinois has codified prior case law that had established a parent's duty to provide for his or her child's education whether the child was of minority or majority age. . . .

. . . In addition, a New York statute permits an award for post-secondary educational expenses when the court determines that the award is appropriate in light of "the circumstances of the case and of the respective parties and the best interests of the child and as justice requires." . . . New York's statute replaces years of case law holding that a college education could be a "special circumstance" meriting support past minority.

. . . Thus, whether based on statute or rooted in the courts' equitable powers in family matters, the efforts of these states to provide for the college educations of children with wealthy parents persuade us that reason and public policy permit the use of a trust fund in this case.

In light of the guidelines' explicit provision for the use of trusts in cases involving high-income parents, the goals promoted by the use of a trust in this instance, and the reasoned support of other state courts and legislatures, we find the use of an educational trust in this case to be proper. As noted in Section I, however, there remains the question of the level at which the trust should be funded in this case. We therefore reverse the judgment of the Court of Appeals, and remand the case to the Juvenile Court for calculation of an award in accordance with this opinion.

Finally, we grant the appellant her attorney's fees and all other costs of the appeal, pursuant to T.C.A. § 36–5–101(i).

Case Questions

1. Based on the facts of this case, do you agree with the court's decision that a biological father has a financial obligation to pay for his child's college education by making contributions to a trust fund?
2. Because parents in intact families have no legal duty to financially fund college educations for their children, why should the law impose that requirement in a case such as this? Should a child's aptitude for college be considered?

Noneconomic Obligations

Parents' noneconomic obligations include nurturing and controlling their children, seeing that they attend school, and protecting them from abuse and neglect. Authorities can intervene if parents fail to perform these duties. Although parents generally have the right to make decisions on their child's behalf about religious training and educational and medical needs, this right is limited. When a child's life is threatened, for example, and the parents' religious beliefs prevent them from seeking necessary medical care, the state will often intervene and ensure that the child receives treatment.

Children also have obligations, the single most important of which is to obey their parents. When children perpetually defy their parents, a judicial CHINS (child in need of supervision) proceeding may be instituted. Many states also statutorily require adult children to provide their parents with necessaries in the event that the parents become unable to provide for themselves.[69]

Parental Immunity from Suit by Child

As we saw in Chapter 6, parents have traditionally been protected from suit by their children for negligence and intentional torts by an immunity. Over the last thirty years, however, many states have created exceptions to this immunity and have permitted suits in cases of child abuse, neglect, serious batteries, and the negligent operation of automobiles. Today, most states have either abolished the immunity or severely limited its use.

ENDING SPOUSAL RELATIONSHIPS

Spousal relationships can be ended through the legal actions of annulment and divorce, and they can be judicially altered by legal separation.

Annulment

An action to *annul* is appropriate when a marriage partner seeks to prove that no valid marriage ever existed. Thus the plaintiff is not seeking to terminate a valid marriage but, rather, to have a court declare that no valid marriage ever occurred. Annulments were historically important, especially during periods when divorces were difficult to obtain. Obtaining an annulment of a marriage was very useful because it could end the spousal relationship without branding either party as being "divorced" and thus enable each to remarry. Today, with the advent of no-fault divorce, actions for annulment are much less popular, except among those who for religious reasons prefer to end a marriage legally without going through a divorce.

Although each state has its own grounds for annulments, common reasons include bigamy (where a person who is already married marries yet again), incest (where a person marries someone who is a close blood relative contrary to law), mental incompetence (such as where the parties were intoxicated at the time of the ceremony),[70] fraud (such as where one party misrepresents a willingness to engage in sexual relations and have children),[71] coercion, and one or both parties' being underage at the time of the marriage.

Because of the serious potential consequences of an annulment, particularly to property rights, many states have declared the children born to parents whose marriage has been annulled to be legitimate.[72] These states provide by statute that child support and custody matters will be determined in the same way as in divorce cases.[73] Many state courts award temporary alimony and some award permanent alimony to dependent spouses.[74] Each party to an annulment recovers the property held prior to the marriage and is considered a co-owner of property acquired during the marriage.

Legal Separations

Many states have statutorily recognized an action for *legal separation*, also called a *mensa et thoro* divorce (from pillow and table).[75] The so-called *mensa* divorce can be granted when lawfully married parties have actually separated and when adequate grounds for a legal separation have been shown. Although states differ on what constitutes sufficient grounds, common reasons include irreconcilable differences, adultery, desertion, cruelty, and nonsupport. If a court grants a legal separation, the parties remain married to each other but live apart. A criminal action can be brought if one spouse interferes with the other spouse's privacy. Unlike a final divorce, neither party to a legal separation is free to remarry. The court, after considering the financial conditions of each party, can require one spouse to support the other and can determine child custody. States differ about whether a property division should occur. During the legal separation, the possibility of reconciliation still exists, as does the option to proceed with a final divorce. The separation period allows the estranged parties to try to work out their difficulties while living apart.

Divorce/Dissolution

From the perspective of the early twenty-first century, it is difficult to understand the degree to which contemporary expectations of marriage differ from those of our ancestors. Historically, absolute divorce under Anglo-American law was very difficult to obtain. In New York, for example, the legislature had to approve each divorce until 1787, when courts were statutorily authorized to grant divorces in cases of adultery, which was New York's only ground for a lawful divorce until 1966![76] In nineteenth-century America it was assumed that persons were married for life.[77] In 1900 women lived an average of only forty-eight years,[78] so people were married for shorter periods of time. The social, legal, and economic circumstances of that era encouraged husbands and wives to remain formally married despite the existence of dysfunctional relationships and irreparable differences between the parties.

Today, people live longer lives and have more choices.[79] There are fewer pressures on people to marry in the first place, and the miserably married are less likely to remain in intolerable relationships.[80] The availability of birth control permits people to be sexually active without conceiving children. Single parenting is common and is no longer considered unusual. Women have more economic opportunities than they did in 1950. The social stigma of being thirty and divorced or unmarried has greatly diminished. People who marry today do so primarily for companionship,[81] a need that can bring people together but can also cause them to follow different paths as their lives evolve with time.

This social transformation has gradually produced legal changes as well. Although many states had liberalized their divorce laws more than New York by the early 1960s, divorces were generally limited—at least theoretically—to plaintiffs who proved that their spouses had engaged in adultery, cruelty (sometimes interpreted very liberally), and/or desertion.[82] The fact that a married couple had irreconcilable differences and were married in name only was not a sufficient basis under the law for a divorce. The fault-based approach was antidivorce and existed because of widely held fears about the social consequences to families and society that would result from what was feared might become divorce on demand. When states began to liberalize their laws to meet the increasing demand for divorce, they often required long waiting periods before a divorce became final. During the waiting period it was unlawful for people to remarry, start new families, and get on with their lives.[83] To get around such restrictions, people often went to Nevada to obtain what were called "quickie divorces," because that state required only a six-week waiting period.[84] Reformers pressed for change, urging lawmakers to focus on the marriage relationship itself and to recognize that the adversarial process of proving fault was making a bad situation worse. It was damaging the parties and making the process of ending a marriage more difficult and painful than it ought to be. It encouraged collusion and caused some parties to perjure themselves, "admitting" things they had not done, just in order to qualify for a divorce.[85] In California, proponents of reform carefully drafted and quietly pursued the legislative process[86] and were rewarded with enactment of the nation's first "no-fault" divorce law, which took effect on January 1, 1970.[87] Once that dam was broken, all states adopted some form of no-fault divorce; the last state acted in 1985.[88] Today, in many states, the plaintiff can choose to proceed either on a no-fault basis or on the traditional fault basis. Proving fault can sometimes be advantageous if it makes it possible to avoid the waiting period that some states require before a divorce becomes final. And in some jurisdictions, proving fault can affect alimony and child custody decisions.

Although state no-fault laws differ, a plaintiff usually has to prove marital breakdown and to prove that the parties have been living separately for a statutorily determined minimum period of time. In most states, a divorce can be granted despite the defendant's objection.[89] As a result of the philosophical changes that have occurred in recent years, the term *divorce* is increasingly being replaced with the more neutral term *dissolution*, which denotes the legal ending of the marital relationship.

Jurisdictional and Procedural Considerations

You will recall the discussions of *in personam* and *in rem* jurisdiction in Chapter 3 and of civil procedure in Chapter 4. Because terminating a marriage often involves some interesting jurisdictional problems and specialized procedures, it is important briefly to revisit these topics as they are related to divorce.

Jurisdiction

If it is determined that a court has granted a divorce, awarded alimony, or determined custody of a child without having jurisdiction, the court's action is void and without effect. Furthermore, this jurisdictional deficiency would make the court's judgment ineligible for full faith and credit in other states. Although constitutional due process often permits the termination of a marriage on the basis of *in rem* jurisdiction, a court must have *in personam* jurisdiction over a person who is to be required to make alimony and child support payments. Thus a court has jurisdiction to grant a divorce decree where at least one marital party has lived within the forum state long enough to satisfy that state's residency requirement. The residency requirement demonstrates a substantial connection with the forum state and helps to establish the *in rem* notion that the marriage itself (the *res*) is physically located within the forum state.

If the plaintiff seeks to have a court decree alimony or to order child support in addition to terminating the marriage, however, *in rem* jurisdiction is insufficient and the minimum contacts requirement of *in personam* jurisdiction must be satisfied.

Procedure

Many states statutorily permit a court to issue temporary support orders once a divorce action is initiated. This order may temporarily require one party to pay for an economically dependent spouse's necessaries, determines child custody and support, and determines who is responsible for paying which debts. This order is limited and is intended only to enable both parties to meet their living expenses while the action is pending. These issues are not permanently decided until the divorce and related claims have been acted on and a final judgment and order are entered in the case.

Although laypeople generally use the term *divorce* to refer to the entire process of concluding and reordering a couple's marital, parental, and economic relationships, this is actually a misnomer. It is common in many states for each of the divorce-related claims to be decided in segments rather than in one long trial. This approach is called *bifurcation*, and it means that child custody, alimony, property division, and marriage dissolution are taken up separately by the court.

Procedural requirements in a divorce action generally vary with the type and complexity of the claims that must be resolved. Thus a contested divorce will generally be more procedurally cumbersome than an uncontested action, and a no-fault action will often be less procedurally complex than a fault-based action. In some states, cooperating parties can privately negotiate a separation agreement that reflects their mutual decision about how property should be divided, the amounts and types of support to be paid, and even proposals about child custody. If the terms of this contract are not unconscionable, the laws of the state can make this agreement binding on the court except as it relates to child custody provisions. Parties to no-fault divorces who have no children and no substantial assets can end their marriages in some states in a matter of minutes.

Allocation of Financial Obligations

When people divorce, in addition to terminating their marital relationship, there is a need to untangle their financial affairs so that each spouse can function independently. This involves determining whether alimony and child support will be paid and allocating the marital assets and liabilities. In some cases the parties are able to negotiate these matters successfully; in others a judge must ultimately make the decision.

Court-ordered Alimony

Virtually all states permit a court to require an economically strong spouse to pay financial support to an economically dependent spouse where it is necessary and appropriate. This payment, which is discretionary with the court, is often referred to as *alimony*, although it is also called spousal support.[90] Some jurisdictions deny it to any spouse whose marriage ended as a result of that person's marital fault.

One form of spousal support is called *permanent alimony* because it continues until the recipient dies or is remarried. This form of alimony is intended to compensate an economically dependent wife who was married in another era, when homemaking was commonly viewed as a career and when it was reasonable to expect that one's husband would provide support for life. Someone who invested many years taking care of her home and her family, rather than working outside the home, is granted alimony when her marriage is terminated so that she receives economic justice. This form of alimony is on the decline, because public policy today favors sexual equality and because women today generally have the skills and education necessary to get a job and to be self-supporting.

Another type of spousal support, called *rehabilitative alimony*, is awarded for a specified period of years and is intended to provide funds so that the recipient can obtain education or training that will strengthen the person's job prospects. In deciding whether to grant rehabilitative alimony, a court takes into consideration many factors, including the payor's earning capacity; the dependent spouse's health status, work history, and present and future prospects for employment; and the likelihood that the person will take advantage of training and educational opportunities.

A court can order that alimony be paid either in a lump sum or periodically, usually on a monthly basis. If conditions materially change over time, either party can petition for modification. The payor, for example, might seek a reduction because of ill health and unemployment and the fact that the recipient, though not remarried, is cohabiting and has less financial need. The recipient, for example, might argue for an increase to offset inflation's impact on purchasing power and the recipient's need to pay for necessary medical treatment.

Enforcing payment of alimony is very problematic, because courts are reluctant to incarcerate defaulters (how can they earn money while in jail?) and because it is often too expensive for recipients to use the normal remedies available for enforcing civil judgments (these remedies were discussed in Chapter 4).

Child Custody and Child Support

The general responsibility of parents to support their children was previously addressed in this chapter. The current discussion focuses on child custody and support in the context of a divorce, annulment, or temporary separation.

Although parents can negotiate an agreement and resolve many issues, they can only recommend whether the court should grant custody to both parents (*joint custody*) or grant custody to only one parent. Although the court has the responsibility to protect children, it usually will incorporate into the final judgment the custodial arrangements that have been agreed to by the parents if the arrangements are reasonable and appropriate. The court's decision is of great importance because of the custodial parent's right to make important decisions regarding a child's upbringing. Although judges historically have granted custody of young children to their mothers,[91] most states have discarded the *"tender years doctrine,"* at least as a rigid rule, in response to increasing challenges from fathers during the 1970s.[92] The "best interest of the child" rule, preferred custody statutes (that favor the primary caretaker), and joint custody have become the most widely accepted standards for determining custody.[93]

The *"best interest of the child"* rule requires judges to show no gender preference and to act in the best interest of each child. When making this decision, the courts consider such matters as each parent's ability to provide, and interest in providing, the child with love, a good home, food, clothing, medical care, and education. Inquiry will be made into the stability of each parent's employment and whether the employment is compatible with the child's needs. Courts also look for instances of parental misconduct (such as substance abuse and sexually and morally questionable behavior), continuity of care,[94] and a sound moral foundation for the child. The following case demonstrates the difficulty of applying the "best interest of the child" rule. Notice how issues of employment, educational and professional accomplishment, and parental bonding bear on the determination of custody.

In re **Marriage of Riddle**
500 N.W.2d 718
Court of Appeals of Iowa
March 30, 1993

Donielson, Judge

Dorothy Riddle appeals from the district court dissolution decree which awarded primary physical custody of the parties' minor child to Michael Riddle.

Dorothy and Michael Riddle were married in August 1986. They have one minor child, Lauren, who was born in January 1987.

Dorothy was born in 1966. At age sixteen, she married Pat Pepples. The marriage lasted only nine months and bore one child, Ashley, in June 1983. Dorothy has sole custody of Ashley. Dorothy married Michael just prior to her sophomore year at Iowa State University. While attending college, Dorothy held a number of part-time jobs. Dorothy has now graduated from Iowa State with a Bachelor of Science degree in nutrition. She is currently employed as the chief clinical dietician at Broadlawns Medical Center in Des Moines and earns a net monthly income of $1560.

Michael was born in 1964. He attends college at Iowa State University and intends to complete his degree in elementary education in about two years. Michael currently works several part-time jobs including assistant coaching duties, handyman work for the Ames School District, and sales for the Fuller Brush Company. His net monthly income is about $1102.

In July 1990, Dorothy filed a petition for dissolution of marriage. The petition was not served on Michael until November 1991. In January 1992, the district court awarded temporary physical custody of Lauren to Dorothy.

In August 1992, following a hearing, the district court issued its dissolution decree. The court determined, among other matters, primary physical custody of Lauren should be awarded to Michael. The court ordered Dorothy to pay $351 per month in child support.

Dorothy now appeals. Dorothy contends the district court erred in awarding primary physical custody to Michael. She specifically claims the district court erred in: (1) finding Lauren's long-term best interests were best served by awarding primary physical custody to Michael; [and] (2) separating Lauren from her half-sister, Ashley. . . .

In child custody cases, the best interests of the child is the first and governing consideration. . . .

The critical issue in determining the best interests of the child is which parent will do better in raising the child. . . . Gender is irrelevant, and neither parent should have a greater burden than the other in attempting to gain custody in a dissolution proceeding. . . .

We agree with the district court's finding that the issue of primary physical custody was a "close call." Both Michael and Dorothy care deeply for Lauren and her welfare. They both clearly offer Lauren a stable environment both emotionally and financially.

We admire Dorothy's diligence in completing her bachelor's degree while helping to raise two children. Dorothy has found a responsible and challenging job which provides her with considerable financial stability. In comparison, we recognize Michael's future plans are not as certain and that his income is less than that of Dorothy's. However, the fact Michael is employed only by several part-time jobs and the fact he has a lower income do not constitute evidence that Michael is unable to offer Lauren stability.

On our review, the record supports the finding that the long-term best interests of Lauren would be better served if Michael were the physical custodian. As Dorothy spent considerable time working and completing her degree, Michael became the primary caretaker for Lauren. Michael has done an excellent job as the primary caretaker to Lauren during the first five years of her life. As a coach, Michael takes Lauren to many of his practices and games. At trial, many witnesses testified to the close bond between Michael and Lauren.

Dorothy asserts she is being "punished" for having assumed the "traditional male duties" of being the family breadwinner. We do not agree. Our decision is based on an examination of which parent had been the child's primary psychological parent and with which parent the child had more closely bonded. . . . Here, the evidence suggests Lauren has consistently demonstrated a greater emotional attachment to her father.

In our decision, we recognize the preference for not separating siblings. . . . Admittedly, Lauren and her half sister, Ashley, are close. However, Michael is not the legal father of Ashley and he has no right to seek physical custody of Ashley in the dissolution. Michael therefore argues it would be unfair to give substantial weight to the preference for keeping siblings together because this gives Dorothy an unfair advantage in the contest for physical care of Lauren.

In *In re Marriage of Orte*, 389 N.W.2d 373, . . . (1986), the supreme court examined the issue of how much weight should be given to the preference for keeping siblings together in the case of half siblings. The court found the general principles governing the separation of siblings should govern, regardless of the advantage given to the parent of the half sibling. . . . The court found, in order to depart from the preference for keeping siblings together, "it must appear that separation 'may better promote the long-range interests of children.'" . . .

Here we find the district court did have a good and compelling reason to separate Lauren and Ashley. Lauren and Michael have a close relationship, and Michael has been the primary caretaker of Lauren throughout her life. There is no evidence that Lauren and Ashley will not be able to continue their close relationship despite the separation. On our review, we find granting Michael primary physical care will better promote the long-range best interests of Lauren.

We remind Michael that liberal visitation rights are in the best interests of the children. Iowa Code §598.41(1) (1991); . . . Both parents, as joint custodians, are charged with maintaining those interests. Unless visitation with the noncustodial parent will in some way injure the child, it is not to be prohibited.

For the reasons stated, we affirm the judgment of the district court.

Affirmed.

Case Questions

1. Are you satisfied with the Iowa Court of Appeals' explanation of the basis for its decision?
2. Do you agree with the trial and appellate courts that a compelling reason had been shown which justified rejecting the Iowa preference for not separating siblings in child custody disputes?

 From your perspective, how should a court ethically weigh the economic contributions of a parent who works outside the home against the contributions of the parent who provides a child with primary care and psychological support?

Preferred Custody Statutes

Preferred custody statutes were enacted because it was uncertain whether judges had sufficient reliable information to predict accurately what would be in a child's best interest.[95] Some states require that preference be given to a child's primary caretaker, when the primary caretaker can be established. Such an approach has the advantage of not favoring either gender, and it provides the child with continuity and stability in the parenting role.

When the statutory preference is for joint custody, the public policy provides that even though the marital relationship between the parents has ended, their parenting roles and responsibilities will continue as before. Both parents will share decision making in regard to their child's upbringing. Joint custody produces no winners and losers of a custody battle. The parents continue to share a family, but not a marriage.[96] When joint custody works, the child benefits from the active involvement of both a mother and a father. But it works only where divorcing parents are willing and able to separate their marital and parental relationships and act cooperatively to benefit their child.[97]

Once a court has determined that one parent should have custody, the noncustodial parent will normally be awarded visitation rights. It is important to encourage the noncustodial parent to continue to play an active role in the child's life. Sometimes the custodial parent wants to relocate, which would have the effect of curtailing the visitation opportunities of the noncustodial spouse. Courts are divided on what standard to apply when the parents disagree about making such a move.[98] Although the initial custody determination can be modified at a future date if material changes in the child's circumstances prove harmful, courts are reluctant to unsettle a child unless compelling reasons are shown.

Child Support

Earlier in this chapter we learned that although parents can formally and informally break up with one another, they cannot divorce their minor children. We also learned that the parental support generally continues until the child reaches the age of majority and, in some circumstances, even beyond. We focus now on the special circumstances that arise in conjunction with a divorce.

When a marriage that involves children is terminated, the court will examine the earning capacity of each parent and the needs of each child, will determine who has custody, and will determine each parent's support obligation. Every state has some guidelines to help judges make this determination. Generally, when custody has been awarded to one parent, the noncustodial parent will be ordered to make support payments. This parent is legally required to make the payments irrespective of side issues such as whether the custodial parent has violated the noncustodial parent's visitation rights or whether the custodial parent is spending the support payment money for other purposes than the children. Although child support is awarded to provide for the needs of the child, courts disagree about the exact meaning of that term. It certainly includes a child's necessaries, and there are cases in which noncustodial parents have been required to pay for their children's college educations.[99] Nevertheless, child support has a theoretically different purpose from that of alimony and property awards, which are intended to benefit a spouse.

When parents divorce, remarry, and establish second families, their support obligation to their first family continues, and many states require that the children from the first family receive priority over the children in the second family. Some states are moving away from this traditional approach and are structuring child support so that it benefits both families.[100] As was previously indicated, states differ about whether stepparents have a support liability or stepchildren.

As is the case with alimony, either party can petition for modification of the support order when there is a substantial change of circumstances.

Property Division

When people divorce, the property that they have accumulated during their marriage is apportioned between them. It is common for married people to concurrently own a house, cars, and other tangible personal property and to have joint accounts at the bank. If they have been married for a long time, they will probably have accumulated much property. States address the distribution problem differently, depending on whether they basically follow the common law/equitable distribution approach or the community property approach.

Common Law/Equitable Distribution Approach

In most states, what is known as equitable distribution has replaced the traditional common law approach to determining property rights. Under the common law, the person who had title to property owned it, and generally this meant the husband. When lawmakers and judges began to look upon marriage as an economic partnership, property acquired during marriage was perceived in different terms. This new perspective produced reforms intended to result in the more equitable distribution of property to each of the divorcing parties. Though not all states that adopt equitable distribution classify property, many do. In those states, property is classified as separate property or as marital property. *Marital property* is nonseparate property acquired during the marriage and is subject to an equitable distribution by a judge. *Separate property*, that which was owned prior to the marriage or was received as a gift or inheritance, is not subject to distribution.

Obviously, the legal definition of property is crucial to any distribution scheme. Many states now treat pensions in which the ownership rights have matured (vested) and medical insurance benefits as also subject to distribution.

Though not all states agree with the holding in the following case, it is looked upon as a landmark decision. In the *O'Brien* case, the court declared that a spouse who has made significant contributions to her husband's medical education and licensing as a doctor was entitled to a property interest in his license at the time of their divorce.

O'Brien v. O'Brien
489 N.E.2d 712
Court of Appeals of New York
December 26, 1985

Simons, Judge

In this divorce action, the parties' only asset of any consequence is the husband's newly acquired license to practice medicine. The principal issue presented is whether that license, acquired during their marriage, is marital property subject to equitable distribution under Domestic Relations Law § 236(B)(5). Supreme Court held that it was and accordingly made a distributive award in defendant's favor. It also granted defen-

dant maintenance arrears, expert witness fees and attorneys' fees. . . . On appeal to the Appellate Division, a majority of that court held that plaintiff's medical license is not marital property and that defendant was not entitled to an award for the expert witness fees. It modified the judgment and remitted the case to Supreme Court for further proceedings, specifically for a determination of maintenance and a rehabilitative award. . . . The matter is before us by leave of the Appellate Division.

We now hold that plaintiff's medical license constitutes "marital property" within the meaning of Domestic Relations Law § 236(B)(1)(c) and that it is therefore subject to equitable distribution pursuant to subdivision 5 of that part. . . .

I

Plaintiff and defendant married on April 3, 1971. At the time both were employed as teachers at the same private school. Defendant had a bachelor's degree and a temporary teaching certificate but required 18 months of postgraduate classes at an approximate cost of $3,000, excluding living expenses, to obtain permanent certification in New York. She claimed, and the trial court found, that she had relinquished the opportunity to obtain permanent certification while plaintiff pursued his education. At the time of the marriage, plaintiff had completed only three and one-half years of college but shortly afterward he returned to school at night to earn his bachelor's degree and to complete sufficient premedical courses and enter medical school. In September 1973 the parties moved to Guadalajara, Mexico, where plaintiff became a full-time medical student. While he pursued his studies defendant held several teaching and tutorial positions and contributed her earnings to their joint expenses. The parties returned to New York in December 1976 so that plaintiff could complete the last two semesters of medical school and internship training here. After they returned, defendant resumed her former teaching position and she remained in it at the time this action was commenced. Plaintiff was licensed to practice medicine in October 1980. He commenced this action for divorce two months later. At the time of trial, he was a resident in general surgery.

During the marriage both parties contributed to paying the living and educational expenses and they received additional help from both of their families. They disagreed on the amounts of their respective contributions but it is undisputed that in addition to performing household work and managing the family finances defendant was gainfully employed throughout the marriage, that she contributed all of her earnings to their living and educational expenses and that her finan-

cial contributions exceeded those of plaintiff. The trial court found that she had contributed 76% of the parties' income exclusive of a $10,000 student loan obtained by defendant. Finding that plaintiff's medical degree and license are marital property, the court received evidence of its value and ordered a distributive award to defendant.

Defendant presented expert testimony that the present value of plaintiff's medical license was $472,000. Her expert testified that he arrived at this figure by comparing the average income of a college graduate and that of a general surgeon between 1985, when plaintiff's residency would end, and 2012, when he would reach age 65. After considering Federal income taxes, an inflation rate of 10% and a real interest rate of 3% he capitalized the difference in average earnings and reduced the amount to present value. He also gave his opinion that the present value of defendant's contribution to plaintiff's medical education was $103,390. Plaintiff offered no expert testimony on the subject.

The court, after considering the lifestyle that plaintiff would enjoy from the enhanced earning potential his medical license would bring and defendant's contributions and efforts toward attainment of it, made a distributive award to her of $188,800, representing 40% of the value of the license, and ordered it paid in 11 annual installments of various amounts beginning November 1, 1982 and ending November 1, 1992. The court also directed plaintiff to maintain a life insurance policy on his life for defendant's benefit for the unpaid balance of the award and it ordered plaintiff to pay defendant's counsel fees of $7,000 and her expert witness fee of $1,000. It did not award defendant maintenance.

A divided Appellate Division . . . concluded that a professional license acquired during marriage is not marital property subject to distribution. It therefore modified the judgment by striking the trial court's determination that it is and by striking the provision ordering payment of the expert witness for evaluating the license and remitted the case for further proceedings. . . .

II

The Equitable Distribution Law contemplates only two classes of property: marital property and separate property (Domestic Relations Law § 236[B][1][c], [d]). The former, which is subject to equitable distribution, is defined broadly as *"all* property acquired by either or both spouses during the marriage and before the execution of a separation agreement or the commencement of a matrimonial action, *regardless of the form in which title is held"* (Domestic Relations Law § 236[B][1][c] [emphasis added]; *see* § 236 [B][5][b], [c]). Plaintiff does not contend that his license is excluded from distribution because it is separate property; rather, he claims that it is not property at all but represents a personal attainment in acquiring knowledge. He rests his argument on decisions in similar cases from other jurisdictions and on his view that a license does not satisfy common-law concepts of property. Neither contention is controlling because decisions in other States rely principally on their own statutes, and the legislative history underlying them, and because the New York Legislature deliberately went beyond traditional property concepts when it formulated the Equitable Distribution Law. . . . Instead, our statute recognizes that spouses have an equitable claim to things of value arising out of the marital relationship and classifies them as subject to distribution by focusing on the marital status of the parties at the time of acquisition. Those things acquired during marriage and subject to distribution have been classified as "marital property" although, as one commentator has observed, they hardly fall within the traditional property concepts because there is no common-law property interest remotely resembling marital property. "It is a statutory creature, is of no meaning whatsoever during the normal course of a

marriage and arises full-grown, like Athena, upon the signing of a separation agreement or the commencement of a matrimonial action. [Thus] [i]t is hardly surprising, and not at all relevant, that traditional common law property concepts do not fit in parsing the meaning of 'marital property.'" . . . Having classified the "property" subject to distribution, the Legislature did not attempt to go further and define it but left it to the courts to determine what interests come within the terms of section 236(B)(1)(c).

We made such a determination in *Majauskas v. Majauskas,* . . . 463 N.E.2d 15, holding there that vested but unmatured pension rights are marital property subject to equitable distribution. Because pension benefits are not specifically identified as marital property in the statute, we looked to the express reference to pension rights contained in section 236(B)(5)(d)(4), which deals with equitable distribution of marital property, to other provisions of the equitable distribution statute and to the legislative intent behind its enactment to determine whether pension rights are marital property or separate property. A similar analysis is appropriate here and leads to the conclusion that marital property encompasses a license to practice medicine to the extent that the license is acquired during marriage.

Section 236 provides that in making an equitable distribution of marital property, "the court shall consider: . . . (6) any equitable claim to, interest in, or direct or indirect contribution made to the acquisition of such marital property by the party not having title, including joint efforts or expenditures and contributions and services as a spouse, parent, wage earner and homemaker, and *to the career or career potential* of the other party [and] . . . (9) the impossibility or difficulty of evaluating any component asset or any interest in a business, corporation or *profession"* (Domestic Relations Law § 236 [B][5][d][6], [9] [emphasis added]). Where equitable distribution of marital property is appropriate but "the distribution of an interest in a business, corporation or *profession* would be contrary to law" the court shall make a distributive award in lieu of an actual distribution of the property (Domestic Relations Law § 236[B][5][e] [emphasis added]). The words mean exactly what they say: that an interest in a profession or professional career potential is marital property which may be represented by direct or indirect contributions of the non-title-holding spouse, including financial contributions and nonfinancial contributions made by caring for the home and family.

The history which preceded enactment of the statute confirms this interpretation. Reform of section 236 was advocated because experience had proven that application of the traditional common-law title theory of property had caused inequities upon dissolution of a marriage. The Legislature replaced the existing system with equitable distribution of marital property, an entirely new theory which considered all the circumstances of the case and of the respective parties to the marriage. . . . Equitable distribution was based on the premise that a marriage is, among other things, an economic partnership to which both parties contribute as spouse, parent, wage earner or homemaker. . . . Consistent with this purpose, and implicit in the statutory scheme as a whole, is the view that upon dissolution of the marriage there should be a winding up of the parties' economic affairs and a severance of their economic ties by an equitable distribution of the marital assets. Thus, the concept of alimony, which often served as a means of lifetime support and dependence for one spouse upon the other long after the marriage was over, was replaced with the concept of maintenance which seeks to allow "the recipient spouse an opportunity to achieve [economic] independence." . . .

The determination that a professional license is marital property is also consistent with the conceptual base upon which the

statute rests. As this case demonstrates, few undertakings during a marriage better qualify as the type of joint effort that the statute's economic partnership theory is intended to address than contributions toward one spouse's acquisition of a professional license. Working spouses are often required to contribute substantial income as wage earners, sacrifice their own educational or career goals and opportunities for child rearing, perform the bulk of household duties and responsibilities and forego the acquisition of marital assets that could have been accumulated if the professional spouse had been employed rather than occupied with the study and training necessary to acquire a professional license. In this case, nearly all of the parties' nine-year marriage was devoted to the acquisition of plaintiff's medical license and defendant played a major role in that project. She worked continuously during the marriage and contributed all of her earnings to their joint effort, she sacrificed her own educational and career opportunities, and she traveled with plaintiff to Mexico for three and one-half years while he attended medical school there. The Legislature has decided, by its explicit reference in the statute to the contributions of one spouse to the other's profession or career . . . that these contributions represent investments in the economic partnership of the marriage and that the product of the parties' joint efforts, the professional license, should be considered marital property.

The majority at the Appellate Division held that the cited statutory provisions do not refer to the license held by a professional who has yet to establish a practice but only to a going professional practice. . . . There is no reason in law or logic to restrict the plain language of the statute to existing practices, however, for it is of little consequence in making an award of marital property, except for the purpose of evaluation, whether the professional spouse has already established a practice or whether he or she has yet to do so. An established practice merely represents the exercise of the privileges conferred upon the professional spouse by the license and the income flowing from that practice represents the receipt of the enhanced earning capacity that licensure allows. That being so, it would be unfair not to consider the license a marital asset.

Plaintiff's principal argument, adopted by the majority below, is that a professional license is not marital property because it does not fit within the traditional view of property as something which has an exchange value on the open market and is capable of sale, assignment or transfer. The position does not withstand analysis for at least two reasons. First, as we have observed, it ignores the fact that whether a professional license constitutes marital property is to be judged by the language of the statute which created this new species of property previously unknown at common law or under prior statutes. Thus, whether the license fits within traditional property concepts is of no consequence. Second, it is an overstatement to assert that a professional license could not be considered property even outside the context of section 236(B). A professional license is a valuable property right, reflected in the money, effort and lost opportunity for employment expended in its acquisition, and also in the enhanced earning capacity it affords its holder, which may not be revoked without due process of law. . . . That a professional license has no market value is irrelevant. Obviously, a license may not be alienated as may other property and for that reason the working spouse's interest in it is limited. The Legislature has recognized that limitation, however, and has provided for an award in lieu of its actual distribution. . . .

Plaintiff also contends that alternative remedies should be employed, such as an award of rehabilitative maintenance or reimbursement for direct financial contributions. . . . The statute does not expressly authorize retrospective maintenance or rehabilitative awards and we have no occasion to decide in this case whether the authority to do so may ever be implied from its provisions. . . . It is sufficient to observe that normally a working spouse should not be restricted to that relief because to do so frustrates the purposes underlying the Equitable Distribution Law. Limiting a working spouse to a maintenance award, either general or rehabilitative, not only is contrary to the economic partnership concept underlying the statute but also retains the uncertain and inequitable economic ties of dependence that the Legislature sought to extinguish by equitable distribution. Maintenance is subject to termination upon the recipient's remarriage and a working spouse may never receive adequate consideration for his or her contribution and may even be penalized for the decision to remarry if that is the only method of compensating the contribution. As one court said so well, "[t]he function of equitable distribution is to recognize that when a marriage ends, each of the spouses, based on the totality of the contributions made to it, has a stake in and right to a share of the marital assets accumulated while it endured, not because that share is needed, but because those assets represent the capital product of what was essentially a partnership entity" (*Wood v. Wood*, . . . 465 N.Y. S.3d 475). The Legislature stated its intention to eliminate such inequities by providing that a supporting spouse's "direct or indirect contribution" be recognized, considered and rewarded (Domestic Relations Law § 236[B][5][d][6]).

Turning to the question of valuation, it has been suggested that even if a professional license is considered marital property, the working spouse is entitled only to reimbursement of his or her direct financial contributions. . . . If the license is marital property, then the working spouse is entitled to an equitable portion of it, not a return of funds advanced. Its value is the enhanced earning capacity it affords the holder and although fixing the present value of that enhanced earning capacity may present problems, the problems are not insurmountable. Certainly they are no more difficult than computing tort damages for wrongful death or diminished earning capacity resulting from injury and they differ only in degree from the problems presented when valuing a professional practice for purposes of a distributive award, something the courts have not hesitated to do. . . . The trial court retains the flexibility and discretion to structure the distributive award equitably, taking into consideration factors such as the working spouse's need for immediate payment, the licensed spouse's current ability to pay and the income tax consequences of prolonging the period of payment . . . and, once it has received evidence of the present value of the license and the working spouse's contributions toward its acquisition and considered the remaining factors mandated by the statute . . . , it may then make an appropriate distribution of the marital property including a distributive award for the professional license if such an award is warranted. When other marital assets are of sufficient value to provide for the supporting spouse's equitable portion of the marital property, including his or her contributions to the acquisition of the professional license, however, the court retains the discretion to distribute these other marital assets or to make a distributive award in lieu of an actual distribution of the value of the professional spouse's license. . . .

III

. . . Accordingly, in view of our holding that plaintiff's license to practice medicine is marital property, the order of the Appellate Division should be modified, with costs to defendant, by reinstating the judgment and the case remitted to the Appellate Division for determination of the facts, including the exercise of that court's discretion (CPLR 5613), and, as so modified, affirmed.

Case Questions

1. When Loretta O'Brien sued her husband Michael for divorce, what claim did she make with respect to the marital property of the couple?
2. What was the basis of her claim?
3. How does the court define marital property in this case?

 What moral principles are reflected in the New York equitable distribution statute?

Determining Fairness

For a distribution to be fair, the court must identify, classify, and determine the value of each spouse's assets—or their detriment, in the case of debts. The court must also consider the circumstances and needs of the parties, the length of their marriage, their marital standard of living, their contributions to the marriage, and other similar factors.

Although it is possible to take such matters to trial and have them decided by a judge, it is often faster—and the parties have more control over the outcome—if they negotiate a property settlement in lieu of fighting it out in court. Property dispute battles can be very expensive. Appraisals and expensive expert witnesses are required to establish the value of assets. Litigation costs can also increase dramatically and diminish the assets ultimately available for distribution. Judges frequently incorporate a negotiated agreement that equitably allocates marital assets and debts into the final judgment.

Community Property Approach

The states of Louisiana, Texas, California, New Mexico, Arizona, Nevada, Washington, Idaho, and Wisconsin have statutorily decided to treat all property that is not separate property and that was acquired during the marriage as presumptively community property that belongs equally to both spouses. Under this approach, it doesn't matter who worked and earned the money for a purchase or who purchased the property. Both spouses have the right to make management decisions regarding community property (such as whether it is leased, loaned, invested, etc.).

If the parties wish to alter the community property presumption, they may do so by agreement, by gift, and by commingling separate and community assets so that separate property loses its character (such as the merger of a separate stamp collection with a community collection or the deposit of birthday money into the community checking account). In the event of a divorce, the court in a community property state makes an equitable division of all community property to each spouse.

Conclusion

Irrespective of whether the issues are negotiated or litigated, at the end of the process the court issues a judgment that dissolves the marriage, distributes the property, and determines claims for alimony, child custody, and child support. The attorneys for the parties then assist the former spouses to implement the orders. Property must be exchanged, ownership rights transferred, money transferred, debts paid, insurance policies obtained, pension rights transferred, and other details wrapped up.

Chapter Questions

1. Define the following terms:

adoption	common law marriage
alimony	community property
annulment	custodial parent
child support	divorce

family	necessaries
foster parent	noncustodial parent
joint custody	open adoption
legal separation	physical custody
marital property	separate property
marriage	separation agreement
natural parent	

2. Andrea Moorehead was abandoned by her birth mother, a crack cocaine user who had tested positive for venereal disease shortly after birth. Andrea was placed with foster parents when she was nine days old. The foster parents, Melva and Robert Dearth, sought to adopt Andrea when she was ten months old. The county's Children's Service Bureau (CSB) opposed this proposed adoption. The Dearths alleged that CSB's decision was predicated on the fact that they were white and Andrea was black. They proved that they lived in an interracial neighborhood, that they attended an interracial church, and that their two children attended an interracial school. They had a stable marriage and financial standing. The Dearths filed a motion for review of this administrative decision in the Common Pleas Court. They requested that CSB's custody be terminated and that permanent custody of Andrea be granted to them. The Court denied the Dearths' motion. The Dearths appealed. The appeals court found that there was clear evidence that CSB had a documented policy of placing black children with white adoptive parents only when no black parents could be found. Under Ohio law, adoption placements are to be made in the "best interests of the child." To what extent can adoption agencies such as CSB consider factors such as race and culture in determining adoption placements? Under the law, can the racial factor outweigh all other considerations?

   In re Moorehead, 600 N.E.2d 778 (1991)

3. Charles Collins and Bethany Guggenheim began living together in 1977. They were not married to each other. Bethany was recently divorced and had two children from the prior marriage. As part of the property settlement, she had received title to a 68-acre farm, and Charles, Bethany, and the children moved there in 1979. They intended to restore the farmhouse (circa 1740). Charles and Bethany jointly became liable for and made payments on a bank mortgage loan, insurance, and property taxes. They maintained a joint checking account to pay for joint expenses as well as individual checking accounts. They jointly purchased a tractor and other equipment, Charles paying two-thirds of the cost and Bethany one-third. Charles also invested $8,000 of his money in additional equipment and improvements for the farm. For several years they jointly operated a small business that made no profit. Despite Charles's contributions, the title to the farm remained at all times with Bethany. The parties experienced personal difficulties, and when they could not reconcile their differences, they permanently separated in 1986. During their cohabitation period, Charles contributed approximately $55,000 and Bethany $44,500 to the farm. Charles filed suit against Bethany.

He claimed that fairness required either that Bethany and he should share title to the farm as tenants in common or that he should receive an equitable distribution of the property acquired during the period of cohabitation. Charles did not allege that Bethany had breached any contract or engaged in any type of misconduct. The trial court dismissed the complaint. What action should a court take in a situation such as this, where unmarried, cohabiting people go their separate ways?

Collins v. Guggenheim, N.E.2d (1994)

4. James Ellam filed suit for divorce against his wife, Ann, on the ground that they had been living separately and apart. Ann counterclaimed against James for desertion. The facts reveal that James moved out of the marital home on July 5, 1972, because of severe marital discord. He moved back to his mother's home in a nearby city, where he slept, kept his clothes, and ate some of his meals. For the next eighteen months, James had an unusual weekday routine. His mother would drive James early in the morning from her home to the marital home so that James could see his dog, check on the house, take his car out of the garage, and go to work, much as he had done before he and Ann "separated." At the end of the day, James would drive to the marital residence, put the car back in the garage, play with the dog, talk with his wife until she went to bed, and watch television until 12:30 A.M., when his mother would pick him up and take him "home." On weekends, James would do chores at the marital home and even socialize with his wife (although the parties had terminated their sexual relationship). James lived this way because he claimed to love his wife and especially the dog, he wanted to maintain the marital home properly, and he did not want the neighbors to know about his marital problems. New Jersey law provides that persons who have lived separate and apart for a statutory period of time may be granted a divorce. Should the trial court have granted a divorce on the grounds that James and Ann had satisfied the statutory requirements by living "separate and apart in different habitations" as permitted under New Jersey law?

Ellam v. Ellam, 333 A.2d 577 (1975)

5. The Washington Revised Code (Section 26.16.205) provides as follows:

> The expenses of the family . . . are chargeable upon the property of both husband and wife, or either of them, and in relation thereto they may be sued jointly or separately. . . .

Should a husband be financially obligated to pay the legal costs resulting from his wife's appeal of criminal convictions?

State v. Clark, 563 P.2d 1253 (1977)

6. Oregon law provides for "no-fault" divorces. Marie and Max Dunn had been married for twenty years when Marie filed for divorce. After Marie presented evidence of irremediable and irreconcilable differences between herself and her husband, the trial court entered a decree dissolving the marriage. The court also awarded Marie custody of their two minor children

and set alimony at $200 per month. Max appealed to the Oregon Court of Appeals on the ground that the trial court's decree was premature and was not supported by adequate proof. Max argued that the court acted without considering the views of both parties to the marriage. The appellate court interpreted the Oregon statute to require only that the trial court determine whether the existing difference "reasonabl[y] appears to the court to be in the mind of the petitioner an irreconcilable one, and based on that difference . . . whether or not . . . the breakdown of that particular marriage is irremediable." What public policy arguments can you identify related to the facts in the above case that would favor "no-fault" divorces? What arguments could be brought to bear against them?

Dunn v. Dunn, 511 P.2d 427 (1973)

7. Two women brought suit against the Jefferson County (Kentucky) Clerk of Courts because the clerk refused to issue them a license to become married to each other. The women alleged that the clerk's refusal denied them various constitutionally protected rights, among these the right to become married, the right to freedom of association, and the right to freedom from cruel and unusual punishment. The trial court ruled that persons seeking to enter into a same-sex marriage were not entitled under the law to a marriage license. The women appealed to the Court of Appeals of Kentucky. The Kentucky statutes do not define the term *marriage*. The appeals court disposed of the case without even reaching the appellants' constitutional claims. Can you surmise on what grounds the appeals court decided the case?

Jones v. Hallahan, 501 S.W.2d 588 (1973)

Notes

1. J. Demos, "A Little Commonwealth: Family Life in Plymouth," in *Family and State*, ed. L. Houlgate (Totowa, NJ: Rowman & Littlefield, 1988), pp. 30–31.
2. Table 57. Family Groups with Children Under 18 Years of Age . . . Statistical Abstract of the United States 2001.
3. B. Yorburg, *The Changing Family* (New York: Columbia University Press, 1973), p. 94.
4. D. Castle, "Early Emancipation Statutes: Should They Protect Parents as Well as Children?" 20 *Family Law Quarterly* 3, 363 (Fall 1986).
5. H. Jacob, *Silent Revolution* (Chicago: University of Chicago Press, 1988) p. 1.
6. M. Grossberg, *Governing the Hearth* (Chapel Hill: University of North Carolina Press, 1985) p. 3.
7. L. Houlgate, *Family and State* (Totowa, NJ: Rowman & Littlefield, 1988).
8. E. Pound, "Individual Interests in Domestic Relations," 14 *Michigan Law Review* 177, 179–181 (1916).
9. L. Wardle, C. Blakeseley, and J. Parker, *Contemporary Family Law,* Sec. 1:02 (Deerfield, IL: Clark Boardman Calaghan, 1988).
10. E. Jenks, *A Short History of English Law* (2nd revised edition) (Boston: Little, Brown & Co., 1922), note 24 at 20–22.
11. Wardle, Blakeseley, and Parker, Sec. 1:02.
12. Ibid., Sec. 1:03.

13. *Wisconsin v. Yoder,* 406 U.S. 205 (1972), 229–230.

14. P. C. Hoffer, *Law & People in Colonial America* (Baltimore: Johns Hopkins University Press, 1982).

15. Grossberg, pp. 3–4.

16. Ibid., p. 5.

17. Ibid., p. 6.

18. R. Melton, "Evolving Definition of 'Family,'" *Journal of Family Law* 504 (1990–1991).

19. *Braschi v. Stahl Association,* 543 N.E.2d 49 (1989) 58.

20. *Braschi,* 543 N.E.2d at 53–54.

21. J. Collier, M. Rosaldo, and S. Yanagisako, "Is There a Family? New Anthropological Views," in *Rethinking the Family: Some Feminist Questions,* eds. B. Thorne and M. Yalon (New York: Longman, 1982), pp. 25–39.

22. M. Farmer, *The Family* (London: Longmans, Green and Co., 1970), p. 17.

23. H. D. Krause, *Family Law* (2nd ed.) (St. Paul: West Publishing, 1986), pp. 31–32.

24. *Maynard v. Hill,* 125 U.S. 190 (1888).

25. Wardle, Blakeseley, and Parker, Sec. 3:02.

26. Alabama, Colorado, the District of Columbia, Iowa, Montana, Oklahoma, Pennsylvania, Rhode Island, South Carolina, Texas, and Utah recognize common law marriages without qualification.

27. Montana Code Annotated 40-1-403 and 23 Pennsylvania Consolidated Statutes Section 1103.

28. *Baehr v. Levin,* 91-1394, (1993).

29. *Baker v. State,* 744 A.2d 864 (1999).

30. *Baehr v. Levin,* p. 79.

31. National Commission for Adoption, *Adoption Factbook* 18 (1989).

32. J. Evall, "Sexual Orientation and Adoptive Matching," 24 *Family Law Quarterly* 349 (1991).

33. Some states require that a petitioner be at least 10 years or older than the person to be adopted, whereas others require that the adoptee not be related to the petitioner. Some states also refuse to allow an adult petitioner to adopt another adult who happens to be the petitioner's homosexual partner, where the parties may be trying to use the adoption law to circumvent the marriage, contract, and probate laws.

34. Krause, p. 163.

35. E. Bartholet, *Family Bonds* (Boston: Houghton Mifflin, 1993), p. 66.

36. Ibid., p. 71.

37. Ibid., pp. 70–72.

38. *Palmore v. Sidoti,* 466 U.S. 429 (1984).

39. *Compos v. McKeithen,* 341 F. Supp.264 (E.D. La. 1972).

40. K. Forde-Mazrui, "Black Identity and Child Placement: The Best Interests of Black and Biracial Children," 92 *Michigan Law Review* 939 (1994).

41. A. McCormick, "Transracial Adoption: a Critical View of the Courts' Present Standards," 28 *Journal of Family Law* 314 (1989–1990); Forde-Mazrui, pp. 925, 929–930.

42. McCormick, pp. 303, 309; E. Bartholet, "Where Do Black Children Belong? The Politics of Race Matching in Adoption," 139 *U.Pa. Law Rev.* 1163. 1183–1200 (1991).

43. L. Schwartz, "Religious Matching for Adoption: Unraveling the Interests Behind the 'Best Interests' Standard," 25 *Family Law Quarterly* 2 (Summer 1991).

44. *Wisconsin v. Yoder,* 406 U.S. 205 (1972), 229–230.

45. Ibid., p. 179.

46. Ibid., p. 189.

47. Ibid.

48. Florida Statutes Annotated Sec. 63.042(3) (West 1985); and New Hampshire Revised Statutes Section 170-B:4 (Supp 1989).

49. J. Evall, "Sexual Orientation and Adoptive Matching," 24 *Family Law Quarterly* 3, 354–355 (1991).

50. *Appeal in Pima County Juvenile Action B-10489,* 727 P.2d 830 (Ariz. App 1986).

51. Evall, pp. 356–357.

52. Bartholet, p. 48.

53. Ibid., p. 55.

54. Ibid., p. 56.

55. Adoption and Foster Care Analysis & Reporting System (AFCARS), *Interim FY 1999 Estimates as of June 2001,* U.S. Dept. of Health and Human Services.

56. U.S. Department of Health and Human Services. (2002). *Safety, permanency, well-being: Child welfare outcomes 1999: Annual Report.*

57. A. Hardin, ed., *Foster Children in the Courts,* Foster Care Project, National Legal Resource Center for Child Advocacy and Protection (Chicago: American Bar Association, 1983), p. 70.

58. *Foster Care Fact Sheet.* Evan B. Donaldson Adoption Institute. (2002).

59. American Public Welfare Association, as quoted in *Newsweek,* April 25, 1994, p. 55.

60. U.S. Department of Health and Human Services' Adoption and Foster Care Analysis and Reporting System (AFCARS). *Report 6 (Fiscal Year 1999)* (June 2001).

61. D. Roberts, *Shattered Bonds: The Color of Welfare (New York: Basic/Civitas Books, 2001).*

62. Jacob, p. 1.

63. States differ as to exactly what level of support must be provided. Some states define necessaries to be essentially the most basic needs, whereas other states are more generous in their construction of that term.

64. C. Hused, "Married Woman's Property Law 1800–1850," 71 *Georgetown Law Journal* 1359, note 4 at 1400 (1983). Also see *Thompson v. Thompson,* 218 U.S. 611 (1910).

65. *Griswold v. Connecticut,* 381 U.S. 479 (1965).

66. *Wisconsin v. Yoder,* 406 U.S. 205 (1972), 229–230.

67. See Kentucky Revised Statutes sec. 205.310, South Dakota Codified Laws Annotated Sec. 25-7-8, and Washington Revised Code Sec. 26.16.205. See also *M. H. B. v. H. T. B.,* 498 A. 2d 775 (1985).

68. See Alaska Statute Sec. 47.25.250, Iowa Code Sec. 252.5, *Estate of Hines,* 573 P.2d 1260 (1978), and Wisconsin Statutes Annotated Sec. 940.27.

69. See Alaska Statute Sec. 25.20.030 and Oregon revised Statute Sec. 109.010.

70. See *Mahan v. Mahan,* 88 SO2d 545 (1956).

71. See *Heup v. Heup,* 172 N.W.2d 334 (1969).

72. Maryland Annotated Code Article 16, Sec 27.

73. New Hampshire Revised Statutes annotated Sec. 458:17, Minnesota Sec. 518.57.

74. 4 *American Jurisprudence* 2d, 513.

75. *Posner v. Posner,* 233 So.2d 381 (1970).

76. Jacob, p. 30.

77. Ibid., p. 4.

78. U.S. Bureau of the Census, *Historical Statistics of the United States, Colonial Times to 1957* (Washington, D.C., 1960), p. 25.

79. This is not to suggest that the amount of choice is equally distributed throughout society and is not affected by considerations of race, gender, and socioeconomic status.

80. It is important to emphasize that, in all eras, spouses and parents have deserted their partners and families without bothering with legal formalities. Note also that the primary victims have been women who devoted their lives to their families and

homes and who were often left destitute and with children. This has contributed to what is often referred to as the feminization of poverty.

81. Jacob, p. 251.

82. Ibid., p. 47.

83. Ibid., pp. 46–47.

84. Ibid., p. 34.

85. Wadlington, "Divorce Without Fault Without Perjury," 52 *Virginia Law Revue,* 32, 40 (1966).

86. Jacob, pp. 60–61.

87. Ibid., p. 59.

88. Ibid., p. 80.

89. *Hagerty v. Hagerty,* 281 N.W.2d 386 (1979).

90. Freed and Walker, "Family Law in the Fifty States: An Overview." 24 *Family Law Review* 309, 355 (1991).

91. A. Shepard. "Taking Children Seriously: Promoting Cooperative Custody After Divorce," 64 *Texas Law Review* 687 (1985).

92. S. Quinn, "Fathers Cry for Custody," *Juris Doctor* 42 (May 1976).

93. R. Cochran, Jr., "Reconciling the Primary Caretaker Preference, and Joint Custody Preference and the Case-by-Case Rule," in *Joint Custody and Shared Parenting,* ed. Jay Folberg (New York: The Guilford Press, 1991), pp. 218–219.

94. J. Goldstein, A. Freud, and A. Solnit, *Beyond the Best Interests of the Child* (New York: The Free Press, 1970), pp. 107–109.

95. Cochran, p. 222.

96. M. Elkin, in *Joint Custody and Shared Parenting,* ed. Jay Folberg (New York: The Guilford Press, 1991), pp. 12–13.

97. Ibid., p. 13.

98. See *Gruber v. Gruber,* 583 A.2d 434 (1990), and *In re Miroballi,* 589 N.E.2d 565 (1992), for cases supporting parent's right to relocate. See *Plowman v. Plowman,* 597 A.2d 701 (1991), for a contrary opinion.

99. See *Fortenberry v. Fortenberry,* 338 S.E.2d 342 (1985), *Toomey v. Toomey,* 636 S.W.2d 313 (1982), and *Neudecker v. Neudecker,* 577 N.E.2d 960 (1991).

100. H. Krause, *Family Law in a Nutshell* (2nd ed.) (St. Paul: West Publishing, 1986), p. 211.

X   Contracts

A BRIEF HISTORY OF AMERICAN CONTRACT LAW

The modern contract action can be traced to the English common law writs of debt, detinue, and covenant, which were created in the twelfth and thirteenth centuries.[1] The *debt* action was used to collect a specific sum of money owed. *Detinue* was used against one who had possessory rights to another's personal property but who refused to return it when requested by the true owner. *Covenant* was initially used to enforce agreements relating to land (especially leases).[2] Later it was employed to enforce written agreements under seal.[3] Gradually, these writs were supplemented by the common law *writ of trespass*, which included trespass to land, assaults, batteries, the taking of goods, and false imprisonment. Each of these acts involved a tortfeasor who directly caused injury to the victim by force and arms and thereby violated the King's peace.

In 1285, Parliament enacted the Statute of Westminster, which authorized the chancery to create a new writ, called *trespass on the case*, to address private wrongs that fell outside the traditional boundaries of trespass.[4] Case, as it came to be called, could remedy injuries that resulted from the defendant's failure to perform a professional duty that in turn resulted in harm to the plaintiff. Thus case would be appropriate where A's property was damaged while entrusted to B, as a result of B's failure to exercise proper skill or care.[5] These early writs were based on property rights and were not based on modern contractual notions such as offer, acceptance, and consideration.

In the fifteenth and sixteenth centuries, some breaches of duty (called undertakings) that had been included within the writ of trespass on the case evolved into a new writ called *assumpsit*.[6] For example, in one early case a ferry operator was sued in assumpsit for improperly loading his boat such that the plaintiff's mare drowned while crossing the Humber River.[7] By the early 1500s, a plaintiff could also sue in assumpsit for nonfeasance (failure to perform a promise).[8]

During the 1560s, plaintiffs bringing assumpsit actions were generally required to allege that undertakings were supported by consideration.[9] Consideration grew in importance, and in the 1700s chancellors began refusing to order specific performance if they thought the consideration inadequate.[10] This development made the enforceability of contracts uncertain because judges could invalidate agreements reached by the parties and could prevent the parties from making their own bargains.

Assumpsit was the principal "contract" action until the early 1800s, when economic changes and widespread dissatisfaction with the technical requirements and expense of common law pleading resulted in an erosion of the common law approach.[11] The 1800s brought a significant shift in thinking away from the old writs and toward the emerging new substantive action, called contract, which included all types of obligations. Contributing to the demise of assumpsit was the old-fashioned notion that courts had a responsibility to ensure that contracting parties received equivalent value from their bargains.[12] It became apparent that commercial prosperity required that courts protect their expectation damages (the return they had been promised in an agreement).[13] When the courts responded to these changes and demands, contract law rapidly developed. New York's replacement of the writ system in 1848 with its newly enacted Code of Civil Procedure established a trend toward modern code pleading that swept the nation.[14]

By 1850, American courts had accepted the notion that contracts are based on the reciprocal promises of the parties.[15] As courts became increasingly willing to enforce private agreements, they began to recognize the customs of each trade, profession, and business rather than general customs. The courts would often disregard existing legal requirements in favor of the rules created by the contract parties. This fragmentation of law was bad for business. The absence of a widely accepted code of contract rules resulted in unpredictability and uncertainty in American society, the economy, and the courts. This caused business firms to press for uniform laws dealing with commercial transactions among states.

In the 1890s, the American Bar Association established the National Conference of Commissioners on Uniform State Laws to encourage states to enact uniform legislation. The Uniform Sales Act and the Negotiable Instruments Law were two products of this movement. During this era, Samuel Williston and Arthur Corbin wrote widely accepted treatises on the law of contracts. Then, in 1928 a legal think tank of lawyers and judges, called the American Law Institute, developed and published the Restatement of Contracts, a proposed code of contract rules that was grounded in the common law.

In 1942, the American Law Institute and the American Bar Association sponsored a project to develop a Uniform Commercial Code (UCC), which was completed in 1952. Pennsylvania was the first state to adopt the UCC in 1953. The code covers sales, commercial paper, bank collection processes, letters of credit, bulk transfers, warehouse receipts, bills of lading, other documents of title, investment securities, and secured transactions. The UCC governs only sales of (and contracts to sell) goods, defined as movables, or personal property having tangible form. It does not cover transactions involving realty, services, or the sale of intangibles. If a contract involves a mixed goods/services sale (for example, application of a hair product as part of a beauty treatment), the courts tend to apply the UCC only if the sale-of-goods aspect dominates the transaction. The UCC has been adopted at least partially in all fifty states and has had the largest legislative impact on the law of contracts.

NATURE AND CLASSIFICATION OF CONTRACTS

A *contract* is a legally enforceable agreement containing one or more promises. Not every promise is a contract—only those promises enforceable by law. Although the word *contract* is often used when referring to a written document that contains the terms of the contract, in the legal sense, the word *contract* does not mean the tangible document, but the legally enforceable agreement itself.

In order to establish an enforceable contract, there must be (1) an agreement (2) between competent parties (3) based on genuine assent of the parties, (4) supported by consideration, (5) that does not contravene principles of law and (6) that must be in writing in certain circumstances. Each of these requirements is discussed in detail in this chapter.

An *agreement* is an expression of the parties' willingness to be bound to the terms of the contract. Usually, one party offers a proposal, and the other agrees to the terms by accepting it. Both parties to the contract must be *competent*. Some people—because of age or mental disability—are not competent and thus do not have, from the legal standpoint, the capacity to bind themselves contractually. *Genuine assent* of both parties is also necessary. It is presumed to exist unless one of the parties is induced to agree because of misrepresentation, fraud, duress, undue influence, or mistake.

Consideration on the part of both parties is an essential element of a contract. One party's promise (or consideration) must be bargained for and given in exchange for the other's act or promise (his consideration). The bargain cannot involve something that is prohibited by law or that is against the best interests of society. And finally, certain contracts, to be enforceable, must be evidenced in writing.

Common law is the primary source of the law of contracts. Many statutes affect contracts, especially specific types of contracts, such as employment and insurance. But the overwhelming body of contractual principles is embodied in court decisions.

Valid, Void, Voidable, and Unenforceable Contracts

Contracts can be classified in terms of validity and enforceability. A *valid contract* is a binding and enforceable agreement which meets all the necessary contractual requirements. A contract is said to be valid and enforceable when a person is entitled to judicial relief in case of breach by the other party.

A *void contract* means no contract, because no legal obligation has been created. When an agreement lacks a necessary contractual element—such as consideration—the agreement is without legal effect, and therefore void.

A *voidable contract* exists when one or more persons can elect to avoid an obligation created by a contract because of the manner in which the contract was brought about. For example, someone who has been induced to make a contract by fraud or duress may be able to avoid the obligation created by the contract. Contracts made by those who are not of legal age are also voidable, at the option of the party lacking legal capacity. A voidable contract is not wholly lacking in legal effect, however, because not all the parties can legally avoid their duties under it.

A contract is *unenforceable* (not void or voidable) when a defense to the enforceability of the contract is present. For example, the right of action is lost in a situation in which a sufficient writing is required and cannot be produced. Also, when a party wanting to enforce a contract waits beyond the time period prescribed by law to bring the court action (statute of limitations), the contract is unenforceable.

Bilateral and Unilateral Contracts

All contracts involve at least two parties. *Bilateral contracts* consist simply of mutual promises to do some future act. The promises need not be express on both sides; one of the promises could be implied from the surrounding circumstances.

A *unilateral contract* results when one party makes a promise in exchange for another person performing an act or refraining from doing something. For example, assume that someone wants to buy an item owned by another for $100. If the buyer promises to pay the owner $100 for the item *if and when* the owner conveys legal title and possession to the buyer, a *uni*lateral contract is created. It is a promise of an act. The contract comes into existence when the act of conveying title and possession is performed. If, however, the buyer promises to pay $100 in exchange for the owner's promise to convey title and possession of the item, a bilateral contract results. A *bi*lateral contract comes into existence when mutual promises are made.

AGREEMENT

In order for a contract to be formed, there must be mutual *agreement* between two or more competent parties who must manifest their intent to be bound to definite terms. The agreement is usually reached by one party making an offer and the other—*expressly or impliedly*—accepting the terms of the offer.

The intention of the parties is the primary factor determining the nature of the contract. This is ascertained not just from the words used by the parties, but also from the entire situation, including the acts and conduct of the parties. In determining the intent of the parties, the courts generally use an objective rather than a subjective test. In an objective test, the question would be "What would a reasonable person in the position of party A think was meant by the words, conduct, or both, of party B?" If a subjective test were used, the question would be "What did party A actually mean by certain expressions?" For example, suppose that one of the parties is not serious about creating a legal obligation, but the other party has no way of knowing this. Under the objective test, a contract would still be created.

In law, invitations to social events lack contractual intention and, when accepted, do not give rise to a binding contract. For example, when two people agree to have dinner together or to go to a baseball game together, each usually feels a moral obligation to fulfill his or her promise. Neither, however, expects to be legally bound by the agreement. An agreement also lacks contractual intent when a party's assent to it is made in obvious anger, excitement, or jest. This is true even when the parties' expressions, if taken literally as stated, would amount to mutual assent. Sometimes it is not obvious that a proposal is made in anger, excitement, or jest. Under the objective test, the surrounding circumstances and context of the expressions would be examined to determine what a reasonably prudent person would believe.

Offer

An *offer* is a proposal to make a contract. It is a promise conditional on a return promise, act, or forbearance being given by the offeree. The return promise, act, or forbearance is acceptance of the offer.

A legally effective offer must be (1) a definite proposal (2) made with the intent to contract and (3) communicated to the offeree. The terms of the offer, on acceptance, become the terms of the contract. An offer must be definite and certain, so that when the offeree accepts, both parties understand the obligations they have created.

It is important to distinguish between a definite proposal, which is an offer, and a solicitation of an offer. A willingness to make or receive an offer is not itself an offer, but an invitation to negotiate. For example, the question "Would you be interested in buying my television set for $100?" is considered an invitation to negotiate. A "yes" response would not create a contract, since there was no definite proposal made (form of payment, when due, etc.).

For an offer to be effective, it need not be made to one specific named person. It can be made to the general public, in the form of an advertisement. These may be circulars, quotation sheets, displays, and announcements in publications. However, the publication of the fact that an item is for sale, and its price, is usually an invitation to negotiate, not an offer.

Termination of an Offer

The offeree can bind the offeror to his or her proposal for the duration of the offer—the time from the moment an offer is effectively communicated to the offeree until it is terminated. An offer can be terminated by (1) revocation by the offeror, (2) lapse of time, (3) subsequent illegality, (4) destruction of the subject matter, (5) death or lack of capacity, (6) rejection, (7) a counteroffer, and (8) acceptance.

An offeror has the power to terminate the offer by revocation at any time before it is accepted. Even when an offeror promises to hold an offer open for a certain period of time, the offeror can revoke the offer before that time, unless consideration is given to hold the offer open. For example, if a seller promises in an offer to give the offeree one week to accept the offer, the seller still retains the power to withdraw the offer at any time.

A contract whereby an offeror is bound to hold an offer open is called an *option*. In an option contract, consideration is necessary in return for the promise to hold the offer open. For example, if the offeree pays the offeror ten dollars to hold an offer open for ten days, the offeror does not have the power to withdraw the offer before the ten-day period is up.

If an offer stipulates how long it will remain open, it automatically terminates with the expiration of that period of time. When an offer does not stipulate a time period within which it may be accepted, it is then effective for a "reasonable" length of time.

An offer to enter into an agreement forbidden by law is ineffective and void, even if the offer was legal when made. If the subject matter of an offer is destroyed, the offer is automatically terminated because of impossibility.

An offer is terminated at the death of either the offeror or the offeree. Adjudication of insanity usually has the same effect as death in terminating an offer. The termination is effective automatically without any need to give notice. For example, if a person offers to sell an item at a stated price, but dies before the offer is accepted, there can be no contract, because one of the parties died before a meeting of the minds took place. If the offeree had accepted the offer before the death, however, there would have been a meeting of minds and the offeror's estate would be responsible under the contract.

An offer is also terminated by a rejection or a counteroffer. When an offeree does not intend to accept an offer and so informs the offeror, the offer is said to have been terminated by rejection. If the offeree responds to an offer by making another proposal, the proposal constitutes a counteroffer and terminates the original offer. For example, if an offer is made to sell merchandise for $300 and the offeree offers to buy this merchandise for $250, the offeree has rejected the original offer by making a counteroffer. However, an *inquiry*, or a request for additional terms by the offeree, is not a counteroffer and does not terminate the offer. Thus, if the offeree had asked whether the offeror would consider reducing the price to $250, this inquiry would not terminate the original offer.

Acceptance

An acceptance is the agreement of the offeree to be bound by the terms of the offer. There is no meeting of the minds until the offeree has consented to the proposition contained in the offer. In order for an acceptance to be effective in creating a contract, there must be (1) an unconditional consent (2) to an open offer (3) by the offeree only, and (4) communicated to the offeror. In addition, there must be some act of manifestation of the intention to contract. This can be in the form of (1) silence or inaction, (2) a promise, (3) an act or forbearance from an act, or (4) any other manner specifically stipulated in the offer.

In most situations, silence or inaction on the part of the offeree does not constitute acceptance. When a person receives goods or services expecting that they will have to be paid for, the act of receiving the goods or services constitutes acceptance of the offer. An offeror is usually not permitted to word the offer in such a way that silence or inaction of the offeree constitutes acceptance. However, silence or inaction *can* do so in situations in which this method of dealing has been established by agreement between the parties or by prior dealings of the parties.

In an offer to enter into a bilateral contract, the offeree must communicate acceptance in the form of a promise to the offeror. The offeror must be made aware, by the express or implied promise, that a contract has been formed. An offer to enter into a unilateral contract requires an acceptance in the form of an act. A mere promise to perform the act is not an effective acceptance.

The offeror has the power to specify the means and methods of acceptance, and the acceptance must comply with those requirements. For example, an oral acceptance of an offer that called for a written acceptance would be ineffective. If nothing is stated, a reasonable means or method of acceptance is effective. An offer can provide that the acceptance is effective only on the completion of specified formalities. In such a situation, all these formalities must be complied with in order to have an effective acceptance.

At common law, an acceptance must be a "mirror image" of the offer. If it changes the terms of an offer in any way, it acts only as a counteroffer and has no effect as an acceptance. Under the UCC (2-207), an acceptance that adds some new or different terms to contracts involving the sale of goods does create a contract. The new terms are treated as proposals that must be accepted separately.

The next case involves a pest control company that sought to require customers wishing to renew their contracts to thereafter arbitrate rather than litigate contractual disputes between the parties. The company subsequently learned to its chagrin that its customer, the Rebars, had, unknown to company officials, transformed the company's proposed renewal contract into a counteroffer in which the company's arbitration clause was deleted.

Because the Rebars carefully read the company's proposed contract, they detected the presence of the arbitration clause. The Rebars, not wishing to give up their right to litigate any contract-related claims, made some changes to the noneconomic portions of the company's proposal and sent the revised document back to the company along with a check (which the company subsequently cashed). The company, not realizing that their proposal had been rejected, proceeded to provide services to the Rebars, believing that they had accepted the proposal containing the arbitration clause. The Rebars' actions went undiscovered until a contractual dispute arose and the Rebars elected to bring the matter to court.

The moral of this story is that a contracting party cannot assume that another contracting party will shine a spotlight on substantive changes it has decided to include in its contract proposals. Every party to a contract needs to take the time to carefully read an offer, and, if possible, compare it with previous agreements in order to identify changes.

Cook's Pest Control, Inc. v. Robert and Margo Rebar

1010897
Supreme Court of Alabama
December 13, 2002

Stuart, Justice

. . . August 28, 2000, Cook's Pest Control and the Rebars entered into a one-year renewable "Termite Control Agreement." Under the agreement, Cook's Pest Control was obligated to continue treating and inspecting the Rebars' home for termites during the term of the agreement, which, with certain limited exceptions, continued so long as the Rebars continued to pay the annual renewal fee. The agreement contained a mandatory, binding arbitration provision.

When the initial term of the agreement was about to expire, Cook's Pest Control notified the Rebars and requested that they renew the agreement for another year by paying the renewal fee. On August 16, 2001, Mrs. Rebar submitted a payment to Cook's Pest Control; with the payment she included an insert entitled "Addendum to Customer Agreement." . . . That addendum provided, in part:

> "Addendum to Customer Agreement:
> To: Cook's Pest Control, Inc. . . .
> Please read this addendum to your Customer Agreement carefully as it explains changes to some of the terms shown in the Agreement. Keep this document with the original Customer Agreement.
> " . . .
>
> "Arbitration.
> Cook's [Pest Control] agrees that any prior amendment to the Customer Agreement shall be subject to written consent before arbitration is required. In the event that a dispute arises between Cook's [Pest Control] and Customer, Cook's [Pest Control] agrees to propose arbitration if so desired, estimate the cost thereof, and describe the process (venue, selection of arbitrator, etc.). Notwith-

standing prior amendments, nothing herein shall limit Customer's right to seek court enforcement (including injunctive or class relief in appropriate cases) nor shall anything herein abrogate Customer's right to trial by jury. Arbitration shall not be required for any prior or future dealings between Cook's [Pest Control] and Customer.

> "Future Amendments.
> Cook's [Pest Control] agrees that any future amendments to the Customer Agreement shall be in writing and signed by Customer and [an] authorized representative of Cook's [Pest Control].
>
> "Effective Date.
> These changes shall be effective upon negotiation of this payment or the next service provided pursuant to the Customer Agreement, whichever occurs first.
> " . . .
>
> "Acceptance be [sic] Continued Use.
> Continued honoring of this account by you acknowledges agreement to these terms. If you do not agree with all of the terms of this contract, as amended, you must immediately notify me of that fact."

The addendum proposed new terms for the agreement and notified Cook's Pest Control that continued service or negotiation of the renewal-payment check by Cook's Pest Control would constitute acceptance of those new terms. After it received the addendum, Cook's Pest Control negotiated the Rebars' check and continued to perform termite inspections and services at the Rebars' home.

On August 30, 2001, the Rebars filed this action against Cook's Pest Control. The Rebars alleged fraud, negligence, breach of contract, breach of warranty, breach of duty, unjust enrichment, breach of the duty to warn, negligent training, supervision and retention of employees, and bad-faith failure to pay and bad-faith failure to investigate a claim. Those claims were based upon Cook's Pest Control's alleged failure to treat and control a termite infestation in the Rebars' home and to repair the damage to the home caused by the termites.

Cook's Pest Control moved to compel arbitration of the Rebars' claims. In support of its motion, Cook's Pest Control relied upon the arbitration provision contained in the agreement; Cook's Pest Control also submitted the affidavit testimony of the president of the company, who testified regarding the effect of Cook's Pest Control's business on interstate commerce.

The Rebars opposed the motion to compel arbitration, asserting, among other things, that a binding, mandatory arbitration agreement no longer existed. The Rebars asserted that a binding, mandatory arbitration agreement no longer existed because the agreement between the parties had been modified when it was renewed in August 2001. The Rebars presented to the trial court a copy of the addendum and a copy of the canceled check they had written to Cook's Pest Control in payment of their renewal fee, which Cook's Pest Control had accepted and negotiated. The Rebars also submitted the affidavit of Mrs. Rebar, who testified that after Cook's Pest Control had received the addendum and had negotiated the check for the renewal fee, Cook's Pest Control inspected the Rebars' home.

On December 18, 2001, the trial court denied Cook's Pest Control's motion to compel arbitration. . . . Cook's Pest Control appeals. . . .

Analysis

Cook's Pest Control argues that the trial court incorrectly found that it accepted the terms included in the addendum by continuing to inspect and treat the Rebars' home after it received the addendum and negotiated the Rebars' check for the renewal fee. Cook's Pest Control argues that, under the terms of the agreement, it was already obligated to continue inspecting and treating the Rebars'

home. Cook's Pest Control also argues that the addendum was an improper attempt to unilaterally modify an existing contract. We reject those arguments.

First, we reject Cook's Pest Control's argument that the Rebars were attempting unilaterally to modify an existing contract. We note that the parties' original agreement was due to expire on August 28, 2001; Cook's Pest Control had already sent the Rebars a notice of this expiration and had requested that the Rebars renew the agreement by submitting the annual renewal fee.

Upon receiving notice that the agreement was up for renewal, the Rebars responded to Cook's Pest Control's offer to renew that contract with an offer of their own to renew the contract but on substantially different terms. This response gave rise to a counteroffer or a conditional acceptance by the Rebars:

> "If the purported acceptance attempts to restate the terms of the offer, such restatement must be accurate in every material respect. It is not a variation if the offeree merely puts into words that which was already reasonably implied in the terms of the offer. But the very form of words used by the offeror is material if the offeror so intended and so indicated in the offer. An acceptance using a different form makes no contract. A variation in the substance of the offered terms is material, even though the variation is slight. . . .
>
> "In the process of negotiation concerning a specific subject matter, there may be offers and counter-offers. One party proposes an agreement on stated terms; the other replies proposing an agreement on terms that are different. Such a counter-proposal is not identical with a rejection of the first offer, although it may have a similar legal operation in part. In order to deserve the name 'counter-offer,' it must be so expressed as to be legally operative as an offer to the party making the prior proposal. It is not a counter-offer unless it is itself an offer, fully complying with all the requirements that have been previously discussed. This does not mean that all of its terms must be fully expressed in a single

communication. Often they can be determined only by reference to many previous communications between the two parties. In this, a counter-offer differs in no respect from original offers. But there is no counter-offer, and no power of acceptance in the other party, unless there is a definite expression of willingness to contract on definitely ascertainable terms.

"If the party who made the prior offer properly expresses assent to the terms of the counter-offer, a contract is thereby made on those terms. The fact that the prior offer became inoperative is now immaterial and the terms of that offer are also immaterial except in so far as they are incorporated by reference in the counter-offer itself. Very frequently, they must be adverted to in order to determine what the counter-offer is. Often, the acceptance of a counter-offer is evidenced by the action of the offeree in proceeding with performance rather than by words.

". . . If the original offeror proceeds with performance in consequence of the counter-offer, there can be no successful action for breach of the terms originally proposed.

"The terms 'counter-offer' and 'conditional acceptance' are really no more than different forms of describing the same thing. They are the same in legal operation. Whether the word 'offer' is used or not, a communication that expresses an acceptance of a previous offer on certain conditions or with specified variations empowers the original offeror to consummate the contract by an expression of assent to the new conditions and variations. That is exactly what a counter-offer does. Both alike, called by either name, terminate the power of acceptance of the previous offer." Joseph M. Perillo, *Corbin on Contracts* §§ 3.32 at 478-80; §§ 3.35 (rev. ed. 1993) (footnotes omitted).

In this case, the Rebars did not accept the terms proposed by Cook's Pest Control for renewal of the agreement but instead proposed terms for the renewal of that contract that were materially different from the terms of the agreement. . . . The Rebars did not accept the arbitration provision proposed by Cook's

Pest Control; they countered with an arbitration provision of their own.

In addition, the Rebars specified in the addendum the method by which Cook's Pest Control could signify its acceptance of those different terms. Had Cook's Pest Control wished to reject those terms, it could have refused to renew the agreement and forgone receipt of the Rebars' renewal check.

In response, Cook's Pest Control argues that it was obligated under the terms of the original agreement to continue servicing and treating the Rebars' home and that its continued service and treatment should not be regarded as acceptance of modifications to that agreement proposed by the addendum. We disagree.

Because the Rebars did not unconditionally accept the renewal contract as proposed by Cook's Pest Control but rather countered with terms that differed materially from those proposed by Cook's Pest Control, Cook's Pest Control had three options upon receipt of the addendum: (1) reject the Rebars' counteroffer and treat the agreement as terminated on August 28, 2001; (2) respond to the Rebars' counteroffer with a counteroffer of its own; or (3) accept the Rebars' counteroffer. Cook's Pest Control did not reject the counteroffer and treat the agreement as terminated; nor did it respond with its own counteroffer; rather, it deposited the Rebars' check and continued to inspect and treat the Rebars' home— the exact method specified by the Rebars for acceptance of the proposed modifications to the agreement. Those actions constituted acceptance of the Rebars' counteroffer.

Cook's Pest Control also argues that the addendum had no effect upon the renewal of the agreement because none of the employees in the office where the Rebars' payment was processed had the authority to enter into a contract on behalf of Cook's Pest Control. Thus, Cook's Pest Control argues, a properly authorized agent never assented to the modifications proposed by the Rebars. Again, we disagree.

"It is well settled that whether parties have entered a contract is determined by reference to the reasonable meaning of the parties' external and objective actions." . . . It is also well settled that an agent with actual or apparent authority may enter into a contract and bind his or her principal. . . .

We note that if Cook's Pest Control wished to limit the authority of its employees to enter into contracts on its behalf, Cook's Pest Control, as the drafter of the original agreement, could have included such limiting language in the agreement. We find nothing in the agreement so limiting the authority of employees of Cook's Pest Control; we find nothing in the agreement requiring that a purported modification to the agreement be directed to any particular office of Cook's Pest Control, and we find nothing in the agreement stating that, to be effective, such a modification must be signed by a corporate officer or by a duly authorized representative of Cook's Pest Control.

Based upon the fact that Cook's Pest Control received the Rebars' proposed modifications to the agreement and that Cook's Pest Control, for some two months thereafter, acted in complete accordance with the Rebars' stated method of accepting those proposed modifications, we conclude that Cook's Pest Control's external and objective actions evidenced assent to the Rebars' proposed modifications. It was reasonable for the Rebars to rely upon those actions as evidence indicating that Cook's Pest Control accepted their proposed changes to the agreement.

We agree with the trial court's conclusion, i.e., that, after receipt of the Rebars' addendum, Cook's Pest Control's continuing inspection and treatment of the Rebars' home and Cook's Pest Control's negotiation of the Rebars' check constituted acceptance of the terms contained in that addendum. Upon acceptance of those new terms, the binding arbitration provision contained in the agreement was no longer in effect. The parties' agreement regarding arbitration had been amended to state:

> "Cook's [Pest Control] agrees that any prior amendment to the Customer Agreement shall be subject to written consent before arbitration is required. In the event that a dispute arises between Cook's [Pest Control] and Customer, Cook's [Pest Control] agrees to propose arbitration if so desired, estimate the cost thereof, and describe the process (venue, selection of arbitrator, etc.). Notwithstanding prior amendments, nothing herein shall limit Customer's right to seek court enforcement (including injunctive or class relief in appropriate cases) nor shall anything herein abrogate Customer's right to trial by jury. Arbitration shall not be required for any prior or future dealings between Cook's [Pest Control] and Customer."

Because the Rebars oppose arbitration of their claims against Cook's Pest Control, the trial court properly denied Cook's Pest Control's motion to compel arbitration. . . .

Affirmed.

Case Questions

1. Why did the Appellate Court conclude that the Rebars' addendum constituted a counteroffer?
2. What steps might Cook's Pest Control take to prevent this from happening in the future?

INTERNET TIP

Students can read a contract formation case entitled *Beaman Pontiac v. Gill,* on the textbook's website. This case involves an oral, bilateral contract, and the opinion discusses issues involving the Uniform Commerical Code, the Mailbox Rule, and the existence of consideration.

REALITY OF CONSENT

Genuine assent to be bound by a contract is not present when one of the parties' consent is obtained through duress, undue influence, fraud, or innocent misrepresentation, or when either of the parties, or both, made a mistake concerning the contract. Such contracts are usually voidable, and the injured party has the right to elect to avoid or affirm the agreement. (These defenses against the enforceability of a contract can also be used against other legal documents, such as wills, trust agreements, and executed gifts.)

An injured party who wishes to avoid or rescind a contract should act promptly. Silence beyond a reasonable length of time may be deemed an implied ratification. An injured party who elects to rescind a contract is entitled to *restitution*—the return of any property or money given in performance of the contract. The injured party must also return any property or money received through the contract.

Duress

Freedom of will of both parties to a contract is absolutely necessary. When one of the parties' will is overcome because of duress, the agreement is voidable. *Duress* is any unlawful constraint exercised on people that forces their consent to an agreement that they would not otherwise have made. Unlike those situations in which people act as a result of fraud, innocent misrepresentation, or mistake, a person acting under duress does so knowingly. Three elements are necessary for duress to exist: (1) coercion, (2) causing a loss of free will, and (3) resulting in a consent to be bound by a contract.

Any form of constraint improperly exercised in order to get another's consent to contract is sufficient for coercion. Exercise of pressure to contract is not enough; it must be exercised wrongfully. Thus advice, suggestion, or persuasion are not recognized as coercive. Likewise, causing a person to fear embarrassment or annoyance usually does not constitute duress. In order to amount to coercion, the constraint must entail threatened injury or force. For duress to exist, the person must enter into the agreement while under the influence of this threat.

The threat need not necessarily be to the person or the property of the contracting party. For example, a threat to injure the child of a contracting party could amount to duress. A threat of criminal prosecution gives rise to duress when fear overcomes judgment and deprives the person of the exercise of free will. Making a threat of civil action, however—with the honest belief that it may be successful—is not using duress. For example, assume that an employee embezzles an undetermined amount of money from an employer. The employer estimates that the theft amounts to about $5,000, and threatens to bring a civil suit for damages unless the employee pays $5,000. Even though the employee takes the threat seriously and pays the $5,000, no duress exists. If the employer were to threaten to bring criminal charges under the same circumstances, duress would take place.

Economic distress or business compulsion may be grounds for duress. The surrounding circumstances of the business setting and the relative bargaining positions of the contracting parties are examined in order to determine whether duress is present.

Undue Influence

Undue influence results when the will of a dominant person is substituted for that of the other party, and the substitution is done in an unlawful fashion, resulting in an unfair agreement. Usually, undue influence is found when there is (1) a confidential relationship that is used to create (2) an unfair bargain.

In determining whether a confidential relationship exists, all the surrounding circumstances are examined to find out whether one of the parties dominates the other to the extent that the other is dependent on him or her. Family relationships, such as husband-wife or parent-child, often give rise to confidential relationships. Some relationships involving a special trust—such as trustee-beneficiary or attorney-client—entail a confidential relationship. Sometimes confidential relationships are created between business associates, neighbors, or friends. A person who is mentally weak—because of sickness, old age, or distress—may not be capable of resisting the dominant party's influence.

Whenever there is dominance in a confidential relationship, the court must determine whether the contract was equitable and voluntary. A contract is not invalid simply because there is a confidential relationship. A contract is voidable if one abuses the confidence in a relationship in order to obtain personal gain by substituting one's own will or interest for that of another. Whether the weaker party has had the benefit of independent advice is an important factor in determining fairness in contractual dealings. A legitimate suggestion or persuasion may influence someone, but it is not undue influence; nor, usually, is an appeal to the affections. When methods go beyond mere persuasion and prevent a person from acting freely, undue influence is present.

Fraud

The term *fraud* covers all intentional acts of deception used by one individual to gain an advantage over another. The essential elements of actionable fraud are (1) the misstatement of a material fact (2) made with knowledge of its falsity, or in reckless disregard of its truth or falsity, (3) with the intention to deceive, (4) inducing reliance by the other party, and (5) that results or will result in injury to the other party.

For fraud, misstatements must be of a fact, a *fact* being something that existed in the past or exists at present. The misstated fact must be material. The often-used definition of a *material fact* is that it is a fact without which the contract would not have been entered into. The speaker, when making the statement of fact, must know that it is false. The stating party must have the intention to deceive, and thereby induce the other party to enter into the contract.

The deceived party's reliance on the misstatement must be justified and reasonable. A party wishing to rescind a contract need not show actual damages resulting from the fraud. However, a party wishing to sue for damages in addition to rescission must prove that actual damage has been sustained. Assume, for example, that Carlotta purchases a dog from Enrique based on his statements that the dog is a purebred with a pedigree from the American Kennel Club. Carlotta can rescind the contract, return the dog, and recover the purchase price from Enrique if she later discovers that the dog actually is a crossbred. Carlotta may also be able to recover for the dog's medical care, food, and supplies, based on their value to Enrique.

Misrepresentation

When a party to a contract misrepresents a material fact, *even though unknowingly,* and the other party relies on and is misled by the falsehood, *misrepresentation* is present. If a contract is induced by misrepresentation, the deceived party has the right of rescission. Fraud and misrepresentation are quite similar. However, the *intent* to deceive is the primary distinction between fraudulent and nonfraudulent misrepresentation. Rescission and restitution are available for both, although damages are not obtainable in cases of misrepresentation.

Mistake

Sometimes one or both of the parties to a contract understand the facts to be other than what they are. If ignorance of a fact is material to the contract, a *mistake* exists and the contract may be voidable. Although a mistake of material fact related to the contract is sufficient for relief, a mistake of law is not. In addition, the mistake must refer to a past or present material fact, not to a future possibility.

When one enters into a plain and unambiguous contract, one cannot avoid the obligation created by proving that its terms were misunderstood. Lack of due diligence, poor judgment, lack of wisdom, or a mistake as to the true value of an item contracted for are not grounds for relief. Relief based on mistake may not be had simply because one party to a speculative contract expected it to turn out differently.

The court in the following case ordered rescission of an executed agreement and restitution because the parties to the contract made a mutual mistake.

Carter v. Matthews
701 S.W.2d 374
Supreme Court of Arkansas
January 13, 1986

Newbern, Justice

This is a real estate sale case in which the chancellor granted rescission in favor of the appellant on the ground of mutual mistake but did not award the money damages she claimed. The damages she sought were for her expenses in constructing improvements which subsequently had to be removed from the land. The appellant claims it was error for the chancellor to have found she did not rely on misrepresentations made by the appellees through their real estate agent, and thus it was error to refuse her damages for fraud plus costs and an attorney fee. On cross-appeal, the appellees contend the only possible basis for the rescission was fraud, not mistake, and the chancellor erred in granting rescission once he had found there was no reliance by the appellant on any active or constructive misrepresentations of the appellees. We find the chancellor was correct on all counts, and thus we affirm on both appeal and cross-appeal.

1. Rescission

The chancellor found that conversations between the appellant and the appellees' agent showed that both parties were under the mistaken impression that the low, flat portion of land in question was suitable for building permanent structures such as a barn, horse corral and fencing. In fact, however, the area where the appellant attempted to build a barn and corral and which she wanted to use as pasture for horses was subject to severe and frequent flooding. The chancellor held there was thus a mutual mistake of fact making rescission proper. While there was evi-

dence the appellees had known of one instance of severe flooding on the land, the evidence did not show they knew it was prone to the frequent and extensive flooding which turned out to be the case.

Other matters not known to the parties were that the low portion of the land, about two-thirds of the total acreage, is in the 100 year floodplain and that a Pulaski County ordinance . . . requires a seller of land lying in the floodplain to inform the buyer of that fact no later than ten days before closing the transaction. The county planning ordinance also requires that no structures be built in the floodplain. If the chancellor's decision had been to permit rescission because of the parties' lack of knowledge of these items, we would have had before us the question whether the mistake was one of law rather than fact and thus perhaps irremediable. . . .

While the chancellor mentions these items, his basis for rescission was the mutual lack of knowledge about the extent of the flooding, and misunderstanding of the suitability of the property, as a matter of fact, for the buyer's purposes which were known to both parties. We sustain his finding that there was a mutual mistake of fact. A mutual mistake of fact as to a material element of a contract is an appropriate basis for rescission. . . .

2. Damages for Fraud

The chancellor refused to allow the appellant any damages for the loss she sustained with respect to the improvements she had placed in the floodplain. He found the appellant had made an independent investigation of the propensity of the property to become flooded and had ascertained, erroneously, that the property was not in the floodplain. Thus, in spite of the legal duty on the part of the appellees to tell the appellant that the land was in the floodplain, and what might have been the resultant constructive fraud upon failure to inform her, he held that fraud may not be the basis of a damages award absent reliance on the misrepresentation. For the same reason the chancellor refused to base his decision on any alleged fraud resulting from the appellees' failure to tell the appellant what they may have known about the land's propensity to flood. He was correct. An essential element of an action for deceit is reliance by the plaintiff on the defendant's misrepresentation. . . . In view of the strong evidence, including her own testimony, that the appellant made her own investigation as to whether the land flooded, the extent to which a creek running through the land was in the floodplain and the feasibility of bridging the creek above the floodplain, we can

hardly say the chancellor's factual determination that the appellant did not rely on the failure of the appellees to give her information known to them or which they had a duty to disclose to her under the ordinance was clearly erroneous. . . .

When rescission is based on mutual mistake rather than fraud, the recoveries of the parties are limited to their restitutionary interests. . . . As the appellant could show no benefit conferred on the appellees from her attempted improvements on the land, she was entitled to no recovery in excess of the return of the purchase price, which was awarded to her by the chancellor, as well as cancellation of her note and mortgage. . . .

Affirmed.

Case Questions

1. The plaintiff-appellant in this case went to court seeking rescission as well as damages. What exactly is the remedy called rescission?
2. Why did the chancellor agree to grant rescission? What was the rationale behind this ruling?
3. Why did the chancellor refuse to allow the appellant any damages for fraud?
4. What recovery was made by the appellant?

CONSIDERATION

Consideration is simply that which is bargained for and given in exchange for another's promise. Each party to a contract has a motive or price that induces the party to enter into the obligation. This cause or inducement is called *consideration*. Consideration usually consists of an act or a promise to do an act. Forbearance or a promise to forbear may also constitute consideration. Forbearance is refraining from doing an act, or giving up a right.

A person must bargain specifically for the promise, act, or forbearance in order for it to constitute consideration. A promise is usually binding only when consideration is given in exchange. If a person promises to give another $100, this is a promise to make a gift, and it is unenforceable since the promise lacked consideration. If, however, the promisee had promised to convey a television set in return for the promise to convey $100, the promise to give $100 would have been supported by consideration and therefore would be enforceable.

Although a promise to make a gift is not enforceable, a person who has received a gift is not required to return it for lack of consideration.

Consideration must be legally sufficient, which means that the consideration for the promise must be either a detriment to the promisee or a legal benefit to the promisor. In most situations both exist. *Benefit* in the legal sense means the receipt by the promisor of some legal right that the person had not previously been entitled to. *Legal detriment* is the taking on of a legal obligation or the doing of something or giving up of a legal right by the promisee.

Assume that an uncle promises to pay a niece $1,000 if she enrolls in and graduates from an accredited college or university. If the niece graduates from an accredited college, she is entitled to the $1,000. The promisee-niece did something she was not legally obligated to do, so the promise was supported by legally sufficient consideration. The legal detriment of the niece certainly did not amount to actual detriment. It can hardly be said that the uncle received any actual benefit either.

Consideration should not be confused with a condition. A *condition* is an event the happening of which qualifies the duty to perform a promise. A promise to give a person $100 if the person comes to your home to pick it up is a promise to make a gift on the condition that the person picks up the money. A promisee who shows up is not legally entitled to the $100.

When one party to an agreement makes what appears at first glance to be a promise but when on examination no real promise is made, this situation is called an *illusory promise*. A contract is not entered into when one of the parties makes an illusory promise, because there is no consideration. For example, a promise to work for an employer at an agreed rate for as long as the promisor wishes to work is an illusory promise. The promisor is really promising nothing and cannot be bound to do anything.

A court will not concern itself with the terms of a contract as long as the parties have capacity and there has been genuine assent to the terms. Whether the bargain was a fair exchange is for the parties to decide when they enter into the agreement. Consideration need not have a pecuniary or money value. If a mother promises her son $100 if he does not drink or smoke until he reaches the age of eighteen, there is no pecuniary value to the abstinence; yet it is a valid consideration.

It is not necessary to state the consideration on the face of the document when an agreement is put in writing. It may be orally agreed on or implied. Although the recital of consideration is not final proof that it exists, it is evidence of consideration that is *prima facie*, or sufficient on its face. Evidence that no consideration existed will overcome the presumption that the recital creates, however. And a statement of consideration in an instrument does not create consideration where it was really never intended or given.

If a promise is too vague or uncertain concerning time or subject matter, it will not amount to consideration. If a promise is obviously impossible to perform, it is not sufficient consideration for a return promise. When a promise is capable of being performed, even though improbable or absurd, it is consideration.

Consideration must be bargained for and given in exchange for a promise. Past consideration is not consideration. If a person performs a service for another without the other's knowledge, and later the recipient of the service promises to pay for it, the promise is not binding, since the promise to pay was not supported by consideration. A promise to do what one is already legally obligated to do cannot ordinarily constitute consideration. For example, a promise by a father to pay child support payments that are already an existing legal obligation determined by a court will not constitute consideration. Similarly, consideration is also lacking when a promise is made to refrain from doing what one has no legal right to do.

The court in the following case found that adequate consideration existed to support enforcement of a restrictive covenant clause in an employment contract.

Modern Laundry and Dry Cleaning v. Farrer
536 A.2d 409
Superior Court of Pennsylvania
January 19, 1988

Popovich, Judge

This is an appeal from the Order entered April 16, 1987, in the Court of Common Pleas of Montgomery County, which dissolved appellant's temporary restraining order and dismissed his petition for a preliminary injunction. Appellant alleges the lower court erred in declaring that the restrictive employment covenant was invalid, and, consequently, it erred in denying the Motion for Preliminary Injunction. For the following reasons, we reverse and remand the case for determination of the remaining issue, i.e., whether the restrictive covenant is reasonably limited in time and territory.

On November 6, 1982, Modern Laundry and Dry Cleaning Company (Modern) hired William Farrer to work as a route salesman. For approximately one month, Farrer trained as a probationary employee under the supervision of an experienced route salesman on company Route Thirty-Six. During this probation period, Farrer worked without an employment contract. Under Modern's training program, Farrer was taught how to handle a

particular route but was not given any responsibility for the route until Modern was satisfied with his performance. Once Modern became confident in Farrer's ability, he was offered full-time employment. In order to assume full-time status, Farrer was required to sign an employment contract. Included in the employment contract was the following restrictive covenant:

"As an inducement to the execution of this agreement, and to any renewal or continuation thereof, it is agreed that in the event Employee shall leave the said employment, or be discharged by Employer, during, or at the expiration of this agreement, or any renewal or extension thereof, the said Employee agrees that he shall not, or will not, directly or indirectly, for the space of one year after ceasing in any manner to be in the employ of the Employer, engage in the laundry business in any form or manner on his own account, or as agent, employee, or in any other capacity, for any other person, firm, company, or corporation, in the route or routes, territory or territories assigned to, covered, or served by him, or within three full squares of any point in or on said territory; and that he will not, directly or indirectly, for himself on his own account, or as driver, canvasser, or in any other capacity, for any other person, persons, firm, company or corporation, or within the route or routes, territory or territories assigned to, covered, or served by him, or within three squares of any point in or on said route or routes, territory or territories, solicit for or do any laundry work, or furnish any laundry service whatsoever, to any customer or customers served by said Employer, whether said customer or customers originally belonged to the Employer or were secured by the Employee, or through his efforts, while in the employ of the Employer."

Once the contract was signed, Farrer assumed complete responsibility for Route Thirty-Six. Farrer continued to service Route Thirty-Six for Modern until January 30, 1987, at which time he notified the company that he was terminating his employment effective immediately.

After Farrer's departure, Modern estimated that from January, 1987, to April, 1987, the company lost approximately 41% of its customers on Route Thirty-Six. In late March, 1987, Modern learned that Farrer had started his own laundry and dry cleaning business and that he was servicing his old route in violation of the restrictive covenant in his employment contract. Modern sought to prevent Farrer from operating his business within his old territory and to gain access to his business records so that the damages to Modern's business could be determined.

On April 7, 1987, Modern filed a Complaint in Equity and a Motion for Temporary Restraining Order and Preliminary Injunction. A temporary restraining order enjoining Farrer from soliciting or servicing any person within "three full squares" of his previous territory was issued. After hearings on April 13, 1987, and April 15, 1987, the lower court ordered the Temporary Restraining Order dissolved and denied the Motion for Preliminary Injunction. This appeal followed.

It is the law of the Commonwealth that for a covenant in restraint of trade to be enforceable, it must meet the following requirements: (1) the covenant must relate to (be ancillary to) a contract for the sale of the good will of a business or to a contract of em-

ployment; (2) the covenant must be supported by adequate consideration; (3) the covenant must be limited in both time and territory. . . . Our courts have consistently held that the taking of employment is sufficient consideration for a restrictive covenant. . . .

In the instant case, the lower court ruled that the employment contract between the parties was not ancillary to his taking of employment, and, therefore, it was invalid and unenforceable. However, the appellant cites cases and the record reveals facts which support appellant's contention that the contract was ancillary to the taking of employment. To be valid the restrictive covenant need not appear in the initial employment contract. . . . Therefore, the fact that Modern and Farrer did not enter into the contract containing the restrictive covenant at the beginning of Farrer's employment does not automatically invalidate the covenant. As long as the restrictive covenant is an auxiliary part of the taking of employment and not a later attempt to impose additional restrictions on an unsuspecting employee, a contract of employment containing such a covenant is supported by valid consideration and is therefore enforceable. . . .

In a case similar to the one *sub judice*, *Morgan's Home Equipment Corp. v. Martucci*, . . . the purchaser of a business retained certain employees on a provisional basis and, one month later, offered them regular employment upon the condition that they sign a covenant not to compete. Our Supreme Court held that because the parties entered into a "regular employment relationship in contradistinction to provisional employment" at the same time the employment contract was signed, the restrictive covenant was ancillary to the employment contract. . . . In the instant case, Farrer began his employment with Modern as a trainee on a strictly provisional basis. After his one month training period, Modern believed Farrer was capable of handling Route Thirty-Six, and, on December 7, 1972, Modern offered Farrer full-time employment, provided he signed an employment contract containing a covenant not to compete. Following the analysis in *Morgan's Home*, the requirement of adequate consideration for the contract is met by Modern's offer of full-time employment coupled with Farrer's signing of the contract containing the covenant not to compete. Consequently, the restrictive covenant would be ancillary to the employment contract and supported by adequate consideration. Thus, the covenant would be valid.

Even if this court had determined that the covenant was not ancillary to the taking of employment, the covenant would still be valid. If an employment contract containing a restrictive covenant is entered into subsequent to employment, it must be supported by new consideration which could be in the form of a corresponding benefit to the employee or a beneficial change in his employment status. . . .

After signing the employment contract, Farrer experienced a significant change in his employment status. He was no longer a provisional employee under the charge of an experienced salesman. Farrer had become his own supervisor solely responsible for the operation of Route Thirty-Six. The case of *M.S. Jacobs & Associates, Inc. v. Duffley* . . . presents facts resembling the case before us. In *M.S. Jacobs*, prior to signing an employment contract, the employee was paid only a salary while working in support of an experienced salesman. But, after signing the employment contract containing the restrictive covenant, the employee was given his own territory and received a commission on his total sales. Our Supreme Court held that the employee

had received a substantial beneficial change in his employment constituting sufficient consideration to support an anticompetition clause in his employment contract. . . . Likewise, Farrer's employment status changed beneficially when the parties reduced their agreement to writing. Hence, the instant restrictive covenant is valid.

In addition to the beneficial change in employment status, Farrer was given the opportunity to increase his earnings substantially. Pursuant to his employment contract, Farrer received 17% of all the cash he collected and paid over to his employer. In addition, Farrer's earnings would increase in direct proportion to the new business he procured on his route. . . . [T]his court [has] ruled that the potential to realize monetary gains due to a change in employment status [is] adequate consideration to support a restrictive covenant entered into after initial employment. . . . Accordingly, Farrer's opportunity to increase his earnings due to his change in employment status is sufficient consideration to support the restrictive covenant in his employment contract.

In conclusion, we hold that the restrictive covenant was ancillary to Farrer's taking of employment and supported by adequate consideration. Therefore, the restrictive covenant is valid and, if the covenant is found to be reasonably limited in time and territory, enforceable. We reverse the lower court decision and remand this case for determination of whether the covenant is reasonably limited in time and territory.

Reversed and remanded. Jurisdiction relinquished.

Case Questions

1. Why did the lower court in this case rule that the restrictive covenant was unenforceable?
2. The Pennsylvania Superior Court ruled that the restrictive covenant was ancillary to the taking of employment. What is the court's rationale?

3. The superior court even goes so far as to say that the covenant would be valid if it had been contained in an employment contract entered into after employment. Why?

4. Why is the presence of consideration so essential to an enforceable agreement?

CAPACITY

In order to create a contract that is legally binding and enforceable, the parties must have the legal capacity to contract. All parties do not have the same legal capacity to enter into a contract, however. Full contractual capacity is met when a person is of legal age without mental disability or incapacity.

It is presumed that all parties to an agreement have full legal capacity to contract. Therefore any party seeking to base a claim or a defense on incapacity has the burden of alleging *and proving* the incapacity. The principal classes given some degree of special protection on their contracts because of their incapacity are (1) minors, (2) insane people, and (3) intoxicated people.

Minors

At common law, people remained minors until they reached the age of twenty-one. Generally, present legislation has reduced this age to eighteen. The law pertaining to minors entering into contracts formerly held that those contracts were void. Now that law has been almost universally changed and holds that such contracts are voidable. This law applies not only to contracts, but also to executed transactions such as sales.

The law grants minors this right in order to protect them from their lack of judgment and experience, limited will power, and presumed immaturity. A contract between an adult and a minor is voidable only by the minor; the adult must fulfill the obligation, unless the minor decides to avoid the contract. Ordinarily, parents are not liable for contracts entered into by their minor children.

Adults contract with minors at their own peril. Thus an adult party frequently will refuse to contract with or sell to minors because minors are incapable of giving legal assurance that they will not avoid the contract.

Transactions a Minor Cannot Avoid

Through legislation, many states have limited minors' ability to avoid contracts. For instance, many states provide that a contract with a college or university is binding. A purchase of life insurance has also been held to bind a minor. Some statutes take away the right of minors to avoid contracts after they are married. Most states hold that a minor engaging in a business and operating in the same manner as a person having legal capacity will not be permitted to set aside contracts arising from that business or employment. Court decisions or statutes have established this law in order to prevent minors from using the shield of minority to avoid business contracts.

Minors are liable for the reasonable value (not the contract price) of any necessary they purchase, whether goods or services, if they accept and make use of it. The reasonable value of the necessaries, rather than their contract price, is specified to protect them against the possibility that the other party to the agreement has taken advantage of them by overcharging them. If the necessaries have not yet been accepted or received, the minor may disaffirm the contract without liability.

In general, the term *necessaries* includes whatever is needed for a minor's subsistence as measured by age, status, condition in life, and so on. These include food, lodging, education, clothing, and medical services. Objects used for pleasure and ordinary contracts relating to the property or business of the minor are not classified as necessaries.

Disaffirmance of Contract

Minors may avoid both *executed* (completed) and *executory* (incompleted) contracts at any time during their infancy. They may also disaffirm a contract for a reasonable period of time after they attain their majority. In this way, former minors have a reasonable time in which to evaluate transactions made during their infancy. What constitutes a reasonable time depends on the nature of the property involved and the surrounding circumstances. As long as minors do not disaffirm their contracts, they are bound by the terms. They cannot refuse to carry out their part of an agreement, while at the same time requiring the adult party to perform.

Disaffirmance of a contract by a minor may be made by any expression of an intention to repudiate the contract. Disaffirmance need not be verbal or written. If a minor performs an act inconsistent with the continuing validity of a contract, that is considered a disaffirmance. For example, if a minor sells property to Gaskins and later, on reaching majority, sells the same property to Ginger, the second sale to Ginger would be considered a disaffirmance of the contract with Gaskins.

Minors may disaffirm wholly executory contracts, that is, contracts that neither party has performed. In addition, if only the minors have performed, they may disaffirm and recover the money or property they have paid or transferred to an adult. A conflict arises, however, if the contract is wholly executed or if only the adult has performed and the minor has spent what he or she has received and therefore cannot make restitution. As a general rule, minors must return whatever they have in their possession of the consideration under the contract; if the consideration has been destroyed, they may nevertheless disaffirm the contract and recover the consideration they have given. For example, suppose Weldon, a minor, purchases an automobile and has an accident that demolishes the car. She may obtain a full refund by disaffirming the contract and also will not be liable for the damage to the car.

A few states, however, hold that if the contract is advantageous to the minor and if the adult has been fair in every respect, the contract cannot be disaffirmed unless the minor returns the consideration. In the preceding example, the minor would have to replace the reasonable value of the damaged automobile before she could disaffirm the contract and receive the consideration she gave for the automobile. These states also take into account the depreciation of the property while in the possession of the minor.

Some states have enacted statutes that prevent minors from disaffirming contracts if they have fraudulently misrepresented their age. Generally, however, the fact that minors have misrepresented their age in order to secure a contract that they could not have otherwise obtained will not later prevent them from disaffirming that contract on the basis of their minority. Most courts will hold minors liable for any resulting damage to, or deterioration of, property they received under the contract. Minors are also generally liable for their torts; consequently, in most states, the other party to the contract could recover in a tort action for deceit. In any case, the other party to the contract may avoid it because of the minor's fraud.

Ratification

Although minors may disaffirm or avoid their contracts before reaching their majority, they cannot effectively ratify or approve their contracts until they have attained their majority. *Ratification* may consist of any expression or action that indicates an intention to be bound by the contract, and may come from the actions of the minor who has now reached majority. For example, if a minor acquired property under a contract and, after reaching majority makes use of or sells the property, he or she will de deemed to have ratified the contract.

Insane People

People are said to be insane when they do not understand the nature and consequences of an act at the time of their entering into an agreement. In such cases, they lack capacity and their contracts are either void or voidable. The contracts of a person who has been judicially declared insane by a court are void. Such a person will have a judicially appointed guardian who is under a duty to transact all business for him or her.

The contracts of insane people who have not been judicially declared insane are generally voidable. Although such people may not ratify or disaffirm a contract during their temporary insanity, they may do so once they regain their sanity. However, if the contract is executed and the sane party to the contract acts in good faith, not knowing that the other party is temporarily insane, most courts refuse to allow the temporarily insane person the right to avoid the contract, unless the consideration that has been received can be returned. On the other hand, if the sane party knows that the other party is mentally incompetent, the contract is voidable at the option of the insane person.

As in the case of minors, the party possessing capacity to contract has no right to disaffirm a contract merely because the insane party has the right to do so. The rule in regard to necessaries purchased by temporarily insane persons is the same as in the case of minors.

Intoxication

If persons enter into a contract when they are so intoxicated that they do not know at the time that they are executing a contract, the contract is voidable at their option. The position of the intoxicated person is therefore much the same as that of the temporarily insane person.

ILLEGALITY

An agreement is *illegal* when either its formation or performance is criminal, tortious, or opposed to public policy. When an agreement is illegal, courts will not allow either party to sue for performance of the contract. The court will literally "leave the parties where it finds them." Generally, if one of the parties has performed, that person cannot recover either the value of the performance or any property or goods transferred to the other party. There are three exceptions to this rule, however.

First, if the law that the agreement violates is intended for the protection of one of the parties, that party may seek relief. For example, both federal and state statutes require that a corporation follow certain procedures before stocks and bonds may be offered for sale to the public. It is illegal to sell such securities without having complied with the legal requirements. People who have purchased securities from a corporation that has not complied with the law may obtain a refund of the purchase price if they desire to do so.

Second, when the parties are not equally at fault, the one less at fault is granted relief when the public interest is advanced by doing so. This rule is applied to illegal agreements that are induced by undue influence, duress, or fraud. In such cases, the courts do not regard the defrauded or coerced party as being an actual participant in the wrong and will therefore allow restitution.

A third exception occurs within very strict limits. A person who repents before actually having performed any illegal part of an illegal contract may rescind it and obtain restitution. For example, suppose James and Richardo wager on the outcome of a baseball game. Each gives $500 to Smith, the stakeholder, who agrees to give $1,000 to the winner. Prior to the game, either James or Richardo could recover $500 from Smith through legal action, since the execution of the illegal agreement would not yet have occurred.

If the objectives of an agreement are illegal, the agreement is illegal and unenforceable, even though the parties were not aware, when they arrived at their agreement, that it was illegal.

On the other hand, as a general rule, even if one party to an agreement knows that the other party intends to use the subject matter of the contract for illegal purposes, this fact will not make the agreement illegal unless the illegal purpose involves a serious crime. For example, suppose Aiello lends money to

Roja, at a legal interest rate, knowing Roja is going to use the money to gamble illegally. After Roja loses her money, she refuses to repay Aiello on the grounds that the agreement was illegal. Aiello can recover her money through court action, even though she knew Roja was going to illegally gamble with the money she lent her.

Contracts Against Public Policy

A contract provision is contrary to public policy if it is injurious to the interest of the public, contradicts some established interests of society, violates a statute, or tends to interfere with the public health, safety, or general welfare. The term *public policy* is vague and variable; it changes as our social, economic, and political climates change. One example is the illegal lobbying agreement, an agreement by which one party uses bribery, threats of a loss of votes, or any other improper means to procure or prevent the adoption of particular legislation by a lawmaking body, such as Congress or a state legislature. Such agreements are clearly contrary to the public interest since they interfere with the workings of the democratic process. They are both illegal and void.

The court in the following case ruled that Iowa's public policy was not violated by an automobile liability insurance policy that excluded from coverage bodily injury to members of the insured owner's family.

**Principal Casualty Insurance Company
v. Blair**
500 N.W.2d 67
Supreme Court of Iowa
May 19, 1993

Schultz, Justice

We must decide in this appeal whether a family exclusion provision contained in a homeowners insurance policy is effective to prevent coverage for personal liability and medical payments to others. The Principal Casualty Insurance Company (Principal) issued a homeowners policy to Stephen and Debbie Blair. Debbie Blair, individually and as mother and next best friend of Michael Blair, commenced an action for damages against her husband, Stephen Blair, for injuries their son Michael sustained when a wheel came off of his bicycle and caused him to fall. In her petition, Debbie alleged that Stephen had

negligently assembled the bicycle. Principal commenced this declaratory judgment action, claiming its policy did not provide liability coverage for Stephen and medical payments coverage for Michael because of its family exclusion clauses. The district court sustained Principal's motion for summary judgment, ruling that there was no insurance coverage. We affirm.

In this case the facts are not in dispute. Our review is to determine whether the district court correctly determined the legal consequences arising from the terms of the insurance policy. . . .

Principal's homeowners policy provides clauses for personal liability protection and for medical payment coverage. The "Personal Liability Coverage" for an insured excludes coverage for bodily injury to "your relatives residing in your household. . . ." The policy clause for "Medical Payment to Others Coverage" pays medical expenses for persons who sustain bodily injury caused by activities of an insured person; however, the clause specifies that the insurer does not cover injury to an "insured person." One of the definitions of an "insured person" is "your relatives residing in your household." Michael Blair, a minor, resides with Stephen and Debbie Blair, the named insureds. Principal named all of the Blairs as defendants in this lawsuit. Hereinafter we shall refer to them as the Blairs.

Principal maintains the exclusion of "relatives residing in your household" (family exclusion), deprives the Blairs of liability coverage and medical payments coverage. The Blairs contend the "family exclusion" is void because it is contrary to public policy. . . .

I. Public Policy

The Blairs present affidavits to the effect that no other Iowa insurers offer coverage to insureds who negligently injure family members residing in the household. The Blairs urge that a significant population is irrationally excluded from insurance coverage contrary to public policy.

The Blairs cite us no case authority to support their position. We find no cases of our own involving the application of the "family exclusion" to a homeowners policy; however, many other jurisdictions have recognized the validity of the exclusion without discussing public policy.

We have stated that the term "public policy" is not susceptible of an exact definition, but "a court ought not enforce a contract which tends to be injurious to the public or contrary to the public good." *Walker v. American Family Mut. Ins. Co.,* 340 N.W.2d 599, 601 (Iowa 1983). Further, we have observed that when a court determines whether a contract is contrary to the public good it must be cautious and act only in cases free from doubt. We must harmonize public policy and the freedom of parties to contract. In *Walker,* we reviewed our statutes and case law and rejected an attempt to nullify a clause in an automobile insurance policy excluding liability coverage for bodily injury to an "insured or any member of the family of the insured residing in the same household as the insured." While *Walker* involved the named insured, we believe the same policy arguments are applicable to a member of the household.

No statutes or court cases have been cited that require a private citizen to obtain homeowners insurance that provides coverage for negligently injuring family members. We disagree with the Blairs' contention that the lack of insurers willing to provide the type of coverage they seek in this case should cause us to act. We believe that this is a policy decision for the legislature, not the judiciary. Further, we believe that we should follow the lead of the jurisdictions that have rejected similar public policy claims. . . .

We affirm the judgment entered by the district court.

Affirmed.

Case Questions

1. The trial and appellate courts were urged to invalidate a clause in a homeowner's insurance policy on public policy grounds. Explain the basis of the public policy argument.
2. What does the Supreme Court of Iowa decide? What is the basis for the decision?

Agreements to Commit Serious Crimes

An agreement is illegal and therefore void when it calls for the commission of any act that constitutes a serious crime. Agreements to commit murder, robbery, arson, burglary, and assault are obvious examples, but less obvious violations are also subject to the rule, depending on the jurisdiction.

Agreements to Commit Civil Wrongs

An agreement that calls for the commission of a civil wrong is also illegal and void. Examples are agreements to slander a third person, to defraud another, to damage another's goods, or to infringe upon another's trademark or patent.

A contract that calls for the performance of an act or the rendering of a service may be illegal for one of two reasons. (1) The act or service itself may be illegal (illegal *per se*), and thus any contract involving this act or service is illegal. Prostitution is a good example. (2) Certain other service contracts are not illegal *per se*, but may be illegal if the party performing or contracting to perform the service is not legally entitled to do so. This latter condition refers to the fact that a license is required before a person is entitled to perform certain functions for others. For example, doctors, dentists, lawyers, architects, surveyors, real estate brokers, and others rendering specialized professional services must be licensed by the appropriate body before entering into contracts with the general public.

All the states have enacted regulatory statutes concerning the practice of various professions and the performance of business and other activities. However, these statutes are not uniform in their working or in their scope. Many of the statutes specifically provide that all agreements that violate them shall be void and unenforceable. When such a provision is lacking, the court will look to the intent of the statute. If the court is of the opinion that a statute was enacted for the protection of the public, it will hold that agreements in violation of the statute are void. If, however, the court concludes that the particular statute was intended solely to raise revenue, then it will hold that contracts entered in violation of the statute are legal and enforceable.

A contract that has for its purpose the restraint of trade and nothing more is illegal and void. A contract to monopolize trade, to suppress competition, or not to compete in business, therefore, cannot be enforced because the sole purpose of the agreement would be to eliminate competition. A contract that aims at establishing a monopoly is not only unenforceable, but also renders the parties to the agreement liable to indictment for the commission of a crime.

When a business is sold, it is commonly stated in a contract that the seller shall not go into the same or similar business again within a certain geographical area, or for a certain period of time, or both. In early times, such agreements were held void since they deprived the public of the service of the person who agreed not to compete, reduced competition, and exposed the public to monopoly. Gradually, the law began to recognize the validity of such restrictive provisions. To the modern courts, the question is whether under the circumstances the restriction imposed upon one party is reasonable or whether the restriction is more extensive than is required to protect the other party. A similar situation arises when employees agree not to compete with their employers should they leave their jobs.

The North Carolina Court of Appeals was asked to determine the validity of a postemployment noncompetition clause which had been signed by former employees at the time of their employment by Redlee/SCS, Inc. Because the employment agreement between the parties contained a choice-of-law clause, the North Carolina Court of Appeals used Texas law to decide the case.

Redlee/SCS, Inc. v. Carl J. Pieper
571 S.E.2d 8
Court of Appeals of North Carolina
October 15, 2002

Thomas, Judge

Plaintiff, Redlee/SCS, Inc., filed an action against defendants seeking to enforce a covenant not to compete. The trial court granted a preliminary injunction in favor of plaintiff, and defendants appeal. . . .

Redlee is in the business of securing contracts with owners or managers of large office buildings to perform janitorial services. It then manages and supervises cleaning subcontractors. Redlee does business throughout the United States, including North Carolina.

On or about 8 September 1997, defendant Carl Pieper began employment with Redlee in its Charlotte office as an area manager. In consideration of his employment and training, Pieper executed an employment agreement at the initiation of his work with Redlee expressly effective for a six-month term. The agreement contained a covenant not to compete with Redlee for a period of two years after termination of his employment. In March of 1998, Pieper executed a second employment agreement that continued his employment with Redlee as an area manager. Additionally, the agreement obligates Pieper to maintain the confidentiality of, and not disclose or use, confidential

information obtained while employed by Redlee "concerning [it's] business clients, methods, operations, financing or services."

Around December 1999 or January 2000, defendant Ben Simon became employed as a district manager with Redlee in its Charlotte office. On or about July 2000, Simon entered into an employment agreement forbidding him to compete with Redlee for two years after the termination of his employment or to disclose any confidential information obtained during his employment.

In January 2000, Pieper resigned from Redlee and began work with defendant Allied International Building Services, Inc. Allied is one of Redlee's direct competitors. In December 2000, Simon resigned from Redlee and also began working for Allied. After learning that Pieper and Simon contacted some of Redlee's customers on behalf of Allied to solicit business, Redlee instituted an action against them as well as Allied.

At the outset, we note the two-year duration of the covenant not to compete. . . . Pieper's covenant not to compete expired in January of 2002. The preliminary injunction is no longer in effect. Therefore, the issues on appeal regarding Pieper are moot. Simon's noncompete agreement, however, expires in December 2002. We proceed only on the assignments of error as to Simon.

By their first and second assignments of error, defendants Simon and Allied contend the trial court improperly granted the preliminary injunction. They argue that: (1) the agreements are not valid; and (2) the trial court erred in concluding Redlee can show "a likelihood of success on the merits" of its case. . . .

A preliminary injunction is interlocutory in nature and therefore not immediately appealable unless it deprives the appellant of a substantial right that he would lose absent immediate review. . . . Our courts have recognized the inability to practice one's livelihood as a substantial right. . . . As a result of the preliminary injunction, Simon has been prevented from managing janitorial services in Mecklenburg County. The granting of Redlee's motion for a preliminary injunction therefore deprived him of a substantial right. . . .

There is no dispute between the parties that the agreement states it will be "governed by and construed in accordance with the laws of the State of Texas." This provision is effective. . . . Since the agreement is, in fact, governed by Texas law, we must next determine whether there is a likelihood that Redlee will prevail on the merits in light of Texas law.

The validity and enforceability of restrictive covenants is governed by the Covenants Not to Compete Act. Tex. Bus. & Com. Code Ann. §§§ 15.50–15.52. . . . Under the Act, a covenant is enforceable if:

(1) it is ancillary to or part of an otherwise enforceable agreement at the time the agreement is made, and
(2) the limitations of time, geographical area and scope of activity are reasonable and do not impose a greater restraint than is necessary to protect the good will or other business interest of the promisee. . . .

In Texas, an agreement to employ for specified terms is an "otherwise enforceable agreement" for the purposes of a convenant not to compete. . . . Simon's agreement provides for a definite twelve-month term of employment. Therefore, the noncompete covenants in it are "part of an otherwise enforce-

able agreement." . . . Moreover, "satisfaction contracts" are recognized:

> In Texas, a contract by which one agrees to employ another as long as the services are satisfactory, or which is otherwise expressed to be conditional on the satisfactory character of the services rendered, gives the employer the right to terminate the contract and to discharge the employee whenever the employer, acting in good faith, is actually and honestly dissatisfied with the work. . . .

Therefore, while an employment-at-will contract allows severance of the employment relationship at any time without cause, "when an employment agreement is a satisfaction contract, there must be a bona fide dissatisfaction or cause for discharge." . . . As a result, a satisfaction contract is an enforceable ancillary agreement that will support a restrictive covenant; an employment-at-will contract will not. . . .

Here, the agreement states that the employee may be terminated for "failure to meet and perform duties of employment to minimum performance standards and expectations of the employer." It further provides: "Employer shall not have the right to terminate this agreement without cause." These limitations on Redlee's right to terminate Simon, as long as he satisfactorily performs his duties, changes the normal at-will relationship. Accordingly, Simon was an employee under a satisfaction contract that supports the restrictive covenant.

We next determine whether the restrictions as to time, scope, and geographic location set forth in the covenants are reasonable . . . Tex. Bus. & Com. Code Ann. §§ 15.51. Section 15.51 provides:

> If the covenant is found to be ancillary to or part of an otherwise enforceable agreement but contains limitations as to time, geographical area, or scope of activity to be restrained that are not reasonable and impose a greater restraint than is necessary to protect the goodwill or other business interest of the

promisee, the *court shall reform the covenant to the extent necessary to cause the limitations contained in the covenant as to time, geographical area, and scope of activity to be restrained to be reasonable* and to impose a restraint that is not greater than necessary to protect the goodwill or other business interest of the promisee and enforce the covenant as reformed, except that the court may not award the promisee damages for a breach of the covenant before its reformation and the relief granted to the promisee shall be limited to injunctive relief. . . .

Our determination is governed by: (1) whether the restriction is greater than necessary to protect the business and goodwill of Redlee; (2) whether Redlee's need for protection outweighs the economic hardship which the covenant imposes on Simon; and (3) whether the restriction adversely affects the interests of the public. . . . "The restrictive covenant must bear some relation to the activities of the employee and must not restrain his activities into a territory into which his former work has not taken him or given him the opportunity to enjoy undue advantages in later competition with his former employer." . . .

Here, the covenant not to compete restricts Simon for a period of two years from: (1) directly competing with Redlee; and (2) soliciting or servicing any customer of Redlee's existing at the time of termination who had been solicited or serviced by Redlee within one year prior to the time of termination, or whose contract expired within one year prior to termination.

The agreement prohibits Simon from working with direct competitors in the business of securing contracts with owners or managers of large office buildings to perform janitorial services and then soliciting or servicing current or recent clients of Redlee at the time of his termination.

We conclude that the restraint created is not greater than necessary to protect Redlee's legitimate interests in its confidential information, particularly its customer and pricing information. Moreover, the necessity of the restraint created was not outweighed by the hardship to the promisors or injury to the public. Thus, the covenant not to compete was reasonable as to the scope of activity restrained. We also find the two-year time period reasonable. . . . ("Two to five years has repeatedly been held a reasonable time restriction in a non-competition agreement.").

The geographical restriction, as reformed by the trial court, is also reasonable. "Texas courts have generally held that a geographical limitation imposed on the employee which consists of the territory within which the employee worked during his employment is a reasonable geographical restriction." . . . The agreement here restricted the geographical area to several counties. The trial court, however, reformed the covenant's territorial limitation to just Mecklenburg County. That was the only county in which Simon had worked during his employment with Redlee. Accordingly, we hold the agreement to be valid under Texas law.

We now turn to the issue of whether Redlee has met its burden of showing a likelihood of success on the merits. The agreement was voluntarily signed by Simon. As set forth above, the time and territory provisions are reasonable and not unduly oppressive. Simon's at-will employment changed to termination only for cause when he signed the agreement, thus constituting valuable consideration.

Under the agreement, Simon agreed to not solicit current or recent clients of Redlee, or "use . . . or possess any of [Redlee's] confidential and proprietary information." Redlee introduced evidence that Simon solicited Redlee's customers on behalf of Allied. Simon actually admits calling a Redlee client, answering questions about Allied, and then delivering an Allied brochure to the client's office. Redlee has met its burden of showing a likelihood of success on the merits.

The next issue is whether Redlee is "likely to sustain irreparable loss unless the injunction is issued, or if, in the opinion of the Court, issuance is necessary for the protection of a plaintiff's rights during the course of litigation." . . . This determination is discretionary and requires the trial court to weigh the equities. We therefore apply North Carolina law. . . . In *QSP, Inc. v. A. Wayne Hair,* . . . (2002), this Court stated:

> "Intimate knowledge of the business operations or personal association with customers provides an opportunity to [a] . . . former employee . . . to injure the business of the covenantee." . . .

In *A.E.P. Industries,* our Supreme Court emphasized that this potential harm warrants injunctive relief:

> "It is clear that if the nature of the employment is such as will bring the employee in personal contact with patrons or customers of the employer, or enable him to acquire valuable information as to the nature and character of the business and the names and requirements of the patrons or customers, enabling him by engaging in a competing business in his own behalf, or for another, to take advantage of such knowledge of or acquaintance with the patrons and customers of his former employer, and thereby gain an unfair advantage, equity will interpose in behalf of the employer and restrain the breach. . ."

Here, Redlee's evidence pertaining to Simon's solicitation of its customers is sufficient to show that Redlee is likely to sustain irreparable loss unless an injunction is issued. . . .

We carefully examined the validity of the covenants under Texas law and, as a result, concluded the covenants to be valid and fully enforceable. Under North Carolina law, we determined that, absent the preliminary injunction, Redlee is likely to sustain irreparable loss. As defendants cite no additional law contrary to our decision that the covenants here are valid and serve a legitimate business interest of Redlee, . . . we affirm the decision of the trial court. . . .

Case Questions

1. List some specific employment examples where a postemployment noncompetition agreement would be enforceable.
2. The employment agreement specifically provided that Texas law should govern. Why would the parties put such a provision in their contract? Could the right to choose and agree on the state law that shall govern a contract be abused?

WRITING

Every state has statutes requiring that certain contracts be in writing to be enforceable. Called the *statutes of fraud,* these statutes are based on "An Act for the Prevention of Frauds and Perjuries," passed by the English Parliament in 1677. Statutes of frauds traditionally govern six kinds of contracts: (1) an agreement by an executor or administrator to answer for the debt of the decedent, (2) an agreement made in consideration of marriage, (3) an agreement to answer for the debt of another, (4) an agreement that cannot be performed in one year, (5) an agreement for the sale of an interest in real property, and (6) an agreement for the sale of goods above a certain dollar amount.

The writing required by the statute need not be in any special form or use any special language. Usually, the terms that must be shown on the face of the writing include the names of the parties, the terms and conditions of the contract, the consideration, a reasonably certain description of the subject matter of the contract, and the signature of the party, or the party's agent, against whom enforcement is sought. These terms need not be on one piece of paper but may be on several pieces of paper, provided that their relation or connection with each other appears on their face by the physical attachment of the papers to each other or by reference from one writing to the other. At least one, if not all, of the papers must be signed by the party against whom enforcement is sought. (The requirements of memorandums involving the sale of goods differ.)

Agreement by Executor or Administrator

A promise by an executor or administrator to answer for the debt of the decedent is within the statute and must be in writing to be enforced. In order for the statute to operate, the executor's promise must be to pay out of the executor's own personal assets (pocket); a promise to pay a debt out of the assets of a decedent's estate is not required to be in writing.

Agreement in Consideration of Marriage

Agreements made in consideration of marriage are to be in writing. Mutual promises to marry are not within the statute, since the consideration is the exchanged promise, not the marriage itself. However, promises made to a prospective spouse or third party with marriage as the consideration are within the statute. For example, a promise by one prospective spouse to convey property to the other, provided the marriage is entered into, is required to be in writing. Similarly, if a third party, say a rich relative, promises to pay a certain sum of money to a prospective spouse if a marriage is entered into, the promise will be unenforceable unless reduced to writing.

Agreement to Answer for the Debt of Another

Agreements to answer for the debt or default of another shall be unenforceable unless in writing. The rationale for this provision is that the guarantor or surety has received none of the benefits for which the debt was incurred and therefore should be bound only by the exact terms of the promise. For example, Bob desires to purchase a new law text on credit. The bookstore is unsure as to Bob's ability to pay, so Bob brings in his friend, Ellen, who says, "If Bob does not pay for the text, I will." In effect, the promise is that the bookstore must first try to collect from Bob, who is primarily liable. After it has exhausted all possibilities of collecting from him, then it may come to Ellen to receive payment. Ellen is therefore secondarily liable. Ellen has promised to answer for Bob's debt even though she will not receive the benefit of the new law text; therefore, her agreement must be in writing to be enforceable.

This situation must be distinguished from those in which the promise to answer for the debt of another is an original promise; that is, the promisor's objective is to be primarily liable. For example, Bob wants to purchase a new law text. When he takes the book to the cashier, his friend Ellen steps in and says, "Give him the book. I will pay for it." Ellen has made an original promise to the bookstore with the objective of becoming primarily liable. Such a promise need not be in writing to be enforceable.

Sometimes it is difficult to ascertain whether the purpose of the promisor is to become primarily liable or secondarily liable. In resolving the issue, courts will sometimes use the leading object rule. This rule looks not only to the promise itself, but also to the individual for whose benefit the promise was made. The logic of the rule is that if the leading object of the promise is the personal benefit of the promisor, then the promisor must have intended to become primarily liable. In such a case, the promise will be deemed to be original and need not be in writing to be enforced.

The question in the following Missouri case involved whether an alleged oral agreement by a promisor to pay another's debt was within or outside the scope of the statute of frauds.

Douglas D. Owens v. Leonard Goldammer

Court of Appeals of Missouri Western District
77 S.W.3d
June 11, 2002

Forest W. Hanna, Judge

Leonard Goldammer is the owner of Golden Accounting Tax and Consultant Service. Mr. Goldammer, and his accounting business, provided accounting services for Centennial Land & Development, Inc., Residential Project, which was a residential real estate development project owned by Barbara Naughton. The Centennial Project consisted of over 500 acres of land located in Clinton County. Sometime before 1995, the plaintiff, Douglas Owens, became a customer of de-fendant, Golden Accounting and Goldammer. Golden Accounting Tax, through Mr. Goldammer, provided accounting, payroll, and some tax audit services for one of Mr. Owens' businesses.

Owens sued Goldammer and his business, alleging in part that Goldammer breached his oral agreement to guarantee a $50,000 loan from Owens to Ms. Naughton. The jury returned verdicts in favor of Owens on his claim for breach of oral contract and his fraud claim, with the actual damages on the contract claim set at $43,042.84, plus $4,814.04 prejudgment interest. The jury found in Goldammer's favor on Owens' negligent misrepresentation and breach of fiduciary duty claims. Both parties appealed. Both parties raise numerous points but the decisive issue on this appeal is cross-appellant

Goldammer's argument that his oral promise to pay the debt of another falls within the statute of frauds.

Owens' hobby shop business had just completed a very profitable year. During discussions about Owens' tax liability, Goldammer and Owens considered various investment opportunities. Goldammer told Owens that he thought that the Centennial Project was a good investment and suggested that Owens consider investing in it. At the time, the IRS and Missouri had tax liens against the property. Owens understood that his money would help clear the liens so that the project could get under way. On February 24, 1995, because of Goldammer's recommendation, Owens sent Ms. Naughton a check payable to her in the amount of $50,000 for the project. Goldammer orally agreed to guarantee the loan with a fifteen percent rate of interest and a fifteen percent return. Naughton was unaware of Goldammer's guarantee. Subsequently, on July 13, 1995, Owens made a second loan for $160,488, secured by a deed of trust on the property.

Neither Goldammer nor his business, Golden Tax, had an ownership interest in the project, however, he and his mother had invested $121,000 in the project, secured by a deed of trust on the project's property. Goldammer had a written agreement with the Centennial Project, which provided that Goldammer negotiate payment of taxes and lien releases with the IRS and the Missouri Department of Revenue, assist Naughton in obtaining finances for the project, and provide consulting and administrative duties for the project. He also assisted in the coordination of the project. In exchange, Goldammer was to receive five percent of the price of each lot sold, which was described as delayed payment for services previously rendered for his work on the IRS and Missouri tax liens. The five percent fee was based on the gross sale of the lot, regardless of whether the sale was profitable or not.

The Centennial Project ultimately failed and Naughton filed bankruptcy. Owens proceeded on his claim for $50,000, plus thirty percent interest against Naughton in the bankruptcy court. Owens received partial satisfaction of his debt when the bankruptcy court distributed Naughton's assets. Subsequently, Owens filed this lawsuit against Goldammer for the difference between the loan, plus interest, minus the amount recovered from the bankruptcy court.

The second loan of $160,488 is not a part of this lawsuit. . . .

There is no written documentation of the loan at issue except the $50,000 check payable to Naughton. There is no promissory note and, of course, no written guaranty from Goldammer to Owens. . . .

Goldammer maintains that the Missouri Statute of Frauds requires that any promise to pay the debt of another must be in writing. Section 432.010, RSMo. Owens argues that Goldammer's promise was an original undertaking placing it outside of the Statute of Frauds and, thus, enforceable. Because the Statute of Frauds requires such a guaranty to be in writing, our inquiry is whether the agreement was an original promise, outside of the statute, or a collateral promise, within the statute. . . .

Section 432.010, RSMo 1978, provides in pertinent part that "[n]o action shall be brought to . . . charge any person upon any special promise to answer for the debt, default or miscarriage of another person . . . unless the agreement upon which the action shall be brought . . . shall be in writing and signed by the party to be charged therewith. . . ." . . . Missouri courts have recognized that "[a] claimed exception to the statute of frauds is 'regarded with the most rigid scrutiny.'" . . . The exception is to be "sparingly invoked." . . .

The original/collateral promise distinction is the standard used in determining whether an oral guarantee is enforceable. . . . An exception to that statute exists if the oral agreement to answer for the debt of another is an original promise, as opposed to a collateral promise. . . . For the oral promise to be an original obligation not covered by the statute of frauds, two elements must be met. First, credit must be given by the promisee to the promisor alone. . . . In addition, the leading or main purpose of the promisor must be to gain some personal advantage for him, rather than to become the mere guarantor or surety of another's debt, and the promise must be supported by a consideration directly beneficial to the promisor. . . . [The cited cases] hold that if the benefit went to the original obligor and the promisee looked to the original obligor for repayment, it is not an original undertaking and the promisor is merely a surety. . . .

In our case, Owens filed his proof of claim in Naughton's bankruptcy proceeding. His claim described the agreement with Naughton as her promise to pay him the principal amount and stated that he was "entitled to a thirty percent rate of return." His proof of claim was for $64,585.50, which included a return on the principal of thirty percent. His documentation was his cancelled check payable to Barbara Naughton for $50,000. The promisee's action in seeking repayment of the debt from Naughton identifies her, as a matter of law, as the original obligor primarily liable on the debt. . . .

When Owens put his money into the Centennial Project, his check was payable and delivered to Naughton, not Goldammer. The money was for the Centennial Project. The project was owned and operated by Naughton, not Goldammer. There was no evidence suggesting, or argument made, that Goldammer had any control over the funds. When Owens demanded his money back, he sought recovery from Naughton, for not only the principal, but thirty percent interest. He pursued his claim under the theory that Naughton was the original debtor who owed him the money and interest. Owens'

court testimony denies his legal argument on appeal. Owens testified that Goldammer guaranteed the loan and, thus, his risk was minimal "because if Barbara Naughton didn't pay it back, Leonard said he would." This testimony is representative of his evidence.

The proof of the promisor's leading or main purpose in guarantying the debt fell short of the mark as well. For the oral promise to be an original obligation the leading or main purpose of the promisor in making the promise must be to gain some advantage for himself, rather than to become the mere guarantor or surety of another's debt, and furthermore, the promise must be supported by a consideration beneficial to the promisor. . . .

The cases which have considered the leading or main purpose rule seek to determine the primary objective of the promisor in making the promise to repay the loan. If the primary purpose is to serve his own interests, either gaining a benefit for himself or inducing a detriment to the promisee, the promise is held to be an original undertaking and enforceable. . . .

To show that the leading or main purpose was for his own purposes, Owens points to Goldammer's investment in the project and the terms of the contract between Goldammer's business and the Centennial Project. Owens claims that Goldammer benefited from the loan because the money was used to pay off the preexisting tax liens, which helped get the project under way, and, thus, increased the prospects for the sale of lots for which he would receive five percent of the sale price of each lot sold. Also, Owens argues that Goldammer received greater protection for his deed of trust on the property in the event of liquidation of the project. . . .

Although Goldammer's prospects for receiving his delayed compensation were improved by the additional money put into the project, and his investment received some degree of protection, notwithstanding that it was secured by a deed of trust, the benefits to

Goldammer were incidental and indirect. The facts relative to Goldammer's arrangements with the Centennial Project do not establish that Goldammer entered into a new or independent undertaking such as to take the oral promise out of the statute. Moreover, there is a lack of new consideration flowing from the creditor to the promisor. Instead, Naughton,

the owner and the original debtor, received the direct benefit of the loan.

The judgment for breach of contract in favor of Owens against Goldammer and Golden Accounting Tax and Consultant Service is reversed and the case is remanded for entry of a judgment in accordance with this opinion.

Case Questions

1. Why did Goldammer believe he was not legally required to pay Naughton's debt owed to Owens?
2. What was Owens' argument regarding an "original promise"?
3. What did the appellate court decide and why?

Agreements Not to Be Performed in One Year

Most statutes require contracts that cannot be performed within one year from the time the contract is formed to be in writing. This determination is made by referring to the intentions of the parties, to the nature of the performance, and to the terms of the contract itself. For example, if Jack agrees to build a house for Betty, the question is whether the contract is capable of being performed within one year. Houses can be built in one year. Therefore, this agreement need not be in writing even if Jack actually takes more than one year to build the house.

It is important to remember that the *possibility* that the contract can be performed within one year is enough to take it out of the operation of the statute regardless of how long performance actually took.

Agreement Conveying an Interest in Real Property

The statute of frauds generally renders unenforceable oral agreements conveying interests in real estate. Most problems center on what an interest in real estate is and whether the agreement contemplates the transfer of any title, ownership, or possession of real property. Both must be involved to bring the statute into effect. Real property has been held to commonly include land, leaseholds, easements, standing timber, and under certain conditions, improvements and fixtures attached to the land.

The landlord in the following case brought suit to enforce a written but unsigned two-year lease. The court ruled that there was no leasehold and that only a month-to-month tenancy existed because the requirements of the statute of frauds were not satisfied.

Mulford v. Borg-Warner Acceptance Corp.
495 N.Y.S.2d 493
Supreme Court of New York,
Appellate Division
November 21, 1985

Harvey, Justice

Appeal from an order and judgment of the Supreme Court at Special Term (Murphy, J.), entered April 19, 1985 in Madison County, which granted defendant's motion for summary judgment dismissing the complaint.

This is an action involving a written lease for certain office space in the Village of Canastota, Madison County, for a period of two years. The lease was never subscribed by anyone on behalf of defendant. Prior to the lease in issue, there were three written leases between these parties involving space in the same office building owned by plaintiff. Each lease expired on March 31, 1983. Prior to the expiration date, plaintiff proposed a new lease for a three-year period involving the same accommodations. Defendant informed plaintiff that it would not lease one of the office suites previously occupied by it and that, as to the remaining space, it would only be interested in a two-year lease. Thereafter, and on the expiration date of the original lease, plaintiff prepared a written two-year lease, subscribed it and delivered it to defendant. Although defendant retained possession of the property described in the document and paid rent at a rate in accordance with the provisions contained therein, it never signed the new lease. On August 2, 1983, defendant notified plaintiff that it was quitting the premises as of August 31, 1983, and paid the rent for that month.

Plaintiff commenced this action alleging that the unexecuted lease was a valid lease and demanded unpaid rent and other expenses alleged to have resulted from defendant's default. After issue was joined, defendant moved ... for summary judgment dismissing the complaint, relying upon General Obligations Law § 5-703(2) as an absolute defense. Special Term granted the motion and this appeal ensued.

General Obligations Law § 5-703(2) provides:

> "A contract for the leasing for a longer period than one year, or for the sale, of any real property, or an interest therein, is void unless the contract or some note or memorandum, is in writing, subscribed by the party to be charged, or by his lawful agent thereunto authorized by writing."

Although plaintiff freely admits that the proposed lease was never subscribed by defendant, he contends that signed checks delivered to plaintiff for monthly rentals in the amounts as would have been required by the proposed lease constitute sufficient memoranda to satisfy the Statute of Frauds. We disagree. The law requires that the memoranda embody all the essential and material parts of the lease contemplated with such clarity and certainty as to show that the parties have agreed on all the material parts of the lease contemplated. . . . The only material factors which could be established by the checks were the fact of possession and the amount of monthly rental. Nothing contained in the checks or any memoranda attached thereto gave any clue as to the term of the lease. The notation on the memo portion of the first check stating "additional rent due for April (new lease)" is consistent with a month-to-month tenancy. This notation is insufficient to establish a tenancy involving all the provisions, including the term, of the proposed written but unsigned lease. We conclude, therefore, that defendant's occupancy of the premises from April 1, 1983 to August 31, 1983 was on the basis of a month-to-month tenancy. . . .

Order and judgment modified, on the law and the facts, without costs, by granting plaintiff judgment for one month's rent for September 1983 . . . and, as so modified, affirmed.

Case Questions

1. What is the rationale behind requiring that contracts for longer than one year satisfy the statute of frauds?
2. The plaintiff argued that the monthly rental checks paid by the defendant to the plaintiff should be held to satisfy the statute of frauds. Why does the appellate court disagree?

Sale of Goods

Generally, a contract for the sale of goods for the price of $500 or more is not enforceable unless there is some writing to serve as evidence that a contract has been entered into. An informal or incomplete writing will be sufficient to satisfy the UCC statute of frauds, providing that it (1) indicates that a contract between the parties was entered into, (2) is signed by the party against whom enforcement is sought, and (3) contains a statement of the quantity of goods sold. The price, time and place of delivery, quality of the goods, and warranties may be omitted without invalidating the writing, as the UCC permits these terms to be shown by outside evidence, custom and usage, and prior dealings between the parties. Thus the provisions that must be included in a writing that will conform with the UCC statute of frauds are substantially less than those necessary in a writing that evidences one of the other types of contracts governed by the statute of frauds. Under the UCC, the contract will be enforced only as to the quantity of goods shown in the writing (UCC 2-201 [1]).

Parol Evidence Rule

After contracting parties have successfully negotiated a contract, they often sign a written document that contains what they intend to be a definitive and complete statement of the agreed-upon terms. Courts will usually presume that such a writing is accurate. Therefore, under the *parol evidence rule*, evidence of alleged prior agreements or terms not contained in the written document will be inadmissible if offered to change the terms of the document.

The parol evidence rule would not apply, however, where the contracting parties have prepared only a partial memorandum or other incomplete writing. In that context the incomplete writing is only partially integrated (i.e., it is intended to be a final and complete statement of the terms addressed in the memorandum but not as to omitted terms that can be proven extrinsically). There are several exceptions to the parol evidence rule. For example, parol evidence can be used to prove fraud or the absence of consideration in the formation of a contract and to explain the meaning of ambiguous words.

Ronald A. Yocca v. The Pittsburgh Steelers Sports, Inc.
806 A.2d 936
Commonwealth Court of Pennsylvania
August 28, 2002

Judge Friedman

This is an appeal from an order of the Court of Common Pleas of Allegheny County (trial court), dated December 28, 2001, which sustained the preliminary objections of The Pittsburgh Steelers Sports, Inc., a National Football League Franchise, . . . d/b/a The Steelers Pittsburgh Football Club (Steelers) and the Sports & Exhibition Authority of Pittsburgh & Allegheny County (Authority) (together, Defendants), and dismissed the third amended class action complaint (Complaint) filed by Ronald A. Yocca . . . , individually and on behalf of all similarly situated persons (Plaintiffs), who purchased "stadium builder licenses" (SBLs) from Defendants. . . .

In their Complaint, Plaintiffs allege that Defendants issued a brochure (SBL Brochure) soliciting Plaintiffs to purchase SBLs for a new professional football stadium, now known as Heinz Field. . . . The SBL Brochure indicates that those who purchased SBLs would be making a one-time contribution to the cost of building the new stadium. In return, the SBL purchasers would be assigned to a particular seating area (Section) in the stadium and would have the right to buy season tickets in that Section for as many seasons as they wished. They also would have the right to determine who gains control of the season tickets for their seats in the future. . . . The actual seat assignments were to be made after the seats were physically installed in the stadium. . . .

The price of the SBLs ranged from $250.00 to $2700.00, depending on which Section the purchaser wished to sit in. . . . The SBL Brochure contained colored diagrams of the planned stadium showing the various Sections and showing the yard-lines of the playing field. The SBL Sections were designated, A, B, C, D, E, F, Club I and Club II. . . .

The penultimate page of the SBL Brochure was headed "Before you sign" and contained the following text:

> Use the application on the next page to order Stadium Builder Licenses (SBLs) or season tickets in non-SBL Sections for the same number or fewer season tickets as you currently hold.
>
> You may apply for any Section you wish as your first preference. To ensure fairness, every application received by the November 30 deadline will be assigned a random computerized priority number and that priority number will be used to assign both sections and seats.
>
> Stadium Builder Licenses (SBLs)
> If you are ordering SBLs, you will be mailed a contract by the end of March 1999, notifying you of your Section assignment. The contract must be signed and returned within 15 days. If the completed contract is not returned as required, your season ticket holder discount, seating priority and deposit will be forfeited.
>
> Same Seating Area Preference
> Current season ticket holders who apply for [an] SBL Section that corresponds with their current seat location in Three Rivers Stadium will be the first assigned to that Section. If that is your choice, we will try to assign seats as close to your current seat location as the new stadium seating configuration will allow. All other seats in a given SBL Section will be assigned using the random priority number. Assignment of your first preference is not guaranteed. . . .

The last page of the SBL Brochure was an application form . . . that interested parties were to fill out, indicating their first, second, and third Section choices. . . . Purchasers were to make payment for the SBLs in three equal installments: a nonrefundable one-third deposit was due with the Application; the second installment was due in October 1999; and the third installment was due in October 2000. . . . Plaintiffs allege that they completed the Application, sent it to Defendants with the required deposit, and completed payment of the SBL fees according to the terms of the contract. . . .

Plaintiffs allege that Defendants mailed two documents to the SBL applicants in October 1999, an "SBL Agreement" and "Additional Terms." The SBL Agreement incorporates by reference the Additional Terms, which, in turn, contains an integration clause, stating that "This Agreement contains the entire agreement of the parties with respect to the matters provided for herein and shall supersede any representations or agreements previously made or entered into by the parties hereto." . . . Plaintiffs allege that they signed the SBL Agreement and paid the remaining installments for their SBLs. . . .

Plaintiffs allege that when they took their seats in Heinz Field for the first time, they realized that Defendants had enlarged some of the SBL Sections, causing their individual seats to be "shifted both horizontally away from the [fifty] yard-line and vertically away from the field." . . . Therefore, their seats were outside the SBL Sections as depicted in the SBL Brochure, upon which they relied when they filled out their Applications.

For example, Representative Plaintiff Ronald A. Yocca applied for and was awarded two SBLs for the Club I Section. Based on the diagram in the SBL Brochure, . . . Plaintiffs allege that Yocca reasonably believed that Club I Section seats would be somewhere between the twenty-yard lines. . . . However, Yocca's seats turned out to be at the eighteen yard-line. . . .

The Complaint alleges that by expanding the size of the Club [I] Section, Defendants have improperly overcharged SBL holders actually sitting in Club [II] the annual seat fee of Club [I]. Subject to verification in discovery, Plaintiffs believe and therefore aver that the additional revenue generated in the [expanded Club I Section] will exceed $650,000.00 per year for the life of the stadium. . . .

In other words, Plaintiffs allege that Yocca is being forced to pay the Club I price for seats that, according to the SBL Brochure, should have been considered part of the Club II Section. Furthermore, this alleged injury to Yocca will continue for as long as he purchases season tickets. . . .

The Steelers and the Authority each filed preliminary objections, which included demurrers and motions to dismiss. The trial court sustained the preliminary objections and dismissed Plaintiffs' Complaint in its entirety. . . .

Plaintiffs now appeal from the trial court's order dismissing their Complaint. . . .

Breach of Contract

Plaintiffs . . . argue that the trial court erred in concluding that their claim for breach of contract is barred by the parole evidence rule. . . .

Under the "parole evidence rule," where the parties to a contract have embodied their agreement in a single memorial, which they regard as the final expression of that agreement, all other utterances, prior to or contemporaneous with the making of the memorial, are immaterial for the purpose of determining the terms of the contract. . . . If an agreement contains an integration clause, the parole evidence rule is particularly applicable. . . .

Here, the trial court concluded that the parole evidence rule barred Plaintiffs' claim for breach of contract because the SBL Agreement contained an integration clause. However, Plaintiffs argue, and we agree, that their contracts with Defendants were not finally embodied in the SBL Agreement. Indeed, their contracts with Defendants were formed well before Defendants mailed out the SBL

Agreement and Additional Terms, and the new provisions contained in those two documents constituted unilateral and, therefore, unenforceable, changes to the contract terms.

A contract is formed when there is an offer, an acceptance of that offer and an exchange of consideration. . . . Once these three elements are present, the contract is formed, even if the parties intend to reduce their agreement to a single writing with additional terms at a later date. . . . Once a contract has been formed, its terms may be modified only if both parties agree to the modification and the modification is founded upon valid consideration. . . . The terms of a contract cannot be modified by unilateral action. . . .

Applying the above principles of contract law to this case, we are struck by one important fact alleged in the Complaint: The SBL Applications had to be accompanied by a non-refundable deposit when they were mailed in. Because the SBL applicants had remitted the first one-third of their payment for the SBLs, and because they could not get that money back, the contract was complete at that point. In other words, the SBL Brochure was the offer, the mailing of the Application was acceptance of the offer, and the non-refundable exchange of money for the SBLs was the consideration.

Even if the SBL Agreement superceded the original contract, Plaintiffs allege that when they accepted that Agreement by signing it and paying their additional installments, such acceptance was still based on the terms set forth in the SBL Brochure. Thus, according to Plaintiffs, the SBL Agreement and Additional Terms, mailed out after the original contract had been formed, contained unilateral, unbargained-for changes to the terms of the contract that cannot be overcome by including an integration clause. . . .

A demurrer is not proper unless the law states with certainty that no recovery is possible on the facts alleged in the complaint. . . . We must accept as true all well-pled allegations of material fact averred in the complaint, as well as all inferences reasonably deduced therefrom. Any doubts must be resolved in favor of overruling the demurrer. . . . Because we do not believe that the parole evidence rule necessarily bars Plaintiffs' count alleging breach of contract, and because we cannot say the Plaintiffs cannot possibly recover on the facts alleged in the complaint, we conclude that the trial court erred in dismissing Plaintiffs' claim for breach of contract.

Accordingly, we reverse that portion of the trial court's decision dismissing Plaintiffs' claim for breach of contract. . . .

Case Questions

1. Why did the trial court dismiss the plaintiff's complaint?
2. For what reason was the trial court reversed on appeal?

ASPECTS OF CONTRACT PERFORMANCE

When parties enter into a contract, they generally expect that each side will fully perform in the manner called for in the agreement. Often, however, problems arise and full performance does not occur, as in the following examples.

Accord and Satisfaction

One party may agree to take something less than full performance to satisfy the agreement. For example, suppose that A asks B to pay a debt for services rendered and B states that he is too poor to pay the full amount. A may agree to accept payment for only half of the debt. In this situation, the parties have worked out an accord and satisfaction. An *accord* is the offer of something different from what was due under the original contract. The *satisfaction* is the agreement to take it. Since the law favors a compromise, courts try to uphold any good-faith modification agreement.

Anticipatory Repudiation

Suppose that A, who is one party to a contract, clearly manifests that she will not perform at the scheduled time. The other party, B, has a choice at common law. B may either sue immediately or ignore A's repudiation and wait for the day of performance. If B waits, A may change her mind and still perform according to the original contract. Under UCC section 2-610, the injured party may not wait until the day of performance. B may wait for a change of mind only for a commercially reasonable period of time after repudiation before taking action.

Warranties

A *warranty* is a contractual obligation that sets a standard by which performance of the contract is measured. If the warranties are created by the parties to the contract, they are *express*. Under UCC section 2-313, express warranties exist whenever a seller affirms facts or describes goods, makes a promise about the goods, or displays a sample model.

If warranties are imposed by law, they are *implied*. There are two types of implied warranties under UCC section 2-314 and section 2-315. (1) When a merchant sells goods that are reputed to be fit for the ordinary purpose for which they are intended and are of average quality and properly labeled and packaged, the merchant is bound by an *implied warranty of merchantability*. (2) When the seller has reason to know some particular (nonordinary) purpose for which the buyer has relied on the seller's skill or judgment in making a selection, the seller is bound by an *implied warranty of fitness* for a particular purpose.

Implied warranties may be disclaimed by a conspicuous disclaimer statement that the goods are being sold "as is." Once an express warranty is created, however, it cannot be disclaimed, and any attempt to do so is void. The Magnuson-Moss Federal Warranty Act is an act requiring that written warranties for consumer products be categorized as "full" or "limited" so that consumers know what type of warranty protection they are getting. In addition, under this act, a consumer may sue under both the federal and state warranties to recover actual damages.

Originally, a warranty was enforceable only by purchasers, but the trend has been to extend the warranty to nonbuyers (such as recipients of gifts) who have been injured by the defective product.

Discharge, Rescission, and Novation

A *discharge* from a duty to perform occurs because of objective impossibility, by operation of law, or by agreement. Thus one party may die or become physically incapable of performing, a statute may be passed that prevents a party from performing, or a duty to perform may be discharged in bankruptcy. Parties can also agree to end their contractual relationship through a rescission. In a *rescission* each party gives up its right to performance from the other; this constitutes sufficient consideration for the discharge. A *novation* occurs when a promisee agrees to release the original promisor from a duty and enters into a new agreement with another party.

Transfers of Duties and Rights

Sometimes one of the original parties to a contract decides to transfer its rights or duties to some third person who was not originally a party to the agreement. The transfer of rights is called an *assignment*, and the transfer of duties is called a *delegation*. An assignor assigns his or her rights to an assignee. For example, a creditor (the assignor) may decide to transfer her right to collect money owed by a debtor to a finance company (the assignee).

In another example, Smith may contract with a builder to construct a garage next to her house using the turnkey method of construction (this means that the developer finances and builds the garage and receives payment when it is completed). The builder would negotiate a bank loan to finance the project, and the bank probably would negotiate a requirement that the contractor transfer his rights to payment to the bank as security for the loan. A right is not assignable if it significantly affects the corresponding duty associated with that right. Thus Smith probably would not be permitted to assign her right (to have the builder construct a garage) to her sister who lives twenty miles away, since the added distance would be a significant detriment to the building contractor.

A person contractually obligated to perform a duty may often delegate that duty to a third person. If Smith contracts with a painter to paint her new garage, the painter could delegate that duty to other painters. A party cannot delegate a duty if there is a personal component involved such that the duty can only be performed by the party to the original agreement. For example, the personal component exists when a person contracts with a famous photographer to take her portrait. The photographer in this situation would not be permitted to delegate the duty to just any other photographer.

An assignee is legally responsible for any claims that were originally available against the assignor. Thus the debtor would be entitled to raise his or her defenses (such as capacity, duress, illegality, or mistake) against the finance agency that were available against the creditor. The rules are similarly strict vis-à-vis the delegation of a duty. Smith's painter would be responsible if the painter to whom he delegated the painting duty (painter #2) performed inadequately. If Smith agrees to a novation, however, the original contracting painter could be relieved of his duty to perform and painter #2 could be substituted.

Statutory provisions generally require that some assignments be in writing. Statutes also prohibit contractual restrictions on most assignments of rights. The following case illustrates what happens when one original contracting party assigns rights and delegates duties over the objection of the other contracting party.

Macke Company v. Pizza of Gaithersburg, Inc.
270 A.2d 645
Court of Appeals of Maryland
November 10, 1970

Singley, Judge

The appellees and defendants below, Pizza of Gaithersburg, Inc.; Pizzeria, Inc.; The Pizza Pie Corp., Inc. and Pizza Oven, Inc., four corporations under the common ownership of Sidney Ansell, Thomas S. Sherwood and Eugene Early and the same individuals as partners or proprietors (the Pizza Shops) operated at six locations in Montgomery and Prince George's Counties. The appellees had arranged to have installed in each of their locations cold drink vending machines owned by Virginia Coffee Service, Inc., and on 30 December 1966, this arrangement was formalized at five of the locations, by contracts for terms of one year, automatically renewable for a like term in the absence of 30 days' written notice. A similar contract for the sixth location, operated by Pizza of Gaithersburg, Inc., was entered into on 25 July 1967.

On 30 December 1967, Virginia's assets were purchased by The Macke Company (Macke) and the six contracts were assigned to Macke by Virginia. In January, 1968, the Pizza Shops attempted to terminate the five contracts having the December anniversary date, and in February, the contract which had the July anniversary date.

Macke brought suit in the Circuit Court for Montgomery County against each of the Pizza Shops for damages for breach of contract. From judgments for the defendants, Macke has appealed.

The lower court based the result which it reached on two grounds: first, that the Pizza Shops, when they contracted with Virginia, relied on its skill, judgment and reputation, which made impossible a delegation of Virginia's duties to Macke; and second, that the damages claimed could not be shown with reasonable certainty. These conclusions are challenged by Macke.

In the absence of a contrary provision — and there was none here—rights and duties under an executory bilateral contract may be assigned and delegated, subject to the exception that duties under a contract to provide personal services may never be delegated, nor rights be assigned under a contract where *delectus personae** was an ingredient of the bargain. . . .

The six machines were placed on the appellees' premises under a printed "Agreement-Contract" which identified the "customer," gave its place of business, described the vending machine, and then provided:

"TERMS

"1. The Company will install on the Customer's premises the above listed equipment in good operating order and stocked with merchandise.

Delectus personae means choice of person.—*Ed.*

"2. The location of this equipment will be such as to permit accessibility to persons desiring use of same. This equipment shall remain the property of the Company and shall not be moved from the location at which installed, except by the Company.

"3. For equipment requiring electricity and water, the Customer is responsible for electrical receptacle and water outlet within ten (10) feet of the equipment location. The Customer is also responsible to supply the Electrical Power and Water needed.

"4. The Customer will exercise every effort to protect this equipment from abuse or damage.

"5. The Company will be responsible for all licenses and taxes on the equipment and sale of products.

"6. This Agreement-Contract is for a term of one (1) year from the date indicated herein and will be automatically renewed for a like period, unless thirty (30) day written notice is given by either party to terminate service.

"7. Commission on monthly sales will be paid by the Company to the Customer at the following rate: . . . "

The rate provided in each of the agreements was "30% of Gross Receipts to $300.00 monthly[,] 35% over [$]300.00," except for the agreement with Pizza of Gaithersburg, Inc., which called for "40% of Gross Receipts."

. . . We cannot regard the agreements as contracts for personal services. They were either a license or concession granted Virginia by the appellees, or a lease of a portion of the appellees' premises, with Virginia agreeing to pay a percentage of gross sales as a license or concession fee or as rent, . . . and were assignable by Virginia unless they imposed on Virginia duties of a personal or unique character which could not be delegated. . . . [T]he agreements with Virginia were silent as to the details of the working

arrangements and contained only a provision requiring Virginia to "install . . . the above listed equipment and . . . maintain the equipment in good operating order and stocked with merchandise." . . . Moreover, the difference between the service the Pizza Shops happened to be getting from Virginia and what they expected to get from Macke did not mount up to such a material change in the performance of obligations under the agreements as would justify the appellees' refusal to recognize the assignment. . . . Modern authorities . . . hold that, absent provision to the contrary, a duty may be delegated, as distinguished from a right which can be assigned, and that the promisee cannot rescind, if the quality of the performance remains materially the same.

Restatement, Contracts § 160(3) (1932) reads, in part:

"Performance or offer of performance by a person delegated has the same legal effect as performance or offer of performance by the person named in the contract, unless,

"(a) performance by the person delegated varies or would vary materially from performance by the person named in the contract as the one to perform, and there has been no . . . assent to the delegation. . . ."

In cases involving the sale of goods, the Restatement rule respecting delegation of duties has been amplified by Uniform Commercial Code § 2-210(5), Maryland Code (1957, 1964 Repl.Vol.) Art 95B § 2-210(5), which permits a promisee to demand assurances from the party to whom duties have been delegated. . . .

As we see it, the delegation of duty by Virginia to Macke was entirely permissible under the terms of the agreements. . . .

Judgment reversed as to liability; judgment entered for appellant for costs, on appeal and below; case remanded for a new trial on the question of damages.

Case Questions

1. When the Virginia Coffee Service sold its assets to the Macke Company, what rights did it assign?
2. What duties were delegated?

Contracts for the Benefit of Third Parties

In some situations, the parties contract with a clear understanding that the agreement is intended to benefit some other, noncontracting person. For example, a son and daughter might contract with a carpenter to repair the back stairs at their elderly mother's house. In another case, a woman might have accidentally damaged a neighbor's fence and agreed to have the fence repaired. The woman might want to discharge this obligation by contracting with a carpenter to repair the damage.

The third person in the first example (the mother) is classified as a *donee beneficiary*, and the third person in the second example (the neighbor) is classified as a *creditor beneficiary*. American law generally permits donee beneficiaries and creditor beneficiaries to sue for breach of contract. The third party's right to sue, however, only exists if that party's rights have "vested," that is, have matured to the point of being legally enforceable. Jurisdictions generally choose one of the following three rules to decide when rights vest: (1) rights vest when the contract is formed, (2) rights vest when the beneficiary acquires knowledge about the contract, or (3) rights vest when the beneficiary relies on the contract and changes his or her position.

The following case illustrates the difficulties encountered by one claiming status as a third-party beneficiary.

Castorino v. Unifast Bldg. Products
555 N.Y.S.2d 350
Supreme Court, Appellate Division,
First Department
May 17, 1990

Memorandum Decision

Order, Supreme Court, New York County (Eugene L. Nardelli, J.), entered November 30, 1988, denying, without prejudice to renewal following discovery, defendant Unifast Building Products Corp.'s motion for summary judgment dismissing plaintiff's amended complaint and all cross-claims against it, unanimously modified, on the law, to dismiss the amended complaint against said defendant, and, except as so modified, affirmed, without costs or disbursements.

In this wrongful death action it is alleged that plaintiff's decedent was assaulted and murdered in her apartment by someone who gained entry either through a window which did not have locking devices or which did not have locking devices in proper working condition. Liability against defendant appellant Unifast, which had contracted with defendant DCI Contracting Corp. to supply and install windows throughout the apartment building in which decedent resided, is predicated on a claim that the window locking mechanisms were defective and that the windows could not be properly closed or locked.

Unifast moved for summary judgment, arguing, *inter alia*, that plaintiff could not recover on a theory of contractual liability since it had no contract with plaintiff's decedent, nor was decedent an intended beneficiary of any contract between Unifast and the landlord. In addition, Unifast urged that there could be no recovery in tort since Unifast had not undertaken any duty to decedent in agreeing to supply windows to the building in which she resided. Finding a question as to whether Unifast owed a duty to the decedent, the [trial] court denied summary judgment, without prejudice to renewal following discovery, since it could not yet be determined whether the windows were manufactured and delivered in a defective condition.

In view of the broad "hold harmless [clause]" included in the contract between Unifast and DCI, the only party whose cross-claims appear in the record, we agree with the [trial] court insofar as it denied Unifast's motion for summary judgment dismissing the cross-claims against it. However, since we find no basis, under principles of either contract or tort law, for a finding of liability against Unifast, we modify to grant Unifast's motion and dismiss the complaint against it.

Plaintiff predicates Unifast's contractual liability on an assertion that the decedent was an intended beneficiary of the contract between Unifast and DCI, the landlord's general contractor. While the law is settled that an intended beneficiary may maintain an action as a third party for breach of contract,

he must establish "(1) the existence of a valid and binding contract between the parties, (2) that the contract was intended for his benefit and (3) that the benefit to him is sufficiently immediate, rather than incidental, to indicate the assumption by the contracting parties of a duty to compensate him if the benefit is lost." . . . Since there is nothing in the subcontract between Unifast and DCI which "evince[s] a discernible intent to allow recovery for the specified damages to the third party that result[ed] from a breach thereof," no cause of action against Unifast can be maintained.

Einhorn v. Seeley, . . . 525 N.Y.S.2d 212, . . . also mandates the conclusion that this theory is unavailable here. *Einhorn* was a personal injury action in which plaintiff was allegedly assaulted and raped in an apartment building and sued, *inter alia*, a locksmith, on a theory that it had improperly installed or repaired the lock on the front door of the building, through which the assailant might have gained access to the premises. We held that the action was "not maintainable in contract on a third-party beneficiary theory since plaintiffs were, at most, incidental rather than intended beneficiaries of any agreement between the landlord and [the locksmith]."

Nor, under *Einhorn*, can defendant be held liable in tort. Rejecting plaintiff's claim against the locksmith for tort liability, the *Einhorn* court held that the locksmith did not undertake a duty to the injured plaintiff when it entered into its relationship with the landlord: "Here we are concerned with a possible liability for an injury to a mere guest of a tenant caused by an unlawful act of a third party. Under these circumstances, to hold a locksmith responsible for the alleged consequences of an allegedly defective lock would be to enlarge the obligations of such artisans far beyond the existing law and beyond sound public policy." . . . Similarly, it would be an unacceptable extension of existing law to hold the supplier/installer of windows responsible for the alleged consequences of an allegedly defective window locking mechanism. It is "the responsibility of courts, in fixing the orbit of duty, 'to limit the legal consequences of wrongs to a controllable degree' [citations omitted], and to protect against crushing exposure to liability [citations omitted]. . . . The courts' definition of an orbit of duty based on public policy may at times result in the exclusion of some who might otherwise have recovered for losses or injuries if traditional tort principles had been applied." . . .

The fact that in this case plaintiff's decedent was a resident of the building in which the attack occurred, while the injured plaintiff in *Einhorn* was merely a guest of a tenant—and was explicitly referred to as such . . . —

does not warrant a contrary conclusion. The decision in *Einhorn* turned not on the fact that plaintiff was a guest but on the rule that "[t]here will ordinarily be no duty thrust on a defendant to prevent a third party from causing harm to another."* . . . It is clear that the result would have been no different if plaintiff had been a tenant.

*An exception to this rule "may occur in the case where a special relationship exists between the defendant and the third person so as to give rise to a duty to control, or alternatively, when a special relationship exists between the defendant and the victim which gives the latter the right to protection [citation omitted]" (*Einhorn, supra.* . . .). This exception is inapplicable here, however, since there is nothing in the record to support the claim in plaintiff's brief that the assailant "is believed to be an employee, contractor, or agent of [Unifast] or its agents."

Case Questions

1. Why did the appellate court reverse the trial court's grant of summary judgment in favor of the defendants?
2. Common law courts were historically opposed to recognizing any third-party rights. Based on your knowledge of contract fundamentals, why do you think there was such judicial resistance?

The Duty to Perform and Breach of Contract

Many agreements include conditions precedent and conditions subsequent that may affect a party's duty to perform. A *condition precedent* exists when some specified event must occur before a duty to perform becomes operative (i.e., obtain a mortgage at a specified rate of interest). A *condition subsequent* exists when a specified event occurs that discharges the parties from their duties.

A breach of contract occurs when a party fails to perform a duty, or inadequately performs what he or she has promised. A breach of contract is a material breach if the nonperforming party totally or substantially fails to perform. Thus a material breach has occurred if a homeowner contracts with a painter to paint a house with two coats of primer and one finish coat, and the painter quits after painting one coat of primer. The homeowner has not received the substantial benefit of his or her bargain.

In the next case an exterminating company breached its contract with a homeowner through inadequate performance of its duty.

Clarkson v. Orkin Exterminating Co., Inc.
761 F.2d 189
U.S. Court of Appeals, Fourth Circuit
May 9, 1985

Haynsworth, Senior Circuit Judge

A jury awarded the plaintiff damages on three separate claims. She claimed breach of a contract to inspect for termites and to treat again if necessary. There was a claim of fraud and of a violation of South Carolina's Unfair Trade Practices Act. § 39–0(a), Code of Laws of South Carolina, 1976.

There was adequate proof that Orkin broke its contract, though an improper measure of damages was applied. There is no evidence in the record, however, to support the finding of fraud or a violation of the Unfair Trade Practices Act. Hence, we reverse in part and affirm in part, but remand the contract claim for an appropriate assessment of damages.

I

In 1976 Mrs. Clarkson purchased a house. Orkin had contracted with her predecessor in title to retreat the house in the event that a termite problem developed. Orkin also promised, for a fee, to inspect the house yearly and, if necessary, retreat it for termites before certifying that the house remained free of termites.

In early 1983, Mrs. Clarkson offered her home for sale. When prospective purchasers noticed evidence of termite infestation, Mrs. Clarkson called Orkin and requested that they inspect the house. Orkin complied with her request and issued a report that the house was free of termites. The report also mentioned the presence of a moisture problem, which had been reported to Mrs. Clarkson on several earlier occasions but which remained uncorrected. For the moisture problem, Orkin had unsuccessfully attempted to sell a protective chemical treatment to Mrs. Clarkson.

The day after Orkin's 1983 inspection, Mrs. Clarkson had the house inspected by the representative of another exterminating company. He found two termite tunnels and damage from water. He attributed the water damage to a drainage problem and expressed the opinion that the water damage would progress unless there were alterations to a porch to prevent drainage of water into the basement.

After a contractor had made the necessary repairs and the recommended alterations, Mrs. Clarkson sought to have Orkin reimburse her for her entire cost of the reconstruction work. She also asked that Orkin reinspect the house and certify that the house was free of termite infestation. Orkin refused both requests.

A jury awarded Mrs. Clarkson $613.47 on the breach of contract claim, $551 on the Unfair Trade Practices Act Claim and $1,148 actual damages and $5,000 punitive damages on the fraud claim. The district judge concluded that the Unfair Trade Practices Act claim was a willful one and tripled the award on that claim and ordered Orkin to pay the plaintiff's attorneys' fees.

II

As proof of a violation of the South Carolina Unfair Trade Practices Act, Mrs. Clarkson points (1) to the fact that Orkin certified in 1983 that the house was free of termites when significant infestation was visible, and (2) the fact that Orkin on several occasions had attempted, though unsuccessfully, to sell to Mrs. Clarkson a "moisture problem treatment package" that would not have been an adequate corrective of an improper drainage problem.

It is abundantly clear that in its 1983 inspection Orkin's representative failed to discover termite infestation which was present and visible. This, however, does not establish a violation of the South Carolina Unfair Trade Practices Act. It shows no more than that Orkin's representative was negligent or incompetent. Mrs. Clarkson had not directed his attention to the area where the infestation was present, though she did direct the attention of the other exterminator to that area. . . .

III

There is enough to support a finding of contract violation. Orkin failed to retreat the house when a termite infestation was present, and it refused Mrs. Clarkson's subsequent request that it reinspect and spray the house after the repairs had been made.

There is no claim that Mrs. Clarkson lost an opportunity to sell the house because of the termite problem. What she claimed was the cost of repairs and alterations. On the breach of contract claim, the jury assessed the damaged at $613.47, which was precisely the cost to Mrs. Clarkson of replacing the wood damaged by the termites. In effect, the jury converted Orkin's retreatment contract into a repair contract.

Orkin offers its customers alternatives. It will promise and guarantee to provide retreatment if there is a later termite infestation. For a higher fee, it will promise and guarantee to effect necessary repairs after a termite infes-

tation has occurred. Mrs. Clarkson's predecessor in title, and she, elected to take the lower option. In Orkin's guarantee to Mrs. Clarkson, there is an express recital of her waiver and release of Orkin from any liability for damage to the structure occasioned by termites. Mrs. Clarkson cannot now claim the benefits of a repair guarantee she chose not to purchase.

Mrs. Clarkson was entitled to a proper performance by Orkin of its contract, which was to inspect and treat again if an infestation was found. That promise was not properly performed, and Mrs. Clarkson is entitled to any damage she suffered by reason of that non-performance. Since she knew of the termite infestation one day after Orkin failed to detect it, her damage would apparently be limited to the cost of inspection by the other exterminator plus the cost of any retreatment she may have procured.

While we agree that the evidence supports a finding of a breach of contract, we remand that claim for further proceedings on damages as may be consistent with this opinion. Judgment in the plaintiff's favor on the unfair trade practice and fraud claims is reversed.

Reversed in part; Affirmed in part, and remanded.

Case Questions

1. In what way did Orkin breach its duty?
2. Why did the court remand the breach of contract claim for further proceedings?

REMEDIES FOR BREACH OF CONTRACT

An injured party who has established a breach of contract is entitled to turn to a court for legal or equitable relief, as discussed in Chapter 7.

Common Law Remedies

In most cases of breach, the injured party is awarded money damages which can be compensatory, nominal, or liquidated.

The following case involves breach of contract claims between homeowners and a building contractor. The homeowners discharged the contractor because of defective work. The contractor filed suit against the homeowners to recover the damages. The Maine Supreme Court vacated the trial court's judgment on the counterclaim because of errors in the jury instructions regarding damages.

Anuszewski v. Jurevic
566 A.2d 742
Supreme Judicial Court of Maine
November 28, 1989

Clifford, Justice

Defendants and counterclaim plaintiffs Richard and Judy Jurevic appeal from a judgment entered after a jury trial in Superior Court.... Because we conclude that the court improperly limited the jury's consideration of damages claimed by the Jurevics, we vacate the judgment on the counterclaim.

In early 1987, the Jurevics contracted with the plaintiff, Robert E. Anuszewski, a contractor doing business as Pine Tree Post & Beam, for Anuszewski to construct a home for the Jurevics in Kennebunkport. The home was to be completed by June 1, 1987, at a cost of $134,000, and the contract called for the Jurevics to make periodic progress payments. The home was only about fifty percent complete on June 1, 1987. In January, 1988, the Jurevics discharged Anuszewski. In March, 1988, Anuszewski brought an action against the Jurevics to recover $39,590.* The Jurevics filed a counterclaim.

At trial, the Jurevics presented evidence that the construction work was defective and testimony in the form of an expert opinion as to the total cost to correct the defects and to complete the house. The testimony indicated that this cost would include a general contrac-

tor markup of fifty percent added to the actual cost of the work to be done for overhead and profit, and that this was a usual and customary practice of the industry. The Jurevics also claimed damages for rental and other incidental expenses caused by Anuszewski's delay in completing the house. The court, however, prohibited the Jurevics from presenting evidence of delay damages beyond January 5, 1988, the date the Jurevics terminated the contract with Anuszewski.

At the conclusion of the evidence, the court, in its jury instructions, precluded the jury from considering the general contractor's markup as follows:

> "[I]f you find that the Jurevics are entitled to recover damages from Mr. Anuszewski for completion of the work not done or for repairing work not performed in a workmanlike manner, any amount of damages that you award must be the cost of doing that work by the various workmen without any markup to a general contractor, such as was testified to by [the Jurevics' expert witness]."

The jury returned a verdict awarding Anuszewski damages of $25,000 on his complaint and awarding $22,000 to the Jurevics on their counterclaim. This appeal by the Jurevics followed the denial of their motions for a mistrial, or in the alternative, for a new trial, and for additur.

We find merit in the Jurevics' contention that the court impermissibly restricted the jury's consideration of the full amount of damages that they were entitled to recover. The purpose of contract damages is to place the injured parties in the position they would have been in but for the breach, by awarding

---

*The $39,500 represented, alternatively, the unpaid part of the contract price, or the value of the labor and materials provided by Anuszewski for which he had not been paid.

the value of the promised performance. . . . Those damages for breach of a construction contract are measured by either the difference in value between the performance promised and the performance rendered, or the amount reasonably required to remedy the defect. . . . The amount reasonably required to remedy the defect may be measured by the *actual* cost of necessary repairs. . . . Those costs may be proven by the presentation of expert testimony, as the Jurevics did here. . . .

The court correctly instructed the jury that the Jurevics' measure of recovery for incomplete or defective work was "the amount reasonably required to remedy the defect" as specifically measured by the actual cost of repair. . . . The court went on, however, to instruct the jury that the cost of repair was to be considered "without any markup to a general contractor." This instruction was given despite testimony from an expert witness that the actual cost to remedy the incomplete and defective construction work of Anuszewski would include a general contractor markup for overhead and profit, and that such a markup was customary and usual in the construction business. Although Anuszewski defends the court's instruction, he did not argue at trial, nor does he now, that the Jurevics were not entitled to have the jury consider their claim that it was reasonable for them to hire a general contractor to supervise the repairs and completion of the house. If the jury concluded that it would be reasonable for the Jurevics to hire a substitute general contractor to supervise the repairs and completion, but was precluded by the court's instruction from considering the award of damages for the reasonable cost of the substitute contractor's overhead, for which the evidence suggests they would be charged as a matter of routine, then the Jurevics could be deprived of full recovery in their breach of contract claim. They would not be placed in the same position they would have been had Anuszewski performed the contract. . . .

In breach of contract cases we have upheld repair or replacement damage awards of the amount required to bring a home into compliance with the contract. . . . In addition, we have affirmed the computation of indebtedness owed a builder by a homeowner that included a contractor's overhead and profit. . . . We see no reason to exclude reasonable and customary profit and overhead of a contractor from the cost of repairs to remedy defects in a breach of contract case.

The entry is:

Judgment on the complaint affirmed. Judgment on the counterclaim vacated.

Remanded to the Superior Court for further proceedings consistent with the opinion herein.

Case Questions

1. According to the Jurevics, what error was committed by the trial judge?
2. What is a counterclaim?

Punitive Damages

You may recall from Chapter 7 that punitive damages are awarded in tort cases to punish defendants for their wanton, reckless, malicious, or oppressive conduct and to deter others from similar antisocial conduct. Traditionally, punitive damages have not been awarded in contract cases. A few courts will deviate from the traditional rule when certain types of contractual breaches have been proven:

1. Breaches that are accompanied by an independent tort (such as where an employee sues her employer for wrongful discharge from employment and slander)
2. Breaches where the conduct that establishes the breach independently establishes a common law tort (such as where a malicious or wanton breach of contract causes the plaintiff to suffer emotional distress)
3. Breaches of insurance contracts by insurance companies
4. Breaches that involve fraud, malice, gross negligence, or oppression, where the public interest would be advanced by the deterrent effect resulting from the imposition of punitive damages (as in the following case)

Hibschman Pontiac, Inc. v. Batchelor
362 N.E.2d 845
Supreme Court of Indiana
May 13, 1977

Givan, Chief Justice

Batchelor brought an action for breach of contract and oppressive conduct by Hibschman Pontiac, Inc. and General Motors Corporation. A trial before a jury resulted in a verdict for Batchelor and against Hibschman Pontiac and General Motors Corporation in the amount of $1,500.00. Further, the jury assessed punitive damages against Hibschman Pontiac, Inc. in the amount of $15,000.00.

The Court of Appeals, Third District, reversed the grant of punitive damages. . . . Batchelor now petitions for transfer.

The record reveals the following evidence: Prior to buying the Pontiac GTO automobile involved in this case, Batchelor inquired of the salesman, the service manager and the vice president as to the quality of Hibschman Pontiac's service department, as it was important that any deficiencies in the car be corrected. The salesman and the service manager responded that the service department at Hibschman Pontiac was above average. Jim Hibschman, the vice president,

assured him that he would personally see that any difficulties would be corrected. Batchelor stated that he relied on the statements of the three men and ordered a 1969 GTO Pontiac automobile.

When Batchelor picked up the new car he discovered several problems with it. As requested by the service manager of Hibschman Pontiac, Batchelor made a list of his complaints and brought the car in for repair a few days later. The service manager attached the list to a work order but did not list the deficiencies on the work order. Later the manager called Batchelor and said that the car was ready. When he picked up the car Batchelor noticed that several items on the list had not been touched. Batchelor testified that there were many occasions when he took the car to Hibschman Pontiac for repairs and the service manager told him that the defects had been fixed when in fact they were not fixed. Batchelor testified that the service manager knew the defects were not corrected, but represented to him that the defects were corrected. Batchelor stated that he relied on the service manager's statements and took the car on several trips, only to have it break down. Some of the deficiencies resulted in abnormal wear of the car and breakdowns after the warranty period had expired.

Batchelor testified that he had taken the car in for repairs five times before he had owned it a month but that the defects had not been corrected. Batchelor had taken the car in 12 times during the warranty period for overnight repair and at least 20 times in all during the period. During the warranty period Batchelor lost use of the car approximately 45 days while it was at Hibschman Pontiac.

Batchelor had appealed to Jim Hibschman on several occasions to take care of his car. Hibschman replied that he realized the repairs were not effected properly but that Hibschman Pontiac would "do everything to get you happy." On another occasion Jim Hibschman responded they had done all they could with the car but that Batchelor was just a particular, habitual complainer whom they could not satisfy and "I would rather you would just leave and not come back. We are going to have to write you off as a bad customer."

On several occasions Batchelor attempted to see Dan Shaules, an area service representative from Pontiac Division, about the car but was kept waiting so long that he had to leave without seeing him. Batchelor did see Shaules in Buchanan, Michigan, when he took the car to an authorized Pontiac dealer there after the warranty had expired. Shaules inspected the car and told Batchelor to return the car to Hibschman Pontiac for repairs.

Hugh Haverstock, the owner of the garage where several of the deficiencies were corrected after the expiration of the warranty, testified that Batchelor was a good customer and paid his bills. He stated that an average transmission man could have corrected the problem with the transmission and that a problem with the timing was discovered and corrected when a tune-up lasted only 800 miles. Haverstock stated that the difference in value of the car without defects and with the defects it had was approximately $1,500.00. Haverstock testified that when a person complains about problems with cars that have not

been fixed by dealerships, word gets out and others do not want to work on the cars.

Arnold Miexel, the service manager for Hibschman Pontiac during the time in question, testified that his representation to Batchelor regarding Hibschman Pontiac service department was based on the fact that the mechanics were factory trained and that he had received no complaints regarding their work. He further stated that he could not check the work of the mechanics. Miexel testified that if their work was unsatisfactory it was done over but no work order was written for it. He stated that it was possible that Batchelor made complaints about the car, but the defects were not corrected. The warranty expired and, as a consequence, later work was not considered under warranty.

Dan Shaules testified that Miexel was an average service manager. He testified that not all of the deficiencies in the car were corrected properly. He further stated that if any defects in the car were brought to their attention within the warranty period, items would be corrected if necessary after the warranty had expired.

Appellant first argues that there was insufficient evidence to permit the issue of punitive damages to go to the jury and that the court should have rendered a directed verdict on the issue of punitive damages on behalf of Hibschman Pontiac. This Court has recently dealt with the question of punitive damages in a contract action. In *Vernon Fire & Casualty Ins. Co. v. Sharp* (1976) . . . the majority restated the general provision that punitive damages are not recoverable in contract actions and went on to state exceptions to this rule. Where the conduct of a party, in breaching his contract, independently establishes the elements of a common law tort, punitive damages may be awarded for the tort.

Punitive damages may be awarded in addition to compensatory damages "whenever the elements of fraud, malice, gross negligence or oppression *mingle* in the controversy." (Emphasis supplied.)

Further, where a separate tort accompanies the breach or the elements of tort mingle with the breach, it must appear that the public interest will be served by the deterrent effect of the punitive damages.

Appellant urges that the evidence presented does not indicate tortious conduct of any sort on its part. While a reasonable inference could be made from the evidence that appellant merely attempted to fulfill its contract and to do not more than that contract required, it is also reasonable to infer that Hibschman Pontiac acted tortiously and in willful disregard of the right of Batchelor. This Court has often stated the maxim that it will not reweigh the evidence nor determine the credibility of witnesses, but will sustain a verdict if there is any evidence of probative value to support it. . . .

A corporation can act only through its agents, and their acts, when done within the scope of their authority, are attributable to the corporation. . . .

Here, the jury could reasonably have found elements of fraud, malice, gross negligence or oppression mingled into the breach of warranty. The evidence showed that requested repairs were not satisfactorily completed although covered by the warranty and capable of correction. Some of these defects were clearly breaches of warranty. Paint was bubbled, the radio never worked properly, the hood and bumper were twisted and misaligned, the universal joints failed, the transmission linkage was improperly adjusted, the timing chain was defective causing improper tune-ups and the carburetor was defective, among other things. Batchelor took the car to the defendant with a list of defects on numerous occasions and picked up the car when told

it was "all ready to go." It was reasonable to infer that the defendant's service manager represented repairs to have been made when he knew that the work had not been done and that in reliance on his representations, Batchelor drove the car on trips and had breakdowns. Before purchasing the car Batchelor was given special representations on the excellence of Hibschman's service department, and the jury could find that Batchelor relied on these in buying the car from the defendant. After having brought the car in on numerous occasions, Batchelor was told by Jim Hibschman, "I would rather you would just leave and not come back. We are going to have to write you off as a bad customer." And he was told by one of Hibschman's mechanics that, "If you don't get on them and get this fixed, they will screw you around and you will never get it done." From these statements the jury could infer that the defendant was attempting to avoid making certain repairs by concealing them during the period of the warranty. Batchelor gave the defendant numerous opportunities to repair the car and the defendant did not do so; instead he tried to convince Batchelor that the problems were not with the car, but rather with Batchelor. We are of the opinion that in this case the jury could have found there was cogent proof to establish malice, fraud, gross negligence and oppressive conduct.

Although fraudulent conduct was not alleged in the complaint, evidence on the subject was admitted. Any inconsistency between the pleadings and proof will be resolved in favor of the proof at trial. . . . Thus there was probative evidence supporting the claim for punitive damages. The trial court did not err in denying a directed verdict as to that issue. . . .

Case Questions

1. Under what conditions can punitive damages be allowed for breach of contract in Indiana?

2. Why do you think courts have been so resistant to the award of punitive damages for routine breaches of contract?

Equitable Remedies

If money damages are deemed to be an inadequate remedy, the court may be persuaded to grant equitable relief. The discussion in Chapter 7 addresses the most common forms of equitable relief in breach of contract cases (injunctions, restitution after the court has granted rescission, and specific performance).

UCC Remedies for Breach of Contract for the Sale of Goods

The Uniform Commercial Code provides special rules for breaches of contracts involving the sale of goods. For example, if a seller breaches his or her contract to deliver goods, the buyer is entitled to (1) rescind the contract, (2) sue for damages, and (3) obtain restitution for any payments made. If the goods are unique such as rare artwork, or custom-made, a court may order specific performance. Replevin also is permitted in some situations. If a buyer breaches a sales contract by not accepting delivery of goods, or wrongfully revokes a prior acceptance, the injured seller is entitled to (1) cancel the contract, (2) stop delivery of goods, and (3) recover money damages from the buyer.

Chapter Questions

1. Define the following terms:

acceptance	offer
accord	option
assignee	parol evidence rule
assignor	promisee
bilateral contract	promisor
breach of contract	rescission
capacity	satisfaction
condition precedent	statute of frauds
condition subsequent	undue influence
consideration	unenforceable
creditor beneficiary	Uniform Commercial Code
discharge	unilateral contract
donee beneficiary	void
duress	voidable
fraud	warranty
novation	

2. Paul Searles, a former basketball player at St. Joseph's College, brought suit against the college, the basketball coach, and the trainer for breach of contract and negligence. Searles alleged that he had sustained basketball-related injuries to his knees and that St. Joseph's had orally contracted to reimburse him for his basketball-related medical costs. Searles asserted in his complaint that the college had promised to pay his medical expenses if he continued to play for the team. His proof was a statement that the coach had approached Searles's parents after a game and expressed a willingness to pay for all of the medical bills. Given the above factual record, does Searles have a contract with St. Joseph's College?

   Searles v. Trustees of St. Joseph's College, 695 A.2d 1206 (1997)

3. S. Allen Schreiber, having tired of receiving unsolicited phone calls from telemarketers in general, received such a call on November 29, 1989, from Olan Mills, a national family portrait chain. Schreiber promptly sent a "Dear Telemarketer" letter to the defendant.

   > Dear Telemarketer:
   >
   > Today, you called us attempting to sell us a product or a service. We have no interest in the product or service that you are selling. Please don't call us again. Please remove us from your telemarketing list and notify the provider of the list to also remove our name and number since we do not appreciate receiving telemarketing phone calls.
   >
   > We rely on the availability of our phone lines which have been installed for our convenience and not for the convenience of telemarketers. We pay for these phone lines and instruments. You do not. Please don't tie up our phone lines.
   >
   > Should we receive any more calls from you or from anyone connected with your firm of a telemarketing nature, we will consider that you have entered into a contract with us for our listening services and that you have made those calls to us and expect us to listen to your message on a "for hire" basis.
   >
   > If we receive any additional telemarketing phone calls from you, you will be invoiced in accordance with our rates which are $100.00 per hour or fraction thereof with a minimum charge. Payment will be due on a net seven (7) day basis.
   >
   > Late payment charge of 1½% per month or fraction thereof on the unpaid balance subject to a minimum late charge of $9.00 per invoice per month or fraction thereof will be billed if payment is not made as outlined above. This is an annual percentage rate of 18%. In addition, should it become necessary for us to institute collection activities, all costs in connection therewith including, but not limited to, attorney fees will also be due and collectible.

   Olan Mill representatives made two additional calls, which resulted in the instant breach of contract suit. Did Olan Mills enter into an enforceable contract with Schreiber?

   Schreiber v. Olan Mills, 627 A.2d 806 (1993)

4. George and Mary Jane Graham were driving in a car insured by State Farm when they were forced off the road by an unidentified motorist. The Graham's vehicle struck a telephone pole and both occupants were injured.

When the Grahams were unable to reach an agreement with their insurer regarding the amount they should be paid pursuant to the uninsured motorist provisions of their automobile insurance policy, they filed suit against State Farm. State Farm responded with a motion for summary judgment on the grounds that the policy called for binding arbitration in lieu of litigation in the event of such a dispute. The Grahams did not know about the arbitration clause at the time they paid the first premium. State Farm pointed out that the Grahams, after receiving a copy of the policy, never complained about the arbitration clause at any time during the following two years. The Grahams responded that this was a "take it or leave it" situation, under which they actually had no opportunity to "leave it" because they were denied the information necessary to make a decision at the time they enrolled with State Farm. The court, they contended, should not compel them to arbitrate their claim. They pointed out that this contract was drafted by the insurance company's lawyers and that the terms were written in a one-sided manner, permitting the powerful insurance company to take advantage of weaker insureds such as the Grahams. Delaware public policy favors the use of arbitration to resolve disputes in situations such as this. Should the court enforce the arbitration clause?

Gram v. State Farm Mutual Co., 565 A.2d 908 (1989)

5. Mr. Lucy and Mr. Zehmer were talking at a restaurant. After a couple of drinks, Lucy asked Zehmer if he had sold the Ferguson farm. Zehmer replied that he had not and did not want to sell it. Lucy said, "I bet you wouldn't take $50,000 cash for that farm," and Zehmer replied, "You haven't got $50,000 cash." Lucy said, "I can get it." Zehmer said he might form a company and get it, "but you haven't got $50,000 to pay me tonight." Lucy asked him if he would put it in writing that he would sell him this farm. Zehmer then wrote on the back of a pad, "I agree to sell the Ferguson Place to W. O. Lucy for $50,000 cash." Lucy said, "All right, get your wife to sign it." Zehmer subsequently went to his wife and said, "You want to put your name to this?" She said no, but he said in an undertone, "It is nothing but a joke," and she signed it. At that time, Zehmer was not too drunk to make a valid contract. The Zehmers refused to convey legal title to the property, and Lucy sued for specific performance. What defense would the Zehmers use in the suit? Who should win the suit?

Lucy v. Zehmer, 196 Va. 493, 84 S.E.2d 516 (1954)

6. National Beverages, Inc., offered to the public prizes to be awarded in a contest known as "Pepsi-Cola Streator-Chevrolet Sweepstakes." The first prize was a Chevrolet Corvair. No order of drawing was announced prior to the close of the contest. After the close of the contest, just prior to the drawing, a sign was displayed stating the order of drawing. The first tickets drawn would receive twelve cases of Pepsi-Cola, and the last ticket drawn would receive the automobile. Walters' ticket was the first ticket to be drawn from the barrel. She claims that her number, being the first qualified number drawn, entitles her to the first prize, the Chevrolet Corvair. She bases her

claim on the wording of the offer, which listed the automobile as the first prize. She accepted the offer by entering the contest. Is Walters entitled to the automobile?

Walters v. National Beverages, Inc., 18 Utah 2d 301, 422 P.2d 524 (1967)

7. Green signed a roofing contract with Clay Tile, agent for Ever-Tite Roofing Company, to have a new roof put on his house. The agreement stated that this contract was subject to Ever-Tite's approval and that the agreement would become binding upon written notice of acceptance or commencement of work. Nine days later, Clay Tile loaded up his truck and drove to Green's house, only to find that someone else was already doing the job. Ever-Tite wishes to sue on the contract for damages. Was Green's offer to Ever-Tite accepted before the offer was revoked?

Ever-Tite Roofing Corporation v. Green, 83 So.2d 449 (La.App. 1955)

8. Workers agreed to work aboard a canning ship during the salmon canning season. The contract, signed individually by each worker, was to last for the length of time it took to sail from San Francisco to Pyramid Harbor, Alaska, and back. Each worker was to receive a stated compensation. They arrived in Alaska at the height of the fishing and canning season. Knowing that every day's delay would be financially disastrous and that it would be impossible to find workers to replace them, the workers refused to work unless they were given substantial wage increases. The owner of the canning ship acceded to their demands. When the ship returned to San Francisco, the owner paid them in accordance with the original agreement. The workers now bring suit to recover the additional amounts due under the second agreement. Will the contract be upheld?

Alaska Packers Association v. Domenico, 117 F.99 (9th Cir. 1902)

9. A little girl found a pretty stone about the size of a canary bird's egg. She had no idea what it was, so she took it to a jeweler, who eventually bought it from her for a dollar, although he too did not know what it was. The stone turned out to be an uncut diamond worth $10,000. The girl tendered back the $1 purchase price and sued to have the sale voided on the basis of mutual mistake. Should mutual mistake be a basis for recovery?

Wood v. Boynton, 64 Wis. 265, 25 N.W. 42 (1885)

10. William E. Story agreed orally with his nephew that if he would refrain from drinking liquor, using tobacco, swearing, and playing cards or billiards for money until he became twenty-one years old, then he, Story, would pay his nephew $5,000 when the nephew reached age twenty-one. The nephew fully performed his part of the agreement. But when he reached age twenty-one, his uncle stated that he had earned the $5,000 and that he would keep it at interest for his nephew. Twelve years later, Story died, and his nephew brought an action to recover the $5,000 plus interest. Was there sufficient consideration to create a contract?

Hamer v. Sidway, 124 N.Y. 538, 27 N.E. 256 (1891)

11. The Kentucky Bankers Association provided a reward of $500 for the arrest and conviction of each bank robber. Three armed men robbed First State Bank. Later in the day, they were apprehended and placed under arrest by three policemen. Two of the policemen were from the county of the bank, and the other was from a neighboring county and out of his jurisdiction. Four employees of the bank gave the officers the details of the crime and described the culprits. The information was used in capturing the robbers. After the conviction of the robbers, the employees of the bank and the policemen wanted to share in the reward. Who would be entitled to the reward?

    Denney v. Reppert, 432 S.W. 647 (Ky. 1968)

12. Robert Rogers turned seventeen, quit high school, and married his home-town sweetheart. To provide her with the style of life with which she had become accustomed, Robert went out in search of employment. He signed an agreement with the Gastonia Personnel Corporation, agreeing to pay a commission of $293 if it was successful in procuring him a job. Gastonia found him a job, but Robert refuses to pay and denies liability on the grounds of minority. Can he avoid payment on this ground?

    Gastonia Personnel Corporation v. Rogers, 276 N.C. 279, 172 S.E.2d 19 (1970)

Notes

1. W. Walsh, *A History of Anglo-American Law* (Indianapolis: Bobbs-Merrill Company, 1932), p. 339; A. W. B. Simpson, *A History of the Common Law of Contract* (Oxford: Clarendon Press, 1975), pp. 12, 53; A. K. R. Kiralfy, *Potter's Historical Introduction to English Law* (London: Sweet and Maxwell Ltd., 1962), pp. 452–457.
2. Kiralfy, p. 456.
3. Ibid., pp. 456–457.
4. Ibid., pp. 305–307; Walsh, p. 344.
5. Walsh, p. 342.
6. Simpson, p. 199; Walsh, p. 344.
7. Simpson, p. 210; Kiralfy, p. 461; Walsh, p. 341.
8. Walsh, p. 340; Simpson, p. 224; T. F. F. Plucknett, *A Concise History of the Common Law.* (Little Brown, 1956) p. 639.
9. Walsh, pp. 345, 351; Simpson, p. 406; Plucknett, pp. 649–656.
10. Kiralfy, p. 626.
11. B. Schwartz, *The Law in America* (New York: McGraw-Hill, 1974), pp. 59–62; W. E. Nelson, *Americanization of the Common Law* (Cambridge: Harvard University Press, 1975), p. 86.
12. M. Horwitz, *The Transformation of American Law, 1780–1860* (Cambridge: Harvard University Press, 1977), pp. 164–180; Nelson, p. 154.
13. Horwitz, pp. 167, 173.
14. Schwartz, p. 72; Nelson, p. 86.
15. Horwitz, p. 185.

XI The Law of Torts

A tort is a civil wrong other than a breach of contract for which courts provide a remedy in the form of an action for damages. Tort law seeks to provide reimbursement to members of society who suffer losses because of the dangerous or unreasonable conduct of others. Each of the fifty states determines its own tort law, which is divided into the following three categories: intentional torts, negligence, and strict liability.

You may recall from Figure 1-2 and the accompanying discussion in Chapter 1, that there are important differences between criminal law and tort law. It was there emphasized that criminal prosecutions are brought by the government to convict and then punish offenders who have committed crimes and thereby harmed society as a whole. You should also remember that the constitution provides defendants in criminal cases with procedural protections that are unavailable in civil litigation. Nevertheless, it is possible for criminal defendants to be sued civilly irrespective of the outcome of a criminal trial. Many readers will recall, for example, that O. J. Simpson was charged with murder and, after a criminal trial, acquitted by the jury. The wrongful death civil action brought by the families against Mr. Simpson is not as well remembered. The state prosecuted Mr. Simpson because it believed he had committed murder under the criminal laws of the state and was deserving of punishment. The families brought their civil actions to obtain compensation for the loss of their loved ones. His acquittal of the criminal charges did not preclude the civil action.

In the civil trial, unlike the criminal prosecution, Simpson was obligated to answer questions at a deposition hearing and testify at trial. He could not remain silent, as he did at the criminal trial. The double jeopardy clause would prevent the government from bringing a second prosecution against Simpson for murder based on his civil testimony. Thus his civil testimony about the events which were the basis of the criminal prosecution could not be self-incriminating.

HISTORICAL EVOLUTION OF AMERICAN TORT LAW

The word *tort* (meaning "wrong") is one of many Norman words that became a part of the English and American legal lexicon. American tort law evolved from the writs of trespass[1] and trespass on the case.[2] Trespass covered a variety of acts, which included trespass to land, assaults, batteries, the taking of goods, and false imprisonment. Each of the acts involved a tortfeasor directly causing injury to a victim. It was commonplace for plaintiffs to use trespass to recover money damages for personal injuries by the end of Henry III's reign.[3] In 1285, Parliament enacted the Statute of Westminster,[4] which authorized the chancery to create new writs to address wrongs that fell outside the boundaries of trespass. Because the new writs were designed to remedy the factual circumstances of a particular case, they were called trespass actions on the case (also called "actions on the case"). From trespass on the case came our contemporary concept of negligence.

One of the major drawbacks of the writ system was that it lacked any comprehensive underlying theoretical base. In the 1800s, as the writ system was being replaced with more modern forms of pleading, American law professors and judges began to develop a basic theory for tort law based on fault.

FUNCTIONS OF TORT LAW

Tort law establishes standards of conduct for all members of society. It defines as civil wrongs these antisocial behaviors: the failure to exercise reasonable care (negligence); intentional interference with one's person, reputation, or property (intentional torts); and in some circumstances, liability without fault (strict liability). Tort law deters people from engaging in behavior patterns that the law does not condone and compensates victims for their civil injuries. It is thus a vehicle by which an injured person can attempt to shift the costs of harm to another person.

Tort law is not static; courts can create new causes of action to remedy an injustice. Thus the argument that a claim is novel does not prevent a court from granting relief when it becomes clear that the law should protect the plaintiff's rights.

INTENTIONAL TORTS

Intentional torts are based on willful misconduct or intentional wrongs. A tortfeasor who intentionally invades a protected interest of another, under circumstances for which there is no lawful justification or excuse, is legally and morally "at fault." The intent is not necessarily a hostile intent or even a desire to do serious harm. A person acts intentionally if he or she has a conscious desire to produce consequences the law recognizes as tortious. A person who has no conscious desire to cause the consequences, but is aware that the consequences are highly likely to follow, can also act intentionally.

Assault

Assault is an intentional tort because as a general proposition, every person should have the right to live his or her life without being placed in reasonable fear of an intentional, imminent, unconsented, harmful, or offensive touching by another person. Assaults occur where the targeted persons's anxiety is the product of the actor threatening conduct, such as by stalking. The law also recognizes that an assault has occurred where a targeted person's fear is the product of the actor's unsuccessful attempt to hit the target with a punch or a thrown object. Mere words alone, however, usually will not constitute an assault, no matter how threatening or abusive they may be. Once an actor has committed an assault, the tort has been committed. An actor cannot avoid civil liability for assaultive conduct already committed against a target through the abandonment of further assaultive conduct.

Battery

In the intentional tort called *battery,* the tortfeasor has violated the target's right to be free from harmful or offensive touchings by another. A battery is defined as an unpermitted, unprivileged, intentional contact with another's person. This tort includes contact that is actually harmful as well as conduct that is merely offensive. The standard used to determine offensiveness is not whether a particular plaintiff is offended, but whether an ordinary person who is not unusually sensitive in the matter of dignity would be offended. It is not essential that the plaintiff be conscious of the contact at the time it occurs.

Assault or battery may occur without the other, but usually both result from the same occurrence. As a result of an assault and battery—as well as other intentional torts—the injured party may bring a civil suit for damages and, as has been previously discussed, seek a criminal prosecution for the same act.

The following case illustrates the intentional torts of assault, battery, and invasion of privacy (discussed on page 530).

Estate of Berthiaume v. Pratt, M.D.
365 A.2d 792
Supreme Judicial Court of Maine
November 10, 1976

Pomeroy, Justice

The appellant, as administratrix, based her claim of right to damages on an alleged invasion of her late husband's "right to privacy" and on an alleged assault and battery of him. At the close of the evidence produced at trial, a justice of the Superior Court granted defendant's motion for a directed verdict. Appellant's seasonable appeal brings the case to this court.

The appellee is a physician and surgeon practicing in Waterville, Maine. It was established at trial without contradiction that the deceased, Henry Berthiaume, was suffering from a cancer of his larynx. Appellee, an oto-laryngologist, had treated him twice surgically. A laryngectomy was performed; and later, because of a tumor which had appeared in his neck, a radical neck dissection on one side was done. No complaint is made with respect to the surgical interventions.

During the period appellee was serving Mr. Berthiaume as a surgeon, many photographs of Berthiaume had been taken by appellee or under his direction. The jury was told that the sole use to which these photographs were to be put was to make the medical record for the appellee's use. . . .

Although at no time did the appellee receive any written consent for taking of photographs from Berthiaume or any members of his family, it was appellee's testimony that Berthiaume had always consented to having such photographs made.

At all times material hereto, Mr. Berthiaume was a patient of a physician other than the appellee. Such other physician had referred the patient to appellee for surgery. On September 2, 1970, appellee saw the patient for the last time for the purpose of treatment or diagnosis. The incident which gave rise to this lawsuit occurred on September 23, 1970. It was also on that day Mr. Berthiaume died.

Although appellee disputed the evidence appellant produced at trial in many material respects, the jury could have concluded from the evidence that shortly before Mr. Berthiaume died on the 23rd, the appellee and a nurse appeared in his hospital room. In the presence of Mrs. Berthiaume and a visitor of the patient in the next bed, either Dr. Pratt or the nurse, at his direction, raised the dying Mr. Berthiaume's head and placed some blue operating room toweling under his head and beside him on the bed. The appellee testified that this blue toweling was placed there for the purpose of obtaining a color contrast for the photographs which he proposed to take. He then proceeded to take several photographs of Mr. Berthiaume.

The jury could have concluded from the testimony that Mr. Berthiaume protested the taking of pictures by raising a clenched fist and moving his head in an attempt to remove his head from the camera's range. The appellee himself testified that before taking the pictures he had been told by Mrs. Berthiaume when he talked with her in the corridor before entering the room that she "didn't think that Henry wanted his picture taken."

It is the raising of the deceased's head in order to put the operating room towels under and around him that appellant claims was an assault and battery. It is the taking of the pictures of the dying Mr. Berthiaume that appellant claims constituted the actionable invasion of Mr. Berthiaume's right to privacy. . . .

The law of privacy addresses the invasion of four distinct interests of the individual. Each of the four different interests, taken as a whole, represent an individual's right "to be let alone." These four kinds of invasion are: (1) intrusion upon the plaintiff's physical and mental solitude or seclusion; (2) public disclosure of private facts; (3) publicity which places the plaintiff in a false light in the public eye; [and] (4) appropriation for the defendant's benefit or advantage of the plaintiff's name or likeness. . . .

"As it has appeared in the cases thus far decided, it is not one tort, but a complex of four. To date the law of privacy comprises four distinct kinds of invasion of four different interests of the plaintiff, which are tied together by the common name, but otherwise have almost nothing in common except that each represents an interference with the right of the plaintiff 'to be let alone.' . . .

"Taking them in order—intrusion, disclosure, false light, and appropriation—the first and second require the invasion of something secret, secluded or private pertaining to the plaintiff; the third and fourth do not. The second and third depend upon publicity, while the first does not, nor does the fourth, although it usually involves it. The third requires falsity or fiction; the other three do not. The fourth involves a use for the defendant's advantage, which is not true of the rest. . . . "

All cases so far decided on the point agree that the plaintiff need not plead or prove special damages. Punitive damages can be awarded on the same basis as in other torts where a wrongful motive or state of mind appears . . . , but not in cases where the defendant has acted innocently as, for example, in the mistaken but good faith belief that the plaintiff has given his consent. . . .

In this case we are concerned only with a claimed intrusion upon the plaintiff's intestate's physical and mental solitude or seclusion. The jury had a right to conclude from the evidence that plaintiff's intestate was dying. It could have concluded he desired not to be photographed in his hospital bed in such condition and that he manifested such desire by his physical motions. The jury should have been instructed, if it found these facts, that the taking of pictures without decedent's consent or over his objection was an invasion of his legally protected right to privacy, which invasion was an actionable tort for which money damages could be recovered.

Instead, a directed verdict for the defendant was entered, obviously premised on the presiding justice's announced incorrect conclusion that the taking of pictures without consent did not constitute an invasion of privacy and the further erroneous conclusion that no tort was committed in the absence of "proof they [the photographs] were published."

Another claimed basis for appellant's assertion that a right to recover damages was demonstrated by the evidence is the allegations in her complaint sounding in the tort of assault and battery. The presiding justice announced as his conclusion that consent to a battery is implied from the existence of a physician-patient relationship. . . .

There is nothing to suggest that the appellee's visit to plaintiff's intestate's room on the day of the alleged invasion of privacy was for any purpose relating to the *treatment* of the patient. Appellee acknowledges that his sole purpose in going to the Berthiaume hospital room and the taking of pictures was to conclude the making of a photographic record to complete appellee's record of the case. From the evidence, then, it is apparent that the jury had a right to conclude that the physician-patient relationship once existing between Dr. Pratt and Henry Berthiaume, the deceased, had terminated.

As to the claimed assault and battery, on the state of the evidence, the jury should have been permitted to consider the evidence and return a verdict in accordance with its fact-finding. It should have been instructed that consent to a touching of the body of a patient may be implied from the patient's consent to enter into a physician-patient relationship whenever such touching is reasonably necessary for the diagnosis and treatment of the patient's ailments while the physician-patient relationship continues. Quite obviously also, there would be no actionable assault and battery if the touching was expressly consented to. Absent express consent by the patient or one authorized to give consent on the patient's behalf, or absent consent implied from the circumstances, including the physician-patient relationship, the touching of the patient in the manner described by the evidence in this case would constitute assault and battery if it was part of an undertaking which, in legal effect, was an invasion of the plaintiff's intestate's "right to be let alone." . . .

We recognize the benefit to the science of medicine which comes from the making of photographs of the treatment and of medical abnormalities found in patients. . . . "The court [also] recognizes that an individual has the right to decide whether that which is his shall be given to the public and not only to restrict and limit but also to withhold absolutely his talents, property, or other subjects of the right of privacy from all dissemination." . . .

Because there were unresolved, disputed questions of fact, which, if decided by the fact finder in favor of the plaintiff, would have justified a verdict for the plaintiff, it was reversible error to have directed a verdict for the defendant. . . .

New trial ordered.

Case Questions

1. Battery is unpermitted, unprivileged, intentional contact with another's person. In a physician-patient relationship, how does a physician receive consent to touch the body of a patient?
2. Could there have been a battery if Dr. Pratt had used rubber gloves in handling Mr. Berthiaume's head in preparation for the pictures? Could there have been a battery if Dr. Pratt had raised Mr. Berthiaume's head by cranking the hospital bed?
3. Could there have been an assault if Mr. Berthiaume was unconscious at the time Dr. Pratt raised his head and placed the blue operating towel under his head?
4. Are plaintiffs able to recover anything in suits for battery if they are unable to prove any actual physical injury?

 Does Dr. Pratt have a moral duty to comply with his patient's request? Does acting morally benefit Dr. Pratt?

Conversion

Conversion is an intentional tort which allows owners of tangible personal property (concepts discussed in Chapter 12 on page 580) to regain possession of their property from other persons who have dispossessed them. Any unauthorized act that deprives an owner of possession of his or her tangible personal property is *conversion*. There may be liability for the intentional tort of conversion even when the defendant acted innocently. For example, D, an auctioneer, receives a valuable painting from X, reasonably believing that X owns it. D sells the painting for X, but it turns out that P owns the painting. D is liable to P for conversion, even though the mistake is honest and reasonable.

Conversion may be accomplished in a number of ways, for example, if a defendant refuses to return goods to the owner or destroys or alters the goods. Even the use of the chattel may suffice. If you lend your car to a dealer to sell and the dealer drives the car once on business for a few miles, it would probably not be conversion. But conversion would result if the dealer drives it for 2,000 miles.

Because conversion is considered a forced sale, the defendant must pay the full value, not merely the amount of the actual harm. However, courts consider several factors in determining whether defendant's interference with plaintiff's property is sufficient to require defendant to pay its entire value. These include dominion, good faith, harm, and inconvenience.

Trespass to Land

Trespass is an intentional tort which protects a lawful owner/occupier's rights to exclusive possession of his or her real property. It occurs when someone makes an unauthorized entry on the land of another. Trespasses to land can occur through either a direct or an indirect entry. A direct entry would occur when one person walks on another person's land without permission. An indirect entry would occur when one person throws an object on another's land or causes it to flood with water.

The law's protection of the exclusive possession of land is not limited to the surface of real property. It extends below the surface as well as above it. Thus a public utility that runs a pipe below the surface of a landowner's property without obtaining an easement or consent can commit a trespass. Similarly, overhanging structures, telephone wires, and even shooting across land have been held to be violations of owners' right to the air space above their land. Although the extent of such rights are still in the process of determination, the legal trend is for landowners to have rights to as much of the air space that is immediately above their property as they can effectively occupy or use. Trespass may also occur to personal property, but most interference with the possession of personal property would be considered conversion.

The plaintiff in the following case brought suit in trespass after sustaining serious injury when an overhanging limb fell from the defendant's maple tree onto the plaintiff's driveway and struck the plaintiff.

Ivancic v. Olmstead
488 N.E.2d 72
Court of Appeals of New York
November 26, 1985

Jasen, Judge

At issue on this appeal is whether plaintiff, who seeks to recover for injuries sustained when an overhanging limb from a neighbor's maple tree fell and struck him, established a prima facie case of negligence and whether Trial Term erred, as a matter of law, in refusing to submit to the jury the cause of action sounding in common-law trespass.

Plaintiff was working on his truck in the driveway of his parents' home located in the Village of Fultonville, New York. Since 1970, defendant has owned and lived on the property adjoining to the west. A large maple tree stood on defendant's land near the border with plaintiff's parents' property. Branches from the tree had extended over the adjoining property. During a heavy windstorm on September 26, 1980, an overhanging limb from the tree fell and struck plaintiff, causing him serious injuries. As a result, plaintiff commenced this action, interposing causes of action in negligence and common-law trespass.

At trial, the court declined to charge the jury on the common-law trespass cause of action or on the doctrine of res ipsa loquitur, submitting the case solely on the theory of negligence. The jury rendered a verdict in favor of the plaintiff in the sum of $3,500. Both parties moved to set aside the verdict, the plaintiff upon the ground of inadequacy, and the defendant upon the ground that the verdict was against the weight of the evidence. The court ultimately . . . ordered a new trial on the issues of both liability and damages.

Upon cross appeals, the Appellate Division reversed, on the law, and dismissed the complaint. The court reasoned that no competent evidence was presented upon which it could properly be concluded that defendant had constructive notice of the alleged defective condition of the tree. The Appellate Division did not address the correctness of the trial court's ruling in declining to charge the jury on the common-law trespass cause of action. . . .

Considering first the negligence cause of action, it is established that no liability attaches to a landowner whose tree falls outside of his premises and injures another unless there exists actual or constructive knowledge of the defective condition of the tree. . . .

Inasmuch as plaintiff makes no claim that defendant had actual knowledge of the defective nature of the tree, it is necessary to consider whether there was sufficient competent evidence for a jury to conclude that defendant had constructive notice. We conclude, as did the Appellate Division, that plaintiff offered no competent evidence from which it could be properly found that defendant had constructive notice of the alleged defective condition of the tree. Not one of the witnesses who had observed the tree prior to the fall of the limb testified as to observing so much as a withering or dead leaf, barren branch, discoloration, or any of the indicia of disease which would alert an observer to the possibility that the tree or one of its branches was decayed or defective.

At least as to adjoining landowners, the concept of constructive notice with respect to liability for falling trees is that there is no duty to consistently and constantly check all trees for nonvisible decay. Rather, the manifestation of said decay must be readily observable in order to require a landowner to take reasonable steps to prevent harm. . . . The testimony of plaintiff's expert provides no evidence from which the jury could conclude that defendant should reasonably have realized that a potentially dangerous condition existed. Plaintiff's expert never saw the tree until the morning of the trial when all that remained of the tree was an eight-foot stump. He surmised from this observation and from some photographs of the tree that water had invaded the tree through a "limb hole" in the tree, thus causing decay and a crack occurring below. However, the expert did indicate that the limb hole was about eight-feet high and located in the crotch of the tree which would have made it difficult, if not impossible, to see upon reasonable inspection. Although there may have been evidence that would have alerted an expert, upon close observation, that the tree was diseased, there is no evidence that would put a reasonable landowner on notice of any defective condition of the tree. Thus, the fact that defendant landowner testified that she did not inspect the tree for over 10 years is irrelevant. On the evidence presented, even if she were to have inspected the tree, there were no indicia of decay or disease to put her on notice of a defective condition so as to trigger her duty as a landowner to take reasonable steps to prevent the potential harm.

Since the evidence adduced at trial failed to set forth any reasonable basis upon which notice of the tree's defective condition could be imputed to defendant, . . . we agree with the view of the Appellate Division that plaintiff failed to establish a prima facie case of negligence.

Turning to plaintiff's claim of error by the trial court in declining to submit to the jury the cause of action sounding in common-law trespass, we conclude that there was no error. The scope of the common-law tort has been delineated in *Phillips v. Sun Oil Co.,* . . . 121

N.E.2d 249, wherein this court held: "while the trespasser, to be liable, need not intend or expect the damaging consequences of his intrusion, he must intend the act which amounts to or produces the unlawful invasion, and the intrusion must at least be the immediate or inevitable consequence of what he willfully does, or which he does so negligently as to amount to willfulness." In this case, there is evidence that defendant did not plant the tree, and the mere fact that defendant allowed what appeared to be a healthy tree to grow naturally and cross over into plaintiff's parents' property airspace, cannot be viewed as an intentional act so as to constitute trespass. . . .

Accordingly, the order of the Appellate Division should be affirmed, with costs.

Case Questions

1. The trial court and the appellate court concluded that the plaintiff was not entitled to an instruction with respect to common law trespass. Why was the instruction refused?
2. Why was the plaintiff's negligence claim rejected?
3. Why should a plaintiff be entitled to recover for a trespass under circumstances where no actual harm has been shown?

Malicious Prosecution

Malicious prosecution is an intentional tort that provides targeted individuals with civil remedies against persons who have filed groundless complaints against the target that result in the target's criminal prosecution. Many states have extended the definition of this tort to permit such suits against individuals who initiate groundless civil actions. The plaintiff in a malicious prosecution case must prove that the defendant maliciously and without probable cause instituted a criminal or civil complaint against the target which resulted in a prosecution or lawsuit, which then resulted in a decision favorable to the target. The target must also establish that he or she suffered legal injury as a result of the groundless charges. Merely threatening to bring a lawsuit against the target is not enough to result in civil liability for malicious prosecution.

In a criminal case, the prosecutor is absolutely immune from malicious prosecution suits. In addition, plea bargaining does not suffice to meet the favorable decision criterion.

False Imprisonment

False imprisonment is an intentional tort that provides targeted individuals with civil remedies against those who unlawfully deprive them of their freedom of movement. Plaintiffs must prove that they were intentionally and unlawfully detained against their will for an unreasonable period of time. The detention need not be in a jail. It may also take place in a mental institution, hospital, restaurant, hotel, store, car, etc. Most courts have held that plaintiffs must be aware of their confinement while suffering it, or if not, then they must suffer some type of actual harm.

The plaintiffs in the following case claimed that they were the victims of false imprisonment by Wal-Mart security personnel.

Debra McCann v. Wal-Mart Stores, Inc.
210 F.3d 51
U.S. Court of Appeals, First Circuit
April 14, 2000

Opinion: Boudin, Circuit Judge.

This case involves a claim for false imprisonment. On December 11, 1996, Debra McCann and two of her children—Jillian, then 16, and Jonathan, then 12—were shopping at the Wal-Mart store in Bangor, Maine. After they returned a Christmas tree and exchanged a CD player, Jonathan went to the toy section and Jillian and Debra McCann went to shop in other areas of the store. After approximately an hour and a half, the McCanns went to a register and paid for their purchases. One of their receipts was time stamped at 10:10 P.M.

As the McCanns were leaving the store, two Wal-Mart employees, Jean Taylor and Karla Hughes, stepped out in front of the McCanns' shopping cart, blocking their path to the exit. Taylor may have actually put her hand on the cart. The employees told Debra McCann that the children were not allowed in the store because they had been caught stealing on a prior occasion. In fact, the employees were mistaken; the son of a different family had been caught shoplifting in the store about two weeks before, and Taylor and Hughes confused the two families.

Despite Debra McCann's protestations, Taylor said that they had the records, that the police were being called, and that the McCanns "had to go with her." Debra McCann testified that she did not resist Tay-

lor's direction because she believed that she had to go with Taylor and that the police were coming. Taylor and Hughes then brought the McCanns past the registers in the store to an area near the store exit. Taylor stood near the McCanns while Hughes purportedly went to call the police. During this time, Debra McCann tried to show Taylor her identification, but Taylor refused to look at it.

After a few minutes, Hughes returned and switched places with Taylor. Debra McCann told Hughes that she had proof of her identity and that there must be some proof about the identity of the children who had been caught stealing. Hughes then went up to Jonathan, pointed her finger at him, and said that he had been caught stealing two weeks earlier. Jonathan began to cry and denied the accusation. At some point around this time Jonathan said that he needed to use the bathroom and Hughes told him he could not go. At no time during this initial hour or so did the Wal-Mart employees tell the McCanns that they could leave.

Although Wal-Mart's employees had said they were calling the police, they actually called a store security officer who would be able to identify the earlier shoplifter. Eventually, the security officer, Rhonda Bickmore, arrived at the store and informed Hughes that the McCanns were not the family whose son had been caught shoplifting. Hughes then acknowledged her mistake to the McCanns, and the McCanns left the store at approximately 11:15 P.M. In due course, the McCanns brought suit against Wal-Mart for false imprisonment. . . .

The jury awarded the McCanns $20,000 in compensatory damages on their claim that they were falsely imprisoned in the Wal-Mart store by Wal-Mart employees. Wal-Mart has now appealed . . . arguing that the McCanns did not prove false imprisonment under Maine law and that the court's jury instructions on false imprisonment were in error. The McCanns have cross-appealed from the district court's pre-trial dismissal of their claim for punitive damages.

Both of Wal-Mart's claims of error depend on the proper elements of the tort of false imprisonment. Although nuances vary from state to state, the gist of the common law tort is conduct by the actor which is intended to, and does in fact, "confine" another "within boundaries fixed by the actor" where, in addition, the victim is either "conscious of the confinement or is harmed by it." Restatement (Second), Torts §§ 35 (1965). The few Maine cases on point contain no comprehensive definition, . . . , and the district court's instructions . . . seem to have been drawn from the Restatement.

While "confinement" can be imposed by physical barriers or physical force, much less will do—although how much less becomes cloudy at the margins. It is generally settled that mere threats of physical force can suffice, . . . ; and it is also settled—although there is no Maine case on point—that the threats may be implicit as well as explicit, see . . . 32 Am. Jur. 2d False Imprisonment §§ 18 (1995) (collecting cases), and that confinement can also be based on a false assertion of legal authority to confine. . . . Indeed, the Restatement provides that confinement may occur by other unspecified means of "duress." . . .

Against this background, we examine Wal-Mart's claim that the evidence was insufficient, taking the facts in the light most favorable to the McCanns, drawing reasonable inferences in their favor, and assuming that the jury resolved credibility issues consistent with the verdict. . . . Using this standard,

we think that a reasonable jury could conclude that Wal-Mart's employees intended to "confine" the McCanns "within boundaries fixed by" Wal-Mart, that the employees' acts did result in such a confinement, and that the McCanns were conscious of the confinement. . . .

The evidence, taken favorably to the McCanns, showed that Wal-Mart employees stopped the McCanns as they were seeking to exit the store, said that the children were not allowed in the store, told the McCanns that they had to come with the Wal-Mart employees and that Wal-Mart was calling the police, and then stood guard over the McCanns while waiting for a security guard to arrive. The direction to the McCanns, the reference to the police, and the continued presence of the Wal-Mart employees (who at one point told Jonathan McCann that he could not leave to go to the bathroom) were enough to induce reasonable people to believe either that they would be restrained physically if they sought to leave, or that the store was claiming lawful authority to confine them until the police arrived, or both.

Wal-Mart asserts that under Maine law, the jury had to find "actual, physical restraint," . . . Taking too literally the phrase "actual, physical restraint" would put Maine law broadly at odds with not only the Restatement but with a practically uniform body of common law in other states that accepts the mere threat of physical force, or a claim of lawful authority to restrain, as enough to satisfy the confinement requirement for false imprisonment (assuming always that the victim submits). It is true that in a diversity case, we are bound by Maine law, as Wal-Mart reminds us; but we are not required to treat a descriptive phrase as a general rule or attribute to elderly Maine cases an entirely improbable breadth.

More interesting is Wal-Mart's claim that the instructions were inadequate. The district court largely borrowed the Restatement formulation by telling the jury that it must find the following:

> One, that the defendant acted intending to confine the plaintiffs within boundaries fixed by the defendant; two, that the acts of the defendant directly or indirectly resulted in such a confinement of the plaintiffs; and third, the plaintiffs were conscious of the confinement or were harmed by it.

The court added that the jury could find for the McCanns if it found that "the plaintiffs reasonably believed they were not permitted to leave the store," and that the plaintiffs did not have to prove that "such restraint was accomplished through actual physical force against their bodies."

In assailing the instructions, Wal-Mart repeats its claims, which we have already rejected, that the district court should have charged that "actual, physical restraint" is required to make out confinement. A somewhat different claim by Wal-Mart, . . . is that the district court's instruction was defective because it did not tell the jury that the restraint must be a physical and not merely a moral influence, and that influencing or convincing another to stay is not actual physical restraint. In substance, Wal-Mart wanted a description of what was not confinement.

We think it is at least arguable that, if a proper instruction were tendered, it might be appropriate or even obligatory (the latter is a nice point that we do not decide) to make clear to the jury that there are outer boundaries to the confinement concept and that a personal plea by the defendant to remain or the defendant's invocation of "moral obligation" alone would not be sufficient to inflict a "confinement." There might be special justification for such a clarification in a case in which the evidence was open to that interpretation.

However, in this case, Wal-Mart did not offer a proper instruction: in arguing for a different instruction, it said to the district court

that the restraint "must be physical and not merely a moral influence," implicating Wal-Mart's incorrect view that actual physical restraint was required; and its further statement that "influencing or convincing another to remain in place is not actual physical restraint" has the same fault and is also open to the criticism that "influencing or convincing" is itself a misleading phrase, at least as presented by Wal-Mart, because one could influence or convince by threats of force or assertions of lawful authority, which do or can constitute false imprisonment. In short, Wal-Mart did not offer a proper instruction. . . .

Finally, the McCanns cross-appeal from the district court's pre-trial dismissal of their claim for punitive damages. The precedents say that punitive damages can only be awarded for tortious conduct where the defendant acts with malice. . . . Under Maine law, malice can be express, as when the defendant is motivated by ill will toward the plaintiff, or implied, where the defendant's actions are "outrageous" and not merely reckless or negligent.

In this case, the McCanns contend that Hughes's refusal to permit Jonathan to use the bathroom was sufficiently outrageous to support a claim for punitive damages. The McCann's testimony was simply that Jonathan said once that he needed to use the bathroom and Hughes told him he could not. At that point, the issue was dropped and neither Jonathan nor his mother said another word to the Wal-Mart employees about it. While we think it was foolish for Hughes to tell the 12-year-old that he could not go to the bathroom, the denial was not "outrageous" given the failure to press the request. We can imagine circumstances where a refusal to allow such a bathroom visit would be outrageous.

The McCanns insist that the refusal must be considered in conjunction with other facts, including an asserted violation by Wal-Mart of its own policy of asking prior shoplifters to leave the store rather than detaining them, Hughes's action of pointing her finger at Jonathan while accusing him of stealing, and her failure to clear up the McCanns' identity at an earlier stage. Whether taken separately or together, these actions may be culpable but are short enough of "outrageous" to permit actual but not punitive damages. To the extent extra harm was done to Jonathan, the jury had no difficulty drawing this distinction; it awarded him $10,000 while awarding his mother and sister only $5,000 each.

Affirmed.

Case Questions

1. What, according to the court, is the "gist" of the tort of false imprisonment?
2. According to the court, must plaintiffs prove that they were physically restrained from leaving the alleged place of confinement?

Defamation

Defamation is an intentional tort that is based on the policy that people should be able to enjoy their good names. This tort provides targeted individuals with remedies against persons who intentionally make malicious statements that injure the target's character, fame, or reputation. A publication is defamatory it it tends to lower a person in other's esteem. Language that is merely annoying cannot be defamatory. Generally, the truth of the statement is a complete defense in a suit for defamation because true statements are not considered to be malicious.

Libel and slander are both forms of defamation. *Libel* is defamation expressed by print, writing, signs, pictures, and in the absence of statutory provisions to the contrary, radio and television broadcasts. *Slander* involves spoken words that have been heard by someone other than the target.

The law treats some defamatory expressions as slanderous per se. Examples of slander per se include falsely accusing another of committing a crime of moral turpitude (rape, murder, or selling narcotics), false accusations that another person has contracted a morally offensive communicative disease (such as leprosy, syphilis, gonorrhea, or AIDS), or defamatory expressions that interfere with another person's trade, business, or profession (saying that a banker is dishonest or that a doctor is a "quack"). In defamation cases, the law requires that special damages such as loss of job, loss of customers, or loss of credit be proven before the plaintiff can recover general damages, such as loss of reputation.[5] However, a plaintiff who proves slander per se is not required to prove special damages because such expressions are almost certain to harm the plaintiff's reputation and produce economic loss. Not having to prove special damages is very helpful to the plaintiff because they are difficult to prove. The defendant can usually lessen the amount of damages awarded by publishing a retraction.

Interference with Contract Relations

The underlying policy reason behind the intentional tort called *interference with contract relations* is the desire to strengthen our economy by promoting the stability of contracts. Strengthening the economy is important to the welfare of Americans both collectively and individually.

The intentional tort of interference with contractual relations takes place when a noncontracting party or third person wrongfully interferes with the contract relations between two or more contracting parties. (See Chapter 10 for a discussion of contracts.) The tort of interference includes all intentional invasions of contract relations, including any act injuring a person or destroying property that interferes with the performance of a contract. For example, this tort occurs when someone wrongfully prevents an employee from working for an employer or prevents a tenant from paying rent to the landlord.

In order to maintain an action against a third person for interference, the plaintiff must prove that the defendant maliciously and substantially interfered with the performance of a valid and enforceable contract. The motive or purpose of the interfering party is an important factor in determining liability.

Infliction of Mental Distress

The intentional tort called *infliction of mental distress,* evolved out of the need to recognize that every person has a right to not be subjected intentionally and recklessly to severe emotional distress caused by some other person's outrageous conduct. A person has a cause of action for infliction of mental distress when the conduct of the defendant is serious in nature and causes anguish in the plaintiff's mind. Because it is difficult to prove mental anguish and to place a dollar amount on that injury, early cases allowed recovery for mental distress only when it was accompanied by some other tort, such as assault, battery, or false imprisonment. Today, the infliction of mental distress is generally considered to be an intentional tort, standing alone.

Recovery for mental distress is allowed only in situations involving extreme misconduct, for example, telling a wife the made-up story that her husband shot himself in the head. Mental worry, distress, grief, and mortification are elements of mental suffering from which an injured person can recover. Recovery is not available for mere annoyance, disappointment, or hurt feelings. For example, the mere disappointment of a grandfather because his grandchildren were prevented from visiting him on account of delay in the transmission of a fax message would not amount to mental distress.

Invasion of Privacy

The law recognizes one's right to be free from unwarranted publicity and, in general, one's right to be let alone. If one person invades the right of another to withhold self and property from public scrutiny, the invading party can be held liable in tort for invasion of the right of privacy. A suit for invasion of privacy may involve unwarranted publicity that places the plaintiff in a false light, intrudes into the plaintiff's private life, discloses embarrassing private facts, or uses the plaintiff's name or likeness for the defendant's gain. Generally, the motives of the defendant are unimportant.

The standard used to measure any type of invasion of privacy is that the effect must be highly offensive to a reasonable person. For example, if a frustrated creditor puts up a notice in a store window stating that a named debtor owes money, this is an invasion of the debtor's privacy.

Technological developments in information storage and communications have subjected the intimacies of everyone's private lives to exploitation. The law protects individuals against this type of encroachment. A person who has become a public figure has less protection, however, because society has a right to information of legitimate public interest.

Although invasion of privacy and defamation are similar, they are distinct intentional torts, and both may be included in a plaintiff's complaint. The difference between a right of privacy and a right to freedom from defamation is that the former is concerned with one's peace of mind, whereas the latter is concerned with one's reputation or character. Truth is generally not a defense for invasion of privacy.

In the next case, the Minnesota Supreme Court explains why it decided to recognize three of the four types of activities that are recognized as constituting the tort of invasion of privacy.

Elli Lake v. Wal-Mart Stores, Inc.
C7-97-263
Minnesota Supreme Court
July 30, 1998

Blatz, Chief Justice

. . . Nineteen-year-old Elli Lake and 20-year-old Melissa Weber vacationed in Mexico in March 1995 with Weber's sister. During the vacation, Weber's sister took a photograph of Lake and Weber naked in the shower together. After their vacation, Lake and Weber brought five rolls of film to the Dilworth, Minnesota Wal-Mart store and photo lab. When they received their developed photographs along with the negatives, an enclosed written notice stated that one or more of the photographs had not been printed because of their "nature."

In July 1995, an acquaintance of Lake and Weber alluded to the photograph and questioned their sexual orientation. Again, in December 1995, another friend told Lake and Weber that a Wal-Mart employee had shown her a copy of the photograph. By February 1996, Lake was informed that one or more copies of the photograph were circulating in the community.

Lake and Weber filed a complaint against Wal-Mart Stores, Inc. and one or more as-yet unidentified Wal-Mart employees on February 23, 1996, alleging the four traditional invasion of privacy torts—intrusion upon seclusion, appropriation, publication of private facts, and false light publicity. Wal-Mart denied the allegations and made a motion to dismiss the complaint . . . for failure to state a claim upon which relief may be granted. The district court granted Wal-Mart's motion to dismiss, explaining that Minnesota has not recognized any of the four invasion of privacy torts. The court of appeals affirmed.

Whether Minnesota should recognize any or all of the invasion of privacy causes of action is a question of first impression in Minnesota. The Restatement (Second) of Torts outlines the four causes of action that comprise the tort generally referred to as invasion of privacy. Intrusion upon seclusion occurs when one "intentionally intrudes, physically or otherwise, upon the solitude or seclusion of another or his private affairs or concerns . . . if the intrusion would be highly offensive to a reasonable person." . . . Appropriation protects an individual's identity and is committed when one "appropriates to his own use or benefit the name or likeness of another." . . . Publication of private facts is an invasion of privacy when one "gives publicity to a matter concerning the private life of another . . . if the matter publicized is of a kind that (a) would be highly offensive to a reasonable person, and (b) is not of legitimate concern to the public. . . . False light publicity occurs when one "gives publicity to a matter concerning another that places the other before the public in a false light . . . if (a) the false light in which the other was placed would be highly offensive to a reasonable person, and (b) the actor had knowledge of or acted in reckless disregard as to the falsity of the publicized matter and the false light in which the other would be placed." . . .

This court has the power to recognize and abolish common law doctrines. . . . As society changes over time, the common law must also evolve:

> It must be remembered that the common law is the result of growth, and that its development has been determined by the social needs of the community which it governs. It is the resultant of conflicting social forces, and those forces which are for the time dominant leave their impress upon the law. It is of judicial origin, and seeks to establish doctrines and rules for the determination, protection, and enforcement of legal rights. Manifestly it must change as society

changes and new rights are recognized. To be an efficient instrument, and not a mere abstraction, it must gradually adapt itself to changed conditions. . . .

To determine the common law, we look to other states as well as to England. . . .

The tort of invasion of privacy is rooted in a common law right to privacy first described in an 1890 law review article by Samuel Warren and Louis Brandeis. . . . The article posited that the common law has always protected an individual's person and property, with the extent and nature of that protection changing over time. The fundamental right to privacy is both reflected in those protections and grows out of them:

> Thus, in the very early times, the law gave a remedy only for physical interference with life and property, for trespass *vi et armis*. Then the "right to life" served only to protect the subject from battery in its various forms; liberty meant freedom from actual restraint; and the right to property to the individual his lands and his cattle. Later, there came a recognition of a man's spiritual nature, of his feelings and his intellect. Gradually the scope of these legal rights broadened; and now the right to life has come to mean the right to enjoy life,—the right to be let alone; the right to liberty secures the exercise of extensive civil privileges; and the term "property" has grown to comprise every form of possession—intangible, as well as tangible. . . .

Although no English cases explicitly articulated a "right to privacy," several cases decided under theories of property, contract, or breach of confidence also included invasion of privacy as a basis for protecting personal violations. . . . The article encouraged recognition of the common law right to privacy, as the strength of our legal system lies in its elasticity, adaptability, capacity for growth, and ability "to meet the wants of an ever changing society and to apply immediate relief for every recognized wrong."

The first jurisdiction to recognize the common law right to privacy was Georgia. . . . [T]he Georgia Supreme Court determined that the "right of privacy has its foundation in the instincts of nature," and is therefore an "immutable" and "absolute" right "derived from natural law." The court emphasized that the right of privacy was not new to Georgia law, as it was encompassed by the well-established right to personal liberty.

Many other jurisdictions followed Georgia in recognizing the tort of invasion of privacy. . . . Today, the vast majority of jurisdictions now recognize some form of the right to privacy. Only Minnesota, North Dakota, and Wyoming have not yet recognized any of the four privacy torts. Although New York and Nebraska courts have declined to recognize a common law basis for the right to privacy and instead provide statutory protection, we reject the proposition that only the legislature may establish new causes of action. The right to privacy is inherent in the English protections of individual property and contract rights and the "right to be let alone" is recognized as part of the common law across this country. Thus, it is within the province of the judiciary to establish privacy torts in this jurisdiction.

Today we join the majority of jurisdictions and recognize the tort of invasion of privacy. The right to privacy is an integral part of our humanity; one has a public persona, exposed and active, and a private persona, guarded and preserved. The heart of our liberty is choosing which parts of our lives shall become public and which parts we shall hold close.

Here Lake and Weber allege in their complaint that a photograph of their nude bodies has been publicized. One's naked body is a very private part of one's person and generally known to others only by choice. This is a type of privacy interest worthy of protection. Therefore, without consideration of the merits of Lake and Weber's claims, we recognize the torts of intrusion upon seclusion, appropriation, and publication of private facts. Accordingly, we reverse the court of appeals and the district court and hold that Lake and Weber have stated a claim upon which relief may be granted and their lawsuit may proceed.

We decline to recognize the tort of false light publicity at this time. We are concerned that claims under false light are similar to claims of defamation, and to the extent that false light is more expansive than defamation, tension between this tort and the First Amendment is increased. . . .

We agree with the reasoning of the Texas Supreme Court. Defamation requires a false statement communicated to a third party that tends to harm a plaintiff's reputation. . . . False light requires publicity, to a large number of people, of a falsity that places the plaintiff in a light that a reasonable person would find highly offensive. . . . The primary difference between defamation and false light is that defamation addresses harm to reputation in the external world, while false light protects harm to one's inner self. . . . Most false light claims are actionable as defamation claims; because of the overlap with defamation and the other privacy torts, a case has rarely succeeded squarely on a false light claim. . . .

We are also concerned that false light inhibits free speech guarantees provided by the First Amendment. As the Supreme Court remarked in *New York Times Co. v. Sullivan*: "Whatever is added to the field of libel is taken from the field of free debate." . . . Accordingly, we do not want to:

> create a grave risk of serious impairment of the indispensable service of a free press in a free society if we saddle the press with the impossible burden of verifying to a certainty the facts associated in news articles with a person's name, picture or portrait, particularly as related to nondefamatory matter. . . .

Although there may be some untrue and hurtful publicity that should be actionable under false light, the risk of chilling speech is too great to justify protection for this small category of false publication not protected under defamation.

Thus we recognize a right to privacy present in the common law of Minnesota, including causes of action in tort for intrusion upon seclusion, appropriation, and publication of private facts, but we decline to recognize the tort of false light publicity. This case is remanded to the district court for further proceedings consistent with this opinion.

Affirmed in part, reversed in part.

Tomjanovich, Justice (dissenting)

I respectfully dissent. If the allegations against Wal-Mart are proven to be true, the conduct of the Wal-Mart employees is indeed offensive and reprehensible. As much as we deplore such conduct, not every contemptible act in our society is actionable. . . .

An action for an invasion of the right to privacy is not rooted in the Constitution. "[T]he Fourth Amendment cannot be translated into a general constitutional 'right to privacy.'" . . . Those privacy rights that have their origin in the Constitution are much more fundamental rights of privacy—marriage and reproduction. . . . We have become a much more litigious society since 1975 when we acknowledged that we have never recognized a cause of action for invasion of privacy. We should be even more reluctant now to recognize a new tort.

In the absence of a constitutional basis, I would leave to the legislature the decision to create a new tort for invasion of privacy.

Case Questions

1. The Minnesota Supreme Court claims that it has a right to judicially establish the tort of invasion of privacy. What is the source of that right?
2. What are the modern sources of the invasion of privacy action in tort?
3. What policy considerations motivate the court to take this step?
4. Why does the court refuse to recognize the tort of false light?

 The Minnesota Supreme Court recognizes in this case a cause of action for invasion of privacy, including publication of private facts. How would you answer dissenting Justice Tomjanovich's question: Should every contemptible act in our society be actionable in a court of law?

NEGLIGENCE

The law recognizes a duty or obligation to conform to a certain standard of conduct for the protection of others against unreasonable risk of harm. If the person fails to conform to the required standard, and that failure causes damage or loss, the injured party has a cause of action for *negligence*. Negligence is the *unintentional* failure to live up to the community's ideal of reasonable care; it is not based on moral fault. The fact that defendants may have suffered losses of their own through their negligent acts does not render them any less liable for plaintiffs' injuries.

An infinite variety of possible situations makes the determination of an exact set of rules for negligent conduct impossible. Conduct that might be considered prudent in one situation may be deemed negligent in another, depending on such factors as the person's physical attributes, age, and knowledge, the person to whom the duty was owed, and the situation at the time. If the defendant could not reasonably foresee any injury as the result of a certain conduct, there is no negligence and no liability.

The elements necessary for a cause of action for the tort of negligence are (1) a duty or standard of care recognized by law, (2) a breach of the duty or failure to exercise the requisite care, and (3) the occurrence of harm proximately caused by the breach of duty. No cause of action in negligence is recognized if any of these elements is absent from the proof.

The plaintiff has the burden of proving, through the presentation of evidence, that the defendant was negligent. Unless the evidence is such that it can reasonably lead to but one conclusion, negligence is primarily a question of fact for the jury. A jury must decide whether the defendant acted as a reasonably prudent person would have under the circumstances—that is, a person having the same information, experience, physique, and professional skill. This standard makes no allowance for a person less intelligent than average.

Children are not held to the same standard as adults. A child must conform merely to the conduct of a reasonable person of like age, intelligence, and experience under like circumstances. This standard is subjective and holds a less intelligent child to what a similar child would do.

Malpractice

The term *malpractice* is a nonlegal term for negligence. Professional negligence takes different forms in different fields. Attorney negligence would include drafting a will but failing to see that it is properly attested; failing to file an answer in a timely manner on behalf of a client, with the result that the plaintiff wins by default; and failing to file suit prior to the running of the statute of limitation, thus barring the client's claim. Accountant negligence would occur if a client paid for an audit but the accountant failed to discover that the client's employees were engaging in embezzlement, exposing the client to postaudit losses that could have been prevented. The case of *Macomber v. Dillman* (Chapter 7) is an example of medical malpractice. In that case, a surgeon improperly performed a tubal ligation and the plaintiff subsequently gave birth to a child.

Plaintiffs in malpractice cases allege that the professional specifically breached a contractual duty (if the suit is in contract) or that the professional breached a duty of care imposed by law (if the suit is in tort). Professionals have a higher degree of knowledge, skills, or experience than a reasonable person and are required to use that capacity. They are generally required to act as would a reasonably skilled, prudent, competent, and experienced member of the profession in good standing within that state. Negligence in this area usually may be shown only by the use of expert testimony.

The plaintiff in the following case sued a supermarket, alleging that the store was negligent in the way it displayed and marketed its green peppers.

Gilhooley v. Star Market Co., Inc.
508 N.E.2d 609
Supreme Judicial Court of Massachusetts
June 8, 1987

O'Connor, Justice

In this tort action, the plaintiff alleges that, due to the defendant's negligence, he sustained personal injuries from slipping on a green pepper in the defendant's supermarket. By a special verdict, the jury found that the defendant had not been negligent. Accordingly, judgment [was] entered for the defendant. On appeal to the Appeals Court, the plaintiff claimed that the judge's instructions to the jury were erroneous because they focused exclusively on the question whether the defendant reasonably should have discovered and removed the pepper before the plaintiff fell. The plaintiff claimed that, as a result, the judge's instructions erroneously "did not permit the jury to find the defendant negligent for the way in which it displayed and marketed its produce." The Appeals Court affirmed the judgment. . . . and this court allowed the plaintiff's application for further appellate review. We, too, affirm the judgment for the defendant. The jury instructions were not erroneous.

We set forth the relevant portions of the jury instructions: "Under our law, the owner, occupant or lessee of premises is under a duty to exercise ordinary care in the management of such premises in order to avoid exposing persons who come thereon, to an unreasonable risk of harm. . . . Negligence is the failure to observe due care, to take due care that someone is not placed in a condition of un-

reasonable risk of harm. So that for definition, I will tell you that the law says that negligence is the failure to use reasonable care. Reasonable care is that degree of care which a reasonably careful person would use under like circumstances, and negligence may consist of either doing something that a reasonably careful person would not do, or omitting to do something that a reasonably careful person would do. . . . Let me say to you this, that the mere unexplained presence of a foreign substance on the premises, and an accident occurring, does not, without more in and of itself establish negligence. If a substance is upon the floor of the defendant's premises, it is up to you to determine whether or not the defendant knew or should have known as to its presence. If he knew, the question is, did he make or did they make or take reasonable precaution to eliminate it. So if he could reasonably foresee its presence, did he take the necessary precautions, or did they take the necessary precautions to eliminate such an event."

At the conclusion of the instructions, the plaintiff objected to the failure of the judge to give certain instructions that the plaintiff had requested. The pertinent portions of the requested instructions are as follows: "You may find that the defendant was negligent for either or both of two grounds: (1) You may find that the defendant was negligent, if you find that the particular piece of produce on which the plaintiff slipped . . . had been on the floor of the defendant's store long enough before the plaintiff slipped on it for the defendant's employees, in the exercise of ordinary care and vigilance, to have noticed it and removed it. . . . (2) You may find that the defendant is negligent if you find that the presence of produce on the floor of the defendant's produce department was a usual, ordinary and foreseeable result of the way in which the defendant conducted its produce business. . . . The second ground does not depend on notice; it does not require that the defendant noticed or should have noticed the green pepper. If you find that the defendant's method of operating its produce department was such that it could be expected that produce would find its way to the floor, or was such that produce finding its way to the floor was an ordinary occurrence, then you may find the defendant negligent, even if it had no notice, actual or constructive, of the particular item on which the plaintiff slipped. . . ."

The requested instructions would have permitted the jury to find the defendant negligent on the basis of foreseeability of risk without the jury's addressing the question whether, despite foreseeable risk, the defendant's conduct met the standard set by an ordinarily prudent person in the same or similar circumstances. The plaintiff was not entitled to such instructions for two reasons: (1) To establish liability for negligence, the critical question is whether the defendant has failed to act as a reasonably prudent person would have acted in all the circumstances, "including the likelihood of injury to others, the seriousness of the injury, and the burden of avoiding the risk." . . . Foreseeability of risk is but one consideration. (2) Although there was evidence of foreseeability of risk, the evidence did not warrant a finding that the pepper had been on the floor as a result of the defendant's failure to display and market its produce according to the standard set by an ordinarily prudent person in the circumstances.

The evidence most favorable to the plaintiff showed that the produce section of the defendant's market was designed for self-service. The peppers were stacked on top of one another in a diagonal fashion in plastic bins on counters. The bins slanted down toward the aisle. Customers and employees sometimes dropped vegetables and fruit onto the floor, and sometimes vegetables and fruit rolled onto the floor when customers or employees touched them. Produce "constantly" had to be taken off the floor. Sweeping was a major concern of the defendant. It was not done according to any schedule, but it was done as often as necessary. It was done "every five minutes, or every minute," if necessary.

The plaintiff argues that self-service creates a risk of spillage, and that the risk may have been enhanced in this case by the peppers' being stacked in a "diagonal" display in bins tilted toward an aisle, the color of which tended to blend with the color of green peppers. We agree with the plaintiff that, in an appropriate case, the keeper of a grocery store may be liable to a customer who slips on produce that is on the floor because of the storekeeper's negligent marketing and display thereof. It is not always necessary for liability that the produce have been on the floor long enough for the storekeeper to have had a reasonable opportunity to have seen and removed it. But, here, there was no evidence of the defendant's failure to comply with industry practices, of inadequate monitoring, or of sloppy or precarious stacking of items. To establish liability, more must be shown than that produce was stacked at an unspecified angle in a self-service area of the defendant's store, and that, as a result of customer and employee activity, produce fell to the floor.

We conclude that, even if the jury instructions be construed to mean that the only theory on which the plaintiff could recover was that the pepper had been on the floor long enough for the defendant reasonably to have seen and removed it, the instructions were correct.

Judgment affirmed.

Case Questions

1. The plaintiff, Gilhooley, appealed because he believed the judges' instructions to the jury to be in error. What was the basis of his argument?
2. Why did the Massachusetts Supreme Judicial Court reject the plaintiff's argument?
3. If the plaintiff believed that a higher standard of care should have been applied to Star Market under the facts of this case, what should he have done to raise that issue?

Duty of Care

There can be no actionable negligence when there is no legal duty. Common law duty is found by courts when the kind of relationship that exists between the parties to a dispute requires the legal recognition of a duty of care. Legislative acts may also prescribe standards of conduct required of a reasonable person. It may be argued that a reasonable person would obey statutes such as traffic laws, ordinances, and regulations of administrative bodies.

In the case of legislative acts, plaintiffs must establish that they are within the limited class of individuals intended to be protected by the statute. In addition, the harm suffered must be of the kind that the statute was intended to prevent. Often the class of people intended to be protected may be very broad. For example, regulations requiring the labeling of certain poisons are for the protection of anyone who may come in contact with the bottle. Many traffic laws are meant to protect other people on the highway. Once it is decided that a statute is applicable, most courts hold that an unexcused violation is conclusive as to the issue of negligence. In other words, it is *negligence per se,* and the issue of negligence does not go to the jury. However, some courts hold that the violation of such a statute is only *evidence* of negligence, which the jury may accept or reject as it sees fit.

Common law provides that one should guard against that which a reasonably prudent person would anticipate as likely to injure another. Damages for an injury are not recoverable if it was not foreseen or could not have been foreseen or anticipated. It is not necessary that one anticipate the precise injury sustained, however.

Courts do not ignore the common practices of society in determining the duty or whether due care was exercised in a particular situation. The scope of the duty of care that a person owes depends on the relationship of the parties. For example, those who lack mental capacity, the young, and the inexperienced are entitled to a degree of care proportionate to their incapacity to care for themselves.

As a general rule, the law does not impose the duty to aid or protect another. However, a duty *is* imposed where there is a special relationship between the parties—for example, parents must go to the aid of their children, and employers must render protection to their employees. In addition, if one puts another in peril, that person must render aid. A person can also assume a duty through contract where the duty would not otherwise exist. Although persons seeing another in distress have no obligation to be Good Samaritans, if they choose to do so they incur the duty of exercising ordinary care. Some states have changed this common law duty by passing Good Samaritan statutes that state that those administering emergency care are liable only if the acts performed constitute willful or wanton misconduct.

The plaintiff in the following case alleged that a radio station's giveaway contest created an unreasonable risk of harm to her husband and thus the station was liable in tort for his death.

Weirum v. RKO General, Inc.
539 P.2d 36
Supreme Court of California
August 21, 1975

Mosk, Justice

A rock station with an extensive teen age audience conducted a contest which rewarded the first contestant to locate a peripatetic disk jockey. Two minors driving in separate automobiles attempted to follow the disc jockey's automobile to its next stop. In the course of their pursuit, one of the minors negligently forced a car off the highway, killing its sole occupant. In a suit filed by the surviving wife and children of the decedent, the jury rendered a verdict against the radio station. We now must determine whether the radio station owed decedent a duty of due care.

The facts are not disputed. Radio station KHJ is a successful Los Angeles broadcaster with a large teen age following. . . . In order to attract an even larger portion of the available audience and thus increase advertising revenue, KHJ inaugurated in July of 1970 a promotion entitled "The Super Summer Spectacular." . . . Among the programs included in the "spectacular" was a contest broadcast on July 16, 1970, the date of the accident.

On that day, Donald Steele Revert, known professionally as "The Real Don Steele," a KHJ disc jockey and television personality, traveled in a conspicuous red automobile to a number of locations in the Los Angeles metropolitan area. Periodically, he apprised KHJ of his whereabouts and his intended destination, and the station broadcast the information to its listeners. The first person to physically locate Steele and fulfill a specified condition received a cash prize. In addition, the winning contestant participated in a brief interview on the air with "The Real Don Steele." . . .

In Van Nuys, 17-year-old Robert Sentner was listening to KHJ in his car while searching for "The Real Don Steele." Upon hearing that "The Real Don Steele" was proceeding to Canoga Park, he immediately drove to that vicinity. Meanwhile in Northridge, 19-year-old Marsha Baime heard and responded to the same information. Both of them arrived at the Holiday Theater in Canoga Park to find that someone had already claimed the prize. Without knowledge of the other, each decided to follow the Steele vehicle to its next stop and thus be the first to arrive when the next contest question or condition was announced.

For the next few miles, the Sentner and Baime cars jockeyed for position closest to the

Steele vehicle, reaching speeds up to 80 miles an hour. . . . The Steele vehicle left the freeway at the Westlake off ramp. Either Baime or Sentner, in attempting to follow, forced decedent's car onto the center divider, where it overturned. Baime stopped to report the accident. Sentner, after pausing momentarily to relate the tragedy to a passing peace officer, continued to pursue Steele, successfully located him, and collected a cash prize.

Decedent's wife and children brought an action for wrongful death against Sentner, Baime, RKO General, Inc. as owner of KHJ, and the maker of decedent's car. Sentner settled prior to the commencement of trial for the limits of his insurance policy. The jury returned a verdict against Baime and KHJ in the amount of $300,000 and found in favor of the manufacturer of decedent's car. KHJ appeals from the . . . judgment. . . . Baime did not appeal.

The primary question for our determination is whether defendant owed a duty to decedent arising out of its broadcast of the giveaway contest. . . . Any number of considerations may justify the imposition of duty in particular circumstances, including the guidance of history, our continually refined concepts of morals and justice, the convenience of the rule, and social judgment as to where the loss should fall. . . . While the question whether one owes a duty to another must be decided on a case-by-case basis, every case is governed by the rule of general application that all persons are required to use ordinary care to prevent others from being injured as the result of their conduct. . . . [F]oreseeability of the risk is a primary consideration in establishing the element of duty. . . .

The verdict in plaintiffs' favor here necessarily embraced a finding that decedent was exposed to a foreseeable risk of harm. . . .

We conclude that the record amply supports the finding of foreseeability. These tragic events unfolded in the middle of a Los Angeles summer, a time when young people were free from the constraints of school and

responsive to relief from vacation tedium. Seeking to attract new listeners, KHJ devised an "exciting" promotion. Money and a small measure of momentary notoriety awaited the swiftest response. It was foreseeable that defendant's youthful listeners, finding the prize had eluded them at one location, would race to arrive first at the next site and in their haste would disregard the demands of highway safety.

Indeed, "The Real Don Steele" testified that he had in the past noticed vehicles following him from location to location. He was further aware that the same contestants sometimes appeared at consecutive stops. This knowledge is not rendered irrelevant, as defendant suggests, by the absence of any prior injury. Such an argument confuses foreseeability with hindsight, and amounts to a contention that the injuries of the first victim are not compensable. "The mere fact that a particular kind of accident has not happened before does not . . . show that such accident is one which might not reasonably have been anticipated." . . . Thus, the fortuitous absence of prior injury does not justify relieving defendant from responsibility for the foreseeable consequences of its acts.

It is of no consequence that the harm to decedent was inflicted by third parties acting negligently. Defendant invokes the maxim that an actor is entitled to assume that others will not act negligently. . . . This concept is valid, however, only to the extent that the intervening conduct was not to be anticipated. . . . If the likelihood that a third person may react in a particular manner is a hazard which makes the actor negligent, such reaction whether innocent or negligent does not prevent the actor from being liable for the harm caused thereby. . . . Here, reckless conduct by youthful contestants, stimulated by defendant's broadcast, constituted the hazard to which decedent was exposed.

It is true, of course, that virtually every act involves some conceivable danger. Liability is imposed only if the risk of harm resulting from the act is deemed unreasonable—i.e., if the gravity and likelihood of the danger outweigh the utility of the conduct involved. . . .

We need not belabor the grave danger inherent in the contest broadcast by defendant. The risk of a high speed automobile chase is the risk of death or serious injury. Obviously, neither the entertainment afforded by the contest nor its commercial rewards can justify the creation of such a grave risk. Defendant could have accomplished its objectives of entertaining its listeners and increasing advertising revenues by adopting a contest format which would have avoided danger to the motoring public. . . .

We are not persuaded that the imposition of a duty here will lead to unwarranted extensions of liability. Defendant is fearful that entrepreneurs will henceforth be burdened with an avalanche of obligations: an athletic department will owe a duty to an ardent sports fan injured while hastening to purchase one of a limited number of tickets; a department store will be liable to injuries incurred in response to a "while-they-last" sale. This argument, however, suffers from a myopic view of the facts presented here. The giveaway contest was no common-place invitation to an attraction available on a limited basis. It was a competitive scramble in which the thrill of the chase to be the one and only victor was intensified by the live broadcasts which accompanied the pursuit. In the assertedly analogous situations described by

defendant, any haste involved in the purchase of the commodity is an incidental and unavoidable result of the scarcity of the commodity itself. In such situations, there is no attempt, as here, to generate a competitive pursuit on public streets, accelerated by repeated importuning by radio to be the very first to arrive at a particular destination. Manifestly, the "spectacular" bears little resemblance to daily commercial activities.

Defendant . . . urges that it owed no duty of care to decedent . . . absent a special relationship, an actor is under no duty to control the conduct of third parties. . . . This doctrine is rooted in the common law distinction between action and inaction, or misfeasance and nonfeasance. Misfeasance exists when the defendant is responsible for making the plaintiff's position worse, i.e., defendant has created a risk. Conversely, nonfeasance is found when the defendant has failed to aid plaintiff through beneficial intervention. . . [L]iability for nonfeasance is largely limited to those circumstances in which some special relationship can be established. If, on the other hand, the act complained of is one of misfeasance, the question of duty is governed by the standards of ordinary care discussed above. . . . [In this dispute,] [l]iability is not predicated on defendant's failure to intervene for the benefit of decedent but rather on its creation of an unreasonable risk of harm to him. . . .

Case Questions

1. Was the exact injury, or result of the contest, foreseeable in this case?
2. Assume that a business entered a float in a commercial parade, and as the float traveled down the street, employees threw candy to the crowd. Children running to collect the candy injured a spectator. Would the injury be foreseeable on the part of the business?
3. Assume that a department store advertises portable television sets at a very low price. There is a limited number to be sold "while they last" after the doors open on a specified day. A customer interested in buying a television

set runs over another customer. On the basis of *Weirum*, would the department store have a duty?

 This case involves an alleged violation of the rule of general application in misfeasance cases that one has a legal duty to exercise ordinary care to prevent others from being injured as a result of one's conduct. How would Immanuel Kant probably react to this legal duty of ordinary care?

Liability Rules for Specialized Activities

The ordinary principles of negligence do not govern occupiers' liability to those entering their premises. For example, the duty the land occupier or possessor owes to a trespasser is less than the duty the possessor owes to the general public under the ordinary principles of negligence. The special rules regarding liability of the possessor of land stem from the English tradition of high regard for land and from the dominance and prestige of the English landowning class. In the eighteenth and nineteenth centuries, owners of land were considered sovereigns within their own boundaries and were privileged to do what they pleased within their domains. The unrestricted use of land was favored over human welfare. Visitors were classified as invitees, licensees, or trespassers. Although English law has since rejected these distinctions, they remain part of the U.S. common law.

An invitee is either a *public invitee* or a *business visitor*. A public invitee is a member of the public who enters land for the purpose for which the land is held open to the public, for example, a customer who enters a store. A business visitor enters land for a purpose directly or indirectly connected with business dealings with the possessor of the land. Thus plumbers, electricians, trash collectors, and letter carriers are classified as business invitees. Invitees are given the greatest protection by the courts. A landowner owes the invitee a duty to exercise ordinary care under the usual principles of negligence liability, and must exercise reasonable care to make the premises safe. This preferred status applies only to the area of invitation.

One who enters or remains on land by virtue of the possessor's implied or express consent is a *licensee*, for example, door-to-door salespeople or social guests. In addition, police officers and firefighters are usually classified as licensees because they often come on premises unexpectedly and it would not be fair to hold possessors to the standard of care applicable to invitees. Licensees must ordinarily accept the premises as they find them and look out for their own welfare. This is based on the principle that land occupiers cannot be expected to exercise a higher degree of care for licensees than they would for themselves. A possessor of land generally owes the licensee only the duty to refrain from willful or wanton misconduct; however, the courts have developed some exceptions to this rule. With respect to active operations, for example, the possessor of land is subject to liability to licensees for injury caused by failure to exercise reasonable care for their safety. What might constitute activities dangerous to licensees depends on the court's interpretation, and knowledge of the nature of the activities normally precludes recovery by the licensee. Generally, the possessor of land is under a duty to give warning of known dangers.

A *trespasser* is one who enters and remains on the land of another without the possessor's expressed or implied consent. Licensees or inviteees may become trespassers when they venture into an area where they are not invited or expected to venture, or if they remain on the premises for longer than necessary. Generally, possessors of land are not liable to trespassers for physical harm caused by their failure either to exercise reasonable care to make their land safe for their reception or to carry on their activities so as not to endanger them. The only duty that is owed to a trespasser by an occupier of land is to refrain from willful or wanton misconduct. However, a duty of reasonable care is owed to an adult trespasser whose presence has been discovered or who habitually intrudes on a limited area. Reasonable care is also owed to the child trespasser whose presence is foreseeable.

Some question the legal and moral justification of a rule that determines the legal protection of a person's life and limb according to this classification scheme. Although courts have been reluctant to abandon the land occupier's preferred position set forth by history and precedent, some courts have replaced the common law distinction with ordinary principles of negligence to govern occupiers' liability to those entering their premises.

The trial court in the next case decided that an invitor-invitee relationship existed between the Detroit Tigers and persons attending Detroit Tigers baseball games. Thus, the Tigers were obligated to make their stadium reasonably safe for fans, like the plaintiff who was injured by a bat fragment. The Tigers appealed this decision to the Michigan Court of Appeals.

Benejam v. Detroit Tigers, Inc.
635 N.W.2d 219
Court of Appeals of Michigan
July 10, 2001, Decided

Bandstra, C. J.

In this case, we are asked to determine whether we should adopt, as a matter of Michigan law, the"limited duty" rule that other jurisdictions have applied with respect to spectator injuries at baseball games. Under that rule, a baseball stadium owner is not liable for injuries to spectators that re-

sult from projectiles leaving the field during play if safety screening has been provided behind home plate and there are a sufficient number of protected seats to meet ordinary demand. . . .

Plaintiff Alyssia M. Benejam, a young girl, attended a Tigers game with a friend and members of the friend's family and was seated quite close to the playing field along the third base line. The stadium was equipped with a net behind home plate, and the net extended part of the way down the first and third base lines. Although Alyssia was behind the net, she was injured when a player's bat broke and a fragment of it curved around the net . . . , [or] traveled in a straight line and bounced off a nearby seat before striking Alyssia. There was no evidence, and plaintiffs do not contend, that the fragment of the bat went through the net, that there was a hole in the net, or that the net was otherwise defective.

Plaintiffs sued the Tigers, claiming primarily that the net was insufficiently long. . . . The Tigers responded with motions before, during, and after trial arguing that, as a matter of law, plaintiffs could not or did not present any viable legal claim. Those motions were all denied by the trial court. Alyssia suffered crushed fingers as a result of the accident and the jury awarded plaintiffs noneconomic damages (past and future) totaling $917,000, lost earning capacity of $56,700 and $35,000 for past and future medical expenses. Damages are not at issue on appeal. . . .

Defendant's argument . . . concern[s] the duty of care . . . applicable in this case. . . .

Defendant argues that although there is no Michigan law directly on point, other jurisdictions have balanced the safety benefits of providing a protective screen against the fact that such screening detracts from the allure of attending a live baseball game by placing an obstacle or insulation between fans and the playing field. The rule that emerges in these cases is that a stadium proprietor cannot be liable for spectator injuries if it has satisfied a "limited duty"—to erect a screen that will protect the most dangerous area of the spectator stands, behind home plate, and to provide a number of seats in this area sufficient to meet the ordinary demand for protected seats. In this case, there is no dispute that the Tigers constructed a protective screen behind home plate, and there was no evidence that the screen was insufficient to meet the ordinary demand for protected seating. . . .

Plaintiffs argue against application of the limited duty doctrine and contend that, under usual principles of premises liability, the cir

cuit court correctly concluded that a jury question was presented. Defendant (an invitor) had a duty to exercise ordinary care and prudence and maintain premises reasonably safe for invitees like Alyssia. Plaintiffs argue that the jury verdict was supported by sufficient evidence that the defendant failed to fulfill this duty because it did not provide a screen extending long enough along the third (and first) base lines.

There is no Michigan case law directly on point. Our review of precedents from other jurisdictions finds overwhelming, if not universal, support for the limited duty rule that defendant advocates. . . .

The logic of these precedents is that there is an inherent risk of objects leaving the playing field that people know about when they attend baseball games. . . . "no one of ordinary intelligence could see many innings of the ordinary league baseball game without coming to a full realization that batters cannot and do not control the direction of the ball." . . . Also, there is inherent value in having most seats unprotected by a screen because baseball patrons generally want to be involved with the game in an intimate way and are even hoping that they will come in contact with some projectile from the field (in the form of a souvenir baseball). . . . "the chance to apprehend a misdirected baseball is as much a part of the game as the seventh inning stretch or peanuts and Cracker Jack." . . . In other words, spectators know about the risk of being in the stands and, in fact, welcome that risk to a certain extent. On the other hand, the area behind home plate is especially dangerous and spectators who want protected seats should be able to find them in this area. Balancing all of these concerns, courts generally have adopted the limited duty doctrine that prevents liability if there are a sufficient number of protected seats behind home plate to meet the ordinary demand for that kind of seating. If that seating is provided, the baseball stadium owner has fulfilled its duty and there can be no liability for spectators who are injured by a projectile from the field. . . .

It seems axiomatic that baseball fans attend games knowing that, as a natural result of play, objects may leave the field with the potential of causing injury in the stands. It is equally clear that most spectators, nonetheless, prefer to be as "close to the play" as possible, without an insulating and obstructive screen between them and the action. In contrast, a smaller number of spectators prefer the protection offered by screening. The most dangerous part of the spectator stands is the area in the lower deck behind home plate and along each of the baselines. Certainly home plate is the center of the most activity on the field. Most notably, it is there that pitched balls, traveling at great speeds in a line that would extend into the stands, are often deflected or squarely hit into those stands. Quite logically, the limited duty rule protects a stadium owner that provides screening for this most dangerous area and, in so doing, accommodates baseball patrons who seek protected seating. Because the limited duty rule is based on the desires of spectators, it further makes sense to define the extent of screening that should be provided behind home plate on the basis of consumer demand.

Plaintiffs do nothing to argue substantively against the limited duty rule, but merely argue that baseball stadium cases should be governed by usual invitor-invitee principles, not any special "baseball rule." Thus, plaintiffs argue that the jury properly determined that defendant failed to exercise "ordinary care" and failed to provide "reasonably safe" premises. However, the limited duty rule does not ignore or abrogate usual premises liability principles. Instead, it identifies the duty of baseball stadium proprietors with greater specificity than the usual "ordinary care/reasonably safe" standard provides. The limited duty precedents "do not eliminate the stadium owner's duty to exercise reasonable care under the circumstances to protect patrons against injury." . . . Rather, these precedents "define that duty so that once the stadium owner has provided 'adequately screened seats' for *all* those desiring them, the stadium owner has fulfilled its duty of care as a matter of law." . . . The limited duty doctrine establishes the "outer limits" of liability and "thereby prevents a jury from requiring a stadium owner to take precautions that are clearly unreasonable." By providing greater specificity with regard to the duty imposed on stadium owners, the rule prevents burgeoning litigation that might signal the demise or substantial alteration of the game of baseball as a spectator sport. . . .

For most fans, the everyday reality of attending a baseball game includes voluntarily subjecting oneself to the risk that a ball or bat might leave the field and cause injury. The limited duty rule comports more nearly with that everyday reality than would usual invitor-invitee principles of liability. While requiring that protected seats be provided for those who want them, the limited duty rule leaves the baseball stadium owner free, without fear of liability, to accommodate the majority of fans who prefer unobstructed and uninsulated contact with the game. Under usual invitor-invitee principles of liability, fear of litigation would likely require screening far in excess of that required to meet the desires of baseball fans.

This case, tried under usual invitor-invitee principles of liability, provides a good example. Plaintiff's expert testified that, on the basis of his review of accidents occurring over time in the spectator stands between first base and third base, reasonable safety precautions would include screening in that entire area. In another case, where an injury occurred farther down the baseline, testimony and argument would likely be adduced to support a further extension as "reasonably necessary" to protect fans. The logical result of having these cases governed by usual invitor-invitee principles of liability would be that warned against in *Akins*, . . . : "Every spectator injured by a foul ball, no matter where he is seated or standing in the ball park, would have an absolute right to go to the jury on every claim of negligence."

Both because the limited duty doctrine represents a good accommodation of the interests that must be balanced in this case . . . , we adopt that doctrine as a matter of Michigan law. Specifically, we hold that a baseball stadium owner that provides screening behind home plate sufficient to meet ordinary demand for protected seating has fulfilled its duty with respect to screening and cannot be subjected to liability for injuries resulting to a spectator by an object leaving the playing field. We do not today hold that a baseball stadium operator that does not provide this level of protection can be held liable. . . . that is not the situation presented on this appeal and we express no opinion regarding the merits of any such argument.

Applying the limited duty rule here, we conclude that plaintiffs have failed to provide any proof sufficient to find that liability could be imposed. Clearly, there was a screen behind home plate and there was no proof whatsoever that persons wanting seats protected by the screen could not be accommodated. To the contrary, uncontested testimony by Tigers ticket personnel established that protected seating is generally open and available to fans who want it. Accordingly, we conclude that the screening provided by defendant was sufficient under the limited duty doctrine applicable in this case. . . .

We reverse and remand. . . .

Case Questions

1. What duty, according to the appeals court, do the Detroit Tigers owe fans attending their games?
2. Why did the appeals court decide to reject the ordinary care standard?

Proximate Cause

For the plaintiff to support a negligence action there must be a reasonable connection between the negligent act of the defendant and the damage suffered by the plaintiff. For tort liability, however, proof of factual causation is not enough. Tort liability is predicated on the existence of *proximate cause*. Proximate cause means legal cause and consists of two elements: (1) causation in fact, and (2) foreseeability. A plaintiff must prove that his or her injuries were the actual or factual result of the defendant's actions. Causation in fact may be established directly or indirectly. Courts usually use a "but for" test to establish causation in fact: but for the defendant's negligence, the plaintiff's injuries would not have occurred. This test is an extremely broad one and could have far-reaching results.

Every event has many contributing causes, even though some may be very remote. The defendant is not relieved from liability merely because other causes have contributed to the result. In many situations, application of the "but-for" test will identify several persons who could be placed on a causation continuum. The question before the court in a negligence case is whether the conduct has been so significant and important a cause that the defendant should be legally responsible. For example, in a nighttime automobile accident, the fact that one of the drivers worked late at the office would be a factual cause of the collision. If she hadn't worked late, she wouldn't have been at the location of the accident. But this cause should not be recognized as a legal cause of the collision. Because cause demands that some boundary be set for the consequences of an act, proximate cause, rather than causation in fact, is used to determine liability.

An individual is only responsible for those consequences that are *reasonably foreseeable*, and will be relieved of liability for injuries that are not reasonably related to the negligent conduct. To illustrate, a driver drives his car carelessly and collides with another car, causing it to explode. Four blocks away, a nurse carrying a baby is startled by the explosion and drops the infant. It is doubtful if any court would hold the driver liable to the infant, even though the driver was negligent and was the factual cause of the infant's injury. The baby's injury is so far removed from the driver that it would be unfair to hold the driver liable. The driver could not reasonably have foreseen the injury sustained by the infant. In other words, the driving would not be the proximate cause of the injury.

If there is more than one cause for a single injury, liability is possible if each alone would have been sufficient to cause the harm without the other. If there are joint tortfeasors of a single injury, each possible tortfeasor's actions must be examined to see if the acts were so closely related to the damage to have proximately caused the plaintiff's injury.

Anglin v. Florida Department of Transportation

472 So.2d 784
District Court of Appeal of Florida
July 2, 1985

Zehmer, Judge

In these consolidated personal injury cases, plaintiffs below appeal a final summary judgment, contending the trial court erred in ruling as a matter of law that appellees were insulated from liability by unforeseeable independent intervening causes. We reverse.*

On the night of September 3, 1979, Cleopatra Anglin, her husband, and her brother

*This opinion also decides the consolidated case of *Anglin v. Seaboard Coast Line Railroad Company.*—Ed.

were traveling through drizzling rain in a 1965 Chevrolet pickup truck. Upon crossing a Seaboard Coastline Railroad track on Alternate U.S. 27 in rural Polk County, they unexpectedly hit an accumulation of water that covered both lanes of travel and was approximately six inches deep. The truck motor was doused with water, sputtered for some distance after hitting the pool of water, and then died. The Anglins attempted to start the motor by pushing the truck down the road and then "popping" the clutch once the truck reached a moderate speed. Approximately fifteen minutes after their truck hit the water, during which time they attempted in vain to push-start the truck several times, a car driven by Edward DuBose passed the Anglin truck heading in the opposite direction. A short distance after passing the truck, which was still on the road and, according to some witnesses, still being pushed, Mr. DuBose turned his car around and headed back toward the truck to render assistance. Unfortunately, Mr. DuBose failed to timely see the truck, hit his brakes, slid into the rear of the truck, and pinned Mrs. Anglin between the two vehicles, causing injury resulting in the amputation of both legs. The distance between the pool of water and the accident scene was estimated by some witnesses as approximately 200 yards, by others up to three-tenths of a mile.

On February 16, 1981, Mrs. Anglin and her husband filed a complaint against the state Department of Transportation and Seaboard Coastline Railroad Company, alleging negligence in the design and maintenance of the road and railroad tracks by allowing the accumulation of water on the roadway immediately adjacent to the railroad tracks. Defendants filed a motion for summary judgment and, in addition to numerous depositions aready taken, plaintiffs filed affidavits in opposition to the motion. A final summary judgment in favor of the defendants was entered on June 9, 1983, upon the trial judge's ruling as a matter of law that the actions of the plaintiffs in attempting to push-start their disabled pickup truck and the actions of Mr. DuBose in negligently losing control of his car and colliding with the plaintiff's truck were independent, efficient intervening causes of the accident that were unforeseeable by the defendants, thereby breaking the chain of causation between the purported negligence of the defendants and the injury.

As a general rule, a tortfeasor is liable for all damages proximately caused by his negligence. The term "proximate cause" (or "legal cause," in the language of the standard jury instructions) consists of two essential elements: (1) causation in fact, and (2) foreseeability. . . . Causation in fact is often characterized in terms of a "but for" test, i.e., *but for* the defendant's negligence, the resulting damage would not have occurred. In the

present case, there is no question as to causation in fact because "but for" the defendants' alleged negligence in causing the pooling of water on the highway, there would have been no accidental stopping of plaintiff's truck and resulting injury.[†]

The second element of proximate cause, foreseeability, is, unlike causation in fact, a concept established through considerations of public policy and fairness whereby a defendant whose conduct factually "caused" damages may nevertheless be relieved of liability for those damages. Thus, proximate cause may be found lacking where the type of damage or injury that occurred is not within the scope of danger or risk created by the defendant's negligence and, thus, not a reasonably foreseeable result thereof. . . . It is not necessary, however, that the defendants "be able to foresee the exact nature and extent of the injuries or the precise manner in which the injuries occur;" all that is necessary to liability is that "the tort feasor be able to foresee that *some* injury will likely result in *some* manner as a consequence of his negligent acts." . . . In the instant case, it cannot be said as a matter of law that an injury to plaintiff was not within the scope of danger or risk arising out of the alleged negligence. In the field of human experience, one should expect that negligently permitting a pool of water on an open highway would likely pose a substantial hazard to motorists because a vehicle crashing unexpectedly into the water is likely to experience a stalled motor or other difficulty causing the vehicle to stop on the highway, thereby subjecting its occupants to the risk of injury from collision by other cars. . . .

Proximate cause may be found lacking, however, where an unforeseeable force or

---

[†]The defendants' negligence in permitting the pooling of water is not an issue on this appeal. The trial court did not find, nor have appellees argued to us, that there was a complete absence of any factual dispute warranting the entry of summary judgment for either side on this issue.

action occurring independently of the original negligence causes the injury or damage. This force or action is commonly referred to as an "independent, efficient intervening cause." . . . For the original negligent actor to be relieved of liability under this doctrine, however, the intervening cause must be "efficient," i.e., truly independent of and not "set in motion" by the original negligence. . . . The trial court's ruling that the conduct of the plaintiffs in pushing their truck down the road was an independent, efficient intervening cause of the accident was error because the existence of the pool of water set into motion the plaintiffs' subsequent actions in attempting to restart the motor that was stalled by driving through the water. These actions, having been "set in motion" by defendants' negligence, did not constitute an independent, efficient intervening cause. Whether the plaintiffs' conduct was negligent and caused the injury should be submitted to the jury under appropriate instructions on comparative negligence.

The trial court correctly characterized Mr. DuBose's negligent operation of his car as an independent intervening cause. The negligent pooling of water did not cause Mr. DuBose to negligently operate his vehicle into collision with the plaintiffs.[‡] The trial court erred, however, in ruling *as a matter of law* that such intervening cause warranted entry of summary judgment for defendants. If an intervening cause is reasonably foreseeable, the negligent defendants may be held liable. . . . Whether an intervening cause is foreseeable is ordinarily for the trier of fact to decide. . . . Only if reasonable persons could not differ as to the total absence of evidence to support any inference that the intervening cause was foreseeable may the court determine the issue as a matter of law. . . . In the circumstance of

this case (the night was dark, it was raining, and the collision occurred in a rural area where traffic customarily moves rapidly), had DuBose come on the scene and collided with plaintiffs' stalled truck immediately after plaintiffs hit the pooled water, the question of foreseeability of that occurrence would most assuredly present a jury issue. The fact that plaintiffs attempted to push-start their stalled truck for approximately fifteen minutes and that Mr. DuBose collided with it while attempting to stop and provide assistance does not change this jury issue as to a question of law. The plaintiffs' exposure to danger was created by defendants' negligence, and the fact that a collision might occur while plaintiffs were extricating themselves from such danger up to fifteen minutes later presents a jury issue on foreseeability. . . . That is so because the defendants need not have notice of the particular manner in which an injury would occur; it is enough that the possibility of some accidental injury was foreseeable to the ordinarily prudent person. . . .

Reversed and remanded.

Booth, Chief Judge, dissenting

We should affirm the summary judgment entered below based on lack of proximate cause. The chain of events here between alleged negligent act and injury is too attenuated and is broken, in fact, by the independent, intervening actions of others.

For the purpose of this appeal, we assume that defendants were negligent in maintaining a depression on a rural roadway, a depression which, in the aftermath of Hurricane David, was filled with six inches of water. It would be foreseeable that a driver who unexpectedly traversed such a depression in the road could lose control of his vehicle, causing an accidental injury to himself or others. Stalling and the immediate consequences thereof are also not unforeseeable. Other results of the puddle could be termed as "foreseeable" in a philosophical, but not a

---

[‡]The result would be otherwise if, for example, Mr. DuBose had driven through the pool of water and failed to stop because his brakes became wet and ineffective.

legal, sense. For example, the disabled vehicle could have been struck by lightning, or the occupants could have been robbed or become ill but unable to seek medical care. In each instance, it could be said that, but for the stalling of their car caused by the defendant these subsequent events would not have occurred. Although there would be cause and effect relationship, such consequences would generally not be within the scope of the risk created by the negligent party who caused the vehicle to become immobile. The law does not impose liability because of the concept of "proximate cause," as stated in *Prosser and Keeton*.§

> "In a philosophical sense, the consequences of an act go forward to eternity, and the causes of an event go back to the dawn of human events, and beyond. But any attempt to impose responsibility upon such a basis would result in infinite liability for all wrongful acts, and would 'set society on edge and fill the courts with endless litigation.' As a practical matter, legal responsibility must be limited to those causes which are so closely connected with the result and of such significance that the law is justified in imposing liability. Some boundary must be set to liability for the consequences of any act, upon the basis of some social idea of justice of policy."

Therefore, I would agree with the majority that there could be a jury question as to causation in fact. But, as to proximate cause, in this case at least, the principle is one of law. In the Prosser and Keeton treatise, it is stated:

> "Once it is established that the defendant's conduct has in fact been one of the causes of the plaintiff's injury, there remains the question whether defendant should be legally responsible for the injury. Unlike the fact of causation with which it is often hopelessly confused, this is primarily a problem of law. It is sometimes said to depend on whether the conduct has been so significant and

important a cause that the defendant should be legally responsible. But both significance and importance turn upon conclusions in terms of legal policy, so that they depend essentially on whether the policy of the law will extend the responsibility for the conduct to the consequences which have in fact occurred. Quite often this has been stated, and properly so, as an issue of whether the defendant is under any duty to the plaintiff, or whether the duty includes protection against such consequences."

In the instant case, the Anglins testified that, after passing through the puddle of water, the engine sputtered and the vehicle was pulled to the side of the road as it came to a stop. At that point, the vehicle was off the road, and there were no injuries. The further events which occurred should not be charged to the act of defendants in allowing a rain-filled depression in the roadway. The Anglins testified that, after some minutes off the road, plaintiffs pushed the truck back onto the roadway and endeavored to push the vehicle down the road on that dark and rainy night.

At this point entered the next intervening force in the form of one Mr. DuBose, who passed, going in the opposite direction, and slowed to ask if plaintiffs would like help. DuBose then continued down the road some short distance and, as plaintiffs testified, "slammed on brakes, slid like and spun around," approached the plaintiffs' vehicle from the rear, and "with the engine roaring" and at a speed approaching 40 miles an hour, slammed into the back of the plaintiffs' truck, striking and seriously injuring Mrs. Anglin. The conduct of DuBose can only be considered gross negligence. . . .

The issue, then, is the scope of the legal duty to protect the plaintiff against intervening causes which are *possible but not probable*. As posed by Prosser and Keeton, *supra*, does defendant's duty include protecting plaintiff against these consequences? Plaintiff's injury occurred more than a quarter of an hour after,

§Prosser and Keeton, *TORTS* 264 (5th ed.).

and three-tenths of a mile down the road from, the puddle. The accident occurred after, and as a result of, negligence of others, each acting independently of defendants.

The law does not impose unlimited liability for all consequences that may result from a puddle of water on the road. This case should illustrate that principle. The trial court correctly held that the injury occurring was not within the scope of danger attributable by law to defendants' conduct, and should be affirmed.

Case Questions

1. Proximate cause consists of two elements—what are they? What is important about each element?
2. What is an independent, efficient, intervening cause?
3. In this case, the trial judge ruled as a matter of law that an independent, efficient, intervening cause existed. According to the appellate court, when is such a decision justified?
4. What position does Chief Judge Booth take in dissent?

 INTERNET TIP

Students visiting the textbook's website will find there a case that discusses both the distinction between invitees and licensees, proximate cause, and foreseeability.

DEFENSES TO NEGLIGENCE

Even after a plaintiff has proved that a defendant was negligent and that the negligence was the proximate cause of his or her injury, the defendant may counter by proving a defense. Contributory negligence and assumption of risk are two such defenses.

Contributory Negligence and Assumption of Risk Defenses

Contributory negligence is a defense that exists when the injured persons proximately contributed to their injuries by their own negligence. This is based on the theory that the plaintiff is held to the same standard of care as the defendant: that is, that of a reasonable person under like circumstances.

To illustrate, D-1 is driving his car and P is his passenger. Both are injured in a collision with D-2's car. If both cars were driven negligently, D-1 could not recover from D-2 because his own negligence contributed to his own injuries.

Yet P could recover from both D-1 and D-2, because they were both joint tort-feasors in causing P's injuries.

The burden of proving contributory negligence is on the defendant.

North Carolina is one of four states that has not adopted the comparative negligence approach. In the next case the plaintiff is denied any recovery from the defendant because she was found to have been contributorily negligent.

Carolyn Alford v. Wanda E. Lowery
COA02-185
Court of Appeals of North Carolina
December 3, 2002

Hunter, Judge

A jury found that Carolyn Alford ("plaintiff") was injured by the negligence of Wanda Evette Lowery ("defendant"). However, plaintiff was barred from recovery because the jury additionally found that plaintiff had been contributorily negligent. Plaintiff appeals from the judgment entered upon the verdict. We affirm for the reasons set forth herein.

This case arises from an automobile accident that occurred on the morning of 2 September 1996 at approximately 6:40 a.m. The accident took place in Mecklenburg County on Hawthorne Lane, which is a two lane road divided by a double yellow line. The evidence tended to show that as plaintiff was driving south on Hawthorne Lane, plaintiff noticed a car ahead of her, driven by defendant, cross the double yellow line and travel towards her in plaintiff's lane of travel. The two vehicles collided head-on. Plaintiff observed that defendant's car was in her lane of travel at least one, and maybe two, blocks away from the location of impact. According to plaintiff, the impact occurred completely in her lane of travel. Neither plaintiff nor defendant blew their horns prior to impact. Plaintiff testified that she did not take any evasive action until just prior to the collision.

Police Officer Kevin L. Weaver testified that when he arrived at the scene of the acci-

dent, both vehicles were straddling the yellow line. Officer Weaver further testified that there were thirty feet of skid marks from plaintiff's vehicle.

Plaintiff filed a complaint on 23 February 1999 alleging that defendant's negligence was a proximate cause of plaintiff's personal injuries and damages. Defendant filed an answer raising the defense of a sudden emergency. Defendant alleged in her answer that as she was proceeding northbound on Hawthorne Lane, an object appeared in the path of her vehicle and caused defendant to swerve to the left in order to avoid colliding with the object. A jury concluded that plaintiff was injured by the negligence of defendant but that plaintiff contributed to her injuries by her own negligence. Judgment was entered upon the verdict and plaintiff recovered nothing since the jury found she had been contributorily negligent. . . .

Plaintiff initially contends that trial court erred in granting defendant's motion to amend her answer to include the affirmative defense of contributory negligence. . . . In the instant case, plaintiff has failed to show that the trial court abused its discretion in allowing defendant's motion to amend her answer. The evidence raises an issue of contributory negligence. Plaintiff testified that she observed defendant's vehicle for at least one, and possibly two, blocks with no visual obstructions traveling towards her in her lane; plaintiff took no evasive action until just prior to impact; the point of impact was entirely within plaintiff's lane; and plaintiff failed to blow her horn in an effort to catch the attention of defendant prior to the accident. In addition, plaintiff was not prejudiced by the grant of this motion since plaintiff's attorney stated that he had been on notice that defendant intended to amend her answer to include the defense of contributory negligence for some time. Therefore, this assignment of error is overruled. . . .

Plaintiff next argues the trial court erred in instructing the jury on the issue of contributory negligence. However, there is no evidence in the record indicating that plaintiff objected to the contributory negligence instruction being submitted to the jury. . . . Therefore, plaintiff has not properly preserved this issue for appeal. . . .

Plaintiff additionally asserts that the jury's finding that she was contributorily negligent was improper since there was no evidence of contributory negligence. We conclude this contention lacks merit. "Contributory negligence . . . is negligence on the part of the plaintiff which joins, simultaneously or successively, with the negligence of the defendant . . . to produce the injury of which the plaintiff complains. . . . The burden is on the defendant to prove contributory negligence. . . . We conclude there was adequate evidence for a jury to find that plaintiff's negligence contributed to her injuries. The evidence showed that plaintiff observed the vehicle driven by defendant for a minimum of one, and a maximum of two, city blocks prior to impact, that plaintiff did not take any evasive action until just prior to impact, that the impact occurred while plaintiff's vehicle was completely within its own lane, and that plaintiff made no attempts prior to the collision to catch defendant's attention. Therefore, the jury's verdict was supported by the evidence and we accordingly conclude plaintiff's argument lacks merit.

The case *sub judice* is representative of the result that often arises from the common law doctrine of contributory negligence. As this Court has previously noted:

The common law doctrine of contributory negligence has been the law in this State since *Morrison v. Cornelius,* . . . (1869). . . . Although forty-six states have abandoned the doctrine of contributory negligence in favor of comparative negligence, contributory negligence continues to be the law of this State until our Supreme Court overrules it or the General Assembly adopts comparative negligence. . . .

For the foregoing reasons, we affirm the judgment of the trial court.

Affirmed.

Case Question

Do you see fairness issues associated with the contributory negligence defense as it was applied in this case?

The defense of *assumption of risk* exists when the plaintiffs had knowledge of the risk and made the free choice of exposing themselves to it. Assumption of risk may be express or implied. In an express assumption of risk, the plaintiff expressly agrees in advance that the defendant has no duty to care for him or her and is not liable for what would otherwise be negligent conduct. For example, parents often expressly assume the risk of personal injury to their children in conjunction with youth soccer, basketball, and baseball programs. Where the assumption of risk is implied, consent is manifested by the plaintiff's continued presence after he or she has become aware of the danger involved. The plaintiffs impliedly consent to take their chances concerning the defendant's negligence. For example, baseball fans who sit in unscreened seats at the ballpark know that balls and even bats may strike them; they implicitly agree to take a chance of being injured in this manner.

Comparative Negligence

When the defense of contributory negligence is used in a noncomparative negligence jurisdiction, the entire loss is placed on one party even when both are negligent. For this reason, most states now determine the amount of damage by comparing the negligence of the plaintiff with that of the defendant. Under this doctrine of *comparative negligence*, a negligent plaintiff may be able to recover a portion of the cost of an injury.

In negligence cases, comparative negligence divides the damages between the parties by reducing the plaintiff's damages in proportion to the extent of that person's contributory fault. The trier of fact in a case assigns a percentage of the total fault to the plaintiff and the plaintiff's total damages are usually reduced by that percentage. For example, a plaintiff who was considered to be 40 percent at fault by the trier of fact would recover $1,200 if the total damages were determined to be $2,000.

The plaintiff in the following case brought suit when his mechanically disabled truck, which was partially on a highway and partially on the shoulder, was struck in the rear by an automobile driven by the defendant.

Stein v. Langer
515 So.2d 507
Court of Appeal of Louisiana, First Circuit
October 14, 1987

LeBlanc, Judge

The issues presented in this personal injury case are the proper allocation of fault among the parties . . .

On the evening of September 5, 1982, plaintiff, David Stein, was driving his truck north on Louisiana Highway 1077, a two-lane rural road in St. Tammany Parish. Upon experiencing a mechanical breakdown, plain-

tiff steered his truck onto the highway shoulder as far as he could and parked. However, the shoulder was not wide enough for him to pull completely off the road. Although exactly how far the truck protruded onto the highway is disputed, it was at least six to eight inches.

Shortly thereafter, Everett Randall Cooper, one of the defendants, who was a friend of the plaintiff, passed in a southbound lane. Recognizing the plaintiff and noting that his truck appeared to be disabled, Cooper turned around and drove back to where plaintiff's truck was parked. Because he thought plaintiff's truck might need a jump-start, he parked his own truck facing south, with the front bumper of his truck several feet from the front bumper of plaintiff's truck. Cooper was unable to pull his truck as far on the shoulder as plaintiff had because of a traffic sign which prevented him from doing so. His truck protruded approximately a foot and a half onto the highway. In this position, one headlight was visible to traffic approaching in the northbound lane. The emergency flashers on Cooper's truck were also on. Once Cooper arrived plaintiff, who was concerned about running his battery down, turned off all the lights on his own truck, leaving it completely unlit.

Several northbound cars passed by the two trucks without incident by moving over partially into the southbound lane to pass. Approximately five minutes later, however, a car proceeding in the northbound lane and driven by defendant, Dianne Langer, struck the rear of plaintiff's truck. The force of the impact pushed plaintiff's truck into the front of Cooper's truck. Plaintiff was standing between the two trucks at the time and sustained injuries to his legs and knees.

Mrs. Langer testified that she saw the headlight of Cooper's truck five to ten seconds before impact, but did not see the plaintiff's black truck prior to hitting it. According to her testimony, she intended to avoid Cooper's vehicle, which appeared to be either a car or motorcycle approaching in her lane of traffic, by going around it on the right shoulder of the highway. She originally was driving approximately 35 mph, but had started to slow down upon seeing the headlight. She testified that her foot was on the brake when she struck plaintiff's truck.

Plaintiff filed suit against Mrs. Langer, [and] her husband, William Langer. . . . Following a jury trial, a verdict was rendered finding Diane Langer fifty-five percent (55%) at fault, plaintiff forty-five percent (45%) at fault and Everett Cooper guilty of no fault. The jury fixed plaintiff's damages at $3,100.00.

Thereafter, on February 13, 1985, the trial court rendered judgment against the Langers and their insurer and in favor of plaintiff for $3,100, subject to a forty-five (45%) reduction. The judgment also dismissed all claims against Cooper. . . . Plaintiff has now appealed the judgment of February 13, 1985, arguing that the jury erred in assessing fault and in awarding him inadequate damages.

Specifically, plaintiff maintains the jury erred in not assessing Mrs. Langer with 100 percent of the fault or, in the alternative, in not finding Cooper guilty of any fault. The standard of review on appeal is that factual findings made by the trier-of-fact are entitled to great weight and will not be overturned unless manifestly erroneous. . . . Since a jury's findings as to percentage of fault are factual in nature, they will not be disturbed unless clearly wrong. . . .

After our thorough review of the record, we find no manifest error in the assessments of fault made by the jury in this case. The fact that plaintiff, as well as Mrs. Langer, was at fault is obvious upon review of the facts. By turning off all the lights on his truck, plaintiff made it much more difficult for motorists to observe the fact that his truck was partially obstructing the highway, thereby greatly increasing the danger of the situation.

Likewise, we find no error in the jury's conclusion that Cooper was not guilty of any fault. In order to give plaintiff's truck a jump-start, Cooper had no choice but to park as he did. Further, Cooper pulled over as far on the shoulder as he could and had both his headlights and emergency flashers turned on. Cooper's actions were reasonable under the circumstances present. In this regard, it is significant that several northbound cars had passed without difficulty before Mrs. Langer's car hit plaintiff's truck. For the above reasons, we affirm the assessments of fault made by the jury.

Case Questions

1. What are the advantages and disadvantages of comparative negligence in comparison with contributory negligence?
2. Under what circumstances will a court disturb a jury's allocation of the percentages of fault?
3. Assume that the jury found the plaintiff to be 51 percent at fault in this case and the defendant 49 percent at fault. If the plaintiff was more at fault than the defendant for this accident, why should the plaintiff recover any damages at all?

Negligence and Product Liability

Plaintiffs can recover in negligence by proving that a manufacturer's conduct violated the reasonable person standard and proximately caused injury. The manufacturer's allegedly tortious conduct could relate to any aspect of product design, manufacturing, quality control, packaging, and/or warnings.

In product liability suits it is often difficult to prove the defendant's act or omission that caused the plaintiff's injury. Thus, in the interests of justice, courts developed the doctrine of *res ipsa loquitur* ("the thing speaks for itself"). This doctrine permits plaintiffs to circumstantially prove negligence if the following facts are proved: (1) the defendant had exclusive control over the allegedly defective product during manufacture, (2) under normal circumstances, the plaintiff would not have been injured by the product if the defendant had exercised ordinary care, and (3) the plaintiff's conduct did not contribute significantly to the accident. From the proved facts, the law permits the jurors to infer a fact for which there is no direct, explicit proof—the defendant's negligent act or omission. The trial judge will instruct the jurors that the law permits them to consider the inferred fact as well as the proved facts in deciding whether the defendant was negligent.

The following case illustrates typical problems associated with a case involving negligent failure to warn. A manufacturer's duty to warn consumers depends on the nature of the product. Warnings are unnecessary for products that are obviously dangerous to everyone (knives, saws, and firearms). However, for products that may contain hazards that are not obvious, manufacturers have a duty to warn if the average person would not have known about a safety hazard. If the plaintiff is knowledgeable about the hazard that the warning would have addressed, the manufacturer's negligent failure to warn would not have proximately caused the plaintiff's injuries. Thus in such cases the extent of the plaintiff's actual knowledge and familiarity with the hazard and the product are relevant to the issue of causation.

Laaperi v. Sears Roebuck & Co., Inc.
787 F.2d 726
U.S. Court of Appeals, First Circuit
March 31, 1986

Campbell, Chief Judge

This is an appeal from jury verdicts totalling $1.8 million entered in a product liability suit against defendants Sears, Roebuck & Co. and Pittway Corporation. The actions were brought by Albin Laaperi as administrator of the estates of his three sons, all of whom were killed in a fire in their home in December 1976, and as father and next friend of his daughter, Janet, who was injured in the fire. Plaintiff's theory of recovery was that defendants had a duty to warn plaintiff that a smoke detector powered by house current, manufactured by Pittway and sold to Laaperi by Sears, might not operate in the event of an electrical fire caused by a short circuit. Defendants contend on appeal that the district court erred in denying their motions for directed verdict and judgment notwithstanding the verdict; that the admission into evidence of purportedly undisclosed expert testimony violated Fed.R.Civ.P. 26(e); and that the award of $750,000 for injuries to Janet Laaperi was excessive and improper. We affirm the judgments in favor of plaintiff in his capacity as administrator of the estates of his three sons, but vacate the judgment in favor of Janet Laaperi, and remand for a new trial limited to the issue of her damages.

I

In March 1976, plaintiff Albin Laaperi purchased a smoke detector from Sears. The detector, manufactured by the Pittway Corporation, was designed to be powered by AC (electrical) current. Laaperi installed the detector himself in one of the two upstairs bedrooms in his home.

Early in the morning of December 27, 1976, a fire broke out in the Laaperi home. The three boys in one of the upstairs bedrooms were killed in the blaze. Laaperi's 13-year-old daughter, Janet, who was sleeping in the other upstairs bedroom, received burns over 12 percent of her body and was hospitalized for three weeks.

The uncontroverted testimony at trial was that the smoke detector did not sound an alarm on the night of the fire. The cause of the fire was later found to be a short circuit in an electrical cord that was located in a cedar closet in the boys' bedroom. The Laaperi home had two separate electrical circuits in the upstairs bedrooms: one which provided electricity to the outlets and one which powered the lighting fixtures. The smoke detector had been connected to the outlet circuit, which was the circuit that shorted and cut off. Because the circuit was shorted, the AC-operated smoke detector received no power on the night of the fire. Therefore, although the detector itself was in no sense defective (indeed, after the fire the charred detector was tested and found to be operable), no alarm sounded.

Laaperi brought this diversity action against defendants Sears and Pittway, asserting negligent design, negligent manufacture, breach of warranty, and negligent failure to warn of inherent dangers. The parties agreed that the applicable law is that of Massachusetts. Before the claims went to the jury, verdicts were directed in favor of the defendants on all theories of liability other than failure to warn.

Laaperi's claim under the failure to warn theory was that he was unaware of the danger that the very short circuit which might ignite a fire in his home could, at the same time, incapacitate the smoke detector. He contended that had he been warned of this danger, he would have purchased a battery-powered smoke detector as a backup or taken some other precaution, such as wiring the detector to a circuit of its own, in order better to protect his family in the event of an electrical fire.

The jury returned verdicts in favor of Laaperi in all four actions on the failure to warn claim. The jury assessed damages in the amount of $350,000 in each of the three actions brought on behalf of the deceased sons, and $750,000 in the action brought on behalf of Janet Laaperi. The defendants' motions for directed verdict and judgment notwithstanding the verdict were denied and defendants appealed.

II

Defendants contend that the district court erred in denying their motions for directed verdict and judgment n.o.v. First, they claim that they had no duty to warn that the smoke detector might not work in the event of some electrical fires. Second, they maintain that even if they had such a duty, there was insufficient evidence on the record to show that the failure to warn proximately caused plaintiff's damages. We address these arguments in turn.

A. Duty to Warn

We must look, of course, to Massachusetts law. While we have found no cases with similar facts in Massachusetts (or elsewhere), we conclude that on this record a jury would be entitled to find that defendants had a duty to warn. In Massachusetts, a manufacturer* can be found liable to a user of the product if the

---

*Defendants make no argument that the duty of Sears is any different from that of Pittway, the actual manufacturer. In the present case, Sears advertised the smoke detector as a "Sears Early One Fire Alarm." Pittway Corp. was not mentioned anywhere in these advertisements nor in the 12-page owner's manual packaged with the detector. Where a seller puts out a product manufactured by another as its own, the seller is subject to the same liability as though it were the manufacturer. . . .

user is injured due to the failure of the manufacturer to exercise reasonable care in warning potential users of hazards associated with use of the product. . . .

The manufacturer can be held liable even if the product does exactly what it is supposed to do, if it does not warn of the potential dangers inherent in the way a product is designed. It is not necessary that the product be negligently designed or manufactured; the failure to warn of hazards associated with foreseeable uses of a product is itself negligence, and if that negligence proximately results in a plaintiff's injuries, the plaintiff may recover. . . .

The sole purpose of a smoke detector is to alert occupants of a building to the presence of fire. The failure to warn of inherent non-obvious limitations of a smoke detector, or of non-obvious circumstances in which a detector will not function, can, we believe, "create an unreasonable risk of harm in that the inhabitants of a structure may be lulled into an unjustified sense of safety and fail to be forewarned of the existence of a fire." . . . In the present case, the defendants failed to warn purchasers that a short circuit which causes an electrical fire may also render the smoke detector useless in the very situation in which it is expected to provide protection: in the early stages of a fire. We believe that whether such a failure to warn was negligent was a question for the jury.

To be sure, it was the fire, not the smoke detector per se, that actually killed and injured plaintiff's children. But as the Second Circuit recently held, the manufacturer of a smoke detector may be liable when, due to its negligence, the device fails to work:

> "Although a defect must be a substantial factor in causing a plaintiff's injuries, it is clear that a 'manufacturer's liability for injuries proximately caused by these defects should not be limited to [situations] in which the defect causes the accident, but should extend to situations in which the

defect caused injuries over and above that which would have occurred from the accident, but for the defective design.'"

It is true that, unlike the above, there was no defect of design or manufacture in this case. But there was evidence from which it could be inferred that the absence of a warning enhanced the harm resulting from the fire. Plaintiff testified that if he had realized that a short circuit that caused an electrical fire might at the same time disable the smoke detector, he would have purchased a back-up battery-powered detector or wired the detector in question into an isolated circuit, thus minimizing the danger that a fire-causing short circuit would render the detector inoperative. We find, therefore, a sufficient connection between the children's deaths and injury and the absence of any warning.

Defendants contend that the district court nevertheless erred in denying their motions because, they claim, the danger that an electrical fire will incapacitate an electric-powered smoke detector is obvious. They point out that anyone purchasing a device powered by house electrical current will necessarily realize that if the current goes off for any reason, the device will not work.

In Massachusetts, as elsewhere, a failure to warn amounts to negligence only where the supplier of the good known to be dangerous for its intended use "has no reason to believe that those for whose use the chattel is supplied will realize its dangerous condition." . . .

Where the risks of the product are discernible by casual inspection, such as the danger that a knife can cut, or a stove burn, the consumer is in just as good a position as the manufacturer to gauge the dangers associated with the product, and nothing is gained by shifting to the manufacturer the duty to warn. Thus, a manufacturer is not required to warn that placing one's hand into the blades of a potato chopper will cause injury, . . . that permitting a three-year-old child to ride on the running board of a moving tractor risks

injury to the child, . . . or that firing a BB gun at another at close range can injure or kill. . . . If a manufacturer had to warn consumers against every such obvious danger inherent in a product, "[t]he list of obvious practices warned against would be so long, it would fill a volume." . . .

Defendants ask us to declare that the risk that an electrical fire could incapacitate an AC-powered smoke detector is so obvious that the average consumer would not benefit from a warning. This is not a trivial argument; in earlier—some might say sounder—days, we might have accepted it. . . .

Our sense of the current state of the tort law in Massachusetts and most other jurisdictions, however, leads us to conclude that, today, the matter before us poses a jury question; that "obviousness" in a situation such as this would be treated by the Massachusetts courts as presenting a question of fact, not of law. To be sure, it would be obvious to anyone that an electrical outage would cause this smoke detector to fail. But the average purchaser might not comprehend the specific danger that a fire-causing electrical problem can simultaneously knock out the circuit into which a smoke detector is wired, causing the detector to fail at the very moment it is needed. Thus, while the failure of a detector to function as the result of an electrical malfunction due, say, to a broken power line or a neighborhood power outage would, we think, be obvious as a matter of law, the failure that occurred here, being associated with the very risk—fire—for which the device was purchased, was not, or so a jury could find.

. . . We think that the issue of obviousness to the average consumer of the danger of a fire-related power outage was one for the jury, not the court, to determine. In the present case, the jury was specifically instructed that if it found this danger to be obvious it should hold for the defendants. It failed to do so.

B. Causation

While, as just discussed, the danger the detector would fail in these circumstances was not so obvious as to eliminate, as a matter of law, any need to warn, we must also consider whether Laaperi's specialized electrical knowledge constituted a bar to his own recovery. . . . [P]laintiff's specialized knowledge is immaterial to whether defendants had a duty to warn, since that duty is defined by the knowledge of the average purchaser. But plaintiff's expertise *is* relevant to whether defendants' failure to warn caused plaintiff's damages. Even though defendants may have been required to provide a warning, plaintiff may not recover if it can be shown that because of his above-average knowledge, he already appreciated the very danger the warning would have described. In such event there would be no connection between the negligent failure to warn and plaintiff's damages.

Defendants here presented considerable evidence suggesting that Laaperi, who was something of an electrical handyman, knew of the danger and still took no precautions. Laaperi, however, offered evidence that he did not know of the danger, and that he would have guarded against it had he been warned. . . .

Self-serving as this testimony was, the jury was free to credit it. In reviewing the denial of a motion for directed verdict or judgment n.o.v., we are obliged to view the evidence in the light most favorable to the verdict winner. . . . In light of this standard, we cannot say that the district court erred in denying defendants' motions for directed verdict and judgment n.o.v., for the jury could have believed Laaperi's testimony in the colloquy quoted above, among other evidence, and concluded that had he been properly warned, Laaperi would have instituted different fire detection methods in his home to protect his family against the danger that his smoke detector would be rendered useless in the event of a fire-related power outage.

IV

. . . Considering Janet's injuries alone, apart from the horrible nature of her brothers' deaths, we find the award of $750,000 was so grossly disproportionate to the injuries of Janet Laaperi as to be unconscionable. It is therefore vacated.

The judgments in favor of Albin Laaperi in his capacity as administrator of the estates of his three sons are affirmed. In the action on behalf of Janet Laaperi, the verdict of the jury is set aside, the judgment of the district court vacated, and the cause remanded to that court for a new trial limited to the issue of damages.

So ordered.

Case Questions

1. What warning should the defendants arguably have given the plaintiffs under the facts of this case?
2. Would the outcome in this case have been different if Albin Laaperi were a licensed electrician?
3. Why didn't the plaintiff base the claim on strict liability?

 What would utilitarians think of the doctrine of res ipsa loquitor?

Imputed Negligence

Although people are always responsible for their own acts, one may be held liable for the negligence of another by reason of some relationship existing between two parties. This is termed *imputed negligence*, or vicarious liability.

Imputed negligence results when one person (the agent) acts for or represents another (the principal) by the latter's authority and to accomplish the latter's ends. A common example is the liability of employers for the torts that employees commit in the scope of their employment.

One should take a liberal view of the scope-of-employment concept, because the basis for vicarious liability is the desire to include in operational costs the inevitable losses to third persons incident to carrying on an enterprise, and thus distribute the burden among those benefited by the enterprise. Generally, an employee would not be within the scope of employment (1) if the employee is en route to or from home, (2) if the employee is on an undertaking of his own, (3) if the acts are prohibited by the employer, or (4) if the act is an unauthorized delegation by the employer.

One is not accountable for the negligent act of an independent contractor. *Independent contractors* are those who contract to do work according to their own methods and are not subject to the control of employers except with respect to the results. The right of control over the manner in which the work is done is the main consideration in determining whether one employed is an independent contractor or an agent. However, there are certain exceptions to this nonliability; for example, an employer who is negligent in hiring a contractor or who assigns a nondelegable duty may be liable.

The plaintiff/appellant in the following case was an employee of the Holt Roofing Company, which had been selected by the Drypers Corporation to be its roofing subcontractor on a building site. Hillabrand claimed that Drypers was vicariously negligent because a dumpster had been improperly positioned on the job site and this was causally related to injuries Hillabrand sustained when he received an electrical shock while throwing metal debris from the roof into the dumpster.

Todd Hillabrand v. Drypers Corporation
9-02-37
Court of Appeals of Ohio
October 10, 2002

Bryant, J.

This appeal is brought by plaintiff-appellant Todd Hillabrand from the judgment of the Court of Common Pleas, Marion County, granting summary judgment to defendant-appellee Drypers Corporation.

The record presents the following facts. On May 3, 1996, Plaintiff-Appellant Todd Hillabrand incurred electrical shock injuries while performing duties in the course and scope of his employment with Holt Roofing Company (Holt Roofing). At the time of the accident, Hillabrand was the supervisor of a job in Marion, Ohio, for which Defendant-Appellee Drypers Corporation (Drypers) had hired Holt Roofing to perform a roof repair on the commercial building they occupied and leased from Willis Day Properties, Inc.

Hillabrand's injuries occurred when he threw a piece of metal debris from the roof, where he stood, intending it to reach a dumpster positioned on the ground below. The debris inadvertently made contact with an uninsulated, energized, electrical power line causing an electrical "flash" which thereafter struck and injured Hillabrand. Hillabrand currently suffers from significant memory loss and does not recall the events leading up to his injuries.

On May 30, 1997, Hillabrand filed suit in the Marion County Court of Common Pleas naming Drypers as a defendant. The complaint alleged, *inter alia,* that Hillabrand's injuries were actually and proximately caused by Drypers' negligence. Specifically, Hillabrand alleged that Drypers had negligently positioned a garbage dumpster, in which Holt Roofing was to discard debris, below energized power lines. On November 27, 2000, after a significant period of discovery and delay, Drypers filed a motion for summary judgment. In the motion, Drypers argued that they owed no duty of care to Hillabrand since at the time of the accident, Hillabrand was performing duties in the scope of his employment with Holt Roofing, an independent contractor. The trial court granted summary judgment to Drypers on June 6, 2002. It is from this ruling that Appellant now appeals. . . .

Appellant asserts three assignments of error each alleging that the trial court erred by granting summary judgment to Appellee. In the first two assignments, Appellant argues that there is an issue of material fact as to whether Drypers owed Appellant a duty of care. Appellant's third assignment of error alleges that the trial court improperly relied on an affidavit that contained inadmissible hearsay, thereby violating Civ.R.56(E). . . .

First Assignment of Error

To establish a claim of negligence, Hillabrand must show that Drypers (1) had a duty to protect him; (2) breached that duty; (3) injury resulted; and (4) that the breach of the duty was the proximate cause of the injury. . . . The question of whether a duty exists is a matter of law, not fact. . . . "In Ohio it is well-established that liability in negligence will not lie in the absence of a special duty owed by the defendant." . . . When faced with Hillabrand's negligence claim against Drypers, that trial court concluded that Hillabrand failed the first prong of the negligence test; to establish that Drypers owed him a duty of care. Thus, the trial court determined that Drypers was entitled to a judgment as a matter of law. In his first assignment of error, Appellant insists that the trial court erred because there was, in fact, a factual dispute as to the existence of Appellee's duty of care. We disagree.

Generally, "where an independent contractor undertakes to do work for another in the very doing of which there are elements of real or potential danger and one of such contractor's employees is injured as an incident to the performance of the work, no liability for such injury ordinarily attaches to the one who engaged the services of the independent contractor." *Wellman . . .* (1953). It is undisputed that at the time of the accident, Appellant was an employee of Holt Roofing, an independent contractor hired by Drypers to repair a roof, in the very doing of which there are elements of real or potential danger, thus the *Wellman* principal applies.

However, in *Hirschbach v. Cincinnati Gas & Elec. Co.* (1983), the Ohio Supreme Court carved out an exception to *Wellman* when it held, "One who engages the services of an independent contractor, and who actually participates in the job operation performed by such contractor and thereby fails to eliminate a hazard which he, in the exercise of ordinary care, could have eliminated, can be held responsible for the injury or death of an employee of the independent contractor." . . . It is the actual participation by one who hires a sub-contractor that is the dispositive issue when applying the *Hirschbach* exception. . . . A general contractor who has not actively participated in a subcontractor's work, does not, merely by virtue of supervisory capacity, owe a duty of care to employees of subcontractor who are injured while engaged in inherently dangerous work. . . .

Here, Appellant alleges that there is dispute of material fact as to whether Drypers actually participated in the roof repair conducted by Holt Roofing by ordering the placement of a dumpster. It is undisputed that the dumpster in question belonged to Drypers, that Drypers volunteered the use of the dumpster to Holt Roofing, and that Jerry Fout, a Drypers employee, moved the dumpster from the inside of the Drypers "shop," and positioned it outside, adjacent to the building after he was asked to "put it out there." The dispute, argues Appellant, is that Fout does not remember *who* told him to move the dumpster and does not remember *why* he chose to position the dumpster where he did. Fout could only speculate that he may have placed the dumpster according to where he was able to maneuver it with a forklift. Appellant argues that if a representative of Drypers, whether it was Fout or his supervisor, ordered or chose the location of the dumpster, Drypers actually participated in the roof repair and Drypers owed Hillabrand a duty of care pursuant to *Hirschbach*.

While we agree with Appellant's summation of the disputed issue, we do not agree that the source of Fout's orders are material to a finding in this matter. Regardless of who told Fout to place the dumpster adjacent to the building, such an act is not sufficient as a matter of law to establish actual participation. "Active participation which gives rise to a duty of care may exist 'where a property owner either directs or exercises control over the work activities of the independent contractor's employees, or where the owner retains or exercises control over a critical variable in the workplace.'" . . .

Here, there is no evidence that Drypers exercised control over Holt Roofing's activities or employees. Appellant does not allege that Drypers demanded that the dumpster be placed in a particular spot for a particular reason. Nor does Appellant allege that Drypers refused to allow Holt Roofing to reposition the dumpster to a safer location, never mind the record is void of any evidence that would suggest Drypers had any interest whatsoever in where the dumpster was placed. Finally, Appellant does not point to any other area over which Drypers exercised control. Accordingly, Appellant does not fall into a valid *Hirschbach* exception and has otherwise failed to establish the first prong of the negligence test; that the defendant owed him a duty of care. . . .

In his second assignment of error, Appellant argues additionally and alternatively that Drypers owes him a duty of care pursuant to R.C. 4101.11 which states:

> "Every employer shall furnish employment which is safe for the employees engaged therein, shall furnish a place of employment which shall be safe for the employees therein and for the frequenters thereof, shall furnish and use safety devices and safeguards, shall adopt and use methods and processes, follow and obey orders, and prescribe hours of labor reasonably adequate to render such employment and places of employment safe, and shall do every other thing reasonably necessary to protect the life, health, safety, and welfare of such employees and frequenters."

The duty owed to frequenters, *i.e.*, including employees of other companies, . . . requir[es] that the premises be kept in a reasonably safe condition, and that warning be given of dangers of which he has knowledge. . . . However, the duty to frequenters of places of employment, as set forth in R.C. 4101.11, does not extend to hazards which are inherently and necessarily present because of the nature of the work performed, where the frequenter is the employee of an independent contractor. . . .

In the case at the bar, Appellant neither argues nor establishes that Drypers and/or Fout had actual or constructive knowledge of any danger presented by the electrical wires. Fout testified that he had no training in electrical safety and had no experience with roofing. Appellant does not allege that Fout knew that Appellant would be tossing metal debris off of the roof. Moreover, Appellant does not allege an "abnormally dangerous" condition. In fact, the proximity to overhead power lines is inherent in roof repair as demonstrated by Appellant's testimony that he had been trained continually throughout his roofing career on the routine dangers of working near electrical wires. Appellant stated that he was trained to recognize electrical dangers and was taught how to implement safety procedures while working in the presence of electrical wires. Consequently, there is no issue of material fact as to Dryper's duty of care pursuant to R.C. 4101.11. Appellant's second assignment of error is overruled. . . .

In conclusion, after construing the evidence most strongly in favor of Appellant, we find no genuine issue of material fact remaining to be litigated regarding a duty of care owed by Appellee. Thus, Appellant has fatally failed to establish the first prong of his negligence claim and Appellee is entitled to a judgment as a matter of law. For the reasons stated it is the order of this Court that the judgment of the Court of Common Pleas, Marion County is affirmed.

Judgment Affirmed.

Case Questions

1. What did the appellate court conclude as to the relationship between Drypers and Holt Roofing's employees?
2. What is the significance of that conclusion?
3. Why did the court reject Hillabrand's argument that a duty existed pursuant to the frequenters rule?

No-Fault Liability Statutes

The greatest number of civil cases in the United States are tort actions, and automobile collision suits account for most of these tort claims. Responding to widespread dissatisfaction with the delay and expense in the litigation of traffic accident cases, several states have passed no-fault liability statutes in an attempt to correct the injustices and inadequacies of the fault system in automobile accident cases. The first such statute was passed by Massachusetts and became effective on January 1, 1971.

Under a no-fault liability statute, parties sustaining damages from automobile accidents are compensated by their own insurance companies rather than by the parties whose negligence caused the accidents, or by those parties' insurers. The goal of the statutes is to reduce the cost of automobile insurance by saving litigation costs, including attorneys' fees, and by allowing little or no recovery for pain and suffering resulting from an automobile accident.

STRICT LIABILITY

In addition to intentional torts and negligence, there is a third type of tort called strict liability or absolute liability. This imposes liability on defendants without requiring any proof of lack of due care. Under the early common law, people were held strictly liable for trespass and trespass on the case without regard to their intentions and whether they exercised reasonable care. Although the breadth of strict liability diminished with the emergence of negligence and intentional torts, strict liability in tort is applied in cases involving what the common law recognized as abnormally dangerous activities and, more recently, in product liability cases.

Abnormally Dangerous Activities

One who is involved in abnormally dangerous activities is legally responsible for harmful consequences that are proximately caused. The possessor of a dangerous instrumentality is an insurer of the safety of others who are foreseeably within the danger zone. Because of jurisdictional differences, it is impossible to formulate a general definition or complete listing of all dangerous instrumentalities. However, poisons, toxic chemicals, explosives, and vicious animals are examples of items that have been found to fall into this category.

The plaintiff in the following case sustained personal injuries when she was bitten by the owner's dog while a guest of the defendant.

Westberry v. Blackwell
577 P.2d 75
Supreme Court of Oregon
April 18, 1978

Howell, Justice

Plaintiff filed this action to recover for personal injuries sustained when she was bitten by defendant's dog. The complaint alleged a cause of action for strict liability and another for negligence. The trial court granted a judgment of involuntary nonsuit on both causes of action. Plaintiff appeals. The evidence is viewed in the light most favorable to plaintiff.

On July 2, 1975, the plaintiff, accompanied by her young son and daughter, visited defendants' home. Plaintiff testified that as she went toward defendants' house from her car in the driveway the defendants' dog, a one-year-old St. Bernard named "Happy" gave her a superficial bite on her right hand. After plaintiff had been in the defendants' home for some time, her 12-year-old son ran into the house complaining that the dog had tried to bite him. The plaintiff further testified that after Mrs. Blackwell assured her of the dog's docility, Mrs. Westberry attempted to walk past the dog to her car in order to leave. As she did so, she was severely bitten two or three times by the dog, requiring stitches to be taken in her left hand.

The issue on this appeal is whether the evidence introduced by the plaintiff is sufficient to present a question of fact for the jury on either of the two charges, strict liability or negligence.

Plaintiff's first cause alleges that the defendants are strictly liable for the damages suffered by the plaintiff from the dog bite. The general rule is that the owner of a dog or other domestic animal is strictly liable for injuries caused by the animal only if the owner knows or has reason to know of the animal's dangerous propensities. . . . The Restatement (Second) of Torts states the rule in § 509:

"(1) A possessor of a domestic animal that he knows or has reason to know has dangerous propensities abnormal to its class, is subject to liability for harm done by the animal to another, although he has exercised the utmost care to prevent it from doing the harm.
"(2) This liability is limited to harm that results from the abnormally dangerous propensity of which the possessor knows or has reason to know." Restatement, supra at 15.

and goes on to apply it to licensees in § 513:

"The possessor of a wild animal or an abnormally dangerous domestic animal who keeps it upon land in his possession, is subject to strict liability to persons coming upon the land in the exercise of a privilege whether derived from his consent to their entry or otherwise." . . .

Thus, in the present case, if a jury could reasonably conclude the defendants knew or had reason to know of their dog's tendency to bite, they would be liable. The knowledge necessary to constitute notice of the dog's dangerous propensity varies. Harper & James note that:

". . . Any knowledge of the animal's propensity to bite or attack, whether in anger or play, is sufficient. If the owner has seen or heard enough to convince a man of ordinary prudence of the animal's propensity to inflict the type of harm complained of, there is such notice or scienter as the law requires, the question being in each case whether the owner, as a fact, had the knowledge from

which he might reasonably anticipate the general kind of harm which occurred." . . .

We have held on a previous occasion that a prior bite by a dog is not conclusive as to the existence of the dog's dangerous propensities nor as to the defendant's knowledge of the propensities. . . . [W]e held that the question of knowledge by the owner was a matter for the jury. We believe that the bite received by the plaintiff in the instant case as she went toward the house, coupled with her son's later statement, could reasonably lead a jury to believe that the dog had dangerous propensities, and that the defendants had knowledge of them.* Thus, the involuntary nonsuit on the strict liability cause was improperly granted.

Plaintiff's second cause of action alleged defendants were negligent in failing to confine the dog. Failure to confine or control such a domestic animal can give rise to a cause of action in negligence. The Restatement (Second) of Torts, § 518, states the rule as follows:

"Except for animal trespass, one who possesses or harbors a domestic animal that he does not know or have reason to know to be abnormally dangerous, is subject to liability for harm done by the animal if, but only if,
"(a) he intentionally causes the animal to do the harm or
"(b) he is negligent in failing to prevent the harm." Restatement, supra at 30.

Here, the evidence indicates that Mrs. Blackwell could have controlled or confined the dog when she knew plaintiff was leaving the premises. She knew the dog had bitten plaintiff on her way into the house. Whether a reasonable person in the exercise of ordinary care would have restrained the dog is properly a question for the jury.

The defendants' motion for a judgment of involuntary nonsuit should not have been

---

*There was evidence that the dog had chased sheep on one occasion; that he once knocked a girl off her bicycle; and that he was usually chained in the back yard.

granted. Viewing the evidence in the light most favorable to the plaintiff, a legitimate question of fact for the jury was presented, both as to the charge in strict liability and the charge in negligence.

Reversed and remanded.

Case Questions

1. What is the general rule regarding an owner's strict liability for injuries caused by an animal?
2. Why was the trial court's judgment of involuntary nonsuit improperly granted?

Strict Liability and Product Liability

A purchaser of tangible, personal property may have a right to recover from the manufacturer for injuries caused by product defects. Product defects include defects in design, manufacturing defects, and warning defects. A person who has been injured by a product defect may be able to recover based on strict liability as well as on breach of warranty (see discussion in Chapter 10) and negligence (see earlier discussion in this chapter).

The use of strict liability in product liability cases occurred because of dissatisfaction with the negligence and warranty remedies. It was very difficult for average consumers to determine whether manufacturers, wholesalers, or retailers of defective goods were responsible for their injuries. Also, the traditional requirement of privity limited the manufacturer's liability in tort and warranty actions to the person who purchased the defective product, often the wholesaler or retailer. Reformers argued that too often consumers assumed the full cost of the losses. They believed that it would be more just and economically wise to shift the cost of injuries to manufacturers, since manufacturers could purchase insurance and could distribute the costs of the premiums among those who purchased their products.

In contrast to breach of warranty and negligence remedies, which focus on the manufacturer's conduct, modern strict liability focuses on the product itself. A plaintiff who relies on strict liability has to prove that the product was unreasonably dangerous and defective and that the defect proximately caused the injury (although the unreasonably dangerous requirement is disregarded by some courts).

The following product liability case involves a Jeep CJ-7 that pitched over while being driven, killing two people and injuring two others. The plaintiffs brought suit, claiming a design defect was responsible for their injuries. Notice how the Ohio Supreme Court refers to Section 402A of the Restatement of Torts and indicates that this section has been adopted as part of Ohio law. You can examine the text of Section 402A in Figure 11-1.

---

§ 402A. Special Liability of Seller of Product for Physical Harm to User or Consumer

(1) One who sells any product in a defective condition unreasonably dangerous to the user or consumer or to his property is subject to liability for physical harm thereby caused to the ultimate user or consumer, or to his property, if

(a) the seller is engaged in the business of selling such a product, and

(b) it is expected to and does reach the user or consumer without substantial change in the condition in which it is sold.

(2) The rule stated in Subsection (1) applies although

(a) the seller has exercised all possible care in the preparation and sale of his product, and

(b) the user or consumer has not bought the product from or entered into any contractual relation with the seller.

FIGURE 11-1   Section 402A of the Restatement (Second) of Torts

Source: Copyright © 1965 by The American Law Institute. Reprinted with the permission of the American Law Institute.

Leichtamer v. American Motors Corp.
424 N.E.2d 568
Supreme Court of Ohio
August 5, 1981

Brown, Justice

This litigation arises out of a motor vehicle accident which occurred on April 18, 1976. On that date, Paul Vance and his wife, Cynthia, invited Carl and Jeanne Leichtamer, brother and sister, to go for a ride in the Vance's Jeep Model CJ-7. The Vances and the Leichtamers drove together to the Hall of Fame Four-Wheel Club, of which the Vances were members. The Vances were seated in the front of the vehicle and the Leichtamers rode in the back. The club, located near Dundee, Ohio, was an "off-the-road" recreation facility. The course there consisted of hills and trails about an abandoned strip mine.

While the Vance vehicle was negotiating a double-terraced hill [proceeding *down* the hill], an accident occurred. The hill consisted of a 33-degree slope followed by a 70-foot-long terrace and then a 30-degree slope. Paul Vance drove over the brow of the first of these two slopes and over the first flat terrace without incident. As he drove over the brow of the second hill, the rear of the vehicle raised up relative to the front and passed through the air in an arc of approximately 180 degrees. The vehicle landed upside down with its front pointing back up the hill. This movement of the vehicle is described as a pitch-over.

The speed that the Vance vehicle was travelling at the time of the pitch-over was an issue of dispute. The Leichtamers, who are the only surviving eyewitnesses to the accident, described the vehicle as travelling at a slow speed. Carl Leichtamer described the accident as occurring in this fashion:

> "Well, we turned there and went down this trail and got to the top of this first hill. . . . And Paul looked back and made sure that everybody had their seat belt fastened. That it was fastened down; and he pulled the automatic lever down in low and he put it in low wheel, four wheel, too. . . . And then he just let it coast like over the top of this hill and was using the brake on the way down, too. We came to the level-off part. He just coasted up to the top of the second hill, and then the next thing I remember is the back end of the Jeep going over. . . . When we got to the top of the second hill, the front end went down like this (demonstrating) and the back end just started raising up like that (demonstrating)."

John L. Habberstad, an expert witness for American Motors Corporation, testified that the vehicle had to be travelling between 15 and 20 miles per hour. This conclusion was based on evidence adduced by American Motors that the vehicle landed approximately 10 feet from the bottom of the second slope, having traversed about 47 feet in the air and having fallen approximately 23.5 feet.

The pitch-over of the Jeep CJ-7, on April 18, 1976, killed the driver, Paul Vance, and his wife, Cynthia. Carl Leichtamer sustained a depressed skull fracture. The tail gate of the vehicle presumably struck Jeanne Leichtamer. Jeanne was trapped in the vehicle after the accident and her position was described by her brother as follows: "She was like laying on her stomach although her head was sticking out the jeep and the—she was laying on her stomach like and the tailgate of the jeep like, was laying lower, just a little bit lower or right almost on her shoulders and then the back seat of the jeep was laying on her lower part of her back. . . . [H]er legs were twisted through the front seat." Jeanne Leichtamer is a paraplegic as a result of the injury.

Carl and Jeanne Leichtamer, appellees, subsequently sued American Motors Corporation, American Motors Sales Corporation and Jeep Corporation, appellants, for "enhanced" injuries they sustained in the accident of April 18, 1976. The amended complaint averred that the permanent trauma to the body of Jeanne Leichtamer and the other injuries to her brother, Carl, were causally related to the displacement of the "roll bar" on the vehicle. Appellees claimed that Paul Vance's negligence caused the accident, but alleged that their injuries were "substantially enhanced, intensified, aggravated, and prolonged" by the roll bar displacement.

Paul Vance purchased his Jeep CJ-7 four-wheel-drive motor vehicle from a duly licensed factory-authorized dealer, Petty's Jeep & Marine, Inc., owned and operated by Norman Petty. Vance purchased the vehicle on March 9, 1976. The vehicle came with a factory-installed roll bar. The entire vehicle was designed and manufactured by Jeep Corporation, a wholly owned subsidiary of American Motors. American Motors Sales Corporation is the selling agent for the manufacturer. Appellees did not claim that there was any defect in the way the vehicle was manufactured in the sense of departure by the manufacturer from design specifications. The vehicle was manufactured precisely in the manner in which it was designed to be manufactured. It reached Paul Vance in that condition and was not changed.

The focus of appellees' case was that the weakness of the sheet metal housing upon which the roll bar had been attached was causally related to the trauma to their bodies. Specifically, when the vehicle landed upside down, the flat sheet metal housing of the rear wheels upon which the roll bar tubing was attached by bolts gave way so that the single, side-to-side bar across the top of the vehicle was displaced to a position 12 inches forward of and 14½ inches lower than its original configuration relative to the chassis. The movement of the position of the intact roll bar resulting from the collapse of the sheet metal housing upon which it was bolted was, therefore, downward and forward. The roll bar tubing did not punch through the sheet metal housing, rather the housing collapsed, taking the intact tubing with it. That this displacement or movement of the intact roll bar is permitted by the thin nature of the sheet metal wheel housing to which it is attached and the propensity of the bar to do so when the vehicle lands upside down is central to appellees' case.

The appellants' position concerning the roll bar is that, from an engineering point of view, the roll bar was an optional device provided solely as protection for a side-roll.

The other principal element of appellees' case was that the advertised use of the vehicle involves great risk of forward pitch-overs. The accident occurred at the Hall of Fame Four-Wheel Club, which had been organized, among others, by Norman Petty, the vendor of the Vance vehicle. Petty allowed the club to meet at his Jeep dealership. He showed club members movies of the performance of the Jeep in hilly country. This activity was coupled with a national advertising program of American Motors Sales Corporation, which included a multimillion-dollar television campaign. The television advertising campaign was aimed at encouraging people to buy a Jeep, as follows: "Ever discover the rough, exciting world of mountains, forest, rugged terrain? The original Jeep can get you there, and Jeep guts will bring you back."

The campaign also stressed the ability of the Jeep to drive up and down steep hills. One Jeep CJ-7 television advertisement, for example, challenges a young man, accompanied by his girlfriend: "[Y]ou guys aren't yellow, are you? Is it a steep hill? Yeah, little lady, you could say it is a steep hill. Let's try it. The King

of the Hill, is about to discover the new Jeep CJ-7." Moreover, the owner's manual for the Jeep CJ-5/CJ-7 provided instructions as to how "[a] four-wheel-drive vehicle can proceed in safety down a grade which could not be negotiated safely by a conventional two-wheel-drive vehicle." Both appellees testified that they had seen the commercials and that they thought the roll bar would protect them if the vehicle landed on its top.

Appellees offered the expert testimony of Dr. Gene H. Samuelson that all of the physical trauma to the body of Jeanne Leichtamer were causally related to the collapse of the roll bar support. These injuries—fractures of both arms, some ribs, fracture of the dorsal spine, and a relative dislocation of the cervical spine and injury to the spinal cord—were described by Samuelson as permanent. He also testified that the physical trauma to the body of Carl Leichtamer was causally related to the collapse of the roll bar.

Appellants' principal argument was that the roll bar was provided solely for a side-roll. Appellants' only testing of the roll bar was done on a 1969 Jeep CJ-5, a model with a wheel base 10 inches shorter than the Jeep CJ-7. Evidence of the test was offered in evidence and refused. With regard to tests for either side-rolls or pitch-overs on the Jeep CJ-7, appellants responded to interrogatories that no "proving ground," "vibration or shock," or "crash" tests were conducted.

The jury returned a verdict for both appellees. Damages were assessed for Carl Leichtamer at $10,000 compensatory and $100,000 punitive. Damages were assessed for Jeanne Leichtamer at $1 million compensatory and $1 million punitive. . . .

I(A)

Appellants' first three propositions of law raise essentially the same issue: that only negligence principles should be applied in a design defect case involving a so-called "second collision." In this case, appellees seek to hold appellants liable for injuries "enhanced" by a design defect of the vehicle in which appellees were riding when an accident occurred. This cause of action is to be contrasted with that where the alleged defect causes the accident itself. Here, the "second collision" is that between appellees and the vehicle in which they were riding.

Appellants assert that the instructions of law given to the jury by the trial court improperly submitted the doctrine of strict liability in tort as a basis for liability. The scope of this review is limited to the question of whether an instruction on strict liability in tort should have been given. For the reasons explained herein, we answer the question in the affirmative.

I(B)

The appropriate starting point in this analysis is our decision in *Temple v. Wean United, Inc.* (1977). In *Temple*, this court adopted Section 402A of the Restatement of Torts 2d, thus providing a cause of action in strict liability for injury from a product in Ohio.

. . . [T]he vast weight of authority is in support of allowing an action in strict liability in tort, as well as negligence, for design defects. We see no difficulty in also applying Section 402A to design defects. As pointed out by the California Supreme Court, "[a] defect may emerge from the mind of the designer as well as from the hand of the workman." A distinction between defects resulting from manufacturing processes and those resulting from design, and a resultant difference in the burden of proof on the injured party, would only provoke needless questions of defect classification, which would add little to the resolution of the underlying claims. A consumer injured by an unreasonably dangerous design should have the same benefit of freedom from proving fault provided by Section 402A as the consumer injured by a defectively manufactured product which proves unreasonably dangerous.

Strict liability in tort has been applied to design defect "second collision" cases. While a manufacturer is under no obligation to design a "crash-proof" vehicle, an instruction may be given on the issue of strict liability in tort if the plaintiff adduces sufficient evidence that an unreasonably dangerous product design proximately caused or enhanced plaintiff's injuries in the course of a foreseeable use. Here, appellants produced a vehicle which was capable of off-the-road use. It was advertised for such a use. The only protection provided the user in the case of roll-overs or pitch-overs proved wholly inadequate. A roll bar should be more than mere ornamentation. The interest of our society in product safety would best be served by allowing a cause in strict liability for such a roll bar device when it proves to be unreasonably dangerous and, as a result, enhances the injuries of the user.

I(C)

We turn to the question of what constitutes an unreasonably dangerous defective product.

Section 402A subjects to liability one who sells a product in a "defective condition, unreasonably dangerous" which causes physical harm to the ultimate user. Comment *g* defines defective condition as "a condition not contemplated by the ultimate consumer which will be unreasonably dangerous to him." Comment *i* states that for a product to be unreasonably dangerous, "[t]he article sold must be dangerous to an extent beyond that which would be contemplated by the ordinary consumer who purchases it, with the ordinary knowledge common to the community as to its characteristics."

With regard to design defects, the product is considered defective only because it causes or enhances an injury. "In such a case, the defect and the injury cannot be separated, yet clearly a product cannot be considered defective simply because it is capable of producing injury." Rather, in such a case the concept of "unreasonable danger" is essential to establish liability under strict liability in tort principles.

The concept of "unreasonable danger," as found in Section 402A, provides implicitly that a product may be found defective in design if it is more dangerous in use than the ordinary consumer would expect. Another way of phrasing this proposition is that "a product may be found defective in design if the plaintiff demonstrates that the product failed to perform as safely as an ordinary consumer would expect when used in an intended or reasonably foreseeable manner."

Thus, we hold a cause of action for damages for injuries "enhanced" by a design defect will lie in strict liability in tort. In order to recover, the plaintiff must prove by a preponderance of the evidence that the "enhancement" of the injuries was proximately caused by a defective product unreasonably dangerous to the plaintiff.

Affirmed.

Case Questions

1. According to the court, when should an instruction have been given on the issue of strict liability in tort?
2. What makes a defective product unreasonably dangerous in design?

Tort Reform

As the country moves into a new century, the battle over tort reform rages on with "reformers" seeking to limit plaintiff's venue choices, increase the immunities available to physicians, pharmacists, and physician assistants, reduce the liability of pharmaceutical manufacturers in product liability cases, and cap noneconomic and punitive damages. Many advocates of reform insist that trial attorney greed is at the core of the problem.

Reform opponents point to a 1999 report published by the Institute of Medicine which indicated that a minimum of 44,000 people die annually in the United States because of medical errors.[6] They argue that reforms ultimately seek to arbitrarily deny injured people the just recovery they are entitled to because of the circumstances and the nature and extent of their injuries. They point out that the damage awards are large only in cases in which the injuries are horrific and the tortfeasor's liability is great. They also argue that corporations must be held fully accountable for their tortious acts or they will not have any economic incentive to act in the public's interest.

The battle has played out at the state level with the enactment of laws intended to lessen recoveries, especially in medical malpractice cases. Reform proposals typically eliminate joint and several liability, limit a plaintiff's choice of venues, cap noneconomic damages, shorten statutes of limitations periods, and cap punitive damages.

Joint and Severable Liability

Under the common law, if Sarah, Jose, and Soyinni commit a tort at the same time and are equally at fault, liability for the entire harm is imposed on each of the tortfeasors jointly and individually. This means that the judgment creditors could recover one-third from each judgment debtor, or the entire judgment from one defendant (who could then seek contribution from the other two). Reformers favor modifying the rule so that a judgment debtor found to be only 10 percent liable could not be required to pay for 100 percent of the judgment. Pennsylvania enacted a new law in 2002 that permits joint and severable liability in negligence cases only where a defendant is found to be at least 60 percent at fault. The effect of this reform is to benefit judgment debtors at the expense of judgment creditors, who will now face a greater likelihood of being unable to collect the full amount of the judgment which they won in court.

Limitations on Venue Choice

Reformers allege that plaintiff's lawyers are taking advantage of jurisdictions that permit forum shopping. In recent years, certain counties in some states have developed a reputation for consistently awarding large verdicts and have been designated "tort hellholes" by reform advocates.[7] Reformers suggest that plaintiffs be limited to filing suit in the county of the state in which the tort occurred.

Caps on Noneconomic Damages

Many states have tried to lower jury awards by statutorily establishing ceilings on recoveries for noneconomic damages such as pain and suffering, loss of consortium, and loss of enjoyment of life (hedonic damages). President Bush in January, 2003, urged Congress to establish a national cap in the amount of $250,000 on noneconomic damages in medical malpractice cases in an attempt to reduce the cost of malpractice insurance for doctors.

Statutes of Limitations

Legislatures often attempt to limit a potential defendant's exposure to tort liability by shortening the statute of limitations. Although this proposal is intended to benefit defendants, it does so at the expense of injured plaintiffs who will be denied the opportunity for their day in court if they fail to file their suits in a timely manner.

Caps on Punitive Damages

Many states have abolished punitive damages unless such awards are specifically permitted by statute. Increasingly, states are requiring that punitive damages be proven clearly and convincingly rather than by a preponderance

of the evidence, and others require bifurcated trials for punitive damages. Reformers urge legislatures to impose dollar ceilings on punitive damage awards
in medical malpractice and product liability cases.

Chapter Questions

1. Define the following terms:

agent	libel
assault	malicious prosecution
assumption of risk	negligence
battery	principal
contributory negligence	proximate cause
conversion	slander
defamation	vicarious liability
false arrest, imprisonment	wanton misconduct
independent contractor	warrant
invitee	

2. Jack McMahon and his wife Angelina decided to take a break from driving
    and stopped at a Mobil mini mart for a take-out coffee. Angelina took the
    plastic lid off the Styrofoam cup as Jack resumed driving. She spilled coffee
    on her lap while trying to pour some of the coffee into another cup, and suf-
    fered second- and third-degree burns. Angelina experienced considerable
    pain for several months and sustained scarring on one of her thighs and
    on her abdomen. The McMahons settled their claims against the manu-
    facturers of the cup and lid, but brought suit against the manufacturer of
    the coffee-making machine, the Bunn-O-Matic Corporation. The plaintiffs
    alleged that the machine was defective because it brewed the coffee at too
    high a temperature, 179 degrees F (the industry average is between 175 and
    185), and that the heat caused the cup to deteriorate. They also claimed that
    Bunn was negligent in failing to warn customers about the magnitude of
    the injuries (second- and third-degree burns) that could result from spilled
    coffee at this temperature. Did Bunn, in your opinion, have a legal duty to
    give plaintiffs the requested warnings?
    McMahon v. Bunn-O-Matic Corp., 3:96-cv-538 RP, U.S.7th Circuit Court of Appeals (1998)

3. Patrick Reddell and Derek Johnson, both eighteen years of age, wanted to
    take part in a BB gun war "game." They agreed not to fire their weapons
    above the waist and that their BB guns would be pumped no more than
    three times, thereby limiting the force of the BB's impact when striking the
    other person. They also promised each other only to fire a BB gun when the
    other person was "in the open." While participating in this activity, John-
    son shot Reddell in the eye, causing seriously impaired vision. Reddell
    sued Johnson for gross negligence and for recklessly aiming his weapon
    above the waist. Johnson answered by denying liability and asserting the

defenses of *assumption of risk* and *contributory negligence*. Both parties then filed motions for summary judgment. How should the trial judge rule on the motions?

Reddell v. Johnson, 942 P.2d 200 (1997)

4. Shannon Jackson was injured while driving her car on a farm-to-market road when her vehicle hit and killed a horse named Tiny that was standing in the road. The force of the collision severely damaged her vehicle, which was totaled. Jackson brought a negligence suit against Tiny's owner, Naomi Gibbs, for failing to prevent Tiny from wandering onto the road. Gibbs defended by saying she owed Jackson no duty on a farm-to market road that was within a "free-range" area. The trial court rejected the defense, and a jury found the defendant negligent and liable for damages of $7,000. The state intermediate appeals court affirmed the trial court, ruling that although there was no statutory duty to keep Tiny off the road, the court recognized a common law duty "to keep domestic livestock from roaming at large on public roads." This was a case of first impression before the state supreme court. Texas courts prior to this case had rejected the English common law rule imposing a duty on the owner of a domestic animal to prevent it from trespassing on a neighbor's property. English common law imposed no corresponding duty to keep an animal from wandering onto a public road unless the animal had "vicious propensities." In light of the above, Texas law generally permitted healthy, nonvicious animals to roam freely, a condition associated with "free range" jurisdictions. An exception to the free range law was statutorily recognized where a "local stock law" was enacted to keep animals off of a state highway. What arguments might be made supporting and opposing the new common law rule recognized by the intermediate court of appeals?

Gibbs v. Jackson, 97-0961, Supreme Court of Texas (1998)

5. The plaintiff became ill in the defendant's store. The defendant undertook to render medical aid to the plaintiff, keeping the plaintiff in an infirmary for six hours without medical care. It was determined that when the plaintiff finally received proper medical care, the extended lapse of time had seriously aggravated the plaintiff's illness. Discuss what action, if any, the plaintiff has.

Zelenka v. Gilbel Bros., Inc., 287 N.Y.S. 134 (1935)

6. Plaintiff came into defendant's grocery store and purchased some cigarettes. He then asked if the store had any empty boxes he could use. The defendant instructed the plaintiff that he could find some in the back room and told the plaintiff to help himself. Plaintiff entered the room, which was dark. While searching for a light switch, the plaintiff fell into an open stairwell and was injured. What is the status of the plaintiff (invitee, licensee, trespasser)? How will the status affect the plaintiff's ability to recover from the defendant, if at all? Do you think the fact that the defendant is operating a business should affect his duty?

Whelan v. Van Natta Grocery, 382 S.W.2d 205 (Ky. 1964)

7. Plaintiff's intestate was killed when the roof of the defendant's foundry fell in on him. Plaintiff alleges that the defendant failed to make proper repairs to the roof, and that such neglect of the defendant caused the roof to collapse. The defendant claims, however, that the roof collapsed during a violent storm, and that, even though the roof was in disrepair, the high winds caused the roof to fall. What issue is raised, and how would you resolve it?
   Kimble v. Mackintosh Hemphill Co., 59 A.2d 68 (1948)

8. The plaintiff's intestate, who had been drinking, was crossing Broadway when he was negligently struck by one of defendant's cabs. As a result of the accident, the plaintiff's intestate was thrown about twenty feet, his thigh was broken, and his knee injured. He immediately became unconscious and was rushed to a hospital, where he died of delirium tremens (a disease characterized by violent shaking, often induced by excessive alcoholic consumption). Defendant argued that the deceased's alcoholism might have caused delirium tremens and death at a later date, even if defendant had not injured him. What is the main issue presented here? Who should prevail and why?
   McCahill v. N.Y. Transportation Co., 94 N.E. 616 (1911)

9. Plaintiff, while a spectator at a professional hockey game, is struck in the face by a puck. The defendant shot the puck attempting to score a goal, but shot too high, causing the puck to go into the spectator area. Plaintiff brings suit, and defendant claims assumption of risk. Who prevails? Suppose the defendant had been angry at crowd reaction and intentionally shot the puck into the crowd. Would the outcome change?

10. Clay Fruit, a life insurance salesman, was required to attend a business convention conducted by his employer. The convention included social as well as business events, and Fruit was encouraged to mix freely with out-of-state agents in order to learn as much as possible about sales techniques. One evening, after all scheduled business and social events had concluded, Fruit drove to a nearby bar and restaurant, looking for some out-of-state colleagues. Finding none, he drove back toward his hotel. On the journey back, he negligently struck the automobile of the plaintiff, causing serious injuries to plaintiff's legs. Was Fruit in the course and scope of his employment at the time of the accident? From whom will the plaintiff be able to recover?
    Fruit v. Schreiner, 502 P.2d 133 (Alas. 1972)

11. John Prater was employed by Roy Goodman as a general handyman in Goodman's music store, particularly to work on piano cases, deliver pianos, and keep the delivery truck in repair. One evening, Goodman told Prater to take the truck home and work on the truck's body over the weekend. On the truck were a few of Goodman's trash cans, which Goodman had asked Prater to empty. The following morning, a Saturday, Prater loaded several of his own cans of garbage onto the truck. On his way back from the dump, Prater made a detour of a few blocks to pick up his daughter. On this detour, he had a collision with a car driven by W. M Leuthold. Prater was later

found to be negligent. Leuthold brought suit against Goodman for Prater's negligence. What issue does this raise, and how would you resolve it?

Leuthold v. Goodman, 22 Wash.2d 583, 157 P.2d 326 (1945)

12. *Reader's Digest*, with a circulation in California alone of almost two million copies, published an article entitled "The Big Business of Hijacking." The purpose of the article was to describe various truck thefts and the efforts being made to stop such thefts. The plaintiff was mentioned by name in connection with a truck hijacking that had happened eleven years earlier in Danville, Kentucky. Nothing in the article indicated when the hijacking occurred. As a result of the publication, the plaintiff's daughter and friends learned of the incident for the first time. The plaintiff, a resident of California, filed suit against Reader's Digest Association for publishing the article, which disclosed truthful but embarrassing private facts about his past life. This case involved what intentional tort?

Briscoe v. Reader's Digest Association, 483 P.2d (1971)

Notes

1. T. F. F. Plucknett, *A Concise History of the Common Law* (Boston: Little, Brown and Co., 1956), p. 372.
2. A. K. R. Kiralfy, *Potter's Historical Introduction to English Law* (4th ed.) (London: Sweet and Maxwell Ltd., 1962), pp. 376–377.
3. R. Walsh, *A History of Anglo-American Law* (Indianapolis: Bobbs-Merrill Co., 1932), p. 323.
4. Kiralfy, pp. 305–307; Walsh, p. 344.
5. More discussion about the different types of damages can be found in Chapter 7.
6. "A tragic error," *Newsweek*, March 3, 2003, p. 22.
7. "Tort Reform Advances in Mississippi (for starters)," *The National Law Journal* (February 3, 2003), pp. A1, A10–A11.

XII Property

Property refers to a person's ownership rights to things and to a person's interests in things owned by someone else. Property includes the rights to possess, use, and dispose of things. These may be tangible objects, such as a car, book, or item of clothing, or they may be intangible—the technology in a camera, a song, or the right of publicity. Although many people refer to the objects themselves as property, "property" actually refers only to ownership rights and interests.

HISTORICAL DEVELOPMENT OF THE REGULATION OF REAL PROPERTY

When we discuss property law, we must remember that the English common law greatly influenced legal thinking in the prerevolutionary colonies and in the new American states.[1] Private property was thought to be essential to individual liberty, a proposition advanced by the English philosopher John Locke (1632–1704). Locke was a "natural law" philosopher who argued that before the creation of governments, people existed in a natural state in which they had total control over their life, liberty, and property. He reasoned that people who established governments retained these inalienable rights and were entitled to resist any government that failed to respect them. Locke's emphasis on the inviolability of private property was reflected in the decisions of colonial legislatures, judges, and political leaders.[2]

Although American law was significantly influenced by the common law, most colonies were willing to take a different path when solutions provided by common law seemed inappropriate. The Puritans in New England, for example, refused to follow a rule of English common law (which was accepted in southern colonies[3]) that prevented a husband from conveying land without his wife's consent. They believed this was a bad social policy because it treated husbands and wives as individuals with separate legal interests rather than as a single, unified entity. They changed the law to allow husbands to make unilateral decisions for the family regarding the sale of real property.[4]

Before the industrial revolution, the economies of America and England were primarily based on agriculture. England's industrial revolution began with the rise of the textile industry in the 1700s. At this time most economic and political power was held by large landowners such as the church, monarchy, military, and landed gentry.[5] There, as in colonial America, the law recognized property owners as having absolute dominion over their land.[6] But no one could use his or her land in a manner that caused injury to any other landowner. For example, a landowner could not divert the natural flow of a navigable river or stream in order to establish a mill if it created a detriment to another landowner.[7] The fact that economic and social benefits would result from the operation of a new mill was of no consequence.[8]

Legal attitudes toward property began to change as America became industrialized in the 1800s and moved toward a market economy. After the Civil War, courts began to recognize that encouraging competition and economic development benefitted the public.[9] When one landowner's property use conflicted with another's, the courts balanced the nature of the infringement against its socially desirable economic benefits, and the developers usually prevailed.[10] This legal preference for development continued throughout the nineteenth and into the twentieth centuries. Although it produced new technology, new products, and an expanding economy, it also resulted in environmental pollution, the exploitation of workers, hazardous work environments, and labor-management conflict. These conditions resulted in legislative reform efforts throughout the century designed to protect society. Around 1900, the U.S. Supreme Court began to strike down state laws that interfered with employer-employee contracts with respect to wages, hours, and working conditions.[11] The Court concluded that these laws exceeded the state's legislative power because they infringed upon the individual's constitutionally protected due process liberty interest in freedom of contract.

Since the 1930s, the individual's property rights in land have declined as legislatures have acted to protect society from irresponsible and harmful uses of private property. Today, for example, zoning laws regulate land use and building codes regulate building construction. Environmental laws prohibit landowners from filling in wetlands and control the discharge of pollutants into the air, ground, and water.

As environmental regulations have increased in number, they have impacted an increasing number of landowners. A heated ongoing national debate has resulted between supporters and opponents of the legal status quo. Opponents have charged that the existing legislation and case law are excessively antidevelopment and that government agencies are overzealous in enforcing environmental protection regulations. Environmental protection, they conclude, is often achieved without regard for the legitimate rights of landowners.

Supporters of current environmental policies maintain that removing the regulations will produce a precipitous decline in habitat for endangered species and, in many instances, will ultimately lead to extinction. They also argue that backsliding from current standards will produce serious environmental hazards to the public's air, water, and land resources. In the 1990s, the Congress, many state legislatures, and federal and state courts have been rethinking whether our nation's environmental laws properly reflect society's dual interests of protecting both the environment and private property rights. We will examine this question in more detail later in this chapter when we discuss takings and eminent domain.

CLASSIFICATIONS OF PROPERTY

Property can be classified as real, personal (tangible or intangible), or fixtures. Property interests can also be classified as either contingent or vested.

Real property, or realty, includes land and things that are attached permanently to land. It is distinguishable from personal property in that real property is immovable.

Practically every person in the United States owns personal property. *Personal property*, or *personalty*, consists of physical objects that are not realty (or fixtures) and all intangible rights, duties, and obligations arising out of the ownership of physical objects. Personal property also includes intangible property, such as money, stocks, and bonds, that are paper substitutes for certain ownership rights. Thus personal property includes not only a physical or representative object, but also the right to own, use, sell, or dispose of it as regulated by law.

Tangible personal property consists of those physical objects that in themselves embody the rights of ownership. Intangible personal property is personal property that is not a physical object. Ownership of *intangible* property is usually evidenced by some type of legal document that sets forth the ownership rights. For example, a bank savings account is personal property. The passbook that the bank issues to the saver represents the savings account. The passbook, therefore, is evidence of the saver's right to title and right to possession of the funds contained in the account. Trademarks, patents, and copyrights are other examples of intangible personal property.

TRADEMARKS, PATENTS, AND COPYRIGHTS

When one normally thinks of personal property, one generally thinks in terms of tangible property—the rights to things that have a physical existence. However, some of the most valuable property rights have no physical attributes. One who owns intellectual property rights (the rights to trademarks, patents, and copyrights) owns intangible personal property.

Trademarks

The distinctive Nike "Swoosh" is a trademark of the Nike Corporation. The company affixes this mark to its many products in order to distinguish them from those of competitors. Customers learn to associate trademarks with quality and style attributes—a matter of great importance to manufacturers and retailers. The name of a type of product such as microwave or DVD cannot be a trademark. Sometimes, however, a company's trademark becomes recognized by the public as the name of the product itself and loses its legal status as a trademark. Aspirin, thermos, and escalator are examples of trademarks that lost their trademark status because they became words used for the product category. The Coca Cola Corporation works diligently to ensure that the term *Coke* does not lose its status as a trademark by becoming a synonym for soft drink. Similarly, the Xerox Corporation is most concerned that its trademark *Xerox* does not become a synonym for photocopy. Trademarks to be used in interstate commerce are required to be registered with the U.S. Department of Commerce's Patent and Trademark Office, pursuant to the Lanham Act of 1946.

An infringement of a trademark occurs, for example, when an infringing mark is so similar to a well-established mark that it is likely to confuse, deceive, or mislead customers into believing that they are doing business with the more established company.

Federal and state statutes create causes of action for trademark infringement. The Lanham Act of 1946 and the Trademark Law Revision Act of 1988 are the principal federal statutes. At the state level, statutes authorize causes of action for trademark infringement and the common law also provides a basis for such suits. Successful plaintiffs can obtain treble damages, injunctive relief, an award of the defendant's profits, damages, costs, and attorney fees in exceptional cases.

The plaintiff in the following case sought to trademark the words "Best Beer in America" and appealed the Trademark Trial and Appeal Board's decision to reject the proposed trademark application.

In re The Boston Beer Company Ltd. Partnership
198 F.3d 1370
U.S. Court of Appeals, Federal Circuit
December 7, 1999

Mayer, Chief Judge

The Boston Beer Company Limited Partnership ("Boston Beer") appeals from a decision of the U.S. Patent and Trademark Office Trademark Trial and Appeal Board affirming the final rejection of trademark application Serial No. 74/464,118 seeking to register "The Best Beer In America" on the principal register. . . .

Background

On November 30, 1993, the Boston Beer Company filed an application to register "The Best Beer In America" on the principal register for "beverages, namely beer and ale," in Class 32. Boston Beer claimed use since 1985 and asserted that the words sought to be registered have acquired distinctiveness under 15 U.S.C. §§ 1052(f). Boston Beer claimed secondary meaning based on annual advertising expenditures in excess of ten million dollars and annual sales under the mark of approximately eighty-five million dollars. Specifically, Boston Beer spent about two million dollars on promotions and promotional items which included the phrase "The Best Beer in America."

In support of its claims, Boston Beer submitted an affidavit of its founder and co-president, James Koch, asserting that the words sought to be registered had developed secondary meaning as a source-indicator for its goods by virtue of extensive promotion and sales of beer under the mark since June 1985. It also submitted an advertisement for a competitor's product, Rolling Rock Bock beer, which included an invitation to sample "the beer that bested 'The Best Beer in America,'" as evidence that Rolling Rock regards "The Best Beer in America" as Boston Beer's trademark. The examining attorney rejected the proposed mark as merely descriptive and cited articles retrieved from the NEXIS database showing the proposed mark used by Boston Beer and others as a laudatory phrase to refer to superior beers produced by a number of different brewers. All of the beers mentioned had either won comparison competitions or had been touted as the best in America by their makers or others. Boston Beer responded by submitting articles showing its use of the proposed mark to refer to its product and in promoting its beer as a winner of the annual beer competition in Denver. Additionally, it argued that if marks such as "Best Products" and "American Airlines" can be registered even though they are also used descriptively, then the proposed mark should be similarly registered. The examining attorney issued a final refusal to register under 15 U.S.C. §§ 1052(e)(1), holding that Boston Beer had failed to establish that the mark had become distinctive.

Boston Beer filed a notice of appeal and attached further exhibits to its appeal brief.

The application was remanded to the examiner on his request for consideration of the new evidence. Another office action was issued denying registration for lack of distinctiveness which noted that the phrase sought to be registered was selected and used after Boston Beer received awards at the Great American Beer Festival. The board then allowed Boston Beer to file a supplemental brief. Action on the appeal was suspended and the board remanded the application.

The examiner concluded that the proposed mark is the name of a genus of goods, namely "beers brewed in America that have won taste competitions or were judged best in taste tests," and included printouts from the Boston Beer Internet web site to show that it had adopted the proposed mark after it had won such competitions. He therefore issued an office action rejecting the proposed mark as generic and thus incapable of registration. Boston Beer submitted a second supplemental brief to respond to the genericness rejection. After the examiner filed his appeal brief, Boston Beer filed a third supplemental brief arguing against genericness and moved to strike portions of the examiner's brief. Boston Beer argued that the examiner was limited to responding to the issues raised in the second supplemental brief, namely genericness, and could not address descriptiveness and acquired distinctiveness. Boston Beer argued that its proposed mark was not generic because there was no single category at the Great American Beer Festival and thus no "best beer in America" award. The board rejected the motion to strike.

The board found the proposed mark to be merely descriptive because it is only laudatory and "simply a claim of superiority, i.e., trade puffery." . . . The proposed mark was found not to be generic because the examiner's characterization of the genus or class of goods as "'beers brewed in America which have won taste competitions or were judged best in taste tests' stretches the limits of our language and is inconsistent with common usage." ... The board held, however, that the proposed mark inherently cannot function as a trademark because such "claims of superiority should be freely available to all competitors in any given field to refer to their products or services." ... Finally, the board said that "even if [it] were to find this expression to be capable of identifying applicant's beer and distinguishing it from beer made or sold by others, [the board] also would find, in view of the very high degree of descriptiveness which inheres in these words, that applicant has failed to establish secondary meaning in them as an identification of source." ... This appeal followed.

Discussion

We review the board's legal conclusions, such as its interpretation of the Lanham Act, 15 U.S.C. §§ 1051-1127, de novo. We uphold the board's factual findings unless they are arbitrary, capricious, an abuse of discretion, or unsupported by substantial evidence. ...

"Marks that are merely laudatory and descriptive of the alleged merit of a product are also regarded as being descriptive. ... Self-laudatory or puffing marks are regarded as a condensed form of describing the character or quality of the goods." 2 J. Thomas McCarthy, *McCarthy on Trademarks and Unfair Competition* §§ 11:17 (4th ed. 1996) (internal quotations omitted). "If the mark is merely descriptive it may nevertheless acquire distinctiveness or secondary meaning and be registrable under Section 1052(f), although ... the greater the degree of descriptiveness the term has, the heavier the burden to prove it has attained secondary meaning." ... To acquire secondary meaning, section 1052(f) requires that the mark must have become "distinctive of the applicant's goods." 15 U.S.C. §§ 1052(f) (1994).

Boston Beer provided evidence of advertising expenditures, an affidavit from its co-president, and an advertisement from a competitor. It argues that the use of the mark by others was either referring to Boston Beer's products or merely descriptive of the goods of others and was not used as a trademark. This argument is unavailing. The examples of use of the phrase by others in its descriptive form support the board's conclusion that the mark had not acquired distinctiveness. Therefore, on the facts of this case, and considering the highly descriptive nature of the proposed mark, Boston Beer has not met its burden to show that the proposed mark has acquired secondary meaning.

Boston Beer does not dispute that "The Best Beer in America" is a generally laudatory phrase. We have held that laudation does not per se prevent a mark from being registrable. ... As Boston Beer correctly notes, there is an assortment of generally laudatory terms that serve as trademarks. But that is not invariably true; the specific facts of the case control. ... As in this case, a phrase or slogan can be so highly laudatory and descriptive as to be incapable of acquiring distinctiveness as a trademark. The proposed mark is a common, laudatory advertising phrase which is merely descriptive of Boston Beer's goods. Indeed, it is so highly laudatory and descriptive of the qualities of its product that the slogan does not and could not function as a trademark to distinguish Boston Beer's goods and serve as an indication of origin. The record shows that "The Best Beer in America" is a common phrase used descriptively by others before and concurrently with Boston Beer's use, and is nothing more than a claim of superiority. Because the board's conclusion of non-registrability is supported by substantial evidence, is not arbitrary and capricious, and is not an abuse of discretion, we agree that "The Best Beer in America" is incapable of registration as a trademark. ...

Accordingly, the decision of the board is affirmed. ...

Case Questions

1. Why did the Court of Appeals affirm the examiner and refuse to grant the trademark?
2. The Court of Appeals referred to a provision in the Lanham Act that permits recognition of a mark if the proposed mark has acquired a secondary meaning. What do you think that means?

 INTERNET TIP ————————————————————

The U.S. Supreme Court, in 2000, had to decide in the case of *Wal-Mart Stores, Inc. v. Samara Brothers, Inc.,* whether a designer of children's clothing was so distinctive that it's design was entitled to protection under the Lanham Act of 1946. You can read this opinion on the textbook's website.

Patents

A patent is a grant of rights to an inventor from the government. The inventor, or owner of the rights, has the exclusive right to make, use, license others to use, and sell an invention for a period of years (twenty years for most inventions). Patents are only granted for inventions that are beneficial, original, and that involve ingenuity. Patents are granted for new machines, methods, uses, and improvements to existing inventions. Patents are also granted for genetically engineered plants.

Copyrights

Authors of literary pieces, musical compositions, dramatic works, photographs, graphic works of various types, video and audio recordings, and computer software can acquire federal legal protection against most unauthorized uses by placing a proscribed copyright notice on publicly disseminated copies of the work. An owner or author of a copyrighted work is required to register with the Copyright Office in Washington, D.C., prior to bringing suit for copyright infringement.

Congress enacted its first copyright statute in 1790 and in that statute provided that authors had exclusive rights to their works for two 14 year periods. Although the law has been amended many times, in recent decades substantial revisions occurred in 1978 and in 1998. In 1978, Congress abolished common law copyrights and federalized the copyright process, and, in most instances extended the length of the copyright protection from a maximum of 56 years after publication to the author's life plus 50 years. In 1998, Congress enacted the

Sonny Bono Copyright Extension Act, which extended copyright protections even further, to the life of the author plus 70 years for works that were produced after 1978 and to a maximum of 95 years for works produced prior to 1978. Proponents argue that extending the length of U.S. copyright protections brings the United States in line with similar provisions in existing international conventions. Opponents contend that a creator's copyright protections were intended by the founders to be limited. Even the most profitable works should ultimately make their way into the public domain (where they could be freely used by anyone without having to pay royalties).

The constitutionality of this statute has been challenged in the federal courts and is presently before the U.S. Supreme Court for decision in the case of *Eldred v. Ashcroft*. The Court is expected to announce its decision in this case during the first half of 2003. After that announcement, it will be made available on the textbook's website.

The plaintiff in the following case claimed that the defendant infringed on his copyrighted design of a children's shirt that contained the following phrase: "Someone Went to Boston and got this shirt because they love me Very Much."

Matthews v. Freedman
157 F.3d 25
U.S. Court of Appeals, First Circuit
October 9, 1998

Boudin, Circuit Judge

Denise Matthews, a fabric designer and wholesale distributor of "soft-good" souvenirs, makes and sells a children's t-shirt with a design entitled, "Someone Went to Boston and got me this shirt because they love me Very much." This phrase appears on a t-shirt surrounded by small drawings of a fish, a sailboat, a lobster, Faneuil Hall, and scattered hearts. Matthews registered this "Someone . . ." t-shirt design with the U.S. Copyright Office, receiving a certificate of registration effective August 9, 1995.

In February 1997, Alan Freedman, a competing souvenir producer, began offering a children's t-shirt with the slogan "Someone Who Loves Me Went to Boston and Got Me this Shirt." This phrase appears on the Freedman t-shirt and is surrounded by small drawings of a fish, a sailboat, a lobster, a swan boat, ducklings, and a smiling sun. Freedman and Matthews both attend the Boston Gift Show, where Freedman had seen Matthews' "Someone . . ." t-shirt displayed.

Matthews filed suit against Freedman for copyright infringement under 17 U.S.C. § 501 . . . in August 1997. The district court held a nonjury trial on January 21, 1998, and issued a memorandum and order dated February 5, 1998, granting judgment in favor of Freedman on the ground that Freedman's t-shirt did not infringe upon the protectible elements of Matthews' design. . . . This appeal by Matthews followed.

To make out a copyright infringement, a plaintiff must show ownership of a valid copyright—not questioned here—and the "copying of constituent elements of the work that are original." . . . As to this latter element, sometimes the dispute concerns the factual question of whether the defendant saw and copied the plaintiff's work; but in other cases, as in this one, the dispute centers around more subtle, related questions: what aspects of the plaintiff's work are protectible under the copyright laws and whether whatever copying took place appropriated those elements.

A major limitation on what is protectible under the copyright laws is capsulized in the notion that copyright protects the original expressions of ideas but not the ideas expressed. . . . The point is that the underlying idea (*e.g.*, the travails of two star-crossed lovers), even if original, cannot be removed from the public realm; but its expression in the form of a play script (such as William Shakespeare's *Romeo and Juliet*) can be protected. Needless to say, the line is a blurry one.

If the idea-expression dichotomy favors copyright-case defendants, a somewhat different notion in copyright law favors the plaintiffs. It is well settled that where the plaintiff has copyrighted an original expression, an infringement can be found to exist even where the defendant does not copy the original expression in a literal manner (word for word or image by image). It is enough to make out infringement—assuming actual copying—if the alleged infringing work is "substantially similar" to the protectible expression in the copywritten work. . . . In other words, if *Romeo and Juliet* were under copyright, the infringer could not escape solely by changing the names of every character and altering a few words in every line.

A potential tension is now obvious. An alleged infringing work taken as a whole may seem "substantially similar" to the copyrighted work taken as whole, but the impression of similarity may rest heavily upon similarities in the two works as to elements that are not copyrightable—because those elements are the underlying ideas, or expressions that are not original with the plaintiff, or for some like reason. . . . Courts have used various formulas to isolate the protectible expression in the copyrighted work to determine whether the alleged in-

fringing work is "substantially similar" to that protectible expression.

That is just what the district court did in the present case. It declined implicitly to give Matthews any protection for the idea that underlies the phrasing on the t-shirt that the t-shirt's purchase represents someone's love of the donee—or the unoriginal notions of having a legend on a t-shirt, using childish lettering, or placing on the t-shirt symbolic emblems reminiscent of a location (here, Boston). The district court then turned its attention to the remaining elements and found that, as to these elements, the differences between the two works precluded a finding of infringement.

In this regard, the district court pointed to differences in the particular icons selected, their arrangement, the colors used and the lettering. Examination of Matthews' and Freedman's t-shirts bears out the district court's conclusion; no one would think the lettering, colors, or particular icons had been literally copied from one t-shirt to the other. For example, the icons are not all of the same subjects, and even where both t-shirts depict a lobster or fish, the drawings are completely different.

Because Matthews does not directly challenge the district court's assessment on an element-by-element basis, we pause only to address the most obvious possible claim: that the expression of the "someone" theme in the two t-shirts is "substantially similar." Obviously, there is a good deal of similarity in the substance of the two competing phrases: "someone went to Boston and got me this shirt because they love me Very much" and "someone who loves me went to Boston and got me this shirt." But most of the similarity rests on the fact that both phrases are seeking to express essentially the same idea.

Admittedly, there is some similarity in the two expressions of the idea, but this is largely because both are expressing the same idea briefly and in straightforward terms and the available variations in wording are quite limited. Even if the sentiment were original with Matthews—which is by no means clear—it would virtually give Matthews a monopoly on the underlying idea if everyone else were forbidden from using a differently worded short sentence to express the same sentiment. . . .

In all events, Matthews' attack on the district court's decision is not based on any refined comparison of individual elements. Rather, Matthews says broadly that the test for copyright infringement is whether the "ordinary observer" would find a substantial similarity between the two works and would be disposed to overlook the disparities as minor. Matthews then argues that the district court, at least if its judgment is reviewed *de novo* (as Matthews urges), erred because the two t-shirts are to the average observer substantially similar "in design and overall aesthetic appeal" and because "both exhibits have similar 'Someone Who Loves Me Went To Boston And Got Me This Shirt' language and display boats, fish, and a lobster in a childlike fashion."

Case law supports the "ordinary observer" test and the disregard of minor differences in favor of major similarity. . . . As for the proper standard of review, there is some difference among the circuits where the question of substantial similarity is based solely on a visual comparison of two items easily available to the reviewing court. But even if we assumed *arguendo* a de novo standard of review, the *protectible elements* here are not substantially similar for reasons already indicated.

Indeed, Matthews' own argument (just quoted) is practically explicit in its refusal to distinguish what is protectible from what is not. Lack of originality to one side, the notion of displaying "boats, fish and a lobster in childlike fashion" is not in itself an expression; and although a particular drawing might be, the two t-shirts in this case do not display similar icons. For reasons already indicated, the "someone" phrasing in the two t-shirts reflects the same sentiment, but the sentiment is not protectible, and Freedman's expression of it was different from Matthews', given the limited options available.

We do not mean to suggest that every element in copyrighted work must be considered apart from all others; a collection of protectible elements may seem substantially similar primarily through the overall impression created by those protectible elements taken together. . . . Even entirely unoriginal expressions taken from others might sometimes be combined in a way that gave rise to a new protectible expression (imagine a collage of newspaper headlines juxtaposed in some highly creative and original fashion). . . . But this case falls into neither of these categories. . . .

Affirmed.

Case Questions

1. What did the plaintiff have to show in order to establish a copyright infringement?
2. Why did the trial and appellate courts regard the similarity of the sentiments displayed on both the appellant's and appellee's t-shirts as immaterial in this case?

An item of personal property can be the subject of both tangible and intangible property rights. For example, suppose that you buy a camera, the design of which is protected by a valid federal patent. Although you have acquired a piece of tangible personal property that you can use and dispose of in any legal manner, the law will recognize that you do not have all the right vis-à-vis the camera. The patent holder, for example, has intangible property rights in the camera's technology that prevent a purchaser from selling duplicates of the product or the technology without permission. Thus both the patent holder and the purchaser have property rights to the same object.

A fixture is a category of property between realty and personalty. For example, a dishwasher is classified as personalty when it is purchased at an appliance store. When it is permanently built into the buyer's kitchen, however, it becomes a fixture.

Property rights are *contingent* when some future event must occur for the right to become *vested* (fully effective). For example, employers often require that employees work for a company for a specified number of years before their pension rights mature. Once pension rights vest, they belong to the employees even if they subsequently leave the company.

These distinctions are based on practical considerations; for example, tax rates may differ for realty, fixtures, and personalty. In addition, the common law of each state governs real property, whereas the Uniform Commercial Code often governs personalty.[12] The outcome of the next case depends on whether the property is classified as a fixture or as personal property.

Far West Modular Home Sales, Inc. v. Proaps
604 P.2d 452
Court of Appeals of Oregon
December 24, 1979

Campbell, Judge

In this replevin action* the plaintiff sought to recover the possession of a modular home. The parties waived a jury, and following trial to the court, judgment was entered for the plaintiff. The defendants have appealed, and we reverse.

In July 1977 the plaintiff contracted to sell a modular home to the defendants. In January 1978 the home was delivered in two sections from plaintiff's factory to the defendants' property. It was of wood construction, and was mounted and secured on a concrete foundation by bolts and nails. It was connected to sewer, water and electric outlets. When the modular home was in place it measured 60 feet by 24 feet and its accommodations included three bedrooms and two baths. The defendants and their family used it as a residence.

A dispute arose over the price and the plaintiff filed this replevin action. The trial court found that the modular home was personal property. The defendants appealed and have assigned as the only error:

> "The court erred in concluding that the modular home should be treated as personal property, thereby subject to replevin, and awarding same to Plaintiff."

*An action to have personal property returned to the original possessor.—*Ed.*

The defendants contend that the modular home was so affixed to their real property that it lost its character as personalty and, therefore, was not subject to replevin.

The test for determining whether property retains its character as personal property, or loses its separate identity and becomes a fixture, is composed of three factors: annexation, adaptation and intention.

The plaintiff in its brief in this court concedes "the modular home was adaptable to the real property upon which it was placed." Therefore we will consider only the questions of annexation and intention.

The degree of annexation necessary to turn a chattel into a fixture depends upon the circumstances of the particular case. Annexation of a chattel to real property may be either actual or constructive. . . .

The plaintiff in effect argues that the physical attachment of the modular home to the real property was so slight that the annexation factor was not satisfied. It points to the testimony of its witnesses that the home could be unbolted, the utilities unhooked, and the entire unit removed from defendants' property in less than an hour. The removal operation would require a crane and two trucks equipped with low-boys at a total cost of $2,500. It would cost an additional $2,200 to remove the concrete foundation and restore the defendants' land to its previous state.

Since there is no requirement that a chattel actually be attached to the real property to satisfy the annexation test, . . . testimony illustrating the ease with which the modular home could be removed is not controlling. Rather, the fact that this chattel is a home, coupled with evidence that it was bolted and nailed to a foundation and connected to all utilities, established that it was annexed to defendants' real property. This conclusion is further supported by the fact that it would cost $4,700 to remove the modular home and restore the land.

The paramount factor in the determination of whether a chattel has become a fixture is the objective intent of the annexor to make the item a permanent accession of the freehold. . . .

The annexor's intent can be inferred from "the nature of the article, the relation (to the realty) of the party annexing, the policy of law in relation thereto, the structure and mode of annexation, and the purpose and use" for which the item was annexed. . . . The annexor's objective, controlling intent, is determined from all the circumstances.

We begin with the presumption that a building or similar structure is a fixture and therefore a part of the real property. . . .

Also, when annexation is made by an owner of realty, an intent to affix may more readily be found. . . . The fact that here the vendor physically placed the unit on defendants' property does not detract from defendants' status as an annexing party. Moreover, the fact that the home was to be manufactured elsewhere in two large sections before being placed on the homesite does not detract from defendants' objective intent to affix the home to their land. . . .

The plaintiff argues "that no reasonable person would intend that a modular home lost its identity as personal property simply by dropping it on the foundation which had been prepared for it." Instead, plaintiff continues, "reasonable people would [intend] that the modular home would become a fixture contemporaneously with the payment of the purchase price." We find it relevant that plaintiff by implication admits that the installed home would become a fixture. However, plaintiff has not cited us a case, and we have been unable to find one, that holds payment of the purchase price is controlling as to the parties' intention.

A modular home has been defined as "a structure which is prefabricated in a factory and delivered to its intended site where it is installed on a foundation." *Prospecting Unlimited,*

Inc. v. Norberg, 376 A.2d 702, 703 (Rhode Island 1977). The *Norberg* court went on to hold:

> "that once the modules were actually incorporated into completed houses, they became part of the real estate just as any other house usually does. When the houses were completed, the modules were not removable without damage to themselves or the realty. Furthermore, they were permanently fastened to their foundations, were intended to remain so, and were adapted for use as housing, as was the realty to which they were attached."

. . . By way of comparison, the Washington Court of Appeals has held that certain mobile homes which had not lost their identity as mobile units remained personal property. In reaching its conclusion, the court noted that "[a]lthough the hitches and wheels were removed, the axles were left on the units. They were placed on blocks rather than permanent foundations, and the utility connections . . . [were] not fixed pipes but flexible hoses which . . . [could] easily be disconnected." . . .

We are of the opinion that in this case the evidence is so clear that the only conclusion that can be drawn therefrom is that the modular home was a fixture of the real property and therefore not subject to an action of replevin.

Reversed.

Case Questions

1. What three factors do courts consider in determining whether personal property has become a fixture?
2. What difference does the classification of the mobile home as personalty or as a fixture make in this case?

Property Ownership

Property can be owned in several different forms, including severalty ownership, concurrent ownership, and community property. Severalty ownership exists when property is owned by one person. Concurrent ownership exists when property is held simultaneously by more than one person. This can occur in one of three ways—joint tenancy, tenancy in common, and tenancy by the entirety.[13] In joint tenancy, each joint tenant takes an equal, undivided interest in the ownership of property from the same source and at the same time. Each joint tenant also has an undivided right of survivorship. Thus in a joint tenancy involving three tenants, the entire tenancy passes to the two survivors upon the death of the third and by-passes the deceased person's will and heirs. Tenancy in common is similar to a joint tenancy; however, there is no automatic passing of the deceased's rights to the surviving tenants. Instead, the deceased's rights pass according to the will. Tenancies in common can be sold, inherited, and given as a gift. Tenancy by the entirety can exist only between legally married husbands and wives and can be ended only through death, divorce, or mutual consent. Upon the death of one of the tenants, title passes to the surviving spouse. If a divorce occurs, the tenancy is converted into a tenancy in common.

The following case requires that the court determine whether a brother and sister hold title to real property as tenants in common or whether the brother holds title as the severalty owner.

In re Estate of Clayton Gulledge
637 A.2d 1278
District of Columbia Court of Appeals
Decided April 4, 1996.

The dispositive facts are undisputed. Clayton and Margie Gulledge owned a house at 532 Somerset Place, N.W. (the Somerset property) as tenants by the entirety. They had three children—Bernis Gulledge, Johnsie Walker, and Marion Watkins. Margie Gulledge died in 1970. Clayton Gulledge remarried the following year, but his second marriage was apparently unsuccessful.

In order to avert the possible loss, in any divorce proceedings, of the Somerset property, Bernis Gulledge advanced to his father the funds necessary to satisfy the second Mrs. Gulledge's financial demands. In exchange, Clayton Gulledge created a joint tenancy in the Somerset property, naming Bernis and himself as joint tenants. Bernis evidently expected that his father would predecease him, and that the right of survivorship which is the essence of a joint tenancy would enable him to acquire the entire property upon his father's death.

In 1988, however, Clayton Gulledge conveyed his interest in the Somerset property to his daughter, Marion Watkins, "in fee simple tenants in common." In 1991, Clayton Gulledge died, and he was survived by his three children. Bernis Gulledge died in 1993 and Johnsie B. Walker died in 1994. In the now consolidated proceedings relating to the estates of Clayton Gulledge, Bernis Gulledge, and Johnsie Walker, appellant Deborah Walker, Bernis' personal represen-

tative claims that when Clayton died, Bernis, as the surviving joint tenant, became the sole owner of the Somerset property. Ms. Watkins, on the other hand, contends that Clayton Gulledge's earlier conveyance of his interest to her severed the joint tenancy, thereby destroying Clayton's right of survivorship, and that Ms. Watkins and Bernis became tenants in common. The trial court agreed with Ms. Watkins. We affirm.

The parties agree that Clayton Gulledge's interest in the joint tenancy was alienable. They disagree only as to the nature of the interest which Clayton transferred to Ms. Watkins. The Estate of Bernis Gulledge (the Estate) argues that an owner cannot convey to a third party a greater interest than his own, . . . and that because Clayton Gulledge's interest was subject to Bernis' right of survivorship, the interest which Ms. Watkins received from Clayton must be similarly restricted. Ms. Watkins contends, on the other hand, that Clayton's conveyance to her converted the joint tenancy into a tenancy in common by operation of law, and that she received from Clayton an undivided one-half interest in the property.

The question whether a joint tenant severs a joint tenancy by ultimately conveying his interest to a third party without the consent of the other joint tenant has not been squarely decided in the District of Columbia. The issue is one of law, and our review is therefore de novo. . . . The applicable rule in a large majority of jurisdictions is that either party to a joint tenancy may sever that tenancy by unilaterally disposing of his interest, that the consent of the other tenant is not required, and that the transfer converts the estate into a tenancy in common. . . .

Although no decision by a court in this jurisdiction is directly on point, the discussion of joint tenancy that can be found in District of Columbia cases is consistent with the majority approach. In *Harrington v. Emmerman* . . . the court explained that "Joint tenancy cannot exist unless there be present unity of interest, title, time *and possession* that is to say, the interests must be identical, they must accrue by the same conveyance, they must commence at the same time and the estate must be held by the same undivided possession." (Emphasis added.) The interests of Bernis Gulledge and Marion Watkins were not created by the same conveyance, nor did they commence at the same time; the conveyance to Ms. Watkins thus destroyed the unities of title and time. . . .

In *Coleman v. Jackson*, . . . the court held that where a marriage was invalid, the deed purporting to convey property to the couple as tenants by the entireties created a joint tenancy instead. Contrasting the two types of estates, the court pointed out that "[o]f course, joint tenancy lacks the feature of inalienability which tenancy by the entireties possesses. . . . [I]nalienability is an incident only of estates by the entireties. . . ."

In *In re Estate of Wall*, the court restated the principle of *Coleman* and distinguished a tenancy by the entireties from a joint tenancy upon the ground that a tenancy by the entireties creates a "unilateral indestructible right of survivorship," while a joint tenancy does not. The court further stated that "survivorship incidental to joint tenancy differs because it may be frustrated . . . by alienation or subjection to debts of a cotenant's undivided share or by compulsory partition."

Although the foregoing authorities do not conclusively settle the question before us, they provide no support for the notion that this court should reject the majority rule. Moreover, "[b]ecause District of Columbia law is derived from Maryland law, decisions of the Court of Appeals of Maryland, and particularly those relating to the law of property, are accorded the most respectful consideration by our courts. . . . Under Maryland law, the transfer of an interest in a joint tenancy by either joint tenant will sever the joint tenancy and cause the share conveyed to become property held as tenants in common with the other cotenants." . . . We adopt the same rule here. Affirmed.

IV

For the foregoing reasons, we conclude that when Clayton Gulledge conveyed his interest to Ms. Watkins, she and Bernis Gulledge both became owners of an undivided one-half interest in the property as tenants in common. Upon Bernis' death, his estate replaced Bernis as a tenant in common with Ms. Watkins. Accordingly, the trial court correctly held that Ms. Watkins and the Estate of Bernis Gulledge are tenants in common, and that each holds an undivided half interest in the Somerset property.

Case Questions

1. What was the nature of the interest that Clayton transferred to his daughter, Marion Watkins?
2. Why didn't Bernis become the severalty owner of the Somerset property upon Clayton's death?
3. How was it possible for Clayton to create a joint tenancy in the property, with himself and his son Bernis as joint tenants?

Community Property

Community property is recognized by the states of Arizona, California, Idaho, Louisiana, Nevada, New Mexico, Texas, Washington, and Wisconsin. In community property states, each spouse is legally entitled to a percentage of what the state defines as *community property* and this varies by jurisdiction. Although states differ, community property is usually defined as including the earnings of both spouses and property rights acquired with those earnings during the marriage. State statutes, however, usually exclude from community property rights acquired prior to marriage, spousal inheritances, and gifts received during the marriage. These are classified as separate property. Community property states differ on whether earnings from separate property should be treated as community property.

Title

Title refers to ownership rights in property. For example, when a student purchases a textbook from a bookstore, he or she is purchasing the seller's *title* to the book. This means that the bookstore is selling all its rights in the book to the student. The bookstore will provide the purchaser with a receipt (bill of sale) to evidence the purchase of these rights and the transfer of ownership. If the student purchased the textbook from a thief, however, the student would not obtain title to the book. The larceny victim would still have the title, and the thief would be an unlawful possessor.[14]

A student who has purchased title to a textbook has many rights vis-à-vis that object. The student may decide to temporarily loan possessory rights to the book to another student. The student also has the right to decide whether to dispose of the book after completion of the course. For instance, the student might decide to make a gift or sell the rights in the book to another student or resell it back to the bookstore.

A bookstore does not have to produce a written document to establish its ownership when it sells a textbook to a student. However, the law does require the use of title documents to provide evidence of title for some property items. A seller of a motor vehicle, for example, must have a valid title document from the state to transfer ownership rights to the purchaser, and purchases of land require a title document called a deed.

GOVERNMENT'S RIGHT TO REGULATE AND TAKE PRIVATE PROPERTY

State government bears the primary responsibility for defining and limiting the exercise of private property rights through the police power. The police power refers to the authority of state legislatures to enact laws regulating and restraining private rights and occupations for the promotion of the public health, welfare, safety, and morals. The police power of the states is not a grant derived from a written constitution; the federal Constitution assumes the preexistence of the police power, and the Tenth Amendment reserves to the states any power not delegated to the federal government in Article I. Limitations on the police power have never been drawn with precision or determined by a general formula. But the Fifth and Fourteenth amendments' due process clauses require that state actions based on the police power be exercised in the public interest, be reasonable, and be consistent with the rights implied or secured in the Constitution. Government uses of the police power with respect to property include zoning, eminent domain, taxation, and nuisance. See Figure 12–1 for an overview of the government's role in regulating private property.

Zoning

State legislatures originally authorized local governments to enact zoning regulations to promote public health and safety by separating housing districts from incompatible commercial and industrial uses. Today, zoning ordinances also preserve a community's historically significant landmarks and neighborhoods and restrict adult entertainment. State and local environmental protection agencies often resort to zoning ordinances in deciding whether to grant licenses to land developers where a proposed land use threatens wetlands or natural habitat and increases air and water pollution. Zoning ordinances can be very controversial, such as where they prohibit trailer parks or require that structures and lots be large (and therefore often unaffordable to low-income people). In the Family Law chapter (Chapter 9) you can see another example of restrictive zoning. In a 1977 case decided by the U.S. Supreme Court entitled *Moore v. City of East Cleveland*, governmental authorities unsuccessfully sought to use a zoning ordinance to prohibit a grandmother from living with her two grandchildren.

Eminent Domain

The government can take private property for a public purpose over the objection of a landowner pursuant to what is called the power of *eminent domain*. The Fifth Amendment provides that whenever the federal government takes property to benefit the public, it must pay just compensation. This constitutional control on government has been incorporated into the Fourteenth Amendment and is also binding on the states. The *Takings Clause* protects individual private property rights by ensuring that taxpayers, rather than targeted private individuals, pay for public benefits.

Government obtains title to private land through condemnation proceedings in which a court ensures that statutory and constitutional requirements are satisfied. In a related proceeding, a court will determine the fair market value of the land that will be paid to the property owner.

The U.S. Supreme Court has been unsuccessful to date in precisely establishing what constitutes a "taking." It has, however, recognized that takings can

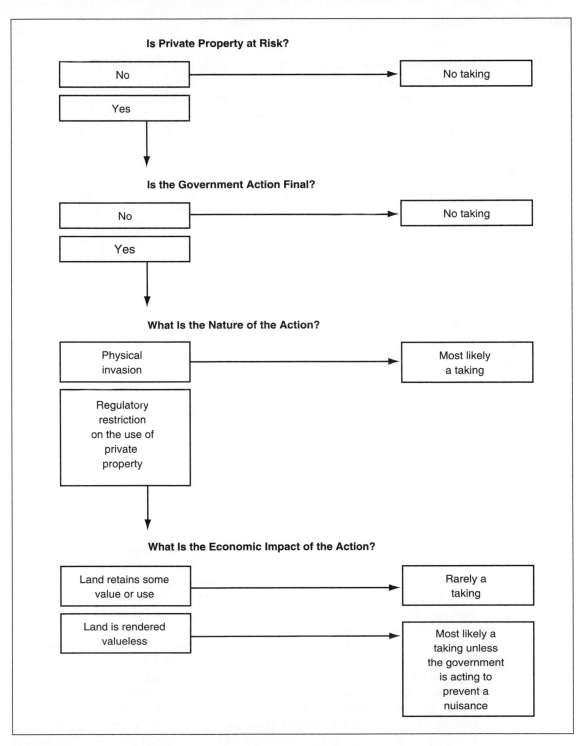

FIGURE 12-1   When Does Government Action Become a Taking of Private Property?

Source: Kathleen C. Zimmerman and David Abelson, "Takings Law: A Guide to Government, Property, and the Constitution," Copyright © 1993 by The Land & Water Fund of the Rockies, Inc.

assume different forms. One obvious example is where the government takes title to land for the purpose of building a public highway. Other takings, however, are less obvious. The Supreme Court found in 1946 that a taking had occurred where low-flying military aircraft created so much noise while flying over a chicken farm that the farm went out of business.[15] The Court ruled that under these circumstances the government had exploited and in effect taken airspace above it for a flight path (a public purpose), to the commercial detriment of the farmer. The farmer, said the Court, was entitled to compensation.

In a 1978 case, the U.S. Supreme Court had to rule whether New York City, as part of a historic landmarks preservation program, could impose limitations on the development of historic buildings such as Grand Central Station. The city wanted to prevent the construction of a large office building above the station. To the developer the restrictions imposed by the Landmark Preservation Law amounted to a taking of private property (the airspace above the station) for a public purpose, for which compensation was due. The Court ruled in favor of the city, largely because the law served a public purpose (improving the quality of life for all New Yorkers) and provided the developer with a reasonable economic return on investment.

Since the ruling in the Grand Central Station case, the concerns of landowners have intensified. One aspect of the dispute that has evolved throughout the 1990s has focused on the point at which taxpayers should be required to compensate property owners whose property values have declined due to governmental environmental regulations.

One widely publicized example of this debate has been the conflict over environmental regulations intended to preserve the habitat of an endangered species called the northern spotted owl. Environmental legislation has been interpreted to prevent owners of land lying within the owl's habitat from commercially logging their own trees. Many landowners have argued that the law is unfairly denying them compensation when their property values fall as a result of governmental restrictions that prevent them from commercially developing their land and its natural resources. Defenders maintain that such regulations are necessary because the cumulative effect of the individual actions of private landowners would likely result in endangered species becoming extinct. Legislative initiatives designed to protect the environment, and preserve aesthetic and cultural landmarks, have generally been upheld by the Supreme Court. Whether this trend will continue is in doubt.

The next case was decided by the U.S. Supreme Court in 1994. It involved a dispute between a property owner/businesswoman and the City of Tigard, Oregon. The Supreme Court had to determine whether the city could require that the property owner dedicate 10 percent of her property for public uses—a public greenway, bike path, and contributions to an improved storm drainage system. In return, the city would grant her permission to replace the building housing her plumbing-supply business with a new and larger structure and to make other commercially valuable improvements to her parcel. The Court had to consider both the proper reach of the city's power to regulate businesses, and the reach of the Fifth Amendment's takings clause.

Dolan v. City of Tigard
114 S.Ct. 2309
U.S. Supreme Court
June 24, 1994

Chief Justice Rehnquist delivered the opinion of the Court.

I

The State of Oregon enacted a comprehensive land use management program in 1973. The program required all Oregon cities and counties to adopt new comprehensive land use plans that were consistent with the statewide planning goals. . . . Pursuant to the State's requirements, the city of Tigard, a community of some 30,000 residents on the southwest edge of Portland, developed a comprehensive plan and codified it in its Community Development Code (CDC). The CDC requires property owners in the area zoned Central Business District to comply with a 15% open space and landscaping requirement, which limits total site coverage, including all structures and paved parking, to 85% of the parcel. . . .

After the completion of a transportation study that identified congestion in the Central Business District as a particular problem, the city adopted a plan for a pedestrian/bicycle pathway intended to encourage alternatives to automobile transportation for short trips. The CDC requires that new development facilitate this plan by dedicating land for pedestrian pathways where provided for in the pedestrian/bicycle pathway plan.

The city also adopted a Master Drainage Plan (Drainage Plan). The Drainage Plan noted that flooding occurred in several areas along Fanno Creek, including areas near petitioner's property. . . . The Drainage Plan also established that the increase in impervious surfaces associated with continued urbanization would exacerbate these flooding problems. To combat these risks, the Drainage Plan suggested a series of improvements to the Fanno Creek Basin, including channel excavation in the area next to petitioner's property. . . . Other recommendations included ensuring that the floodplain remains free of structures and that it be preserved as greenways to minimize flood damage to structures. . . .

The Drainage Plan concluded that the cost of these improvements should be shared based on both direct and indirect benefits, with property owners along the waterways paying more due to the direct benefit that they would receive. . . . CDC Chapters 18.84, 18.86 and CDC § 18.164.100 and the Tigard Park Plan carry out these recommendations.

Petitioner Florence Dolan owns a plumbing and electric supply store located on Main Street in the Central Business District of the city. The store covers approximately 9,700 square feet on the eastern side of a 1.67-acre parcel, which includes a gravel parking lot. Fanno Creek flows through the southwestern corner of the lot and along its western boundary. The year-round flow of the creek renders the area within the creek's 100-year floodplain virtually unusable for commercial development. The city's comprehensive plan includes the Fanno Creek floodplain as part of the city's greenway system.

Petitioner applied to the city for a permit to redevelop the site. Her proposed plans called for nearly doubling the size of the store to 17,600 square feet, and paving a 39-space parking lot. The existing store, located on the opposite side of the parcel, would be razed in sections as construction progressed on the new building. In the second phase of the project, petitioner proposed to build an additional structure on the northeast side of the site for complementary businesses, and to provide more parking. The proposed expansion and intensified use are consistent with the city's zoning scheme in the Central Business District. . . .

The City Planning Commission granted petitioner's permit application subject to conditions imposed by the city's CDC. The CDC establishes the following standard for site development review approval:

> "Where landfill and/or development is allowed within and adjacent to the 100-year floodplain, the city shall require the dedication of sufficient open land area for greenway adjoining and within the floodplain. This area shall include portions at a suitable elevation for the construction of a pedestrian/bicycle pathway within the floodplain in accordance with the adopted pedestrian/bicycle plan." . . .

Thus, the Commission required that petitioner dedicate the portion of her property lying within the 100-year floodplain for improvement of a storm drainage system along Fanno Creek and that she dedicate an additional 15-foot strip of land adjacent to the floodplain as a pedestrian/bicycle pathway. The dedication required by that condition encompasses approximately 7,000 square feet, or roughly 10% of the property. In accordance with city practice, petitioner could rely on the dedicated property to meet the 15% open space and landscaping requirement mandated by the city's zoning scheme.

The city would bear the cost of maintaining a landscaped buffer between the dedicated area and the new store.

Petitioner requested variances from the CDC standards. . . . The Commission denied the request.

The Commission made a series of findings concerning the relationship between the dedicated conditions and the projected impacts of petitioner's project. First, the Commission noted that "[i]t is reasonable to assume that customers and employees of the future uses of this site could utilize a pedestrian/bicycle pathway adjacent to this development for their transportation and recreational needs."

The Commission noted that the site plan has provided for bicycle parking in a rack in front of the proposed building and "[i]t is reasonable to expect that some of the users of the bicycle parking provided for by the site plan will use the pathway adjacent to Fanno Creek if it is constructed." . . . In addition, the Commission found that creation of a convenient, safe pedestrian/bicycle pathway system as an alternative means of transportation "could offset some of the traffic demand on [nearby] streets and lessen the increase in traffic congestion." . . .

The Commission went on to note that the required floodplain dedication would be reasonably related to petitioner's request to intensify the use of the site given the increase in the impervious surface. The Commission stated that the "anticipated increased storm water flow from the subject property to an already strained creek and drainage basin can only add to the public need to manage the stream channel and floodplain for drainage purposes." . . . Based on this anticipated increased storm water flow, the Commission concluded that "the requirement of dedication of the floodplain area on the site is related to the applicant's plan to intensify development on the site." The Tigard City Council approved the Commission's final order. . . .

Petitioner appealed to the Land Use Board of Appeals (LUBA) on the ground that the city's dedication requirements were not related to the proposed development, and, therefore, those requirements constituted an uncompensated taking of their property under the Fifth Amendment. . . . Given the undisputed fact that the proposed larger building and paved parking area would increase the amount of impervious surfaces and the runoff into Fanno Creek, LUBA concluded that "there is a 'reasonable relationship' between the proposed development and the requirement to dedicate land along Fanno Creek for a greenway." . . .

With respect to the pedestrian/bicycle pathway, LUBA noted the Commission's finding that a significantly larger retail sales building and parking lot would attract larger numbers of customers and employees and their vehicles. It again found a "reasonable relationship" between alleviating the impacts of increased traffic from the development and facilitating the provision of a pedestrian/bicycle pathway as an alternative means of transportation. . . .

The Oregon Court of Appeals affirmed. . . . We granted certiorari. . . .

II

The Takings Clause of the Fifth Amendment of the United States Constitution, made applicable to the States through the Fourteenth Amendment, . . . provides: "[N]or shall private property be taken for public use, without just compensation." One of the principal purposes of the Takings Clause is "to bar Government from forcing some people alone to bear public burdens which, in all fairness and justice, should be borne by the public as a whole." . . .

Without question, had the city simply required petitioner to dedicate a strip of land along Fanno Creek for public use, rather than conditioning the grant of her permit to redevelop her property on such a dedication, a taking would have occurred. . . . Such public access would deprive petitioner of the right to exclude others, "one of the most essential sticks in the bundle of rights that are commonly characterized as property."

. . . On the other side of the ledger, the authority of state and local governments to engage in land use planning has been sustained against constitutional challenge. . . .

. . . "Government hardly could go on if to some extent values incident to property could not be diminished without paying for every such change in the general law." *Pennsylvania Coal Co. v. Mahon*, . . . (1992). A land use regulation does not effect a taking if it "substantially advance[s] legitimate state interests" and does not "den[y] an owner eco-nomically viable use of his land." *Agins v. Tiburon*, . . . (1980).

The sort of land use regulations discussed in the cases just cited, however, differ in two relevant particulars from the present case. First, they involved essentially legislative determinations classifying entire areas of the city, whereas here the city made an adjudicative decision to condition petitioner's application for a building permit on an individual parcel. Second, the conditions imposed were not simply a limitation on the use petitioner might make of her own parcel, but a requirement that she deed portions of the property to the city. In *Nollan v. California Coastal Comm'n*, we held the governmental authority to exact such a condition was circumscribed by the Fifth and Fourteenth Amendments. Under the well-settled doctrine of "unconstitutional conditions," the government may not require a person to give up a constitutional right—here the right to receive just compensation when property is taken for a public use—in exchange for a discretionary benefit conferred by the government where the property sought has little or no relationship to the benefit. . . .

Petitioner contends that the city has forced her to choose between the building permit and her right under the Fifth Amendment to just compensation for the public easements. Petitioner does not quarrel with the city's authority to exact some forms of dedication as a condition for the grant of a building permit, but challenges the showing made by the city to justify these exactions. She argues that the city has identified "no special benefits" conferred on her, and has not identified any "special quantifiable burdens" created by her new store that would justify the particular dedications required from her which are not required from the public at large.

III

In evaluating petitioner's claim, we must first determine whether the "essential nexus" exists between the "legitimate state interest" and the permit condition exacted by the city. . . . If we find that a nexus exists, we must then decide the required degree of connection between the exactions and the projected impact of the proposed development. We were not required to reach this question in *Nollan*, because we concluded that the connection did not meet even the loosest standard. . . . Here, however, we must decide this question.

A

We addressed the essential nexus question in *Nollan*. The California Coastal Commission demanded a lateral public easement across the Nollan's beachfront lot in exchange for a permit to demolish an existing bungalow and replace it with a three-bedroom house. . . . The public easement was designed to connect two public beaches that were separated by the Nollan's property. The Coastal Commission had asserted that the public easement condition was imposed to promote the legitimate state interest of diminishing the "blockade of the view of the ocean" caused by construction of the larger house.

We agreed that the Coastal Commission's concern with protecting visual access to the ocean constituted a legitimate public interest. . . . We also agreed that the permit condition would have been constitutional "even if it consisted of the requirement that the Nollans provide a viewing spot on their property for passersby with whose sighting of the ocean their new house would interfere." . . . We resolved, however, that the Coastal Commission's regulatory authority was set completely adrift from its constitutional moorings when it claimed that a nexus existed between visual access to the ocean and a permit condition requiring lateral public access along the Nollan's beachfront lot. . . . How enhancing the public's ability to "traverse to and along the shorefront" served the same governmental purpose of "visual access to the ocean" from the roadway was beyond our ability

to countenance. The absence of a nexus left the Coastal Commission in the position of simply trying to obtain an easement through gimmickry, which converted a valid regulation of land use into "an out-and-out plan of extortion." . . .

No such gimmicks are associated with the permit conditions imposed by the city in this case. Undoubtedly, the prevention of flooding along Fanno Creek and the reduction of traffic congestion in the Central Business District qualify as the type of legitimate public purposes we have upheld. . . . It seems equally obvious that a nexus exists between preventing flooding along Fanno Creek and limiting development within the creek's 100-year floodplain. Petitioner proposes to double the size of her retail store and to pave her now-gravel parking lot, thereby expanding the impervious surface on the property and increasing the amount of stormwater run-off into Fanno Creek.

The same may be said for the city's attempt to reduce traffic congestion by providing for alternative means of transportation. In theory, a pedestrian/bicycle pathway provides a useful alternative means of transportation for workers and shoppers: "Pedestrians and bicyclists occupying dedicated spaces for walking and/or bicycling . . . remove potential vehicles from streets, resulting in an overall improvement in total transportation system flow." . . .

B

The second part of our analysis requires us to determine whether the degree of the exactions demanded by the city's permit conditions bear the required relationship to the projected impact of petitioner's proposed development. . . .

The city required that petitioner dedicate "to the city as Greenway all portions of the site that fall within the existing 100-year floodplain [of Fanno Creek] . . . and all property 15 feet above [the floodplain] boundary."

In addition, the city demanded that the retail store be designed so as not to intrude into the greenway area. The city relies on the Commission's rather tentative findings that increased stormwater flow from petitioner's property "can only add to the public need to manage the [floodplain] for drainage purposes" to support its conclusion that the "requirement of dedication of the floodplain area on the site is related to the applicant's plan to intensify development on the site." . . .

The city made the following specific findings relevant to the pedestrian/bicycle pathway:

> "In addition, the proposed expanded use of this site is anticipated to generate additional vehicular traffic thereby increasing congestion on nearby collector and arterial streets. Creation of a convenient, safe pedestrian/bicycle pathway system as an alternative means of transportation could offset some of the traffic demand on these nearby streets and lessen the increase in traffic congestion." . . .

The question for us is whether these findings are constitutionally sufficient to justify the conditions imposed by the city on petitioner's building permit. Since state courts have been dealing with this question a good deal longer than we have, we turn to representative decisions made by them. . . . Despite any semantic differences, general agreement exists among the courts "that the dedication should have some reasonable relationship to the needs created by the [development]."

We think the "reasonable relationship" test adopted by a majority of the state courts is closer to the federal constitutional norm than either of those previously discussed. But we do not adopt it as such, partly because the term "reasonable relationship" seems confusingly similar to the term "rational basis" which describes the minimal level of scrutiny under the Equal Protection Clause of the Fourteenth Amendment. We think a term such as "rough proportionality" best encapsulates what we hold to be the requirement of the Fifth Amendment. No precise mathematical calculation is required, but the city must make some sort of individualized determination that the required dedication is related both in nature and extent to the impact of the proposed development. . . . It is axiomatic that increasing the amount of impervious surface will increase the quantity and rate of storm-water flow from petitioner's property. . . . Therefore, keeping the floodplain open and free from development would likely confine the pressures on Fanno Creek created by petitioner's development. In fact, because petitioner's property lies within the Central Business District, the Community Development Code already required that petitioner leave 15% of it as open space and the undeveloped floodplain would have nearly satisfied that requirement. . . . But the city demanded more—it not only wanted petitioner not to build in the floodplain, but it also wanted petitioner's property along Fanno Creek for its Greenway system. The city has never said why a public greenway, as opposed to a private one, was required in the interest of flood control.

The difference to petitioner, of course, is the loss of her ability to exclude others. As we have noted, this right to exclude others is "one of the most essential sticks in the bundle of rights that are commonly characterized as property." It is difficult to see why recreational visitors trampling along petitioner's floodplain easement are sufficiently related to the city's legitimate interest in reducing flooding problems along Fanno Creek, and the city has not attempted to make any individualized determination to support this part of its request. . . .

Admittedly, petitioner wants to build a bigger store to attract members of the public to her property. She also wants, however, to be able to control the time and manner in which they enter.

. . . By contrast, the city wants to impose a permanent recreational easement upon petitioner's property that borders Fanno Creek. Petitioner would lose all rights to regulate the time in which the public entered onto the Greenway, regardless of any interference it might pose with her retail store. Her right to exclude would not be regulated, it would be eviscerated.

If petitioner's proposed development had somehow encroached on existing greenway space in the city, it would have been reasonable to require petitioner to provide some alternative greenway space for the public either on her property or elsewhere.

. . . We conclude that the findings upon which the city relies do not show the required reasonable relationship between the floodplain easement and the petitioner's proposed new building.

With respect to the pedestrian/bicycle pathway, we have no doubt that the city was correct in finding that the larger retail sales facility proposed by petitioner will increase traffic on the streets of the Central Business District. The city estimates that the proposed development would generate roughly 435 additional trips per day. Dedications for streets, sidewalks, and other public ways are generally reasonable exactions to avoid excessive congestion from a proposed property use. But on the record before us, the city has not met its burden of demonstrating that the additional number of vehicle and bicycle trips generated by the petitioner's development reasonably relate to the city's requirement for a dedication of the pedestrian/bicycle pathway easement. The city simply found that the creation of the pathway "could offset some of the traffic demand . . . and lessen the increase in traffic congestion." . . .

As Justice Peterson of the Supreme Court of Oregon explained in his dissenting opinion, however, "[t]he findings of fact that the bicycle pathway system 'could offset some of the traffic demand' is a far cry from a finding that the bicycle pathway system will, or is likely to, offset some of the traffic demand." No precise mathematical calculation is required, but the city must make some effort to quantify its findings in support of the dedi-

cation for the pedestrian/bicycle pathway beyond the conclusory statement that it could offset some of the traffic demand generated.

Cities have long engaged in the commendable task of land use planning, made necessary by increasing urbanization particularly in metropolitan areas such as Portland. The city's goals of reducing flooding hazards and traffic congestion, and providing for public greenways, are laudable, but there are outer limits to how this may be done. "A strong public desire to improve the public condition [will not] warrant achieving the desire by a shorter cut than the constitutional way of paying for the change."

The judgment of the Supreme Court of Oregon is reversed, and the case is remanded for further proceedings consistent with this opinion.

It is so ordered.

Justice Stevens, with whom Justice Blackmun and Justice Ginsburg join, dissenting

The record does not tell us the dollar value of petitioner Florence Dolan's interest in excluding the public from the greenway adjacent to her hardware business. The mountain of briefs that the case has generated nevertheless makes it obvious that the pecuniary value of her victory is far less important than the rule of law that this case has been used to establish. It is unquestionably an important case.

Certain propositions are not in dispute. The enlargement of the Tigard unit in Dolan's chain of hardware stores will have an adverse impact on the city's legitimate and substantial interests in controlling drainage in Fanno Creek and minimizing traffic congestion in Tigard's business district. That impact is sufficient to justify an outright denial of her application for approval of the expansion. The city has nevertheless agreed to grant Dolan's application if she will comply with two conditions, each of which admittedly will mitigate the adverse effects of her proposed development. The disputed question is whether the city has violated the Fourteenth Amendment to the Federal Constitution by refusing to allow Dolan's planned construction to proceed unless those conditions are met.

The Court is correct in concluding that the city may not attach arbitrary conditions to a building permit or to a variance even when it can rightfully deny the application outright. I also agree that state court decisions dealing with ordinances that govern municipal development plans provide useful guidance in a case of this kind. Yet the Court's description of the doctrinal underpinnings of its decision, the phrasing of its fledgling test of "rough proportionality," and the application of that test to this case run contrary to the traditional treatment of these cases and break considerable and unpropitious new ground.

I

Candidly acknowledging the lack of federal precedent for its exercise in rulemaking, the Court purports to find guidance in . . . "representative" state court decisions. To do so is certainly appropriate. The state cases the Court consults, however, either fail to support or decidedly undermine the Court's conclusions in key respects. . . .

II

It is not merely state cases, but our own cases as well, that require the analysis to focus on the impact of the city's action on the entire parcel of private property. In *Penn Central Transportation Co. v. New York City*, . . . we stated that takings jurisprudence "does not divide a single parcel into discrete segments and attempt to determine whether rights in a particular segment have been entirely abrogated." . . . Instead, this Court focuses "both on the character of the action and on the nature and extent of the interference with rights in the parcel as a whole." *Andrus v. Allard* . . .

reaffirmed the nondivisibility principle outlined in *Penn Central*, stating that "[a]t least where an owner possesses a full 'bundle' of property rights, the destruction of one 'strand' of the bundle is not a taking, because the aggregate must be viewed in its entirety."

Although limitation of the right to exclude others undoubtedly constitutes a significant infringement upon property ownership, restrictions on that right do not alone constitute a taking, and do not do so in any event unless they "unreasonably impair the value or use" of the property.

The Court's narrow focus on one strand in the property owner's bundle of rights is particularly misguided in a case involving the development of commercial property. As Professor Johnston has noted:

> "The subdivider is a manufacturer, processer, and marketer of a product; land is but one of his raw materials. In subdivision control disputes, the developer is not defending hearth and home against the king's intrusion, but simply attempting to maximize his profits from the sale of a finished product. As applied to him, subdivision control exactions are actually business regulations." Johnston, Constitutionality of Subdivision Control Exactions: The Quest for A Rationale, 52 Cornell L.Q. 871, 923 (1967).

The exactions associated with the development of a retail business are likewise a species of business regulation that heretofore warranted a strong presumption of constitutional validity.

In Johnston's view, "if the municipality can demonstrate that its assessment of financial burdens against subdividers is rational, impartial, and conducive to fulfillment of - authorized planning objectives, its action need be invalidated only in those extreme and presumably rare cases where the burden of compliance is sufficiently great to deter the owner from proceeding with his planned development." . . . The city of Tigard has demonstrated that its plan is rational and impartial and that the conditions at issue are "conducive to fulfillment of authorized planning objectives." Dolan, on the other hand, has offered no evidence that her burden of compliance has any impact at all on the value or profitability of her planned development. Following the teaching of the cases on which it purports to rely, the Court should not isolate the burden associated with the loss of the power to exclude from an evaluation of the benefit to be derived from the permit to enlarge the store and the parking lot.

The Court's assurances that its "rough proportionality" test leaves ample room for cities to pursue the "commendable task of land use planning," . . . even twice avowing that "[n]o precise mathematical calculation is required," . . . are wanting given the result that test compels here. Under the Court's approach, a city must not only "quantify its findings," . . . and make "individualized determination[s]" with respect to the nature *and* the extent of the relationship between the conditions and the impact, . . . but also demonstrate "proportionality." The correct inquiry should instead concentrate on whether the required nexus is present and venture beyond considerations of a condition's nature or germaneness only if the developer establishes that a concededly germane condition is so grossly disproportionate to the proposed development's adverse effects that it manifests motives other than land use regulation on the part of the city.

III

Applying its new standard, the Court finds two defects in the city's case. First, while the record would adequately support a requirement that Dolan maintain the portion of the floodplain on her property as undeveloped open space, it does not support the additional requirement that the floodplain be dedicated to the city. . . . Second, while the city adequately established the traffic increase that the proposed development would

generate, it failed to quantify the offsetting decrease in automobile traffic that the bike path will produce.

IV

The Court has made a serious error by abandoning the traditional presumption of constitutionality and imposing a novel burden of proof on a city implementing an admittedly valid comprehensive land use plan. Even more consequential than its incorrect disposition of this case, however, is the Court's resurrection of a species of substantive due process analysis that it firmly rejected decades ago. . . .

It applied the same kind of substantive due process analysis more frequently identified with a better known case that accorded similar substantive protection to a baker's liberty interest in working 60 hours a week and 10 hours a day. See *Lochner v. New York,* . . . (1905).

Later cases have interpreted the Fourteenth Amendment's substantive protection against uncompensated deprivations of private property by the States as though it incorporated the text of the Fifth Amendment's Takings Clause. . . . There was nothing problematic about that interpretation in cases enforcing the Fourteenth Amendment against state action that involved the actual physical invasion of private property. . . . Justice Holmes charted a significant new course, however, when he opined that a state law making it "commercially impracticable to mine certain coal" had "very nearly the same effect for constitutional purposes as appropriating or destroying it." *Pennsylvania Coal Co. v. Mahon,* . . . (1922). The so-called "regulatory takings" doctrine that the Holmes dictum kindled has an obvious kinship with the line of substantive due process cases that *Lochner* exemplified. Besides having similar ancestry, both doctrines are potentially open ended sources of judicial power to invalidate state economic regulations that Members of this Court view as unwise or unfair.

This case inaugurates an even more recent judicial innovation than the regulatory takings doctrine: the application of the "unconstitutional conditions" label to a mutually beneficial transaction between a property owner and a city. The Court tells us that the city's refusal to grant Dolan a discretionary benefit infringes her right to receive just compensation for the property interests that she has refused to dedicate to the city "where the property sought has little or no relationship to the benefit." . . .

Dolan has no right to be compensated for a taking unless the city acquires the property interests that she has refused to surrender. Since no taking has yet occurred, there has not been any infringement of her constitutional right to compensation. . . .

The Court has decided to apply its heightened scrutiny to a single strand—the power to exclude—in the bundle of rights that enables a commercial enterprise to flourish in an urban environment. . . .

In its application of what is essentially the doctrine of substantive due process, the Court confuses the past with the present. On November 13, 1922, the village of Euclid, Ohio, adopted a zoning ordinance that effectively confiscated 75 percent of the value of property owned by the Ambler Realty Company. Despite its recognition that such an ordinance "would have been rejected as arbitrary and oppressive" at an earlier date, the Court (over the dissent of Justices Van Devanter, McReynolds and Butler) upheld the ordinance. Today's majority should heed the words of Justice Sutherland:

> "Such regulations are sustained, under the complex conditions of our day, for reasons analogous to those which justify traffic regulations, which, before the advent of automobiles and rapid transit street railways, would have been condemned as fatally arbitrary and unreasonable. And in this there is

no inconsistency, for while the meaning of constitutional guaranties never varies, the scope of their application must expand or contract to meet the new and different conditions which are constantly coming within the field of their operation. In a changing world, it is impossible that it should be otherwise." *Euclid v. Ambler* . . . (1926).

In our changing world one thing is certain: uncertainty will characterize predictions about the impact of new urban developments on the risks of floods, earthquakes, traffic congestion, or environmental harms. When there is doubt concerning the magnitude of those impacts, the public interest in averting them must outweigh the private interest of the commercial entrepreneur. If the government can demonstrate that the conditions it has imposed in a land-use permit are rational, impartial and conducive to fulfilling the aims of a valid land-use plan, a strong presumption of validity should attach to those conditions. The burden of demonstrating that those conditions have unreasonably impaired the economic value of the proposed improvement belongs squarely on the shoulders of the party challenging the state action's constitutionality. That allocation of burdens has served us well in the past. The Court has stumbled badly today by reversing it.

I respectfully dissent.

Justice Souter, dissenting

This case, like *Nollan v. California Coastal Comm'n*, . . . (1987), invites the Court to examine the relationship between conditions imposed by development permits, requiring landowners to dedicate portions of their land for use by the public, and governmental interests in mitigating the adverse effects of such development. *Nollan* declared the need for a nexus between the nature of an exaction of an interest in land (a beach easement) and the nature of governmental interests. . . .

I cannot agree that the application of *Nollan* is a sound one here, since it appears that the Court has placed the burden of producing evidence of relationship on the city, despite the usual rule in cases involving the police power that the government is presumed to have acted constitutionally. Having thus assigned the burden, the Court concludes that the City loses based on one word ("could" instead of "would"), and despite the fact that this record shows the connection the Court looks for. Dolan has put forward no evidence that the burden of granting a dedication for the bicycle path is unrelated in kind to the anticipated increase in traffic congestion, nor, if there exists a requirement that the relationship be related in degree, has Dolan shown that the exaction fails any such test. The city, by contrast, calculated the increased traffic flow that would result from Dolan's proposed development to be 435 trips per day, and its Comprehensive Plan, applied here, relied on studies showing the link between alternative modes of transportation, including bicycle paths, and reduced street traffic congestion. . . . *Nollan,* therefore, is satisfied, and on that assumption the city's conditions should not be held to fail a further rough proportionality test or any other that might be devised to give meaning to the constitutional limits. As Members of this Court have said before, "the common zoning regulations requiring subdividers to . . . dedicate certain areas to public streets, are in accord with our constitutional traditions because the proposed property use would otherwise be the cause of excessive congestion." . . .

. . . The bicycle path permit condition is fundamentally no different from these.

In any event, on my reading, the Court's conclusions about the city's vulnerability carry the Court no further than *Nollan* has gone already, and I do not view this case as a suitable vehicle for taking the law beyond that point. The right case for the enunciation of takings doctrine seems hard to spot.

Case Questions

1. What test did the Supreme Court adopt in deciding this case?
2. Can you see any consequences that might flow from this decision in the future?
3. The Court's decision in this case was supported by five of the justices. Why did four justices dissent?

 The Supreme Court adopted as its legal standard the "rough proportionality test" for determining whether a zoning regulation has intruded on property rights to such a degree as to constitute a "taking" under the Fifth Amendment. Is this test workable in your opinion? Does it meaningfully guide lower courts toward reaching just outcomes in subsequent cases?

Taxation

A property owner is usually required to pay taxes to the government based on the value and use of the property. Failure to pay these taxes can result in the filing of a lien and eventually in the public taking of the property to satisfy the taxes. Government frequently uses tax concessions to encourage property uses it favors.

Nuisance

A nuisance exists when an owner's use of his or her property unreasonably infringes on other persons' use and enjoyment of their property rights. Nuisances are classified as public, private, or both. A *public nuisance* exists when a given use of land poses a generalized threat to the public. It is redressed by criminal prosecution and injunctive relief. Examples of public nuisances include houses of prostitution, actions affecting the public health (such as water and air pollution), crack houses, and dance halls. A *private nuisance* is a tort that requires proof of an injury that is distinct from that suffered by the general public. (It differs from trespass because the offensive activity does not occur on the victim's property.) A party injured by a private nuisance can obtain both damages and injunctive relief.

Gloria Lane, the plaintiff in the following case, sustained significant damages to her home caused by branches falling from a neighbor's tree and tree roots that penetrated her sewer pipe. Lane's nuisance suit against the neighbor was dismissed by the trial court. After the intermediate appellate court affirmed the trial court's decision, she appealed to the state supreme court.

Gloria B. Lane v. W. J. Curry & Sons
No. W2000-01580-SC-R11-CV
Supreme Court of Tennessee
December 19, 2002

Frank F. Drowota, III

We granted review in this case to determine whether a landowner can bring a nuisance action against an adjoining landowner when tree branches and roots from the adjoining landowner's property encroach upon and damage the neighboring landowner's property. . . .

Factual and Procedural Background

This case involves a dispute between adjacent property owners over harm caused by encroaching tree branches and roots. The plaintiff, Gloria Lane, owns a house in Memphis located next door to a house owned by the defendant, W. J. Curry & Sons. The plaintiff, who is 47-years old and unemployed, has lived in the house all of her life. Her disabled brother lives with her. The defendant's house is used as rental property and is occu-

pied. The houses in the parties' neighborhood are at least fifty-years old and are situated close together.

The defendant has three large, healthy oak trees located on its property near the common boundary line with the plaintiff. The trees are much taller than the parties' houses and have limbs, described as "extremely protruding," that hang over the plaintiff's house. The defendant's trees were described as "overshadowing the [plaintiff's] entire house." The plaintiff has had problems with the trees' limbs and roots encroaching upon her property for many years. Her roof, for example, had to be replaced in the late 1980s because the overhanging branches did not allow the roof to ever dry, causing it to rot. The plaintiff testified that prior to that time "every roof and wall in [her] house had turned brown and the ceiling was just falling down. We would be in bed at nighttime and the ceiling would just fall down and hit the floor."

In 1997, a large limb from one of the defendant's trees located between the parties' houses broke off and fell through the plaintiff's roof, attic, and kitchen ceiling, causing rainwater to leak into the interior of her home. It appears based on photographs contained in the record that the limb came from a tree that was only a few feet from the plaintiff's house. The water ruined the plaintiff's ceilings, floor, and the stove in her kitchen. The plaintiff is not physically able to cut the limbs back that hang over her house, and she cannot afford to hire someone else to do it. Nor can she afford to repair the damage to the exterior and interior of her home, including the hole in her roof.

In addition to the harm caused by the overhanging branches, roots from the defendant's trees have infiltrated and clogged the plaintiff's sewer line, causing severe plumbing problems. The plaintiff has tried to chop the encroaching roots over the years, but they keep growing back and causing more plumbing problems. The plaintiff has not been able to use her toilet, bathtub, or sink in two years because of the clogged sewer pipes. She must go to a neighbor's house to use the restroom. Raw sewage bubbles up into her bathtub, and her bathroom floor has had to be replaced because her toilet continually backs up and water spills onto her floor. . . .

After the defendant's branch fell through her roof, the plaintiff contacted Judith Harris, the owner of defendant W. J. Curry & Sons, to complain about the encroaching trees and to inform Harris of the damage caused by the fallen limb. Harris sent a tree trimming company to the property to cut back the overhanging limbs, but this proved unsatisfactory because branches high up in the trees were not cut, and those that were cut grew back. Harris eventually told the plaintiff that she, the plaintiff, could trim the branches or roots, but that Harris no longer felt any responsibility to remedy the situation.

The plaintiff subsequently filed suit. . . . The General Sessions Court found in favor of the defendant. . . . conclud[ing] that the plaintiff's sole remedy was self-help and that the defendant's trees could not constitute an actionable nuisance. . . .

On appeal, the Court of Appeals agreed. . . . Accordingly, the Court of Appeals affirmed the trial court's dismissal of the case.

Analysis

I. Granberry v. Jones

In finding that the plaintiff's only remedy was self-help . . . , both lower courts relied on this Court's decision in *Granberry v. Jones, . . .* (Tenn. 1949).

This Court held in *Granberry* that the plaintiff "had the legal right to cut any branches or foliage which to any extent hung over his soil from the hedge growing upon the adjoining land." . . . In reaching this conclusion, we relied on the then prevailing rule that "no landowner has a cause of action from the mere fact that the branches of an innoxious tree, belonging to an adjoining landowner, overhang his premises, his right to cut off the overhanging branches being considered a sufficient remedy." . . .

However, we . . . left open the possibility of the injured landowner recovering damages, or at least expenses, after the landowner availed himself to self-help remedies. . . .

II. Approaches Taken in Other Jurisdictions

We begin our analysis of this case by observing that since *Granberry* was decided in 1949, states considering the question of encroaching vegetation have taken a number of different approaches. The courts uniformly hold that a landowner has a remedy of self-help, meaning that the landowner has the right to cut encroaching branches, roots, and other growth to the property line, but may not enter the adjoining property to chop down the tree or plant or cut back growth without the adjoining property owner's consent. . . . Thus, jurisdictions that have considered the matter, including Tennessee, permit the landowner whose property is encroached by overhanging branches and roots to trim them to the extent of the encroachment. . . . Some states apply this rule even if the encroaching limbs and roots are not causing any harm to the adjoining property. . . . These courts reason that from "ancient times" it has been the accepted rule that a landowner has the exclusive right to possess and use all of the landowner's property, including the air space above the ground, and therefore the redressable harm caused by encroaching trees is that of the trespass onto the neighboring property, not physical damage done to the neighboring land. . . .

Several jurisdictions have adopted the "Hawai'i rule," which holds that living trees and plants are ordinarily not nuisances, but can become so when they cause actual harm or pose an imminent danger of actual harm to adjoining property. . . . Under this approach, "when overhanging branches or protruding roots actually cause, or there is imminent danger of them causing, [substantial] harm to property other than plant life, in ways other than by casting shade or dropping leaves, flowers, or fruit, the damaged or imminently endangered neighbor may require the owner of the tree to pay for the damages and to cut back the endangering branches or roots, and if such is not done within a reasonable time, the . . . neighbor may cause the cutback to be done at the tree owner's expense." . . . However, the injured landowner "may always, at his own expense, cut away only to his property line above and below the surface of the ground any part of the adjoining landowner's tree or other plant life" that encroach upon the property. . . . The Hawai'i approach thus addresses the flood of litigation concern expressed by some courts over the natural processes and cycles of trees, roots, and other vegetation, by imposing a requirement of actual harm or imminent danger of actual harm to the adjoining property. Hence, the mere fact that tree limbs or roots extend to another's property does not by itself constitute an actionable nuisance. . . . At the same time, the rule provides a meaningful remedy in deserving cases, i.e., those involving actual harm or imminent danger of actual harm. The rule has been described as "realistic and fair" because the "owner of the tree's trunk is the owner of the tree, [and therefore] he bears some responsibility for the rest of the tree. . . ."

Permitting a cause of action every time a tree or plant so much as drops a leaf or casts shade upon another's land could well subject landowners to the "annoyance, and the public to the burden, of actions at law, which would be likely to be innumerable and, in many instances, purely vexatious." . . .

The Rule We Adopt

After carefully considering the various approaches of other jurisdictions and our own decision in *Granberry*, we have decided to join the growing number of states that have adopted the Hawai'i approach. . . . As stated by one court, "this approach voices a rational and fair solution, permitting a landowner to grow and nurture trees and other plants on his land, balanced against the correlative duty of a landowner to ensure that the use of his property does not materially harm his neighbor." . . . We agree that since the "owner of the tree's trunk is the owner of the tree, he [should] bear some responsibility for the rest of the tree." . . . [W]e are persuaded that the Hawai'i approach is stringent enough to discourage trivial suits, but not so restrictive that it precludes a recovery where one is warranted. Although some courts express the concern of spawning numerous lawsuits, we note that states which do not limit a plaintiff's remedy to self-help have apparently not suffered any such flood of litigation. Imposing a requirement of actual harm or imminent danger of actual harm to the adjoining property is a sufficient and appropriate gatekeeping mechanism. Third, we agree with the notion that limiting a plaintiff's remedy to self-help encourages a "law of the jungle" mentality because self-help replaces the law of orderly judicial process as the exclusive way to adjust the rights and responsibilities of disputing neighbors. It seems that more harm than good can come from a rule that encourages angry neighbors to take matters into their own hands. Fourth, the Hawai'i rule does not depend upon difficult to apply or unworkable distinctions, . . . We do not wish to place our courts in the difficult, and sometimes impossible, position of having to ascertain the origin of a particular tree or other vegetation. Nor should landowners who allow their property to run wild be shielded from liability while those who maintain and improve their land be subject to liability. The law should not sanction such an anomaly. Fifth, the Hawai'i approach is consistent with the principle of self-help embraced in *Granberry*. The rule is also consistent with *Granberry's* recognition that a landowner may recover the "expense to which he may be put now or hereafter in cutting the overhanging branches or foliage," assuming the encroaching vegetation constitutes a nuisance. . . . Finally, the rule we adopt today is in keeping with the aim of the law to provide a remedy to those who are harmed as a result of another's tortious conduct. . . .

Accordingly, we hold that encroaching trees and plants are not nuisances merely because they cast shade, drop leaves, flowers, or fruit, or just because they happen to encroach upon adjoining property either above or below the ground. However, encroaching trees and plants may be regarded as a nuisance when they cause actual harm or pose an imminent danger of actual harm to adjoining property. If so, the owner of the tree or plant may be held responsible for harm caused by it, and may also be required to cut back the encroaching branches or roots, assuming the encroaching vegetation constitutes a nuisance. We do not, however, alter existing Tennessee law that the adjoining landowner may, at his own expense, cut away the encroaching vegetation to the property line whether or not the encroaching vegetation constitutes a nuisance or is otherwise causing harm or possible harm to the adjoining property. Thus,

the law of self-help remains intact as it has since 1949 when *Granberry* was decided. It is important to note, however, that dead or decaying trees that cause harm are in a category of their own and require a different analysis. Unlike the cases involving harm caused by live trees, which are based on nuisance or trespass principles, cases involving dead or decaying trees are typically analyzed according to negligence concepts. Thus, liability usually turns on whether the defendant landowner lived in an urban or rural area, and whether the defendant knew or should have known that the tree was dead or decaying and therefore was on notice that the tree might fall. . . . The trees involved in the present case are live, healthy trees. Thus, we do not reach the question in this case of whether or to what extent liability may be imposed for harm caused by a dead or decaying tree. That subject must await an appropriate case.

B. Private Nuisance

As indicated above, the plaintiff asserts that the defendant's trees constitute a private nuisance. Tennessee courts have defined a private nuisance as "anything which annoys or disturbs the free use of one's property, or which renders its ordinary use or physical occupation uncomfortable . . . [and] extends to everything that endangers life or health, gives offense to the senses, violates the laws of decency, or obstructs the reasonable and comfortable use of property." . . . Depending on the surroundings, activities that constitute a nuisance in one context may not constitute a nuisance in another. Whether a particular activity or use of property amounts to an unreasonable invasion of another's legally protectable interests depends on the circumstances of each case, such as the character of the surroundings, the nature, utility, and social value of the use, and the nature and extent of the harm involved. . . .

Tennessee's definition of private nuisance is typical of how most states have defined the tort, both now and in the past. . . . Indeed, actions based on the unreasonable interference with another's interest in the private use and enjoyment of property date back to the twelfth century in England. . . . Nuisance law has since developed over the centuries to the point where a nuisance may now consist of a physical condition on the land itself (i.e., vibrations, pollution, or flooding), cause discomfort or inconvenience to the occupants of the property (i.e., odors, dust, smoke, noise), or consist of a condition on adjoining property which impairs the occupier's tranquility (i.e., conducting an unlawful business or keeping diseased animals). . . . So "long as the interference is substantial and unreasonable, such as would be offensive or inconvenient to the normal person, virtually any disturbance of the enjoyment of the property may amount to a nuisance." . . . Thus, nuisance does not describe a defendant's conduct, but a type of harm suffered by the plaintiff. . . .

A party who has been subjected to a private nuisance may be entitled to several types of remedies. Since at least the mid-1800s, courts in Tennessee have had the authority to order the nuisance abated. . . . Thus, a plaintiff may be entitled to injunctive relief, especially where the nuisance is likely to continue. . . . Further, in cases involving a temporary private nuisance, which is one that can be corrected, damages may be awarded for the cost of restoring the property to its pre-nuisance condition, as well as damages for inconvenience, emotional distress, and injury to the use and enjoyment of the property. . . . The typical way of measuring injury to the use and enjoyment of the property is the decrease in rental value of the property while the nuisance existed. . . . (noting that the measure of damages is the "injury to the value of the use and enjoyment of the property, which is usually shown by evidence of the extent that the rental value of the property is diminished by the nuisance"). Accordingly, courts provide an appropriate remedy in the form of either damages or injunctive relief or both.

C. Application to this Case

Applying the principles we have adopted to the present case, it is clear that the defendant's trees satisfy Tennessee's definition of a private nuisance, i.e., "anything which annoys or disturbs the free use of one's property, or which renders its ordinary use or physical occupation uncomfortable. . . . [and] extends to everything that endangers life or health, gives offense to the senses, violates the laws of decency, or obstructs the reasonable and comfortable use of property." . . . When asked about the condition of her home, the plaintiff replied, "everything is all messed up. I can't bathe. I can't cook. I don't want people coming to my house because it has odors in it, fleas, flies, bugs. It has just been awful for me." These circumstances have understandably taken a toll on the plaintiff. She is under the care of a psychiatrist and takes medication for emotional problems. She testified that she may have to move out of her house because she "just can't take too much more." Clearly, the defendant's encroaching trees have adversely affected the plaintiff's reasonable and ordinary use and occupation of her home, not to mention posing hazards to the plaintiff's health and safety. Accordingly, we reject the defendant's assertion that its trees do not constitute a nuisance.

Conclusion

After carefully considering the record and relevant authorities, we conclude that the lower courts erred in finding that the plaintiff's sole remedy was self-help. . . . We further find that the record in this case is sufficient to establish liability for nuisance. Accordingly, the judgment of the Court of Appeals affirming the trial court's dismissal of the case is reversed. The case is remanded to the trial court for a determination of damages and other appropriate relief, such as ordering the nuisance abated (i.e., order the trees removed). . . .

Case Questions

1. What is required to change a private nuisance into a public nuisance?
2. Does the existance of a nuisance depend on the nature of the conduct or the nature of the harm caused to the plaintiff? Explain.

REAL PROPERTY

The laws that govern real property in America have their origins in medieval England. Under feudal law all land was derived from the king; thus people could own estates in land but not the actual land itself. Estates were classified according to their duration, a practice that continues in American law today.

Estates in Land

The word *estate* is derived from the Latin word for status. An estate in land, therefore, is the amount of interest a person has in land. Some estates in land can be inherited. A person who holds an estate in what is known as fee simple can pass his or her interest on to heirs. This represents the maximum ownership right to land that is permissible by law. A person who has an estate in land for the duration of his or her life has a life estate in land. Life estates cannot be passed on to heirs. A person who leases real property has only a possessory interest in land called a leasehold. Leaseholds allow tenants to obtain possessory interests in real property for a month, a year, or even at will.

A landowner has the right to minerals that exist beneath the surface of the land. Landowners also have the right to control and use the airspace above their land. Governmental regulations regarding the height of buildings, as well as engineering limitations that are associated with a particular property, often limit the exercise of this right.

Easements

Easements and licenses are interests in land that do not amount to an estate but affect the owner's use of land. An *easement* is a nonpossessory property right in land; it is one person's right to use another person's land. For example, B might grant A an easement that permits her to use a private road on B's property. Because B continues to own the land, B can grant similar easements to persons C and D. B can grant these additional easements without having to obtain permission from A, because A lacks possessory rights on B's land. Easements are often classified as affirmative or negative. An affirmative easement would exist where land-owner A conveys to B the right to lay a pipeline across A's land. A negative easement would exist where A conveys part of her land to B and retains an easement that forbids B to burn trash or plant trees within five yards of A's property line.

An easement also may be created by eminent domain. In such a case, the landowner is constitutionally entitled to receive just compensation. Easements often are created by deed, and usually have to be in writing to be legally enforceable. They can be limited to a specific term or event or they can be of infinite duration. It is commonly said that easements "run with the land," meaning that the burden or benefit of the easement is transferred with the land to the subsequent owners.

Licenses

A *license* is a temporary grant of authority to do specified things on the land of another, for example, hunt or fish. A license can be oral because it is not an actual estate in land and therefore is not subject to the statute of frauds (see Chapter 10). Licenses can generally be revoked at will.

Covenants

To protect themselves from sellers who don't have title, purchasers of land often require the seller to make certain promises in the deed that are called *covenants*. The grantor's covenants ensure that he or she has possessory rights to the premises and that the title is good and is free and clear of encumbrances. The grantor will further promise to defend this title against the claims and demands of other people.

Other covenants that affect land use are those that run with the land. Historically, restrictive covenants have discriminated against people because of race, religion, and national origin. Today such covenants are illegal and contrary to public policy and would not be enforced in any court. Courts will, in appropriate cases, enforce nondiscriminatory covenants that run with the land and that create contractual rights in property. Although easements have traditionally been used to affect land use, lawyers began to resort to covenants to augment the kind of restrictions sellers could require of purchasers beyond the scope of easements. A baker, for example, might be willing to sell an adjacent lot that he owns; however, he might protect his business by requiring the purchaser to covenant that the premises conveyed will not be used for the operation or maintenance of a bakery, lunchroom, or restaurant.

Covenants that run with the land are regulated closely by courts because they restrict the use of property. For a covenant to run with the land and bind successive landowners, the original grantor and grantee must have intended that the restrictions on the covenant go with the land. In addition, a close, direct relationship known as *privity of estate* must exist between a grantor and a grantee. The privity requirement is satisfied, for example, when land developer A deeds part of her land to B, and B covenants not to put up a fence on B's land without A's written approval. Finally, covenants must "touch and concern" land; they may not be promises that are personal and unrelated to land. Successors in interest to the original grantor and grantee will be bound by the terms of a properly created covenant that runs with the land.

Adverse Possession

A person who has no lawful right of possession can obtain title to another's land by complying with the rules for *adverse possession*. The law requires property owners to ensure that no one else uses the land without permission, and a person who fails to use or protect his or her land for many years may one day lose title to an adverse possessor. In order to obtain title by adverse possession, the adverse possessor must take actual possession of the land, the possession must be hostile (without the consent of the owner), the possession must be adverse (against the owner's interest), the possession must be open and notorious (obvious and knowable to anyone who is interested), and the possession must be continuous for a statutorily determined period of time, often twenty years. A successful adverse possessor cannot sell the land because he or she does not have a marketable title (clear ownership of the land). The adverse possessor would have to file what is called a quiet title action and have the court determine who is entitled to title. If the court rules in favor of the adverse possessor, he or she will receive a marketable title.

The Recording System

The *recording system* gives purchasers of land notice of claims against real property. It also helps resolve questions of priority if, for example, a seller deeds land to one person and then deeds the same land to a second person. In every county there is a governmental office called the registry of deeds usually located in the county courthouse. There the registrar of deeds maintains an index of documents relating to all real property transactions. These include deeds, easements, options, and mortgages. The recording system permits buyers of real property to evaluate the quality of the seller's title. In addition, the purchaser's attorney or a bank's attorney may obtain a document called a title abstract or an insurance company's agreement to insure the title. The abstract is a report that summarizes all the recorded claims that affect the seller's title. If a dispute arises between competing claimants, the recording statutes help the courts resolve who the law will recognize as having title to the property.

PERSONAL PROPERTY

There are many ways by which title to personal property is acquired. These include purchase, creation, capture, accession, finding, confusion, gift, and inheritance. In addition, one person may acquire the personal property of another, though not the title to that property, through bailment.

Purchase

The purchase or sale of goods is the most common means of obtaining or conveying ownership rights to personal property. Most purchases involve an exchange of money for the ownership rights to goods. This is a contractual relationship and is governed by the Uniform Commercial Code.

Creation

A person who manufactures products out of raw materials through physical or mental labor has title to the items created. Thus a person who builds a boat, writes a song, makes a quilt, or develops a software program will have title to that item. A person who is employed to produce something, however, will not have title; ownership rights will belong to the employer.

Capture

A person who acquires previously unowned property has title to the items captured. For example, a person who catches fish on the high seas has title by way of *capture*. Such captures usually require the purchase of a fishing or hunting license. This license authorizes the holder to take title by way of capture according to established regulations that define the size of the daily catch and determine the season, for example.

Accession

A person can take title to additions that occur to his or her property because of natural increases. This means that the owner of animals has title to the offspring by way of *accession*. Similarly, the owner of a savings account has title to the interest that is earned on that account by way of accession.

Finding

A finder of lost property has title that is good against everyone except the true owner. Some states provide that a finder of a lost item above some designated dollar value has a duty to turn the item over to an agency (often the police) for a period of time. If the true owner fails to claim the item, the finder takes title and the true owner's ownership rights are severed. A finder has a duty to make reasonable efforts to locate the true owner, although no expenses must be incurred to satisfy this obligation. Lost property differs from mislaid and abandoned property. If you inadvertently leave your jacket in a classroom after a class, you have mislaid it. As we see in the next case, a finder who is a trespasser acquires neither possessory nor ownership rights.

Favorite v. Miller
407 A.2d 974
Supreme Court of Connecticut
December 12, 1978

Bogdanski, Associate Justice

On July 9, 1776, a band of patriots, hearing news of the Declaration of Independence, toppled the equestrian statue of King George III, which was located in Bowling Green Park in lower Manhattan, New York. The statue, of gilded lead, was then hacked apart and the pieces ferried over Long Island Sound and loaded onto wagons at Norwalk, Connecticut, to be hauled some fifty miles northward to Oliver Wolcott's bullet-molding foundry in Litchfield, there to be cast into bullets. On the journey to Litchfield, the wagoners halted at Wilton, Connecticut, and while the patriots were imbibing, the loyalists managed to steal back pieces of the statue.

The wagonload of the pieces lifted by the Tories was scattered about in the area of the Davis Swamp in Wilton and fragments of the statue have continued to turn up in that area since that time.

Although the above events have been dramatized in the intervening years, the unquestioned historical facts are: (1) the destruction of the statue; (2) cartage of the pieces to the Wolcott Foundry; (3) the pause at Wilton where part of the load was scattered over the Wilton area by loyalists; and (4) repeated discoveries of fragments over the last century.

In 1972, the defendant, Louis Miller, determined that a part of the statue might be located within property owned by the plaintiffs. On October 16 he entered the area of the Davis Swamp owned by the plaintiffs although he knew it to be private property. With the aid of a metal detector, he discovered a statuary fragment fifteen inches square and weighing twenty pounds which was embedded ten inches below the soil. He dug up this fragment and removed it from the plaintiffs' property. The plaintiffs did not learn that a piece of the statue of King George III had been found on their property until they read about it in the newspaper, long after it had been removed.

In due course, the piece of the statue made its way back to New York City, where the defendant agreed to sell it to the Museum of the City of New York for $5500. The museum continues to hold it pending resolution of this controversy.

In March of 1973, the plaintiffs instituted this action to have the fragment returned to them and the case was submitted to the court on a stipulation of facts. The trial court found the issues for the plaintiffs, from which judgment the defendant appealed to this court. The sole issue presented on appeal is whether the claim of the defendant, as finder, is superior to that of the plaintiffs, as owners of the land upon which the historic fragment was discovered.

Traditionally, when questions have arisen concerning the rights of the finder as against the person upon whose land the property was found, the resolution has turned upon the characterization given the property. Typically, if the property was found to be "lost" or "abandoned," the finder would prevail, whereas if the property was characterized as "mislaid," the owner or occupier of the land would prevail.

Lost property has traditionally been defined as involving an involuntary parting, i.e., where there is no intent on the part of the loser to part with the ownership of the property.

Abandonment, in turn, has been defined as the voluntary relinquishment of ownership of property without reference to any particular person or purpose; i.e., a "throwing away" of the property concerned; . . . while mislaid property is defined as that which is intentionally placed by the owner where he can obtain custody of it, but afterwards forgotten.

It should be noted that the classification of property as "lost," "abandoned," or "mislaid" requires that a court determine the intent or mental state of the unknown party who at some time in the past parted with the ownership or control of the property.

The trial court in this case applied the traditional approach and ruled in favor of the landowners on the ground that the piece of the statue found by Miller was "mislaid." The factual basis for that conclusion is set out in the finding, where the court found that "the loyalists did not wish to have the pieces [in their possession] during the turmoil surrounding the Revolutionary War and hid them in a place where they could resort to them [after the war], but forgot where they put them."

The defendant contends that the finding was made without evidence and that the court's conclusion "is legally impossible now after 200 years with no living claimants to the fragment and the secret of its burial having died with them." While we cannot agree that the court's conclusion was legally impossible, we do agree that any conclusion as to the mental state of persons engaged in events which occurred over two hundred years ago would be of a conjectural nature and as such does not furnish an adequate basis for determining rights of twentieth century claimants.

The defendant argues further that his rights in the statue are superior to those of anyone except the true owner (i.e., the British government). He presses this claim on the ground that the law has traditionally favored the finder as against all but the true owner, and that because his efforts brought the statue to light, he should be allowed to reap the benefits of his discovery. In his brief, he asserts: "As with archeologists forever probing and unearthing the past, to guide man for the betterment of those to follow, explorers like Miller deserve encouragement, and reward, in their selfless pursuit of the hidden, the unknown."

There are, however, some difficulties with the defendant's position. The first concerns the defendant's characterization of himself as a selfless seeker after knowledge. The facts in the record do not support such a conclusion. The defendant admitted that he was in the business of selling metal detectors and that he has used his success in finding the statue as advertising to boost his sales of such metal detectors, and that the advertising has been financially rewarding. Further, there is the fact that he signed a contract with the City Museum of New York for the sale of the statuary piece and that he stands to profit thereby.

Moreover, even if we assume his motive to be that of historical research alone, that fact will not justify his entering upon the property of another without permission. It is unquestioned that in today's world even archeologists must obtain permission from owners of property and the government of the country involved before they can conduct their explorations. Similarly, mountaineers must apply for permits, sometimes years in advance of their proposed expeditions. On a more familiar level, backpackers and hikers must often obtain permits before being allowed access to certain of our national parks and forests, even though that land is public and not private. Similarly, hunters and fishermen wishing to enter upon private property must first obtain the permission of the owner before they embark upon their respective pursuits.

Although few cases are to be found in this area of the law, one line of cases which have dealt with this issue has held that except where the trespass is trivial or merely technical, the fact that the finder is trespassing is sufficient to deprive him of his normal preference over the owner of the place where the property was found. The presumption in such cases is that possession of the article found is in the owner of the land and that the finder acquires no rights to the article found.

The defendant, by his own admission, knew that he was trespassing when he entered upon the property of the plaintiffs. He admitted that he was told by Gertrude Merwyn, the librarian of the Wilton Historical Society, *before* he went into the Davis Swamp area, that the land was privately owned and that Mrs. Merwyn recommended that he call the owners, whom she named, and obtain permission before he began his explorations. He also admitted that when he later told Mrs. Merwyn about his discovery, she again suggested that he contact the owners of the property, but that he failed to do so.

In the stipulation of facts submitted to the court, the defendant admitted entering the Davis Swamp property "with the belief that part of the 'King George Statue' . . . might be located within said property and with the intention of removing [the] same if located." The defendant has also admitted that the piece of the statue which he found was embedded in the ground ten inches below the surface and that it was necessary for him to excavate in order to take possession of his find.

In light of those undisputed facts the defendant's trespass was neither technical nor trivial. We conclude that the fact that the property found was embedded in the earth and the fact that the defendant was a trespasser are sufficient to defeat any claim to the property which the defendant might otherwise have had as a finder.

Where the trial court reaches a correct decision but on mistaken grounds, this court has repeatedly sustained the trial court's action if proper grounds exist to support it. The present case falls within the ambit of that principle of law and we affirm the decision of the court below.

There is no error.

Case Questions

1. On what grounds did the trial court hold for the plaintiff?
2. Why did the Supreme Court of Connecticut disagree with the lower court's reasoning?

 Why, in your opinion, should anyone be expected to act "ethically" unless it is in the person's self interest to do so?

Confusion

Confusion involves the blending or intermingling of fungible goods—goods of a similar character that may be exchanged or substituted for one another; for example, wheat, corn, lima beans, and money. Once similar items are mingled, it is impossible to separate the original owner's money or crops from those of others. In such cases each depositor owns an equivalent tonnage or number of bushels of the crop in an elevator or an equivalent dollar amount on deposit with a bank.

Gift

A person who has title to an item can make a gift by voluntarily transferring all rights in the item to another. A person making a gift is called a donor and the recipient of the gift is called a donee. The donor has donative intent—he or she is parting with all property rights and expects nothing (except love or appreciation) in return. The law requires that a donor make an actual or constructive delivery of the item. This means that if the donor is making a gift of a car, for example, the donor must bring the car to the donee (actual delivery) or present the car keys to the donee (constructive delivery). The donee must accept for a valid gift to occur.

Rick Kenyon believed himself to be the owner of a very valuable painting which he had purchased for twenty-five dollars at a Salvation Army Thrift Store. But Claude Abel, the painting's previous owner, claimed that he was still the rightful owner, because the painting had been inadvertently packed and unintentionally shipped with items being donated to the Salvation Army. The Wyoming Supreme Court had to determine who had title to the painting.

Rick Kenyon v. Claude Abel
36 P.3d 1161
Supreme Court of Wyoming
December 27, 2001

Hill, Justice

This dispute concerns the ownership of a painting by the noted Western artist Bill Gollings. Rick Kenyon (Kenyon) purchased the painting, valued between $8,000 and $15,000, for $25 at a Salvation Army thrift store. Claude Abel (Abel) filed suit against Kenyon seeking return of the painting, which had belonged to his late aunt. Abel claimed that the Salvation Army mistakenly took the painting from his aunt's home when the box in which it was packed was mixed with items being donated to the thrift store. Kenyon appeals the district court's decision awarding the painting to Abel. . . .

Abel's aunt, Rillie Taylor (Taylor), was a friend of the artist Bill Gollings, whose works were known for their accurate portrayal of the Old West. Sometime before his death in 1932, Gollings gave a painting to Taylor depicting a Native American on a white horse in the foreground with several other Native Americans on horses in the background traveling through a traditional western prairie landscape. The painting remained in Taylor's possession at her home in Sheridan until her death on August 31, 1999.

After Taylor's death, Abel traveled from his home in Idaho to Sheridan for the funeral and to settle the estate. Abel was the sole heir of Taylor's estate so he inherited all of her personal belongings, including the Gollings painting. Abel and his wife sorted through Taylor's belongings selecting various items

they would keep for themselves. Abel and his wife, with the help of a local moving company, packed those items into boxes marked for delivery to their home in Idaho. Items not being retained by Abel were either packed for donation to the Salvation Army or, if they had sufficient value, were taken by an antiques dealer for auction. The scene at the house was apparently one of some confusion as Abel attempted to vacate the residence as quickly as possible while attempting to make sure all of the items went to their designated location. The painting was packed by Abel's wife in a box marked for delivery to Idaho. However, in the confusion and unbeknownst to Abel, the box containing the Gollings painting was inadvertently picked up with the donated items by the Salvation Army. The painting was priced at $25.00 for sale in the Salvation's Army Thrift Store where Kenyon purchased the painting.

After returning to Idaho, Abel discovered that the box containing the painting was not among those delivered by the moving company. Through local sources, Abel learned that the painting had gone to the Salvation Army and was then purchased by Kenyon. . . . Abel sought possession of the painting through two causes of action: replevin and conversion. Kenyon countered that he was a "good faith purchaser" of the painting under the Uniform Commercial Code (UCC). The district court concluded that Abel was entitled to possession of the painting under either the common law doctrines of gift or conversion or the statutory provisions of the UCC. Kenyon now appeals. . . .

The key to resolving this dispute, under either common law or the UCC, is determining whether or not the painting was voluntarily transferred from Abel to the Salvation

Army. The district court concluded that Abel had no intent to give the painting to the Salvation Army. This is a factual conclusion that we will reverse only upon a showing that it is clearly erroneous. Our review convinces us that the district court's conclusion that Abel did not voluntarily transfer the painting to the Salvation Army is supported by the record and is not, therefore, clearly erroneous.

Abel's testimony during the trial disclosed the following facts. Abel's aunt received the painting as a gift from the artist. Abel testified that his aunt often expressed to him the importance of the painting to her and her desire that it remain in the family's possession. He indicated that the painting had a lot of value to him and the family beyond its monetary worth because of his family's personal relationship with the artist. The aunt rejected at least one offer to buy the painting for about $5,000. After inheriting the painting, Abel's wife packed it in a box marked for delivery to their home in Idaho. On the day the painting was packed for moving, there was much confusion around the house as Abel and his wife tried to sort through all of the items and designate them for delivery to the appropriate location. In that confusion, the Salvation Army came to the house to pick up various items. The Salvation Army apparently took the painting, along with the items specifically donated to it. Abel testified that he did not intend to include the painting with the goods that were meant to go to the Salvation Army and, at that time, he had no idea that the painting had been taken by them. According to Abel, he did not learn that the painting was missing until after the moving company had delivered all of the boxes to Idaho. Upon finding that the painting was missing, Abel testified that he immediately contacted an acquaintance in Sheridan who was able to trace the painting from the Salvation Army to Kenyon. Thereupon, Abel attempted to contact Kenyon about the painting's return.

Kenyon rebuffed Abel's attempts to discuss the painting thus leading to this action.

The testimony of Abel is sufficient to support the district court's conclusion that the transfer of the painting to the Salvation Army was involuntary. Abel specifically denied any intent to make such a transfer. That denial is supported by reasonable inferences that could be drawn from the painting's acknowledged sentimental value to Abel and his family and from Abel's actions in attempting to recover the painting immediately upon discovery of its loss. Under these circumstances, the district court's conclusion was not clearly erroneous. . . .

The district court awarded Abel possession of the painting on the basis of two common law doctrines: the law of gifts and the law of conversion. A valid gift consists of three elements: (1) a present intention to make an immediate gift; (2) actual or constructive delivery of the gift that divests the donor of dominion and control; and (3) acceptance of the gift by the donee. . . . The pivotal element in this case is the first one: whether an intention to make a gift existed. As we noted above, we have upheld the district court's conclusion that Abel did not have any intent to donate the painting to the Salvation Army. Therefore, the district court correctly ruled that the transfer of the painting to the Salvation Army did not constitute a valid gift. . . .

. . . The district court held that the sale of the painting constituted conversion by the Salvation Army. The record supports the district court's decision: (1) as the heir to his aunt's estate Abel had legal title to the painting; (2) Abel possessed the painting at the time it was removed from his aunt's residence; (3) the Salvation Army exercised dominion over the property in such a manner that denied Abel the right to enjoy and use the painting, i.e., it sold the painting; (4) Abel demanded the return of the painting from Kenyon, who effectively refused by denying any knowledge of it; and (5) Abel has suffered damages through the loss of a valuable asset without compensation. As a good faith purchaser of converted property, Kenyon is also a converter and must answer in damages to the true owner. . . . This is true because a converter has no title whatsoever (*i.e.,* his title is void) and, therefore, nothing can be conveyed to a bona fide purchaser for value. . . .

UCC

Kenyon seeks to escape the consequences of the common law doctrines of gifts and conversion by arguing that the UCC is the applicable law in this instance. For purposes of resolving this case, we will assume that the UCC applies to the transaction between Kenyon and the Salvation Army because, as we shall see, it does not provide the benefit to Kenyon he claims it will.

The district court correctly noted that a distinction exists between a "void" and a "voidable" title. Section 2-403(1)(d) [of the UCC] provides, in effect, that a voidable title is created whenever the transferor voluntarily delivers goods to a purchaser even though that delivery was procured through fraud punishable as larcenous under the criminal law. . . . [T]his subsection is predicated on the policy that where a transferor has voluntarily delivered the goods to purchaser, he, the transferor, ought to run the risk of the purchaser's fraud as against innocent third parties. . . .

It should be noted that Section 2-403(1)(d) does not create a voidable title where the goods have been wrongfully taken, as by theft or robbery. If the goods have been stolen, the thief acquires no ownership and has no power, except in rare cases of estoppel, to pass a good title to a bona fide purchaser. Nothing in Section 2-403 changes this common-law rule. Section 2-403(1)(d) does not create a situation where the goods are wrongfully taken, as contrasted with delivered voluntarily because of the concepts of "delivery" and "purchaser" which are necessary preconditions. "Delivery" is defined . . . to mean "voluntary transfer of possession." By analogy, it should be held that goods are not delivered for purposes of Section 2-403 unless they are voluntarily transferred. Additionally, Section 2-403(1)(d) is limited by the requirement that the goods "have been delivered under a transaction of purchase." "Purchase" is defined . . . to include only voluntary transactions. A thief who wrongfully takes goods is not a purchaser within the meaning of this definition, . . . The Salvation Army, of course, did not steal the painting from Abel. However, the key here is the voluntariness of the transfer from the original owner. . . .

The Salvation Army did not acquire the painting in a voluntary transaction from Abel. A third party purchaser could only acquire rights in the painting to the extent of the interest possessed by the Salvation Army. Since the Salvation Army possessed a void title, the original owner was entitled to recover the painting from the third party purchaser. Accordingly, the district court's order granting possession of the painting to Abel is affirmed.

Case Question

Why wouldn't the appellate court recognize Abel's title to the painting which he purchased from the Salvation Army, which had obtained possession of the painting from Rick Kenyon?

INTERNET TIP

The Pennsylvania Supreme Court majority decided to adopt a no-fault approach in a case posing the question of who is entitled to the ring when one party decides to call off the wedding. You can read the majority opinion and two dissenting opinions from this case on the textbook's website.

Inheritance

A person can acquire property from the estate of a deceased person. This is called an inheritance. When a person making a will (a testator or testatrix) makes a bequest of property, the title to the item will be transferred from a deceased's estate. If the person died without a will (intestate), property is transferred according to a statutory plan enacted by the state legislature (called a statute of descent).

BAILMENTS

A *bailment* relationship exists when one person (called the bailor) delivers personal property to another person (called the bailee) without conveying title. Although the possession of the object is transferred in a bailment, the bailor intends to recover possession of the bailed object, and thus does not part with the title. When a person borrows, loans, or rents a videotape or leaves one's lawn mower or car for repair, for example, a bailment is created.

Some bailments primarily benefit only one person, either the bailee or the bailor. These are called gratuitous bailments. For example, the bailee primarily benefits when he or she borrows a lawn mower from a neighbor. Other bailments primarily benefit the bailor, for example, when he or she asks to leave a motor vehicle in the bailee's garage for a month. Some bailments are mutually beneficial, such as when the bailor leaves shoes for repair at a shoe repair shop or takes clothes to the dry cleaners.

Some bailments are created by contract, such as when a person rents a car from a car rental company. Other bailments are created by a delivery and acceptance of the object, such as when one student loans a textbook to another student. Here there is no contract, because there is no consideration.

All types of bailments involve rights and obligations. In a mutual benefit bailment, the bailee has the duty to exercise reasonable care toward the bailed object. The bailee is not allowed to use the bailed object for his benefit, but may work on the object for the benefit of the bailor. The bailor's duties include paying the bailee and warning the bailee of any hidden dangers associated with the bailed object.

With a gratuitous bailment for the benefit of the bailor the bailee must exercise at least slight care and store the bailed object in the agreed-upon manner. There is no compensation or quid pro quo involved.

With respect to a bailment for the benefit of the bailee a bailee must exercise a high degree of care. Since the bailor is acting solely out of friendship and is not receiving any benefit and the bailee is allowed to use the bailed object without charge, the bailee must use the bailed object in the proper manner and return it in good condition when the bailment period ends. The bailee is responsible in negligence for any damages caused to the bailed object. As we see in the next case, the bailor can end the bailment period at any time and ask for the return of the bailed object.

James Croskey and Leach Brothers Automobile Services entered into a contract pursuant to which the Leach Brothers were to install an engine and transmission into Croskey's 1985 Buick. When Croskey discovered that the Buick had been stolen and damaged while in the Leach Brother's possession, he brought suit, claiming the breach of a mutual benefit bailment. The Leach Brothers lost at trial and appealed to the Ohio Court of Appeals.

James W. Croskey v. Carl Leach
C-010721
Court of Appeals of Ohio
October 18, 2002

Painter, Presiding Judge

Plaintiff-appellee James W. Croskey left his car at a repair shop for installation of an engine and transmission after a first attempted repair failed, only to have his car stolen from the shop's lot twice. The owners of the repair shop, defendants-appellants, Carl Leach and Joe Leach, d/b/a Leach Brothers Automotive Services and d/b/a Joe Leach Service Center, appeal a Hamilton County Municipal Court judgment in Croskey's favor. The court found the Leaches liable for failure to redeliver Croskey's car due to their failure to exercise ordinary care to protect against loss or damages, further ruling that the Leaches had violated the Ohio Consumer Sales Practices Act. The court awarded treble damages plus reasonable attorney fees to Croskey. . . .

A Failed Repair—And Two Thefts

In June 1999, Croskey and his aunt, Ruth St. Hilaire, took Croskey's 1985 Buick to the Leaches for replacement of the engine and transmission. St. Hilaire agreed to pay for the repairs to Croskey's Buick, with the understanding that Croskey would pay her back over time. The Leaches put in a used engine and transmission, and St. Hilaire paid the $2077.60 bill in cash.

Within two weeks, Croskey brought the Buick back to the Leaches because of noise and leaking fluid from the new transmission. The Leaches added transmission fluid and supplied Croskey with additional quarts of fluid, but otherwise refused to service the car until Croskey could produce the receipt for the previous work. Because St. Hilaire had the receipt and was out of town, Croskey continued to drive the Buick and to replace the leaking transmission fluid. The engine soon died, and the car was towed back to the Leaches' business.

Upon St. Hilaire's return to the city, either the 17th or 18th of August 1999, she delivered the receipt to the Leaches. The Leaches agreed to replace the engine and transmission with used parts. Carl Leach told Croskey and his aunt that he did not have a 1985 Buick engine in his inventory and that he would have to wait until he received one, but they had no knowledge or appreciation of the length of the ensuing delay.

During the delay, which lasted until December 1999, the car was stolen twice from the Leaches' lot. The first time, in September, the North College Hill Police Department contacted Croskey and Carl Leach to inform them that someone had stolen Croskey's Buick, driven it into the wall of the store next door, and then fled from the scene. The police investigation revealed that the Leaches had left the keys in the Buick after closing hours. The car had damage to the bumper and fender, and it was returned to the Leaches' lot.

On October 2, 1999, the Leaches' business was again broken into, and this time keys to customer automobiles were taken. It was not until December 2, however, that either Leach or Croskey realized that Croskey's car had been stolen. On December 2, Croskey, tired of the delay, came to the Leaches' business to retrieve his car. When they could not find the car, Croskey called the police and reported it stolen. The police soon located the stripped Buick and stored it at an impoundment lot.

Croskey sued the Leaches, alleging that they had breached a bailment and violated the Ohio Consumer Sales Practices Act, R.C. Chapter 1345. The trial court ruled that the Leaches were liable for their failure to redeliver Croskey's automobile because they had failed to exercise ordinary care to protect the car from damage or loss, and that the Leaches had breached their repair and services agreement by failing to install an operable transmission and engine. The court also held that the Leaches had engaged in several unfair and deceptive acts under the Ohio Consumer Sales Practices Act. The court ordered the Leaches to pay treble damages of $6,232.80, plus reasonable attorney fees of $3,450, for a total award of $9,682.80.

A Failed Bailment

In their one assignment of error, the Leaches . . . argue that the trial court's judgment was contrary to the manifest weight of the evidence. . . .

The trial court concluded that the transaction between the Leaches and Croskey was, in law, a mutual-benefit bailment. The court then found that the Leaches were liable for their failure to redeliver Croskey's automobile, because they had failed to exercise ordinary care to protect the car from loss or damages.

Where one person delivers personal property to another to be held for a specific purpose, a bailment is created; the bailee must hold the property in accordance with the terms of the bailment. When a bailor delivers property to a bailee and the bailee fails to redeliver the property undamaged, the bailor has a cause of action against the bailee, in either contract or tort. To establish a prima facie case in contract, a bailor must prove (1) the contract of bailment, (2) delivery of the bailed property to the bailee, and (3) failure of the bailee to redeliver the bailed property undamaged at the termination of the bailment.

The record indicates that Croskey left his car with the Leaches after the initial repair failed, with the understanding that the Leaches would install another used engine and transmission. Carl Leach testified that, after the first break-in and robbery of the repair shop, the Leaches took no new or extra precautions to protect the keys from theft, because they believed they were not responsible for cars parked on their outer lots.

After the second theft, the Leaches did not inventory the cars on their lots to determine if Croskey's car had been stolen, and they did not inform Croskey about the theft of his car key. When Croskey finally discovered that his car had been stolen and that it was in the police impoundment lot, the Leaches denied responsibility for recovering it or returning it to their lot.

There is competent and credible evidence in the record to support the trial court's judgment that the Leaches were liable for failing to redeliver Croskey's car. The evidence also supports the court's conclusion that the Leaches had failed to provide minimum security to protect the keys from theft, and that they had breached their agreement to install an operable engine and transmission. . . .

For . . . the foregoing reasons, the Leaches' . . . assignment of error is not well taken. The trial court's judgment is accordingly affirmed.

Case Questions

1. Why was this bailment a mutual benefit bailment?
2. What duty did the Leach Brothers fail to meet in this case? What should they have done but didn't do?

Chapter Questions

1. Define the following terms:

accession	grantor
adverse possession	intangible
bailment	leasehold
bailor	license
capture	life estate
covenant	nuisance
creation	personalty
easement	police power
eminent domain	realty
estate	recording system
fee simple	tangible
fixture	vested
grantee	

2. C/R TV, Inc. is a cable television company that sought to provide its services to a private housing subdivision (Shannondale). The subdivision had contracted with Mid-Atlantic Cable Services, Inc., one of C/R's competitors, to provide exclusive cable services to Shannondale. C/R, however, believed it had a lawful right to string cable on existing telephone poles in the subdivision pursuant to a 1972 licensing agreement with Potomac Edison. Shannondale had granted easements to Potomac Edison for electrical and telephone services in most of the subdivision in 1955 and in part of the development in

1991. The Shannondale president threatened a trespass action against C/R TV when he learned that the company had installed over six miles of cable wiring in the subdivision. C/R TV responded by bringing a declaratory judgment action against Shannondale. The trial judge ruled in favor of Shannondale, concluding that the 1955 easements were not "sufficiently broad to provide for television cable facilities." The trial court did rule that the part of the subdivision covered by the 1991 easements could be serviced by the plaintiff. C/R TV appealed. Should the 1955 easements which were granted to Potomac Edison "for the purpose of installation, erection, maintenance, repair and operation of electric transmission and distribution pole lines, and electric service lines, with telephone lines thereon" be interpreted so as to permit Potomac Edison's licensee the right to install cable-television wiring over Shannondale's objections?

C/R TV, Inc. v. Shannondale, Inc., 27 F.3d (1994)

3. Tracy Price took her English Bulldog to Dr. Nancy Brown, a veterinarian, for a surgery, which was performed on August 30, 1991. When Tracy visited her dog the next evening at the veterinary hospital, the animal appeared groggy and was panting heavily. Tracy requested that the dog be monitored all day and night and was assured that this would be done. The dog died on the morning of September 1. Tracy filed suit on May 4, 1993. She claimed that she had entrusted her dog to Dr. Brown based on Brown's assurances that appropriate surgery would be performed and the dog returned to her in a healthy condition. Tracy demanded damages in the amount of $1,200, the fair market value of the animal. She claimed that her dog had been entrusted to the veterinarian for surgical treatment and that it had died while in the doctor's care as a result of the doctor's negligence. Has Tracy stated a cause of action for breach of a bailment agreement?

Price v. Brown, 680 A.2d 1149 (1996)

4. The Kingsmen, a rock band formed in 1958, recorded a rock classic entitled "Louie Louie." The band members contracted with Spector Records in 1968, which provided that the band would received 9 percent of the future licensing fees and profits generated by the song. Spector subsequently assigned its rights under the agreement to Gusto Records and G.M.L., Inc. In 1993, the Kingsmen sued Gusto, G.M.L., and Highland Music for recission of the contract and back royalties calculated from the date that the suit was filed. They sought recission because that would result in the restoration of their title to and possession of the master. The band alleged that the defendants and their predecessors in title had for thirty years failed to pay the band its contracted share of royalties. The defendants argued that the action was barred by the four-year statute of limitations and that the plaintiffs were not entitled to income produced pursuant to licenses that preexisted the recission. The trial court ruled in favor of the Kingsmen. The defendants appealed to the U.S. Court of Appeals (9th Circuit). Should the Kingsmen prevail on appeal?

Peterson v. Highland Music, Nos. 95-56393, 97-55597, and 97-55599 (1998)

5. Hiram Hoeltzer, a professional art restorer, sought declaratory relief to quiet title to a large mural that once was affixed to the walls of the Stamford High School. This mural had been painted as part of the Works Progress Administration (WPA) in 1934. Workers removed the mural when the high school was renovated in the summer of 1970. They cut it into thirty pieces and placed it on top of a heap of construction debris, adjacent to a dumpster. This was done despite oral and written requests from school officials that the mural be taken down and preserved. A 1970 graduate of Stamford High, recognizing the value of the mural, placed the mural pieces into his car and took them home. The student took the mural to Karel Yasko, a federal official responsible for supervising the restoration of WPA artwork. Yasko suggested that the mural be taken to Hiram Hoeltzer. In 1980, city officials and other interested people began contacting Hoeltzer about the mural. In 1986, the city formally wrote to Hoeltzer and claimed title. Hoeltzer, however, who had retained possession of the mural for ten years, claimed that he was the rightful owner of the mural. Who has legal title to the mural? Why?

   Hoeltzer v. City of Stamford, Conn., 722 F.Supp. 1106 (1989)

6. Leonard and Bernard Kapiloff are stamp collectors. In 1976 they purchased two sets of stamps worth $150,400. Robert Ganter found the stamps in a dresser he had purchased for $30 in a used furniture store in 1979 or 1980. Ganter had taken the stamps to an auction house, and they were listed for sale in a nationally distributed catalogue that was read by the Kapiloff brothers. The brothers contacted Ganter and demanded the return of the stamps. Ganter refused. The brothers then contacted the FBI, which took physical possession of the stamps. The brothers then brought a replevin action against Ganter for the stamps and asked the court for a declaratory judgment that they were the true owners of the stamps. The person who originally sold the brothers the stamps supported the brothers' allegations that the stamps Ganter found were the same stamps that had belonged to the Kapiloffs. Who is the owner of the stamps?

   Ganter v. Kapiloff, 516 A.2d 611 (1986)

7. The case of *Clevenger v. Peterson Construction Company* turned on the question of whether forty-four mobile trailers should be classified as personal property or fixtures. The trailers had axles, although they were without hitches or wheels. They were positioned on concrete blocks and not on permanent foundations, and were connected to utilities with flexible hoses. Which classification is more appropriate?

   Clevenger v. Peterson Construction Company, Inc., 542 P.2d 470 (1975)

8. The District of Columbia enacted an ordinance that made it unlawful for any hotel to exclude any licensed taxicab driver from picking up passengers at hotel taxicab stands. The Washington Hilton did not have to operate a taxicab stand on its property but elected to do so for the convenience of its guests. The hotel was dissatisfied with the quality of service provided

by some of the taxicab drivers and with the cleanliness of some of their vehicles. The hotel wanted to discriminate against some taxis in favor of others. It wanted to require cab drivers to obtain permits and pay an annual fee to use the hotel's taxicab stand. The city's attorney was consulted about these plans and ruled that they violated the Taxicab Act. Does this ordinance constitute a taking of the hotel's property by the district?

Hilton Washington Corporation v. District of Columbia, 777 F.2d 47 (1985)

9. Terry Bohn presented Tommie Louise Lowe with a ring in 1974 when they became engaged to be married. Tommie had a continuing series of strokes over the next ten years, and the marriage never took place. She still possessed the engagement ring at the time of her death in 1984. After her death, Terry brought suit against Tommie's estate to recover the engagement ring. Who has title to the ring?

A Matter of Estate of Lowe, 379 N.W.2d 485 (1985)

10. Robert Lehman and Aki Eveline Lehman were married in 1964. They separated in 1971. They became divorced in 1976. At the time of the separation, Aki retained possession of forty-three art objects that were in the house. Robert and Aki each claimed ownership rights to these objects. Robert claimed that forty-two of the items were either purchased by him or given to him by his father. One item was given to him by Aki. Aki claimed ownership of the items as a result of her purchases made with joint funds, as well as a result of gifts from Robert and Robert's father. Aki took all forty-three items to Paris when she and their children moved there in 1972. Robert demanded that Aki return his property. When she refused, he filed suit against Aki for replevin, conversion, and breach of bailment. At the time the lawsuit was filed, only thirteen items were still in Aki's possession. Aki testified at trial that she didn't know what had happened to the thirty missing items. The court determined that Robert was the exclusive owner of forty of the forty-three items, and Robert and Aki jointly owned the remaining three items. What relief will the court order? Why?

Lehman v. Lehman, 591 F.Supp 1523 (1984)

11. Michael and Albina Kloss purchased a tract of land from John and Anne Molenda in 1950. No land survey was conducted to determine the precise boundary line between the two properties. Instead, John and Michael paced off the lot and placed stakes in the ground to mark the boundary. The Klosses built a house on their lot and installed a concrete sidewalk along the property which extended to the boundary stake. They also installed a concrete driveway that came within thirty inches of the boundary line separating their property from the Molendas'. They put topsoil in the thirty-inch strip of land between the driveway and the boundary line, and planted this area with grass. They continuously maintained this grassy strip for over thirty years. The Molendas planted a hedge on their side of the staked property line. John Molenda died in 1983 and a survey of the land was completed. The surveyor found that the thirty-inch grassy strip

was actually on Molenda property. Anne Molenda thereupon installed a fence along the edge of the Kloss driveway. The Klosses filed suit, claiming ownership of the grassy strip. Who should own the strip of land? Why?

Kloss v. Molenda, 513 A.2d 490 (1986)

12. Toby and Rita Kahr were the owners of twenty-eight pieces of sterling silver that Rita's father had given them as a wedding present twenty-seven years previously. Each piece of silver was engraved with the letter "K." On April 5, 1983, the Kahrs brought used clothing to Goodwill Industries and told Goodwill personnel that they wanted to make a donation of clothing. Unknown to Toby and Rita, the sterling silver, along with a wallet containing their credit cards, were included in the sacks. The Kahrs called Goodwill two hours later when they realized what had happened, and were told that the silver had been sold for $15 to Karen Markland. The Kahrs alleged that the silver had a value of $3,791. The Kahrs brought a replevin action against Goodwill and Markland to recover the silver. Markland claimed that she had purchased the silver from a merchant who deals in that kind of goods and that she was the lawful owner of the silver. Should the court order replevin? Was the silver abandoned by the Kahrs?

Kahr v. Markland, 543 N.E.2d 579 (1989)

Notes

1. P. C. Hoffer, *Law and People in Colonial America* (Baltimore: Johns Hopkins University Press, 1982), pp. 19–24; D. H. Flaherty, *Essays in the History of Early American Law* (Chapel Hill: Institute of Early American History and Culture, 1969), pp. 272–273; B. Schwartz, *The Law in America* (New York: McGraw-Hill Book Co., 1974), pp. 8–18; M. Horwitz, *The Transformation of American Law 1780–1860* (Cambridge: Harvard University Press, 1977), pp. 4–6.
2. Horwitz, pp. 7–9, 84.
3. L. Salmon, *Women and the Law of Property in Early America* (Chapel Hill: The University of North Carolina Press, 1986), pp. 18–22.
4. Ibid., pp. 14–15, 22–25.
5. W. Hurst, *Law and the Conditions of Freedom in the Nineteenth Century* (Madison: The University of Wisconsin Press, 1967), p. 8.
6. W. E. Nelson, *Americanization of the Common Law* (Cambridge: Harvard University Press, 1975), p. 47; Horwitz, p. 102.
7. Horwitz, p. 35.
8. Nelson, p. 159; Horwitz, p. 36.
9. Horwitz, p. 102; Hurst, pp. 28–29.
10. Hurst, pp. 24–25.
11. *Lochner v. New York*, 198 U.S. 45 (1905).
12. The Uniform Commercial Code is not uniformly adopted from state to state. Each state legislature decides whether to adopt the Uniform Commercial Code and the extent to which they accept or modify its terms. Other differences can arise from judicial interpretations.

13. Many jurisdictions only recognize the tenancy by the entirety in conjunction with real property.
14. There are two exceptions to this general rule. A good faith purchaser of bearer bounds can take title from a thief, and a buyer in the ordinary course of business who purchases goods from a merchant can take title even if the merchant obtained the items from a thief. Public policy reasons support these exceptions because it is very important to the economy that people who buy goods from merchants can rely on the seller's claims of title to the goods.
15. *U.S. v. Causby*, 328 U.S. 256 (1946).

 # Administrative Law and Administrative Agencies

A discussion of the U.S. legal system would not be complete without an examination of the government's use of statutory law and administrative rules to regulate business practices. This chapter addresses administrative law and the role of administrative agencies.

THE RISE OF ADMINISTRATIVE AGENCIES

Administrative agencies have existed at the federal level since the early 1800s, when Congress created the U.S. Patent Office (1802),[1] the Bureau of Indian Affairs (1824),[2] and the Army Corps of Engineers (1824).[3] The greatest growth occurred after 1900, however, when approximately two-thirds of current agencies were created.[4] Before President Franklin Roosevelt's New Deal, this country operated on the premise that the federal government should be kept relatively small. That model of government changed during the 1930s in response to the serious social and economic problems associated with the Great Depression. Newly created agencies included the Federal Deposit Insurance Corporation (1933), the Tennessee Valley Authority (1933), the Federal Communications Commission (1933), the Securities and Exchange Commission (1934), and the National Labor Relations Board (1935). More recently, Congress has created agencies to address important social and public welfare goals, such as the Equal Employment Opportunity Commission (1965), the Occupational Safety and Health Review Commission (1970), and the Environmental Protection Agency (1970). These and a multitude of other commissions, boards, authorities, and departments administer legislation that affect many aspects of daily life (see Figure 13-1).

Many regulatory bodies also exist at the state and local levels of government. State administrative agencies monitor environmental pollution, license

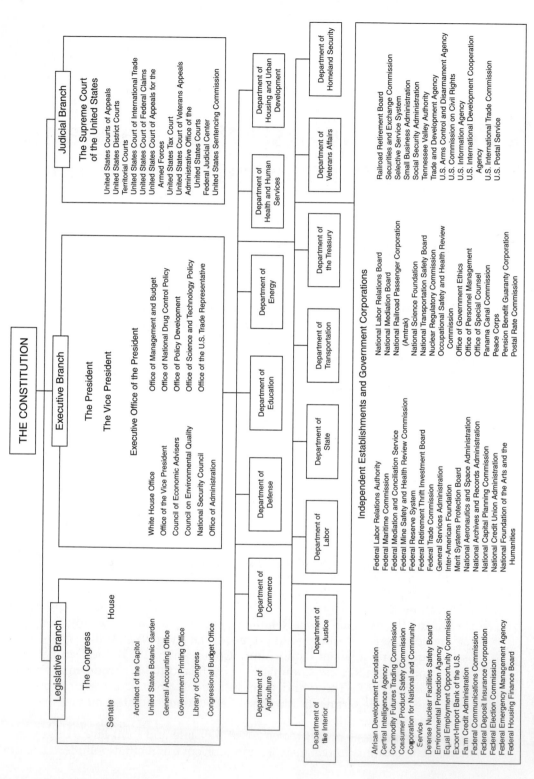

FIGURE 13-1   The Government of the United States

Source: Office of the Federal Register, National Archives and Records Administration, U.S. Government Manual, 2001–2002, p. 22.

drivers, determine automobile insurance rates, and oversee public utilities. They also regulate a wide range of professions and occupations, including hairdressers, barbers, teachers, doctors, lawyers, and psychologists. At the local level, administrative agencies operate zoning boards, housing authorities, water and sewer commissions, and historical commissions.

This chapter is concerned with the legal framework for administrative law. It does not include political analyses of the role that ideology and resources play in agency decision making. Nor does this chapter focus on process questions, such as how administrative agencies decide which of competing policy alternatives will be adopted. These most interesting issues are often addressed in conjunction with political science courses.

ORGANIZATION AND CLASSIFICATION OF FEDERAL AGENCIES

Administrative agencies are commonly classified in terms of their organizational structure. Agencies that are organized into commissions and boards and directed by commissioners include the Federal Maritime Commission (FMC), the Federal Reserve Board (FRB), the Interstate Commerce Commission (ICC), the National Labor Relations Board (NLRB), the Nuclear Regulatory Commission (NRC), and the Securities and Exchange Commission (SEC). (See, for example, the SEC organizational chart in Figure 13-2.) Agencies that are structured as cabinet-level departments or administrations and are headed by secretaries or administrators include the Department of the Interior, the Department of Agriculture, the Department of Labor, the Department of Homeland Security, and executive agencies such as the Environmental Protection Agency (EPA). (The EPA organizational chart can be seen in Figure 13-3.)

Commissioners, cabinet-level secretaries, and agency head administrators are nominated by the president and are subject to Senate confirmation. In general, commissions and boards are considered to be independent agencies because the commissioners do not serve at the pleasure of the president and can only be removed for cause, such as neglect of duty or inefficiency. In addition, Congress often requires that these agencies be bipartisan. The SEC, for example, has five members. The chairman is chosen by the president and normally is of the president's party. Because the SEC is a bipartisan agency, two Democrats and two Republicans will be chosen for the remaining four seats. Each commissioner serves a five-year staggered term; one term expires each June. Agencies headed by cabinet secretaries and head administrators are not independent, and their leaders serve at the pleasure of the president.

Functions of Administrative Agencies

Administrative agencies came into existence because legislative bodies recognized that they could not achieve desired economic and social goals within the existing governmental structure. Although legislatures could provide general

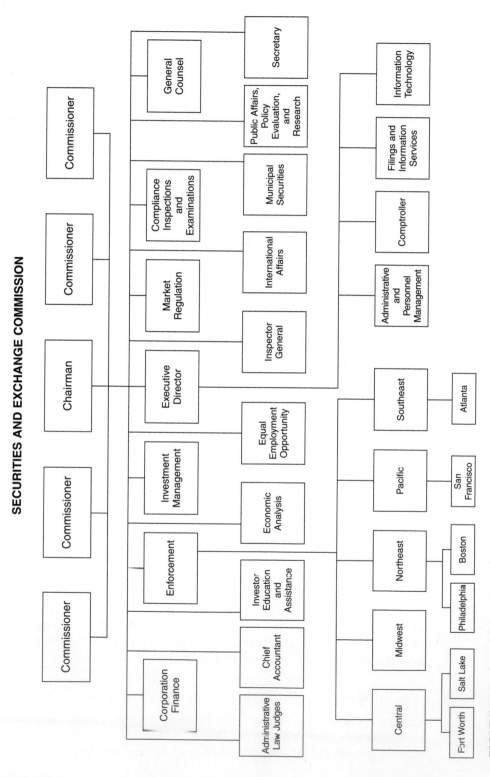

FIGURE 13-2 Securities and Exchange Commission

Source: Office of the Federal Register, National Archives and Records Administration, U.S. Government Manual, 2001–2002, p. 514.

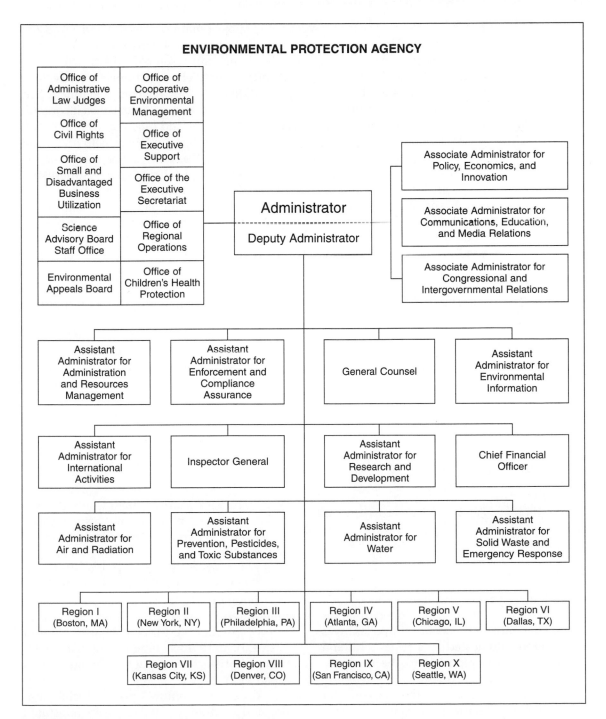

FIGURE 13-3   Environmental Protection Agency

Source: Office of the Federal Register, National Archives and Records Administration, U.S. Government Manual, 2001–2002, p. 384.

policy direction, they possessed limited subject matter expertise and could not devote continuing attention to the multitude of problems that confront our modern society. Agencies, on the other hand, can assemble experts who focus on one area and work toward achieving legislatively determined objectives.

Legislatures establish an administrative agency by enacting a statute called an *enabling act*. In addition to creating the agency, this act determines its organizational structure, defines its functions and powers, and establishes basic operational standards and guidelines. These standards and guidelines help reviewing courts control the abuse of discretion. Courts also use written directives to assess whether an agency is operating according to the legislature's intent. Administrative agencies can also be created by executive orders authorized by statute.

Agencies perform a variety of functions. For example, they monitor businesses and professions in order to prevent the use of unfair methods of competition and the use of deceptive practices; they help ensure that manufacturers produce pure medications and that food products are safe to consume; and they function to protect society from environmental pollution and insider stock-trading practices. Since the 1960s, several agencies have been created to protect citizens' rights in the work place and to ensure equal employment opportunity. Although there have been many notable achievements by administrative agencies, a lack of funding and political support, inadequate knowledge, and corruption have in some instances undermined agency effectiveness.

The plaintiff in the following case brought suit against the Commissioner of Public Safety for refusing to reinstate his driving privileges because of his non-driving-related use of alcohol.

Askildson v. Commissioner of Public Safety
403 N.W.2d 674
Court of Appeals of Minnesota
April 7, 1987

Leslie, Judge

Appellant's driving privileges were reinstated after revocation, conditioned upon his total abstinence from alcohol. Appellant was later found intoxicated in a restaurant, and the incident was reported to the Commissioner. His driving privileges were again revoked, and he petitioned to the trial court for reinstatement. The trial court denied all relief and dismissed the petition, and appellant brings an appeal from the order. We affirm.

Facts

Appellant Rick Marven Askildson's driving privileges were revoked at various times under the DWI and implied consent statutes as a result of violations occurring on August 30, 1975, April 24, 1976, January 6, 1984, and June 24, 1984. In addition, on July 26, 1984, all driving privileges were also cancelled and indefinitely denied as "inimical to public safety" pursuant to Minn.Stat. §§ 171.14 and 171.04(8), until such time as appellant submitted satisfactory evidence of successful rehabilitation.

Appellant submitted proof of rehabilitation and his driving privileges were reinstated effective December 18, 1985. As a part of his reinstatement, he signed a form agreeing to total abstinence as a condition for receipt of driving privileges and stating that any use of alcohol coming to the attention of the Commissioner would subject him to immediate cancellation and denial of driving privileges. He was issued a "B Card" with his driver's license which indicated that any use of alcohol or controlled substances invalidated the license.

On April 18, 1986, at 11:53 P.M., a police officer responded to a complaint of an intoxicated person at a restaurant. The officer found appellant "extremely intoxicated" and "passed out" inside one of the restaurant's booths. The officer took appellant to a detoxification center and sent a report of the incident to the Commissioner of Public Safety. The Commissioner, acting on that report, summarily cancelled and denied appellant's driving privileges effective May 2, 1986.

Appellant petitioned the trial court for reinstatement of his driving privileges. He did not challenge the fact that he was using alcohol, but claimed the Commissioner exceeded his authority in requiring abstention and in cancelling driving privileges when the reported use of alcohol was not directly related to driving a motor vehicle. Appellant also claimed there had been no findings that his use of alcohol made him "inimical to public safety," or that rehabilitation is required. The trial court dismissed appellant's petition for reinstatement, and denied the relief requested. The appellant brings an appeal from the trial court order.

Issues

1. Did the Commissioner exceed his authority and act in an arbitrary and capricious manner when he required appellant to abstain from the use of alcohol as a condition of reinstatement of driving privileges?

2. Was the Commissioner's cancellation and denial of appellant's driving privileges supported by adequate findings?

Analysis

1. The Commissioner cancelled appellant's driving privileges pursuant to Minn.Stat. §§ 171.04(8) and 171.14. Minn.Stat. § 171.04(8) (1986) states that the department shall not issue a driver's license "when the commissioner has good cause to believe that the operation of a motor vehicle on the highways by [a] person would be inimical to public safety or welfare." Minn.Stat. § 171.14 allows the commissioner to "cancel the driver's license of any person who, at the time of the cancellation, would not have been entitled to receive a license under the provisions of section 171.04."

Appellant petitioned for judicial review pursuant to Minn.Stat. § 171.19 (1984), seeking reinstatement of his driving privileges. In such proceedings, the petitioner has the burden of proving he is entitled to reinstatement. . . . The decision to cancel or deny driving privileges rests with the Commissioner of Public Safety. Minn.Stat. § 171.25 (1986). There is a presumption as to the regularity and correctness of these administrative acts. . . . In general, we will not reverse the decision of an administrative agency unless the decision is fraudulent, arbitrary, unreasonable, or not within the agency's jurisdiction and power. . . . These principles apply to review of driver's license proceedings. . . .

Appellant contests the Commissioner's authority to require total abstinence as a continuing condition for retaining a driver's license, and his authority to cancel and deny driving privileges for non-driving related use of alcohol. Appellant claims this is an attempt to control his private life. He asserts that without specific legislative authority, the Commissioner had no power to regulate non-driving use of alcohol; that the Commissioner's action here was arbitrary and capricious.

The legislature may delegate power to an administrative agency if the statute provides a reasonably clear policy to guide the administrative officers, so the law takes effect by its own terms, rather than according to the whim or caprice of the administrative officers. . . .

[I]n the present case, the Commissioner had the discretion to decide what conduct would render a driver "inimical to public safety." Administrative regulations promulgated by the Commissioner provide that he shall cancel and deny the driver's license of a person when there is sufficient cause to believe that he has consumed alcohol after completing rehabilitation. . . . It was not arbitrary or capricious for the Commissioner to regulate non-driving related alcohol consumption in this case.

We have upheld the Commissioner's authority to require total abstinence from alcohol as a condition of reinstatement or a period of abstinence from alcohol prior to reinstatement. . . .

In *Mechtel v. Commissioner of Public Safety*, . . . we explained that the Commissioner partially discharges his duty to minimize the risk to the public by drunken motorists "by requiring repeating offenders to prove abstinence and sobriety for a prescribed period of time.". . .

The abstinence requirement is not an attempt to control appellant's private life; instead, as the Commissioner states, it presented appellant with the choice of drinking or driving. Further, the fact that appellant was found intoxicated in a restaurant rather than a motor vehicle is irrelevant. It does not diminish the fact that appellant did not abide by the abstention requirement. . . . The Commissioner was within his discretion in requiring a driver with appellant's record to maintain abstinence from alcohol as a condition for retaining his driver's license. The determination that appellant was "inimical to public safety," justifying cancellation and denial of appellant's driver's license, was also within the Commissioner's discretion.

2. Appellant contends the Commissioner's decision to cancel driving privileges for non-driving related use of alcohol was arbitrary and capricious. He claims the Commissioner failed to make the necessary finding that appellant was "inimical to public safety" or in need of rehabilitation. However, under the circumstances of this case, the Commissioner's summary cancellation and denial of driving privileges was appropriate. Appellant signed a written agreement wherein he agreed to abstain from alcohol and controlled substances for so long as he lived. He did this as a condition of reinstatement of his driving privileges. Appellant fully understood that any use of alcohol that was brought to the attention of the Commissioner would be grounds for an immediate cancellation of his privilege to drive. No finding that appellant was inimical to public safety was required. A violation of a condition of reinstatement is sufficient to support cancellation and these facts were subsequently verified at the district court proceeding.

Minn.Stat. § 171.19 provides that the trial court is to "take testimony and examine into the facts of the case to determine whether the petitioner is entitled to a license or is subject to revocation, suspension, cancellation, or refusal of license, under the provisions of this chapter. . . ." The trial court made this determination, and the Commissioner's decision to cancel and deny appellant's driving privileges for his failure to abide by the abstinence requirement, was not arbitrary and capricious. The Commissioner's requirement of rehabilitation prior to license reinstatement is clearly based upon the appellant's record and violation of the abstinence requirement, . . . and the Commissioner's rationale has been adequately explained. . . .

Decision

The order of the trial court is affirmed.
    Affirmed.

Case Questions

1. What factors did the court say an appellant must show in order to overcome the presumption of regularity and correctness of the commissioner's discretionary decisions regarding reinstatement?
2. Is an administrative agency a distinct branch of government?
3. According to the court, why must the legislature provide reasonably clear policy guidelines within the enabling act?

ADMINISTRATIVE AGENCY POWERS

Regulatory agencies interfere with individual and business decision making by exercising legislatively delegated rule-making, investigative, and adjudicative powers. Although the separation of powers doctrine states that the legislative, executive, and judicial functions of government should not exist in the same person or group of persons, the courts have ruled that combining such functions within a single agency does not conflict with the doctrine. Even though a wide range of powers may be delegated to an agency in its enabling act, there are checks on its activities. The creator of the agency, which is generally the legislature, retains the power to eliminate it or to alter the rules governing it. In addition, agency decisions are subject to judicial review, although this right in practice is very limited.

The 1946 Administrative Procedure Act (APA) was enacted to improve and strengthen the administrative process and to preserve the basic limits on judicial review. APA procedures address both the rule-making and adjudication functions. For example, the APA requires that rule making follow notice and comment procedures. This means that agencies are required to publish notice of proposed rule making in the *Federal Register*. This notice gives interested parties a right to participate in the rule-making process by submitting written data or arguments. The opportunity for oral presentation may or may not be granted by the agency. In addition, publication of a substantive rule in the *Federal Register* is required not less than thirty days before its effective date. The APA requires that agency adjudication processes include trial-type procedures such as the administration of oaths, the issuance of subpoenas, the taking of depositions, and the use of settlement conferences. The APA applies to federal administrative agencies, unless Congress provides otherwise in each agency's enabling act. Most states have similar legislation.

Rule-making Power

Rule making is often referred to as the quasi-legislative function of administrative agencies. Agencies that have been granted rule-making powers are authorized to make, alter, or repeal rules and regulations only if they are so permitted by the terms of their enabling statutes. The statutes set the general standards, authorize the agencies to determine the content of the regulations, and provide general sanctions for noncompliance with the rules. The rule-making power of administrative agencies covers a vast range of business and government functions.

The next case involves a challenge to an Environmental Protection Agency regulation on the grounds that its adoption was not in conformity with the requirements of the Administrative Procedures Act.

Ethyl Corporation v. Environmental Protection Agency

U.S. Court of Appeals, District of Columbia Circuit
306 F.3d 1144
October 22, 2002

Williams, Senior Circuit Judge

Title II of the Clean Air Act, 42 U.S.C. §§ 7521 et seq. (1955), sets up a program for the regulation of both motor vehicles and their fuels in order to reduce harmful emissions. Section 206 charges the Environmental Protection Agency with testing new motor vehicles to ensure that each vehicle's emissions will comply with federal emissions standards throughout its "useful life." . . . Section 206(d) says that the agency "shall *by regulation* establish methods and procedures for making tests under this section." . . . (emphasis added).

In a rulemaking pursuant to §§ 206, the EPA adopted a Compliance Assurance Program or "CAP 2000." . . . CAP 2000 does not, however, set out "methods and procedures for making tests." Rather, it establishes a framework for automobile manufacturers to develop their own tests, to be used once the EPA gives approval, case-by-case, after private proceedings with each manufacturer.

Petitioner Ethyl manufactures and markets fuel and lubricant additives for use in motor vehicles. It argues that CAP 2000 violates the Act because it provides for test procedures and methods to be vetted in individual

closed proceedings rather than in a notice-and-comment rulemaking. And it claims to be injured because the mechanism adopted by the EPA deprives it of the opportunity to observe the rulemaking process and thus gain information useful in its efforts both to develop and improve its products and to key them to the certification tests. For the reasons given below we grant the petition.

Before a manufacturer may introduce a new motor vehicle into commerce, it must obtain an EPA certificate indicating compliance with the requirements of the Act and applicable regulations. It submits an application containing test data and other information specified by the EPA, which issues a certificate if the manufacturer has shown, among other things, that the vehicle's emissions control systems will achieve compliance with emissions standards over the vehicle's full useful life. . . .

Critical here is the question of the control systems' possible deterioration over time. Before 1993 EPA had had a durability test that called for prototype vehicles to be driven over a 50,000-mile course known as the Automobile Manufacturers Association ("AMA") driving cycle. . . . In 1993 it adopted a "revised durability program" or "RDP" that retained that test "as the standard EPA-defined procedure." . . . But the RDP regulations also permitted automobile companies to develop alternative test methods and procedures provided that they (a) obtained EPA approval for each such test and (b) performed in-use testing to verify the accuracy of the emissions deterioration predictions made by their tests. . . . The EPA did not adopt these tests through rulemaking but simply approved them on a case-by-case basis.

In May 1999 the EPA replaced RDP with CAP 2000. These regulations eliminate the AMA driving cycle as an EPA-defined test method. Instead, the program available as an alternative in 1993–99, under which manufacturers are to develop their own emissions durability test methods and procedures, has become the sole method. Thus, rather than promulgating methods and procedures for durability testing itself, the EPA now requires, through CAP 2000, that "the manufacturer shall propose" a durability program. . . . Each manufacturer is required to obtain EPA approval for its tests, and must verify its results through in-use testing.

Manufacturer-proposed tests under CAP 2000 must (a) "effectively predict the expected deterioration of candidate in-use vehicles over their full and intermediate useful life," and (b) be "consistent with good engineering judgment." . . . Within these criteria, the manufacturer-developed mileage accumulation procedures are to be

> based upon whole-vehicle full-mileage accumulation, whole-vehicle accelerated mileage accumulation (e.g., where 40,000 miles on a severe accumulation cycle is equivalent to 100,000 miles of normal in-use driving), bench aging of individual components or systems, or other approaches approved by the Administrator. . . .

The "bench aging" referred to is a system whereby components are removed from the vehicle and tested for durability separately. . . .

In adopting this system of individualized test approval, the EPA explicitly found that "rulemaking for each durability program is not required." . . . It also said, in a response to petitions for reconsideration by Ethyl, that public participation in the certification process would interfere with the process of reviewing manufacturers' submissions "because of the large amount of information claimed confidential" and that, because the process was annual, the use of notice-and-comment procedures would be "administratively burdensome." August 23, 2001 Response to Ethyl Corporation Petitions Denying Reconsideration of Three EPA regulations: CAP 2000, Heavy Duty Gasoline, and OBD/IM, EPA Air Docket A-96-50, No. VI-C-03, 39.

Ethyl challenges not only CAP 2000 but also regulations governing the certification of heavy duty vehicles and engines, 65 Fed. Reg. 59,896 (2000), which incorporate the CPA 2000 regulations by reference, and EPA's denial of its various petitions for reconsideration, 66 Fed. Reg. 45,777 (2001).

The EPA argues that we need not reach the merits because, it says, Ethyl lacks both Article III and "prudential" standing. We think it has both. . . .

On to the merits: As we said, §§ 206(d) of the Act states that the administrator "shall by regulation establish methods and procedures for making tests under this section." . . . Although special provisions govern review under the Act, here the relevant provisions are the same as under the Administrative Procedure Act. We are to reverse the challenged EPA actions if they are "arbitrary, capricious, an abuse of discretion, or otherwise not in accordance with law" or "in excess of statutory jurisdiction, authority, or limitations." . . .

CAP 2000 does not, as §§ 206 directs, "establish methods and procedures for making tests," and it is the only "regulation" in the picture. Instead, it provides criteria for individual automobile manufacturers to develop their own test methods and procedures, which the EPA approves in a process that does not involve rulemaking.

Conceivably §§ 206(d)'s requirement that EPA use regulation to "establish methods and procedures for making tests" could be squared with the record by reading "making tests" as referring to *devising* the tests rather than *conducting* them. Thus Congress would be mandating that the EPA use regulations merely to set up a system for picking tests (which might then be picked any old way) rather than mandating the use of regulations to decide how the tests themselves should be conducted. But nothing in the context of the provision suggests that the "establishment" under §§ 206(d) is to be so remote from the actual process of conducting tests, and it is hard to see any congressional purposes that would be served by such a requirement. Indeed, neither in the administrative proceedings nor before us has the EPA invoked such a reading.

Rather, the EPA seeks to defend CAP 2000 by treating the issue as involving simply the level of specificity or generality at which it was supposed to act, citing *American Trucking Associations v. Department of Transportation,* . . . (D.C. Cir. 1999) (agency to promulgate by regulation safety rating "requirements" and means to determine whether carriers had met the requirements), and *New Mexico v. EPA,* . . . (D.C. Cir. 1997) (agency to promulgate "criteria" for a certification process). In those cases, as Congress had not specified the level of specificity expected of the agency, we held that the agency was entitled to broad deference in picking the suitable level. . . . But here Ethyl's challenge is not that the EPA was too general in establishing test procedures by regulation, but that it didn't establish them by regulation at all.

EPA's failure to act by regulation is thus similar to, and controlled by, our decision in *MST Express v. Department of Transportation,* . . . (1997), which preceded *American Trucking* and involved the same statutory requirement of proceeding by regulation in setting safety requirements for common carriers. Rather than promulgate regulations stating the means for determining whether carriers met the safety fitness requirements, the agency had simply required a carrier to "demonstrate

that it has adequate controls in place" to ensure compliance with the substantive requirements, and had developed a "safety fitness rating methodology." . . . This methodology provided agency inspectors with detailed guidelines for evaluating a motor carrier's safety rating—but it was *not* the product of notice-and-comment rulemaking. . . . We found that the agency had "failed to carry out its statutory obligation to establish by regulation a means of determining whether a carrier has complied with the safety fitness requirements." . . . EPA's error here is similar.

There may, of course, be cases in which it is hard to distinguish between promulgations of (1) vaguely articulated test procedures (which would be reviewed deferentially under such cases as *American Trucking)* and (2) procedures for later development of tests (invalid under *MST Express).* Both, after all, necessarily imply a later (or at least different) proceeding in which the agency will fill in details. In this case, however, one can distinguish on the basis of the language used by the agency. With CAP 2000, the EPA does not claim to have itself articulated even a vague durability test. Rather, CAP 2000 requires that "the manufacturer shall propose a durability program" for EPA approval. . . . It thus falls on the forbidden side of the line.

The EPA also defends CAP 2000 on grounds that seem to flout the evident congressional purpose. First, it argues that because it has chosen to approve test procedures only for one model year at a time, proceeding by regulation would be administratively burdensome. Obviously this cannot overcome a clear congressional command. Further, it is true only in the sense that an *open* procedure—the very thing mandated by Congress—is less convenient than a closed one. It may be. Other parties may raise questions or find fault in procedures that look fine to the agency and the auto makers. But Congress has already made the trade-off. Nothing in our opinion requires that EPA use only a "one-size-fits-all" test method. All that is required is that it establish its procedures, no matter how variegated, "by regulation."

Finally, both EPA and the auto manufacturers who intervene on its behalf argue that the approach of CAP 2000 is necessary because of the presence of what the manufacturers believe to be "confidential business information" ("CBI"). If the EPA were to establish test methods and procedures by regulation, they say, important CBI might become public, allowing competitors to "back engineer" their products. . . . Moreover, they argue that the sheer "amount of claimed confidential business information would significantly reduce the usefulness of public notice and an opportunity to comment upon manufacturers' durability programs." . . .

It is hard to know what to make of this argument. First and foremost, §§ 208(c) provides that the administrator may protect the confidentiality of "methods or processes entitled to protection as trade secrets." . . . Especially given this available remedy, it seems

to us a complete non sequitur to suggest that because a procedure (the rulemaking mandated by §§ 206(d)) may involve some protectable CBI, the entire procedure should be short-circuited and replaced with a cluster of closed bargaining sessions between the EPA and each manufacturer. Congress obviously expected that rulemakings would proceed despite the existence of CBI that would require protection under §§ 208(c). Plainly the theory provides no basis for disregarding the congressional command.

CAP 2000, rather than constituting an EPA establishment "by regulation" of "methods and procedures for making tests," as required by §§ 206(d), is instead a promulgation of criteria for the later establishment of such methods and procedures by private negotiation between the EPA and each regulated auto maker. So it is "not in accordance with law." We therefore vacate the CAP 2000 program and remand the case to the EPA with instructions to establish test methods and procedures by regulation. So ordered.

Case Questions

1. What was the Ethyl Corporation's complaint about the EPA's Compliance Assurance Program 2000?
2. What legal conclusions did the Court of Appeals reach as to the legality of the Compliance Assurance Program 2000?

Executive Power

Agencies cannot operate without access to facts for intelligent regulation and adjudication. Thus the investigative power is conferred on practically all administrative agencies. As regulation has expanded and intensified, the agencies' quest for facts has gained momentum.

Statutes commonly grant an agency the power to use several methods to carry out its fact-finding functions, such as requiring reports from regulated businesses, conducting inspections, and using judicially enforced subpoenas.

The power to investigate is one of the functions that distinguishes agencies from courts. This power is usually exercised in order to properly perform another primary function. However, some agencies are created primarily to perform the fact-finding or investigative function. Like any other power or function of the government, it must be exercised so as not to violate constitutionally protected rights.

The Inspector General of the U.S. Department of Agriculture is statutorily charged with auditing federal programs and exposing fraud and abuse in federal disaster relief programs. In the following case, the Inspector General served Ann Glenn and others with subpoenas to turn over specified records, documents, and reports. Glenn and the others, believing that the Inspector General did not have the right to subpoena such information, sought relief in the Eleventh Circuit U.S. Court of Appeals.

Inspector General of U.S. Department of Agriculture v. Glenn
No. 96-8686
U.S. Court of Appeals, Eleventh Circuit
Sept. 18, 1997

Floyd R. Gibson,
Senior Circuit Judge

I. Background

In 1993, in response to a hotline complaint alleging questionable disaster program payments to program participants in Mitchell County, Georgia, the United States Department of Agriculture's ("USDA") Inspector General audited the Consolidated Farm Service Agency's ("CFSA") Mitchell County disaster program. The Inspector General sought to determine whether CFSA program participants were complying with regulatory payment limitations. As a result of the audit, the Inspector General determined that $1.3 million in questionable disaster payments were awarded to Mitchell County program participants. As part of the audit, the Inspector General requested various information from appellants to determine their compliance with the payment limitations. When appellants repeatedly refused to provide the requested information, the Inspector General issued subpoenas to require production of the

information. The Inspector General sought summary enforcement of the subpoenas in the United States District Court for the Middle District of Georgia. The district court ordered enforcement, and appellants challenge that order on appeal.

II. Discussion

Due to a concern that fraud and abuse in federal programs was "reaching epidemic proportions," . . . Congress created Offices of Inspectors General in several governmental departments "to more effectively combat fraud, abuse, waste and mismanagement in the programs and operations of those departments and agencies," . . . 5 U.S.C. app. §§ 1–12 (1994). The Inspector General Act of 1978, . . . enables Inspectors General to combat such fraud and abuse by allowing "audits of Federal establishments, organizations, programs, activities, and functions," and by authorizing broad subpoena powers, . . . We will enforce a subpoena issued by the Inspector General so long as (1) the Inspector General's investigation is within its authority; (2) the subpoena's demand is not too indefinite or overly burdensome; (3) and the information sought is reasonably relevant. . . .

Although appellants recognize that the scope of the Inspector General's subpoena power is broad, they contend that the USDA's

Inspector General exceeded the scope of this power when he subpoenaed information as part of a payment limitation review. Appellants argue that a payment limitation review is a "program operating responsibilit[y]" which section 9(a)(2) of the IGA prohibits agencies from transferring to the Inspector General. . . .

The IGA specifically directs Inspector General to coordinate "activities designed . . . to prevent and detect abuse" in departmental programs. . . . To enable the Inspector General to carry out this function, the IGA authorizes the Inspector General to conduct "audits," . . . for the purpose of promoting "efficiency" and detecting "fraud and abuse," . . . The IGA's legislative history suggests that audits are to have three basic areas of inquiry:

> (1) examinations of financial transactions, accounts, and reports and reviews, compliance with applicable laws and regulations,
> (2) reviews of efficiency and to determine whether the audited is giving due consideration to economical and efficiency management, utilization, and conservation of its resources and to minimum expenditure of effort, and
> (3) reviews of program results to determine whether programs or activities meet the objectives established by Congress or the establishment. . . .

To enable the Inspector General to conduct such audits in an effective manner, the IGA provides the Inspector General with broad subpoena power which is "absolutely essential to the discharge of the Inspector . . . General's functions," for "[w]ithout the power necessary to conduct a comprehensive audit the Inspector . . . General could have no serious impact on the way federal funds are expended." . . .

This case illustrates the necessity of the Inspector General's auditing and subpoena powers. The Inspector General received a hotline complaint regarding questionable payments in the CFSA's Mitchell County disaster program. The Inspector General appropriately began an investigation of the program to detect possible abuse. As part of the audit, the Inspector General requested information from program participants to determine whether the payments they received were warranted. When appellants, who were program participants, refused to produce the requested information, the Inspector General utilized its subpoena powers to acquire the necessary information. Without this ability to issue subpoenas, the Inspector General would be largely unable to determine whether the program and its benefit recipients were operating in an appropriate manner. Thus, an abuse of the system, which the Inspector General was specifically created to combat, could possibly go undetected, and government waste and abuse could continue unchecked. The subpoena power, which the Inspector General appropriately invoked in this case, is vital to the Inspector General's function of investigating fraud and abuse in federal programs.

Appellants contend that the Inspector General is only authorized to detect fraud and abuse within government programs, and that program administrators are responsible for detecting abuse among program participants. While we agree that IGA's main function is to detect abuse within agencies themselves, the IGA's legislative history indicates that Inspectors General are permitted and expected to investigate public involvement with the programs in certain situations. Congressman Levitas, a co-sponsor of the IGA, stated that the Inspector General's "public contact would only be for the beneficial and needed purpose of receiving complaints about problems with agency administration and in the investigation of fraud and abuse by those persons who are misusing or stealing taxpayer dollars." . . . From this statement, we conclude that the Inspector General's public contact in this case was appropriate because it occurred during the course of an investigation into alleged misuse of taxpayer dollars. In sum, we conclude that the subpoenas issued by the Inspector General did not exceed the statutory authority granted under the IGA.

Appellants also claim that the subpoenas were too indefinite and were unduly burdensome. CFSA regulations require participants to retain records for a period of two years following the close of the program year. . . . Appellants argue that the Inspector General cannot subpoena records which predate the required retention period. We do not agree with appellants' argument. While appellants are not required to retain records beyond the two-year period, no indication exists that records created prior to the retention period should be free from the Inspector General's subpoena powers.

Appellants further contend that the subpoenas are unduly burdensome because the 1990 and 1991 records sought by the Inspector General "were maintained and controlled by [appellant] J. C. Griffin, Sr., who had no

mental capacity to explain the record-keeping system utilized in 1990 and 1991 in his dealings with the USDA during [that] time period." . . . We do not believe that Mr. Griffin's mental incapacity has any bearing on the enforceability of the Inspector General's subpoenas. At this stage, the Inspector General is merely requesting information from appellants as part of a large investigation involving many program participants in Mitchell County. The Inspector General has not requested that Griffin explain the contents of his records or his system for maintaining them. Consequently, we are unable to conclude that subpoenas create an undue burden upon Griffin or any of the other appellants. . . .

III. Conclusion

For the reasons set forth in this op we AFFIRM the district court's decision to enforce the Inspector General's subpoenas.

Case Questions

1. What argument did Glenn make to the appellate court regarding the Inspector General's statutory authority?
2. How did the appeals court rule, and why?
3. Why do you think that the appellants were unsuccessful with their claims that the subpoenas were both indefinite and unduly burdensome?

Adjudicative Power

When an agency's action involves the rule-making function, it need not make use of judicial procedures. The *adjudicative function* of administrative agencies, however, involves a determination of legal rights, duties, and obligations, and adjudicatory hearings resemble a court's decision-making process. Thus, when an agency is intent on obtaining a binding determination or adjudication that affects the legal rights of an individual or individuals, it must use some of the procedures that have traditionally been associated with the judicial process.

Before sanctions can be imposed, an alleged violator is entitled to an administrative hearing that is conducted according to APA procedures (or the procedures specified in the enabling act) and that complies with the due process requirements of the Fifth and Fourteenth Amendments. This means that the accused has to receive notice and a fair and open hearing before an impartial and competent tribunal. Parties affected by the agency action must be given the opportunity to confront any adverse witnesses and present oral and written evidence on their own behalf. An agency may confine cross-examination to the essentials, thus avoiding the discursive and repetitive questioning common to courtroom cross-examinations.

Administrative agencies employ administrative law judges (ALJs) to conduct adjudicatory hearings. Like judges, ALJs decide both questions of fact and issues of law, and they are limited to the evidence that is established on the record. ALJs are authorized to issue subpoenas, administer oaths, make evidentiary rulings, and conduct hearings. ALJs are not, however, members of the federal judiciary. They perceive their function as that of implementing and administering a legislative purpose rather than as judges impartially deciding between two litigants. In some agencies ALJs are quite active in questioning witnesses so that a thorough record of the proceedings is developed for the benefit of the agency's administrator or board.

However, administrative law judges *are* empowered to make findings of fact and to recommend a decision. The recommendation is sent to the board of final review in the administrative agency which retains the power to adopt, alter, or reverse it.

In theory, the decision of an administrative law judge is thoroughly reviewed before the agency's board of final review adopts it as its opinion. In reality, however, because of a board's heavy workload, the review may be delegated to members of its staff, and board members may never even read the administrative law judge's opinion. Although this has been challenged as a lack of due process for the defendant, the courts often permit delegation of review to agency staff members. The courts require only that the board members make decisions and understand the positions taken by the agency.

JUDICIAL REVIEW

Judicial review is a relatively minor aspect of administrative law. In part, this is because judges lack expertise in the very technical and specialized subject area that are subject to agency regulation. The sheer volume of agency adjudications also makes it unrealistic to expect the judiciary to review more than a small percentage of such decisions. Thirdly, the expense of obtaining judicial review is a barrier to many potential appellants.

Courts and administrative agencies are collaborators in the task of safeguarding the public interest. Thus, unless exceptional circumstances exist, courts are reluctant to interfere with the operation of a program administered by an agency. As the courts' respect of the administrative process increases, judicial self-restraint also increases.

Timing of Review

Parties must address their complaints to administrative tribunals and explore every possibility for obtaining relief through administrative channels (*exhaust administrative remedies*) before appealing to the courts. The courts will generally not interrupt an agency's procedure until it has issued a final decision because when the administrative power has not been finally exercised, no irreparable harm has occurred—the controversy is not ripe.

The courts will hear a case before a final agency decision if the aggrieved party can prove that failure to interrupt the administrative process would be unfair. To determine the extent of fairness, the court will consider (1) the possibility of injury if the case is not heard, (2) the degree of doubt of the agency's jurisdiction, and (3) the requirement of the agency's specialized knowledge.

The requirements of exhaustion of administrative remedies and ripeness are concerned with the timing of judicial review of administrative action, but the two requirements are not the same. Finality and exhaustion focus on whether the administrative position being challenged has crystallized and is, in fact, an institutional decision. Ripeness asks whether the issues presented are appropriate for judicial resolution. Although each doctrine has a separate and distinct aim, they frequently overlap.

Sturm, Ruger & Company attempted to litigate claims against the Occupational Safety and Health Administration without having first exhausted all of their administrative remedies. The U.S. District Court dismissed their complaint for lack of subject matter jurisdiction, based on this failure, and Sturm appealed that decision to the U.S. Court of Appeals for the District of Columbia Circuit.

Sturm, Ruger & Co., Inc. v. Elaine Chao, Sec., U.S. Dept. of Labor
300 F.3d 867
U.S. Court of Appeals, District of Columbia Circuit
August 23, 2002

Garland, Circuit Judge

Sturm, Ruger & Company, Inc. filed a complaint in the United States District Court for the District of Columbia, challenging the Occupational Safety and Health Administration's Data Collection Initiative as unlawful. The court concluded that it lacked subject matter jurisdiction over the complaint, and that the company must pursue its claims through the review process prescribed by the Occupational Safety and Health Act. We agree. . . .

We begin with a description of the statutory framework and of prior proceedings involving Sturm Ruger. . . .

The Occupational Safety and Health Act (OSH Act) authorizes the Secretary of Labor to promulgate workplace safety and health standards, 29 U.S.C. §§ 655(b), as well as regulations "necessary or appropriate for the enforcement of [the Act] or for developing information regarding the causes and prevention of occupational accidents and illnesses," . . . It further directs the Secretary to "prescribe regulations requiring employers to maintain accurate records of, and to make periodic reports on, work-related deaths, injuries and illnesses." . . . And it gives the

Secretary enforcement power, authorizing her to issue citations and to assess penalties for violations of the Act and of the standards and regulations promulgated thereunder. . . . The Secretary has delegated the bulk of these statutory responsibilities and authorities to the Occupational Safety and Health Administration (OSHA).

While the OSH Act charges the Secretary with rulemaking and enforcement, it gives the task of "carrying out adjudicatory functions" to an independent entity, the Occupational Safety and Health Review Commission (OSHRC or the Commission). . . . Under the Act, employers may contest OSHA citations before OSHRC. . . . Such contests are heard first by an ALJ [administrative law judge], whose decision becomes the final order of the Commission unless the Commission decides to hear the case. . . . Both employers and the Secretary may seek review of OSHRC orders in the courts of appeals. . . .

In 1996, OSHA launched an annual survey called the Data Collection Initiative (DCI). . . . Under the DCI, OSHA requires selected employers to report the number of workers they employed and the number of hours their employees worked during a specified period, as well as the number of work-related injuries and illnesses their employees suffered during that period. . . . From this information, OSHA calculates injury/illness incidence rates, which it uses to identify establishments to target for inspection. . . . When the DCI was first implemented in 1996, OSHA had in effect regulations requiring employers to maintain logs of work-related injuries and illnesses, . . . and to provide these logs to OSHA upon its request, . . . OSHA did not, however, have a regulation that required employers to respond to the DCI survey. Several employers filed suit against the Secretary, seeking an injunction against its implementation. *See American Trucking Ass'ns, Inc. v. Reich*, . . . (D.D.C. 1997). In January 1997, the district court granted summary judgment

for the employers, holding that OSHA "must promulgate a regulation before purporting to command employers to file reports like the one at issue here." . . . The Secretary did not appeal that decision, and the next month, to "clarify OSHA's authority," OSHA adopted 29 C.F.R. §§ 1904.17, which we discuss below. . . . Since the filing of Sturm Ruger's complaint, OSHA has revised 29 C.F.R. pt. 1904, and the regulation concerning the DCI now appears at 29 C.F.R. §§ 1904.41. . . . Reg. 5916 (Jan. 19, 2001) . . .

In April 1997, OSHA sent Sturm Ruger a DCI survey, requiring it to provide information regarding its Pine Tree Castings Division, a New Hampshire facility that manufactures steel investment castings. Sturm Ruger complied and returned the completed survey to OSHA. In June 1998, based on information in the survey, two OSHA compliance officers arrived at Pine Tree to inspect the facility. . . . Sturm Ruger refused to consent to the inspection, prompting OSHA to obtain a search warrant. . . . When OSHA officers arrived to execute the warrant, Pine Tree employees prevented them from doing so. On the same day, Sturm Ruger moved to quash the warrant, arguing that the data used to target Pine Tree for inspection was derived from a survey that was not authorized by regulation, and that the warrant violated the Fourth Amendment.

. . . [T]he district court denied the motion to quash and enforced the warrant. . . . Sturm Ruger appealed . . . , and sought a stay of execution of the warrant pending appeal. The First Circuit denied the stay, and OSHA executed the warrant. After inspecting the Pine Tree facility, OSHA announced that it was considering issuing citations for violations of safety and health standards discovered during the inspection. . . .

In August 1999, the First Circuit dismissed Sturm Ruger's appeal for failure to exhaust administrative remedies. Noting that the OSHA inspection had already occurred and that citations could soon issue, the court of appeals held that Sturm Ruger had to pursue its challenge by contesting the citations through the review process established by the OSH Act. The court noted that this process "would involve initial review by an administrative law judge, discretionary review by the Occupational Safety and Health Review Commission, and eventual review by this court." . . .

The First Circuit reached its conclusion notwithstanding Sturm Ruger's insistence that its claim "involved a 'purely legal' issue consisting of a 'facial' challenge" to the DCI. . . . The court found that Sturm Ruger had "not suggested that its claims cannot be adequately adjudicated in the . . . anticipated enforcement proceeding," . . . , and that in fact "a successful appeal following exhaustion of administrative remedies" would vindicate its rights, . . . Moreover, the court held that, while the company had "not shown that requiring exhaustion would subject it to irreparable harm," permitting the district court to hear the claim would interfere with "agency autonomy." . . .

On September 2, 1999, OSHA issued citations to Sturm Ruger based on its inspection of the Pine Tree facility. In accordance with the OSH Act's review provisions, the company contested those citations before an ALJ appointed by OSHRC. . . . At the outset of the proceeding, Sturm Ruger moved to suppress the evidence obtained during the Pine Tree inspection, arguing that no regulation authorized OSHA to collect the survey data that it used to target employers for inspection, and that the use of the data violated the Fourth Amendment. The ALJ denied the motion on the ground that, by responding to the survey, Sturm Ruger had waived the right to challenge its legality. . . .

After the ALJ issued a final decision on the merits, Sturm Ruger petitioned for, and the Commission granted, discretionary review. Sturm Ruger's petition argued that the cita-

tions should be vacated because they were discovered in an inspection based on data collected through an unlawful and unconstitutional survey. . . . The DCI was unlawful under the OSH Act and the Administrative Procedure Act (APA), . . . the company contended, because no regulation required employers to maintain the data sought by the survey. . . . And it was unconstitutional because Sturm Ruger had "a privacy interest protected by the Fourth Amendment in the information that the survey form compelled it to produce." . . . Sturm Ruger's case is currently pending before the Commission. . . .

On May 9, 2000, two months before the ALJ denied its motion to suppress, Sturm Ruger filed a complaint against the Secretary of Labor and the Assistant Secretary responsible for OSHA in the United States District Court for the District of Columbia. . . . Like its filings before the Commission, the company's complaint alleged that the DCI was unlawful under the OSH Act, the APA, and the Fourth Amendment. It sought both a declaratory judgment and an injunction barring OSHA from compelling compliance with the DCI survey, from conducting inspection programs that rely on survey data, and from "pursuing enforcement proceedings under the unlawful targeting inspection programs." . . .

In its complaint, Sturm Ruger made the same argument now pending before the Commission. . . . The company rested its argument on a section of the OSH Act that states:

> On the basis of the records made and kept pursuant to section 657(c) of this title, employers shall file such reports with the Secretary as he shall prescribe by regulation. . . .

Sturm Ruger did not dispute that OSHA had satisfied the requirement of the final clause of the section with 29 C.F.R. §§ 1904.17, a regulation that requires employers to file reports in response to annual DCI surveys. . . . But it argued that the first clause of the section only permits the agency to compel employers to provide information that is contained in "records made and kept pursuant to section 657(c)." Section 657(c), in turn, provides:

> Each employer shall make, keep and preserve, and make available to the Secretary . . . , such records regarding his activities relating to this chapter as the Secretary . . . may prescribe by regulation. . . .

Sturm Ruger claimed that, . . . no regulation required them to create and maintain the employment data also demanded by the survey. Thus, the company argued, the DCI's requirement that employment data be reported was unlawful under the OSH Act, . . . and consequently under the APA because it was not "in accordance with law," . . . Finally, like its pleadings before the Commission, Sturm Ruger's complaint also contended that employers "have a privacy interest protected by the Fourth Amendment in the information that the survey form seeks to compel them to produce." . . .

The Secretary of Labor moved to dismiss Sturm Ruger's complaint on the ground that "the administrative review process established by the OSH Act is the exclusive means by which plaintiff may challenge the DCI's legality." . . . The district court agreed and granted the motion. . . . [concluding] that the OSH Act established a comprehensive review procedure that precluded district court jurisdiction. . . .

On appeal, we . . . first consider whether the OSH Act has a statutory review structure like that of the statute at issue in *Thunder Basin*, . . . We then address whether Sturm Ruger's claims "are of the type Congress intended to be reviewed within this statutory structure." . . .

In *Thunder Basin*, the Supreme Court considered a pre-enforcement challenge filed by a mine operator against the Secretary of Labor. . . .

The Court held that the statutory review scheme of the Mine Act deprived the district court of subject matter jurisdiction over the operator's complaint. It declared that "in cases involving delayed judicial review"— that is, where appeal can be taken to the court of appeals after completion of administrative proceedings—"we shall find that Congress has allocated initial review to an administrative body where such intent is 'fairly discernible in the statutory scheme.' . . . The Court found that intent discernible in the following elements of the Mine Act's statutory review procedure.

First, the Court noted that the "Act establishes a detailed structure for reviewing violations" of . . . [administrative] standards and regulations. . . . The Court further noted that under the Act, "mine operators may challenge adverse Commission decisions in the appropriate court of appeals, whose jurisdiction 'shall be exclusive and its judgment and decree shall be final' except for possible Supreme Court review." . . . Courts of appeals must "uphold findings of the Commission that are substantially supported by the record." . . . In addition, "the statute establishes that the Commission and the courts of appeals have exclusive jurisdiction over challenges to agency enforcement proceedings," and its "comprehensive review process does not distinguish between pre-enforcement and post-enforcement challenges, but applies to all violations of the Act and its regulations." . . . Finally, the "Act expressly authorizes district court jurisdiction in only two provisions . . . , which respectively empower the Secretary to enjoin habitual violations of health and safety standards and to coerce payment of civil penalties." . . .

In the instant case, the district court concluded, and we agree, that "the administrative and judicial review procedures in the OSH Act are 'nearly identical' to those in the Mine Act." . . . This is hardly surprising since, as we have previously noted, the Mine Act's review process was written to conform to the review process of the OSH Act. . . . Like the Mine Act, the OSH Act gives employers a limited period to contest a citation issued by OSHA, and provides that if no contest is brought within that period, the citation is "deemed a final order . . . not subject to review by any court or agency." . . . Contests to OSHA citations are brought before an independent adjudicatory commission (OSHRC), where they are heard first by an ALJ and then reviewed by the Commission, at its discretion. . . . Only the Commission has authority to impose civil penalties proposed by the Secretary, which the Commission reviews de novo. . . .

As under the Mine Act, employers may appeal adverse Commission decisions to the appropriate court of appeals, whose jurisdiction "shall be exclusive and its judgment and decree shall be final," but which must uphold the Commission's findings of fact if "supported by substantial evidence." . . . Finally, also like the Mine Act, the OSH Act expressly grants district courts jurisdiction over specified actions, . . . but those do not include actions brought by employers.

In short, in every relevant respect the statutory review provisions of the OSH Act parallel those of the Mine Act, and we therefore join the First and Sixth circuits in concluding that *Thunder Basin*'s analysis of review under the Mine Act is fully applicable to the OSH Act. . . .

. . . We must also consider whether Sturm Ruger's claims "are of the type Congress intended to be reviewed within this statutory structure." . . .

Like the statutory claims at issue in *Thunder Basin,* Sturm Ruger's claim that the DCI violates the OSH Act because it is not authorized by regulation is not "wholly collateral" to the OSH Act's review provisions. . . . Rather, it "requires interpretation of the parties' rights and duties" under the Act and its regulations, and therefore "falls squarely within the Commission's expertise." . . . As for the company's claim that the DCI violates

the Fourth Amendment, we note that the same factors that persuaded the *Thunder Basin* Court that the constitutional challenge at issue there should be raised within the statutory review structure are present here: (1) "the reviewing body is not the agency itself but an independent Commission"; (2) the Commission has addressed constitutional claims in previous enforcement proceedings, . . . ; and (3) the employer's claims can still "be meaningfully addressed in the Court of Appeals" after the Commission has rendered a decision. . . .

. . . [B]arring district court review in this case will not deprive employers of the opportunity to obtain judicial review. An employer can, for example, refuse to answer the survey, draw a citation from OSHA, and then contest the citation through the statutory review procedure that ultimately ends in a court of appeals. . . . Sturm Ruger contends that this review option is not meaningful because, faced with the threat of OSHA sanctions, employers will not risk ignoring the survey. . . . But the Court rejected a similar argument in *Thunder Basin,* . . . Moreover, in this case Sturm Ruger has already triggered the review process that ultimately will bring it to a court of appeals, by contesting the citations its Pine Tree facility received as the allegedly tainted product of a search based on information obtained through the DCI. . . .

Finally, we consider our recent decision in *National Mining Ass'n v. Department of Labor,* . . . (D.C. Cir. 2002), in which this court held that, notwithstanding the rule of *Thunder Basin,* a district court had jurisdiction to hear a "generic" challenge to regulations issued by the Secretary of Labor under the Black Lung Benefits Act (BLBA), 30 U.S.C. §§ 901 *et seq.* That decision is inapplicable to Sturm Ruger's challenge. . . .

For the foregoing reasons, the judgment of the district court, dismissing the complaint for lack of subject matter jurisdiction, is

Affirmed.

Case Question

What is the policy basis for the exhaustion of remedies rule?

Recognition of Administrative Competence and Scope of Review

In general, courts are willing to defer to an agency's competence. Courts will uphold administrative findings if they are satisfied that the agency has examined the issues, reached its decision within the appropriate standards, and followed the required procedures.

It is impossible for a reviewing court to consider more than the highlights of the questions actually argued before an administrative agency since the fact situations are often complex and technical, and the time available for argument short. Instead, courts rely on an agency's expertise. Even when a court holds an original determination invalid, it usually remands the case for further consideration by the agency, rather than making its own final decision.

The courts have established standards as to the scope of judicial review. In general, questions of law are ultimately determined by courts and questions of fact are considered only to a very limited extent. Questions of law must be reserved for the courts because the power of final decision on judicial matters involving private rights cannot constitutionally be taken from the judiciary. However, this does not mean that courts will review every issue of law involved in an administrative determination.

Agency findings with respect to questions of fact, if supported by substantial evidence on the record considered as a whole, are conclusive. Substantial evidence exists when the agency's conclusion is reasonably supported by the facts of record. Legal conclusions are judicially reversed only because of arbitrariness, capriciousness, an abuse of discretion, or a denial of due process.

INTERNET TIP

Students may wish to read a case involving the judicial review of a final decision by the Occupational Safety and Health Review Commission to issue citations to one of the contractors involved in the "Big Dig" project in downtown Boston. This case includes discussions of many of the topics addressed in this chapter in the context of an actual dispute. The case is *Modern Continental Construction Co. Inc v. Occupational Safety and Health Review Comm.*, and it can be found on the textbook's website.

The health care provider in the next case claimed to have been a victim of agency arbitrariness and capriciousness perpetrated by the U.S. Department of

Health and Human Services. Maximum Home Care, Inc. claimed that it had been wrongfully denied reimbursement for sums paid to Diversified Health Management Company.

Maximum Home Health Care, Inc. v. Donna E. Shalala
272 F.3d 318
U.S. Court of Appeals, Sixth Circuit
November 15, 2001

Merritt, Circuit Judge

This case arises under Title XVIII of the Social Security Act (the "Medicare Act"), . . . as a challenge to the denial of reimbursement of costs for providing health care to Medicare patients. Plaintiff Maximum Home Health-care, Inc. ("Maximum") appeals the district court's judgment affirming the denial of Medicare reimbursements by Department of Health and Human Services Secretary Donna Shalala ("Secretary" or "Defendant"), in the amounts of $58,272 and $79,354 for the fiscal years 1990 and 1991, respectively. Maximum argues that the denial of reimbursement is arbitrary and capricious, or in the alternative, is not supported by substantial evidence. . . .

Facts

Maximum is a certified home health care agency that provides medical care to Medicare patients. Diversified Health Management Company ("Diversified") provides management and consulting services to home health care agencies. In 1988, Maximum entered into a contract with Diversified to provide management services. For the fiscal years in question, Diversified charged $13.00 in 1990 and $13.60 in 1991, for each visit by Maximum to a Medicare patient. Under the Medicare Act, the Secretary contracts with a fiscal intermediary (the "Intermediary") to process and audit reimbursements to providers such as Maximum. . . . In this case, Blue Cross and

Blue Shield of South Carolina was the intermediary. After reviewing Diversified's fees, the intermediary determined that the average per visit rate was $9.74 for comparable companies during both 1990 and 1991. As a result, the intermediary found that Diversified's fees were substantially out-of-line with market values. Because the Medicare Act requires that costs not be substantially out-of-line from costs of comparable institutions, the Secretary denied reimbursement of Diversified's fees for amounts above $9.74 per visit. . . .

. . . Maximum appealed the intermediary's determination to the Provider Reimbursement Review Board (the "review board"). The review board reversed the intermediary and awarded full reimbursement to Maximum. In its reversal of the intermediary, the review board found that the intermediary's study was flawed because the companies to which Maximum was compared had been chosen arbitrarily and there was no evidence that the services offered by Maximum were identical to the other companies. In addition, the review board also found that a study done by the independent accounting firm KPMG Peat Marwick was more persuasive than the intermediary's study. . . . The KPMG study found an average cost of $11.38 per visit, with a standard deviation of $2.93. Because Maximum's costs fell within the standard deviation, the review board found that they were reasonable and not substantially out-of-line with the market.

The intermediary then appealed to the Administrator of the Health Care Financing Administration, acting on behalf of the Secretary. The Administrator reversed the review board, and reinstated the decision of the intermediary. In finding that Maximum was not entitled to reimbursement in excess of

$9.74 per visit, the Administrator looked for guidance from the Medicare Provider Reimbursement Manual (the "manual"). Relying on the manual, the Administrator held that Maximum was not a prudent buyer, and as a result, held that its costs were not reasonable. . . . Specifically, the Administrator found fault with Maximum's failure to follow the manual's suggested procedures and solicit competitive bids before entering into a contract with Diversified. . . . In addition, the Administrator relied on the survey by the intermediary and discounted the survey by KPMG, noting that the KPMG study did not name the comparable companies used in its survey. Relying on the prudent buyer principle and following the reasoning of the Administrator, the district court affirmed the decision of the Administrator by issuing a judgment on the administrative record. Maximum timely appealed the decision of the district court.

Discussion

The question before the Court is whether the Administrator's denial of reimbursement to Maximum was arbitrary and capricious, contrary to law, or unsupported by substantial evidence. . . . The Medicare Act provides that reimbursements are to be made where the costs claimed are reasonable. . . . The Medicare Act defines reasonable cost as "the costs actually incurred . . . and shall be determined in accordance with regulations establishing the method or methods to be used, and the items to be included, in determining such costs." . . . Both the regulations and the manual provide additional guidance in determining what constitutes reasonable cost. The regulations mandate applying the substantially out-of-line standard, and the manual advocates using the prudent buyer standard. . . . Neither the regulations nor the manual make clear how these two standards should be reconciled.

The Plaintiff argues that the Administrator's reliance on the prudent buyer standard is misplaced because it is inconsistent

with the substantially out-of-line standard, and a regulation trumps a manual provision. On their face, the substantially out-of-line standard and the prudent buyer provision as articulated in PRM §§§ 2102.1, 2103A appear to be reconcilable. The Secretary could reasonably require the Plaintiff to act as a prudent buyer to avoid charging excess fees which are substantially out-of-line with the market valuation of the services. . . .

The Administrator, however, reads the prudent buyer concept as including a competitive bidding or similar market survey requirement. . . . the Administrator found that, to act as a prudent buyer, a provider must meet the additional requirement of engaging in a competitive bidding process or otherwise making an undefined search of the marketplace. Insofar as it adds the requirement of competitive bidding or equivalent process, we find that the Administrator's interpretation of the prudent buyer principle is inconsistent with the substantially out-of-line test.

Because the Administrator relied on a manual provision that was inconsistent with an administrative regulation, we hold that his denial of full reimbursement to Maximum was arbitrary and capricious. The purpose of a regulatory scheme such as Medicare is to provide uniform rules by which all participants may be treated equally. . . . Where an administrative agency creates manual provisions that are inconsistent with the governing regulations, it creates for itself a kind of open-ended discretion in its administrative investigations, and opens the door to disparate treatment of interested parties. By adding the requirement of competitive bidding in the manual, the Secretary leaves the provider to guess as to what rule will be applied. It undermines the clear congressional purpose underlying the requirement that significant rules be established by regulations.

A fundamental requirement of the Administrative Procedures Act is that interested persons be given notice of proposed "substantive" or "legislative" regulations, and an opportunity to comment. . . . Because the competitive bidding requirement is a rule that creates a significant new burden on the provider, the rule should be subject to the rule-making procedures. If the Secretary wants to add a competitive bidding requirement consistent with the Administrator's interpretation, she should do so, absent emergency or other justification, in accordance with the notice and comment rulemaking procedures mandated by 5 U.S.C. §§ 553. . . . Until such an amendment is made, application of the manual provisions to require competitive bidding and as a result disallow costs that are not substantially out-of-line with comparable institutions cannot be sustained. . . .

Lastly, it is important to note that although the district court relied on several cases to support the proposition that the prudent buyer principle can be employed to de-

termine reasonable cost, none of the cited cases established that the prudent buyer principle is a legitimate method of disallowing costs independent of the substantially out-of-line test. . . .

Because the actions of the Administrator in imposing the competitive bidding requirement informally were arbitrary and capricious, we do not reach the question of whether the Administrator's decision was supported by substantial evidence. It is clear that the Plaintiff is entitled to all of its costs so long as they are not substantially out-of-line with comparable companies. Thus, the holding of the district court is REVERSED, and the case is REMANDED to the district court with instructions to return the case to the Administrator to determine whether the Plaintiff's costs were substantially out-of-line with comparable companies.

Case Questions

1. Why did the Administrator of the Health Care Financing Administration reverse the review board's decision in favor of Maximum Health Care, Inc.?
2. What, according to the Court of Appeals, was the legal significance of the Administrator's reliance on his interpretation of the prudent buyer standard?

ADMINISTRATIVE AGENCIES AND THE REGULATION OF BUSINESS

Congress has neither the time nor the expertise to regulate business. Congress has also decided that the judicial process is not well suited to the task. Instead it has entrusted the day-to-day responsibility for regulating business to administrative agencies. The following material focuses on three administrative agencies and how they perform this function.

Occupational Safety and Health Administration

Historically, the common law provided an employee injured on the job with little recourse against an employer who could use the assumption of risk and contributory negligence defenses or who invoked the fellow servant doctrine.

With little incentive for employers to reduce employment-related injuries, the number of industrial injuries increased as manufacturing processes became more complex. Legislation was passed to improve job safety for coal miners during the late 1800s, and most states had enacted job safety legislation by 1920. Maryland and New York were the first states to establish workers' compensation laws, which have now been adopted in all fifty states. Although these laws modified the common law to enable injured employees to recover, they didn't change the practices that caused the dangerous conditions. Furthermore, state legislatures were reluctant to establish strict safety regulations, fearing that such actions would cause industry to move to other, less restrictive states.

In response to the problem, in 1970 Congress passed the Occupational Safety and Health Act to improve employees' safety and working conditions. The act established the National Institute of Occupational Safety and Health to conduct research in the area of employee health and safety. The act also created an administrative agency, called the Occupational Health and Safety Administration (OSHA), to set and enforce environmental standards within the work place.

An employee who suspects that there is a safety violation at his or her place of work can contact the local OSHA office. An OSHA inspector makes an unannounced visit to the premises and conducts an inspection. If the inspection reveals violations, appropriate citations—either civil or criminal—are issued.

For civil citations, OSHA may impose fines up to seventy thousand dollars for each willful and repeated violation and seven thousand dollars for less serious violations. As we saw earlier in this chapter in the case of *Sturm, Ruger & Co., Inc. v. Elaine Chao, Sec., U.S. Dept. of Labor,* an employer may contest an OSHA citation at a hearing before an administrative law judge. The ALJ's decision is appealable to the Occupational Health Review Commission, whose decision is appealable to the U.S. Court of Appeals.

Criminal prosecutions for OSHA violations are rare, however when brought they are tried in federal district court. Convicted offenders can be fined up to $500,000 for each count and sentenced to a maximum of six months in prison.

OSHA inspectors also have the right to post a job site as imminently dangerous and obtain injunctions where necessary to shut down a work site because of the existence of dangerous working conditions.

Federal Trade Commission and Consumer Credit Protection

The first multiuse credit cards, Visa and MasterCard, came into existence only in 1959. Initially, businesses that extended credit to consumers were subject to few regulations. They often imposed unduly high interest charges, failed to disclose their interest rates and associated credit charges, and mailed unsolicited credit cards to potential users. Because debt collection practices were unregulated, consumers were often harassed and threatened at home and at work. As a result, in 1968 Congress passed the Consumer Credit Protection Act (CCPA).

Designed to promote the disclosures of credit terms and to establish the rights and responsibilities of both creditors and consumers, the CCPA is much more protective of the consumer than was the common law. Although several agencies share authority for enforcing and controlling the CCPA, the Federal Trade Commission bears primary responsibility for the CCPA enforcement.

Under the CCPA, many early credit card and loan practices became illegal. Issuers of credit cards, for example, were no longer permitted to mail unsolicited cards. Many of the questions about the apportionment of duties between the merchants who accepted credit cards and the card-issuing banks were clarified. For example, under the CCPA, a bank may not withdraw funds from a card-holder's savings or checking accounts to cover a credit card charge without the cardholder's authorization. Also, under the CCPA a cardholder's liability for unauthorized charges is limited to fifty dollars in most cases.

The CCPA is extremely lengthy and complex and is better known under its various subsections. Title 1 of the CCPA is known as the Truth in Lending Act. The Fair Credit Reporting Act was added in 1970, the Equal Credit Opportunity Act was added in 1974, the Fair Credit Billing Act in 1975, and the Fair Debt Collection Practices Act in 1977.

The Truth in Lending Simplification and Reform Act was signed into law in 1980. It primarily regulates the disclosure of credit terms and conditions in conjunction with household purchases and common real estate transactions. Congress intended to make it easier for consumers to shop for credit. Before the passage of this act, many lenders did not disclose interest rates, finance charges, or other charges in ways that could be easily compared with their business competitors. Under the Truth in Lending Act, creditors must disclose informa-tion about interest rates and other finance charges in a highly regulated and uniform manner. A knowing and willful violator of the Truth in Lending Act may be criminally prosecuted and penalized with fines and incarceration. However, the most effective and most commonly used method of enforcing this act is through private suit. A successful plaintiff can recover a fine, an award of compensatory damages and an order that the creditor pay the consumer's attorney's fees.

The Fair Credit Reporting Act of 1970, (FCRA), is designed to ensure that consumers are treated fairly by credit-reporting agencies and medical informa-tion businesses. Prior to its enactment, agencies that investigated individuals in order to provide companies with credit, insurance, employment, or other consumer reports were subject to few restraints. Individuals not only had no right to know the contents of the report, but businesses had no duty to disclose the fact that a report even existed. Hence many individuals were denied credit, employment, or other benefits without knowing that an investigation had been made. Consumers now have the right to know the contents of any adverse report used by a business, the name of the agency that compiled the report, and when such information has resulted in an adverse decision that has been made based on such a report. Consumers may also require compiling agencies to investigate disputed facts, correct the report, or include a consumer's own explanation of disputed facts as part of its report. Investigating agencies must follow "reasonable procedures" in compiling the report, and comply with provisions intended to protect the consumer's privacy.

The Fair Credit Billing Act (FCBA) provides that a credit cardholder is financially responsible only for the first $50 of unauthorized charges. Many credit card issuers, as a matter of company policy, will even waive a bona fide customer's obligation to make this payment. The FCBA also addresses a cardholder's rights vis-à-vis a creditor where the cardholder has discovered that items purchased with a credit card were received in damaged condition or were of poor quality. In general, (and there are exceptions), the FCBA provides a cardholder with the same remedies against the creditor as exist under state law in the cardholder's state (which will frequently include the right to withhold payment) if certain requirements are met. First, the credit card purchase must have cost more than $50; second, the purchase must have been made either in the cardholder's own state or within 100 miles of his or her home; third, the cardholder must have attempted to resolve the dispute with the merchant; and fourth, the cardholder must have given the credit card issuer a detailed written explanation of the facts within sixty days of receiving the credit card bill containing the disputed charge.

The Equal Credit Opportunity Act (ECOA) of 1974 is designed to eradicate discrimination in the granting of credit when the decision to grant it or refuse it is based on an individual's sex, marital status, race, color, age, religion, national origin, or receipt of public assistance. The major effect of this act had been to eliminate sex discrimination. Under the ECOA, a married woman can now obtain credit in her own name. A prospective creditor may not ask about an individual's marital status, childbearing plans, spouse or former spouse, or other similar criteria. Questions regarding alimony and child support are proper only if the applicant will rely on those sums to repay the obligation.

Because the ECOA is modeled after the Equal Employment Opportunity Act, facially neutral practices that have the effect of discriminating against a protected class are also prohibited.

The ECOA requires creditors to notify consumers of any decision about the extension or denial of credit, along with the creditor's reasons or a statement indicating that the individual is entitled to know the reasons. An individual may bring suit against a creditor for noncompliance with the ECOA to recover actual and punitive damages.

As previously stated, the Federal Trade Commission bears primary responsibility for the CCPA enforcement. We see an example of the FTC attempting to enforce one of the various consumer protection acts for which it is responsible, in the following case. Trans Union, the appellant, is one of the nation's largest credit reporting companies. What follows is its appeal of an FTC determination that the Fair Credit Reporting Act prohibits credit reporting agencies from compiling and selling certain types of information that have been collected for purposes of credit-worthiness determinations to marketing firms who deal directly with consumers.

Trans Union Corporation v. Federal Trade Commission

245 F.3d 809

U.S. Court of Appeals, District of Columbia Circuit

April 13, 2001

Tatel, Circuit Judge

Petitioner, a consumer reporting agency, sells lists of names and addresses to target marketers—companies and organizations that contact consumers with offers of products and services. The Federal Trade Commission determined that these lists were "consumer reports" under the Fair Credit Reporting Act and thus could no longer be sold for target marketing purposes. Challenging this determination, petitioner argues that the Commission's decision is unsupported by substantial evidence and that the Act itself is unconstitutional. . . .

I

Petitioner Trans Union sells two types of products. First, as a credit reporting agency, it compiles credit reports about individual consumers from credit information it collects from banks, credit card companies, and other lenders. It then sells these credit reports to lenders, employers, and insurance companies. Trans Union receives credit information from lenders in the form of "tradelines." A tradeline typically includes a customer's name, address, date of birth, telephone number, Social Security number, account type, opening date of account, credit limit, account status, and payment history. Trans Union receives 1.4 to 1.6 billion records per month. The company's credit database contains information on 190 million adults.

Trans Union's second set of products—those at issue in this case— are known as target marketing products. These consist of lists of names and addresses of individuals who meet specific criteria such as possession of an auto loan, a department store credit card, or two or more mortgages. Marketers purchase these lists, then contact the individuals by mail or telephone to offer them goods and services. To create its target marketing lists, Trans Union maintains a database known as MasterFile, a subset of its consumer credit database. MasterFile consists of information about every consumer in the company's credit database who has (A) at least two tradelines with activity during the previous six months, or (B) one tradeline with activity during the previous six months plus an address confirmed by an outside source. The company compiles target marketing lists by extracting from MasterFile the names and addresses of individuals with characteristics chosen by list purchasers. For example, a department store might buy a list of all individuals in a particular area code who have both a mortgage and a credit card with a $10,000 limit. Although target marketing lists contain only names and addresses, purchasers know that every person on a list has the characteristics they requested because Trans Union uses those characteristics as criteria for culling individual files from its database. Purchasers also know that every individual on a target marketing list satisfies the criteria for inclusion in MasterFile.

The Fair Credit Reporting Act of 1970 ("FCRA"), . . . regulates consumer reporting agencies like Trans Union, imposing various obligations to protect the privacy and accuracy of credit information. The Federal Trade Commission, acting pursuant to its authority to enforce the FCRA, . . . determined that Trans Union's target marketing lists were "consumer reports" subject to the Act's limitations. . . .

. . . Finding that the information Trans Union sold was "collected in whole or in part by [Trans Union] with the expectation that it would be used by credit grantors for the purpose of serving as a factor in establishing the consumer's eligibility for one of the transactions set forth in the FCRA," and concluding that target marketing is not an authorized use of consumer reports . . . the Commission ordered Trans Union to stop selling target marketing lists, . . .

Trans Union petitioned for review. In *Trans Union Corp. v. FTC*, . . . (D.C. Cir. 1996) ("*Trans Union I*"), we agreed with the Commission that selling consumer reports for target marketing violates the Act. . . . We nevertheless set aside the Commission's determination that Trans Union's target marketing lists amounted to consumer reports. . . . The Commission, we held, failed to justify its finding that Trans Union's lists, by conveying the mere fact that consumers had a tradeline, were communicating information collected for the purpose of determining credit eligibility. We found that the Commission had failed to provide evidence to support the proposition that "the mere existence of a tradeline, as distinguished from payment history organized thereunder," was used for credit-granting decisions or was intended or expected to be used for such decisions. . . .

On remand, following extensive discovery, more than a month of trial proceedings, and an initial decision by an Administrative Law Judge, the Commission found that Trans Union's target marketing lists contain information that credit grantors use as factors in granting credit. Accordingly, the Commission concluded, the lists are "consumer reports" that Trans Union may not sell for target marketing purposes. . . . The Commission also rejected Trans Union's argument that such a restriction would violate its First Amendment rights. Applying intermediate scrutiny, the Commission found that the government has a substantial interest in protecting private credit information, that the FCRA directly advances that interest, and that the Act's restrictions on speech are narrowly tailored. . . . The Commission thus ordered Trans Union

to "cease and desist from distributing or selling consumer reports, including those in the form of target marketing lists, to any person unless [the company] has reason to believe that such person intends to use the consumer report for purposes authorized under Section [1681b] of the Fair Credit Reporting Act." *In re Trans Union Corp.*, Final Order, No. 9255 (Feb. 10, 2000). Trans Union again petitions for review.

II

As we pointed out in *Trans Union I*, the first element of the FCRA's definition of consumer report—"bearing on a consumer's credit worthiness, credit standing, credit capacity, character, general reputation, personal characteristics, or mode of living," 15 U.S.C. §§ 1681a(d)(1)—"does not seem very demanding," for almost any information about consumers arguably bears on their personal characteristics or mode of living. . . . Instead, Trans Union does not challenge the Commission's conclusion that the information contained in its lists meets this prong of the definition of consumer report.

Whether the company's target marketing lists qualify as consumer reports thus turns on whether information they contain "is used or expected to be used or collected in whole or in part for the purpose of serving as a factor in establishing the consumer's eligibility for [credit]." . . . According to the Commission, "a factor in establishing the consumer's eligibility for [credit]," *id.*, includes any type of information credit grantors use in their criteria for "prescreening" or in "credit scoring models." . . . "Prescreening" involves selecting individuals for guaranteed offers of credit or insurance. . . . "Credit scoring models" are statistical models for predicting credit performance that are developed by observing the historical credit performance of a number of consumers and identifying the consumer characteristics that correlate with good and bad credit performance. . . . Applying its prescreening/credit scoring model standard, the Commission found that Trans Union's lists contain the type of information "'used' and/or 'expected to be used' . . . as a factor in establishing a consumer's eligibility for credit." . . .

Trans Union urges us to reject the Commission's interpretation of the Act in order to avoid what the company calls "serious constitutional questions." . . . But as we demonstrate in Section III, *infra*, Trans Union's constitutional arguments are without merit, so we have no basis for rejecting the Commission's statutory interpretation on that ground.

Nor has Trans Union offered a basis for questioning the Commission's statutory interpretation on other grounds. . . .

We have the same reaction to the brief's occasional suggestions that the Commission's decision was arbitrary and capricious. . . . [T]he list of issues presented for review neither mentions the arbitrary and capricious standard nor otherwise questions the reasonableness of the Commission's decision.

We thus turn to the one non-constitutional argument that Trans Union clearly mounts: that the Commission's decision is unsupported by substantial evidence. . . .

Instead of challenging the Commission's findings regarding specific target marketing products, Trans Union points to evidence relating to the general question of whether the information in its target marketing lists is used to determine credit worthiness. This is not the question before us. As we indicate above, the Commission interprets "factors in establishing the consumer's eligibility for credit," . . . to include any information considered by lenders in prescreening, which, as two witnesses testified, can involve consideration of criteria other than credit worthiness, e.g., whether a given consumer is likely to respond to an offer of credit. Because Trans Union has not challenged the Commission's

interpretation of the statute, its argument that the information the company sells is not actually used to determine credit worthiness is beside the point. Moreover, Trans Union cites no testimony refuting the Commission's finding that the information in its target marketing lists is used in prescreening.

. . . Trans Union [has] thus failed to mount a proper substantial evidence challenge to the Commission's finding that lenders take list information into account in credit models and prescreening, but we have no doubt that the decision does find support in the record. Consider, for example, Trans Union's "MasterFile/Selects" product line, which allows marketers to request lists based on any of five categories of information: (1) credit limits (e.g., consumers with credit cards with credit limits over $10,000), (2) open dates of loans (e.g., consumers who took out loans in the last six months), (3) number of tradelines, (4) type of tradeline (e.g., auto loan or mortgage), and (5) existence of a tradeline. The Commission cites testimony and other record evidence that support its finding that lenders consider each of these five categories of information in prescreening or credit scoring models. . . . To support its finding that information about the number of tradelines in a consumer's credit file is a consumer report, the Commission cites the testimony of a vice president in charge of direct mail processing for a bank's credit card department who explained that, in its credit making decisions, her bank considers the number of tradelines consumers possess. . . . The Commission also points to record evidence demonstrating that Trans Union itself uses the number of tradelines as a predictive characteristic in its credit scoring models. . . . As to the type of tradeline, the Commission cites the testimony of representatives of companies that design credit models who explained that some credit scoring models, including two used by Trans Union, take into account possession of a bank card. . . . One witness testified that Trans Union scoring models also consider possession of a finance company loan to be a predictive characteristic. Another witness, this one representing a credit card company, testified that his company's scoring models assign points for possession of a mortgage, retail tradeline, or bank card. . . .

The record also contains sufficient evidence to support the Commission's resolution of the issue remanded by *Trans Union I:* whether mere existence of a tradeline is "a factor in credit-granting decisions." . . . An employee of a bank that issues credit cards testified that to be eligible for credit, an individual must have at least one tradeline. . . . The vice president of credit scoring at another credit card issuer testified that the very first question her company asks in prescreening is whether the consumer has a tradeline that has been open for at least a year. Challenging the implications of this testimony, Trans Union argues that banks ask whether consumers have tradelines not because the existence of a tradeline is itself a factor in determining credit eligibility, but because banks want to determine whether there is enough information in consumer files to make credit eligibility determinations. This may be true. But as we explain above, our task is limited to determining whether substantial record evidence supports the Commission's finding that banks consider the existence of a tradeline as a factor in prescreening or credit models. Because the record contains such evidence, we have no basis for questioning the Commission's decision. . . .

III

Trans Union's constitutional challenge consists of two arguments. It claims first that the FCRA is vague, thus running afoul of the due process guarantee of the Fifth Amendment. Trans Union also argues that the statute violates the free speech guarantee of the First Amendment because it restricts its ability to disseminate information.

Beginning with the Fifth Amendment challenge, we are guided by *Village of Hoffman Estates v. Flipside, Hoffman Estates, Inc.,* . . . (1982). "Laws," the Court said, must not only "give the person of ordinary intelligence a reasonable opportunity to know what is prohibited," but in order to prevent "arbitrary and discriminatory enforcement," they must also "provide explicit standards for those who apply them." . . . Emphasizing that these principles should not "be mechanically applied," the Court held that "economic regulation is subject to a less strict vagueness test because its subject matter is often more narrow, and because businesses, which face economic demands to plan behavior carefully, can be expected to consult relevant legislation in advance of action." . . . The "regulated enterprise," the Court added, "may have the ability to clarify the meaning of the regulation by its own inquiry, or by resort to an administrative process." . . . Finally, "the consequences of imprecision are qualitatively less severe" when laws have "scienter requirements" and "civil rather than criminal penalties." . . .

Applying this standard, we see no merit in Trans Union's vagueness argument. To begin with, because the FCRA's regulation of consumer reporting agencies is economic, it is subject to "a less strict vagueness test." . . . Moreover, Trans Union has "the ability to clarify the meaning of the [FCRA]," . . . , through the Commission's advisory opinion procedures. *See* 16 C.F.R. §§§ 1.1-1.4 (establishing general procedures for obtaining advisory opinions); *id.* §§ 2.41(d) (establishing procedures for obtaining guidance regarding compliance with FTC orders). . . .

Trans Union's First Amendment challenge fares no better. Banning the sale of target marketing lists, the company says, amounts to a restriction on its speech subject to strict scrutiny. Again, Trans Union misunderstands our standard of review. In *Dun & Bradstreet, Inc. v. Greenmoss Builders, Inc.,* . . . (1985), the Supreme Court held that a consumer reporting agency's credit report warranted reduced constitutional protection because it concerned "no public issue." . . . "The protection to be accorded a particular credit report," the Court explained, "depends on whether the report's 'content, form, and context' indicate that it concerns a public matter." . . . Like the credit report in *Dun & Bradstreet,* which the Supreme Court found "was speech solely in the interest of the speaker and its specific business audience," . . . the information about individual consumers and their credit performance communicated by Trans Union target marketing lists is solely of interest to the company and its business customers and relates to no matter of public concern. Trans Union target marketing lists thus warrant "reduced constitutional protection." . . .

We turn then to the specifics of Trans Union's First Amendment argument. The company first claims that neither the FCRA nor the Commission's Order advances a substantial government interest. The "Congressional findings and statement of purpose" at the beginning of the FCRA state: "There is a need to insure that consumer reporting agencies exercise their grave responsibilities with . . . respect for the consumer's right to privacy." . . . Contrary to the company's assertions, we have no doubt that this interest

—protecting the privacy of consumer credit information—is substantial.

Trans Union next argues that Congress should have chosen a "less burdensome alternative," i.e., allowing consumer reporting agencies to sell credit information as long as they notify consumers and give them the ability to "opt out." . . . Because the FCRA is not subject to strict First Amendment scrutiny, however, Congress had no obligation to choose the least restrictive means of accomplishing its goal.

Finally, Trans Union argues that the FCRA is underinclusive because it applies only to consumer reporting agencies and not to other companies that sell consumer information. But given consumer reporting agencies' unique "access to a broad range of continually-updated, detailed information about millions of consumers' personal credit histories," . . . , we think it not at all inappropriate for Congress to have singled out consumer reporting agencies for regulation. . . . To survive a First Amendment underinclusiveness challenge, . . . "neither a perfect nor even the best available fit between means and ends is required." . . . The FCRA easily satisfies this standard. . . .

IV

Having considered and rejected Trans Union's other arguments, we deny the petition for review.

So Ordered.

Case Questions

1. What consumer interest was the FTC seeking to protect in ruling as it did vis-à-vis Trans Union?
2. Why did the appeals court uphold the agency's determination that Trans Union's actions were contrary to the requirements of the Fair Credit Reporting Act?

Environmental Protection Agency

The Environmental Protection Agency (EPA) was created by Congress in 1970 to replace the fifteen federal agencies that previously were responsible for enforcing the laws regulating environmental pollution. The EPA is charged with controlling water, air, noise, and radiation pollution; solid and hazardous waste treatment, storage, and disposal; and pesticides and toxic substances.

History of Pollution Control

Prior to the late 1960s, controlling pollution was a matter primarily governed by state legislation and the law of torts. Among the earliest examples of federal legislation is the Rivers and Harbors Act of 1886.[5] Although clean water legislation was enacted at the state level in the 1930s and 1940s,[6] Congress waited until the late 1940s to enact the Federal Insecticide, Fungicide, and Rodenticide Act (1947) and the Federal Water Pollution Control Act (1948). Although common law tort actions could be based on nuisance, trespass, negligence, and, more recently, strict liability, common law remedies were inadequate to protect the public, because what was deemed tortious was decided by judges on a case-by-case basis in response to particular factual conditions.

In 1969, Congress recognized that the pollution problem was too large and complex to be adequately addressed by the states and enacted the National Environmental Policy Act (NEPA). NEPA, which took effect on January 1, 1979, required federal agencies to develop environmental impact statements (EIS) whenever their actions were likely to have significant consequences for the environment. In the 1970s Congress became very active in pollution control by amending previously existing legislation and by enacting new laws. Although political gridlock prevented most environmental legislation during the 1980s,[7] the passage of the Clean Air Act of 1990 was a major legislative attempt to protect the public health. A brief summary follows of some of the most important environmental statutes concerning air pollution, water pollution, pesticide control, and hazardous wastes control.

Air Pollution

The Clean Air Act of 1990 was intended to substantially reduce acid rain, urban smog, air pollution, and automobile exhaust emissions and to phase out the use of chemicals that harm the ozone layer. Air quality is determined by measuring the levels of ozone, carbon monoxide, nitrogen dioxide, sulphur dioxide, inhalable particulate matter, and lead in the air. These are the pollutants that adversely affect public health. Air pollution contributes to thousands of bronchitis cases and deaths per year,[8] and it injures crops, animals, wilderness areas, historic buildings, and monuments.[9] The CAA required the EPA to develop detailed regulations for reducing the amount of harmful toxins that industrial plants emitted into the air to the lowest achievable level given the limitations of existing technology. This legislation also debuted the use of market-based incentives to induce utility companies to reduce their sulfur dioxide emissions. A power plant that operates with clean fuel or purchases new technology is permitted to accumulate unused sulfur dioxide allowances, which can then be sold to other utilities that have exceeded their own allowances.[10] This "environmental dividend" amounts to a new form of capital that companies can use to help pay for their investments in technology. The total amount of emissions permitted under the law in the year 2000 is over 1 million tons less than what was allowed in 1990. There is evidence that air quality in the United States has improved since 1975, with the greatest progress occurring in ozone protection and acid rain reduction.[11]

Local and state governments are required to become active partners with the EPA in the control of air pollution. States with severe pollution problems, for example, are required to develop plans that include incentives to encourage carpooling and public transportation.[12] Enormous controversy has surrounded the EPA's rule-making efforts based on economic, legal, and political considerations.[13] The EPA, partly in response to political changes in Congress, has actively sought to negotiate its rule making with environmental, industrial, and labor associations.[14] The controversies have produced uncertainty, confusion, resistance, and delay in implementation.

Water Pollution

In 1972 Congress overrode President Nixon's veto and enacted the Clean Water Act.[15] Its goals included restoring water quality, so that it supports fish and wildlife and recreational uses, and eliminating the discharge of pollutants.[16] The act applies to publicly owned treatment works as well as private enterprises. When toxic chemicals, many originating from landfills and underground storage tanks, were found to have contaminated the drinking water, Congress responded by enacting the Safe Drinking Water Act in 1974. Pursuant to these acts, the EPA developed technical policies and effluent regulations for each industry.[17] These policies and regulations are enforced with a permit system. One of the conditions of obtaining a permit is that the EPA has the right to enter the premises of the discharger to inspect records and monitor compliance with federal law and EPA regulations. In 1987 Congress enacted a new Clean Water Act and required that states establish standards for removing harmful pollutants from fresh water.[18] Many states have chosen to play the leading role in CAA enforcement. The EPA encourages this where state standards equal or exceed federal requirements.

Pesticide Control

Congress enacted the Federal Insecticide, Fungicide, and Rodenticide Act (FIFRA) in 1947. This act was amended in 1972 and 1978 by the Federal Environmental Pesticide Control Act. These statutes provide that a pesticide cannot be distributed through interstate commerce unless its container displays cautionary warnings and the product has been registered with the EPA.[19] These acts also require pesticide manufacturers to undertake studies that demonstrate the effect their products have on humans.[20] The EPA is authorized to restrict public access to any product that is hazardous to humans. It may, for instance, require that certain products only be applied by certified applicators.[21] The EPA can also cancel registrations if a pesticide is found to unreasonably harm the environment. Civil and criminal fines and criminal jail sentences can be imposed on people who knowingly violate these acts.

Hazardous Wastes Disposal

The Resource Conservation and Recovery Act of 1976 (RCRA) was enacted to replace the Solid Wastes Disposal Act of 1965. Prior to RCRA, many producers of hazardous waste merely dumped their contaminated matter on their own property and in landfills. Despite the production of millions of tons of hazardous waste, the government could not determine what waste was being disposed, where it was disposed, and whether it was being disposed of properly. Under RCRA, dischargers are required to maintain detailed records regarding waste disposal. This information is vital to prevent the recurrence of situations such as Love Canal in New York.[22]

The act also requires operators of active hazardous waste disposal sites to operate their facilities in compliance with EPA regulations. EPA promulgates standards that regulate the generation, transportation, and disposal of hazardous wastes.[23] These standards require labeling, record maintenance, the use of environmentally appropriate receptacles, and reporting procedures.[24] The EPA relies on a permit system to track hazardous waste from its point of origin to its final destination. RCRA was amended in 1984 to regulate small quantities of hazardous waste and to prevent the land disposal of heavy metals such as lead, mercury, and nickel in amounts above EPA-approved concentrations.[25]

Although RCRA addressed active hazardous waste disposal sites, it did not confront the problem of inactive sites containing abandoned hazardous wastes.[26] Congress responded to this problem in 1980 when it enacted the Comprehensive Environmental Response, Compensation and Liability Act (CERCLA), also known as the Superfund law. This law, as amended, provides funds to be used by the EPA to clean up abandoned hazardous waste sites and spills. Amendments made to CERCLA in 1986 required users of hazardous wastes to report releases of regulated harmful substances into the environment, and they provided the public with a legally protected right to know the type and amount of toxic chemicals that are present in local communities.[27]

Enforcement of Environmental Laws

Those who violate the Clean Air Act, Clean Water Act, and RCRA are subject to administrative fines, civil fines, or criminal fines and imprisonment. Congress has also provided individual citizens with the right to sue, thereby creating pressure on business and the EPA to aggressively enforce the law.[28]

Chapter Questions

1. Define the following terms:

   adjudication   final decision
   Administrative Procedure Act   hearing
   burden of proof   license
   delegate   notice
   discretion   record
   exhaustion of administrative   ripe
      remedies   rule-making power
   Federal Register   separation of powers

2. The Secretary of Commerce, pursuant to rule-making authority contained in the Atlantic Tunas Convention Act of 1975 (the "ATCA"), adopted regulations regarding the use of "spotter aircraft" by fishing permit holders. The purposes of the ATCA included preventing the overfishing of the Atlantic Bluefin Tuna (ABT), setting quotas on the ABT catch per country, and increasing ABT scientific research. The regulations prohibited persons holding "general" category fishing permits from using "spotter" aircraft to locate Atlantic Bluefin Tuna (ABT), but permitted the use of such planes by persons licensed to catch ABT with harpoons or seine nets. The ABT is a very valuable fish, each one being worth up to $50,000. The Atlantic Fish Spotters Association brought suit, maintaining that this regulation should be overturned. What standard will the plaintiffs have to meet to persuade the U.S. District Court to overturn the regulation? What type of evidence will the plaintiffs need to produce to be successful?
   Atlantic Fish Spotters Association v. Dailey, 8 F. Supp.2d 113 (1998)

3. Faustino Ramos, Michael Beal, and Francisco Murillo were employees of Mavo Leasing, Inc. Mavo and the Production Workers Union of Chicago were parties to a collective bargaining agreement that required that all employees pay union dues to the PWU. Mavo discharged the above-named employees for not paying their union dues in accordance with a clause in the collective bargaining agreement. The three employees claimed that the union had not given them notice of their right to challenge certain union expenditures which were not made in furtherance of collective bargaining. They argued that they did not have to pay dues for nonrepresentation expenses. The employees complained about this lack of notice to the National Labor Relations Board (NLRB). An ALJ heard the complaint and ruled that the Union did not have an affirmative obligation to provide the employees with the requested notice. An NLRB three-member appeals panel ruled in favor of the employees and interpreted the National Labor Relations Act as requiring the union to affirmatively provide the employees with notice of the right to object to paying dues to fund nonrepresentation expenditures,

prior to discharge from employment for nonpayment of union dues. The issue was appealed to the U.S. Court of Appeals for the Seventh Circuit. How should the Court decide this appeal and why?

Production Workers Union of Chicago v. N.L.R.B., 161 F.3d 1047 (1998)

4. The Fertilizer Institute (TFI) is a trade organization that represents members of the fertilizer industry. TFI filed suit in U.S. District Court against the EPA, contesting the agency's decision to list nitrate compounds on the toxic release inventory that is compiled by the EPA pursuant to the "Emergency Planning and Community Right to Know Act of 1986." The EPA listed these compounds because there was evidence that they posed a chronic health threat to human infants. TFI argued that the record did not support the EPA's decision. What evidence would the trial court need to conclude that the EPA had acted arbitrarily in reaching its decision? Why?

Fertilizer Industry v. Browner, 163 F.3d 774 (1998)

5. New York's Aid to Families with Dependent Children (AFDC) program, stressing "close contact" with beneficiaries, requires home visits by caseworkers as a condition for assistance "in order that any treatment or service tending to restore [beneficiaries] to a condition of self-support and to relieve their distress may be rendered and . . . that assistance or care may be given only in such amount and as long as necessary." Visitation with a beneficiary, who is the primary source of information to welfare authorities about eligibility for assistance, is not permitted outside working hours, and forcible entry and snooping are prohibited. The appellee was a beneficiary under the AFDC program. Although she had received several days' advance notice, she refused to permit a caseworker to visit her home. Following a hearing and advice that assistance would consequently be terminated, she brought suit for injunctive and declaratory relief, contending that home visitation is a search and, when not consented to or supported by a warrant based on probable cause, would violate her Fourth and Fourteenth amendment rights. The district upheld the appellee's constitutional claim. Was the district court correct? Why or why not?

Wyman v. James, 400 U.S. 309 (1971)

6. Columbia East, Inc., the owner of 34.3 acres of farmland, wanted the zoning changed in order to develop a mobile home park. The board of zoning appeals granted a preliminary approval of the application for a special exception to develop a mobile home park in the area zoned as agricultural. Final approval by the board of zoning appeals could only be granted after the plans and specifications for the development of the proposed trailer court had been completed and approved by the appropriate agencies. Neighboring landowners filed a suit in court challenging the board's preliminary approval, claiming the decision was made without adequate provision for sewage treatment. What should the court decide?

Downing v. Board of Zoning Appeals, 274 N.E.2d 542 (Ind. 1971)

7. The Occupational Safety and Health Act empowers agents of the Secretary of Labor to search the work area of any employment facility within the act's jurisdiction. No search warrant or other process is expressly required under the act. An OSHA inspector entered the customer service area of Barlow's, Inc., an electrical and plumbing installation business, and stated that he wished to conduct a search of the working areas of the business. Barlow, the president and general manager, asked the inspector whether he had received any complaints about the working conditions and whether he had a search warrant. The inspector answered both questions in the negative. The inspector was denied entry into the working areas. Marshall, Secretary of Labor, argued that warrantless inspections to enforce OSHA regulations are reasonable within the meaning of the Fourth Amendment, and relied on the act, which authorizes inspection of business premises without a warrant. Should the court accept Marshall's argument?

   Marshall v. Barlow's, Inc., 436 U.S. 307 (1978)

8. The city of Denver was authorized by its charter to make local improvements and to assess the cost on the property specifically benefited. However, there first had to be notice by publication, and any interested person's comments were required to be heard. Then the city council had to approve. After completion of a project, the total cost of the improvement had to be published, and the share of the cost for each piece of land determined. Objections had to be heard by the city council before it could pass an ordinance assessing the cost of the improvement. Following this procedure, an improvement was made. The complainants filed objections, challenging the creation of the assessment district, the method of carrying out the improvement, and the final assessments against each piece of property. However, the city council adopted a resolution that "no complaint or objection had been filed or made against the apportionment of said assessment . . . but the complaints and objections filed deny wholly the right of the city to assess any district or portion of the assessable property of the city of Denver." Therefore, the council enacted an ordinance approving the proposed assessments. Was there a violation of complainants' rights of due process of law? Why or why not?

   Londoner v. Denver, 210 U.S. 373 (1908)

9. The owner of some real estate in Denver brought a suit to enjoin the State Board of Equalization, the Colorado Tax Commission, and the assessor of Denver from effecting a 40 percent increase in the state tax valuation of all taxable property in Denver. The plaintiff claimed that he had been given no opportunity to be heard, and that his property would therefore be taken without due process of law, contrary to the Fourteenth Amendment of the Constitution. The Supreme Court of Colorado sustained the order of the board and directed the suit to be dismissed. Compare the tax proposal with the subject matter of the procedure in Question 6. What are the differences? Was the Colorado Supreme Court correct?

   Bi-Metallic Investment Co. v. State Board of Equalization, 239 U.S. 441 (1915)

10. Under the U.S. Community Health Centers Act, the Secretary of the Department of Health, Education, and Welfare was empowered to award monetary grants to health centers that complied with federal regulations. Temple University received funds under the act and was therefore required to meet the federal regulations. In addition, the Pennsylvania Department of Public Welfare and the County Mental Health and Retardation Board were charged with the responsibility of administering county health programs. In 1970, the Temple University Mental Health Center was required to cut back services and impose strict security measures because of campus riots. Members of the surrounding community brought suit against Temple University, charging that the center was not providing required services and that members of the community were deprived of access to the facility. What should the court's decision be?

North Philadelphia Community Board v. Temple University, 330 F.Supp. 1107 (1971)

Notes

1. *Federal Regulatory Directory* (Washington, D.C.: Congressional Quarterly, Inc., 1990), p. 621.
2. Ibid., p. 687.
3. Ibid., p. 2.
4. Ibid., p. 3.
5. K. M. Mackenthun and J. I. Bregman, *Environmental Regulations Handbook* (Boca Raton: Lewis Publishers, 1991), p. 2.
6. Ibid.
7. G. Bryner, *Blue Skies, Green Politics: The Clean Air Act of 1990* (Washington, D.C.: 1993), pp. 90–93.
8. M. Freedman and B. Jaggi, *Air and Water Pollution Regulation* (Westport, CT: Quorum Books, 1993), p. 17.
9. Bryner, p. 6.
10. Freedman and Jaggi, p. 6.
11. Ibid., p. 16.
12. J. W. Waks and C. R. Brewster, "Clean Air Requires Commuting Options," *The National Law Journal* 4, 18 (October 1993).
13. R. S. Frye and L. S. Ritts, "State Clean Air Act Programs Undefined," *The National Law Journal* 21, 28 (June 1993).
14. G. Bryner, *Blue Skies, Green Politics: The Clean Air Act of 1990,* 2nd ed. (Washington, D.C.: Congressional Quarterly Inc. 1995), p. 211.
15. Mackenthun and Bregman, p. 9; Freedman and Jaggi, p. 21.
16. Mackenthun and Bregman, p. 12.
17. Freedman and Jaggi, pp. 21–22.
18. Ibid.
19. Mackenthun and Bregman, p. 17.
20. Ibid.
21. Ibid., p. 18.
22. Love Canal refers to an environmental and social tragedy that occurred during the late 1970s in a residential neighborhood in Niagara Falls, New York. The Love Canal

neighborhood had been constructed on land that was heavily contaminated by toxic chemicals in the early 1950s. The chemical migrated below the surface of the land and allegedly caused community residents to suffer illnesses and even genetic damage. Over seven hundred families had to be moved from their homes and relocated at government expense because their properties had become unmarketable.

23. S. J. Buck, *Understanding Environmental Administration and Law* (Washington, D.C.: Island Press, 1991), p. 106.
24. Mackenthun and Bregman, pp. 21–22.
25. Ibid., pp. 22, 175–176.
26. Ibid., p. 23.
27. Ibid., p. 24.
28. Ibid., pp. 217–228.

XIV Alternative Dispute Resolution

Litigation is not the only mechanism available for the resolution of a dispute. Disputants who are unable to negotiate a solution to a pending conflict but who wish to avoid a public court trial can choose what is currently called alternative dispute resolution (ADR). ADR has gained in popularity largely because many people are dissatisfied with the workings of the traditional legal system. This dissatisfaction has many origins. Plaintiffs, in particular, dislike litigation's snail-like pace and complain about the volume of cases clogging up the court system and producing gridlock.[1] In federal district courts, for example, 250,907 civil cases were filed in 2001.[2]

Dissatisfaction also results when lawyers adopt a strategy of winning by exhausting an opponent's financial resources. Although case preparation generally will not compensate for a weak case, sometimes a weak case can be won if the client has vastly superior resources. An attorney may take such a case to trial in order to drag out the proceedings, dramatically increase the opponent's litigation expenses, and force the opponent to settle the case on unfavorable terms.

As a factual matter, a very small percentage of cases filed actually go to trial. The data from federal courts is illustrative. Of the 259,234 civil cases terminated in U.S. district courts during 2000, only 2.2 percent actually went to trial.[3] The percentage of federal cases reaching trial has actually been cut in half during the last twenty years.

Many attorneys, while acknowledging that few cases are actually resolved at trial, continue to prepare each case as if it will. They overprepare for a variety of professional and strategic reasons. Because litigation is an adversarial process, lawyers assume that opponents will resort to every legal device to win. Attorneys anticipate a continuing series of battles with the opponent at the pretrial, trial, and appellate stages of a process that can take years to determine an ultimate winner. They know that there are many ways to lose a case, and they worry about malpractice claims. Trial victories require more than good facts and sound legal arguments; they result from careful preparation and thorough discovery. Discovery also consumes large amounts of an attorney's time, which often translates into billable hours paid by the client.

The fact that lawyers become heavily involved in preparing attacks upon their client's opponent often means that they avoid looking at possible weaknesses in their own cases until just before trial. Lawyers often view themselves as their client's champion, and they frequently engage in posturing and puffery. Some refuse to initiate settlement discussions with the opponents because they fear that this might be interpreted by their clients as well as their client's opponents as a sign of weakness. If settlement discussions do occur, neither side is likely to be candid and reveal the amount that would be accepted in settlement of the case. Further, a tactical advantage can be gained by responding to an opponent's proposal rather than being the first to suggest a settlement figure. This gamelike approach to litigation only compounds costs in money and time as the parties prepare for a trial that statistically is unlikely to occur.

Many litigants often find the judicial system's traditional "winner-take-all" approach unsatisfactory because it produces a pyrrhic victory. Both parties can lose when the disputants have an ongoing relationship, as in business, labor-management, or child custody cases, and one party clobbers the other in court. Because ADR methods can often resolve disputes more satisfactorily than trials—at less expense and in less time—some lawyers are required to explain the existence of options to litigation to their clients.[4]

Businesses have been looking for ways to resolve disputes that avoid class action lawsuits and jury trials, which expose them to the possibility of high damage awards. Congress's enactment of the Alternative Dispute Resolution Act (1998), has increased judicial interest in ADR. In the ADRA, Congress explicitly required the federal district and courts of appeals to implement ADR procedures. Its reasoning is clearly explained in the excerpt found in Figure 14-1.

State courts also have been looking for cost-efficient ways to reduce the length of their burgeoning dockets, given the low percentage of their civil cases that are actually tried. California, Florida, and Texas, for example, have established statewide systems. Other states permit local jurisdictions to experiment with ADR if they wish to do so. Some jurisdictions offer a menu of ADR options; others focus on a preferred procedure, such as mediation or arbitration.[5]

Disputants participate in ADR either because they have been required to do so by legislation or court rule (court-annexed ADR).

VOLUNTARY ADR

When parties to a dispute decide to avoid the negative aspects of a court trial, they may voluntarily choose to resort to ADR, because it can often produce a fair result faster and at less cost than a public court trial. In fact, several major

---

Sec. 651. Authorization of alternative dispute resolution

(a) Definition.—For purposes of this chapter, an alternative dispute resolution process includes any process or procedure, other than an adjudication by a presiding judge, in which a neutral third party participates to assist in the resolution of issues in controversy, through processes such as early neutral evaluation, mediation, minitrial, and arbitration as provided in sections 654 through 658.

(b) Authority.—Each United States district court shall authorize, by local rule adopted under section 2071(a), the use of alternative dispute resolution processes in all civil actions, including adversary proceedings in bankruptcy, in accordance with this chapter, except that the use of arbitration may be authorized only as provided in section 654. Each United States district court shall devise and implement its own alternative dispute resolution program, by local rule adopted under section 2071(a), to encourage and promote the use of alternative dispute resolution in its district.

(c) Existing Alternative Dispute Resolution Programs.—In those courts where an alternative dispute resolution program is in place on the date of the enactment of the Alternative Dispute Resolution Act of 1998, the court shall examine the effectiveness of that program and adopt such improvements to the program as are consistent with the provisions and purposes of this chapter.

(d) Administration of Alternative Dispute Resolution Programs.—Each United States district court shall designate an employee, or a judicial officer, who is knowledgeable in alternative dispute resolution practices and processes to implement, administer, oversee, and evaluate the court's alternative dispute resolution program. Such person may also be responsible for recruiting, screening, and training attorneys to serve as neutrals and arbitrators in the court's alternative dispute resolution program. . . .

FIGURE 14-1   Excerpt from the Alternative Dispute Resolution Act of 1998. Public Law 105-315, 105th Congress

corporations will contract only with vendors who agree to participate in ADR. Disputants often prefer ADR because they can choose the procedure that seems most appropriate to their needs. They may also like having their dispute resolved by a person or persons who have particular expertise in that subject area.

When parties voluntarily participate in ADR, they negotiate a contract that sets forth the rules that will govern the proceedings. There are several agencies to which they can turn for model ADR rules and procedures. This is helpful because attorneys who are inexperienced with ADR are sometimes reluctant to negotiate an ADR agreement with a more seasoned opponent. Model rules are even-handed, and their terms provide either side with an advantage. They establish reasonable and simplified discovery rules and simplified rules of evidence that allow the parties to introduce documents that might otherwise be inadmissible hearsay. The rules also can provide for confidentiality: businesses and individuals often would prefer to deny competitors, the general public, and the news media access to private and potentially embarrassing information that would be revealed in conjunction with public court litigation.[6]

ADR practitioners and firms often advertise in trade publications and list themselves in many metropolitan-area telephone directories under "arbitration." To attract customers, increasing numbers of automobile manufacturers, local home contractors, businesses, and professionals advertise that they participate in ADR. The American Arbitration Association, and the Federal Conciliation and Mediation Service are prominent examples of institutions that maintain panels of arbitrators and impartial third parties (called neutrals) who can be engaged to provide ADR services. National dispute resolution firms have offices in major cities, have employed hundreds of retired judges (even state supreme court justices), and have annual revenues exceeding $40 million.[7]

COURT-ANNEXED ADR

Participation in ADR is legislatively or judicially authorized in many jurisdictions. The federal Alternative Dispute Resolution Act, for example, provides for ADR programs in both the U.S. District Courts and the U.S. Courts of Appeals.

Where federal and state judges claim authority to compel ADR participation, they usually promulgate court rules. Such rules are justified as being necessary and an appropriate exercise of a court's inherent power to manage its docket. Local rules often require that parties participate in nonbinding, court-annexed ADR programs before they are permitted access to a jury trial. Such programs encourage settlements, reduce court dockets, and lessen the financial burdens on taxpayers, who pay for the operation of the public judicial systems. The Alternative Dispute Resolution Act requires every federal district court to adopt at least one ADR method by local rule.

Most ADR methods are undertaken in the expectation that such programs will result in reducing the number of cases that are tried to juries. Any proposals to deny plaintiffs pursuing common law relief access to a trial by jury will clearly collide with the traditional right to a jury trial enshrined in the Seventh Amendment to the U.S. Constitution. The scope of the Seventh Amendment's jury trial right is deeply rooted in our history. Under our law, the right to a jury trial is recognized for all actions that were tried by English juries at the time of the Constitution's ratification and for other actions that are closely related to common law claims. There is no jury trial right for litigants who seek equitable relief or for actions that were unknown to the common law. Compulsory ADR has been structured so that there is no infringement of the right to a jury trial. Litigants are required to participate in pretrial ADR, but they can reject ADR solutions and then proceed to a trial by jury.

In the following case, the petitioner, Atlantic Pipe Corporation (APC), petitioned for a writ of prohibition from the district court's ruling that APC was required to participate in, and share in the cost of, court-annexed mediation, conducted by a neutral appointed by the court.

In Re Atlantic Pipe Corporation
304 F.3d 135
U.S. Court of Appeals, First Circuit
September 18, 2002

Selya, Circuit Judge

. . . January 1996, Thames-Dick Superaqueduct Partners (Thames-Dick) entered into a master agreement with the Puerto Rico Aqueduct and Sewer Authority (PRASA) to construct, operate, and maintain the North Coast Superaqueduct Project (the Project). Thames-Dick granted subcontracts for various portions of the work, including a subcontract for construction management to Dick Corp. of Puerto Rico (Dick-PR), a subcontract for the operation and maintenance of the Project to Thames Water International, Ltd. (Thames Water), and a subcontract for the fabrication of pipe to Atlantic Pipe Corp. (APC). After the Project had been built, a segment of the pipeline burst. Thames-Dick incurred significant costs in repairing the damage. Not surprisingly, it sought to recover those costs from other parties. In response, one of PRASA's insurers filed a declaratory judgment action in a local court to determine whether Thames-Dick's claims were covered under its policy. The litigation ballooned, soon involving a number of parties and a myriad of issues above and beyond insurance coverage. . . .

. . . Thames-Dick asked that the case be referred to mediation and suggested Professor Eric Green as a suitable mediator. The district court granted the motion over APC's objection and ordered non-binding mediation to proceed before Professor Green. . . . The court also stated that if mediation failed to produce a global settlement, the case would proceed to trial.

After moving unsuccessfully for reconsideration of the mediation order, APC . . . alleged that the district court did not have the authority to require mediation. . . . and, in all events, could not force APC to pay a share of the expenses of the mediation. We invited the other parties and the district judge to respond. . . . Several entities . . . opposed the petition. Two others . . . filed a brief in support of APC. We assigned the case to the oral argument calendar and stayed the contemplated mediation pending our review. . . .

The Merits

There are four potential sources of judicial authority for ordering mandatory non-binding mediation of pending cases, namely, (a) the court's local rules, (b) an applicable statute, (c) the Federal Rules of Civil Procedure, and (d) the court's inherent powers. Because the district court did not identify the basis of its assumed authority, we consider each of these sources.

A. The Local Rules.

A district court's local rules may provide an appropriate source of authority for ordering parties to participate in mediation. . . . In Puerto Rico, however, the local rules contain only a single reference to any form of alternative dispute resolution (ADR). That reference is embodied in the district court's Amended Civil Justice Expense and Delay Reduction Plan (CJR Plan). . . .

The district court adopted the CJR Plan on June 14, 1993, in response to the directive contained in the Civil Justice Reform Act of 1990 (CJRA), . . . Rule V of the CJR Plan states:

> Pursuant to 28 U.S.C. §§ 473(b)(4), this Court shall adopt a method of Alternative Dispute Resolution ("ADR") through mediation by a judicial officer. Such a program would allow litigants to obtain from an impartial third party—the judicial officer as mediator—a flexible non-binding, dispute resolution process to facilitate negotiations among the parties to help them reach settlement.

. . . In addition to specifying who may act as a mediator, Rule V also limns the proper procedure for mediation sessions and assures confidentiality. . . .

The respondents concede that the mediation order in this case falls outside the boundaries of the mediation program envisioned by Rule V . . . because it involves mediation before a private mediator, not a judicial officer. . . . APC argues that the . . . court exceeded its authority . . . by issuing a non-conforming mediation order (i.e., one that contemplates the intervention of a private mediator). The respondents counter by arguing that the rule does not bind the district court because, notwithstanding the unambiguous promise of the CJR Plan (which declares that the district court "shall adopt a method of Alternative Dispute Resolution"), no such program has been adopted to date.

This is a powerful argument. APC does not contradict the respondents' assurance that the relevant portion of the CJR Plan has remained unimplemented. . . . Because that is so, we conclude that the District of Puerto Rico has no local rule in force that dictates the permissible characteristics of mediation orders. Consequently, APC's argument founders. . . .

B. The ADR Act.

There is only one potential source of statutory authority for ordering mandatory non-binding mediation here: the Alternative Dispute Resolution Act of 1998 (ADR Act), 28 U.S.C. §§§§ 651–658. Congress passed the ADR Act to promote the utilization of alternative dispute resolution methods in the federal courts and to set appropriate guidelines for their use. The Act lists mediation as an appropriate ADR process. . . . Moreover, it sanctions the participation of "professional neutrals from the private sector" as mediators. . . . Finally, the Act requires district courts to obtain litigants' consent only when they order arbitration, . . . not when they order the use of other ADR mechanisms (such as non-binding mediation).

Despite the broad sweep of these provisions, the Act is quite clear that some form of the ADR procedures it endorses must be adopted in each judicial district by local rule. . . . (directing each district court to "devise and implement its own alternative dispute resolution program, by local rule adopted under [28 U.S.C.] section 2071(a), to encourage and promote the use of alternative dispute resolution in its district"). In the absence of such local rules, the ADR Act itself does not authorize any specific court to use a particular ADR mechanism. Because the District of Puerto Rico has not yet complied with the Act's mandate, the mediation order here at issue cannot be justified under the ADR Act. . . .

Although the ADR Act was designed to promote the use of ADR techniques, Congress chose a very well-defined path: it granted each judicial district, rather than each individual judge, the authority to craft an appropriate ADR program. In other words, Congress permitted experimentation, but only within the disciplining format of district-wide local rules adopted with notice and a full opportunity for public comment. . . . To say that the Act authorized each district judge to disregard a district-wide ADR plan (or the absence of one) and fashion innovative procedures for use in specific cases is simply too much of a stretch. . . .

We add, however, that . . . we know of nothing in either the ADR Act or the policies that undergird it that can be said to restrict the district courts' authority to engage in the case-by-case deployment of ADR procedures. Hence, we conclude that where, as here, there are no implementing local rules, the ADR Act neither authorizes nor prohibits the entry of a mandatory mediation order.

C. The Civil Rules.

The respondents next argue that the district court possessed the authority to require mediation by virtue of the Federal Rules of Civil Procedure. They concentrate their attention on Fed. R. Civ. P. 16, which states in pertinent part that "the court may take appropriate action with respect to . . . (9) settlement and the use of special procedures to assist in resolving the dispute when authorized by statute or local rule. . . ." . . . Because there is no statute or local rule authorizing mandatory private mediation in the District of Puerto Rico, . . . Rule 16(c)(9) does not assist the respondents' cause. . . .

D. Inherent Powers.

. . . [D]istrict courts have substantial inherent power to manage and control their calendars. . . . This inherent power takes many forms. . . . By way of illustration, a district court may use its inherent power to compel represented clients to attend pretrial settlement conferences, even though such a practice is not specifically authorized in the Civil Rules. . . .

Although many federal district courts have forestalled . . . debate by adopting local rules that authorize specific ADR procedures and outlaw others, . . . [because] the District of Puerto Rico is not among them . . . , we have no choice but to address the question head-on.

We begin our inquiry by examining the case law. In *Strandell v. Jackson County*, . . . (7th Cir. 1987), the Seventh Circuit held that a district court does not possess inherent power to compel participation in a summary jury trial. . . . In the court's view, Fed. R. Civ. P. 16 . . . prevented a district court from forcing "an unwilling litigant [to] be sidetracked from the normal course of litigation." . . . But the group that spearheaded the subsequent revision of Rule 16 explicitly rejected that interpretation. . . . Thus, we do not find *Strandell* persuasive on this point. . . .

. . . [T]he Sixth Circuit also has found that district courts do not possess inherent power to compel participation in summary jury trials. . . . The court thought the value of a summary jury trial questionable when parties do not engage in the process voluntarily, and

it worried that "too broad an interpretation of the federal courts' inherent power to regulate their procedure . . . encourages judicial high-handedness." . . .

The concerns articulated by these two respected courts plainly apply to mandatory mediation orders. When mediation is forced upon unwilling litigants, it stands to reason that the likelihood of settlement is diminished. Requiring parties to invest substantial amounts of time and money in mediation under such circumstances may well be inefficient. . . .

The fact remains, however, that none of these considerations establishes that mandatory mediation is always inappropriate. There may well be specific cases in which such a protocol is likely to conserve judicial resources without significantly burdening the objectors' rights to a full, fair, and speedy trial. Much depends on the idiosyncrasies of the particular case and the details of the mediation order.

In some cases, a court may be warranted in believing that compulsory mediation could yield significant benefits even if one or more parties object. After all . . . negotiations could well produce a beneficial outcome, at reduced cost and greater speed, than would a trial. While the possibility that parties will fail to reach agreement remains ever present, the boon of settlement can be worth the risk.

This is particularly true in complex cases involving multiple claims and parties. The fair and expeditious resolution of such cases often is helped along by creative solutions—solutions that simply are not available in the binary framework of traditional adversarial litigation. Mediation with the assistance of a skilled facilitator gives parties an opportunity to explore a much wider range of options, including those that go beyond conventional zero-sum resolutions. Mindful of these potential advantages, we hold that it is within a district court's inherent power to order non-consensual mediation in those cases in which that step seems reasonably likely to serve the interests of justice. . . .

E. The Mediation Order.

Our determination that the district courts have inherent power to refer cases to non-binding mediation is made with a recognition that any such order must be crafted in a manner that preserves procedural fairness and shields objecting parties from undue burdens. We thus turn to the specifics of the mediation order entered in this case. . . .

As an initial matter, we agree with the lower court that the complexity of this case militates in favor of ordering mediation. At last count, the suit involves twelve parties, asserting a welter of claims, counterclaims, cross-claims, and third-party claims predicated on a wide variety of theories. The pendency of nearly parallel litigation in the Puerto Rican courts, which features a slightly different cast of characters and claims that are related to but not completely congruent with those asserted here, further complicates the matter. Untangling the intricate web of relationships among the parties, along with the difficult and fact-intensive arguments made by each, will be time-consuming and will impose significant costs on the parties and the court. Against this backdrop, mediation holds out the dual prospect of advantaging the litigants and conserving scarce judicial resources.

In an effort to parry this thrust, APC raises a series of objections. . . . APC posits that the appointment of a private mediator proposed by one of the parties is per se improper (and, thus, invalidates the order). We do not agree. The district court has inherent power to "appoint persons unconnected with the court to aid judges in the performance of specific judicial duties." . . . In the context of non-binding mediation, the mediator does not decide the merits of the case and has no authority to coerce settlement. Thus, in the absence of a contrary statute or rule, it is perfectly acceptable for the district court to appoint a qualified and neutral private party as

a mediator. The mere fact that the mediator was proposed by one of the parties is insufficient to establish bias in favor of that party. . . .

We hasten to add that the litigants are free to challenge the qualifications or neutrality of any suggested mediator (whether or not nominated by a party to the case). APC, for example, had a full opportunity to present its views about the suggested mediator both in its opposition to the motion for mediation and in its motion for reconsideration of the mediation order. Despite these opportunities, APC offered no convincing reason to spark a belief that Professor Green, a nationally recognized mediator with significant experience in sprawling cases, is an unacceptable choice. When a court enters a mediation order, it necessarily makes an independent determination that the mediator it appoints is both qualified and neutral. Because the court made that implicit determination here in a manner that was procedurally fair (if not ideal), we find no abuse of discretion in its selection of Professor Green. . . .

APC also grouses that it should not be forced to share the costs of an unwanted mediation. We have held, however, that courts have the power under Fed. R. Civ. P. 26(f) to issue pretrial cost-sharing orders in complex litigation. . . .

The short of the matter is that, without default cost-sharing rules, the use of valuable ADR techniques (like mediation) becomes hostage to the parties' ability to agree on the concomitant financial arrangements. This means that the district court's inherent power to order private mediation in appropriate cases would be rendered nugatory absent the corollary power to order the sharing of reasonable mediation costs. To avoid this pitfall, we hold that the district court, in an appropriate case, is empowered to order the sharing of reasonable costs and expenses associated with mandatory non-binding mediation.

. . . [A] mediation order[,] [however,] must contain procedural and substantive safeguards to ensure fairness to all parties involved. The mediation order in this case does not quite meet that test. In particular, the order does not set limits on the duration of the mediation or the expense associated therewith. . . .

. . . As entered, the order . . . does not set forth either a timetable for the mediation or a cap on the fees that the mediator may charge. The figures that have been bandied about in the briefs—$900 per hour or $9,000 per mediation day—are quite large and should not be left to the mediator's whim. Relatedly, because the mediator is to be paid an hourly rate, the court should have set an outside limit on the number of hours to be devoted to mediation. Equally as important, it is trite but often true that justice delayed is justice denied. An unsuccessful mediation will postpone the ultimate resolution of the case—indeed, the district court has stayed all discovery pending the completion of the mediation—and, thus, prolong the litigation. For these reasons, the district court should have set a definite time frame for the mediation. . . .

To recapitulate, we rule that a mandatory mediation order issued under the district court's inherent power is valid in an appropriate case. We also rule that this is an appropriate case. We hold, however, that the district court's failure to set reasonable limits on the duration of the mediation and on the mediator's fees dooms the decree.

IV. Conclusion

We admire the district court's pragmatic and innovative approach to this massive litigation.

Our core holding—that ordering mandatory mediation is a proper exercise of a district court's inherent power, subject, however, to a variety of terms and conditions—validates that approach. We are mindful that this holding is in tension with the opinions of the Sixth and Seventh Circuits in NLO and Strandell, respectively, but we believe it is justified by the important goal of promoting flexibility and creative problem-solving in the handling of complex litigation.

That said, the need of the district judge in this case to construct his own mediation regime ad hoc underscores the greater need of the district court as an institution to adopt an ADR program and memorialize it in its local rules. In the ADR Act, Congress directed that "each United States district court shall authorize, by local rule under section 2071(a), the use of alternative dispute resolution processes in all civil actions. . . ." 28 U.S.C. §§ 651(b). While Congress did not set a firm deadline for compliance with this directive, the statute was enacted four years ago. This omission having been noted, we are confident that the district court will move expediently to bring the District of Puerto Rico into compliance.

We need go no further. For the reasons set forth above, we vacate the district court's mediation order and remand for further proceedings consistent with this opinion. The district court is free to order mediation if it continues to believe that such a course is advisable or, in the alternative, to proceed with discovery and trial.

Vacated and remanded. . . .

Case Questions

1. Should a court have the power to compel litigants to participate in (and pay for) mediation before permitting a jury trial? Isn't this a waste of time and money?
2. Did reading this case expose any problems with the Alternative Dispute Resolution Act?

3. What exactly did the Sixth Circuit Court of Appeals decide in this case? How did the court justify its decision?

ADR TECHNIQUES

The demand for trial-avoidance methods to resolve disputes has resulted in increasing reliance on settlement conferences, arbitration, and mediation—three of the oldest and the most popular ADR options—as well as the development of newer techniques such as private trials, mini-trials, and summary jury trials.

Settlement Conferences

Rule 1 of the Federal Rules of Civil Procedure states that judges are expected to promote "the just, speedy, and inexpensive determination of every action." This very general charge gives judges considerable flexibility in determining how they will achieve this goal. Many judges use settlement conferences, which are a traditional step in the litigation process, as an informal method for resolving a dispute without a trial.[8]

A judge who is willing to be assertive can help parties explore a lawsuit's settlement potential. The judge can initiate the process or respond to a request for assistance from one or more of the parties. This intervention can be helpful when neither of the opposing attorneys is willing to make the first move toward a settlement. The parties, however, often leap at an opportunity to discuss settlement if the judge broaches the subject. An assertive judge may personally convene a settlement conference, carefully review the case, and emphasize each side's weaknesses and strengths. This is important because the evidence is frequently inconclusive. A judge who is knowledgeable about the relevant law can be very influential. He or she can point out the costs of going to trial and emphasize the risks each side incurs by trying the matter to an unpredictable jury.[9] The judge may know about recent verdicts in similar cases that went to trial and may suggest ADR options that could help each side avoid the necessity of a trial. Some judges, if requested by the parties, will propose a settlement figure. Judges who have the time, skill, and interest to function as mediators may meet privately with each side, or with only the clients. They may even request that the clients meet without their attorneys being present. The judge's participation is the key ingredient. It is one thing for an attorney to engage in puffery with a client or an opponent. It is another matter to refuse to acknowledge the weaknesses of one's case to an experienced trial judge. Many judges, however, don't define their role in this way, believing that settlement is a matter to be decided solely by the parties without judicial involvement.

Serious issues arise regarding the judge's proper role in the settlement conference. Many lawyers are concerned that a party who refuses to settle may encounter bias if the matter is subsequently set for trial before the settlement judge. They fear that the judge might rule against the "uncooperative" party on motions and evidence admissibility at trial. One solution to this problem is to make sure that the judge conducting the settlement conference does not sit as the trial judge. Another is to use a lawyer-mediator instead of the judge at the settlement conference.

The Indiana Court of Appeals in the next case had to determine whether a trial judge had acted improperly in the conduct of a settlement conference between the parties.

Estate of John Skalka v. Mark Skalka
751 N.E.2d 769
Court of Appeals of Indiana
July 10, 2001

Mattingly-May, Judge

John "Jay" Skalka, Joseph Skalka, and Laura Ostergren appeal the trial court's order enforcing a settlement agreement made between them and Mark Skalka on November 16, 1999. . . .

Facts and Procedural History

John Skalka passed away on September 7, 1996. John "Jay" Skalka, Joseph Skalka, Laura Ostergren, and Mark Skalka are his surviving children. Prior to his death, John Skalka created a revocable living trust agreement in order to bequeath fifty acres of property, including a lake, to his children. The disposition of that lake property is the subject of this appeal.

Jay, Joseph, and Laura were unable to agree with Mark regarding the use of the property. Therefore, the three of them together filed a petition to partition the property with intent to sell it or buy Mark out should a complete partition not be successful. In a pretrial conference held on November 16, 1999, the parties discussed settlement. During that conference, the trial judge spoke with the parties in chambers for a period of time without their attorneys; then the attorneys joined their clients in chambers to make notes regarding an agreement reached by the parties. That agreement provided that Mark was to have ten of the fifty acres as well as an easement to use the lake; Jay, Joseph, and Laura were to share the remaining forty acres and also have use of the lake. Later that day, the attorney for Jay, Joseph, and Laura submitted to the court and to Mark's attorney a draft of the agreement for signing. The parties never signed the agreement.

In a status conference held on May 10, 2000, the trial judge reiterated his recollection of the agreement reached by the parties in chambers on November 16, 1999. Jay, Joseph, and Laura denied reaching that agreement, but Mark was in accord with the agreement. The trial judge took the matter under advisement, allowing the parties time to file trial briefs. The judge issued an order on August 25, 2000, putting in writing the agreement he reiterated on the record during the May 10, 2000, status conference. Jay, Joseph, and Laura objected, claiming they never agreed to the settlement during the pretrial conference and claiming that the trial judge's recollection of what occurred during the conference was inaccurate. This appeal followed. . . .

Discussion and Decision

The trial court made the following finding in its order dated August 25, 2000:

> 9.) That in the course of this litigation, the parties reached an oral settlement agreement at a pretrial conference held on . . . November 16, 1999 . . . in the presence of this Court as to the partition of the real estate and the disputes regarding estate (trust) assets and the payment of estate (trust) expenses and that the agreement was made part of the record of this Court. . . .

It is this finding with which Jay, Joseph, and Laura first take issue. They argue that the record is devoid of evidence that they accepted the settlement, and they suggest that the judge exerted pressure on them to accept the settlement when he met with them in chambers without their attorney present. "The acceptance of the trial court's recollection as a basis for enforcing an alleged settlement agreement is tantamount to the judge testifying against the Appellants and then making a finding of fact based on his own testimony." . . . They assert they were denied their day in court, as the agreement was entered as a final order without them having an opportunity to have an evidentiary hearing on the matter before the trial court.

The record contains sufficient evidence to support the trial court's finding that an agreement was reached at the pretrial conference. We note initially that the lack of a transcript of the settlement conference does not render the agreement unenforceable. Generally, a settlement agreement is not required to be in writing. . . . Here, the trial judge was present during the settlement discussions, and thus he heard the parties agree to the settlement. In addition, we find it particularly compelling that Jay, Joseph, and Laura's own counsel drafted a written version of the agreement that very afternoon after the conference and provided it to all parties and to the trial court. Thus, we are not persuaded by Jay, Joseph, and Laura's argument that the trial court's inaccurate memory is the only evidence in support of the agreement. . . .

Jay, Joseph, and Laura next argue that the judge improperly acted as a mediator during the pretrial conference on November 16, 1999. They note that the ADR rules prevent a judge from acting as a mediator. They also argue the pretrial conference agreement was nothing more than a failed attempt at mediation and thus should be considered under the Alternative Dispute Resolution rules. They point to the following statement by the judge in support of their argument:

> You know, we sat in my chambers, people, and you walked out of my office in agreement. Alright. I did as much as I could possibly do to resolve the conflict. But if you people want to continue fighting, I'm no longer going to be the *mediator* here, I'm going to be a judge. You are going to go through the cost of this thing. It's going to be financially draining and I can tell you you're going to wind up losing the property. . . .

However, we find that this statement merely indicates the trial judge was attempting, in his role as judge, to assist the parties in reaching a settlement of their disputes, not that he was seeking to act as a mediator in a mediation governed by the Alternative Discipline Resolution (ADR) rules. Mark's brief contains an especially apt description of the trial court's actions: the trial judge was simply "entertaining settlement discussion at a pretrial conference." . . . Generally, the purpose of a pretrial conference is to narrow the issues for trial; in this case, all the issues were resolved at the pretrial conference. As this was a pretrial conference and not a mediation, the judge did not act improperly. The case before us brings into relief the potential for conflict between a judge's traditional role as decision-maker and a court's well-intentioned attempts to encourage and facilitate less-formal resolution of disputes by the parties themselves. A court's readiness to take advantage of the various options offered by the Indiana Alternative Dispute Resolution rules might help to avoid situations like this one where, as a result of a judge's diligent efforts to bring about settlement among the parties, "no good deed goes unpunished." . . .

Next, Jay, Joseph, and Laura note that the trial judge met with the parties in chambers for a period of time without their attorneys present; after a settlement was reached, the judge called the attorneys into his chambers to review the agreement along with their clients. They suggest they were subjected to undue pressure from the trial judge to settle during this meeting. While this method of attempting to resolve a dispute is perhaps somewhat unorthodox, we find no impropriety . . . in this action by the court. Indeed, Jay, Joseph, and Laura's attorney drew up settlement documents immediately following the conference, an action we imagine he would not have taken had he suspected any undue influence had been exerted on his clients. . . .

Affirmed.

Case Questions

1. Jay, Joseph, and Laura alleged that the trial judge acted improperly in conducting the settlement conference. What was the nature of the wrongful conduct?
2. How did the appellate court rule and why?

Arbitration

Arbitration is the most used form of ADR[10] and was in existence long before the emergence of the English common law.[11] It was well known in the eighteenth century, and George Washington's will even contained an arbitration clause in the event that disputes arose between his heirs.[12] American courts were traditionally opposed to arbitration awards because the parties had rejected the judicial system and had chosen to settle their disputes privately. Many judges believed that people who chose arbitration over the judicial system should not be entitled to come to the judiciary for enforcement of nonjudicial decisions. In the 1925 Federal Arbitration Act, however, Congress established a national policy favoring the arbitration of commercial transactions. In the act, Congress provided that arbitration contracts "shall be valid, irrevocable, and enforceable save upon such grounds as exist at law or equity for the revocation of any contract" and required that courts enforce most arbitration awards.[13] The Labor Management Relations Act of 1947 extended the use of arbitration to disputes arising out of collective bargaining, and the U.S. Supreme Court has gone along with Congress and the executive branch in generally supporting the expansion of this and other forms of ADR.[14]

INTERNET TIP ————————————————————————————————

But the Court has also shown its willingness to deviate from its pro-arbitration policy on occasion. The recently decided case, *Equal Employment Opportunity Commission v. Waffle House, Inc.* (2002), can be read on the textbook's website.

Some disputants end up in arbitration because it is required by a court-annexed program or as a condition of being employed. In other instances, parties contract to submit their disputes to an arbitrator for resolution.

Voluntary Arbitration

Voluntary arbitration is increasingly used to resolve business disputes because it provides prompt decisions at a reasonable cost. The voluntary arbitration process is very different from the judicial process. In voluntary arbitrations, for example, the arbitrator makes a binding decision on the merits of the dispute and can base his or her decision on a lay or business sense of justice rather than on the rules of law that would be applied in court. A private arbitration proceeds pursuant to a contract in which the parties promise to bind themselves to arbitrate their controversy and abide by the arbitrator's decision (which is called an *award*). Because a person who chooses to arbitrate waives the right to a jury trial, arbitration agreements must be in writing to be enforceable in court. Some parties agree to arbitrate their agreements prior to the existence of any dispute.[15] Contracts between unions and management, investors and stock brokers,[16] and banks and their customers,[17] often include arbitration clauses. Many major corporations routinely include arbitration clauses in contracts they make with their suppliers. Arbitration agreements can also be negotiated after a controversy has arisen.

Arbitrators are selected by agreement of the parties. The nonprofit American Arbitration Association has been a supplier of arbitrators since 1926.[18] Arbitrators in business disputes are often chosen because of their expertise in a specific field. This better enables them to render a reasonable and proper decision. This should be contrasted with the trial decisions that are made by a randomly selected judge and jury. The parties can choose a person who they believe will conduct the proceedings fairly and with integrity. However, the legal continuity of the judicial system is not necessarily present in a voluntary arbitration. Arbitrators, for example, do not have to follow precedent in their decision-making process, nor do they have to prepare written explanations for their award (although they often do both).

Each arbitration hearing is convened for the sole purpose of deciding a particular dispute. Arbitration hearings are often conducted in hotels, motels, and offices and, unlike court trials, are generally not open to the public. Although the formalities of a court proceeding need not be followed, arbitration hearings usually follow the sequence of opening statements by the opposing parties, direct and cross-examination of the witnesses, introduction of exhibits, and closing arguments. Arbitrators base their decisions on the evidence and the arguments made before them. However, they are generally not bound by the rules of evidence used in litigation.

Although the parties to an arbitration usually comply with the terms of the arbitrator's award, judicial enforcement action can be taken against a party who reneges.

Shelly Sullivan, the plaintiff at trial, sought to litigate rather than arbitrate her claims against a pest control company. The company contended that Sullivan had contractually agreed to arbitrate any claims she might have and thus the lawsuit should be abated.

Sears Authorized Termite and Pest Control, Inc. v. Shelly J. Sullivan
816 So. 2d 603
Supreme Court of Florida
May 2, 2002

Wells, C. J.

We have for review the . . . issue of whether a provision requiring arbitration in an agreement to provide exterminating services for pests, including spiders, includes claims for personal injury allegedly caused by being bitten by spiders which were to be eradicated in the performance of the agreement. . . .

In this case, petitioner Sears Authorized Termite & Pest Control, Inc. (Sears) and respondent Shelly Sullivan (Sullivan) executed a pest control agreement in which Sears agreed to provide services for the control of various pests, including spiders. Sullivan filed suit, essentially alleging in her complaint that Sears treated and retreated for spiders but failed to control the population of spiders at her residence. The failure to control the population of spiders resulted in Sullivan being bitten by spiders, causing her personal injuries and damages. Sears responded by moving to abate and compel arbitration based upon the following arbitration provision in the pest control agreement:

Arbitration

The purchaser and . . . Sears Authorized Termite & Pest Control agree that any controversy or claim between them arising out of or related to the interpretation, performance or breach of any provision of this agreement shall be settled exclusively by arbitration. This contract/agreement is subject to arbitration pursuant to the Uniform Arbitration Act of the American Arbitration Association. The arbitration award may be entered in any court having jurisdiction. In no event shall either party be liable to the other for indirect, special or consequential damages or loss of anticipated profits.

The trial judge held a hearing and entered an order granting Sears' motion. In his order the trial judge stated:

The key case seems to be *Seifert v. U.S. Home Corporation*, ... The two closest cases to the present case are *Terminix International Company v. Michaels*, . . . (Fla. 4th DCA 1996), and *Terminix International Company v. Ponzio*, . . . (Fla. 5th DCA 1997).

The present case hinges on an arbitration provision in a pest control customer agreement. The Court's view of the pertinent portion of the agreement is that: regarding any provision of this contract for which a controversy exists concerning its interpretation, performance or breach, arbitration is required. The Court analyzes the pertinent provisions of the contract to require the pest control company to provide necessary service for the control of spiders. The allegations in this complaint are essentially that the pest control company treated and retreated for spiders but failed to control the spiders. The counts are counts for breach of warranty which are clearly contractual counts and counts for negligence, fraud in the inducement, fraud, and negligent misrepresentation.

This case differs from *Michaels* in that *Michaels* had to do with the use of ultra hazardous chemicals. A general duty is imposed on the producer and distributor of hazardous chemicals which is independent of and unrelated to any contractual obligations. Personal injuries claimed in that case were the result of poisoning from these ultra hazardous chemicals. In the present case the cause of action is based on the inability of the pest control services to effectively poison the spiders. In *Michaels* the duty to avoid poisoning persons with ultra hazardous chemicals existed whether or not there was a contract between the parties.

Ponzio is factually like the present case in that it was a lawsuit on a pest control contract for failure to eradicate brown recluse spiders, the same spiders in the present case. Like *Ponzio* . . . the allegations of the present complaint are that the pest control service had a duty to control certain pests and that it failed to do so resulting in bodily injury. There is no assertion of strict liability or of a failure to warn and the claims and controversy herein derive from the contract.

Seifert is the most important case. It involves an inherently dangerous design of an air conditioning system so that carbon monoxide gas from a vehicle in the garage circulated through the house and killed Mr. Seifert. The court held that the tort claim related to duties wholly independent of the agreement by the builder to construct the house. *Seifert* recognized that carbon monoxide poisoning was not related to any of the contemplated terms of the contract. In the present case the contemplated

terms of the contract call for the control of spiders. The issue is whether the spiders were properly controlled or not. This at least, raises some issue, the resolution of which requires a reference to or construction of a portion of the contract, namely the portion that obligates the pest control service to control the pests. It involves a disagreement or a controversy relating to the performance or breach of this requirement of the contract as well as the interpretation of how much treatment was necessary in order to effectuate control of the pests.

Unlike an ultra hazardous chemical, or a latent fatally dangerous condition in a home, the present condition is not one imposed by general law or public policy but arises from the contract in question. The obligation is based on a new duty that did not exist without the contract. The tort claims are therefore directly related to the contract. The contract explicitly refers to the control of spiders. It is not necessary to stretch the scope of the arbitration clause in order to encompass these claims. Consequently the arbitration clause is not interfering with a right to jury trial since arbitration clauses are enforceable and favored when the disagreement falls within the scope of the arbitration agreement. . . .

. . . [T]he . . . Court of Appeal . . . reversed. . . . [I]t . . . found that *Seifert* and *Michaels* should be read to mean that Sullivan's claim for personal injuries and damages resulting from the spider bites were not covered by the arbitration provision. . . .

In this case, it is clear that the intent of the agreement was to "control" spiders, among other "pests." Thus, Sullivan's cause of action rests upon the failure to perform the agreement. The plain language of this arbitration clause covers the "performance" of the agreement. This clearly is distinct from *Seifert*, in which we specifically held: "The tort claim filed in this case neither relies on the agreement nor refers to any provision within the agreement. Rather, the petitioner's tort claim relates to duties wholly independent from the agreement." . . . We likewise find this case to be distinguishable from the Fourth District Court of Appeal's decision in *Michaels,* in which the factual allegation was based on the use of ultra-hazardous chemicals. . . . Rather, we find this case to be similar to the Fifth District Court of Appeal's decision in *Ponzio.*

Accordingly, we quash the Fourth District Court of Appeal's decision in Sullivan, approve *Ponzio* to the extent it is consistent with this opinion, and remand this case with instructions that the trial court's order compelling arbitration be affirmed.

It is so ordered.

Case Questions

1. Why does the Florida Supreme Court reverse the Court of Appeals?
2. How were the *Seifert* and *Michaels* cases distinguished on their facts from the facts of the *Sullivan* case?

Judicial Review of Arbitration Awards

Either party to an arbitration may institute a court action seeking *confirmation* (judicial enforcement) or modification of the award. Federal and state laws provide for jurisdiction in specified courts to (1) recognize and enforce arbitration, (2) provide standards of conduct for arbitration hearings, (3) make arbitration agreements irrevocable, and (4) provide that court action cannot be initiated until the arbitration has concluded.

Courts have limited powers when reviewing an arbitration award. They will usually confirm the award unless the arbitrator violated the terms of the arbitration contract, the arbitration procedures offended fundamental due process, or the award violated public policy. The reviewing court will not review an arbitrator's findings of fact.

The arbitration agreement in the following case contained a clause which permitted either party to seek judicial review of the legal and factual sufficiency of the arbitrator's award.

Ronald Crowell v. Downey Community Hospital Foundation
B148291.
Court of Appeal of California
January 28, 2002

agreement validly agree that an arbitration award is subject to judicial review to determine whether the award is supported by law and substantial evidence? . . .

Factual and Procedural Background

Doi Todd, J.

This appeal presents an important question of first impression: Can parties to an arbitration

Ronald Crowell, M.D., a professional corporation, appeals from a judgment of dismissal pursuant to an order granting defendant

Downey Community Hospital Foundation's (DCHF) general demurrer without leave to amend his complaint. The complaint sought a declaration of rights as to the enforceability of an arbitration provision which explicitly required that (1) the arbitrator make findings of fact and conclusions of law, (2) the award be supported by law and substantial evidence, and (3) the merits of the award be subject to court review.

Crowell and DCHF entered into an "Agreement to Provide Hospital Emergency Department Services" effective January 1, 1996 through December 31, 1997. The agreement required arbitration of certain disputes in accordance with the provisions of the California Arbitration Act (Act), . . . except that the arbitrator was required to prepare written findings of fact and conclusions of law which "shall be supported by law and substantial evidence." The parties agreed that the decision of the arbitrator was to be final and binding except that "upon the petition of any party to the arbitration, a court shall have the authority to review the transcript of the arbitration proceedings and the arbitrator's award and shall have the authority to vacate the arbitrator's award, in whole or in part, on the basis that the award is not supported by substantial evidence or is based upon an error of law. . . ."

In March 1998, DCHF notified Crowell to cease operations. Crowell demanded arbitration pursuant to the agreement. Although contending the agreement had expired, DCHF nonetheless expressly agreed in writing "to arbitrate the disputes identified in [Crowell's letters demanding arbitration] under the terms specified in the expired agreement."

The arbitration was not immediately initiated. Instead, after an unexplained lapse of more than two years, Crowell filed a complaint for declaratory relief seeking a judicial determination that the arbitration agreement was "valid and enforceable" and that the par-

ties were "obligated, forthwith, to arbitrate in accordance with their agreement."

DCHF demurred to the complaint on the grounds that the arbitration agreement was "void and unenforceable as a matter of law" and because declaratory relief was "not necessary or proper under all the circumstances pursuant to [section] 1061." It argued that judicial review of private arbitration awards was limited to cases where statutory grounds existed to vacate or correct the award and that declaratory relief was unnecessary "to enforce an illegal contract."

The trial court sustained the demurrer without leave to amend, issuing the following minute order: "Defendant contends that the parties agreed to do something that does not exist, conduct a Code of Civil Procedure Section 1280 et seq. arbitration with a guaranteed right of judicial review of the merits, making the arbitration clause at issue unenforceable. The relief requested by Plaintiff is neither 'necessary nor proper' under Code of Civil Procedure 1061."

Judgment of dismissal of the complaint was subsequently entered and a timely notice of appeal from that judgment filed.

Contentions

Appellant contends that binding arbitration is essentially a matter of contract between the parties, and that while sections 1286.2 and 1286.6 specify grounds on which a court may vacate or correct an arbitration award, these are merely default provisions which control when the parties do not agree otherwise. Respondent contends that the arbitration agreement is void and unenforceable as a matter of law because jurisdiction to review arbitration awards is conferred by the Act, which provides the exclusive grounds on which courts are authorized to vacate or correct an award, and the parties cannot broaden review by agreement. Both parties find support for their claims in the Supreme

Court's decision in *Moncharsh v. Heily & Blase* (1992) . . . (*Moncharsh*).

Discussion

A. The Agreement Provided for Court Review of the Arbitration Award on the Merits.

Private arbitration is a matter of agreement between the parties and is governed by contract law. . . . Arbitration agreements are to be construed like other contracts to give effect to the intention of the parties. . . . "In cases involving private arbitration, '[t]he scope of arbitration is . . . a matter of agreement between the parties.' . . ."

Here, there is no dispute that the parties agreed to an arbitration process that required findings of fact and conclusions of law and purported to authorize judicial review on the merits.

B. The Parties Cannot Expand the Trial Court's Jurisdiction to Review Arbitration Awards by Agreement.

Because the parties clearly agreed to the arbitration provision here, the issue we must decide is a narrow one: Can the parties expand the scope of judicial review of an arbitration award by agreement? We have found no California case deciding this issue, but there is substantial support in the Act and in cases interpreting the Act that they cannot.

Moncharsh

The Supreme Court's most expansive discussion of the scope of judicial review of arbitration awards is contained in *Moncharsh*. Although it does not specifically deal with an arbitration provision allowing judicial review of the merits of an award, *Moncharsh* provides guidance in resolving this issue.

In *Moncharsh [v. Heily & Blase]*, Moncharsh, an attorney, was hired by a law firm

and signed an employment agreement that provided for the allocation of legal fees in the event he left the firm. The agreement contained an arbitration clause that provided: "Any dispute arising out of this Agreement shall be subject to arbitration under the rules of the American Arbitration Association. No arbitrator shall have any power to alter, amend, modify or change the terms of this agreement. The decision of the arbitrator shall be final and binding on Firm and Employee-attorney." . . . Moncharsh subsequently left the firm, and a dispute arose as to the allocation of fees he received from former firm clients who left the firm with him. The parties invoked the arbitration provision and submitted the matter to an arbitrator, who ruled in the firm's favor, stating his conclusions in the award.

Moncharsh petitioned the superior court to vacate the award, and the law firm petitioned to confirm it. The superior court ruled that "'[t]he arbitrator's findings on questions of both law and fact are conclusive. A court cannot set aside an arbitrator's error of law no matter how egregious.'" . . . While the court acknowledged an exception for error appearing on the face of the award, it found no such error. . . . The Court of Appeal affirmed.

The Supreme Court recognized that the Act "represents a comprehensive statutory scheme regulating private arbitration in this state." . . . "'The policy of the law in recognizing arbitration agreements and in providing by statute for their enforcement is to encourage persons who wish to avoid delays incident to a civil action to obtain an adjustment of their differences by a tribunal of their own choosing.'" . . . "Expanding the availability of judicial review of such decisions 'would tend to deprive the parties of the arbitration agreement of the very advantages the process is intended to produce.' . . . Ensuring arbitral finality thus requires that judicial intervention in the arbitration process be minimized." . . .

The court expressed a strong concern that judicial intervention in the arbitral process be minimized to ensure that the benefits of arbitration were not lost. It surveyed nearly 150 years of the legal history of arbitration in California. It observed that "because an arbitrator is not ordinarily constrained to decide according to the rule of law, it is the general rule that, 'The merits of the controversy between the parties are not subject to judicial review.' . . . More specifically, courts will not review the validity of the arbitrator's reasoning. . . . Further, a court may not review the sufficiency of the evidence supporting an arbitrator's award. . . ."

The court noted that at early common law, in the absence of statutes, courts sitting as courts of equity would set aside arbitration awards for mistakes of fact or law. After adoption of the first statute, in 1851 which did not permit review, the courts "concluded the grounds for vacating an award were exclusively those set forth by statute" with a narrow exception for errors "'spread upon the record'" affecting a "'palpable and material point.'" . . .

The 1927 amendments to the Act provided several additional grounds for vacating an arbitrator's award. . . . The cases after the amendments continued to hold that "The merits of the controversy between the parties are not subject to judicial review." . . . In *Crowfoot v. Blair Holdings Corp.* (1953) . . . , the court concluded that after the 1927 amendments to the Act, written agreements to arbitrate were governed exclusively by statute and there was "no field for a common law arbitration to operate." . . . After noting differences between common law and statutory arbitration, *Crowfoot* concluded that "by the adoption of the 1927 statute, the Legislature intended to adopt a comprehensive all-inclusive statutory scheme applicable to all written agreements to arbitrate, and that in such cases the doctrines applicable to a common law arbitration were abolished." . . .

Moncharsh concluded that the statutory bases for vacating and correcting arbitration awards are exclusive. Permitting parties to expand that review by agreement would undermine the benefits of arbitration and the goals of the Act to reduce expense and delay in resolving disputes. The Act clearly "limit[s] judicial review of private arbitration awards to those cases in which there exists a statutory ground to vacate or correct the award." . . .

The California Arbitration Act

The Act also suggests that limitation on judicial review was intended by the Legislature. Sections 1286.2 and 1286.6 set forth grounds for vacating and correcting arbitration awards. Former section 1286.2 provided: "Subject to Section 1286.4, the court shall vacate the award if the court determines any of the following:

(a) The award was procured by corruption, fraud, or other undue means.
(b) There was corruption in any of the arbitrators.
(c) The rights of the party were substantially prejudiced by misconduct of a neutral arbitrator.
(d) The arbitrators exceeded their powers and the award cannot be corrected without affecting the merits of the decision upon the controversy submitted.
(e) The rights of the party were substantially prejudiced by the refusal of the arbitrators to postpone the hearing upon sufficient cause being shown therefore or by the refusal of the arbitrators to hear evidence material to the controversy or by other conduct of the arbitrators contrary to the provisions of this title.
(f) An arbitrator making the award was subject to disqualification upon grounds specified in Section 1281.9 but failed upon receipt of timely demand to disqualify himself or herself as required by that provision." . . .

Section 1286.6 provides that the court shall correct an award if it determines:

"(a)There was an evident miscalculation of figures or an evident mistake in the description of any person, thing or property referred to in the award;

(b) The arbitrators exceeded their powers but the award may be corrected without affecting the merits of the decision upon the controversy submitted; or

(c) The award is imperfect in a matter of form, not affecting the merits of the controversy."

None of the grounds for vacating or correcting an award suggests that a court can review the merits of an award for errors of law or lack of adequate supporting evidence.

There is further evidence the Legislature did not intend that an arbitration award could be reviewed on its merits, even by the parties' agreement. Section 1296, under title 9.2, headed "Public Construction Contract Arbitration," PROVIDES: "The parties to a construction contract with a public agency may expressly agree in writing that in any arbitration to resolve a dispute relating to the contract, the arbitrator's award shall be supported by law and substantial evidence. If the agreement so provides, a court shall, subject to Section 1286.4, vacate the award if after review of the award it determines either that the award is not supported by substan-

tial evidence or that it is based on an error of law." Here, the Legislature specifically authorized the parties to agree to a review of the merits of a construction contract arbitration. No such review is authorized for other forms of arbitration in the Act. This suggests the legislative intent that parties cannot agree to a review on the merits. If that were not the case section 1296 would be superfluous. . . .

Furthermore, with respect to the scope of the arbitration and the procedures applicable to the actual arbitration, the Legislature has explicitly provided that the parties can agree for themselves on the powers of arbitrators . . . , the conduct of arbitration proceedings . . . , discovery . . . , and time for making an award. . . .

Because the Legislature clearly set forth the trial court's jurisdiction to review arbitration awards when it specified grounds for vacating or correcting awards in sections 1286.2 and 1286.6, we hold that the parties cannot expand that jurisdiction by contract to include a review on the merits.

Disposition

The judgment is affirmed.

Case Question

Why did the California Supreme Court rule that the parties to a private arbitration cannot by contract confer jurisdiction on any court to judicially review arbitration awards beyond what is provided for by statute? Does this ruling seem consistent with the earlier discussion of subject matter jurisdiction in Chapter 3?

Court-Annexed Arbitration

Court-annexed arbitration includes both voluntary and mandatory procedures. Mandatory arbitrations, however, for reasons founded in the right to jury trial contained in both federal and state constitutions, can only produce nonbinding decisions. The type of cases that can be arbitrated is increasingly determined by statute, but in many jurisdictions is determined pursuant to local court rules. Traditionally, arbitrations are most common in commercial, personal injury, and property damage cases, in which the amount does not exceed a designated sum. That sum, called the jurisdictional amount, varies by jurisdiction.

The rules of arbitration often provide for limited discovery and modified rules of evidence. In brief, trial-like hearings lasting only a few hours, attorneys offer documentary evidence, present witness testimony, and cross-examine opposing witnesses. Arbitrators, often retired judges and local attorneys, are selected in various ways. In some courts, the clerk of court randomly assigns arbitrators. In other jurisdictions the parties, themselves, participate in the selection process.

Arbitrators listen to the presentations, ask questions of the presenters, and determine the liability and damages issues. They generally do not make findings of fact or conclusions of law (as would judges in bench trials), and depending on local practice, may or may not attempt to mediate the dispute, critique the parties, or propose settlement terms.

An arbitrator's award becomes a final judgment unless the parties reject it within a prescribed period of time and demand a traditional jury trial (called a *trial de novo*). Unless the trial judgment exceeds the arbitration award, a party demanding a trial de novo often will be penalized and required to pay the arbitration costs.

The following case contains a discussion of the rights of the parties to a court-annexed arbitration proceeding to reject the arbitrator's decision and insist on a trial de novo.

**Allstate Insurance Company v.
    A. William Mottolese**
803 A.2d 311
Supreme Court of Connecticut
August 20, 2002

Sullivan, C. J.

This case is before us on a writ of error brought by the named plaintiff in error, Allstate Insurance Company (plaintiff), . . . the insurer of the defendant in the underlying action, seeking reversal of an order of the trial court, *Mottolese. J.,* the defendant in error (trial court), imposing sanctions against the plaintiff pursuant to Practice Book §§ 14-13. The dispositive issue in this case is whether a party's proper exercise of its right to a trial de novo . . . following a nonbinding arbitration proceeding may serve as the grounds for the imposition of sanctions under Practice Book §§ 14-13. . . .

The plaintiff claims that the trial court's order of sanctions against it is void because it is not a party to the underlying action and never consented to the court's personal jurisdiction over it. Further, the plaintiff contends that: (1) the trial court violated its due process rights by failing to give notice that that court would be considering whether to impose sanctions upon the plaintiff for its refusal to increase its settlement offer; and (2) the order of sanctions was an improper attempt by the trial court to coerce and intimidate the plaintiff to settle the underlying defendant's case and, as such, violated the underlying defendant's constitutional right of access to the courts. We agree that, under the circumstances of this case, the plaintiff's conduct, which was grounded in its insured's exercise of his right to a trial de novo, cannot serve as the basis for an order of sanctions, and we reverse the order sanctioning the plaintiff.

The record discloses the following relevant facts and procedural history. In December, 1997, Robert Morgan filed the underlying action against David Distasio, the plaintiff's insured, to recover damages for injuries sustained in a December 5, 1995 automobile accident. . . . After a pretrial conference at which no settlement was reached, the trial court referred the case to nonbinding arbitration . . . the court annexed arbitration program. In December, 1999, the arbitrator issued a memorandum of decision in which he found . . . that Distasio negligently had rear-ended Morgan's vehicle, that Morgan had sustained minor physical injuries and property damage, and that judgment should be rendered in favor of Morgan in the amount of $2450. Distasio thereafter timely filed a claim for a trial de novo . . . requesting that the trial court vacate the arbitration award and restore the case to the jury trial list.

On April 4, 2001, a pretrial conference was held before the trial court, Mottolese, J. The trial court continued the conference to April 11, 2001, with the instruction that Distasio produce his insurance claims representative on that date. On April 11, 2001, Distasio, Morgan and their respective counsel, along with the claims representative for the plaintiff, Stephen Coppa, appeared before the court in accordance with a written notice of pretrial conference. Coppa acknowledged that the plaintiff had made its initial settlement offer of $2050 to Morgan after evaluating the case, and that, at the time the offer was made, he had told Morgan that the offer was final. After discussion, the trial court found that the plaintiff's refusal "to pay anything more than $2050 . . . is conduct which may fairly be characterized as unfair and in bad faith." The trial court further stated that "this court deems [the plaintiff's] refusal to participate in a resolution of this case in a reasonable manner as the functional equivalent of a failure to attend a pretrial," and that "it's unreasonable for any insurance carrier, any tortfeasor, to require judicial resources to be put in place and for thousands and thousands of taxpayers' money to be expended in order to save you, [the plaintiff], $400.00." The trial court held that the plaintiff's conduct was an "unwarranted imposition upon scarce judicial resources . . . a gross abuse of the civil justice system; and [that it made] a mockery of Connecticut's court annexed arbitration program." Accordingly, pursuant to Practice Book §§ 14-13, . . . the trial court awarded Morgan attorney's fees of $250 for the April 4 pretrial conference and $250 for the April 11 hearing.

Distasio moved for articulation, requesting that the trial court clarify whether the ruling on attorney's fees was directed at the plaintiff, Distasio or Distasio's counsel. In response, the trial court appointed H. James Pickerstein, an attorney, "as a special master to conduct discovery on behalf of the court and to assist the court in preparing its articulation." The court ordered that the scope of discovery was to include, but not be limited to, the plaintiff's settlement policies and practices as they related to the underlying case, the extent to which Distasio's counsel had participated in the settlement process, and the policies and practices of the court annexed arbitration program and de novo trials. . . .

. . . Distasio filed an appeal in the Appellate Court challenging the appointment of the special master.

In the meantime, the plaintiff moved for permission to amend the writ to address the sanction order. . . .

The plaintiff claims that the order of sanctions was an improper attempt to coerce and intimidate it into settling the matter, thereby violating its constitutional right to a trial by jury. Specifically, the plaintiff argues that Distasio's assertion of his statutory right to a trial de novo following the court-ordered nonbinding arbitration proceeding preserved his right to a trial by jury guaranteed by the Connecticut constitution, and that a party's decision not to be bound by an arbitrator's decision regarding settlement cannot be the basis for the imposition of sanctions under Practice Book §§ 14-13.

Conversely, the trial court argues that, because the arbitrator's award of $2450 in damages was a mere $400 more than the plaintiff was originally willing to pay, the plaintiff took a defiant approach to the settlement process that was interpreted by the trial court as being disrespectful to it, harmful to the opposing party and implicitly contemptuous. The trial court further argues that it is within that court's inherent authority to sanction all who appear before it whose actions may be characterized as unfair and in bad faith.

We agree with the plaintiff and conclude that Distasio's exercise of his right to file for a trial de novo after the completion of arbitration proceedings cannot provide the basis for sanctions pursuant to Practice Book §§ 14-13. Accordingly, we conclude that the trial court abused its discretion when it sanctioned the plaintiff. . . .

We begin with a review of the nonbinding arbitration program. Section 52-549u permits the judges of the Superior Court to refer certain civil actions to an arbitrator for nonbinding arbitration. The arbitrator's decision, however, is not binding on the parties and does not limit either party's access to a trial. . . . Pursuant to §§ 52-549z (d) and Practice Book §§ 23-66 (c), a party that participated in nonbinding arbitration may appeal from the arbitrator's decision by requesting a trial de novo, in which case the arbitrator's decision becomes null and void.

The statutory right to a trial de novo has its underpinnings in the Connecticut constitution. "Article IV of the amendments to the constitution of Connecticut provides, inter alia, that the right of trial by jury shall remain inviolate. It is clear that the right to a jury trial may not be abolished as to causes triable to the jury prior to the constitution of 1818, and extant at the time of its adoption. . . . Nevertheless, such a right may be subjected to reasonable conditions and regulations. . . . The provision by the legislature for an alternative means of dispute resolution through the use of arbitrators to hear cases claimed

for jury trial was but part of an effort to alleviate court congestion. . . . The right to a trial by jury in these cases is preserved inviolate by General Statutes §§ 52-549z and Practice Book §§ [23-66]. Each of these sections provides for a claim for a trial de novo within twenty days of the filing of the arbitrator's decision. Once a claim for trial de novo is filed in accordance with the rules, a decision of an arbitrator becomes null and void." . . .

Although both parties to the arbitration have an inviolable right to a trial de novo, that right is subject to reasonable conditions and regulations. . . . Attendance at a pretrial hearing is one such condition. Thus, Practice Book §§ 14-13 provides in relevant part that "when a party against whom a claim is made is insured, an insurance adjuster for such insurance company shall be available by telephone at the time of such pretrial session unless the judge . . . in his or her discretion, requires the attendance of the adjuster at the pretrial. If any person fails to attend or to be available by telephone pursuant to this rule, the judicial authority may make such order as the ends of justice require, which may include the entry of a nonsuit or default against the party failing to comply and an award to the complying party of reasonable attorney's fees. . . ."

We further recognize, as the trial court claimed, that "our courts have long been recognized to have an inherent power, independent of any statute, to hold a defendant in contempt of court. . . . The purpose of the contempt power is to enable a court to preserve its dignity and to protect its proceedings." . . . The sanction created by Practice Book §§ 14-13 and relied upon by the trial court in this case, however, was intended to serve a different function, namely to ensure the insurer's presence to assist in the settlement of the case.

Public policy favors and encourages the voluntary settlement of civil suits. . . . *Krattenstein v. G. Fox & Co.,* . . . (1967) ("It is a proper exercise of the judicial office to suggest the expediency and practical value of adjusting differences and compromising and settling suits at law. The efficient administration of the courts is subserved by the ending of disputes without the delay and expense of a trial, and the philosophy or ideal of justice is served in the amicable solution of controversies. Our rules specifically provide for the procedure to be followed in pretrial sessions designed to encourage the settlement of cases.") We view with disfavor, however, all pressure tactics, whether employed directly or indirectly, to coerce settlement by litigants, their counsel and their insurers. The failure to concur with what a trial court may consider an appropriate settlement should not result in the imposition of any retributive sanctions upon a litigant, his or her counsel or his or her insurer. As our sister state, New York, has recognized, "the function of courts is to provide litigants with an opportunity to air their differences at an impartial trial according to law. . . . [The court should not be able] to exert undue pressure on litigants to oblige them to settle their controversies without their day in court." . . .

We recognize that Practice Book §§ 14-13 grants the trial court the authority to sanction an insurance company for its failure to attend or be available by telephone at a pretrial session. In this case, however, the plaintiff was not unavailable or otherwise absent from the proceedings. Moreover, its actual presence, through its agent, . . . cannot be transformed into the functional equivalent of an absence, as the trial court ruled, . . . simply because the insurer decided not to abide by the arbitrator's assessment of damages and to insist, as its insured's agent, on the insured's right to a trial.

Although we sympathize with the trial court's concern that merely attending a pretrial conference while refusing, at the same time, to participate meaningfully in the negotiation or settlement process is not within the spirit of the settlement process, the plaintiff's refusal, on the basis of a validly exercised right to a trial de novo, to abide by the arbitrator's nonbinding decision that the plaintiff should pay $400 more than its original offer does not fall within the parameters of sanctionable behavior under §§ 14-13. To conclude otherwise would undermine the insured's constitutional right to a trial of the claims. Practice Book §§ 14-13 authorizes the court to use its discretion to require an insurer to be present or available because the insurer's presence might assist in the settlement of the case. Under these circumstances, however, the failure to negotiate is not equivalent to the failure to appear in court. Distasio indicated, by requesting a trial de novo, that he wanted his dispute to be resolved by trial. The plaintiff's rejection of the arbitration award evidences the same preference, in accordance with §§ 52-549z (d) and Practice Book §§ 23-66 (c). Accordingly, because Distasio properly exercised his statutory right to a trial de novo and the plaintiff properly complied with the trial court's request to be present at the pretrial hearing, we conclude that the trial court abused its discretion when it imposed sanctions. . . .

The writ of error is granted and the matter is remanded with direction to vacate the order of sanctions. . . .

Case Questions

1. What was the arbitrator's decision in this case?
2. Why did Judge Mottolese want to sanction the insurance company in this case for contempt of court?
3. Why did the the state supreme court order that the order of sanctions be vacated?

JOINTLY USED ADR METHODS

Mediation, mini-trials, and arbitration are used with both court-annexed and voluntary ADR. The following discussion briefly examines each of these methods.

Mediation

Mediation is a technique in which one or more neutral parties, called mediators, help disputants to find ways to settle their dispute.[19] Parties often attempt to resolve their disagreements by mediation before participating in binding arbitration or litigation. Informal, unstructured, and inexpensive, mediation focuses on settlement, not on victory at trial. Mediators have no formal power to make a decision: their role is that of facilitator, and different mediators use different styles and techniques to help parties come to an agreement. There is no formal hearing in a mediation. Instead, using joint meetings and private caucuses, mediators (1) help the parties identify their real goals, (2) narrow the issues, (3) look for alternatives and options as well as areas of common interest, and (4) prevent the parties from focusing on only one solution.

Court-annexed mediation often involves using trial attorneys as mediators. Mediators in some jurisdictions are paid and in others are volunteers. The theory is that neutral, experienced trial attorneys will be able to persuade litigants to look at their cases realistically and moderate their monetary demands. These are important hurdles that often stand in the way of a settlement.

Court-annexed mediation procedures vary. Lawyer-mediators are used in some jurisdictions and three-person panels in others. In complex cases, the court may appoint a person called a special master to serve as a mediator. Mediators vary in their approaches, but they tend to evaluate each case and predict what would happen if the case went to trial. They also indicate what they believe to be the settlement value of the case. These two determinations serve as a catalyst in starting settlement discussions between the parties.

In some jurisdictions the court refers most cases to mediation. In other jurisdictions mediation occurs pursuant to stipulation or a suggestion from the court. Mediation is nonbinding, and parties retain their rights to attempt other ADR methods and to go to trial.

There is a big difference in the focus of a trial and mediation. Trials exist to produce a winner and a loser. Mediation exists to help the parties settle their dispute in an amicable and expeditious manner. The objective is to find a solution to the dispute that is more acceptable to each party than going to trial. Mediation is more flexible than a trial and can produce a result that is more attuned to the underlying facts. Another advantage to mediation is that there are fewer enforcement problems. Because mediation produces an agreement between the parties, many problems that result when a judgment creditor attempts to enforce a judgment are avoided.

As states have begun to implement court-annexed mediation, questions have arisen regarding the procedures to be employed when using the ADR method. The following case from Tennessee is illustrative.

Team Design v. Anthony Gottlieb

M1999-00911-COA-R3-CV
Court of Appeals of Tennessee
July 18, 2002

William C. Koch

This appeal raises important issues regarding the permissible range of court-annexed alternative dispute resolution procedures available under Tenn. S. Ct. R. 31. . . .

Michael J. Bonagura and Kathie Baillie Bonagura perform country music in a group known as "Baillie and the Boys." When the transactions giving rise to this lawsuit arose, they were managed by Anthony Gottlieb, who did business as Morningstar Management. On January 22, 1996, the Bonaguras signed an "Exclusive Artist Agreement" with Intersound Entertainment, Inc. ("Intersound"), a Minnesota corporation whose principal place of business was in Roswell, Georgia. This agreement obligated Intersound to be responsible for the artwork and graphic design for the Baillie and the Boys albums.

With Intersound's knowledge and consent, the Bonaguras hired Harris Graphics, Inc. and Team Design to develop the artwork and graphics for an upcoming album called "Lovin' Every Minute." They believed that Intersound would be responsible for paying for this work. However, unbeknownst to the Bonaguras, Mr. Gottlieb had delivered a letter to Intersound agreeing that the Bonaguras would be responsible for paying for the artwork and graphic design for this album.

When Harris Graphics and Team Design were not paid for their work, they filed suit in the Davidson County General Sessions Court against Intersound and Mr. Gottlieb seeking payment and an injunction against the use of their work until they were paid. The general sessions court later permitted Harris Graphics and Team Design to add the Bonaguras as defendants. Following a hear-

ing, the general sessions court granted Team Design a $4,086.75 judgment against Intersound and the Bonaguras. It also granted Harris Graphics a $2,200 judgment against Intersound and a $2,760 judgment against the Bonaguras.

All the parties perfected de novo appeals to the Circuit Court for Davidson County. . . .

The trial was originally set for September 1998 but, at the trial court's initiative, was continued twice to February 16, 1999. Approximately one month before trial, the lawyer representing the Bonaguras requested his fellow lawyers to agree to preserve the Bonaguras' trial testimony by taking their depositions because Cactus Pete's in Jackpot, Nevada had declined to release them from a previous contractual commitment that conflicted with the rescheduled court date. The lawyers agreed, and the Bonaguras' depositions were scheduled for January 19, 1999. However, before the depositions could be taken, Mr. Gottlieb changed his mind and insisted that the Bonaguras be present at the trial. On January 21, 1999, the Bonaguras filed a motion seeking a continuance and an order enforcing the agreement permitting them to present their testimony by deposition. Team Design and Harris Graphics agreed to the use of the depositions at trial but objected to another continuance.

The trial court conducted a hearing on the Bonaguras' motion on February 5, 1999. . . . After the trial court agreed to the Bonaguras' request for a continuance, the lawyers and the trial court began discussing another trial date. During this discussion, the trial court offered the alternative of "binding mediation" and stated that it would be available to conduct the mediation on March 11, 1999. The record contains no indication that the trial court informed the parties of the specific procedures that would be used for this mediation or the legal consequences of their agreement to participate in the mediation. . . . The lawyers for all the parties accepted the court's offer, and on February 16, 1999, the trial court entered an order referring the case to "binding mediation before this Court" on March 11, 1999.

Thereafter, the trial court directed the parties to submit confidential statements outlining their respective positions. When the parties returned to court on March 14, 1999, . . . a clerk explained the procedure the trial court intended to follow which consisted of separate meetings with each of the parties and their lawyers in chambers. Over the next four hours, the trial court met separately with each of the parties and their lawyer. According to one of the lawyers, the trial court "made no attempt to seek a mutual agreement as to a resolution of the issues among the parties, but, after the final interview, announced that she would make a decision and enter an order reflecting her decision." On March 19, 1999, the trial court entered an order awarding Team Design a $4,086.75 judgment against Intersound and awarding Harris Graphics a $5,044.45 judgment against Intersound. The trial court also awarded Intersound a judgment against Mr. Gottlieb for one-third of the total amount of Team Design's and Harris Graphics' judgments to be paid from moneys he received from the "Lovin' Every Minute" album. Likewise, the trial court awarded Intersound a judgment against the Bonaguras for one-third of the of Team Design's and Harris Graphics' judgments to be paid from the royalties generated from their "Lovin' Every Minute" album.

On March 31, 1999, Intersound filed a . . . motion based on its lawyer's assertion that he had understood that the "binding mediation" offered by the trial court would be the sort of mediation authorized by Tenn. S. Ct. R. 31 in which he had previously participated in other cases. He also asserted that he never would have agreed to mediation had he understood the procedure that the court planned to follow. Team Design, Harris Graphics, and Mr. Gottlieb opposed the motion. They ar-

gued (1) that all the parties had agreed to "binding mediation," (2) that Intersound had not objected to the procedure prior to the entry of the March 19, 1999 order, and (3) that it would be unfair to permit Intersound to object to the proceeding at this point. The trial court entered an order on April 29, 1999, denying Intersound's post-trial motion. Intersound has perfected this appeal.

II.

The Trial Court's Authority to Conduct Binding Mediation

We turn first to the question of a Tennessee trial court's authority to conduct "binding mediation." Intersound asserts that any sort of mediation conducted by a trial court in Tennessee must be consistent with Tenn. S. Ct. R. 31. In response, Team Design, Harris Graphics, and Mr. Gottlieb assert that the parties and the trial court may, by agreement, agree upon an alternative dispute procedure that does not meet all the requirements of Tenn. S. Ct. R. 31 and that the trial court and the parties did precisely that. We have determined that all court-annexed alternative dispute resolution procedures must be consistent with Tenn. S. Ct. R. 31 and that the "binding mediation" procedure used in this case was not consistent with Tenn. S. Ct. R. 31.

A.

Public policy strongly favors resolving disputes between private parties by agreement. Private parties may, of course, decide to submit their disputes to the courts for resolution; however, a broad range of other formal and informal alternatives are available before they resort to litigation. These procedures are, as a practical matter, limited only by the parties' imaginations because the parties themselves may agree on virtually any mutually satisfactory procedure that is not illegal or contrary to public policy. Thus, alternative dispute resolution procedures may range from formal procedures such as arbitration under Tennessee's version of the Uniform Arbitration Act . . . to far less formal procedures such as "splitting the difference," flipping a coin, or, for that matter, arm wrestling. At least with regard to formal agreements to resolve disputes, the courts will require the parties to follow their agreed-upon dispute resolution procedure as long as they are competent and are dealing at arm's length. When the parties have agreed to be bound by the outcome of their agreed-upon procedure, the courts will require them to accept the result by declining to try their dispute de novo and by limiting the scope of judicial review of the outcome. . . .

The parties' ability to manipulate the contours of the procedure to resolve their disputes narrows considerably once they submit their dispute to the courts for resolution. Judicial proceedings must be conducted in accordance with the ancient common-law rules, applicable constitutional principles, statutes, and court rules.

In Tennessee prior to 1995, traditional litigation was the only procedure available to parties who turned to the courts for resolution of their disputes. The trial courts lacked express authority to provide judicial oversight over pending cases other than the sort of oversight traditionally provided by American judges. They certainly did not have express authority to offer or require the use of alternative dispute resolution procedures. This changed on July 1, 1995, when amendments to Tenn. R. Civ. P. 16 greatly expanded the trial courts' case management authority. For the first time, Tenn. R. Civ. P. 16.03(7) specifically empowered trial courts to discuss "the possibility of settlement or the use of extrajudicial procedures, including alternative dispute resolution, to resolve the dispute." These amendments did not, however, empower trial courts to require the parties to engage in any sort of

alternative dispute resolution procedure or to participate in any such procedure themselves. These changes were to come five months later.

On December 18, 1995, the Tennessee Supreme Court filed Tenn. S. Ct. R. 31 establishing procedures for court-annexed alternative dispute resolution in Tennessee's trial courts. . . . The original version of the rule represented an incremental approach to court-annexed alternative dispute resolution. The procedures . . . were intended to be alternatives, not replacements, to traditional litigation. . . .

Under the original version of the rule, . . . [ADR] procedures became available only after "all parties are before the court." . . . At that time, any or all of the parties could request authorization to engage in an alternative dispute resolution procedure. . . . The rule also permitted the trial court, even without the parties' request or consent but after consultation with the lawyers and the parties, . . . to require the parties to participate in a judicial settlement conference, a mediation, or a case evaluation. . . . In addition, with the consent of all parties, the trial court could refer the case for "non-binding arbitration, mini-trial, summary jury trial, or other appropriate alternative dispute resolution proceedings." . . .

The original version of Tenn. S. Ct. R. 31, like the current version, specifically defined each of the alternative dispute resolution methods contemplated by the rule. Consistent with the Commission's recommendation that court-annexed alternative dispute proceedings should be non-binding, . . . each of these methods were intended to promote negotiated settlements between the parties themselves. They were not intended to require the parties to relinquish their decision-making right to any third party who would make the decision for them.

The fact that all proposed alternative dispute resolution methods are non-binding is an essential attribute of the court-annexed procedures. . . . The rule specifically defines mediation as "an informal process in which a neutral person . . . conducts discussions among the disputing parties designed to enable them to reach a mutually acceptable agreement among themselves on all or any part of the issues in dispute." . . . The arbitration permitted by the rule must be "non-binding." . . . Likewise, a "case evaluation" is advisory only; a "mini-trial" envisions that "the parties or their representatives [will] seek a negotiated settlement of the dispute;" . . . and a "summary jury trial" envisions only an "advisory verdict" followed by a "negotiated settlement." . . . In 1996, the Tennessee Supreme Court reaffirmed that all court-annexed alternative dispute resolution proceedings permitted by Tenn. S. Ct. R. 31 were premised on the principle of "self-determination." . . .

Another essential attribute of alternative dispute resolution is the neutrality and impartially of the mediators, arbitrators, or other neutral persons conducting the process. . . . The importance of neutrality is reflected in the fact that Tenn. S. Ct. R. 31 refers to persons conducting court-annexed alternative dispute resolution proceedings as "dispute resolution neutrals." . . . It is also reflected in the Standards of Professional Conduct for Rule 31 Mediators adopted by the Tennessee Supreme Court . . . which state that "integrity, impartiality, and professional competence are essential qualifications of any mediator." . . .

A third essential attribute of the court-annexed procedures . . . is confidentiality. All parties in a mediation proceeding trust that the proceeding will be confidential because these proceedings permit them to "bare their soul" to the mediator and provide them the opportunity to vent which, in some instances, is all that stands in the way of a negotiated settlement. . . . Accordingly, a vast majority of the proponents of alternative dispute resolution view confidentiality of the proceedings as a central issue. . . .

The Tennessee Supreme Court recognized the importance of confidentiality when it first authorized court-annexed alternative dispute resolution. Tenn. S. Ct. R. 31, . . . required that a "mediator, settlement judge, or other dispute resolution neutral shall preserve and maintain the confidentiality of all alternative dispute resolution proceedings except where required by law to disclose the information." . . .

The principles of self-determination, neutrality, and confidentiality influenced the Tennessee Supreme Court's view of the role trial judges should properly play in court-annexed alternative dispute resolution proceedings. While the court gave trial courts the authority to require litigants, with or without their consent, to participate in a case evaluation, mediation, or judicial settlement conference, . . . the court carefully limited the trial court's role in these proceedings. First, the court permitted trial judges to participate only in judicial settlement conferences. All other proceedings being presided over by a "neutral person" or a "neutral panel." . . . Secondly, with regard to judicial settlement conferences, the court stated clearly that judges presiding over a pending case could not also conduct the judicial settlement conference. The definition of "judicial settlement conference" makes it clear that these proceedings must be "conducted by a judicial officer other than the judge before whom the case will be tried." . . .

The policy reasons for not permitting the trial judge who could eventually try the case to preside over the mediation or other alternative dispute resolution procedure . . . are evident and compelling. A judge who presides over a judicial settlement conference is not acting as a judge but as a neutral. . . . The success of the settlement "depends largely on the willingness of the parties to freely disclose their intentions, desires, and the strengths and weaknesses of their case" with the neutral. . . . Thus, a judge conducting a settlement conference becomes a confidant of the parties, . . . with whom the parties share information that would normally be shared only with their lawyers.

Generally, knowledge gained in a prior judicial proceeding is not a sufficient ground to require the recusal or disqualification of a trial judge in a later judicial proceeding. . . . However, much of the information imparted during a mediation is not the sort of information that would normally be disclosed to the other parties or the court. Accordingly, should the judge who conducts the judicial settlement conference later be called upon to decide the issues of liability or damages, it is impossible to avoid questions as to whether he or she can disregard the matters disclosed during the conference or put aside any opinions or judgments already formed based on this information. . . .

The Tennessee Supreme Court recognized these confidentiality and predisposition concerns in its September 1996 revisions to Tenn. S. Ct. R. 31. The court added a provision to the rule stating:

> A person serving as a Rule 31 dispute resolution neutral in an alternative dispute resolution proceeding shall not participate as attorney, advisor, judge, guardian ad litem, master or in any other judicial or quasi-judicial capacity in the matter in which the alternative dispute resolution proceeding was conducted. . . .

B.

The "binding mediation" proceeding at issue in this case did not comply with . . . Tenn. S. Ct. R. 31 as it stood in early 1999 in four fundamental particulars. First, [it] . . . did not authorize "binding mediation" . . . as a method for court-annexed alternative dispute resolution. . . . Second, the procedure actually used by the trial court bore no resemblance to a judicial settlement conference or mediation because the parties' decision-making rights

were supplanted by the trial court, and there was no apparent effort to assist the parties in reaching their own voluntary settlement of their differences. . . . Third, the proceeding was conducted by the trial judge to whom the case had been assigned notwithstanding the clear requirement . . . that it be "conducted by a judicial officer other than the judge before whom the case will be tried." Fourth, the judge who conducted the alternative dispute resolution proceeding entered a final order disposing of the parties' claims even though it did not have the authority to do so. . . .

These departures are not just minor deviations from Tenn. S. Ct. R. 31. Each of them is inconsistent with one or more of the fundamental principles that impelled the Tennessee Supreme Court to authorize court-annexed alternative dispute resolution in the first place. They undermined the principles carefully designed to preserve the parties' right of self-determination. They also raised the specter of possible repercussions for the parties who objected to referring the case to alternative dispute resolution or who objected to its outcome. Accordingly, we have concluded that these deviations are substantive and material and that they affected the outcome of this proceeding.

A judgment is considered void if the record demonstrates that the court entering it lacked jurisdiction over either the subject matter or the person, or did not have the authority to make the challenged judgment. . . . A void judgment lacks validity anywhere and is subject to attack from any angle. . . .

A trial court cannot exercise authority it has not been granted expressly or by necessary implication. . . . At the time of this proceeding, Tenn. S. Ct. R. 31 did not permit the judge who conducted the judicial settlement conference to enter an order disposing of the case. Accordingly, the order disposing of the parties' claims entered on March 19, 1999, by the judge who conducted the mediation was void, . . . and the trial court erred when it declined to grant Intersound's . . . motion. . . .

We vacate the March 19, 1999 and April 29, 1999 orders and remand the case to the trial court for further proceedings consistent with this opinion. We tax the costs to Team Design; Harris Graphics, Inc.; Anthony Gottlieb; and Intersound Entertainment, Inc. and its surety for which execution, if necessary, may issue.

Case Questions

1. What was the mediator's decision in this case?
2. Why did the state court of appeals vacate the trial court's orders?

MINI-TRIALS

The mini-trial, used primarily to resolve business disputes, actually isn't a trial at all. It is a process in which each party makes an abbreviated presentation to a panel, generally consisting of a senior manager or decision maker from each side and a judge (in the case of a court-ordered mini-trial) or jointly selected neutral (in the case of a voluntary mini-trial). The theory behind this process is that the presenters for each side will educate the managers about the dispute.[20] The strength of this process is that the business managers, rather than lawyers, judges, and juries, make the decisions. The managers can often design creative solutions that make it possible to resolve the dispute. They are not restricted to the types of relief that courts can award after a trial. If the managers fail to agree, mini-trial rules often require a judge or neutral to forecast what he or she believes would happen if the case were to go to trial and indicate what he or she believes to be a reasonable settlement proposal. The parties in a court-annexed mini-trial can reject the judge's proposal but may incur a penalty. A party who insists on a trial but fails to recover a judgment more favorable than the judge's proposal may be assessed a substantial fine for each day that it takes to try the case.[21] The parties in a voluntary mini-trial can reject the neutral's proposal without a penalty.

Some courts schedule mini-trials only after the parties agree to participate. Other courts require parties to take part. Mini-trials are primarily used in complex, time-consuming cases where the substantial savings of money and time realized by limiting discovery and presentations are strong incentives. Mini-trials are most likely to succeed when both parties are serious about resolving the underlying issues with a minimum of acrimony.

The parties in a mini-trial have control over the procedures and can disregard the formal rules of civil procedure and evidence that apply in litigation. For example, they can set their own rules regarding the nature and scope of discovery and determine whether position papers will be exchanged prior to the hearing. They can also determine the procedures to be used at the hearing. For example, they can decide whether written summaries will be submitted in lieu of witness testimony, how many hours each side will have to present its case, how long opening statements will be, and whether cross-examination will be allowed.

The typical procedures for a mini-trial include an abbreviated presentation of each side's case to a panel of decision makers selected by the parties and the neutral. The decision makers then meet privately after the presentations have concluded and work to negotiate a solution to the dispute.

Summary Jury Trials

An Ohio federal district court judge developed the summary jury trial (SJT) process in 1980 as a court-annexed, mandatory procedure. It operates pursuant to local court rules and is used in cases that have proved difficult to settle—primarily damage cases. The key elements in the typical SJT are an advisory jury, an abbreviated, two-hour hearing, and a nonbinding verdict. The SJT procedure can be helpful when parties agree on the defendant's liability but disagree about the damages. In such cases, the plaintiff's attorney doesn't want to settle for less than what he or she estimates a jury will award. Similarly, the defendant's lawyer will not want to settle for more than what a jury would probably require.

SJT procedures are similar to those at trial.[22] A judge presides, and each side has one or two hours to present its case. Case presentations include oral summaries of the evidence and the reading of witness depositions. Each side also has an opportunity to argue the case to the jury, which consists of five or six jurors. The judge gives the jury abbreviated oral instructions. The SJT juries are composed of persons summoned to court but not chosen to sit on a regular trial jury that day.

After the judge's instructions, the SJT jurors retire and deliberate on both liability and damages. The jurors often are asked to discuss the case with the attorneys and clients after they return with a nonbinding verdict. The process works best when the client or some person with settlement authority attends the SJT and participates in this settlement conference.

The SJT process allows the attorneys to have a practice trial and the opportunity to see how a group of regular jurors reacts to each side's presentation. It also gives the parties "a day in court," which helps to satisfy some litigants' emotional needs. The fact that neutral jurors establish a damage figure is an additional plus. The SJT has had an impact on insurance companies as well as the attorneys and parties. Insurance companies are often more willing to settle after they have seen an SJT jury's verdict because they then have a dollar figure that can serve as a basis for settlement negotiations. If the parties are unable to settle the dispute, the case remains on the calendar for a regular trial.

One criticism of summary jury trials is that SJT presentations compress cases to such an extent that the jurors can't absorb the evidence and argument. In response, a few judges now allow one-week summary "trials." Others permit the use of live witness testimony.

Private Trials

Parties that have failed to resolve their dispute with mediation and/or arbitration may choose to litigate in a private court system. Provided by commercial firms that employ retired federal, state, and local judges, such trials are held in hotels, law schools, and even office buildings in which courtrooms that replicate public courtrooms have been constructed. These firms exist to provide timely, confidential, and affordable trials. In thirteen states the parties can employ jurors selected from the public jury rolls to hear the case. The private trial system allows the parties to select a judge who has experience appropriate to the case. It also allows the parties to conduct their trial in private, an important advantage in many contract, employment rights, professional liability, and divorce actions. The parties to a private trial often contract to use simplified evidentiary and procedural rules and to cooperate with discovery, saving time and money for both parties. The parties also decide whether the decision of the private judge or jury will be final or appealable, and some private court systems even provide for private appeals.

Critics of the private court system maintain that it allows the wealthy to avoid the delays and conditions that others must endure in the public court system. They also express concern that the higher compensation that is paid to private judges could result in a two-tier system of justice. The best judges would handle the litigation of the wealthy in the private sector, while others would litigate before less able judges in underfunded, overworked, public sector courts.

Does ADR Really Work?

The question as to the extent to which ADR programs have produced the benefits that were advertised remains unresolved. In 1996, the Rand Corporation evaluated ten ADR pilot programs created pursuant to the Civil Justice Reform Act. Rand found no statistical evidence that the pilot programs had been more successful than ten comparison districts in reducing cost or delay.[23] A 1997 study conducted by the Federal Judicial Center, however, was more favorable and encouraged continued federal participation.[24] Students interested in reading an excellent article summarizing the effectiveness of ADR in federal district courts and critiquing its use by federal administrative agencies should read a 1997 article in the *Duke Law Journal* written by Judge Patricia M. Wald of the U.S. Court of Appeals for the District of Columbia. This brief and very informative article can be found on the Internet.[25]

Chapter Questions

1. Define the following terms:

   alternative dispute resolution   arbitration agreements
   arbitration   arbitration award

court-annexed	settlement conference
mediation	Seventh Amendment
mini-trial	summary jury trial
private trial	trial *de novo*

2. Frances J. Vukasin was employed by D. A. Davidson & Co. in August 1979. The company implemented an annual performance review in 1985 which rated her performance in each of six areas, gave her an overall rating, and indicated a recommended salary increase. Included in Vukasin's 1986 and 1987 performance reviews, directly above the employee's signature line, was a provision that read "Employment with D. A. Davidson & Co. is subject to arbitration." The review also provided that she or her employer could terminate employment at any time for any reason. There was also a statement that "I [the employee] . . . acknowledge and agree that any controversy between myself and the Company arising out of my employment or the termination of my employment with the Company for any reasons whatsoever shall be determined by arbitration." On December 12, 1988, Vukasin filed a complaint in a state court against the company. She alleged in the complaint that another employee had assaulted and battered her at the company's offices on April 30, 1988. She claimed damages for mental and emotional distress, pain and suffering, loss of wages, and various medical and therapy expenses. Is the allegation of assault and battery outside the scope of the arbitration clause and appropriate for litigation?
Vukasin v. D. A. Davidson & Co., 785 P.2d 713 (Mont. 1990)

3. James Clawson contracted with Habitat, Inc., to build a retaining wall and driveway at his home. The contract contained an arbitration clause. A dispute arose regarding the construction, and the matter was submitted to binding arbitration. The parties continued negotiation throughout the arbitration process. When it appeared that they were close to a settlement, they entered into a new agreement. The new agreement provided that the parties would retract the arbitration if they could negotiate a settlement by 3:00 P.M. on October 21, 1988. Clawson and Habitat disagreed about whether an agreement had been reached by that date. The arbitrator's decision was released on November 1, 1988. Both parties filed motions in the circuit court, Habitat to confirm the award, and Clawson to vacate the award. Should the circuit court confirm the award?
Clawson v. Habitat, Inc., 783 P.2d 1230 (Hawai'i 1989)

4. The Medford (Oregon) Firefighters Association and the City of Medford reached a stalemate while negotiating a collective bargaining agreement. They unsuccessfully tried to mediate their dispute. Pursuant to state law, the Oregon Employment Relations Board appointed an arbitrator, who held a hearing, prepared an agreement, and submitted it to the parties. The firefighters petitioned the circuit court for a writ of *mandamus* when the city refused to sign the agreement. The city claimed that the state law providing

for binding arbitration was unconstitutional. Can the state legislature constitutionally delegate legislative power to a private person as an arbitrator?

Medford Firefighters Association v. City of Medford, 595 P.2d 1268 (1979)

5. Roger Lockhart, a teenager, lost the sight in one of his eyes. He alleged that this was due to the negligence of Dr. Ramon Patel. A summary jury trial was conducted, and the advisory jury awarded the plaintiff $200,000. The court held several formal and informal settlement conferences following the SJT. The court directed that the defense attorney attend a settlement conference on November 3, 1986, and that he bring with him a representative of Dr. Patel's liability insurance carrier, who possessed authority to settle the case. The defense attorney appeared on November 3, but the insurance representative with settlement authority did not. The insurance carrier sent an adjuster instead. The court responded by (1) striking the defendant's pleadings, (2) declaring the defendant in default, (3) setting the trial for the following day, limited to the question of damages, and (4) set a hearing to show cause why the insurance carrier should not be punished for criminal contempt of the court. Does the court have the right to strike the defendant's pleadings because of the insurance carrier's failure to send a representative to attend the settlement conference?

Lockhart v. Patel, 115 F.R.D. 44 (E.D.Ky. 1987)

6. Elizabeth Garfield brought suit against her former employer, Thomas McKinnon Securities, Inc., claiming that McKinnon had discharged her on account of her age in violation of the Age Discrimination in Employment Act. McKinnon moved to dismiss the complaint and compel arbitration because Garfield had agreed to arbitrate any controversy arising out of her employment. Garfield responded that she and all registered brokers are required to execute arbitration agreements as a condition of employment. She maintained that Congress did not intend to permit persons to waive their statutory right to sue for ADEA violations in federal court via the execution of an arbitration agreement. Should the court dismiss the complaint and compel arbitration?

Garfield v. Thomas McKinnon Securities, Inc., 731 F.Supp. 841 (N.D.Ill. 1988)

7. Irmis Achong was hired as a nursing attendant by the Cabrini Medical Center. He became a member of Local 1199 of the Drug, Hospital and Health Care Employees Union, which was party to a collective bargaining agreement. On November 4, 1986, a disoriented and distraught patient kicked Achong as he walked by her stretcher. Cabrini claimed that Achong, who had a perfect performance record at the time, responded by cursing the patient and striking her on the leg. Cabrini discharged Achong for abusing the patient. The collective bargaining agreement provided for binding arbitration whenever the union and Cabrini disagreed upon whether an employee was discharged for just cause. Achong's dismissal was submitted to arbitration. The arbitrator made careful and detailed findings and conclusions. He ruled that just cause did not exist for Achong's discharge, because Cabrini

failed to establish how hard Achong touched the patient. He believed that summary discharge was too harsh a penalty under the circumstances and based on the limited evidence. He ruled that Achong should be reinstated without back pay (thereby imposing a forfeiture of nine months' pay) and given a warning against future conduct. Cabrini brought an action in federal court to set aside the award, and the union brought an action in state court to confirm. Cabrini removed the state action to federal court, where the two actions were consolidated. Cabrini argued that the award violated public policy based on a statutory provision that patients "shall be free from mental and physical abuse." Should the award be confirmed?

Cabrini Medical Center v. Local 1199 Drug, Hospital and Health Care Employees Union, 731 F.Supp. 612 (S.D.N.Y. 1990)

Notes

1. R. Samborn, "In Courts: Caseloads Still Rise," *The National Law Journal* (July 5, 1993).
2. Administrative Office of U.S. Courts. *Judicial Caseload Profile Report: All District Courts.* September 30, 2001.
3. Administrative Office of the U.S. Courts. *Statistical Table for the Federal Judiciary,* Table C-4A, September 30, 2000.
4. As early as 1991, for example, Colorado amended its Code of Professional Responsibility and required lawyers to advise their clients of this option.
5. Massachusetts Supreme Judicial Court Rule 1:18, May 1, 1998.
6. W. H. Schroeder, Jr., "Private ADR May Offer Increased Confidentiality," *The National Law Journal,* C14-16 (July 25, 1995).
7. J. H. Kennedy, "Merger Aimed at Settling Out of Court," *Boston Globe,* May 16, 1994, pp. 18–19.
8. D. M. Provine, *Settlement Strategies for Federal District Judges* (Federal Judicial Center, 1986).
9. H. N. Mazadoorian, "Widespread Disgust with Civil Justice Is Boon to ADR," *Corporate Legal Times,* 17 (April 1994).
10. Ibid.
11. J. W. Keltner, *The Management of Struggle* (Cresskill, NJ: Hampton Press, Inc., 1994), p. 152.
12. J. W. Cooley, "Arbitration vs. Mediation—Explaining the Differences," *Judicature,* 69, 264 (1986).
13. Federal Arbitration Act, 9 U.S.C. Sec. 1.
14. See *Eastern Associated Coal Corp v. United Mine Workers,* 531 U.S. 57 (2000) and *Circuit City Stores, Inc. v. Adams,* 99–1379 (2001).
15. Some states have, in the past, refused to enforce arbitration agreements entered into before the existence of any dispute.
16. *Shearson Lehman Hutton v. McMahon,* 482 U.S. 220 (1987).
17. R. C. Reuben, "Decision Gives Banking ADR a Boost," *American Bar Association Journal* 32 (December 1994), pp. 32–33.
18. Mazadoorian, p. 17.
19. Cooley, p. 266.

20. J. Davis and L. Omlie, "Mini-trials: The Courtroom in the Boardroom," *Willamette Law Review*, 21, 531 (1985).

21. The extent to which judges can order parties to participate in a mini-trial remains a hotly contested issue.

22. "Mandatory and Summary Jury Trial Guidelines for Ensuring Fair and Effective Process," *Harvard Law Review*, 103, 1086 (1993).

23. J. S. Kakalik, *Implementation of the Civil Justice Reform Act in Pilot and Comparison Districts*, Rand Institute for Civil Justice (1996).

24. Federal Judicial Center, *Report to the Judicial Conference Committee on Court Administration and Case Management: A Study of the Five Demonstration Programs Established Under the Civil Justice Reform Act of 1990* (1997).

25. P. M. Wald, "ADR and the Courts: An Update," 46 *Duke Law Journal* 1445 (1997), www.law.duke.edu/journals/dlj/articles/dlj46p1445.

Appendix

THE CONSTITUTION OF THE
UNITED STATES

GLOSSARY OF SELECTED TERMS FROM
THE LAW DICTIONARY

The Constitution of the United States

We the people of the United States, in order to form a more perfect union, establish justice, insure domestic tranquility, provide for the common defense, promote the general welfare, and secure the blessings of liberty to ourselves and our posterity, do ordain and establish this Constitution for the United States of America.

ARTICLE I

Section 1.
All legislative powers herein granted shall be vested in a Congress of the United States, which shall consist of a Senate and House of Representatives.

Section 2.

1. The House of Representatives shall be composed of members chosen every second year by the people of the several States, and the electors in each State shall have the qualifications requisite for electors of the most numerous branch of the State Legislature.

2. No person shall be a representative who shall not have attained to the age of twenty-five years, and been seven years a citizen of the United States, and who shall not, when elected, be an inhabitant of that State in which he shall be chosen.

3. Representatives and direct taxes[1] shall be apportioned among the several States which may be included within this Union, according to their respective numbers, which shall be determined by adding to the whole number of free persons, including those bound to service for a term of years, and excluding Indians not taxed, three fifths of all other persons.[2] The actual enumeration shall be made within three years after the first meeting of the Congress of the United States, and within every subsequent term of ten years, in such manner

---

[1] Altered by the 16th Amendment.

[2] Altered by the 14th Amendment.

as they shall by law direct. The number of representatives shall not exceed one for every thirty thousand, but each State shall have at least one representative; and until such enumeration shall be made, the State of New Hampshire shall be entitled to choose three, Massachusetts eight, Rhode Island and Providence Plantations one, Connecticut five, New York six, New Jersey four, Pennsylvania eight, Delaware one, Maryland six, Virginia ten, North Carolina five, South Carolina five, and Georgia three.

4. When vacancies happen in the representation from any State, the executive authority thereof shall issue writs of election to fill such vacancies.

5. The House of Representatives shall choose their speaker and other officers; and shall have the sole power of impeachment.

Section 3.

1. The Senate of the United States shall be composed of two senators from each State, chosen by the legislature thereof,[3] for six years; and each senator shall have one vote.

2. Immediately after they shall be assembled in consequence of the first election, they shall be divided as equally as may be into three classes. The seats of the senators of the first class shall be vacated at the expiration of the second year, of the second class at the expiration of the fourth year and of the third class at the expiration of the sixth year, so that one third may be chosen every second year; and if vacancies happen by resignation, or otherwise, during the recess of the legislature of any State, the executive thereof may make temporary appointments until the next meeting of the legislature, which shall then fill such vacancies.[4]

3. No person shall be a senator who shall not have attained to the age of thirty years, and been nine years a citizen of the United States, and who shall not, when elected, be an inhabitant of that State for which he shall be chosen.

4. The Vice President of the United States shall be President of the Senate, but shall have no vote, unless they be equally divided.

5. The Senate shall choose their other officers, and also a president pro tempore, in the absence of the Vice President, or when he shall exercise the office of the President of the United States.

6. The Senate shall have the sole power to try all impeachments. When sitting for that purpose, they shall be on oath or affirmation. When the President of the United States is tried, the chief justice shall preside: And no person shall be convicted without the concurrence of two thirds of the members present.

7. Judgment in cases of impeachment shall not extend further than to removal from office, and disqualifications to hold and enjoy any office of honor, trust or profit under the United States: But the party convicted shall nevertheless be liable and subject to indictment, trial, judgment and punishment, according to law.

---

[3] Superseded by the 17th Amendment.

[4] Altered by the 17th Amendment.

Section 4.

1. The times, places, and manner of holding elections for senators and representatives, shall be prescribed in each State by the legislature thereof: But the Congress may at any time by law make or alter such regulations, except as to the places of choosing senators.

2. The Congress shall assemble at least once in every year, and such meeting shall be on the first Monday in December, unless they shall by law appoint a different day.

Section 5.

1. Each House shall be the judge of the elections, returns and qualifications of its own members, and a majority of each shall constitute a quorum to do business; but a smaller number may adjourn from day to day, and may be authorized to compel the attendance of absent members, in such manner, and under such penalties as each House may provide.

2. Each House may determine the rules of its proceedings, punish its members for disorderly behavior, and, with the concurrence of two thirds, expel a member.

3. Each House shall keep a journal of its proceedings, and from time to time publish the same, excepting such parts as may in their judgment require secrecy; and the yeas and nays of the members of either House on any question shall, at the desire of one fifth of those present, be entered on the journal.

4. Neither House, during the session of Congress, shall, without the consent of the other, adjourn for more than three days, nor to any other place than that in which the two Houses shall be sitting.

Section 6.

1. The senators and representatives shall receive a compensation for their services, to be ascertained by law, and paid out of the Treasury of the United States. They shall in all cases, except treason, felony, and breach of the peace, be privileged from arrest during their attendance at the session of their respective Houses, and in going to and returning from the same; and for any speech or debate in either House, they shall not be questioned in any other place.

2. No senator or representative shall, during the time for which he was elected, be appointed to any civil office under the authority of the United States, which shall have been created, or the emoluments whereof shall have been increased, during such time; and no person holding any office under the United States shall be a member of either House during his continuance in office.

Section 7.

1. All bills for raising revenue shall originate in the House of Representatives; but the Senate may propose or concur with amendments as on other bills.

2. Every bill which shall have passed the House of Representatives and the Senate, shall, before it become a law, be presented to the President of the United States; If he approves he shall sign it, but if not he shall return it, with his objections, to that House in which it shall have originated, who shall

enter the objections at large on their journal, and proceed to reconsider it. If after such reconsideration two thirds of that House shall agree to pass the bill, it shall be sent, together with the objections, to the other House, by which it shall likewise be reconsidered, and if approved by two thirds of that House, it shall become a law. But in all such cases the votes of both Houses shall be determined by yeas and nays, and the names of the persons voting for and against the bill shall be entered on the journal of each House respectively. If any bill shall not be returned by the President within ten days (Sundays excepted) after it shall have been presented to him, the same shall be a law, in like manner as if he had signed it, unless the Congress by their adjournment prevent its return, in which case it shall not be a law.

3. Every order, resolution, or vote to which the concurrence of the Senate and the House of Representatives may be necessary (except on a question of adjournment) shall be presented to the President of the United States; and before the same shall take effect, shall be approved by him, or being disapproved by him, shall be repassed by two thirds of the Senate and House of Representatives, according to the rules and limitations prescribed in the case of a bill.

Section 8.

The Congress shall have the power

1. To lay and collect taxes, duties, imposts, and excises, to pay the debts and provide for the common defense and general welfare of the United States; but all duties, imposts, and excises shall be uniform throughout the United States;

2. To borrow money on the credit of the United States;

3. To regulate commerce with foreign nations, and among the several States, and with the Indian tribes;

4. To establish an uniform rule of naturalization, and uniform laws on the subject of bankruptcies throughout the United States;

5. To coin money, regulate the value thereof, and of foreign coin, and fix the standard of weights and measures;

6. To provide for the punishment of counterfeiting the securities and current coin of the United States;

7. To establish post offices and post roads;

8. To promote the progress of science and useful arts, by securing for limited times to authors and inventors the exclusive right to their respective writings and discoveries;

9. To constitute tribunals inferior to the Supreme Court;

10. To define and punish piracies and felonies committed on the high seas, and offenses against the law of nations;

11. To declare war, grant letters of marque and reprisal, and make rules concerning captures on land and water;

12. To raise and support armies, but no appropriations of money to that use shall be for a longer term than two years;

13. To provide and maintain a navy;

14. To make rules for the government and regulation of the land and naval forces;

15. To provide for calling forth the militia to execute the laws of the Union, suppress insurrections and repel invasions;

16. To provide for organizing, arming, and disciplining the militia, and for governing such part of them as may be employed in the service of the United States, reserving to the States respectively, the appointment of the officers, and the authority of training the militia according to the discipline prescribed by Congress.

17. To exercise exclusive legislation in all cases whatsoever, over such district (not exceeding ten miles square) as may, by cession of particular States and the acceptance of Congress, become the seat of the government of the United States, and to exercise like authority over all places purchased by the consent of the legislature of the State in which the same shall be, for the erection of forts, magazines, arsenals, dockyards, and other needful buildings; and

18. To make all laws which shall be necessary and proper for carrying into execution the foregoing powers, and all other powers vested by the Constitution in the government of the United States, or any department or officer thereof.

Section 9.

1. The migration or importation of such persons as any of the States now existing shall think proper to admit, shall not be prohibited by the Congress prior to the year one thousand eight hundred and eight, but a tax or duty may be imposed on such importation, not exceeding ten dollars for each person.

2. The privilege of the writ of habeas corpus shall not be suspended unless when in cases of rebellion or invasion the public safety may require it.

3. No bill of attainder or ex post facto law shall be passed.

4. No capitation, or other direct, tax shall be laid, unless in proportion to the census or enumeration hereinbefore directed to be taken.[5]

5. No tax or duty shall be laid on articles exported from any State.

6. No preference shall be given by any regulation of commerce or revenue to the ports of one State over those of another: Nor shall vessels bound to, or from, one State be obliged to enter, clear, or pay duties in another.

7. No money shall be drawn from the treasury, but in consequence of appropriations made by law; and a regular statement and account of the receipts and expenditures of all public money shall be published from time to time.

8. No title of nobility shall be granted by the United States: And no person holding any office of profit or trust under them, shall, without the consent of

[5]Superseded by the 16th Amendment.

the Congress, accept of any present, emolument, office, or title, of any kind whatever, from any king, prince, or foreign State.

Section 10.

1. No State shall enter into any treaty, alliance, or confederation; grant letters of marque and reprisal; coin money; emit bills of credit; make any thing but gold and silver coin a tender in payment of debts; pass any bill of attainder, ex post facto law, or law impairing the obligation of contracts, or grant any title of nobility.

2. No State shall, without the consent of the Congress, lay any imposts or duties on imports or exports, except what may be absolutely necessary for executing its inspection laws: And the net produce of all duties and imposts laid by any State on imports or exports, shall be for the use of the treasury of the United States; and all such laws shall be subject to the revision and control of the Congress.

3. No State shall, without the consent of the Congress, lay any duty of tonnage, keep troops, or ships of war in time of peace, enter into any agreement or compact with another State, or with a foreign power, or engage in war, unless actually invaded, or in such imminent danger as will not admit of delay.

ARTICLE II

Section I.

1. The executive power shall be vested in a President of the United States of America. He shall hold his office during the term of four years, and, together with the Vice President, chosen for the same term, be elected as follows:

2. Each State shall appoint, in such manner as the legislature thereof may direct, a number of electors, equal to the whole number of senators and representatives to which the State may be entitled in the Congress: But no senator or representative, or person holding an office of trust or profit under the United States, shall be appointed an elector.

   The electors shall meet in their respective States, and vote by ballot for two persons, of whom one at least shall not be an inhabitant of the same State with themselves. And they shall make a list of all the persons voted for, and of the number of votes for each; which list they shall sign and certify, and transmit sealed to the seat of the government of the United States, directed to the president of the Senate. The president of the Senate shall, in the presence of the Senate and House of Representatives, open all the certificates, and the votes shall then be counted. The person having the greatest number of votes shall be President, if such number be a majority of the whole number of electors appointed; and if there be more than one who have such majority, and have an equal number of votes, then the House of Representatives shall immediately choose by ballot one of them for President; and if no person have a majority, then from the five highest on the list the said House shall in like manner choose the President. But in choosing the President, the votes shall be taken by States, the representation from each State having one vote; a quorum for this purpose shall consist of a member or members from two thirds of the States, and a majority of all the States shall be necessary to a choice. In every case, after the choice of the President, the person having the greatest number of votes of the electors shall be the Vice President. But if there should remain two or more who have equal votes, the Senate shall choose from them by ballot the Vice President.[6]

3. The Congress may determine the time of choosing the electors, and the day on which they shall give their votes; which day shall be the same throughout the United States.

4. No person except a natural born citizen, or a citizen of the United States, at the time of the adoption of this Constitution, shall be eligible to the office of President; neither shall any person be eligible to that office who shall not have attained to the age of thirty-five years, and been fourteen years a resident within the United States.

5. In case of the removal of the President from office, or of his death, resignation, or inability to discharge the powers and duties of the said office, the same shall devolve on the Vice President, and the Congress may by law provide for the case of removal, death, resignation or inability, both of the President and Vice President, declaring what officer shall then act as President, and such officer shall act accordingly, until the disability be removed, or a President shall be elected.

6. The President shall, at stated times, receive for his services a compensation, which shall neither be increased nor diminished during the period for which he shall have been elected, and he shall not receive within that period any other emolument from the United States, or any of them.

7. Before he enter on the execution of his office, he shall take the following oath or affirmation: "I do solemnly swear (or affirm) that I will faithfully execute the office of President of the United States, and will to the best of my ability, preserve, protect, and defend the Constitution of the United States."

Section 2.

1. The President shall be commander in chief of the army and navy of the United States, and of the militia of the several States, when called into the actual service of the United States; he may require the opinion, in writing, of the principal officer in each of the executive departments, upon any subject relating to the duties of their respective offices, and he shall have power to grant reprieves and pardons for offenses against the United States, except in cases of impeachment.

2. He shall have power, by and with the advice and consent of the Senate, to make treaties, provided two thirds of the senators present concur; and he shall nominate, and by and with the advice and consent of the Senate, shall appoint ambassadors, other public ministers and consuls, judges of the Supreme Court, and all other officers of the United States, whose appointment are not herein otherwise provided for, and which shall be established by law: But the Congress may by law vest the appointment of such inferior officers, as they think proper, in the President alone, in the courts of law, or in the heads of departments.

---

[6]Superseded by the 12th Amendment.

3. The President shall have power to fill up all vacancies that may happen during the recess of the Senate, by granting commissions which shall expire at the end of their next session.

Section 3.

He shall from time to time give to the Congress information of the state of the Union, and recommend to their considerations such measures as he shall judge necessary and expedient; he may, on extraordinary occasions, convene both Houses, or either of them, and in case of disagreement between them with respect to the time of adjournment, he may adjourn them to such time as he shall think proper; he shall receive ambassadors and other public ministers; he shall take care that the laws be faithfully executed, and shall commission all the officers of the United States.

Section 4.

The President, Vice President, and all civil officers of the United States, shall be removed from office on impeachment for, and conviction of, treason, bribery, or other high crimes and misdemeanors.

ARTICLE III

Section 1.

The judicial power of the United States shall be vested in one Supreme Court, and in such inferior courts as the Congress may from time to time ordain and establish. The judges, both of the Supreme and inferior courts, shall hold their offices during good behavior, and shall, at stated times, receive for their services, a compensation, which shall not be diminished during their continuance in office.

Section 2.

1. The judicial power shall extend to all cases, in law and equity, arising under this Constitution, the laws of the United States, and treaties made, or which shall be made, under their authority;—to all cases affecting ambassadors, other public ministers and consuls;—to all cases of admiralty and maritime jurisdiction; — to controversies to which the United States shall be a party;[7] — to controversies between two or more States; — between a State and citizens of another State; — between citizens of different State; — between citizens of the same State claiming lands under grants of different States, and between a State, or the citizens thereof, and foreign States, citizens or subjects.

2. In all cases affecting ambassadors, other public ministers and consuls, and those in which a State shall be party, the Supreme Court shall have original jurisdiction. In all the other cases before mentioned, the Supreme Court shall have appellate jurisdiction, both as to law and fact, with such exceptions, and under such regulations as the Congress shall make.

3. The trial of all crimes, except in cases of impeachment, shall be by jury; and such trial shall be held in the State where the said crimes shall have been committed; but when not committed within any State, the trial shall be at such place or places as the Congress may by law have directed.

---

[7]Cf. the 11th Amendment.

Section 3.

1. Treason against the United States shall consist only in levying war against them, or in adhering to their enemies, giving them aid and comfort. No person shall be convicted of treason unless on the testimony of two witnesses to the same overt act, or on confession in open court.

2. The Congress shall have power to declare the punishment of treason, but no attainder of treason shall work corruption of blood, or forfeiture except during the life of the person attained.

ARTICLE IV

Section 1.

Full faith and credit shall be given in each State to the public acts, records, and judicial proceedings of every other State. And the Congress may by general laws prescribe the manner in which such acts, records and proceedings shall be proved, and the effect thereof.

Section 2.

1. The citizens of each State shall be entitled to all privileges and immunities of citizens in the several States.[8]

2. A person charged in any State with treason, felony, or other crime, who shall flee from justice, and be found in another State, shall on demand of the executive authority of the State from which he fled, be delivered up to be removed to the State having jurisdiction of the crime.

3. No person held to service or labor in one State under the laws thereof, escaping into another, shall in consequence of any law or regulation therein, be discharged from such service or labor, but shall be delivered up on claim of the party to whom such service or labor may be due.[9]

Section 3.

1. New States may be admitted by the Congress into this Union; but no new State shall be formed or erected within the jurisdiction of any other State; nor any State be formed by the junction of two or more States, or parts of States, without the consent of the legislatures of the States concerned as well as the Congress.

2. The Congress shall have power to dispose of and make all needful rules and regulations respecting the territory or other property belonging to the United States; and nothing in this Constitution shall be so construed as to prejudice any claims of the United States, or of any particular State.

Section 4.

The United States shall guarantee to every State in this Union a republican form of government, and shall protect each of them against invasion; and on application of the legislature, or of the executive (when the legislature cannot be convened) against domestic violence.

[8]Superseded by the 14th Amendment, Sec. 1.
[9]Voided by the 13th Amendment.

ARTICLE V

The Congress, whenever two thirds of both Houses shall deem it necessary, shall propose amendments to this Constitution, or, on the application of the legislatures of two thirds of the several States, shall call a convention for proposing amendments, which in either case shall be valid to all intents and purposes, as part of this Constitution, when ratified by the legislatures of three fourths of the several States, or by conventions in three fourths thereof, as the one or the other mode of ratification may be proposed by the Congress; Provided that no amendment which may be made prior to the year one thousand eight hundred and eight shall in any manner affect the first and fourth clauses in the ninth section of the first article; and that no State, without its consent, shall be deprived of its equal suffrage in the Senate.

ARTICLE VI

1. All debts contracted and engagements entered into, before the adoption of this Constitution, shall be as valid against the United States under this Constitution, as under the Confederation.

2. This Constitution, and the laws of the United States which shall be made in pursuance thereof; and all treaties made, or which shall be made, under the authority of the United States, shall be supreme law of the land; and the Judges in every State shall be bound thereby, any thing in the Constitution or laws of any State to the contrary notwithstanding.

3. The senators and representatives before mentioned, and the members of the several State legislatures, and all executives and judicial officers, both of the United States and of the several States, shall be bound by oath or affirmation to support this Constitution; but no religious test shall ever be required as a qualification to any office or public trust under the United States.

ARTICLE VII

The ratification of the conventions of nine States shall be sufficient for the establishment of this Constitution between the States so ratifying the same.

Done in Convention by the unanimous consent of the States present the seventeenth day of September in the year of our Lord one thousand seven hundred and eighty-seven, and of the independence of the United States of America the twelfth. In witness thereof we have hereunto subscribed our names. [Names omitted.]

•   •   •

Articles in addition to, and amendment of, the Constitution of the United States of America, proposed by Congress, and ratified by the legislatures of the several States, pursuant to the fifth article of the original Constitution.

AMENDMENT I [First ten amendments ratified December 15, 1791]

Congress shall make no law respecting an establishment of religion, or prohibiting the free exercise thereof; or abridging the freedom of speech, or of the press; or the right of the people peaceably to assemble, and to petition the government for a redress of grievances.

AMENDMENT II

A well regulated militia, being necessary to the security of a free State, the right of the people to keep and bear arms, shall not be infringed.

AMENDMENT III

No soldier shall, in the time of peace be quartered in any house, without the consent of the owner, nor in time of war, but in a manner to be prescribed by law.

AMENDMENT IV

The right of the people to secure in their persons, houses, papers, and effects, against unreasonable searches and seizures, shall not be violated, and no warrants shall issue, but upon probable cause, supported by oath or affirmation, and particularly describing the place to be searched, and the persons or things to be seized. *criminal law*

AMENDMENT V

No person shall be held to answer for a capital, or otherwise infamous crime, unless on a presentment or indictment of a grand jury, except in cases arising in the land or naval forces, or in the militia, when in actual service in time of war or public danger; nor shall any person be subject for the same offense to be twice put in jeopardy of life or limb; nor shall be compelled in any criminal case to be a witness against himself; nor be deprived of life, liberty, or property, without due process of law; nor shall private property be taken for public use, without just compensation.

AMENDMENT VI

In all criminal prosecutions, the accused shall enjoy the right to a speedy and public trial, by an impartial jury of the State and district wherein the crime shall have been committed, which district shall have been previously ascertained by law, and to be informed of the nature and cause of the accusation; to be confronted with the witnesses against him; to have compulsory process for obtaining witnesses in his favor, and to have the assistance of the counsel for his defense.

AMENDMENT VII

In suits at common law, where the value in controversy shall exceed twenty dollars, the right of trial by jury shall be preserved, and no fact tried by a jury shall be otherwise reexamined in any court of the United States, than according to the rules of the common law.

AMENDMENT VIII

Excessive bail shall not be required, nor excessive fines imposed, nor cruel and unusual punishments inflicted.

AMENDMENT IX

The enumeration in the Constitution of certain rights shall not be construed to deny or disparage others retained by the people.

AMENDMENT X

The powers not delegated to the United States by the Constitution, nor prohibited by it to the States, are reserved to the States respectively, or to the people.

AMENDMENT XI [Ratified January 8, 1798]

The judicial power of the United States shall not be construed to extend to any suit in law or equity, commenced or prosecuted against one of the United States by citizens of another State, or by citizens or subjects of any foreign State.

AMENDMENT XII [Ratified September 25, 1804]

The electors shall meet in their respective States, and vote by ballot for President and Vice President, one of whom, at least, shall not be an inhabitant of the same State with themselves; they shall name in their ballots the person voted for as President, and in distinct ballots, the person voted for as Vice President, and they shall make distinct lists of all persons voted for as President and of all persons voted for as Vice President, and of the number of votes for each, which lists they shall sign and certify, and transmit sealed to the seat of the government of the United States, directed to the President of the Senate; — The President of the Senate shall, in the presence of the Senate and House of Representatives, open all the certificates and the votes shall then be counted; — The person having the greatest number of votes for President, shall be the President, if such number be a majority of the whole number of electors appointed; and if no person have such majority, then from the persons having the highest numbers not exceeding three on the list of those voted for as President, the House of Representatives shall choose immediately, by ballot, the President. But in choosing the President, the votes shall be taken by States, the representation from each State having one vote; a quorum for this purpose shall consist of a member or members from two thirds of the States, and a majority of all the States shall be necessary to a choice. And if the House of Representatives shall not choose a President whenever the right of choice shall devolve upon them, before the fourth day of March next following, then the Vice President shall act as President, as in the case of the death or other constitutional disability of the President. The person having the greatest number of votes as Vice President shall be the Vice President, if such number be a majority of the whole number of electors appointed, and if no person have a majority, then from the two highest numbers on the list, the Senate shall choose the Vice President; a quorum for the purpose shall consist of two thirds of the whole number of Senators, and a majority of the whole number shall be necessary to a choice. But no person constitutionally ineligible to the office of President shall be eligible to that of Vice President of the United States.

AMENDMENT XIII [Ratified December 18, 1865]

Section 1.
Neither slavery nor involuntary servitude, except as punishment for crime whereof the party shall have been duly convicted, shall exist within the United States, or any place subject to their jurisdiction.

Section 2.

Congress shall have power to enforce this article by appropriate legislation.

AMENDMENT XIV [Ratified July 28, 1868]

Section 1.

All persons born or naturalized in the United States, and subject to the jurisdiction thereof, are citizens of the United States and of the State wherein they reside. No State shall make or enforce any law which shall abridge the privileges or immunities of citizens of the United States; not shall any State deprive any person of life, liberty, or property, without due process of law; nor deny to any person within its jurisdiction the equal protection of the laws.

Section 2.

Representatives shall be apportioned among the several States according to their respective numbers, counting the whole number of persons in each States, excluding Indians not taxed. But when the right to vote at any election for the choice of electors for President and Vice President of the United States, representatives in Congress, the executive and judicial officers of a State, or the members of the legislature thereof, is denied to any of the male inhabitants of such State, being twenty-one years of age, and citizens of the United States, or in any way abridged, except for participating in rebellion, or other crime, the basis of representation therein shall be reduced in the proportion which the number of such male citizens shall bear to the whole number of male citizens twenty-one years of age in such State.

Section 3.

No person shall be a senator or representative in Congress, or elector of President and Vice President, or hold any office, civil or military, under the United States, or under any State, who having previously taken an oath as a member of Congress, or as an officer of the United States, or as a member of any State legislature, or as an executive or judicial officer of any State, to support the Constitution of the United States, shall have engaged in insurrection or rebellion against the same, or given aid or comfort to the enemies thereof. But Congress may by a vote of two thirds of each House, remove such disability.

Section 4.

The validity of the public debt of the United States, authorized by law, including the debts incurred for payment of pensions and bounties for services in suppressing insurrection or rebellion, shall not be questioned. But neither the United States nor any State shall assume or pay any debt or obligation incurred in aid of insurrection or rebellion against the United States, or any claim for the loss or emancipation of any slave; but all such debts, obligations, and claims shall be held illegal and void.

Section 5.

Congress shall have power to enforce, by appropriate legislation, the provisions of this article.

AMENDMENT XV [Ratified March 30, 1870]

Section 1.

The right of citizens of the United States to vote shall not be denied or abridged by the United States or by any State on account of race, color, or previous condition of servitude.

Section 2.

The Congress shall have power to enforce this article by appropriate legislation.

AMENDMENT XVI [Ratified February 25, 1913]

The Congress shall have power to lay and collect taxes on incomes, from whatever source derived, without apportionment among the several States, and without regard to any census or enumeration.

AMENDMENT XVII [Ratified May 31, 1913]

The Senate of the United States shall be composed of two senators from each State, elected by the people thereof, for six years; and each senator shall have one vote. The electors in each State shall have the qualifications requisite for electors of the most numerous branch of the State legislature.

When vacancies happen in the representation of any State in the Senate, the executive authority of such State shall issue writs of election to fill such vacancies: *Provided,* That the legislature of any State may empower the executive thereof to make temporary appointments until the people fill the vacancies by election as the legislature may direct.

This amendment shall not be so construed as to affect the election or term of any senator chosen before it becomes valid as part of the Constitution.

AMENDMENT XVIII[10] [Ratified January 29, 1919]

After one year from the ratification of this article, the manufacture, sale, or transportation of intoxicating liquors within, the importation thereof into, or the exportation thereof from the United States and all territory subject to the jurisdiction thereof for beverage purposes is thereby prohibited.

The Congress and the several States shall have concurrent power to enforce this article by appropriate legislation.

This article shall be inoperative unless it shall have been ratified as an amendment to the Constitution by the legislature of the several States, as provided in the Constitution, within seven years from the date of the submission hereof to the States by Congress.

AMENDMENT XIX [Ratified August 26, 1920]

The right of citizens of the United States to vote shall not be denied or abridged by the United States or by any State on account of sex.

Congress shall have the power to enforce this article by appropriate legislation.

AMENDMENT XX [Ratified January 23, 1933]

Section 1.

The terms of the President and Vice President shall end at noon on the 20th day of January, and the terms of Senators and Representatives at noon on the 3d day of January, of the year in which such terms would have ended if this article had not been ratified; and the terms of their successors shall then begin.

---

[10]Repealed by the 21st Amendment.

Section 2.

The Congress shall assemble at least once in every year, and such meeting shall begin at noon on the 3d day of January, unless they shall by law appoint a different day.

Section 3.

If, at the time fixed for the beginning of the term of President, the President-elect shall have died, the Vice President-elect shall become President. If a President shall not have been chosen before the time fixed for the beginning of his term, or if the President-elect shall have failed to qualify, then the Vice President-elect shall act as President until a President shall have qualified; and the Congress may by law provide for the case wherein neither a President-elect nor a Vice President-elect shall have qualified, declaring who shall then act as President, or the manner in which one who is to act shall be selected, and such person shall act accordingly until a President or Vice President shall have qualified.

Section 4.

The Congress may by law provide for the case of the death of any of the persons from whom the House of Representatives may choose a President whenever the right of choice shall have devolved upon them, and for the case of the death of any of the persons from whom the Senate may choose a Vice President whenever the right of choice shall have devolved upon them.

Section 5.

Sections 1 and 2 shall take effect on the 15th day of October following the ratification of this article.

Section 6.

This article shall be inoperative unless it shall have been ratified as an amendment to the Constitution by the legislatures of three-fourths of the several States within seven years from the date of its submission.

AMENDMENT XXI [Ratified December 5, 1933]

Section 1.

The Eighteenth Article of amendment to the Constitution of the United States is hereby repealed.

Section 2.

The transportation or importation into any State, Territory, or possession of the United States for delivery or use therein of intoxicating liquors in violation of the laws thereof, is hereby prohibited.

Section 3.

This article shall be inoperative unless it shall have been ratified as an amendment to the Constitution by conventions in the several States as provided in the Constitution, within seven years from the date of the submission thereof to the States by the Congress.

AMENDMENT XXII [Ratified March 1, 1951]

No person shall be elected to the office of the President more than twice, and no person who has held the office of President, or acted as President, for more than two years of a term to which some other person was elected President shall be elected to the office of President more than once.

But this article shall not apply to any person holding the office of President when this article was proposed by the Congress, and shall not prevent any person who may be holding the office of President, or acting as President, during the term within which this article becomes operative from holding the office of President or acting as President during the remainder of such term.

This article shall be inoperative unless it shall have been ratified as an amendment to the Constitution by the legislature of three-fourths of the several States within seven years from the date of its submission to the States by the Congress.

AMENDMENT XXIII [Ratified March 29, 1961]

Section 1.
The District constituting the seat of Government of the United States shall appoint in such manner as the Congress may direct:

A number of electors of President and Vice President equal to the whole number of Senators and Representatives in Congress to which the District would be entitled if it were a State, but in no event more than the least populous State; they shall be in addition to those appointed by the States, but they shall be considered, for the purposes of the election of President and Vice President, to be electors appointed by a State; and they shall meet in the District and perform such duties as provided by the twelfth article of amendment.

Section 2.
The Congress shall have power to enforce this article by appropriate legislation.

AMENDMENT XXIV [Ratified January 24, 1964]

Section 1.
The right of citizens of the United States to vote in any primary or other election for President or Vice President, for electors for President or Vice President, or for Senator or Representative in Congress, shall not be denied or abridged by the United States or any State by reason of failure to pay any poll tax or other tax.

Section 2.
The Congress shall have power to enforce this article by appropriate legislation.

AMENDMENT XXV [Ratified February 10, 1967]

Section 1.
In case of the removal of the President from office or of his death or resignation, the Vice President shall become President.

Section 2.
Whenever there is a vacancy in the office of the Vice President, the President shall nominate a Vice President who shall take office upon confirmation by a majority vote of both Houses of Congress.

Section 3.
Whenever the President transmits to the President pro tempore of the Senate and the Speaker of the House of Representatives his written declaration that he is unable to

discharge the powers and duties of his office, and until he transmits to them a written declaration to the contrary, such powers and duties shall be discharged by the Vice President as Acting President.

Section 4.
Whenever the Vice President and a majority of either the principal officers of the executive departments or of such other body as Congress may by law provide, transmit to the President pro tempore of the Senate and the Speaker of the House of Representatives their written declaration that the President is unable to discharge the powers and duties of his office, the Vice President shall immediately assume the powers and duties of the office as Acting President.

Thereafter, when the President transmits to the President pro tempore of the Senate and the Speaker of the House of Representatives his written declaration that no inability exists, he shall resume the powers and duties of his office unless the Vice President and a majority of either the principal officers of the executive departments or of such body as Congress may by law provide, transmit within four days to the President pro tempore of the Senate and the Speaker of the House of Representatives their written declaration that the President is unable to discharge the powers and duties of his office. Thereupon Congress shall decide the issue, assembling within forty-eight hours for that purpose if not in session. If the Congress, within twenty-one days after receipt of the latter written declaration, or, if Congress is not in session, within twenty-one days after Congress is required to assemble, determines by two-thirds vote of both Houses that the President is unable to discharge the powers and duties of his office, the Vice President shall continue to discharge the same as Acting President; otherwise, the President shall resume the powers and duties of his office.

AMENDMENT XXVI [Ratified July 1, 1971]

Section 1.
The right of citizens of the United States, who are eighteen years of age or older, to vote shall not be denied or abridged by the United States or by any State on account of age.

Section 2.
The Congress shall have powers to enforce this article by appropriate legislation.

AMENDMENT XXVII [Ratified May 7, 1992]

No law varying the compensation for the services of the senators and representatives shall take effect until an election of representatives shall have intervened.

Glossary of
Selected Terms from
*The Law Dictionary**

ACCORD An agreement between two (or more) persons, one of whom has a right of action against the other that the latter should do or give, and the former accept, something in satisfaction of the right of action. When the agreement is executed, and satisfaction has been made, it is called accord and satisfaction, and operates as a bar to the right of action. Accord, Restatement (Second) of Contracts § 281(1).

ACT OF STATE DOCTRINE The principle that the courts will not examine the validity of a taking of property by a foreign government within its own territory, if the foreign government is extant and recognized by the United States at the time of the suit, in the absence of a treaty or other unambiguous agreement regarding controlling legal principles, even if the complaint alleges that the taking violates customary international law. The act in question must be public, and not commercial in nature. Expropriation claims may be heard as set-offs in some circumstances, however.

ADJUDICATION A judgment or decision. (2) Of bankruptcy, the declaring a debtor bankrupt.

ADMINISTRATIVE PROCEDURE ACT An act to establish a uniform system of administering laws by and among the agencies of the United States government, and to provide for administrative and judicial review of the decisions of those agencies. 5 U.S.C. §§ 1001 *et seq.*; 60 Stat. 237 (1946).

ADVISORY OPINION In some jurisdictions, the formal opinion of a higher court concerning a point at issue in a lower court. (2) The formal opinion of a legal officer, e.g., Attorney General, concerning a question of law submitted by a public official. (3) In some jurisdictions, the opinion of a court concerning a question submitted by a legislative body.

AFFIDAVIT A written statement of fact, signed and sworn to before a person having authority to administer an oath.

The Law Dictionary (Cochran's Law Lexicon, 6/e), revised by Wesley Gilmer, Jr. Anderson Publishing Co., Cincinnati. Reprinted by permission.

AFFIRM   To make firm; to establish. (1) To ratify or confirm the judgment of a lower court. (2) To ratify or confirm a voidable contract. (3) To declare or verify as a substitute for an oath.

AGE DISCRIMINATION IN EMPLOYMENT ACT OF 1967   An act to prohibit age discrimination in employment. 29 U.S.C. §§ 3322, 8335, 8339, 92 Stat. 189 (1978).

AGENT   A person authorized by another (the principal), to do an act or transact business for him, and to bind the principal within the limits of that authority. An agent may be general, to do all business of a particular kind; or special, to do one particular act. The agent's power to bind the principal is according to the scope of his authority.

ANSWER   In pleading, a statement of the defenses on which a party defending a lawsuit intends to rely. (2) A statement under oath, in response to written interrogatories, i.e., questions, or oral questions.

ANTI-TRUST ACTS or ANTITRUST ACTS   Various federal and state statutes intended to protect trade and commerce from unlawful restraints and monopolies.

APPELLANT   A person who initiates an appeal from one court to another.

APPELLATE JURISDICTION   The authority of a superior court to review and modify the decision of an inferior court.

APPELLEE   The party in a lawsuit against whom an appeal has been taken.

ARBITRATION   The voluntary submission of a matter in dispute to the nonjudicial judgment of one, two, or more disinterested persons, called arbitrators, whose decision is binding on the parties.

ARBITRATION AND AWARD   The voluntary settlement of a controversy by mutually agreeing to submit the controversy to arbitration, so that the decision in the arbitration is binding on the parties. (2) An affirmative defense which seeks to avoid a claim because it was previously submitted to arbitration and an award was established.

ARRAIGN   To bring an accused person to court for the purpose of having him answer the charge against him.

ARREST   The seizing of a person and detaining him in custody by lawful authority. (2) Taking of another into the custody of the actor for the actual or purported purpose of bringing the other before a court, or of otherwise securing the administration of the law. Restatement (Second) of Torts § 112. (3) The seizure and detention of personal chattels, especially ships and vessels libeled in a court of admiralty.

ASSAULT   Strictly speaking, threatening to strike or harm. (2) A threatening gesture, with or without verbal communication. If a blow is struck, it is battery (*q.v.*). (3) Attempting to cause or purposely, knowingly, or recklessly causing bodily injury to another, or negligently causing bodily injury to another with a deadly weapon, or attempting by physical menace to put another in fear of imminent serious bodily injury; also called simple assault. Model Penal Code § 211.1(1).

ASSUMPTION OF RISK   A defense to a claim for negligent injury to a person or property, i.e., a person who voluntarily exposes himself or his property to a known danger may not recover for injuries thereby sustained. Accord, Restatement (Second) of Torts § 496A.

BAIL   To set at liberty a person arrested or imprisoned, on written security taken for his appearance on a day, and at a place named. The term is applied, as a noun, to the persons who become security for the defendant's appearance; to the act of delivering such defendant to his bondsmen; and also to the bond given by the sureties to secure his release. A person who becomes someone's bail is regarded as his jailer, to whose custody he is committed. The word "bail" is never used with a plural termination.

BAILEE   A person to whom personal property (*q.v.*) is entrusted for a specific purpose. See also *Bailment.*

BAILMENT   A broad expression which describes the agreement, undertaking, or relationship which is created by the delivery of personal property by the owner, i.e., the bailor, to someone who is not an owner of it, i.e., the bailee, for a specific purpose, which includes the return of the personal property to the person who delivered it, after the purpose is otherwise accomplished. In a bailment, dominion and control over the personal property usually pass to the bailee. The term is often used to describe, e.g.: (1) The gratis loaning of an automobile for the borrower's use. (2) The commercial leasing of an automobile for a fee. (3) The delivery of an automobile to a repairman for the purpose of having it repaired. (4) The delivery of an automobile to a parking attendant for storage, when the keys are left with the attendant.

BAILOR   A person who commits goods to another person (the bailee) in trust for a specific purpose.

BATTERY   An unlawful touching, beating, wounding or laying hold, however, trifling, of another's person or clothes without his consent.

BILATERAL CONTRACT   An agreement in which two parties mutually promise to fulfill obligations reciprocally toward each other, e.g., one party promises to convey a house and lot and the other party promises to pay the agreed price for it.

BREACH OF CONTRACT   A flexible term for the wrongful failure to perform one or more of the promises which a person previously undertook when he made a contract, e.g., failure to deliver goods.

BURDEN OF PROOF (ONUS PROBANDI)   The duty of proving facts disputed on the trial of a case. It commonly lies on the person who asserts the affirmative of an issue, and is sometimes said to shift when sufficient evidence is furnished to raise a presumption that what is alleged is true. The shifting of the burden of proof is better characterized as the creation of a burden of going forward with the evidence; however, because the total burden of proof is not thereby changed, the burden of going forward with the evidence is apt to revert to the other party and change from time to time.

CASE LAW   Judicial precedent generated as a by-product of the decisions which courts have made in resolving unique disputes, as distinguished from statutes and constitutions. Case law concerns concrete facts. Statutes and constitutions are written in the abstract.

CASES AND CONTROVERSIES   A generic phrase denoting bona fide disputes or lawsuits in which something is decided either affirmatively or negatively. Controversy is usually descriptive of civil proceedings and cases usually include both criminal prosecutions and civil proceedings. Article III of the United States Constitution uses the terms, cases and controversies, to define the judicial power of the United States. (2) The difference between an abstract question and a case or controversy is one of degree and is not discernible by any precise test. The basic inquiry is whether the conflicting contentions of the parties present a real, substantial controversy between parties having adverse legal interests, a dispute definite and concrete, not hypothetical or abstract.

CAUSE OF ACTION   A flexible term, the definition of which is occasionally controversial. (1) An aggregation of facts which will cause a court to grant relief, and therefore entitles a person to initiate and prosecute a lawsuit. (2) The concurrence of a right belonging to a plaintiff, and a wrong committed by a defendant, which breaches the right and results in damage. Under modern rules of civil procedure, the term has been partly superseded by claim for relief.

CERTIORARI   Lat., "to be more fully informed," an original writ or action whereby a cause is removed from an inferior to a superior court for review. The record of the proceedings is then transmitted to the superior court. (2) A discretionary appellate jurisdiction that is invoked by a petition for certiorari, which the appellate court may grant or deny in its discretion. A dominant avenue to the United States Supreme Court. 28 U.S.C. §§ 1257(3), 2103.

CIVIL ACTION   A lawsuit which has for its object the protection of private or civil rights or compensation for their infraction.

CIVIL LAW   The law compiled by the Roman jurists under the auspices of the Emperor Justinian, which is still in force in many of the nations in Europe.

CLAYTON ACT   An act to supplement earlier laws, including the Sherman Act, against unlawful restraints and monopolies. 15 U.S.C. §§ 12 *et seq.,* 18 U.S.C. §§ 402 *et seq.,* 29 U.S.C. §§ 52, 53; 38 Stat, 730 (1914).

COLLUSION   A secret agreement between persons apparently hostile, to do some act in order to defraud or prejudice a third person, or for some improper purpose.

COMITY   The practice by which one court follows the decisions of another court on a like question, though not bound by the law of precedents to do so.

COMMON LAW   An ambiguous term. (1) A system of jurisprudence founded on principles of justice which are determined by reasoning and administration consistent with the usage, customs and institutions of the people and which are suitable to the genius of the people and their social, political and economic condition. The rules deduced from this system continually change and expand with the progress of society. (2) That system of law which does not rest for its authority upon any express statutes, but derives its force and authority from universal consent and immemorial usage, and which is evidenced by the decisions of the courts of law, technically so called, in contradistinction to those of equity and the ecclesiastical courts.

COMPENSATORY DAMAGES   Such as measure the actual loss; not exemplary or punitive.

COMPLAINT   The charge made before a proper officer that an offense has been committed by a person named or described. (2) Under modern rules of civil procedure, a pleading which must be filed to commence an action.

CONDITION PRECEDENT   A qualification, restriction, or limitation, which suspends or delays the vesting or enlargement of an estate in property, or a right until a specified event has occurred. This terminology is not used in the Restatement (Second) of Contracts.

CONDITION SUBSEQUENT   A condition which, if not performed, defeats or diverts a right or estate existing or vested; this terminology is not used in the Restatement (Second) of Contracts.

CONFLICT OF LAWS   The variance between the laws of two states or countries relating to the subject matter of a suit brought in one of them, when the parties to the suit, or some of them, or the subject matter, belong to the other. See also *lex loci.*

CONSENT AGREEMENT   The meeting of minds. It presupposes mental capacity to act. It may be express, i.e., by word of mouth or in writing, or implied from acts, inaction, or silence which are consistent only with assent. If obtained by fraud or duress, it is not binding.

CONSIDERATION   The price, motive or matter of inducement of a contract, which must be lawful in itself. The term is flexible and includes that which is bargained for and paid in return for a promise, the benefits to the party making the promise and the loss or detriment to the party to whom the promise is made. A contract derives its binding force from the existence of a valuable consideration between the parties. Consideration may be *executed,* i.e., past or performed; *executory,* i.e., to be performed; or *continuing,* i.e., partly both. Good or meritorious consideration is that originating in relationship and natural affection. Valuable consideration is that which has a money value. A performance or a return promise which is bargained for. Restatement (Second) of Contracts § 71(1).

CONSTITUTION   The fundamental and basic law of a state or nation which establishes the form and limitation of government and secures the rights of the citizens. The constitution of the United States was adopted in a convention of representatives of the people, at Philadelphia, September 17, 1787, and became the law of the land on the first Wednesday in March, 1789. Each of the states composing the United States has a constitution of its own. Constitutions usually prescribe the manner in which they may be amended.

CONTEMPT   A willful disregard or disobedience of public authority. Courts may punish one who disobeys the rules, orders or process, or willfully offends against the dignity and good order of the court, by fine or imprisonment. Similar authority is exercised by each house of the Congress of the United States, by state legislatures and in some instances by administrative agencies. The contempt power is usually subject to judicial review.

CONTRACT   An agreement between competent parties, upon a legal consideration, to do or to abstain from doing some act. It is usually applied to simple or parol contracts, including written as well as verbal ones. Contracts may be *express,* in which the terms are stated in words; or *implied,* i.e., presumed by law to have been made from the circumstances and the relations of the parties; *mutual* and *dependent,* in which the performance by one is dependent upon the performance by the other; *independent,* when either promise may be performed without reference to the other; *entire,* in which the complete performance by one is a condition precedent to demanding performance of the other; *severable,* in which the things to be performed are capable of separation, so that on performance of part the party performing may demand a proportionate part of the consideration from the other; *executed*, in which the things each agrees to perform are done at the time the contract is made; *executory*, in which some act remains to be done by one or both of the parties; *personal*, i.e., depending on the skill or qualities of one of the parties; *contracts of beneficence*, by which only one of the contracting parties is to be benefited, e.g., loans and deposits. (2) The total legal obligation which results from the parties' agreement as affected by the U.C.C. and any other applicable rules of law. U.C.C. § 1–201(11). (3) A promise or a set of promises for the breach of which the law gives a remedy, or the performance of which the law in some way recognizes as a duty. Restatement (Second) of Contracts § 1.

CONTRIBUTORY NEGLIGENCE   The failure to exercise care by a plaintiff, which contributed to the plaintiff's injury. Even though a defendant may have been negligent, in the majority of jurisdictions, contributory negligence will bar a recovery by the plaintiff. (2) Conduct on the part of a plaintiff which falls below the standard to which he should conform for his own protection, and which is a legally contributing cause cooperating with the negligence of the defendant in bringing about the plaintiff's harm. Restatement (Second) of Torts § 463.

CONVERSIONS   A flexible term. (1) The wrongful appropriation of the goods of another. (2) An intentional exercise of dominion or control over a chattel which so seriously interferes with the right of another to control it that the actor may justly be required to pay the other the full value of the chattel. Restatement (Second) of Torts § 22A(1).

COUNTERCLAIM   The defendant's claim against the plaintiff, which most courts permit him to set up in his response to the complaint.

COURT   An institution for the resolving of disputes. (2) A place where justice is administered. (3) The judge or judges when performing their official duties. Courts may be classified as courts of record, those in which a final record of the proceedings is made, which imports verity and cannot be collaterally impeached, and courts not of record, in which no final record is made, though it may keep a docket and enter in it notes of the various proceedings; courts of original jurisdiction, in which suits are initiated, and which have power to hear and determine in the first instance, and appellate courts, which take cognizance of causes removed from other courts; courts of equity or chancery, which administer justice according to the principles of equity; and courts of law, which administer justice according to the principles of the common law; civil courts which give remedies for private wrongs; criminal courts, in which public offenders are tried, acquitted or convicted and sentenced; ecclesiastical courts, which formerly had jurisdiction over testamentary and matrimonial causes; courts of admiralty, which have jurisdiction over maritime causes, civil and criminal; courts-martial, which have jurisdiction of offenses against the military or naval laws, committed by persons in that service. In numerous instances, the various classifications of courts have been consolidated. The same court may serve as a court of equity, a court of law, a civil court, a criminal court and a court of admiralty. It may qualify as a court of record and be a court of original jurisdiction.

COVENANT   An agreement or unilateral contract such as is contained in a deed. See also *Contract*. The principal covenants in a deed conveying land are seisin, right to convey, for quiet enjoyment, against encumbrances, and for further assurances. A covenant is said to run with the land (or the reversion) when the benefit or burden of it passes to the assignee of the land. (2) Formerly one of the forms of action

CRIMINAL LAW   Jurisprudence concerning crimes and their punishment.

CROSS-EXAMINATION   The questioning of a witness by the party opposed to the party which called the witness for direct examination. This usually occurs after the direct examination but on occasion may be otherwise allowed. The form of the questions on cross-examination is designed for the purpose of eliciting evidence from a hostile witness. (2) Cross-examination should be limited to the subject matter of the direct examination and matters affecting the credibility of the witness. The court may, in the exercise of discretion, permit inquiry into additional matters as if on direct examination. Fed. R. Evid. 611(b).

DAMAGES   A flexible term for the reparation in money which is allowed by law on account of damage. They may be general, such as necessarily and by implication of law arise from the act complained of; or special, such as under the peculiar circumstances of the case arise from the act complained of, but are not implied by law; compensatory, sufficient in amount to cover the loss actually sustained; exemplary, punitive, or vindictive, when in excess of the loss sustained and allowed as a punishment for torts committed with fraud, actual malice, or violence; nominal, when the act was wrong, but the loss sustained was trifling; substantial, when the loss was serious; liquidated, fixed by agreement of the parties, as when it is agreed beforehand what amount one shall receive in case of a breach of contract by the other.

DE NOVO   Lat., "anew; afresh." A trial de novo is a trial which is held for a second time, as if there had been no former decision.

DECLARATORY JUDGMENT, or DECLARATORY DECREE   A determination or decision by a court, which states the rights of the parties to a dispute, but does not order or coerce any performance relative to those rights. The procedural and substantive conditions of the usual action must be present. The relief which the court grants is the distinguishing characteristic.

DEFAMATION   A flexible term for the uttering of spoken or written words concerning someone, which tend to injure that person's reputation and for which an action for damages may be brought. (2) To create liability for defamation there must be (a) a false and defamatory statement concerning another, (b) an unprivileged publication to a third party, (c) fault amounting at least to negligence on the part of the publisher, and (d) either actionability of the statement irrespective of special harm or the existence of special harm caused by the publication. Restatement (Second) of Torts § 558. See also *Libel; Slander.*

DEFAULT   A flexible term for the omission of that which a person ought to do. (2) The failure to plead or otherwise defend an action, by a party against whom a judgment for affirmative relief is sought.

DEFENDANT   A person against whom an action is brought, a warrant is issued or an indictment is found.

DELEGATE   A person authorized to act for another. (2) A person elected to represent others in a deliberative assembly, such as a political convention.

DEPOSITION   A written record of oral testimony, in the form of questions and answers, made before a public officer, for use in a lawsuit. They are used for the purpose of discovery of information, or for the purpose of being read as evidence at a trial, or for both purposes.

DICTUM, or OBITER DICTUM   Lat., a statement by a judge concerning a point of law which is not necessary for the decision of the case in which it is stated. Usually, dictum is not as persuasive as its opposite, i.e., holding (*q.v.*).

DIRECT EXAMINATION   The initial questioning of a witness by the party who calls him.

DIRECTED VERDICT   A determination by a jury made at the direction of the court, in cases where there has been a failure of evidence, an overwhelming weight of the evidence, or where the law, as applied to the facts, is for one of the parties.

DISCHARGE   A flexible term that connotes finality, e.g., cancellation, rescission, or nullification. (2) The court order by which a person held to answer a criminal charge is set free. (3) The court order by which a jury is relieved from further consideration of a case.

DISCOVERY   A pliant method by which the opposing parties to a lawsuit may obtain full and exact factual information concerning the entire area of their controversy, via pretrial depositions, interrogations, requests for admissions, inspection of books and documents, physical and mental examinations and inspection of land or other property. The purpose of these pretrial procedures is to disclose the genuine points of factual dispute and facilitate adequate preparation for trial. Either party may compel the other party to disclose the relevant facts that are in his possession, prior to the trial. Fed. R. Civ. P. 26–37.

DISCRETION   The use of private independent judgment; the authority of a trial court which is not controlled by inflexible rules, but can be exercised one way or the other as the trial judge believes to be best in the circumstances. It is subject to review, however, if it is abused. (2) Ability to distinguish between good and evil.

DOCTRINE   A principle of law, often developed through court decisions; a precept or rule.

DONEE BENEFICIARY   A person to whom a gift is made or a power of appointment is given.

DURESS   Imprisonment; compulsion; coercion. (2) Threats of injury or imprisonment.

EASEMENT   A privilege or intangible right, which the owner of one parcel of real property, called the dominant tenement, has concerning another parcel of real property, called the servient estate, by which the owner of the latter is obligated not to interfere with the privilege. The most common easements are in the nature of passageways, e.g., road, walkway, railroad, pole line or pipeline. It is technically classified as an incorporeal hereditament.

EJECTMENT   Formerly a mixed action at common law, which depended on fictions in order to escape the inconveniences in the ancient forms of action. It was a mixed action, because it sought to recover both possession of land (a real property claim), and also damages (a personal property claim). Various statutory proceedings for the recovery of land, some of which bear the same name, have taken place in most of the United States.

EQUITY   Fairness. A type of justice that developed separately from the common law, and which tends to complement it. The current meaning is to classify disputes and remedies according to their historical relationship and development. Under modern rules of civil procedure, law and equity have been unified. Fed. R. Civ. P. 2. Historically, the courts of equity had a power of framing and adapting new remedies to particular cases, which the common law courts did not possess. In doing so, they allowed themselves latitude of construction and assumed, in certain matters such as trusts, a power of enforcing moral obligations which the courts of law did not admit or recognize. (2) A right or obligation attaching to property or a contract. In this sense, one person is said to have a better equity than another.

ESTATE The condition and circumstance in which a person stands with regard to those around him and his property. (2) The quantum or quality of the interest which a person has in property. Estates in property may be: legal or equitable; real or personal; vested or contingent; in possession or in expectancy; absolute, determinable, or conditional; sole, joint, or in common; of freehold or less than freehold. (3) Includes the property of a decedent, trust, or person whose affairs are subject to the Uniform Probate Code, as originally constituted and as it exists from time to time during administration. Uniform Probate Code § 1–201(11).

EX PARTE Lat., "of the one part"; an action which is not an adverse proceeding against someone else.

EXECUTION The writ, order or process issued to a sheriff, directing him to carry out the judgment of a court, e.g., to make the money due on the judgment out of the property of the defendant.

EXEMPLARY, or PUNITIVE, or VINDICTIVE DAMAGES An award of money given because of torts committed through malice or with circumstances of aggravation, which is in addition to compensation for the injury inflicted.

EXPRESS Something which is stated in direct words, and not left to implications, e.g., an express promise, express trust.

FALSE ARREST, or FALSE IMPRISONMENT A tort consisting of restraint imposed on a person's liberty, without proper legal authority. (2) False imprisonment is a misdemeanor consisting of knowingly restraining another unlawfully so as to interfere substantially with his liberty. Model Penal Code § 212.3.

FEDERAL QUESTION An issue of law or controversy cognizable by the United States courts because it involves the construction of the Constitution, a federal law, or treaty.

FEE SIMPLE A freehold estate of inheritance, absolute and unqualified. This is the highest and most ample estate known to the law, out of which all others are carved. An owner in fee has absolute power of disposition.

FELONY A type of crime which is of a relatively serious nature, usually various offenses in various jurisdictions, for which the maximum penalty can be death or imprisonment in the state penitentiary, regardless of such lesser penalty as may in fact be imposed. Occasionally defined by various state statutes. (2) Formerly, every offense at common law which caused a forfeiture of lands or goods, besides being punishable by death, imprisonment or other severe penalty.

FINAL DECISION, or FINAL ORDER A decree or judgment of a court, which terminates the litigation in the court which renders it. Cf. *Interlocutory.* (2) The United States Courts of Appeals have jurisdiction of appeals from certain final decisions of

United States District Courts (28 U.S.C. § 1291), but the courts have had difficulty defining final decision in that context. A decision may be final, even if it does not terminate the litigation, if the issue which is decided is fundamental to the further conduct of the case. (3) An order is a final judgment for purposes of United States Supreme Court jurisdiction if it involves a right separable from, and collateral to, the merits.

FIXTURE   Formerly, an article which was a personal chattel, but which, by being physically annexed to a building or land, became accessory to it and part and parcel of it. It was treated as belonging to the owner of the freehold, and passed with it to a vendee, and, though annexed by a tenant for his own convenience in the occupation of the premises, could not be removed by him. The rule has been modified by statute in many of the states, and is significantly relaxed in practice, especially as between landlord and tenant. Trade fixtures and ornamental fixtures may usually be removed by the tenant at the end of his term, provided he does no material injury to the freehold. Written leases often make specific provisions concerning the matter.

FOREIGN LAWS   Those enacted and in force in a foreign state, or country.

FORUM   Lat., a court of justice; the place where justice must be sought. (2) Formerly, an open space in Roman cities, where the people assembled, markets were held, and the magistrates sat to transact their business.

FORUM NON CONVENIENS   Lat., an inconvenient court.

FULL FAITH AND CREDIT   The requirement that the public acts, records and judicial proceedings of every state shall be given the same effect by the courts of another state that they have by law and usage in the state of origin. U.S. Const., Art. IV, Sec. I. Congress has prescribed the manner in which they may be proven. Cf. *Comity*.

GENERAL VERDICT   The decision of the jury, when they simply find for the plaintiff or defendant, without specifying the particular facts which they found from the evidence.

GRAND JURY   A body of persons, not less than twelve, nor more than twenty-four, freeholders of a county, whose duty it is, on hearing the evidence for the prosecution in each proposed bill of indictment, to decide whether a sufficient case is made out, on which to hold the accused for trial. It is a body which is convened by authority of a court and serves as an instrumentality of the court. It has authority to investigate and to accuse, but it is not authorized to try cases. It is a creature of the common law which was instituted to protect the people from governmental oppression. In a few states, it has been partially abolished, but in others it exists by constitutional mandate. No person shall be held to answer for a capital or otherwise infamous federal crime, unless on a presentment or indictment of a grand jury, except in cases arising in the land or naval forces, or in the militia, when in actual service in time of war or public danger; U.S. Const., Amendment V.

GUARDIAN   A person appointed by a court, to have the control or management of the person or property, or both, of another who is incapable of acting on his own behalf, e.g., an infant or a person of unsound mind. (2) Guardians ad litem are appointed by the court to represent such persons, who are parties to a pending action. (3) A person who has qualified as guardian of a minor or incapacitated person pursuant to testamentary or court appointment, but excludes one who is merely a guardian ad litem. Uniform Probate Code § 1-201(16). (4) A person who has qualified as a guardian of a minor or incapacitated person pursuant to parental or spousal nomination or court appointment, and includes a limited guardian, but excludes one who is merely a guardian ad litem. Uniform Probate Code § 5–103(6).

HABEAS CORPUS Lat., "that you have the body," words used in various writs, commanding one who detains another to have, or bring, him before the court issuing the same.

HEARING A flexible term for a court proceeding or the trial of a suit. (2) The examination of witnesses incident to the making of a judicial determination as to whether an accused person shall be held for trial.

HEARSAY EVIDENCE Statements offered by a witness, based upon what someone else has told him, and not upon personal knowledge or observation. Usually, such evidence is inadmissible, but exceptions are made, e.g., in questions of pedigree, custom, reputation, dying declarations, and statements made against the interest of the declarant. (2) A statement other than one made by the declarant while testifying at the trial or hearing, offered in evidence to prove the truth of the matter asserted. Fed. R. Evid. 801(c).

HOLDING The principle which reasonably may be drawn from the decision which a court or judge actually makes in a case; the opposite of dictum (*q.v.*). (2) The resolution of the unique dispute which is before a judge or court in a specific case. (3) A broad term for something which a person owns or possesses.

IMPEACH To charge a public official with crime or misdemeanor, or with misconduct in office. (2) To prove that a witness has a bad reputation for truth and veracity, and is therefore unworthy of belief.

IMPLIED CONTRACT Contract presumed by law to have been made from the circumstances and the relations of the parties.

IN PERSONAM Lat., against the person.

IN REM Lat., against the thing; opposed to *in personam*.

INDEPENDENT CONTRACTOR A person who agrees with another to do something for him, in the course of his occupation, but who is not controlled by the other, nor subject to the other's right to control, with respect to his performance of the undertaking, and is thereby distinguished from an employee.

INDICTMENT (DIT) A written accusation that one or more persons have committed a crime, presented upon oath, by a grand jury. The person against whom the indictment is found is said to be indicted.

INJUNCTION A flexible, discretionary process of preventive and remedial justice, which is exercised by courts that have equity powers. Courts issue injunctions when it appears that the ordinary remedy usually provided by law is not a full, adequate and complete one. Injunctions are preventive, if they restrain a person from doing something, or mandatory, if they command something to be done. They are preliminary, provisional or interlocutory, if they are granted on the filing of a bill, or while the suit is pending, to restrain the party enjoined from doing or continuing to do the acts complained of, until final hearing or the further order of the court. They are final, perpetual or permanent, if they are awarded after full hearing on the merits, and as a final determination of the rights of the parties.

INSURANCE   The act of providing against a possible loss, by entering into a contract with a licensed corporation that is willing to bind itself to make good such loss, should it occur. The instrument by which the contract is made is called a policy; the consideration paid to the insurer, who is sometimes called an underwriter, is called a premium. Fire and marine insurance is usually by way of indemnity, i.e., only such sum is paid by the insurer as is actually lost, and, on making such payment, he is entitled to stand in the place of the assured. (2) In the case of life or accident insurance, the insurer undertakes, in consideration of a premium, to pay a certain sum to the insured, or his legal representatives, on his death or injury by an accident. (3) There are many various types of insurance, each of which is defined by the respective policies which evidence the agreements between the parties, e.g., automobile insurance, creditor life insurance, homeowner insurance, owner, landlord, and tenant insurance, and workmen's compensation insurance.

INTANGIBLES   A kind of property which is nonphysical and not subject to being sensed, e.g., touched or felt, but which exists as a concept of people's minds. E.g., promissory notes, bank accounts and corporate stock.

INTERROGATORIES   Written questions propounded on behalf of one party in an action to another party, or to someone who is not a party, before the trial thereof. The person interrogated must give his answers in writing, and upon oath. Fed. R. Civ. P. 26, 33. (2) Verbal questions put to a witness before an examiner, and answered on oath. (3) Questions in writing, annexed to a commission to take the deposition of a witness, to be put to and answered by the witness under oath, whose answers are to be reduced to writing by the commissioner.

INVITEE   A person who goes upon land or premises of another by invitation, express or implied. (2) Either a public invitee or a business visitor: (a) Public invitee is a person who is invited to enter or remain on land as a member of the public for a purpose for which the land is held open to the public. (b) Business visitor is a person who is invited to enter or remain on land for a purpose directly or indirectly connected with business dealings with the possessor of the land. Restatement (Second) of Torts § 332.

ISSUE   A flexible term for offspring or lineal descendants. (2) All of a person's lineal descendants of all generations, with the relationship of parent and child at each generation being determined by the definitions of child and parent. Uniform Probate Code § 1–201(21). (3) The point or points which are left to be resolved by the jury or the court, at the conclusion of the pleadings. Issues may be of fact or of law. To join issue, is a technical phrase for closing the pleadings. To issue a writ or process, is for the proper officer to deliver it to the party suing it out, or to the officer to whom it is directed.

JUDGE   A public official with authority to determine a cause or question in a court of justice and to preside over the proceedings therein.

JURISDICTION   The authority of a court to hear and decide an action or lawsuit. (2) The geographical district over which the power of a court extends. Jurisdiction is limited when the court has power to act only in certain specified cases; general, or residual, when it may act in all cases in which the parties are before it, except for those cases which are within the exclusive jurisdiction of another court; concurrent, when the same cause may be entertained by one court or another; original, when the court has power to try the case in the first instance; appellate, when the court hears cases only on appeal, certiorari, or writ of error from another court; exclusive, when no other court has power to hear and decide the same matter. (3) Subject-matter jurisdiction defines the court's authority to hear a given type of case. (4) Personal jurisdiction requires that the court personally summon the defendant within its geographical district, or that it summon the defendant under the authority of a long-arm statute. This protects the individual interest that is implicated when a nonresident defendant is haled into a distant and possibly inconvenient court.

JURISPRUDENCE   Law. (2) A body of law. (3) Philosophy of law.

JURY   A body of citizens sworn to deliver a true verdict upon evidence submitted to them in a judicial proceeding. They are respectively called, jurymen or jurors. A grand jury is one summoned to consider whether the evidence presented by the state against a person accused of crime, warrants his indictment. A petty or petit jury is the jury for the trial of cases, either civil or criminal. It usually consists of twelve persons, but by various statutes in many of the states, and in England, a lesser number may constitute a jury in some courts. A special or struck jury is one selected especially for the trial of a given cause, usually by the assistance of the parties.

KNOWINGLY   In criminal prosecutions, knowledge that one is acting in violation of some law or regulation; knowledge that the act done is illegal.

LACHES   Negligence, or unreasonable delay, in pursuing a legal remedy, concurrent with a resultant prejudice to the opposing party, whereby a person forfeits his right.

LARCENY   The unlawful taking and carrying away of personal property without color of right, and with intent to deprive the rightful owner of the same. Larceny is commonly classified as grand or petty, according to the value of the thing taken. Usually defined and classified by various state statutes.

LEASEHOLD   Land held under a lease.

LEX FORI   Lat., the law of the country where an action is brought. This regulates the forms of procedure and the nature of the remedy to be obtained.

LEX LOCI   Lat., the law of the place where a contract is made, i.e., Lex loci contractus; or thing is done, i.e., Lex loci actus; tort is committed, i.e., Lex loci delicti; or where the thing, i.e., real estate, is situated, i.e., Lex loci rei sitae. It is usually applied in suits relating to such contracts, transactions, torts, and real estate.

LIBEL   Defamatory writing; any published matter which tends to degrade a person in the eyes of his neighbors, or to render him ridiculous, or to injure his property or business. It may be published by writing, effigy, picture, or the like. Cf. *Slander.* (2) Broadcasting of defamatory matter by means of radio or television, whether or not it is read from a manuscript. Id. § 568A.

LICENSE   Permission or authority to do something, which would be wrongful or illegal to do, if the permission or authority were not granted. The permission or authority may pertain to a public matter, e.g., the privilege of driving a motor vehicle on the public highways, or to a private matter, e.g., the privilege of manufacturing a patented article. In public matters, licenses are often required in order to regulate the activity.

LIEN   A security device, by which there is created a right (1) to retain that which is in a person's possession, belonging to another, until certain demands of the person in possession are satisfied; or (2) to charge property in another's possession with payment of a debt, e.g., a vendor's lien. It may be either (a) particular, arising out of some charge or claim connected with the identical thing; (b) general, in respect of all dealings of a similar nature between the parties; or (c) conventional, by agreement, express or implied, between the parties, e.g., a mortgage; or (d) by operation of law, e.g., a lien for taxes or an attorney's lien.

LIFE ESTATE   An interest in property which has a termination date concurrent with someone's death. The interest may be measured by the lifetime of the owner, who is called a life tenant, or by someone else's lifetime.

LIQUIDATED DAMAGES   The exact amount, which the parties to a contract expressly agree must be paid, or may be collected, in the event of a future default or breach of contract.

MALICIOUS ARREST   Imprisonment or prosecution, a malicious setting in motion of the law, without probable cause, whereby someone is wrongfully and maliciously accused of a criminal offense or a civil wrong, and by reason of which that person sustains damage.

MAXIM   An axiom; a general or leading principle.

MEDIATION   The settlement of disputes by the amicable intervention of an outside party who is a stranger to the controversy.

MENS REA   Criminal intent; evil intent; guilty intent.

MERGER   In real property, an absorption by operation of law, of a lesser right or estate in a greater right or estate, upon the union of their ownership in the same person. It takes place independently of the will of the party. (2) A consolidation of corporations, in which only one of two or more former corporations survives the consolidation, or which brings into existence a new corporation and destroys the former corporations.

MISDEMEANOR   Any crime or offense not amounting to a felony (*q.v.*).

MONOPOLY   An exclusive privilege of buying, selling, making, working, or using a particular thing. (2) The absolute and exclusive control by a person, or combination of persons, of the sale of a particular commodity. (3) A combination of producers or dealers to raise commodity prices via the more or less exclusive control of the supply or the purchasing power.

MOOT   Descriptive of something which is not genuine or concrete, something which is pretended. (2) A meeting, especially for the purpose of arguing points of law by way of exercise.

NEGLIGENCE   A flexible term for the failure to use ordinary care, under the particular factual circumstances revealed by the evidence in a lawsuit. (2) Conduct which falls below the standard established by law for the protection of others against unreasonable risk of harm. It does not include conduct recklessly disregardful of an interest of others. Restatement (Second) of Torts § 282.

NOLO CONTENDERE   Lat., no contest; a plea in criminal cases whereby the defendant tacitly admits his guilt by throwing himself on the mercy of the court.

NOMINAL DAMAGES   A token sum awarded, where a breach of duty or an infraction of plaintiffs' rights is shown, but no substantial injury is proven to have been sustained.

NOTICE   Information given to a person of some act done, or about to be done; knowledge. Notice may be actual, when knowledge is brought home to the party to be affected by it; or constructive, when certain acts are done in accordance with law, from which, on grounds of public policy, the party interested is presumed to have knowledge. It may be written, or oral, but written notice is preferable as avoiding disputes as to its terms. (2) A person has notice of a fact when he has actual knowledge of it, or he has received a notice or notification of it, or from all the facts and circumstances known to him at the time in question, he has reason to know that it exists. U.C.C. § 1–201(25).

NOVATION   The substitution of a new obligor or obligation for an old one, which is thereby extinguished, e.g., the acceptance of a note of a third party in payment of the original promisor's obligation, or the note of an individual in lieu of that of a corporation. Accord, Restatement (Second) of Contracts § 280.

NUISANCE   A flexible and imprecise term for various activities which annoy, harm, inconvenience or damage other persons, under the particular facts and circumstances proven in a lawsuit or criminal prosecution. It may be (a) private, as where one uses his property so as to damage another's or to disturb his quiet enjoyment of it; or (b) public, or common, where the whole community is annoyed or inconvenienced by the offensive acts, e.g., where a person obstructs a highway, or carries on a business that fills the air with noxious and offensive fumes.

PARDON   the remission, by the chief executive of a state or nation, of a punishment which a person convicted of crime has been sentences to undergo.

PAROL EVIDENCE RULE   A significant provision in American law, that when dealings between parties are reduced to an unambiguous written instrument, e.g., a deed, contract or lease, the instrument cannot be contradicted or modified by oral evidence. The rule is subject to various limitations and exceptions, however.

PAROLE   Supervised suspension of the execution of a convict's sentence, and release from prison, conditional upon his continued compliance with the terms of parole. (2) A regular part of the rehabilitation process. Assuming good behavior, it is the normal expectation in the vast majority of cases. Statutes generally specify when a prisoner will be eligible to be considered for parole and detail the standards and procedures applicable.

PER SE   Lat., by itself; alone.

PERSONALTY   Personal property.

PETITION   A request made to a public official or public body that has authority to act concerning it. The right to petition the government for a redress of grievances is secured to the people by the U.S. Const., Amendment I. (2) Under some codes of civil procedure, the written statement of the plaintiff's case which initiates a lawsuit. (3) A written request to the court for an order after notice. Uniform Probate Code § 5–103(15).

PLAINTIFF   A person who initiates a lawsuit.

PLEADINGS   The alternate and opposing written statements of the parties to a lawsuit. Under the Federal Rules of Civil Procedure, and analogous state rules of civil procedure, the pleadings consist of a Complaint and an Answer; a Reply to a Counterclaim denominated as such; an Answer to a Cross-claim, if the Answer contains a

Cross-claim; a Third-party Complaint, if a person who was not an original party is summoned; and a Third-party Answer, if a Third-party Complaint is served. No other pleadings shall be allowed, except that the court may order a Reply to an Answer or a Third-party Answer. Fed. R. Civ. P. 7(a). Pleadings consist of simple, concise and direct averments of claims for relief, defenses and denials. Matters which constitute an avoidance or affirmative defense must be set forth affirmatively. Id. 8.

POLICE POWER   A flexible term for the authority of federal and state legislatures to enact laws regulating and restraining private rights and occupations for the promotions of public health, safety, welfare and order.

PRE-TRIAL CONFERENCE, or PRE-TRIAL HEARING   A meeting between the judge and counsel for the parties, preliminary to the trial of a lawsuit. Under modern rules of civil procedure, in any lawsuit, the court may in its discretion direct the attorneys for the parties to appear before it for a conference, to consider any matters that may aid in the disposition of the lawsuit. Fed. R. Civ. P. 16.

PRICE DISCRIMINATION   As prohibited by the Robinson-Patman Act (*q.v.*), the making of a distinction in price between customers, for reasons which do not reflect differences in cost of manufacture, transportation or sale.

PRIMA FACIE   At first view; on the first aspect.

PRIMA FACIE EVIDENCE   Proof of a fact or collection of facts, which creates a presumption of the existence of other facts, or from which some conclusion may be legally drawn, but which presumption or conclusion may be discredited or overcome by other relevant proof.

PRINCIPAL   The leading, or most important; the original; a person, firm or corporation from whom an agent derives his authority; a person who is first responsible, and for whose fulfillment of an obligation a surety becomes bound; the chief, or actual, perpetrator of a crime, as distinguished from the accessory, who may assist him; the important part of an estate, as distinguished from incidents, or accessories; a sum of money loaned, as distinguished from the interest paid for its use.

PRIVILEGE   An exceptional right, or exemption, It is either (a) personal, attached to a person or office; or (b) attached to a thing, sometimes called real. The exemption of ambassadors and members of Congress from arrest, while going to, returning from, or attending to the discharge of their public duties, is an example of the first. (2) The fact that conduct which, under ordinary circumstances, would subject an actor to liability, under particular circumstances does not subject him to liability. A privilege may be based upon (a) the consent of the other affected by the actor's conduct, or (b) the fact that its exercise is necessary for the protection of some interest of the actor or of the public which is of such importance as to justify the harm caused or threatened by its exercise, or (c) the fact that the actor is performing a function for the proper performance of which freedom of action is essential. Restatement (Second) of Torts § 10.

PRIVITY   Participation in knowledge or interest. Persons who so participate are called privies. Privity in deed, i.e., by consent of the parties, is opposed to privity in law, e.g., tenant by curtesy.

PROBABLE CAUSE   A reasonable ground for suspicion, supported by circumstances sufficiently strong to warrant a cautious man to believe that an accused person is guilty of the offense with which he is charged. (2) Concerning a search, probable cause is a flexible, common-sense standard. It merely requires that the facts available to the officer would warrant a person of reasonable caution in the belief that certain items may be contraband or stolen property or useful as evidence of a crime; it does not demand any showing that the belief is correct or more likely true than false. A practical, nontechnical probability that incriminating evidence is involved is all that is required.

PROCESS The means whereby a court enforces obedience to its orders. Process is termed (a) original, when it is intended to compel the appearance of the defendant; (b) mesne, when issued pending suit to secure the attendance of jurors and witnesses; and (c) final, when issued to enforce execution of a judgment. (2) In patent law, the art or method by which any particular result is produced, e.g., the smelting of ores or the vulcanizing of rubber.

PROMISEE A person to whom a promise is made. Accord, Restatement (Second) of Contracts § 2(3).

PROMISOR A person who makes or gives a promise. Accord, Restatement (Second) of Contracts §2(2).

PROSECUTOR A person who brings an action against another, in the name of the government. A public prosecutor is an officer appointed or elected to conduct all prosecutions in behalf of the government. A private prosecutor is an individual who, not holding office, conducts an accusation against another. Occasionally, an aggrieved person will employ a private attorney to serve as such a prosecutor.

PROXIMATE CAUSE Something which produces a result, and without which, the result could not have occurred. (2) Any original event, which in natural unbroken sequence, produces a particular foreseeable result, without which the result would not have occurred.

PUBLIC POLICY A highly flexible term of imprecise definition, for the consideration of what is expedient for the community concerned. (2) The principle of law which holds that no person can do that which has a tendency to be injurious to the public, or against the public good. (3) The statutes and precedents, and not the general considerations of public interest.

PUNITIVE DAMAGES Damages in excess of the loss sustained and allowed as a punishment for torts committed with fraud, actual malice, or violence.

QUASH To annul or suppress, e.g., an indictment, a conviction, or an order.

QUASI Lat., as if; almost. Often used to indicate significant similarity or likeness to the word that follows, while denoting that the word that follows must be considered in a flexible sense.

QUASI-CONTRACT An obligation which arises without express agreement between the parties; an implied contract.

REAL PROPERTY, REAL ESTATE, or REALTY All land and buildings, including estates and interests in land and buildings which are held for life, but not for years, or some greater estate therein. (2) Real property includes land and any interest or estate in land. Uniform Partnership Act § 2.

RECOGNIZANCE, or RECOGNIZANCE BOND An obligation, or acknowledgment of a debt, in a court of law, with a condition that the debt shall be void on the performance of a stipulated undertaking, e.g., to appear before the proper court, to keep the peace, or to pay the debt, interest and costs that the plaintiff may recover.

RECORD   A written memorial of the actions of a legislature or of a court. (2) The copy of a deed or other instrument relating to real property, officially preserved in a public office.

REFORMATION, or RECTIFICATION   The correction of a written instrument, via a lawsuit, so as to make it express the true agreement or intention of the parties.

REMAND   To recommit a person to jail or prison. (2) To send a lawsuit back to the same court from which it came, for trial or other action.

REMEDY   The legal means to declare or enforce a right or to redress a wrong. (2) Any remedial right, to which an aggrieved party is entitled, with or without resort to a tribunal. U.C.C. § 1–201(34).

REPLEVIN   A form of lawsuit which is used to recover possession of specific chattels, which have been unlawfully taken from, or withheld from, the plaintiff. It may be brought by a general owner, who has the right to immediate possession, or by someone who has a special property in the chattel, e.g., a creditor whose claim is secured by the chattel. Usually defined by various state statutes. Occasionally called claim and delivery or order of delivery.

RES JUDICATA   Lat., a controversy already judicially decided. The decision is conclusive until the judgment is reversed. In litigation, the judgment of a court of competent jurisdiction on the merits of a case is a bar to a new lawsuit involving the same cause of action (q.v.) between the same parties, before the same court or any other court, because it is in the interest of the state and individuals that there should be some end to litigation.

RESCISSION   The cancellation of, or putting an end to, a contract by the parties, or one of them, e.g., for any reason mutually acceptable to the parties, or on the ground of fraud.

RESPONDENT   A party against whom a motion is filed in the course of a lawsuit; analogous to a defendant or an appellee.

RESTITUTION   The restoring of property, or a right, to a person who has been unjustly deprived of it. A writ of restitution is the process by which a successful appellant may recover something of which he has been deprived under a prior judgment.

ROBINSON-PATMAN ACT   An act to amend the Clayton Antitrust Act, to prevent price discrimination (q.v.) and other discriminatory practices, 15 U.S.C. §§ 13 et seq.; 49 Stat. 1526 (1936).

SANCTION   The power of enforcing a statute, or inflicting a penalty for its violation. (2) Consent.

SATISFACTION   The payment of money owing.

SECONDARY BOYCOTT   Variously, a combination to refrain from dealing with a person, or to advise or by peaceful means persuade his customers so to refrain, or to exercise coercive pressure upon such customers, actual or prospective, in order to cause them to withhold or withdraw patronage.

SERVICE   The act of bringing a judicial proceeding to the notice of the person affected by it, e.g., by delivering to him a copy of a written summons or notice. (2) The relationship of an employee, or servant, to his employer, or master. (3) Formerly, the duty which an English tenant owed to his lord by reason of his estate, e.g., rent.

SHERMAN ACT, or SHERMAN ANTI-TRUST ACT.   An act to protect trade and commerce against unlawful restraints and monopolies. 15 U.S.C. §§ 1 *et seq.;* 26 Stat. 209 (1890).

SLANDER   The malicious defamation of a person, in his reputation, profession, or business, by spoken words. To impute a criminal offense, or misconduct in business, is actionable without proof of special damage, but in any case, proof of special damage arising from the false and malicious statements of another is a sufficient ground of action. Usually, the truth of the words spoken is a defense. Occasionally defined by various state statutes. Cf. *Libel* (1). (2) Publication of defamatory matter by spoken words, transitory gestures, or any form of communication other than written words or embodiment in physical form or any other form of communication that has the potentially harmful qualities characteristic of written or printed words. Restatement (Second) of Torts § 568(2).

SOVEREIGN IMMUNITY   A rule of law holding that a nation or state, or its political subdivisions, is exempt from being sued, without its consent, in its own courts or elsewhere. Often criticized as being erroneously conceived, anachronistic and unjust. Occasionally modified by court decisions, and various state and federal statutes, e.g., Tort Claims Act.

SOVEREIGNTY   The supreme authority of an independent nation or state. It is characterized by equality of the nation or state among other nations or states, exclusive and absolute jurisdiction and self-government within its own territorial limits, and jurisdiction over its citizens beyond its territorial limits.

SPECIAL DAMAGES   Reparation in money awarded for any peculiar injury sustained by the party complaining, beyond the general damages presumed by law.

SPECIFIC PERFORMANCE   The actual carrying out of a contract in the particular manner agreed upon. Courts of equity will compel and coerce specific performance of a contract in many cases, where damages payable in money, the usual remedy at law, would not adequately compensate for its nonperformance, e.g., in the case of contracts concerning land, or for the sale of a unique chattel.

STARE DECISIS   Lat., to stand by decided cases; to follow precedent. A flexible doctrine of Anglo-American law that when a court expressly decides an issue of law, which is generated by the facts of a unique dispute, that decision shall constitute a precedent which should be followed by that court and by courts inferior to it, when deciding future disputes, except when the precedent's application to a particular problem case is unsuitable to the character or spirit of the people of the state or nation, and their current social, political and economic conditions.

STATUTE OF FRAUDS   Various state legislative acts, patterned after a 1677 English act, known by the same name. E.g., U.C.C. § 2–201. Because of the variations in each state, reference must be made to the specific state statutes. The main object was to take away the facilities for fraud, and the temptation to perjury, which arose in verbal obligations, the proof of which depended upon oral evidence. Its most common provisions are these: (a) all leases, excepting those for less than three years, shall have the force of leases at will only, unless they are in writing and signed by the parties or their agents; (b) assignments and surrenders of leases and interests in land must be in writing; (c) all declarations and assignments of trusts must be in writing, signed by the party (trusts arising by implication of law are, however, excepted); (d) no action shall be brought upon a guarantee, or upon any contract for sale of lands, or any interest in or concerning them, or upon any agreement which is not to be performed within a year, unless the agreement is in writing and signed by the party to be charged or his agent; (e) no contract for the sale of goods for a certain price or more, e.g., $500,000, U.C.C. § 2–201, shall be good, unless the buyer accept part, or give something in part payment, or some memorandum thereof be signed by the parties to be charged or their agents.

STATUTE OF LIMITATIONS   Various periods of time, fixed by different state and federal statutes, called statutes of limitations, within which a lawsuit must be commenced, and after the expiration of which, the claimant will be forever barred from the right to bring the action. Generally, a statute of limitations is a procedural bar to a plaintiff's action which does not begin to run until after the cause of action has accrued and the plaintiff has a right to maintain a lawsuit.

SUBSTANTIVE LAW   The positive law of duties and rights.

TAFT-HARTLEY ACT, or LABOR MANAGEMENT RELATIONS ACT OF 1947   An act to amend the National Labor Relations Act, to provide additional facilities for the mediation of labor disputes affecting commerce, and to equalize legal responsibilities of labor organizations and employers. 29 U.S.C. §§ 141 *et seq.*; 61 Stat. 136 1947.

TANGIBLE   Descriptive of something which may be felt or touched; corporeal.

TITLE VII (CIVIL RIGHTS ACT OF 1964)   An act to enforce the constitutional right to vote, to confer jurisdiction upon the district courts of the United States to provide injunctive relief against discrimination in public accommodations, to authorize the Attorney General to institute suits to protect constitutional rights in public facilities and public education, to extend the Commission on Civil Rights, to prevent discrimination in federally assisted programs, to establish a commission on Equal Employment Opportunity, and for other purposes. 28 U.S.C. § 1447; 42 U.S.C. §§ 1971, 1975–d, 2000a–200h—6; 78 Stat. 241 (1964).

TORT   Any one of various, legally recognized, private injuries or wrongs, which do not arise as the result of a breach of contract.

TRADE SECRET   A plan, process, tool, mechanism, or compound, known only to its owner, and those of his employees to whom it is necessary to confide it, in order to apply it to the uses intended. It is distinguishable from a patent, in that it may be used by anyone who is able to discover its nature.

TRESPASS   Any transgression of the law, less than treason, felony, or misprision of either. (2) Especially, trespass quare clausum fregit, i.e., entry on another's close, or land without lawful authority. (3) Trespass on the case, or Case, is a general name for torts which formerly had no special writ or remedy. (4) Criminal trespass is entering or surreptitiously remaining in a building or occupied structure, or separately secured or occupied portion thereof, knowing that he is not licensed or privileged to do so. Model Penal Code § 221.2(1). (5) Defiant trespass is entering or remaining in any place as to which notice against trespass is given, knowing that he is not licensed or privileged to do so. The notice against trespass must be given by actual communication to the actor, posting in a manner prescribed by law or reasonably likely to come to the attention of intruders, or fending or other enclosure manifestly designed to exclude intruders. Model Penal Code § 221.2(2).

UNENFORCEABLE CONTRACT A contract (*q.v.*) for the breach of which neither the remedy of damages nor the remedy of specific performance is available, but which is recognized in some other way as creating a duty of performance, though there has been no ratification. Restatement (Second) of Contracts § 8.

UNIFORM COMMERCIAL CODE A proposal by the American Law Institute, and the National Conference of Commissioners on Uniform State Laws, for comprehensive legislation relating to commercial transactions, i.e., sales, commercial paper, bank deposits and collections, letters of credit, bulk transfers, warehouse receipts, bills of lading, other documents of title, investment securities, and secured transactions. It has been adopted in each of the states of the United States, except Louisiana, and in the District of Columbia and the Virgin Islands.

UNILATERAL CONTRACT A one-sided contract (*q.v.*); an agreement in which only one party makes a promise and on the other side of which the consideration has been fully performed, e.g., a promise to repay a loan of money. (2) Occasionally, an agreement which is void because only one party is bound by it and it therefore lacks mutuality of obligation.

UNJUST ENRICHMENT The doctrine which places a legal duty of restitution upon a defendant who has acquired something of value at the expense of the plaintiff.

VENUE (*ven'u*) or VISNE (*ven*) The neighborhood; the county in which a particular lawsuit should be tried; the county from which the jury is taken for the trial of a lawsuit. Often regulated by various state and federal statutes. A change of venue is the sending of a lawsuit to be tried before a jury of another county, e.g., when circumstances render it impossible to have an impartial trial in the county where the cause of action arose.

VICARIOUS LIABILITY Substituted or indirect responsibility, e.g., the responsibility of an employer for the torts committed by his employee within the scope of his employment.

VOID Of no force or effect; absolutely null.

VOIDABLE Descriptive of an imperfect obligation, which may be legally annulled or cured or confirmed, at the option of one of the parties, e.g., the contract of an infant with an adult.

WAIVER A positive act by which a legal right is relinquished.

WANTON MISCONDUCT Such behavior as manifests a disposition to perversity. It must be under such circumstances and conditions that the party doing the act, or failing to act, is conscious that his conduct will, in all common probability, result in injury.

WARRANT Written authority. (2) An order from a court, to an officer, directing the officer to arrest a person.

WARRANTY A guaranty concerning goods or land, which is expressly or impliedly made to a purchaser by the vendor.

WITHOUT PREJUDICE Free of any prejudgment, or bias which interferes with a person's impartiality and sense of justice.

WRIT A written court order, or a judicial process. It is issued by authority of a court, and directed to the sheriff, or other officer authorized by law to execute the same. He must return it, with a brief statement of what he has done in pursuance of it, to the court or officer who issued it. Writs are either (a) prerogative, when the granting of them is in the discretion of the court, as in the case of habeas corpus; or (b) of right, when the applicant is entitled as of course. The latter class includes original writs, by which an action is commenced, e.g., a summons, and judicial writs; under which head almost all writs at present fall, e.g., writs in aid, and writs of execution. (3) An action, e.g., the writs of waste and partition.

ZONING The division of a city or county into separate areas, and the application to each area of regulations which limit the various purposes to which the land and buildings therein may be devoted.

Indexes

CASE INDEX

SUBJECT INDEX

Case Index

Subject Index